The Evolution of Military Law in India

The Evolution of Military Law in India

Including the Mutiny Acts and Articles of War

Wg Cdr (Dr) U C Jha

Vij Books India Pvt Ltd
New Delhi (India)

Published by

Vij Books India Pvt Ltd
(Publishers, Distributors & Importers)
2/19, Ansari Road
Delhi – 110 002
Phones: 91-11-43596460, 91-11-47340674
Mob: 98110 94883
e-mail: contact@vijpublishing.com

ISBN: 978-81-94285-10-6 (Hardback)
ISBN: 978-81-94285-12-0 (ebook)

Contents

List of Appendices

Preface

Militaries all over the world are governed by a unique disciplinary system. The system strives to ensure both discipline amongst the members and justice to those who have been wronged. It is this system which *makes* an army different from a *mob*.

The rules governing the conduct of a soldier have undergone tremendous change over time. In the case of England, for example, the Articles of War that were valid during conflicts in the 1600s, provided for severe punishments of death or loss of limb for almost every crime—something that is unthinkable today. To cite a specific example, the Laws and Ordinances of War of the Earl of Essex in 1643 provided for death penalty for almost every military offence and for branding of the tongue with a red hot iron for blasphemy.

In India, the history of a modern army may be traced back to the establishment of the Presidencies of Bombay, Madras and Calcutta under the East India Company. These establishments were guarded by a small number of European soldiers. There was no specific legal instrument to govern their conduct. The British Articles of War, as suited, were used to discipline them. In due course of time, Indians were recruited to enhance the dignity of the officers of the Company and to guard the Company's assets.

Major Stringer Lawrence of the British Army is regarded as 'the father of the Indian Army'. It was he who formed the first military units of the East India Company in Madras in 1748. The need for such a measure arose because by then the hostilities between England and France had extended to India. The recruitment of troops of this class was recognized by the Statutes of 1754 and 1760. However, disciplinary power was conferred on the Company only in 1813 by the East India Company Act. Later, the Government of India Act, 1833 conferred disciplinary powers on the Governor General of India in Council for formulating Articles of War and laying down regulations for the holding of courts martial. Under the powers conferred by the Act of 1833, the Indian Legislature for the first time provided a common code for the native armies in 1845, which was repealed by the Act of 1847.

After the Mutiny of 1857, the administration of the military forces was transferred from the Company to the Crown. In 1860, with the passing of the European Forces (India) Act, the British and native forces were merged in the regular forces of the Crown. Further reforms in the military legal system were undertaken prior to the First World War. The Commander-in-Chief in India was given the power to mitigate or remit any punishment awarded by courts martial even after they were confirmed by the proper military authority. The Indian Articles of War drawn under Act V of 1869 was substituted by the Indian Army Act, 1911. This remained the main source of law governing the British Indian Army till 1947, when it was revised in keeping with the constitution of the country.

The Indian Army raised by the East India Company and later transferred to the British Crown, was essentially a mercenary force. Its peasant-soldiers left their villages to supplement their meager income from small land holdings. They enlisted not to win battle honour or show loyalty to the British Kingdom, but to secure a regular salary and pension, and if possible the grant of fertile land. They were governed by laws made for European soldiers, and not by laws specifically drafted for them.

This book, divided into seven chapters, is about the evolution of the military legal system in India from the establishment of the East India Company till India gained independence from the British rule i.e., from 1600-1947. The first chapter deals with the origin and growth of the East India Company (EIC), a trading company, which quickly got entangled in local intrigues and power play. The EIC needed an organized military machine to compete in the power arena. To achieve this, by 1805, the EIC had trained up an army of 150,000 men, almost twice the size of the British military. The second chapter describes the militarization of the EIC and the growth of the Indian military. The third chapter covers the induction of officers, soldiers and natives in the military service of the Company and the conditions of their employment under the Company and the British Government. It may be of surprise to many that Commission in His Majesty's Army was allowed to be disposed of by sale.

Britain had no permanent force or standing army till 1660. Military forces were raised only when required to wage a war or put down a rebellion, and these men were retainers of the Crown rather than servants of the State. For each such army the King would either himself make or authorize the Commander to make Ordinances or Articles of War for its governance. Chapter four covers the evolution of the military legal system in Britain through Acts of Parliament and Articles of War. It includes the laws governing the Navy, Air Forces, Reservists, Military Nursing Services and volunteer forces raised by the British Government. Chapter five looks into the issue of military discipline, particularly in the case of serious offences such as drunkenness, gambling, desertion and mutiny. It also deals with the ill-treatment of native soldiers and the mechanism of grievance redressal. The natives followed the military legal system without even understanding its intricacy. However, they protested and reacted spontaneously whenever they felt that their masters were trying to interfere in their religious affairs or being unjust in paying their dues. There were several mutinies in the Indian Army under the Company. Chapter six covers a few of these. It deals briefly with the trial of Muhammad Bahadur Shah, Titular King of Delhi, by a Military Commission. Chapter seven, the last chapter, describes the functioning of the military tribunals and the award and execution of various punishments under the military legal system.

Various Acts of Parliament and Articles of War issued from time to time have been included in the Appendix section of the book. The language used in the Acts and Articles as well as the names of places and persons have not been changed.

I am thankful to Aditya for providing me a comfortable environment to undertake research work for this project during my stay at Natick, Massachusetts, USA. I am grateful to Sqn Ldr RTS Chhina, MBE (Retd), Secretary, Centre for Armed Forces Historical Research at the United Service Institution, New Delhi and the Vice President of the Indian Military Historical Society, UK for his guidance on the subject and material assistance. I am grateful to Gp Capt R K Srivastava for having gone through drafts of few chapters of this book. I have accessed a number of archived military documents and books on the web at http://books.google.com/ for which I remain obliged. I sincerely thank Vij Books India Private Limited for their professional assistance in bringing out this edition.

– U C Jha

Chapter I

The Origin and Growth of East India Company (1600-1858)

Towards the end of the fifteenth century rapid discoveries in mathematics, physics, and astronomy facilitated distant navigation. Portuguese explorer Vasco da Gama, in an expedition that began in July 1497, became the first person to sail around the Cape of Good Hope to reach India. His revolutionary route proved that it was possible to reach India without hazardous journeys through the Mediterranean and Arabia. The Portuguese fleets brought lucrative Indian spices to Europe from the East-Indies and filled the treasury of the State. It lowered the price of eastern commodities in the Italian markets, and created a spirit for distant navigation and commerce among the rising maritime states in the north of Europe.[1] When the Portuguese acquired seats of trade and dominions on the East and West coasts of the Indian peninsula, they found it necessary to establish guards at their factories, to protect the territories which had been ceded to them by the Native Powers.

In 1588, the British acquired naval supremacy after defeating the Spanish Armeda.[2] This encouraged a few merchants of London to form a company for trade in the East.[3] Queen Elizabeth

1 Discovery of Sea-route to India by European countries was one of the most important events in modern times. The wealth of India was an attraction. The Europeans knew about the wealth since ancient time out of the trade link that India established with Greece and Rome. Indian traders used to carry Indian goods for sale in European markets through Afghanistan, Persia, Arab, Egypt and Turkey with hardship. All these trade routes were closed for the Europeans during medieval period. The Muslims of Arab countries monopolized the trade and prevented others for that trade profit. Gradually the relation of the western people with the Muslims became bitter. With the discovery of the Sea-route, a new chapter in the history of India began. European traders started coming to India for trade. Among the Europeans the English, the French, the Dutch, the Spaniards, the Portuguese marched for creating a mark of their commercial supremacy in India. Available at: http://www.historydiscussion.net/history-of-india/how-did-the-europeans-discover-the-sea-route-to-india/2543. Also see: *Annals of the Honourable East-India Company*, Vol. I, London: Black, Parry and Kingsbury, 1810, p. 3-4.

2 The Spanish Armada was an enormous 130-ship naval fleet dispatched by Spain in 1588 as part of a planned invasion of England. Following years of hostilities between Spain and England, King Philip II of Spain assembled the flotilla in the hope of removing Protestant Queen Elizabeth from the throne and restoring the Roman Catholic faith in England. Spain's "invincible Armada" set sail in May 1588, but it was outfoxed by the English, then battered by storms while limping back to Spain with at least a third of its ships sunk or damaged. The defeat of the Spanish Armada led to a surge of national pride in England and was one of the most significant chapters of the Anglo-Spanish War.

3 On the 24 September 1599, a general meeting of these merchants was held, the result of which was, a resolution to apply to the Queen, for her royal assent to a project, intended for the honor of their native country, and the

I of England accepted the proposal to send ships to the Indian Ocean, where Spain was not dominant. A Charter was issued by the Queen on 31 December 1600 which granted the merchants' newly formed organization: "The Governor and Company of Merchants of London, trading to the East-Indies"[4] to purchase lands, and to dispose thereof, and to have a common seal, to ratify and make public their acts. The management of the Company was placed under a Governor and a Committee of twenty-four men, who were to have the direction of voyages, provisions of shipping and sale of merchandize for fifteen years, from Christmas 1600, provided that such trade should not be to any place in possession of any Christian prince in amity with the Queen.

During the initial years of its existence the Company undertook 'separate voyages' and distributed the profits from each voyage among the subscribers.[5] The first effort for regular trade with India was made in 1608 when British Captain Hawkins tried to obtain permission from the Mughal emperor Jahangir to establish a factory at Surat.[6] British merchants in the service of the East India Company would gladly have traded on the same sea-board, which was known as the coast of Malabar, but they were shut out by the Portuguese fortresses. Accordingly they sailed further northward, and tried to get a footing in the Mogul port of Surat. This port was a centre of the Mohammedan religion and an emporium of Mogul trade. It was the starting point for all pilgrims going to Mecca, and the point to which they returned when their pilgrimage was over. At Surat, however, the British were thwarted by the Portuguese. The Nawab of Surat was told that British were pirates. The merchants of Surat were threatened with the capture of their ships if they had any dealings with the British. Fighting was the only way of meeting the difficulty. Accordingly the British attacked a Portuguese fleet outside the bar of Surat. The news of battle and the roar

advancement of trade and merchandize within the realm of England; and to set forth a voyage this year to the East-Indies, and other islands and countries thereabouts. This project was general, and intended for opening a trade, at any of the ports in the East-Indies, at which it might be practicable to sell European or purchase Indian produce.

4 The company was founded by 101 Englishmen who made investments in the company, and each was entitled to an equal share of its value, making it an early joint-stock company. The royal charter gave the founders and the newly formed organization, which would become the East India Company, a monopoly over trade in the East Indies for 15 years. Royal charters were not uncommon during the colonial period, as they were mutually beneficial to both the Crown and those they were granted. The first Charter for erecting an the Company was dated 31 December, 1600; a second Charter was granted to the original Company on 31 May, 1609; a third, 3 April, 1661; a fourth, 5 October, 1677; a fifth, 9 August, 1683; a sixth, 12 April, 1686; a seventh, 7 October, 1693; and an eighth, 13 April, 1698. In addition to these Charters, the Company obtained a grant, dated 27 March, 1669, of the Island of Bombay, and another, 16 December, 1674, of the Island of St. Helena.

5 The Company started in 1600 by buying four vessels second-hand, and continued to purchase old craft down to 1609. But it found vessels constructed for short European voyages unsuited to the armed trade of the east, and in 1607 it resolved to build ships of its own. It leased great dock of its own at Deptford and on 30 December 1609, the King launched Company's first two ships. The system of building its own ships continued for 25 years encouraged by the royal bounty of five shillings a ton. It was this class of vessels that broke the Portuguese power in the Asiatic seas and enable the Company to struggle, ship for ship, with the Dutch. Wilson Sir, William, 1900, *A History of British India*, Vol. II, London: Longmans, p. 168-169.

6 Jahangir (1605-1627), ascended the throne after the death of his father Akbar. The British Captain William Hawkins met Jahangir in the Mughal court, and attempted to obtain permission to open a factory at Sural in India. Hawkins and Jahangir got on so well, that Hawkins stayed there for more than six months and married a woman of Jahangir's choice. However, Jahangir only gave permission in 1613 for an English factory to be set up at Surat, after much bribery and persuasion from the Company for nearly 7 years.

of cannon brought the Nawab, the merchants, and half the population of Surat to the sea-shore. The British sunk and burnt several Portuguese ships until the residue of the fleet steered back to Goa. The Moguls were fascinated by the victory. They saw that the British had superior military strength. The Nawab of Surat feasted the conquerors in his tents on the sands, and the Surat merchants eagerly bought British cargoes and supplied Indian commodities to the men who had beaten the Portuguese.

Surat and Bombay: In 1613 the English succeeded in securing permission from Jahangir to establish their first factory at Surat. [7] The Company officials set up a factory in a large Indian house and named it "English-House" having warehouses and offices below and chambers and refection-rooms above.[8] Not only British travellers, but Italians, Germans, and Frenchmen, were heartily welcomed by the factors at Surat. All were impressed with the order and regularity of the establishment, in which decorum and discipline were as strictly maintained. An English chaplain read prayers every morning and evening, and preached two sermons on Sundays. An English surgeon attended the sick factors, and the Mogul authorities and other grandees often applied for his services, and thus enabled him to promote the Company's interests on important occasions. The chief of the factory was known as the President, but all business was transacted by the President with the help of four or five senior merchants, who met twice a week in council. This management of affairs by a President in Council survived for nearly three centuries.

In 1615 Thomas Roe was instructed by James I to visit the Moghul emperor Jahangir. The purpose of this mission was to arrange for a commercial treaty that would give the company exclusive rights to reside and build factories in Surat and other areas. In return, the company offered to provide goods and rarities from the European market to the emperor. This mission was highly successful as the Company succeeded in securing from the Mughal emperor certain privileges including the right to erect factories in certain parts of the empire. By virtue of this concession the English established factories at Agra, Ahmedabad and Broach within the next four years. These factories were placed under the supervision of the President and the Council of Surat factory.

In order to improve on the general treaty, Thomas Roe made proposals to Sultan Churrum (future Shah Jahan), to enter into an alliance, for resisting the pretensions of the Portuguese. After long discussions with Prince, the treaty was concluded, and the following were its leading articles:—that the prince should take the English under his protection;—that the Governor of Surat should lend ships to the English, to be employed in the defence of the port; the English, however, to be allowed to land only ten armed men at one time, but the resident merchants might wear arms;—that the English might build a house in the city, but distant from the castle;—that the Governor

7 Wheeler J. Talboys, 1886, *India Under British Rule: From the Foundation of the East India Company*, London: Macmillan and Co., pp. 2-5.

8 In the British factory at Surat (White House) the British merchants, factors, and writers lodged and boarded together like members of one family. Native brokers or banyans were employed to buy cotton goods, silks, indigo, and other Indian commodities ; whilst public auctions were held in the factory for the sale of British broadcloths, glass and cutlery, especially sword-blades, and also for the sale of lead, copper, quicksilver, and other European commodities. In those early days no British ladies were allowed to reside in India. If a servant of the Company happened to be married he was obliged to leave his wife in England. The English House was thus a bachelor establishment, without ladies, but not without Surat punch or Persian wine.

of Surat should receive the Ambassador and his suite, with marks of honour;—that the English should enjoy the free exercise of their own religion, and be governed by their own laws;—that in any disputes between the English and the natives, reference was to be made to the Governor and his officers, who should decide, speedily and justly; but disputes, among themselves, were to be decided by their own factory;—that liberty of trade should be granted to the English, in its fullest extent, on payment of the usual duties on landing the goods, from which pearls, jewels, etc. were to be exempted;—that freedom of speech should be granted to the English linguists and brokers, in all matters regarding the trade of their employers;—and, lastly, that all presents, intended for court, should be opened and examined at the custom-house at Surat, and then sealed and delivered to the English, to pass, duty free; but, if such presents were not made, the articles were to be liable to pay duty. The *firman*, ratifying and confirming this treaty, was signed, sealed, and delivered to Thomas Roe.[9]

By 1647 the company had 23 factories and 90 employees in India. The major factories became the walled forts of Fort William in Bengal,[10] Fort St. George in Madras, and the Bombay Castle. The 1660 charter empowered the Company to send ships of war, men, and arms to their factories for defence of the same, and to make peace or war with any people not Christians. Authority was also granted for the fortification of St. Helena, which since 1651 had become the port of call on the voyage to India, and stringent provision was made for the maintenance of the Company's monopoly.

On 21 May 1662, the marriage treaty of Charles II of England and Catherine of Braganza, daughter of King John IV of Portugal, placed Bombay in possession of the British Empire, as part of dowry of Catherine to Charles. After the treaty, some villages in Bombay remained under Portuguese possession, but many were later acquired by the British. Sir Abraham Shipman, who was appointed as first Governor and General of Bombay on 19 March 1662, was sent out with 400 soldiers to take possession of the island. He arrived with his fleet at Bombay on 18 September 1662 and demanded the cession of the island and its dependencies, conformably to the treaty between the King of England and the Crown of Portugal. Shipman demanded not only the island and harbour of Bombay, but also the island of Salsette, believing it to be included in the dependencies of Bombay. The Portuguese Governor of Bombay contended that the island

9 *Annals of the Honourable East-India Company*, 1600 to 1708, Vol. I, London: Black, Perry and Kingsbury, 1810, p. 203-205

10 Jahan Ara, twenty-seven-years-old, was the most trusted adviser of her father, Emperor Shah Jehan, in matters of war and peace. In 1644, there was a great commotion in the palace of the Great Mughul at Agra. The clothes of Jahan Ara had caught fire, and the princess had been severely burnt before the flames could be extinguished. The leading practitioners of traditional Greek and Indian medicine were summoned to cure her wounds; but the recovery of the princess was very slow and the wounds refused to heal. The Emperor learnt of an expert physician on board the HMS Hopewell, one of the British ships anchored at Surat. He approached the officials of the East India Company to make the services of this physician available to him. The Company fetched Dr. Gabriel Boughton from the ship. He treated the Princess and was able to restore her to a working routine. The Emperor was delighted and offered his benefactor any reward he might choose to name – within the limits of the imperial power. The selfless doctor, however, replied that he needed nothing for himself. Instead he pleaded with the Emperor that his Company was having a hard time expanding trade in India and requested permission for it to trade duty-free through all the sea ports in his realm. This ensured the Company to establish a factory at Pipili and for the first time as well as free trade with Bengal.

of Bombay alone had been ceded, and on the ground of some alleged irregularity in the form of the letters patent, he refused to give up even Bombay. The Viceroy of Portuguese India declined to interfere. Shipman thus left Bombay and landed on the island of Anjediva, near Goa on 12 December 1662.[11] In 1664 they were transferred to Madras, in view of the war with Holland; but by the end of the year Shipman and a vast number of the men had fallen sick and died; and when at last they landed in Bombay, in March 1665, the four hundred had dwindled to one officer and one hundred and thirteen men.[12]

In 1668 Charles transferred Bombay[13] together with the whole of its military stores, to the Company for a rent of ten pounds a year. In course of time Bombay became a flourishing commercial city and gained more importance as compared to Surat and was made the headquarters of the Company in India.[14]

Madras: On the east coast also the English set up a number of factories. In fact they had established their first factory on the East coast at Masulipatam in 1611.[15] They established another factory at Armagoan, few miles from the Dutch settlement of Pulicat in 1628. In 1639 a British merchant named Day bought a strip of territory on the Coromandel Coast, about 300 miles to the south of Masulipatam. It was within the dominions of a Hindu Raja, and was about six miles long

11 When the British forces that had been sent to take possession of the Island of Bombay evacuated Anjediva (Goa), that island was left without a possessor. Soon after the Conde de Alvor arrived in India he took possession of that place on behalf of the Crown of Portugal, and erected there a strong fortress, the foundation stone of which building was laid with some ceremony on the 5th of May, 1682. Amaro Simoes was appointed the first Governor of Anjediva, and a Hindu temple that existed there was replaced by a Catholic Church. In later years the island was used as a penal settlement whither felons from Goa, Daman, and Diu were transported. Frederich Charles Danvers, 1894, *The Portuguese in India: Being a History of the Rise and Decline of Their Eastern Empire*, Vol. II, London: W, Waterloo Place, p. 366. Also see: J. Gerson Da Cunha, The Origin of Bombay, *The Journal of the Bombay Branch of the Royal Asiatic Society*, Extra Number, 1900, p. 243.

12 Fortescue John William, 1899, A History of the British Army, Vol. II, London: Macmillan and Co Limited, p.171.

13 It was during Aurangzeb's reign (1658-1707) that the Company gained the city of Bombay (Mumbai), which was part of the dowry given to Charles II. Aurungzeb was involved in a series of costly wars including a war with the English. Aurangzeb was given many fine presents by the East India Company, mostly of gold and silver. But even these did not always ensure that the Company got what it wanted. In 1701 Aurangzeb was presented with gifts of cannons, horses, glassware and cartloads of cloth. The gifts were presented at a grand ceremony to the sound of trumpets, drums and bagpipes. Aurangzeb was not impressed, and kept Sir William Norris (the Company's ambassador to the Mughal Empire) waiting. When Norris left without permission he was brought back and forced to pay a fine. The whole affair cost the Company a staggering £80,000.

14 Bombay was nearly two hundred miles to the south of Surat, and hedged around by the Mahrattas, but being an island it was well protected, and included both a fortress and a town. Moreover, it had a magnificent harbour, and the valuable trade with the Persian Gulf could be better carried on from this harbour than over the bar of Surat at the mouth of the river Tapty. Accordingly the East India Company secretly resolved on leaving Surat for ever, and removing the British factors and their trade to the island of Bombay. Wheeler J. Talboys, 1886, *India under British Rule: From the Foundation of the East India Company*, London: Macmillan and Co., pp. 4-6; Fortescue John William, 1899, A History of the British Army, Vol. II, London: Macmillan and Co Limited, p.171-172.

15 In 1611, an English vessel touched at Point de Galle, sailed up the Coromandel, or eastern, coast of India as far as Masulipatam and founded the nucleus of a factory at Petapolee, the germ from which was to spring the trade of England in the Bay of Bengal. The jealousy of Dutch and Portuguese had by this time risen so high that the Company was obliged to employ force against them. Fortescue John William, 1899, *A History of the British Army*, Vol. II, London: Macmillan and Co., Limited, p. 170.

and one mile inland. It included a small island, which faced the sea and was defended on the land side by a river. Mr. Day agreed to pay the Raja a rent of 500 pounds a year in native coin known as pagodas, and the transaction was duly engraved on a plate of gold. A factory of brick was built upon the island, and mounted with cannon, and called Fort St. George. The Raja was perfectly content. He was too glad to get a rent of 500 pounds a year to raise any difficulty as regards fortifications or cannon. This factory was the germ of the city of Madras, on the coast of Coromandel. Weavers, washers, painters, and hosts of other Hindu artisans, flocked to the spot and eagerly entered the service of the British, and began to set up their looms and to weave, wash, and paint their cotton goods in the open air beneath the trees. Villages of little huts of mud and bamboo soon grew up on the sandy soil to the north of the island and factory. Each avocation formed a caste, which generally had its own quarters and its own head-man. In this manner a Hindu settlement grew up by the side of Fort St. George and was known as Black Town; and the whole locality, including Fort St. George and Black Town, was called Madras, and was the first territory acquired by the East India Company in India. In the next forty years of the building of the British factory, Madras was the pride and glory of the East India Company. Fort St. George, or White Town, was a European city in miniature. The whole of White Town was environed by an outer wall, sufficiently fortified to keep off an Indian army. Only Britons, or Europeans under British protection, were permitted to reside in White Town. This ultimately became the headquarters of the company's settlements on the Coromandel Coast. The garrison consisted of two companies of European soldiers, and a large number of native guards, who were known as peons.[16] In 1660 pagodas were coined at the mint at Fort St. George, under the agency of Sir Edward Winter, from bullion received from Europe.

Calcutta: In Bengal the East India Company had established a factory at Hooghly, by the dismantled Portuguese fortress; but were exposed to insolence and extortion from the Mogul authorities. The trade was enormously profitable, and had helped to defray the cost of the fortifications at Madras and Bombay. Saltpetre had been in large demand ever since the breaking out of the civil war between Charles the First and his parliament. Raw silk and opium were equally marketable, and all three products could be brought from Patna to Hooghly by the river Ganges. At Dacca, the old capital of Bengal, very fine quality of muslins was manufactured. It was said that every young lady in the British Isles who aspired to be a bride was anxious to be led to the altar in a cloud of Dacca muslin.[17]

---

16 Justice was administered by two English gentlemen, who sat twice a week in Black Town in a building known as the Choultry. The Justices of the Choultry tried all offences and disputes amongst the Hindus, and fined, flogged, or imprisoned at discretion. The old English punishments of the stocks, the pillory, and the gallows were also in full force in Black Town, but no Hindu was executed without the confirmation of the Governor and Council. The Justices of the Choultry were bound by no code of laws; they were simply instructed by the Directors of the Company in England to decide all cases, civil and criminal, according to "equity and good conscience," guided by English law and their own experiences of Hindu customs and usages. A Hindu superintendent of police was appointed under the title of "Pedda Naik," or elder chief, who was bound to maintain a certain numer of constables known as peons, and keep the peace in the town. Wheeler J. Talboys, 1886, *India under British Rule: From the Foundation of the East India Company*, London: Macmillan and Co., pp. 7-13.

17 Wheeler J. Talboys, 1886, *India under British Rule: From the Foundation of the East India Company*, London: Macmillan and Co., p. 11.

In 1651 the Company opened factories at Patna and Kasimbazar. Permission to fortify Hooghly, frequently solicited, was persistently refused by the Mogul Emperor, and the armed force of the agency limited to an ensign and thirty men (Europeans) to do honour to the principal agent. This small body of men may be regarded as the nucleus of the Bengal army. In 1669, Bengal was still subordinate to Madras, but was allowed a chief agent and six members of council, similar to those at the latter agency. Trade was then so flourishing that a pilot service for the intricate navigation of the river Hooghly was established. In 1675 the Company placed the three agencies, Surat, Madras, and Hooghly on an equal footing, and similar gradation was granted to its servants. The importance of the Bengal agency, which, among its other factories, now included Malda and Dacca, rapidly increased, and in 1681 the stock allotted for its trade alone amounted to 230,000. Its agent was dignified by the title of Governor, and it was declared independent of Madras. By 1682, the Mogul Emperor started oppressing the flourishing Company and ordered 3.5 per cent, to be levied on all the goods as customs. In 1683, Mr. Gyfford was appointed agent at Fort St. George with the title of President over both the settlements of Madras and Bengal. Thus Bengal became again subordinate to Madras. Though the permission to raise fortifications in Bengal was still refused by the Great Mogul; a war ship of 72-guns was consequently dispatched from England to cruise the Bay of Bengal. In 1690 the Company secured the city of Calcutta from the Nawab of Bengal against the payment of rupees 1,200 per year.

The three Presidencies of Bombay, Madras and Calcutta were established by the end of the seventeenth century. From 1708 all English factories were placed under these Presidencies. Each Presidency was under a separate President who was also the Commander-in-Chief of military forces.

During the initial years the Company followed the policy of peaceful trade, advocated by Thomas Roe. It avoided all attempts for gaining territorial possessions, because it felt that it could prove ruinous to the English interests in India. However, towards the close of the eighteenth century a change took place in the policy of the English. Taking an advantage of the downward trend in the law and order situation in India, they began entertaining political ambitions and gradually adopted the policy of territorial acquisition. Due to the increasing disorder in the country the Company was obliged to make necessary arrangements for its own defence. In view of the changed circumstances Gerald Aungier, President of the factory of Bombay, informed the Court of Directors that "the times now require you to manage your, general commerce with the sword in your hands." Accordingly, Josiah Child, the President of the Board of Directors of the Company approved of a change in Company's policy in 1687. The British in India were advised to establish such a politic of civil and military power and create and secure such a large revenue to secure both as may be the foundation of a large well grounded sure English dominion in India for all times to come. As a result of this change in the policy of the Company, its activities began to acquire political nature and its trade interests also continued to expand.

The prosperity that the employees of the Company enjoyed allowed them to return to their country with the ability to establish sprawling estates and businesses and obtain political power. Consequently, the company developed for itself a lobby in the British parliament. However, under pressure from ambitious tradesmen and former associates of the company, who wanted to establish private trading firms in India, a deregulating Act was passed in 1694. This act allowed any English firm to trade with India, unless specifically prohibited by act of parliament, thereby annulling the charter that was in force for almost one hundred years. By an Act in 1698, a new "parallel" company, titled the "English Company Trading to the East Indies" was floated under a state-backed indemnity of £2 million. However, the powerful stockholders of the old company quickly subscribed a sum of £315,000 in the new concern, and dominated the new body. The two companies wrestled with each other for some time, both in England and in India, for a dominant share of the trade. But it quickly became evident that in practice the original company scarcely faced any measurable competition. Both companies finally merged in 1702, by a tripartite indenture involving the state and the two companies.[18] Under this arrangement, the merged company lent to the treasury a sum of £3,200,000, in return for exclusive privileges for the next three years—after which the situation was to be reviewed. The amalgamated company became the "United Company of Merchants of England Trading to the East Indies" (henceforth the "East India Company").

In 1715 the English secured from the Mughal emperor Farrukhsiya a *firman*,[19] granting the company the privilege of trading in Bengal free of all duties on an annual payment of Rs. 3,000. The Company was also permitted to rent additional territory around Calcutta, and to retain its privilege of trading in the province of Hyderabad free of duty. The Company was exempted from all customs and other duties at Surat in return for the payment of an annual sum of Rs.10,000. The Company was permitted to mint its own coins, which were to have currency in the Mughal empire as well. Within few years of the issue of the Farman of 1716-17 the English fortified the city of Bombay as a measure of defence against the attacks of the Marathas and the Portuguese. The Company increased the number of its armed ships and entered into an alliance with the Peshwa to defeat the Angrias, who had dominated the Western coast from Bombay to Goa. The

18 On the 22 July, 1702, an Indenture Tripartite was made between Queen Anne of the first part; the old Company of the second part; and the new Company of the third part. The object of this was the union of the two Companies at the end of seven years. By the seventeenth article, the Queen granted that the General Courts of both Companies and their Sub-managers shall have the sole government of their forts; that they may coin foreign money in India; and that the old Company may convey Bombay and Saint Helena to the new Company. By the other articles the old Company Covenant to surrender their Charters in two months after the expiration of the said seven years into the Queen's hand, and the Queen engages to accept of such surrender; and from thenceforth the new Company is to be called *The United Company of Merchants of England trading to the East-Indies*, whose affairs shall be conducted by their own sole Directors, agreeable to their Charter of the tenth of King William the Third. And lastly, the Queen declares that this Indenture shall be construed in the most favourable sense for the advantage of both Companies.

19 The word *firman* comes from the Persian meaning "decree" or "order". A *firman* is an official, irrevocable decree issued by a Mughal monarch. Emperor Farrukhsiyar issued the British East India Company such a *firman* in 1717. It allowed the Company to live and trade for free in Mughal India, especially in the Mughal subha of Bengal, Bihar and Orissa. The Company got the freedom to export and import their goods in Bengal without paying taxes. The Nawabs of Bengal, however, showed scant regard for the imperial *firman*. The *firman* of 1717 had far reaching consequences on the subsequent history of the subcontinent. It was a great diplomatic success for the East India Company. It paved the way not only for the expansion of the Company's trade in the province of Bengal but also an increase of the influence of the English in the political arena of the country. Termed as the 'Magna Carta' of the English trade in Bengal, the *firman* granted undue advantages to the English over other traders. It also proved to be a serious drain upon the imperial revenue. Despite the rapid increase in the volume of the company's trade, the amount of the peshkash payable to the government was not raised.

Company captured Suvamdurg, a stronghold of the Angrias in 1755 and their capital Gheria next year

On 20 June 1756, the forces of Siraj-ud-Daulah, the Nawab of Bengal, destroyed the English factory at Calcutta's Fort William. After ransacking the factory, 146 Europeans were confined in a small unventilated prison-cell (known as Black Hole) for a whole night in the hot summer month of June. Within hours of their imprisonment, 123 prisoners were suffocated to death. The Black Hole became a legend for the atrocities committed by the natives of India against the 'heroic' traders of the EIC. According to British historian, the Battle of Plassey— fought a year later between the Nawab and the East India Company—was a direct outcome of the Black Hole.[20]

In 1757, Robert Clive led EIC forces against French-backed Siraj-ud-Daulah to victory at the Battle of Plassey,[21] thereby snuffing out the last known resistances in Bengal.[22] Siraj was betrayed by Mir Jafar in the battle, who was subsequently installed as the titular Nawab Nazim. This victory estranged the British and the Mughals, who had been served by Siraj as an autonomous ruler. But the Mughal Empire was already on the wane after the demise of Aurangzeb, and was breaking up into pieces and enclaves. After the Battle of Buxar, [23] the ruling emperor Shah Alam gave up the administrative rights over Bengal, Bihar, and Orissa.

20 There is a detailed account of incident of 'Black Hole' of Calcutta in Holwell J.Z., 1778, *A Genuine Narrative of the Deplorable Deaths: 20 June 1756*, London: Strand, pp. 56; by one of the survivors. However, his account has not been found absolutely reliable by a number of researchers. There is nothing in the Holwell's work that suggests that Siraj-ud-Daulah committed the act deliberately, though he did not take the trouble to see that they were looked after properly. Mason Philip, 2004, *A Matter of Honour: An Account of the Indian Army, Its Officers and Men*, Dehradun: Natraj Publishers, p. 117.

21 The victory of Plassey, which gave the conspirators (Robert Clive and Mir Jafar, a general in the Siraj- Ud-Daulah's army) success, has been considered as the date of the foundation of the British Empire in India; for it gave the throne of Bengal to a man who owed everything to the English, and whom their support could alone sustain in power. Holms T. Rive, 1904, *A History of the Indian Mutiny*, London: Macmillan and Co. Limited, p. 4. However, according to Malleson, " ... no unbiassed Englishman, sitting in judgment on the events which passed in the interval between the 9th February 1757 and the 23rd June 1757, can deny that the name of Siraju'd daulah stands higher in the scale of honour than does the name of Clive. He (Siraju'd daulah) was the only one of the principal actors in that tragic drama who did not attempt to deceive." Malleson G.B., 1914, *Decisive Battles of India*, third edition, London: Reeves & Turner, p. 71.

22 In the battle of Plassy on 23 June 1757, Robert Clive with 2,000 EIC Indian soldiers and 800 European infantry and artillerymen defeated Siraj-ud-Daulah's army of 50,000. The key to his victory was the treacherous defections of three of the Nawab's commanders, Mir Jafar, Lutuf Khan and Rai Durlabh, all heavily bribed in a series of duplicitous negotiations which reflected no credit on anyone involved. For Clive personally, victory brought all the power, glory and money he had craved. Mir Jafar, to whom Clive had promised the throne of Bengal if he turned against Siraj-ud-Daulah, rewarded him lavishly on becoming Nawab. After Clive led the defence of Mir Jafar's lands against an invasion by the son of the Mughal emperor, Mir Jafar rewarded him with further, by no means unsolicited, large presents including a personal land grant. The EIC appointed Clive Governor of the East India Company Presidency in Bengal and from this period he began to advocate that the Company should take control of territory as well as trade in the region.

23 After the battle of Buxar in 1764, a treaty was signed between the defeated Nawab Shuja-ud-daulah of Awadh and the East India Company on 16 August 1765. The Company put a clause (Article 8) in the treaty which stated that, "His Highness shall allow the English Company to carry on a trade, duty free, throughout the whole of his dominions". [A copy of the treaty can be seen in the Appendix of this book]. Nawab had resented this clause as he feared a repeat in Aawdh of the abuses and dislocation caused by the Company's traders in Bengal. However, Clive

In 1765, Clive became the first British Governor of Bengal. In the due course, Mysore fell to the company forces in 1799, with the slaying of Tipu Sultan.[24] With the gradual weakening of the Maratha Empire in the aftermath of the three Anglo-Maratha wars, the British also secured Bombay and the surrounding areas. Thus, the British had secured the entire region of Southern India (with the exception of small enclaves of French and local rulers), Western India, and Eastern India. The last vestiges of local administration were restricted to the northern regions of Delhi, Oudh, Rajputana, and Punjab, where the company's presence was ever increasing amidst the infighting and dubious offers of protection against each other. Coercive actions, threats, and diplomacy aided the company in preventing the local rulers from putting up a united struggle against it.[25]

By early summer of 1769, the stock price of the EIC crashed and many of London's influential power brokers lost fortunes. In the meantime, corruption had become endemic as men of the EIC sought to line their pockets, make a fortune and retire. The purpose of the EIC was to make money. Now that the EIC was to financially administer the region and tax it, the Company could literally extract revenue from the inhabitants. The role of the Company in Indian politics and society could change but it was very difficult to change the Company's initial purpose, which was to make a large profit. These twin elements, revenue maximization and corruption were the reasons for the massive Bengali famine of 1770. In 1770 the annual summer monsoons came six months late and the region parched in the heat and crops failed. With little money or wealth left,

persuaded Shuja to allow merchants and their agents, holding the Company *dastaks* to freely pursue their trade in Awadh. Jain Shalin, East India Company's Trading Interests an Awadh: 1764-1787, *Proceedings of the Indian History Congress*, Vol. 62, 2001, pp. 390-399.

24 The first of the Anglo Mysore Wars saw the crushing defeat of an allied army of the Marathas, British and the Nizam of Hyderabad at the hands of Hyder Ali from 1766 to 1769. The second, fought between 1780 and 1784, saw the ascent of Tipu Sultan after Haider Ali's death in 1782. In the Battle of Pollilur (1780), the British were defeated at the hands of Tipu's forces that were armed with rockets. The major defeat in Pollilur was inflicted upon Colonel Bailey when his army's ammunition was destroyed after being shot at by a barrage of rockets. The invasion of Travancore by Tipu Sultan initiated the third Anglo Mysore War and resulted in the Treaty of Seringapatam, after its siege by the English. The signatories of the Seringapatam treaty (signed on 18 March 1792) included Lord Cornwallis on behalf of the East India Company, representatives of the Nizam of Hyderabad, and the Maratha Empire, and Tipu Sultan, the ruler of Mysore. Mysore ceded about one-half of its territories to the other signatories. The Peshwa acquired territory up to the Tungabhadra River; the Nizam was awarded land from the Krishna to the Penner River and the forts of Cuddapah and Gandikota. The East India Company received a large portion of Mysore's Malabar Coast territories between the Kingdome of Travancore and the Kali River as well as the Baramahal and Dindigul districts. Tipu Sultan, unable to pay an indemnity of 330 lakhs of rupees, was required to surrender two of his three sons as hostages of war. The fourth and last war saw the loss of the Mysore to the British and the death of Tipu Sultan in 1799.

25 After Clive defeated the Nawab of Bengal at Plassey, the Company quickly installed Mir Jafar – a general who had betrayed the defeated Nawab – as the first of a series of puppet rulers of Bengal. Plassey was followed by the systematic looting of Bengal's treasury. In a powerful symbol of the transfer of wealth that had begun, the Company loaded the treasury's gold and silver onto a fleet of over a hundred boats and sent them downriver to Calcutta. In one stroke, Clive had netted £2.5 million for the Company and £234,000 for himself. Today this would be equivalent to a £262 million corporate windfall and a cool £24.5 million success fee for Clive. Historical convention views Plassey as the first step in the creation of the British Empire in India. It is perhaps better understood as the East India Company's most successful business deal. Robins Nick, 2012, *The Corporation that Changed the World*, London: Pluto Press, p. 3.

the populace could not even afford what little food could be found. Finally, six months late, the monsoon came and swept through the drought ridden land as rivers overflowed and flooded the region. Hundreds of thousands of impoverished Bengalis died from hunger, disease, and floods. In all, as much as a third of the Bengali population died because of the Company's negligence, incompetence and greed.[26] For the officers of the East India Company, corruption was a lucrative way to amass personal profit.

These East India businessmen, called *nabobs* (a corruption of the Persian word for governor, *nawab*)[27] were widely caricatured, lampooned and vilified in the British press. British society also viewed the nabobs' massive wealth as potentially corrupting influences. For instance, Adam Smith, a Scottish, criticized the Company for its behaviour and its monopoly and accused the EIC of oppressing and dominating the East Indies. He argued that the Company's trade monopoly caused the famine in Bengal and labeled the EIC, a nuisance and a misfortune for all countries which fall under their government. And Adam Smith was one of many critics. This change in public opinion would not have been such a problem were it not for the fact that the Company faced enormous financial strain in the early 1770s.

In 1767 a committee of the House of Commons investigated the EIC's recent conduct of a military campaign in India, led by Robert Clive, in which it defeated a Mughal force and got control of an entire province, Bengal. Clive received £234,000, and the EIC in total, over £1,200,000, to place a puppet on the throne at Bengal. In the end, however, the issue was "settled" by the company agreeing to pay £400,000 a year to the government. However, in 1772, it told the government that not only could it not afford to pay the money, but it asked for a loan of £1,400,000. The EIC had to turn to Parliament for a bailout of an astounding £1,000,000 to avoid bankruptcy. The Parliamentarians were outraged as the Company, in their eyes guilty of pillaging and looting much of India for the personal enrichment of a band of rogues and adventurers, was asking for

26 As early as 1693, it appeared from Parliamentary inquiries, that the annual expenditure of the EIC, under the head of "gifts" to men in power, which had rarely amounted to above £1,200 before the revolution, reached the sum of £90,000. The Duke of Leeds was impeached for a bribe of £5,000, and the virtuous King himself convicted of having received £10,000. Besides these direct briberies, rival Companies were thrown out by tempting Government with loans of enormous sums at the lowest interest, and by buying off rival Directors. Marx, K., *The East India Company–Its History and Results*, New-York Daily Tribune, 11 July 1853.

27 The servants of EIC who came to India were without lands or high titles, bur when returned; they bought themselves into the high nobility and lived a life of luxury previously reserved only for monarchs. These British who reaped the wealth of India assumed the derogatory title 'Nabobs', a play on the princely Indian title. These servants of the EIC acquired and held their wealth through a combination of illegal trade and myriad forms of corruption which riddled the Company at every level. When one of these men—Warren Hastings—was put on trial by Edmund Burke, it brought the Company's exploits to the attention of the public. However, through the trial and after, the British government transformed public understanding of the Company's corrupt actions by creating an image of a vulnerable India that needed British assistance. For more details see: Noonan, John T. Jr, The Bribery of Warren Hastings: The Setting of a Standard for Integrity in Administration *Hofstra Law Review*, 1982, Vol. 10, Issue 4, Article 5, pp. 1073-1120. For more details see: Marshall, P. J., 1965, *The Impeachment of Warren Hastings*, New York: Oxford University Press; Holzman, James M., 1926, *The Nabobs in England: A Study of the Returned Anglo-Indian, 1760–1785*, New York: Columbia University Press.

money from the nation's purse. Parliament now had a golden opportunity to reform the Company and bring it under some form of oversight.[28]

Parliament's bailout of the EIC provided the impetus to regulate the EIC. It was part of the unintended legacy of the Seven Years War. Beginning in the 1770s a reform effort began to regulate and reform the Company. The movement was not a single act but a series of three major Acts of Parliament between the 1770s and the early 1790s. In 1773 Sir John Burgoyne, MP and British general succeeded in passing a motion for Parliament to begin investigations into the Company's corruption and mismanagement. This set the ball rolling for the first of two acts. The first was a bailout of the EIC, and the second was the Regulating Act of 1773.[29] It was the first major Parliamentary reform of the EIC. It raised the qualification to vote in the Proprietor's Court from £500 to £1000, established a board of directors who would serve six year terms, and established that the governor general of the Bengal presidency, located at Fort William, would have supervisory powers over the other two presidencies at Madras and Bombay. Finally, the act established a supreme court consisting of a chief justice and three associate justices.

Warren Hastings was made Governor General of Bengal at the age of 40 years, who remained in this position until his resignation and return to England in February 1785. For thirteen years he was the most important holder of political power in Bengal. He had to deal with a variety of Indian rulers, already dependent to varying degrees on the British, and had to face their insubordination or revolts. Hastings supplied Company's army to the ruler of Awadh in exchange for a considerable sum. In 1775, he took a large sum of money from the Raja of Benares which was earlier being paid to the King of Awadh. From the family of the Nawab Wazir of Awadh, Asaf-ud-daula, Hastings was successful in forcibly extracting a huge wealth. He was considered as one of the most corrupt Governor and faced a trial at London, but was finally acquitted.[30]

By the Charter Act of 1793, the Company's commercial privileges were extended for a further period of twenty years.[31] Lord Cornwallis was given special power at the time of his appointment,

28 See generally: Adam Smith, 1937, *An Inquiry into the Nature and Causes of the Wealth of Nations,* New York: Modern Library.

29 The Regulating Act of 1773 [An Act for Establishing Certain Regulations for the Better Management of the Affairs of the East India Company, as well in India as in Europe, 13 Geo. 3, c. 63.]

30 He "did not only give and receive bribes accidentally." He formed plans and systems of government for the very purpose of accumulating bribes and presents to himself. He descended into the muck and filth of peculation and corruption. He was not only a public robber himself, but the head of a system of robbery, the captain-general of the gang. E. Burke, Speech in General Reply (14 June 1794), The Works of Edmund Burke, p. 235, 295. Also see: Noonan, John T. Jr., The Bribery of Warren Hastings: The Setting of a Standard for Integrity in Administration, *Hofstra Law Review*, Vol. 10, Issue 4, Article 5, 1982. Available at: http://scholarlycommons.law.hofstra.edu/hlr/vol10/iss4/5.

31 By the East India Company Act, 1793 (13 Geo. III, c. 63), the Parliament of Britain clearly established its sovereignty and ultimate control over the company. The act recognized the company's political functions and clearly established that the acquisition of sovereignty by the subjects of the Crown is on behalf of the Crown and not in their own right. The Act introduced substantial governmental control and allowed the land to be formally under the control of the Crown, but leased to the company at £40,000 for two years. Under this provision, the governor of Bengal, Warren Hastings (1732–1818) was promoted to the rank of Governor General, having administrative powers over all of British India. Hastings was entrusted with the power of peace and war.

to override his Council but it was not extended to all Governors or Governors-General by the Charter. Greater emphasis on the power of the Governor-General over the other two Presidencies, Bombay and Madras, was given in the Charter. The Governor-General was given the power to appoint a Vice-President to act in his place during his absence from Bengal, from amongst the civilian members of his Council. When the Governor-General would be present in Bombay or Madras he was to supersede the local Governor as the head of the administration during the period of his stay there. The Charter Act of 1793 also effected some change in the Home Government. The Board of Control was to consist of a senior member who was designated as President and two other junior members were not necessarily to be members of the Privy Council. All members of the Board of Control were to be paid their salaries from the Indian revenues and not out of the British Exchequer.

The year 1803 is a good symbolic date for the start of empire. General Gerard Lake defeated the Marathas, perhaps the most important Indian power, and entered Delhi, the Mughal capital. By this time the emperor was mostly a figurehead, but symbolically important. He now became a pensioner of the British, with his realm reduced to the Red Fort. A British official, referred to as the Resident, became de facto ruler of Delhi. Company soldiers protected the city and commercial interests.

On the eve of the renewal of the Charter Act in 1813 a controversy was raised as to whether the Company should continue to enjoy commercial monopoly in India. English traders demanded a share in the Indian trade, particularly in view of loss of trade in the Continent due to the Continental System of Napoleon Bonaparte who sought to cripple England commercially. The English traders wanted to compensate their loss by sharing the Indian Trade. It was also thought if the East India Company which had vastly extended its territories in India should be allowed to continue as a monopolistic trading Company besides its political responsibility; it was ultimately decided that the Company's commercial monopoly should go and by the Charter Act of 1813 the Company was deprived of its commercial monopoly and laid down 'the undoubted sovereignty of the Crown' in and over the possessions of the East India Company.

The East India Company was, however, allowed to enjoy the monopoly of China trade and trade in tea. The share-holders of the East India Company vehemently opposed abolition of Company's commercial monopoly and ultimately a guarantee of 10 percent dividend out of the revenues of India was given them should the commercial account fail to provide this amount. Separate accounts were to be maintained of the territorial revenues and commercial transactions and gains.

The Charter Act of 1813 devised as well as extended the power of direction and superintendence of the Board of Control. One of the most important clause of the Charter Act of 1813 was that a sum of rupees one lakh annually was provided for the revival and improvement of literature and encouragement of the learned natives of India and for the introduction and promotion of knowledge of the sciences among the inhabitants of the British territories in India. This was the first step towards acceptance of the principle of State responsibility for education. Needless to say, that this clause was one of the most significant steps taken by the British Government with regard to India. The evangelicals forced the Company, by getting included in the Charter Act of 1813 to appoint a bishop whose headquarters were to be in Calcutta and his see the whole of British India. The whole of the country (India) was to be open to the Christian missionaries.

Before the time of the renewal of Charter arrived great changes had taken place in Great Britain. The result of the Industrial Revolution showed itself in the coming of Machine Age in Britain and unprecedented hugeness of production of finished goods which were being exported to foreign countries. There was a great influx of wealth through export trade. The labouring class began to agitate for improvement of their economic condition. With the coming of the Whigs to power in 1830 the way for the triumph of liberal principles was opened. Laissez Faire was accepted as the principle of government's attitude towards industrial enterprise. The liberal movement resulted in the Reform Act of 1832. In this atmosphere of liberalism and reforms the Parliament was called upon to renew the Charter in 1833. There was a winding up of the Company and the British Crown should take over the administration of India. But majority opinion in the Parliament did not share this opinion which agreed with Lord Macaulay's contention that the Company would continue to exist with certain changes in matters of control and the renowned historian James Mill, a Benthamite, was also associated with the India House. The Charter Act of 1833 is replete with their personal influence.

The Charter gave another lease of life for twenty years to the East India Company which was to administer the Indian territories "in trust for His Majesty, his heirs and successors". The Company's commercial privileges were all abolished and henceforth it was to function as a political organisation. India was to pay the Company's debts and the Company's share-holders were to receive 10.5 percent dividend per annum till 1874 as compensation for the abolition of the Company's Commercial privileges.

Under the Charter Act of 1833, the President of the Board of Control became Minister for Indian affairs. Other members of the Board were not to continue but the Minister was to have two Assistant Commissioners who were not to be his colleagues but only his assistants. The Secretary to the Minister occupied considerable power as he represented and spoke in the House of Common on behalf of his boss when the latter sat in the House of Lords. All this was a prelude to the appointment of the Secretary of State for India. The Directors of the Company were to act as expert advisers to the President of the Board of Control. The Charter centralised the Indian administration and the Governor-General of Bengal was now made the Governor-General of India. The Governor-General in Council was empowered to superintend, control and direct both the civil and military affairs of the Company.

The Presidencies of Calcutta, Bombay and Madras and other territories of the Company were placed under the fullest control of the Governor-General in Council and all revenues were to be raised under the authority of the Governor-General in Council and expenditure was also to be controlled by the same body. All powers—administrative and financial—were centralised in the hands of the Governor-General in Council.

Before the Charter Act of 1833 there was much confusion in the administration of law and justice as there were diverse laws of conflicting nature in force. For instance, the Acts passed by the British Parliament, the Charter Acts, laws made by the Governors-in-Council of different Presidencies, orders of the Supreme Court which differed in many respects and were even conflicting in some cases and there was no uniformity between the laws passed by different Presidencies. All this created much confusion in the administration of law and justice. The result was utter chaos and confusion in administering criminal law in particular. Influx of a large number of Europeans who settled in different parts of India made it all the more necessary that a uniform system of law should be introduced. The Charter Act of 1833, therefore, provided that the Governor-General in Council would make laws for India, and the former law-making powers of the Bombay and Madras Presidencies were abolished.

The laws passed by the Governor-General in Council were to be enforced by all courts in British Indian territories. The Governor-General in Council was also empowered to amend, repeal or otherwise modify laws passed hitherto before as also make laws for all the servants of the Company, whether residing within the Company's territories or in the territories under the native Princes in alliance with the Company.[32]

The Charter Act of 1833 enlarged the Executive Council of the Governor-General by adding to it a fourth member—Law Member, for legislative purposes only and the fourth member was to give professional advice to the Council in matters of law-making, and could cast his vote only for the purpose. A special arrangement was, however, made in case of Lord Macaulay who was the first Law Member and he was permitted to attend all meetings of the Governor-General in Council. A Law Commission was formed for the purpose of consolidating, codifying and improving the Indian Laws.

One of the most important provisions of the Charter Act of 1833 was that it removed the distinction between Indian and the natural born subject of the British Crown residing in India and no one would be disqualified for any place in the Company's service by reason of his religion, place of birth, descent, or colour. As the Directors pointed out the aim of this provision was not to ascertain qualification but to remove disqualification. There was to be no governing caste in British India and whatever might be the test of qualification, "distinction of race or religion shall not be there". Fitness would be only criterion of eligibility. The Act of 1833 also enjoined upon the Government of India to take measures for the abolition of slavery and improvement of the condition of the slaves.

The Charter Act of 1853 was the last Act passed for East India Company on expiry of the Act 1833. The charter was renewed but no substantial changes were made. However, this was for the first time, that this charter act, unlike other charter acts, did not fix any limit for the continuance of the administration of the company in India. The act provided that the Indian territories will remain under the Governance of the company, until the parliament otherwise directed. The revolt of 1857-58 offered the opportunity as the demand for divesting the Company of its authority over the Company's territories. There were decisive changes as a result of 1857. The Mughal dynasty

32 Code of Military conduct and discipline, Articles of War as well as making provisions for the administration of justice were all placed within the powers of the Governor- General in Council which was not, however, empowered to alter the constitution of the Company or amend the Charter Act, nor could it alter the prerogatives of the Crown nor enact against laws passed by the Parliament or do anything that would militate against the authority of the Parliament. The Mutiny Act was also beyond the Governor-General in Council.

was terminated, as was the Company. The British government took over direct rule, replacing the Company's administrative apparatus with an Indian Civil Service (which became the Indian Administrative Service after independence). In 1858, by the Act for the Better Government of India, the Crown assumed all governmental responsibilities held by the company, and its 24,000-man military force was incorporated into the British army. In 1877, Queen Victoria was proclaimed Empress of India, a symbolic exclamation point. Governor-Generals, referred to as Viceroys (after 1858), came and went, but the direction remained clear: Imperial rule for the profit of Britain, not for the welfare of the people of India—this was shown even in the governmental response to famines, and India became represented as the Jewel in the Crown.[33]

In the beginning of the seventeenth century, when the British came to India, it contained one-fifth of the world's population; it was a civilization rich in wealth, philosophy, literature, religion and art. India was a far greater industrial and manufacturing nation than any in the Europe. The East India Company was basically a business enterprise and its main concerns were those of merchants, ensuring profit for shareholders, while maintaining good relations with the British government and local rulers in the India who authorized them to trade. The Company, under the patronage of British Kingdom invaded and pillaged India through the power of their artillery and the cynicism of their amorality. In 1686, the Company's directors had declared their intentions to establish a large, well-grounded, English dominion in India for all time to come. They displaced nawabs and maharajas for a price, emptied their treasuries as it pleased them and stripped farmers of their land they tilted for generations.[34] A trading company became a garrison state and expanded its territories enormously. It issued coins, passed laws, shifted wealth from Asia to Europe and commanded an army of occupation. The servants of EIC traded, cheated and plundered the country; what British committed was a rape of a Continent.[35]

33 The British had a ruthless economic agenda when it came to operating in India and that did not include empathy for native citizens. Under the British Raj, India suffered countless famines. But the worst hit was undivided Bengal. Under the Mughal rulers, when famines had hit the country, the rulers were quick with useful responses to avert major disasters. After taking over from the Mughal, the British had issued widespread orders for cash crops to be cultivated. These were intended to be exported. Thus, farmers who were used to growing paddy and vegetables were now being forced to cultivate indigo, poppy and other such items that yielded a high market value for them but could be of no relief to a population starved of food. The natural causes that had contributed to the drought were commonplace and there was no backup of edible crops in case of a famine. It was the single-minded motive for profit that wrought such devastating consequences. No relief measure was provided for those affected. Rather, taxation was increased to make up for any shortfall in revenue. The deadliest famine to occur after 1771 was in 1943, when three million people died and others resorted to eating grass and human flesh in order to survive. Winston Churchill, the hallowed British War prime minister was callous about the roaring famine that was swallowing Bengal's population. He casually diverted the supplies of medical aid and food that was being dispatched to the starving victims to the already well supplied soldiers of Europe. When entreated upon, he said, "Famine or no famine, Indians will breed like rabbits." The Delhi Government sent a telegram to him painting a picture of the horrible devastation and the number of people who had died. His only response was, "Then why hasn't Gandhi died yet?" For more details see: Rakhi Chakraborty, The Bengal Famine: How the British engineered the worst genocide in human history for profit, available at: https://yourstory.com/2014/08/bengal-famine-genocide.

34 Tharoor S., 2017, *Inglorious Empire: What British did to India*, London: Hurts and Company, p. 2.

35 See: Durant Will, 1930, *The Case for India*, New York: Simon and Schuster, p. 10.

Chapter II

The Military in British India (1600-1947)

During the seventeenth and early eighteenth centuries, the prominent foreign traders in India included the Portuguese, the Dutch East India Company and the London-East India Company. Amongst them, the Portuguese were the most militarized,[1] followed closely by the Dutch,[2] and the English Company did not have any significant armed forces.[3] During the initial phases of expansion of their trade, the London-EIC used their fortifications to defend existing settlements and avoid conflict whenever possible. In 1611, an English vessel sailed up the Coromandel (Eastern coast at Masulipatam) and founded the nucleus of a factory at Petapolee. The jealousy of Dutch and Portuguese had by this time risen high that the London-Company was obliged to employ force against them. In November 1612, Captain Best defeated a superior Portuguese fleet in the Bay of Surat. Impressed with the outcome of conflict, the reigning Mogul disallowed the Portuguese claim to a monopoly of the trade and agreed to a treaty granting important privileges to the English. An English ambassador was also allowed at the Mogul Court. This was perhaps the first offensive use of military by the EIC in the region. By 1650s, a supreme presidency was established at Surat with special charge of the Persian trade, a subordinate presidency at Madras with control of the factories on the eastern coast and in Bengal, and a third presidency at Bantam for direction of the traffic with the Eastern Islands.

1 Portuguese were the first of the European nations to gain a footing in the East Indian peninsula in 1490s. In 1493 Bartholemew Diaz doubled the Cape of Good Hope, and five years later Vasco da Gama arrived on the Western or Malabar Coast, and after a second voyage obtained permission to establish a factory at Calicut. His work was continued by Albuquerque, under whose care the Portuguese power in India was more widely extended. During his time Goa was made the chief centre of Portuguese influence and Ceylon (Sri Lanka) became tributary to Portugal's king. The Portuguese personnel engaged in trade in India were a militarized arm of the government.

2 In 1595, a Dutchman, James Houtmann, sailed from the Texel, and presented himself as the first rival of the Portuguese by the establishment of a factory at Bantam in Java. Nearly half of employees in the Dutch Company were military personnel. The governor-general of the Dutch Company was of the view that trade without war, and war without trade cannot be maintained.

3 The two first voyages of the London-EIC followed the track of the Dutch to Sumatra and Java, but in the third the ships were driven by stormy weather into Sierra Leone, whence one of them under Captain Hawkins sailed direct to Surat, and found there good promise of opening trade. In 1609 Hawkins visited Agra in person and obtained privileges from Jehangir, the reigning Mogul (eldest son of Akbar); but his influence was soon undermined by Portuguese Jesuits.

Military Forces of the East India Company

The East India Company dispatched the first expedition to Bengal consisting of two ships in 1640. The Company decided to further their trading interest and finally established a factory at Hooghly. The Bengal settlements were dependent on that of Fort St. George, while their trade was subject to the control of the Native government of Bengal. The Company was forbidden to have any military beyond "an ensign and thirty men" for honour to the principal agents.

The new charter of 1660 empowered the Company to send ships of war, men, and arms to their factories for defence of the same, and to make peace or war with any people not Christians. Authority was also granted for the fortification of St. Helena, which since 1651 had become the port of call on the voyage to India, and stringent provision was made for the maintenance of the Company's monopoly. In 1662 Sir Abraham Shipman was accompanied by 400 soldiers to take possession and to remain as governor of Bombay. However, finally when they landed in Bombay, in March 1665, the four hundred had dwindled to one officer and 113 men.

In 1668, when the King leased Bombay to the East India Company, its garrison consisted of 20 commissioned and non-commissioned officers, 124 privates and 54 Topasses.[4] This force eventually became the nucleus of the 1st Bombay European Regiment. Authority was also given for the Company to enlist officers and men for their own service, as well as to call in certain garrisons of the King's troops at Bombay and Madras to fill up vacancies.[5] The men and officers of the King's troops took service with the Company under its own military code and articles of war, and thus was founded the first military establishment in Bombay. The men agreed to serve for three years only, which gave them an additional interest as the first English soldiers ever enlisted for short service. Between 1669 and 1677, Gerald Aungier served as both the President of Surat and Governor of Bombay. He recognized the military importance of Bombay and ordered the construction of a fort within the city and raised a local militia in 1670. In 1672, he obtained sanction for the supply of uniforms for the whole of his troops to be of one colour for the greater awe of the adversary. In 1677, the Court of Directors empowered Aungier to employ force where necessary for the observation of treaties and grants. In 1684, the Bombay garrison was augmented by the enrolment of two companies of Rajputs as auxiliary force. The order to enroll two companies of "Rajputs from the main" to be commanded by their own officers but

4 The Topasses were Christians, generally of mixed blood, but claiming Portuguese origin. They were armed, clad, and disciplined after the European style, and incorporated among the English Companies. From wearing a hat (topie), instead of the turban, as generally used by the natives, these half-caste troops acquired the nickname of "Topasses," and were generally considered inferior in courage to the higher caste of natives and the Mohamedans of India.

5 Bombay was the first territorial possession of the British Crown in India, after the King had in 1668 ceded its ownership to the East India Company. It was the most important and strongest place in the Company's possession and thus had preference over the settlements in Madras and Bengal. The first Governor General of the British possession in India was appointed in the person of Sir John Child in 1686 in Bombay, though this precedence was short lived. Bombay was exposed to threats from the fleets of England's European rivals, the France and the Dutch, and from the country powers, the Moguls Empire and the Maratha Kingdom. Cadell Sir Patrick, 1938, *History of the Bombay Army*, London: Longmans, Green & Co., p. 3.

to share duties with European soldiers probably indicates the first attempt at organization of the Indian soldiers.[6] Finally, in 1684 Bombay was made the headquarters of the Company in India.

In 1681 Bengal became independent of Madras and Mr. Hedges arrived as the Company's "Agent and Governor in the Bay of Bengal and the factories subordinate." The first Governor took with him from Madras a party of a corporal and 20 soldiers, which was increased in 1683 to 100 soldiers, together with arms and accoutrements sufficient for another company.

When the British first began to raise Indian troops for the defence of their trading stations, it was to the jemadari system that they turned, as the normal local way of finding soldiers. The first such men were a company of Rajputs, commanded by their own officers and armed with their own weapons, raised at Madras in 1664.[7] Similar Rajput companies were raised in Bengal in 1682. All these companies probably deployed Purbias by the middle of the following companies. The Indian officers when recruiting gave preference to the members of their own families and would have been thought by members of their own society to have behaved disgracefully had they acted otherwise. The Purbias soldiers were thus continued to be deployed in the expanding British Indian Army, especially in the Bengal which was stationed nearest to their home area.[8]

The traders of the Company had been subject to the jealous repression and exactions of the Native government for many years. Owing to the smallness of their numbers to enforce their claims, the Company's ventures had been thwarted and their trade impoverished to such a degree that the Company decided to equip an expedition of sufficient strength to assert the rights of their agents and to make definite terms with the Emperor Aurangzeb and Nawab Shaistah Khan, the Governor of Bengal. This expedition consisted of a fleet of ten ships bearing six complete companies of infantry, which were augmented by the seamen to ten companies (1,000 men). It was further increased by a force of 400 men from Madras, and a company of Portuguese infantry (called Topasses) raised by Job Charnock, the chief agent at Hooghly.

However, when the expedition arrived at the mouth of the Hooghly the fleet had already lost a third of its strength due to adverse winds and weather conditions. Several months were passed in desultory fighting and negotiations, until the British forces were reduced to the utmost straits by the effects of the climate, and found themselves hemmed in by overwhelming numbers and obliged to make their last stand on the fever-stricken island of Ingelli. At this crisis an offer of further negotiations was gladly accepted by Charnock. In August 1687 a treaty was finally

6 See generally: Haig, Lt Col Wolesley, The Armies of the East India Company, in Dodwell, H. H. (ed.), *The Cambridge History of India, Vol. VI*, London: Cambridge University Press, 1932, p.153-166.

7 No statistical information is available on the militarization of EIC in Madras in the 18th century. A quasi-military force of Indians was maintained at all the principal settlements on the Coromandel Coast. Portuguese, Dutch, English, Danes and French had kept bodies of peons in pay. In times of crisis these peons were largely augmented. Such temporary levies were called "Poligars peons" who belonged to local sub-castes which claimed to be hereditary soldiers. Few writers have claimed that these men were trained in European methods of fire and tactics. However, the peons employed on the Coromandel Coast were never considered as a serious military force until near the middle of the 18th century and even long after that, their military value remained very uncertain. Dodwell H., 1922, Sepoy Recruitment in the Old Madras Army, Calcutta: Government Printing Press, pp. 76.

8 Heathcote T.A., 2013, *The Military in British India: The Development of British Land Forces in South Asia 1600-1947*, South Yorkshire: The Praetorian Press, p. 25.

concluded with Nawab Shaistah Khan, by which the English regained their former rights and received assurances for the future.

However, within a year the oppressions of the Nawab recommenced. Charnock again took recourse to negotiations; but while these were in progress, an armed frigate bearing 160 men under the command of Captain Heath, arrived from England. It was sent by the Court of Directors to carry into execution the orders which had been given to the leaders of the former expedition. Captain Heath, an impatient and hot-tempered man, immediately had recourse to hostilities, seized and pillaged Balasore and made a demonstration before Chittagong. On finding that his violence or negotiations were not of much avail, Heath carried of the whole of the Company's troops, servants and portable property to Madras.

In August 1690, terms having been again agreed on with the Emperor, and Shaistah Khan having been succeeded by Ibrahim Khan as Nawab of Bengal, Charnock, with the Company's servants, returned to the Hooghly and established themselves at Sutanati. For some years the settlement continued to increase rapidly without further retribution from the Native government. However, in 1695 the rebellion of Suba Singh, a zemindar of Burdwan, threatened the safety of the Company's settlements. In order to protect their interest, the Company enlisted Native soldiers for the protection of their property and the fortifications of their trading centres at Chinsura, Chandernagore, and Calcutta. In 1660s, the East India Company had been permitted to enlist troops for the defence of its factories. The charter of the new Company, granted in 1698, empowered that company to 'raise, train, and muster such military forces as shall and may be necessary for the defence of the said forts, places and plantations'.[9] The British army in those days faced serious issues of indiscipline relating to drunkenness and desertion. The earliest armies were regulated by Articles of War issued on the prerogative of the Crown and valid only during the duration of any given conflict.

In 1699 Bengal was made a Presidency. Sir Charles Eyre was appointed President; and the fort at Calcutta, which was named Fort William, in honour of King William III. The military force at this time amounted to some 130 men, exclusive of a small party of artillerymen called "the Gunner and his Crew." For many years the trade and prosperity of Calcutta continued to increase rapidly; and although the military establishment appears to have kept pace with that of other branches of the service, yet no serious danger threatened the settlement until the year 1742, when the Mahrathas devastated the whole province and sacked the town of Hooghly. At this juncture

9 The Company to have the government of all their forts, &c. and to appoint governors and other officers: And we do, of our more especial grace, certain knowledge and mere motion, for us, our heirs and successors, give and grant unto the said English Company trading to the East Indies, that the said Company, for the time being, shall and may have the ordering, rule, and government of all such forts, factories, and plantations, as shall be, at any time hereafter, settled by or under the said English Company, within the East-Indies, and parts before mentioned, and shall and may name and appoint governors, and officers, from time to time, in and for the said forts, factories, and plantations, and them to remove and displace at their will and pleasure; and that such governors, and officers, shall and may, according to the directions of the same Company, raise, train, and muster such military forces as shall or may be necessary for the defence of the said forts, places, and plantations respectively; the sovereign right, power, and dominion, over all the said forts, places, and plantations, to us, our heirs and successors, being always reserved. Regulated by various Acts of Parliament, especially 33 Geo. 3, cap. 52. Sec. 9: 53 Geo. 3, cap. 155, sec. 80, 81: 3 & 4 Wm. 4, cap. 85, sec. 25, 42, 58.

the European and Armenian inhabitants were, for the first time, regularly embodied into a militia; a number of lascars were also inducted to help the gun-room crew in working the guns, and the so-called Mahratha Ditch[10] was commenced round the settlement; however, the Mahrathas did not advance, and the latter work was abandoned.

The inadequacies of native soldiers were revealed when the town of Madras was easily captured by the French in 1746. It was the French who first realized the advantages of training Indian soldiers on European lines. In 1746, an engineer officer in the French service, Paradis, with 230 French soldiers and 700 sepoys, had successfully attacked and defeated forces of an Indian prince consisting of 10,000 soldiers and strongly posted with guns.[11] In view of increasing French threat to English possessions in India, in 1748, Major Stringer Lawrence was given command of all the East India Company's forces. He followed the French example and raised the first few companies of Indian soldiers who were trained and equipped in English style. These sepoys were commanded by their own "Subedars," but were led by European officers. Soon after Major Lawrence's reforms in Madras, changes were made in Bombay and Bengal Presidencies. The war with France had revealed the shortcomings of the organization of the "gunner and his crew" in British artillery. Therefore orders were issued to the three Presidencies that each was to maintain one company of artillery with one second Captain, one Captain Lieutenant, one 1st Lieutenant, one Fire-worker and one 2nd Fire-worker. The rank and files included 4 sergeant bombardiers, 4 corporal bombardiers, 2 drummers and 100 gunners, all of British origin. They also appointed a captain and engineer to command all three artillery companies. As far as the artillery was concerned no Indian, foreigner, person of mixed breed, or any Roman Catholic was inducted for the service.[12]

In the beginning of 1750s, sixty-eight foreigners, of whom fifty were Germans, deserted from the French to Company's army camp near Trichinopoly, and were divided equally amongst the

10 When the Bargis (as the Marathas were known locally), started plundering the Bengal countryside, the Nawab was still powerful, and the British were in the process of developing their trading outpost at Calcutta (now known as Kolkata) in West Bengal, India. Maratha Ditch (archaic Maratta Ditch) was a three-mile long moat was excavated around Calcutta in 1742, as a protection against possible attacks by marauding Bargis. The Bargis, however, never came to the city. Later, the ditch proved to be useless when the Nawab of Bengal, Siraj ud-Daulah, came and ransacked the British settlement in 1756. The ditch was never completely built. It was mostly filled up in 1799 to build the Circular Road and the remainder was filled up in 1892–93. The area bound by the ditch was considered to be the original town of Kolkata.

11 The English appealed to Anwar-uddin the Nawab of Carnatic, for protection and assistance and the latter requested Dupleix, the French Governor to raise the seige of Madras. But the French did not accede to his request. Since the Nawab had no naval fleet, he was not in a position to intervene effectively. Yet he felt that he could teach the French a lesson on land and therefore sent an army against the French troops besieging Madras. Despite its impressive size his troops suffered an ignominious defeat at the hands of the French. This battle of San Thome was the first occasion of many which proved that a resolute attack by properly trained men could easily defeat the force ten times as numerous.This was an eye-opener for the Europeans in India; it revealed that even a small disciplined European force could easily defeat a much larger Indian army. This knowledge was invaluable to them in future dealings with Indian princes. Also see: Mason Philip, 2004, *A Matter of Honour: An Account of the Indian Army, Its Officers and Men,* Dehradun: Natraj Publishers, p. 29-30.

12 The *Army in India and its Evolution,* The Government of India, Handbook, Calcuttta, 1924, p.7.

English and Swiss Companies of Infantry.[13] The Company was also facing problems of desertions as the German and Swiss mercenaries were insisting on maintaining their own separate code of discipline.[14] They were inclined to desert to French or any country power which might offer better wages. Certain concessions were granted to them by the Company. The Mutiny Act of 1754 replaced the old Articles of War as the basis for military discipline in British India.[15] The Mutiny Act also provided that the officers of the British army were to have seniority over officers of the Company's service in the same rank. However, this provision being unreasonable became a source of grievance in India, since it failed to consider the seniority within each rank. During this period the Company's military authorities gradually replaced the 'peon' or 'watchmen' by new kind of Indian soldiers or sepoys.[16] They were trained by the European officers and sergeants, armed and dressed in the European style and promised pay in the European way, i.e. cash at the end of each month. Sepoys were formed into companies on the European model, each headed by its own subedar and commanded by a British officer. [17]

In 1756 the Nawab Siraj-ud-Daulah succeeded to the Government of Bengal. According to the British historians, the Nawab had deep-rooted hatred against the English which culminated into open hostilities against the Company's settlements. Having attacked and taken the factory of Kasimbazar, with its little garrison of two officers (Lieutenant Elliot and Surgeon Forth) and 42 regular soldiers (of whom less than half were Englishmen), he advanced on Calcutta with his whole army, and crossed the Hooghly on the 15 June 1756. The fort was ill-arranged and had poor defences; the ammunition was scanty and inferior; the guns dismounted and use less, and

13 Wilson Lieutenant Colonel W. J., 1882, *History of Madras Army*, Vol. I, Madras: E Keys, Government Press, p. 70.

14 In June 1752 the Captains of the Swiss mercenary companies claimed certain privileges which included: constituting a Council of War within themselves having authority to pronounce sentence of life and death on the criminals brought before them; using their discretion, and inflict their own particular punishments, at the will and pleasure of the Commander; having a specific uniform, different from the national troops, and also a particular manner of beating the drum; exempting them from the duties laid by the Sovereign on certain commodities, such as wine and provision. However, the Government declined to grant any distinction between the English and Swiss troops. The Swiss protested and took up the matter with Governor Suanders. About this time Major Lawrence returned from England, and by his advice the certain privileges were granted to the Swiss Captains were granted. This included: (i) To chastise and inflict from their own private authority over corporal punishment as judged necessary by the Captain, in regard to the soldiers and the Serjeants and Corporals of the Swiss company; to keep them in prison as without being obliged to explain the reasons for it to any one; whipping of criminals before the parade must be with the consent of superior. Wilson Lieutenant Colonel W. J., 1882, *History of Madras Army*, Vol. I, Madras: E Keys, Government Press, p. 64-69.

15 In 1754 the first legislative enactment for the regulation of the Company's military force was passed, and under it Articles of War were framed which, with slight modification, continued to guide the service for many years. The regular military establishment at this time appears to have consisted of five companies of infantry and one of artillery.

16 The first Native foot soldiers in the service of Government were known as Peons. In February 1747, about 3,000 peons were employed at Fort St. David, of whom about 900 were armed with muskets. Being wholly undisciplined, and officered exclusively by natives they were of little use for some time, but they gradually replaced, owing to the care taken in the selection of their Commandants and to their being employed in the field with European troops. Wilson Lieutenant Colonel W. J., 1882, *History of Madras Army*, Vol. I, Madras: E Keys, Government Press, p. 72.

17 Heathcote T.A., 2013, *The Military in British India: The Development of British Land Forces in South Asia 1600-1947*, South Yorkshire: The Praetorian Press, p. 23.

the garrison amounted only to some 500 men, of whom but 174 were Englishmen. As the hostility commenced, the Native soldiers deserted, the Commandant and a large number of the officers of militia, embarked in the available boats, went on board a Company's ship which was lying in the river and dropped down to Govindpur, leaving the unfortunate remnant of the garrison to their fate. On 20 June the fort was captured by Nawab and that night the incident of the "Black Hole" took place.

The survivors of the British inhabitants, together with a re-enforcement of three ships from Bombay, took refuge at Palta. In August 1756, they were joined in by some 230 men from Madras under Major Kilpatrick, while a volunteer company was also formed, including a number of civil servants, among whom was the future Governor General, Warren Hastings. Further re-enforcements were solicited from Madras which reached Palta in the end of December 1757. Clive, with a force of about 2,400 men, [18] advanced from Palta on 27 December, and, after some fighting, took the fort of Budge-Budge on the 29th. The forts of Tannah and Aligarh were abandoned by the Nawab's troops without a shot being fired, and in January 1758 Fort William was recaptured by the Comapany. Hooghly was re-taken on 17 January by a force detached under Major Kilpatrick; and on a large body of about 5,000 of the Nawab's forces were defeated at Gongi, near Bandel, by 50 British soldiers and 100 sepoys under Captain Eyre Coote.

Whilst these expeditions were in progress, Clive turned his attention toward securing the footing just regained by the English in Bengal. He found his small army confronted on the one side by the forces of the Nawab, with whom all attempts at negotiation proved useless, and on the other, by the French settlers[19] of Chandernagore. There was a pressing need for re-enforcements by the formation of a battalion of sepoys. The native troops (called Buxarries, and in Madras Telingas or Peons) which had been employed so far were wholly undisciplined, and were armed and equipped in Native style; even the more carefully trained Madras and Bombay sepoys adhered to Native dress and equipment. Clive, however, tried the experiment of assimilating them as nearly as possible to European troops. Having raised some three or four hundred picked men, he furnished them not only with arms but also with dress of European pattern, drilled and disciplined them as regular troops, and appointed a British officer and non-commissioned officers to command and instruct them. This, the earliest Bengal Native regiment, was for many years known as the Lal Paltan (platoon), on account of its equipment.[20] At the end of January re-enforcements arrived in Bengal of artillery and stores: and on the 5 February Clive attacked and defeated the Nawab's army, which had advanced within the Company's territory, near Cossipore.[21] A treaty of

18 The expedition now comprised 250 men of His Majesty's 39th Regiment, 570 of the Madras European infantry, 1,200 Madras sepoys, some details of artillery, 230 Bengal European infantry, and 70 volunteers, making a total of about 2,400 men.

19 During this time in the Europe, the war had been declared between England and France.

20 Later 'Lal Paltan' went by the name of Gilliez-ki-pallan, from Captain Primrose Galliez, who obtained command of it in 1763 and held that post for many years. It became the 2nd Battalion of the 12th Bengal Native Infantry in 1796.

21 The British loss (including the Royal Navy) was 57 killed and 117 wounded, of whom 18 of the killed and 35 of the wounded were sepoys; that of the enemy was reckoned at 1,300. The total casualties in action up to this period, in

peace with Siraj-ud-Daulah was the result of the battle. [Copy of treaty] Clive's won the French settlement of Chandernagore on 23 February.

This success induced a large numbers of Natives to apply for service in EIC's army, and Clive's newly raised battalion of sepoys was largely augmented. Meantime, while perfecting the drill and discipline of these troops, Clive was also negotiated with Mir Jafar Khan, the Nawab's principal officer in Bengal. On 16 June the army reached Patli, and on the 18 June, Major Eyre Coote, with a force of 200 Europeans and 500 sepoys, attacked and captured Katwa. Clive advanced from his position on the 22 June and arrived at Plassey next day morning.

The Battle of Plassey was a decisive victory of the British Company over the Nawab of Bengal and his French allies on 23 June 1757. The battle consolidated the Company's presence in Bengal, which later expanded to cover much of India over the next hundred years. The battle took place at Plassey (Palashi) on the banks of the Hoogley River, south of Murshidabad then capital of Bengal. The belligerents were the Nawab Siraj-ud-Daulah, the last independent Nawab of Bengal, and the British East India Company commanded by Robert Clive. Siraj-ud-Daulah had become the Nawab of Bengal the year before, and he ordered the English to stop the extension of their fortification. Siraj-ud-Daulah had a numerically superior force and made his stand at Plassey.[22] The British, worried about being outnumbered, formed a conspiracy with Siraj-ud-Daulah's demoted army chief Mir Jafar, along with others, who assembled their troops near the battlefield but made no move to actually join the battle. Robert Clive has bribed Mir Jafar, the commander-in-chief of the Nawab's army, and also promised him to make him Nawab of Bengal. Siraj-ud-Daulah's large army was defeated by 3,000 soldiers of Robert Clive, albeit deceitfully. The battle ended in 11 hours. The EIC forces were successful in killing Nawab's commander Mir Madan Khan. The Nawab fled the battlefield on a camel escorted by 2,000 horsemen. Mir Jafar was duly installed in power as a British puppet.

Siraj-ud-Daulah arrived at Murshidabad at midnight on the 23 June and next day fled the city. Clive entered Murshidabad on 29 June and placed Mir Jafar Khan on the seat of Nawab. On 3 July, Siraj-ud-Daulah was brought back a captive to Mir Jafar, and on the same night was ruthlessly murdered by order of Miran, the son of the new Nawab. For two months after the victory of Plassey, Clive was occupied in exacting from Mir Jafar Khan the indemnity previously agreed upon, and in settling the disputes which arose amongst the British officers, military and naval, over the partition of the same. At the same time he turned his attention to the increase of the military forces of Bengal, and enlisted men for a second regular battalion of sepoys. He formed the corps on drafts from the old battalion. Meanwhile a small force of French under Monsieur Law, which had marched from Bhagalpur to the assistance of Siraj-ud-Daulah, on hearing of

the Army, appear to have amounted to 41 Europeans (including 6 officers) and 18 Natives killed, and 78 Europeans (including 9 officers) and 55 Natives wounded,—192 in all.

22 The strength of the forces engaged were: British artillery, including 50 sailors, 150 men, with 8 six-pounder guns and two small howitzers; British infantry (detachments of the 39th Foot, and of the Bengal, Madras and Bombay European infantry), 750; Topasses, 200; Native infantry, Madras and Bengal, 2,100. The Nawab Siraj-ud-Daulah's army is said to have numbered 50,000 foot and 18,000 horses, with a very powerful train of artillery. The French had sent artillerymen to bolster the Nawab's cannon to more than fifty guns. The balance of forces seemed to make a British victory impossible.

the overthrow of that prince, made towards Patna with the intention of joining the Rajah Ram Narayan. In order to prevent his junction, a detachment was dispatched under Major Coote, on 6 July, consisting of 220 British troops and 500 sepoys, with a detail of artillery. On their march occurred the first recorded instance of a Native court-martial in Bengal, when a sepoy was tried for conniving at the escape of a prisoner, and sentenced, by a court composed of Subadars and Jemadars of the detachment, to receive 500 lashes and be dismissed from the service.

On 17 November Clive marched from Calcutta, and joined the Nawab at Murshidabad; with him was a force of 550 British, some details of artillery, and 1,500 sepoys; while the Nawab was accompanied by a force of 40,000 men. Following the route by which Coote had advanced in July, the combined force arrived at Patna on 4 February 1758. Robert Clive raised a third battalion of sepoys, composed, for the most part, of men enlisted in the Bhojpur district. During this time the new fort at Govindpur, the present Fort William, was completed. In July he accepted the post of President of the newly re-organised local Government, and forthwith set about measures of considerable importance to the military strength of Bengal. Instead of sending back to their presidencies the British detachments from Madras and Bombay, all who volunteered for service in Bengal were formed into a Bengal European battalion, into which also were received a number of volunteers, both officers and men, from His Majesty's 39th Regiment; and a fourth battalion of sepoys was raised in September 1768. The command of this corps was soon afterwards conferred upon Lieutenant Hugh Grant, from whom it became known as *Grant-ki-paltan.* [23]

Expedition to Vishakhapatnam: Meanwhile, the French successes in the Carntic were becoming more and more pronounced, and the Madras Government appealed to Bengal for assistance. On 12 October 1758, a strong detachment was sent by Clive under Lieutenant-Colonel Francis Forde, the Commandant in Bengal, with orders to proceed by sea to Vizagapatam, and, by creating a diversion there, to render assistance to the Madras Government. With this detachment were five companies of the Bengal European Battalion, the 2nd Artillery Company, the 1st and 2nd Bengal Native Battalions, and a battalion of Madras sepoys (who had come to Bengal in 1756). This was the first occasion on which Bengal sepoys were sent by sea on active service.

Battle of Condore and the Siege of Masulipatam: Colonel Forde met the French army of the Northern Circars, under the Marquis de Conflans, on 8 December 1758 at Condore, about forty miles from Rajahmundry, and defeated them.[24] Colonel Forde advanced on 9 December, accompanied by the Rajah Anandiraj of Vizianagram; while a detachment was sent in advance under Captain Knox seized the town and fort of Rajahmundry on the 10th. After some delay, on 6 February 1759 the English force occupied Ellore. After seizing the French factory of Narsipur, Forde advanced and stormed the fort of Konkale on 3 March. He continued his march to Masulipatam. On the morning of 8 April, the French commander de Conflans surrendered

23 In the re-organisation of 1796 it became the 1st battalion of the 2nd Regiment.

24 As Forde's forces advanced to the attack, the two Bengal Native battalions, which were on the flanks, were fully exposed to view, while the European Battalion, which formed the centre, was completely concealed by high standing crops: the French, moving obliquely to their right to attack the Native battalion forming the left of the British line, exposed their left flank to the British centre; thrown into great confusion by a deadly volley from the British battalion, they fell back hastily, and the volley being succeeded by a charge, they were, after a short but severe combat, driven from the field with loss.

and fort of Masulipatam came to the Company. These successes of the Company lowered the morale of the Nizam, who had previously been lending aid to the French, and he opened negotiations with Colonel Forde. By December 1759, the effectiveness of the French on the east coast had diminished. The 40 years succeeding the Battle of Plassey were marked by extension of Company's territory in every direction. In 1760, Clive went home to Englnad where he was feted and admired. He was granted King's commission as a lieutenant colonel. The Prime Minister, Pitt described him as a "heaven-born general."

The expansion of the Company's armed forces did not end with the conclusion of the Seven Years War in 1763. Faced with the withdrawal of the royal troops (the 84th Regiment of Foot were ordered home in October 1763) and the need to maintain a firm hold on recently acquired territories, the directors of the Company were of the view that the advantages gained during the previous decade 'could not be preserved without a respectable military Force'. The military expert military like Generals Stringer Lawrence and John Caillaud and Engineer John Call recommended that this force should consist of 2,500 to 3,000 European infantry, 200 cavalry, 300 artillery and 5,000 native sepoys at each of the Presidencies of Fort William and Fort St. George.

During the 1760s and 1770s the EIC was in the process of transforming itself from a trade-focused commercial enterprise into a landholding quasi-state within the broader British Empire. There was a massive expansion of the EIC armies in the Bengal and Madras Presidencies. The restructuring of the military establishment resulted in the expansion of the Company's forces throughout the seventeen-sixties. The total number of troops employed by the Company rose from 55,052 in 1766 to 64,192 in 1771, with a marked rise occurring at Fort William: from 9,921 in 1763 to 27,762 in 1768. At this time the officers of the Indian troops were selected from among the officers of the European regiments, and were chosen, not only for their soldierly qualities, but also from the point of view of their suitability for serving with the Indian troops. With the increase in the strength of the Indian forces in all three Presidencies the British military officers of the Company faced a number of organizational issues. They enjoyed many advantages, but on the other hand they found themselves in position subordinate to those younger officers of the King's troops. This implied inferiority was resented and these officer asserted their rights and demanded equity of treatment.[25] This resulted in the reorganization of the Company's armies which took place in 1796.[26] At this time the European soldiers in India, including both the Kings and Company's, were 13,000, while the number of India troops were 57,000 (Bengal 24,000, Madras 24,000 and Bombay 9,000). This reorganization reduced the strength of the native armies, but there was a great increase in the establishment of British officers in unit.[27] The Indian

25 Cardew Alexander, 1929, The White Mutiny: A Forgotten Episode in the History of the Indian Army, London: Constable & Co Ltd, p. 11.

26 In 1794 memorials were presented to the Court of Directors by 500 European officers of the Bengal Army, and by numerous officers of the Madras and the Bombay Armies, setting forth their grievances. The whole position of the Indian Armies was then elaborately examined and discussed. These issues were considered in providing various welfare measures life furlough, retirement benefits and pension to the officers. Ibid., p. 6.

27 Previous to this reorganization the establishment of British officers in a battalion had been a commandant and adjutant besides 10 subalterns commanding companies, a total of 12. In the 1796 reorganization, besides the Colonel commanding the regiment, each battalion was given an establishment of 1 lieutenant colonel, 1 major, 4 captains, 11 lieutenants, 5 ensigns (besides 1 British NCO), a total of 23 British officers. Ibid., p. 12.

infantry regiments were formed by linking existing battalions and amalgamating half-battalions of reduced regiments with them. In selecting the units to be amalgamated, no regard was paid to considerations of sentiments or community of tradition. This new organization, which was not completed till 1804, improved the prospects for promotion of the British officer. In addition, establishment of general officers was instituted and furlough regulations and pension rules were introduced. At the same time, these reforms decreased the dignity and authority of the Indian officers in the Company's service. By 1805, the strength of the Presidency armies was as shown in the table below:

	British Troops	Indian Troops	Total
Bengal	7,000	57,000	64,000
Madras	11,000	53,000	64,000
Bombay	6,500	20,000	26,500
Total	24,500	130,000	154,500

The East India Company Act of 1813 [53 Geo. III. Cap. 155] gave power to the Government of the three Presidencies to make laws; regulations and Articles of War to govern the activities of all officers and soldiers 'within the limits of the said Company's Charter.

The Government in India empowered to make laws, regulations, and articles of war, for the native troops; and to hold courts-martial

XCVI. And whereas doubts have been entertained whether the several governments of the said Company have sufficient power in all cases to make laws and regulations and articles of war, for the order and discipline of officers and soldiers, being natives of the East-Indies, or other places within the limits of the said Company's Charter, in the service of the said Company, and for the administration of justice by courts-martial to be holden upon such officers and soldiers; and it is expedient that such doubts should be removed: be it therefore enacted and declared, that the several governments of Fort William, Fort Saint George, and Bombay,[28] have and shall, during the continuance of the term hereby granted to the said Company, be deemed and taken to have full power and authority to make all such laws and regulations and articles of war, as they may think fit, for the order and discipline of all officers and soldiers, natives of the East-Indies, or other places within the limits of the said Company's Charter, in their respective services, and for the administration of justice by courts-martial to be holden on such native officers and soldiers, and for the constitution and manner of proceeding of such courts-martial, and for all other purposes relating to or in any manner concerning such native officers and soldiers, in as full and ample a manner as the said governments respectively may make any other laws or regulations for the government of the natives of the several territories subject to the said presidencies respectively, any Act of Parliament, or other matter or thing, to the contrary notwithstanding: provided always, that all laws, regulations, and articles of war, hereafter to be made respecting any of the matters aforesaid, whereby the rights, persons, or property of any such native officers or soldiers may be affected, shall be made and promulgated in every respect in the same

28 The Governor-general in Council was the only local authority at this time possessing the power of legislation.

> manner as other regulations affecting the rights, persons, or property of natives or other individuals amenable to the provincial courts of the presidency of Fort William in Bengal, are directed to be made by virtue of an Act passed in the thirty-seventh year of his Majesty's reign, intituled, "An Act for the better Administration of Justice at Calcutta, Madras, and Bombay, and for preventing British Subjects from being concerned in Loans to the Native Princes in India."

Later it was clarified that the rules framed originally for the maintenance of discipline in the British Army were applicable to all the rank and file of the native army too. In fact there was no clearly codified law to administer the native army. This was also highlighted by the Judge-Advocate-General of Bombay stating that none of the three Presidencies has as yet established Laws, Regulations or Articles of War for the better government of the Native Troops. Thus, the Act of 1824, confirmed that in the absence of such laws, the legislation meant for the British Army should apply to the native army of each Presidency. Under the statutory provisions of the Acts of 1813 and 1824, a new military code was framed in the Madras Presidency to enforce discipline in the native army. The Act of 1833 empowered the Governor-General-in-Council to enact laws applicable to all native officers and soldiers. In consequence of the powers conferred upon the Governor-General-in-Council by the Act of 1833, a common code called the 'Articles of War for the Native Armies' was enacted in 1845, which was replaced by the Act XIX of 1847.

The 1857 Mutiny and Subsequent Reforms

From May 1857 onwards, a spontaneous uprising swept parts of northern India. The British termed it as the Indian Mutiny, others as the Indian Uprising of 1857, and for a substantial section of Indians it was a full-fledged revolt against an exploitative British Raj.[29] The native army as a whole did not join the revolt but a considerable section actively fought on the side of the government. By an estimate, nearly 70,000 soldiers joined the uprising at various times and most were either disarmed or deserted the service.[30] The Indian soldiers, who took part in the 1857 Mutiny, inflicted violence not only against the British military personnel, but also on civilians and women. According to one of the British officer who fought in the 1857 Mutiny, about one fifth of the European inhabitants were killed by the mutineers. The rebels also destroyed property

29 1857 Mutiny: There is no universally agreed name for the events of this period. In India and Pakistan it has been termed as the "War of Independence of 1857" or "First War of Indian Independence", but it is not uncommon to use terms such as the "Revolt of 1857". The classification of the Rebellion being "First War of Independence" is not without its critics in India. The use of the term "Indian Mutiny" is considered by some Indian politicians as belittling the importance of what happened and therefore reflecting an imperialistic attitude. Others dispute this interpretation. In the UK and parts of the Commonwealth it is commonly called the "Indian Mutiny", but terms such as "Great Indian Mutiny", the "Sepoy Mutiny", the "Sepoy Rebellion", the "Sepoy War", the "Rebellion of 1857", "the Uprising", and the "Revolt of 1857" have also been used. "The Indian Insurrection" was a name used in the press of the UK and British colonies at the time.

30 The 1857 Uprising was one the major events in the colonial India. A large section of the Bengal army, which garrisoned Bengal and North India, revolted. There were troops who remained loyal during the course of 1857. They were Punjab troops (80,000), Bombay Army (36,710), Madras Army (59, 391), Nepal troops (10,000), British troops (24,263 which later increased to about 80,000). Menezes Lt Gen S.L., 1999, *Fidelity and Honour: The Indian Army form Seventeenth to the Twenty-first Century*, Delhi: Oxford University Press, p. 198-201.

and houses inhabited by the British. In fact all the symbols of state institutions were attacked.[31] The British military officers and the troops under their command also attacked unarmed Indian civilians.[32] No mercy was shown to a deserter or mutineer by the Company's military authorities. A "pandy" deserter,[33] caught red handed was hanged to the nearest tree or death at the cannon's mouth was assured. No trials under the military law were held, and this penalty was imposed to a large number of deserters/mutineers. At some instances, men were placed along the edge of the precipice overhanging a river and were shot one by one.[34] A British military officer contributed the success of its military in containing the 1857 Mutiny to their 'racial superiority'.[35]

During the Mutiny only a remnant of the Bengal army remained faithful to the Company. All the contingents connected with it joined, sooner or later, in the rebellion. The Punjab Frontier Force—which formed a separate army, recruited from a different country, and which was brought into contact with the regular army, came to the aid of the British force in the Punjab, and took a highly prominent role in the suppression of the rebellion. The Bombay army, although recruited to some extent from Upper India, generally escaped the contamination. In the Madras Army, which was recruited entirely in Southern India, one regiment only of cavalry showed a mutinous spirit, and was disbanded.[36]

The Mutiny of 1857 gave the death-blow to the system of 'double government', with its division of powers and responsibilities. The Government of India Act, 1858 declared that India was to be

31 The 1857 Mutiny in the Bengal Army was mainly caused by service issues coupled with interference in religious and social customs. The cartridge issue was used by some sepoys, mainly the ringleaders, as a pretext to oppose the state. The Bengal Army had become an interconnected brotherhood because sepoys were recruited from a restricted area and among too few castes. These sepoys had little outlet for ambition, the discipline of the Bengal Army as a whole had become too lax and the power of commanding officers to punish and reward them had diminished. The best British officers had abandoned their regiments for more attractive civil employment and those who commanded the native companies exhibited poor leadership qualities. David Saul, 2009, *The Bengal Army and the Outbreak of the Indian Mutiny*, New Delhi: Manohar, pp. 15-32.

32 When James Neel with the Madras Fusiliers marched from Benaras to Allahabad, he systematically executed nearly 6,000 Indians. The men killed were shopkeepers, artisans, peddlers and porters. They were hanged on the branches of trees. The favourite phrase amongst the white soldiers was "to bag the niggers." Their objective was to frighten the people into submission and docility. The dead bodies hanging at the market place and roads were visible symbol of the British atrocity. Roy Kaushik, "The Beginning of 'People's War in India," in *1857: Essays form Economic and Political Weekly*, Hyderabad: Orient Longman, 2008, pp. 135-160.

33 Mutineers were called "Pandy". It originated from the word "Pandey," one of the commonest surnames among the Oudh Brahmins in northern India.

34 For more details see: Menezes Lt Gen S.L., 1999, *Fidelity and Honour: The Indian Army form Seventeenth to the Twenty-first Century*, Delhi: Oxford University Press, p. 144-187.

35 He writes: "It was a question of race. This race of ours has been gifted by Providence with the qualities of manliness, of endurance, of a resolution which never flags. It has been its destiny to conquer and to maintain. It never willingly lets go. Its presence in England is a justification of its action all over the world. Wherever it has conquered, it has planted principles of order, of justice, of good government. And the Providence which inspired the race to plant these great principles, endowed it with the qualities necessary to maintain them wherever they had been planted." Malleson Colonel G.B., 1891, *The Indian Mutiny of 1857*, London: Seelay and Co. Limited p. 410.

36 Chesney General Sir George, 1894, *Indian Polity: A view of the system of administration in India*, London: Longmans, Green and Co., pp. 222.

governed directly by and in the name of the Crown, acting through a Secretary of State, to whom were to be transferred the powers formerly exercised either by the Court of Directors or by the Board of Control. Power was given to appoint a fifth principal Secretary of State for this purpose. The Secretary of State was to be aided by a council of fifteen members, of whom eight were to be appointed by the Crown and seven elected by the directors of the East India Company. The major part both of the appointed and of the elected members were to be persons who had served or resided in India for ten years, and, with certain exceptions, who had not left India more than ten years before their appointment. The members of the council were to hold office during good behaviour, but to be removable on an address by both Houses of Parliament, and were not to be capable of sitting or voting in Parliament. The council was charged with the duty of conducting, under the direction of the Secretary of State, the business transacted in the United Kingdom in relation to the government of India and the correspondence with India. The Secretary of State was to be the president of the council, with power to overrule in case of difference of opinion, and to send, without reference to the council, any dispatches which might under the former practice have been sent through the secret committee. The property of the Company was transferred to the Crown. The Board of Control was formally abolished. With respect to contracts and legal proceedings, the Secretary of State in Council was given a quasi-corporate character for the purpose of enabling him to assert the rights and discharge the liabilities devolving upon him as successor to the East India Company.

Reforms in the Armed Forces

It was observed that under the authority given by various Acts, the Company raised and maintained separate military forces. The troops belonging to these forces, whilst in India, were governed by a separate Mutiny Act, perpetual in duration, though re-enacted from time to time with amendments.[37] The Company also had a small naval force, once known as the Bombay Marine, afterwards as the Indian Navy, and now represented by the Royal Indian Marine.

The Act of 1858 transferred to the service of the Crown all the naval and military forces of the Company, retaining, however, their separate local character, with the same liability to local service and the same pay and privileges as if they were in the service of the Company. Many of the European troops refused to acknowledge the authority of Parliament to make this transfer. They demanded re-engagement and bounty as a condition of the transfer of their services, and, failing to get these terms, were offered their discharge. In 1860 the existence of European troops as a separate force was brought to an end by an Act (23 & 24 Vict. c. 100) which, after reciting that it is not expedient that a separate European force should be continued for the local service of Her Majesty in India, formally repealed the enactments by which the Secretary of State in Council was authorized to give directions for raising such forces. In 1861 the officers and soldiers formerly belonging to the Company's European forces were invited to join, and many of them were transferred to, the regular army under the authority of an Act of that year (24 & 25 Vict. c. 74). Thus the European army of the late East India Company, except a small residue, became merged in the military forces of the Crown. The naval force of the East India Company was

37 The first of these Acts was an Act of 1753 (27 Geo. II, c. 9), and the last was an Act of 1857 (20 & 21 Vict. c. 66), which was repealed in 1863 (26 & 27 Vict. c. 48).

not amalgamated with the Royal Navy, but came to an end in 1863, when it was decided that the defence of India against serious attack by sea should be undertaken by the Royal Navy, which was also to provide for the performance of the duties in the Persian Gulf which had been previously undertaken by the Indian Navy.[38] The change effected by the Government of India Act, 1858, was formally announced in India by the Queen's Proclamation of 1 November 1858. Thus, the Indian Army came under the direct responsibility of the Queen.

On 15 July 1858, a Royal Commission (Chairman Major-General Jonathan Peel) had been set up in London to inquire into the organization of the Indian Army.[39] The Peel Commission was asked to respond to eleven questions regarding the future organization of the army. Six questions (numbers 1,3,7,9,10,11) related with the involvement of the natives, including the terms of the Indian Army's transfer to the Crown, the proportion of European to native troops, the possibility of mixing European and native troops in regiments or brigades, etc., the remaining five questions (numbers 2,4,5,6 and 8) were exclusively about European troops.[40]

1. On what terms should those in Company's army be transferred to the service of the Crown?
2. How many European troops should be permanently stationed in India once the Mutiny campaign was over?
3. What should be the proportion of European to native troops in the cavalry, artillery and infantry respectively?
4. Was the European element to be made of troops from the British Army serving limited tours of duty in India, or should it be raised for permanent local service there?
5. What was the best means of regularly relieving the former, or maintaining the efficiency of the latter?
6. Would it be possible to consolidate the Company's European forces with the British Army and allow subsequent exchanges, with justice to all Company officers?
7. Should European and Indian troops be mixed at either regimental or brigade level?

38 Ilbert Sir Courtenay, 1922, *The Government of India: A brief Historical Survey of Parliamentary Legislation Relating to India*, Oxford: Claredon Press, pp. 94-112.

39 The Chairman of the Commission, Major-General Jonathan Peel was the Secretary of State for War and brother of the late Prime Minister. His ten co-members were: Lord Stanley, Commissioner for Indian Affairs (and later Secretary of State for India); the Duke of Cambridge, Commander-in-Chief of the British Army; General the Marquess of Tweeddale, the former Governor and Commander-in Chief of Madras; Lieutenant-General Sir George Wetherall, Adjutant-General of the British Army; Lieutenant-General Sir Harry Smith, a veteran of the Peninsula, Waterloo and Ist Sikh War; Major-General Viscount Melville, commander of a Bombay cavalry brigade in the 2nd Sikh War; Major-General Henry Hancock, the former Adjutant-General of the Bombay Army; Major-General Patrick Montgomery; Colonel William Burlton; and Colonel Thomas Tait, the Commandant of the 3rd Bengal I. C. and the only member still a serving officer in the Indian Army.

40 Stephen P. Cohen, "The Untouchable Soldier : Caste, Politics and the Indian Army," *Journal of the Asian Studies*, XXVIII, 3 May, 1969, p. 34

8. Should troops for any European forces by kept up by Drafts and Volunteers from the British units in India or should be, as at present, separately recruited in Great Britain?
9. Should colonial troops be raised for service in India?
10. Should the native Indian forces or organized on the regular of irregular system, and in what proportion to each other?
11. Should the native component include artillery?
12. Should cadets for the native Army be attached to European units?

The important aspects of the responses of Commissioners on the questions were as follows: (i) No change should be made in the terms of employment for existing Company officers (i.e., rates of pay, pensions and promotion by seniority), but new regulations could be applied to future officers; (ii) The total number of Europeans necessary for the security of India should be about 80,000; of which 50,000 would be required for Bengal, 15,000 for Madras, and 15,000 for Bombay; (iii) The Native force should not have a greater proportion to the European, in Cavalry and Infantry, than two to one for Bengal, and three to one for Madras and Bombay respectively; (iv) The Local force should be abolished on the grounds that it caused professional jealousies and was less disciplined; (v) The European officers of the junior ranks (second lieutenants, cornets, and ensigns) be allowed to exchange from one Branch of the service to the other; (vi) Mixing of the European and native troops, would be detrimental to the efficiency and discipline of both; (vii) Recruitment to a Local European force should be kept up by drafts from England and "volunteers from the regiments of the Line" leaving India. (viii) All Bengal native cavalry should be on the "irregular system" (with a commandant, an adjutant, a medical officer and one European officer per squadron; (ix) Artillery should be mainly a European force; (x) and European cadets for native corps should be thoroughly drilled and instructed in their military duty in Britain before they were sent out to India.[41] To avoid unity amongst native soldiers, the Peel Commission recommended that 'the Native Army' should be composed of different nationalities and castes, and as a general rule, mixed promiscuously through each regiment. The establishments of the three Presidencies Armies remained the same but some changes took place in dress, equipment and armament.

The Commissioners made following additional recommendations: (i) The Native Amy should be composed of different nationalities and castes, and as a general rule, mixed promiscuously through each regiment; (ii) Men of the regular Native Army should be enlisted for general service; (iii) Modification should be made in the uniform of the Native troops making it more suitable to the climate; (iv) Europeans should, as far as possible, be employed in the scientific branches of the service, but that Corps of pioneers be formed, for the purpose of relieving the European sappers from those duties which entail exposure to the climate; (v) The Articles of War, which govern the Native Amy, be revised, and that the power of commanding officers be increased; (vi) Promotion of Native commissioned and non-commissioned officers should be efficiency based; (vii) The officers commanding regiments should have the power to promote noncommissioned officers,

41 David Saul, 2009, *The Bengal Army and the Outbreak of the Indian Mutiny*, New Delhi: Manohar, p. 311.

as exercised by the officers commanding regiments of the line; (viii) As far as practicable, fixed scales of allowances for the troops in garrison or cantonments and the field be provided; and (ix) The Commander-in-Chief in Bengal be styled the Commander-in-Chief in India, and that the General Officers commanding the armies of the minor Presidencies be Commanders of the Forces.[42]

General Grant was convinced that the absence of officers in the Bengal Army was central to the outbreak of mutiny. In a memorandum to Lord Canning, during his brief stint as Commander-in-Chief in Bengal after the death of General Anson in May 1857, Grant identified a "want of officers in whom the sepoy could confide" as one of the four factors that had given rise to a feeling of "dissatisfaction and distrust" among the Bengal sepoys long before their religious fears were played upon by conspirators. This, in turn, was caused by the fact that only few officers were present with their regiments. Further, "these officers are discontented only looking forward to leaving their regiments for some more pleasant employment, ... and never, as a general rule, mix or converse with their men; but, on the contrary, too often refuse to listen to their complaints, at the best telling them to go to the adjutant, and not infrequently, "Go to hell – don't bother me". Similar sentiments were expressed by many of the officers who gave written or oral evidence to the Peel Commission.

An important area of military reforms was an increase in the powers of commanding officer to punish and reward. In 1861, the Articles of War were revised, which went a long way in reforming the disciplinary system of the army. Article 3 gave commanding officers the summary power to reduce Non-commissioned officers (NCO) to the ranks and to discharge NCOs and soldiers by punishment. Every such dismissal or discharge carried with it a mandatory forfeiture of claim to pension. Article 67 gave commanding officers the option to try offences (except mutiny) normally applicable to a District Court Martial by a Regimental Court-Martial, albeit with the approval of officer commanding the Division.[43] Article 74 empowered the Commander-in-Chief of the Presidency to try native troops by courts martial who were subject to the Articles of War but not attached to the forces of any Presidency. Article 81 empowered the commanding officers to hold summary trials of native NCOs and soldiers and, on conviction, to carry out sentences without confirmation from higher authorities, as long as the sentences were not more severe than could be awarded by District Courts Martial.[44] Article 83 affirmed commanding officer's summary power

42 Only few recommendations of the Commission made any attempt to redress the type of professional grievances that many believed were responsible for the mutiny. This was mainly because the questions themselves were drafted with any such intention in mind. They were more concerned with the deterrent value of an enlarged European force, and therefore concentrated on its size and organization vis-à-vis Indian counterpart. David Saul, 2002, *The Indian Mutiny 1857*, New Delhi: Penguin Books, p. 400.

43 Articles of War of 1861, Article 67: When the Officer Commanding a Regiment or Corps considers that any Soldier under his command, who is charged with any offence declared by the foregoing Articles to be triable by a District or Garrison Court Martial, should be tried by a Regimental Court Martial, he may order the offender to be tried by such Court Martial, and shall report the case to the Officer Commanding the Division, stating the reason, for such order.

44 Article 81 provided, "The Commanding Officer any Regiment or Corps may summarily try any offence against these Articles of War committed by any person subject to these Articles (not being a Commissioned Officer,) and, on conviction, may sentence the offender and carry out such sentence without confirmation or any further authority;

to award minor sentences.[45] In an effort to increase the authority of the commanding officer, the Peel Commission recommended that efficiency should replace seniority as the dominant factor in the promotion of Indian native troops. Thus the vicious systems of promotion by seniority, which were sufficient to destroy the discipline in an army, had been abolished, and by new Articles of War, the commanding officers were vested with considerable powers, both for rewards and punishments. Three Acts of great importance to the civil administration were passed in the year 1861.[46]

As a result of the reorganization the establishment of the Indian forces in 1865 was as follows: [47]

provided that such sentence shall not exceed the sentence which a District or Garrison Court Martial might pass. A Commanding Officer holding a trial under this Article shall be deemed a Court Martial, and the words "Court Martial" in these Articles of War shall be deemed to include a Commanding Officer holding a trial. The proceedings on such trials by the Commanding Officer shall be conducted in the presence of two or more European or Native Commissioned Officers and shall be recorded in the English language, and the evidence shall be taken on oath or affirmation, and interpreted by an interpreter upon affirmation. The Commanding Officer shall record the finding and sentence, and the proceedings shall then be signed by such Commanding Officer, and by the Officers in whose presence the trial is held, and shall, without delay, be forwarded to the Officer Commanding the Division, who is hereby authorized to set aside the trial for reasons based on the merits of the case, but not on any merely technical grounds. Every sentence so awarded by a Commanding Officer may be carried out without waiting for its approval by the reviewing Officer." This system of court martial is akin to today's summary court martial.

45 Articles of War, 1861, Article 83 dealing with punishment of light offences provided: "For light offences, a commanding officer may, without the intervention of a Court Martial, award extra drill, restriction to barrack limits or within the lines of the, Regiment or Camp, confinement in the Quarter Guard or Defaulters Room or in Solitary Cell, removal from Staff situations, or acting appointments; or may order any soldier to be employed in piling and unpiling shot, and in cleaning accoutrements of men in hospital." Further, "The Commander-in-Chief of the Presidency shall prescribe the period not exceeding which offenders shall be liable to drill or confinement or restriction to local limits, as authorized by this Article."

46 These were: (i) The Indian Civil Service Act, 1861 (24 & 25 Vict. c. 54) which validated all the civil irregular appointments in the past, but scheduled a number of appointments which, in the future, were to be reserved to members of the covenanted civil service; (ii) The Indian Councils Act, 1861 (24 & 25 Vict. c. 67), which modified the constitution of the governor-generals executive council and remodelled the Indian legislatures. A fifth ordinary member was added to the governor general's council. Of the five ordinary members, three were required to have served for ten years in India under the Company or the Crown, and one was to be a barrister or advocate of five years' standing. Power was retained to appoint the commander-in-chief an extraordinary member; and (iii) The Indian High Courts Act, 1861 under which the Queen was empowered to establish, by letters patent, high courts of judicature in Calcutta, Madras, and Bombay, and on their establishment the old chartered supreme courts and the old 'Sadr Adalat Courts' were to be abolished, the jurisdiction and the powers of the abolished courts being transferred to the new high courts. Each of the high court's was to consist of a chief justice and not more than fifteen judges, of whom not less than one-third, including the chief justice, were to be barristers, and not less than one-third were to be members of the covenanted civil service. All the judges were to be appointed by and to hold office dicing the pleasure of the Crown. The high courts were expressly given superintendence over, and power to frame rules of practice for, all the courts subject to their appellate jurisdiction.

47 *The Army in India and its Evolution, Including an Account of the Establishment of the Royal Air Force in India,* (Reorganization in the Army After the War of 1914-18), 1924, Calcutta: Superintendent Government Printing, p. 19.

	Cavalry Regiment	Artillery Batteries	Infantry Regiments	Sappers and Miners
Bengal Army	19	-	49	1
Madras Army	4	-	40	1
Bombay Army	7	5	30	1
Punjab Frontier Force	6	4	12	-
Hyderabad Contingent	4	-	6	-

Table: The Indian Forces in 1865

The Commanding officers were given extra power in 1873, by which they could deprive good conduct pay to non-commissioned officers and sepoys. In the conduct of the Afghan War of 1878-1880, a number of defects in the Indian military system emerged. In 1879 an Army Organization Commission was assembled by Lord Lytton to reduce the military expenditure and recommend measures to improve the efficiency of the army in war. During this time the total strength of the Presidency armies was approximately 200,000 of which British troops were 65,000 and the remaining were the Indian. The immediate effect of the Commissions' recommendation was that one British officer was added to Indian cavalry and infantry regiments, and the reduction of the strength of the Indian armies by 4 cavalry regiments and 18 infantry regiments. However, the most important recommendation of the commission was to abolish the Presidency Armies, which was finally implemented sixteen years later. Certain other important changes were also made during this time. In 1884, the three ordnance departments were united under Government of India. In 1886 the Punjab Frontier Force was transferred from the control of the Government of Punjab to that of the Commander-in-Chief of India.[48] In 1886-87, for the first time, a reserve for the Indian armies was formed. The term of reserve services were of two types, an active and a garrison reserve. Service in the reserve was voluntary for men of not less than 5 years and not more than 12 years' colour. The garrison reserve was for men who were pensioned at 21 years' colour service or who had completed a combined colour and reserve service amounting to that period. The active service reserve was to be called up for one month training every year, and the garrison reserve for one month training every alternate year.

In the year 1895, all the three Presidencies armies were amalgamated to create the Indian Army, headed by a Commander-in-Chief (C-in-C).[49] Under the C-in-C there were four commands: the Madras Command (including Burma), the Bombay Command (including Sind, Quetta and

48 *The Army in India and its Evolution, Including an Account of the Establishment of the Royal Air Force in India*, (Reorganization in the Army After the War of 1914-18), 1924, Calcutta: Superintendent Government Printing, p. 22.

49 The Presidency Armies were abolished with effect from 1 April 1895 by a General Order of the Government of India in the Army Department, No. 981 dated 26 October 1894.

Aden), the Bengal Command, and the Punjab Command (including the North West Frontier and Punjab Frontier Force), each headed by a Lieutenant General.[50]

On 28 November 1902, Lord Kitchener took up the appointment of Commander-in-Chief in India and commenced the re-organization and redistribution of the army in India. On 1 January 1903, the designation, "Indian Staff Corps" was abolished and the officers belonging to the corps were designated, "Officers of the Indian Army". The title "Indian Army" was used officially from 1 January 1903.[51]

In order to reduce the extra expenditure, 9 Divisional Commands were established and the Madras Command, which was superfluous to the scheme, was abolished. Ina further redistribution in 1905, the distribution of Indian Army was done under the three Commands: Northern, Western and Easter. By 1908 the Army in India was again divided into Northern and Southern Commands which in turn were divided into various divisions under the control of Army Headquarters. The First World War revealed inadequacies in Kitchener's organizational scheme. Since there was too much centralization in Army Headquarters, the system proved a failure during the War.

During the First World War large number of troops, British as well as Indian were sent out of India to support the British war efforts in France and Flanders, in Egypt, Eats Africa and Mesopotamia (Iraq). The Indian troops also served in Salonica, Russia, Iran and elsewhere. On the eve of First World War in 1914, the Indian Army had a total of 190,140 combatants, accounting for three-quarters of the Army in India. The Indian Army's active soldiers were 152,500 and its reservists 35,000. The army was led by British officer corps of 2,600 active members and 40 reservists. By the end of war the number of Indian personnel under arms had risen 573,484. However, deployment of Indian forces in this war was not appreciated by the Government of India due to excessive pressure exerted by the War Officer India's limited military resources. In addition, Indian army's war losses were not easy to replace. The system of reserve which the scientific school of reformers had pressed upon India army for the previous thirty years failed. Most of the reservists who were recalled in August 1914 were unfit for active duty and recruiting new replacements also became difficult.

A number of cases of self-inflicted injuries were reported in the First World War. At First Ypres, the Indian Corps' medical staff estimated that of its total 1,848 Indian troops wounded between

50 The following local corps which were under the control of the Government of India but did not belong to any Command: (i) The Hyderabad Contingent, (ii) The Malwa Bhil Corps, (iii) The Bhopal Battalion, (iv) The Deoli Irregular Troops, (vi) The Erinpura Irregular Force, (viii) The Meywar Bhil Corps, and (ix) The Merwara Battalion. The Army in India and its Evolution, Including an Account of the Establishment of the Royal Air Force in India, 1924, Calcutta: Superintendent Government Printing, p. 24-25.

51 The additional reforms were: (1) On 9 January 1903 the Burma 1st Class District was separated from the Madras Command and constituted a separate independent Command, designated the Burma Command. (2) With effect from 1 April 1903, the Hyderabad contingent was broken up and delocalized. One cavalry regiment, the 3rd Lancers, Hyderabad Contingent, was absorbed into the other three, which were transferred to the Bombay Command, while the 6 infantry regiments of the Contingent were transferred to the Madras regiment. (3) The Punjab Frontier Force and its territorial areas were distributed between the Peshawar, Kohat and Derajat Districts. (4) In an Indian Army order No. 181 dated 2 October 1903, the new designations and numbers of all units of the Indian Army were published.

23 October and 3 November, 1049 had hand wounds, mostly on the left hand. The self-inflicted wounds were largely among particular battalions that went into action first. The soldiers probably believed that if they wounded themselves they could be sent home, in keeping with pre-war India army custom. General James Willcocks, the British military commander took serious action to deter further Indian self-infliction of wounds. Through summary general court martial, two of the Indian soldiers who had deliberately wounded themselves were sentenced to death and executed by firing squads.[52] A number of other soldiers were awarded imprisonment for 14 years. He imposed the new rule that the Indians having minor injuries, including those with hand wounds must return to duty once passed fit. Because of this measure, the hand-wounds rates amongst the Indian soldiers dropped.[53] Indian soldiers' grievance and resentments in France and Belgium caused a few of them to malinger in their hospitals, but there was no Indian mutiny on the western front. Indian discipline during the War was generally good. From October 1914 to February 1915, nearly 2.7 percent of the British Corps received court martial convictions, but the Indian rate was only 0.3 percent. James Willcocks, shortly before he left the Indian Corps, reported to Buckingham Palace, ".... The Truth is that the Indians have done well, beyond all expectations; they have stood a long test which indelibly stamps them as worthy of their Sovereign's uniform. .... They have freely given their lives, health, and most cherished ideas for England. Can man do more?"[54]

Initially Indian public had supported the war efforts; however, by 1916 the mood had changed. The world influenza epidemic had killed five million Indians and left many more millions depressed and distressed financially. Apparently, Mahatma Gandhi, champion of passive resistance and leader of the struggle for Indian home rule, played an active role in the recruitment of Indian soldiers during World War I, writing later that If we would improve our status through the help and cooperation of the British, it was our duty to win their help by standing by them in their hour of need. The strength of combatant troops of the Indian Army as on 11 November 1918 is shown in the table as follows:

52 Morton-Jack George, 2015, *The Indian Army on the Western Front: India's Expeditionary Force to France and Belgium in the First World War*, New Delhi: Cambridge University Press, p. 173. However, according to Corrigan (2015), official statistics of the war show that no sentence of death on a member of the Indian Corps on the Western Front was carried out (except in one case where a *Sowar* of the 16th Cavalry was shot by a firing squad of his own regiment in 1917 for the murder of an Indian officer). See: Corrigan Gordon, 2015, *Sepoys in the Trenches: The Indian Corps on the Western Front 1914-1915*, UK: Spellmount, p. 136. The statement by Corrigan appears incorrect because he has relied upon *Statistics of the Military Effort of the British Empire during the Great War 1914-1920,* War Office, HMSO, London, 1922. According to Oram (2000), the figure mentioned in the War Office document does not include Indian troops or civilians. See: Oram, Gerard Christopher, What alternative punishment is there? Military Executions During World War I, Ph D thesis, The Open University, 2000, p. 4.

53 Morton-Jack George, 2015, *The Indian Army on the Western Front: India's Expeditionary Force to France and Belgium in the First World War*, New Delhi: Cambridge University Press, p. 171-186.

54 Morton-Jack George, 2015, *The Indian Army on the Western Front: India's Expeditionary Force to France and Belgium in the First World War*, New Delhi: Cambridge University Press, p. 305.

	Indian Army			
	BRITISH		Indian Ranks	Grand Total Indian Army
	Officers	Other Ranks		
Cavalry	975	-	52,277	53,252
Artillery	166	-	10,469	10,635
Sappers & Miners	342	365	22,556	23,263
Signals	193	2,930	7,120	10,243
Infantry	5,422	-	470,669	476,091
Total	7,098	3,295	563,091	573,484*

* Exclusive of Indian Combatants in British Artillery and British Machine Gun Companies.
Source: The Army in India and Its Evolution, p. 219.

In 1919 there were fears that the second Indian mutiny which the British had guarded against for almost 60 years was about to break out. The threat of a breakdown in British control was serious in Punjab, which had a large number of ex-soldiers. The killing of hundreds of unarmed civilians in Jalian-wala-bagh by General Dyer's violated all the military norms on the use of force. Therefore, as soon as war ended, the Indian Office proposed setting up of a committee to the military system of India.

The public opinion expected the conditions of service of Indian soldiers must be improved up to the level of those in the Western countries. It was felt by the Government of India that an army well-equipped, well-paid, well-clothed, and well-housed, would be much more efficient and more contended. After the First World War, the next major reorganization of the Army was undertaken in 1922. The main aim was to improve the system of reserves and reinforcements. The government introduced major reductions in personnel and equipment in order to save money. The Indian infantry was re-organized into 20 regiments, each with an average of five combat battalions and a training battalion. The Gurkha battalion had 10 regiments each of two battalions and a depot. The cavalry regiments were reduced by amalgamating the existing regiments from 39 to 21. The total combat strength, including pioneers amounted to 107 battalions. Artillery, apart from mountain batteries was kept exclusively in the hands of British. These reductions allowed comparable cuts in the number of British units without disturbing the ration of British to India troops.

The following table shows the ratio of British to Indian troops from 1794 to 1939.

Ratio of British to Indian troops in British India: 1794-1939

Year	Number of troops: British	Number of troops: India	Indian soldiers per British soldier
Before the Mutiny			
1793	18,768	88,429	4.7
1805	24,891	167,674	6.7
1815	31,611	195,572	6.2
1857	45,522	232,224	5.1
After the Mutiny			
1863	62,000	125,000	2.0
1878	66,343	123,254	1.9
1901	66,086	142,831	2.2
1903	76,878	142,087	1.8
1905	78,370	150,410	1.9
1923	66,106	139,719	2.3
1939	43,000	177,000	4.1

The number of British/Indian troops mentioned in various sources differ: The figures of 1903 and 1923 are from *The Army in India and its Evolution, Including an Account of the Establishment of the Royal Air Force in India*, 1924, Calcutta: Superintendent Government Printing, p. 217 and 219. The Figures for 1939 are from Farwell Byron, 1989, *Armies of the Raj: From the Great Indian Mutiny to Independence, 1858-1947*, London: Viking, p. 51; while the remaining figures are from Omissi David, 1994, *The Sepoy and The Raj: The Indian Army, 1860-1940*, London: Macmillan, p. 132; Michael Duffy, "World-wide War and British Expansion, 1793-1815, P. J. Marshall (ed.), 1998, *The Eighteenth Century,* Vol. II, *The Oxford History of the British Empire,* Oxford: Oxford University Press, p. 202.

The Army was divided into four commands, each under a General Officer Commanding-in-Chief. The forces in various Commands were to be localized for service in those Commands, and the Indian units included in them retained the numbers and designations which they held in the old Presidency armies.

At the same time a Retrenchment Committee (headed by the earl of Inchcape) ordered savings regardless of the commitments of the Indian Army. In 1923 further reductions in the strength of the army was undertaken by disbanding an entire regiment rather than a single battalion from several regiments. The other deductions included a ten percent reductions in artillery, savings on expenditures on hospitals, transport, training establishments, sale of reserve equipments, and reductions in messing. The result of this policy was that in 1927 the Army in India was declared by its Commander-in-Chief to be ineffective for war. An extra amount of Rupees ten crores was sanctioned with a view to re-equip it in the next four years.

The Government of India Act, 1935 was a significant step in bringing further reforms in Indian self-government, but the British still controlled the defence, law and order, and foreign policy.[55] The Indian Army Department was changed to Defence Department, headed by the Commander-in-Chief in India. Burma ceased to be the part of the Indian Empire and the 20th Burma Rifles was no longer the part of the Indian Army.

A modernization committee headed by Major General Auchinleck of Indian Army in 1938 reported that the Indian Army was unfit to be called a modern army as it was even lagging behind the forces of minor states such as Egypt, Iraq and Afghanistan. It was unfit to fight against land or air forces equipped with modern weapons. Most of the combat unit relied upon animals for its transport and most of the drafts joining the units with obsolete weapons.[56] the Indian politicians also did not agree for to India paying for the expensive modernization of the British contingents in India while India units were left un-modernized. In view of Auchinleck, the relegation of the Indian Army to the role of a glorified constabulary would destroy its morale and make it useless for wider imperial uses. In Auchinleck's view the Army in India was to undertake five functions: (i) frontier defence, (ii) coastal defence, (iii) internal security, (iv) a general reserve, and (v) the conduct of operations beyond India's borders. However, before Auchinleck's proposal to modernize the Indian Army could take shape, the British government set up a committee headed by Admiral of the Fleet Lord Chatfield to examine the best way of rearming and reorganizing the military forces in India. His terms of reference drew attention to the increased cost of modern weapons and to the limited resources which were available for the defence forces in India.

Chatfield submitted his report in February 1939. His tour to India was boycotted by the Indian political parties on the grounds that the cost of the British contingent in India was an unfair burden on Indians. Further, the British contingent was an army of occupation and was not required for the protection of India. Chatfield, however, was of the opinion that the British military and naval forces were necessary for the protection of India and also for the maintenance of the internal law and order. Further, if the British gave up the control of defence, the result would be disastrous for the India. Chatfield introduced a new term 'external defence' for the use of troops, on the Indian establishment, in overseas campaign.

Governor General Lord Linlithgow, issued a proclamation on 3 September 1939 that India was at war with Germany without having any consultation with the Indian political leaders. In March 1940 Congress resolved to give no support to the war unless the British promised to grant independence without further delay. In 1942 the British forces were defeated in Malaya and

55 Article 11 of the Government of India Act, 1935 [26 Geo. 5.] dealing with provisions as to defence, ecclesiastical affairs, external affairs and the tribal areas stated:, "The functions of the Governor-General with respect to defence and ecclesiastical affairs and with respect to external affairs, except the relations between the Federation and any part of His Majesty's dominions, shall be exercised by him in his discretion, and his functions in or in relation to the tribal areas shall be similarly exercised. To assist him in the exercise of those functions the Governor-General may appoint counsellors, not exceeding three in number, whose salaries and conditions of service shall be such as may be prescribed by His Majesty in Council."

56 Mechanization in the Indian Army had proceeded only to ht extent that four British cavalry regiments were being re-equipped with light tanks and two Indian ones with armoured cars. While the British Army elsewhere has begun to modernize, in India it had not. Heathcote T.A., 2013, *The Military in British India: The Development of British Land Forces in South Asia 1600-1947*, South Yorkshire: The Praetorian Press, p. 198.

Burma. In March 1942, a Cabinet mission led by Sir Stafford Cripps offered to give every seat in the Council to Indians except that of the Commander-in-Chief, and to divide the responsibility of the Defence Department between the Commander-in-Chief as 'War Member' and an Indian Defence Minister. Though the Cripps mission failed in its main aim, but division of Defence Department was implemented. In August-September 1942, fifty-seven battalions of the army were used the control wide-spread disruption caused by Quit-India movement.

The British Indian Army was the largest volunteer force during the Second World War. Without resorting to conscription, the British were able to recruit 2.5 million Indians in the Indian Army. The Indian Army fought the three major Axis powers (Japan, Italy, and Germany) from Hong Kong in the east to Italy in the west. It displayed tactical virtuosity and fought in varying terrains, from the swamps and jungles of Malaya and Burma to the rocky terrain of Eritrea, the sandy desert of North Africa, and the mountains of central Italy. These campaigns cost the lives of over 87,000 Indian servicemen, while another 34,354 were wounded, and 67,340 became prisoners of war. Their valour was recognized with the award of 4,000 decorations, and 18 members of the Indian Army were awarded the Victoria Cross or the George Cross. The Indian Army experienced very few mutinies during the war.[57]

The Second World War ended in August 1945. On 05 July 1947 an Armed Forces Reconstitution Commission was set up to set out the principles on which partition would take place. The Indian Independence Act received the royal assent on 18 July 1947. At the beginning of August new commander-in-chiefs were appointed to the Armies of Pakistan and for the Republic of India. British India Empire came to an end on 15 August 1947.[58]

During the post-Mutiny era till the First World War, no major battles were fought by the British Indian Army. All the conflicts and wars involving troops from India were either expeditions of the army against weak neighbouring areas (Afghanistan, Burma, Tibet) or overseas against Ethiopians, Sudanese, Arabs or Chinese. There were more than 70 expeditions against the tribes from 1850 to 1922, in tribal areas of NWFP bordering Afghanistan, an average of one expedition per year. The major army operations included Chitral 1896, Malakand 1897, the Waziri tribe 1901-2, 1919 and 1937, the Mahsuds 1925, and the Mohmands 1933. This demonstrates that the Indian military in general and the native forces in particular were used not only external security but also internal order to prolong and firm the establishment of the British Raj.[59]

57 Barua Pradeep P, 2005, *The State at War in South Asia*, Lincoln: University of Nebraska Press; Johnson Rob, "Making a Virtue out of Necessity: The Indian Army, 1746–1947" In *The British Indian Army: Virtue and Necessity*, 2014, Rob Johnson (ed.), UK: Cambridge Scholars, pp. 1-14; Marston Danie, "A Force Transformed: The Indian Army and the Second World War" in Daniel P. Marston and Chandar S. Sundaram (ed.), 2007, *A Military History of India and South Asia: From the East India Company to the Nuclear Era*, 2007, Westport, CT: Praeger, p. 207-222.

58 Heathcote T.A., 2013, *The Military in British India: The Development of British Land Forces in South Asia 1600-1947*, South Yorkshire: The Praetorian Press, pp. 199-205.

59 Syed Hussain Shaheed Soherwordi, 'Punjabisation' in the British Indian Army 1857-1947 and the Advent of Military Rule in Pakistan, Edinburgh Papers in South Asian Studies, Number 24, 2010, School of History & Classics, University of Edinburgh, pp. 34.

The demand for the Indianization of the forces did not end with the submission of the Skeen report. The issue was taken up once again during the Round Table conference when its sub-committee on military affairs made a demand on similar lines, including setting up a military college in India on the Sandhurst model. Finally, the struggle was accomplished in the shape of the establishment of an Indian Military Academy at Dehra Dun in October 1932. Its first batch, commissioned in 1935, was called Indian Commissioned Officers (ICOs). After the Second World War, the Eight Unit Scheme was brought to an end, and all the branches of the army were opened to Indian officers. Training facilities at Dehra Dun were expanded. A large number of officers were recruited on short and long courses (short and emergency commissions). By early 1947, out of 9,500 Commissioned Officers, about 500 were pre-war KCOs and ICOs.

The army was always a very special and private concern of the British in India. They kept it away from any kind of politics. Rather, in case of any clash between the country's politics and security, they favoured the latter. Even as late as 1946, the Viceroy's civilian Executive council had no powers over defence and the defence budget. The British Indian Army was kept free from a strong influence on Indian politics as there was no synthesis between the two. Defence had nothing to do with the politics of the country. Thus the British-Indian Army proved an autonomous entity. Their training (discipline and professionalism) and separation from the society strengthened their organisational ties and loyalty to the British authority.

On 2 September 1946 an interim government took the place of the Governor General's Council, with Jawahar Lal Nehru as Vice President and Member for External Affairs and Sardar Baldev Singh became Member for Defence and post of war Member previously held by the Commander-in Chief was abolished. By this time, the Indian Army had also become more politically aware. The Indian soldiers drawn from various background during the WW II had been exposed to modern political views. On 20 February 1947 Lord Louise Mountbatten, the King's cousin was appointed Viceroy of India. Indian independence Act received royal ascent on 18 July 1947. Mountbatten administered the transfer of power from Britain to the newly independent nations of India and Pakistan at the partition of the subcontinent that took effect at midnight August 14–15, 1947. And British India ended on 15 August 1947. Partition of India also caused partition of its armed forces.[60] The details of division of manpower and units of the Armed Forces were drawn up by the Army, Navy and Air Force Sub-Committees of the Armed Forces Reconstitution Committee (AFRC). Since the Navy and the Air Force were small services, their reconstitution was completed by the end of October 1947. The plan for the division of army units was drawn up by the Army Sub-Committee under Major General Irwin as the Chairman. In all cases, the recommendations of the three Sub-Committees for reconstitution had been unanimous and received prompt approval from the AFRC.

60 The Armed Forces of the British Raj, which was built over the past 300 years, had to be reconstituted within a short period of less than two months. The outbreak of communal disturbances and lack of cooperation between the Congress and Muslim League leaders had made the task of division of the forces difficult. Lord Ismay, who was Mountbatten's Chief of Staff, described the division as 'the biggest crime and the biggest headache.' He was of the opinion that it would destroy the old Indian Army and had remarked, "It is just possible that two really good armies will emerge from the process. It is true that they will not in sum total be equal to the single army out of which they have been fashioned." Alan Campbell-Johnson, 1951, *Mission with Mountbatten*, New York: Dutton, p.137.

Chapter III

Recruitment and Living Conditions

From the early days of the East India Company, when it hired few guards for the Presidencies, until 1 November 1858, when armies, soldiers, civil servants, power and territories of the Company were transferred to the Crown, the Indian Army was the largest mercenary army in the world. It was the property of a chartered British trading company which was engaged in expanding the Company's territory.[1] During the initial stages, a number of natives were hired by the Company's establishments at Madras and Bombay as watchmen and doorkeepers. Major Stringer Lawrence was responsible for forming the first military units of the Company in Madras in 1748 and immediately after that two other presidencies formed their own armies. Bengal Presidency began with "an ensign and thirty men" in addition to "a gunner and its crew".[2] In Bombay, arrival of a detachment of the British forces made the beginning of the Army. Because of the large distance separating these presidencies, and lack of communication facilities, their armies developed separately along different lines, but all were initially a mixture of sailors who had jumped ships, men from the disbanded French units, Swiss, prisoners of war, and other white-men in search of a livelihood.[3]

In 1748, when Lawrence had formed companies of Europeans, the French in India raised several battalions of Indian troops. Thereafter, Lawrence also recruited Indians in the army. In 1754, the first British regulars, the 39th Foot arrived and thus caused an amalgamation of East India Company's Indian Army composed of both European and Indian troops and Royal British regulars who were rented from the Crown. All, the British and Indian Companies and Royal troops, were officered by British Officers. Each presidential army developed its own characteristics and traditions. By the last quarter of the eighteenth century the role of the Indian army expanded

1 Farwell Byron, 1989, *Armies of the Raj: From the Great Indian Mutiny to Independence, 1858-1947*, London: Viking, p. 18.

2 In 1651-52, the East India Company was given *firman* for the establishment of a Factory at Hooghly and an Agency at Patna, the establishment of armed retainer was strictly limited to "An Ensign of 30 men to do honour to the principal Agents" which could be called as the nucleus of the future extensive army maintained by the Company in the Bengal Presidency. The Bengal establishment was subordinate to Madras, on which it was directed to rely for counsel and assistance in any cases of difficulty. Broom, Captain Arthur, 1850, *History of the Rise and Progress of the Bengal Army*, Volume I, Calcutta: W. Thacker and Co., p. 5-6.

3 Farwell Byron, 1989, *Armies of the Raj: From the Great Indian Mutiny to Independence, 1858-1947*, London: Viking, p. 25.

beyond the maintenance of the Company's power in India; it became the strategic reserve for the entire British position in the East. In the following decades, India proved a source of cheap manpower to fight for the Imperial designs at the cost of the Indian revenues.[4] This chapter covers the induction of commissioned, non-commissioned officers and the natives in the military service of the Company and conditions of their service under the Company and the British rule.

Purchase of Commission: Officers

The officers of the His Majesty service were placed in higher position in relation to the officers of the Company's forces. In the Crown's service, commission could be purchased in higher ranks up to Lieutenant Colonel. The purchase of commission was never legalized or regulated in the armies of the Company as it was in the case of Crown's service. The Commission in the His Majesty's Army were allowed to be disposed of by sale, and the following table shows their established rates of value. The officers selling out commission were entitled to receive the sum to which they may be respectively entitled under the Regulations. In order to avoid the possibility of communication between the Parties, the purchasers were directed to lodge his money for his promotion to higher commission, the seller being afterward selected by the Commander in Chief from the list registered in His Royal Highness's office.[5]

Table: Established Prices of Commission

Corps	Ranks	Full price of Commissions £
Life Guard	Lieutenant Colonel	7250
	Major	5350
	Captain	3500
	Lieutenant	1785
	Cornet	1260
Royal Regiment of Horse Guards	Lieutenant Colonel	7250
	Major	5350
	Captain	3500
	Lieutenant	1600
	Cornet	1200

4 Sandhu Amna Mahmood, The Royal Indian Army, Evolution and Organization: An appraisal, *Margalla Papers 2011*, pp. 49-72.

5 In all cases the officers desirous of purchasing promotion were required to give reference to a house agency in India for payment of regulated purchase money or difference. No officer was promoted to the rank of Captain, until he has served two years as an effective subaltern. No officer was promoted to the rank of major, until he has been six years in the service. Jephson George, 1839, The Orders and Regulations of the Bengal Army, Part I, Calcutta: WM Thacker and Company, pp. 408-410.

Dragon Guards and Dragons	Lieutenant Colonel	6175
	Major	4575
	Captain	3225
	Lieutenant	1190
	Cornet	840
Foot Guards	Lieutenant Colonel	9000
	Major with rank of Lt Colonel	8300
	Captain with rank of Lt Colonel	4800
	Lieutenant with rank of Captain	2050
	Ensign with rank of Lieutenant	1200
Regular Regiment of Infantry	Lieutenant Colonel	4500
	Major	3200
	Captain	1800
	Lieutenant	700
	Ensign	450
In Regiments of Fusiliers	1st Lieutenant	700
	2nd Lieutenant	500

The minimum age for holding a commission in the His Majesty's Army was sixteen years. All recommendations for commissions were to certify the eligibility of the person recommended, in respect to education, character, connexions, and bodily health, and that he is prepared immediately to join army Regiment to which he may be appointed. His Christian name and place of address must also be particularly stated. When an officer was desirous of retiring from the service, and of obtaining leave to sell his commission, he was required to send his resignation through the Commanding Officer of the Regiment to his Colonel, who would transmit the same to the Commander in Chief through his Military Secretary.[6]

Any trade in the obtaining or sale of commission was prohibited and punishable by court martial. The standing orders specified, "An officer who takes, accepts or receives or agrees to pay, any larger sum of money, directly or indirectly, than what is allowed by the regulations made by His

6 The most valuable source of recruitment was the Royal Army. Officers of king's regiments leaving India were permitted to volunteer for the Company's service, in which they usually received a step in rank, and when peace in Europe led to the reduction of regiments there was always a number of officers on half-pay and in reduced circumstances who were glad to accept employment under the East India Company. Such officers improved the efficiency, the social status and the military spirit of the officers in the Company's armies. When service in those armies became attractive the directors discouraged local appointments, and took the military patronage, as it became more valuable, into their own hands. Haig Lt Col Wolesley, "The Armies of the East India Company," in Dowell H. H. (ed.), *The Cambridge History of India, Vol. VI*, London: Cambridge University Press, 1932, pp. 153-166.

majesty in relation to the purchase, sale or exchange of commissions in His Majesty Forces; or who pays or cause to be paid any sum of money to any agent or broker or other person for negotiating the purchase, sale, or exchange of any such commission, shall on being convicted thereof by a general court martial, forfeit his commission and be cashiered."[7]

By an act of Parliament of 1754, officers of the Crown serving in India always took precedence over the officers of the same rank serving in the Company's army. A captain of the King's army, even if he was a captain of one day's standing, was considered senior over the senior-most captain of the Company's army in India. In addition, promotions in the Royal Army were also faster. For instance, in 1750s, an officer in the Crown service got promoted to the rank of Colonel after completing 25 years of service, whereas an Officer in the Company's service could become only Captain in this length of service. This preferential treatment raised vehement protest from the Company's officers who only obtained redress in 1788, when, with the sanction of the Parliament, royal commissions were locally granted to the Company's officers which allowed them to equal privileges with their colleagues in the royal regiments.[8]

The Medical Staff Officers of Regiments and Offices of Civil Department attached to the Army were classed with military ranks, but were not authorized to exercise command over the troops. Amongst Regimental Staff Officers, Surgeons were appointed in the rank of Captain, Assistant Surgeons as Lieutenant; Veterinary Surgeons during the first ten years service were appointed as Cornets, after 10 years as Lieutenant, and after 20 years of service as Captain. Amongst the Medical Staff appointments, Members of the Medical Board were granted the rank of Brigadier General and Superintending Surgeons wore the rank of Lieutenant Colonel.[9] The British officers had perception that they were of superior race, had certain character---a supreme combination of incorruptibility, intelligence, fairness and other leadership traits--- supposedly unique of their Anglo-Saxon race.

Duties of the Officers in the Regiment: The Officers entrusted with the Command of a regiment were responsible for maintaining discipline and the conduct of troops in all situations. The Regulations provided, "Unanimity and good understanding amongst the officers, as connected with the character and discipline of a Regiment are objects peculiarly deserving the attention of the Commanding Officer. His timely interference to prevent disputes, his advice to the young and inexperienced, his protection and favour to the deserving, and his immediate notice and reprehension of any misconduct likely to interrupt the harmony of the Corps, and the best means of securing these desirable objects, towards the attainment of which he has a right to demand, and ought to receive, the assistance of every officer." The provisions were also made in the Articles of War for this important object and attention of Commandants and officers in general.

7 Regulations for the Guidance of Officers Selling out, retiring from, or purchasing promotion in His Majesty's Army: Jephson George, 1839, The Orders and Regulations of the Bengal Army, Part I, Calcutta: WM Thacker and Company, pp. 405-407.

8 Barat Amiya, 1962, *The Bengal Native Infantry: Its Organization & Discipline 1796-1852*, Calcutta: Firma K. L. Mukhopadhyay, pp. 99-100.

9 General Regulations of the Madras Army, Adjutant General Office, Fort St George, 1849, Madras: Military Male Orphan Asylum Press, p. 64-65.

In the punishment of offences, the Commanding Officers were guided by the Standing Orders and General Regulations of the Service, applying the punishments which they were authorizes to inflict, according to the nature and degree of the offence, and with due regard to the character and previous conduct and services the individual. They were not empowered to inflict punishments which were not authorized in the orders and regulations. The regulations provided, "In all first offences not of an aggravated character, or committed by young and inexperienced soldiers, mild reproof and admonition should be tried---nor should punishment be restored to until a repetition of the offence may have shown that the milder treatment has failed. Soldier's should be taught to know that it is wished to avoid punishment if discipline can be maintained without it." Further, "Officers should be cautious of reproving Non-commissioned Officers for any irregularity, neglect of duty, or awkwardness, in the presence of hearing of the soldiers, lest they should thereby weaken their authority and respectively in the eyes of their subordinates." The Commanding Officer were to ensure that sentences of corporal punishments were invariably inflicted in the presence of Medical Officer, and were not to be carried into effect on Sundays, except in cases of urgent necessity requiring an immediate example. [10]

Command and Control: All Commands in the Regular Forces belonged to the Eldest Officers, whether of Cavalry, Artillery, Engineers, or Infantry. In case two Commissions of the same date interfered, a retrospect was to be had to former Commissions. When Regiments or Detachments were united; either in Camp, Garrison, or Quarters, the Eldest Officer, whether by brevet or otherwise, was to command the whole. During the absence of the Commander-in-Chief, the Command of the Troops at the Presidency devolved on the next senior Officer, unto whom the usual Reports and Returns were to be made; but this did not include the Command of the Fort and Garrison of Bombay, the nomination to this Station resting entirely on the pleasure of the Governor, as long and to such extent, as he considered it fit to devolve the detail of that duty on another.[11] The General Officer, when beyond his limits, was to leave all matters of usual Routine and Detail to the next in Command; but he retained the power of giving such Orders on matters of discipline and general control, as deemed expedient to him. An Officer in the temporary command of a Regiment was not authorized to issue any Standing Order, or contradict, or alter, those issued by the permanent Commanding Officer.[12]

The Officers Commanding regiments and garrisons were responsible for the upkeep of public property. An extract from Hon'ble Court's Military Letter to Bengal, dated 9 September 1812 provided: "We hold the Commanding Officers of all Military Posts, to be personally responsible for the enforcement of the general Regulations of Government, with regard to the custody and preservation of all Public Property within the limits of their respective Commands. It is their duty to take care that all Barrack Masters, Commissaries of Ordnance, or others, under their Command, specially entrusted with the conservation of public Property, do their duty to the Public, and in

10 General Regulations of the Madras Army, Adjutant General Office, Fort St George, 1849, Madras: Military Male Orphan Asylum Press, p. 96-99.

11 Aitchison Captain John William, 1824, *A General Code of the Military Regulations in force under the Presidency of Bombay*, Calcutta: Mission School Press, p. 105.

12 General Regulations of the Madras Army, Adjutant General Office, Fort St George, 1849, Madras: Military Male Orphan Asylum Press, p. 117.

the event of any neglect in those Officers, to report it to the Military Board and to Government; and we direct that any Officer Commanding a Garrison, or Post, who shall fail in his duty in this instance, be removed from his Command, as well as the inferior Officers more immediately responsible for the neglected property."[13] The right of Command of a Battalion belonged to the Lieutenant Colonel alone, and Officers under that rank who could be senior present with a Corps, were in all circumstances, designated as "in charge," and signed themselves accordingly.

Recruitment of European Soldiers

For the recruitment of European soldiers, there was no standard method was followed in England. In Britain, during the sixteenth century, and for a long time after, the recruitment for army depended chiefly upon the Captains of companies, each Captain recruiting for his company. When the recruitment of an establishment completed, he was allowed the pay of two soldiers in time of peace, and five during a period of war, to enable him to keep up the numbers, and to preserve its efficiency. Immediately after the recruitment, the recruit was brought before the Muster-master, or Commissary of Musters of the Army, and an Oath was administered to him, which was taken by commissioned officers as well as by soldiers. After this attestation, the Captain received a certificate that the recruit had been entered in the Muster-master's roll; and this certificate entitled him to draw pay for him. Any soldier who enlisted with two Captains at the same time, or who left one and enlisted with another was liable to the punishment of death. [14]

During 1640s, the English faced great difficulty in procuring the volunteers to join the army for service in Ireland upon the breaking out of the rebellion in that part of the kingdom. From 1781 to 1799, the Company enlisted its own European troops, is the Company was authorized to keep in depot 2,000 men in war time and half that number in peace. The European element of the Company's Army included European of almost every nationality.

The East India Company recruited its own private European army for which recruitment depots were opened in England. Article XXXII of the Act of 1781 [21 Geo II. III. Cap. LXV] authorized the Company to recruit soldiers in England and maintain a military force in the East-Indies not exceeding two thousand at any one time in time of war, and one thousand at any time in time of peace. This number was increased in the due course of time. Most of the recruits who joined the Company's army were of tender age. The dregs of British society joined the British army. Most of them were criminals and tricked into joining the British army. A considerable proportion of the British Army was consisting either of orphans, or children deserted by their parents; and nearly

13 Aitchison Captain John William, 1824, *A General Code of the Military Regulations in force under the Presidency of Bombay*, Calcutta: Mission School Press, p. 106.

14 I, A.B., do swear and promise to do all loyal, true, and faithful service unto the Queen of England, Her Most Excellent Majesty, and unto the provinces and cities united in these countries, and their associates, under the charge of the Right Excellent the Earl of Leicester, Governor-General of the said provinces and cities, and their associates, and of Her Majesty's army and forces within the same; and all lawful and due obedience unto the said Governor, and to any other superior that shall have charge under him for government in this army. And further, I do promise to endeavour myself to fulfil and keep all such lawful ordinances as his Excellency hath or shall set forth and establish for the better ordering of this army, as much as concerns me, so long as I shall serve in the same under him. So help me God by Jesus Christ. Marshall Henry, 1846, *The Military Miscellany; Comprehending a History of the Recruiting of the Army, Military Punishments*, London, p. 13.

thirty to fifty per cent of the men who enlisted were "unable to read with profit and satisfaction, or at any rate without difficulty." It was considered opinion that the soldier's life is wholly unsuited to young men of good principles and good habits. [15] Those who joined the Company's army were no better and fell prey to scurvy and malnutrition during their voyage to India.[16] The British mess culture in colonial India encouraged excessive drinking, which cause a number of deaths. In comparison, India soldiers were healthier and must cheaper to the Company when compared to white troop. A number of general Orders were issued by the Commanders-in-Chief to control the drunkenness amongst the officers and soldiers.[17] The regimental commanders were given the power to deal with crime of drunkenness in the army by infliction of summary fines. These fines were to be awarded in accordance with the scale were to be strictly and rigidly adhered to.

---

15 Marshall on Improving the Condition of Soldiers, TAITS, Edinburg Magazine for 1846, Vol. XIII, London: William Tait, p. 381-382.

16 Roy Kaushik, "The Armed Expansion of the English East India Company: 1740-1849," in Marston Daniel P. and Chandar S. Sundaram (ed.), 2007, *A Military History of India and South Asia: From the East India Company to the Nuclear Era*, London: Praeger Security International, p. 4-5.

17 On 11 January 1850, Captain William Charles Hollings of the 47th Native Infantry was tried by General Court Martial at Cawnpore. There were three charges against him: 1st: For having at Cawnpore, on 6 November 1849, when Superintending Officer of a Native Court of Requests, attended the Court in a state of intoxication, which rendered him incapable of properly conducting the proceedings. 2nd: For highly unbecoming conduct, in having, at Cawnpore, on the same occasion, addressed abusive language to, and struck Dheraj Mahajun, a party to suits before the Court, and in having addressed himself in familiar and obscene language to persons present in Court. And 3rd: For having, at Cawnpore, on 17 November 1849, been drunk at an inspection parade of the Regiment. The Court found him 'Guilty' of 1st charge; 'Not Guilty' of 2nd; and on the 3rd charge, the Court found him Guilty of been partially intoxicated at inspection parade of the Regiment, but not 'drunk," of which the Court acquitted him. With regard to the 3rd charge, the Court was of the opinion that the matter was disposed of by the competent authority and did not pass any sentence against it. The Court awarded him sentence of suspension from rank, pay and allowances for six months.

The proceedings were returned for revision by the Commander in Chief on 7 February 1850, with the remarks, "The Court is directed to read over the first charge on which it has convicted the prisoner, and then to read the 76th Article of War; it will see that it has no power to pass any other sentence than that of "cashiering" which it must therefore do, or stand a prosecution for passing an illegal sentence. With regard to the second charge, the finding of the Court is in the face of the evidence, and I have directed the Judge Advocate General to point this out to the Court. With regard to the third charge, the Court has erroneously assumed that the crime was disposed of previously by competent authority. The Judge Advocate General will also explain this error to the Court, and that a refusal to pass sentence upon a criminal will expose the President and Members of the Court to the charge of disobedience of orders in refusing to do its duty; I therefore recommend the Court to read the 42nd Article of War."

The Court, after revision awarded sentence of "To be cashiered"; but made the following recommendation, "As it appears from the remarks of His Excellency the Commander in Chief, that there is no discretionary power as to the punishment in this case, the Court unanimously and respectfully beg leave to recommend the prisoner to the merciful consideration of the Commander in Chief, on the grounds of the weak state of health he was in when he committed the offences, his long service, and high character." The Commander in Chief approved and confirmed the sentence on 2 March 1850, with the remarks, "It is a matter of surprise to me that the Court should recommend the prisoner to pardon! I must refer the Court to the charges against the prisoner, of which the Court have found him guilty, and I ask if a person guilty of such conduct can be described as an Officer of "high character" and pardoned upon such grounds? Certainly not, and I should do a gross injustice to the Company's service were I to pardon the prisoner.

In 1799, the Company was authorized by the His Majesty [39 George III. Cap. CIX.] to recruit the Company's European army in England and four recruiting stations were established. Certain fixed number of recruits, between the age group of 20 and 30, were provided annually to the Company. These recruits were subjected to military law applicable in the Great Britain previous to their embarkation and during their passage to, the places where the said United Company are entitled to maintain and keep such militia force. The Act also prescribed a particular form of oath to be administered to recruits thus raised. The European soldiers were engaged to serve for ten years after their arrival in India, and at the expiry of the engagement, they were at the liberty to re-enlist for the service for another term of five years or return to England at the Company's expense. They remained subject to the Mutiny Acts for the Crown's Forces whilst they remained in India.

The European Non-Commissioned Officer of a Regiment of Native Infantry exercised authority over the Native Commissioned Officers. The Commander in Chief had issued directions that a Regiment must never to be paraded without an European Officer. However, in the event of so improbable a contingency as the absence of all the European Officers, the Sergeant Major, and not the Senior Native Officer is to assume the command the parade and to receive reports from them.[18]

Recruitment of Natives in the Company's Forces

The recruits for the Company's army in India were enlisted under the orders of Adjutant General. For the recruitment of natives parties were sent out in districts with the sanction of the Commander in Chief. Native officers and sepoys were also instructed while proceeding of leave or furlough to bring with them prospective recruits for enlistment in the Company's service. The recruiting parties for the enlistment consisted of European or Native officers, detached from the Headquarters of a regiment or from recruiting depots in India. The officer-in-charge of a recruiting party, on arrival in a particular district, generally divided his party in smaller groups and sent them to different villages. In case the recruiting party also included a medical officer, the interested individuals, if found within permissible height and age, were medically examined for enlistment. If passed by the medical officer as fit for the service, his name was entered in a Roll (Form No. 4), and he was considered as listed from that date. In addition men presenting themselves for enlistment at Regimental Headquarters, were if approved by the Commanding Officer were sent for medical examination and if found fit for the service, were enlisted. During medical examination, a candidate was made to walk, run, leap, hop upon one leg alternatively and put through the "Extension Motion", in order to ascertain that he has the free use of his limbs. He was also vaccinated, if required on the enlistment. The first four Articles of War were read and carefully explained to every recruit by the recruiting officer, for which purpose copies in Hindoostanee and other local language were provided.[19]

18 Letter from Adjutant General's Officer, Head Quarters, Simlah, dated 3 August 1831 addressed to Lt Col Gomess, 24th Regiment N.I. See: Abstracts of General Orders 1840 to 1847.

19 Recruiting Regulations, General Regulations of the Madras Army, Adjutant General Office, Fort St George, 1849, Madras: Military Male Orphan Asylum Press, p. 368-378.

Every native sepoy who volunteered to enlist himself in the Company service took the following oath, as provided in the Articles of War, at the time of his so enlisting:

> I .... AB... do swear to serve the Honourable Company faithfully and truly against their all enemies, while I continue to receive their pay and eat their salt. I do swear to obey all the Orders I may receive from my Commanders and Officers, never to forsake my post, abandon my Colours or turn my back to my enemies and that I will in all things behave myself like a good and faithful sepoy in perfect obedience at all times to the rules and customs of war.

The natives, usually drawn from the agricultural class, rose to the non-commissioned grade by length of service in his Regiment.[20] The selection of men for promotion in the Native army for the rank of Lance Naik was left to the Captain or Officer in charge of the troop or Company, unless particular circumstances dictated individual variation from this rule. No Naik was promoted to the rank of Havildar, without previously going through the grade of Naik. Promotions in Non-commissioned ranks were made by the authority of the Officer Commanding the Regiment. Havildars and Naiks could be reduced to rank or ranks only by the authority of a court martial.[21]

In the Company's army, there were Indians also who occupied an officer rank below the British officers and above the Indian troops. Advancement to the officer ranks of native officer, and promotion from the lower to the higher grade in that rank was regulated in the same way, by pure seniority, the senior havildar of the Regiment having a recognized claim to succeed to a vacancy among the 'Jemadars' and the senior Jemadar becoming in turn 'Subadar'. Promotion to the rank of native officer was usually made by selection from the non-commissioned ranks; but Government had the power of bestowing direct commissions on gentlemen of position.[22] Native Commissioned, Non-commissioned Officers and men were entitled to superior allowances from the date casualty causing the promotion. Under the Regulations of 1796 a native officer could expect to achieve the ultimate rank of Subadar in his regiment through a promotion strictly regulated by seniority.

In 1813, the Bengal Government observed that once Native Officers have attained the rank of Subadar they had nothing more to look to, and having got all that they could get, they have no further inducement and are dissatisfied. It was suggested that there ought to be some higher object kept in their view to which by diligence and fidelity they may still attain. It was therefore recommended that one Subadar in each regiment of native cavalry and one in each battalion of native infantry should be granted the rank of Subadar-Major and be made entitled to an extra

20 For a sepoy, knowledge of reading and writing in the vernacular was required for promotion, but subject to this small qualification the senior private, if of good character, was entitled by custom to become a naik and then havildar in order of seniority in succession to vacancies.

21 The pay of a native soldier being from two to three times the amount of wages of an agricultural labourer in India, admission into the ranks became an object of competition, and dismissal one of severe punishment. Old soldiers, who retired to their villages with their small pensions were admired and respected, even envied. Marshall Henry, 1846, *The Military Miscellany; Comprehending a History of the Recruiting of the Army, Military Punishments*, London, p. 99.

22 Rivett-Carnac, Colonel S., 1890, *The Presidential Armies of India*, London: W. H. Allen & Co, p. 420-421.

allowance of twenty five rupees per month.[23] The Home authorities sanctioned the proposal and ordered that the rank of Subadar-Major should be awarded on the most distinguished and deserving Subadar and an allowance of twenty five rupees per month in addition to the pay and allowance as a Subadar would be attached to this post.[24] A Subadar-Major was not entitled to any specific superior authority in the Corps to which he belonged. However, when employed upon any general duty with Officers of other Corps, he was entitled to the benefit of his Army Rank as Subadar Major, upon the same principle as was available to Brevet Rank with European Officers.[25]

After 1858, the Native Offiers holding the rank of Jemadar, Subadar, and Subadar-Major were known as "Viceroy Commissioned Officers" (VCOs). The special tier of rank for Indian native officer did not exist in any other army in the world. Their commission came from Viceroy rather than British sovereign and they formed a vital link between British officers and native Indian soldiers in a battalion. Every battalion had 20 VCOs, who performed the duties of company officers and platoon commanders. There VCO ranks: the Jemadar, who functioned roughly as today's Naib Subedar; the Subedar; and the Subedar Major,[26] who was the senior VCO of the battalion or regiment. In Indian cavalry units, they were called Daffadar, Rissaldar, and Rissaldar Major. During the early Company army, the rank of Native Commandant existed, but was abolished during the reorganization in 1760s.[27] The VCOs did not undergo any specific training

23 For the selection of Subadar Major, Commanding Officer was to select the most distinguished and deserving Subadar, without respect to seniority, it being of importance that this honourable rank should be conferred only upon officers of acknowledged character and service. Except under provisions of the 93d Article of War, a Subadar Major was not entitled to any superior authority as such in the Corps to which he belonged, but continued to perform his duty as usual with his Troop or Company. Native Officers, General Regulations of the Madras Army, Adjutant General Office, Madras: Military Male Orphan Asylum Press, 1849, p. 354-355.

24 However, a condition was imposed by the Court of Directors that the post of Subadar-Major should be recommended by the officers commanding regiments to the Commander-in-Chief and that the rank should "not continue after his (the Subadar-Major) transfer to the invalid establishment." The Governor-General in his reply dated 21 July 1818 suggested that "the pay of the Subadar Major should accompany him in his retirement and if this stipend so dearly purchased, so honourably earned by a whole life of meritorious service on the part of a few selected veteran officers was not to be continued to them, during the short remainder of their lives and when age and infirmities did but augment their claims on the state, whom they served in their days of youth and vigour, the whole scope and object of the institution would be defeated. That admirable regulation would indeed become worse than nugatory." But the Court did not approve the proposal on the ground of cost. Sen Amiya, The Structure and Organization of the Bengal Native Infantry with Special Reference to Problems of Discipline (1796-1852), Ph D thesis, University of London, 1961, pp. 242-244.

25 General Regulations of the Madras Army, Adjutant General Office, Fort St George, 1849, Madras: Military Male Orphan Asylum Press, p. 354.

26 For the rank of Subadar Major, Commanding Officers were to select the most distinguished and deserving Subadar, without respect for seniority, it being of importance that this honourable rank should be conferred only upon Officers of acknowledged character and service. A Subadar Major was not entitled to any specific superior authority in the Corps to which he belonged. However, when employed upon any general duty with Officers of other Corps, he was entitled to the benefit of his Army Rank as Subadar Major, upon the same principle as was available to Brevet Rank with European Officers. General Regulations of the Madras Army, Adjutant General Office, Fort St George, 1849, Madras: Military Male Orphan Asylum Press, p. 354.

27 Sundaram Chander S., "Grudging Concessions: The Officer Corps and Its Indianization, 1817-1940" in Marston Daniel P. and Chandar S. Sundaram (ed.), 2007, *A Military History of India and South Asia: From the East India*

and were not commissioned in the usual sense. They rose from the ranks in the units they had first joined as ordinary sepoys or sowars. The time it took to become a Subedar was far too long for most sepoys to aspire to, for this promotion was seldom given until after forty years' service. The oldest and most senior VCOs ranked below the most junior British officer and they were addressed as "sahib". Though many British authors have stated that the VCOs were treated with respect and the British Officers took care not to offend them,[28] the reality may not be so.[29]

In a Regiment, the native officer of the rank of Subadar Major worked as confidential officer of the British commandant. Next below him in rank was the second in command, who was the senior wing or squadron commander. Wing and squadron commanders were answerable for the appearance, discipline, and officering of their half battalions or squadrons, and for the instruction of their officers, European and native. The quartermaster of a native regiment was responsible for all the public buildings used, and generally for the lines and bazar. Subedars commanded their troops or companies on parade, instruct them in drill, and were responsible for their order in lines and barracks, and the due intimation to them of all legitimate orders. Jemadars were the native subalterns, taking their turn of duty with the Subedars as regimental officer of the day.

Silladar System

In 1796, the East India Company raised first of the three, European styled, native cavalry regiment in Bengal Army. By 1842 there were 11 regiments of Bengal Light Cavalry with British officers and Indian troopers. They were effectively used by the British to put down the 1857 Mutiny. The so-called irregular cavalry, which formed the main part of the Bengal Cavalry Regiment was organised on a different footing.[30] It was recruited from a higher class, mostly landholder, each man bringing his horse with him and depositing a substantial sum in the regimental chest. Against

Company to the Nuclear Era, London: Praeger Security International, pp. 88-101.

28 Farwell Byron, 1989, *Armies of the Raj: From the Great Indian Mutiny to Independence, 1858-1947*, London: Viking, p. 29.

29 Sita Ram, a native in the Service of Company' army and then under the British rule, was promoted to *Subedar* at the age of 65 years after completing forty-eight years of service. He writes, "I was an old man of sixty-five years of age and had attained the highest rank to be gained in the Native Army. What could I do now at the head of my Company? How could I double-march, or perform Light Infantry drill? But I was expected to be as active as ever and no allowance was made for my forty-eight Years' service. No one bothered to remember that I had carried a musket for thirty years and had been present in as many battles as most of the officers had lived years. I was shouted at by the Adjutant as if I was a bullock, and he a mere boy, young enough to be my grandson. I was abused by the Commanding Officer, and called a fool, a donkey, and an old woman! Finally, I was taken before the Commander-in-Chief and reported on as being utterly useless---a man the Commanding Officer could do nothing with. I was taken before the Invaliding Committee which agreed my discharge, and I acquired the pension of a *Subedar*. Had any attention been paid to my rights, I should have received this pension years before." James Lunt (ed.), *From Sepoy to Subedar*, Being the Life and Adventures of Subedar Sita Ram, a Native Officer of the Bengal Army written and related by himself, Translated and First Published by Lieutenant-Colonel Norgate, Bengal Staff Corps at Lahore, 1873, p. 172.

30 Irregular cavalry regiment system was based on the concept of Silladar. The word Silladar means "bearer of arms" in Persian and it was the name given to native cavalrymen who would join the irregular regiments. A recruit was supposed to provide his horse, stabling attendant, forage, camp equipment, clothing and weapons. (later Government started providing weapons and ammunition to bring uniformity.) For this, Silladar would receive a higher pay than his equivalent in the regular regimen.

this he was debited with the cost of his uniform and equipment, and credited in turn with their value on leaving the regiment, when the balance of his deposit was repaid to him. The rate of pay included the cost of maintaining the soldier's horse which was provided by the soldier himself. Originally a native gentleman or a man of substance on enlisting might bring a certain number of relatives or retainers with him, and he drew pay for them, the portion distributed in turn to them being a matter of private arrangement. Later on this individual footing was gradually altered to a regimental system, under which the horse as well as the forage was found by the regiment, which was self-contained and self-managed, both as to the supply and up-keep of horses and equipment. The Government merely issued gross pay per head and leaving all arrangements for maintenance and equipment to be managed regimentally. [31]

Irregular units had few British Officers, usually the Commandant, Second-in-Command, Adjutant and Medical Officer. Therefore native officers had higher status and more authority than there equivalents in the regular units. In a regular unit, a native officer would always be outranked by most junior Cornet whereas in irregular unit, he could become a squadron commander. The weapons, uniform and role of light cavalry suited the nature and customs of native cavalrymen. These reasons attracted men of highest quality towards the irregular regiments. Irregular Cavalry regiments used to organize Regimental darbar chaired by the Commandant and attended by all ranks. These darbars were held at regular intervals, sometimes as frequently as once a week. Every person had the right to speak on matters like discipline, training, administrations, leave, weapons etc. All the matters were decided by the Commandant with the advice of his officers; the British and native alike. This system strengthened the feeling of a large family in the regiment where every sowar saw his interest in the interest of the regiment.[32] Promotions in the Silladar system of the service were made by selection on the nomination by the commanding officer; the commissioned ranks were filled partly by direct appointment of natives from the military class, and partly by promotions from the non-commissioned grade, in which were generally serving many men of good family.

Living Conditions in Military Camps

The East India Company did not construct any barracks of earmarked any building for the Indian native troops at military cantonments. Instead of barracks, certain ground was allotted in a cantonment for the residence of the native regiments. On this allotted ground a native soldier had to build a hut for himself. The Madras and Bombay native soldiers received hutting money for the erection of new huts,[33] but the Bengal sepoys never enjoyed any such privilege. In order to equalize the service conditions of the three Presidential armies, in 1846, hut-allowance was

31 Chesney General Sir George, 1894, *Indian Polity: A view of the system of administration in India*, London: Longmans, Green and Co., p. 409.

32 Sumit Walia, Origin of Cavalry in Indian Army and the Silladar System, Indian Defence Review, available at: http://www.indiandefencereview.com/origin-of-cavalry-in-indian-army-and-the-silladar-system/.

33 In Madras Presidency, public accommodation not being provided for the families of Native Troops while in Garrison, following allowance was granted to all native Effective and Non-effective Troops, including those permanently attached to European Corps: Subadar Rs 24, Jemadar Rs 12, Havildar Rs 4, and others categories Rs 3. Hutting money was allowed on every final change of station. These allowances were paid on bills duly counter-signed by the Quarter Master General. When a Corps was on permanent march, the owners were allowed to dispose

granted to the Bengal sepoys, but only on their changing stations.[34] Each native sepoy was allotted a space of 30 x 12 feet and the non-commissioned officers (30x20) and commissioned officers were allotted slightly larger plots (30x40). In the ground allowed to a regiment, lines were marked out and divided into ten rows, one per company, with a street between those of each company and a broader one to separate the two sections. Those huts belonging to native sepoys and non-commissioned officers in a cantonment consisted of quadrangular buildings with mud walls generally surmounted by thatch of grass or palmyra leaves, with a small enclosed yard or compound in front. The huts of the native officers were attached to the company lines. The native troops had no lavatories, no baths, no kitchens, and no sanitary supervision of any kind. They used the ground round them as privies without hindrance.

The public buildings attached to a native line consisted of a barrack for arms, the stores, the Sergeant's quarter and the congee house. A barrack or Bell of Arms was built immediately in front of the line of each company. The arms and accoutrements of the native soldiers were lodged in this building and a native non-commissioned officer was placed in charge. A guard-room and a prisoner's cell were also attached to the Bell of Arms. The colours and cash chest were lodged in the guard-room while prisoners, under trial by court martial, were confined in the prisoners' room.

In the Bombay Army, the men's lines were subject to the supervision of the quartermaster, but each of the company authorities were responsible, through him and by constant inspection, to the commanding officer as to their general cleanliness and neatness. No strangers were allowed to live in the lines without (through the company authorities) the permission of the commanding officer. In the Bombay army the men were never separated from their arms, accoutrements, and ammunition, either in quarters, on the march, or service, except at sea; when, according to the Bombay army rules for such occasions, they were lodged in the places pointed out for the purpose by the vessel's authorities. The "fatigue duty" in garrison, field, or board ship was regularly performed in the Bombay Native Army, which were always performed by the sepoys with readiness and cheerfulness. The adjutant of the regiment was responsible to the commanding officer for every detail of the regiment connected with drill, duty, and discipline. He was expected to be on the drill (recruit) ground or parade every morning and evening. His immediate subordinates were the native adjutant, havildar major; and the staffs of drillmasters (in proportion to the number of recruits) were selected by him for efficiency and smartness, and without any reference to caste.[35]

Each regiment of the British Indian Army had its religious instructor: maulvis for Muslims, pundits for Hindus and granthis for Sikhs. In a mixed regiment all three were present. Except when their unit was on active service, they were to subject to military law, but a commanding officer could dismiss them. Similarly each regiment had its own contractor who was responsible for organizing the bazaar at each station and at each camp site. Before WWI, they marched with

of their huts. Hutting Rule, General Regulations of the Madras Army, Adjutant General Office, Madras: Military Male Orphan Asylum Press, 1849, pp. 312-323.

34 G.O.C.C. 15 July 1845, Bengal Military Cons, 15 July 1845, No.68.

35 Rivett-Carnac, Colonel S., 1890, *The Presidential Armies of India,* London: W. H. Allen & Co, p. 442.

the regiment and regularly set up shops to supply the troops with necessities and basic luxuries.[36] The Army Act, 1950 still caters for subjugation of such followers to the military law.[37]

To look after the health of the native soldiers the Army administrators had attached two native doctors with one surgeon and one surgeon's mate to each sepoy regiment. These men regulated the hospital service attached to the unit in all situations. The native soldiers while in hospital had to pay for medical service.[38] For a soldier wounded in action or on service, however, there was no hospital stoppage. During the time of a war or in a distant campaign, general field hospitals were also established whenever necessary.

In addition to the systems of reward and pension, the native soldiers while in the Company's service also enjoyed certain privileges in civil life. From 1796 to 1815, in any civil court of justice both in the Company's territories and those of Oudh, a sepoy's representation for any wrong done to him or his family found precedence over all other cases. This preference may have been granted by the Company while it was busy fighting the Indian powers and could ill afford to sanction frequent or long leave of absence to its sepoys. To the small landholders however this facility was considered to be as great a privilege as any and they were anxious to have their sons or relations in the Company's native army so that they might secure it. With a sepoy in their family they expected to gain some influence over the collectors and other civil authorities in pushing through their own law suits. This measure was considered as an interference by the civil authorities and in 1815 the Directors ordered the Bengal Government to issue an ordinance prohibiting army officers" from furnishing native officers and soldiers going on furlough with any letter or other writing to the Magistrate in whose districts their families reside with a view to an early adjustment of and Punjab wars, however, when desertion in the native infantry regiments increased to a great extent, the Court, in its anxiety to make its military service as attractive as it used to be, retracted this order and asked the Bengal Government to reintroduce the privilege of early hearings for sepoys in the civil courts.[39] In 1899, Lord Robert revived the dormant order granting soldier's precedence in the hearing of civil suits. This provision still exists in the Indian

36 Farewell Byron, 1989, *Armies of the Raj: From the Great Indian Mutiny to Independence, 1858-1947*, London: Viking, p. 36.

37 Section 2 (1) (i) of the Army Act, 1950 provides that persons not otherwise subject to military law who, on active service, in camp, on the march or at any frontier post specified by the Central Government by notification in this behalf, are employed by, or are in the service of, or are followers of, or accompany any portion of, the regular Army. Note to AA s. 2 (1)(i) states "Persons commonly known as 'followers' are not ordinarily subject to the Army Act unless they have been enrolled under it, but in the interest of discipline and security it is obviously necessary that they and other civilians who accompany any portion of the regular Army should be subject to military discipline on active service and in certain other circumstances.

38 The charges for a day were four annas (one rupee was divided into sixteen annas) for a subadar, two annas for a jamadar, a havildar or a naik and one anna for a sepoy, this sum being recovered from their pay. Since complaints were often received that native soldiers in order to avoid duty, pretended illness and tried to get admission into the hospital, in 1840, the Government increased the hospital charges and the daily rate for native soldiers was raised to eight annas for a commissioned officer, three annas for a non-commissioned officer and two annas for a sepoy.

39 Sen Amiya, The Structure and Organization of the Bengal Native Infantry with Special Reference to Problems of Discipline (1796-1852), Ph D thesis, University of London, 1961, pp. 247-248

military law, however, rarely honoured in the corrupt judicial system prevailing today.[40] The First World War introduced additional measures in the form of preferential government employment, free education to the wards of disabled or dead soldiers. The British administrative system in India also worked hard to trace beneficiaries of dead soldiers because it fostered contentment and helped in new recruitments.

Discharge from the Service

The Non-commissioned officers and Sepoys on expiration of period of contract were eligible for discharge from the service. The European soldiers were also permitted to purchase their discharge after paying certain amount of money.[41] The commanding officers had the power to discharge soldiers who were unfit for the service from physical causes, sickness, or accident and were incapable of performing the duties of a soldier.[42] They were also authorised to dismiss a native solider who from awkwardness at the drill appeared that was unlikely to become a smart soldier. However, such cases were to be forwarded to the Commander in Chief for the sanction of discharge. All native soldiers convicted of the crime of theft, before a court martial or a magistrate, were to be discharged from the service, without a reference to headquarters, as such persons were considered a disgrace to the military profession.[43] The native soldiers to whom corporal punishment was awarded, be means of a Regimental Order or court martial were to be discharged from the service, if the General or Officer Commanding the division considered it

40 Section 32 of the Army Act, 1950, dealing with priority in respect of army personnel's litigation, states, "On the presentation to any court by or on behalf of any person subject to this Act of a certificate from the proper military authority of leave of absence having been granted for the purpose of prosecuting or defending any suit or other proceeding in such court, the court shall, on the application of such person, arrange, so far as may be possible, for the hearing and final disposal of such suit or other proceeding within the period of the leave so granted or applied for." Further, "The certificate from the military authority shall state the first and last day of the leave or intended leave, and set forth a description of the case with respect to which the leave was granted or applied for. No fee shall be payable to the court in respect of the presentation of any such certificate, or of any application by or on behalf of any such person, for priority for the hearing of his case. Where the court is unable to arrange for the hearing and final disposal of the suit or other proceeding within the period of such leave or intended leave as aforesaid, it shall record its reasons for its inability to do so, and shall cause a copy thereof, to be furnished to such person on his application without any payment whatever by him in respect either of the application for such copy or of the copy itself."

41 Soldiers under 7 years of service; Rs 400 or £ 40; above 7 years of service Rs 360 or £ 40; above 10 years of service Rs 300 or £ 30; above 12 years of service Rs 200 or £ 20; above 14 years of service Rs 100 or £ 10; above 15-17 years of service Rs 60 or £ 6; and above 17 years of service free.

42 A number of cases were reported where in order to claim disability-pension, number of native Non-commissioned Officers and Sepoys were found malingering, showed false assertion of inability to perform their duty, retarded their cure, or aggravated their sickness. In order to check such mischievous practice, such individual were examined by special medical board and were dismissed from the service. Jephson George, 1847, The Orders and Regulations of the Bengal Army, Part II, Calcutta: WM Thacker and Company, pp. 588.

43 No soldier could be discharged from the service of the Company except by authority of the Commander in Chief, with the following exceptions: (i) those not permanently enlisted; (ii) those recruited on temporary basis like Puckallies, Bhisties and Artificer, (iii) those discharged by sentence of a court martial duly confirmed, and (iv) those individuals convicted of disgraceful conduct involving discharge or was sentenced to Imprisonment with hard labour by the civil or military court and such sentence was duty confirmed. General Regulations of the Madras Army, Adjutant General Office, Fort St George, 1849, Madras: Military Male Orphan Asylum Press, p. 89-91.

proper to order the punishment of flogging. By an order dated 19 May 1834, it was directed that a native Non-commissioned Officers or Sepoys should not be discharged from the service after having suffered corporal punishment, unit he have fully recovered from the effects of it and duly certified by the medical officer.

No application for the discharge of a soldier "at his own request" was forwarded to the Headquarters, unless such Soldier had clearly and explicitly stated to the Officer in charge of his troop or company and repeated in the presence of Officer Commanding the Corps, that his request to be discharged is perfectly voluntary. Before any soldier was recommended for discharge on medical grounds, a certificate on specified form was required form the medical officer. Every soldier on being discharged was furnished with a discharge certificate, printed on whole sheet of Foolscap paper, both in English and the Vernacular of the man discharged. Every man was minutely examined prior to his discharge and not only any marks, but also peculiarity of features, expressions, make, in short anything which would facilitate his being identified was noted in his roll. Whenever a discharged man was re-enlisted, his Discharge Certificate was taken from him and destroyed in his presence.[44]

The Commanding Officers of the Corps were to issue the certificate of discharge to those who whose contracted time of service has expired and were not desirous of continuing in the service.[45] The European soldiers whose contractual period of the Company service has completed and they desired to remain in India were subject to Military Law pending the completion of arrangements for their discharge. In the cases of Irregular Horse, for misconduct, duffadars and private could be discharged from the service, upon their being pronounced unworthy or unfit by five native officers of the Corps, whose opinion, was to be recorded.[46] When soldiers obtained their discharge, every article of dress and ornament appertaining to it, became their property, except the coats in wear, and they were allowed to take them or leave them with their Company, receiving from the Quarter Master just consideration in money. The Non-commissioned officers and soldiers were not to be dismissed from the service, except by the sentence of a general court martial, or on special order of the Governor General in Council or Commander in Chief. Every discharge of Non-commissioned officers and sepoys was to be published in the Regimental Orders.[47]

Whenever orders were given to discharge a soldier with ignominy, they were carried into effect in the following manner: The Regiment being paraded, and the man about to be discharged brought forward, the several crimes and irregularities of which he had been guilty were to be recapitulated, and the order for his dismissal from the Service to be read. The buttons, facings, lace and any other distinctions were stripped from his clothing, his jacket turned, and he was then to be marched down the rank, and trumpeted or drummed off the parade of the Corps.

44 General Regulations of the Madras Army, Adjutant General Office, Fort St George, 1849, Madras: Military Male Orphan Asylum Press, p. 89-91.

45 Every native soldier, after expiry of three years of service was entitled to his discharge in time of peace, if his Company was not ten men short of its complement. Native Infantry Standing Order 1828, section 18.

46 A.G.'s letter to Company Commander, Irregular Horse dated 21 June 1809.

47 Jephson George, 1847, *The Orders and Regulations of the Bengal Army*, Part II, Calcutta: WM Thacker and Company, pp. 585-587.

Chapter IV

Evolution of Military Legal System

The British Military Legal System

Britain, in early times was divided under the feudal system into many fiefs, and as and when required, each of fiefs furnished forces to the crown.[1] Troops were thus raised for a particular service and were disbanded upon the cessation of hostilities. There was no permanent military force or standing army. Military forces existed only in time of war and these men were retainers of the Crown rather than servants of the State. The Crown under its prerogative made rules and regulations, with the advice of the Constable, or of the Peers, and other experienced persons, for the government and discipline of its troops during their embodiment and service. These rules were known as "Articles of War".[2] These could also be enacted by the Commander-in-Chief in pursuance of an authority for that purpose given in his commission from the Crown. The earlier articles of war were of excessive severity, inflicting death for almost every crime. These Articles or War or Ordinances, however, remained in force only during the service of the troops for whose government they were issued, and ceased to operate on the conclusion of peace.

The earliest complete code seems to have been the "Statutes, Ordinances, and Customs" of Richard II, issued by him to his army in the ninth year of his reign (1385), and probably on the occasion of the war with France.[3] These are followed by the statutes of Henry V made by him during his conquest of France[4]. In 1642, Lord Essex, the leader of the Parliamentary forces, under

1 England under William the Norman was entirely a military establishment. The kingdom was divided into 62,215 military fiefs or portions of land. The subjects were tied down to the military service at the command of the Crown. Every possessor of a Knight's fief was bound to furnish a soldier to attend the King in his wars, during forty days in every year. Thus the king had, at his absolute command, and free from all expense, an army of more than 62,000 men. As the Crown, however, during the peace, was more in want of money than of men, it became customary to take pecuniary commutations in lieu of personal service; though in reality the military part of the feudal system was understood to be strictly constitutional, till it was formally abolished at the Restoration. Jackson Tatlow, 1862, *Martial Law: What it is? Who can declare it*, Philadelphia, John Campbell Booksellers, p. 4.

2 McLean Ridley, Historical Sketch of Military Law, *Journal of Criminal Law and Criminology*, Vol. 8, May 1917-March 1918, p. 27-32.

3 Manual of Military Law, War Office, 1907, London: His Majesty's Stationery Office. p. 6-7.

4 For more details see: Grose Francis, 1788, *Military Antiquities Respecting A History of English Army: From The Conquest to the Present Time*, Vol. I and II, London: S. Hooper, pp. 412/621.

authority given by an ordinance of the Lords and Commons, issued Articles of War almost in the same language as the Royal Articles of War.

During the Charles I regime, the army was ill-paid and undisciplined, and when employed committed serious outrages. In order to repress such wrongs, the King gave commissions to the Lords Lieutenants and their deputies, to proceed against all soldiers, mariners, and other disorderly persons joining with them, who should be guilty of felonies, robberies, murders, or other misdemeanors, and to execute all such persons immediately as in time of war. In the interval between the King's fourth and fifth parliament, the Scots having invaded England, an army of 21,000 men was raised by Charles for the necessary defence of the kingdom. An ordinance was passed in August 1644 by both Houses, which had the following principal heads and clauses:

> The Earl of Essex, captain-general of the Parliamentary forces, together with the Earls of Northumberland, Kent, Pembroke, Salisbury, Manchester, Denbigh, and forty-nine others of the nobility, gentry, and principal officers, or any twelve of them, are appointed commissioners, with full power to hear and determine all such causes as "belong to military cognizance," according to the following articles; and to try, condemn, and execute all offenders against them, or otherwise punish them according to the nature of their offences:
>
> Art. I. No person whatever shall go from London and Westminster, or any part of the kingdom under the power of the Parliament, to hold any communication whatever either personally, by letters, or messages, with the King, Queen, or Lords of the Council abiding with them, without consent of both Houses, or their committee for managing the war, or the Lord General or officer commanding in chief, on pain of death, or other corporal punishment at discretion.
>
> II. Whosoever shall plot, contrive, or endeavour the betraying or surrendering to the enemy, or shall actually betray and surrender, contrary to the rules of war, any cities, towns, forts, magazines, or forces under the power of the Parliament, shall be punished with death.
>
> III. No person whatsoever; not under the power of the enemy, shall voluntarily relieve any person being in arms against the Parliament, knowing him to be so, with money, victuals, or ammunition, on pain of death, or other corporal punishment at discretion; nor shall voluntarily harbour any such, on pain of such discretionary punishment.
>
> IV. No officer or soldier shall make any mutinous assemblies, or be assisting thereunto, on pain of death.
>
> V. No guardian or officer of any prison, shall willfully suffer any prisoner of war to escape, on pain of death; or negligently, on pain of imprisonment, and further punishment at discretion.
>
> VI. Whosoever shall voluntarily take up arms against the Parliament, having taken the national covenant, shall die without mercy.
>
> VII. Whatsoever officer or commander shall desert his trust, and adhere to the enemy, shall die without mercy.

> Further, the said commissioners, or any twelve of them, shall be authorized to sit, as often as they shall think fit, or shall be ordered by both or either House of Parliament, in some convenient place in London or Westminster, or lines of communication; and to appoint a Judge-Advocate, a Provost Marshal, and all other necessary officers.
>
> And further, all mayors, sheriffs, justices, constables, bailiffs, etc. are required to aid the said commissioners in the execution of the premises.
>
> Provided, that no member of either House of Parliament, or assistants of the House of Peers, shall be subject to the authority of the said commissioners without consent of both Houses; And the endurance of this ordinance is limited to four months, from eight days after the publication of the same.

Many trials by Court Martial were held under the Ordinance of 1644.[5] Sir Alexander Carew was tried for a design to deliver up the garrison of Plymouth to the King, condemned, and beheaded. Sir John Hotham, formerly governor of Hull, was tried by the same court on five several charges: (1) Betraying his trust, and adhering to the enemy. (2) His refusal to supply the Lord Fairfax with ammunition, to the great prejudice of the Parliament. (3) His scandalous words against the Parliament. (4) His endeavour to betray Hull to the enemy. (5) His correspondence with the Queen, and his seeking to escape. He was condemned, on the testimony of thirty witnesses, and the evidence of his own letters, to be beheaded on Tower-hill. However, the House of Lords, on a petition from himself and his son, voted him a pardon. The Commons declared this procedure of the Lords to be most illegal; then sent their own order to the Lieutenant of the Tower for immediate execution; and the prisoner was accordingly beheaded. Mr. L'Estrange was tried under the same ordinance, by the city Court Martial of London, on the charge of his coming as a spy, without drum, trumpet, or pass, from the King's quarters at Oxford, and tampering with the lieutenant-governor of Lynne-Regis, to deliver up that garrison to the King. He was condemned to death, but later escaped and got beyond the seas.[6]

Articles of War were also issued by Charles II in 1666, when the first Dutch war was declared, and in 1672, upon the outbreak of the second Dutch war; and by James II in 1685, on the occasion of Monmouth's rebellion. Military law, in time of peace, did not come into existence till the

5 The military power, in the hands of the Parliament, was exemplified in a variety of orders issued from time to time for the conduct of the war; and among others, a regulation was made, that all soldiers and officers of the city's marching regiments should instantly repair to their posts, under pain of immediate death to the common men, and a trial by Martial law to the officers; an ordinance of a singular spirit from, the same men who had denied the competency of punishing, by the Martial law, (unless when actually in sight of an enemy), even the most atrocious act of mutiny, namely, soldiers murdering their officers. On the expiration of the ordinance under which these trials were held, another was framed nearly to the same purpose, but with the additional proviso, that all the officers of the army should be nominated and approved of by both Houses, and should, within twenty days of their appointment, subscribe the national League and Covenant. By this ordinance 40 officers, specially named, together with some civilians and common lawyers, or any twelve or more of them, were appointed a Court Martial within London and Westminster, to try all offenders against any of its regulations. For more details see: Tytler Alexander Fraser, 1814, *An essay on Military Law and the Practice of Courts Martial*, London: Military Library, pp. 423.

6 Tytler Alexander Fraser, 1814, *An essay on Military Law and the Practice of Courts Martial*, London: Military Library, pp. 75-77.

passing of the first Mutiny Act in 1689.[7] The Mutiny Act provided that, "Every person mustered and in pay as an Officer or Soldier in the King's Army found guilty by Court Martial of exciting, causing, or joining in any mutiny or sedition, or of desertion from the Army, should suffer death or such other punishment as that Court should award." The effect of the Act was, therefore, to leave all ordinary Military /offences to be dealt with, as heretofore, by the Crown alone, but to give Parliamentary sanction to the infliction of Capital Punishment for certain specified offences which, whether regarded as Military or Political, it was expedient should be summarily punished by Courts-martial. Direct authority was then given to the King or to the General of the Army to grant his Warrant to Officers (not under the rank of Colonel) for assembling Courts-martial from time to time for the punishment of offenders. These Statutory (as distinguished from Prerogative) Courts were never to consist of less than thirteen Officers—of the rank of Field Officers for the trial of Field Officers, or of Captains for the trial of other offenders. In all cases they were to have the power of swearing witnesses giving evidence before them, and the life of the accused was guarded by other securities laid down in the Statute: thus, "where the offender may be punished with death," the Judges were to be sworn upon the Holy Evangelists "well and truly to try and determine according to the evidence the matters then pending between the King and the Prisoner:" —they were to proceed in the trial "but between the hours of 8 AM and 1PM," and nine of them at least were to concur in the sentence. Lastly, the life of the Act was limited to seven months from 12 April to 10 November 1689.

On 19 October 1689, Parliament re-assembled and a second Mutiny Act was passed which came into effect on 20 December 1689, thus an interval of more than a month occurred between the lapse of the first Act and the coming into force of the second Act. Successive Mutiny Acts, with certain exceptions of short intervals were passed annually from the year 1690 to 1878. From 1698 to 1702, the nation was at peace and the Mutiny Act was allowed to lapse. On renewal of hostilities in 1702, the Mutiny Act was revived and extended to Ireland. In the next renewal of the Act, new clauses were added for the better enforcement of discipline abroad and certain offences committed abroad could be tried in England. The Crown was also given power to grant commissions for holding court martial within the realm.

The system of governing troops on active service by Articles of War issued under the prerogative power of the Crown, whether issued by the King himself or by the Commander-in-Chief or other officers holding commissions from the Crown, continued from the time of the Conquest till long after the passing of annual Mutiny Acts, and did not actually cease till the prerogative power of issuing such Articles was superseded, in 1803, by a corresponding statutory Power [43 Geo. III, c. 20].

Under the Mutiny Act, power was granted to the Sovereign, to make the Articles of War for the better government of his Majesty's forces, and of constituting Courts Martial, with power to try, hear, and determine any crimes or offences by such Articles of War, and inflict such penalties

7 The effect of the Act was to leave all ordinary military offences to be dealt with, by the Crown alone, but to give Parliamentary sanction to the infliction of capital punishment for certain specified offences which, whether regarded as military or political, it was expedient should be summarily punished by Courts-martial. Clode Charles M., 1874, *The Administration of Justice under Military and Martial Law*, London: John Murray, Albemarle Street, pp. 21.

as the articles direct.[8] However, this extensive power had its limits; and these were of such a nature as to bar every possible exertion of a tyrannical authority, or arbitrary infringement of the valuable rights of the subject. While the right of framing Articles of War, and inflicting penalties, is declared to belong to the Sovereign, at the same time it provided, "That no officer or soldier shall, by such Articles of war, be subjected to any punishment extending to life or limb, for any crime which is not expressed to be so punishable by the Mutiny Act." The penalties, which were authorized for the Sovereign to decree by his own authority, were of a very slight and subordinate nature, and meant merely for the enforcement of good discipline; since the greater crimes, and their appropriate punishments, were defined and regulated by the Mutiny Act, and the penalty of death could not be inflicted by any articles of war, unless for such crimes were expressed to be so punishable by the Mutiny Act.

The Mutiny Act and Articles of War which contained the rules of military discipline, were framed, by the joint will and co-operation of the two houses of British Parliament and of the Sovereign, the legislative and executive powers of the state; and the observance of these rules were enforced, either by plain, specific, and fixed penalties appropriated to each offence, where the crime is of a positive nature, admitting of no gradations; or the offence is left, in certain cases where it admits of degrees of criminality, to the decision of a jury, in other words, of a court martial.

In 1803, The Mutiny Act brought out major constitutional changes. With the Mutiny Act of 1803 the power of the Crown to make any Articles of War became statutory and the former prerogative was merged in the Act of Parliament. On the resumption of hostilities, the Act and statutory Articles were applied in 1813 towards the close of the peninsular war to the troops and the prerogative power of making Articles of War in time of war was thus finally superseded by a statutory power. The settled law thus continued thereafter and the British army was governed by the Mutiny Act and statutory Articles until the year 1879. In 1881, the earlier law was updated by making certain amendments in the Army Act of 1881. When Royal Air Force was founded as separate Service in 1918 it adopted a legal and disciplinary system based upon that of the Army.[9] After the revision of the Army and Air Force Acts (Transitional Provisions), two new Acts came into force: The Army Act 1955 and the Air Force Act, 1955.

For discipline of the fleet, the first record of instructions is found in an Ordinance of 1190 issued by King Richard I for the Third Crusade Fleet wherein the King appointed certain high ranking

8 **The Mutiny Act** was an Act of Parliament passed by both Houses of Parliament, and approved by the Queen annually. It was entitled "An Act for the punishment of Mutiny and Desertion, and for the better payment of the Army and their Quarters." The duration of the Mutiny Act is for twelve months. The Mutiny Act, being a regular Act of Parliament, binds civilians as well as soldiers, on such points as are therein especially declared to be applicable to the former. Therefore, all questions concerning civilians must be provided for in the Mutiny Act, e. g., billets, recruiting, apprehension of a deserter, compulsory attendance of a civilian witness, recruit deserting before becoming liable to military law, etc. **The Articles of War** were ordinances framed by the Sovereign under the authority of the Mutiny Act for the government of the Army. They were permanent till altered by the Sovereign, i. e., they were not framed afresh annually, but remained in force till any alteration in them was made and published by the order of the Sovereign. The Articles of War were binding on soldiers only. Gorham Major, 1887, *A Short Course of Military Law as Applicable to Persons Subject to the Mutiny Act*, Calcutta: Thacker, Spink, and Co., pp. 5-6.

9 Blackett Jeff, 2009, *Rant on the Court Martial and Service Law*, Oxford: Oxford University Press, p. 4.

officers to be judiciaries over the combined fleet of England, Normandy, Britanny, and Pictou and listed a number of offences and their punishments. A copy of the ordinance was to be nailed to the foremost of each ship and disciplinary powers were delegated to the captains of the ships, with the commander having the sole powers over more serious offences. In the Royal Navy, the disciplinary system evolved through the eighteenth and nineteenth centuries. Because of the need to maintain discipline in harsh conditions of the ship of that era and voyages lasting for years, the captains in the navy were given more summary powers over their men. In 1886, under a new Navy Discipline Act certain judicial reforms were introduced and rules and procedures were updated. The power of a captain was reduced to a maximum of three months of imprisonment. The Judge Advocate General of the Fleet supervised legal proceedings of the Royal Navy and reviewed all legal proceedings and rulings.

In the UK, each of the three services has its own disciplinary code—the Army Act, 1955; the Air Force Act, 1955; and the Naval Discipline Act, 1957—together known as Service Discipline Acts (SDA). The SDAs enable the service authorities to try service offenders for offences, whether committed in the UK or abroad. They have to be renewed by Parliament every five years by means of amendments, known as Armed Forces Acts, which incorporate changes and update them. In 1996, in the context of several cases relating to the operation of military justice that had been referred to the European Court of Human Rights (ECHR),[10] the British authorities set about significantly reforming the system of military justice. In 2006, the SDAs were repealed and replaced by the Armed Forces Act 2006 established the standing Court Martial to administer justice in the three services of the Armed Forces. [11]

II. The Military Law in India

A. Army

Military law in India originated from a union between classical Indian traditions and the culture imposed by the British Army.[12] The history of military law in India is co-extensive with that of the Indian Army created by the British.[13] The East India Company (EIC) had established factories or trading posts at Surat, Masulipacam, Armagon, Madras, Hooghly and Balasore in the first half of the seventeenth century. These factories were initially guarded by Europeans

10 The most well-known case was of *Findlay v The United Kingdom* (1997) 24 EHRR 221 ECHR, judgment dated 25 February 1997. The other cases were *Coyne v The United Kingdom*, judgment dated 24 September 1997, Case No 124/1996/734/942; *Hood v The United Kingdom*, judgment dated 18 February 1999, Communication No 27267/95; and *Cable and Ors v The United Kingdom*, judgment dated 18 February 1999, Communications 24436/1994 and *Grieves v. UK* [2003] ECHR 57067/00.

11 Blackett Jeff, 2009, *Rant on the Court Martial and Service Law*, Oxford: Oxford University Press, p. 5-7.

12 Clemmons, Byard Q, 'Military Justice in India and the United States: A Comparison', *Strategic Analysis*, May 1989, p. 205.

13 In 1608, William Hawkins landed at Surat with the 300-ton ship *Hector*. The ship *Hector* was chartered by the Company of Merchants of London, trading to the East Indies under a charter granted eight years earlier by Queen Elizabeth I. Hawkins' purpose was to establish a trading station or a factory. Finding that permission to do so could be obtained only from the Mughal Emperor at Agra, he set off for the capital on 1 February 1609. He hired 50 Pathans as escort, the first military force to be raised by the British in India.

recruits. Subsequently, Indians were enrolled as armed guards or peons with the dual objective of protecting the factories of the EIC and lending dignity to its principal functionaries. As the factories grew in size and importance, the peons were organised in a semi-military structure, and gradually, improvements were made in their organisation. The Company also recruited a few local armed troops for defending assets at their post at Bombay. In certain cases special restrictions were placed by treaty on their strength, so as to prevent their acquiring any military importance. The organisation of these guards was later improved and from them emerged East India Company's European and native troops. Both of these steadily increased in numbers.

The rise of Native Army, may be traced to the year 1748, when owing to the hostilities between England and France which had by that time extended to India, a small body of sepoys were enlisted at Madras in defence of the British settlement of Fort St. George.[14] The recruitment by the Company of troops of this class was afterwards recognized by two Statutes of 1754 and 1760 respectively.

An Act was passed for the discipline of the East India Company's troops in 1754, entitled, "for punishing Mutiny and Desertion of officers and soldiers in the service of the United Company of Merchants of England trading to the East-Indies; and for the Punishment of Offences committed in the East-Indies, or at the Island of Saint Helena.[15] Section 8 of this Act empowered the King to make Articles of War for the government of these troops, and such articles were accordingly made and published.[16] The terms of the Act were wide enough to cover both European and native troops, but the language of these articles themselves shows that they were originally intended for Europeans only. In the absence of any other code, however, the Governments of Bengal, Madras, and Bombay seem to have applied these articles, with such modifications and omissions as appeared necessary, to the bodies of native troops maintained by them. During these years of British dominion over India, a military commander's authority to punish was virtually unfettered.[17]

In 1786, an important change also took place in Bengal army as regard the native officers, who, for the first time, got commissions signed by the commander-in-chief; until that year they only had warrants signed by the officer commanding the brigade to which they belonged; and there used to be eight or nine battalions in a brigade. About the same time a sergeant major and quarter-master sergeant (Europeans) were added to each native corps. The issue which came up was whether a native officer, who has a commission (which he can only be deprived by the sentence

14 Carnduff, H.W.C., 1904, *Military and Cantonment law in India*, Calcutta: S.K. Lahiri & Co. p. i.

15 27 George II Cap. IX and 1 George III, Cap. XIV.

16 Article VIII: The King may make Articles of War, "Provided always, and be it enacted, That it shall and may be lawful to and for his Majesty to form, make, and establish Articles of War, for the better Government of the said United Company's Forces, and for bringing Offenders against the same to Justice; and to erect and constitute Courts-martial, with Power to try, hear, and determine any Crimes or Offences by such Articles of War, and inflict Penalties by Sentence or Judgment of the same, as well within the said United Company's Limits of Trade, as in the said Island of Saint Helena."

17 Speaking of the power of life or death held by the Commander-in-Chief in India, Sir James Mac-Donald justified it in these remarkable words: 'That if he held not this power, he might find himself in any *moment*—instead of commanding an Army—in command of an *armed* mob.' Clode, Charles M, *Military Forces of the Crown; Their Administration and Government*, Vol II, John Murray, London, 1869, p 354.

of the government, the commander-in-chief, or a general court martial), shall be obliged to report to, or receive orders from a European, who has no commission, or written authority, authorizing him to command native officers. Further, in case it should so happen that all the European officers with a native corps were to fall, who should take the command of that corps, whether a native officer who has a commission as subedar-major, or a European with the rank of serjeant-major. In most regiments the native officers were made to receive orders from the European Serjeants and were never authorized to command the troops.[18]

The disciplinary power over the Native troops was conferred initially by section 96 of the East India Act, 1813 (53 George III, c. 155).[19] This Act gave power to the Government of the three Presidencies to make laws; regulations and Articles of War to govern the activities of all officers and soldiers within the limits of the said Company's Charter.

> **The Government in India empowered to make laws, regulations, and articles of war, for the native troops; and to hold courts-martial**
>
> And whereas doubts have been entertained whether the several governments of the said Company have sufficient power in all cases to make laws and regulations and articles of war, for the order and discipline of officers and soldiers, being natives of the East-Indies, or other places within the limits of the said Company's Charter, in the service of the said Company, and for the administration of justice by courts-martial to be holden upon such officers and soldiers; and it is expedient that such doubts should be removed: be it therefore enacted and declared, that the several governments of Fort William, Fort Saint George, and Bombay,[20] have and shall, during the continuance of the term hereby granted to the said Company, be deemed and taken to have full power and authority to make all such laws and regulations and articles of war, as they may think fit, for the order and discipline of all officers and soldiers, natives of the East-Indies, or other places within the limits of the said Company's Charter, in their respective services, and for the administration of justice by courts-martial to be holden on such native officers and soldiers, and for the constitution and manner of proceeding of such courts-martial, and for all other purposes relating to or in any manner concerning such native officers and soldiers, in as full and ample a manner as the said governments respectively may make any other laws or regulations for the government of the natives of the several territories subject to the said presidencies respectively, any Act of Parliament, or other matter or thing, to the contrary notwithstanding: provided always, that all laws, regulations, and articles of war, hereafter to be made respecting any of the matters aforesaid, whereby the rights, persons, or property of any such native officers or soldiers may be affected, shall be made and promulgated in every respect in the same manner as other regulations affecting the rights, persons, or property of natives or other individuals amenable to the provincial courts of the presidency of Fort William in Bengal, are directed to be made by virtue of an Act passed in the thirty-seventh year of his Majesty's reign, intituled, "An Act for the better Administration of Justice at Calcutta, Madras, and Bombay,

18 Badenach Walter, 1826, *Inquiry into the State of the Indian Army*, London: William Clowes, p. 142-143.

19 53 Geo. III. Cap. 155.

20 The Governor-General-in-Council was the only local authority at this time possessing the power of legislation.

> and for preventing British Subjects from being concerned in Loans to the Native Princes in India."

Later it was clarified that the rules framed originally for the maintenance of discipline in the British Army were applicable to all the rank and file of the native army too. In fact there was no clearly codified law to administer the native army. This was also highlighted by the Judge-Advocate-General of Bombay stating that none of the three Presidencies has as yet established Laws, Regulations or Articles of War for the better government of the Native Troops. Thus, the Act of 1824, confirmed that in the absence of such laws, the legislation meant for the British Army should apply to the native army of each Presidency. Under the statutory provisions of the Acts of 1813 and 1824, a new military code was framed in the Madras Presidency to enforce discipline in the native army.

Eventually section 73 of the Government of India Act, 1833 (3 & 4 Will. c. 85)[21] empowered the Governor-General-in-Council to enact laws applicable to all native officers and soldiers and lay down regulations for the holding of courts martial.[22] The regulations, entitled 'Rules and Articles for the better government of the officers and soldiers in the service of the East India Company from the 1st day of January 1841', shifted much of the power to punish from the sole discretion of the military commander to a court-martial panel of officers.[23] A commander wishing to impose substantial punishment was forced to convene a court-martial. The court-martial consisted of 13 commissioned officers, led by a non-lawyer president, who could seek counsel from an appointed legal advisor. There was no judge advocate, and the president controlled the proceedings with regard to both issues of fact and law. The Commander in Chief, the officer convening the court martial had the power to sent back the proceedings for revision to the same court, if he disagreed with the findings and sentence of a court martial.

Under the powers conferred upon it by the Act of 1833 the Indian Legislature for the first time provided a common code for the Native Armies of India in 1845, "Articles of War" for those armies being enacted by the Governor General in Council as Act XX of that year. This Act was shortly after repealed and replaced by Act XIX of 1847.

---

21 Prior to this, three different systems of military laws operated in India: of the Queen's troops, that of the Company's Europeans, and that of the Company's troops who were "Natives of the East Indies or other places within the limits of the Company's Charter". By section 73 of the Government of India Act, 1833, the power to legislate for the Native army was restricted to the Governor General in Council, and laws so made were given general application to all "native officers and soldiers" wherever serving.

22 The effect of British of military law on the natives of India was considered beneficial by the British officers. One such officer comments, ".... a strong inducement for us to extend it further, as it almost entirely changes their habits, and corrects that part of their conduct in which they are most apt to go wrong. The contrast between two native brothers, educated in the same way, becomes, after the one has been a sepoy, and the other employed in civil situations for a short time, as great as possibly can be. The sepoy fulfils every reasonable hope we can expect from him, whilst in the other we are as generally disappointed, and the reason is very obvious, for while the sepoy's good conduct entitles him to reward, bad conduct makes him fully as certain of punishment." Badenach Walter, 1826, *Inquiry into the State of the Indian Army*, London: William Clowes, pp. 87-88.

23 Singh MP, *The Indian Army Under the East India Company,* Sterling Publishers Pvt Ltd, New Delhi, 1976.

The 1857 Mutiny caused reconstruction both of British administration and of the British military system in India.[24] The territories directly administered by the East India Company were transferred to the Crown under a Viceroy. The Company's army was incorporated into the British army.[25] During the period of May 1857 to December 1859, various temporary Acts were passed to deal with the mutineers and other law & order issues faced by the Government.[26]

The Act of 1847 was again supplemented by Act VI of 1860. The Act of 1847 which, having been frequently amended in the intervening period, was repealed by Act XXIX of 1861.[27] The Act of 1861 consolidated and amended the Articles of War.[28] The revised Articles of War gave commanding officers the summary power to reduce non-commissioned officers (NCO) to the ranks and to discharge NCOs and soldiers (a punishment that carried with it a mandatory loss of pension). They were also given the authority to hold summary trials of NCOs and soldiers, and, on conviction of such NCOs and soldiers, to carry out sentences without confirmation from the higher authorities, as long as they were not more severe than those that could be awarded by the district court-martial.

24 On 15 July 1858, a Royal Commission was set up in London 'to inquire into the organization of the Indian Army'. This body, known as the Peel Commission—after its chairman Major General Jonathan Peel, Secretary of State for War—was asked to respond to eleven questions regarding the army's future organisation. Report of Commission Appointed to Enquire into the Organisation of the Army (Peel Commission), London, 1859.

25 Barnett, Correlli, 1970, *Britain and Her Army 1509-1970: A Military, Political and Social Survey*, Allen Lane, The Penguin Press, London, p. 175.

26 These include: Act VIII of 1857 for the trial and punishment of offences against the Articles of War for the Native Army; Act XI of 1857 for the trial of persons who rebel, or wage war against the Queen or the Government of the East India Company; Act XIV of 1857 to make further provision for the trial and punishment of certain offences relating to the Army, and of offences against the State; Act No XVI of 1857 to make temporary provision for the trial and punishment of heinous offences in certain Districts; Act No XVII of 1857 to provide temporarily for the apprehension and trial of Native Officers And Soldiers for Mutiny and Desertion; Act No XXXII of 1857 to amend the Articles of War for the Native Army (Marking of those accused of desertion and mutiny with letters D and M respectively); Act XXIII of 1858 to authorize in certain cases the transportation of offenders sentenced to imprisonment; Act XXVI of 1858 to make further provision for the trial and punishment of offences against the State; and Act XXVII of 1859 for further continuation of Acts XIV of 1857, XVI of 1857, and XVII of 1857.

27 An Act to consolidate and amend the Articles of War for the government of the Native Officers and Soldiers in Her Majesty's Indian Army; Act No XXIX of 1861, passed by the Legislative Council of India, which received the assent of the Governor-General on the 7th September 1861.

28 In 1858, a questionnaire to bring reforms in the military code and rules of discipline in the Bengal Native Infantry was circulated amongst senior military officers of the British Army in India. The first five questions were: 1. Can you suggest improvement in the Articles of War in use? 2. Should the special rules regulating punishment in the native Army be made, or should they be assimilated to the rules which obtain in the British Army? 3. Does the system of native Court Martial work satisfactorily? 4. What measures are adopted to acquaint the Native Troops of Bengal in the military code under which they live and are governed? 5. What proportions of the Native troops can read for themselves, in the Vernacular dialect, the Articles of War? The remaining three questions were related to maintaining the discipline in Police Corps. The suggestions were: a thorough revisions of the Articles of War; increase in the powers of the Brigade Commander to dismiss a native soldier having less than five years of service; increase in the powers of the commanding officer to award punishment to a native soldier; and the abolition of the native regimental court martial system. Precise of the Replies to the Questions of Infantry: Military Code and Rules of Discipline, compiled by Lt Col H.M. Durand, 1858.

The Act of 1861 was amended twice, once in 1863 and a second time in 1865, and by the year a number of shortcomings were observed that it was decided to codify the whole law on the subject. The result was The Indian Articles of War, Act V of 1869. In the preamble to this Act reference was for the first time made to "native officers, soldiers, and other persons in Her Majesty's Indian Army," thus recognizing the existence of 'followers' in the categories of other persons. The Act 1869 (the Indian Articles of War) vested considerable powers in the commanding officers with regard to reward and punishment. By 1873, the commanding officers could also deprive soldiers of good conduct badge pay.[29] The Act of 1869 remained in India statue book until 1894.[30]

The amalgamation of the three native armies in 1895 necessitated significant amendments to the Indian Articles of War. These amendments were made by Act XII of 1894. No new military offences were created, but some of those existing were more clearly defined. The provisions were also made for the trial by court martial of crimes of violence committed by Native Officers and Soldiers on other military men, these having formerly been triable by ordinary criminal courts alone, and in general law was simplified and improved. The Indian Articles of War, as altered by the Act of 1894 and various minor amending acts, formed the statutory basis of the Indian Military Code until 1911, when the amendment of the Indian Articles of War was taken up again and the Indian Army Act, 1911 was passed. It came into force on 1 January 1912, repealing all previous acts on the subject. This act was subsequently altered by various amending Acts.[31] During the World War I, incidents of depression and self-inflicted injuries did occur. During the period 1886-1930, there were at least 14 incidents of mutiny in the British Indian Army. However, most of these mutinies had religious background or when an officer violated the implicit contract between the Indian sepoy and British commanders. In certain instance unpopular commanding officers were held accountable for the dissents were also removed. [32]

The Indian Army (Suspension of Sentences) Act, 1920: During the First World War (1914-18) temporary Acts were passed to provide for the suspension of sentences. These measures were found to be beneficial to the British Government, and on 23 March 1920 a permanent Act to provide for the suspension of sentences of imprisonment or transportation passed by courts-

29 David, Saul, *The Indian Mutiny 1857*, Viking, London, 2002.

30 By the Madras and Bombay Armies Act, 1893 (56 & 57 Vict., c. 62) the offices of the Provincial Commander-in-Chief of Madras and Bombay were abolished and certain duties and powers were transferred to the Government of India; and thereupon legislation was moved to Pass the Indian Articles of War Amendment Act, 1894.

31 As time went on, the Indian Army began to take its share in the imperial responsibilities of the British Army. It was found that an Act originally framed for three separate local forces, each serving as a rule in its own Presidency, failed to provide adequately for the discipline and administration of that army under modern conditions. Owing also to the mass of amendments super-imposed on the original articles, these were often difficult to understand, and sometimes even self-contradictory. See: Acts of Governor General in Council, XV of 1914, X of 1917, XI of 1918, XVIII of 1919, II of 1920, XXII of 1923, VIII of 1930, XXXIII of 1934 and VII of 1935. Army Department Notification No 911 dated 3 November 1911, Part IV.

32 The 3 Gurkha, for example, mutinied in 1886 when their colonel reduced their customary rice Batta. The protest of men to light a number of related grievances relating to food, costly fuel, absence of suitable place for cooking in barracks; so the sepoy had to go hungry when it rained. The native officers did not heed the men's complaints and new commanding officer, a colonel was unpopular. Two companies of the 17 Bombay Infantry mutinied for similar reasons. David Omissi, 1994, *The Sepoy and the Raj: The Indian Army, 1860-1940*, London: Macmillan Press, p. 140-147.

martial on persons subject to the Indian Army Act, which repealed the temporary Acts, came into force.[33]

B: The Naval Forces

The East India Company, in 1612, maintained a naval force of frigates and small cruising craft as Company's Marine.[34] In 1615 the Portuguese assault force that attacked Goa included 6,000 Indians and 2,600 Europeans. The Dutch had a large naval force in place in the East during 1620s, with roughly sixty-six ships actively engaged in various military actions across ports. The British, in contrast, had only two small vessels to protect coastal English trade in 1669; which made for the modest beginning of the Company's first naval force, the Bombay Marine. By 1686, with British commerce having shifted predominantly to Bombay, the name of this force was changed to Bombay Marine. Beginning in 1690 the British Royal Navy provided assistance to the Company by escorting ships through the Atlantic as a safeguard against pirates and hostile combatants in times of war.[35] This force rendered unique service, fighting not only the Portuguese, Dutch and French, but also interlopers and pirates of various nationalities. The Bombay Marine was involved in combat against the Marathas and the Sidis and participated in the Burma War in 1824. In 1830 the Marine was renamed the Indian Navy but did not long survive as a fighting service the end of the East India Company's rule. In 1863, the remaining ships and men were reorganized into the Bombay Marine, renamed Her Majesty's Indian Marine in 1877. At this time, the Marine had two divisions, the Eastern Division based at Calcutta under the Superintendent, Bay of Bengal, and the Western Division at Bombay under the Superintendent, Arabian Sea.

In recognition of the services rendered during various campaigns, its title was changed to Royal Indian Marine in 1892, by which time it consisted of over 50 vessels.[36] The Marine was formally re-designated as the Royal Indian Marine (RIM) in 1892. This, however, meant little change in its size or in its dedication to surveying, trooping and local security work around India and within the Persian Gulf. The RIM played an active part in the First World War, but its limitations became

33 The provisions of this Act were incorporated in the Indian Army Act, 1950. For more details see Chapter XIV of the Army Act, 1950 on "Pardons, Remissions and Suspensions".

34 The history of the Indian Navy can be traced back to 1612 when Captain Best encountered and defeated the Portuguese. This encounter, as also the trouble caused by the pirates, forced the British East India Company to maintain a small fleet at Swally, near Surat (Gujarat). The First Squadron of fighting ships arrived on 5 September 1612, forming what was then called the Honourable East India Company's Marine. It was responsible for the protection of the East India Company's trade in the Gulf of Cambay and the river mouths of the Tapti and Narmada. From its origins in 1612 as the East India Company's Marine, the Navy underwent various changes, including changes to its name. Over time it was named the Bombay Marine (1686), the Bombay Marine Corps (1829), the Indian Navy (1830), Her Majesty's Indian Navy (1858), the Bombay and Bengal Marine (1863), the Indian Defence Force (1871), Her Majesty's Indian Marine (1877) and the Royal India Marine (1892). It was finally named the Royal Indian Navy (RIN) in 1934. However, it remained a relatively small force until the World War II, when it was greatly expanded.

35 Emily Erikson, 2014, *Between Monopoly and Free Trade: The English East India Company, 1600–1757*: Princeton University Press, pp. 8-10.

36 An Indian Harbour Defence Squadron was created in 1871, but this had an idle and uneventful existence at Bombay with a pair of armoured coast defence ships and a handful of torpedo craft. Manned by a mix of Royal Navy and Indian Marine personnel, it did not survive past 1903.

very clear, particularly during the abortive Mesopotamian campaign of 1915-16, which resulted in the British surrender at Kut. The first Indian to be granted a commission was Sub Lieutenant D.N. Mukherji who joined the Royal Indian Marine as an engineer officer in 1928. In 1934, the Royal Indian Marine was re-organised into the Royal Indian Navy, and was presented the King's Colour in 1935 in recognition of its services. At the outbreak of the Second World War, the Royal Indian Navy (RIN) consisted of eight warships. The RIN remained a force of escorts, minesweepers and light units throughout the Second World War. By the end of the war, its strength had risen to 117 combat vessels and 30,000 personnel who had seen action in various theatres of operations. On India attaining Independence, the RIN consisted of 32 ageing vessels suitable only for coastal patrol, along with 11,000 officers and men. The senior officers were drawn from the Royal Navy. The prefix 'Royal' was dropped on 26 January 1950 with India being constituted as a Republic.[37]

The Legal System of the Navy

The evolution of naval law, so far as today's Indian Navy is concerned, owes its origin to the laws and customs of the sea which formed the original body of rules for the day-to-day maintenance of order and discipline afloat in the British Royal Navy. Originally the discipline of the British Navy rested in the hands of the Lord High Admiral, who, through his Court of Admiralty and the Judge presiding there, exercised Jurisdiction in respect of all Crimes and Offences committed upon the Sea, the Coast, or in the main stream of great rivers.[38]

Sometimes during the fifteenth century, the Lord High Admiral became a permanent officer of state. The admiral was a commander of naval forces in war and performed the functions which on land were performed by the Constables and the Marshal. The admiral applied the law himself or through his delegates. In 1644 an ordinance for the government of the fleet was drafted by the House of Lords, and was passed the Commons in the following year. Power to hold Courts Martial was given to a General Council of War. Further powers were given in 1648 and in 1652, and the "Laws of War" were issued. In 1653 the Admirals and Generals at Sea, Blake, Monk, Desborough and Penn issued their instructions for the formation of Courts Martial in future. They gave flag officers power to hold a court in their respective fleets, or divisions of a fleet, with a "Council of War" which must not consist of less than three persons. A sentence which entailed loss of life or limb must be referred to the Admirals and Generals "the criminal being still secured," together with minutes of the evidence by the Judge Advocate of the fleet. The Judge Advocate was an officer of the old Admiralty Court, and his presence serves to connect Court Martial with the ancient general jurisdiction of the Admiral. A divisional Court Martial could not cashier a captain without reference to the Admirals and Generals, or a master without the approval of the general of that fleet to which it belonged. Similar powers were vested in the commander of a detachment of not less than three ships. Every captain of a ship belonging to, or in the service of

37 For more details see: Goldrick James, 1997, *No Easy Answers: The Development of the Navies of India, Pakistan, Bangladesh and Sri Lanka 1945—1996*, Papers in Australian Maritime Affairs, No. 2, New Delhi: Lancer Publishers, pp. 269; Hastings Commander D.J., 1988, *The Royal Indian Navy, 1612-1950*, Macfarland & Co., Jefferson, North Carolina, pp. 28-32; Sridharan, Rear Admiral K., 1982, *A Maritime History of India*, Ministry of Information and Broadcasting, New Delhi: Government of India, New Delhi.

38 15 Eich. II, c. 3. For more details see: Clode Charles M., 1874, *The Administration of Justice under Military and Martial Law*, London: John Murray, Albemarle Street, pp. 41.

the Commonwealth was empowered to hold a court with his lieutenant, if he had one, his master, master's mates, the purser, gunner, boatswain, and carpenter, for the trial of offenders belonging to that vessel, subject to the obligation to refer all sentences of life or limb, and for the cashiering of any commissioned or warrant officer to the commander of the party or to the flag commander of the division. These orders of the Admirals and Generals expressly authorized Courts Martial to try and to punish offences committed on shore in any place or harbour.

The limitations in the jurisdiction of a court martial to offences specified in the Act of 1661 by the 13th Charles II[39] and clumsy wording of certain clauses invited serious objections. During the next 90 years several attempts were made to correct these errors and omissions. In 1720 a clause was inserted into an Act, which authorised a court martial to try all who were in actual service and pay for offences against the articles of war committed beyond the jurisdiction of the Admiral. In 1722, the jurisdiction of court martial was further extended. A clause authorizing it to try captains who were found to have merchandize on board their ships (other than bullion which was often shipped in men-of-war for safety's sake) was inserted in an Act for the better suppression of piracy. The collocation is startling, but the real reason for the insertion of the clause was not that navy captains had played the pirate, but that some of them smuggled or interloped within the charter of the East India and the South Sea Companies.

The two Acts of 1746 and 1748 [40] contained the 36 Articles of War, in which almost every possible offence was explicitly set down, and the punishment thereof annexed, or left to the discretion of court martial. It also included sundry clauses of express rules and orders for assembling and holding courts for the trial of any of the offences specified in the Act. The Commanders of the ships were to ensure that they were also to be red over once in every month, in the presence of the officers and seamen, immediately after the articles of war are read, hence no officer or seaman could plead ignorance of the penalties and punishments, to which he was liable, from neglect or disobedience, nor can he be unacquainted with encouragements and benefits, to which seamen were entitled, by a due and faithful performance of their duty.[41] The Articles of War of 1749, as amended by an Act passed in the nineteenth year of George III's reign, constituted the fundamental code by which discipline was maintained in the British navy during the age of Nelson. This code was eminently suited to the exigencies of maritime existence. It provided a flexible system of justice which lasted for well over a century.

The 1749 Articles of War defined four types of crime: (i) relating to contraventions against religion and morality; (ii) against the king and his government; (iii) relating to infringements of the rights

39 The 13th Charles II, c. 89 of 1661: An Act for establishing articles and orders for the regulation and better government of His Majesty's Navies, Ships of War, and forces at sea.

40 In 1748 the Act [19 Geo. III. c.17] was passed to reinforce and extend the Act 1746 [22 Geo. II. c. 33]. The two contained much the same provisions as to the constitution of court martial as the Act of 1749. The naval reform of that year was carried on parallel to a considerable change in the Mutiny Act of the army. In the 19th year of George III, 1779, an Act was passed to authorize a lesser penalty than death for offences against article 10 and 12, and to exempt members of court martial from the obligation to remain on board the ship in which trial was held until the proceedings were completed.

41 McArthur John, 1792, *A Treatise of the Principles and Practice of Naval Courts Martial*, London: Whieldon and Butterworth, pp. 25-26.

of individuals; and (iv) relating to naval infractions. In the first category of offences, officers were admonished to observe the Sabbath according to the rites of the Church of England. Under the Articles, all members of the fleet were expected to maintain a high standard of decorum. Thus, profane oaths, cursing, execrations, Drunkenness, uncleanness, or other scandalous actions, in derogation of God's honour and corruption of good manners were prohibited. Since these offences were considered misdemeanors, the penalties attached to them were left to the discretion of the court. The only crime in this category, the unnatural and detestable sin of buggery or sodomy with a man or beast, was punishable with the mandatory death sentence.

Most crimes in the second category were of more serious nature than those in the first category and were capital. All unauthorized communication with an enemy or rebel was punished with death. Any member of the fleet guilty of failing to report intercourse with an enemy or rebel/ spying, or aiding and abetting an enemy or rebel was liable to death or "such other punishment as the nature and degree of the offence" deserved. All persons convicted of mutiny, mutinous or seditious expressions, or striking a superior officer received a compulsory death sentence. Those who incited disturbances, disobeyed lawful orders, or concealed mutinous plots could be sentenced to death if the court so decided. The members of the fleet who unlawfully destroyed naval property were also punished with death. For other offences in this category, for instance attempts to defraud the government (i.e., embezzlement, signing false musters, etc.) the sentence was left to the discretion of the court.

The third category of offences dealt with infringements of the rights of individuals. Like the clauses dealing with most economic crimes, these Articles gave the court wide discretionary powers. Only murder carried a mandatory death sentence. In cases of theft the court had the option of taking the offender's life or imposing on him a lesser penalty "upon consideration of circumstances." Similarly, the court was granted considerable latitude in determining the sentence for quarrelling and fighting. The fourth category of offences dealt with strictly naval infractions. While the sections punishing crimes against individuals were relatively mild, those of a purely naval character were not. Most of the clauses concerned with naval questions were aimed at the officer corps. Articles X to XIV, enjoined officers to adopt an aggressive posture when engaging an enemy and were to do their utmost to take or destroy them. Those who failed to provide "every possible assistance" to a friendly vessel in peril, or did not pursue a retreating foe was liable to death or such lesser punishment as a court martial thought fit to impose. Under Article XXXIII, officers guilty of behaving in a scandalous, infamous, cruel, oppressive, or fraudulent manner were to be dismissed from the service. Article XVIII prohibited the reception on board the king's ships of any goods or merchandizes whatsoever, other than for the sole use of the ship or vessel, except gold, silver, or jewels, and except the goods and merchandizes belonging to any merchant, or other ship or vessel which may be Shipwrecked, or in imminent danger of being shipwrecked, either on the high seas, or in any port, creek, or harbour, in order to the preserving them for their proper owners. Finally, because the navy was constantly in need of men, especially in time of war, officers were prone to accept deserters from other ships to fill out their complements without reporting them to their former captains.

However, there was confusion relating to power which could be exercised by the commander of a ship over the troops who were on board British warships. Naval commanders maintained their right to punish soldiers stationed in their ships. The case of Lieutenant General Fitzgerald[42] raised certain dissatisfaction as this restriction was considered against the principles of the naval service and in direct contradiction to the statute for the government of His Majesty's ships, vessels and forces by sea. By Section XXIII of the military Articles of 1812,[43] the officers and soldiers embarked on board naval vessels were expected to "conform themselves to the laws and regulations established for the government and discipline of the said ship, and .... consider themselves .... as under the command of the senior officer of that particular ship, as well as of the superior officer of the fleet (if any) to which such ship belongs."

The Articles of War were read publicly at the commissioning of new ships, at least once a month, usually when church was rigged on Sunday, when an offender's punishment warrant was read to the ship's company and at timely intervals by the Captain to the Ship's Company. In the British Navy during the age of sail, flogging was the most common of all punishments. When a disciplinary offence was committed by a member of the Ship's Company and was serious enough to warrant more severe punishment than the captain was authorised to award, notice of the offence would be forwarded to the Admiralty where a 'Warrant Punishment' would be initiated and then sent back to the ship or naval installation for reading and sentencing. Warrant punishments were 'read' publicly while the offender stood to attention in front of the formally mustered ship's company, or if received on board at an unusual hour in front of the fallen in Duty Watch.

The Articles of War of 1749, as amended by an Act passed in the nineteenth year of George III's reign, constituted the fundamental code by which discipline was maintained in the British navy during the age of Nelson. This code was suited to the exigencies of maritime existence. It provided a flexible system of justice which lasted for well over a century. In these Articles almost every possible offense that can be committed in the royal navy is set down in explicit terms, and the punishment thereof annexed. This harsh criminal code was designed to preserve the authority of the ruling classes who administered it by providing these men with legal devices of horror which could be used at the appropriate moments to intimidate the lower orders into accepting

42 In July 1795, Lieutenant Gerald Fitzgerald of the Eleventh Regiment of Foot, then serving on board the Diadem in the Mediterranean, was court-martialled for contempt and dismissed from His Majesty's service and also rendered incapable of ever serving His Majesty, his heirs and successors, in any military capacity. Protesting the legality of the trial, Fitzgerald petitioned the Duke of York, then commander in chief of the army, for redress. In response to the lieutenant's predicament, the Duke, in order to avoid a recurrence of such incident, issued a controversial set of regulations defining the relationship of members of the army to the Articles of War. These regulations stripped naval officers of virtually all power to discipline troops at sea. The second paragraph stated quite clearly the proposed restrictions: "In case any officer or soldier of his Majesty's land forces ..... shall be guilty of any offences against. the laws and regulations established for the government and discipline of the ship on board of which he may have been received/ the commanding officer of such ship is to cause him to be put under arrest or to confine him as a close prisoner, if circumstances and the naval articles shall require it, and if necessary to detain him in either of these situations as long as he shall remain on board, transmitting a report of the charges against him to his superior officer, or to the commander-in-chief of the land forces under whom he may be then placed in order that he may be proceeded against according to law, in case the offences of which he may be accused are such as are cognizable by military courts-martial."

43 52 Geo. III. C. 22.

their dominion. The Articles were intended to maintain the power of admirals and captains to command obedience which was considered the essence of the naval discipline.[44]

The Regulations and Instructions of 1806 gave naval commanders more latitude in matters of discipline.[45] However, certain checks were introduced. After 1806 the Board took several steps to restrict their powers. Four months after the revised manual was issued the Lords Commissioners abolished the penalty of running the gauntlet in which a culprit was scourged by the entire crew. In 1809, the practice of starting, or beating a man with a rope's end, was prohibited. After March 1811 captains were required to transmit quarterly to the Admiralty precise records of punishments. The punishment books were to include the name of the offender, his crime, the date it was committed, the length of his confinement, and the date and type of punishment he received. During the review of the punishment books of period ending July 1812, it revealed the general prevalence of "excessive flogging'. Necessary directions were issued by their Lordships to do everything "to check a practice fraught with consequences so injurious to His Majesty's service".

The Act of 1840 [46] empowered the general or other officer commanding-in-chief of the forces belonging to the presidencies of Fort William, Fort Saint George, and Bombay to appoint general Courts-martial anywhere beyond 120 miles from the presidencies of Fort William, Fort Saint George, and Bombay, except Prince of Wales' Island, Singapore, and Malacca, for trial of capital offences. Under Article XLIII, the Governor General in Council was empowered to make laws and regulations for securing discipline and punishing offences in the India Navy.

The Naval Discipline Act [29 & 30 Vict., c.109] of 10 August 1866[47] streamlined punishments which could be awarded by court martial. It provided that in case of corporal punishment not more than 48 lashes shall be inflicted. Further, no officer shall be subject to corporal punishment and no petty or non-commissioned officer shall be subject to corporal punishment, except in

44 According to John Delafons, who had served as a deputy judge advocate at numerous trials, suggests: "Undoubtedly, men who are amenable to military jurisdiction, submit to many privations, perhaps hardships; but these privations and hardships are indispensably necessary to the welfare of the country, in whose defense they are engaged. Whenever, discipline shall become relaxed; whenever officers shall no longer be competent to assert the power with which they are invested, for the maintenance of subordination and diligence; then, and not till then, will the British Navy, which has hitherto enforced respect and awe on surrounding nations, instead of proudly constituting the bulwark and glory of these kingdoms, become baneful at home, and despicable abroad;— the scourge of their own country, and the derision of their enemies." John Delafons, 1805, *Treatise on Naval Courts Martial*, London: P. Steel, pp. ix-x.

45 Regulations and Instructions Relating to His Majesty's Service at Sea, (2nd ed.), London, 1806, p. 160.

46 The Act to consolidate and amend the Laws for punishing Mutiny and Desertion of officers and Soldiers in the Service of the East-India Company, and for providing for the Observance of Discipline in the Indian Navy, and to amend the Laws or regulating the Payments of regimental debts, and the Distribution of the Effects of Officers and Soldiers Dying in Service, dated 4 August 1840. [3&4 Vict. cap. XXXVII].

47 The Articles of War, as revised in 1749, were replaced by the Naval Discipline Act in 1860, which, subsequently, was replaced by those of 1861, 1864 and 1866. The Act of 1866 incorporated the earlier Acts and remained in force until 1957. Corporal punishment was still permitted but no more than 48 lashes could be inflicted at any one time. Later, a circular letter issued by the Admiralty in 1871 directed that corporal punishment could be inflicted only for mutiny or violence towards a superior officer. In 1899, another letter directed that no Commanding Officer could award a sentence of more than 25 lashes. In March 1949, an Order in Council removed all authority to award corporal punishment.

case of mutiny.[48] During the First World War, Naval law was derived predominantly from two sources, the Naval Discipline Act (NDA), which was also known as the Articles of War, and King's Regulations and Admiralty Instructions (King's Regulations).[49] Elements of these two publications were combined to form the Manual of Naval Law and Court Martial Procedure. Copies of the NDA and King's Regulations were carried on all naval ships, and were theoretically available for consultation by any member of the ship. The NDA comprised 101 different articles in the 1866 edition, with amendments following regularly. In 1913 King's Regulations (in two volumes) covered topics as diverse as 'ceremonies and distinctions' and 'physical training'. Whilst the majority of areas covered by King's Regulations should be considered as guidelines for behaviour, transgression from which would not necessarily result in court martial, there were certain articles which could be seen as offences against naval discipline and which were tried and punished accordingly. All offences against the NDA could theoretically be taken to courts martial; however, in practice, this was not always done, and many officers demonstrated great discretion in dealing with offenders. Regulations covered every area of a serviceman's life.

In 1934, the Indian Legislature passed the Indian Naval (Discipline) Act, 1934 with the Royal Indian Marine becoming the Royal Indian Navy. In order to give effect to this Act, the Regulations for the Indian Navy were framed and promulgated in 1938 as the Regulations for the Navy.[50]

C: The Air Force and its Legal System

In 1909, M. Bleriot, by flying across the English Channel awakened a new interest in aviation in England; and in 1910 Commander-in-Chief in India received the first official application from an officer of the Indian Army for employment as an airman. The request was not granted, and, for the next four years more and flying in India remained in the hands of private enterprise.

In 1912 an officer of the Royal Artillery attended army manoeuvres at Rawalpindi with an early type of Farman biplane and a French pilot. Both the pilot and the machine had been imported into India at the officer's private expense. The few flights that were made, were the first flights in India, but ended in disaster to the aeroplane. However, they bore fruit in directing serious attention to the military potentialities of the new arm. Very soon a decision was taken to establish an Indian Flying School. Accommodation for the school was created in the barracks of the deserted cantonment of Sitapur. The staff was provided by officers of the Indian Army, who, having learnt to fly at their own expense while on leave in England, had afterwards completed a course with the Royal Flying Corps at Farnborough. Mechanics and aeronautical material were provided from England. It was proposed to commence the first course of instruction at Sitapur in September 1914.

48 Article 52 and 53, the Naval Discipline Act of 1866.

49 The King's Regulations and Admiralty Instructions for the Government of His Majesty's Naval Service, London: HMSO, 1913.

50 The law relating to discipline in the Indian Navy was contained in the Indian Navy (Discipline) Act, 1934, passed in pursuance of Section 66 of the Government of India Act, 1919 which was later replaced by Section 105 of the Government of India Act, 1935. The Government of India Acts of 1919 and 1935 empowered the Indian Legislature to apply to title naval forces raised in India, the provisions of the British Naval Discipline Act, 1866 which was set forth in the First Schedule to the Indian Navy (Discipline) Act, 1934.

The outbreak of the First World War, however, delayed the training. It was not possible at that time to anticipate the duration of the war, or the enormous demand for trained aviators; thus the school at Sitapur could not start and its staff and aircraft equipment were devoted to active service in the field. This Indian flying unit, which, may be regarded as the embryo of the Royal Air Force in India, first saw active service with the Indian Expeditionary Force dispatched to Egypt. It performed valuable service in reconnaissance connected with the Turkish attack on the Suez Canal. After the failure of the attack, the unit was relieved by a squadron of the Royal Flying Corps, and its personnel were released for service in Mesopotamia.

The nucleus of the air force required for the Mesopotamia Expeditionary Force, consisted of an air contingent provided by the Commonwealth of Australia. This was supplemented partly by trained men from India, and partly by the Indian Army airmen released from Egypt. The Imperial Government provided aircraft and aviation stores. The composite body thus formed did excellent work in Mesopotamia, but suffered the loss of a great part of its stores, and some of its personnel, in the retreat to Kut and in the siege.

By the middle of 1915 insistent calls for more air squadrons came from every fighting front. It became evident that, in meeting these demands, the best results would be achieved if the air organization for the war were centralized and controlled by single authority. The rapid technical developments made on the European fronts justified a policy of concentration in the hands of the Imperial Government. Thus, the winter of 1915 saw the demise of the Indian Flying Corps as a separate body. In December 1915, the first detachment of the Royal Flying Corps arrived in India. It consisted of No. 31 Squadron and the nucleus of an Aircraft Park, a unit designed for the storage and supply of technical equipment for the squadron. The whole formation was first located at Nowshera, and subsequently at Risalpur (now in Pakistan).

The period of 1916 to 1918 saw witnessed intensive training in the RAF. No large air operations were undertaken, but from time to time flights were detached for operations on the North West frontier. The experience thus gained led to a decision to add to the strength of the air force in India and in 1918 a second squadron was formed. The total strength of the Air Force in India was increased to 80 officers and 600 men. In 1919 four more air squadrons were added, and in 1920, two single-seater squadrons were added. The Air Force was then a body of considerable strength. It consisted of 8 squadrons, two for distant reconnaissance and bombardment, four were equipped for co-operation with troops, and two scout or fighting squadrons. The distribution of the force ranged from Bangalore to Peshawar and Quetta; and its organization received expert advice from the Air Force authorities in the United Kingdom.

The First World War also caused financial constraints and adversely affected the growth of the Air Force. Both the new scout squadrons were dispensed with in 1921, one being transferred to Iraq and the other disbanded. A special inquiry was also made in 1922 into the state of the Air Force in India, conducted by an officer of the Royal Air Force, who visited India on his way to assume command of His Majesty's forces in Iraq. This resulted in further reform of the Royal Air Force in India. The number of existing six squadrons was not increased, but, by certain economic measures were undertaken to attain higher standard of efficiency. Lord Inchcape's Retrenchment

Committee of 1922-23 did not recommend any reduction of the Royal Air Force in India as thus reconstituted.

The Royal Air Force in India was controlled by the Commander-in-Chief in India as part of the defence services of the Indian Empire. The Air Force budget was incorporated in the army estimates. The Commander of the Air Force, the Air Officer Commanding in India, was an Air Vice Marshal and the headquarters of the Air Force was closely associated with Army Headquarters. The Air Officer Commanding has a headquarters staff, constituted in three branches, namely, air staff, personnel, and technical and stores. The system of staff organization was similar to the staff system functioning in the Indian army. The formations subordinate to the RAF Headquarters were (i) Wing Commands, which in turn, comprised the squadrons of aeroplanes; (ii) The Aircraft Depot; and (iii) The Aircraft Park. The three Wing Commands in India, commanded by an officer of the rank of wing commander, were located at Peshawar, Risalpur and Quetta. The total establishment of the Air Force consisted of 218 officers, 1757 British non-commissioned officers and airmen and 138 Indians. The RAF also had its own medical service, which consisted of eleven medical officers and twenty-one medical other ranks. The Indian Air Force was officially established in 1932, when Act No. XIV was passed by the Indian Legislature and received the assent of the Governor General on the 8 April 1932. The Act was similar to the existing Army Act.[51]

After independence, three separate acts came into force for the governance of the three services—the Army Act, 1950;[52] the Air Force Act, 1950;[53] and the Navy Act, 1957.[54] The Army Act and Air Force Act were virtually a continuation of the existing Indian Army Act, 1911. No procedural or other reforms were made in these Acts. The Navy Act adopted a few procedural reforms suggested by the Pilcher Committee[55] on the administration of justice in the UK.[56]

51 The Army in India and its Evolution: Including an Account of the Establishment of the Royal Air Force in India, 1924, Calcutta: Government Printing Press, p. 241.

52 The Army Act, 1950 was passed by the Parliament of India on 22 May 1950 and came into force on 22 July 1950. The Army Rules, 1950 made under section 191 of the Act were subsequently replaced by the Army Rules, 1954. Army Rules are in the nature of procedural laws, such as the Code of Criminal Procedure. Certain amendments were incorporated in the Army Act and in the Army Rules in 1992 and 1993 respectively. SRO 484, dated 27 November, 1954; The amendments were incorporated in the Army Act, 1950 vide Army Amendment Act 37 of 1992, and in the Army Rules vide S.R.O. 17E, dated 6 December 1993.

53 The Air Force Act, 1950 (Act 45 of 1950), was passed by the Parliament in 1950 and came into force on 22 July 1950. The Air Force Rules, 1969, were made as per the provisions of Section 189 of the Air Force Act, SRO No. 123 dated 22 July 1950, Gazette of India, Part II, Section 4, p 87.

54 The Navy Act, 1957 was finally passed by Parliament on 27 December 1957, and came into effect from 1 January 1958. Unlike the Army and the Air Force, the Indian Navy does not have Navy Rules. However, in accordance with the power conferred under Section 184 of the Navy Act, the Central Government has made regulations for the governance, command, discipline and regulation of the naval forces, and for carrying into effect the provisions of the Navy Act. SRO. No. 11-E Extra Ordinary Gazette of India dated 31 December 1957, part II, section 4.

55 The Committee appointed to consider the Administration of Justice under the Naval Discipline Act (1949), commonly known as the Pilcher Committee.

56 Consequent to the passage of the Navy Act, 1957, three earlier Acts were repealed. These were the Indian Navy (Discipline) Act, 1934 (XXXIV of 1934), the Indian Naval Reserve Forces (Discipline) Act, 1939, and the Naval Forces (Miscellaneous Provisions) Act, 1950 (LVII of 1950).

D: Indian Military Nursing Service

The Military Nursing Service[57] was formally established in the present form through the Indian Military Nursing Service Ordinance, 1943. The Section 5 of the ordinance ordained that, all members of the Indian Military Nursing Service shall be of commissioned rank and shall be appointed as officers of the Indian Military Nursing Service by the Central Government by notification in the Official Gazette. The Section 9 (1) provides that provisions of the Indian Army Act, 1911 (now Army Act, 1950), shall, to such extent and subject to such adaptations and modifications as may be prescribed, apply to Officers of the Indian Military Nursing Service as they apply to Indian commissioned officers, unless they are clearly inapplicable to women. The modifications and adaptations of the Indian Army Act 1911, as applicable to Officers of Indian Military Nursing Service were published in the War Department notification no. 923 dated 13 Jun 1944. After the independence of our country, through a special gazette of India notification, the Army Act 1950 was subsequently made applicable to the Officers of Military Nursing Service with suitable modification and adaptation. These adaptations and modifications are contained in Army Order 197/59. These modifications and adaptations of Army Act, 1950 are only pertaining to Military Offences, otherwise, the rest of the Army Act in its entirety is applicable to MNS Officers. The Sections of Army Act dealing with offences (at that time) were modified for the Military Nursing Service, because it was constituted as an all women force. The Nursing Service Officers were the only women serving in the Indian armed forces during the Second World War.

Military Nursing Service (India) Rules, 1944: The Central Government, under the powers conferred by Section 10 of Indian Military Nursing Service Ordinance, 1943, framed the Military Nursing Service (India) Rules, 1944. The Rule 3(a) lays down that the provisions of the Indian Army Act, 1911, shall apply to officers of the Nursing Services mentioned in Sub Section 1 of Section 9 of the Ordinance, as if they were Indian Commissioned Officers, and Sub Rule (b) stipulates that, the provisions of the Army Act shall apply to officers of the Nursing Service mentioned in Sub Section (2) of the said Section, as if they were Officers of the Regular Forces. The Rules 5 and 6 gives the specific adaptations and modification as ordained in Section 9(1)

57 The Indian Military Nursing Service is a corps or regiment of the Indian Army, first formed when under British rule in 1881. The Military Nursing Service stands out as one of the oldest services where women have contributed directly to the nation's war effort by providing care to the sick and wounded soldiers. This is also true for all the armed forces of the world. The Military Nursing Service Indian Army has its origin from the Army Nursing Service formed in 1881 part of the British Army. The force went through many changes in its 126 years of glorious existence. In 1893, it was designated as Indian Army Nursing Service. The force went through further changes in 1902, when the Indian Nursing Service and the Army Nursing Service were combined and on 27 March 1902, it was redesignated to Queen Alexandra's Imperial Military Nursing Service. At the outbreak of World War in 1914 there were just fewer than 300 nurses in the QAIMNS, by the end of the war this had raised to 10,404. The Army nurses served in Flanders, the Mediterranean, the Balkans, the Middle East and onboard hospital ships. Of the 200 plus army nurses died on active service, many were Indians. After, the war on 1st October 1926, the Nursing Services was granted permanent status in Indian Army. This date is formally recognised as the formation day of Military Nursing Service. With the outbreak of second world war, nurses once again found themselves serving all over the world, including Singapore, Burma, Italy, Mesopotamia, Ceylon, Egypt and Western Africa. During the middle of the war in 1943, the Indian arm of the Nursing Services was separated through Indian Military Nursing Service Ordinance, 1943 and redesignated it, thereby constituting the Military Nursing Service (MNS) in its present form.

of the Ordinance. As a whole, the Rules lay down the modalities for the implementation of the Ordinance. Post Independence, the Military Nursing Service is an integral part of the Armed Forces Medical Services (AFMS). The AFMS consists of Army Medical Corps (AMC), Army Dental Corps (ADC) and Military Nursing Service (MNS).

E: Volunteer Force

In the early days of the East India Company, the Company's servants and the Christina residents of their factories were required to serve in the militia. In 1756, this militia was unsuccessfully used to defend the Fort William with the help of European Auxiliary. In 1820, an Act of British Parliament (I Geo. 4, c. 99) authorized the Company to raise and maintain a corps of volunteer infantry. However, only in 1854, Lord Dalhousie formally sanctioned the enrolment of volunteers in the Straits Settlements, which were then under the Indian Government. During the 1857 Mutiny, these volunteers the Europeans and Eurasian formed into military corps and helped the Company to restore the normalcy. Volunteer Guards were raised first in Calcutta, and then at Madras, Meerut, Agra and Allahabad. The Act XXIII of 1857 regulated the discipline of the volunteer corps as they became subject to the Articles of War applicable to European officers and soldiers of the Company. Later the Indian Volunteers' Act, 1869 (XX of 1869) introduced certain changes in it. Section 24 of the Act provided that any member of a volunteer corps, when on duty, may prevent any disturbance of public peace, and may disperse any persons whom he finds assembled together, to the number of five or more, without reasonable cause, between sunset and sunrise in any public place; and further he may apprehended and handed over to the police any person reasonably suspected of having committed any offence against the State or of having abetted, or being about to abet, any other person in commission of such an offence.

The Act of 1869 was modified by the Act of 1896. The preamble of this Act provided that, "many loyal subjects of Her Majesty" had volunteered their services for the protection of life and property and the preservation of pace, and had with the sanction of the Government, associated and enrolled themselves as military corps under officers appointed to command them. The volunteer forces were thus composed of British only and they were recruited from the European and Eurasian population of India. The Army Regulation, India provided that only natural borne or naturalized British subjects of European descents may be enrolled as volunteers, although in special cases Natives of India may be enrolled as honourary members.

In 1901, the number of volunteers in the force increased to nearly 32,500 non-military Europeans, who were between the age group of 18 to 55. With the appointment of an Inspector General of Volunteers, the terms and conditions of their service were improved and the award of decoration and long service medal was also extended to them. For a minor military offence, a volunteer could be fined or dismissed by a general court martial. A volunteer who neglected to attend drill or parade could be tried by a regimental court martial. No sentence passed on a volunteer by court martial, could be put into execution until after a report of the whole proceedings was made to, and the sentence was confirmed by the Local Government, which was vested with the power to commute any sentence into one of less severity or to pardon the offender altogether.

F: Reserve Forces

The Indian Reserve Forces Act, 1888 (IV of 1888) was enacted by the Indian Legislatures for the natives who retired from the active military service but could rejoin the colours in the cases of emergency. A native soldier could join the reserve after five years' service; and in certain cases even after only three years in the regular army, and a reservist could re-enlist at any time. Under section 2 of the Indian Reserve Forces Act, 1888, the reserve forces consisted of the regular or active Reserves and the supplementary or garrison Reserves. A person belonging to the regular Reserve Forces was liable to serve anywhere and the members of later within the British India only. Every reservist was to inform his address, and any change of such address, to the commanding officer. By Article 183 of the Indian Articles of war (Act V of 1869), every person belonging to the Indian reserves, when called out for, or engaged upon, or returning from training or service as an officer or soldier was given the benefits and privileges of a regular army officer/soldier. Every reservist was made subject to Indian Army Act, 1911 until duly discharged or dismissed. When a reservist of the Native Army was sentenced by an ordinary criminal court to transportation or imprisonment for a term exceeding three months, the court was to report the fact to the officer commanding the concerned Reserve Centre. The Indian Reserve Forces Act, 1888 and the Indian Reserve Forces Rules of 1925 made under it still govern the reservists' members of the armed forces.

G: Auxiliary Forces

In 1920, the Auxiliary Force Act to constitute an auxiliary force for service In India was passed. The classes of persons who could be enrolled under this Act included, (i) European British subjects as defined in the Code of Criminal Procedure, 1898, (ii) British subject of European descent in the male line, or (iii) Not being a British subject, who satisfied the conditions prescribed for enrolment of persons of that class. Such person must have attained the age of 16 years and must not be and is not a member of His Majesty's regular naval, military or air forces or of His Majesty's Royal Indian Marine.[58] Certain provisions of the Auxiliary Force Act were amended in 1928.

H: Territorial Army

Sir Charles Monro, the Commander-in-Chief introduced a Bill in the Indian Legislative Council on 27 August 1920 to constitute an Indian Territorial Force. The "Statement of Objects and Reasons" of the bill provided that the Indian Defence Force formed in 1917 was an experimental measure; and on account of the paucity of trained personnel and that owing to the heavy demand on the Regular Force, the success of the scheme could not be attained. The Indian Territorial Force was aimed at forming a second line to the Regular Amy and in this way to expand the fighting forces of British India to provide more adequately for her protection against foreign attack. The Indian Territorial Force would be liable to general service within India, and in extreme necessity, in case of its employment beyond the frontiers of India, it would require the special sanction

58 Sections 4 and 5 of the Auxiliary Force Act, 1920.

of the Government of India.[59] The Act No. XLVIII of 1920 to constitute the Indian Territorial Force came into force on 1 October 1920 and it extended to all the Provinces of India.[60] After Independence Territorial Army Act, 1948 replaced the Act of 1920.

The Territorial Army is part of Regular Army [61] and its role is to relieve the Army from static duties and assist civil administration in dealing with natural calamities and maintenance of essential services in situations where life of the communities is affected or the Security of the Country is threatened and to provide units for Regulars Army as and when required. The Territorial Army has strength of 40,000 personnel comprising of Departmental TA units such as Railway, IOC, ONGC, Telecommunication and General Hospital and the non Departmental TA units of Infantry Bn (TA), Ecological Bn (TA) affiliated to various Infantry Regiments and Engineer Regiment (TA) for maintenance of Line of Control Fencing.

59 Gazette of India - 1920, Part V, page 174.

60 The Territorial Army initially had various types of units such as Armed Regt (TA), Infantry Battalion (TA), Air Defence (TA), Med Regt (TA), Engineers Field Park Coy (TA), Signal Regiment (TA), EME Workshop (TA), Coast Battery (TA), ASC GT Coy (TA), ASC Compo Platoon (TA), AMC Field Ambulance (TA), by 1972 these units have either been disbanded or converted to Regular Army except Infantry Bn (TA).

61 The Regulations for Army, 1987, paragraph 1 provides that the Indian Army is composed of those who have undertaken a definite liability for military service, viz., combatant troops, administrative services/ departments and enrolled non-combatants. The Army comprises of (i) the Regular Army, (ii) the Army Reserve, and (iii) the Territorial Army.

Chapter V

Military Discipline: European and Indian Forces

The instances of indiscipline reported amongst the European soldiers in India, as compared to native soldiers, were very high. Most of the European soldiers were drawn from Britain's poorest sections. Vagabonds, thieved and other disreputable individuals were recruited in the army. As late as 1900, the regular British Army was considered as the last resort for the social drags. Unemployed and unskilled persons from the working class entered the army due to bleak prospects in the civil society. Most of the time cash incentives were given to attract them to join the army service. Once they arrived in India, they spent most of their money on drink and deserted to enlist again for getting cash bounty. [1]

The rules for the governance of the native soldiers were cumbersome. These rules were in line with the Articles of War of the Royal Army. Known as "Articles of War", these were printed in English and translated in Persian and Hindustani and were read out to all the serving sepoys of the regiment.[2] While few were read every month, the rest were read quarterly. The Hindustani version of the Articles of War, had a great deal of Arabic and Persian words in it, made it difficult even for a lettered sepoy to understand. The suitability of these rules to regulate the activities of the native troops was open to question because the regulation of the Royal Army in England and the Company's sepoy army in India were two widely different matters and the regulations which suited one might not be suitable for the other. The formal reading of the Articles of War was criticized because to a native soldier it meant practically nothing and left him confused. A native soldier never understood the intricacies of English military law, nor was he capable of doing so.[3] In spite of these intricacies, the incidents of indiscipline and disobedience amongst

1 Roy Kaushik, Spare the Rod, Spoil the Soldier? Crimes and Punishments in the Army of India, 1860-1913, *Journal of the Society for Army Historical Research*, Vol. 84, 2006, pp. 9-33.

2 Bengal Army G.O. 21 December 1796: The translation of a selection of the Articles of War in Persian and Hindoostanee being completed and printed, copies thereof will be transmitted to the several Native Corps of the army. It being the intention of the Government, in causing this publication to be made, that Native Officers and Sepoys shall be acquainted with the laws by which they are governed as soldiers; the obedience and duties required of them, and the punishment to which they are liable for certain offences. These articles are to be read in Hindoostanee language, every month at the head of each Native regiment or Battalion in the service, immediately after muster.

3 Almost all the European officers of the Indian army, who gave evidence before the Army Commission, questioned the utility of the Articles of War in the native army. According to them, these Articles of War were beyond the comprehension of a native soldier. They raised vague notions of some ill understood rights which some unknown

native soldiers were quite negligible. A table shown below gives details of trials of European Non-commissioned officers and soldiers of the Queen's and Company troops of Bengal Army for the period of 1834-1837.

Offences	**Year**			
	1834	1835	1836	1837
Absent without leave	1	8	1	-
Attempt to kill, or wound	-	-	3	-
Burglary	1	-	1	-
Desertion	6	17	23	16
Disabling himself	-	-	1	-
Drunkenness	1	-	-	5
Insubordinate, and threatening conduct	3	4	-	4
Manslaughter	1	-	1	3
Murder	1	-	2	1
Mutinous conduct	14	13	6	10
Mutiny	13	8	3	3
Post, or guard, leaving or sleeping on	4	5	3	3
Robbery	6	4	-	3
Stabbing	1	-	2	-
Stabbing, Intent to murder	-	-	-	1
Striking, NCO, on duty	23	11	15	7
Theft	4	4	3	-
Threat, if evidence given	-	-	-	1
Wounding	-	2	2	2
Total	79	76	66	59

Table showing Trial of Crimes: European Non-commissioned officers and soldiers, Queen's and Company's troops, Bengal Army; 1834-1837

[Source: Hough Major William, 1839, *Military Law Authorities*, Calcutta: W Thacker and Co., pp. 255]

authority was apparently suspected of wishing to subvert, and created a vague feeling of suspicion and discontent. Authorities like Henry Lawrence and John Jacob were even of the opinion that the reading of these Articles before the new sepoys put into their minds ideas of desertion, mutiny and disobedience by the constant occurrence of references to them in these Articles. They argued that instead of preventing the men from committing these offences, the reading of these Articles corrupted them. Sen Amiya, The Structure and Organization of the Bengal Native Infantry with Special Reference to Problems of Discipline (1796-1852), Ph D thesis, University of London, 1961, pp. 260-262.

During the period 1834 to 1837, a total of 43 cases of indiscipline were reported in the Bengal Native Army sepoys. During the same period 296 cases of indiscipline were reported amongst the European soldiers. Between 1825 and 1833 not a single Native Bengal Army sepoy was tried for drunkenness which shows the higher moral standards of the native sepoys.[4] The Bengal Government in an effort to root out the evil adopted flogging and other forms of severe and degrading punishment. This practice was strongly criticized by the Enquiry Committee of 1824 as being an impediment to recruiting. The Court when informed of this criticism ordered, the Bengal Government not to inflict severe punishment for desertion and also to enquire into the causes of the desertion which had occurred in the Bengal Army in 1824.[5]

In the short period of about 18 months (7 May 1849 to November 1950), during which Sir Charles Napier was at the head of the Indian Army, 14 officers of Her Majesty's regiments in India and 36 officers of the Bengal Military Service were tried by General Court Martial. Only one of the former and two of the latter were acquitted. During this period, only 8 European non-commissioned officers were brought to trial; of these two were acquitted and two received pardon. A total of 80 European private soldiers were tried by General Court Martial, of whom ten were acquitted, one was pardoned, and in two cases the Commander-in-Chief annulled the proceedings by refusing his confirmation. In comparison, during this period, 28 Native commissioned officers, 12 non-commissioned officers and 23 sepoys were tried by General Court Martial.[6] In this chapter issues relating to the discipline and other investigative bodies and the grievance redressal system are covered.

Drunkenness and Gambling

The European Officers and Soldiers of the East India Company were often involved in gambling, incurring debts, drunkenness and unbecoming conduct. These were considered serious military offences and those involved in them were brought to trial before Court Martial. On 25 June 1849, Private Owen McAteer of HM 29th Foot was tried by General Court Martial at Ferozepore on the charges of 'Being drunk in barracks; and having twice struck his superior officer, Corporal John Walker'. He was found 'Guilty' and awarded the sentence of 'Fifty lashes and one year imprisonment', which was approved and confirmed by the Commander-in-Chief on 6 July 1849.[7]

4 Hough Major William, 1839, *Military Law Authorities*, Calcutta: W Thacker and Co., p. xiv.

5 The Bengal Council in its letter of 1830 informed the Court that the Bengal Sepoys had been ordered in 1824 to march from the northern regions of India to the north of Bengal proper to invade Cachar, Assam and Arakan. This marching order was the main reason for the increased desertion as in those days of slow communications the Bengal infantrymen were reluctant to march to so great a distance from their families in Bihar or Oudh. Besides, the Bengal sepoys were recruited from wheat eating regions and they disliked service in the eastern provinces of India where rice was the staple food and the climate was humid and unsuitable. Sen Amiya, The Structure and Organization of the Bengal Native Infantry with Special Reference to Problems of Discipline (1796-1852), Ph D thesis, University of London, 1961, p. 265.

6 Mawson John, 1851, *Records of the Indian Command of General Sir Charles James Napeir*, Calcutta: R. C. Lepage and Company, p. 2-4.

7 For this and other cases mentioned in this chapter see: Mawson John, 1851, *Records of the Indian Command of General Sir Charles James Napeir*, Calcutta: R. C. Lepage and Company, pp. 244 + Appendix.

In another case, Lieutenant George John Ashton of H.M. of the 53rd Foot was tried by General Court Martial at Ruwal Pindee on 14 August 1849 of the charges of scandalous conduct: 1st, in having been in a state of intoxication in quarters; and 2nd, in having on the same occasion violently assaulted and repeatedly struck Lieutenant W. H. Grubbe, of the H. M. 53rd Foot. He was found guilty and sentenced 'to be dismissed the service'. The Court recommended for merciful consideration of the case. The Commander in Chief approved and confirmed the proceedings on 30 August 1849 with the following remarks:

> There are few things that are more painful than to refuse mercy, but it is my duty to support discipline in the vast Army of India, and discipline cannot be upheld if Officers, who are, by Law, the Judges that try Private Soldiers, for drunkenness, set an example of the crime! This Lieutenant Ashton has done; and though it is by far the worst part of the delinquent's conduct, it is not all. The being intoxicated after dinner, however unbecoming and disgraceful it is to the character of a well-bred gentleman, may still have the pretext of conviviality for a thoughtless, but culpable, excess in a young man. This, however, is not the crime of the prisoner. His has been deliberate drunkenness; a glaring disregard of decency in the broad face of day; an act destructive to all society, all discipline, all moral feelings, and calculated to make the uniform of a British Officer a bye-word and a shame! The Court has recommended Lieutenant Ashton to mercy, but it has offered no reason for this recommendation. The above are mine for refusing a recommendation which has no apparent foundation; and therefore, while it adds much to the pain of performing a distressing duty, cannot divert me from the paramount object of a Commander in Chief; namely, that of supporting the integrity of Military discipline and the high character of British Officers. I will not pardon Lieutenant Ashton.

Gunner William Baker of the 3rd Company, 2nd Battalion Artillery was tried by General Court Martial at Lahore on 29 November 1850 for the offences relating to drunkenness and misbehaviour. The Court Martial tried him on the following five charges on 29 November 1850.

> 1st: For insubordinate conduct, at Lahore, on the night of 9 October 1850, in having refused to return to his cot when ordered by his superior Officer, acting Staff Sergeant Hedley of the same company.
>
> 2nd: For insubordinate conduct, in having, at the same time and place, made use of highly abusive language to the said acting Staff Sergeant Hedley, drawn a bayonet on the escort ordered to convey him to the guard room, and threatened to stab any one who approached him.
>
> 3rd: For having, at the same place, on 13 October 1850, been drunk when a prisoner in the Artillery division quarter guard.
>
> 4th: For having, at the time and place last stated, thrown two glass bottles at, and with one of them struck, his superior Officer, Corporal J. Hill, of the 2nd Battalion of Artillery, being in the execution of his office.

5th: For having, at the time and place last stated, thrown a brick at, and therewith struck Gunner R. Savage, of the 2nd Battalion of Artillery, on duty at the said guard, and one of an escort ordered to place him in close confinement.

The Court found the accused guilty of all the five charges and sentenced him to fifty lashes and eight months' imprisonment; which was approved and confirmed by the Commander in Chief on 7 December 1850.

Lieutenant Edward Cookson of the 68th N.I. was tried by General Court Martial at Delhi on 11 January 1850. There were seven charges against the accused:

1st: For having gone to the mess of the Regiment in a state of intoxication, at Delhi, on the evening of 2 December 1849 and there conducted himself in a highly unbecoming manner.

2nd: For having gone to the mess of the Regiment, at breakfast, in a state of intoxication, at Delhi, on the morning of 4 December 1849 and there endeavoured to provoke Ensign Alexander, of the same Regiment, into a quarrel with him.

3rd: For having gone to the mess of the Regiment in a state of intoxication, at Delhi, on the evening of 4 December 1849, and dressed in a shooting jacket, in direct disobedience of Regimental Orders, dated Delhi, 17 November 1849.

4th: For having, at Delhi, on 6 December 1849, behaved with unbecoming levity and great disrespect to a Regimental Court of Inquiry assembled to inquire into his conduct, as alleged in the foregoing charges; Lieutenant Cookson being at the time under the influence of drink.

5th: For having attended the same Court of Inquiry, at Delhi, on 8 December 1849, in a state of intoxication.

6th: For having, at Delhi, on 12 December 1849, broken his arrest, and proceeded to the mess house of the Regiment and to the tent of Ensign Montagu on the same premises.

7th: For having, at the same time and place, conducted himself outrageously towards Lieutenant and Adjutant Gibbs, of the same Regiment; threatening him with personal violence when endeavouring to persuade him, Lieutenant Cookson, to return to his own quarters: for having shortly afterwards proceeded in a shameful state of intoxication to the house of Captain Bryant, of the same corps, and thence, in the same state, proceeded to the tent of Ensign Montagu, of the same corps, where he behaved with much violence and subjected himself to the disgrace of being taken back to his own quarters by force, under a guard of the Regiment.

The Court found the accused Guilty of all the charges, with the exception of the words "having gone to the mess of the Regiment in a state of intoxication," in the third charge, which the Court do not consider proved. He was sentenced "To be dismissed the service;" which was approved and on 26 January 1850 by the Commander in Chief, the confirming officer.

A General Order issued by the Commanding-in-Chief on 20 April 1869 dealt with the issue of drunkenness. Order No. 46 clarified that under the Article of War of 1869; power was given to commanding officer to deal with crime of drunkenness in the army by infliction of summary fines. These fines were to be awarded in accordance with the scale and must be strictly and rigidly adhered to. These fines were progressive in amount on the repetition of acts of drunkenness, but, on the other hand, were subject to reduction in proportion to the length of time elapsing between the offences; thereby holding out strong inducements to the soldier to abstain. The fines were to be enforced by an actual daily stoppage, and not by a mere debit in the monthly account. When the fine amounts to ten shillings or a second dine has been incurred, before a former one is paid, the daily stoppage will be 4 pence. But it is never to be less than 3 pence. The fines for a second offence, while the soldier is already undergoing stoppage for a former act of drunkenness, will commence when the first is paid. The soldier in every case of fine has the right to appeal to a court-martial.

In case of drunkenness, confinement to barrack at the discretion of the commanding officer, subject to the regulated limitations, may be combined with fine for drunkenness, should the aggravated nature of the case seem to demand such a course. It shall be considered a rule that in all cases after the commission of an act of drunkenness, a soldier shall, where practicable, be kept in barracks or camp for 24 hours without punishment drill. Imprisonment in the garrison cells shall not in any case be combined with fine for simple acts of drunkenness, though it may be added for serious offences in connection with drunkenness.

All awards for fine were to be entered in the regimental defaulters book, and published in regimental orders. Absence from tattoo to reveille the following morning is to be considered as equivalent to an act of drunkenness in calculating the amount of fine imposed by the scale. The scale of fine to be placed in a conspicuous position in every barrack rooms. The amount accruing from the fines will be formed into a general fund, to be applied under the direction of the Secretary of State of War to objects tending the benefit of the soldiers of the army generally. The number of men, who have been fined for drunkenness during the month---the number of fines---and the total amount of fines, are to be shown at the foot of the return of court-martial.

Scale of Fines for Drunkenness:

First and Second Acts: Admonition or confinement to barracks at the discretion of the commanding officer.

For every subsequent act of drunkenness:

If within 3 months of former act	If over 3 and within 6 months	If over 6 and within 9 months	If over 9 and within 12 months	If over 12 months	When the 4 preceding acts have been committed in 12 months
7s.6d.[8]	5s.	2s.6d.	Company entry	To be treated as the first act	2s.6d. to be added to the foregoing amount.

Drunkenness was not only inimical to professional efficiency, but was also related to subsequent unlawful conduct and misbehaviour. Sheer boredom amongst the European officers and soldiers also encouraged them to resort to excessive drinking. Till the nineteenth century, the punishment for being dismissal was generally dismissal, however in the first decade of the twentieth century sentences of court martial became more lenient.[9]

Gambling

The gambling transactions, particularly in the European military lines were quite rampant. In one of the gambling session, a young British officer was stripped of nearly whole of a considerable patrimony bequeathed to him shortly before. A General Order of the Commander in Chief, Head Quarters, Calcutta dated 25 September 1820, thus stated, "Instances of gambling in the Army having come within the notice of the Commander in Chief, His Lordship earnestly calls upon Officers at the head of Corps to use their active exertions in discouraging so pernicious a practice. It is hereby enjoined as a duty on each Commanding Officer, to report to the Commander in Chief any case where a Superior Officer may game with Subalterns. An Officer of any standing ought to feel himself called upon by every principle, to warn the inexperienced against the fatal consequences of the practice, instead of endeavouring to strip a young brother soldier of his scanty means and reduce him to penury, if not to irremediable ruin."

On 18 October 184, First Lieutenant T. W. Pulman, Artillery was tried by General Court Martial on the following charges:

> First charge: For conduct disgraceful to an Officer and a Gentleman, in the following instances:
>
> > 1st. In having, at Lahore, on 5 April 1849, before the Military Court of Requests there held, attempted to defraud Adam Ali, Native Merchant of Lahore, of his just claim

8 Under the British system, there were 12 pence in a shilling and 20 shillings (or 240 pence), in a pound. The symbol's' for shilling and 'd' for pence derive from the Latin solidus and denarius used in the Middle Ages and symbol '£' was used for a pound. A £1 coin was called a Sovereign and was made of gold. A paper pound often was called a quid.

9 Roy Kaushik, 2009, *Brown Warriors of the Raj: Recruitment and the Mechanics of Command in the Sepoy Army 1859- 1913*, Delhi: Manohar, p. 271.

against him, by deposing on his oath, that the signature to a voucher produced in support of the said claim was not his, although he well knew that his signature had been affixed thereto with his consent on or about 21 December 1848, by Lieutenant J. G. Batten, of the 37th Regiment Native Infantry; and in further falsely deposing on his oath, that he had never received the articles charged to him in the said claim of Adam Ali, and that he had no knowledge of the debt.

2nd. In having, on the same occasion, and at the same place, attempted to defraud Cashmeeree Loll, Native Merchant of Lahore, of his just claim against him, by falsely declaring that he had never heard of, or employed, any such person as Cashmeeree Loll; and in having further falsely denied having received some of the articles charged to him in the claim of the said Cashmeeree Loll.

3rd. In having, at the same time and place, in behalf of Lieutenant J. G. Batten, of the 37th Regiment Native Infantry, a defendant in an action before the said Court of Requests, at the suit of Emambux and Company, Native Merchants of Lahore, for soda water furnished on 21 September 1849 to him, Lieutenant Batten, voluntarily stated that he would swear that the initials J. G. B. to a voucher for the soda water were not signed by Lieutenant Batten, the object of Lieutenant Pulman in so doing, being to assist in defrauding the said Emambux and Company of their just claim against Lieutenant Batten.

Second charge: For having, at Lahore, on 5 April 1849, appeared before the Military Court of Requests there held, in a shameful state of intoxication.

The Court was of opinion that the prisoner Lieutenant Thomas Walter Pulman, was guilty of the 1st charge, on first instance; second instance, guilty of having "falsely denied having received some of the articles charged to him in the claim of the said Cashmeeree Loll;" but not guilty of the remainder, and acquitted him. On the third instance, the Court found him guilty to preamble of the first charge and not guilty to the 2nd charge. He was sentenced to dismissal from the service. The proceedings were approved and confirmed by the Commander in Chief on 2 November 1849 with the following remarks,

"I never confirmed the sentence of a Court Martial that gave me more pain than I feel in confirming this, which dismisses from the service a young man, of whose abilities I had formed a high opinion, when (some years ago) he served under my command in the field! The service has lost a clever Officer, an honorable family is thrown into deep affliction, and a young man of great promise is utterly ruined in his profession by a vice which has ruined three others since my arrival in India! It is therefore impossible for me not to call upon all who have common sense, resolution and respect for their uniform, to join in the endeavour which I am making to repress those destructive vices which are so unfortunately prevalent in the European portion of the armies in India---drunkenness and gambling. Courts Martial are ready to show all practicable mercy to a prisoner; but they will not, and cannot sacrifice the honor of the military profession to indulgent feelings for an individual, and so cause the ruin of numbers! Their sentences shall be carried into effect!"

A General Court Martial assembled at Lahore, on 28 September 1849, to try Major Thomas Cooke of the 17th Regiment N.I. on the following charges:

First. For un-officer-like conduct, especially unbecoming an Officer commanding a Regiment, in having, at Jugraon and at Mullickpore, in the months of February and March 1849, played at chess and at cards with Captain L. G. DaCosta, of the 58th Regiment Native Infantry, for large stakes and bets, in the course of which play he lost to Captain DaCosta the sum of twenty six thousand Rupee; such conduct being in direct disobedience of repeated General Orders prohibiting gambling in the Army, viz., General Orders by the Commander in Chief, dated 25 September 1820, 16 August 1831, and 26 June 1845.

Second. For conduct unbecoming an Officer and a Gentleman, in having, at Mullickpore, about 17 March 1849, and at Lahore, about 21 April and 21 May 1849, tried to evade the payment of the large sum he had lost to Captain DaCosta, by endeavouring to induce him to accept a much smaller amount on various pretences; by offering Captain DaCosta, whatever money he, Major Cooke, might win at Simla in the present year; and by declaring that he could never pay the whole sum he had lost and in having further demurred to pay on account of certain calumnious reports to the prejudice of Captain DaCosta's character, which he, Major Cooke, had spread about; for spreading which he afterwards, about 23 May 1849, apologized to Captain DaCosta.

Third. For conduct unbecoming an Officer and a Gentleman, in having, in a letter addressed to the Major of Brigade at Lahore, dated Lahore, 21 July 1849, given inaccurate statements of the transactions between himself and Captain DaCosta, in the following instances:

1st. In having, in the said letter, made a false statement in the following words: "Merely as an amusement we did play together at chess and at cards for one Rupee per game; afterwards, when under excitement, some large bets were made, ending in my having lost 26,000 Rupees, this being a larger sum than I could immediately command, I requested Captain DaCosta to wait till I could draw the money from England, when the debt should be paid, but he replied that he would prefer half paid down, and it ended by my giving a bill for 10,000 Rupees, a buggy and horse, and cash, equalling together 13,000 Rupees," whereas, in truth, the parties played for large stakes, besides making large bets, and Captain DaCosta did not state he would prefer half paid down, neither was any prompt payment either offered or agreed to in respect of the greater part of the amount; but he was induced to agree to the specified arrangement by Major Cooke declaring on his honor, that he would never be able to pay more of the debt he had incurred than the said sum of thirteen thousand Rupees, and further induced thereto by Major Cooke retracting and apologizing for the calumnious reports he had spread about regarding him.

2nd. In having, in the said letter, disingenuously and falsely stated as follows: "He (Captain DaCosta) then considered his character injured by me, and applied to his commanding Officer, who applied to me, and expressed himself in writing perfectly satisfied, but Captain DaCosta was not so, and referred the case to Brigadier Godby,

> but subsequently recalled the reference of his own accord;" thereby insinuating, that Captain DaCosta had no ground for making that complaint, whereas he, Major Cooke, had injured the character of Captain DaCosta, and the commanding Officer of the 58th Native Infantry did not express himself satisfied till Major Cooke had expressed his regret, while Captain DaCosta, who still pressed his complaint upon the attention of superior authority, was at length induced to withdraw it solely by Major Cooke's subsequent retraction of all that he had said to the prejudice of Captain DaCosta, and making an apology for it.

The Court found that the prisoner Major Thomas Cooke, was 'guilty' of the 1st and 2nd charge, but not guilty of the third charge and acquitted him. The proceedings were returned for review with the remarks of the Commander in Chief, "I cannot approve of the finding of acquittal on the 1st instance of the 3rd charge, which appears to me to be sufficiently proved." On review, the accused was found guilty of all the three charges and sentenced to dismissal from the service. The Court however, made the recommendations of mercy on the following grounds: 1st. Because the prisoner showed a disposition to pay, as evinced by his attempt to borrow from 18 to 20,000 Rupees from the North-Western Bank Agency on 21 April 1849. 2nd. Because he did not originate the reports against Captain DaCosta. 3rd. On account of the excellent character Major Cooke has hitherto borne, as shown by the handsome testimonials which have been placed before the Court. The Commander in Chief, while confirming the proceedings on 11 October 1849, remarked, "It is with pain that I express my inability to discover any just grounds for disturbing the sentence pronounced by the Court."

Desertion

Alongside cowardice and *mutiny*, *desertion* was regarded as the most serious *military* offence; it was punishable with death. A large of death sentences and executions were imposed on *the* soldiers accused for the crimes of desertion, mutiny and cowardice. The offence of desertion amongst the Native soldiers occurred only under special circumstances. Increased desertion was seen in the Bengal native infantry when the troops were placed under the uncertainty in regard to their future destination. The Officers in Command of European Regiments or Detachments were required to send to the Civil Authorities of the neighbouring Districts, a Descriptive Report of soldiers who have deserted. The Officers Commanding Native Corps were also required to forward a Descriptive Report of every Deserter to the Authorities at or nearest to the particular station at which the individuals were enlisted or to which they may be supposed to have gone. For apprehension of deserters' suitable award was declared.

Private Michael Kelly of the H. M. 61st Foot was tried by General Court Martial at Peshawur on 20 August 1849 on the charges of (i) Desertion; (ii) Having taken away a musket and brought it back in an unserviceable state, and having lost or made away with regimental appointments and necessaries. He was found guilty of the charges and sentenced to transportation for seven years. The Commander in Chief, while confirming the findings and sentence on 29 August 1849 made the following remarks, "The prisoner carried away many articles of necessaries as well as his musket, and he came back without these necessaries. I cannot understand why the Court should limit the finding of "Guilty" on this 2nd charge to taking away his musket only? The Court should, in my opinion, have convicted him fully on that charge. Where the prisoner was taken, and if by force, and other evident matters ought to have been investigated, because the want of this investigation gives some degree of plausibility to the defence."

On 2 October 1849, Gunner James Fitzpatrich, of 3rd Company 4th Battalion Artillery was tried by General Court Martial at Umballah on the charge of 'desertion from camp at Jugraon'. He was found guilty and sentenced to transportation for seven years, and branding with the letter 'D' in the usual manner. The sentence was confirmed on 10 October 1849.

The Government and General Order (GGO) of 3 July 1793 specified that for apprehending European deserters, an award of 10 rupees each be allowed. This amount was to drawn upon indent on the paymasters, signed by the town major at the Presidency, by the Fort Adjutant at subordinate garrisons, and by the senior staff officer, in the field or cantonments. Upon the apprehension or surrender of a deserter at any Station at a distance from Regimental Headquarter, he was sent under a suitable escort of the non-commissioned officer.[10] A soldier was liable to be tried for the crime of desertion without reference to the number of days he may have been absent.[11] The act of desertion cancelled every claim that a Soldier may at the time have upon the service---and no arrears of pay, clothing, prize money, nor any allowance whatever can be drawn an account of a deserter, or paid to him.

No soldier was to be struck off the strength of any Corps as a deserter until he was absent without leave for a period of twenty-one days. The Officers Commanding Divisions and Forces were empowered to direct the re-admission on the strength of Corps of deserters, or of men returned absent without leave, without reference to Army Headquarters, except in cases where such Deserters were in excess of the established complement, when application must be made for the sanction of the Commander in Chief. In the case of Regiments stationed at the Presidency, the Commander in Chief's authority for the re-admission of deserters was necessary. The service of a soldier who deserted was calculated only from the date his re-admission on the strength of his Corps, unless otherwise specifically ordered by the Commander in Chief.[12]

Mutiny

Mutiny has remained one of the gravest military crimes, punishable with death in most militaries across the world. Sometimes the purpose of this serious punishment was to act as a warning or deterrent to others, with the justice of sentences passed on individuals of less importance than

10 Regulations and Orders for General Officers, General Regulations of the Madras Army, Adjutant General's Office, Fort St George, Madras: Military Male Orphan Asylum Press, 1849, p. 84-85.

11 Article 82 of the Articles of War prescribed that when a soldier absents illegally from his duty for a space of two months, a regimental court of inquiry shall assemble. After having received proof of the fact of illegal absence, declare such absence, and period thereof, and the officer commanding the corps shall record such absence, and the declaration of such court of inquiry in the regimental book. If such soldier was apprehended or surrenders before such record has been entered, or subsequently apprehended or surrender, he shall be tried by a court martial empowered to try deserters. Hough Captain William, 1834, *The Practice of Courts-Martial and Other Military Courts,* Calcutta: Thacker and Co., pp. 133-134.

12 Regulations and Orders for General Officers, General Regulations of the Madras Army, Adjutant General's Office, Fort St George, Madras: Military Male Orphan Asylum Press, 1849, p. 84-85.

the disciplinary needs of the army. Even at early dates the Army in India was not unfamiliar with the crime of mutiny. In the East India Company's Bengal Army the first native court martial was assembled in July 1757, under the orders of Robert Clive, but it was not till 1764 that such a court martial was called upon to deal with mutinous regiment.

After a series of very inconclusive events on the borders of Oudh and Bihar, which occupied the first half of 1764, Major Hector Munro, of the 89th, arrived from Bombay and took command of the Company's Army on 13 August 1764. Munro learnt that the Sepoys were deserting and even threatening to seize their officers and deliver them up to the enemy, if they did not get an increase of pay, and prize-money promised them by Meer Jaffier. The very next day, Munro inspected the main body of the army and issued a general order in which it was said that "regular discipline and strict obedient to orders is the only superiority European possesses in this country over the natives." He followed this with long code of orders, enjoining far stricter attention to duty by the officers. Among other points, the Articles of War, forming the code of military discipline, were to be read in each corps once a fortnight. His orders, the manner in which they were expressed and the steps he took to enforce them carried immediate conviction to the Europeans. But to the sepoys, who were not used to such elaborate instructions appeared a routine affair and made no effect.

Munro issued another order on 24 August, which was to be read to all the sepoys of the army and explained to them. This order announced his firm resolution to treat the sepoys in every respect as soldiers, to give them all their just rights when they behave well and their just punishment when they violated any the law. He also clarified on the issue of "prize-money" and firmly stated that there could be no alteration on that issue.[13] Any sepoy having a grievance must put them to their officers in a decent and obedient manner, which will be a correct way of obtaining redressal. However, a number of mutinous incidents occurred in several battalions which showed that discontent over "prize-money" was still active:

> On 8 September 1764, the men of 9th Battalion, the oldest corps in the service, assembled without orders, and said they would serve no longer as promises have been broken. They did not lay down their arms but used them to imprison their officers and sergeants. Next day, however, they released them and let them go. They perhaps imagined that their officers would come and plead them as before, and they would then extort some more prize-money.
>
> A detachment of Marines and the 10th Bengal Native Infantry found the Red Battalion in a mango grove. They were taken by surprise and surrendered. The personnel of the Red Battalion were deprived of their arms made prisoners and marched back to Chapra. They reached in the morning of 13 September, where Major Munro had the entire garrison

13 Major Pemble, in command of the Patna sepoys restored the issue of full 'batta' and persuaded the Government to sanction the measure. However, there were complaints that the prize money had not been equitably shared. It was clarified that the "prize money" was an indulgence that none had a right to ask and it had been divided according to the approbatip of the Nawab who gave it. It was further added that indulgence such as prize money will never be permitted again in any army in India and the sepoys and the soldiers will be treated on the same footing and that it expected the sepoys to behave soldier-like. Sen Amiya, The Structure and Organization of the Bengal Native Infantry with Special Reference to Problems of Discipline (1796-1852), Unpublished Ph D Thesis, University of London, 1961, p.46-47.

drawn up to meet them. He ordered the commanding officer of the mutinous corps to pick fifty ringleaders. Then from those fifty, 24 were selected. They were tried on the spot be drumhead court-martial of native officers of two other battalions, one being the battalion which arrested them. Munro addressed the officers of the court, explaining the nature of the offence and penalties under the Articles of War. All the 24 men were found guilty and sentenced to death by blowing away from guns. The punishment was confirmed by Munro. This form of punishment was commonly used by the Mughals and borrowed for the military purposes, by both the French and the British.

There were four six-pounder present on the parade. Munro ordered that four of the condemned should be bound to the guns for immediate execution. But before guns could be fired, four others of the condemned step forward; they were grenadiers and said, it was their privilege to lead in the death as they had in life. Major Munro accepted their plea; the four men from the companies of the line were untied and the four grenadiers took their place. On a signal from their commander, the matches were put and four guns fired. Sixteen men were further blown away, four at a time. Four were reserved to suffer the same fate in the presence of other battalions who had shown sign of discontent.[14]

Subadar Shekh Madar Buksh of the 66th N.I. was tried by General Court Martial at Govindgurh on 14 February 1850 on the charge of, "For having, at Govindgurh, on or about 2 February 1850, when on duty at the gate guard of the Fort, and being present at a mutiny of the Sepoys of the said guard, not used his utmost efforts to suppress the same." He was found guilty and sentenced to dismissal from the service." The Court however, made the recommendation of mercy of the Commander in Chief, founded on the prisoner's length of service. The Court was of the view that he may not be, in his old age, entirely deprived of the benefits of a lengthened service." The Commander in Chief, while confirm the sentence on 24 February, commented, "I reject the recommendation of the Court, with this caution to all Native Officers, that they shall do their duty or lose their commissions. I repeat that mutineers shall have no mercy from me.

Jemadar Gunga Singh of the 66th N.I. was tried by the same Court Martial on 16 February 1850. There were two charges against him: 1st. For having, at Govindgurh, on or about 2 February 1850, when being present and aware that the Sepoys of his company were mutinously arming and accoutring themselves, failed to give information thereof to his Commanding Officer; and 2nd. For conduct unbecoming an Officer, in having, then and there falsely stated to Major H. Troup, commanding his Regiment, that he, Gunga Singh, Jemadar, was not aware that the Sepoys of the grenadier company were arming and accoutering themselves without orders. The Court found him guilty of both the charges and awarded sentenced of dismissal from the service. The proceedings were returned by the Commander in Chief on 23 February for revision on the grounds that the sentence is inadequate to the crime. The Court pronounced revised sentence of transportation for life, which was commuted on 14 March 1850. While doing so, the Confirming Officer, the Commander in Chief remarked, "I revised the former proceedings, because I thought that the

14 For more detalis see: Keightley Thomas, 1847, *A History of India from the earliest Times to the Present Day*, London: Whittaker and Co., p. 89; Mason Philip, 2004, *A Matter of Honour: An Account of the Indian Army, Its Officers and Men*, Dehradun: Natraj Publishers, pp. 106-109.

sentence was too lenient. The present sentence I consider to be just; but I nevertheless commute it to dismissal and fourteen years' imprisonment, because no mutineer of the 66th Regiment has been punished with such severity as transportation; and as his crime was less than that of the men of the gate guard, I do not think it would be just that his punishment should be greater."

According to Article 7 of the Indian Articles of War [Act No V of 1869], "Any person subject to these Articles, who (i) begins, excites, causes or joins in any mutiny or sedition in any regiment, corps, detachment, or guard; or (ii) being present at any mutiny or sedition, does not use his utmost endeavours to suppress the same; or (iii) knowing or having reason to believe in the existence of any mutiny, or of any intention to mutiny, or, of my conspiracy against the State; does not, without delay, give information thereof to his Commanding or other Superior Officer would be guilty of the offence of mutiny. The prescribed punishment for mutiny, as contained in Article 24 was the death or transportation for life.

Cruelty and Ill-treatment of Native Soldiers

The military has always been a mixture composed of the good, the bad, and the indifferent, --- the orderly and the disorderly. There were a number of instances when native sepoys or civilians were ill-treated by the European officers and other ranks. A General Order of 20 January 1764 specified: "....no soldier belonging to the honorable company's troops be seen in the streets with sticks or bamboos in their hands upon any account whatever, on pain of being brought to a court martial and tried for disobedience of orders." European soldiers were also prevented from using native soldiers as servants. In 1768 a very necessary injunction imposed penalties for any European non-commissioned officer commanding guards striking an Indian officer.

General Order of 25 September 1768 stated, "The native officers in general commanding the sepoys, having complained to the commanding officer of the garrison, that several of their people have been often beaten and abused by the European non-commissioned officers commanding guards. It is positively ordered in future that no non-commissioned officer strike or abuse any of those useful people, who are to be considered, in every respect, as other soldiers are, and when guilty of disorders or neglects are to be confined and tried by their own courts martial. The commissioned officers whose guards are composed partly of sepoys will therefore see that this order is complied with, and confine such who disobey it."

A General Order dated 11 December 1768 clarified: "In conformity to an order from the honorable the Governor and Council to the commanding officer, no officer in the garrison is permitted in future to have a man to attend him in quality of a servant, who is mustered on the rolls."Another General Order of 17 February 1769 further clarified that no sepoy shall be employed on any menial services whatever, or sent on messages that do not immediately relate to the public service.

On 16 June 1770, a General Order was issued which warned the European officers about their ill-treatment and unbecoming character. The Order stated:

> Repeated complaints having been made of several young officers for beating the inhabitants, especially those who come to demand payment of their just debts, the commanding officer is sorry to observe such a licentious spirit prevails, and so unbecoming the character of officers

> and gentlemen, who have any regard to their honor, more especially as they have the civil magistrates to complain to, who will redress them if those people behave impertinently. The commanding officer therefore expressly forbids in future any officer, non-commissioned officer, drummer, or private man to abuse or maltreat any inhabitant on any pretence, under the penalty of being confined and tried by a general or regimental court martial for disobedience of orders.

In an incident, European Officer Lieutenant X had beaten a native Subahee, resulting in the death of the native, by whom he suspected himself to have been robbed. The accused officer was tried by Court martial and dismissed from the service and sent back to Europe immediately. In another incident a serious complaint was received by the Court of Directors from different natives residing at or near Titalya against an officer of the rank of Captain belonging to the Company. A Commission consisting of a gentleman of the civil service and the Officer Commanding the troops was constituted to investigate the matter. It was brought out that Captain X caused five villagers to be seized by a party of sepoys and brought to his house, from which they were conducted to the Military Bazar of the station, and were there, by his order, and in his presence, tied up and flogged, and afterwards subjected to the ignonimous punishment of having one side of the head, and one half of the beard, publicly shaved. In view of the General Order dated 14 April 1813, "to dismiss from the service every Officer guilty of cruelty to any native either by violently and illegally beating or otherwise maltreating him;" Captain was suspended from the exercise of his professional functions and the matter was reported to the Court of Directors for further action. In yet another reported case an officer of the rank of Lieutenant Colonel, was charged with striking and using improper language to the native soldiers under his command. He was transferred to the Pension establishment, in compliance with his own wishes before the report on his case was sent home.

A General Order by the Commander in Chief highlights the malaise,[15]

> As we consider it to be our duty to protect, as far as in us lies, all the Natives of India from injustice, cruelty, and oppression, we direct you to notify in GO to the army our resolution to dismiss from our service every Officer who shall be proved to have been guilty of cruelty to any native, either by violently and illegally beating, or otherwise maltreating him; and we desire that you will be very particular in bringing to out notice any instances of that kind that may hereafter occur.

In another incident reported from Benares on 12 April 1830, a European Ensign of the Native Infantry has assaulted Sepoy Goordayal Sing without any cause and beat him in a cruel manner; the Ensign was immediately suspended and was later dismissed from the service. [16] The Court of Director gave further orders on the issue of cruelty to native soldiers vide their letter of 2 June 1930: "We have frequently exhorted you, and now again very earnestly call upon you to use your best exertions to check, both in our civil and military services, this offensive, and in some cases,

15 Published vide GGO, 18 September 1813; Jephson George, 1847, The Orders and Regulations of the Bengal Army, Part II, Calcutta: WM Thacker and Company, pp. 577-912.

16 Jephson George, 1847, The Orders and Regulations of the Bengal Army, Part II, Calcutta: WM Thacker and Company, pp. 579-581.

inhuman behaviour; and we trust, that if such an instance of unjustifiable and disgraceful conduct shall occur in any branch of our service, you will immediately make a severe example of the offender, without regard to his rank and standing, and we assure you, that in such instances you shall receive the fullest support from our authority."

Unbecoming Conduct

Lieutenant R. F. Fanshawe of Invalid Establishment and Adjutant and Quarter Master of the European Invalids at Chunar was tried by General Court Martial at Benares on 29 October 1850. The five charges against him were:

> 1st. For un-officer-like conduct and direct disobedience of the standing General Order of 30 December 1823, in having, at Chunar, at various times between 16 May 1848 and the 2 August 1848, borrowed several sums of money, amounting in all to nine hundred and twenty-two Rupees and eight Annas, (922-8-0) from Sergeant George Hind, of the European Invalids at Chunar.
>
> 2nd. For highly unbecoming conduct, in having, at Chunar, between 6 January 1849 and 28 May 1 849, occupied and kept possession of a house belonging to a widow named Zinut (commonly called French) without her consent and contrary to her wish; and for having withheld from her the rent of the said house, 50 Rupees per month, for the whole or a great part of the period of his occupation, until forced to pay it by awards of Courts of Request at the suit of Mrs. French, the rent for February, March, April and May, 1849, being still unpaid to Mrs. French.
>
> 3rd. For highly unbecoming conduct, in having, at Chunar, between 26 June 1848 and 29 May 1849, inclusive, or for various periods respectively within that time, withheld just wages of 15 servants in his employ; thereby causing distress and loss to these individuals.
>
> 4th. For having, at Chunar, between 18 April 1849 and 3 June 1849, fraudulently misapplied the sum of one hundred and thirty-four rupees and one pie, (Rs. 134-0-1) or thereabouts, being the aggregate of the estates of Bombardier P. Burke, Gunner W. Brown and Private T. Barron, deceased, with which he, Lieutenant Fanshawe, was entrusted for the purpose of distribution to the heirs of the deceased, as the Officer in charge of the companies to which the deceased men belonged.
>
> 5th. For having, between 1 March 1848 and 3 June 1849, fraudulently misapplied the sum of thirty-four rupees, or thereabouts, drawn by him, as Adjutant of the European Invalids, which ought to have been paid, and is still due, to School Master Sergeant Walter Law, of the European Invalids.

The Court found the accused guilty of the first charge; of the second charge, guilty, with the exception of certain the word; of the 3rd charge, not guilty, and acquits him thereof. The Court found that the prisoner did owe the wages to the servants as stated in the charge, but under the peculiar circumstances of the case, attach no guilt to the fact. On the fourth charge, he was found guilty with the exception of the word "fraudulently". Of the fifth charge, guilty, with the exception of the word "fraudulently:" and sentenced him "To be very severely reprimanded." The

Commander in Chief, while confirming the sentence on 27 November 1850, made the following remarks:

> I am unable to understand upon what principle the Court found Lieutenant Fanshawe guilty of the first charge and yet fails to cashier this Officer? An Officer who is capable of writing a begging letter (asking for money) to a Sergeant under his command, is unfit to hold a commission, even had this act not been a direct breach of the General Orders, and had been the only one of which he has been convicted!
>
> I am equally unable to understand upon what grounds the Court acquits the prisoner on the third charge? The Court finds that he, a British Officer, did owe money to his servants; it is also proved that these poor men were much distressed thereby and, in consequence, were obliged to borrow money! Moreover, while Lieutenant Fanshawe did not pay these men their wages, this Officer kept three horses (for I am warranted in taking it for granted that he did not keep three grooms without he kept three horses) his duty being confined to the Fort of Chunar!
>
> I do not know to what "peculiar circumstances" the Court can possibly refer, to excuse such an act of dishonesty and want of feeling? The only "peculiar circumstance" I can find, is that Lieutenant Fanshawe chose to contract debts which he well knew that he could not pay! I cannot agree with the Court in its extraordinary opinion that "no guilt attaches to the fact" of not paying servants their just wages and forcing them to borrow money in their distress! I am inclined to believe that if the Government kept the Members of this Court eight months or a year out of their pay, we should hear very different sentiments expressed.
>
> Reprimand.—Lieutenant Fanshawe! your sentence is to be "*severely reprimanded.*" I cannot understand why the Court Martial did not cashier you, as, in my opinion, it ought to have done. Public duty makes me regret that you have escaped from a just punishment, but I shall rejoice if the very lenient punishment inflicted may improve your conduct as a British Officer.

In another case, Rissaldar Khodayar Khan of the 5th Irregular Cavalry was tried by General Court Martial at Mooltan on 26 November 1850. The only charge against him was, "Highly unbecoming conduct, in having, at Mooltan, on 22 October 1850, when on parade with the Regiment and checked by the Commanding Officer for being out of his proper place, disrespectfully replied to his Commanding Officer; and in having, when told if he spoke in that way he would be placed under arrest, insolently taken off his sword and thrown it down in front of his Commanding Officer, repeatedly saying "place me in arrest," and then, quitting the parade, without leave, proceeded to the lines of the Regiment. The accused was found guilty and sentenced to "suspension from rank, pay and allowance for three months." The Court also made the recommendation of mercy, "The Court having performed the painful duty of awarding punishment in strict conformity to an Article of War, beg, unanimously, and respectfully, to recommend the case of Ressaidar Khodayar Khan, of the 5th Irregular Cavalry, to the merciful consideration of His Excellency the Commander in Chief, on the grounds of the prisoner's long and faithful service of 36 years, the favorable testimonials he has produced, and in consideration of the prisoner's age, which may palliate infirmity of temper though it cannot altogether excuse it.

On 7 December 1850, the Commander in Chief while pardoning the accused, made the following remarks:

> 1st. I have great pleasure in attending to the recommendation of the Court in favour of this old and distinguished Officer, but he is to be told that such unjustifiable ebullitions of ill temper cannot be submitted to, and if he again transgresses, he will not again be pardoned. He is to return to his duty.
>
> 2nd. The last witness for the prosecution states, in substance, that when a junior Officer is a more sharp and clever man than a senior Officer, the junior is given the command of the squadron while the senior commands the troop on parade. This may be, and I believe is the system in many Irregular Regiments, and a very good one to make a show, but not to make a Regiment fit for service. It is well calculated to injure discipline and produce Courts Martial, as it has done in the present case.

On 25 November 1850, Private William McKenzie of the 1st European Bengal Fusiliers was tried by General Court Martial at Lahore on the charges of:

> 1st. For insubordinate conduct, in having, at Lahore, on 9 October 1850, declared on parade that he would not parade for inspection, which he had been directed to do as a punishment for previous misconduct; and in having, in pursuance of that determination, fallen out of the ranks and thrown his musket and accoutrements on the ground.
>
> 2nd. For gross insubordination, in having, at Lahore, on 12 October 1850, at the orderly room of the Regiment, after having been warned for trial by a District Court Martial, said to the Adjutant of the Regiment "you may as well give me a General Court Martial, for I will not shoulder a firelock again in the Regiment," or used words to that effect.

The Court found the accused guilty of the charges and sentenced him to fifty lashes and six months' imprisonment. The Commander in Chief, approved and confirmed the proceedings on 4 December 1850, but pardoned the accused. His remarks were, "First: I pardon the prisoner and desire his Commanding Officer to admonish him as to his future behaviour, and that this sort of sulky conduct cannot be permitted. Second: I desire that the Commanding Officer of the Regiment will be so good as to inform me: (a) Why the Officer commanding the company, to which the prisoner belonged, did not tell off his own company? (b) What Officers were on the parade? (c) Why the Officer of the company did not speak to, and warn the prisoner of the danger he was incurring by his loss of temper and consequent insubordination? (d) Why the Commanding Officer did not himself speak to the prisoner and admonish him, or if he did, why was not this stated on the prosecution by the Prosecutor? All these matters ought to have been elicited by the Court, as the Prosecutor omitted to do so. It is the duty of a Commanding Officer to do all in his power to prevent crime by admonition; and it is the duty of a Court, by questions, to ascertain how far a prisoner is really guilty in spirit as well as in fact. As far as I am informed by the proceedings, I think that the prisoner was guilty in fact, but that a little admonition and cool reasoning with him by the Commander of his company or of the Regiment would have put him right; and therefore I have pardoned him in the belief that he will see his conduct was wrong, and in future that he will conduct himself so as to prove my leniency has not been misplaced."

On 27 June 1849, Ensign William Henry Hanker of 38th N.I. was tried by General Court Martial at Lucknow on the charge of 'Highly unbecoming conduct'; in that he retained and fraudulently appropriated to his own use, the sum of 21 Rupees, sent by Captain Knyvett, of the same regiment, to another officer of the 66th Regiment of N.I. deceiving Captain Knyvett into the belief that the money had duly reached its destination. He was found 'Guilty' and awarded sentence of Dismissal from the service. The Court recommended for the merciful consideration of sentence in the hope that clemency may have a beneficial effect on his future conduct.

The conforming officer while approving court sentence on 9 July 1849 remarked:

> ...... I now refer the Officers who have recommended Ensign Hankey to mercy; a proceeding which does so little credit to the Court, that I cannot believe it to have been unanimously voted. What! pardon and turn back among the Officers of the Indian army, a man convicted of felony! On what grounds does the majority of this Court cast upon the Commander in Chief the pain of refusing pardon? On the grounds of youth! Has he not been nearly a year and a half in the army? Has he not a commission? Is he not, by the rules of the service, deemed old enough to sit, and has he not sat as an Officer in judgment, and as a Magistrate to try and punish others? Is he not old enough to be entrusted, and has he not been entrusted with the command of men? with a Subaltern's command in peace and in war? and when men's lives and safety depend upon the conduct of a Subaltern? Has not that glorious uniform, which he has disgraced by two infamous actions, sufficed, by its recognized honour, to introduce him into the best society, even into the presence of the Sovereign? And would the majority of the Court wish me to leave it on the back of such a man as the prisoner? Has he been tempted by misfortune and distress! No! He avows his wealth; he has had the education of a gentleman; his misconduct seems to be the result of innate moral turpitude! Had the prisoner been horror struck at the enormity of his guilt, avowed his crime, and cast himself, repentant and conscience smitten, upon the mercy of the Court, I could have understood the feelings of those who recommended him to mercy. But such is not the case. On the contrary, while conscious of his guilt, he deliberately adds to his crime by the effrontery, the sophistry, and the falsehood of his defence! To pardon such an offender would be an insult to the army, and I will not do it.

Unlawful Associations and Assemblies

Any form of assembly for discussion of military related issues or sending joint memorials to the higher authorities was prohibited. An extracts form a letter from the Court of Directors, dated 1 May 1810 provides, "We direct that all associations and meeting of Officers, or Soldiers, in our service, for the purpose of discussing, remonstrating, or petitioning against the Regulations, or Orders, of the Government, and of their Superiors, be strictly prohibited, as well as, the writing or circulating any combined or joint memorial, and petitions for these purposes; and we further direct, that if any Officer, or Soldier, shall be proved to the satisfaction of the Government, to have been guilty of wilful obedience of this order, he shall be brought to trial, by a Court Martial for such disobedience, or be immediately suspended the Service, and sent to Europe at the discretion of Government."

The Order further stated, "Every Officer and Soldier has a regular and easily accessible channel for laying his just and individual claims before his Superiors, and if necessary before Government; but all combinations and associations of Military Men, whether in the higher or lower ranks of the Army, are not only irregular but illegal and subversive of the first principles of military subordination and of the supremacy of the Civil Power, as declared and sanctioned by the authority of the Legislature. The Commander in Chief of the British Forces had notified to His Majesty's Army, the strong sense of disapprobation and displeasure with which he has viewed an assembly of Military men, for the purpose of even of complimenting a Superior Officer upon his promotion. The circumstances of inferiors of any class of Military men assembling for the purpose of bestowing praise and public marks of approbation on their superiors, implies a power of deliberation of their conduct which belongs to the King alone, or to those Officers to whom His Majesty may be pleased to entrust the command and discipline of his Troops. It is a procedure equally objectionable whether in the higher or lower ranks of the Army, and as the Commander in Chief cannot but regard it as in principle subversive of all military discipline, he trusts it is a practice which will be forever banished from the British Service, as deserving of the highest censure, and he directs Officers in Command, to act accordingly."[17]

General Regulation on Military Discussion stipulated that deliberations or discussion, among any class of Military men, having the object of conveying praise, censure, or any mark of approbation towards their superiors, or others, are strictly prohibited, as being subversive of discipline, and an assumption of power which belong to the King alone, or to those Officers to whom His Majesty may be pleased to entrust the command and discipline of his Troops. Deliberations, or discussions, among any class of Military men, having the object of conveying praise, censure, or any mark of approbation, towards their Superiors, or others, was strictly prohibited, as being subversive of discipline, and an assumption of power which belongs to the Government alone, or to those Officers to whom may be entrusted the command and discipline of the Troops. A General Order of 16 October 1839 on Giving/Accepting Presents form subordinates: "Lord Hill finds it necessary to refer to the Army General Order of 18 January 1810, as well as to the General Regulations and Orders, and to declare, that His Lordship will hold every Officer responsible for a breach thereof, who shall allow himself to be complimented by Officers, Non-commissioned Officers or Soldiers, who are serving or have served, under his Command, by means of presents of Plate, Swords, etc, or by any collective expression of their opinion."

Punishment to Natives only by a court martial

Most British military officers and administrators believed themselves to be culturally superior to the races of India, with both a duty and a right to rule over them. Many British authorities felt that they were inherently superior in the character and education, which have them a greater capacity to rule than it did to those of races or nationalists. Many Britons made no attempt to conceal their

17 General Regulations of the Madras Army, Adjutant General's Office, Fort St George, Madras: Military Male Orphan Asylum Press, 1849, pp. 434-436.

disdain for most of the native races of India, a disdain which the Mutiny exacerbated. One of the Briton, writing home in December 1857 complains: "It is very dull here, now and then a sepoy hung or blown away, a cricket match or two and a little quail shooting….." British officers and men exploited Indian illiteracy and poverty. On a number of occasions the British officers used to humiliate or degrade native soldiers. [18] It has been said, with some truth, that the British in India knew only servants and maharajas, though most officers did get to know their pheasant soldiers.

There were a few instanced where Company Officers had reduced native Havildars and Naiks to the ranks, and deliberately inflicted corporal punishments on sepoys without any form of trial. It was specified in the Orders that a native non-commissioned officer or sepoy could not be punished except by the sentence awarded by a court martial, except in cases when an immediate example was necessary to be made and when delays be attended with dangerous consequences to the service.[19] By G.O. dated 27 February 1791 in was stated that such practices of award of illegal punishment were not warranted by the Regulations of the service and might tend to the subversion of justice. The commanding officers and other officers were cautioned and asked to discontinue such illegal practices in the future.

For a minor offence a native soldier was punished with either extra drills or extra guards. The commanding officer of a company could punish his men by ordering ten days of extra drill or four extra guards. In case, an offence demanded more severe punishment, a report was required to be sent to the Commanding Officer of the Regiment for a trial by a court-martial. This procedure of trial by military courts, though prevalent in some form or other before 1796, was formally established and promulgated in the reforms of that year. By the regulations of 1796, three types of courts-martial were established for the accused native soldiers: These were the regimental, the district or garrison, and the general courts martial. Native officers were selected to sit with European officers as judges in these courts. This honour was given only to those native officers who had qualified themselves in an examination in the Articles of War governing the native soldiers and had obtained certificates to that effect from the Adjutant-General of the native army. A general court martial was the only tribunal before which a native commissioned officer could be tried, the other two being authorised to try sepoys and non-commissioned officers only. Only a general court martial had the power of awarding the penalties of death or dismissal from the service. Every soldier brought for trial before any native court-martial was at liberty to ask to be tried only by European judges. But in that case no appeal was to be allowed from one court to another. The composition of these courts was as follows:

(a) A native general court martial was to be consists of not less than nine native officers of the rank of Subadars or Jemadars, unless such court martial were held under a warrant from the Commander in Chief in the situations where such number of officers were not

18 People come out to India with but very indifferent ideas regarding the natives. They think that because a man is black he is to be despised. And …. young officers talk about "those horrible black nigger" or, as "good-for-nothing black sepoys." They look down upon them as brute beasts; they make use of opprobrious language towards them; and lower themselves so far even as to curse and swear at them!" Hervey Capt Albert, 1850, *Ten Years in India or The Life of a Young Officer*, Vol. I, London: W. Shoberi, p. 278.

19 M.C., 7 May 1781; Jephson George, 1839, The Orders and Regulations of the Bengal Army, Part I, Calcutta: WM Thacker and Company, pp. 466.

available. In cases of general courts martial so held, when number of nine officer cannot, in the judgement of the Officer convening the same, be conveniently assembled, any number of native officers of the rank of Subadars and Jemadars, not less than five were competent to form such general court martial for the trial of native officers and soldiers belonging to such detachments. But no sentence of death could be passed by such courts martial, unless two thirds of the members, or four where the court consisted of five concurred therein.

(b) Garrison courts-martial were also similarly composed, with the exception that their officer members were drawn from the different native regiments in the garrison.

(c) Regimental courts-martial were appointed by the Commanding Officer of a regiment and tried all crimes that were not capital,, This Court consisted of five to nine native officers under the superintendence of a subaltern officer.

The Officers of Her Majesty's Services were not detailed as Members of European Courts martial held, under the Provisions of the Native Articles of War, for the trial of Native Officers and Soldiers; except in the cases of emergency when other Officers may not be available.[20] Lawfully, there was no objection to a Commanding Officer presiding at a General Court Martial for the trial of a man of his own Corps; however, it was considered practicable to avoid this situation. Because, if a Commanding Officer has pre-examined the case he would not considered an unbiased Juror in giving his opinion on the guilt of the accused.[21] At all native court martial, a European Lieutenant or Captain of the Corps was detailed to superintend the proceedings. His duty was to regulate the court martial so that the prosecution and the evidence in support of the charge, with the defence are carried on in due form. He was to countersign the proceedings, and to deliver or forward them to the person, by whose authority the court was assembled. [22] The superintending officer so appointed was to take oath, to be administered to him by the Commanding Officer or Adjutant of his Corps, previously to his entering on the functions of his officer.[23] In subsequent period European Officers were additionally appointed as interpreter of at native courts martial; and an oath of office was also administered to them.

Whenever charges were preferred against any native officer or Soldier, or other Native of India, subject to military law, a certified translation of charges were prepared and the same was read and delivered to the accused in presence of the Staff Officer of the Station, or Commanding Officer

20 Native Courts Martial, para V: General Regulations of the Madras Army, Adjutant General's Office, 1849, Madras: Military Main Orphan Asylum Press, p. 441.

21 GOCC, 8 September 1841.

22 Regulations II, 1809, passed 14 February 1809; see Jephson George, 1839, The Orders and Regulations of the Bengal Army, Part I, Calcutta: WM Thacker and Company, pp. 526-527.

23 The form of oath: "I, A.B., do swear that I will conduct the proceedings of the native court-martial of which I here sit as superintending officer, according to the best of my abilities, the Rules and Articles of War, and the Regulations of the Service; that I will conscientiously and faithfully interpret and record the proceedings and sentence of the said court, and further, that I will not communicate or discover the proceedings, or sentence of the court, until the same have been approved by the competent authority." C.G.O. 19 June 1813; see Jephson George, 1839, The Orders and Regulations of the Bengal Army, Part I, Calcutta: WM Thacker and Company, pp. 534.

of the Regiment, at least 24 hours before trial.[24] In most native courts martial when the courts was to pronounce judgement, it was a practice to allow the members to consult among them and a general verdict was given through the president of court martial. It was found that the practice was not consistent with the mode laid down in the Articles of War. By G.O. of 24 June 1793, it was clarified that when a verdict of court martial to be given, the question, "Guilty" or "Not Guilty" be put separately to each member, beginning with the youngest; the procedure followed even today. Whenever there was a difference of opinion among the members of a court-martial on any material point, the judge advocate or superintending officer were to make a memorandum of the opinion of each individual member, which was to be preserved in case required by the due authority. In cases where the Articles of war did not specify the penalty, the courts martial were competent to award a punishment corresponding to its nature, as far as possible, with the character of the offence.[25]

The courts martial functioned more like an administrative disciplinary proceeding than a judicial proceeding. Decisions of the regimental and garrison courts could be approved and carried out by the Commanding Officer the Regiment, who had to convey this information to the Headquarters. The decision of a general court martial had to be approved by the Commander-in-Chief before it could be carried out. Native courts-martial were authorized to deal out any form of punishment ranging from simple imprisonment, corporal punishment or even capital punishment depending upon the gravity of the crime. Native courts martial could be considered a farce because native members were always guided by the superintending European officer. The European officer exerted great influence on the native officers, who could readily give their assent to his findings and conclusions.

In cases of European soldiers awarded death sentence, most of these punishments were later commuted to transportation. A European soldier awarded punishment of transportation was sent to New South Wales. The Courts were lenient while awarding punishment to Europeans as compared to native officers and soldiers. The case on Thompson is noteworthy in this regard.

> Thompson was appointed as ensign in the East India Company's Bombay Army on 27 March 1821 and arrived in India in August that year. He was promoted to the rank of Lieutenant in the European Regiment on 10 June 1822. An uneventful spell of ten years' service passed. However on 22 April 1831 the commanding officer of the regiment suddenly ordered an immediate inspection of the money bags and account books of each company. Thompson was paymaster of his company but was unable to attend the audit as he was unwell. He ordered his Pay Sergeant to make out the men's accounts and to insert a debt of Rs 707 owed by Thompson. Later that day, Thompson was arrested. He tendered money to pay the debt but this was refused. On 9 June 1831 he was court martial held in camp near Deesa. Thompson was charged for conduct unbecoming the character of an officer and a

24 Native Courts Martial, para X: General Regulations of the Madras Army, Adjutant General's Office, 1849, Madras: Military Main Orphan Asylum Press, p. 441.

25 G.O. 9 May 1831; see Jephson George, 1839, The Orders and Regulations of the Bengal Army, Part I, Calcutta: WM Thacker and Company, pp. 538.

gentleman in having embezzled monies entrusted to him for the payment of the men of the 6th Company under his charge.

The Court Martial found Thompson guilty of embezzlement but without intent to defraud. It acquitted him of un-gentleman like conduct. He was sentenced to be dismissed from East India Company service and was ordered to make good the deficiency. The verdict was accompanied by a unanimous appeal for mercy as the members of the Court felt that the punishment they were compelled to award was disproportionate to the degree of offence committed. Major General J S Barns, Commander of the Forces, confirmed the punishment but put on record his marked disapprobation of the Court's finding that the embezzlement of public money was not conduct unbecoming the character of a gentleman. Thompson was struck off the strength and ordered to take passage to England. In November 1832 Thompson wrote to the Company Directors in London asking to be restored to the service. On 29 January 1833 his request was rejected. But the Company decided to grant him an annual allowance of £50 because of the Court Martial recommendation for mercy, the strength of testimonials produced by Thompson, and his distressed situation.

Since the infliction of corporal punishment caused much resentment amongst the native soldiers, the Commander-in Chief of the Bengal army, recommended to the Directors in 1826, that the punishment of flogging be entirely abolished. He succeeded in winning the approval of the Home authorities and in 1827 ordered that in future no native soldier should be sentenced to corporal punishment unless for the crime of stealing, marauding or gross insubordination, where the individuals were deemed unworthy to continue in the ranks of the army.[26] It was also laid down that in case of an award of corporal punishment, the divisional commander should be referred to and given every detail of the prisoner before the sentence was carried into effect and if he confirmed it and did not see cause to remit the punishment he would at the same time direct the man to be dismissed from the service. This was the first restrictive step taken to curtail the award of corporal punishment. In 1832, the Commander-in-Chief, retraced the step, and the power to sanction the sentence of corporal punishment was no longer confined to the divisional commander. Instead, the officer who assembled the court-martial was permitted to confirm the proceedings and then to carry the sentence into effect or to remit it altogether. [27]

The Legislative Council, however, referred the issue of award of corporal punishment for detailed investigation to three Presidential Committees. These Committees were unanimous in their opinion that though there must be some restriction in inflicting corporal punishment upon the sepoys, the punishment howsoever degrading and injurious, could not be entirely be abolished. Bentinck's humanitarian views were not satisfied with the finding. He criticized the observation of these committees and stated that an insuperable terror appears to reign over the imagination of all and like the native superstition which sees in some charm or amulet the only protection against all evils that can affect the body or haunt the mind, so corporal punishment is venerated as the sole security against every military distemper and as the sole guarantee for the efficiency and good regulation of the army. Advancing his reasons for the total abolition of corporal punishment,

26 G.O.C.C. 19 March 1827; Bengal Military Cons. 19 March 1827. No. 71.

27 G.O.C.C. 15 June 1832; Bengal Military Cons. 1832, No. 65.

Bentinck argued that the Bengal native soldiers were already subordinate to all superior authority and were proverbially faithful to their salt. According to Bentinck, discharge from the service was the most complete substitute for corporal punishment. The Directors were convinced by the argument of Bentinck and approved the total abolition of corporal punishment. An order was accordingly issued in 1835 discontinuing the practice of punishing native soldiers by using the cat-o-nine-tails or rattan.[28] It was also ruled that a soldier was to be sentenced to dismissal from the service for any offence which might now be punished by flogging. However, during this time a British soldier in the military service could still be sentenced to 300 lashes.[29] In the British Army flogging had been partially abolished in 1867 following the death of Private Robert Slim from such punishment, but it remained available as a punishment during peacetime for crimes of mutiny or insubordination involving violence and during wartime it was extended to cover desertion and even drunkenness. For a decade the British army used flogging sparingly, but its re-emergence as a common punishment in Zululand in 1879 attracted the attention of Liberal politicians, including Gladstone, who rejected the 'necessary deterrent' argument and denounced the practice as anachronistic. The number of lashes was initially reduced by Parliament before its final abolition in 1881.[30]

In early 1840s, an increase in the number of mutinous incidents and consequent courts-martial in the Bengal native army were noticed and it was felt that this unsatisfactory state of things had mainly occurred because of the abolition of corporal punishment. It was also suggested that a Sepoy who was merely dismissed could manipulate an exit from the service whenever he desired and could enlist with a hostile state. In October 1844, Governor-General Hardinge drafted set of Indian Articles of War that would apply across the three Presidency armies. He reintroduced flogging to the native army on the grounds that as it was now used in the British army was not a disgraceful infliction. According to him, it was the best sort of punishment for the prompt suppression of the serious military offences that soldiers committed in the native army. Hence, with the approval of the Directors, an order was issued in 1845 by the Governor-General Sir Henry Hardinge to reintroduced corporal punishment for the "native" army in India. On restoration to the native army, the maximum number of lashes was put at 200.

28 On 24 February 1835, Governor-General and Commander-in-Chief in India, Lord Bentinck passed a General Order discontinuing the practice of punishing soldiers of the native army by the cat-o'nine tails or rattan, and directed their dismissal from service in such cases. Papers relating to Corporal Punishments, East Indies, *Parliamentary Papers, House of Commons*, Vol. 40, 1836.

29 During this time in the British Parliament, Bentinck's order was being criticized over the use of corporal punishment in the British military service. The questions raised were, why was the British soldier still subject to the lash, when the Negro slave and the Native Indian sepoy had been emancipated? Critics, accused Bentinck of passing the order without consultation with the home government and on the eve of his departure from India to build up steam for the reform campaign in Britain. In 1868, flogging had been restricted, with some exceptions, to offences on active service for the British soldier. The British soldier also remained vulnerable to a punishment considered archaic, because up to 1871 the letter "**D**" for deserter or "**BC**" for Bad Character could be marked indelibly on his body. Singha Radhika, The Rare Infliction: The Abolition of Flogging in the Indian Army, circa 1835-1920, *Law & Hist. Rev.*, Vol. 34, 2016, p. 785-789.

30 Oram, Gerard Christopher, What alternative punishment is there? Military Executions During World War I, PhD thesis The Open University, 2000, pp. 354.

After the 1857 Mutiny in India, the military legal system redrafted giving more powers to the Commanding Officers. Under the Indian Articles of War (Act V of 1869) any court-martial, including the SCM convened by the commanding officer, could sentence any personnel below the rank of warrant officer to corporal punishment not exceeding fifty lashes. In camp or any frontier post, the commanding officer could award up to twelve strokes of the rattan to a 'menial' follower without holding a court martial, and in the field and on the line of march the provost-marshal could order the summary infliction of up to fifty lashes on anyone below the rank of a warrant officer.[31] Act XII of 1894 introduced another form of extraordinary court-martial to Indian military law, namely the Summary General Court Martial (SGCM) designed to facilitate trials in military detachments during active service when stiffer sentences were required than were possible by the SCM. The SGCM consisting of three officers could pass any sentence including the death. The use of capital punishment increased during the First World War;[32] and in 1920 flogging was completely abolished in the native army.

Review of Court Martial Proceedings

The Officers Commanding the Division or field force, and the Officers Commanding the District or Brigade, while approving sentences for execution, were to give due consideration to the proceedings of court martial. They were empowered to direct the release of prisoners where the trial was void from illegality, or unauthorized sentence was awarded, or where the verdict was not sustained by the evidence. In case the proceedings of any Regimental or other Court Martial required any special consideration, these officers were required to forward the proceedings to the Judge Advocate General for the purpose of being placed before the Commander in Chief.[33]

Trial of Retainers, Servants and Others in a Military Garrison and Cantonment

There were a number of native retainers and followers attached to military establishments and dependents of the army at every establishment of the Company. In order to make them subject to military law, the regulations were framed in 1810.[34] Titled, "A Regulation for Subjecting persons attached to the military establishment to martial law in certain cases, and for the Better Government of the retainers and dependents of the Army receiving Public Pay on Fixed Establishment," These regulations provided punishment for petty offences by a military tribunal. It provided that all persons serving with any part of the army, and receiving public pay, drawn by

31 Act V of 1869, articles 76, 166, 169.

32 At the time of the First World War, corporal punishment had been abolished - senior commanders all too readily fell back on capital punishment as the sole means of maintaining discipline rather than exploring alternatives. During the World War, a total of 359 executions of men serving with the British Army are recorded in official documents (twenty-nine of which were carried out after the armistice): 321 for military offences such as desertion and cowardice etc., the remaining forty for murder. Additionally, an unknown number of Indian soldiers were also executed, however their records are not be traced. Oram, Gerard Christopher, What alternative punishment is there? Military Executions During World War I, PhD thesis The Open University, 2000, pp. 354.

33 The Rules for the review of the proceedings of court martial framed by the Commander in Chief in Modification of General Orders of 6 November 1818, issued vide G.O.C.C. 23 September 1845.

34 Regulation XX of 1810 passed by the Governor General in Council on 29 December 1810; see Jephson George, 1839, The Orders and Regulations of the Bengal Army, Part I, Calcutta: WM Thacker and Company, pp. 518-519.

any Officer in charge of public department appertaining to the army, whether as lascars, magazine men, khalassies, native doctors, writers, bheesties, puckallies, syces, grass-cutters, mahouts, or other subordinate servants attached to public cattle in any capacity, shall be subject to be tried by a court-martial for all breaches of their respective duties, and for all disorders and neglects to the prejudice of good order and of local regulations established by the Commanding Officer or other competent authority, in the cantonment, garrison, station , or other places where the troops to which they are attached, may be serving. Menial servants of officers within the precincts of any cantonment, garrison, or military station, or military bazaar were also subject to these regulations for the maintenance of good order in the cantonment. The military courts martial were authorised to award sentence to persons of the above description but not heavier than lawfully inflicted on enlisted soldiers of the army under the Articles of War. The Courts martial were authorises to award maximum of fifty lashes with a cat-o'-nine-tails, or fourteen days' confinement, or in aggravated cases, both these punishments. The persons attached to military bazaars of Corps or Station Bazars, who were petty dealers; in the first instance, for breach of local Regulations could be sentenced to a maximum of sicca rupees one hundred, which could be levied under the written orders of the Commanding Officers. If not paid forthwith, the amount of fine could be recovered by seizure and public sale f good of the offender as may be found within the limits of the cantonment, garrison or bazaar. If sufficient goods are not found within the limits of cantonment or bazaar, the offender may be arrested by a written order of the Commanding Officer and confined for one month. Native court martial were also empowered to award sentence of imprisonment for a term not exceeding twenty days or imposing a fine not exceeding fifty sicca rupees, or corporal punishment not exceeding fifty lashes with a cat-o'-nine-tail. The person not subject to this regulation, if accused of a crime, were arrested on the orders of the Commanding Officer and handed over to the magistrate for trial under the existing provisions.

Redress of Grievance and Complaints

For the first time, the Articles of War published in 1765 provided mechanism for the redress of service wrongs in the army. An officer or solider who deems himself wronged by any superior or commanding officer may complain to the higher authorities for the redress of his grievances. Section XII of the Articles dealing with the "Redressing Wrongs", provided that if any Officer thinks himself to be wronged by his Colonel, or the Commanding Officer of the Regiment, and shall, upon due Application made to him, be refused to be redressed, he may complain to the General, Commanding in Chief, of Forces, in order to obtain justice. The General Officer was required to examine into the said complaint; and either himself, or by the Secretary at War, to make his report to the Government thereupon, to receive the further directions in the matter.

The procedures for making complaints was provided vide a General Order of the Commander in Chief in 1793. It stated that when any number of Officers belonging to different Corps or Brigades, are desirous to state a real or supposed grievance to Government, or the Commander-in-Chief, the Senior Officer of that number will first make application to the Commander-in-Chief, through the Adjutant General, for permission to hold a Meeting for that purpose; and his Excellency's sanction to the Meeting being obtained, the Representation or Memorial agreed upon, shall be signed by the Senior Officer only of those who may think themselves aggrieved; and such Officer is to transmit to the Commander-in-Chief, (through the Adjutant General in a separate paper, enclosed in the Memorial) a list of the names of all those who may have given sanction to his signature. But the Senior Officer, in all such cases, will be held particularly responsible, both for the matter itself, and for the manner in which complaints may be stated in those Remonstrance and Representations. In Detachments, or at Stations, where the Commander-in-Chief was not present, applications for the Meeting, as above mentioned, was to be made in a similar manner, to the Commanding Officer of the Detachment or Station, who would forward the Representation to the Adjutant General, to be laid before the Commander-in-Chief.[35]

As regards persons below the officer rank, the provisions stated, if any inferior officer or soldier thinks himself wronged by his Captain, or other Officer commanding the Troop or Company to which he belongs, he is to complain thereof to the Commanding Officer of the Regiment, who was to summon a Regimental Court-martial, for the doing justice to the complainant; from which Regimental Court-martial either party may, if he thinks himself still aggrieved, appeal to a General Court-martial. However, upon a second hearing, if the appeal appears to be vexatious and groundless, the person so appealing shall be punished at the discretion of the said General Court Martial.[36]

When the Non-commissioned Officers or men of a Regiment, troop or Company, had just cause of complaining, they were to apply for redress through their Commanding Officers. First, the Captain or Commanding Officer of the troop or company, to which they belong; second, the Commanding Officer of the Regiment; and finally, the General Officer in command of the district, who will forward their representation, if proper, to the Commander in Chief. Such applications for redress could be signed and delivered by two or three aggrieved men; but any assemblage of the Regiment, troop or Company, without due authority, was considered a high breach of discipline, and punished accordingly.[37] The Officers Commanding His Majesty's Corps in India, were requested to explain to the soldiers serving under them, that the Captains or Officers Commanding their respective Companies are the persons to be approached in the first instance, if they were desirous of petitioning the Commander in Chief upon any subject.[38]

According to the Artillery Standing Orders of 1828, all complaints from the men of the troops or Company were to be laid before the Captain previous to being submitted to the Commanding Officer, and a free access should exist between them, without any intermediate authority. The Captain or Officers commanding the troop was to make efforts to settle all complaints which come within their cognizance; or else refer them to their superiors. He could also reject applications which were frivolous and groundless, but must permit the party to forward any appeal against his own decision, which should, therefore, be well weighed, so that he may be looked up to by his en as their immediate patron and protector. According to the Articles of War, (Section 10, Article 2), direct appeal to higher authority from aggrieved Non-commissioned Officer or soldier was

35 CGO dated 7 June and 28 June 1793

36 Jephson George, 1839, The Orders and Regulations of the Bengal Army, Part I, Calcutta: WM Thacker and Company, pp. 494-495.

37 General Order of 9 August 1807.

38 G.O.H.M.T. of 6 September 1821.

not permitted, until the aggrieved person has failed in procuring redress, on a reference of his complaint through the regular channel.

Native Infantry Standing Order of 1828 emphasised that the European Officers should themselves attend to the complaints of the men, and not allow this duty to devolve on a native officer, a Havildar, or a servant. The officer, who permits this part of his duty to be performed by another, deprives himself of the best opportunity to securing the respect and attachment of the native soldier. It should be impressed on the young officers, that grievances, which to him may appear frivolous, are of serious import, when connected with the religious prejudices of the men; and that even when the redress of such grievances is impracticable, it is still his power to listen with patience to the soldier's statement, and to convince him, that his feelings have not been disregarded.

The Order stated that the Native Officers should not be permitted to interfere with men wishing to make any complaint or reference to their European Officers; that they may accompany the men, but should not make any previous investigation; and it should be fully explained to them, that any attempt, on their part, to suppress a complaint, or to prevent a sepoy from going to his European Officer, would be considered as disobedience or orders, and dealt with accordingly. The privilege of communicating wishes or requests of the men to the Commanding Officer was to be confined to matters connected with their religious prejudices and ceremonies. When a Non-commissioned Officer or soldier thinks that he has cause of complaint, he will make his representation in a respectful manner, through the Officer Commanding his Company; and although on inquiry, the complaint may prove to be groundless, he is not to be rebuked for the mistake he has committed. Should the complaint be well founded, no delay is to take place in redressing the grievance complained of.

The Order clarified that the soldiers who have any representation to make, are to take opportunity of making it, when they are not on duty; but any man who murmurs, or even speaks on parade, or at drill, unless it be in answer to a question put to him by a superior officer, shall liable to punishment. If any sepoy, considering himself ill-treated by a Non-commissioned Officer, shall in return, make use of threatening or provoking words or actions, or abusive language, instead of taking the proper means for obtaining redress, he shall be liable to punishment for this breach of discipline, although, on inquiry, it may appear that the Non-commissioned Officer's conduct was responsible, in the first instance. This rule was to apply in all disputes between any Non-commissioned Officer and another of higher rank.

Certain responsibilities relating to the submitting grievance applications were allocated to the interpreters. The interpreters were to consider it their duty, to make out petitions of all kinds for the men. Any native commander, non-commissioned officer or sepoy, requiring a petition to be prepared, was to apply to his Officer Commanding his Company, who was to give him a letter to the interpreter mentioning his request. The interpreter was to sign all petitions, as examined, and submit them to the Commanding Officer for signature.

Native Infantry Standing Orders, 1828 prohibited all meetings and assemblies of the Native Officers and their instituting an investigation into alleged complaints, or examining individuals.

Those implicated in such proceedings were to be brought immediately to the notice of the Commander in Chief. In case any meeting of the Native Officers or other ranks were held, the Native Officer of the Day had a duty to report about such meetings to the European Officer of the day. Any neglect in this duty was deemed a disobedience of orders, and dealt with accordingly. Native Non-Commissioned officer, though not on duty were to check irregularities and neglects which were prejudicial to good order and discipline. In whatever Company, or portion of the Corps, the discontent may show itself, on it coming t o the knowledge of a non-commissioned officer, he was to report it immediately to the superior European Officer.

The General Order by the Governor General of 19 August 1824 further clarified that all Officers, having native servants, public or private, under the denomination of peons, chuprassies, etc, attached to them, are to consider it their duty to warn such servants that they are, on no account, to prevent ingress to persons who wish to make representation or present urzees (applications). It is consequently directed, that on a breach of this order coming to the knowledge of the Officer, he is instantly to confine the offender and bring his before a court martial for trial. The intention of the Government in this regard must be known to the inhabitants of military bazaars and cantonment. It was directed that the said CGO to be translated and transcribed in the local and Persian character, and affixed on some conspicuous part of the chubootra (courtyard), in every military cantonment under this Presidency.

A General Order of 11 July 1837 (No. 129) by the Commander in Chief stated, "We highly disapprove and strictly prohibit our Officers and Soldiers from writing or publishing anonymous complaints against their Superiors or against each other, such conduct being disgraceful to themselves, subversive of Military discipline as well as destructive of private harmony"

Grievances against Superiors: The Right to Demand a Trial before a Court Martial

Under the Articles of War,[39] a Non-commissioned officer (NCO), or soldier, who considered himself wronged by his captain, or other officer commanding the troop or company to which he belonged had a right of demanding trial, in the first place before a Regimental Court Martial, and afterwards a right of appeal to a General Court. It was provided under Article 2 of the 12th section of the Articles of War, that such NCO or soldier who thinks himself so wronged, "is to complain thereof to the commanding officer of the regiment, who is hereby required to summon a Regimental Court Martial for the doing justice to the complainant; from which Regimental Court Martial either party may, if he thinks himself still aggrieved, appeal to a General Court-Martial. But if, upon a second hearing, the appeal appeared to be vexatious and groundless, the person so appealing would be punished at the discretion of the said General Court Martial." In all such cases of alleged wrong or injustice committed by superior officers towards their inferior officers or private men, the right of appeal could not be refused, but was granted, by the Commander in Chiefs by appointing a General Court-Martial to take cognizance of the matter. The only check against rash and ill-founded applications in cases of the above nature was a certification that an adequate punishment would be awarded for an unjust or groundless appeal.

39 Tytler Alexander Fraser, 1806, *An essay on Military Law and the Practice of Courts Martial*, London: Military Library, pp. 334-339.

The reason why a power of appeal was declared as absolute right to NCO or soldiers complaining of being wronged by their superior or commanding officer, was that a regimental or garrison Court Martial had no power of inflicting any punishment on commissioned officers. Such inferior courts could only express their opinion, that the complaint is just, or the contrary, and restore the sufferer against any existing grievance; and the injury complained of, however flagrant, must therefore have remained un-redressed, if an appeal to a General Court Martial had not been declared to be a matter of right to the party aggrieved.[40]

Complaints against superior officers

Article 111 of the Articles of War [41] dealing with complaint against superior officer provided, "Any Officer or Soldier thinking himself wronged by his superior or other Officer is to complain thereof to the Commanding Officer of his Troop or Company, by whom, if the grievance be not redressed, such Officer, Non-Commissioned Officer, or Soldier, may complain to the Commanding Officer of his Regiment, who is hereby required to examine into such complaint, or remit it to his superior authority as the circumstances may require; but if the complaint should appear to be frivolous or groundless, the party preferring it shall be liable to be punished according to the sentence of a General or other Court-martial in manner hereinbefore mentioned; provided that such offender shall not be liable to be sentenced to Dismissal, nor to suffer Corporal Punishment or Imprisonment with Hard Labour.

Under the Indian Articles of War (Act V of 1869) the grievance redressal procedure was modified. Article 167 of the Act of 1869 provided, "Any person subject to these Articles, who deems himself wronged by any superior or other officer, may, if not attached to a troop or company, complain to the Officer under whose command or orders he is serving; and may, if attached to a troop or company, complain to the Officer Commanding the same. When the Officer complained against is the Officer to whom any other complaint should, under this Article, be preferred, the aggrieved person shall complain to such Officer's nest superior office. No such complaint shall be made to any Officer other than those indicated in the former part of this Article. Every officer receiving any such complaint shall examine into it, and, when necessary, refer it to superior authority.

40 The procedure before a General Court Martial in cases of appeal from a regimental or garrison court was as follows. The court being constituted by proper authority, the parties in the trial were summoned to attend, together with all the necessary allegations. The appellant sustains, in conjunction with the Judge-Advocate, the part of prosecutor, and the party in whose favour the inferior court had given its judgment, was defendant in the cause; the charges on the original trial being the matter at issue, on the truth or falsehood of which the court of appeal is to decide. The witnesses examined before the regimental court were duly sworn by the Judge Advocate. The whole of the evidence was taken down in writing by the Judge-Advocate as recorder; and the court deliberates thereon, and pronounces its opinion and sentence, in the same manner as in ordinary trials. The general regulation of the Articles of War applied to sentences pronounced on appeal, as well as to all others, viz. that no sentence of a general Court-Martial was to be put in execution, till after a report made to His Majesty of the whole proceedings, or to the officer commanding in chief, or some person duly authorized under the Royal sign-manual, to confirm the same. The Court could be asked to revise it decision by the commander, who was authorized to approve the sentence.

41 Act No. XIX. of 1847; Article 158 of the same Articles of War provided that Article 111 (along with few other Articles, viz., 2, 4, 75, 78, 80, 102, and 103) to be translated into the several languages of the different Presidencies, and to be read once every three months at the head of every Regiment, Troop, or Company mustered in the service and to every Recruit at the period of his attestation.

Every such complaint shall be preferred through such channels as may be from time to time prescribed by proper authority; and any person preferring a frivolous or groundless complaint shall be liable trial by any Court Martial competent to try him, and to such punishment, other than dismissal, corporal punishment, or imprisonment with hard labour, as the Court is empowered by these Articles to award."[42]

The King's Regulations, Articles 8 and 9, dealt with the redress of grievances in the Royal Navy and read: "Every person subject to this Act who shall have any cause of complaint, either of the unwholesomeness of the victuals or upon any other just ground, shall quietly make the same known to his superior, or captain, or commander-in-chief, and the said superior, captain, or commander-in-chief shall, as far as he is able, cause the same to be presently remedied; and no person subject to this Act upon any pretence whatever shall attempt to stir up any disturbance, upon pain of such punishment as a court-martial may think fit to inflict, according to the degree of offence." King's Regulations laid down the way in which a complaint could be brought. In the first instance, after a lapse of 24 hours from the alleged incident, the complainant could request to see the Captain to whom he would make his complaint verbally. Should the Captain refuse to or be unable to remedy the complaint the complainant could 'respectfully request' that his complaint be given in writing and forwarded to the officer commanding the squadron in which he served. He would then be given another 24 hours to reconsider his decision and was allowed the advice and assistance of an officer. This officer would, at the same time, warn the complainant that 'should there be no reasonable grounds for his complaint, he is liable to be treated as having made a frivolous or vexatious complaint, which is an act to the prejudice of good order and naval discipline.' Should the officer commanding the squadron in which the man was serving refuse to or be unable to remedy the complaint, the complainant could subsequently forward his complaint to the Commander-in-Chief and finally to the Secretary of the Admiralty. The Article offered one small consolation: 'Although the superior authority to whom the matter has been submitted may not see fit to alter the ruling of the Captain, the latter is not justified in dealing with the appeal as a breach of discipline, and is only to do so when expressly authorised by such superior authority.' According to Article 9, only the method set down in Article 8 would be recognised as a legitimate method of representation. Neither ratings nor officers were permitted to look to outside sources to vent grievances which remained within the boundary of established and legal service procedure.

Courts of Inquiry and Inquests:

Courts of Inquiry, in most instances, were ordered to enable the Commander in Chief to judge whether, or not, there may be matter to render trial by Court Martial necessary. All officers holding commands had the power to order the assembly of a Court of Inquiry, and to direct them to investigate any matter that may be laid before them, and may also direct the Court to revise its proceedings as often as may be considered necessary, and to receive further evidence. A Court of Inquiry was not be considered a judicial body. The main object is to receive and methodize information, so as to enable the authority convening the Court to arrive at a correct conclusion as to the necessity or otherwise of a Court Martial. The Officers and soldiers, whose testimony

42 The existing provisions for the redress of grievance in the Indian Army (contained in section 26/27 of the Army Act, 1950 and the Regulations paragraph 364) are similar.

may be called in a court of inquiry, were duty bound to give it; and their refusing to do so was considered as gross neglect of duty, contempt of authority, and direct disobedience of orders. In all cases where it was necessary to direct the assembly of Native Court of Inquiry, a European Superintending Officer and an Interpreter were invariably attached to the same, in like manner as to Native Courts Martial inferior to General. Courts of Inquiry usually consisted of 3 or 5 officers, of any rank, which however, if possible should not be inferior to that of the Officer whose conduct or character may be implicated in the investigation; and in choosing the members, care was to be taken that none are named who would requires in the event of a court martial arising out of the proceedings. The Court was to give its opinion on any matter if specially ordered to do so. It had no power to administer an oath or to compel the attendance of civil witnesses. The controlling power over military men which enforced their attendance came from the orders of a superior officer, and not from the authority which Courts of Inquiry possessed of themselves.

Under ordinary circumstances when a Court of Inquiry was assembled for the purposes of examining witnesses, with the view of ascertaining if grounds existed for a Court Martial, the individual accused was to be permitted in the Court, and it was his duty to attend if warned to do so. He has no right to cross-examine witnesses. He was not obliged to take part in any proceedings, and may decline to make any statement, or to call evidence. It is a closed court, to which the general public cannot claim admission as they can to a Court Martial. The Court was not restricted to the ordinary rules of evidence and could also record hearsay, for information of the authority by which it was assembled. Neither party (the accuser or accused) could demand a copy of the Proceedings, which were only intended for the Officer convening the Court. The Proceedings of the Court was to be signed by all the members of the Court, and by the Judge Advocate, in cases where one was appointed to it.[43]

In the cases of unnatural deaths, where the civil authorities when requisitioned by the Officer in Command of a Military Station, could not undertake an inquest; the Commanding Officers were competent to convene a Court of Inquest to investigate the causes of sudden deaths. Such Courts of Inquest were composed of not less than three European Officers, with a Captain, when practicable, as President; and a Medical officer as member. Where European Officers were not available, Native Officers could also be detailed as members. The completed proceeding of Court of Inquest was required to be forwarded by the Commanding Officer to the Adjutant General of the Army.[44]

Military Courts of Requests for Native Officers and Soldiers

Under the Act No XI of 1841, the Military Courts of Request could be constituted within the territories of the East India Company for actions of debts and other personal actions against Native Officers, Soldiers, and other persons amenable to the Articles of War for the Native Forces in the Service of the East India Company. It was necessary that the affected individuals were carrying on any trade or business in the Military Bazar and the value of dispute in question

43 Courts of Inquiry, General Regulations of the Madras Army, Adjutant General Office, Madras: Military Male Orphan Asylum Press, 1849, pp. 460-461.

44 Ibid., pp. 461-464.

did not exceed two hundred rupees. The Officers Commanding any Station, or Cantonment, or any portion of Troops were authorised to convene such courts, consisting of not less than three Native Commissioned Officers, with an European Officer of not less than five years standing to superintend and record the proceedings. Such military Courts were constituted monthly and were held on some convenient day before the issue of the pay for each month. The forms of proceedings of such Courts to conform to the usages observed on trials before Courts Martial held for the native troops in the service of the East India Company. Such Courts had the power of summoning the witness as was possessed by Courts Martial. The witnesses omitting to attend, refusing to give evidence, or committing perjury, and persons suborning witnesses to commit perjury, were to be tried and punished if amenable to Articles of War, by a Court Martial; and if not amenable to Articles of War, they could be tried and punished in the nearest Court of the East India Company for administration of Criminal Justice in like manner as if such offences had been committed in regard to any trial before such nearest Court. A record was kept of the proceedings in every case tried before any Military Court of Request. It was lawful for the Commanding Officer to whom the proceedings were forwarded for approval, to return the same for revision either by the same or another Military Courts of Request. In the case of any new trial, the Court may receive evidence which was not adduced at the first trial. The judgement of the Military Courts of Requests was final and the Commanding Officer could neither disapprove the award, nor refuse to carry into execution.[45] It was competent for the court of request to make deductions from wages, when sued for in the court, for articles proved to have been lost, or wilfully damaged, through the negligence of the complainant. The decree of the Military Courts of Request was to be published in the Station Orders before its execution. No more than one half of the pay and allowances of any commissioned officer, or more than one fourth of the pay and allowances of any Non-commissioned Officer or Soldier could be stopped in one month for honouring the decree of the Military Courts of Request.[46]

By GOCC of 1 January 1848, new rules or standing Orders were framed for the conduct of European and native Courts of request. Under this Order, the Native Courts of request were to assemble at the different Military stations on the 5th of every month, or should that fall on a Sunday, on the following day. A proclamation was required to be made through all lines and bazaars at noon, on the last day of each month, of the time and place where the next Native Court of Request will assemble. Parties desirous of instituting suits before these Courts, were to prefer these claims in writing to the Station Staff Officer; who in turn will prepare a schedule according to prescribed format and sent it at least two days before the assembly of the Court to Adjutants of Corps or heads of departments. A competent interpreter was to be appointed to Court of Requests where the defendants were natives. In cases of absolute necessity, the Superintending Officer could also act as interpreter. The proceedings of Native Courts of request were published in Station Orders after the perusal of commanding officer. The Commanding Officer of the stations had the power to order revision of an award, but only once.

45 Clarifications issued vide A.G. Circular No. 528 of 1 May 1829.

46 General Regulations of the Madras Army, Adjutant General's Office, Fort St George, Madras: Military Male Orphan Asylum Press, 1849, p. 487-490.

Chapter VI

Mutiny in the East India Company Army

Mutiny is almost as old as military. It could be defined as any overt act of defiance or attack upon military (including naval) authority by two or more military persons subject to such authority. Mutiny was regarded as a most serious offence, especially aboard ships at sea. Because the safety of the ship was thought to depend upon the submission of all persons on board to the will of the captain, wide disciplinary powers were given to the commanding officer, including the power to inflict the death penalty without a court martial. In East India Company and the British military some of the causes of mutiny have been due to dissatisfaction over the salary and allowances, undue interferences in religious feelings, sub-standard or poor quality of food, and serious injustice.

The mutiny amongst the Madras sepoys in Vellore in 1806 was due to the contemptuous orders of the military authorities as regards caste marks and turbans, and above all by the jeers of the locals who taunted them with becoming Christians. While the Indian Rebellion of 1857 had diverse political, economic, military, religious and social causes; the main being the hurting the religious sentiments of Hindu and Muslim sepoys that the cartridges used in Enfield rifles was filled with the fat of cow and pig. The action of Mangal Pandey, a sepoy of Barrackpore near Calcutta on 29 March 1857 led to the mutiny of sepoys in the beginning which precipitated the revolt of the people. Mangal Pandey's action was not a spontaneous outburst against the British officer but it was a culmination of a simmering discontent brewing in the sepoys. Mangal Pandey was a representative of the totality of the sepoys' wrath against the British.[1] Some of the important

1 It may be presumed that the revolt of 1857 was the result of a culmination of popular dissatisfaction that had been simmering for a long time against the policies of the British in India – expansion, exploitation and economic drain and humiliation of the Indian spirit by advocating the white-man's civilizing mission – factors of multiple dimension of direct and indirect, long run and short run and of immediate nature led to the revolt of 1857. Added to the political and administrative distrust and hatred, the economic exploitation, the social and religious discrimination of superiority complex viewing the Indians as racially inferior and culturally backward and their belief that God had created the white men to civilize the Indians and intolerance of the idolatry of the Hindus by the Christian missionaries also created distrust between the natives and the British. The British were so arrogant and haughty, that a police regulation published by a magistrate at Agra categorically states "Every native, whatever his pretended rank may be, ought to be compelled, under heavy penalties, to salaam all English gentlemen in the streets and if the native is on horseback or in a carriage, to dismount and stand in a respectful attitude until the European has passed him." Top 4 Causes of the Revolt of 1857 In India, available at: http://www.historydiscussion.net/history-of-india/top-4-causes-of-the-revolt-of-1857-in-india/2083.

instances of mutiny which took in the East India Company and the British Indian Army and trials of Mangal Pandey and Bahadur Shah Zafar are discussed in this chapter.

Vellore Mutiny

While there have been a number of mutinies in the British Army before 1857, the Vellore mutiny of 1806 is most significant. It was the first big revolt by the native Sepoys against the East India Company. In November 1805, the Commander-in-Chief of the Madras Army, Lt. General Sir J.F. Craddock, issued a change in regulations by which the troops were to wear a turband (round-hat) instead of a turban and it would have a feather in it and a leather cockade. The regulation made the following observations: "It is ordered by the regulations that a native soldier should not have painted mark on his face to denote his caste or wear earrings, when dressed in his uniform and it is further clean shaved on the chin. It is directed also that uniformity shall as far as practicable be preserved in regard to the qualification and shape of the hair upon the lip."[2]

The new 'hat' was ordered on the ground that those in wear were heavy and inconvenient, and also because there was no uniformity in the turban as worn in different regiments. During the months of April-June 1806, new pattern turbands were sent to each Regiment, and commanding officers were directed to cause new turbands to be made up in conformity therewith, and to be issued to the men.[3]

The native Officers and sepoys resented this new dress regulation. Both Hindus and Muslims were attached to their own customs and manners, habit and opinions. A Muslim would not shave his beard, which was commonly associated with his faith. Similarly, a caste Hindu had the habit of making his forehead to symbolize his religious sect. They were also prohibited to wear earrings. The new turban was considered highly objectionable for a variety of reasons. It was like a European hat and secondly, it contained a leather cockade expected to be made from the skin of cows, which was a taboo to the Hindus. In India, the hat was particularly associated with Christians who were referred to as *Topi-Wallahs* or Hat-Wearers (worn by the East Indian drummers). Consequently, the Sepoy felt that the introduction of the new regulations was the first step to convert them into Christianity.[4]

While imposing this condition very little care was taken to respect the sentiments of the native soldiers. So these stipulations were viewed as measures calculated to hurt the religious feelings

2 The British authorities at Madras had introduced an obnoxious head-dress resembling a European hat, in the place of the old time-honoured turban, and had, moreover, forbidden the sepoys to appear on parade with earrings and caste marks.

3 Wilson Lieutenant Colonel W. J., 1883, *History of Madras Army, Vol. III*, Madras: E Keys, Govt Press, p. 170.

4 Anyone with knowledge on India would have known that a hat is quite different from a turban and that a 'hat-wearer' was a common name used for a native Christian. Also leather of any kind was an abomination to a Hindu and regarded with suspicion by a Muslim, because it may be of pig-skin. Beard was of special significance to a Muslim as an outward sign of his faith. Earring were also linked with family rights in childhood and worn till death. The marks on the forehead of many Hindus were not, as the British called them 'caste-marks', but were rather indication of the sect a man followed and his having recently gone through the ceremonies of his religion. Mason Philip, 2004, *A Matter of Honour: An Account of the Indian Army, Its Officers and Men*, Dehradun: Natraj Publishers, p. 238.

of the native Sepoys and enforce an inferior social status on them based on race and colour. However, the military administration had different opinions on the matter. The military officials felt that the old turban was inconvenient and they favoured its replacement by a lighter one which would foster a better appearance for the soldier.

The dissatisfaction of the sepoy was not long concealed when the orders regarding wearing the new turban came in May 1806. There was a discontent and uneasiness about the offensive order.[5] The 2nd Battalion of the 4th Regiment of Native Infantry refused to wear the turban sent for their use. The objections expressed by the 2nd/4th at Vellore were reported but met with a reply that any objection with dress was absolutely uncompromising; the orders have to be carried out at one. Further, the ring leaders should be confined and sent to Madras for a trial by Court Martial.

The actions of the 2nd Battalion were followed by several other battalions who also started defying the dress regulations. A squadron of HM 19th Dragoons was dispatched to Vellore to act as escort to any prisoners who were to be brought o the Presidency for trial in May 1806. There were 21 prisoners of whom two were sentenced to 900 lashes and dismissal; 19 were sentenced to 500 lashes each, but were pardoned on making a full apology. The 2nd/4th were moved to Madras and their promotion stopped. The charges, sentences, and orders of the Commander-in-Chief of 29 June, were published on 2 July.

On 17 June 1806, a sepoy Mustafa Beg, warned his commanding officer Lt Colonel Forbes that a mutiny was being planned but, his story was referred for investigation to a board of native officers who were involved in the plot. Mustafa was punished for being a trouble maker.[6]

However, the discontent continued to simmer. The mutiny at Vellore broke out at 3am on Sunday, the 10 July 1806. The garrison at Vellore consisted of about 400 Europeans and 1500 sepoys. At midnight, without warning, the sepoys rose in mutiny. One body fired on the European barracks until half the soldiers were killed or wounded. Another body fired on the houses of the British officers, and shot them down as they rushed out to know the cause of the uproar. In the outbreak at Vellore, 14 British officers were killed and 115 other ranks of His Majesty's 69th were killed or died of wounds. Inside the fort, Tipu's old flag was hoisted. Hearing the news of mutiny, Colonel Rollo Gillespie, the Commander at Arcot reached Vellore within two hours. Mutineers were trapped in the fort and lacking any leadership of their own made practically no resistance. In the ensuing action, 400 were killed in the fort, and of the remainder were tried by a drumhead court martial. Six were blown away from the guns, five shot by musketry, eight hanged, and five transported. About 600 men, who had not taken part in mutiny, but remained bystanders,

5 The fallen families of Hyder Ali and Tippu were lodged in this Vellore fortress, and many of Tippu's old soldiers were serving in the garrison. These people taunted the sepoys about wearing hats and becoming Christians, whilst some secret intriguing was going on for restoring Mohammedan ascendency in Southern India, under the deposed dynasty of Mysore. Wheeler J. Talboys, 1886, *India under British Rule: From the Foundation of the East India Company*, London: Macmillan and Co., p. 100.

6 Heathcote T.A., 2013, *The Military in British India: The Development of British Land Forces in South Asia 1600-1947*, South Yorkshire: The Praetorian Press, p. 50.

were dismissed. Finally, the dress regulations were withdrawn in order to respect the religious sentiments of the native soldiers and the old headgear was restored. [7]

On 15 April 1807, the Court of Directors sent an order for the removal of Lord William Bentinck from the post of Governor and Lt. General Sir J.F. Craddock from the post of Commander-in-Chief for their inability to manage the situation. The failure of the local authorities to initiate prompt measures was viewed as a failure, because it had led to the rebellion of the company's most well-behaved and distinguished corps.

The White Mutiny of 1809

There were many instances of indiscipline and insubordination amongst the European Officers of the East India Company.[8] The Officers of the Company's Army were aware about their strength and position and extorted substantial concessions from the unwilling Company. In 1794 memorials were presented to the Court of Directors by 500 officers of the Bengal Army, and by numerous officers of the Madras and of the Bombay Armies, setting forth their grievances. The whole position of the Indian Armies was then elaborately examined and discussed. During the reorganization of the Army in 1796, a revised system of pay, pension and furlough was introduced. It recognized the claim of officers to furlough, up to a maximum of three years, after not less than ten years' service in India, and for the first time it conferred retiring allowance to the Indian Army. With this, irregular and improper allowances, which were intended to supply the absence of a regular pension, were discontinued. The Court decided also ordered that the Bazar allowance, the grant of double batta, and other objectionable forms of remuneration were to cease. It was expected that this liberal and generous measure of reform would put an end once and for all to discontent and agitation in the Army.

The Company's expectation that its concessions would immediately produce complete content in their Native Army was disappointing. Some legitimate grievances remained, and others, less legitimate, were soon discovered. The agitation still went on, especially in the Madras army. One reasonable ground of complaint which the reorganization of 1796 did not deal with was the difference between the allowances granted in Bengal and in Madras. Bengal was a wealthy Province and could afford to be liberal in the matter of house-rent and other allowances which were denied in Madras. What made the hardship greater to the Madras officer was that the cost of living was really higher in Madras than in Bengal. The matter was represented to the Court of

7 For more details see: Wheeler J. Talboys, 1886, *India under British Rule: From the Foundation of the East India Company*, London: Macmillan and Co., pp. 312.

8 In Madras Presidency a serious incident of indiscipline took place in August 1776. The Governor, Lord Pigott, was engaged in a dispute with the members of his Council. Pigott ordered the arrest of the Commander-in-Chief, Sir Robert Fletcher, on a charge of inciting the troops to mutiny, and offered the command to Colonel Stuart. This officer was, however, in league with the Governor's opponents in the Council. He dissembled his intentions, attended a meeting of the Council and accepted the Governor's invitation to supper. But while they were driving back together in the Governor's carriage, it was stopped by officers posted by Colonel Stuart; Governor Pigott was treacherously arrested and was carried off to St. Thomas' Mount, where he was held a close prisoner for many months. He eventually died in confinement in March 1777. Cardew Alexander, 1929, *The White Mutiny: A Forgotten Episode in the History of the Indian Army*, London: Constable & Co Ltd, p.5.

Directors, but it declined to admit the principle that such allowances as these must be on the same scale throughout India. The Madras officer felt that in this he was badly treated.

From the beginning of the 1807, the officers of the Madras Army had shown discontent over a few issues like the higher allowances granted to the officers of the Bengal Army and the undue proportions of most lucrative command position were bestowed upon the officers of the Royal Army.[9] This feeling was aggravated by the discontinuation, in July 1807, of certain allowances paid to officers commanding districts, stations, and cantonment, out of the duties levied in military bazars;[10] and by the abolition of the tent contract[11] in May 1808.[12] The withdrawal of

9 In the early days of the Company's Army, a King's officer was entitled to supersede and take command of any officer of the Company of the same rank, however senior in age and standing. A Captain in the Company's service, grown grey with age and hard service, though in command of his regiment, might find himself superseded by some boy in a King's regiment only a few years out of school. In 1788 orders were issued giving officers of the Company equality in rank with those in the King's regiments, but the matter had not been fully settled even as late as 1807. Cardew Alexander, 1929, *The White Mutiny: A Forgotten Episode in the History of the Indian Army*, London: Constable & Co Ltd, p. 9.

10 The discontinuance of the allowances from the bazaar fund was justified by the Court of Directors as being in strict conformity with the Articles of War, which prohibited the levy of duties by Military Officers on any article of consumption. It was the opinion of the Government that such taxations for the benefit of those command them may give rise to feeling of discontent amongst the soldiers. It was further observed that in India the amount of the collections in military bazaars was always depended, principally, on the extension of spirituous liquors to the troops. Moreover, the abolition of this allowance was not confined to Madras, but was carried out in the other Presidencies also, and it affected the officers of the Royal army as well as those of the Company. Wilson Lieutenant Colonel W. J., 1883, History of Madras Army, Vol. III, Madras: E Keys, Govt Press, p. 243.

11 Lieutenant-General Stuart, when Commander-in-Chief, devised a plan for the provision and conveyance of camp tent equipage, and regimental stores, with the object of avoiding the serious losses which had been sustained by Government in consequence of the frequent capture of public cattle and tents during the wars with Hyder and Tippoo. This resulted in the issue of a regulation in 1802, which, in consideration of a certain monthly sum to be drawn by officers commanding regiments of cavalry, battalions of infantry, companies of artillery, and the corps of pioneers, made it obligatory upon them to provide and maintain, in constant readiness for the fields camp equipage and carriage for their respective corps on a scale laid down in the regulation, besides carriage for regimental stores, and hutting accommodation for the men when not encamped. The allowance in question was to meet all expenses for cover to the native troops in the field, in cantonment, or in garrison, in peace or war. This regulation came into operation shortly before the Mahratta War of 1808, and was found to answer remarkably well; but shortly after the peace in 1806, Government, in compliance with instructions from England, commenced to reduce the military expenditure, and Sir John Gradock, at that time Commander-in-Chief, called upon Major Munro, the Quartermaster-General, for information regarding the working of the tent contract. That officer accordingly submitted a report, in which, for reasons assigned, the abolition of the contract was recommended, and the Commander-in-Chief, concurring, laid the report before Government in June 1807. The recommendation, having been duly considered, was approved, and, having received the sanction of the Supreme Government, the contract was ordered to be abolished from May 1808. Wilson Lieutenant Colonel W. J., 1883, *History of Madras Army*, Vol. III, Madras: E Keys, Govt Press, pp. 243-244.

12 The relative status of the officers of the King's and the Company's services had long been a thorny question, and the case for the Company's officers was thus moderately stated by Colonel (afterwards Major-General Sir John) Malcolm, writing in 1811, "If it [the British Empire in India] cannot afford to give high pecuniary rewards, it should purchase the services of men of birth and education; and remunerate the great sacrifices which they make in entering the native army of India by approbation, rank, and honours; and, instead of leaving them in a state of comparative obscurity, depressed by the consideration that they are an inferior service, and that military fame, and the applause of their King and country, are objects placed almost beyond their hopes; their minds should

Bazar allowances was bitterly resented. Men who had been used for years to the enjoyment of the Bazar allowance faced the immediate loss. The abolition of the Bazar allowance and tent contract was therefore a prominent cause of grievance.

In the Madras Army the total number of officers, which was only 87 in 1755, had risen to 652 in 1800 and to 1200 in 1809. There was serious doubt whether many of the young men who had joined the Army since the reorganization would ever rise above the rank of Captain. This approaching block in promotion doubtless had an effect on the spirits and outlook of the junior ranks.

In 1806, a new appointment of Inspector of Cavalry was created and Colonel R. R. Gillespie, who had saved many lives during the Vellore mutiny, was appointed to this post. However, Colonel Gillespie was junior in standing to Lieutenant-Colonel St. Leger; he was also an officer of the King's service, and on both accounts St. Leger considered his position as Inspector of Cavalry as a personal affront. The Commander-in-Chief of Madras at the time was Sir John Craddock, himself an officer of the King's service; but he could not redress the grievance of Col Leger.[13] Dissatisfied with the rejection of his petitions, Col Leger sent a lengthy memorial to the Government in India on 28 August, highlighting his position as, "under the most severe and degrading position an officer can be placed in." He made himself the mouthpiece of the officers and to ventilate their complaints as well as his own. In subsequent action, on 1 May, few ring-leaders were selected for disciplinary action (suspension from command, removal or dismissal from the service) against them.

Once the order of the 1 May became public, the discontent amongst the Company's officers resulted into mutiny. A large number of the officers openly defied the orders of the Government and announced their resolution to contribute towards the support of suspended offices, as well as to join in any legal measures to remove the cause of the existing discontent. The mutiny spread to Secunderabad/Hyderabad, Jaulna, Bellary, Cumbum, Ellore, Trichinopoly, Dindigul, Madras, Pallamcottah, Quilon and Seringapatam, the troops in the last-named place rising in arms against the government. Treasure was seized, acts of violence were committed, and the intention of the mutineers appeared to be the subversion of the civil government. Near Seringapatnam, the forces under the command of the mutineers were attacked by the Mysore Horse. Amongst the European officers, Captain McIntosh was wounded and taken a prisoner and Lieutenant Best of 8th regiment died of fatigue. A large number of the silladar horses were killed. The actual

be studiously elevated to these objects; and they should be put upon a footing which would make them have an honourable pride in the service to which they belong. This they never can have (such is the nature of military feeling), while they consider themselves one shade even below another, with which they are constantly associated."

13 The Commander-in-Chief of Madras was anxious both on personal and family grounds to show all possible consideration to Colonel St. Leger, and when the latter came to see him to represent his grievances, Sir John Craddock did all he could to pacify him. He pointed out that as the appointment of Colonel Gillespie had been made while Colonel St. Leger was absent from India, it could not be construed as conveying the slightest reflection on the latter. He exhorted the Colonel to wait a little while until some opportunity should occur of providing him with a more suitable post, and meantime to resume command of his regiment, the 6th Native Cavalry. However, this counseling had no effect of Col Leger, and he sent a petition to the Governor in Council. His petition did not find any favour from the Governor in Council. Cardew Alexander, 1929, *The White Mutiny: A Forgotten Episode in the History of the Indian Army*, London: Constable & Co Ltd, p. 15.

casualties in the silladar horse, 8th and 15th both, were 126 men, and 150 horses killed and nearly 281 were missing. Many of those declared as "missing" were supposed to have been killed. In addition, few camp followers were also killed and wounded in the fort.

After the mutiny was brought under control, a general order was issued on 25 September, whereby general amnesty was given to all concerned except a few ringleaders. On 30 September an order was issued by which all officers who had been removed from the military service, were permitted to rejoin their respective Corps on signing the declaration, a proffer which was universally accepted.

Finally, 21 Officers were selected for punishment, as examples to the rest. On the 1st November, a General Court Martial, of which Major-General Warde was President, and which was composed of an equal number of officers of each service, assembled at Bangalore for the trial of Lieutenant Colonel Bell and others. The charges against Bell were:

> Lieutenant-Colonel John Bell, of the Madras artillery, and late commanding the fort and garrison of Seringapatam, charged by the officer commanding the army with having, in subversion of all good order and military discipline, and in violation of the rules and articles of war for the better government of the Company's forces, joined in and headed a most dangerous and alarming mutiny and sedition, which took place in the said garrison on and betwixt the 30th day of July last and 23d of August following, during which period the garrison fired on the troops of his Majesty and those of the Company, and their ally the Rajah of Mysore, and seized on the public treasury; and he, Lieut. Col. John Bell, declared his resolution not to deliver up the fort and garrison to the proper authorities.

Amongst the officers who faced trial by court martial, one died, four were cashiered, and sixteen were dismissed from the service. With the exception of Lieutenant-Colonel John Bell,[14] and the Commandants of the battalions which had marched from Chittledroog, every surviving officer who had been suspended, dismissed, or cashiered, was ultimately restored to the service.[15] The historiography of the 'White Mutiny' of 1809 implicitly denies the reality of its sepoy casualties. Sepoys died because their officers mutinied. Why the officers were leniently treated afterwards has never been explained. In fact, when the crisis was over and the danger removed, every attempt was made to obscure the issue.[16]

14 Colonel Bell was found guilty on the 9th December 1809, and sentenced to be cashiered. The proceedings were returned for revision, but the Court adhered to their original sentence. The Commander-in-Chief, when confirming it, remarked that the punishment awarded to the prisoner bore no proportion to the atrocity of the crime. See: Proceedings of a General Court Martial Held at Bangalore on the Trial of Lieut. Col. John Bell on the Madras Artillery, London: T.C. Savill, 1837, p. 288.

15 Major Storey was sentenced to be cashiered. This sentence was also returned for revision, but the Court having declined to make any alteration, it was confirmed by the Commander-in-Chief without remark. Lieutenant-Colonel Munro was sentenced to be cashiered, which sentence was duly confirmed. Major Kenny was also sentenced to be cashiered, and the sentence was confirmed. Lieutenant-Colonel Doveton was charged with having marched from Jaulna without authority, and with mutinous designs and was suspended from the service.

16 Cardew Alexander, 1929, *The White Mutiny: A Forgotten Episode in the History of the Indian Army*, London: Constable & Co Ltd, p. (v).

The Barrackpore Mutiny

In November 1824, the Native soldiers mutinied when the East India Company was fighting the First Anglo-Burmese war under William Amherst. During that time sepoys of Bengal Army were not bound to undertake a journey by sea. The mutiny had its roots in British insensitivity towards Indian cultural sentiments. In October 1824, the 26th, 47th and 62nd Regiments of the Bengal Native Infantry were ordered to march a distance of 800 km from Barrackpore to Chittagong in preparation for entering Burmese territory. The regiments had just marched almost 1,600 km from Mathura to Barrackpore and were reluctant to undertake another long march, this time against the Burmese, an unknown enemy. Their feeling was aggravated by the fact that the government had failed to supply bullocks for baggage and ordered that all sepoys would provide their own bullocks. The order was felt unjustified because there was a shortage of bullocks. which had already been purchased by the government and the prices had risen very high. The few bullocks that were available were of inferior quality and cost exorbitant rates beyond the means of the sepoys, who requested that the government should provide the bullocks or pay them double batta to cover the cost of purchasing them.

These requests were disregarded and the sepoys were instead advised to carry whatever they could in their knapsacks and to leave the rest behind. To resolve the situation, the Commander offered a 4,000 rupee advance to each regiment. The sepoys turned down this offer as it still meant paying baggage charges out of their own pocket. The situation was escalated by threats from a Muslim Subedar Major, that if they did not stop complaining about the bullocks, they would be sent by sea.

The lack of transport for personal effects and cultural concerns about being transported by sea caused apprehension and when troops from the 47th Native Infantry appeared on parade, the troops refused to march towards Chittagong, unless their grievances were remedied. Attempts to resolve the dispute failed and dissent spread to elements of the 26th and 62nd Regiments. The Commander in Chief, General Edward Paget, ordered the troops to lay down their arms before considering their requests for redress.

On the morning of 2 November, the reinforcements and the loyal members of the 26th and 62nd Regiments moved into position. They secretly surrounded the sepoy camp ground and a final message was sent to the mutineers, demanding that they lay down arms before any discussion on grievances but it is said that only ten minutes were offered to make up their minds. The sepoys either hesitated or rejected the ultimatum and Paget ordered two cannons to fire on the rebels, followed by an attack from the rear by the secretly placed horse artillery. Surprised by this sudden assault, the sepoys tried to flee but the rest of the British regiments attacked from all directions. Some of the sepoys jumped into the Hooghly River to escape and drowned, others entered local households for shelter but the loyalists chased them in and killed them with bayonets. Many bystanders, including women and children who were in the neighbourhood, were killed during the operation.

Of about 1,400 mutineers, 180 were killed during the attack, although the death toll is disputed. In the aftermath, eleven sepoys were identified as the ring leaders and received a swift trial, where they were sentenced to death by hanging. Around 52 sepoys were sentenced to fourteen years' hard labour; while numerous others were sentenced with lesser terms of penal servitude. The 47th Regiment was disbanded on 4 November by a General Order and its Indian officers dismissed, while its European officers were transferred to other regiments. On 9 November, Sepoy Bindee Yadav, who was considered as a ring-leader was arrested nearby, and suffered the especially harsh punishment of being hung in chains on the next day. His body was left to rot for months in open public display. No disciplinary measures were taken against Paget or any other officer of the Company's army. The incident was largely suppressed in the media, with only limited information being released to the public but there was Parliamentary criticism of the Company's government for its heavy-handedness in dealing with the genuine grievances of native soldiers.

The 1857 Mutiny

The expansionist and annexationist policies of the British power in India made all the Indian rulers, big and small, Hindu and Muslim look with suspicion and develop hatred towards the British power in India. Failure on the part of the East India Company in honouring the provision of 1833 Charter Act that "no Indian shall by reason of his faith, place of birth, descent, complexion or any of them, be disabled from holding any place, office or employment under the East India Company", convinced the educated Indians of the arrogant racial hatred of the British towards the natives of India. The Mutiny of 1857 or revolt was the result of a culmination of popular dissatisfaction that had been simmering for a long time against the policies of the British in India.

In 1857, the mutiny broke out in the Bengal Army. The reason for revolt was the introduction of the new Enfield rifle. To load it, the sepoys had to bite off the ends of lubricated cartridges. Apparently the grease used to lubricate the cartridges was a mixture of pigs' and cows' fat; thus, to have oral contact with it was an insult to both Muslims and Hindus. There is no conclusive evidence that either of these materials was actually used on any of the cartridges in question. However, the perception that the cartridges were tainted added to the larger suspicion that the British were trying to undermine Indian traditional society. For their part, the British did not pay enough attention to the growing level of sepoy discontent.[17] In late March 1857, Sepoy Mangal Pandey (Mungul Pandy) attacked British officers at the military garrison in Barrackpore. He was arrested and tried by a native court martial.

17 In August 1856, greased cartridge production was initiated at Fort William, Calcutta, following a British design. The grease used included fat supplied by the Indian firm of Gangadarh Banerji & Co. By January 1857, the rumours were abroad that the Enfield cartridges were greased with animal fat. Company officers became aware of the rumours through reports of an altercation between a high-caste sepoy and a low-caste labourer at Dumum. The labourer had taunted the sepoy that by biting the cartridge, he had himself lost caste, although at this time such cartridges had been issued only at Meerut and not at Dumdum. On 27 January 1857, Colonel Richard Birch, the Military Secretary, ordered that all cartridges issued from depots were to be free from grease, and that sepoys could grease them themselves using whatever mixture they may prefer. A modification was also made to the drill for loading so that the cartridge was torn with the hands and not bitten. This, however, merely caused many sepoys to be convinced that the rumours were true and that their fears were justified.

Trial of Mangal Pandey

On Sunday, the 29 March 1857, a Non-commissioned Officer came in the afternoon to the quarters of Lieutenant Baugh, Adjutant of the 34th Native Infantry (NI), and reported that Sepoy Mungul Pandy had turned out in front of the quarter-guard of the regiment and fired at the sergeant-major. Having put on his uniform, Baugh reached to the lines duly armed. He had scarcely pulled up at the quarter-guard when a shot was fired and his horse fell under him. As soon as he could disentangle himself, he drew his pistol from the left holster, and, seeing that Mungul Pandy was reloading; he fired, but missed. Mungul Pandy stopped loading. Baugh drew his sword and rushed in to secure him. The sergeant-major came to the assistance of his officer. Mungul Pandy held both his assailants at bay, and severely wounded them with his sword. A blow by another sepoy knocked down the sergeant-major, and at the same time Baugh was brought to the ground. However, Sepoy Shaik Pultoo, rushed forward and held Mungul Pandy until the two wounded men had time to rise and make good their retreat. During this time, with the exception of Shaik Pultoo, no man advanced from the quarter-guard or from the lines to assist their officers or arrest Mungul Pandy. When the Adjutant, maimed and bleeding, was retiring from the conflict, he passed the lines of his regiment and reproached the men assembled there with having allowed their officers to be cut down before their eyes without offering to assist them; they made no reply, but turned their backs, and moved sullenly away. Meanwhile a sepoy had rushed to the quarters of the General, and informed him that "all the sepoys of the brigade were turning out on their parades."

The General then mounted his horse, and, accompanied by his two sons, galloped down to the parade ground of the 34th Native Infantry (N.I.). On arriving there he saw that eighty or ninety paces in front of the quarter-guard, Mungul Pandy striding up and down and vehemently calling upon his comrades to join him to defend and die for their religion and caste. The General immediately rode towards the quarter-guard accompanied by his two sons and Major Eoss, the Assistant Adjutant-General. Immediately after, Mungul Pandey fired, and the whistle of the bullet was heard by the guard. Then they saw Mungul Pandy fall to the ground. At the last moment he had turned the muzzle to his breast and discharged it by the pressure of his foot. On reaching him they found him covered with blood, and his clothes burning and smoking. The fire was quickly put out, and he was conveyed to hospital.

Two days after the incident, the 19th N.I. marched into Barrackpore and disbanded. General hearsey told the men that Government, though he had punished them by summary dismissal from the service, did not wish to disgrace them by stripping them of their uniform. He also informed them that, as a reward for their penitence and good conduct on the march from Berhampore, they would be provided at the public cost with carriage to carry them to their homes. Six days after the disbandment of the 19th Regiment of N.I., Mungul Pandy was brought to trial.

On 6 April 1857, a Native Court Martial assembled in the 34th Regiment Mess House to try Sepoy Mangal Pandey. Presiding officer of the court was Subadar-Major Jowahir Lal Tewary, with fourteen other native Subadars as members of the court. The Judge-Advocate was Captain G C Hatch and Lt. James Vallings of 19th NI undertook the interpretation duties. During the trial,

Mangal Pandey was under medical treatment. The report of doctor read, "Sepoy Mungul Pandy has not improved in health since he came under my charge; he has been gradually becoming weaker, and is now much debilitated. The wound also presents an unhealthy appearance. I still, however, consider him fit to be removed the mess house of 34th Regiment, Native Army."[18] James Allen, Assistant Surgeon, 34th Regiment, NI, certified that Mungul Pandy was is a fit state to undergo his trial. The charges against Mungul Pandey were following:

> 1st – For mutiny, in having at Barrackpore, on 29 March 1857, gone on to the parade ground in front of the quarter-guard of his regiment armed with a sword and musket, and then and there used words intending to incite the men of his regiment to turn out and join him in resistance to lawful authority.
>
> 2 nd– For having, on the occasion set forth in the first charge, used violence against his superior officers Sergeant-Major James Thornton Hewson and Lieutenant and Adjutant Bempde Henry Baugh, of the 34th Regiment, Native Infantry, by discharging at them, severally, his loaded musket, and then and there striking and wounding with his sword the said Lieutenant B. H. Baugh and Sergeant-Major Hewson.

Mangal Pandey pleaded not-guilty to the charges, his hand-cuffs were removed and the prosecution started with the first witness, Lt. Col Wheeler, the Commanding Officer. He testified in general about what he observed happen on 29 March. He was asked if he had observed anything unusual among the sepoys lately. He responded, "Towards the latter end of January, there was much talk among the sepoys, I understood, of the new cartridges being made up, and in consequence they had an idea that we were going to make them Christians by force." The second witness was Sergeant-Major Hewson who testified while lying on a *charpoy* still wounded. The bulk of his testimony was about the conduct of sepoys while Mangal Pandey was inciting them. They had done nothing to help him subdue Mangal Pandey and had just stood there "talking between themselves". Mangal Pandey refused cross-examination.

Lt. Baugh was sworn in as the third witness. Baugh pointed out that no one except Sheikh Pultoo had lifted a finger to help him. Baugh was also severely hurt so he retired. The fourth witness was Drummer John Lewis who had been told by Mungul Pandy to sound the assembly. He saw Pandy extort another sepoy nearby, "Why are you not getting ready? It is for our religion". He further testified that the Jamadar had not made any move or given any order to stop Mungul Pandy. Drummer John Lewis affirmed that the prisoner had fired his musket at the adjutant, and hit the horse. The fifth and the last witness was Havildar Shaikh Pultoo; who was given double promotion for restraining Mungul Pandy, and saving life of two British officers. He affirmed that the prisoner was restrained by him in causing further injuries to the two British Officers. [19]

The prosecution rested and the prisoner was called upon to present his defence. These are the only words directly attributed to him in this history: "I did not know who I wounded and who I did not; what more shall I say? I have nothing more to say. I have no evidence." The Court Martial

18 Signed on 6 April 1857 by T. B. Reid, Asst-Surgeon, 53th Regiment.

19 Sarup Leela, 2007, *The Trial of Mangal Pandey: State Papers*, New Delhi: Neogi Books, pp. 114-128.

found Mungul Pandy guilty, and sentenced him to be hanged. The native officers who tried him were unanimous in their verdict, and eleven out of fourteen passed the sentence of death. At the time of the award of punishment, Mungul Pandy was twenty six years two months and nine days and had seven years, two months and nine days of service. He had no previous convictions and his character in the military was assessed as 'Good'.

On the morning of 8 April, Mungul Pandy was hanged on the Parade ground at Barrackpore soon after gun-fire. The gallows was erected in the centre of the parade ground, and the troops were drawn up so as to form three sides of a square. Mungul Pandy was carried to the ground, accompanied by a detachment of the guard. When the detachments were marched up in front of the gallows, General Hearsey addressed the 34th N. I., in a few words, alluding in particular to the Articles of War which they had all sworn to obey. At a given signal the platform was withdrawn, and almost without a struggle, the Mungul Pandy was launched into eternity. Some difficulty had arisen the day previous for a hang man, and two domes and two mehters were called from Calcutta. The troops were then marched off the ground, the 34th N.I., seeming but too happy to be released; but the men in the guard belonging to this corps to the number of nineteen, who rendered no assistance at the time of the affray, and who were supposed to have been concerned in the attack, were still in close confinement, awaiting the result of the Court-Martial then pending.[20]

On the 10 April, two days after the execution of Mungul Pandy, Jemadar Issuree Pandy the native officer, who had incited the sepoys of the quarter-guard to refrain from assisting their officer, was brought to trial, and also sentenced to be hanged. The sentence, however, could not be immediately carried out owing to a legal difficulty. A week elapsed before it was approved and confirmed by the Commander-in-Chief, who wrote, "The extreme punishment of military law has been justly awarded…." On 21 April, Issuree Pandy was duly hanged by the neck at six o'clock, in presence of all the troops at the station. [21]

The ball set rolling from the arsenal at Barrack-Dumdum soon assumed monstrous dimensions in the cantonment at Barrackpore. The sepoys blindly accepted the conclusion that Her Majesty the Queen and Lord Canning had arranged a secret scheme for converting them all to Christianity. The greased cartridges, they decided, must have been manufactured expressly to destroy their religion; to compel them to become Christians. Wild fictions were talked over as matters of fact, by the ignorant sepoys.[22] The revolt of 1857 began as a mutiny of sepoys of the East India Company's army in the town of Meerut,[23] and soon erupted into other mutinies and civilian rebellions remained largely confined to northern Indian Gangetic Plain and central India.

20 For more details see: *The Trial of Mangal Pandey: State Papers*, Ed. Leela Sarup; New Delhi: Niyogi Books, 2007; Ainslie Embree, *1857 in India: Mutiny or War of Independence*, Boston: D.C. Heath & Co., 1963, p. 2.

21 Forrest, G. W., 1904, *A History of Indian Mutiny*, Vol. I, London: William Blackwood and Sons, p. 507.

22 Wheeler J. Talboys, 1886, *India under British Rule: From the Foundation of the East India Company*, London: Macmillan and Co., pp. 196-197.

23 The military cantonment at Meerut covered an area of five miles, and was the largest in India. At one end were the lines of three sepoy regiments, two of infantry and one of cavalry, whilst the bungalows of the European officers were scattered about. At the other end of the cantonment were the European barracks, in which a European force was quartered strong enough to have routed four times the number of sepoys. There was a regiment of Dragoon

On 24 April 1857, ninety men of the 3rd Native Cavalry were paraded to practice tearing instead of biting off the end of the cartridge, a change intended to allay suspicion; but all except 5 refused to receive the ammunition. The delinquents were arrested and tried by a native court martial. They were all convicted of mutiny; eighty were sentenced to imprisonment with hard labour for ten years, and the remaining five to a like imprisonment for six years. All were recommended to the mercy of General Hewitt, but the recommendation was ignored, and it was determined to carry out the sentence at once in accordance with orders received by telegram from Lord Canning.

The mutineers were placed under a strong European guard, consisting of two companies of the 60th Rifles and twenty-five men of the Carabineers. The parade for punishment was held at daybreak on 9 May, Saturday. The three regiments of sepoys were drawn up to behold the disgrace of the delinquents; and the men of the sepoy cavalry also were brought out to look on the degradation of their comrades. The Carabineers and Rifles were on the ground, and were ordered to load and be ready. The batteries of artillery were in position, and received the same orders. The slightest movement of disaffection or revolt would have been followed by a terrible slaughter. Not a sepoy stirred from the ranks. The prisoners were brought on the ground, stripped of their uniforms and accoutrements, and put in irons. They were utterly broken in spirit. They put up their hands and cried for mercy, and were then led away, cursing their comrades for not coming to their rescue. This incident precipitated the Mutiny, which by an understanding known only to three or four men in each corps throughout the Bengal army had been arranged for Sunday, 31 May 1857.

The sepoys who were sentenced, were kept for three days under a strong guard of European soldiers, were made over to the civil authorities, and lodged in the civil jail, only two miles from the cantonments, under the charge of Native warders. The consequence was that the sepoys brooded over the fate of their comrades, and secretly determined on rescuing them from the jail, and murdering their European officers. The Europeans went to church on Sunday morning and prepared for church in the evening. Meanwhile there had been agitation in the sepoy lines, but nothing to excite alarm. The native women of the bazaar taunted the sepoys of the cavalry with not having rescued their comrades.

On 31 May, at about five o'clock the sepoys seized their arms and ammunition, and rushed out of their lines, with loud shouts and discharges of musketry. A detachment of sepoy cavalry galloped off to the jail, and liberated not only their eighty-five comrades, but all the other prisoners, 1,500 in number. The whole body then returned to the cantonment and joined the sepoys, who were burning down bungalows, and murdering every European they met, regardless of sex and age. Ladies riding in carriages, and officers driving in their buggies, were assaulted and fired at as they drove along. Then with the cavalry they fired the cantonment, and having murdered every European, male and female, whom they met, they marched for Delhi.

Guards, known as the Carabineers; a battalion of the 60th Rifles; two troops of horse artillery, and a light field battery. The European barracks were thus at a long distance from the sepoy cantonments, and the interval was occupied by shops, houses, and gardens. Wheeler J. Talboys, 1886, *India under British Rule: From the Foundation of the East India Company*, London: Macmillan and Co., p. 205.

The Trial of Bahadur Shah Zafar

In September 1857, on the collapse of the Mutiny in Delhi after five months, Bahadur Shah Zafar, the King took shelter at his ancestor Emperor Humayun's tomb, rejecting advice to accompany rebel forces to Oudh to continue the war from there. But Mirza Ilahi Baksh, father-in-law of one of his sons, advised surrender. Captain William Hodson negotiated the surrender through emissaries. The only condition which Bahadur Shah stipulated was that his life and the lives of the Queen, Zinat Mahal and their son, Jawan Bakht, be spared, and that the pledge should be made to him by Hodson himelf. Capt Hodson agreed to these conditions and the King surrendered on 21 September 1857.

Major Hodson also arrested the King's sons, Mirza Mughal and Mirza Khizr Sultan, and his grandson, Mirza Abu Bakr and rejected their plea that their lives be spared as well. A mob followed the bullock cart which carried the princes. Once their followers were disarmed near the tomb, Hodson galloped and overtook the cart about a mile from Delhi Gate and shot the princes in cold blood.[24]

On 30 May 1857, the State Offences Act (XI of 1857) containing only two articles, was passed. It provided,

> I. All persons owing allegiance to the British Government who, after the passing of this Act shall rebel, or wage war against the Queen or the Government of the East India Company, or shall attempt to wage such war, or shall instigate or abet any such rebellion or the waging of such war, or shall conspire so to rebel or wage war, shall be liable, upon conviction, to the punishment of death, or to the punishment of transportation for life, or of imprisonment with hard labour for any term not exceeding fourteen years; and shall also forfeit all their property and effects of every description.
>
> II. All persons who shall knowingly harbour or conceal any person who shall have been guilty of any of the offences mentioned in the preceding Section shall be liable to imprisonment, with or without hard labour, for any term not exceeding seven years, and shall also be liable to fine.

A week later, Act XIV of 1857 was enacted to provide for the trial and punishment of persons who instigated 'mutiny and sedition' among the Forces of the East India Company and also for trial of offences against the State. The Governor-General could empower officers in command to set up 'General Courts Martial' to try offences punishable under both the Acts. Alternately, the

24 Near the city gate before entering Delhi, suddenly Hodson ordered the three princes to get off the cart and remove their top garments in the presence of a huge gathering around them. No sooner had their signet rings, turquoise arm-bands and bejeweled swords been removed, than in a flash, without any scruples, Hodson took a carbine from one of his troopers and shot them dead without any inquiry or trial. A cold blooded murder had been committed right before the people who stood there frozen. Hodson had the bodies of three Mogul princes displayed in front of a *Kotwali* as a warning to the future rebels. It was a dirty display of military power and arrogance and thus Hodson took the credit (rather discredit) of felling the last Mogul ruler Bahadur Shah's legal heirs to the throne. Overnight, Major Hodson, a well-trained military cum civilian officer became an assassin. The gate near the place where they were killed is still called the Khooni Darwaza or Bloody Gate.

Government could set up 'a Commission' for the trial of persons charged under these Acts. The Commissioners could 'hold a court' for trying the accused. Its orders were final and the Act XIV was not applicable to the Europeans.

These laws envisaged either a Court Martial or a Commission to try cases. It did not authorise a 'Military Commission' to conduct a fact-finding inquiry in the guise of a criminal trial. The Military Commission was set up by order of Major-General Penny on the orders of Sir John Lawrence, Chief Commissioner of the Punjab, and Court Martial procedure was followed. It purported to function under Act XIV of 1857. The President of the Commission was Lt Col Dawes of the Artillery. The other three members were army officers of the rank of Major whereas one member was Captain. The Deputy Judge-Advocate General who conducted the prosecution was Major F J Harriott.

There were four charges against the Emperor, to all of which he pleaded 'not guilty'. The first was that he 'being a pensioner of the British Government in India' encouraged Mohammad Bakht Khan, *Subedar* of the Regiment of Artillery, and other soldiers of the Company, to mutiny. The second charge was that he encouraged his son, Mirza Mughal, and others, to wage war against the State; the third was that he proclaimed himself 'the reigning King and sovereign of India', and took 'unlawful possession of the City of Delhi.' The last charge was that on 16 May, within the precincts of the Palace, he caused or abetted the murder of 49 persons, 'chiefly women and children of European and mixed European descent,' and during the mutiny encouraged others to commit similar outrages.[25]

25 The Charges were: **1st**: For that he, being a pensioner of the British Government in India did at Delhi, at various times between the 10 May and 1 October 1857, encourage, aid and abet Muhammad Bakht Khan, Subadar of the Regiment of Artillery and divers others, native commissioned officers and soldiers unknown, of the East India Company's army, in the crimes of Mutiny and Rebellion against the State. **2nd**. For having at Delhi, at various times between the 10 May and 1 October 1857, encouraged, aided and abetted Mirza Mughal, his own son, a subject of the British Government in India, and others unknown, inhabitants of Delhi, and of the North-West Provinces of India, also subjects of the said British Government, to rebel and wage war against the State. **3rd.** For that he, being a subject of the British Government in India, and not regarding the duty of his allegiance, did, at Delhi, on the 11 May 1857, or thereabouts, as a false traitor against the State proclaim and declare himself the reigning King and sovereign of India, and did then and there traitorously seize and take unlawful possession of the city of Delhi; and did, moreover, at various times between the 10 May and 1 October 1857, as such false traitor aforesaid, treasonably conspire, consult and agree with Mirza Moghal, his own son, and with Muhammad Bakht Khan, Subadar of the Regiment of Artillery, and divers others false traitors unknown, to raise levy, and make insurrection, rebellion, and war against the State, and further to fulfil and perfect his treasonable design of overthrowing and destroying the British Government in India, did assemble armed forces at Delhi, and send them forth to fight and wage war against the said British Government. **4th**. For that he, at Delhi, on the 16th of May 1857, or thereabouts, did, within the precincts of the palace at Delhi, feloniously cause, and become accessory to the murder of 49 persons, chiefly women and children of European and mixed European descent; and did, moreover, between the 10 May and 1 October 1857, encourage and abet divers soldiers and others in murdering European officers, and other English subjects, including women and children, both by giving and promising such murderers service, advancement, and distinctions; and further, that he issued orders to different native Rulers having local authority in India, to slay and murder Christians and English people, whenever and wherever found on their territories; the whole or any part of such conduct being an heinous offence under Act XIV of 1857 of the Legislative Council in India.

The trial began in the *Diwan-e-Khas* of the Red Fort on 27 January 1858 and lasted twenty-one days. After the accused's plea was recorded, the Judge-Advocate opened the case for the prosecution. In his opening words, he made plain his intention to let in all manner of evidence, regardless of whether it bore on the guilt of the Emperor or not.[26] He said that the rules of evidence would not be followed; that documents would be tendered without direct proof of having come from those to whom they were attributed; but, they should not be rejected 'merely because some unimportant formula cannot be complied with.'[27]

The royal prisoner was resigned to his fate and took little interest in the proceedings. Bahadur Shah tottered into the court, supported on one side by his only remaining son Jawan Bakht and on the other by one of his attendants. A place was assigned to him between the President and the Prosecutor and he seated himself there on the cushion placed for his accommodation, Jawan Bakht standing on his left. Now and then, he would come to life and challenge some evidence or cross-examine a witness. The Prosecutor read before the Court a mass of documents designed to show that `following the mutiny the King had indeed begun to rule as Emperor.' The documents were of varied quality. They bore autographed orders and signatures of the King written in pencil at the top. Most of them were petitions addressed to *Jahan-panah* (protector of the world) and sought various favours or protection. On 9 March, the twenty-first day of the trial, Bahadur Shah submitted a written statement in his defence. He forcefully denied charges of complicity in the murders and pleaded his helplessness.

The Commission did not deliver reasoned judgment. The Court pronounced a terse finding on 9 March 1858: "The Court, on the evidence before them, are of opinion that the Prisoner Muhammad Bahadur Shah, Ex-King of Delhi, is guilty of all and every charges preferred against him." This was approved and confirmed by Major General R. Pennny, Commanding Meerut Division on 2 April 1858. The Commission had violated the very statute which established it and under which it professed to act. The death sentence was ruled out. Yet, no other sentence was pronounced, either. That lay in the sole discretion of the government.

The proceedings were forwarded to Sir John Lawrence, Chief Commissioner for the Punjab, who recommended transportation overseas of the ex-King. His wife Zinat Mahal and son Jiwan

26 See: Judge Advocate's address to the Court, "Before proceeding further in this case, it may be necessary to mention that evidence will be submitted to you which may not bear strictly on the charges that have just been perused. It is deemed that all the circumstances connected with the late rebellion, even though not in direct relation to the indictment, may be here appropriately recorded; indeed, up to a late date it had been decided that as the king's life had been guaranteed, this investigation should not be accompanied by charges at all, or even assume the form of a trial, but should embrace all such matters as the discovered correspondence and other reliable sources of information might indicate. .... it must be clearly understood, that the scope of the investigation is not in any way confined by the observance of technicalities, such as belong to a more formal and to a regular trial." Selections from the records of the Government of Punjab and its Dependencies, New Series, Vol VII, Trial of Muhammad Bahadur Shah, Titular King of Delhi and of Mogul Beg, and Hajee, all of Delhi for rebellion against the British Government, and Murder of Europeans during 1857, Punjab Printing Company, 1870, pp. 332.

27 For more details see: Garrett H.L.O., 2007, *The Trial of Bahadur Shah Zafar*, New Delhi: Roli Books, pp. 450.

Bakht were to be given the option to accompany him or of being confined in Bengal, they chose to follow the Emperor. In October 1858, accompanied by Zinat Mahal and Jiwan Bakht, the King departed from Delhi for Calcutta, where they were placed on board a warship and taken to Rangoon.[28] The King died in 1862 at the age of 87 and was buried in Rangoon.

The trial of Bahadur Shah was probably the first of the victor's trials in modern history. His trial ended on 9 March 1858, while the Mutiny still raged fiercely in other parts of India. The proceedings were conducted by military officers, who constituted neither a court martial, nor a Commission of Inquiry but a 'European Military Commission.' A fundamental flaw vitiated the entire proceedings and rendered the trial devoid of legitimacy. Bahadur Shah was himself a sovereign and not a British subject. He was not amenable to the jurisdiction of a British Court. The prosecutor himself referred to him as 'the titular majesty of Delhi.'[29] As a sign of surrender, the Emperor had handed over his arms, including two swords, one with the name 'Nadir Shah' and the other with the seal of Jahangir engraved upon it. Hodson later presented them to Queen Victoria as war trophy.

The Mutiny of 1857 posed a considerable threat to East India Company power in India, and was contained only with the fall of Gwalior on 20 June 1858. The rebellion led to the dissolution of the East India Company in 1858. It also led the British to reorganize the army, the financial system and the administration in India. The country was thereafter directly governed by the Crown as the new British Raj.

28 The final disposal of the ex-King of Delhi became a question of some difficulty, in consequence of the sentence of the court by which he was tried, indicating Andaman Island as his place of exile; as the inlands having been chosen as penal stations for the rebels taken in arms. However, it was considered injudicious to place the deposed King, in immediate proximity of them. After considerable discussion, a station in British Burma, named Tonghoo, some 500km inland from Rangoon, and represented as the most desolate and forlorn district of the whole country was finally selected for him. In early October 1858, an order of the government directed the removal of ex-King and his family to Calcutta, where his final destination was to be made known to him. Departure of the cortege took place at an early hour in the morning of 7 October 1858 in the following order: a squadron of lancers as an advance guard: a palanquin carriage, in which were the diposed king and two of his sons, Jumma Bukht and Shah Abbas (the latter a mere child); the carriage was surrounded by lancers; a second carriage contained the begum, Zeenal Mahal, and some ladies of the zenana; a third carriage the Taj Mahal begum (a second wife of the ex-King), and female attendant. The convoy was followed by five magazine store carts, in which there were 20 of the male and female attendance of the prisoner. The whole closely guarded by lancers, a strong party of whom formed the rear of the cavalcade. In this order, the escort, with its charge proceeded towards Allahabad via Cawnpore (Kanpur). Upon reaching Allahabad, the prisoner with his family was placed on board a river-flat, for conveyance to Calcutta. The *Soorma* flat, in tow of the *Koyle* steam-tug reached Diamond Harbour on the 4 December, where her Majesty's ship Megora, which has recently arrived from the Cape with troops, was found ready to receive the prisoner and convey him to Rangoon, where he arrived on 9 December 1958. Ball Charles, 1812, *The History of the Indian Mutiny*, Vol. II, London: The London Printing and Publishing Company Limited, p. 629-630.

29 Also see: https://frontline.thehindu.com/static/html/fl2412/stories/20070629003302400.htm.

Mutiny in the British Indian Army

There were 14 mutinies in the Indian Army between 1886 and 1930, as shown in the table below.

S. No.	Date	Unit	Place	Troops Involved
1.	12 April 1886	3 Gurkhas	Almorah	Most of the Battalion
2.	3 May 1894	17 Bengal Infantry	Agra	A and E Companies
3.	Oct 1894	25 Madras Infantry	Burma	4 Hindu Companies
4.	13 Sept 1897	14 Bombay Infantry	Bareilly	170 Konki Mahrattas
5.	18 Sept 1897	27 Madras Infantry	Moulmein, Burma	30 Men
6.	1 Nove 1897	17 Bombay Infantry	Bhuj	One Company
7.	11 April 1910	76 Punjabis	Tientsin, China	200 Men
8.	January 1915	130 Baluchis	Rangoon, Burma	Three Pathan Companies
9.	15 February 1915	5 Light Infantry	Singapore	Half Battalion
10.	23 February 1916	15 Lancers	Basra, Mesopotamia	429 Men
11.	2-4 April 1917	3 Brahmans	Mesopotamia	120 Men
12.	22 June 1918	18 Infantry	China	20 Men
13.	1-3 July 1918	30 Dogras	Jhelum	Hill Brahmin Companies
14	24 April 1930	2/18 Royal Garhwal Rifles	Peshawar	Two Platoons

Table: Indian Army Mutinies, 1886-1930[30]

Unlike military uprising of 1857, they were all relatively minor. In the midst of World War I, on 15 February 1915, the Rajput of the 5th Light Infantry (Indian Army) which was stationed in Singapore, revolted, killing more than 40 British officers, British residents and local civilians. The mutiny was originally referred to as the Mutiny of the 5th Light Infantry, but became known later as the Singapore Mutiny. The troops had been stationed to guard military prisoners from the German ship, *Emden*, at Tanglin Barracks. With their duties completed, they were slated to

30 For more details on mutiny see: Omissi David, 1994, *The Sepoy and The Raj: The Indian Army, 1860-1940*, London: Macmillan, pp. 113-152.

leave for Hong Kong by 16 February 1915. However, rumours spread among the troops that they were to be ferried to fight against Muslim Turkey instead. The misunderstanding led to greater disaffection and some 800 soldiers broke out of their barracks on the afternoon of 15 February and killed several British officers before moving on to other areas of the city. The mutiny took the British authorities by surprise because it was a public holiday and most officers and men were away on leave. By the time the revolt was quashed, about 10 days later, 44 British officers, soldiers and civilians, as well as three Chinese and two Malay civilians, were killed in the mutiny. In the course of the fighting, 56 sepoys were killed.

A Court of Inquiry was held on 23 February 1915, first in secret. It then continued publicly, and lasted until May.[31] A total of 47 mutineers were executed, including two Indian officers, six havildars and 39 sepoys. The executions were carried out at Outram Prison. Two of the mutineers were executed on the day of the first trial on 23 February while the others were executed in public executions, witnessed by a large crowd of 15,000 on one occasion. A further 165 mutineers were sentenced to transportation or imprisonment.[32]

Mutiny, including any endeavour to seduce the personnel of the armed forces from duty, is a capital offence under the three service Acts in India. Section 37 of the Army Act, 1950 states that any person subject to the Act who commits any of the following offences, shall, on conviction by court martial, be liable to suffer death or such less punishment as is mentioned in the Act: (a) Begins, incites, causes, or conspires with any other persons to cause any mutiny in the military, naval or air forces of India or any forces co-operating therewith; (b) Joins in any such mutiny; (c) Being present at any such mutiny, does not use his utmost endeavours to suppress the same; (d) Knowing or having reason to believe in the existence of any such mutiny, or of any intention to mutiny or of any such conspiracy, does not, without delay, give information thereof to his commanding or other superior officer; or (e) endeavours to seduce any person in the military, naval or air forces of India from his duty or allegiance to the Union.[33] The Navy Act, 1957 defines the term "Mutiny" as: "any assembly or combination of two or more persons subject to naval law, the Army Act, or the Air Force Act, or between persons two at least of whom, are subject to naval law or any such Act:

I. To overthrow or resist lawful authority in the Navy, regular Army or Air Force or any part of any one or more of them or any forces cooperating therewith or any part thereof; or

31 The men of the Light Infantry had their own idea of the First World War (1914-18) and they considered the meaning of this European conflict and the meaninglessness of their sacrifice for it. The mutiny in Singapore was an expression of their reluctance to go to the war front, or of their anti-war feeling. Letters written by the men to their home in India on the eve of the outbreak bear witness to their feelings. Those men who did not join the revolt, but were terrified at the scene of the mutiny, and ran away to the jungle, had also shared something common with the men who revolted. This gave the real strength to the mutiny. Sho Kuwajima, Indian Mutiny in Singapore, 1915, *New Zealand Journal of Asian Studies*, Vol. 11 No. 1, June 2009, p. 375-84.

32 For more details see: Harper R.W.E. and Miller H., 1984, *Singapore Mutiny*, Singapore: Oxford University Press, pp. 254.

33 Section 37 of the Air Force Act, 1950, and section 43 of the Navy Act, 1957 contain similar provisions.

II. To disobey such authority in such circumstances as to make the disobedience subversive of discipline or with the object of avoiding any duty or service against, or in connection with operations against, the enemy; or

III. To show contempt to such authority in such circumstances as to make such conduct subversive of discipline; or

IV. To impede the performance of any duty or service in the Navy, regular Army or Air Force or any part of any one or more of them or any forces co-operating therewith or any part thereof."

Collective petitions/representations or the submission of a petition through the medium of any association in respect of military matters are forbidden. Sections 131 and 132 of the Indian Penal Code, 1860, punish abetment of mutiny and attempt to seduce armed forces personnel from duty.[34]

34 The Indian Penal Code 1860, Section 131: Abetting mutiny, or attempting to seduce a soldier, sailor or airman from his duty: "Whoever abets the committing of mutiny by an officer, soldier, sailor or airman, in the Army, Navy or Air Force of the Government of India or attempts to seduce any such officer, soldier, sailor or airman from his allegiance or his duty, shall be punished with imprisonment for life, or with imprisonment of either description for a term which may extend to ten years, and shall also be liable to fine." Section 132 dealing with abetment of mutiny (if mutiny is committed in consequence thereof) provides: "Whoever abets the committing of mutiny by an officer, soldier, sailor or airman, in the Army, Navy or Air Force of the Government of India, shall, if mutiny be committed in consequence of that abetment, be punished with death or with imprisonment for life, or imprisonment of either description for a term which may extend to ten years, and shall also be liable to fine."

Chapter VII

Military Courts and Punishments

The Mutiny Act of 1689[1] made peacetime desertion, mutiny, and sedition by military personnel in Britain crimes triable by court martial and punishable by death. [2] The Act of 1689 and all subsequent Mutiny Acts had duration of one year and so a new act was passed annually until 1879. The Mutiny Acts (a creation of Parliament) were modified to provide for courts-martial of military personnel for acts prohibited by the Articles of War (a creation of the Crown) as long as the Articles conformed to the then current Mutiny Act. The Articles of War issued by the Crown in 1718 gave the power to regimental and general court martial for inflicting penalty or corporal punishment for the violations of the various articles. For most of the offences listed in the Articles specified punishment was death. In cases where punishment was not specified the accused could be punished according to the nature of his offence, by the judgment of a regimental or general court-martial. For instance Article VIII provided that if any officer or soldier refuses to obey the

1 The Mutiny Act of 1689 has a curious background. Edward I (1239-1307) created the Court of Chivalry, which was given authority over cases involving military law, chivalry, heraldry, and murder/high treason overseas. The king, working through the Court of Chivalry, created a special law governing the military called the Articles of War. This type of law was operative only during war and fell into abeyance once peace prevailed. With the start of each new war, a fresh set of Articles of War, specifically tailored to the circumstances of the new conflict, were promulgated. As the Court of Chivalry developed and grew, so did the parallel Courts of Chancery and Common Law, which had authority over the civilian population, but not the military. Eventually, British kings, especially the Tudors and Stuarts, began to invoke the Articles of War against civilians even in times of peace, trying people by courts-martial rather than in the common law courts. This abusive expansion of military law led to Parliament's passing the Petition of Right (1627), which barred courts-martial from having jurisdiction over: (a) civilians; or (b) soldiers and officers, residing in Britain during times of peace. During the "Glorious Revolution" (1688) when William III ousted King James II from the British throne, Scottish troops loyal to James refused to obey King William, marching home to Scotland instead, and since the mutinous troops were located in Great Britain and it was technically a time of peace, Courts-martial had no jurisdiction over them. Only the Courts of Chancery and Common Law had jurisdiction, but they were not empowered to enforce any sanction against mutiny.

2 The Mutiny Act of 1689 was the first of a series of Mutiny Acts, re-enacted with only a few short intervals from year to year until 1879. The Act of 1689, although confining itself to the offences of mutiny and desertion, marked the beginning of an era, as it made these offences statutory and prescribes to some extent the requirements of the court-martial to try offenders, Before the passing of the Army Act, 1881, the Crown continued to make Articles of War, but they were only valid in so far as they were consistent with the Mutiny Act in force at the time. Stuart-Smith James, Military Law: Its History, Administration and Practice, *Military Law Review: Bicentennial Issue*, September 1975, p. 25-27 (originally published in *Law Quarterly Review*, Vol. 85, 1969).

lawful orders of his superior officer, he shall be punished with death, or otherwise, as a general court-martial shall think fit.

The Act of 1754[3] specified that the King may grant a Commission or Warrant to the Court of Directors of the East India Company, who, by virtue of such Commission or Warrant, shall have the power to authorise and empower their President and Council at their principal Settlements to appoint Courts-Martial. Such Commissions could also be issued to empower the Commander in Chief employed in the Company's Service, to appoint Courts-Martial for the trial of any of the officers or soldiers under their respective commands. The Act further provided that a General Court-Martial shall consist of not less than nine officers, except in the case at Saint Helena, where it shall not consist of less than five officers. Two-third of the Officers present in the Court were to concur in all sentence of death.[4] The Articles of War published in 1765,[5] further specified that the Commissioned Officers of every Regiment could hold Regimental Courts-Martial for the enquiring into any disputes, or criminal matters for inflicting corporal punishments for small offences. Such Courts, consisting of not less than five officers and in exceptional conditions by three officers, were to give judgment by the majority; but no sentence was to be executed till the Commanding Officer (not being a Member of the Court-Martial) or the Governor of the Garrison confirmed the same.[6]

The Articles of War made under the Act No. XIX. of 1847, provided the punishment of death, transportation, corporal punishment or dismissal for the offences of mutiny and seditions (Article 5), striking a superior officer (Article 6), Disobedience of lawful command of superior officer (Article 7), desertion (Article 8), sentry sleeping on post at the time of war or plundering (Article 9), shamefully abandoning a post (Article 10), treacherously divulging pass-word (Article 11), illegal corresponding with enemy (Article 12), assisting an enemy, allowing an enemy to escape, misbehaviour before enemy, and shamefully casting his arms (Articles 13- 16), leaving commanding officer in time of action and going in search of plunder (Article 17), violence against a person bringing supplies to military camp (Article 18), discharging fire arms (Article 19), releasing state prisoner without authority (Article 20), and being a sentry quitting his post (Article 21). Capital punishment was available for a wide range of offences, both military and criminal. However, the inclusion of certain criminal offences such as housebreaking or plunder had ceased to be capital crimes in the future military codes.

An officer accused of above crimes was awarded punishments of death, or transportation for life, or be dismissed the Service; whereas a soldier on conviction, in addition to above, could be awarded corporal punishment, imprisonment, with or without hard labour including solitary confinement. For other minor offences, not in the face of enemy, the military officers and soldiers could be awarded punishments of dismissal, reduction, corporal punishment, or simple imprisonment (with or without solitary confinement) and reprimand. An officer or soldier, found guilty of

3 27 Geo. II, cap. IX.

4 Article V, The Act of 1754 [27 Geo. II, cap. IX].

5 The Articles of War passed by the Parliament applicable to any portion of the Company's Forces were published in 1765.

6 Article XII and XIII, The Act of 1754 [27 Geo. II, cap. IX].

wilfully and knowingly giving false evidence on oath or affirmation on any trial before any Court Martial,[7] or any Military Court could be dismissed from the service, and further subjected to fine, or imprisonment which may extend to three years. The military courts, viz., General Court Martial, District or Garrison Court Martial and Regimental Court Martial had varying powers to award punishments. A General Court Martial could sentence any officer or soldier to death or transportation, for crimes expressly made liable to sentence of death or transportation in the Articles of War. The Commander-in-Chief had power to commute a sentence of transportation passed on a soldier, to imprisonment (with or without hard labour). They could also commute a sentence of corporal punishment to dismissal from the service passed on a soldier.

A district or garrison Court Martial could sentence any Non-commissioned officer to be reduced to the ranks,—or may sentence any Noncommissioned officer or soldier to be dismissed from the service; may sentence any soldier to suffer corporal punishment not exceeding fifty lashes; or imprisonment, with or without hard labour, not exceeding one year, and to be kept in solitary confinement for certain duration. A regimental Court Martial could sentence any Non-commissioned officer to be reduced to the ranks;—or may sentence any Non-commissioned officer or soldier, to be dismissed from the service; or may sentence any soldier to suffer corporal punishment not exceeding fifty lashes; or imprisonment, with or without hard labour, for any period not exceeding six calendar months; and to be kept in solitary confinement for certain specific duration. Under Article 69, for offences committed on the Line of March, or on board any Ship or other Vessel, the officer in Command of the Troops was authorized to try any soldier by a Regimental, or Detachment Court Martial, and to confirm and execute the sentence on the spot; provided, that such sentence did not exceed the power of a Regimental Court Martial and the proceedings held in such cases were transmitted for the information of the Commander-in-Chief. Minor punishments which could be awarded by court martial in Native Corps are shown in the table below.

7 In Britain, the courts, sometimes known as the Court of Honour or Court of Chivalry, exercised jurisdiction over military offences, against the ordinances issued by or under authority of the King when an army was embodied. It enjoyed also a permanent jurisdiction over offences of murder and high treason committed abroad and, in its capacity as a court of honour, over questions of chivalry such as coat armour and precedence. The judges of the court were the High Constable and Earl Marshal of England who attended the King in his Wars: The High Constable as the commander-in-chief under the King and the Earl Marshal as his deputy and, in modern terms, Adjutant and Quartermaster General. The offices of Constable and Marshal were military officers. When these officers of state, the High Constable and Earl Marshal, did not accompany an army, this judicial function was exercised by the Constable and Marshal of the army concerned. The court was responsible for the trial of military offences until 1521, when the then holder of the office of Lord High Constable was beheaded, having come into conflict with the King, and the office was not re-bestowed. The court, however, continued to exercise jurisdiction under the Earl Marshal alone for a further century, although its function passed gradually to courts or committees of officers. These continued to be known as Courts of the Marshal and, in course of time, Courts-Martial. Stuart-Smith James, Military Law: Its History, Administration and Practice, *Military Law Review: Bicentennial Issue*, September 1975, p. 28 (originally published in *Law Quarterly Review*, Vol. 85, 1969).

Table: Minor Punishment awardable without Court Martial in Native Corps[8]

Punishments	By Commanding Officer	By Troop or Company Officer	Portion involving prospecting exclusion from Good Conduct Pay	Remarks
For Non-commissioned Rank and File including Gun Lascars and Ordnance Drivers				
I. Removal from Staff appointment	--	--	--	By Regimental Commanding Officers only
II. Reduction from Lance appointments	--	--	--	
III. Piling and Unpiling shots	No limit	5 days	--	
IV. Mid-day Grooming	--	Until Horse or Bullock is brought into proper condition.	--	Never to be awarded except for bad condition of the individual's Horse or Bullock and then always until the animal is brought into proper condition.
V. Cleaning Arms and Accoutrements in Hospital	No limit	5 days	--	
VI. Drill without pack	15 days	5 days	--	
VII. Drill with pack	15 days	--	8 days	
VIII. Restriction to Barracks, or for Ordnance Drivers, restrictions to Bullock lines, simple	15 days	7 days	8 days	Taking all Duties and attending all Drills of the Regt., Troop or Company
IX. Restriction for Barrack, or for Ordnance Drivers, restriction to Bullock Lines with Drill	15 days	5 days	8 days	Taking all Duties in course and punishment Drill without Pack, at other times twice a day.

8 Regulations and Orders for General Officers, General Regulations of the Madras Army, Adjutant General's Office, Fort St George, Madras: Military Male Orphan Asylum Press, 1849, p. 124-125.

Punishments	By Commanding Officer	By Troop or Company Officer	Portion involving prospecting exclusion from Good Conduct Pay	Remarks
X. Confinement in Defaulter or Guard Room	7 days	--	4 days	--Do--
XI. Confinement in Conjee House	7 days	--	4 days	Taking neither Drill nor Duty
XII. Confinement in Solitary Cell	7 days	--	2 days	

Punishment for the European Corps was little different form for the Native Corps. The punishment number I and II only were allowed to be awarded to Non-commissioned Officers and other punishments were unsuitable for them. When a heavier punishment was required to be imposed, they were brought to trial by court martial. A Native Officer in command of a detached portion was allowed to award punishments awardable by a Troop or Company Officer. The term staff appointment included Regimental or Troop Havildar Majors; Drill Havildar; Pay and Hospital Havildars; Trumpet, Bugle, Drum and Fire Major, etc. For the punishment of Drill, with or without pack, two hours of drill constituted a day's punishment. In the punishment of "Drill with Pack", the weight of pay was not to exceed 17 pounds in weight, slings and al included.

The European Corps could be awarded an additional punishment of "Stoppage of Coffee Room or Canteen Liberty" for 30 days by the Regimental Commanding Officers and for 15 days by the Troop or Company Officer, during which the individuals were debarred from entering Coffee Room or Canteen. A list of all regimental defaulters was to be made out every month by Troops or Companies and read aloud at the head of the Regiment, Corps or Detachment. It was expected, that it would tend to excite a spirit of emulation among the men to endeavour to have the smallest number of Defaulters in their respective Troops or Companies. [9]

Punishments were designed in theory to fit the crime. However the time and place were also significant determining factors. In times of war, punishments became harsher and military justice grew more subjective as the need to send a message sometimes overrode the search f or guilt or innocence. The 'desire' of the commanding officers had been invisible president of many courts martial and his wishes swayed many decisions.[10]

9 Regulations and Orders for General Officers, General Regulations of the Madras Army, Adjutant General's Office, Fort St George, Madras: Military Male Orphan Asylum Press, 1849, p. 126-127.

10 Henderson Robert, "Terror of Example" Crime and Punishment in the British Army in 1812, Part One: Capital Punishment, available at: http://www.warof1812.ca/punish1.htm.S-96.

Composition of Court Martial

The Articles of War [made under the Act No. XIX of 1847] provided that a General Court-Martial consisted of not less than thirteen Commissioned Officers, unless it was held out of the East India Company's Territories, where such Court-Martial could consist of seven Commissioned Officers, if a greater number cannot be conveniently assembled. A sentence of a General Court-Martial could not be put in execution until after a report has been made of the whole proceedings to the Commander-in-Chief, or to some other person duly authorized to confirm the same, and until his directions have been issued.[11] A District or Garrison Court-martial was to consist of not less than seven Commissioned Officers, except in situations where that number cannot be conveniently assembled, when such Court could consist of not less than five Commissioned Officers. When a District or Garrison Court Martial for the trial of a Native Soldier was composed of less than seven Commissioned Officers, a Memorandum by the officer convening the Court Martial was to be addressed to the officer conducting the Court, and to be attached to the proceedings. Similarly, whenever a Regimental Court Martial consisted of less than five officers, Memorandum form the Commanding officer of the offender's Regiment was to be attached to the proceedings of the Court, stating the reasons that rendered it impracticable to assemble the regulated number of members.

Whenever charges were preferred against any Native Officer or Soldier, or other Native of India, subject to Military Law, a certified translation thereof was prepared without delay, and the same read and delivered to the Prisoner in the presence of the Staff Officer of the Station, or Commanding Officer of the regiment, Detachment or Guard as the case may be, at least 24 hours before trial. Native Court Martial were always superintended by an European Officer. When a Superintending Officer of a Native Court Martial performed the duty of Interpreter also, a Memorandum, under the authority of the Officer Commanding the Station, was attached to the Proceedings of the Court stating that the services of an Interpreter or other competent person were not available at that Station. Under the provisions of the Native Articles of War all descendants of Europeans professing the Christian religion, whether born in wedlock or illegitimate, were entitled to claim trial as Europeans, by a European Court Martial.[12]

Detailed guidelines for the constitution, jurisdiction and practice of court martial were provided in the Presidencies. No Native Officer was eligible to sit as Member of any Court Martial until he has passed a satisfactory examination in the Native Articles of War—a Certificate to which effect was given to each signed by the Adjutant and countersigned by the Commanding Officer.[13] Section LVIII guidelines provided, "the duties attached to Officers employed on Courts Martial, are of most grave and important nature, and in order to discharge them with justice and propriety, it is incumbent on all officers to apply themselves diligently to the acquirement of a complete knowledge of Military Law, and to make themselves acquainted with all orders and regulations,

11 Article 74, the Act No. XIX of 1847.

12 General Regulations of the Madras Army, Adjutant General's Office, Fort St George, Madras: Military Male Orphan Asylum Press, 1849, p. 440-442.

13 Native Officers, General Regulations of the Madras Army, Adjutant General Office, Madras: Military Male Orphan Asylum Press, 1849, p. 356.

and with the practice of Military Courts. With this view, the Officers Commanding Regiments were to require all officers on their entrance into the Army, and before they are nominated to the Members of Court martial, to attend proceedings of such Courts, until the Commanding Officers may deem them competent for the performance of so important duty."[14] A District or Garrison Court-martial could sentence any Non-Commissioned Officer to be reduced to the ranks,—or may Sentence any Non-Commissioned Officer or Soldier to be dismissed from the Service; or could sentence any soldier to suffer Corporal Punishment not exceeding fifty lashes; or Imprisonment, with or without Hard Labour, not exceeding one year, and to be kept in Solitary Confinement.

Summary Court Martial

By the Act V of 1869, the commanding Officers were empowered to hold Summary Court Martial for the trial of native non-commissioned officers and sepoys. The Summary Court Martial was peculiar to the Indian Army, and the one most frequently used in India even in the modern time. The European commanding officer of a Native Regiment presided as judge and jury over the Court Martial and could award a wide range of sentences, including corporal punishment of up to fifty lashes, and these sentences could be implemented forthwith, without confirmation from higher authority. If the commanding officer was of less than five years' standing, he could not carry into effect any sentence by Summary Court Martial, until it has received the approval of the nearest superior Military Officer holding a command of not less than a regiment. A Summary Court Martial was also attended by two commissioned officers, whether European or Native, whose role was not specified in the Act. A Non-commissioned officer could be sentenced to a flogging only if he was reduced to ranks. This composition of summary court martial is valid even today under the Army Act, 1950, except that two officers who attend the proceedings of court martial could be commissioned or junior commissioned officer and it cannot award sentence of flogging.

Summary General Court Martial

The Indian Articles of War were further amended by Act of 1894 and new kind of court martial, i.e., Summary General Courts Martial was added.[15] Under Article 90, the following authorities had the power to convene a Summary General Court-Martial:-

(a) In any place, whether or within or beyond British India, by an officer empowered in this behalf by an order of the Governor General in Council or of the Commander-in-Chief in India or of the general officer of the Command.

(b) By an officer commanding any detached portion of Her Majesty's troops upon active service when, in his opinion, it was not practicable, with due regards to discipline and the exigencies of the service, that an offence should be tried by an ordinary general court-martial.

14 Constitution, Jurisdiction and Practice of Courts Martial, General Regulations of the Madras Army, Adjutant General's Office, Fort St George, Madras: Military Male Orphan Asylum Press, 1849, p. 454.

15 Thus, five kinds of courts-martial could be held, namely (1) General courts-martial, (2) District courts-martial, (3) Regimental courts-martial, (4) Summary general courts-martial, and (5) Summary courts-martial. The first three courts-martial were called ordinary courts-martial, while the last two were called extra-ordinary courts-martial.

A Summary General Court-Martial was to consist of not less than three officers, who may be either British or Native, or both British and Native officers, as the officer convening the court thinks fit. A Summary General Court Martial had all powers of a general court-martial, and subject to any instructions contained in the order convening the court, its sentence was to be valid, and may be carried out forthwith in case it does not exceed that which a district court-martial is empowered to pass, and in any other case when confirmed by the authority convening the court. In case a native court martial consisted only of Native officer and not attended by the judge advocate, a British officer of not less than four years' service was to be appointed to superintendent the proceedings.[16]

The Indian Army Act, 1911 made a number of changes in the law relating to the Indian British Army. Section 43 of the Act listed for the first time the punishments which could be awarded by a court martial, according to the scale as follows:

(i) Death;

(ii) Transportation for life or for any period not less than seven years;

(iii) Imprisonment [either rigorous simple][17], for any term not exceeding 14 years;

(iv) Dismissal from the service;

(v) In the case of officers and warrant officers, suspension from rank, pay and allowances for a period not exceeding two months;

(vi) Reduction, in the case of a warrant officer, to a lower grade or class, and in the case of a Non-commissioned officer, to a lower grade or to the ranks;

(vii) In the case of officers, warrant officers and non-commissioned officers, forfeiture of seniority of rank;

(viii) In the case of officers, reprimand or severe reprimand;[18]

(ix) Forfeitures and stoppages. [19]

16 Para 32, the Indian Articles of War (Amendment Act, 1894) Act No. XII of 1894. The summary general court martial is still a part of Army Act, 1950 and three lay officers may award any punishment, which a General Court Martial can award. Only solace is that the punishment of the death has to be confirmed by the Central Government.

17 These words were substituted for the words and brackets "(with or without solitary confinement) by s. 11(1) of the Indian Army (Amendment) Act, 1918 (11 of 1918).

18 This clause was added by s. 11 of the Indian Army (Amendment) Act, 1918 (11 of 1918).

19 This included the following: (a) Forfeiture of service for the purpose of promotion, increased pay, pension or any other prescribed purpose; (b) Forfeiture of any military decoration or military reward; (c) Forfeiture, in the case of a person sentenced to dismissal from the service of all arrears of pay and allowances and other public money due to him at the time of such dismissal; (d) Stoppages of pay and allowances until any proved loss or damage occasioned by the offence of which he is convicted is made good; and (e) On active service forfeiture of pay and allowances for a period not exceeding three months. Last clause was added by s. 11 of the Indian Army (Amendment) Act, 1918 (11 of 1918).

Punishment of flogging, not exceeding 30 lashes, could be awarded under section 45 of the Indian Army Act, 1911. By an amendment to section 45 issued in 1920, flogging was replaced by the field punishment. It provided, "Where any person, subject to this Act and under the rank of warrant officer, on active service is guilty of any offence, it shall be lawful for a court-martial to award for that offence any such punishment, other than flogging as may be prescribed as a field punishment. Field punishment shall be of the character of personal restraint or of hard labour but shall not be of a nature to cause injury to life or limb." For the purpose of commutation, field punishment was placed next below dismissal.

During the First World War, the Indian officers and soldiers were governed by the Indian Article of War, 1911. The Articles defined offences and laid down punishments. The possible punishments were draconian, and included death penalty for the following offences: Shamefully abandoning a post (only applicable to officer or NCO in command of the post); Castings away his arms and ammunition in the presence of an enemy, or inducing other to do so; Cowardice; Communicating with the enemy and not reporting it; Treacherously giving away the password; Assisting the enemy with victuals or money; Giving a false alarm on active service; Spreading reports calculated to crate alarm or despondency; Being a sentry in time of war, sleeping upon his post; As a sentry quitting his post in time of war; Leaving a post to go in search of plunder in time of action; Desertion; Leaving a post without being regularly relieved; Looting in time of war; Mutiny, including failing to suppress it and failing to report it; Assaulting a superior; Disobeying a lawful command; Allowing, assisting or permitting a prisoner to escape; and Releasing a state prisoner without proper authority.

In wartime, to try a native accused for the above offences, the officer commanding the forces in field or a detachment commander could convene a Summary General Court Martial.[20] The presiding officer was always a British Officer, with two British or Natives officers as members. During the First World War, Summary General Courts Martial were more frequently convened than General Court Martial. Summary General Court Martial allowed a considerable simplification of procedural matters and requirements, supposedly in the interests of military expediency, but not justice. The trials were carried out in improvised accommodation, with the battalion adjutant acting as prosecutor. The charges were read and the accused was asked to plead "guilty or not guilty"? The Court had the power to award death sentence, transportation for from seven years to life, imprisonment for up to 14 years, dismissal from the service and other minor punishments. When death penalty was awarded, the method of execution, shooting or hanging was decided by the Court.

The Judge Advocate General's Department

Under the East India Company, the Judge Advocate General's department consisted of three Judge Advocates General, viz.: One to each of the Armies of Bengal, Madras, and Bombay, and twenty deputies. The 20 deputy judge advocates were distributed as follows:

20 Section 62 and 63, the Indian Articles of War, 1911.

- In the Bengal and Agra Presidencies there was a Deputy Judge Advocate to each of the following divisions of the army: Meerut, Saugor, Dinapoor and Benares, the Presidency, Sirhind, Caunpore, and the Meywar Field Force (Total 7).
- In the Madras Presidency, there was a Deputy Judge Advocate to each of the following divisions of the army: Nagpore Subsidiary Force, Jaulna, Secunderabad, Northern Mysore, Malabar and Canara, Ceded Districts, Centre Presidency and St. Thomas Mount, Southern and the Tenasserim Provinces (Total 9).
- In the Bombay Presidency, there was a Deputy Judge Advocate to each of the following divisions of the army: Southern, Northern, Poona, and the Scinde Field Force (Total 4).

The Judge Advocate General of the Bengal Army being also Judge Advocate to Her Majesty's Forces in India, held the brevet rank of lieutenant colonel, and the Judge Advocates General of the Madras and Bombay Armies held the brevet rank of major, should they not have attained that rank regimentally. All Deputies Judge Advocate General were to vacate their appointments, and leave the Department on attaining the rank of major regimentally. [21]

All proceedings of Courts Martial which require confirmation of the Commander in Chief were to be forwarded to the Judge Advocate General for that purpose. The Judge Advocate General was to decide on all questions of military law and instruct the Deputies therein; but whenever it was necessary to introduce any change that could affect either the practice, custom or discipline of the Army, it was previously be published in General Orders or communicated to the Army by the Adjutant General in such way as the Commander in Chief may direct. The proceedings of all Minor Courts martial were supervised by the Deputies Judge Advocate General and reports thereof made to the Judge Advocate General as prescribed by the General Orders of the Army.[22]

The Indian Army Act of 1911 provided that every general court-martial shall, and every district court-martial may, be attended by a judge advocate, who shall be either an officer belonging to the department of the Judge Advocate General in India, or, if no such officer is available, an officer appointed by the convening officer.

21 The pay of Judge Advocates General in India was different for the three Presidencies. The staff salary of the Judge Advocate General of the Bengal Army was Rs 1,450; of the Madras Army was Rs 1,000 and that of the Bombay Army was Rs 600 per month. In addition they were authorized a monthly horse allowance of Rs 60. The staff salary of all Deputies Judge Advocate General was Rs 350 every month. The above staff salaries were exclusive of contingent allowances for stationery. All the Deputies Judge Advocate General drew a monthly allowance of Rs 50 for writers, stationery, and other contingent expenses, and when on field service draw Rs 7.5 for office tent allowance. A judge advocate attending a court martial was allowed additional allowances. A General Order (GO) of 5 February 1794 stated, "....that lieutenant Robert Lewis be allowed four Rupees a day for the days the courts martial sat to which he officiated as judge advocate from the 1st of January to 1st June 1793, and likewise to have batta for the days he was travelling to attend those courts martial. In respect to his application for an establishment he is to receive 100 Rupees per month from the 1st of June for a clerk, peon, stationary, office rent and in lieu of every contingency. Aitchison Captain John William, 1824, *A General Code of the Military Regulations in force under the Presidency of Bombay*, Calcutta: Mission School Press, p. 74.

22 Regulations and Orders for General Officers, General Regulations of the Madras Army, Adjutant General's Office, Fort St George, Madras: Military Male Orphan Asylum Press, 1849, p. 5.

Provost Marshal

There was no permanent police in the army and only during war would a provost marshal, an officer of field rank, be charged to "secure deserters, and all other criminals." The provost marshal or his deputies/ subordinates, were to "go round the army, hinder the soldiers from pillaging, indict offenders, execute the sentence pronounced, and regulate the weights and measures used by the army in the field."[23] Bruce Alexander has (1717) described the duties and functions of Provost Martial as follows:[24]

> As to a Provost Martial, his power and trust is so great, "That all officers and soldiers are prohibited to hinder to him, his Lieutenant or Servants, in the Execution of their Office, upon pain of death, or such other punishments as a Court Martial shall think fit. And all Captains, Officers and soldiers, are ordered to do their utmost to apprehend, and bring to Punishment all offenders, and to assist the other Offices and Forces therein, especially the said Provost Martial, his Lieutenants and Servants. And if the Provost Martial, or his Officers require the assistance of any officer or soldier, in apprehending any person, declaring to them that it is for a capital crime, and the party escape for want and of Aid and Assistance, the Party or Parties refusing to aid or assist, is to suffer such Punishment as a Court Martial shall inflict. Lastly, the Provost martial of every regiment is to have the same Privileged in his own Regiment, as the Provost Martial General hath in the Army or Camp; and such fees also as the Court Martial shall allow.
>
> But, for preventing all abuses of this power, it is further ordered, First, That No Provost martial shall refuse to receive or keep prisoner committed to his charge by Authority, or shall dismiss him without Order, upon Pain of an arbitrary punishment. And if the offence for which the prisoner was apprehended, deserved Death, the Provost martial refusing to receive and keep him as aforesaid, is declared liable to the same punishment. Secondly, If any Person be committed by Provost Martial's own authority, without other Command, he is ordained to acquaint the General or other Chief Commander with the Cause, within twenty four hours, and the Provost is thereupon ordained to dismiss him, unless he have order to the contrary. Thirdly, It is left to general Court Martial to appoint and limit his fees, as they shall think fit.

The Indian Articles of War made under the Act No. V of 1869, provided, "For the prompt and instant repression of irregularities and offences committed in the field or on the line of march, Provost Marshals shall be appointed by the Commander-in-Chief of the Presidency, or the Officer Commanding the Forces in the field; and the powers and duties of such Provost Marshals shall be regulated according to the established custom of war and the rules of the service. The duties of a Provost Marshal so appointed were to take charge of prisoners confined for offences of a general description, to preserve good order and discipline, and to prevent breaches of the same

23 Grodzinski John R., Bloody Provost: Discipline During the War of 1812, *Canadian Military History*, Vol. 16: Issue 4, Article 3, 2007, p. 27.

24 Bruce Alexander, 1717, *The Institution of Military Law: Ancient and Modern*, Edinburgh, [Gale Ecco, Print Editions, 27 May 2010], pp. 336, at p. 305-306.

by persons belonging or attached to the Army.[25] The Provost Marshal could punish, corporally, then and there, any person amenable to these Articles below the rank of Warrant Officer, who, in his view or in the view of any of his assistants, committed any breach of good order and military discipline. If the actual commission of the offence was not witnessed by the Provost Marshal, or any of his assistants, but sufficient proof could be obtained of the offender's guilt, he was to report the case to the Commander of the Troops, who could deal with the case as he may deem most conducive to the maintenance of good order and military discipline.[26]

Under section 23 of the Indian Army Act of 1911, Provost Martial could be appointed for the prompt and instant repression of irregularities and offences committed in the field or on the march, by the Commander-in-Chief in India or an officer commanding an army, army corps, division or independent brigade or an officer commanding the forces in the field. The powers and duties of such provost-marshals were to be regulated according to the established custom of war and the rules of the service.[27]

Manipulation of System of Court Martial

The system of court martial always remained under manipulation and exploitation by the British in particular where the natives were involved. The descendants of Europeans professing the Christian religion were entitled to claim trial as Europeans, by a European Court Martial. The Court Martial constituted by the British officers had the freedom to award desired punishment to a European or Native accused. In case victim was a native, apparently lenient punishments were awarded by such courts. For instance, Private Thomas Walley of HM 60th Foot was tried by General Court Martial at Wuzeerabad on 24 May 1849 on the charge of murdering Sepoy Sewraj Sing Sepoy, by rifle shot. The Court found the accused 'Not Guilty'. The Commander in Chief made the following remarks while confirming the proceedings on 12 June 1849: "I cannot say approved, for I never read such inefficient proceedings in my life. Court, officiating Judge Advocate, and evidence, all inefficient! The prisoner must return to his duty." In another case, Gunner Hugh McInnis of the 3rd Company 1st Battalion Artillery was tried by General Court Martial at Peshawur on 24 January 1850. The charge against him was, "Having feloniously and unlawfully killed Salaroo, camp follower, by throwing a tent peg at his head." The Court found him guilty but awarded him a mild sentence of imprisonment for one year. Interestingly, this case

25 Article 100 of the Articles of War [Act No. XIX of 1847] provided, "The duties of Provost Marshals being limited to the punishment of offenders whom they may detect in the actual commission of any crime, the General Commanding the Forces in the Field will cause them to exercise the powers entrusted to them in such manner and under such circumstances as he may consider best calculated to prevent and instantly to repress crimes injurious to the discipline of the East India Company's Army and the Public Service."

26 Articles 168 and 169 of the Indian Articles of War (Act No. V of 1869).

27 The duties of the provost martial, specified under section 24 of the Act of 1911 and further amended by s. 3 of the Indian Army (Amendment) Act, 1920, were as follows: (1) To take charge of prisoners confined for offences of a general description, to preserve good order and discipline, and to prevent breaches of the same by persons belonging or attached to the army. He could at any time arrest and detain for trial any person subject to the Act who committed an offence and may also carry into effect any punishments to be inflicted in pursuance of the sentence of a court-martial. (2) To award punishment to any 'follower' or 'menial servant' who were accused of any breach of good order and military discipline on active servic. These punishments were specified under section 22 of the Act.

was not sent by the Commander in Chief for revision, who while approving the proceedings on 2 February 1850 remarked, "I only confirm this sentence, because I think it too lenient."

In cases where Native Court Martial were constituted, a British military Officer was detailed to superintendent the proceedings. In sensitive cases, when it was expected that the India Officers constituting a Native Court Martial would be sympathetic to an accused, the British Officer gave an advance briefing to the court. Proceedings were recorded by the British officer or judge advocate in English. In a typical regimental court martial held by native officers, the members of court martial remained in a state of mesmerism during the whole of the proceedings. When finally called upon for their opinion, invariably answer the superintending officer with "Jo apkee khooshee (what your honour pleases)" and could seldom be induced to give any other reply.[28] The Commander-in-Chief had the final say in the outcome of a court martial as the findings and proceedings were not final unless confirmed by him. He had the prerogative to send the proceedings back to the same court for revision with his comments. However, there were a few instances where the Court remained adhered to its verdict in revision.

Private John Walsh of the H.M. 80th Foot was tried by General Court Martial at Dinapore on 24 October 1850. There were four charges against him.[29] The Court found the accused guilty of all the charges, with exception to the words in the first charge "while in the act of raising it to take aim at Color Sergeant John Bish, 80th Regiment, with intent to injure that non-commissioned Officer." Since the accused had no former convictions and general good character; he was sentenced to imprisonment for six months, with solitary confinement for the first fourteen days of the 1st, 2nd, 3rd and 4th months; and stoppages for the musket and other articles damaged, lost, or made away with. The proceedings were returned to the Court for revision with the following remarks of the Commander in Chief:

> The prisoner loaded his musket, and must have had some object in committing this dangerous and grave breach of discipline? He then came out of his barrack room, and instantly fixed his eyes upon Sergeant Bish, whom he singled out among the three non-commissioned Officers that were there.—He was in a state of agitation, showing thereby that he meditated some mischief. With his eyes still fixed on Sergeant Bish he raised his firelock and discharged it, as he raised it, in the direction of Sergeant Bish.—His finger must therefore have been on the trigger; he then dashed his musket on the ground in a rage, and fled! All this is sworn to by those present, who all give it as their opinion that he intended to fire at the Sergeant!

28 Hodgson, Col. John Studholme, 1857, *Opinions on the Indian Army: originally published at Meerut in 1850, under the title of Musings on Military Matters*, London, p. 136.

29 The Charges were: 1st: For highly un-soldier-like conduct in having, in barracks, at Dinapore, on or about 23 September 1850, discharged a musket loaded with powder and ball, while in the act of raising it to take aim at Color Sergeant John Bish, 80th Regiment, with intent to injure that non-commissioned Officer; 2nd: For having, then and there, destroyed one round of balled ammunition issued to him for the public service; 3rd: For having, then and there, by wilful violence rendered unserviceable a musket issued to him for the public service; and 4th: For having, at or about the time and place specified in the preceding charges, lost through neglect, or designedly made away with, the following articles of Regimental necessaries, viz.; one pair of white trowsers, one pair of blue trowsers, one white shirt, one flannel shirt, one pair of braces, and two pairs of boots.

> The questions which naturally arise are: Why did the prisoner load his musket? Why did he cock it? Why did he turn towards Sergeant Bish when he came out of his barrack room? Why did he fix his eyes upon Sergeant Bish, who was lying down? Why did he raise his musket towards Sergeant Bish, with his eyes still fixed upon the Sergeant? Why did he fire his musket? Why did all present think he intended to shoot Sergeant Bish? The prisoner makes no defence whatever. He meets all accusations by silence! Yet the Court acquit him of "an intent to injure that non-commissioned Officer." For my part, I am obliged by the evidence which is here recorded to consider that Private Walsh made a deliberate attempt to murder Sergeant Bish, and that he only failed because his agitation made him press the trigger too strongly as he raised his weapon to accomplish his murderous purpose. Such is the view I take of the evidence, and I therefore beg of the Court to reconsider its finding and sentence.

In revision, the Court remained adhered to their former finding and sentence. The Commander in Chief disapproved but confirmed the proceedings on 3 December 1850 and remarked: "The finding and sentence appear to me to be so in the face of evidence that I am unable to understand them, or on what ground the Court based them."

On 7 January 1850, Shaick Fucqueera Bux, Dulmust Khan, and Hemnarain Sing, Sepoys, of the 32nd N.I. were tried by a Native Court Martial at Wuzeerabad on the charge of exciting a mutiny in their Regiment and quitting their guard without leave. The Court found Dulmust Khan and Hemnarain Sing guilty and sentenced them to imprisonment with hard labour for 14 years. The Commander in Chief returned the proceedings for revision with following strong remarks:

> "I call on this Court Martial to do its duty to the State. It has found the prisoners guilty of having "begun and excited a mutiny in their Regiment;" of an infamous attempt to dictate to the Government what amount of pay it should give to the Soldiers of the 32nd Regiment of Native Infantry!
>
> These prisoners had voluntarily enlisted in the service of the East India Company for a certain fixed rate of pay; they swore to serve that Company for that rate of pay. When food becomes dear the Government generously pays the extra expense when above a certain reasonable price, so that the Sepoy may not suffer when his duty takes him into provinces of the empire where circumstances make food increase in price. The Sepoy is found in clothing, in lodging, in pay beyond what he could earn were he not a Sepoy. He is also honorably treated in every way. Should a Sepoy commit any serious crime, his punishment is, ordinarily, simply dismissal from this noble army; and the dread of such a misfortune reigns in the bosom of every Sepoy! What higher compliment can be paid by Soldiers to their Government? What greater proof can be offered of that Government's justice and generosity? None! The nobleness of the Sepoy army, and the advantages which it enjoys are known to the whole world: pensions for long service ; pensions for wounds received in battle; pensions to the bereaved families of those whose gallant fathers have fallen in action; increased pay for service to those who are yet robust and fit to do duty; Orders of Merit and medals for valour in fight; hospitals for the sick; and, finally, these excellent Soldiers are led by European Officers, all proud of, and glorying in their men! These are all

> great advantages. They crowd on the mind of the Sepoy who reflects upon the conduct of the generous Government which he serves: his reason and his heart make him true to those glorious standards under which he and his father have ever fought and conquered? I ask the Officers composing this Court Martial, whether they, as honorable Soldiers, think that 14 years' imprisonment, with hard labour, is an adequate punishment for the ruffians whom this Court has, itself, convicted of trying to subvert that order, that discipline, that justice, that generosity, (which the Court well knows I have described without exaggeration) and thus turn the whole into dire confusion and despair, depriving veterans of their pensions, widows and orphans of their support, and the good Sepoys of the 32nd Native Infantry of their pay, by forcing the Government to strike this brave Regiment from the service of the East India Company for ever? For this must have happened if the machinations of these culprits had succeeded? The prisoners, like infamous agitators as they are, have been convicted by the Court of having gone from company to company exciting their comrades to mutiny and administering unlawful oaths; and I revise the sentence passed upon them, as inadequate to the magnitude of their crime. I beg of the Court to re-consider its sense of the consequences which may result from the crime of these heinous offenders. Let it sentence a punishment commensurate with their damnable projects."

The revised sentence of "death by hanging" awarded by the Court was approved and confirmed by the Commander in Chief on 16 January 1850.

There were many instances where the Court Martial made recommendation of mercy while awarding sentences. The Commander in Chief, in a number of cases gave considerations to such recommendations, while in a few he completely rejected them. Jemadar Diaram Opediah of 2nd N. I., (Grenadiers) was tried by General Court Martial at Umballah, 28 May 1849 on the charge of 'Giving false evidence before a Regimental Court Martial' and was found 'Guilty'. He was sentenced to dismissal from the service, and forfeiture of arrears. The Court made following recommendations, "on account of the Jemadar's long service and high standing, and also on account of the many months he has been in confinement, to recommend him to the favorable consideration of the Commander in Chief." The Commander-in-Chief while confirming the proceedings on 13 June 1849 commented: "When an honourable soldier commits a military crime, not of a disgraceful nature, I always feel disposed to favour him; and, in such a case, a Court Martial is sometimes justified in recommending such a man to mercy, and the Court's recommendation is then of great weight. But when an Officer perjures himself as a witness before a Court Martial, (as the Jemadar has been proved to have done) the Court which convicted him of this heinous offence, has no right whatever to recommend him to mercy; to do so is to insult the army, and I reject their recommendation with the condemnation which it deserves."

Punishments

Since military units were sometimes isolated from other units and the civilian population, it was necessary that court-martial authority be decentralized, with lower echelon commanders possessing the power to convene a court-martial and staff it with their own officers so that a determination could be made quickly and the unit could get back to its main task. The court-martial had to follow relatively simple proceedings, with few legal formalities, sometimes conducted in the field with a drum as a desk, hence the term "drum-head justice". There was little pretence at providing an impartial and adversary "judicial" hearing. The purpose was to determine the facts and administer a punishment which would provide deterrence to other men and, if possible, return the individual to his role as a functioning soldier as quickly as possible. Thus, it was not uncommon for crimes which would draw a prison sentence today, such as assault with a deadly weapon, to be punished only by corporal punishment, while crimes which threatened disciplinary order often resulted in harsh sentences, including death. No one blushed in admitting that the court-martial was not a real trial; that the commander used it to enforce his disciplinary policies and inculcate military values in his men; that it was administered by officers alone; that there was no right to review; and that the penalties were calculated to set an example and not to provide equal justice.[30]

The frequency of 'crime' within Indian native troops was much lower when compared to Europeans. Figures from military authorities of the time, and the observations from British officers in India, reveal that compared with the European rank and file, Native Sepoys were rarely implicated in criminal activities. Of 484,160 sepoys in the Bengal service between 1825 and 1833, district and general courts martial tried only eleven deserters, one guilty of absence without leave, and one embezzler. Sepoys in the Bombay Army were similarly docile in comparison to the European rank and file. Sir Jasper Nicolls' testimony to a parliamentary inquiry revealed that during his three years tenure at Meerut, only three sepoys were tried for drunkenness, yet of the Europeans, liquor was a factor in eight out of every ten courts martial.[31] In spite of better discipline amongst the native troops, the punishment awarded to them by court martial were much more severe when compared to those awarded to European officers and soldiers.

There was as little consistency in the awarding of punishments by court martial as there was in the framing of the charges. Similar crimes were often punished with remarkably dissimilar punishments; in some cases disobedience was punished with fifty lashes, in others it resulted in three hundred lashes. One soldier convicted of slapping his officer was condemned to death; a month later, in a different station, a soldier found guilty of stabbing his officer with the intention of killing him was given only six months' imprisonment. Perhaps the most glaring example of this was uncovered in Bombay in 1827. A Court of Inquiry had been held to discover why one sepoy regiment was on the verge of mutiny. It found that the main grievance of sepoy was that their regimental commander had blatantly failed to conduct himself according to the Articles of War. This officer had awarded punishments that were not sanctioned by the Articles of War, such as ordering on two occasions that the lash be applied 'to the bare posterior'. He had also punished several sepoys with dishonourable discharge for crimes where discharge was not among the punishments permitted by the Articles of War.

Military punishments could be divided into capital, corporal, degradatory, cashiering, imprisonment, suspension, pecuniary, and reprimand: of these some affected commissioned

30 Sherman Edward F., The Civilianization of Military Law, *Maine Law Review*, Vol. 22, 1970, p. 3-103.

31 Peers Douglas M., Sepoys, Soldiers and the Lash: Race, Caste and Army Discipline in India, 1820–50, *The Journal of Imperial and Commonwealth History*, 1995, Vol. 23:2, p. 211-247.

officers alone; some commissioned and non-commissioned officers and soldiers; and others the non-commissioned officers and soldiers only.

Execution of Sentence

The sentence of a court-martial having been confirmed, the next step was to carry it into execution. The execution of sentence was marked by solemnities and ceremonies.[32] Various methods of execution followed by the East India Company and the British commander in India are discussed herewith.

I. Capital Punishment

In most militaries in the world, obedience was attainable only through traditional concepts of punishment based on fear and deterrence. The harsh nature of military discipline in Britain owed much to tradition.[33] Military punishments were divided into capital, corporal, pecuniary, derogatory, cashiering, imprisonment, suspension and reprimand: of these some affect commissioned officers alone; some commissioned and non-commissioned officers and soldiers; and others the non-commissioned officers and soldiers only. The most serious sentence available to a court martial was death by hanging or shooting. However, on a number of occasions, the military accused as well as civilians were blown from a gun, a practice followed by Mughal rulers in India.

Hanging

When capital punishment was to be inflicted, great ceremony was observed. Whenever sentences of court martial on European or Native Non-commissioned officers or soldiers were executed, the Corps to which they belonged was under arms and attended by all officers.[34] When death by hanging was to be inflicted, the troops were formed in square on the gallows as a centre. The prisoner, with the escort, having arrived at their respective places, the charge, sentence, and warrant are read aloud, and the executioner, under the direction of the provost marshal, performs his office. The troops marched off the ground at common time; the provost marshal with the

32 For more details see: De Hart William C., 1859, Observations on Military Law and Constitution and Practice of Courts Martial, New York: Wiley and Halsted, pp. 244-249.

33 Grose Francis (1788) has described various military punishments prevailing in the English Army during that period. In many instances, where a corps or a considerable body of men were guilty of a crime for which the established punishment was death, to prevent too great a weakening of the army, the delinquents were decimated, that is, only every tenth man was taken; the common mode of decimation was this: a number of billets equal to that of the body to be decimated, were put into a helmet, every tenth billet being marked with the letter D or some other character signifying death. The helmet was then shaken, in order to mix them, and the soldiers filing off singly from the right, passed by the commanding officer, before whom, on a table, stood the helmet: as they passed each drew a billet and presented it to an officer placed to receive them. If the billet had the fatal mark, the soldier was seized and marched into the rear, if it proved a saving one, he continued his march, and fell in with the other men that had passed before him. Grose Francis, 1788, *Military Antiquities Respecting A History of English Army: From The Conquest to the Present Time*, Vol. II, London: S. Hooper, pp. 195-204.

34 G.O. 15 May 1787; Jephson George, 1839, The Orders and Regulations of the Bengal Army, Part I, Calcutta: WM Thacker and Company, p. 467.

escort, remaining until the body was taken down.[35] The execution of Private Flanagan offers an insight into the faulty process of military legal system.

> Private Flanagan was a fine soldier, about six feet one inch in height. He had excellent natural talents, and had received a tolerably good education. He had acquired knowledge of Latin, and could speak the French language. When the regiment went to India, he was in a short time able to communicate with the natives in several of the languages of the country. Although Flanagan was a smart clever soldier, he used to commit slight breaches of military discipline, and his name was consequently sometimes entered in the Regiment's Defaulter Books.
>
> Being a man of high spirit and violent temper, Flanagan could ill bear the reproaches of the Adjutant, who repeatedly censured him for his irregularities. On one occasion he became so irritated with the rebuke he was receiving, that he impatiently pushed the Adjutant from him with the back of his arm. Flanagan was forthwith tried by a court-martial for offering violence to the Adjutant, and sentenced to suffer death. When the sentence was communicated to him, he simply observed that he thought the award of the court was severe.
>
> On the day of the execution Flanagan preserved the most remarkable firmness, and conducted himself with the strictest decorum. The square having been formed, he, by permission, addressed the company to which he belonged. Having reached the fatal spot, the Fort-Adjutant commenced to read the proceedings of the court-martial; but having lost self-possession, his tongue faltered, which being observed by Flanagan, he addressed him by saying, "I see, sir, that you are agitated; pray allow me to read the proceedings for you." No notice was, of course, taken of this offer. He then begged that he should not be blindfolded, and that he might be permitted to give the word of command to the execution party; both of which requests were granted. He finally gave the word of command, with as firm a voice as a Sergeant-Major is accustomed to do on a drill parade.
>
> Flanagan's untimely fate took place in June, 1828, at Trichinopoly — he having, in all probability, fallen a victim to the unwise, injudicious, and harassing treatment of a superior officer.[36]

Shooting

When a criminal was to be put to death by shooting, the troops to witness the execution were formed on three sides of a square. The prisoner, escorted by a detachment, was brought on the ground. The provost marshal led the procession, followed by the band or field music of the regiment to which the convict belongs, drums muffled, playing the dead march. The party detailed

35 Hanging was also performed on a kind of portable gallows, which was set up for the occasion, and a spike driven into it, so that the sufferer hangs with his feet very near the ground; a small stool being set he stood on it till the cord was fixed by a noose over the spike, and the stool being pulled away he was turned off. Grose Francis, 1788, *Military Antiquities Respecting A History of English Army: From The Conquest to the Present Time*, Vol. II, London: S. Hooper, pp. 195-204.

36 Marshall Henry, 1846, *The Military Miscellany; Comprehending a History of the Recruiting of the Army, Military Punishments*, London, p. 118.

to fire, consisting usually of eight to twelve men, came next; then four bearers with the coffin, and immediately after the prisoner attended by a chaplain; the escort closed the rear. The procession passed in front and along the three sides of the square facing inwards. On arriving at the flank of each regiment the band of that regiment played the dead march, and continued until its front was cleared. When the procession had reached the open space, the music ceased; the prisoner was placed on the fatal spot where the coffin has been put down, and the charge, sentence, and order for the execution read aloud. The chaplain engaged in prayer with the condemned, retired. The execution party formed at about six paces from the prisoner, and the word was given by the provost marshal. When the firing party formed, the escort moved by the right flank and took position in rear of that party, at ordered arms. Should the fire not prove instantaneously fatal, it was the duty of the provost marshal, or a file which has been reserved for such duty, to complete the sentence. The execution being over, the troops break into column by the right and moved past the corpse in slow time.[37]

A soldier belonging to one of the regiments serving in India, fired at a Sergeant on the parade ground of the corps, and killed him. The delinquent was tried and sentenced to suffer death. Unusual care was taken to render his execution as solemn and impressive as possible. At the execution, he was completely dressed in white, with a rosette of black ribbon on his breast, for the purpose of serving as a target for the men to fire at. Nothing was omitted which seemed calculated to intimidate others, and to deter them from following the example of the criminal. A few weeks after this man was executed, a private of the same Corps shot the Adjutant through the head on parade, of which wound he died in a moment. The soldier was seized, tried by court martial and sentence to suffer death. Before his execution, it was suggested to the Commanding Officer, that as the pompous ceremonial which attended the former execution should be avoided and another mode of carrying the sentence into effect might be tried. The Commanding Officer benefited by the suggestion he had received, and the criminal was privately hanged at a little distance from the cantonments of the corps, and afterwards hung in chains. No similar delinquency followed the execution.[38]

In Bengal Presidency, British authorities were embarrassed on one occasion when Native sepoy sentenced to be executed by firing squad was not hit by a single musket ball from what was obviously a very sympathetic firing party, and one that stood only eight paces from the condemned man. The Provost Marshal had to intervene and carry through the sentence with a shot to the man's skull.

Blowing from Gun

Blowing from a gun was a method of execution in which the victim was tied to the mouth of cannon which was then fired.[39] Blowing from a gun was a reported means of execution followed

37 De Hart William C., 1859, Observations on Military Law and Constitution and Practice of Courts Martial, New York: Wiley and Halsted, pp. 244-249.

38 Marshall Henry, 1846, *The Military Miscellany; Comprehending a History of the Recruiting of the Army, Military Punishments*, London, p. 249.

39 The prisoner was generally tied to a gun with the upper part of the small of his back resting against the muzzle. When the gun is fired, his head is seen to go straight up into the air some forty or fifty feet; the arms fly off right

during the Mughal Empire in India and was used by the British until the 20th century. There have been numerous incidents where Native soldiers were executed in this manner. In March 1764, a Native officer (subedar), who was accused of enticing the troops, was court-martialed and blown from a gun in front of the troops. In September the same year, Major Hector Munro had executed 24 "ring leaders" who were accused of desertion and mutiny. In 1782, three mutineers were sentenced to death by the court in Barrackpore, two of them were blown from a gun, the last to be hanged.

In 1819, six deserters who had joined the ousted rajah of the annexed Kingdom of Nagpur were apprehended by the British and were blown from the guns on 7 February. In 1832, six native soldiers were convicted at Bangalore of having been engaged in a conspiracy, which had for its object the subversion of the British supremacy in Mysore. Four of them were sentenced to be blown from guns, and two to be shot with musketry, the former mode of execution being deemed the nobler, or rather the less ignominious of the two. In this instance, the men who were to be blown from guns were tied to stakes driven into the ground, when the guns, six or nine pounders, loaded with blank cartridge, were run close up to them. After the explosion, the guns were found bespattered with blood and brains, while the legs, and a portion of the trunk of some of the criminals, were still attached to the stakes to which they had been bound, the other parts of the bodies having been scattered far and wide over the dusty plain.[40]

Following the Mutiny of 1857, blowing-from-a-gun was a method the British used for executing rebels as well as for those natives found guilty of desertion. On 10 June 1857, 40 Native soldiers from the 54th Regiment, were blown from guns at Ludhiana. Things did not always worked out according to plan at such executions. At a mass execution at Firozpur in 1857, there was an order that blank cartridge should be used, but some guns were loaded with grapeshot instead. Several of the spectators facing the cannons were hit by the grapeshot and some had to have limbs amputated as a result. In addition, some of the soldiers had not been withdrawn properly and sustained injuries from being hit by whizzing pieces of flesh and bone. The Rebellion of 1857 was not the last time that British military used blowing from a cannon as an execution method. In 1871, for example, 65 members of the Sikh sect Kukas (Namdhari) were executed by the British military, by being blown from guns.[41]

During the First World War, the number of executions in the British army exceeded 400.[42] However, this figure does not include Indian troops for whom no official record is maintained in the War Office. During the period of World War I when corporal punishment had been abolished, the senior commanders resorted to capital punishment as the sole means of maintaining discipline

and left, high up in the air, and fall at, perhaps, a hundred yards distance; the legs drop to the ground beneath the muzzle of the gun; and the body is literally blown away altogether, not a vestige being seen.

40 Marshall Henry, 1846, *The Military Miscellany; Comprehending a History of the Recruiting of the Army, Military Punishments*, London, pp. 249-250.

41 For more details see: Bhai Nahar Singh and Bhai Kirpal Singh, 1995, *Rebels Against the British Rule*, New Delhi: Atlantic Publishers, p. 902.

42 This figure is based on the War Office publication Statistics of the Military Effort of the British Empire in the Great War 1914-1920 (HMSO, London, 1922), p. 648.

rather than exploring alternatives.[43] When the British Army went into action in the summer of 1914, a number of offences were punishable with death. This included mutiny, cowardice before the enemy, self-inflicted wounds, disobedience of a lawful order, desertion or attempted desertion, sleeping or being drunk on post, striking a superior officer, casting away arms or ammunition in the presence of the enemy, leaving a post without orders, abandoning a position, and treacherously communicated with or in any way assisting the enemy. A survey of the registers of courts-martial kept by the British army has cast doubt on the accuracy of the official number of condemnations which, it appears, have been slightly under-estimated.[44] To punish one man for the purpose of deterring some other unknown person from the commission of crime, can hardly be defended upon the principles of justice, even if it was demonstrated that exemplary punishments are beneficial.[45] In the Army Act, 1950, hanging as well as shooting are both listed as official methods of execution. [46]

II. Flogging

In the earlier days in Britain, soldiers could be flogged an unlimited number of times for almost any misdemeanour.[47] The disciplinary codes of the British Army and the Royal Navy were harsh because bloody campaigns placed great strain on officers' authority. If unquestioning obedience from ordinary soldiers was not forthcoming, swift and brutal summary justice was administered. During wartime, soldiers were subject to capital punishment. In 1792,Serjeant George Samuel Grant was sentenced a "thousand lashes," in addition to his loss of rank and pay as a serjeant, "for the crime of having been instrumental in the enlisting for the service of the East India Company, two drummers, knowing them at the same time to belong to the foot guards.[48] In 1828, two NCOs from Kilkenny Barracks were sentenced to 1,000 lashes for writing deceitful letters. During campaign in India, British military commanders flogged and hanged men to restore discipline. This was exemplary justice, intended to subdue and terrorize the men in equal measure.

The flogging was designed to humiliate and degrade an offender and therefore considered most effective punishment. Many of its defenders were of the firm opinion that the punishment was

43 Oram, Gerard Christopher, 2000, What alternative punishment is there?: Military Executions During World War I, Ph D thesis, The Open University.

44 Oram, Gerard, The administration of discipline by the English is very rigid: British Military Law and the Death Penalty (1868-1918), *Crime, History & Societies*, Vol. 5, No. 1, 2001, pp. 93-110.

45 Marshall Henry, 1846, *The Military Miscellany; Comprehending a History of the Recruiting of the Army, Military Punishments*, London, p. 128.

46 Section 166 of the Act provides, "In awarding a sentence of death a court- martial shall, in its discretion, direct that the offender shall suffer death by being hanged by the neck until he be dead, or shall suffer death by being shot to death." A person sentenced by court martial to death remains subject to Army Act until the sentence is carried out. In India, since Independence no military accused has been executed. Death punishments awarded by court martial were commuted to life imprisonment by the Government or higher courts.

47 Burroughs Peter, Crime and Punishment in the British Army, 1815-1870, *The English Historical Review*, Vol. 100, No. 396, July 1985, pp. 560-1.

48 For more details see: Napier Charles J., 1837, *Remarks on Military Law and the Punishment of Flogging*, London: T. and W. Boone, p. 276.

intended to deter observers rather than reform offenders. As the British government explained in 1834, 'The object of the punishment was, to strike terror into others by the example.' James Charles Napier, General of the British Empire, in his *Remarks of Military Law*, wrote that sentences of thousands lashes were common at the end of the eighteenth century. These were divided into installments: when the skin had started to heal it was time to whip again. Flogging in the military, navy, schools and private homes was a common disciplinary measure in the nineteenth century. In order to discipline the mind it was considered necessary to discipline the body. Then, the skin was intended as a body's shield.

Flogging Ritual: In awarding the sentence of flogging, a court-martial commonly stated, that the infliction shall be "on the bare back, with a cat-o'-nine-tails, in the usual manner;" but the last four words were formerly sometimes omitted, as is alleged, for the purpose of conveying to the officer ordering the execution of the sentence, a power to inflict the punishment on the back or breech, at his discretion. The mode of inflicting corporal punishment was usually as follows: The brigade, garrison, regiment, or detachment, being arms, is formed into a square in some retired spot, often in the ditch of an outwork of fortified places or posts, to receive the prisoner, who is brought by an escort to the centre of the brigade. The Commanding Officer, the Adjutant, the medical officer, the band, and the Drum-Major, with the drummers, next take their respective stations within the square. The Town-Major, or Adjutant, as the case may be, proceeded to read aloud the charges, sometimes the proceedings;—but invariably the sentence of the court, and the approval of the competent officer, the prisoner being uncovered, and advanced a pace or two in front of the escort. The delinquent was then directed by the Commanding Officer to strip, which he does to the waist: he was forthwith tied to a machine termed a triangle, which consists of three legs or poles, connected by a belt at top, and separate about four feet at bottom; to two of the legs a bar is fixed, at a convenient height, that the prisoner's chest may rest against it. The hands being pulled up to the top of the triangle, were there secured with cords by the drummers, who also tied him to the triangle round the upper part of the thighs and the ankles. Halberts were sometimes rigged out, to serve the purpose of triangles, leading to the common saying, "bringing a man to the halberts," which is synonymous with bringing him to corporal punishment. At other times the prisoner was lashed to a gun-wheel, or to a tree. A cartouche belt, which was held by a drummer, was usually thrown over the man's head, and rests on the back of his neck, by which means his head was kept steady.[49]

49 Marshall Henry, 1846, *The Military Miscellany; Comprehending a History of the Recruiting of the Army, Military Punishments*, London, pp. 251-252.

The description of Cat to be used in all Corps, whether European or Native, was as follows:[50]

Length of the Wooden Handle	Length of the Cords	Number of Cords	Number of Knots upon each Cord	Quality of the Materials of which the Cords are made.
18 inches	24 inches	9	3	Thin Europe Whip Cord

The Drum-Major was presumed to see that the ends of the cords of the cats are not entangled during the infliction, so as to produce a more serious blow than intended, but that they are disengaged from time to time; should the cords become heavy with coagulated blood, they are sometimes washed with water. As nine of every ten of the drummers are right-handed, and consequently stand on the left of a delinquent, the right shoulder suffers much more severely than the left. Left-handed drummers appear, as has already been observed, to inflict more pain than right-handed punishers, in consequence of the cat being applied to a sound and sensible part of the skin of the back. The Drum-Major stands behind the inflicting drummer with a cane in his hand, and his eyes fixed on the sufferer's back, ready to lay it hard and heavy on the shoulders or thighs of the punisher, should he think he is laying on lightly or unfair.[51] An ex-drum-boy, who rose to the rank of a commissioned officer, narrates his manual experience in the following terms:

> From the very first day I entered the service as drum-boy, and for eight years after, I can venture to assert, that, at the lowest calculation, it was my disgusting duty to flog men at least three times a week. From this painful task there was no possibility of shrinking, without the certainty of a rattan over my own shoulders by a Drum-Major, or of my being sent to the black-hole. When the infliction is ordered to commence, each drum-boy, in rotation, is ordered to strip, for the purpose of administering twenty-five lashes (slowly counted by the Drum-Major) with freedom and vigour. After a poor fellow had received about 100 lashes, the blood would pour down his back in streams, and fly about in all directions with every additional blow of the cat, so that by the time he had received 300, I have found my clothes all over blood from the knees to the crown of the head. Horrified at my disgusting appearance, I have, immediately after parade, run into the barrack-room, to escape from the observations of the soldiers, and to rid my clothes and person of my comrade's blood.[52]

According to General Napier, when he was a subaltern, he frequently witnessed 600, 700, 800, 900, and 1000 lashes inflicted on military accused after they were sentenced by regimental courts-martial. He states, "I have heard of 1200 having been inflicted, but never witnessed such an execution. I then often saw the unhappy victim of such barbarous work brought out from the hospital three and four times to receive the remainder of his punishment, too severe to be borne

50 General Regulations of the Madras Army, Adjutant General's Office, Fort St George, Madras: Military Male Orphan Asylum Press, 1849, p. 129.

51 Marshall Henry, 1846, *The Military Miscellany; Comprehending a History of the Recruiting of the Army, Military Punishments*, London, pp. 256.

52 Ibid., p. 255.

without danger of death at one flogging; and sometimes I have witnessed this prolonged torture applied for the avowed purpose of adding to its severity. On these occasions it was terrible to see the new tender skin of the scarcely healed back again laid bare to receive the lash. I declare that, accustomed as I was to such scenes, I could not on these occasions bear to look at the first blows; the feeling of horror which ran through the ranks was evident,—and all soldiers know the frequent fainting that took place among recruits when they first see a soldier flogged."[53] General Sir Charles Napier has described the physical consequence of large punishments upon delinquents, and the moral effect upon the spectators:

> I have seen many hundreds of men flogged, and have always observed, that when the skin is thoroughly cut up or flayed off, the great pain subsides. Men are frequently convulsed and screaming during the time they receive one lash to 300 lashes, and then they bear the remainder, even to 800 or 1000 lashes, without a groan; they will often lie as if without life, and the drummers appear to be flogging a lump of dead raw flesh. Now, I have frequently observed, that in these cases, the faces of the spectators assumed a look of disgust; there was always a low whispering sound, scarcely audible, issuing from the apparently stern and silent ranks,—a sound arising from lips that spoke not; but that sound was produced by hearts that felt deeply, and this too, when the soldier believed in its justice, and approved of the punishment, when the willing drummers had, up to that moment, laid on the lash with great asperity. This low and scarcely audible sound spoke aloud to my mind, that the punishment had become excessive, that the culprit had disappeared and the martyr taken his place.[54]

A sense of shame was associated with public whippings since early modern times, when offenders were beaten through the streets. Public corporal punishment was intended to deter the observers and shame the offender in equal measure. However, the numbers of public whippings declined in the course of the eighteenth and nineteenth centuries, matched by a rise in the rate of private whippings, administered behind prison walls. Thus flogging was inextricably linked with criminality and deviance.

Robert Southey, in *Letters from England by Don Manuel Alvarez Espriella* (1814) has described the military punishments of Britain, "The martial laws of England are the most barbarous which at this day exist in Europe. The offender is sometimes sentenced to receive a thousand lashes—a surgeon stands by to feel his pulse during the execution, and determine how long the flogging can be continued without killing him. When human nature can stand no more he is remanded to prison (hospital),—his wound, for from the shoulders to the loins it leaves him one wound, is dressed, and as soon as it is sufficiently healed to be laid open in the same manner, he is brought out to undergo the remainder of his sentence. And this is repeatedly and openly practised in a country where they read in their churches and in their houses that Bible, in their own language, which saith, 'Forty stripes may the judge inflict upon the offender, and not exceed.'"[55] By this

53 Marshall Henry, 1846, *The Military Miscellany; Comprehending a History of the Recruiting of the Army, Military Punishments*, London, p. 263.

54 Ibid., p. 255.

55 Robert Southey, 1814, *Letters from England by Don Manuel Alvarez Espriella*, London: Longman, p. 109-110.

time popular opinion had in some measure become adverse to severe and degrading punishment of flogging in the British army. A soldier, who was punished in this manner, received the popular sympathy of a martyr, rather than the degradation of a culprit.

It is impossible to say how many men died from flogging, since the army's interests were not served by recording such a cause of death. A flogging was inflicted under medical supervision; if the regimental doctor believed the man would die, it was halted. However, men still died as a consequence of flogging and when newspapers reported these cases, they caused a public sensation. Even non-fatal floggings could arouse public anger, as happened when Private John Henderson received 300 lashes in Charing Cross Barracks, London. It was reported that 'The sufferings of this man were dreadful; and his shrieks so loud and piercing that drums were beat in order to drown out the sound. The heat of the weather added dreadfully to the severity of the flogging.' Public feeling was outraged and the government decided to appoint a royal commission to inquire into military discipline. The flogging of soldiers often became the subject of discussion in the press and attracted public attention, especially if a soldier died in the process. In most cases, soldiers were hospitalized as a result of flogging. In 1833, the number of crimes punishable by flogging was reduced and also the number of lashes was commuted to 300-500.

The members of the Royal Commission on Military Punishments (1835-6) were more in favour of the status quo than reform but, coincidentally, 2 men died after being flogged while the commission was sitting. Press coverage of their deaths made it impossible for the commission to ignore the deleterious effects of corporal punishment. Subsequently, the maximum number of lashes that could be awarded by a general court martial was limited to 200. However, most minor offences were tried by regimental court martial, where the punishment was restricted to 100 lashes. Even after these 'reforms', men died as a result of flogging. In 1846, a young British soldier Private Frederick John White died after a punishment of flogging. It provoked a national outcry. The details of incident are as follows:

> In June 1846, Private Frederick John White of the 7th Queen's Own Hussars, under the effects of alcohol had had an argument with his sergeant and, during the fight he had stroked the sergeant's chest with a metal bar. As a result, the Martial Court had sentenced White to 150 lashes. After Farrier-Major Critton struck the 150th lash on the back of Private White, at the end of the disciplinary session at Hounslow Barracks, West London, the soldier walked himself to the infirmary to have his wounds dressed. His skin healed promptly, but 4 weeks later, he was found dead in his dormitory. The army medical officers, after performing an autopsy, reached the conclusion that the soldier had died from inflammation of internal organs but excluded any connection with flogging. This version of facts did not convince the coroner for Middlesex.
>
> White's body was just about to be buried when the coroner for Middlesex decided to hold a judicial inquiry. The coroner was Thomas Wakley, a surgeon, medical journalist and anti-flogging campaigner. After 3 more weeks of inquiry and 2 more postmortem examinations, the famous dermatologist Erasmus Wilson contradicted the army officers by affirming that the soldier had indeed died from the effects of flogging as the analysis of the cutaneous lesions and underneath would demonstrate. The inquest into the Hounslow case sparked a

national outcry. The postmortem examination of the soldier's corpse, extensively reported by the Victorian press, provoked a burning political and medical debate on the effects of flogging on the health of a human being.

As one of the witnesses told the coroner during the inquiry, blood had appeared between White's shoulders after twenty lashes had been given. A regimental farrier kept on flogging until the fiftieth; he then handed over to his colleague so that he could have a rest. After fifty more had been given he took the whip again and inflicted the final fifty lashes. The farriers used the cat o' nine tails, a tool made up of nine knotted thongs of cotton that could be found in veterinary shops. The punishment lasted half an hour: one lash every twelve seconds. The colonel and the regiment's doctor stood with their arms folded. Neither of them checked the soldier's pulse. A reader of the *Times* wrote to the editor that had the regimental doctor put his fingers on White's wrist he would have found that at each lash his pulse faltered.

The coroner asked many questions to find out how many lashes a human being can endure. This was not because he thought that this number could be established but only to show the jury and the reporters that the number could not be quantified. It was unpredictable, and depended on variables such as the type of whips, the number of knots that the whips may form and, the external temperature. According to the press, 1846 recorded an unusually hot summer and this might have impaired the ability of White to recover. The experience of the floggers also matters. They often undertook a training to learn how to flog, using a tree trunk as a body. They were not supposed to break the skin and, as the *Lancet* reported, experienced hands knew that the lash should have fallen in the small area between the shoulders only. But as a Victorian pamphlet recited: "performers and skin materially differ, accidents sometimes happen".

Dermatologist Erasmus Wilson was called by Wakley to perform a third autopsy on the body of White. Wilson, by analysing the cutaneous layer and the organs underneath, argued, in times prior to the discovery of the effects of bacteria in the bloodstream, that there was a connection between the external lacerations caused by the lashes and the internal state of the organs. According to Wilson, the injuries resulting from flogging were confined to the skin but the flogging was followed by inflammation of the internal organs and pulpy softening of muscles. The jury's verdict, given on 4 August 1846, was that Frederick John White died from the mortal effects of the flogging that he had received at Cavalry Barracks in Hounslow.

On returning the verdict the jury called upon the public to send petitions to the British Legislature for the abolition of this form of military punishment. Less than a week after the end of the inquest, the Duke of Wellington established a limit of fifty lashes to be given for military corporal punishment. John White was not the only person who had died after a flogging but this was the occasion on which the explanation for a dynamic relationship between superficial marks and injuries left on the body and internal organs of the punished was used as a political argument against corporal punishment. The back of the soldier furnished the script for marking advancement in the history of the anti-flogging campaign in Britain.

Flogging was partially abolished in 1867 following the death of Private Robert Slim from such punishment,[56] but it remained available as a punishment during peacetime for crimes of mutiny or insubordination involving violence and during wartime it was extended to cover desertion and even drunkenness. The incidence of flogging declined gradually as part of army discipline; and finally in 1881, the Army Discipline and Regulation Act completely abolished it.

The average number of floggings per regiment per year in India between 1801 and 1808 was 7.59 in Bengal, 23.79 in Madras and 36.54 in Bombay.[57] By an Order dated 24 February 1835, The Governor General of India in Council directed that the practice of punishing soldiers of the native army by cat-o'-nine tails or rattan, be discontinued at all Presidencies, and soldiers be sentenced to dismissal from the service, for any offence for which such soldiers might now be punished by flogging, provided such sentence of dismissal shall not be carried into effect unless confirmed by the General or other Officers Commanding the Division.[58] However, the punishment of

56 In February 1867, an inquest jury of 12 Limerick men met in the hospital of the New Barracks, to investigate the death of Private Robert Sim 'then and there lying dead' before them. According to the military surgeon Charles John White, Private Sim, of the 74th Highland Regiment had died 2 days earlier, from 'congestion of the brain, occasioned by erysipelas (an acute bacterial infection of the skin). During that time, inquests were convened when the coroner had doubts about the cause of death, and these suspicions were generally aroused by a report from a clergyman, a policeman or a local government official. 17 days before his death, Sim had been taken the barrack square, tied to the halberds and lashed fifty times with the cat o' nine tails. Limerick Coroner John Gleeson called the inquest on Sim's body because he, and others in the city, suspected that the Private's death was something out of the ordinary. The inquest called 5 military witnesses: two Non-commissioned officers (NCOs) responsible for running the military prison and hospital respectively and three regimental surgeons. The officer commanding the regiment, Colonel William Kelty McLeod, was also present and participated. The jurors questioned each witness, their inquiries revealing their collective concerns about the medical care offered to Private Sim after the flogging. The NCOs were asked about the practice of sending flogged men to jail rather than prison, while the surgeons were asked about whether doctors supervised floggings and if military prisoners were visited daily by medical officers. Sim's body was also examined by a civilian doctor, Dr Jonathan Elmes. He agreed with the diagnosis of erysipelas. His verdict on Sim's death was 'irritative fever, with the concomitant congestion of the brain', which was in agreement with Surgeon White. However, under questioning from the jury, Elmes offered a medical opinion at odds with White's: 'I have no doubt but that the punishment the deceased underwent led to the train of symptoms which led to his death.' The jury now had two contradictory assertions from medical professionals who agreed erysipelas had killed Sim, but differed on whether the flogging had affected his health. They had viewed the body, listened to the evidence and questioned the witnesses. The jury of 12 Limerick men reached a startling conclusion; that Sim died from fever 'accelerated from corporal punishment he received, as the result of a district court martial.' This finding blamed the death of Private Sim not on any medical deficiency in his care but on the flogging he received 17 days before he died. After the inquest, the body of Private Sim was taken from the New Barracks to be buried in the military graveyard. The knowledge of the soldier's punishment and death was not confined to the coroner. The next day, the verdict was reported in the press, and over the next few weeks the story featured in other newspapers in provincial Ireland. The fate of Robert Sim had not escaped the notice of the British Members of Parliament who were opposed to flogging, and who annually challenged the Mutiny Bill clause on corporal punishment. The death of Robert Sim in Limerick and the jury's determination to condemn flogging had a direct effect on the abolition of flogging in the British army.

57 Peers Douglas M., Sepoys, Soldiers and the Lash: Race, Caste and Army Discipline in India, 1820–50, *The Journal of Imperial and Commonwealth History*, 1995, Vol. 23:2, p. 230.

58 The Governor General of India in Council vide latter 24 February 1835 directed, "...that the practice of punishing soldiers of the native army by the cat-o'-nine tails or rattan, be discontinued at all Presidencies; and that it shall henceforth be competent to any Regimental, detachment, of Brigade Court Martial, to sentence a soldier of the native army to dismissal from the service, for any offence for which such soldier might be punished by flogging,

flogging was re-introduced in the British Indian Army. It was only on 2 September 1920, that an amendment to the Indian Army Act [Act XXXVII of 1920] abolished corporal punishment for the Indian soldier and follower and introduced field punishment as a substitute on active service. This freedom from torturous and humiliating punishment came approximately 40 years after flogging had been abolished for the British soldier by the Army Discipline and Regulation Act, 1881.[59]

III. Transportation

The punishment of transportation for life, which involved sending of a convict into banishment or exile, was authorized as one form of punishment for serious crimes by the East India Company's Government under the General Regulations. There was a close nexus between the demand for prison labour in colonies and the award of transportation by the military or civil court. British made extensive use of convict transportation to assist the wider process of colonization. As the demand for labour increased, more offences were made punishable by transportation.[60] From 1787, the East India Company shipped Indian convicts to Bencoolen, a short-lived British outpost on the island of Sumatra (in the East Indies), and from 1790 to the newly conquered territories in the Straits Settlements. By the early nineteenth century it had become Company policy to send Europeans convicted in Indian courts to the Australian penal colonies and Asian convicts to destinations within the wider Indian Ocean world.[61]

The general or other officer Commanding in Chief the forces of the Presidencies of Fort William, Fort Saint George, and Bombay were empowered to appoint general Courts Martial, and issue

provided such sentence of dismissal shall not be carried into effect unless confirmed by the General of Other Officer Commanding a division. There were a number of cases in the Bengal Presidency where natives were tried by court martial and dismissed from the service on account of mutinous conduct, intoxication, insubordination conduct towards Commanding Officer, scandalous and disgraceful conduct, disrespectful towards superior officers. Three native Doctors employed in 50th and the 10th Regiment of Native Infantry were tried for scandalous and disgraceful conduct in that they demanded and received money from the soldiers of the Regiments (for having extorted money from men proceeding on sick leave, that if such sums were not paid the men will not get medical certificate) who were proceeding on sick leave. They were tried by a native court martial and dismissed from the service. The application for reinstatement in the service on the account of past good service was considered from one of the native doctor and he was granted pardon and taken back of the strength of the Army. GC dates 14 July 1836, Jephson George, 1847, The Orders and Regulations of the Bengal Army, Part II, Calcutta: WM Thacker and Company, p. 589.

59 Singha Radhika, The Rare Infliction: The Abolition of Flogging in the Indian Army, circa 1835-1920, *Law & Hist. Rev.*, Vol. 34, 2016, p. 783-818.

60 Act 3 & 4 Vict., Cap. 37 (4 August 1840) provided the punishment of death or transportation by a court martial for certain offences which included mutiny; sedition; casting away of arms or ammunition; misbehaviour before the enemy; shamefully abandoning fortress or post; violence to any person bringing provisions or other necessaries of the forces; forcing a safeguard; striking or using violence against superior officer; disobeying any lawful command of superior officer; or deserting the service, etc.

61 By a statute passed in the reign of Elizabeth, it was enacted, that "such rogues as were dangerous to the inferior people should be banished the realm." Transportation was not brought into common operation until after the sixth year of the reign of George I. Under the statutes of George I, transportation to America lasted from 1718 till the commencement of the War of Independence, in 1775. Transportation was resumed by a statute, 24th Geo. III.; and in the month of May 1787, the first band of convicts left England, which in the succeeding year founded the colony of New South Wales.

their warrant to any general or other officer not below the degree of a field officer, for the trial of any person under their command, accused of having committed wilful murder or any other capital crime, or of having used violence or committed any offence against the person or property of any subject of her Majesty, and award punishment of death, or transportation for life or for a term of years, or to such other punishment which could be awarded according to the nature and degree of the offence.[62] Most native soldiers were seen as 'having nothing but their bodies', which made fines pointless or hard to administer; transportation was often seen as preferable to service in India. A district court martial had no the power of passing sentence of death or transportation. During the period 1789–1939 the British Empire had transported more than one lakh Indian, which included military and civil accused, to various destinations, as shown in the table below.

Origin	Destination	Period	Number
Bengal and Madras Presidencies	Amboyna and Bencoolen	1787-1823	2,823
Bengal Presidency	Andaman Islands	1793-1796	265
Bengal, Bombay and Madras Presidencies; and Princely States of Mysore and Hyderabad	Straits Settlements (Penang, Malacca and Singapore after 1826)	1789-1860	11,919
Bengal and Madras Presidencies	Burma	1830-1860	6,518
British India and Ceylon	Mauritius	1815-1836	1,462
Bombay Presidency	Aden	1841-1848	140
British India inc. Burma, and Mysore and Hyderabad	Andaman Islands	1858-1939	83,313
Total			106,440

Table: Convict (both military and civilian) Transportation during the British Empire[63]

Transportation had no other recommendation as a punishment for soldiers, but that it got rid of offenders. Even in civil life it had little or no effect as an example, partly because the culprit himself considered it a punishment, and partly because the distance caused both him and his crime to be forgotten as completely as if he were removed by death. When the sentence was passed on men, they sometimes said, "Thank you, my Lord;" but, in the army, the punishment

62 Article III, Act 3 & 4 Vict., Cap. 37 (4 August 1840) provided that the punishments of death and transportation could not executed until confirmed by the general or other officer Commanding-in-Chief at the Presidency, with the concurrence of the Governor General in Council, or Governor in Council of the respective Presidency.

63 Source: Clare Anderson, Transnational Histories of Penal Transportation: Punishment, Labour and Governance in the British Imperial World, 1788–1939, *Australian Historical Studies*, Vol. 47:3, 2016, pp. 381-397.

of transportation may became an incitement to the commission of military offences. A number of Europeans who were serving the East India Company committed smaller crimes or mutilated themselves, for the express purpose of becoming convicts, and transferred to New South Wales for undergoing punishment. The men appeared to balance the advantages and disadvantages of being a convict, with the advantages and disadvantages of being a soldier, and give the preference to the condition of a convict.

The British had experimented with a penal colony in the Andaman Islands in 1793–1799, shipping nearly 300 convicts. However, this settlement was devastated by disease and abandoned. The islands again became a destination for convicts following the 1857 Rebellion and received a further 80,000 convicts up to 1940.[64] The British on occasion substituted convicts for slaves, enabling colonial administrators to engage in the rhetoric of abolition while securing an alternative source of labour.[65] During the initial stages of colonisation convicts were often deployed in 'frontier' zones. These covered culturally unfamiliar, uninhabited and densely forested lands, littorals and islands. In these years, attempts were made to isolate the convict from neighbouring communities, whether comprising indigenous people or migrant settlers. The labour services that convicts performed were diverse and could encompass land clearance; infrastructural work, including the building of barracks, fortifications, jails, roads and bridges; airfields, agriculture and cultivation of rubber, silk and salt; mining; working as personal servants or grooms; policing, or military related works.

During the period of transportation, convicts were encouraged to marry, formed connections in the place and found many inducements to remain there that they practically became colonists. For instance, Indian convicts sent to Singapore Penal Settlement were under no restraint and received no support and were allowed to provide for themselves. They differed in no respect from free population of the place, excepting that they had to give security for appearance whenever required.[66]

---

64 Between 1858 and 1939, the British government of India transported around 83,000 Indian and Burmese convicts to the penal colony of the Andamans. In terms of the total number of convicts received, this renders the Andamans the largest penal colony in the entire British Empire. The British government subsequently transferred European transportation convicts to Andaman penal colony to act as supervisors on an extra wages of fifty rupees per month. A number of European overseer prisoners availed this opportunity and took up their post, which ensured better discipline in the penal colony. Anderson Clare, The Andaman Islands Penal Colony: Race, Class, Criminality, and the British Empire, *IRSH*, Vol. 63 (2018), Special Issue, pp. 25–43.

65 The longevity of penal transportation as a system of securing cheap labour to aid colonial expansion can be ascribed to four inter-related factors: (i) Convict transportation attracted remarkably little comment from elites of the society or colonial interlocutors since it could be argued that, unlike slaves, convicts were the agents of their own demise; (ii) Convict transportation was flexible in that it provided a means of securing a cheap, controllable and easily replaceable form of labour, and convicts could be forced to go to places where free labourers would not settle; (iii) Penal transportation delivered an effective tool for policing colonial populations, i.e., public management of labour in the age of imperial expansion; and (iv) Transportation was perceived as less costly than the other penal alternative. Clare Anderson and Hamish Maxwell-Stewart, Convict Labour and the Western Empires, 1415–1954, available at: https://www.researchgate.net/publication/276418150_Convict_labour_and_the_Western_Empires_1415-1954.

66 For more details see: Gokhale Nishant, Life Imprisonment in India: A Short History of A Long Sentence, *NUJS Law Review*, Vol. 11, No. 3, 2018, pp. 1-21; Malik Balwant Singh, The Law of punishments of transportation for life and imprisonment for life - a Critical appraisal, (1999) 5 SCC (Jour), 4.

The Indian Law Commissioner in its draft of the Indian Penal Code, 1837 had preferred transportation for most offences instead of life imprisonment. It observed, ""“Prolonged imprisonment may be more painful in the actual endurance: but it is not so much dreaded beforehand; nor does a sentence of imprisonment strike either the offender or the by-standers with so much horror as a sentence of exile beyond what they *(Indians)* call the Black Water. This feeling, we believe, arises chiefly from the mystery which overhangs the fate of the transported convict. The separation resembles that which takes place at the moment of death. The convict is taken for ever from the society of all who are acquainted with him, and conveyed by means of which the natives have but an indistinct notion over an element which they regard with extreme awe, to a distant country of which they know nothing, and from which he is never to return.” The Committee recommended further that transportation in all cases, should be for life. A sentence which thrived on the fear of the unknown would serve little purpose if people who were sentenced to it, were to return within a few years. After independence, the punishment of transportation was reserved for grave offences, for some of which the only prescribed penal alternative was the death penalty. In 1955, the punishment of transportation for life was substituted with the ‘life imprisonment’ in the Indian Penal Code, 1860, and other penal statutes including the Army Act, 1950.[67]

IV. Branding

Flogging was not the only way that the nineteenth-century army left permanent marks upon soldiers bodies. It is shocking to today’s sensibilities, but miscreant soldiers were branded or forcibly tattooed.[68] Men had been branded with a hot iron in the seventeenth century. But by the nineteenth century, the hot iron had been abandoned. A new device was created to mark the soldiers’ skin with ink, or even gunpowder. The large, blunt points of the device caused pain as a spring mechanism forced these points into the skin. Regimental doctors described the practice as ‘cupping’.

A soldier could also be marked with the letters ‘BC’ meaning ‘bad character’, if he was found to have deserted with premeditation. Until 1829, any soldier could be branded but after this year this punishment was reserved for deserters. A man who deserted his regiment could, upon conviction by a court-martial, be branded with a ‘D’. In the mid-1840s over two-third of those convicted of absconding were branded. By the early 1850s some 400 men a year were banded, but between 1855 and 1868 the annual figure ranged from 1136 to 2642.[69]

67 Section 53A, The Indian Penal Code, 1860.

68 The practice of branding was also strongly associated with criminality. Until 1789, a convicted criminal could be branded on the thumb with ‘T’ for theft, ‘F’ for felon or ‘M’ for murder. While the parallels between criminal and military punishment outraged public opinion in the case of flogging, branding did not arouse the same feelings. Politicians expressed surprise that branding even existed, suggesting that awareness of it was relatively low. Being a shorter and necessarily quieter punishment than flogging, civilians were unlikely to hear the cries of soldiers being marked. It may be that the earlier cessation of branding in a criminal context meant that it quickly fell from public knowledge.

69 Peter Burroughs, Crime and Punishment in the British Army, 1815-1870, English Historical Review, Vol. 100, No. 396, July 1985, p. 570.

Supporters of the practice claimed that this was not actually a punishment, but a means for the army to prevent fraud.[70] A portion of men were serial enlisters who joined up, then quickly deserted time after time. In the 1860s, it was argued that since flogging for desertion was no longer permitted, it was impossible to tell during a medical examination if a man was a deserter or a genuine fresh recruit. Without the marks of the lash on his back, a man could reenlist as many times as he liked. Desertion was rife among young men and new recruits. Unfortunately for those who changed their mind after enlisting, they had signed over their bodies to the state and escape was difficult. In 1871, the War Office abandoned this punishment to popularize the enlistment in the army.

V. Field Punishment

On 2 September 1920, an amendment to the Indian Army Act abolished corporal punishment for the Indian soldier and introduced field punishment as a substitute on active service. This field punishment remained in Indian Army Act, 1950 until 1993, when it was completely abolished. However, this punishment is still part of the Air Force Act, 1950, but rarely awarded. A court-martial or commanding officer exercising authority under the Act may, for the purpose of awarding field punishment under the Act, sentence an offender below the rank of Non-commissioned officer for a period not exceeding, in the case of a court-martial, three months, and in the case of commanding officer, 28 days, to one of the following punishments, namely: Field Punishment No. 1, or Field Punishment No. 2.[71]

Where an offender was sentenced to field punishment No. 1, he would be during the continuance of his sentence, be punished as follows: (a) He may be kept in irons, that is to say, in fetters or hand cuffs or both fetters and hand-cuffs, and may be secured so as to prevent his escape; (b) When in irons, he may be attached for a period or periods not exceeding two hours in any one day to a fixed object, but he must not be so attached during more than three out of any four consecutive days, not during more than twenty-one days in all; (c) Straps or ropes may be used for the purpose of these rules in lieu of irons.

The offender must be attached so as to be standing firmly on his feet which, if tied, must not be more than twelve inches apart, and it must be possible, for him to move each foot at least three inches. If he is tied around the body there must be no restriction of his breathing. If his arms or wrists are tied, there must be six inches of play between them and the fixed object. His arms must swing either by the side of his body or behind his back. For the purpose of field punishment, irons should be used when available, but straps or ropes may be used in lieu of them when necessary. Any straps or ropes used for the purpose must be of sufficient width to inflict

70 In a bid to stamp out the heinous and flourishing crime of desertion, the punishment of 'branding' or tattooing was introduced and gained popularity amongst military authorities. Though critics of this punishment were of the view that this was a humiliating punishment, military authorities continue to justify it as a cheap, quick method of identifying deserters and unmanageable rogues, preventing fraudulent enlistment and protecting public from criminals. Burrough Peter, Crime and Punishment in the British Army, 1815-1870, *The English Historical Review*, Vol. 100, No. 396, July 1985, pp. 545-571.

71 Rules for Field Punishment, Maunal of Military Law (War Office) 1907, London: His Majesty's Stationery Office, p. 598-599.

no bodily harm and leave no permanent mark on the offender. The accused may be subjected to the like labour, employment and restraint and dealt with in like manner as if he were undergoing a sentence of rigorous imprisonment. Where an offender is sentenced to field punishment No. 2, he was not be liable to be attached to a fixed object. Every portion of a field punishment shall be inflicted in such a manner as is calculated not to cause injury or leave any permanent mark on the offender; and a portion of a field punishment must be discontinued upon a report by a responsible Medical Officer that the continuance of that portion be prejudicial to the offender's health. Filed punishment was carried out within the unit to which offender belonged or was attached so long as that unit was actually on the move, but when the unit was halted at any place where there is a provost marshal, or an assistant provost marshal, the punishment was carried out under the orders of that officer.

VI. Gagging

Gagging has been described as a mode of punishment to prevent insolent language during confinement for drunkenness or other misconduct. A punishment of gagging was performed in the following manner: A piece of wood or iron, various in diameter and length, is introduced into the mouth; exactly in the way a bit is introduced into the mouth of a horse, so that a portion of it shall project from each side. It is retained in this position by means of a cord passed over the projecting extremities and behind the head. In 1835, gagging was still used in the East India Company army, as means of silencing talkative soldiers.[72] In the year 1815, a captain was tried by a court-martial on the charged of cruelty and oppression. The victim/accused had suffered a dislocation of the jaws, from the severe punishment of gagging, inflicted on him by the directions of captain. The piece of wood to which the victim was successively gagged was of fir, about 6-7 inches long, and of the thickness of the thumb. The victim bit through one or more pieces of wood successively; and when he had bitten through the third piece, he appeared to have hurt himself, and upon examination by the medical officer, it was found that his jaw was completely dislocated. The court while acquitting captain, gave the following decision: "The Court is of the opinion that the dislocation of the victim's jaw was occasioned by his own violence in biting the piece of wood through, and *by a facility which he had of putting the jaw out and in himself*, and not from the punishment of gagging."[73]

VII. Solitary Imprisonment

For placing an individual in solitary confinement, the Commanding Officers were to strictly follow the following instructions: Only one prisoner was to be placed in a confinement in a cell. The prisoners, previous to being placed in a cell were to be carefully examined to ascertain that they do not have knives, or anything of an objectionable nature. The prisoners were fatigue clothing while in solitary confinement and his Regimental clothing and his kit was to be kept in the store. As a general rule, the diet of prisoners under solitary confinement was restricted to

72 *Asiatic Journal*, Vol. XVIII, Part ii, p. 156.

73 Marshall Henry, 1846, *The Military Miscellany; Comprehending a History of the Recruiting of the Army, Military Punishments*, London, pp. 373-374.

bread and water, subject to such additions as the Medical Officer may at any time certify to be necessary. The prisoners were allowed only religious or prayer book during the confinement. The solitary cells were opened once daily, in the presence of the officer on duty, in order to admit of the Cells being cleaned, the prisoner being washed, his clothing changed, and his daily supply of food given to him. Only one Cell is to be opened at the same time for the above purposes. The Officer on duty so attending will be careful to ascertain that the Cells have been perfectly cleaned, and that the cleanliness of the prisoners has been properly attended to, and will certify the same in his report upon coming off duty. He will also ascertain that during the process of cleaning out the Cell, no conversation is carried out with the prisoner by the persons so employed. Sentries over Solitary Cells are to be instructed to prevent all persons from approaching the Cells, or conversing with the prisoners; and are themselves to be confined for a breach of order if detected carrying out conversation with men in confinement. Solitary Cells are not to be opened otherwise, unless in case of sickness or by the express order of the commanding officer; anf then in the presence of the Officer on duty. In case of sickness, the Medical Officer in charge is to inspect the prisoner himself, and to report to the Commanding Officer what measures the requisite medical treatment may call far. The keys of Solitary Cells are to be kept in the Guard House under the orders of the Officer on duty. The Guard over Solitary Cells was invariably to be composed of Native troops.[74]

Congee-House Confinement

During the punishment of "Confinement in Conjee House,"[75] the individual was confined within a convenient room receiving only "Conjee" diet. Congee-House confinement, not exceeding one week for one offence, could be awarded for small crimes by the Commanding Officer of Brigades, Battalions or detachments, they being field officers, but not by other officers in such command, unless particular permission was given by the Commanding Officers of Brigades, Battalions, or the by the Headquarters of which the detachments belongs.[76] Soldiers and women guilty of drunkenness or irregularities could also be confined in the Congeee-house, by order of the Officer Commanding, the troops in garrison; the Town-Major or Fort Adjutant; Heads of Department, or officers commanding Corps, Battalions or detachments, quartered in garrison. European soldiers who were awarded Congee-House confinement were fed on bread and water, at the rate of one brown loaf of bread, weighing one pound for twenty-four hours, and water as much as they could drink. Non-commissioned officers were not committed to the congee-house; those who deserved such punishments, were could not be worthy of their rank, and were previously reduced to the ranks. [77]

Sentence to congee-house varied from one week to twelve months, and was sometimes qualified by hard labour or solitary confinement. Typical sentences were one month's solitary confinement

74 General Regulations of the Madras Army, Adjutant General's Office, Fort St George, Madras: Military Male Orphan Asylum Press, 1849, p.128-129.

75 The name was derived from the reduced diet of prisoners, 'congee' being the water in which rice had been boiled with salt, but without any other condiments.

76 A.G. Circular No. 6114, 5 March 1821.

77 Jephson George, 1839, The Orders and Regulations of the Bengal Army, Part I, Calcutta: WM Thacker and Company, pp. 576.

for being drunk on parade and insolent to an officer, and three hundred lashes remitted to six weeks of confinement for being absent from Guard or returning drunk. Stoppage of pay was occasionally added to these sentences, but only to pay for damages or loss incidental to the crime, not as additional punishment. Native soldiers sentenced to imprisonment without hard labour, and who were again to return to their duty at the expiration of their sentences, were not sent to any gaol to undergo their sentence, but imprisonment in such cases is to be inflicted under the best arrangement that can be made by the military authorities on the spot.

VIII. Riding Wooden Horse

Riding the wooden horse was a punishment used in different services. The wooden horse was formed of planks nailed together, so as to form a sharp ridge or angle about eight or nine feet long, this ridge represented the back of the horse, it was supported by four posts or legs, about six or seven feet long, placed on a stand made moveable by trucks; to complete the resemblance, a head and tail were added. When a soldier was sentenced by a court martial, or ordered by the commanding officer of the corps, to ride this horse, his hands were tied behind, and frequently, to increase the punishment, had muskets tied to his legs, to prevent, as it was jocularly said, their horse from kicking them off; this punishment being chiefly inflicted on the infantry, who were supposed unused to ride. Prolonged riding the wooden horse having been found to injure the men physically and it was left off.[78]

IX. Dismissal

General Orders by the Commander-in-Chief of the 5th of January, 1797, declared that no sepoy or trooper of our native army shall be dismissed from the service by the sentence of any but a general court martial. General Orders by the Commander-in-Chief, Lord Combermere, of 19 March, 1827, declared that his Excellency was of opinion that the quiet and orderly habits of the native soldiers are such that it can very seldom be necessary to have recourse to the punishment of flogging, which might be almost entirely abolished with great advantage to their character and feelings; and directs that no native soldier shall in future be sentenced to corporal punishment unless for the crime of stealing, marauding, or gross insubordination, where the individuals are deemed unworthy to continue in the ranks of the army. No such sentence by a regimental, detachment, or brigade court martial was to be carried into effect till confirmed by the general officer commanding the division. By Act 23 of 1839, passed by the Legislative Council of India on the 23rd of September, it was made competent for courts martial to sentence soldiers of the native army in the service of the East India Company to the punishment of dismissal, and to be imprisoned, with or without hard labour, for any period not exceeding two years, if the sentence be pronounced by a general court martial; and not exceeding one year, if by a garrison or line court martial; and not exceeding six months, if by a regimental or district court martial. Imprisonment for any period with hard labour, or for a term exceeding six months without hard labour, to

78 Grose Francis, 1788, *Military Antiquities Respecting A History of English Army: From The Conquest to the Present Time*, Vol. II, London: S. Hooper, pp. 199-200.

involve dismissal. Act 2 of 1840 provides for such sentences of imprisonment being carried into execution by magistrates or other officers in charge of the gaols.

X. Cashiering

The punishment of cashiering signified a dishonourable dismissal of an officer or soldier, and in the former had three degrees; the first was simply a dismissal of an officer from his employment, by a letter from the secretary of war to him signifying that His Majesty has no farther occasion for his services, or by the sentence of a court martial whereby he was sentenced to be cashiered. The second was dismissal an officer from the service, and rendering him incapable of serving for the future in any military capacity; a sentence which seems rather an infringement on the royal prerogative; perhaps a declaration that the court deem him unworthy for the future to hold any such office. The third was dismissal with infamy, and degradation from the rank of a soldier and a gentleman. A sentence of third kind was for cowardice and was inflicted in the following manner.

The line being ordered out under arms, the prisoner was brought to the head of the eldest brigade, completely accoutered, when his sentence being read, his commission was cancelled, his sword broken over his head, his sash cut in pieces and thrown into his face, and lastly the provost-martial's servant giving him a kick on the posteriors, turned him out of the line. A similar to this was the ceremony of dismissing a soldier sentenced to be drummed out of the regiment with a halter about his neck. The corporal punishment commonly accompanying this sentence being over, and the regiment turned out, with or without arms, the prisoner was brought to the right of it, under an escort of a corporal and six men, with bayonets fixed: the halter was then put round his neck, and frequently a label on his back signifying his crime, a drummer then takes hold of the end of the rope, and leads him along the front, the drums following and beating the rogues march; when they have passed the left, the procession moves to the rear, if in camp, or if in quarters, to the end of the town, where the drummer giving him a kick on the breech dismisses him with the halter for his perquisite.[79] This punishment is now called 'cashiering' under the Army Act and the Air Force Act, and 'dismissal with disgrace from naval service' under the Navy Act and can be awarded only to officers. However, the procedure as described above is not observed.

XI. Reprimand

A reprimand at the head of the regiment, was sometimes ordered by a court martial, and sometimes only in the presence of the officers of the corps; this was generally given by one of the field officers. It was usually given in the following manner: Captain or Lieutenant A. B. you have been tried for —, and were found guilty by the general court martial and sentenced to be reprimanded at the head of the regiment; the disagreeable task of doing it is assigned to me. I therefore do hereby reprimand you, and hope that it may prevent your falling again into the like error. Non-commission-officers were sometimes though not frequently, ordered to be

79 Grose Francis, 1788, *Military Antiquities Respecting A History of English Army: From The Conquest to the Present Time*, Vol. II, London: S. Hooper, pp. 195-204.

reprimanded. [80] Lieutenant Thomas Latter of the 67th N.I. was tried by General Court Martial at Dinapore on 12 March 1850 on the charge of, "For highly unbecoming conduct, in having, at Dinapore, on 19 December 1849, when Regimental Officer of the day, and visiting the Hospital guard of the Regiment, struck with a cane, and grossly abused Usdully Khan, Sepoy, of the same Regiment, who was sentry at the Hospital guard." The Court found him guilty of the charge, with the exception of the words "struck with a cane" and "grossly." He was sentenced, "To be reprimanded in such manner as the Commander in Chief may direct."

The Commander in Chief, while confirming the sentence made the following remarks on 27 March 1850: "Ist, When an Officer so forgets the sacred character of a sentry as to abuse the Soldier on his post, that Officer must be prepared to receive such punishment as the protection of sentries may demand. Lieutenant Latter, without any just cause for such improper conduct, rode up to and abused Usdully Khan, Sepoy, when that Soldier was on sentry and pushed the Soldier's cap straight with a cane, which he, Lieutenant Latter, had in his hand; such treatment would have warranted the sentry to have kept Lieutenant Latter off with his bayonet! Lieutenant Latter must learn that sentries are not to be insulted. If a sentry deserves a reprimand, it is to be given in a proper manner and not with a cane, nor with such language as Lieutenant Latter used, for which he is hereby reprimanded according to the sentence of the Court. 2nd. Brigadier General Young will order the foregoing reprimand to be translated into Hindoostanee and read at the head of the 67th Regiment N.I., after which Lieutenant Latter is to return to his duty.

Punishments in Royal Navy

In 1779, An Act for amending, explaining, and reducing into one act of Parliament, the laws relating to the government of His Majesty's ships, vessels, and forces by sea; and in the nineteenth year of George III, another Act was passed, which modified and amended the Act of 1779. These two Acts of Parliament[81] contained, with the requisite modifications, all the rules, articles, and orders, for the regulating and better government of Her Majesty's ships, vessels, and forces by sea. In above naval penal code, there were nine articles, or branches of articles, referring to common seamen, which, on conviction, expressly inflict death, without alternative, or leaving any discretionary power to the members of a court-martial to award a milder punishment; and there are about twelve articles which inflict the punishment of death, or "such other punishment as the nature and degree of an offence shall be found to deserve," and which a court in its discretion may award. In about ten other articles the word death is omitted, and the punishment to which a man may be sentenced is left, both in kind and degree, wholly to the discretion of a court-martial; and as these articles are for the punishment of offences not of so flagrant a nature as in the former two classes of articles, it may be presumed that the Legislature meant to exclude the power of a court-martial to inflict a capital punishment for any of the offences therein specified. In these cases it is left wholly to the discretion of a court-martial to discriminate the shades of guilt, and to inflict a punishment, in quality and amount, proportionate, in their opinion, to the offence, but

80 Grose Francis, 1788, *Military Antiquities Respecting A History of English Army: From The Conquest to the Present Time*, Vol. II, London: S. Hooper, pp. 195-204.

81 Act 22 Geo. II, c. 33 of 1779 and Act 19 Geo. III, c. 17.

not affecting life or limb. In the British legal system, relating to the Army and the Navy, awarding death sentence has been at all times lawful in cases of mutiny.

In early times, and even during the eighteenth century, punishments were very severe. It was not then uncommon for an offender, guilty of desertion, to be adjudged to suffer death, or to be punished with 1,000 lashes. The punishments which were in the power of naval courts-martial to inflict, were various in their nature and degree. They varied from death, the greatest and highest, descending in various shades down to mild reprimand and gentle admonition. Articles 36 of the Articles of War (1779) provided, "All other crimes not capital committed by any person or persons in the fleet, which are not mentioned in this act, or for which no punishment is hereby directed to be inflicted, shall be punished by the laws and customs in such cases used at sea." [82] For anomalous offences old standing customs and usages of the service were restored to as a kind of unwritten law which replaced to written statute.[83]

In the Royal navy, courts-martial were ordered either by the Admiralty or by the Commanding Officer of a station. The punishments to which seamen were liable by the sentence of a court-martial were death and flogging round the fleet. The summary punishments frequently inflicted at the discretion of a Captain or Commanding Officer were: (i) Flogging at the gangway; (ii) Running the gauntlet; (iii) Starting; (iv) Keelhauling; (v) Ducking; (vi) Gagging; (vii) The spread eagle; (viii) The wooden collar; (ix) The barrel pillory; (x) Carrying a capstan bar; and (xi) The black list.

Execution of the sentence of Death:

The most severe corporal punishment inflicted in the Royal Navy was death. When the King was pleased to approve of the sentence of death, the warrant for execution was transmitted by the Admiralty to the officer commanding the ships and vessels at the place for the time being, who issued the necessary orders; and, in pursuance thereof, preparations were made. Although high ranking officers were brought before a firing squad, the standard method of execution for seamen was hanging from a yard-arm. All executions were held publicly as a dreadful spectacle and an

82 Early in the month of March 1797, a mutiny broke out in the fleet at Portsmouth, the principal subjects of discontent among the seamen being the smallness of their pay, and of the Greenwich pensions, the very unequal distribution of prize money, the excessive harshness and severity of the discipline, and the haughty and tyrannical behaviour of many of the officers. The seamen obtained all their demands, and forthwith returned to their duty. Among the officers charged with oppression, and discarded by the men, were one Admiral, four Captains, twenty-nine Lieutenants, seventeen Master's Mates, twenty-five Midshipmen, five Captains of Marines, three Lieutenants of Marines, four Surgeons, and about thirteen petty officers. The men refused to receive on board those tyrannical officers, whom they had sent on shore; and Lord Howe, who had been commissioned to settle all matters of dispute, found himself obliged to comply with the decided resolution of the men. Marshall Henry, 1846, *The Military Miscellany; Comprehending a History of the Recruiting of the Army, Military Punishments*, London, p. 375.

83 During May 1797, a mutiny broke out at the Nore, and the mutineers petitioned against the naval code containing their list of grievances. According to petition, the Articles of War, as were enforced, required various alterations, several of which required to expunged; thereby expressing an opinion, that the system of discipline and the Articles of War were unnecessarily severe and required relaxation, in order to disabuse seamen in general of the prejudice against the navy. In the letter which the mutineers at the Nore sent to the King, they urged, "that no punishment should be inflicted on board a King's ship, until the offender had been previously tried and convicted by a jury of seamen." Ibid., p. 355.

example to provide those who observed them with a grim lesson about the fatal consequences that could accompany serious violations of the Articles of War. Therefore, hangings were staged with great ceremony. On the appointed day a yellow flag, "the signal of death," was flown from the masthead of the ship on which the execution was to take place. A party under armed guard from each vessel in the squadron was dispatched to attend the punishment. Meanwhile, the rest of the ships' companies were turned out on deck in formation to witness the spectacle. Once assembled, their commanding officers read the Articles of War to them and explained the crime for which the prisoner was to forfeit his life. Upon completion of these rituals the crews stood in silence as the condemned man was made ready to meet his demise. When the fatal moment had arrived, a gun was fired and the unfortunate mariner was run up a yard-arm. As was the practice at hangings on shore, the corpse remained suspended for several hours as a warning to deter others from the commission of similar crimes.[84]

Flogging Round the Fleet:

Flogging round the fleet was often used by courts martial as a substitute for execution. Like executions, floggings round the fleet were conducted publicly according to a solemn, formalized ritual designed to make horrible examples of the victims and leave lasting impressions on those who witnessed them. On the morning of the day of the punishment, a yellow flag was unfurled from the foremast of the commanding officer's ship. In response to this signal, each vessel in the squadron sent a boat manned by a party of seamen and a detachment of armed mariners under the direction of a lieutenant to participate in the proceedings.

The delinquent having been put into a launch, attended by Assistant-Surgeon, he was forthwith stripped naked to the waist, and tied up with his arms extended upon a frame of wood, when he received a specified number of lashes. The Master-at-Arms stood beside him with a drawn sword, and reckons the lashes as they are inflicted; a drummer and fifer stand in the bow: a Lieutenant and the Surgeon of the ship accompanying the launch in another boat. The whole flotilla of boats then formed into line, taking in tow the launch containing the culprit. The fifer stroked up the Rogue's March, accompanied by the drum, muffled, and the procession moves on at a slow rate, following a light gig, called the dispatch-boat, which went forward to announce the delinquent's approach to those ships where he was to receive his punishment. The prisoner having reached the ship, the crews cover the sides and channels upon that side where the procession halted. The sentence of the court-martial was read aloud, after which two Boatswain's Mates were sent from the ship, who inflicted that portion of the punishment which has been directed to be given alongside of it, the amount of lashes being divided among the number of ships belonging to the fleet. A blanket was then thrown over the man's shoulders, the flotilla of boats again take the launch in tow, the music strikes up, the dispatch-boat proceeds to the next ship as before, and thus the culprit was slowly dragged from one vessel to another, for a period extending some times to

84 For more details see: Byrn, John D. Jr, Crime and Punishment in the Royal Navy: Discipline on the Leeward Islands Station, 1784-1812 (England), 1987, LSU Historical Dissertations and Thesis, 4345; McArthur John, 1805, *Principles and Practice of Naval and Military Courts Martial*, Vol. I & II, London: J Butterworth, pp. 450 & 573.

several hours, till the sentence has been carried into effect, or the punishment was suspended by the recommendation of the Surgeon.[85]

In 1811, certain judicious measures were adopted by the Admiralty to abolish cruelty and restrain severity of punishments in the Royal Navy. Each Captain was directed to forward a quarterly report of punishments inflicted by his order, specifying the nature of offence and the number of lashes inflicted, explaining the cases where the punishment had exceeded four dozen lashes.[86] The Corporal punishment inflicted in the Royal Navy from 1839-1843 on the orders of Captain, showing the highest and lowest number of lashes at each time are reflected in the table below.[87]

	1839	**1840**	**1841**	**1842**	**1843**
Total number of punishments	2,007	2,026	2,066	2,472	2,170
Total number of lashes inflicted	59,341	60,302	61,669	71,024	63,985
Highest number inflicted at one time	60	48	50	100	60
Lowest number inflicted at one time	3	1	2	1	3

Table: Corporal punishment (Lashes) inflicted in the Royal Navy from 1839-1843

In the Royal Navy, flogging was more severe as compared to the Army. It was estimated that 'Forty-eight lashes in the Navy were equal to 100 lashes ashore', or even that a naval flogging was 'four times as heavy as in the army'. One reason was that the naval cat was heavier than that of the army; another, the flogging in the Navy was administered by a succession of boatswain's mates, experienced and in all likelihood strong in the arm, in the army it was done by the drummer boys who, one assumes, would be unable to 'lay on' with quite the same effect.[88]

85 The punishment of flogging round the fleet was not abolished in the Royal Navy as in the case of British Army. On 5 January 1844, a court-martial was held on board Her Majesty's ship Minden, at Hong-Kong, to try two seamen for desertion. The Court Martial was presided by Rear-Admiral Sir Thomas Cochrane, which held the accused guilty and each was sentenced to receive 100 lashes. On the morning of 9 January the yellow flag, the signal of punishment, was displayed from the Agincourt, the gun was fired, and fourteen boats, manned and armed, assembled to attend the punishment, which was executed in the usual barbarous manner. Marshall Henry, 1846, *The Military Miscellany; Comprehending a History of the Recruiting of the Army, Military Punishments*, London, pp. 363-364.

86 Some Captains of ships kept their cats steeped in brine, to make their horrid punishments still more cruel but this was unusual, and always reprobated. Ibid., p. 369.

87 Ibid., pp. 367-368.

88 Peers Douglas M., Sepoys, soldiers and the Lash: Race, Caste and Army Discipline in India, 1820–50, *The Journal of Imperial and Commonwealth History*, 1995, Vol. 23, No. 2, p. 232; Dacam, John H., 'Wanton and Torturing Punishments': Patterns of Discipline and Punishment in the Royal Navy, 1783-1815, Unpublished Ph D Thesis, the University of Hull, September 2009, pp. 266.

Flogging at the Gangway

This punishment was severe in the Royal Navy when compared to the Army. Floggings at the gangway could be ordered by captains summarily. The punishment usually took place at half-past eleven o'clock in the morning, (seven bells) and the infliction was executed in the following manner: The carpenters were ordered to "rig the gratings," that is, to fasten two gratings at the gangway, in such a manner that the culprit stands upon one, to which his feet are fastened, and leans forward against the other, to which his hands are secured. The officers appear in their cocked-hats and side-arms, and the marines are "under arms;" the ship's company stood on the opposite side of the deck. Near the gratings the delinquent stood, and close to him the Master-at-Arms, with his sword drawn. The Boatswain and Boatswain's Mates complete the line round him. One of the Mates was commonly standing ready with a cat-o'-nine-tails, half concealed under his jacket. These arrangements being made, the First Lieutenant reported the same to the Captain, who usually came upon deck forthwith. The Captain sometimes addressed the crew, together with the culprit, and concluded by ordering him to "strip." When he has stripped, the Captain says, "Seize him up," and he was instantly fastened to the gratings. An Article of War, relative to the punishment, was then read by the Captain, who concluded by ordering the Boatswain's Mate to "give him a dozen." While the Article of War is being read, the officers, including the Midshipmen, stand uncovered. The punisher, who is usually a powerful man, having separated the cords with the fingers of the left hand, throws the cat over his right shoulder, and then brings it down upon the culprit's back, apparently with all his strength. It would appear that in some ships a Sergeant of Marines was employed to reckon the lashes, and regulate the time of infliction, by means of a sand-glass of a quarter of a minute. At the conclusion of a dozen another Boatswain's Mate is called, for the purpose of inflicting an equal number, and so on until the Captain suspends the punishment.

Running the Gauntlet

The punishment of 'running the gauntlet' was alternative forms of punishment in the Royal Navy. It was awarded for 'for minor offences' like theft, fraud, sodomy or attempted sodomy.

The whole ship's crew was disposed in two rows, standing face to face, on both sides of the deck, so as to form a lane whereby to go forward on one side and aft on the other, each person being furnished with a small twisted cord or rope called a knittle, having two or three knots upon it. The delinquent, stripped naked above the waist, was brought to the gangway, where he received one dozen from a Boatswain's Mate. Next followed what may be called a procession, which took place between the two rows of men in the following order: 1st: A drummer, plating the Rogue's March. 2nd: The Master-at-Arms, having a drawn cutlass under his arm, with the point directed behind him towards the delinquent. 3rd: The culprit. 4th: The Surgeon's Mate. The delinquent passed forward between the two rows of men on one side, and aft on the other, a certain number of times, rarely exceeding three, during which every person lays on him with their knittles. All the officers were present, and when the Captain sees fit, he directed the punishment to cease. The ordinary effects of the gauntlet were, excessive tumefaction of the shoulders and ribs; the parts do not usually ulcerate, but the sufferer was commonly some time on the sick list, being unfit for duty. As a punishment, this could be fatal, and it was banned in 1806 after some deaths resulted.[89]

Starting

Starting (the beating of a seaman with a rope's end) was a severe punishment which could be awarded summarily. This punishment was formerly used on board ships, which was inflicted on the seamen by the Boatswain's Mate with a rope's end (or, a colt or rattan), by order of the Commanding Officer. Starting was frequently inflicted upon men who were a few minutes late for muster when their watch was called; also in hoisting in beer and water, and in performing similar duties. In many cases, the punishment of starting resulted in bruises to the man's head and arms as well as to his back and shoulders.[90] As part of the effort to ameliorate the condition of seamen, the practice was abolished by an Admiralty directive in 1809.

Keelhauling

Among several extreme methods of punishment on the sea during Age of Sail, no punishment was so brutal and unforgiving as the practice of Keelhauling. Developed very early in the history of navy, this punishment, and execution method managed to survive and remained in use from 9th century BC, to mid 19th century. Its extreme consequences and the fear of its use while on sea managed to solidify its presence in popular culture long after keelhauling stopped being actually used. Keelhauling was also one of the most gruesome methods of in the age of piracy.

In keelhauling, accused sailor was stripped and tied so that he could not swim, with chains or cannonball being tied to his body (usually legs). He was fastened with two ropes; one from his back to the yard-arm (the widest point of the horizontal structure of the main mast), and other that went from sailor all the way under the ship to the other side of yard-arm. When sailor was dropped in the water the weight pulled him under the waves, but to prevent him going too much under, the crew (sometimes entire crew of the ship) would pull on the second rope, forcing the sailors to move under the ship and touching the hull, eventually raising him up on the other side

89 Dacam, John H., 'Wanton and Torturing Punishments': Patterns of Discipline and Punishment in the Royal Navy, 1783-1815, Unpublished Ph D Thesis, the University of Hull, September 2009, pp. p.102-103; Marshall Henry, 1846, *The Military Miscellany; Comprehending a History of the Recruiting of the Army, Military Punishments*, London, p. 371

90 One victim graphically described the punishment of starting in the following manner: It was on one occasion, that I received one of the blows across my shoulders, which sent the blood at once whizzing and boiling back upon my heart; for the blow seemed to fall through my bones into my breast, so ponderous was the stroke. I reeled, and became sick and faint; this gave him opportunity for repeating the blow, and it was too delicious a pleasure to be lost; my limbs bowed under me as if they were rushes, and I sank down on deck, senseless; and I felt, then, nothing of the kick with which he sent my body out of the way of those who were following, and I know not who, or how many, trampled on me. But I do remember that an hour after I recovered, there was a dismal drumming in my ears, my brain seemed compressed within hard bandages, and a hoop of iron was welded round my brow, and I stood in stupor gazing down towards the deck, trying to look at something which was not there. Dacam, John H., 'Wanton and Torturing Punishments': Patterns of Discipline and Punishment in the Royal Navy, 1783-1815, Unpublished Ph D Thesis, the University of Hull, September 2009, pp. 119-120.

of the ship.[91] The punishment was not focused only on the prospect of drowning (which was a real possibility) but more on the injuries the sailor received while hitting the bottom hull of the ship that was often overgrown with barnacles and other sea life. The cuts received from such close contact could not only cause severe injuries and blood loss, but also the loss of limbs and even in some cases decapitation. If the captain of the ship was not satisfied with the victim's injuries, the entire process was repeated. The Royal Navy adopted keelhauling in the 11th century. While the widespread use of keelhauling stopped in mid 19th century, isolated events of keelhauling persisted until the 20th century.

Ducking

This punishment used to be inflicted in the Royal Navy for uncleanness, blasphemy, or scandalous actions. The French Navy inflicted it on those who were convicted of desertion, or persons who were alleged to be seditious. The punishment was inflicted in the following manner: The delinquent was placed astride on a short thick batten, fastened to the end of a rope, which passed through a block hanging at one end of the yard-arm. This fixed, he was hoisted suddenly up to the yard, and the rope being slackened at once, he was allowed to fall into the sea. This chastisement was repeated several times, and by having double-headed shot fastened to his feet during the punishment, he would sink a considerable depth before he was hoisted up again.

Gagging

In the Royal Navy, as in the case of army, gagging was a punishment for answering back or to prevent insolent language during confinement for drunkenness or other misconduct. It was, in fact a form of torture in which a wooden or iron bolt was put across a man's open mouth and secured by tying behind his head.[92] It was introduced into the mouth, exactly in the way a bit

91 The speed of movement while underwater was often crucial in determining how much injury sailor will get. If the rope was pulled more slowly, weight on the sailor would cause him to go deeper and narrowly miss the barnacles on the hull. But if he was pulled faster, the sailor would remain in contact with the hull during entire underwater travel, causing incredible injuries. During times when underwater sections of the hull were not covered with sea life (if the ship was new or recently cleaned during repairs) or of the ship was too small, keelhauling was done from front to back of the ship. This prolonged the duration the sailor was held underwater. Victims of this grueling torture method were usually not brought back on the ship immediately, and instead were left hanging on the yard-arm as a warning to other sailors.

92 In the year 1815, Captain J.T. of His Majesty's sloop M....., was tried by a court-martial on charges of cruelty and oppression. The first charge stated, that "Thomas Payne, belonging to His Majesty's sloop M, had suffered a dislocation of the jaw, from the severe punishment of gagging, inflicted on him by direction of Captain J.T." The pieces of wood with which Payne was successively gagged were of fir, about six or seven inches long, and of the thickness of the finger or thumb. Payne bit through one or more pieces of wood successively; and when he had bitten through the third piece, he appeared to have hurt himself, and upon examination by the Surgeon, it was found that his jaw was completely dislocated. The dislocation was shortly after reduced; but next day, or the day after, the Surgeon discovered that the jaw was again in a state of dislocation, and his repeated attempts to reduce it were ineffectual. The distortion and disfigurement was disgusting and humiliating, conveying the impression of idiotism. However, the decision of the court was as follows: "The court is of opinion that the dislocation of Thomas Payne's jaw was occasioned by his own violence in biting the piece of wood through, and by a facility which he had of putting the jaw out and in himself, and not from the severe punishment of gagging." The prisoner, Captain J.T., was accordingly acquitted. Marshall Henry, 1846, *The Military Miscellany; Comprehending a History of the Recruiting of the Army, Military Punishments*, London, pp. 372-373.

is introduced into the mouth of a horse, so that a portion of it shall project from each side. The punishment of gagging was used in the East India Company's army, as a means of silencing talkative soldiers. It was used as a punishment for other offences as well, because it continued until at least 1867 when a George Addison, of the *Favourite*, was gagged for drunkenness and violence, and died within two hours.[93]

Amongst other corporal punishments, spread-eagle was inflicted on a man while he was in a state of inebriety. The 'spread-eagle' consisted of tying a man by his outstretched hands and feet to the rigging of the mizenmast. Ducking entailed putting a culprit on a small batten with his feet weighted down by shot and hoisting him rapidly up one of the yard arms only to drop him suddenly into the sea. In this state the delinquent remained until the officer of the watch directed him to be taken down. The wooden collar, as its name suggests, called for a delinquent to wear a cumbersome lumber yoke laden with approximately sixty pounds of cannonballs (weight was decided according to the nature of the crime or the pleasure of the Commanding Officer) for a few hours in a conspicuous part of the vessel. In the punishment of barrel pillory two large barrels were placed on the quarter-deck, in which the culprits were placed several hours during the day, wearing a cap (designated the fool's cap). In front of the cask was written the nature of the offence committed, and in this manner they were subjected to the gaze of the curious who visit the ship, as well as the ridicule of their comrades. The punishment of 'Carrying a Capstan Bar,' consisted in a man being obliged to carry a heavy beam of wood, and to walk fore and aft upon the weather gangway, for the period of a watch, or about four hours. The 'Black List' was composed of men who were guilty of venial offences, commonly some trivial neglect of duty, and were placed on the black list of the First Lieutenant. The black-listed delinquents, when their duty was over for the day, carried their hammocks on their shoulders up and down the quarter-deck, at every six feet placing a rope about three feet from the deck, and making who followed one another like sheep, step over each rope. The punishment caused physical exertion. In addition to these corporal punishments, the Royal Navy administered an array of nonphysical penalties; which included dismissal from the service, dishonourable discharge (drumming out of the fleet), penal deductions, reprimand and admonition.

The punishments authorized under the existing military justice system are more severe than those under the prevailing civil-criminal justice system. The basic jurisdiction for punishment is prescribed by the threes service Act as an integral part of each offence. With the maximum punishment prescribed by the section, the court martial has the discretionary power to apportion punishment according to the degree of guilt of the accused. Those convicted of offences in relation to the enemy, mutiny or desertion on active service could be awarded punishment of death or such less extreme punishment as is prescribed in the Act. All other offences are punishable either with imprisonment or cashiering or dismissal from service or lower punishment. The table of punishment includes death; life imprisonment; imprisonment, rigorous or simple, up to 14 years; cashiering (in case of officers); dismissal from service; reduction to the ranks; forfeiture of seniority or service; reprimand; and forfeiture or stoppage of pay and allowances.[94] The

93 Dacam, John H., 'Wanton and Torturing Punishments': Patterns of Discipline and Punishment in the Royal Navy, 1783-1815, Unpublished Ph D Thesis, the University of Hull, September 2009, p. 103.

94 Section 71, Army Act, 1950; Section 71, Air Force Act; and Section 81 the Navy Act 1957.

punishment awarded by court martial cannot be executed unless confirmed by the designated confirming authority. The punishment of death can be confirmed only by the Central Government. However, under the Navy Act, in the case of mutiny in times of war or on active service, the punishment of death can be executed without confirmation.[95]

95 Section 82(2), the Navy Act, 1957.

Epilogue

The British military justice system, conceived with the aim of 'disciplining' a mercenary force is the progenitor of the Indian military legal system. To preserve the continuity of the legal system, the Indian Independence Act, 1947 as passed by the British Parliament, provided that the existing laws of British India, including the services' laws, would continue to operate in the new country until superseded by subsequent legislation. The then existing military laws with respect to the army and the air force were replaced by the Army Act, 1950, and the Air Force Act, 1950, respectively. The Indian Navy Act was passed in 1957. These three systems differ on various counts as to the rights of a military accused. In essence, the existing military laws are replicas of the British-Indian Army Act of 1911.

In 1992/93 certain changes were made in the Army Act and the Rules, to keep the system in tune with the updated civilian criminal justice system. Similar changes were not made in the Air Force Act and the Navy Act for reasons best known to the Ministry of Defence. A few minor changes were made in the Navy Act in 2005. Under the Air Force Act, which is the most primitive, the commanding officer still retains the power to award field punishment, which is against human rights norms.

There is a perception amongst members of the civil society that in a trial by court martial, the convening officer exercises 'command influence' over the court members while seeking the desired findings and sentences. Trial by a summary court martial has come under heavy criticism by the Supreme Court recently and there is need to take a *de novo* look whether we still need this post-1857 system that empowered a British officer to deprive a native non-commissioned officer of livelihood and freedom. The procedure for a summary trial before the commanding officer is quite different from a trial in a magistrate's court. The accused is not entitled to legal representation, he does not plead to the charge, laws of evidence need not apply and the proceedings are not open to the public. Where a commanding officer, after hearing the case, considers that the accused is guilty, he may impose a penalty that involves imprisonment, loss of pay or promotions. There is no right of appeal against summary punishments. The proceedings may be reviewed by the superior authority, who are empowered to cancel, vary or remit an illegal, unjust or excessive punishment. The process of review, however, remains a closed-door exercise and the affected person has no right of hearing.

In 2009, the Armed Forces Tribunal was set up to reduce the hardships faced by the members of the armed forces. A large number of cases relating to the members of the armed forces were pending in the courts and there was no independent adjudicatory forum for hearing complaints of defence personnel relating to the service matters and appeals against the judgment of Court Martial. However, the Tribunal suffers from a few congenital defects in that it has no jurisdiction over certain service matters and cannot enforce its orders and decisions. Besides, the functioning of the tribunal and its benches have been criticized on various counts. The major one being that it is de facto subordinate to the Ministry of Defence, and lacks power of 'civil' contempt. By an amendment brought out in 2017, the government can appoint anyone *having special knowledge and professional experience of 20 years* as administrative member. How the presence of such a person, with no knowledge of service functioning and ethos would be beneficial has not been explained by the government. Currently, 195 out of the 593 posts of the Tribunal are vacant. These include Group A, B and C posts as well as Members. Retired high court judges do not find the appointment of 'judicial member' lucrative enough, so a number of courts of the Tribunal remain non-functional. As on 30 November 2018, a total number of 11,705 cases were pending with the Tribunal.[1] Incidentally, the Tribunal was created because the government was concerned over the pendency of nearly 9,430 cases involving military personnel in various high courts and the Supreme Court.

The government has recently announced the creation of the post of the Chief of Defence Staff. However, it has not made any reforms in the military justice system on the basis of the emerging human rights norms or the prevailing civilian criminal justice system. Many key elements of the Indian military justice system are controversial in a constitutional sense. The armed forces in India are being deprived of the benefit of world-wide developments in the fields of human rights, jurisprudence and judicial process. A rigorous, honest and informed review of the military justice system is the need of the hour. The system should be common to all the three services.

1 Armed Forces Tribunal, Ministry of Defence, posted on 02 January 2019, available at: http://pib.nic.in/PressReleseDetail.aspx?PRID=1558132.

Appendices

List of Appendices

Treaty between the Nabob Shujah-ul-Dowla, the Nabob Nudjum-ul-Dowla, and the English Company, executed at Illiabad—the 16th of August 1765.

(Sealed and approved by the King)

Whereas, the Right Honourable Robert, Lord Clive, Baron Clive of Plassey, Knight Companion of the Most Honourable Order of the Bath, Major General and Commander of the Forces, President of the Council, and Governor of Fort William, and of all the Settlements belonging to the United Company of Merchants of England trading to the east Indies, in the Provinces of Bengal , Behar, and Orissa; and John Carnac, Esq., Brigadier-General, Colonel in the service of the said Company, and Commanding Officer of their Forces upon the Bengal Establishment, are invested with full and ample powers on the behalf of the His Excellency the Nabob Nudjum-ul-Dowla, Soubahdar of Bengal, Behar, and Orissa, and likewise on the behalf of the United Company of Merchants of England trading to the East Indies, to negotiate, settle, and finally to conclude a form and lasting peace with His Highness the Nabob Shujah-ul-Dowla, Vizier and the Empire : Be it known to all those to whom it may or shall in any manner belong, that the above-named Plenipotentiaries have agreed upon the following Articles with His Highness:--

ARTICLE 1

A perpetual and universal peace, sincere friendship, and firm union shall be established between His Highness Shujah-ul-Dowla and his heirs, on the one part, and His Excellency Nudjum-ul-Dowla, and English East India Company on the other ; so that the said contracting powers shall give the greatest attention to maintain between themselves, their dominions, and their subjects this reciprocal friendship, without permitting, on either side, and kind of hostilities to be committed, from henceforth, for any cause, or under any pretence whatsoever, and everything shall be carefully avoided which might hereafter prejudice the union now happily established.

ARTICLE 2

In case the dominion of His Highness Shujah-ul-Dowla shall at any time be hereafter be attacked, His Excellency Nudjum-ul-Dowla and the English Company shall assist him with a part or the whole of their forces, according to the exigency of his affairs, and so far as may consistent with their own security : and if the dominion of His Excellency Nudjum-ul-Dowla or the English Company, shall be attacked, His Highness shall, in like manner, assist them with a part or the whole of his forces. In the case of the English Company's forces being employed in His Highness's service, the extraordinary expense of the same is to be defrayed by him.

ARTICLE 3

His Highness solemnly engages never to entertain or receive Cossim Ally Khan, the late Soubahdar of Bengal, &c, Sombre, the assassin of the English, nor any of the European deserters, within his dominions, nor to give the least countenance, support, or protection to them. He likewise solemnly engages to deliver up to the English whatever Europeans may be future desert from them into his country.

ARTICLE 4

The King Shah Aalum shall remain in full possession of Cora, and such part of the Province of Illiabad as he now possesses, which are ceded to His Majesty, as a royal demesne, for the support of his dignity and expenses.

ARTICLE 5

His Highness Shujah-ul-Dowla engages, in a most solemn manner, to continue Bulwant Sing in the zemindarries of Benares, Ghazepore, and all those districts he possessed at the time he came over to the late Nabob Jaffier Ally Khan and the English, on condition of his paying the same revenue as heretofore.

ARTICLE 6

In consideration of the great expense incurred by the English Company in carrying on the late war, His Highness agrees to pay them (50) fifty lakhs of rupees in the following manner; viz., (12) twelve lakhs in money, and a deposit of jewels of the amount of (8) eight lakhs, upon the signing of this Treaty; (5) five lakhs one month after, and the remaining (25) twenty-five lakhs by monthly payments, so as that the whole may be discharged in (13) thirteen months from the date hereof.

ARTICLE 7

It being firmly resolved to restore to His Highness the country of Benares, and the other districts now rented by Bulwant Sing, notwithstanding the grant of the same from the King to the English Company, it is therefore agreed that they shall be ceded to the His Highness in manner following, viz., they shall remain in the hands of the English Company, with their revenue, till the expiration of the Agreement between Bulwant Sing and the Company, being on the 27th of the November next ; after which His Highness shall enter into possession, the Fort of Chunar excepted, which is not to be evacuated, until the 6th Article of this Treaty shall be fully complied.

ARTICLE 8

His Highness shall allow the English Company to carry on a trade, duty free, throughout the whole of his dominions.

ARTICLE 9

All the relations and subjects of His Highness, who in any manner assisted the English during the course of the late war, shall be forgiven, and no ways molested for the same.

ARTICLE 10

As soon as this Treaty is executed, the English forces shall be withdrawn from the dominions of His Highness, excepting such as may be necessary for the garrison of Chunar, or for the defence and protection of King in the city of Illiabad, if His Majesty should require a force for that purpose.

ARTICLE 11

His Highness the Nabob Shujah-ul-Dowla, His Excellency the Nabob Nudjum-ul-Dowla, and the English Company promise to observe sincerely and strictly all the Articles contained and settled in the present Treaty; and they will not suffer the same to be infringed, directly or indirectly, by their respective subjects: and the said contracting powers, generally and reciprocally, guarantee to each other all the stipulations of the present treaty.

Signed, sealed, and solemnly sworn to, according to their respective faiths, by the contracting parties, at Illiabad, the 16th day of August, in the year of Our Lord 1765 in the presence of us.

EDMUND MASKELYNE, CLIVE
ARCHIBALD SWINTON, JOHN CARNAC
GOERGE VANSITTART,

SHUJAH-IL-DOWLA'S SEAL

and ratification

MIRZA KOSSIM KHAN

RAJA SHITABROY

MEER MUSHALA

Fort William, September 30th, 1765.

The Charter of King Richard I made in the first year of his reign AD 1189, and chiefly meant to prevent disputes between the soldiers and sailors, in their voyage to the Holy Land

Charter of King Richard I for the Government of those going by Sea to the Holy Land[1]

RICHARD, by the grace of God, king of England, duke of Normandy, and earl of, &c. &c. To all his men going by sea to Jerusalem, greeting. Know ye, that by the common council of all good men, we have made the underwritten ordonances. He who kills a man on shipboard, shall be bound to the dead man, and thrown into the sea: if the man is killed on shore, the slayer shall be bound to the dead body, and buried with it. Anyone convicted by lawful witnesses of having drawn his knife to strike another, or who shall have drawn blood of him, to lose his hand. If he shall have only struck with the palm of the hand, without drawing blood, he shall be thrice ducked in the sea. Anyone who shall reproach, abuse, or curse his companion, shall for every time he is convicted thereof, give him so many ounces of silver. Anyone convicted of theft, shall be shorn like a champion,[2] boiling pitch shall be poured on his head, and down of feathers shaken over it, that he may be known; and he shall be set on shore at the first land at which the ship touches,

Witness myself at Chinon.

The Ordonnances (Ordinances) of Richard II are the next in the chronological order, that I have been able to search.

These are the Statutes, Ordonnances and Customs to be observed in the Army, ordained and made by good consultation and deliberation of our most Excellent Lord the King Richard, John Duke of Lancaster, Seneschall of England, Thomas Earl of Essex, and Buckingham Constable of England, and Thomas de Mowbray Earl of Notingham, Mareschall of England, and other Lords, Earls, Barons, Bannereotts, and experienced knights, whom they have thought proper to call unto them; then being at Durham the 17th day of the Month of July, in the ninth year of the Reign of our Lord the King Richard II.[3]

I. FIRSTLY. That all manner of persons, of what nation, state or condition they may be, shall be obedient to our lord the king, to his constable and mareschall (Marshal), under penalty of everything they can forfeit in body and goods.

1 Grose Francis, 1788, *Military Antiquities Respecting A History of English Army: From The Conquest to the Present Time*, Vol. II, London: S. Hooper, p. 59.

2 Champions hired to fight legal duels, in cases of murther or homicide, had their hair clipt or shorn close to their heads.

3 Grose Francis, 1788, *Military Antiquities Respecting A History of English Army: From The Conquest to the Present Time*, Vol. II, London: S. Hooper, p. 59-65.

II. ITEM, that none be so hardy as to touch the body of our lord, nor the vessel in which it is contained, under pain of being drawn, hanged and beheaded.

III. ITEM, that none be so hardy as to rob and pillage the church, nor to destroy any man belonging to holy church, religious or otherwise, nor any woman, nor to take them prisoners, if not bearing arms; nor to force any woman, upon pain of being hanged.

IV. ITEM, that no one be so hardy to go before, or otherwise than in the battail (battle) to which he belongs, under the banner or pennon of his lord or master, except the herbergers, whose names shall be given in by their lords or masters to our constable and mareschall, upon pain of losing their horses.

V. ITEM, that no one take quarters, otherwise than by the assignment of the constable and mareschall and the herbergers; and that after the quarters are assigned and delivered, let no one be so hardy as to remove himself, or quit his quarters, on any account whatsoever, under pain of forfeiture of horse and armour, and his body to be in arrest, and at the king's will.

VI. ITEM, that everyone be obedient to his captain, and perform watch and ward, forrage, and all other things belonging to his duty, under penalty of losing his horse and armour, and his body being in arrest to the mareschall, till he shall have made his peace with his lord or master, according to the award of the court.

VII. ITEM, that no one be so hardy as to rob or pillage another of money, victuals, provisions, forage or any other thing, on pain of losing his head; nor shall any one take any victuals, merchandise, or any other thing whatsoever, brought for the refreshment of the army, under the same penalty; and any one who shall give the names of such robbers and pillagers to the constable and mareschall, shall have twenty nobles for his labour.

VIII. ITEM, no one shall make a riot or contention in the army for debate of arms, prisoners, lodgings, or any other thing what so ever, nor cause any party or assembly of persons, under pain (the principals as well as the parties) of losing their horses and armour, and having their bodies in arrest at the king's will, and if it a boy or page he shall lose his left ear. Any person conceiving himself aggrieved, shall make known his grievance to the constable, and mareschall, and right shall be done him.

IX. ITEM, that no one be so hardy as to make a contention or debate in the army on account of any grudge respecting time past or for anything to come, if in such contest or debate any one shall be slain, those who were the occasion shall be hanged; and if any one shall proclaim his own name, or that of his lord or master, so as to cause a rising of the people, whereby an affray might happen in the army, he who made the proclamation shall be drawn and hanged.

X. ITEM, that no one be so hardy as to cry "havoc" [4] under pain of losing his head, and that he or they that shall be the beginners of the said cry, shall likewise be beheaded, and their bodies after wards be hanged up by the arms.

4 Havok was the word given as a signal for the troops to disperse and pillage; and that on the word havok being cried, every one might seize his part. This probably was only a small part of the licence supposed to be given by that word.

XI. ITEM, that no one make the cry called mounte, [5] or any other whatsoever in the army, on account of the great danger that may thereby happen to the whole army; which God forbid! And that on pain, if he be a man at arms, or archer on horseback, of losing his best horse, and if he be an archer on foot or boy, he shall have his left ear cut off.

XII. ITEM, if in any engagement whatsoever an enemy shall be beat down to the earth, and he who shall have thus thrown him down shall go forwards in the pursuit, and any other shall come afterwards, and shall take the faith or parole of the said enemy, he shall have half of the said prisoner, and he who overthrew him the other half, but he who received his parole shall have the keeping of him, giving security to his partner.

XIII. ITEM, if any one takes a prisoner, and another shall join him, demanding a part, threatening that otherwise he will kill him (the prisoner) he shall have no part, although a share be granted to him; and if he kills the said prisoner, he shall be in arrest to the mareschall, without being delivered till he has satisfied the party, and his horses and armour shall be forfeited to the constable.

XIV. ITEM, that no man go out on an expedition by night or by day, unless with the knowledge and by the permission of the chieftain of the battail in which he is, so that they may be able to succour him, should occasion require it, on pain of losing horse and a armour.

XV. ITEM, that for no news or affray whatsoever, that may happen in the army, any one shall put himself in disarray in his battail, whether on an excursion or in quarters, unless by assignment of his chieftain, under pain of losing horse and armour.

XVI. ITEM, that every one pay to his lord or master, the third of all manner of gains of arms, herein are included those who do not receive pay, but only have the benefit of quarters, under the banner or pennon of arms of a captain.

XVII. ITEM, that no one be so hardy as to raise a banner or penon of St. George or any other, to draw together the people out of the army, to go to any place whatsoever, under pain, that those who thus make themselves captains shall be drawn and hanged, and those who follow them be beheaded, and all their goods and heritages forfeited to the king.

XVIII. ITEM, that every man, of what estate, condition or nation he may be, so that he be of our party, shall bear a large sign of the arms of St. George before, and another behind, upon peril that if he be hurt or slain in default thereof, he who shall hurt or slay him shall suffer no penalty for it: and that no enemy shall bear the said sign of St. George, unless he be a prisoner, upon pain of death.

XIX. ITEM, if any one shall take a prisoner, as soon as he comes to the army, he shall bring him to his captain or master, on pain of losing his part to his said captain or master; and that his said captain or master shall bring him to our lord the king, constable or mareschall as soon as he well can, without taking him elsewhere, in order that they may examine him concerning news and intelligence of the enemy, under pain of losing his third to him who may first make it known to

5 Mounte, i. e. montez, to horse; probably this was either a mutinous cry, calling on the cavalry to take horse and leave the army, or might be the method of calling to arms from a supposed approach of the enemy, and was what would now be called, raising a false alarm.

the constable or mareschall; and that every one shall guard, or cause to be guarded by his soldiers, his said prisoner, that he may not ride about at large in the army, nor shall suffer him to be at large in his quarters, without having a guard over him, lest he espy the secrets of the army, under pain of losing his said prisoner; reserving to his said lord the third of the whole, if there is not a partner in the offence; and the second part to him that shall first take him; and the third part to the constable. On the like pain, and also of his body being in arrest, and at the king's will, he shall not suffer his said prisoner to go out of the army for his ransome, nor for any other cause, without leave of the king, constable and mareschall, or the commander of the battle in which he is.

XX. ITEM, that every one shall well and duly perform his watch in the army, and with the number of men at arms and archers as is assigned him, and that he shall remain the full limited term, unless by the order or permission of him before whom the watch is made, on pain of having his head cut off.

XXI. ITEM, that no one shall give passports or safe conduit to a prisoner nor any other, nor leave to any enemy to come into the army, on pain of forfeiture of all his goods to the king, and his body in arrest and at his will; except our lord the King, Monsieur de Lancaster, seneschall, the constable and marshall: and that none be so hardy as to violate the safe conduit of our lord the king, up on payne of being drawn and hanged, and his goods and heritage forfeited to the king; nor to infringe the safe-conducts of our aid lord of Lancaster, seneschall, constable and mareschall, upon pain of being beheaded.

XXII. ITEM, if any one takes a prisoner, he shall take his faith, and also his bacinet, or gauntlet, to be a pledge and in sign that he is so taken, or he shall leave him under the guard of some of his soldiers, under pain, that if he takes him, and does not do as is here directed, and another comes afterwards, and takes him from him (if not under a guard) as is said, his bacinet or right gauntelet in pledge, he shall have the prisoner, though the first had taken his faith.

XXIII. ITEM, that no one be so hardy to retain the servant of another, who has covenanted for the expedition, whether soldier, man at arms, archer, page or boy, after he shall have been challenged by his master, under pain that his body shall be in arrest till he shall have made satisfaction to the party complaining, by award of the court, and his horses and armour forfeited to the constable.

XXIV. ITEM, that no one be so hardy to go for forage before the lords or others, whosoever they may be, who mark out or assign the places for the foragers, if it is a man at arms, he shall lose his horses and harness to the constable, and his body shall be arrested by the marischal, and if it is a valet or boy, he shall have his left ear cut off.

XXV. That none be so hardy as to quarter himself otherwise than by the assignment of the herbergers, who are authorised to distribute quarters, under like penalty.

XXVI. ITEM that every lord whatsoever cause to be delivered to the constable and marischal, the names of their herbergers, under penalty, that if any one goes forward and takes quarters, and his name is not delivered in to the constable and mareschall, he shall lose his horses and armour.

The Statutes of Henry V in time of War, 1421[1]

The clemency of the great Creator disposes those under him to be modest, peaceable and chaste; nevertheless because unbridled avarice, the enemy of peace, daily generates so many new causes for disturbance and litigation, that unless its efforts are repressed by the force of justice, and the sense and intricacy of its questions resolved, all Christian rules for our army would be destroyed, and that common good for which we live and reign, extinguished.

Therefore law and constitutions are ordained, that noxious appetites may be confined under the rule of justice, by which mankind are informed how to live honestly, without injuring each other, rendering to every one their right. And that our army, as well in peace as war, may be led in the proper path, and the said common good preserved entire; and also on the other part that the constable and mareschal of our said army may judge and determine the more prudently in the causes daily brought before them. We have with the advice of our peers, lords and nobles, made certain constitutions, promulgating the same in our army, by public proclamation, enacting that all and every one of the captains in our said army shall have these our said constitutions in writing, that our publication may be considered as a sufficient warning, and that all those concerned may not pretend ignorance of the said constitutions.

Of Churches, and Preserving the Sacrament of the Eucharist in its proper State

AND because holiness becomes the house of God, we have ordained, that the church shall universally be maintained in its state, and if any one shall be found to have presumed, without the approbation of the constable of our army, to take away, or remove any goods of the church, such as vestments, chalices, books, trinkets or relicks, found in any churches, chapels or monasteries, he shall on his apprehension and conviction before the constable or marischal of our army, be hanged, and the said goods, as soon as possible, be restored to the churches from whence they were taken: we moreover ordain, that no one, under pain of death, shall dare irreverently to touch the sacrament of the Eucharist, nor the pyx or box in which the said sacrament is contained.

The Persons of Ecclesiastics and Women not to be seized

PRIESTS daily serving God and ministering to him at the altar, shall always enjoy their privileges, any one laying violent hands on the said priests, or slaying them, shall be capitally punished; which punishment, it is our will, shall be extended to ravishers of women, wheresoever they are found; further directing that no one have the temerity to touch any religious men, or veiled or religious women whatsoever, they wearing, without fraud, the habit of their order, nor shall any

1 Grose Francis, 1788, *Military Antiquities Respecting A History of English Army: From The Conquest to the Present Time*, Vol. II, London: S. Hooper, p. 66-85.

one dare to make them prisoners, they not appearing in arms, nor openly nor privately making war, under penalty of imprisonment, their body there to remain during our will.

What Persons all are bound to obey

MOREOVER, we ordain, that all persons remaining with our army, of what state, dignity, nation, order or condition soever, shall in all things lawful and honest, obey our constable and mareschal, as ourselves, under penalty of forfeiture of body and goods. Also we direct, that soldiers, and other persons receiving wages from us, or our kingdom, shall be obedient to their immediate captain or masters, in all things legal and honest, keeping watch and ward imposed on the said soldiers, or reasonably to be imposed. Nor shall they quit the said watch or ward in any manner, without the especial licence of their said captains or master, under pain of arrest of body and goods, until, according to the discretion and disposition of our mareschal, the first captain or master shall be fully satisfied. Also, if a scarcity of victuals, or dearth of forage should happen, and it shall be judged necessary by the captains to send to the neighbouring villages for the said victuals and forage, we direct all soldiers, according to the order of their captains or masters, humbly to be ready to go, either on horseback or on foot, for the said victuals; any one disobeying this order shall incur the penalties mentioned in the preceding statute.

Also merchants, either travelling with the army, or buying and selling in our markets, shall obey our constable and mareschal, and even the clerk of the market, as ourselves. Also all contracts, crimes and suits shall be heard and finally determined in our court, by the judgement of our constable and mareschal; or, in the absence of our constable, in the presence of our mareschal, if one or both of contractors, delinquents or suitors, are belonging to our army, whether soldiers or merchants, or handycrafts, such as shoemakers, taylors, barbers, physicians or washer-women, and also our scouts especially appointed.

Of observing Watches and Guards

WHEREAS disturbances frequently happen in our army, as well by day as night, which by daily and diligent watches and proper guards are prevented; wherefore we ordain, that our mareschal shall appoint a daily guard, portioned to the number of armed men, of which our army shall consist; and every captain shall in turn assist in performing the said watches and guards. Nor shall any captain, either of horse or foot, being as is premised, duly warned and ordered for guard, dare to be deficient in the number of men of arms or archers, or to quit the said guard or watch in any manner, till the limited time, without the special licence of him by whom the said guard was appointed, under pain of decapitation. We moreover ordain, that all our captains of our army shall keep a sufficient watch in their quarters, as well by night as day, whether on an expedition, or besieging castles, forts or towns, under penalty of arrest of their bodies, to be severely punished at our will.

Of Public Musters

AND that the said watch may be always duly preserved without fraud, it is our will that every captain of our army, without any fraud or reserve whatsoever, shall make a muster or shew of all his soldiers, as well men of arms as archers, fully and perfectly, according to his assigned number, before us or our commissaries, as often as the said captain shall by us, or our commissaries be duly and legally thereunto required; also, that the captains shall shew only their own soldiers, with whom they have agreed for the expedition, and no others, under pain of perpetual reprobation, and the loss of their wages for the said expedition. We also prohibit any one from retaining in his service any soldier, servant or boy, who was lately in the service of another, without the consent and permission of his prior captain or master: we moreover direct and command, that all our commissaries in the aforesaid musters do diligently enquire after, and see that the soldiers shew their proper arms, without fraud; and this we also would have more especially observed respecting the bows and arrows; and, if necessary, it is our will, that respecting this our commissaries may compel the captain or master to answer upon oath.

Of Disturbances and Public Cries

MOREOVER, it is our will, that no one, of what condition, nation, degree or dignity soever, shall dare to make any clamour or disturbance, by which we or our army may any ways be disturbed, and especially that clamour we call "mountee;" or that any person or persons shall in future dare to make any other irrational clamour, under pain that the beginner shall be arrested, and with his horse or horses put in custody of the constable or mareschal, to be punished without favour, until he shall have duly satisfied the said constable and mareschal for his offence; and the discoverer, informer, or accuser of the said beginner, shall receive an hundred shillings of Tours, to wit, ten shillings of English money for his labour, from the said constable or mareschal.

ALSO if any one shall proclaim his own name, or that of his lord or master, by which proclamation a gathering or assembly of the people shall be made to the disturbance of the army, any one so offending, and convicted thereof before the constable or mareschal shall be publickly hanged; also if any one shall be found to have in any manner begun the clamour called "havock," without our especial licence, he shall be punished with death, and his followers with arrest of body and goods, and to be diligently kept in the custody of the constable and mareschal, till they have fined with them for the offence.

ALSO, if any alarm or clamour of a coming enemy should suddenly arise in our army, we direct and command, that every captain with his men shall immediately repair to our person, or that of our principal captain, leaving certain persons appointed by the said captains, for the safe keeping of the quarters, those captains only excepted, near whose quarters the said disturbance or alarm has arisen, whom we command to remain with their companies to defend their quarters, which we would have fully to be observed in our absence for this voyage, in the person of every principal captain whatsoever; and also when we ride out on an expedition, we expressly prohibit any one whatsoever, to dare to leave our army without our especial licence, whereby disturbances or clamors might arise in our said army, under pain of forfeiture of goods to be put in custody of the constable or mareschal, and arrest of body at our will and favour, and in our absence, at the will of the principal captain of the army by us ordained.

Of General Equitations

No one in our army shall dare to cause any assembly or meeting by any means for the purpose of equitating from our said army, to any neighbouring country, town or fortress, without our especial leave, or that of the principal captain of our army, for succour, under pain of arrest of body and goods during our will.

ALSO, if it should happen that any such general equitation should be made by our especial licence, we then ordain and will, that no one shall dare to recede from the company and society of the captain of the said equitation, without the especial licence of the said captain, under pain of arrest at our will, and loss of booty by him so acquired that day, nevertheless the third part of the said booty to be reserved entire to his immediate master, and two other parts of the said booty being likewise reserved out of the said booty, for the captain of the said equitation. This our statute we direct shall at all times be inviolably observed by all men, as often as such equitation shall be made. We also prohibit any one to dare to erect our standard, that of any lords, or of Saint George, in order to call together any part of our army, to equitate or cross over to any country, town or fortress whatsoever, without our especial licence, on pain of hanging and drawing for the captains so presuming, and beheading for every one of their followers, with forfeiture of hereditaments and goods.

WE also ordain, that no captain, of what condition, state or dignity soever, shall make equitations, or dare to grant leave to others so to do, without our special licence, under pain of our perpetual indignation, and arrest of body, to be severely punished at our will.

ALSO, if we shall have assigned an equitation to be made by any particular persons, we expressly prohibit, under pain of death, any one to dare to burn any building, house or houses, or to put fire to them, without our especial mandate.

Of taking and assigning Quarters

WE moreover direct, that no one shall go before our army in any manner, our own quarter-master and those of other lords or captains excepted, whose names have first been delivered in to the constable or mareschal, and by him declared in writing, under pain of arrest of body and goods, to be put into the custody of our constable or marshal, until the said delinquent has fined sufficiently for his offence to the said constable or mareschal.

ALSO, that no person of what state, dignity soever, shall presume to quarter himself, it being our will that, in all matters respecting quarters, all persons should obey our quarter master general as our selves, under pain of arrest of body and goods; we also direct under the aforesaid penalties, that no one having his quarters assigned him as above directed, shall quit the said quarters without the special licence of his captain or master.

Also should it happen that any one should find any victuals, either in or about his quarters, it is our will that the said finder should decently enjoy the said victuals, by using it moderately, and if any should remain, he should bestow the same on others standing in need thereof, without any abuse or destruction whatsoever, under pain of arrest of body and forfeiture of his horses, or horse if he shall have only one, and also of his arms, untill he shall have fined sufficiently to the constable or mareschal.

WE also prohibit any one, of what state, condition or dignity he may be, to presume to dispute about his quarters, or those of his followers, or to dare to make any combination or assembly of his people, in order to cause any dispute within his quarters, or those of any other person, under pain of arrest of body during our pleasure, and of his horses and arms, untill he shall have fined to the constable and mareschal for his offence; and if the delinquent shall be a boy or youth, he shall be punished by the cutting off his left ear; and if the offence shall be greater, the offender shall be more severely punished at the discretion of the constable and mareschal.

We moreover prohibit any one either within or out of his quarters, to begin any disturbance with any person, on account of any injury, grudge, or quarrel, past or future, by which dispute, the death of either party may be caused or happen, under penalty of forfeiture of body and goods; and if death should really ensue, all so offending shall be hanged.

Of Prisoners

BECAUSE in battles and other warlike actions, prisoners are frequently taken, and through fear of the enemy rallying, the captor cannot sometimes attend to the care of his prisoner; we have thought it proper to lay down a certain rule in writing, whereby we declare, that he to whom the prisoner has surrendered, shall have the said prisoner, although he shall not have been able to superintend the custody of the said prisoner to the end of the conflict, provided the said prisoner shall not afterwards be found defending himself in the same engagement: also, if any one shall beat down his enemy to the ground, and another shall take his surrender, the prisoner so taken, shall be the joint-property of both, and the person to whom he surrendered shall have the keeping of the said prisoner, giving sufficient security to his partner, for his part of the ransom of the before-named prisoner; also, when a prisoner is taken, and another person coming up and demanding a part, a part shall be granted to him, with the consent of the captor; but if by chance the party demanding a share, shall threaten he will otherwise kill the prisoner, he shall have no part in the said prisoner, although a part should have before been granted him; and if he should actually kill the aforesaid prisoner, he shall be arrested by the constable and mareschal, and remain in prison till he shall have fined to the party aggrieved at the discretion of our constable and mareschal of our army.

WE also direct, that as soon as a prisoner is taken, the taker of the said prisoner shall bring him to our army, and present him without delay to his captain or master, under penalty of losing the said prisoner, to be adjudged to his immediate master; and if the prisoner so taken shall be his superior in one part of the army, and shall have from his sovereign permission to display his standard; or if the prisoner shall be of the blood royal, a duke, a marquis, earl, or chief captain, then the said captive, he be whom he may, shall be the prisoner of the chief captain of that part of our said army, unless the taker of such prisoner shall be his equal, or superior in arms or dignity, or such baron or notable soldier, who shall have before displayed his banner; the chief captain in that case, shall agree with the taker, giving him a sufficient reward for the captive.

WE also will, that the captain or master, receiving a prisoner from his lanceman or archer as is aforesaid, shall within eight days, faithfully present him to us, our principal captain or constable, or the mareschal of our army, under penalty of lofing such part of the said prisoner, he would otherwise have been entitled to, which part we give to anyone notifying to us, the constable or mareschal of our army, the secreting of such prisoner; we farther ordain, that no one shall presume to suffer their prisoner to straggle about, or go at large, or ride about at his liberty, or to remain unguarded in his quarters, under penalty of the loss of the said prisoner; but one third part of the ransom of the prisoner so negligently guarded, to be reserved to the captain or master of the captor, provided the said captain or master shall not be chargeable with any part of the said neglect; the other part of the aforesaid ransom we adjudge to the accuser: we also assign to the constable and mareschal of our army, the third part of the said ransom, as also the body of the delinquent in arrest, as has been before said, to be severely punished at our mercy.

WE also will and ordain, that no one shall suffer his prisoner to leave our army without our safe conduct, or that of the commander of our army, first obtained for the said prisoner, under the penalties of the last statute: we also ordain, that no one shall dare to sell his prisoner, or to take ransom for him, without the licence of his captain, indented with us, under hand and seal for the expedition, under penalty of losing such prisoner, to be adjudged to the said captain, and arrest of the person so offending: we moreover will, that the purchasers shall be punished with the loss of their prisoners so purchased.

Of Thirds

THE soldiers of every captain, all armed shield-bearers and archers whatsoever, are bound to pay to their captain, or immediate master, without fraud, of what state or condition, or dignity soever, one third part of their acquisitions made by war, under penalty of losing the whole of the principal sum so gotten, and arrest of body, until he shall fined with his aforesaid master.

IT is also our pleasure, that all persons with us in our army, whether serving under our standard, or following the army, although they do not receive wages from us or our kingdom, such as physicians, merchants, barbers, and many like, shall be bound to pay to us, or the principal captain of our army, one third of the goods obtained by them in the war, such as prisoners, and other moveables acquired in like manner.

Against Plundering

We farther ordain, that none under pain of death, shall dare to rob or spoil any merchant or merchants, or presume to take away from them, any goods, especially victuals; the same we direct to be observed towards physicians and barbers; nor shall any soldier dare to spoil any provisions or forage whatsoever bought by them, or acquired by any just manner, under pain of death ; and we prohibit any soldier, or other, of what state or degree whatsoever, to presume to steal, spoil, or carry away from another, any goods, that he by his just labours may have acquired from the enemy ; such as victuals, hay, straw, oats, wheat, wine, oil or the like, under pain of arrest of the body of the delinquent, to be punished at our will.

Of Assaults

WE also ordain, that no assault shall be made against any castle or fortress whatsoever, by archers, or other common soldiers, without the presence of some captain especially appointed to the same, under pain of imprisonment; and in fact, if any such premised as fault is made, and a publick prohibitory proclamation has been issued by us, or the principal captain, or constable, or mareschal of our army, those disobeying shall be punished with imprisonment, and loss of goods there acquired.

Of safe Conduct

NOR shall any of our inferior captains, the general of our army only excepted, presume to give licence to any enemy or prisoners to come into our army, or pass through, or leave it, without our special licence, and with our safe conduct, or that of the constable of our army, if his commission extend so far, under pain of forfeiture of body and goods: we also prohibit any one, of what state, degree, condition, or dignity soever, to presume to give or grant safe conduct to any one by his own authority, either under his proper seal or that of another, our constable only excepted, if he has received such powers from us: also that none dare to break, or violate in any manner, any safe conduct granted by us or our constable as aforesaid, under pain of hanging and drawing, and confiscation of hereditaments and goods.

Of turning out the common Whores

MOREOVER we order that publick and common whores, are by no means permitted to remain with the army, and especially during the sieges of towns, castles, or fortresses of any sort, but that they shall be stationed together afar off from the army, at the distance of a league at least, which we will also have observed in all cities, castles, and fortresses, taken by us or our forces, or yielded to us or our forces, or hereafter to be taken or yielded to us, or others in our name, to wit, that no one shall remain in the said castle or fortress, or shall maintain house whether small or great, under pain of fracture of the left arm of the said whore, if after one admonition she be found publickly or privately in the said prohibited place.

THE orders of King Henry V to the captain of Rouen, or his lieutenant, exhibit a specimen of the garrison regulations of that king; they are printed in Rymer; similar orders were at the same time issued to thirty-six other captains.

The king to the captain of Rouen or his lieutenant greeting: Whereas many captains of town and fortresses, and their lieutenants in the dutchy of Normandy, usurp greater powers than the king has invested them with, or than is proper, oppressing and plundering his subjects, both of money and provisions, and committing divers enormities and excesses, and permitting the same to their soldiers, stipendiaries and servants; wherefore, the following articles are laid down, specifying in what manner they are to regulate themselves, under the penalties therein named, or others at his pleasure.

ALL soldiers and stipendiaries to obey the captain, and to attend to every thing that may conduce to the safety of the garrison; and the said captain and his officers minutely to attend, both day and night, the gates, sally-ports, ditches, walls, and watches of the said place; and to punish all delinquents respecting these or other transgressions, abstaining from all exactions under pretence of neglect of the night-watches, or any other colour.

THE captain to have the determination of all disputes between the garrison, respecting booty arising from excursions made by the said garrison.

THAT both the captain and his soldiers, &c. be in all things humbly obedient and assisting to the king's lieutenant for Normandy, chancellor, treasurer, seneschall, bailiff, &c. and other his officers, assisting him with their arms, if duly required.

NO impositions, exactions, &c. to be made by himself or his soldiers, or the inhabitants of any town, village, parish, &c. either in taking grain or cattle, as they will answer to the said, king and his subjects.

ITEM; because some of the soldiers of the king's garrisons and their followers, and servants, neither fearing God, nor reverencing men, keep, as the king is informed, women in concubinage, and what is worse, in adultery, or other unlawful connections, and not having means of obtaining their voluptuous allurements, (which require and demand an immoderate expence) they rob and plunder his faithful subjects, thereby provoking the divine wrath, and causing great danger and prejudice to the government and subjects:

HE therefore directs, that no soldier, stipendiary, &c. be permitted to keep a woman in concubinage, nor to have any prohibited or illicit connexion with one; and if anyone is found offending in these matters, all favor being set aside, he be imprisoned for a month at least, or longer, according to the nature of his offence; for which month, or other time of imprisonment, he shall lose his wages, nor be released from prison, until he shall have given reasonable security, under a penalty by the said captain to be fixed, that he shall live and converse well and honestly for the future.

AND to the end, that neither captain, soldier, nor stipendiary, may in future plead ignorance of these matters, the king has sent certain inclosed articles, which according to their tenor and form, he would have observed, and besides, ordered to be publickly proclaimed; further directing and commanding, under pain of his indignation, that his captains and lieutenants to whom it is directed, do attend to the premises, and that they do not by any means, usurp or encroach on the ordinary jurisdiction belonging to his bayliffs and other justices.

Signed: given at our castle of Rouen, 25th day of April, 1421.

In the next month, the following commission of enquiry was issued by the king to Sir John Radcliff, Knight, giving him power and authority to enter and visit, all and every of his towns, castles and fortresses, by which he should happen to pass, and diligently to enquire, or to use other ways and means whereby he might know, or be more fully informed, of the discipline and government of the captains, lieutenants, governors, constables, mareschals, porters, and others officers and soldiers, for, and relative to, the safe keeping and wholesome government of the towns, fortresses, &c. assigned to them.

ALSO, to learn in what manner the said captains, governors, constables, officers, and soldiers behave to all, as well towards the king in the careful keeping and good government of these places, as to the people thereof, and the king's other liege subjects of the parts adjacent.

AND particularly to enquire respecting extortions, pillagings, robberies, impositions, appaticisements,[2] and other undue actions, by them as it is said, done, and perpetrated; and whether the said captains, &c. &c. have done, or attempted anything, contrary to the king's admonitions, prohibitions, ordonnances, and mandates, so repeatedly directed to them; and also, many times proclaimed by the bailiffs.

And what jurisdiction or authority in criminal cases; and also in transgressions by their soldiers or others, they have exercised contrary to our ordonnances, or more than they are legally entitled to do; and all things respecting the king's advantage and honour, for the preservation of these places; or concerning the king's liege subjects in any manner.

ALSO, of all attempts offered and improperly perpetrated, and the steps taken for amending, correcting, and reforming such abuses, or causing emendations, &c. to be made therein, punishing and imprisoning the attemptors, delinquents, and those who shall disobey and neglect these ordonnances, edicts, &c. of what state and condition soever, without favor, as the cause shall require, or as directed in the said ordonnances.

ALL things necessary respecting these orders to be attended to, although they should require a more especial mandate, to which all are commanded to be attentive ; and all and every of the king's captains, and other liege subjects, whom these presents may concern, are directed to obey the said mandate, and assist if necessary in the execution thereof.

Dated at the castle of Rouen, 5 May 1421.

2 Appaticisements: contributions, or money paid by the enemy, in compensation for their towns being protected from the ravages of war.

The Laws and Ordinances of Warre of the Earl of Essex 1643[1]

The laws and ordinances of warre established by the Earl of Northumberland for the army of King Charles I, AD 1640 is the next authentic military code available today. This was shortly after followed, namely, in 1643, by that of the Earl of Essex for the government of the parliamentary forces,[2] in most articles they are literally the same, and as the articles and ordinances of war for the Scots army of the same year, though not immediately pertaining to my subject, serve to elucidate the military history of those times.

LAWES and ordonnances of warre established for the better conduct of the service in the Northern parts, by his excellence the earl of Northumberland, Lord General of his Majestie's armie and fleete.

ALGERNOUN, earl of Northumberland, lord of the honors of Cockermouth and Petworth, Lord Percy, Lucie, Poynyngs, Fitz pain; Brian, and Latimer, lord high admirall of England, knight of the most noble order of the garter, one of his majestie's most honourable privie councell, and captain generall of his majestie's armie and fleete employed in this present expedition.

TO all officers of the armie, colonels, lieutenant colonels, serjeant majors, captains, other officers and souldiers of horse and foot; and all his majestie's subjects and others whom these laws and ordinances ensuing shall concern ; which laws and ordinances hereby published, all the said persons respectively and severally are required and commanded to swear unto, and observe and keep, on the pains and penalties therein expressed.

OF DUTIES TO GOD

I. Blasphemy

FIRST, let no man presume to blaspheme the holy and blessed Trinitie, God the Father, God the Son, and God the Holy Ghost, nor the known articles of Christian faith, upon pain to have his tongue boared with a red hot iron.

1 Grose Francis, 1788, *Military Antiquities Respecting A History of English Army: From The Conquest to the Present Time*, Vol. II, London: S. Hooper, p. 106-127.

2 ENTITLED, "Laws and Ordinances of Warre established for the better conduct of the armie by his excellency the earl of Essex, lord general of the forces raised by the authoritie of the parliament for the defence of king and kingdom, and now enlarged by command of his excellency, and printed by his authoritie, London, for Luke Fawne 1643.

II. Cursing

UNLAWFUL oaths and execrations and scandalous acts in derogation of God's honour, shall be punished with losse of pay and other punishments at discretion.

III. Profaning of Churches

IN the same manner shall be punished, all those who abuse and profane places and utensils dedicated to God's public worship, or wrong his ministers. (d)

IV. Neglecting Divine Service

ALL those who often and wilfully absent themselves from sermons, and morning and evening prayer, shall be proceeded against at discretion: and all such who shall violate places of publike worship, shall undergo severe censure.

OF DUTIES TO KING AND STATE

I. Traiterous Words

NO man shall use any traiterous words against his majesty's sacred person, or royall authority, upon paine of death.

II. Intelligence with the Enemy

ALL such as shall practise and entertain intelligence with the enemy, by any manner of means or slights, or have any communication with them, without direction from my lord generall, shall be punished as traitours and rebels.

III. Relief of the Enemy

NO man shall relieve the enemy with money, victuall, ammunition; neither harbour, or receive any such, upon pain of death.

IV. Yielding up of Forts

WHOSOEVER yieldeth up any town, fort, magazine, victuals, armes, ammunition, or that motioneth any such thing, but upon extremity, and that to the governor, or in councell, shall be executed as a traitor.

V. Careless Service

WHOSOEVER shall be convicted to do his majesty's service negligently and carelessly shall be punished at discretion.

VI. Violating of Safeguard

WHOSOEVER shall presume to violate his majesty's saveguard, shall die without mercy.

OF DUTIES TOWARDS SUPERIORS AND COMMANDERS

I. Violating of the Lord General

WHOSOEVER shall use any words tending to the life or dishonour of the lord generall, shall be punished with death.

II. Quarrelling with Officers

NO man shall presume to quarrel with his superior officer, upon pain of cassering (discharging with infamy or cashiering) and arbitrary punishment, nor to strike any such, upon pain of death.

III. Departing from Captains and Masters

No souldier shall depart from his captain, nor servant from his master, without licence, though he serve still in the army, upon payne of death.

IV. Silence in the Army

EVERY private man and souldier, upon pain of imprisonment, shall keep silence when the army is to take lodging, or when it is marching or embattayling, so as the officers may be heard, and their commandments executed.

V. Resisting against Correction

NO man shall resist, draw, lift, or offer to draw or lift, his weapon against an officer correcting him orderly for his offence, upon pain of death.

VI. Unlawful Assemblies

NO persons shall make any unlawfull assembly, or be present, or assisting thereunto, or in or by them demand their pay, upon pain of death.

VII. Resisting of the Provost Marshall

NO man shall resist the provost marshall, or any other officer, in the execution of his office, or break prison, upon pain of death.

VIII. Seditious Words

NONE shall utter any words tending to sedition and uprore, or mutinie, upon paine of death.

IX. Concealing of mutinous Speeches

THE same punishment shall be inflicted upon them, who after they have heard mutinous speeches, acquaint not their commanders with them.

X. Revenging of Injuries

WHOSOEVER shall receive an injurie, and shall take his own satisfaction, shall be punished by imprisonment, and as it shall be thought fit by the marshall court: but he that is injured shall be bound, if he do not forgive the injury, to seek reparation by complaint to his captain or colonell, or other superior officer, and it shall be given him in ample manner.

OF DUTIES MORALL

I. Drunkenness

DRUNKENNESSE in an officer shall be punished with losse of place. In a common souldier, with such penalties as a court marshal shall think fit.

II. Unnatural Abuses

RAPES, ravishments, unnaturall abuses, shall be punished with death.

III. Adultery

ADULTERY, fornication, and dissolute lasciviousnesse, shall be punished at discretion, according to the quality of the offence.

IV. Theft

THEFT and robbery, exceeding the value of 12d, shall be punished with death.

V. Provocation

NOE man shall use reproachfull or provoking words or acts to any, upon pain of imprisonment, and such further punishment as shall be thought fit to be inflicted upon enemies of discipline and service.

VI. Seizing on dead Men's Goods

NO man shall take or spoile the goods of him that dieth or is killed in service, upon pain of restoring double the value, and arbitrarie punishment.

VII. Murther

MURDER shall be expiated with the death of the murtherer.

OF A SOULDIER'S DUTY TOUCHING HIS ARMES

I. Full Armour

ALL souldiers coming to their colours, to watch, or to be exercised, shall come fully armed, upon pain of severe correction.

II. Slovenly Armour

NONE shall presume to appear with their armes un-fix or undecently kept, upon paine of arbitrarie correction.

III. Loosing of Horses or Armes

IF a trooper shall loose his horse or hackney; or a footman any part of his armes by negligence or lewdnesse, by dice or cards; he or they shall remaine in qualitie of pioners and scavengers, till they be furnished with as good as were lost, at their own charge.

IV. Pawning of Armes

NO town or countreyman shall presume to buy or take to pawn, an horse, or armes, or furniture of tents and hutts, of any souldier, upon pain of forfeiting the double value thereof, and to be punished at discretion: and the souldier giving them to pawn shall suffer a severe punishment.[3]

V. Wilful Spoiling of Horses

IF a trooper shall spoile his horse willingly, of purpose to be rid of the service, he shall lose his horse, and remain in the camp for a pioner.

VI. Borrowed Arms

IF one borrows arms of another to pass the muster withall: the borrower shall be rigorously punished, and the lender shall forfeit his goods.

VII. Imbezeling of Ammunition

NONE shall presume to spoil, sell or carry away, any ammunition delivered unto him upon pain of death.

3 No souldier shall give to pawn, or sell his armour, upon pain of imprisonment and punishment at discretion; and wheresoever any armour shall be found so sold or pawned, they shall be brought again into the army.

OF DUTIE IN MARCHING

I. Waste and Extortion

NONE on their march thorow the countreys, under his majestie's obedience, shall waste, spoil, or extort any victuals, money, or pawn from any subject, upon no pretence of want whatsoever: but shall pay for their meat and drink the usuall rates, upon pain of death.

II. Taking Horses out of the Plough

NO souldier shall presume, upon no occasion whatsoever, to take an horse out of the plough, or to wrong the husbandmen in their persons or cattell, or goods, upon pain of death.

III. Straggleing from the Colours

NO souldier either horse or foot, shall presume in marching to straggle from his troop or company, or to march out of his rank upon pain of death.

IV. Spoiling of Trees

NO souldier shall presume in marching or lodging to cut down any fruit trees, or to deface or spoil walks of trees, upon pain of severe punishment.

DUTIES IN CAMP AND GARRISON

I. Swarving from the Camp

NO man shall depart a mile out of the army or camp without licence, upon pain of death.

II. Going in or out by by-ways

NO man shall enter or go out of the army but by ordinary wayes, upon pain of death.

III. Drawing of Sword after Setting of the Watch

NO man shall presume to draw his sword without order after the watch is set, upon pain of death.

IV. Giving a false Alarm

NO man shall give a false alarm, or discharge a peece in the night, or make any noise without a lawfull cause, upon pain of death.

V. Drawing of Swords in a Quarrel

NO man shall draw any sword in private quarrel within the camp, upon pain of death.

VI. Revealing the Watch Word

HE that makes known the watch word without order, or gives any other word but what is given by the officer, shall die for it.

VII. Offering Violence to Victuallers

NO man shall do violence to any that bring victuals to the camp, upon pain of death.

VIII. Speaking with the Enemies Messengers

NONE shall speak with a drum or trumpet, or any other sent by the enemy, without order, upon pain of punishment at discretion.

IX. A Sentinell asleep or drunk

A SENTINELL or perdue found asleep, or drunk, or forsaking their place before they be drawn off, shall die for the offence without mercy.

X. Failing at the Rendezvous

NO man shall faile wilfully to come to the rendezvous or garrison appointed him by the lord generall, upon pain of death.

XI. Remaining unrolled in the Army

NO man that carrieth armes and pretends to be a souldier, shall remain three days in the army without being enrolled in some company, upon pain of death.

XII. Departing without Leave

NO man that is enrolled shall depart from the army or garrison, or from his colours, without licence, upon pain of death.

XIII. Outstaying a Passe

NO private souldier shall outstay his passe without a certificate of the occasion under the hand of a magistrate, at the next muster, upon pain of losing his pay during all the time of his absence.

XIV. Absenting from the Watch

HE that absents himself when the sign is given to set the watch, shall be punished at discretion, either with bread and water in prison, or with the wooden horse.

XV. Discontented with their Quarters

WOSOEVER shall expresse his discontent with the quarter given him in camp or garrison, shall be punished as a mutineer.

XVI. Lying or Supping out of the Quarter

NO officer of what quality soever, shall go out of the quarter to dinner or supper, or lie out all night, without making his superior officer acquainted, upon pain of casseering.

XVII. Keeping the Quarters clean

ALL officers whose charge it is, shall see the quarters kept clean and sweet, upon pain of severe punishment. [4]

OF DUTIES IN ACTION

I. Repairing to the Colours upon an Alarme

NO man shall faile immediately to repair unto his colours, (except upon evident necessity) when an alarme is given, upon paine of death.

II. Flying

NO man shall abandon his colours or flie away in any battell, upon pain of death.

III. Flinging away defensive Arms

IF a pikeman throw away his pike, or a muskettier his musket or bandalier, he or they shall be punished with death.

IV. Burning and wasteing

NO man shall burn any house or barn, or spoile any corn, hay, or straw in stacks in the fields, or any ship, boat, carriage, or anything that may serve for provision of the army, neither at home nor in the enemies countrey, without order, upon pain of death.

V. Killing an enemy who yeelds

NONE shall kill an enemy who yeelds and throws down his arms, upon pain of death.

VI. Saving Men armed with offensive Arms

NONE shall save a man that hath his offensive arms in his hand, upon pain of losse of his prisoner.

4 The parliamentary ordinnances had the two following articles: XVIII. NONE shall presume to let their horses feed in sown grounds whatsoever, or to endamage the husbandmen any way, upon severest punishment. XIX. WHOSOEVER shall in his quarter, abuse, beat, fright his landlord, or any person else in the family, or shall extort money or victual by violence from them, shall be proceeded against as a mutineer and an enemy to discipline.

VII. Flinging away Powder

WHOSOEVER in skirmish shall fling away his powder out of his bandeleers, that he may the sooner come off, shall be punished with death

VIII. Imbezeling of the Prey

NO souldier shall imbeazell any parte of the preye, till it be disposed of by the Lord Generall, or others authorized, upon pain of death.

IX. Concealing of Prisoners

NO officer or souldier shall ransom or conceal a prisoner, but within twelve hours, shall make the same known to the Lord Generall, or others authorized, upon pain of death.

X. Pillaging without Licence

NO man upon any good successe shall fall a pillaging before licence, or a sign given, upon pain of death.

XI. Retreating before handy Blowes

A REGIMENT or company of horse or foot that chargeth the enemy, and retreats before they come to handy strokes, shall answer it before a councel of warr, and if the fault be found in the officers, they shall be banished the camp; if in the souldiers, then every tenth man shall be punished at discretion, and the rest serve for pioners and scavengers, till a worthy exploit take off that blot.

OF THE DUTIES ON COMMANDERS AND OFFICERS IN PARTICULAR

I. Commanders must see God duly served

ALL commanders are straitly charged to see Almighty God reverently served, and sermons and praiers duly frequented.

II. Commanders must acquaint my Lord General with dangerous Humours

ALL commanders and officers that finde discontented humours, apt to mutinies, or any swarving from directions given, or from the policy of the army set down, shall straightway acquaint the lord Generall therewith, or others authorized, as they will answer their neglect.

III. Defrauding of Souldiers Pay

ANY officer that shall presume to defraud the souldiers of their pay, or any part of it, shall be casseered.

IV. Stopping of Duellers

NO corporall or other officer commanding the watch, shall wittingly suffer a souldier to go forth to a duell or private fight, upon paine of death.

V. Drunken and Quarrelsome Officers

WHAT officer soever shall come drunk to his guard, or shall quarrel in the quarter, or commit any disorder, shall be casseered without mercy; and the next officer under him shall have his place, which he may pretend to as his right, and it shall not be refused to him.

VI. Careles, Captains

A CAPTAINE that is carelesse in the training and governing of his company, shall be displaced of his charge.

VII. Officers outstaying their Pass

ALL captains or officers that shall out-stay their passe, shall be punished at the Lord Generall his discretion.

VIII. All Officers bound to part Quarrels

ALL officers of what condition soever, shall have power to part quarrels and fraies, or sudden disorders betwixt the souldiers, though it be in any other regiment or company, and to commit the disordered to prison for the present, untill such officers as they belong unto are acquainted with it; and what souldier soever shall resist, disobey, or draw his sword against such an officer, although he be no officer of his regiment or company, shall be punished with death.

IX. Officers non-residents in Garrison

A CAPTAIN or officer non-resident in the place assigned him for garrison without licence, shall have one moneth's pay defaulked for the first offence; and two moneths for the second; upon the third offence he shall be discharged of his command.

X. Casseering of Souldiers

AFTER the armie is come to the general rendezvous, no captain shall casseere any souldier that is inrolled, without special warrant of the Lord Generall.

XI. Mustering of false and counterfeit Troopers

NO captaine of a troope shall present in the musters, any but reall troopers, such as are bound by their oath and pay to follow the troope, upon pain of death without mercy: and if any towns or countreymen, victualler, freebooter, enterloper or souldier whatsoever, of any other troop or company, shall present himself or his horse in the muster, to mislead the muster-master, to defraud his majestie, and to betray the service, the same shall be punished with death.

XII. Inhabitants of Garrisons must not be Soulders there

NO captain of a troop or company, shall take into his troop or company, any inhabitant of that place where the troop or company is in garrison, upon pain of severe punishment. (m)

XIII. Commissaries of Victuals and Ammunition must be true

NO provider, keeper, or officer of his majestie's victual or ammunition, shall embeazel or spoil any part thereof, or give any false account to the Lord Generall, upon pain of death.

OF THE DUTY OF THE MUSTER-MASTER

I. Muser-master conniving at Counterfeits

NO muster-master shall wittingly let any passe in the musters, but such as are really of the troop or company presented, upon pain of death.

II. Captains must send a Roll of their Men to the Lord Generall

ALL captains shall cause their troops and companies to be full and compleat; and two days after the general mustering, they shall send to the Lord Generall a perfect list or roll of all the officers of their troops and companies, and likewise of all the troopers and souldiers that are in actual service, putting down distinctly on the head of each man his monethly pay.

III. Every Pay-day

THE like roll or list shall the captains send to the Lord General, and to the treasurer of the armie, upon every pay-day during the service, with a punctual expression at the bottom of the said roll, what new troopers or souldiers have been entertained since the last pay-day, in lieu of such as are either deceased or casseered, and likewise the day whereon they were so casseer'd and entertain'd.

IV. Subscribed by all the Officers of the Top or Company

WHICH said list or roll shall be subscribed, not onely by the captain, his lieutenant and cornet, or ensign, but also by the serjeants and corporals respectively, who shall declare upon their oaths, that the troopers and soldiers enrolled in the said list, are reall and actual troopers and soldiers of the respective troopes and companies; and whosoever shall be convicted of falshood in any of the premises, shall be punished with death.

V. Muster-Masters must use no other Rolls

NO muster-master shall presume to receive or accept of any roll to make the musters by but the fore-mentioned rolls, upon paine of the losse of his place, and other punishment at discretion.

VI. Counterfeit Names in the Rolls

NO man shall presume to present himself to muster, or to be enrolled in the muster-rolls, by a counterfeit name, or surname, or place of birth, upon paine of death.

OF VICTUALLERS

I. Victuallers issuing neughtie Victuals

NO victualler shall presume to issue or sell unto any of the army, unfound, unfavorie, or unwholesome victuals, upon paine of imprisonment, and further arbitrary punishment.

II. No Souldier must be a Victualler

NO souldier shall be a victualler without the consent of the Lord Generall, or others authorized, upon pain of punishment at discretion.

III. Unseasonable Hours kept by Viciuallers

NO victualler shall entertain any souldiers in his house, tent, or hutt, after the warning-piece at night, or before the beating of the ravalee in the morning.

OF ADMINISTRATTION OF JUSTICE

I. Summarie Proceedings

ALL controversies between souldiers and their captains, and all others, shall be summarily heard and determined by the councell of warre, except the weightinesse of the cause require further deliberation.

II. The Provost Marshall must look to his Prisoners

NO provost marshall shall refuse to keep a prisoner committed to his charge, nor dismisse him being once received, upon paine of being liable to the same punishment which should have been inflicted upon the partie dismissed. [5]

5 In Essex's Ordinance: All officers and others, who shall send up any prisoners unto the marshall generall of the army, shall likewise deliver unto the marshall, the cause and reason of the imprison ment; and without such cause and reason shewn, the marshall is expressly forbid to take charge of the prisoner. III. When a prisoner is committed to the charge of the marshall generall, the information of the crime which he stands committed for, is to be given in to the advocate of the army within forty-eight hours after the commitment, or else for default thereof, the prisoner to be released, except good cause be shewn, wherefore the information cannot be ready within that time.

III. Goods of the Defunct

THE goods of such as die in the armie or garrison, or be slain in the service, if they make any will by word or writing, shall be disposed of according to their will: if they make no will, then shall go to their wives or next of kinde: if no wife nor kindred appear within one year after, shall be disposed of by the appointment of the lord generall, according to the laws civill and militarie.

IV. Civil Magistrates imprisoning of Souldiers

No magistrate of town or countrey shall presume without licence to imprison any souldier, unlesse for capitall offences.

V. For Debt and small Offences

IN matters of debt, or trespasse, or other inferior causes, the magistrate shall not lay hands upon the souldier, but shall acquaint his captain, or other chief officer therewith: who is to end the matter, with the consent of the complainant, or to leave the partie grieved, to take his remedie by due course of law; and if the officer faile of his dutie herein, the lord generall upon complaint of the partie grieved, will not onely see him righted, but the officer punished for his neglect in this behalfe.

VI. Braving the Court of justice

NO man shall presume to use any braving or menacing words, signes or gestures, while the court of justice is sitting, upon paine of death.

VII. Receiving of Runaways

NO inhabitant of citie, towne or countrey, shall presume to receive any souldier into his service; or conceale or use means to conveigh such run-aways; but shall apprehend all such, and deliver them over to the provost marshall, upon pain of punishment at the discretion of the lord generall.

VIII. Detecting of Offenders

ALL captains, officers, and souldiers, shall do their endeavours to detect, apprehend and bring to punishment all offenders, and shall assist the officers of the army for that purpose, as they will answer their slacknesse in the marshal's court.

IX. Offences whatsoever punished by the Laws of Warre

ALL other faults, disorders and offences, not mentioned in these articles, shall be punished according to the generall customes and laws of warre. [6]

6 In Essex's Ordinance: X. If the marshall shall dismisse without authority any prisoner committed unto his charge, or suffer him to make an escape, he shall be lyable to the same punishment due unto the dismissed or escaped offendour.

OF THE SOULDIERS OATH

ALL souldiers that are really and actually in his majestie's service, shall take this ensuing oath.

> "I PROMISE and swear to be true and faithfull to my Soveraigne Lord King Charles. To obey my lord generall, and the commanders and officers under him. To observe the lawes and ordinances of warre established by him. To watch and ward, and work in the service. To wait on my colours, and to follow them. To endure, suffer, and fight to the last, as God shall help me."[7]

AND to the end that these lawes and ordinances be made more publike and known as well to the officers, as to the common souldiers: every colonell and captain is to provide one of these books.

And within a short time after that the army shall come to the general rendezvous, these laws in every severall regiment, in the presence of all the officers, are plainly and distinctly to be read by the marshals of the severall regiments, assisted by the marshall generall. In the horse quarters, by sound of trumpet, and amongst the foot by beat of drum. And weekly afterwards, upon the pay day every captain is to cause the same to be read to his own company, in presence of his officers. And also upon every main guard, the captain is to do the like, that none may be ignorant of the duties required, and thereafter govern themselves. (q)

Given under my hand, the 25th of November 1643

7 Articles and Ordinances of War for the Expedition of the Army of the Kingdom of Scotland, issued by the Committee of Eftates, and his Excellency the Lord General of the Army in 1643 contained the following form of oath: "I, N. N. promise and swear to be true and faithful in this service, according to the heads sworn by me, in the solemn league and covenant of the three kingdoms: to honour and obey my lord general, and all my superior officers and commanders, and by all means to hinder their dishonour and hurt: to observe carefully all the articles of war and camp discipline; never to leave the defence of this cause, nor flee from my colours so long as I can follow them: to be ready to watching, warding, and working, so far: as I have strength; to endure and suffer all distresses; and to fight manfully to the uttermost, as I shall answer to God, and as God shall help me."

Articles of War James II (1688)[1]

RULES AND ARTICLES FOR THE BETTER GOVERNMENT OF HIS MAJESTIES LAND FORCES IN PAY

ARTICLE I.

All Officers and Soldiers (not having just Impediment) shall diligently frequent Divine Service and Sermon, in such Places as shall be appointed for the Regiment, Troop, or Company, wherein they serve; and such as either willfully or negligently Absent themselves from Divine Service or Sermon, or else, being present do behave themselves undecently or irreverently during the same; If they be Officers, They shall be severely reprehended at a Court-Martial; But if private Soldiers, they shall for every such First Offence forfeit each man Twelve Pence, to be deducted out of their next Pay; And for the Second Offence, shall forfeit Twelve Pence, and be laid in Irons for Twelve Hours; and for every like offence afterwards, shall suffer and pay in like manner.

ARTICLE II.

If any Sutler or Seller of Ale, Beer, Wine, or any sort of Drinks, Bread, Victuals or other Commodities or Merchandise whatsoever, attending His Majesties Forces, shall during the time of Divine Service, or Sermon, set any such thing to sale, he shall forfeit the full value thereof, for the use of the Poor.

ARTICLE III.

Whosoever shall use any unlawful Oath or Execration (whether Officer or Soldier) shall incur the Penalties exprest in the first Article.

ARTICLE IV.

If any Officer or Soldier shall presume to Blaspheme the Holy and Undivided Trinity, or the Persons of God the Father, God the Son, or God the Holy Ghost; Or shall presume to speak against any known Article of the Christian Faith, he shall have his Tongue Bored through with a Red-hot Iron.

---

1 Winthrop William, 1920, *Military Law and Precedents*, Washington: Government Printing Office, pp. 920-930.

ARTICLE V.

If any Officer or Soldier shall Abuse or Profane any Place Dedicated to the Worship of God, or shall offer Violence to any Chaplain of the Army, or any other Minister of God's Word, he shall suffer such Punishment as shall be inflicted on him by a Court-Martial.

And whosoever shall take any of the Utensils or Ornaments belonging or Dedicated to God's Worship, in any Church or Chappel, shall suffer Death for the Fact.

ARTICLE VI

All Officers of what Quality or Condition soever, shall take the following Oath, which shall be Administered to them, by such Person or Persons, and in such Places as His Majesty, His General, Lieutenant General, or Commander in Chief of the Forces for the time being, shall appoint.

THE OATH OF FIDELITY TO BE TAKEN BT EVERY OFFICER AND SOLDIER IN THE ARMY

I, A. B., Do Swear to be true and faithful to my Sovereign Lord King JAMES, and to His Heirs and Lawful Successors; and to be Obedient in all things to His General, Lieutenant General, or Commander in Chief of His Forces, for the time being. And will behave myself obediently towards my Superior Officers In all they, shall command me for His Majesty's Service. And I do further Swear That I will be a true, faithful, and obedient Servant and Soldier, every way performing my best Endeavours for His Majesty's Service, Obeying all Orders, and Submitting to all such Rules and Articles of War, as are or shall be Established by His Majesty; and I do likewise Swear, That I believe, That it is not lawful upon any Pretence whatsoever, to take Arms against the King; and that I do Abhor that Traiterous Position of taking Arms by His Authority against His Person, or against those that are Commissioned by Him. *So help me God.*

ARTICLE VII

No Officer or Soldier shall use any Traiterous Words against the Sacred Person of the King's Most Excellent Majesty upon Pain of Death.

ARTICLE VIII

Whosoever shall hold correspondence with any Rebel or Enemy of His Majesty, or shall give them Advice or Intelligence either by Letters, Messages, Signs, or Tokens, or in any manner of way whatsoever, shall suffer Death. And whatever Regiment, Troop, or Company shall Treat with such Rebels or Enemies, or enter into any Condition with them without His Majesties Leave, or Leave of the General, Lieutenant General, or of the Chief Commander in his absence; and the officers of such Regiment, Troop, or Company who are found guilty shall die for it; and of the Soldiers who shall consent thereunto, every tenth Man by Lot shall be Hanged, and the rest punished at the Discretion of the General Court-Martial; But whatsoever Officers or Soldiers can prove that they did their utmost to resist and avoid such a Treaty, and were no Partakers of the Crime, they shall not only go free, but shall also be Rewarded for their Constancy and Fidelity.

ARTICLE IX

Whosoever shall go about to Entice or Persuade either Officer or Soldier to join or engage in any Traiterous or Rebellious Act, either against the Royal Person of the King or Kingly Government, shall suffer Death for it; And whoever shall not reveal to his Superior Officer such a conspiracy as soon as ever it shall come to his knowledge, shall be judged equally guilty with the Contrivers of such a Plot or Conspiracy, and consequently shall suffer the same Penalty.

ARTICLE X

If any Officer or Soldier shall behave himself disrespectfully towards the General, Lieutenant General, or other Chief Commander of the Army, or speak words tending to his Hurt or Dishonor, he shall be punished according to the Nature and Quality of the Offence by the Judgment of the General Court-Martial.

ARTICLE XI

Whosoever shall presume in the Presence of the General, Lieutenant General, or other Commander in Chief, to draw his Sword with a purpose to do any Officer, or any of his fellow Soldiers mischief, shall suffer such Punishment as a Court-Martial shall think fit to Inflict upon him for the said Offence.

ARTICLE XII

Whoever shall presume to violate any Safe Conduct or Protection given by His Majesty, the General, Lieutenant General, or other Commander In Chief (knowing the same) shall suffer Death, or such other punishment as shall be inflicted on him by the General Court-Martial.

ARTICLE XIII

No Man shall presume so far as to raise or cause the least Mutiny or Sedition in the Army, upon Pain of Death, or such other Punishment as a Court-Martial shall think fit. And if any number of Soldiers shall presume to assemble to take Councel amongst themselves for the demanding their Pay, any Inferior Officers accessory thereunto, shall suffer Death for it, as the Heads and Ring-leaders of such Mutinous and Seditious Meetings; And the Soldiers shall be punished either with death, or otherwise at the Discretion of the General Court-Martial: And if any Captain being privy thereunto shall not suppress the same, or complain of it, he shall likewise be punished with Death, or such other Punishment as the General Court-Martial shall think fit.

ARTICLE XIV

No Officer or Soldier shall utter any words tending to Sedition or Mutiny upon pain of suffering such Punishment as shall be inflicted on him by a Court-Martial.

And whosoever shall hear any Mutinous or Seditious Words spoken, and shall not with all possible speed reveal the same to his Superiour Officers, shall be punished as a Court-Martial shall think fit.

ARTICLE XV

If any Inferior Officer or Soldier shall refuse to obey his Superior Officer, or shall quarrel with him, he shall be Cashiered, or suffer such Punishment as a Court-Martial shall think fit.

But if any Officer or Soldier shall presume to resist any Officer in the Execution of his Office, or shall strike, or lift up his hand to strike, or shall draw, or offer to draw, or lift up any Weapon against his Superior Officer upon any pretence whatsoever, he shall suffer Death, or such other Punishment as the General Court-Martial shall think fit.

ARTICLE XVI

Every Soldier shall keep silence when the Army is Marching, Embattelling, or taking up their Quarters, (to the end that their Officers may be heard, and their Orders executed) upon Pain of Imprisonment, or such other Punishment as a Court-Martial shall think fit, according to the Circumstance and Aggravation of the Fact.

ARTICLE XVII

All murders and wilful killing of any Person shall be punished with Death.

ARTICLE XVIII

All Robbery and Theft committed by any Person in or belonging to the Army, shall be punished with Death, or otherwise as the Court-Martial upon consideration of the Circumstances shall think fit.

ARTICLE XIX

Whoever shall in danger draw his Sword whilst his Colours are flying either in Battel, or upon the March, unless it be against the enemy, shall suffer such Punishment as a Court-Martial shall think fit.

ARTICLE XX

When any March is to be made, every Man who is sworn shall follow his Colours; and whoever shall without leave stay behind, or depart above a Mile from the Camp, or out of the Army without Licence, shall suffer such Punishment as shall be inflicted on him by a Court-Martial.

ARTICLE XXI

No person shall extort Free quarter, or shall commit any Waste or spoil or deface Walks of Trees, Parks, Warrens, Fishponds, Houses or Gardens, tread down, or otherwise destroy Standing Corn in the Ear, or shall put their Horses into Medows without Leave from their Superior Officer, upon pain of Severe Punishment; But if any Officer or Soldier shall exact Money, or willfully Burn any House, Barn, Stack of Corn, Hay or Straw, or any Ship, Boat or Carriage, or anything which may serve for the Provision of the Army, without Order from the Commander in Chief, he shall suffer Death for it.

ARTICLE XXII

Whoever shall run from his Colours, or doth not defend them to the utmost of his Power, shall suffer Death.

ARTICLE XXIII

If any Officers or Soldiers, Regiment, Troop, or Company, or Commanded Party, shall not behave themselves in Fight against an Enemy as they ought to do, they shall suffer such Punishment as the General Court-Martial shall inflict.

ARTICLE XXIV

When it shall please God that his Majesty's Forces shall beat the Rebels, or Enemy, every Man shall follow his Officer in the Chase; but whoever shall presume to Pillage or Plunder till the Rebels, or Enemy be entirely beaten, he shall suffer Death, or such other Punishment as shall be pronounced against him by the General Court-Martial; and the Pillage so gotten shall be forfeited to the use of the sick and maimed Soldiers.

ARTICLE XXV

In What Place soever it shall please God that the Rebels or Enemy shall be subdued or overcome, all the Ordnance, Ammunition and Victuals that shall be there found, shall be secured to his Majesties use, and for the better Relief of the Army; and one-tenth part of the Spoil shall be laid apart towards the Relief of the sick and maimed Soldiers.

ARTICLE XXVI

All Officers whose Charge it is shall see the Quarters kept clean and neat upon pain of severe Punishment.

ARTICLE XXVII

No Officer shall lie out all Night from the Camp or Garison without his Superior Officer's Leave, upon pain of being punished for it as a Court-Martial shall think fit; Nor shall any Soldier or Officer go any By-way to the Camp, or other than the Common Way laid out for all, upon pain of being punished as aforesaid.

ARTICLE XXVIII

No Soldier shall presume to make any alarm in the Quarters by shooting of his Musket in the Night after the Watch is Set, unless it be at an Enemy; upon pain of suffering such Punishment as a Court-Martial shall inflict.

ARTICLE XXIX

No Soldier shall in anger draw his Sword in any Camp, Post, or Garison, upon, pain of suffering such Punishment as a Court-Martial shall inflict upon him for the same.

ARTICLE XXX

When warning is given for Setting the Watch, by Beat of Drum, or Sound of Trumpet, if any Soldier shall absent himself without reasonable Cause, he shall be punished by Riding the Wooden Horse, or otherwise at the Discretion of the Commander.

And whoever shall fail at the Beating of a Drum, or sound of a Trumpet, or upon an Alarm given, to repair to his Colours, with his Arms decently kept, and well fixed (unless there be an evident necessity to hinder him from the same) he shall either be put in Irons for it, or suffer such other Punishment as a Court-Martial shall think fit.

ARTICLE XXXI

Whoever makes known the Watchword without Order, or gives any other Word but what is given by the Officer, shall suffer Death, or such other punishment as the General Court-Martial shall think fit.

ARTICLE XXXII

A Centinel who shall be found sleeping in any Post, Garrison, Trench or the like, (while he should be upon his Duty) shall suffer Death, or such other Punishment as the General Court-Martial shall inflict for the same.

And if a Centinel or Perdue shall forsake his Place, before he be relieved or drawn off; or upon discovery of an Enemy, shall not give Warning to his Quarters, according to Direction, he shall suffer Death, or such other Punishment as the General Court-Martial shall think fit.

And if any Soldier employed as a Scout, shall not go upon that Service so far as he is commanded, or having discovered an Ambush, or Approach of the Enemy, shall not return forthwith to give Notice or Warning to his Quarters; of if he enter into any House, and there or elsewhere be found sleeping or drunk, whilst he should have been upon Service, he shall suffer Death, or such other Punishment as shall be inflicted upon him by the General Court-Martial.

ARTICLE XXXIII

Whoever shall do violence to any who shall bring Victuals to the Camp or Garrison, or shall take his Horse or Goods, shall suffer Death, or such other Punishment as the General Court-Martial shall inflict.

If any shall presume to beat or abuse his Host, or the Wife, Child, or Servant of his Host, where he is Quartered, he shall be put in Irons for it: And if he do it a second time, he shall be further punished; and the party wronged shall in both Cases have amends made him.

And whoever shall force a Woman to abuse her (whether she belong to the Enemy, or not) and the fact be sufficiently proved, shall suffer Death for it.

ARTICLE XXXIV

No Soldier or Officer shall use any reproachful or provoking Speech or Act to another upon pain of Imprisonment, and such further punishment as a Court-Martial shall think fit.

Nor shall any Officer or Soldier presume to send a Challenge to any other Officer or Soldier to fight a Duel; neither shall any Soldier or Officer up-raid another for refusing a Challenge; And we do acquit and discharge all men that have Quarrels offered, or Challenges made to them, of all Disgrace, or opinion of Disadvantage, since they but do the Duties of Soldiers who ought to subject themselves to Discipline; and they that provoke them, shall be proceeded against as Breakers of Discipline, and Enemies to Our Service: And whoever shall offend in either of these Cases, if it be an Officer, he shall be Cashiered; and if a private Soldier, he shall Ride the Wooden Horse, and be further punished as a Court-Martial shall think fit. And if any Corporal or other Officer Commanding a Guard, shall willingly or knowingly suffer either Soldiers or Officers to go forth to a Duel, he shall be punished for it by the Sentence of a Court-Martial.

And all Officers of what Condition soever, have power to part and quell all Quarrels, Frays, or sudden Disorders between Soldiers and Officers, those of another Company, Troop or Regiment, and to commit the disorderly Persons to Prison, until their proper Officers be acquainted therewith. Whoever shall resist such an Officer (though of another Company, Troop, or Regiment) or draw his Sword upon him, shall be severely punished as the General Court-Martial shall appoint.

And if two or more going into the Field to Fight a Duel, shall draw their Swords or other Weapons and Fight, though neither of them fall upon the Spot, nor die afterwards of any Wound there received, yet if they be Officers, they shall be cashiered; and if common Soldiers, they shall be punished with Riding the Wooden Horse, or suffer such other Punishment as a Court-Martial shall direct.

And lastly, in all Cases of Duels, the Seconds, and Carriers of Challenges, shall be taken as Principals, and punished accordingly.

ARTICLE XXXV

All Passes and Licenses for being absent, shall be brought to the Muster-Master, who is required to enter the same in a Book fairly written, to prevent Collusion; And whoever is absent longer than the time limited in his Pass for his absence, shall be respited, and not allowed the Muster, without order from his Majesty, the General, or other Commander in Chief of his Majesties Forces.

ARTICLE XXXVI

If any Soldier be sick, wounded, or maimed in his Majesties Service, he shall be sent out of the Camp to some fit Place for his Recovery, where he shall be provided for by the Officer appointed to take care of sick and wounded Soldiers, and his Wages or Pay shall go on and be duly paid till it do's appear that he can be no longer serviceable in the Army, and then he shall be sent by Pass to his Countrey, with Money to bear his Charges in his Travel, or such other Provision shall be made for him, as his Majesty shall direct.

ARTICLE XXXVII

All Commissions granted by his Majesty, the General, or Commander in Chief of his Majesties Forces, to any Officer in Pay, shall be brought to the Commissary of the Musters, and Secretary at War, who are to receive and Enter the same in a Book fairly written; and no Commission-Officer shall be allowed in Muster, without a Commission from his Majesty, or the Commander in Chief for the time being, and the same Entered with the Commissary-General of the Musters, or his Deputies, and Secretary at War.

ARTICLE XXXVIII

No Commission Officer after Enrollment and being Mustered, shall be Dismissed or Cashiered without order from his Majesty, the General or Commander in Chief for the time being, or a General Court-Martial: But the Captains with the approbation of their Colonels, or of the Governour of the Garison where they are, may discharge any Non-Commission Officer, or Private Soldier when they find cause, taking other Non-Commission Officers or Soldiers in their Places; Provided that such Colonel or Governour shall forthwith certifie the Commissary General of the Muster, That (by their approbation) such Non-Commission Officers or Soldiers were discharged, and others taken into their Places respectively. And in Quarters and Garisons where they are only single Troops or Companies, the Captains certificates are forthwith to be sent and accepted by the Commissary-General, expressing the Day of each Non-Commission Officers or Soldiers Discharge or Death, and who has been entertained in his Place.

ARTICLE XXXIX

All Captains shall use their utmost Endeavours to have their Troops and Companies compleat and full, and no Soldiers Duty, either of Horse or Foot, shall be done by any other than the Soldier himself; But in case of Sickness or Disability, or other necessary Cause, his Captain may dispence with his absence, without obliging him to find another to Serve in his stead.

ARTICLE XL

If any Trooper or Dragoon shall lose or spoil his Horse, or any Foot Soldier his Arms, or any part thereof by Negligence or Gaming, he shall remain in the quality of a Pioneer or Scavenger, till he be furnished at his own Charge, with as good as were lost; and if he be not otherwise able, the one half of his Pay shall be deducted and set apart for the providing of it till he be re-furnished.

Nor shall any Soldier sell, or negligently or wilfully break his Arms, or any part thereof, or any Hatchets, Spades, Shovels, Pickaxes, or other Necessaries of War, upon pain of severe punishment, at the discretion of the General Court-Martial. And where Arms, or other Necessaries aforesaid shall be pawned, they are to be forfeited, and seized on for his Majesties use.

ARTICLE XLI

All Officers and Soldiers, and also the Muster-Master, not duly observing these Orders and Instructions, and every of them respectively, shall be Cashiered, or liable to such other Punishments as his Majesty, or Commander in Chief of the Forces, or a Court-Martial shall appoint.

ARTICLE XLII

None shall presume to spoil, sell, or convey away any Ammunition delivered unto him, upon pain of suffering death, or such other punishment as the General Court-Martial shall think fit.

ARTICLE XLIII

No Officer, Provider or Keeper of the Victuals or Ammunition for his Majesties Forces shall imbezel or willingly spoil or give a false Account of any part thereof to whom he is to make his Account, upon pain of suffering Death, or such other Punishment as the General Court-Martial shall think fit.

ARTICLE XLIV

No Commissary or Victualler shall bring or furnish unto the Camp any unsound or unsavory Victuals of what kind soever, whereby sickness may grow in the Army, or the Service be hindred; and if upon Examination before the General Court-Martial he shall be found guilty, he shall suffer such Punishment as they shall direct.

ARTICLE XLV

No Officer or Soldier shall be a Victualler in the Army upon pain of being punished at discretion.

ARTICLE XLVI

No Victualler or seller of Beer, Ale, or Wine belonging to the Army, shall Entertain any Soldier in his House, Booth, Tent or Hutt after the Warning- Piece, Tattoe or Beat of the Drum at night, or before the Beating of the Reveilles in the morning; Nor shall any Soldier within that time be anywhere but upon his Duty, or In his Quarters, upon pain of Punishment both to the Soldier and Entertainer at the Discretion of a Court-Martial.

ARTICLE XLVII

The Commission-Officers of every Regiment may hold a Court-Martial for that Regiment upon all necessary Occasions.

The Provost-Martial of every Regiment shall have the same priviledge in his own Regiment as the Provost-Martial General hath in the Army or Camp, and such Fees also as the Court-Martial shall allow.

ARTICLE XLVIII

Such who are Judges in a General Court-Martial or in a Regimential Court-Martial, shall hold the same Rank in those Courts as they do in the Army for Orders sake, and they shall take an Oath for the due Administration of Justice according to these Articles, or (where these Articles do not assign any special Punishment) according to their consciences, the best of their Understandings, and the Custom of War in the like Cases; and shall demean themselves orderly in the hearing of Causes, and before giving of Sentence every Judge shall deliver his Vote or Opinion distinctly, and the Sentence is to be according to the plurality of Votes, and if there happen to be in equality of Votes, the President is to have a casting Voice.

And when Sentence is to be given, the President shall pronounce it; and after that the sentence is pronounced the Provost-Martial shall have Warrant to cause Execution to be done according to Sentence.

ARTICLE XLIX

At a General Court-Martial there shall be a Clerk who Is to be sworn to make true and faithful Records of all the Proceedings of that Court, and there shall be also such other Officers appointed both for that, and also for the Regimental Court-Martial as shall be necessary; and the General Court-Martial may appoint and limit the Fees of the Provost-Martial-General as they shall think fit.

ARTICLE L

All controversies either between Soldiers and their Captains or other Officers, or between Soldier and Soldier relating to their Military Capacities, shall be summarily heard and determined at the next Court-Martial of the Regiment.

ARTICLE LI

If in any Matter which shall be Judged in any of the aforesaid Regimental Courts-Martial either or the Parties shall find himself aggrieved, he may appeal to the General Court-Martial, who are to take care that if the Party appealing make not good his Suggestion, Recompence be made to the other for the trouble and Charge of such an Appeal.

ARTICLE LII

In all Criminal Causes which concern the Crown, His Majesties Advocate-General or Judge-Advocate of the Army, shall inform the Court and prosecute on his Majesties behalf.

ARTICLE LIII

No Oflicers or Soldiers shall presume to hinder the Provost-Martial, his Lieutenant or Servant in the Execution of their Office upon pain of Death or such other Punishment as a Court-Martial shall think fit; And all Captains, Officers and Soldiers shall do their utmost to apprehend and bring to punishment all Offenders, and shall assist the Officers of His Majesties Army or Forces therein, especially the said Provost-Martial, His Lieutenant and Servants; and if the Provost-Martial or his Officers require the assistance of any Officer or Soldier in apprehending any Person, declaring to them that it is for a Capital Crime, and the Party escape for want of Aid and Assistance, the Party or Parties refusing to Aid or Assist shall suffer such Punishment as a Court-Martial shall inflict.

ARTICLE LIV

If any Officer or Soldier who shall presume to draw his Sword in any place of judicature while the Court is sitting, he shall suffer such punishment as shall be inflicted on him by a Court-Martial. And the Provost-Martial of his Majesties Army is hereby empowered and directed by his own authority to apprehend such Offenders.

ARTICLE LV

If any Soldier being committed for any Offence shall break Prison, the said Provost-Martial-General shall by his own Authority apprehend him, and the Offender shall suffer Death.

ARTICLE LVI

If any Fray shall happen within the Camp or place of Garison in any of the Soldiers Lodgings, or where they meet, it shall be inquired into by the Officers of the Regiment, and the Beginners and pursuers thereof punished according to the quality of the Offence.

ARTICLE LVII

If any Inferiour Officer either of Horse or Foot, be wronged by his Officer, he may complain to his Colonel, or other Superiour Officer of the Regiment, who is to redress the same upon due Proof made of the Wrong done him: But if he fail therein, the Party grieved is to apply to the General Officer for redress; And if the Accusation be false, the Complainant is to be punished at the discretion of a Court-Martial.

ARTICLE LVIII

If any Colonel or Captain shall force or take any thing away from a private Soldier, such- Colonel or Captain shall be punished according to the quality of the Offence, by the Judgment of a General Court-Martial.

And if a Soldier shall be wronged, and shall not appeal to the Court, or his Superiour Commander, but take his own Satisfaction for it, he shall be punished by the Judgment of a Court-Martial.

ARTICLE LIX

If any Soldier die, no other shall take or spoil his Goods, upon pain of restoring double the value to him to whom they belong, and of such further Punishments as a Court-Martial shall think fit. But the Captain of the Company of which such a Soldier was, shall take, the said Goods into his custody, and dispose of them for paying his Quarters, and to keep the overplus (if any be) for the use of those to whom they belong, and who shall claim the same within Three months after his Death.

And if any Captain or Officer die the Chief Commander shall take care of reserving his Estate in like manner.

ARTICLE LX

No Provost-Martial shall refuse to receive or keep a Prisoner committed to his Charge by Authority, or shall dismiss him without Order, upon pain of such Punishment as a Court-Martial shall think fit.

And if the Offence for which the Prisoner was apprehended deserved Death, the Provost-Martial failing to receive and keep him as aforesaid shall be liable to the same Punishment.

ARTICLE LXI

If any Person be committed by the Provost-Martial's own Authority without other Command, he shall acquaint the General or other Chief Commander with the Cause within twenty-four hours, and the Provost-Martial shall thereupon dismiss him unless he have Order to the contrary.

ARTICLE LXII

No man shall presume to use any Braving or Menacing Words, Signs or Gestures where any of the aforesaid Courts of Justice are sitting, upon pain of suffering such Punishment as the Court-Martial shall think fit.

ARTICLE LXIII

Whatever is to be published or generally made known, shall be done by Beat of Drum, or the sound of Trumpet, That no man may pretend ignorance thereof: And if afterwards any one shall be found disobedient or transgressing what is so Published, he shall be punished according to these Articles, or the quality of the Fact.

ARTICLE LXIV

All other faults, misdemeanours and Disorders not mentioned in these Articles, shall be punished according to the Laws and Customs of War, and discretion of the Court-Martial; Provided that no Punishment amounting to the loss of Life or Limb, be inflicted upon any Offender in time of Peace, although the same be allotted for the said Offence by these Articles, and the Laws and Customs of War.

The First Mutiny Act 1689 (1 William & Marry, CAP. 5)

"An Act for punishing Officers and Soldiers who shall Mutiny or Desert their Majesty Service.

"WHEREAS, the raising or keeping a standing Army within his kingdom in time of peace unless, it be with consent of Parlyament is against law. And whereas it is judged necessary to their Majestyes and this present Parlyament. That during this time of Danger severall of the Forces which are not on foote should be continued and others raised for the Safety of the Kingdom for the common defence of the Protestant Religion and for the reduceing of Ireland:

"And whereas noe man may be forejudged of Life or Limbe, or subjected to any kind of punishment by Martial Law, or in any other manner than by the judgement of his Peeres, and according to the knowne and Established Laws of this Realme. Yet neverthelesses, it being for retaineing such Forces as are or shall be raised during this exigence of Affaires in their Duty an exact Discipline be observed, And that Soldiers who shall Mutiny or Stirr up Sedition, or shall desert Their Majestyes Service be brought to more exemplary and speedy Punishment than the usuall Forms of Law will allow:

"Bee it therefore Enacted by the King and Queenes most Excellent Majestyes by and with the Advice and Consent of the Lords Spiritually and Temporall and Commons in the present Parlyament assembled, and by authoritie of the same, That from and after the Twelfth day of April in the years of Our Lord One thousands six hundred eighty-nine every person being in Their Majestyes Service in the Army, and being mustered and in pay as an Officer or Soldier, who shall at any time before the Tenth day of November in the yeare of our Lord One thousand six hundred eighty-nine, excite, cause, or joyne in any mutiny or sedition in the Army or shall desert Their Majestyes Service in the Army, shall suffer death or such other punishment as a Court-Martiall shall be inflicted.

"3. And it is hereby further enacted and declared. That Their Majestyes or Generall of their Army for the time being, may by virtue of the Act have full power and authoritie to grant Commissions to any Lieftnants, Generall or other Officers, not under the degree of Collonells, from time to time to call and assemble Court-Martialls for punishing such offences as aforesaid.

"4. And it is hereby further enacted and declared, That noe Court-Martiall which have power to inflict any punishment by virtue of the Act for the offences aforesaid shall consist of fewer that thirteen, whereof none to be under degree of Captaines.

"5. Provided always, That no field officer be tried by other than field Officers. And that such Court-Martiall shall have power and authoritie to administer an oath to any witness in order to the examination or tryall of the offences aforesaid.

"6. Provided alwayes, That nothing in this Act contained shall extend or be construed to exempt any officer or soldier whatsoever from the ordinary processe of Law.

"7. Provided alwayes, That this Act, or anything therein contained, shall not extend or by any wayes construed to extend to or concern any of the Militia Forces of this Kingdome.

"8. Provides alsoe, That this Act shall continue and be in force until the said Tenth day of November in the said yeare of our Lord One thousand six hundred eighty-nine and noe longer.

"9. Provided always, and bee it enacted, That in all tryalls of offenders by Court-Martiall to be held by virtue of this Act, where the offence may be punished by Death, every officer present at such tryall, before any proceeding be had thereupon, shall take an oath upon the Evangelists before the Court (and the Judge Advocate or his Deputy shall, and hereby respectively authorised to administer the same) in these words, that is to say:

" 'You shall well and truly try and determine according to your evidence the matter now before you between Out Soveraigne Lord and Lady the King and Queen's Majestyes and the Prisoner to be tried,

"Soe helpe your God."

"10. And noe Sentence of Death shall be given against any offender in such case by any Court-Martiall unlesse nine of thirteene officers present, then the judgement shall passé by the concurrence of the greater part of them soe sworne, and not otherwise; and noe Proceedings, Tryall, or Sentence of Death shall be had or given against any offender but betweene the houres of eight in the morning and one in the afternoone."

The British Articles of War of 1718[1]

I. All officers and soldiers (not having just impediment) shall diligently frequent divine service, in such places as shall be appointed for the regiment, troop, or company to which they belong; and such as either wilfully or negligently absent themselves from divine service or sermon, or else being present, do behave themselves undecently or irreverently during the same, if they be officers, they shall be severely reprehended at a court-martial; but if private soldiers, they shall for every such first offence, forfeit each man i.e., to be deducted out of their next pay; and for the second offence shall forfeit, and be laid in irons for twelve hours; and for every like offence afterwards, shall suffer and pay in like manner; and the money so forfeited shall be applied to the relief of the sick soldiers of such troop or company to which the offender does belong.

II. If any sutler, in any of the forts, garrisons, camps, barracks, or guards shall, during divine service or sermon, presume to sell any beer, brandy, wine, or other liquors, or any kind of victuals, or other merchandise, he shall be delivered over to the civil magistrate, to be punished according to law.

III. Whosoever shall use any unlawful oath or execration (whether officer or soldier) shall incur the penalties expressed in the first article.

IV. If any officer or soldier shall presume to blaspheme the holy and undivided Trinity, or the persons of God the Father, God the Son, or God the Holy Ghost, or shall presume to speak against any known article of the Christian Faith, he shall be delivered over by the commanding officer to the civil magistrate to be punished according to law.

V. If any officer or soldier shall abuse or profane any place dedicated to the worship of God, or shall offer violence to any chaplain of the army, or any other minister of God's word, he shall be liable to such penalty or corporal punishment as shall be inflicted on him by a court-martial.

1 The British Articles of War of 1718, promulgated by the Crown under the Act of 4 Geo. I, c. 4. The articles of 1718 marked an epoch in the history of English military law. The military law, as a branch of the law of the land, legally operative in the time of peace, was then in its infancy. Only twenty-eight years before this date Parliament first recognized the necessity of providing by law for the punishment of certain military offences in time of peace. This legislative act, however, was very defective, and its defects were supplied by the Articles of War promulgated by the Crown, but it was not until the session of 1717-18 that the power of the Crown to issue such articles, to be in force at home in time of peace, was recognized by Parliament. The articles of 1718 were the first issued by the Crown by virtue of this legislative authorization; and it does not seem that there was at that time any dread of the consequences of a recognition of such a prerogative power; for the debate in Parliament did not run on this subject, but on the power of courts-martial to punish mutiny and desertion with death—a question with reference to which there was much difference of opinion, and which was at first carried by a majority of eighteen only.
The Articles of War were reproduced in "The Journal of the Military Service Institution" June 1886, p. 217-220.

VI. If any officer or soldier shall presume to use any traitorous or disrespectful words against the sacred person of his Majesty, his Royal Highness the Prince of Wales, or any of the royal family, or shall behave himself with contempt or disrespect toward the General or other commander-in-chief of the forces, or speak words tending to his hurt and dishonor, he shall be punished according to the nature of his offence, by the judgment of a regimental or general court-martial.

VII. If any officer or soldier shall excite, cause, or join in any mutiny or sedition in the company, troop, or regiment to which he belongs, or in any other company, troop, or regiment in his Majesty's service, or on any party or post where the duty is done by detachment from several regiments or otherwise, in the army, he shall suffer death, or such other punishment as a general court-martial shall inflict.

And if any officer, non-commissioned officer, or soldier shall hear any words tending to mutiny or sedition, or being anyway privy thereto, do not immediately use his utmost endeavors to suppress the same, as also to discover it to his superiors, if an officer, he shall be cashiered; if a non-commissioned officer or soldier, he shall be severely punished at the discretion of a court-martial.

VIII. If any officer or soldier shall refuse to obey the lawful orders of his superior officer, he shall be punished with death, or otherwise, as a general court-martial shall think fit.

X. All officers and soldiers who have received pay, or have been duly listed in our service, and shall desert the same, either in the field, upon a march, in quarters, or in garrison, and be convicted thereof before a general court-martial, shall suffer death, or such other punishment, as by the said court shall be inflicted.

XII. If any officer or soldier shall persuade or advise any other officer or soldier to desert our service, he shall suffer such punishment as shall be inflicted by the sentence of a general court-martial.

XVI. If any officer, non-commissioned officer, or soldier, shall be accused of any capital crime, or of any violence or offence against the person, estate, or property of any of our subjects, which is punishable by the known laws of the land, the commanding officers of every regiment, troop, or company, are hereby required to deliver over such accused person to the civil magistrate, so soon as applied to; and are also to be aiding and assisting to the officers of justice in the seizing and apprehending such offender, in order to bring him to trial, under pain of our highest displeasure.

XIX. No officer or soldier shall use any reproachful or provoking speeches or gestures to another, upon pain of imprisonment, and asking pardon of the party offended, in presence of his commanding officer.

Nor shall any officer or soldier presume to send a challenge to any other officer or soldier to fight a duel, upon pain of being cashiered, if he be an officer; or suffering the severest corporal punishment, if a non-commissioned officer or private soldier. And if any officer or non-commissioned officer, commanding a guard, shall wittingly and knowingly suffer any person whatever to go forth to fight a duel he shall be punished as above; and all seconds also, and carriers of challenges in order to duels, shall be taken as principals, and punished accordingly.

All officers of what condition soever, have power to part and quell all quarrels, frays, and other disorders, though of another company, troop, or regiment; and to command officers to arrest, and soldiers to prison, until their proper officers be acquainted therewith.

And whoever shall refuse to obey such officers (though of inferior rank) or draw his sword upon him, shall be punished as a general court-martial shall appoint.

Nor shall any officer or soldier upbraid another for refusing a challenge, since, according to these our orders, they but do the duty of soldiers, who ought to subject themselves to discipline; and we do acquit and discharge all men who have quarrels offered, or challenges sent to them, of all disgrace or opinion of disadvantage in the obedience hereunto; and whosoever shall upbraid them, and offend in this case, shall be punished as a challenger.

XXI. Every non-commissioned officer and soldier who shall enlist himself in our service, shall, at the time of his so enlisting, or within a month afterwards at the farthest, be taken before a Justice of Peace by the enlisting officer, or the officer commanding the troops or company into which he has listed, and shall there take the following oath:

> I swear to be true to our Sovereign Lord King George, and to serve him honestly and faithfully in defence of his person and dignity, against all his enemies and opposers whatsoever, and to observe and obey his Majesty's orders, and the orders of the Generals and officers set over me by his Majesty. So help me God.

XXVIII. All officers and soldiers are to behave themselves orderly in quarters and on the march; and whoever shall commit any waste or spoil, either on walks or trees, parks, warrens, fish-ponds, houses or gardens, corn-fields, inclosures or meadows, or shall maliciously destroy any property whatever belonging to any of our subjects, or belonging to any person whatever, unless by order of the then commander-in-chief of our forces, to annoy rebels, or other enemies in arms against us, he or they, that shall be found guilty of offending therein, shall (besides such penalties as they are liable to by law) be punished according to the nature and degree of the offence, by the judgment of a regimental or general court-martial.

XXIX. No officer shall demand billets for quartering of more than his effective men, nor quarter any women or children in the house assigned him for the quartering of officers and soldiers, without the consent of the owner, nor shall take money for freeing of landlords from quartering of officers or soldiers, under pain of being cashiered for it.

XXX. Every officer commanding a regiment, troop, company, or party, whether in settled quarters or on the march, shall see his own quarters, and the quarters of every officer and soldier under his command, paid, according to the rate specified in the act of Parliament now in force.

And upon every payment to be made in quarters, the said officer shall give public notice thereof to the landlords, in order to see them satisfied as aforesaid. And in case any such regiment, troop, company, or party, shall be ordered to march, before money may be come to the hands of the commanding officer as aforesaid, he is hereby required before his departure out of any town or village, to make up the accounts with all persons concerned in money due to them in quartering of officers or soldiers, for what time soever he shall have happened to remain there; and grant to every such party a signed certificate for the same, therein specifying the name of the regiment, troop, or company such officers or soldiers do belong to, under pain of being cashiered for it, upon proof of having wilfully offended herein.

XXXI. On marches, the commanding officers are to apply to the proper magistrates for the carriages necessary for the service, and to pay for them according to the Act of Parliament in that behalf, taking care not to abuse, nor to suffer any under their command, to beat or abuse the wagoners, or other persons attending such carriages, nor to put more than twenty hundred weight on any wain or wagon so furnished to them by the country.

And whatever officer shall be convicted of offending herein, or of refusing to grant certificates in case of failure of money, as in the preceding article, shall, by the judgment of a general court-martial, be cashiered or otherwise punished, according to the degree of his offence.

XXXII. All officers commanding in garrisons, in quarters, or on marches, shall keep good order, and redress all such abuses or disorders as may happen to be committed by any officer or soldier under their command; and if on complaint made to any such commanding officer, of beating of landlords, or extorting of more from them than they are obliged by law to furnish; of soldiers disturbing of fairs or markets, or committing any other kind of riot, to the disturbing or disquieting our people, he, the said commander, who shall refuse or omit to see justice done to the offender, and reparation made to the party injured, so far as part of the offender's pay can enable him, he shall, upon proof thereof, be punished by a general court-martial, as if he himself had personally committed the crimes or disorders complained of.

XXXVII. If any officer shall protect any person from his creditors, otherwise than is allowed by the present act of Parliament, or anyone who does not actually serve in the ranks, and consequently do all the duties of a soldier (according to the true intent and meaning of the said act), he shall be cashiered for it.

XLIV. In case any officer, non-commissioned officer, or soldier be accused of any violence against the person, estate, or property of any of our subjects, punishable by any of our civil courts or magistrates, the officers to whom such accusation is brought shall not proceed to the trial of such offender or offenders by a court-martial within the space of eight days, unless at the desire of the person or persons injured; and in case no application be made to the commanding officer in quarters during the space of eight days by the person or persons injured, the offender or offenders may be tried by a court-martial for any offence mentioned in these articles, provided that, within the space of the said eight days, the person injured hath not proceeded to the prosecution of such offender before a civil court or magistrate, and notice given thereof to the officer commanding in the quarters where such offence shall be committed.

XLV. These, our rules and articles, are to be observed by, and do in all respects regard, our troops and regiments of horse- and foot-guards, as well as our other forces.

XLVI. The aforegoing rules and articles shall be read and published at the head of every regiment, troop, and company mustered, or to be mustered, in our service, once every two months at furthest, and are to be duly observed by all officers and soldiers in our service, and also by our companies of gunners, and other military officers of our trains of artillery, with such alterations only as relate to the payment of soldiers' quarters and carriages, which in the kingdom of Ireland are to be regulated by the Lord-Lieutenant thereof, and in our islands, provinces, and garrisons beyond the seas, by the respective governors of the same, according as the nature of the thing shall require; and notwithstanding it is expressed in the sixteenth article of these, our rules and orders, that every commissioned officers is required to deliver up to the civil magistrate all such persons (under his command) as shall be accused of any crimes which are punishable by the known laws of the land, yet in our garrison of Gibraltar, island of Minorca, forts of Placentia, and Annapolis-Royal, where our forces now are, or in any other place beyond the seas to which any of our troops may hereafter be commanded, and where there is no form of our civil judicature in force, the governors or commanders respectively are to appoint general courts-martial to be held, who are to punish criminals by their sentence, as has been practised heretofore and authorized by former articles of war.

An Act for punishing Mutiny and Desertion of Officers and Soldiers in the Service of the United Company of Merchants of England trading to the East-Indies; and for the Punishment of Offences committed in the East-Indies, or at the Island of Saint Helena, 1754

27 GEORGE II Cap. IX

For Further Powers to hold Courts-martial (see Geo. 3. C. 14.); Every officer or Soldier in the Company's Service, who, alter Publication of this Act; Shall Mutiny, or Desert, &c.; or list in any other regiment; Or shall be found sleeping on, or shall desert his Post or correspond with the Enemy; Or shall strike, or not obey his superior Officer; shall suffer Death, or such Punishment as a Court-martial shall inflict.

WHEREAS the United Company of Merchants of England trading to the East-Indies, are possessed of several principal Settlements in the East-Indies, and of several Settlements or Factories subordinate to such principal Settlements, and are also possessed of the Island of Saint Helena: And for the Safety and Protection of the said Settlements and Places, and for the better carrying on of their Trade to the Advantage of this Nation, the said United Company, at their own Costs and Charges, do maintain and keep a Military Force for the Garrison and Defence of the said Settlements, Factories, and Places; and it being requisite for

the retaining of such Forces in their Duty, that an exact Discipline be observed, and that Soldiers who shall Mutiny, or stir up Sedition, or shall desert the said Company's Service, be brought to a more exemplary and speedy Punishment than the usual Forms of the Law do allow; be it therefore enacted the King's most Excellent Majesty, by and with the Advice and Consent of the Lords Spiritual and Temporal, and Commons, in this present Parliament assembled, and by the Authority of the same, That from and after the twenty-fifth Day of March, one thousand seven hundred and fifty four (27 March 1754), if any Person being mustered or in pay as an Officer, or who is or shall be listed, or in the said Company's pay as a Soldier in any of their Settlements, or in the said Island of Saint Helena, respectively, shall, at any Time after the Publication of this Act, in their principal Settlements, in the said Island of Saint Helena, respectively, and within such Time as such Officer or Soldier shall have contracted and agreed to serve the said United Company, begin, excite, cause, or join in, any Mutiny or Sedition in the Company, Troop, or Regiment whereto he doth belong, or in any other Company, Troop, or Regiment in the said United Company's Service; or shall not use his utmost Endeavours to suppress the same, or coming to the Knowledge of any Mutiny, or intended Mutiny, shall not without Delay give Information thereof to his commanding Officer; or shall desert the said United Company's Service; or being a Soldier actually listed in any Regiment, Troop, or Company, shall list himself in any other Regiment, Troop, or Company, without a Discharge produced in Writing from the Officer commanding in chief the Regiment,

Troop, or Company, in which he last served as a listed Soldier; or shall be found sleeping upon his Post, or shall leave it before relieved; or if any Officer or Soldier in the said United Company's Service shall, either upon Land, or upon the Sea, hold Correspondence with any Rebel to his Majesty, or with any Enemy of his Majesty, or of the said United Company; or give them Advice or Intelligence cither by Letters, Messages, Signs, or Tokens, in any Manner or Way whatsoever; or shall treat with such Rebels or Enemies, or enter into any Condition with them without the Licence of the said United Company, or of the said United Company's President and Council, at any of their said principal Settlements, or of the said United Company's Governor and Council at Saint Helena, or without the Licence of the General, Lieutenant General, or Chief Commander of the said Company's Forces; or shall strike or use any violence against his superior Officer, being in the Execution of his Office; or shall disobey any lawful Command of his superior Officer; all and every Person and Persons so offending in any of the Matters before-mentioned shall suffer Death, or such other Punishment as by a Court-martial shall be inflicted.

The King may grant a Commission to hold Courts-martial, &c.

II. And be it further enacted by the Authority aforesaid, That his Majesty may grant a Commission or Warrant under his Royal Sign Manual, unto the Court of Directors of the said

United Company, who, by Virtue of such Commission or Warrant, shall have Power under the Seal of the said United Company to authorise and empower their President and Council for the Time being, at their said principal Settlements respectively, or the major Part of them, and their Governor and Council for the Time being at the said Island of Saint Helena, or the major Part of them, from Time to Time to appoint Courts-martial; and to authorise and empower the Commander in Chief of any Detachment of any of the Officers or Soldiers employed in the said Company's Service, to appoint Courts-martial for the Trial of any of the Officers or Soldiers under their respective Commands; in which Courts-martial all the Offences above-mentioned, and all other Offences herein-after specified, shall be tried and proceeded against in such Manner as by this Act shall be hereafter directed.

The Commander-in-Chief to appoint Courts-martial

III. Provided always, and be it enacted, That when and so long as any of his Majesty's Forces shall be employed to act in defence of any of the said Company's Settlements, or to assist against any of their Enemies in the East-Indies, the Power of appointing Courts-martial, or authorising such Appointment as aforesaid, shall be in the Commander in Chief of such his Majesty's Forces for the Time being, over such of the said Company's Officers and Soldiers as shall belong to the principal Settlement where or from whence such Forces shall be employed.

Immoralities or neglect of Duty, punishable by Courts-martial

IV. And be it also further enacted, That it shall and may be lawful to and for such Courts-martial, by their Sentence or Judgment, to inflict corporal Punishment on any Soldier for Immoralities, Misbehaviour, or neglect of Duty.

General Courts-martial trial not to consist of less than nine; President of the Court; General Court-martial at Saint Helena not to consist of less than five; President of each Court-martial may administer Oath; Two-third of the Officers present to concur in all sentence of death.

V. And it is hereby further enacted, That no general Court-martial which shall have Power to sit by Virtue of this Act, or by any Authority from the Commander in Chief of his Majesty's Forces, or by Appointment of the President and Council of any of the said United Company's principal Settlements, or the major Part of them, shall consist of a less Number than nine; whereof none to be under the degree of a Commission Officer; and the President of such general Courts-martial shall neither be the Commander-in-Chief, or Governor of the Garrison where the Offender shall be tried, nor under the Degree of a Captain; and that no general Court-martial, which shall have Power to sit by Virtue of this Act, by Appointment from the Governor and Council of Saint Helena, or the major Part of them, shall consist of a less Number than five, whereof none to be under the Degree of a commissioned Officer; and the President of such general Court-martial shall neither be the Commander-in-Chief, or Governor of the Garrison where the Offender shall be tried, nor under the Degree of a Lieutenant; and that such Courts-martial shall have Power and Authority, and are hereby required to take and administer such Oaths, and to proceed in such Manner as his Majesty shall from Time to Time think fit to order and direct, by any Rules or Orders under his Royal Sign Manual; and no Sentence of Death shall be given against any Offender in such Case by any general Court-martial, unless two-thirds of the Officers present shall concur therein; and no Proceeding or Trial shall be had upon any Offence, but between the Hours of eight of the Clock in the Morning and three in the Afternoon, except in Cases which require an immediate example.

Judge Advocate to transmit to the Commander in Chief the original proceedings

VI. Provided always, and it is hereby enacted by the Authority aforesaid, That every Judge Advocate, or Person officiating as such at any general Court-martial, do, and he is hereby required to transmit, with as much Expedition as the Opportunity of Time and Distance of Place can admit, the original Proceedings and Sentence of such Court-martial to his Majesty's Commander-in-Chief for the Time being, in case such Court-martial shall be held by Virtue of his Warrant or Authority as aforesaid, or to the President and Council of such of the said United Company's principal Settlements, by Virtue of whose Warrant or Authority the same shall be held; or unto the Governor and Council at Saint Helena, if the same shall be held within their Jurisdiction; which said original Proceedings and Sentence shall be carefully kept and preserved by such Commander in Chief, or by such President and Council, or Governor and Council respectively; to the End that the Persons intitled thereto may be enabled, upon Application to them, to obtain Copies thereof according to the true Intent and Meaning of this Act.

No Person to be tried a second Time for the same offence

VII. Provided also, and it is hereby declared and enacted, That no Officer or Soldier being acquitted or convicted of any Offence, be liable to be tried a second Time by the same or any other Court-martial for the same Offence; and that no Sentence given by any Court-martial, and signed by the President thereof, be liable to be revised more than once.

The King may make Articles of War

VIII. Provided always, and be it enacted, That it shall and may be lawful to and for his Majesty to form, make, and establish Articles of War, for the better Government of the said United Company's Forces, and for bringing Offenders against the same to Justice; and to erect and constitute Courts-martial, with Power to try, hear, and determine any Crimes or Offences by such Articles of War, and inflict Penalties by Sentence or Judgment of the same, as well within the said United Company's Limits of Trade, as in the said Island of Saint Helena.

No punishment to extend to Life of Limb in Pace, except by this Act

IX. Provided always, That no Person or Persons shall be adjudged to suffer any Punishment extending to Life or Limb, by the said Articles, in Time of Peace, except for such Crimes as are expressed to be so punishable by this Act.

Capital Crimes cognizable by the civil Magistrate punishable by cashiering

X. Provided also, That no Person or Persons being acquitted, or convicted of any capital Crimes, Violences, or Offences, by the civil Magistrate, shall be liable to be punished by a Court-martial for the same, otherwise than by cashiering.

Offenders against the Laws to be delivered up to the civil Magistrate; Officers neglecting to deliver up such Offenders; Disabled to hold any Military Office, Conviction thereof to be affirmed at the Quarter Sessions, and a Certificate transmitted to the President and Council

XI. Provided also, That if any Officer, Non-commission Officer, or Soldier, shall be accused of any capital Crime, or of any Violence or Offence against the Person, Estate, or Property of any of his Majesty's Subjects, which is punishable by the known Laws of the Land, the Commanding Officer or Officers of every Regiment, Troop, Company, or Party, is and are hereby required to use his utmost Endeavours to deliver over such accused Person to the civil Magistrate, shall also be aiding and assisting to the Officers of Justice in the seizing and apprehending such Offender, in order to bring him to trial: And if any such commanding Officer shall wilfully neglect or refuse, upon Application made to him for that Purpose, to deliver over any such accused Person to the civil Magistrate, or to be aiding and assisting to the Officers of Justice in apprehending such Offender; every such Officer so offending, and being thereof convicted before two or more Justices of the Peace for the Settlement or Place where the Fact is committed, by the Oath of two credible Witnesses, shall be cashiered, and shall be utterly disabled to have or hold any Military Office or Employment in the said United Company's Service in the East-Indies; provided the said Conviction be affirmed at the next Quarter Sessions of the Peace for the said Settlement or Place, and a Certificate thereof be transmitted to the President and Council of such principal Settlement, who are hereby obliged to certify the same to the next Court-martial.

Person employed in the trains of Artillery included

XII. And whereas it may otherwise be doubted whether the Officers and Persons employed in the several Trains of Artillery be within the Intent and Meaning of this Act; it is hereby enacted by the Authority aforesaid, That the Officers and Persons employed, or that shall be employed in any of the Trains of Artillery, be deemed in all Respects whatsoever within the Intent and Meaning of this Act.

Offences committed by the Company's President, Council or Governors; May be enquired of in the Court of King's Bench or before Commissioners appointed by his Majesty in England

XIII. And be it further enacted by the Authority aforesaid, That if any of the said United Company's Presidents or Council, at their respective principal Settlements, or any of them, or their Governor or Council at the said Island of *Saint Helena*, shall, after the said twenty-fifth Day of March, one thousand seven hundred and fifty-four (25 March 1754), be guilty of Oppressing any of his Majesty's Subjects beyond the Seas, within their respective Jurisdictions or Commands, or shall be guilty of any other Crime or Offence contrary to the Laws of that Part of Great Britain called *England*, or in Force within their respective Jurisdictions or Commands; such Oppression, Crimes, and Offences, may be enquired of, heard, and determined in his Majesty's Court of King's Bench, within that Part of Great-Britain called *England*; or before such Commissioners, and and in such County of that Part of Great-Britain called *England*, as shall be assigned by his Majesty's Commission, and by good and lawful Men of the same County; and such Punishment shall be inflicted on such Offenders, as are usually inflicted for Offences of the like Nature committed in that Part of Great-Britain called *England*.

The Articles of War passed by the Parliament applicable to any portion of the Company's Forces were published in 1765.

British Articles of War of 1765[1]

RULES AND ARTICLES FOR THE BETTER GOVERNMENT OF OUR FORCE AND FOOT GUARDS, AND OTHER FORCES IN OUR KINGDOMS OF GREAT BRITAIN AND IRELAND, DOMINIONS BEYOND THE SEAS, AND FOREIGN PARTS

Section I: Divine Worship

George R.

Article I.

All Officers and Soldiers, not having just Impediment, shall diligently frequent Divine Service and Sermon, in the Places appointed for the assembling of the Regiment, Troop, or Company, to which they belong; such as wilfully absent themselves, or, being present, behave indecently or irreverently, shall, if Commissioned Officers, be brought before a Court-Martial, there to be publickly and severely reprimanded by the President; if Non-commissioned Officers, or Soldiers, every Person so offending shall, for his First Offence, forfeit Twelve Pence, to be deducted out of his next pay; for the Second Offence he shall not only forfeit Twelve Pence, but be laid in Irons for Twelve Hours; and for every like Offence, shall suffer and pay in like Manner: Which Money so forfeited, shall be applied to the Use of the sick Soldiers of the Troop or Company to which the Offender belongs.

Article II.

Whatsoever Officer or Soldier shall use any unlawful Oath or Execration, shall incur the Penalties expressed in the First Article.

Article III.

Whatsoever Officer or Soldier shall presume to speak against any known Article of the Christian Faith, shall be delivered over to the Civil Magistrate, to be proceeded against according to Law.

Article IV.

Whatsoever Officer or Soldier shall profane any Place dedicated to Divine Worship, or shall offer Violence to a Chaplain of the Army, or to any other Minister of God's Word; he shall be liable to such Penalty or corporal Punishment as shall be inflicted on him by a Court-martial.

1 Winthrop William, 1920, *Military Law and Precedents*, Washington: Government Printing Office, pp. 931-945.

Article V.

No Chaplain who is commissioned to a Regiment, Company, Troop, or Garrison, shall absent himself from the said Regiment, Company, Troop, or Garrison (excepting in case of Sickness or Leave of Absence) upon Pain of being brought to a Court-Martial, and punished as their Judgment and the Circumstances of his Offence may require.

Article VI.

Whatsoever Chaplain to a Regiment, Troop, or Garrison, shall be guilty of Drunkenness, or of other scandalous or vicious Behaviour, derogating from the Sacred Character with which he is invested, shall upon due Proofs before a Court-martial, be discharged from his said Office.

Section II: Mutiny

Article I.

Whatsoever Officer or Soldier shall presume to use traiterous or disrespectful Words against the Sacred Person of his Majesty, or any of the Royal Family; if a Commissioned Officer, he shall be cashiered; if a Non-commissioned Officer or Soldier, he shall suffer such Punishment as shall be inflicted upon him by the Sentence of a Court-martial.

Article II.

Any Officer or Soldier who shall behave himself with Contempt or Disrespect towards the General, or other Commander in Chief of Our Forces, or shall speak Words tending to his Hurt or Dishonour, shall be punished according to the Nature of his Offence, by the Judgment of a Court-martial.

Article III.

Any Officer or Soldier who shall begin, excite, cause, or join in, any Mutiny or Sedition, in the Troop, Company or Regiment, to which he belongs, or In any other Troop or Company in Our Service, or in any Party, Post, Detachment, or Guard, on any Pretence whatsoever, shall suffer Death, or such other Punishment as by a Court-martial shall be inflicted.

Article IV.

Any Officer, Non-commissioned Officer, or Soldier, who being present at any Mutiny or Sedition, does not use his utmost Endeavour to suppress the same, or coming to the Knowledge of any Mutiny or intended Mutiny, does not without Delay give Information thereof to his Commanding Officer, shall be punished by a Court-martial with Death, or otherwise according to the Nature of the Offence.

Article V.

Any Officer or Soldier, who shall strike his superior Officer, or draw, or offer to draw, or shall lift up any Weapon, or offer any Violence against him, being in the Execution of his Office, on any Pretence whatsoever, or shall disobey any lawful Command of his superior Officer, shall suffer Death, or such other Punishment as shall, according to the Nature of his Offence, be inflicted upon him by the Sentence of a Court-martial.

Section III: Of Inlisting Soldiers

Article I.

Every Non-commissioned Officer and Soldier, who shall inlist himself in Our Service, shall, at the Time of his so Inlisting, or within Four Days afterwards, have the Articles against Mutiny and Desertion read to him, and shall, by the Officer who inlisted him or by the Commanding Officer of the Troop or Company into which he was inlisted, be taken before the next Justice of the Peace, or Chief Magistrate of any City or Town Corporate (not being an officer of the Army) or in Foreign Parts, where Recourse cannot be had to the Civil Magistrate, before the Judge Advocate, and in his presence shall take the following Oath:

> I Swear to be true to our Sovereign Lord King GEORGE, and to serve him honestly and faithfully, in Defence of his Person, Crown, and Dignity, against all His Enemies or Opposers whatsoever: And to observe and obey His Majesty's Orders, and the Orders of the Generals and Officers set over me by his Majesty.

Which Justice or Magistrate is to give the Officer a Certificate signifying that the Man inlisted did take the said Oath, and that the Articles of War were read to him, according to the Act of Parliament.

Article II.

After a Non-commissioned Officer or Soldier shall have been duly inlisted and sworn, he shall not be dismissed Our Service without a Discharge in Writing; and no Discharge granted to him shall be Allowed of as sufficient, which is not signed by a Field Officer of the Regiment into which he was inlisted; or Commanding officer, where no Field Officer of the Regiment is in *Great Britian.*

Section IV: Musters

Article I.

Every Officer commanding a Regiment, Troop, or Company, shall, upon the Notice given to him by the Commissary of the Musters, or from One of his Deputies, assemble the Regiment, Troop, or Company under his Command, in the next convenient place for their being mustered.

Article II.

Every Colonel or other Field Officer commanding the Regiment, Troop, or Company, and actually residing with it, may give Furloughs to non-commissioned Officers and Soldiers, in such Numbers, and for so long a Time, as he shall judge to be most consistent with the Good of Our Service; but no Non-commissioned Officer or Soldier shall by Leave of his Captain, or inferior Officer commanding the Troop or Company (his Field Officer not being present) be absent above Twenty Days in Six Months, nor shall more than Two private Men be absent at the same Time from their Troop or Company, excepting some extraordinary Occasion shall require it, of which Occasion the Field Officer present with, and commanding the Regiment, is to be the Judge.

Article III.

At every Muster the Commanding Officer of each Regiment, Troop, or Company there present, shall give to the Commissary Certificates signed by himself, signifying how long such Officers who shall not appear at the said Muster have been absent, and the Reason of their Absence; in like Manner the Commanding Officer of every Troop or Company shall give Certificates, signifying the Reasons of the Absence of the Non-commissioned Officers and private Soldiers; which Reasons and Time of Absence shall be inserted in the Muster-rolls opposite to the Names of the respective absent Officers and Soldiers: The said Certificates shall, together with the Muster-rolls, be remitted to Our Commissary's Office within Twenty Days after such Muster being taken; on the Failure thereof, the Commissary so offending shall be discharged from Our Service.

Article IV.

Every Officer who shall be convicted before a General Court-martial of having signed a false Certificate, relating to the Absence of either Officer or private Soldier, shall be cashiered.

Article V.

Every Officer who shall knowingly make a false Muster of Man or Horse, and every Officer or Commissary who shall willingly sign, direct, or allow the signing of the Muster-rolls, wherein such false Muster is contained, shall, upon Proof made thereof by Two Witnesses before a General Court-Martial, be cashiered, and suffer such other Penalty as by the Act of Parliament is for that Purpose inflicted.

Article VI.

Any Commissary who shall be convicted of having taken Money by way of Gratification on the mustering any Regiment, Troop, or Company, or on the signing the Muster-rolls, shall be displaced from his Office, and suffer such other Penalty as by the Act of Parliament is inflicted.

Article VII.

Any Officer who shall presume to muster any Person as a Soldier, who is at other Times accustomed to wear a Livery, or who does not actually do his duty as a Soldier, shall be deemed guilty of having made a false Muster, and shall suffer accordingly.

Section V: Returns.

Article I.

Every Officer who shall knowingly make a false Return to Us, to the Commander in Chief of our Forces, or to any his superior Officers authorized to call for such Returns, of the State of the Regiment, Troop, or Company, or Garrison, under his Command, or of Arms, Ammunition, Clothing, or other Stores thereunto belonging, shall by a Court-martial be cashiered.

Article II.

The Commanding Officer of every Regiment, Troop, or Independent Company, or Garrison in *South Britain*, shall, in the Beginning of every Month, remit to the Commander in Chief of Our Forces, and to Our Secretary at War, an exact Return of the State of the Regiment, Troop, Independent Company, or Garrison under his Command, specifying the Names of the Officers not then residing at their Posts, and the Reason for, and Time of, their Absence: Whoever shall be convicted of having, through Neglect or Design, omitted the sending such Returns, shall be punished according to the Nature of his Crime by the Judgment of a General Court-Martial.

Article III.

Returns shall be made in like Manner of the State of Our Forces in Our Kingdom of *Ireland*, to the Chief Governor or Governors thereof, as likewise of Our Forces in North Britain, to the Officer there commanding in Chief; which Returns shall from time to time be remitted to Us, as it shall be best for Our Service.

Article IV.

It is Our Pleasure, That exact Returns of the State of Our Garrisons at *Gibraltar* and *Port Mahon*, and of Our Regiments, Garrisons, and Independent Companies in *America*, be by their respective Governors or Commanders there residing, by all convenient Opportunities, remitted to Our Secretary at War, for their being laid before Us.

Section VI: Desertion

Article I.

All Officers and Soldiers, who having received Pay, or having been duly inlisted in Our Service, shall be convicted of having deserted the same, shall suffer Death, or such other Punishment as by a Court-martial shall be inflicted.

Article II.

Any Non-commissioned Officer or Soldier, who shall, without Leave from his Commanding Officer, absent himself from his Troop or Company, or from any Detachment with which he shall be commanded, shall, upon being convicted thereof, be punished according to the Nature of his Offence at the Discretion of a Court-martial.

Article III.

No Non-commissioned Officer or Soldier shall inlist himself In any other Regiment, Troop, or Company, without a regular Discharge from the Regiment, Troop, or Company, in which he last served, on the Penalty of being reputed a Deserter, and suffering accordingly: And in case any officer shall knowingly receive and entertain such Non-commissioned Officer or Soldier, or shall not, after his being discovered to be a Deserter, immediately confine him, and give Notice thereof to the Corps In which he last served, he the said Officer so offending shall by a Court-Martial be cashiered.

Article IV.

Whatsoever Officer or Soldier shall be convicted of having advised or persuaded any other Officer or Soldier to desert Our Service, shall suffer such Punishment as shall be inflicted upon him by the Sentence of a Court-martial.

Section VII: Quarrels and Sending Challenges

Article I.

No Officer or Soldier shall use any reproachful or provoking Speeches or Gestures to another, upon Pain, if an Officer, of being put in Arrest; if a Soldier, imprisoned, and of asking Pardon of the Party offended, in the Presence of his Commanding Officer.

Article II.

No Officer or Soldier shall presume to send a Challenge to any other Officer or Soldier, to fight a duel, upon Pain, if a Commissioned Officer, of being cashiered; if a Non-commissioned Officer, or Soldier, of suffering corporal Punishment, at the Discretion of a Court-martial.

Article III.

If any Commissioned or Non-commissioned Officer commanding a Guard shall knowingly and willingly suffer any Person whatsoever to go forth to fight a Duel, he shall be punished as a Challenger: And likewise all Seconds, Promoters, and Carriers of Challenges, in order to Duels, shall be deemed as Principals, and be punished accordingly.

Article IV.

All Officers, of what Condition soever, have power to part and quell all Quarrels, Frays, and Disorders, though the Persons concerned should belong to another Regiment, Troop, or Company; and either to order Officers into Arrest, or Non-commissioned Officers or Soldiers to Prison, till their proper superior Officers shall be acquainted therewith; and whosoever shall refuse to obey such Officer (though of an inferior Rank) or shall draw his Sword upon him, shall be punished at the discretion of a General Court-martial.

Article V.

Whatsoever Officer or Soldier shall upbraid another for refusing a Challenge, shall himself be punished as a Challenger; and We hereby acquit and discharge all Officers and Soldiers of any Disgrace, or Opinion of Disadvantage, which might arise from their having refused to accept of Challenges, as they will have only acted in Obedience to Our Orders, and done their Duty as good Soldiers, who subject themselves to Discipline.

Section VIII: Suttling

Article I.

No Suttler shall be permitted to sell any Kind of Liquors or Victuals, or to keep their Houses or Shops open, for the Entertainment of Soldiers, after Nine at Night, or before the Beating of the Reveilles, or upon *Sundays*, during Divine Service or Sermon, on the Penalty of being dismissed from all future Suttling.

Article II.

All Officers, Soldiers, and Suttlers, shall have full Liberty to bring into any of Our Forts or Garrisons, any Quantity or Species of Provisions, eatable or drinkable, except where any Contract or Contracts are or shall be entered into by Us, or by Our Order, for furnishing such Provisions, and with respect only to the Species of Provisions so contracted for.

Article III.

All Governors, Lieutenant Governors, and Officers commanding in Our Forts, Barracks, or Garrisons, are hereby required to see, that the Persons permitted to Suttle shall supply the Soldiers with good and wholesome Provisions at the Market Price, as they shall be answerable to Us for their Neglect.

Article IV.

No Governors, or Officers, commanding in any of Our Garrisons, Forts, or Barracks, shall either themselves exact exhorbitant Prices for Houses or Stalls let out to Suttlers, or shall connive at the like Exactions in others; nor by their own Authority, and for their private Advantage, shall they lay any Duty or Imposition upon, or be Interested in the Sale of such Victuals, Liquors, or other Necessaries of Life, which are brought into the Garrison, Fort, or Barracks, for the use of the Soldiers, on the Penalty of being discharged from our Service.

Section IX: Quarters

Article I.

No Officer shall demand Billets for Quartering more than his effective Men; nor shall he quarter any Wives, Children, Men or Maid Servants, in the Houses assigned for the Quartering of Officers or Soldiers, without the Consent of the Owners; nor shall he take Money for the freeing of Landlords from the Quartering of Officers or Soldiers: If a Commissioned Officer so offending, he shall be cashiered; if a Non-commissioned Officer, he shall be reduced to a private Centinel, and suffer such corporal Punishment as shall be inflicted upon him by the Sentence of a Court-martial.

Article II.

Every Officer commanding a Regiment, Troop, or Company, or Party, whether in settled Quarters, or upon a March, shall take Care that his own Quarters, as also the Quarters of every Officer and Soldier under his Command, be regularly cleared at the End of every Week, according to the Rules specified by the Act of Parliament now in Force; but in case any such Regiment, Troop, or Company or Party be ordered to march before Money may be come to the Hands of the Commanding Officer aforesaid, he is hereby required to see that the Accounts with all Persons who shall have Money due to them for the Quartering of Officers and Soldiers, be exactly stated; specifying what Sum is then justly due to him, as likewise the Regiment, Troop, or Company to which the Officers and Soldiers so indebted to him belong, and is, by the first Opportunity, to remit Duplicates of the said Certificates to Our Paymaster General: Any Commanding Officer who shall refuse or neglect the making up such Accounts, and certifying the same as is above directed, shall be cashiered.

Article III.

The Commanding Officer of every Regiment, Troop, or Company, or Detachment, shall, upon their first coming to any City, Town, or Village, where they are to remain in Quarters, cause publick Proclamation to be made, signifying, That if the Landlords or other Inhabitants suffer the Non-commissioned Officers or Soldiers to contract Debts beyond what their daily Subsistence will answer, that such Debts will not be discharged; he, the said Commanding Officer shall, for refusing or neglecting so to do, be suspended for Three Months; during which Time his whole Pay shall be applied to the discharging such Debts as shall have been contracted by the Non-commissioned Officers or Soldiers under his Command, beyond the Amount of their daily Subsistence: If there be any Overplus remaining, it may be returned to him.

Article IV.

If, after publick Proclamation to be made, the Inhabitants shall notwithstanding suffer the Non-commissioned Officers and Soldiers to contract Debts beyond what the Money issued out, or to be issued out for their daily Subsistence will answer, it will be at their own Peril, the Officers not being obliged to discharge the said Debts.

Article V.

Every Officer commanding in Quarters, Garrisons, or on a March, shall keep good Order, and to the utmost of his Power redress all such abuses or disorders which may be committed by any Officer or Soldier under his Command if, upon Complaint made to him of Officers or Soldiers beating, or otherwise ill-treating of their Landlords, or of extorting more from them than they are obliged to furnish by Law; of disturbing Fairs or Markets, or of committing any Kind of Riots, to the disquieting of Our People; he the said Commander who shall refuse or omit to see Justice done on the Offender or Offenders, and Reparation made to the Party or Parties injured, as far as Part of the Offender's Pay shall enable him or them, shall, upon Proof thereof, be punished by a General Court-martial, as if he himself had committed the Crimes or Disorders complained of.

Section X: Carriages

The Commanding Officer of every Regiment, Troop, Company or Detachment, which shall be ordered to march, is to apply to the proper Magistrates for the necessary Carriages, and is to pay for them as is directed by the Act of Parliament; taking Care not himself to abuse, nor to suffer any Persons under his Command to beat or abuse the Waggoners, or other Persons attending such Carriages ; nor to suffer more than Thirty hundred Weight to be loaded on any Wain or Waggon so furnished, or in Proportion on Carts or Carrs; not to permit Soldiers (except such as are sick or lame) or Women to ride upon the said Carriages; Whatsoever Officer shall offend herein, or, in case of Failure of Money, shall refuse to Grant Certificates, specifying the Sums due for the Use of such Carriages, and the Name of the Regiment, Troop, or Company in whose Service they were employed, shall be cashiered, or be otherwise punished according to the Degree of his Offence by a General Court-martial.

Section XI: Of Crimes Punishable by Law

Article I.

Whenever any Officer or Soldier shall be accused of a capital Crime, or of having used Violence, or committed any Offence against the Persons or Property of Our Subjects, such as is punishable by the known Laws of the Land, the Commanding Officer and Officers of every Regiment, Troop, or Party, to which the Person or Persons so accused shall belong, are hereby required, upon Application duly made by or in behalf of the Party or Parties injured, to use his utmost Endeavours to deliver over such accused Person or Persons to the Civil Magistrate; and likewise to be aiding and assisting to the Officers of Justice, in apprehending and securing the Person or Persons so accused, in order to bring them to a Trial: If any Commanding Officer or Officers shall willfully neglect or shall refuse, upon the Application aforesaid, to deliver over such accused Person or Persons to the Civil Magistrates, or to be aiding and assisting to the Officers of Justice in apprehending such Person or Persons, the Officer or Officers so offending shall be cashiered.

Article II.

No Officer shall protect any Person from his Creditors on the Pretence of his being a Soldier, nor any Non-commissioned Officer or Soldier who does not actually do all Duties as such, and no farther than is allowed by the present Act of Parliament, and according to the true Intent and Meaning of the said Act: Any Officer offending herein, being convicted thereof before a Court-martial, shall be cashiered.

Section XII: Of Redressing Wrongs

Article I.

If any Officer shall think himself to be wronged by his Colonel, or the Commanding Officer of the Regiment, and shall, upon due Application made to him, be refused to be redressed, he may complain to the General, commanding in Chief, of Our Forces, in order to obtain Justice; who is hereby required to examine into the said Complaint; and either by himself, or by Our Secretary at War, to make his Report to Us thereupon, in order to receive Our further Directions.

Article II.

If any inferior Officer or Soldier shall think himself wronged by his Captain, or other Officer commanding the Troop or Company to which he belongs, he is to complain thereof to the Commanding Officer of the Regiment, who is hereby required to summon a Regimental Court-martial, for the doing Justice to the Complainant; from which Regimental Court-martial either Party may, if he thinks himself still aggrieved, appeal to a General Court-martial: But if, upon a Second Hearing, the Appeal shall appear to be vexatious and groundless, the Person so appealing shall be punished at the Discretion of the said General Court-martial.

Section XIII: Of Stores, Ammunition, &c.

Article I.

Whatsoever Commissioned Officer, Store-keeper, or Commissary shall be convicted at a General Court-martial of having sold (without a proper Order for that Purpose) embezzled, misapplied, or wilfully, or through neglect, suffered any of Our Provisions, Forage, Arms, Clothing, Ammunition, or other Military Stores, to be spoiled or damaged, the said Officer, Storekeeper, or Commissary so offending, shall, at his own Charge, make good the Loss or Damage, and be dismissed from Our service, and suffer such other Penalty as by the Acts of Parliament is inflicted.

Article II.

Whatsoever Non-commissioned Officer or Soldier shall be convicted at a Regimental Court-martial of having sold, or designedly, or through Neglect, wasted the Ammunition delivered out to him to be employed in Our Service, shall, if a Non-commissioned Officer, be reduced to a private Centinel, and shall besides suffer corporal Punishment, in the same Manner as a private Centinel so offending, at the Discretion of a Regimental Court-martial.

Article III.

Every Non-commissioned Officer or Soldier who shall be convicted at a Court-martial of having sold, lost, or spoiled, through Neglect, his Horse, Arms, Clothes, or Accoutrements, shall undergo such Weekly Stoppages (not exceeding the Half of his Pay) as a Court-martial shall judge sufficient for repairing the Loss or Damage; and shall suffer Imprisonment, or such other corporal Punishment, as his crime shall deserve.

Article IV.

Every Non-commissioned Officer who shall be convicted at a General or Regimental Court-martial, of having embezzled or misapplied any Money, with which he may have been intrusted for the Payment of the Men under his Command, or for inlisting Men Into Our Service, shall be reduced to serve in the Ranks as a private Soldier, be put under Stoppages until the Money be made good, and suffer such corporal Punishment (not extending to Life or Limb) as the Court-martial shall think fit.

Article V.

Every Captain of a Troop or Company, is charged with the Arms, Accoutrements. Ammunition, Clothing, or other warlike Stores belonging to the Troop or Company under his Command, which he is to be accountable for to his Colonel, in case of their being lost, spoiled, or damaged, not by unavoidable Accidents, or on actual Service.

Section XIV: Of Duties in Quarters, in Garrison, or in the Field.

Article I.

All Non-commissioned Officers and Soldiers, who shall be found One Mile from the Camp, without Leave in Writing from their Commanding Officer, shall suffer such Punishment as shall be inflicted upon them by the Sentence of a Court-martial.

Article II.

No Officer or Soldier shall lie out of his Quarters, Garrison, or Camp without Leave from his superior Officer, upon Penalty of being punished according to the Nature of his Offence by the Sentence of a Court-Martial.

Article III.

Every Non-commissioned Officer and Soldier shall retire to his Quarters or Tent at the Beating of the Retreat; in Default of which, he shall be punished according to the Nature of his Offence, by the Commanding Officer.

Article IV.

No Officer, Non-commissioned Officer, or Soldier shall fail of repairing, at the time fixed, to the Place of Parade of Exercise, or other Rendezvous appointed by his Commanding Officer, if not prevented by Sickness, or some other evident Necessity; or shall go from the said Place of Rendezvous, or from his Guard, without Leave from his Commanding Officer, before he shall be regularly dismissed or relieved, on the Penalty of being punished according to the Nature of his Offence, by the Sentence of a Court-martial.

Article V.

Whatever Commissioned Officer shall be found drunk on his Guard, Party, or other Duty, under Arms, shall be cashiered for it; any Non-commissioned Officer or Soldier so offending, shall suffer such corporal Punishment as shall be inflicted by the Sentence of a Court-martial.

Article VI.

Whatever Centinel shall be found sleeping upon his Post, or shall leave it before he shall be regularly relieved, shall suffer Death, or such other Punishment as shall be inflicted by the Sentence of a Court-martial.

Article VII.

No Soldier belonging to any of Our Troops or Regiments of Horse or Foot Guards, or to any other Regiment of Horse, Foot, or Dragoons in Our Service, shall hire another to do his Duty for him, or be excused from Duty, but in case of Sickness, Disability, or Leave of Absence; and every such soldier found guilty of hiring his Duty, as also the Party so hired to do another's Duty, shall be punished at the next Regimental Court-martial.

Article VIII.

And every Non-commissioned Officer conniving at such Hiring of Duty as aforesaid, shall be reduced for it; and every Commissioned Officer, knowing and allowing of such ill Practices in Our Service, shall be punished by the Judgment of a General Court-martial.

Article IX.

Any Person belonging to Our Forces employed in Foreign Parts who, by discharging of Fire Arms, drawing of Swords, beating of Drums, or by any other Means whatsoever, shall occasion false Alarm in Camp, Garrison, or Quarters, shall suffer Death, or such other Punishment as shall be ordered by the Sentence of a General Court-martial.

And whosoever shall be found guilty of the said Offence in *Great Britain* or *Ireland*, shall be punished at the Discretion of a General Court-martial.

Article X.

Any Officer or Soldier, who shall, without urgent Necessity, or without the Leave of his superior Officer, quit his Platoon or Division, shall be punished according to the Nature of his Offence by the Sentence of a Court-martial.

Article XI.

No Officer or Soldier shall do Violence to any Person who brings Provisions or other Necessaries to the Camp, Garrison, or Quarters of Our Forces employed in Foreign Parts, on Pain of Death.

Article XII.

Whatsoever Officer or Soldier shall misbehave himself before the Enemy, or shamefully abandon any Post committed to his Charge, or shall speak words inducing others to do the like, shall suffer Death.

Article XIII.

Whatsoever Officer or Soldier shall misbehave himself before the Enemy, and run away, or shamefully abandon any Port, Post, or Guard, which he or they shall be commanded to defend, or speak Words inducing others to do the like; or who, after Victory, shall quit his Commanding Officer, or Post, to plunder and pillage; every such Offender, being duly convicted thereof, shall be reputed a Disobeyer of Military Orders; and shall suffer Death, or such other Punishment as by a General Court-martial shall be Inflicted on him.

Article XIV.

Any Person belonging to Our Forces employed in Foreign Parts, who shall cast away his Arms and Ammunition, shall suffer Death, or such other Punishment as shall be ordered by the Sentence of a General Court-martial.

And whosoever shall be found guilty of the said Offence in *Great Britain* or *Ireland*, shall be punished at the discretion of a General Court-martial.

Article XV.

Any Person belonging to Our Forces employed in Foreign Parts, who shall make known the Watch Word to any Person who Is not entitled to receive it according to the Rules and Discipline of War, or shall presume to give a Parole or Watch Word different from what he received, shall suffer Death, or such other Punishment as shall be ordered by the Sentence of a General Court-martial.

And whosoever shall be found guilty of the said Offence in *Great Britain* or *Ireland*, shall be punished at the Discretion of a General Court-martial.

Article XVI.

All Officers and Soldiers are to behave themselves orderly in Quarters, and on their March; and whosoever shall commit any Waste or Spoil, either in Walks of Trees, Parks, Warrens, Fish-ponds, Houses, or Gardens, Cornfields, Enclosures, or Meadows, or shall maliciously destroy any Property whatsoever belonging to any of our subjects, unless by Order of the then Commander In Chief of Our Forces to annoy Rebels, or other Enemies in Arms against Us, he or they that shall be found guilty of offending herein, shall (besides such Penalties as they are liable to by Law) be punished according to the Nature and Degree of the Offence, by the Judgment of a Regimental or General Court martial.

Article XVII.

Whosoever of Our Forces employed in Foreign Parts shall force a Safeguard, shall suffer Death.

Article XVIII.

Whosoever shall relieve the Enemy with Money, Victuals, or Ammunition, or shall knowingly harbour or protect an Enemy, shall suffer Death, or such other Punishment as by a Court-martial shall be inflicted.

Article XIX.

Whosoever shall be convicted of holding Correspondence with, or giving Intelligence to, the Enemy, either directly or indirectly, shall suffer Death, or such other Punishment as by a Court-martial shall be inflicted.

Article XX.

All Public Stores taken in the Enemies Camp, Towns, Forts or Magazines, whether of Artillery, Ammunition, Clothing, Forage, or Provisions, shall be secured for Our Service; for the Neglect of which Our Commanders in Chief are to be answerable.

Article XXI.

If any Officer or Soldier shall leave his Post or Colours to go in Search of Plunder, he shall, upon being convicted thereof before a General Court-martial suffer Death, or such other Punishment as by a Court-martial shall be inflicted.

Article XXII.

If any Governor or Commandant of any Garrison, Fortress, or Post, shall be compelled by the Officers or Soldiers under his Command to give up to the Enemy, or to abandon it, the Commissioned Officers, Non-commissioned Officers, or Soldiers, who shall be convicted of having so offended, shall suffer Death, or such other punishment as may be inflicted upon them by the Sentence of a Court-martial.

Article XXIII.

All Suttlers and Retainers to a Camp, and all persons whatsoever serving with Our Armies in the Field, though no inlisted Soldiers, are to be subject to orders, according to the Rules and Discipline of War.

Article XXIV.

Officers having Brevetts, or Commissions of a prior Date to those of the Regiment in which they now serve, may take Place in Courts-martial and on Detachments, when composed of different Corps, according to the Ranks given them in their Brevetts, or dates of their former Commissions; But in the Regiment, Troop, or Company, to which such Brevett Officers, and those who have Commissions of a prior Date, do belong, they shall do Duty, and take Rank both on Courts-martial and on Detachments, which shall be composed only of their own Corps, according to the Commissions by which they are mustered in the said Corps.

Article XXV.

If upon Marches, Guards, or in Quarters, any of Our Troops of Horse Guards, Grenadier Guards, or Regiment of Horse Guards, shall happen to join or do Duty together, the eldest Officer by Commission there, on Duty or in Quarters, shall command the Whole, and give out Orders for what is needful to Our Service; Regard being always had to the several Ranks of those Corps, and the Posts they usually occupy.

Article XXVI.

And in like Manner also, if any Regiments, Troops, or Detachments of Our Horse or Foot Guards shall happen to march with, or be encamped or quartered with any Bodies or Detachments of Our other Troops, the eldest Officer, without Respect to Corps, shall take upon him the Command of the Whole, and give the necessary Orders to Our Service.

Article XXVII.

When Our Regiments of Foot Guards, or Detachments from Our said Regiments, shall do Duty together, unmixed with other Corps, they shall be considered as One Corps; and the Officers shall take Rank and do Duty according to the Commissions by which they are mustered.

Section XVI.—-Administration of Justice

Article I.

A General Court-martial in Our Kingdoms of *Great Britain* or *Ireland*, shall not consist of less than Thirteen Commissioned Officers, and the President of such Court-martial shall not be the Commander in Chief, or Governor of the Garrison, where the Offender shall be tried, nor be under the Degree of a Field Officer.

Article II.

A General Court-martial, held in Our Garrison of *Gibraltar*, Island of *Minorca*, or in any other Place beyond the Seas, shall not consist of less than Thirteen Commissioned Officers; nor shall the President of such General Court-martial be the Commander in Chief, or Governor of the Garrison, where the Offender shall be tried, nor under the Degree of a Field Officer, unless where a Field Officer cannot be had, in which Case the Officer next in Seniority to the Commander, not being under the Degree of a Captain, shall preside at such Court-martial.

Article III.

Whereas these Our Rules and Articles are to be observed by, and do in all Respects regard Our Troops and Regiments of Horse and Foot Guards, as well as Our other Forces; and that several Disputes have arisen, and may arise, between the Officers of Our Horse and Foot Guards, in relation to their holding of Courts-martial, and also among the Officers of Our Troops of Horse Guards, Grenadier Guards, and Regiment of Horse Guards, on that and other Points of Duty; we do therefore herein declare it to be Our Will and Pleasure, That when any Officer or Soldier belonging to Our said Troops of Horse Guards, Grenadier Guards, or Regiment of Horse Guards, shall happen to be brought before a General Court-martial, for Differences arising purely among themselves, or for Crimes relating to Discipline, or Breach of Orders, such Courts-martial shall be composed of Officers serving in any or all of those Corps of Horse Guards (as they may then happen to lie for their being most conveniently assembled) where the Officers are to take Post according to the Dates and Degrees of Rank granted them in their respective Commissions, without Regard, to the Seniority of Corps, or other formerly pretended Privileges.

Article IV.

In like Manner also, the Officers of Our Three Regiments of Foot Guards, when appointed to hold Courts-martial for Differences or Crimes as aforesaid, shall of themselves compose Courts-martial, and take Rank according to their Commissions; but for all Disputes or Differences which may happen between Officers or Soldiers belonging to Our said Corps of Horse Guards, and other Officers and Soldiers belonging to Our Regiments of Foot Guards, or between any Officers or Soldiers belonging to either of those Corps of Horse or Foot Guards, and Officers and Soldiers of Our other Troops, the Courts-martial to be appointed in such Cases shall be equally composed of Officers belonging to the Corps in which the Parties complaining and complained of do then serve; and the President to be ordered by Turns, beginning first by an Officer of One of Our Troops of Horse Guards; and so on in Course out of the other Corps.

Article V.

The Members both of General and Regimental Courts-martial shall, when belonging to different Corps, take the same Rank which they hold in the Army; but when Courts-martial shall be composed of Officers of One Corps, they shall take their Ranks according to the Dates of the Commissions by which they are mustered in the said Corps.

Article VI.

The Judge Advocate General, or some Person deputed by him, shall prosecute in His Majesty's Name; and in all Trials of Offenders by General Courts-martial, administer to each Member the following oaths:

> You shall well and truly try and determine, according to your Evidence, the Matter now before you, between our Sovereign Lord the King's Majesty, and the Prisoner to be tried.
>
> I A. B. do swear, That I will duly administer Justice according to the Rules and Articles for the better Government of His Majesty's Forces, and according to an Act of Parliament now in Force for the Punishment of Mutiny and Desertion, and other Crimes therein mentioned, without Partiality, Favour, or Affection; and if any doubt shall arise, which is not explained by the said Articles or Act of Parliament, according to my Conscience, the best of my Understanding, and the Custom of War in the like Cases. And I do further swear, That I will not divulge the Sentence of the Court, until it shall be approved by His Majesty, the General, or Commander in Chief; neither will I, upon any account, at any Time whatsoever, disclose or discover the Vote or Opinion of any particular Member of the Court-martial, unless required to give Evidence thereof, as a Witness, by a Court of Justice, in a due Course of Law.

And as soon as the said Oath shall have been administered to the respective Members, the President of the Court shall administer to the Judge Advocate, or Person officiating as such, an Oath in the following words:

> I A. B. do swear, That I will not, upon any account, at any Time whatsoever, disclose or discover the Vote or Opinion of any particular Member of the Court-martial, unless required to give Evidence thereof, as a Witness, by a Court of Justice in a due Course of Law.

Article VII.

All the Members of a Court-martial are to behave with Decency; and in the giving of their Votes are to begin with the youngest.

Article VIII.

All Persons who give Evidence before a General Court-martial, are to be examined upon Oath; nor shall any Sentence of Death be given against any offender by any General Court-martial, unless Nine Officers present shall concur therein: And if there be more than Thirteen, then the Judgment shall pass by the Concurrence of Two-thirds of the Officers present.

Article IX.

No Field Officer shall be tried by any Person under the Degree of a Captain; nor shall any Proceedings or Trials be carried on excepting between the Hours of Eight in the Morning, and of Three in the Afternoon, except In Cases which require an immediate Example.

Article X.

No sentence of a General Court-martial shall be put in Execution, till after a Report shall be made of the whole Proceedings to Us, or to Our General or Commander in Chief, and Our or his Directions shall be signified thereupon; excepting in Ireland, where the Report is to be made to the Lord Lieutenant, and to Our Chief Governor or Governors of that Kingdom, and his or their Directions be received thereupon.

Article XI.

For the more equitable Decision of Disputes which may arise between Officers and Soldiers belonging to different Corps, whether they be of Our Troops, or Regiment of Horse Guards, Our Three Regiments of Foot Guards, or Our other Regiments of Horse or Foot, We direct, That the Courts-martial shall be equally composed of Officers belonging to the Corps in which the parties in question do then serve; and that the Presidents shall be taken by Turns, beginning with that Corps which shall be eldest in Rank.

Article XII.

The Commissioned Officers of every Regiment may, by the Appointment of their Colonel or Commanding Officer, hold Regimental Courts-martial for the enquiring into such Disputes, or Criminal Matters, as may come before them, and for the inflicting corporal Punishments for small Offences, and shall give Judgment by the Majority of Voices; but no Sentence shall be executed till the Commanding Officer (not being a Member of the Court-martial) or the Governor of the Garrison shall have confirmed the same.

Article XIII.

No Regimental Court-martial shall consist of less than Five Officers, excepting in Cases where that Number cannot be conveniently assembled, when Three may be sufficient; who are likewise to determine upon the Sentence by the Majority of Voices; which Sentence is to be confirmed by the Commanding Officer, not being a Member of the Court-martial.

Article XIV.

Every Officer commanding in any of Our Forts, Castles, or Barracks, or elsewhere, where the Corps under his Command consists of Detachments from different Regiments, or of Independent Companies, may assemble Courts-martial for the Trial of Offenders in the same manner as if they were Regimental, whose Sentence is not to be executed till it shall be confirmed by the said Commanding Officer.

Article XV.

No Commissioned Officer shall be cashiered or dismissed from Our Service, excepting by an Order from Us, or by the Sentence of a General Court-martial, approved by Us, or by such General or Commander in Chief, who shall by Our Authority appoint the same to be held; but

Non-commissioned Officers may be discharged as private Soldiers, and, by the Order of the Colonel of the Regiment, or by the Sentence of a Regimental Court-martial, be reduced to private Centinels.

Article XVI.

No Person whatever shall use menacing Words, Signs, or Gestures, In the Presence of a Court-martial then sitting, or shall cause any Disorder or Riot, so as to disturb their Proceedings, on the Penalty of being punished at the Discretion of the said Court-martial.

Article XVII.

To the end that Offenders may be brought to Justice, We hereby direct, That whenever any Officer or Soldier shall commit a Crime deserving Punishment, he shall, by his commanding Officer, if an Officer, be put in Arrest; if a Non-commissioned Officer or Soldier, be imprisoned till he shall be either tried by a Court-martial, or shall be lawfully discharged by a proper Authority.

Article XVIII.

No Officer or Soldier who shall be put in Arrest or Imprisonment shall continue in his Confinement more than Eight Days, or till such time as a Court-martial can be conveniently assembled.

Article XIX.

No Officer commanding a Guard, or Provost-martial, shall refuse to receive, or keep any Prisoner committed to his Charge, by any Officer belonging to Our Forces; which Officer shall, at the same Time, deliver an Account in Writing, signed by himself, of the Crime with which the said Prisoner is charged.

Article XX.

No Officer commanding a Guard, or Provost-martial, shall presume to release any Prisoner committed to his Charge, without proper Authority for so doing; nor shall he suffer any Prisoner to escape, on the Penalty of being punished for it by the Sentence of a Court-martial.

Article XXI.

Every officer or Provost-martial to whose charge Prisoners shall be committed, is hereby required, within Twenty-four Hours after such Commitment, or as soon as he shall be relieved from his Guard, to give In Writing to the Colonel of the Regiment to whom the Prisoner belongs (where the Prisoner is confined upon the Guard belonging to the said Regiment, and that his Offence only relates to the Neglect of Duty in his own Corps) or to the Commander in Chief, their Names, their Crimes, and the Names of the Officer who committed them, on the Penalty of his being punished for his Disobedience or Neglect, at the Discretion of a Court-martial.

Article XXII.

And if any Officer under Arrest shall leave his Confinement, before he is set at Liberty by the Officer who confined him, or by a superior Power, he shall be cashiered for it.

Article XXIII.

Whatsoever Commissioned Officer shall be convicted before a General Court-martial, of behaving in a scandalous Infamous Manner, such as is unbecoming the Character of an Officer and a Gentleman, shall be discharged from Our Service.

Section XVI: Entry of Commissions

All Commissions granted by Us, or by any of Our Generals having Authority from Us, shall be entered in the Books of Our Secretary at War, and Commissary General, otherwise they will not be allowed of at the Musters.

Section XVII: Concerning the Effects of Deceased Officers and Soldiers.

Article I.

When any Commissioned Officer shall happen to die, or be killed in Our Service, the Major of the Regiment, or the Officer doing the Major's Duty in his Absence, shall immediately secure all his Effects or Equipage then in Camp or Quarters; and shall before the next Regimental Court-martial make an Inventory thereof, and forthwith transmit the same to the Office of Our Secretary at War, to the end that his Executors may, after Payment of his Debts in Quarters, and Interment, receive the Overplus, if any be, to his or their Use.

Article II.

When any Non-commissioned Officer or Private Soldier shall happen to die, or to be killed in Our Service, the then Commanding Officer of the Troop or Company shall, in the Presence of two other Commissioned Officers, take an Account of whatever Effects he dies possessed of, above his Regimental Clothing, Arms, and Accoutrements, and transmit the same to the Office of Our Secretary at War; which said Effects are to be accounted for, and paid to the Representative of such deceased Non-commissioned Officer or Soldier. And in case any of the Officers, so autorized to take care of the Effects of dead Officers and Soldiers, should, before they shall have accounted to their Representatives for the same, have Occasion to leave the Regiment, by Preferment or otherwise, they shall, before they be permitted to quit the same, deposit in the Hands of the Commanding Officer, or of the Agent of the Regiment, all the effects of such deceased Non-commissioned Officers and Soldiers, in order that the same may be secured for and paid to, their respective Representatives.

Section XVIII: Artillery.

Article I.

All Officers, Conductors, Gunners, Matrosses, Drivers, or any other Persons whatsoever receiving Pay or Hire in the Service of Our Artillery, shall be governed by the aforesaid Rules and Articles, and shall be subject to be tried by Courts-martial, in like Manner with the Officers and Soldiers of Our other Troops.

Article II.

For Differences arising amongst themselves, or in Matters relating solely to their own Corps, the Courts-martial may be composed of their own Officers; but where a Number sufficient of such Officers cannot be assembled, or in Matters wherein other Corps are interested, the Officers of Artillery shall sit in Courts-martial with the Officers of Our other Crops, taking their Rank according to the Dates of their respective Commissions, and no otherwise.

21 George II III., Cap. LXV (1781)

AN ACT for establishing an Agreement with the United Company of Merchants of England trading to the East-Indies, for the Payment of the Sum of 400,000 pounds for the use of the Public, in full discharge and satisfaction of all claims and demands of the Public from the time the Bond Debt of the said Company was reduced to one million five hundred thousand pounds, until the first day of March, one thousand seven hundred and eighty-one, in respect of the territorial acquisitions and revenues lately obtained in the East Indies; and also for securing to the Public in respect thereof, for a term therein mentioned, a certain part or proportion of the clear revenues and profits of the said Company; and for granting to the said Company, for a further term, the sole and exclusive Trade to and from the East-Indies, and limits therein mentioned; and for establishing certain Regulations for the better Management of the Affairs of the said Company, as well in India as in Europe, and the recruiting the Military Forces of the said Company.

Regulations relative to raising recruits for the Company's service in India

XXXII. And whereas it is necessary for the said United Company to keep and maintain a military force in the East-Indies, and the present method of obtaining recruits to keep up the same hath been found very inconvenient and defective; be it therefore enacted by the authority aforesaid, that it shall and may be lawful to and for the said United Company, by licence from his Majesty for that purpose, from time to time to enlist such number of men, being his Majesty's subjects, and of such ages, and for such time, as shall be expressed in such licence, to serve them as soldiers in the East-Indies, and to deposit and keep such men, not exceeding 2,000 at any one time in time of war, and one thousand at any time in time of peace, at such place or places, in any part of his Majesty's dominions in Europe, as shall be approved of for that purpose by his Majesty, until they can be sent to India; and in case any person or persons so enlisting and engaging, after he shall have signed an agreement for that purpose, and shall have declared before a magistrate, at the distance of twenty-four hours at the least after his first enlisting, that he freely and voluntarily signed such agreement, and is willing to go and serve the said United Company as a soldier in the East-Indies, shall desert from the place appointed for him to reside at till the time of his embarkation to go to the East Indies, or shall refuse to perform his agreement, it shall be lawful for any person or persons to apprehend such person or persons, and convey him before a magistrate; and it shall be lawful for such magistrate, on proof of the case, to commit such person or persons to gaol, there to be kept in safe custody, and maintained at the expense of the said United Company, until such person can be sent to India; and it shall be lawful for the said United Company to cause such person or persons to be conveyed in custody on shipboard, to be carried to the East-Indies, in such service as aforesaid.[1]

1 Vide 39 Geo. 3, cap. 109; 50 Geo. 3, cap. 87; 57 Geo. 3, cap. 57; 3 & 4 Vict. cap. 37; and 5 Vict, sess. 2, cap. 12.

39 GEORGII III. Cap. CIX.

An Act for better Recruiting the Forces of the East-India Company

[12 July 1799]

Preamble

Whereas the United Company of Merchants of England trading to the East-Indies are by law entitled to maintain and keep up, and at their own costs and charges do maintain and keep up, a military force in their settlements abroad, for the defence and protection of the territorial acquisitions and revenues of which they are in possession, and for the defence and protection of their trade; and by an Act of Parliament made in the twenty-first year of the reign of his present Majesty, intituled, "An Act for establishing an Agreement with the United Company of Merchants of England trading to the East-Indies, for the payment of the Sum of Four hundred thousand Pounds, for the Use of the Public, in full Discharge and Satisfaction of all Claims and Demands of the Public, from the time the Bond Debt of the said Company was reduced to one million five hundred thousand Pounds, until the First Day of March one thousand seven hundred and eighty-one, in respect of the Territorial Acquisitions and revenues lately obtained in the East-Indies; and also for securing to the Public in respect thereof, for a Term therein mentioned, a certain part or Proportion of the clear Revenues and Profits of the said Company; and for granting to the said Company, for a further Term, the sole and exclusive Trade to and from the East-Indies, and Limits therein mentioned; and for establishing certain Regulations for the better Management of the Affairs of the said Company, as well in India as in Europe, and the recruiting the Military Forces of the said Company,"[21 G. 3, c. 65] certain regulations are established for the said Company's raising recruits in Great Britain, but no provision is made, by virtue of which such recruits can be trained, arrayed, exercised, or disciplined, during their abode in this kingdom, or whereby they can be subjected to military law previous to their embarkation for, and during their passage to, the places where the said United Company are entitled to maintain and keep such militia force: and whereas it is expedient that his Majesty's officers should be authorized in certain cases to enlist recruits for service, either in his Majesty's troops or in the forces of the said United Company, as his Majesty shall think fit to direct; and that all recruits so raised and transferred over to, or enlisted by officers in the service of the said United Company, should be trained, arrayed, exercised, and disciplined in the use of arms, previous to their departure for places abroad; and that they should be subjected to military law during their abode in this kingdom, and during their passage to, and before their arrival at such places: may it therefore please your Majesty that it may be enacted; and be it enacted by the King's most excellent Majesty, by and with the advice and consent of the Lords spiritual and temporal, and Commons, in this present Parliament assembled, and by the authority of the same, that it shall and may be lawful to and for his Majesty, his heirs and successors, to order and cause such of his officers as he shall see fit, to levy, enlist, and raise such number of men as from time to time his Majesty shall think fit, for the special purpose of serving in the East-Indies, either in his Majesty's troops, or in the forces of the said United Company.

[The Act goes on to prescribe a particular form of oath to be administered to recruits thus raised, and the second section directs the Justice before whom the recruit shall appear to tender the oath; but by 5 Vict. sess. 2, cap. 12, sec. 36, (the annual Mutiny Act) the forms prescribed therein, and no other are to be used during the continuance of that Act.]

His Majesty, on petition of the Court of Directors, may cause recruits to be transferred to the service of the Company

III. And be it further enacted, that it shall and may be lawful to and for his Majesty, his heirs and successors, upon the petition of the Court of Directors of the said United Company, to cause so many recruits or soldiers, who shall have been raised by his Majesty' officers for the special purpose hereinbefore mentioned, as the said Court of Directors shall petition for, and as his Majesty, his heirs or successors, shall see fit to grant, to be transferred over to the service of the said United Company, which transfer shall be made by such recruits or soldiers being delivered over by such officer in his Majesty's service, who shall have the command of them, at such place as his Majesty shall think proper to appoint, to such person or persons as the said Court of Directors shall appoint to receive them.

Company not obliged to receive invalids

IV. Provided always, and be it enacted, that the said United Company shall not be obliged to receive into their service any recruit or soldier who shall be an invalid, or who shall have any bodily infirmity.

Company to pay such sum as shall be agreed upon for such recruits, and their subsistence, from enlistment

V. And be it further enacted, that the said United Company shall pay person or persons for the use of his Majesty, as shall be appointed for that purpose in writing by the Commissioners of his Majesty's Treasury, or any three or more of them, or by the Lord High Treasurer for the time being, such sum and sums of money as from time to time shall be agreed upon between one of his Majesty's principal Secretaries of State on behalf of his Majesty, and the said Court of Directors, to reimburse the expense of raising such recruits and soldiers as shall be transferred into the service of the said United Company in manner hereinbefore mentioned; and that, over and above such sum, the said United Company shall in like manner pay to such person or persons as aforesaid, the costs of the subsistence of each recruit, from the time of his enlistment to the time of his being delivered over to the said United Company, as hereinbefore mentioned.

Company may train men enlisted under recited Act, and transferred under this, in Great Britain, or Jersey and may make drafts to be sent abroad

VI. And be it further enacted, that the said United Company shall and may deposit, keep, maintain, pay, train, and exercise in the use of arms, such men as they may from time to time enlist and engage in their service, under and by virtue of the authority of the said Act of the twenty-first year of his Majesty's reign, and such men as shall be transferred over to their service in manner herein mentioned, in any of his Majesty's garrisons, or at such other place or places within Great Britain, or the Islands of Guernsey or Jersey, as shall be approved of by his Majesty; and that the said United Company, or their Court of Directors, may, from the men so enlisted or transferred as aforesaid, make drafts of non-commissioned officers and soldiers, to be from time to time sent abroad in the said United Company's service, as they shall think proper and necessary.

Court of Directors, with the approbation of His Majesty, may appoint officers holding commission from His Majesty and the Company, for disciplining the men, out of whom thay may appoint serjeants, etc.

VII. And be it further enacted, that for the purpose of raising, receiving, keeping, training and exercising the men so enlisted by license from His Majesty as aforesaid, it shall may be lawful for the Court of Directors of the said United Company, with the approbation of his Majesty, signified under the handwriting of one of his Majesty's principal Secretaries of State, to appoint, from and amongst such officers in the service of the said United Company, as may be in England, on furlough, or by leave of absence, from their duty in India, or who have retired from the service of the said Company, and shall hold and have commissions from his Majesty as well as from the said United Company, one commanding officer, and such other commissioned officers, of such ranks and with such commissions as shall be necessary for the training, exercising, and disciplining such men so enlisted or transferred as aforesaid, until they shall be sent abroad; and that it shall also be lawful for the said Court of Directors to appoint, from the number of men so enlisted or transferred as aforesaid such number of serjeants, corporals, drummers, and fifers, as shall be necessary for the same purpose.

Company not to enlist above a certain number of men, nor appoint more than the necessary number of commissioned officers

Officers not to have any power longer than they hold commissions from His Majesty

No more than a certain number of men enlisted, and not transferred, shall be maintained within the realm

VIII. Provided always, and be it enacted, that it shall not be lawful for the said United Company to enlist or have in pay at any one time, or to train or discipline at any one time, by virtue of this Act, any greater number of non-commissioned officers and private men than two thousand, nor shall it be lawful for the Court of Directors of the said Company to appoint any greater number of commissioned officers than the number of men to be so raised and disciplined shall require; nor shall the officer so appointed to command, or any other commissioned officer to be appointed as aforesaid, be continued in the said appointment, or have any power or authority to command, train, or discipline the said men so enlisted, longer than he shall continue to hold a commission from his Majesty, his heirs or successors; and his or their said appointment, powers, authorities, and commands, shall cease and determine, and become utterly void, from and immediately after the said commission shall be revoked, determined, or otherwise made void by his Majesty, his heirs or successors: provided also, that from and after the passing of this Act, and until the twenty-fifth day of March one thousand eight hundred, no greater number than three thousand of men enlisted for the special purpose aforesaid, and not transferred by his Majesty to the service of the said Company, shall, at any one time, be maintained by his Majesty within this realm ; and that, from and after the said day, no greater number of such men shall be so maintained than shall be specially included within the provisions of such Act or Acts of Parliament as may, from time to time, be made and be in force for the punishment of mutiny and desertion, or for the discipline and government of his Majesty's forces in Great Britain.

Company with the approbation of His Majesty, may appoint quarter-masters, etc.

IX. Provided also and be it further enacted, that it shall and may be lawful for the said Company, with his Majesty's approbation so signified as aforesaid, to appoint such quarter-masters, pay-masters, and other persons, as may be necessary for disciplining and training, attending, and otherwise taking care of, the said men so enlisted and transferred, over and above the number of commissioned officers hereinbefore mentioned, whether the said persons shall be in their service or not.

Rates of Pay to be allowed to the commissioned, non-commissioned, and staff officers

X. Provided also, and be it further enacted, that it shall not be lawful for the said United Company to pay or allow any greater pay, or other sums, to the commissioned and non-commissioned and staff officers to be appointed to raise, receive, train, exercise, and discipline, the said men, than after the rates following: that is to say, not more than ten shillings per day to each captain, not more than five shillings per day to each subaltern officer, over and above the pay, according to their rank, which they shall be entitled to during their being in this country on furlough or leave of absence, or retired from their service; nor more than five shillings per day to each quarter-master, one hundred and twenty pounds per annum to each paymaster, two shillings per day to each serjeant, one shilling and sixpence per day to each corporal, five shillings per day to each surgeon, and one hundred pounds per annum to one chaplain; such last-mentioned sums to be the full allowance to which in any case such officers shall be entitled (save and except the regimental pay which such officers may be entitled to, according to their respective ranks, and save and except such barrack allowances as are usual to be given to officers in his Majesty's service when quartered in barracks).

Pay to be in full of all emoluments; and clothing, etc, to be provided asn the Directors shall think best

XI. And be it further enacted, that the said pay, so to be made to the said officers respectively as aforesaid, shall be in full satisfaction of all emoluments whatsoever; and that the clothing for the said men, and all other things whatsoever, necessary to be provided for them, or for the place in which they shall be deposited and kept, shall be provided by the said United Company, upon the best terms, and in such manner as shall appear to the Court of Directors of the said Company to be best suited to that purpose.

Officers and men to be subject to the commandants of garrisons or barracks, and to partake in the duties

XII. And be it further enacted, that in case the said men, so to be enlisted into, or transferred over to, the service of the said United Company, shall be deposited and kept at any of his Majesty's garrisons or barracks, all such recruits and soldiers, and the commissioned and non-commissioned officers having the command of, or being employed in the training, exercising, and arraying such recruits or soldiers, shall at all times be subject to the command and orders of the commandant of such garrison or barracks, or in his absence to the senior officer in his Majesty's service, or the officer for the time being commanding in such garrison or barracks; and that the commissioned and non-commissioned officers, to be appointed by the said United Company to the command of, or for the training, exercising, or arraying such recruits as aforesaid, shall at all times partake in and perform the duties of any of his Majesty's garrisons or barracks in which they may be stationed.

Orders of the Company to be given through such commandants

XIII. And be it further enacted, that all orders which shall be given by the said United Company, or their Court of Directors, to their officers so stationed at any of his Majesty's garrisons or barracks, shall be given and passed through the commandant or senior officer commanding at such garrisons or barracks.

Deserter may be apprehended and confined as from His Majesty's service

XIV. And be it further enacted, that if any person who shall be enlisted and engaged by the said United Company, under the authority of the said Act of the twenty-first year of his Majesty's reign, or who shall be transferred over to the service of the said United Company as herein mentioned, shall afterwards desert, or be found wandering, or otherwise illegally absenting himself from the service of the said United Company, it shall and may be lawful for any constable, headborough, or tythingman, of the town or place where any such person who may be reasonably suspected to be a deserter, shall be found, to apprehend or cause him to be apprehended in the same manner as if he were a deserter from his Majesty's service; and every constable, headborough, tythingman, justice of the peace, or magistrate shall have the same power and authority, and proceed in the same manner as he or they would have had, or as he or they would have proceeded in, if the person had been a deserter from His Majesty's service; and every keeper of any gaol, house of correction, or prison, to which such person shall be committed, shall be entitled to receive the full subsistence of such deserter, during the time he shall remain in their custody, for the maintenance of such deserter and shall receive and confine him or them in the same manner as if he or they had been a deserter from his Majesty's service.

Persons apprehending deserters to be entitled to such rewards only as the Company may give

XV. Provided always, that nothing in this Act contained shall extend, or be construed extend to authorize any justice to pay or cause to be paid any reward to any person or persons, who shall apprehend or cause to be apprehended any person or persons who shall desert from the service of the East-India Company, nor shall the person or persons apprehending the same be entitled to any other reward than the East-India Company may voluntarily give for such apprehension.

Officers and soldiers until embarkation, to be subject to the Mutiny Laws

XVI. And be it further enacted, that all such officers and soldiers as shall be raised and enlisted by virtue of this Act shall, at all times and until their embarkation, be subject to the provisions and regulations of the said Act, made in the present session of Parliament, intituled, "An Act for punishing mutiny and desertion, and for the better payment of the arm and their quarters," during the continuance of the same Act in Great Britain, and after the expiration thereof to such other Act or Acts of Parliament, provisions, and regulations, as shall from time to time be made and be in force for the discipline and government of his Majesty forces in Great Britain.

[This section goes on to provide that recruits after embarkation shall be subject to 27 Geo. 2, cap. 9, but that Act was repealed by 4 Geo. 4 cap. 81, which Act was also repealed by 3 & 4 Vict. cap. 37, by which last Act the law on the subject was amended and consolidated.]

Majesty may grant commissions for holding general courts martial

XVIII. And whereas for more effectually suppressing mutiny and desertion, and for the punishment of other offences committed by officers and soldiers in the service of the said United Company, during the time of their being trained and disciplined by virtue of this Act, or by any of the officers or non-commissioned officers employed on that service, it may be necessary that his Majesty should be enabled to convene courts martial, or to authorize the same to be convened, consisting either in the whole or in part of officers in the service of the East-India Company who hold commissions from his Majesty: be it enacted that it shall and may be lawful for his Majesty from time to time to grant a commission for the holding of general courts martial for the trial of offences committed by officers or soldiers in the service of the said United Company, during the time of their being so employed, and trained and exercised under the authority of this Act, which courts martial may either consist of officers appointed to train and discipline the said men, or of such other officers in the service of the East-India Company, holding commissions from his Majesty, as may be in Great Britain upon furlough, or by leave of absence, or of officers in his Majesty's service in Great Britain, or of such numbers and proportions of each, as to his Majesty shall seem meet; and such courts martial shall in all other respects be convened, and have the same powers and authorities, and their sentences shall be carried into execution, as if they were courts martial respecting his Majesty's forces. [Vide 50 Geo.3, cap. 87, sec. 7.]

Regimental courts martial may be convened

XIX. And be it further enacted, that regimental courts martial, or courts martial to be composed of officers of different corps, with the same powers as regimental courts martial, may be convened for inquiring into such disputes or criminal matters as may come before them, touching any of the non-commissioned officers or soldiers in the service of the said United Company during the time of their being so employed and trained and exercised as aforesaid, and for awarding corporal or other punishments for small offences; and such courts martial shall be constituted and proceeded, and their sentences shall be carried into execution, in like manner as if they were courts martial respecting his Majesty's forces. [Vide note on section 18.]

[Section 20 provides for the punishment of offences committed after embarkation, under 27 Geo. 2, cap. 9, which Act has been repealed, (see note on sec. 16). For the existing law on the subject, see 3 & 4 Vict, cap. 37, sec. 39, and 5 Vict. sess. 2, cap. 12, sec. 32.]

Court of Directors to transmit a report of the number of men levied, etc, to the secretary of State, and the Commander-in-Chief

XXI. And be it further enacted, that the Court of Directors of the said United Company shall, and they are hereby required and directed, twice in every year, to make out a report of the number of men levied and subsisted by virtue of this Act, and of all the orders issued, and every other matter or thing done or directed to be done by them in the execution of this Act, and to transmit one copy of the same to one of his Majesty's principal Secretaries of State, and chief another to the Commander-in-chief of his Majesty's forces.

Public Act

XXII. And be it further enacted, that this Act shall be deemed to be a public Act, and shall be taken notice of as such, by all judges and justices whomsoever, without specially pleading the same.

45 GEORGII III. Cap. XXXVI

An Act to enable the East-India Company to appoint the Commander-in-Chief on the Bengal Establishment to be a Member of the Council of Fort William in Bengal, notwithstanding the Office of Governor-general of Fort William, and the Office of Commander-in-chief of all the Forces in India, being vested in the same Person.

[10 April 1805]

The Court of Directors may appoint the commander of the forces of the Company on the Bengal establishment to be a member of the Council of Fort William, notwithstanding the office of Governor-general and Commander-in-Chief to be vested in the same person

I. Whereas it is expedient that the Court of Directors of the United Company of Merchants of England trading to the East-Indies should be authorized and empowered, if they shall think fit, to appoint the commander of the military forces of the said United Company on the Bengal establishment to be a member of the Supreme Council of Fort William in Bengal, notwithstanding the office of Governor-general of Fort William aforesaid, and the office of Commander-in-chief of all the forces in India, shall be vested in the same person; may it therefore please your Majesty that it may be enacted ; and be it enacted by the King's most excellent Majesty, by and with the advice and consent of the Lords spiritual and temporal, and Commons, in this present Parliament assembled, and by the authority of the same, that it shall and may be lawful to and for the Court of Directors of the said United Company specially to authorize and appoint the commander of the military forces of the said United Company on the Bengal establishment to be a member of the said Supreme Council of Fort William aforesaid, notwithstanding the office of Governor-general of Fort William aforesaid, and the office of Commander-in-chief of all the forces in India, shall be vested in the same person.

And such commander shall have rank at the Board next to the Governor-general but shall not succeed to the government in case of vacancy, unless provisionally appointed to supply the same.

II. And be it enacted, that when any such commander of the military forces of the said United Company on the Bengal establishment shall be appointed a member of the said Supreme Council, such commander shall have rank and precedence at the Council Board next to the Governor-general, but he shall not succeed to the government of such presidency on the happening of a vacancy in the office of Governor-general, unless such commander of the military forces of the said United Company on the Bengal establishment shall have been provisionally appointed to supply the same; but such vacancy shall be supplied by the counsellor next in rank at the Council Board to such commander of the military forces of the said United Company on the Bengal establishment, anything contained in an Act, passed in the thirty-third year of the reign of his present Majesty, intituled, "An Act for continuing in the East-India Company for a further term the Possession of the British Territories in India, together with their exclusive Trade, under certain Limitations; for establishing further Regulations for the Government of the said Territories, and the better Administration of Justice within the same; for appropriating to certain Uses the Revenues and Profits of the said Company; and for making Provision for the good Order and Government of the Towns of Calcutta, Madras, and Bombay;" or any other law, usage, or custom, to the contrary thereof in anywise notwithstanding.[1]

Such commander so appointed a member of the Council shall be subject to recall

III. Provided always, and be it enacted, that any commander so to be appointed a member of the said Supreme Council as herein-before is mentioned shall be subject to recall by the same persons and in the same manner, and shall have the same powers, franchises, and authorities, in all respects as a Member of Council, as if he had been appointed thereto as Commander-in-chief of all the forces in India.

1 The two sections above are in substance re-enacted, as affects the Supreme Council of India, by 3 & 4 Wm. 4, cap. 85, secs. 40 and 62.

50 George III. Cap. LXXXVII

An Act to amend Two Acts, relating to the raising Men for the Service of the East-India Company, and the Quartering and Billetting such Men; and to Trials by Regimental Courts-Martial [15 June 1810]

His Majesty may order any of his officers to enlist the number of men specified in recited Act of 39 G,3, c. 109, to serve in the Company's forces in India for life or limited times

I. Whereas an Act passed in the thirty-ninth year of the reign of his present Majesty, intituled, "An Act for the better recruiting the Forces of the East-India Company;" [39 G. 3. C. 109] and whereas an Act passed in the twenty-seventh year of the reign of his late Majesty King George the Second, intituled, "An Act for punishing Mutiny and Desertion of Officers and Soldiers in the Service of the United Company of Merchants of England trading to the East-Indies, and for the punishment of Offences committed in the East-Indies or at the Island of Saint Helena:" and whereas it would tend to the more speedy recruiting of the forces of the East-India Company, if men were permitted to enlist for a limited time in the service of the said Company, without engaging to serve in his Majesty's forces; and provision must in such case be made for quartering and billeting the men so raised ; and whereas it is also expedient that the provisions of the said recited Act of his late Majesty King George the Second, as to trials by regimental courts-martial, should be amended in relation to the members and witnesses being sworn, as now required on such trials in his Majesty's regular forces; be it therefore enacted by the King's most excellent Majesty, by and with the advice and consent of the Lords spiritual and temporal, and Commons, in this present Parliament assembled, and by the authority of the same, that it shall be lawful for his Majesty, his heirs and successors, to order and cause such of his officers as he shall see fit, to levy, enlist, and raise such number of men, either for life or limited service, as his Majesty shall from time to time think fit, not exceeding the number of men specified in the said recited Act of the thirty-ninth year of the reign of his present Majesty aforesaid, (1) for the special purpose of serving in the East-Indies in the forces of the said United Company only; and the recruits to be raised for such special purpose, instead of taking the oath of fidelity appointed to be taken by the said recited Act of the thirty-ninth year aforesaid, or by any Act in force for the punishment of mutiny and desertion, shall take the oath specified in the Schedule to this Act annexed, marked (A); and instead of the oath of service prescribed by any Act in force for the punishing of mutiny and desertion, shall take the oath in the Schedule to this Act annexed, marked (B); which oaths shall be administered by all justices of the peace and magistrates before whom any such recruits shall be carried for the purpose of being attested; and the certificate given upon such attestation shall be in the form in the Schedule to this Act annexed, marked (C).

Soldiers to be subject to the Mutiny Act till their embarkation, then to be subject to the recited Act 27 G. 2, c. 9

II. And be it further enacted, that all soldiers enlisted into the service of the said United Company of Merchants shall be trained and disciplined and subject to such command and regulations, and at all times and until their embarkation be subject to all the provisions of any Act in force for the punishment of mutiny and desertion, and the better payment of the army and their quarters, and after their embarkation, to the provisions of the said recited Act of the twenty-seventh year aforesaid,[1] (1) in like manner as is prescribed in the said recited Act of the thirty-ninth year aforesaid; and all the powers, authorities, provisions, clauses, rules, regulations and restrictions, penalties and forfeitures, contained and prescribed in the said recited Act of the thirty-ninth year aforesaid, shall extend and be in full force as to all soldiers enlisted under and after the passing of this Act into the service of the said United Company of Merchants, as fully and effectually, as if the same were severally and respectively repeated and re-enacted in this Act and made part thereof.

Powers of Acts relating to quartering etc to extend to this Act

III. And be it further enacted, that all the powers, authorities, provisions, clauses, rules, regulations, and restrictions, and penalties, and forfeitures, contained and prescribed in any Act or Acts of Parliament in force for the time being, in relation to the quartering and billeting and provisioning of, and allowances in respect of such quartering and billetting of soldiers and officers in his Majesty's service, and to the providing of carriages for the use of soldiers, shall, from and after the passing of this Act, extend to all soldiers enlisted for or transferred into the service of the said United Company of Merchants, as fully and effectually as if the same were severally and separately repeated and re-enacted in this Act, and made part thereof; anything in the said Act of the thirty-ninth year aforesaid, or any other Act or Acts of Parliament to the contrary notwithstanding.

Men may enlist for twelve years

IV. And whereas it is expedient to allow men to enlist in the service of the said United Company for twelve years; be it therefore enacted, that it shall be lawful for any person enlisting for limited service in the service of the said United Company, to enlist for twelve years, if at the time of such enlisting he shall be of the age of eighteen years and upwards, and if he shall be under eighteen years of age, then for such further period beyond twelve years as shall be equal to the difference between eighteen years and the age of the person so enlisting.

After the expiration of the first period the men may re-enlist

V. Provided always, and be it further enacted, that it shall be lawful for all persons who shall have been enlisted for limited service in the forces of the said United Company, after the expiration of the first period for which they shall have been severally enlisted, to re-enlist for such further

1 The 27 Geo. 2, cap. 9, here referred to, was repealed by 4 Geo. 4, cap. 81. The laws for punishing mutiny and desertion of officers and soldiers in the service of the East-India Company were consolidated in 3 & 4 Vict. cap. 37.

period as shall be allowed and appointed by any order of the Governor general in Council in Bengal.

Men serving in the local militia may enlist

VI. And be it further enacted, that it shall be lawful for any person ballotted or enrolled to serve or serving in the local militia, to enlist or enter into the service of the United Company of Merchants trading to the East-Indies, in like manner and at such times as any such person might or may enlist or enter into his Majesty's regular forces.

His Majesty may direct the manner of trials by courts-martial

VII. And be it further enacted, that all regimental and garrison and other courts-martial which shall be held for the trial of any offences committed by the troops in the service of the said United Company, shall have full power and are hereby authorized and required to take and administer such oaths, and to proceed in such manner in the trial of offences, as his Majesty shall from time to time think fit to order and direct.

The Government of India Act, 1833

[Act 85 of 1833]

(3 & 4 Will. 4, c. LXXXV)

[28 August, 1833]

An Act for effecting an Arrangement with the East India Company, and for the better Government of His Majesty's Indian Territories, till the thirtieth day of April one thousand eight hundred and fifty-four.

THE BRITISH TERRITORIES IN INDIA TO REMAIN UNDER THE GOVERNMENT OF THE COMPANY TILL 30 APRIL 1854; REAL AND PERSONAL PROPERTY OF THE COMPANY TO B EHELD IN TRUST FOR THE CROWN, FOR THE SERVICE OF INDIA

Whereas by an Act passed in the Fifty-third Year of the Reign of His Majesty King George the Third, intituled "An Act for continuing in the East India Company for a further Term the Possession of the British Territories in India, together with certain exclusive Privileges; for establishing further Regulations for the Government of the said Territories, and the better Administration of Justice within the same; and for regulating the Trade to and from the Places within the Limits of the said Company's Charter" [53 G. 3, c. 155], the Possession and Government of the British Territories in India were continued in the United Company of Merchants of England trading to the East Indies for a Term therein mentioned: And whereas the said Company are entitled to or claim the Lordships and Islands of St. Helena and Bombay under Grants from the Crown, and other Property to a large Amount in Value, and also certain Rights and Privileges not affected by the Determination of the Term granted by the said recited Act: And whereas the said Company have consented that all their Rights and Interests to or in the said Territories, and all their Territorial and Commercial, Real and Personal Assets and Property whatsoever, shall, subject to the Debts and Liabilities now affecting the same, be placed at the Disposal of Parliament in consideration of certain Provisions herein-after mentioned, and have also consented that their Right to trade for their own Profit in common with other His Majesty's Subjects be suspended during such Time as the Government of the said Territories shall be confided to them: And whereas it is expedient that the said Territories now under the Government of the said Company be continued under such Government, but in Trust for the Crown of the United Kingdom of Great Britain and Ireland, and discharged of all Claims of the said Company, to any Profit therefrom to their own Use, except the Dividend herein-after secured to them, and that the Property of the said Company be continued in their Possession and at their Disposal, in Trust for the Crown, for the Service of the said Government, and other Purposes in this Act mentioned: Be it therefore enacted by the King's most Excellent Majesty, by and with the Advice and Consent of the Lords Spiritual and Temporal, and Commons, in this present Parliament assembled, and by the Authority of the same, That from and after the Twenty-second Day of April One thousand eight hundred and thirty-four the Territorial Acquisitions and Revenues mentioned or referred to in the said Act of the Fifty-third Year of His late Majesty King George the Third, together with the Port and Island of Bombay, and all other Territories now in the Possession and under the Government of the said Company, except the Island of St. Helena, shall remain and continue under such Government until the Thirtieth Day of April One thousand eight hundred and fifty-four; and that all the Lands and Hereditaments, Revenues, Rents, and Profits of the said Company, and all the Stores, Merchandize, Chattels, Monies, Debts, and Real and Personal Estate whatsoever, except the said Island of St. Helena, and the Stores and Property thereon herein-after mentioned, subject to the Debts and Liabilities now affecting the same respectively, and the Benefit of all Contracts, Covenants, and Engagements, and all Rights to Fines, Penalties, and Forfeitures, and other Emoluments whatsoever, which the said Company shall be seised or possessed of or entitled unto on the said Twenty-second Day of April One thousand eight hundred and thirty-four, shall remain and be vested in, and be held, received, and exercised respectively, according to the Nature and Quality, Estate and Interest of and in the same respectively, by the said Company, in Trust for His Majesty, His Heirs and Successors, for the Service of the Government of India, discharged of all Claims of the said Company to any Profit or Advantage therefrom to their own Use, except the Dividend on their Capital Stock, secured to them as herein-after is mentioned, subject to such Powers and Authorities for the Superintendence, Direction, and Control over the Acts, Operations, and Concerns of the said Company as have been already made or provided by any Act or Acts of Parliament in that Behalf, or are made or provided by this Act.

SECTION 38: PRESIDENCY OF FORT WILLIAM IN BENGAL TO BE DIVIDED INTO TWO PRESIDENCIES; THE COURT TO DECLARE THE LIMITS FROM TIME TO TIME OF THE SEVERAL PRESIDENCIES

And be it enacted, That the Territories now subject to the Government of the Presidency of Fort William in Bengal shall be divided into Two distinct Presidencies, one of such Presidencies, in which shall be included Fort William aforesaid, to be styled the Presidency of Fort William in Bengal, and the other of such Presidencies to be styled the Presidency of Agra; and that it shall be lawful for the said Court of Directors, under the Control by this Act provided, and they are hereby required, to declare and appoint what Part or Parts of any of the Territories under the Government of the said Company shall from Time to Time be subject to the Government of each of the several Presidencies now subsisting or to be established as aforesaid, and from Time to Time, as Occasion may require, to revoke and alter, in the whole or in part, such Appointment, and such new Distribution of the same as shall be deemed expedient.

SECTION 39: GOVERNMENT OF INDIA VESTED IN GOVERNOR GENERAL AND COUNSELLORS

And be it enacted, That the Superintendence, Direction, and Control of the whole Civil and Military Government of all the said Territories and Revenues in India shall be and is hereby vested in a Governor General and Counsellors, to be styled "The Governor General of India in Council."

SECTION 40: THERE SHALL BE FOUR ORDINARY COUNCILLORS, THREE OF WHOM SHALL BE SERVANTS OF THE COMPANY; NO MILITARY OFFICER TO HOLD ANY COMMAND WHILST A MEMBER; THE FOURTS MEMBER NOT TO BE APPOINTED FROM COMPNY'S SERVANTS

And be it enacted, That there shall be Four Ordinary Members of the said Council, Three of whom shall from Time to Time be appointed by the said Court of Directors from amongst such Persons as shall be or shall have been Servants of the said Company; and each of the said Three Ordinary Members of Council shall at the Time of his Appointment have been in the Service of the said Company for at least Ten Years; and if he shall be in the Military Service of the said Company, he shall not during his Continuance in Office as a Member of Council hold any Military Command, or be employed in actual Military Duties; and that the Fourth Ordinary Member of Council shall from Time to Time be appointed from amongst Persons who shall not be Servants of the said Company by the said Court of Directors, subject to the Approbation of His Majesty, to be signified in Writing by His Royal Sign Manual, countersigned by the President of the said Board; provided that such last-mentioned Member of Council shall not be entitled to sit or vote in the said Council except at Meetings thereof for making Laws and Regulations; and it shall be lawful for the said Court of Directors to appoint the Commander-in-Chief of the Company's Forces in India, and if there shall be no such Commander-in-Chief, or the Offices of such Commander-in-Chief and of Governor General of India shall be vested in the same Person, then the Commander-in-Chief of the Forces on the Bengal Establishment, to be an Extraordinary Member of the said Council, and such Extraordinary Member of Council shall have Rank and Precedence at the Council Board next after the Governor General.

SECTION 43: THE GOVERNOR GENERAL IN COUNCIL EMPOWERED TO LEGISLATE FOR INDIA, EXCEPT AS TO MATTERS HEREINAFTER MENTIONED

And be it enacted, That the said Governor General in Council shall have Power to make Laws and Regulations for repealing, amending, or altering any Laws or Regulations whatever now in force or hereafter to be in force in the said Territories or any Part thereof, and to make Laws and Regulations for all Persons, whether British or Native, Foreigners or others, and for all Courts of Justice, whether established by His Majesty's Charters or otherwise, and the Jurisdictions thereof, and for all Places and Things whatsoever within and throughout the whole and every Part of the said Territories, and for all Servants of the said Company within the Dominions of Princes and States in alliance with the said Company; save and except that the said Governor General in Council shall not have the Power of making any Laws or Regulations which shall in any way repeal, vary, suspend, or affect any of the Provisions of this Act, or any of the Provisions of the Acts for punishing Mutiny and Desertion of Officers and Soldiers, whether in the Service of His Majesty or the said Company, or any Provisions of any Act hereafter to be passed in anywise affecting the said Company or the said Territories or the Inhabitants thereof, or any Laws or Regulations which shall in any way affect any Prerogative of the Crown, or the Authority of Parliament, or the Constitution or Rights of the said Company, or any Part of the unwritten Laws or Constitution of the United Kingdom of Great Britain and Ireland whereon may depend in any Degree the Allegiance of any Person to the Crown of the United Kingdom, or the Sovereignty or Dominion of the said Crown over any Part of the said Territories.

SECTION 46: RESTRICING THE POWER OF PUNISHING WITH DEATH EUROPEAN SUBJECTS

Provided also, and be it enacted, That it shall not be lawful for the said Governor General in Council, without the previous Sanction of the said Court of Directors, to make any Law or Regulation whereby Power shall be given to any Courts of Justice, other than the Courts of Justice established by His Majesty's Charters, to sentence to the Punishment of Death any of His Majesty's natural born Subjects born in Europe, or the Children of such Subjects, or which shall abolish any of the Courts of Justice established by His Majesty's Charters.

SECTION 65: THE GOVERNOR GENERAL IN COUNCIL TO HAVE CONTROL OVER THE PRESIDENCIES

And be it further enacted, That the said Governor General in Council shall have and be invested by virtue of this Act with full Power and Authority to superintend and control the Governors and Governors in Council of Fort William in Bengal, Fort Saint George, Bombay, and Agra, in all Points relating to the Civil or Military Administration of the said Presidencies respectively, and the said Governors and Governors in Council shall be bound to obey such Orders and Instructions of the said Governor General in Council in all Cases whatsoever.

SECTION 71: THE NEW PRESIDENCY OF AGRA NOT TO AFFECT THE SUCCESSION OF COMMANDS AND OFFICES IN BENGAL AND AGRA

And be it enacted, That there shall not, by reason of the Division of the Territories now subject to the Government of the Presidency of Fort William in Bengal into Two Presidencies succession as aforesaid, be any Separation between the Establishments and to Commands Forces thereof respectively, or any Alteration in the Course and Order of Promotion and Succession of the Company's Servants in the same Two Presidencies respectively, but that all the Servants, Civil and Military, of the Bengal Establishments and Forces, shall and may succeed and be appointed to all Commands and Offices within either of the said Presidencies respectively as if this Act had not been passed.

SECTION 72: PRESIDENCYOF FORT WILLLIAM TO BE ENTIRE FOR THE PURPOSES OF THE MUTINY ACT

And be it enacted, That for the Purposes of an Act passed in the Fourth Year of the Reign of His late Majesty King George the Fourth, intituled "An Act to consolidate and amend the poses of the Laws for punishing Mutiny and Desertion of Officers and Soldiers in Mutiny Act, the Service of the East India Company, and to authorize Soldiers and Sailors in the East Indies to send and receive Letters at a reduced Rate of Postage", and of any Articles of War made or to be made under the same, the Presidency of Fort William in Bengal shall be taken and deemed to comprise under and within it all the Territories which by or in virtue of this Act shall be divided between the Presidencies of Fort William in Bengal and Agra respectively, and shall for all the Purposes aforesaid be taken to be the Presidency of Fort William in Bengal in the said Act mentioned.

SECTION 73: ARTICLES OF WAR TO BE MADE BY GOVERNOR GENERAL IN COUNCIL

And be it enacted, That it shall be lawful for the said Governor General in Council from Time to Time to make Articles of War for the Government of the Native Officers and Soldiers in the Military Service of the Company, and for the Administration of Justice by Courts-martial to be holden on such Officers and Soldiers, and such Articles of War from Time to Time to repeal or vary and amend; and such Articles of War shall be made and taken notice of in the same Manner as all other the Laws and Regulations to be made by the said Governor General in Council under this Act, and shall prevail and be in force, and shall be of exclusive Authority over all the Native Officers and Soldiers in the said Military Service, to whatever Presidency such Officers and Soldiers may belong, or wheresoever they may be serving: Provided nevertheless, that until such Articles of War shall be made by the said Governor General in Council any Articles of War for or relating to the Government of the Company's Native Forces, which at the Time of this Act coming into operation shall be in force and use in any Part or Parts of the said Territories, shall remain in force.

SECTION 74: HIS MAJESTY MAY REMOVE ANY OFFICER OF THE COMPANY IN INDIA

And be it enacted, That it shall be lawful for His Majesty, by any Writing under His Sign Manual, countersigned by the President of the said Board of Commissioners, to remove or dismiss any Person holding any Office, Employment, or Commission, Civil or Military, under the said Company in India, and to vacate any Appointment or Commission of any Person to any such Office or Employment; provided that a Copy of every such Writing, attested by the said President, shall within Eight Days after the same shall be signed by His Majesty be transmitted or delivered to the Chairman or Deputy Chairman of the said Company.

SECTION 75: THE POWER OF THE DIRECTORS TO REMOVE THEIR SERVANTS PRESERVED

Provided always, and be it enacted, That nothing in this Act contained shall take away the Power of the said Court of Directors to remove or dismiss any of the Officers or Servants of the said Company, but that the said Court shall and may at all Times have full Liberty to remove or dismiss any of such Officers or Servants at their Will and Pleasure; provided that any Servant of the said Company appointed by His Majesty through the Default of Appointment by the said Court of Directors shall not be dismissed or removed without His Majesty's Approbation, as herein-before is mentioned.

SECTION 78: DIRECTORS TO MAKE REGULATIONS FOR THE DISTRIBUTION OF PATRONAGE IN INDIA

And be it enacted, That the said Court of Directors, with the Approbation of the said Board of Commissioners, shall and may from Time to Time make Regulations for the Division and Distribution of the Patronage and Power of Nomination of and to the Offices, Commands, and Employments in the said Territories, and in all or any of the Presidencies thereof, among the said Governor General in Council, Governor General, Governors in Council, Governors, Commander in Chief, and other Commanding Officers respectively appointed or to be appointed under this Act.

SECTION 79: DEPARTURE OF GOVERNOR GENERAL ETC., FOR EUROPE, TO BE A RESIGNATION

And be it enacted, That the Return to Europe or the Departure from India with Intent to return to Europe of any Governor General of India, Governor, Member of Council, or Commander in Chief, shall be deemed in Law a Resignation and Avoidance of his Office or Employment, and that no Act or Declaration of any Governor General, or Governor, or Member of Council, other than as aforesaid, excepting a Declaration in Writing under Hand and Seal, delivered to the Secretary for the Public Department of the Presidency wherein he shall be, in order to its being recorded, shall be deemed or held as a Resignation or Surrender of his said Office; and that the Salary and other Allowances of any such Governor General or other Officer respectively shall cease from the Day of such his Departure, Resignation, or Surrender; and that if any such Governor General or Member of Council of India shall leave the said Territories, or if any Governor or other Officer whatever in the Service of the said Company shall leave the Presidency to which he shall belong, other than in the known actual Service of the said Company, the Salary and Allowances appertaining to his Office shall not be paid or payable during his Absence to any Agent or other Person for his Use; and in the event of his not returning, or of his coming to Europe, his Salary and Allowances shall be deemed to have ceased on the Day of his leaving the said Territories, or the Presidency to which he may have belonged; provided that it shall be lawful for the said Company to make such Payment as is now by Law permitted to be made to the Representatives of their Officers or Servants who, having left their Stations intending to return thereto, shall die during their Absence.

(Sections of the Charter relevant to the subject of this book have only been included)

ACT XXIII of 1839[1]

An Act for authorizing Sentences of Imprisonment, with or without Hard Labour, by Courts-martial, in certain cases Passed by the Honourable the President of the Council of India in Council, on 23 September 1839

Soldiers sentenced to dismissal may be imprisoned with or without labour

It is hereby declared and enacted, that in all cases in which, by a general order of the Governor-General of India in Council, dated the 24th of February, in the year of our Lord 1835, it is made competent for courts-martial to sentence soldiers of the native army in the service of the East-India Company to the punishment of dismissal from such service, it is and shall be lawful to sentence such soldiers to be imprisoned with or without hard labour for any period not exceeding two years, if the sentence be pronounced by a general court-martial ; or not exceeding one year, if the sentence be pronounced by a garrison or line court-martial ; or not exceeding six months, if the sentence he pronounced by a regimental or detachment court-martial. And every soldier so sentenced to imprisonment with hard labour for any period whatever, or to imprisonment without hard labour for any period exceeding six months, shall, after confirmation of his sentence, be dismissed from such service ; provided always, that all sentences under this Act pronounced by any court-martial inferior to a general court-martial shall require the confirmation of the general or other officer commanding the division or field force to which the person convicted belongs.

ACT II of 1840 [2]

An Act for regulating the Execution of Sentences of Imprisonment passed by Courts-martial in certain cases: Passed by the Honourable the President of the Council of India in Council, on the 10th February, 1840.

Civil officers to give effect to sentences of imprisonment of courts-martial under Act XXIII of 1839

I. It is hereby declared and enacted, that whenever, under Act No. XXIII of 1839, any sentence of a court-martial shall adjudge imprisonment, or imprisonment with labour, for any offence, it shall be the duty of every judge, magistrate, sheriff, or other officer in charge of any gaol, to give effect to such sentence on the offender being delivered into his custody, and on being furnished with a

1 The provisions of this Act, as well as those of Acts II of 1840, and XXVIII of 1841, may perhaps be held to be superseded by the Articles of War in Act XIX 1847.

2 The provisions of this Act as well as those of Acts XXIII of 1839 and XXVIII of 1841 may perhaps be held to be superseded by the Articles of War contained in Act XIX of 1847: see Article 84 of that Act.

copy of the sentence by the officer commanding the division, garrison, regiment, or detachment, as the case may be, to which the offender belongs.

Act No. XXVIII of 1841

Passed by the Governor-General of India in Council on 15 November 1841

An Act for extending Act No XXIII of 1839 to Camp Followers

It is hereby enacted, that in cases in which an offender, being a Soldier, is punishable under Act No. XXIII of 1839 any offender amenable to any Articles of War for the East India Company's native forces, not being a Commissioned Officer, shall be punishable according to that Act, as well as otherwise according to law; and Act No. II of 1840 shall be applicable to offenders imprisoned under this Act.

Act No. XXXVI. of 1850

Passed by the Honourable the President of the Council of India in Council, on the 4th October 1850

An Act to amend the 113th Article of War for the Native Army

Whereas it is expedient that Native Soldiers, when imprisoned, should be treated as European Soldiers are in the like case, as respects subsistence and clothing; It is enacted as follows :—

I. From and after the First day of December 1850, so much of the 113th Article of War for the Government of the Native Officers and Soldiers in the Military Service of the East India Company as provides for the forfeiture of allowances, and the subsistence of such Officers and Soldiers when in imprisonment under the sentence of any Court Martial or of any Court or Criminal Judicature, is repealed.

II. From and after the said First day of December 1850, no Native Officer or Soldier, or public Follower in the Military Service of the East India Company shall be entitled to pay or allowances, when imprisoned under the sentence of a Court Martial or a commuted sentence, or under the sentence of a Court of Criminal Judicature; but shall be clothed and subsisted at such rates, or in such manner, as the Governor General of India in Council may from time to time order.

3 & 4 VICTORIAE Cap. XXXVII

(3 & 4 Vic. Cap. 37)

4th August, 1840

AN ACT to consolidate and amend the Laws for punishing Mutiny and Desertion of officers and Soldiers in the Service of the East-India Company, and for providing for the Observance of Discipline in the Indian Navy, and to amend the Laws or regulating the Payments of regimental debts, and the Distribution of the Effects of Officers and Soldiers Dying in Service.

Punishment for Mutiny, desertion, and divers other military crimes

Whereas an Act was passed in the fourth year of the reign of his late Majesty King George the Fourth, intituled, "*An Act to consolidate and amend the Law for punishing Mutiny and Desertion of Officers and Soldiers in the Service of the East-India Company, and to authorize Soldiers and sailors in the East-Indies to send and receive letters at a reduced rate of Postage*," [4 G. IV, c.81] and it being requisite for the retaining of such forces in their duty, that an exact discipline be observed, and that soldiers who shall mutiny or sir up sedition, or shall desert the said Company's service, be brought to a more exemplary and speedy punishment than the usual forms of the law; be it therefore enacted by the Queen's most excellent Majesty, by and with the advice and consent of the Lords spiritual and temporal, and Commons, in the present parliament assembled, and by the authority of the same, that if any person who is or shall be commissioned or in pay as an officer, or who is or shall be listed or in pay as non-commissioned officer or soldier in the service of the said Company, shall at any time during the continuance of this Act, begin, excite, cause, or join in any mutiny or sedition in the land or marine forces of her Majesty or of the said Company, or shall not use his utmost endeavours to suppress the same, or coming to the knowledge of any mutiny or intended mutiny shall not, without delay, give information thereof to his commanding officer; or shall cast away his arms or ammunition, or otherwise misbehave himself before the enemy; or shall shamefully abandon or deliver up any garrison, fortress, post, or guard committed to his charge, or which he shall be commanded to defend ; or shall compel the governor or commanding officer of any garrison, fortress, or post to deliver up to the enemy or to abandon the same; or shall speak words or use any other means to induce such governor or commanding officer, or others, to misbehave towards the enemy, or shamefully to abandon or deliver up any garrison, fortress, post, or guard committed to their respective charge, which he or they shall be commanded to defend ; or shall treacherously make known the watchword; or shall intentionally occasion false alarms in action, camp, garrison, or quarters; or shall leave his post, for plunder or otherwise, before relieved, or shall be found sleeping on his post; or shall hold correspondence with or give advice or intelligence to any rebel or enemy of her Majesty or the said Company, either by letters, messages, signs, or tokens, in any manner or way whatsoever; or shall knowingly harbour or protect such rebel or enemy, or shall treat or enter into any terms with such rebel or enemy, without the licence of the said Company or of the said Company's Governor-general in Council, or Governor in Council at any of their presidencies, or without the licence of the general or chief-commander; or who shall do violence to any per son bringing provisions or other necessaries to the quarters of the forces; or shall force a safe guard; or shall strike or shall use or offer any violence against his superior officer, being in the execution of his office; or shall disobey any lawful command of his superior officer; or shall desert the said Company's service; all and every person and persons so offending in any of the matters before mentioned, whether such offence shall be committed within the dominions of her Majesty or the possessions or territories which are or may be under the government of the said Company, or in foreign parts, upon land or upon the sea, within or without the limits of the Charter of the said United Company, shall suffer death, transportation, or such other punishment as by a Court-martial shall be awarded.

Power to appoint general courts-martial anywhere beyond 120 miles from the presidencies of Fort William, Fort Saint George, and Bombay, except Prince of Wales' Island, Singapore, and Malacca, for trial of capital offences

II. And be it enacted, that the general or other officer commanding in chief the forces of or belonging to the presidencies of Fort William, Fort Saint George, and Bombay respectively for the time being may appoint general Courts-martial, and issue his warrant to any general or other officer not below the degree of a field officer, having the command of a body of troops of her Majesty, or of the said Company, empowering them respectively to appoint general Courts-martial, as occasion may require, to be holden within the territories of any foreign state, or in any country under the protection of her Majesty or the said Company, or at any place (other than Prince of Wales' Island, Singapore, and Malacca), in the territories under the government of the said Company, and situated above one hundred and twenty miles from the said presidencies respectively, for the trial of any person under his command, accused of having committed wilful murder or any other capital crime, or of having used violence or committed any offence against the person or property of any subject of her Majesty, or any other person entitled to her Majesty's protection, to the protection of the respective governments of the East India Company, or of any state in alliance with the said Company, within the territories of any foreign state, or in any country under the protection of her Majesty or the said Company, or at any place, other than Prince of Wales Island, Singapore, or Malacca, in the territories under the government of the said Company, situated above one hundred and twenty miles from the said presidencies respectively; and the persons accused, if found guilty, shall suffer death, or be liable to transportation for life or for a term of years, or to such other punishment, according to the nature and degree of the respective offences, as by such sentence of any such general Court-martial shall be awarded: provided always, that any such person so tried shall not be liable to be tried for the same offence by any other Court whatsoever.

Sentences of death or transportation not to be carried into execution till confirmed by the officer commanding-in-chief, with the concurrence of the governor of the presidencies

III. And be it enacted, that in every case wherein a sentence of death or transportation shall be pronounced, or a sentence of death shall be commuted to transportation, for any such capital offence committed at any place situated above one hundred and twenty miles from the presidencies of Fort William, Fort Saint George, and Bombay respectively, and being within territories under the government of the said Company, such sentence, whether original, revised, or commuted, shall be by carried into execution until confirmed by the general or other officer commanding-in-chief at the presidencies, with the concurrence of the Governor-general in Council, or Governor in Council of the presidencies in the territories subordinate to which the offender shall have been tried, although such offender may belong to the forces of another presidency: provided always, that such sentence shall have been regularly reported to and approved and confirmed by the general or other officer commanding-in-chief of the forces of the presidencies to which such offender shall belong, and by whom or under whose authority the Court-martial by which such offender shall have been tried was appointed.

Such offender, if apprehended by the civil authorities, to be delivered over for trial by court-martial

IV. And be it enacted, that if any person liable to be tried by a Court-martial for any such offence alleged to have been committed within the territories of any foreign state, or in any country under the protection of her Majesty or the said Company, or at any place (other than Prince of Wales' Island, Singapore, or Malacca,) in the territories under the government of the said Company situate above one hundred and twenty miles from the said Presidencies of Fort William, Fort Saint George, and Bombay respectively, and for which no proceeding shall have been commenced in any Court of competent jurisdiction, shall be apprehended by the authority of or brought before any magistrate for any such offence, such magistrate shall deliver over such accused person to the commanding officer of the regiment, corps, or detachment to which such accused person shall belong, or to the commanding officer of the nearest military station, for the purpose of his being tried by a Court-martial for such offence as hereinbefore is provided in that behalf.

The ordinary course of law not to be interfered with; After trial by the civil power on other punishment than cashiering

V. And be it enacted, that nothing in this Act contained shall be construed to exempt any officer or soldier from being proceeded against by the ordinary course of law; and any commanding officer who shall wilfully neglect or refuse, when application is made to him for that purpose, to deliver over to the civil magistrate any officer or soldier accused of any capital crime, or of any violence or offence against the person, estate, or property of any of her Majesty's subjects, or any other person entitled to her Majesty's protection, or to the protection of the respective governments of the East-India Company, or of any state in alliance with the said Company, which is punishable by the ordinary course of law, or shall wilfully neglect or refuse to assist the officers of justice in apprehending such offender, shall, upon conviction thereof in any prosecution in any of her Majesty's Courts of Record in India, be deemed to be ipso facto cashiered, and shall be utterly disabled to have or hold any civil or military office or employment in the said Company's service in the East-Indies: and a copy of the record of such conviction, subscribed and attested by the clerk of the crown or other proper officer of the Court in which such conviction shall take place, shall, within two months from the time of such conviction, be transmitted to the Judge Advocate General of the army to which such offender shall belong; provided that nothing herein contained shall extend to require the delivery over to the civil magistrate of any such person accused of any offence who shall have been tried for such offence by any Court-martial in manner hereinbefore provided in respect of offences committed within the territories of any foreign state, or in any country under the protection of her Majesty or the said Company, or at any place in or out of the territories of the said Company situate above one hundred and twenty miles from the said presidencies of Fort William, Fort Saint George, and Bombay respectively, or against whom any effectual proceeding shall have been taken or ordered to be taken, for the purpose of bringing such person to trial by such Court-martial as aforesaid; provided also, that no person or persons, being acquitted or convicted of any capital crime, violence, or offence, by the civil magistrate or the verdict of a jury, shall be liable to be punished by a Court-martial for the same otherwise than by cashiering.

No soldier liable to arrest for debt, unless amounting to 300 Company's rupees; Plaintiff may enter a common appearance

VI. And be it enacted, that no person whatever enlisted into the Company's service as a soldier shall be liable to be arrested or taken therefrom, by any process or execution whatever, other than for some criminal matter, unless an affidavit (for which no fee shall be taken) shall be made by the plaintiff, or someone on his behalf, before a judge of the Court out of which such process or execution shall issue, or before some person authorized to take affidavits in such Courts, of which affidavit a memorandum shall, without fee, be endorsed upon the back of such process, that the original debt for which the action has been brought or execution sued out amounts to the value of three hundred Company's rupees at the least, over and above all costs of suit in the action or actions on which the same shall be grounded; and any judge of such Court may examine into any complaint thereof made by a soldier or by his superior officer, and by warrant under his hand discharge such soldier without fee, he being shown to be duly enlisted, and to have been arrested contrary to the intent of this Act, and shall award reasonable costs to such complainant, who shall have for the recovery thereof the like remedy that the person who takes out the said execution might have had for his costs, or the plaintiff in the like action might have had for the recovery of his costs, in case judgment had been given for him with costs, against the defendant in the said action; provided that any plain tiff, upon notice of the cause of action first given in writing or left at such soldier's last quarters, may file a common appearance, in any action to be brought for or upon account of any debt whatsoever, and proceed therein to judgment according to the course of the Court, and have execution other than against the body.

The Queen may make articles of war, of which all courts shall take judicial notice, and copies to be transmitted to judges and governors

VII. And be it enacted, that it shall be lawful for her Majesty to make articles of war for the better government of the said Company's Forces, which articles of war shall be judicially taken notice of by all judges and in all Courts whatsoever; and copies of the same, printed by the Queen's printer, shall, as soon as conveniently may be after the same shall have been made and established by her Majesty, be transmitted by her Majesty's Secretary-at-War, signed with his own hand and name, to the Judges of her Majesty's superior Courts at West minster, Dublin, Edinburgh, and in India respectively, and also to the Governors of her Majesty's dominions abroad, and the territories within the limits of the Charter of the said Company; provided that no person shall by such articles of war be subject to any punishment extending to life or limb or transportation within the dominions of her Majesty, or the pos sessions or territories which are or may be under the government of the said Company, for any crime committed within one hundred and twenty miles distance from either of the presidencies of Fort William, Fort Saint George, or Bombay, which is not expressed to be so punishable by this Act; provided also, that nothing in this Act contained shall in any manner impeach or affect any articles of war, or any matters enacted or in force, or which hereafter may be enacted by the Government of India, respecting officers or soldiers being natives of the East-Indies, or other places within the limits of the said Company's Charter, and to whom the present Act is declared not to be applicable. [vide 53 Geo. 3, cap. 155, secs. 96 & 97, and 3 & 4 Wm. 4, cap. 85, sec. 73.]

Trial of native officer or soldier

VIII. And be it enacted, that on the trial of all offences committed by any native officer or soldier, or follower, reference shall be had to the articles of war, framed by the Government of India for such native officers, soldiers, or followers, and to the established usages of the service.

The Queen may authorize the Court of the east India Company to empower the Indian government and their commanding field officers to appoint Courts-martial

IX. And be it enacted, that her Majesty may from time to time grant a commission or warrant under her royal sign manual unto the Court of Directors of the said Company, who, by virtue of such commission or warrant, shall have power under the seal of the said Company to authorize and empower their Governor-general in Council and Governor in Council for the time being at the presidencies of Fort William, Fort Saint George, and Bombay respectively, from time to time to appoint Courts-martial, and to authorize and empower the general or other officer commanding any body of the forces employed in the said Company's service to appoint general Courts-martial, as well as to authorize any officer under their respective commands, not below the degree of a field officer, to convene general Courts-martial, as occasion may require, for the trial of offences committed by any of their forces under their several commands, whether the same shall have been so committed before or after such officer shall have taken upon himself such command, all which Courts-martial shall be constituted and shall regulate their proceedings according to the several provisions hereinafter specified; provided that, whenever any of her Majesty's forces shall be employed to act under the authority of any of the said Company's presidencies in the East-Indies, the power of appointing Courts-martial, or authorizing the appointment of Courts-martial, for the trial of any officer or soldier of the said Company of or belonging to such presidencies, shall be in the officer for the time being commanding in chief at such presidency.

The Queen may authorize the convening of Courts-martial for trying offences against articles of war

X. And be it enacted, that for bringing to justice offenders against such articles of war as may be framed by her Majesty as hereinbefore provided, it shall be lawful for her Majesty to grant her commission or warrant to the persons and in the manner herein mentioned and ex pressed for convening, and authorizing any officer under their respective commands not below the degree of a field officer to convene Courts-martial, as well in the possessions or territories which are or may be under the government of the Company, as elsewhere, where the troops of the Company are or may be employed, as occasion may require, for the trial of offences com mitted by any of the forces under their several commands, whether the same shall have been committed before or after such officer shall have taken upon himself such command.

Offender may be tried and punished in places other than where the offence have been committed

XI. And be it enacted, that any person subject to the provisions of this Act who shall, in any part of her Majesty's dominions, or the possessions or territories under the government of the East-India Company, or elsewhere, commit any offence for which he may be liable to be tried by Court-martial by virtue of this Act, may be tried and punished for the same in any part of her Majesty's dominions, or the possessions or territories which are or may be under the government of the said Company, or elsewhere where he may have come after the commission of the offence, in the same manner as if the offence had been committed where such trial shall take place.

Composition and constitution of general Courts-martial

XII. And be it enacted, that all general Courts-martial held under the authority of this Act shall consist of not less than thirteen commissioned officers, except the same shall be holden in any place out of her Majesty's dominions, or of the possessions or territories which are or may be under the government of the said Company, or at Prince of Wales' Island, Singapore, or Malacca, at which places such general Court-martial may consist of any number not less than five; and no judgment of death shall pass without the concurrence of two-thirds at least of the officers present; and the president shall in no case be the officer commanding in chief or Governor of the garrison where the offender shall be tried, nor under the degree of a field officer, unless where a field officer cannot be had, nor in any case whatsoever under the degree of a captain.

Powers of General Courts-martial

XIII. And be it enacted, that a general Court-martial may sentence any soldier to imprisonment, with or without hard labour, in any public prison or other place which the Court or the officer commanding the regiment or corps to which the offender belongs or is attached shall appoint, and may also direct that such offender shall be kept in solitary confinement for any portion or portions of such imprisonment, not exceeding one month at a time, or three months at different times, with intervals of not less than one month between such times in one year of such imprisonment with hard labour, or may sentence any soldier to corporal punishment, not extending to life or limb, for immorality, misbehaviour, or neglect of duty; and a general Court-martial may, in addition to any such punishment as aforesaid, sentence any offender to forfeiture of all advantage as to additional pay and pension on discharge; and whensoever any Court-martial by which any soldier shall have been tried and convicted of any offence punishable with death shall not think the offence deserving of capital punishment, such Court-martial may, instead of awarding a corporal punishment or imprisonment, adjudge the offender, according to the degree of the offence, to be transported as a felon for life or for a certain term of years, or may sentence him to general service as a soldier in any corps of the said Company's forces, and in any country or place (such country or place being within the limits of the said Company's Charter, and under the said Company's Government), which the officer commanding in chief at the presidency to which the offender belongs shall thereupon direct, or may, if such offender shall have enlisted for a limited number of years, sentence him to serve for life as a soldier in any corps of the said Company's forces which such officer commanding in chief shall direct; and the Court may, in addition to any other punishment, sentence such offender to forfeit all advantage as to increase of pay or as to pension on discharge which might otherwise have accrued to such offender; provided that in all cases where a capital punishment shall have been awarded by a general Court-martial it shall be lawful for the officer commanding in chief the forces of the presidency to which the offender shall belong, instead of causing such sentence to be carried into execution, to order the offender to be transported as a felon, either for life or for a certain term of years, as shall seem meet to the officer commanding as aforesaid.

The Queen empowered to appoint or to authorize the Indian Government to appoint place of transportation; Indian Government to execute sentences of transportation

XIV. And be it enacted, that her Majesty may, by any order or orders, to be by her from time to time made, with the advice of her Privy Council, appoint, or by any such order or orders in Council authorize the Governor-general of India in Council, and the Governor in Council of Fort Saint George and Bombay respectively, to appoint any place or places beyond the seas within her Majesty's dominions to which felons and other offenders may be conveyed; and that when such offenders shall be about to be transported from any of the said presidencies to such place of transportation, the Governor of such presidency shall give orders for his intermediate custody and removal to the ship to be employed for his transportation, and shall empower some person to make a contract for the effectual transportation of the offender to the place so appointed, and shall direct security to be given for such transportation.

Transports to be subject to the convict laws of the place of transportation

XV. And be it enacted, that so soon as such offender shall be delivered to the Governor of the colony, or other person or persons to whom the contractor or other person appointed for that purpose as aforesaid shall be so directed to deliver him, every such person shall, within the place or places to which, under or in pursuance of any such order or orders in Council, they shall be sent or transported, be subject and liable to all such and the same laws, rules and regulations as are or shall be in force in any such place or places with respect to convicts trans ported from Great Britain.

Trial and punishment for embezzlement and similar offences

XVI. And be it enacted, that every paymaster or other commissioned officer, or any person employed in the ordnance or commissariat department, or in any manner in the care or distribution of any money, provisions, forage, or stores, who shall embezzle or fraudulently misapply, or be concerned in or connive at the embezzlement, fraudulent misapplication, or damage of any money, provisions, forage, clothing, ammunition, or other military stores, belonging to her Majesty's forces, or for her use, or belonging to the East-India Company, or for their use, may be tried for the same by a general Court-martial, which may adjudge any such offender to be transported as a felon for life, or for any certain term of years, or to suffer such punishment of fine, imprisonment, dismissal from the said Company's service, and in capacity of serving the East-India Company in any office, civil or military, as such Court shall think fit, according to the nature and degree of the offence; and every such offender shall, in addition to any other punishment, make good at his own expense the loss and damage sustained, which shall have been ascertained by such Court-martial; and the loss and damage so ascertained as aforesaid shall be a debt to her Majesty or the East-India Company, as the case may be, and may be recovered accordingly.

Composition and powers of district or garrison Courts-martial

XVII. And be it enacted, that a district or garrison Court-martial shall consist of not less than five commissioned officers, and may sentence any soldier to any imprisonment, with or without hard labour, in any public prison or other place which such Court or the officer commanding the regiment or corps to which the offender belongs or is attached shall appoint, and may also direct that such offender shall be kept in solitary confinement for any portion or portions of such imprisonment, not exceeding one month at a time, or three months at different times with intervals of not less than one month between such times in one year, of such imprisonment with hard labour, or may sentence any soldier to corporal punishment, not extending to life or limb, for immorality, misbehaviour, or neglect of duty; and such Court may, in addition to either of the said punishments, sentence a soldier to forfeiture of all advantage as to additional pay, and to pension on discharge, for disgraceful conduct.

In wilfully maiming or injuring himself, or any other soldier, at the instance of such soldier, with intent to render himself or such soldier unfit for service;

In tampering with his eyes;

In malingering, feigning disease, absenting himself from hospital whilst under medical care, or other gross violation of the rules of any hospital, thereby wilfully producing or aggravating disease or infirmity, or wilfully delaying his cure;

In purloining or selling stores, the property of the Crown or of the East-India Company;

In stealing any money or goods, the property of a comrade, or of any military or regimental mess;

In producing false or fraudulent accounts or returns: In embezzling or fraudulently misapplying money intrusted to him, belonging either to the Crown or the East-India Company;

Or in committing any petty offence of a felonious or fraudulent nature, to the injury of or with intent to injure any person, civil or military;

Or for any other disgraceful conduct, being of a cruel, indecent, or unnatural kind;

And such offender may be further put under stoppages, not exceeding two-thirds of his daily pay, until the amount be made good of any loss or damage arising out of his misconduct; and if any soldier shall be convicted of any such disgraceful conduct, and shall be sentenced to forfeiture of his claim to pension, the Court may further recommend him to be discharged with ignominy from the service; and any such Court shall deprive a soldier, if convicted of a charge of habitual drunkenness, of his liquor when issued in kind, or of his allowance in lieu of beer or liquor, or of such proportion thereof, or of such portion of his additional or regular pay, for such period, not exceeding two years, as may accord with her Majesty's articles of war for the Company's troops, subject to restoration on subsequent good conduct; and in addition to any such punishment, the Court may, if it shall think fit, sentence such offender to imprisonment or to corporal punishment; provided that in all the foregoing cases the sentences of a district or garrison Court-martial shall be confirmed by the general officer, governor, or senior officer in command of the district, garrison, or island; and the president of every Court-martial, other than a general Court-martial, not being under the rank of captain, shall be appointed by the officer convening such Court-martial; provided that such Court-martial shall not have power to pass any sentence of death or transportation.

Certain offences may be tried and punished by regimental Courts-martial

XVIII. And be it enacted, that in cases of mutiny and gross insubordination, or any offences committed on the line of march, the offence may be tried by a regimental Court-martial, and the sentence confirmed and carried into execution on the spot by the officer in the martial. immediate command of the troops, provided that the sentence shall not exceed that which a regimental Court-martial is competent to award; and a regimental Court-martial may try any soldier for habitual drunkenness, and may sentence any soldier to imprisonment, with or without hard labour, for any period not exceeding forty days, and to solitary confinement for any period not exceeding twenty days; and whenever any such Court-martial shall sentence any soldier to imprisonment as aforesaid it may (if it shall think fit) direct that he be kept in solitary confinement for a certain portion or portions of the period of such imprisonment: provided always, that when such Court shall direct the imprisonment to be part solitary and part otherwise, the whole period of such imprisonment, including the solitary part thereof, shall not exceed twenty days, and shall be divided into periods not exceeding ten days each; and a regimental Court-martial may sentence any soldier for being drunk when on or for duty or parade, or on the line of march, to be deprived of a penny a day of his pay for any period not exceeding thirty days, in addition to any other punishment which such Court may award; and any such Court shall deprive a soldier, if convicted of a charge of habitual drunkenness, of his liquor, when issued in kind, or of his allowance in lieu of beer or liquor, or of such pro portion thereof, or of such portion of his additional or regular pay for such period, not exceeding six months, as may accord with her Majesty's Articles of War for the Company's troops, subject to restoration on subsequent good conduct.

Additional punishments

XIX. And be it enacted, that every soldier who shall be found guilty of desertion by a general or district or garrison Court-martial, where such findings shall be duly approved, or of felony in any Court of civil judicature, shall thereupon forfeit all advantage as to additional pay, and to pension on discharge, in addition to any punishment which such Court may award; and it shall be lawful for any Court-martial empowered to try the crime of desertion, in addition to any other punishment, to direct that the offender be marked on the left side, two inches below the arm-pit, with the letter '**D**', such letter not to be less than an inch long, and to be marked upon the skin with some ink or gunpowder, or other preparation, so as to be visible and conspicuous, and not liable to be obliterated.

Officer in command of troops serving in foreign countries, not in alliance with the East India Company, may assemble Courts-martial

XX. And be it enacted, that it shall be lawful for any officer commanding any district, or any portion of thesaid Company's troops which may at any time be serving in any place out of her Majesty's dominions, or of the possessions or territories which are or may be under the government of the said Company, or of the territories of those states in alliance with the said Company in which the said Company's forces are permanently stationed, upon complaint made to him of any offence committed against the property or person of any inhabitant of or resident in any such countries, by any person serving with or belonging to the Company's army, being under the immediate command of any such officer, to summon and cause to assemble a Court-martial, which shall consist of not less than three officers at the least, for the purpose of trying any such person, notwithstanding any such officer shall not have received any warrant empowering him to assemble Courts-martial; and every such Court-martial shall have the same powers in regard to summoning and examining witnesses, trial of and sentence upon any such offenders, as are granted by this Act to general Courts-martial; provided that no sentence of any such Court-martial shall be executed until the general commanding in chief of the army to which the division, brigade, detachment, or party to which any person so tried, convicted, and adjudged to suffer punishment shall belong, shall have approved and confirmed the same.

How proceedings shall be regulated in cases of conjunction of Queen/s and Company's officers on Courts-martial

XXI. And be it enacted, that officers of her Majesty's land forces, and of the forces in the service of the East-India Company may, whenever it shall be necessary, sit in conjunction on Courts-martial, which shall be regulated in like manner as if consisting wholly of officers of her Majesty's land forces, or wholly of officers in the service of the said Company; except that upon the trial of any person in her Majesty's land forces, the provisions of the Act which shall exist at the time for the punishment of mutiny and desertion in her Majesty's forces shall be applicable; and on the trial of any officer or soldier in the service of the said East-India Company, the provisions of this Act shall be applicable, notwithstanding any officer in the actual service of the said Company may have a commission from her Majesty or any of her royal predecessors.

Courts-martial may be wholly composed of Queen's officers

XXII. And whereas it may sometimes happen that officers in the service of the said Company cannot conveniently be had to compose the whole or part of a Court-martial; be it enacted, that any officer or soldier, or person subject to the provisions of this Act, may be tried by a general Court-martial composed of officers in her Majesty's service alone; provided always, that the officer convening such Court-martial shall specify in his warrant that no officer in the service of the said Company could conveniently be had.

Oath or solemn declaration to be administered

XXIII. And be it enacted, that all general and other Courts-martial shall administer an oath, or, in case of natives of India, an oath or solemn declaration, as circumstances may require, to every person who shall be examined before such Court in any matter relating to any proceedings before the same.

Members of general Courts-martial and officiating Judge Advocate to take oaths mentioned in the schedule; Protection to witnesses; Witness not attending or refusing to give evidence liable to be attached

XXIV. And be it enacted, that in all trials by general Courts-martial to be held by virtue of this Act the President and every member assisting at such trial, before any proceedings be had thereon, shall take the oaths in the schedule to this Act annexed, before the Judge Advocate or his deputy, or person officiating as such, and on trials by other Courts-martial before the President of such Court, who are hereby respectively authorized to administer the same, and any sworn member may administer the oath to the President; and as soon as the said oaths shall have been administered to the respective members, the President of the Court shall administer to the Judge Advocate, or the person officiating as such, the oath in the schedule to this Act annexed; and no proceeding or trial shall be had but between the hours appointed by the officer commanding where the Court-martial is held, except in cases which require an immediate example: provided also, that every witness duly summoned or warned to attend any Court-martial shall during his necessary attendance on such Court, and in going to and returning from the same, be privileged from arrest, and shall, if arrested in breach of such privilege, be discharged by such Court-martial, or any Court of law, or Judge of any such Court, according as the case shall require, upon its being made appear to such Court martial, Court of law, or Judge, by affidavit in a summary way, that such witness was arrested in going to or returning from or attending upon such Court-martial; and that every witness so duly summoned or warned to attend as aforesaid who shall not attend on such Court, or who attending shall refuse to give evidence, on oath or solemn declaration, or to answer all such questions as the Court may legally demand, shall be liable to be attached in the Courts of law, upon complaint made, in like manner as if such witness had neglected to attend on any trial in any such Court.

A second trial to be had only on appeal from a regimental to a general Court-martial, and no revision more than once

XXV. And be it enacted, that no officer or soldier, being acquitted or convicted of any offence, shall be liable to be tried a second time by the same or any other Court-martial for the same offence, unless in the case of an appeal from a regimental to a general Court-martial; and that no finding, opinion, or sentence given by any Court-martial, and signed by the President thereof, shall be liable to be revised more than once; and no witness shall be examined nor shall any additional evidence be received by the Court on such revision.

Original proceedings, sentence, &c. to be transmitted to the Judge Advocate General of the Army in which such court shall be held

XXVI. And be it enacted, that every Judge Advocate, or person officiating as such at a general Court-martial, shall transmit, with as much expedition as circumstances will admit, the original proceedings, and the sentence, finding, or opinion of such Court-martial, to the Judge Advocate-general of the army in which such Court-martial shall be held, in whose office they are to be carefully preserved; and any person tried by a general Court-martial, or any person in his behalf, shall be entitled, on demand, to a copy of such sentence, finding, or opinion, and proceedings, (paying reasonably for the same,) whether such sentence shall be approved or not, at any time not sooner than three months if the trial took place on the continent of India, or six months if beyond seas; provided that such demand as aforesaid shall have been made within the space of three years from the date of the approval or other final decision upon the proceedings before such general Court-martial.

Indian Governments may suspend proceedings

XXVII. And be it enacted, that the Government of any of the said presidencies in India may suspend the proceedings of any Court-martial which may at any time be holden within such presidencies respectively.

Offences against former Mutiny Act punishable as if committed against this Act, and all existing proceedings continued; Limitation as to trial of offence

XXVIII. And be it enacted, that all crimes and offences which have been committed against the said Act of the fourth year of the reign of his Majesty King George the Fourth, or against any of the Articles of War made and established by virtue of the same, may, during the continuance of this Act, be inquired of and punished in like manner as if they had been committed against this Act; and every warrant for holding any Court-martial under the said Act of the fourth year of the reign of his Majesty King George the Fourth shall remain in full force, notwithstanding the repeal of such Act, and all proceedings of any Court-martial upon any trial begun under the authority of such former Act shall not be discontinued by the repeal of the same: provided always, that no person shall be liable to be tried and punished for any offence against the said Act or this Act, or the Articles of War made or to be made by virtue of the same Acts, or either of them, which shall appear to have been committed more than three years before the issuing of the commission or warrant for such trial, unless the person accused, by reason of his having absented himself, or of some other manifest impediment, shall not have been amenable to justice within that period, in which case such person shall be liable to be tried under such commission or warrant at any time not exceeding two years after the impediment shall have ceased; or unless the conduct of the person accused shall have been submitted to the consideration of the Court of Directors of the East-India Company by the Government of the presidency to which such person shall belong, in which case such person shall be liable to be tried under such commission or warrant at any time not exceeding five years after his offence shall have been committed.

Desertion shall be punishable, notwithstanding any circumstance of enlistment; Admissibility of evidence of former offence

XXIX. And be it enacted, that every soldier shall be liable to be tried and punished for desertion from any corps into which he may have enlisted, or from her Majesty's service, notwithstanding that he may of right belong to some corps from which he shall have originally deserted; and if such person shall be claimed as a deserter by the corps to which he originally belonged, and be tried as a deserter therefrom, or shall be tried as a deserter from any other corps into which he may have enlisted, or if he shall be tried while actually serving in some corps for desertion from any other corps, every desertion previous or subsequent to that for which he shall be under trial, as well as every previous conviction for any other offence, may be given in evidence against him; and in like manner in the case of any soldier tried for any offence whatever, any previous convictions may be given in evidence against him; provided that no such evidence shall in any case be received until after the prisoner shall have been found guilty of such offence, and then only for the purpose of affixing punishment; and provided also, that after he shall so have been found guilty, and before such evidence shall be received, it shall be proved to the satisfaction of the Court that he had previously to his trial received notice of the intention to produce such evidence on the same; and provided further, that the Court shall in no case award to him any greater or other punishment or punishments than may by this Act, and by the Articles of War to be framed by her Majesty by virtue of this Act, be awarded for the offence of which he shall have been found guilty.

A person acknowledging himself to be a deserter to be deemed duly enlisted and dealt accordingly

XXX. And be it enacted, that any person who shall voluntarily deliver himself up as a deserter from any regiment or corps of the said Company's forces, or who, upon being apprehended for desertion or any other offence, shall, in the presence of the magistrate or of the commanding officer of the place, confess himself to be a deserter from any such regiment or corps, shall be deemed to have been duly enlisted and to be a soldier, and shall be liable to serve in any such corps of the said Company's forces as the commander of the forces of the said Company shall think fit to appoint, whether such person shall have been ever actually enlisted as a soldier or not.

Punishment for inducing or assisting in desertion

XXXI. And be it enacted, that every person who shall directly or indirectly persuade any soldier to desert shall suffer such punishment by fine or imprisonment, or both, as the Court before which the conviction may take place shall adjudge; and every person who shall assist any deserter, knowing him to be such, in deserting or in concealing himself, shall forfeit for every such offence the sum of eight hundred Company's rupees, and be further liable to imprisonment, not exceeding twelve months.

Regulations for musters and penalties on false musters

XXXII. And be it enacted, that musters shall be taken of every regiment, troop, or company in thesaid Company's service at such times as shall be appointed; and no soldier shall be absent from such musters unless properly certified to be employed on some other duty, or to be sick, or in prison, or on furlough; and every person who shall give or procure to be given any untrue certificate whereby to excuse any soldier for his absence from any muster or any other service which he ought to attend or perform, or shall make any false or untrue muster of man or horse, or shall wittingly or willingly allow or sign the muster-roll wherein such false muster is contained, or any duplicate thereof, or who shall directly or in directly take or cause to be taken any money or gratuity for mustering any soldiers, or for signing any muster-rolls or duplicates thereof, or shall knowingly muster any person by a wrong name, upon proof thereof upon oath made by two witnessess before a general Court-martial, shall for such offence be forthwith cashiered, and shall be thereby utterly disabled to have or hold any civil or military office or employment within the territories under the government of the East-India Company, or in her Majesty's service or the service of the said Company; and if the person giving such untrue certificate shall not have any military commission he shall forfeit for every such offence the sum of five hundred Company's rupees; and any person who shall falsely be mustered or offer himself to be mustered, or lend or furnish any horse to be falsely mustered, shall, upon oath made by two witnesses before some magistrate residing near the place where such muster shall be made, forfeit the sum of two hundred Company's rupees; and the informer, if he belong to the Company's service, shall, if he demand it, be forthwith discharged.

Suspension and forfeiture of pay

XXXIII. And be it enacted, that any soldier who shall absent himself without leave, or who shall desert, shall, on conviction by a general or other Court-martial, in addition to any punishment awarded by such Court, forfeit his pay for the days on which he has so absented himself without leave, or on which he has been absent by such desertion; and that no soldier shall be entitled to pay, or to reckon service, rewards, pay, or pension, when in confinement under any sentence of any Court, or during any absence from duty by commitment on a charge of any offence cognizable by a civil or criminal Court, or by reason of any arrest for debt, or as a prisoner of war, or while in confinement under any charge of which he shall after wards be convicted; and if any soldier shall absent himself without leave for any period not exceeding five days, and shall not account for the same to the satisfaction of the commanding officer, it shall be lawful for the said commanding officer (if he shall think fit) to order and direct that, in addition to such other punishment as he has authority to inflict, such soldier shall also suffer forfeiture of his pay for the day or days on which he has so absented himself, and thereupon such pay shall be forfeited, and such soldier shall not be liable to be afterwards tried by a Court-martial for the said offence: provided always, that any soldier who shall be so ordered to forfeit his pay shall have a right to insist on being tried by a Court-martial for his offence instead of submitting to such forfeiture; and provided also, that any soldier acquitted of any offence for which he had been committed shall, upon return to his duty in his corps, be entitled to receive all arrears of pay growing due, and to reckon service during his absence or confinement; and upon rejoining the service from being a prisoner of war due inquiry shall be made by a Court-martial, and if it shall be proved to the satisfaction of such Court that the said soldier was taken prisoner without wilful neglect of duty on his part, and that he hath not served with or under or in any manner aided the enemy, and that he hath returned as soon as possible to the service, he may thereupon be recommended by such Court to receive either the whole of such arrears of pay, or a proportion thereof, and to reckon service during his absence; provided also, that it shall be lawful for the government under which any soldier is serving to order or withhold the payment of the whole or any part of the pay of any such soldier during the period of absence by any of the causes aforesaid.

Soldiers entitled to discharge may claim to be sent home, free of expense

XXXIV. And be it enacted, that every soldier entitled to his discharge under any orders or any regulations made by the said Company, or upon the expiration of any period for which he shall have engaged to serve, or under this Act, shall be entitled to be sent to Great Britain or Ireland free of expense, and be entitled on his return to have and receive marching money from the place of his being landed to the parish or place in which he shall have been originally enlisted, or at which he shall at the time of arrival in Great Britain or Ireland decide to take up his residence, such place not being at a greater distance from the place of his landing than the place of his original enlistment, such marching money being at the rate and reckoning per diem fixed for victualling soldiers in her Majesty's service on the march: provided always, that every such soldier entitled to and claiming his discharge, and to be sent to Great Britain or Ireland, shall, until his arrival and debarkation in Great Britain or Ireland, be subject to the provisions of this Act, and the Articles of War framed, or to be framed by her Majesty for the better government of the Company's forces.

No paymaster to receive fee, or to make unusual deductions out of pay or to detain pay; Punishment for so doing; Indian Government may give orders to withhold pay in cases of absent without leave

XXXV. And be it enacted, that no paymaster or other person shall receive any fees or make any deductions whatsoever out of the pay or allowances of any officer or soldier (without his consent be obtained thereto), other than the usual deductions or such other necessary deductions as shall from time to time be required to be made according to the regulations of the service; and every paymaster or other officer having received any officer's or soldier's pay and allowances, who shall unlawfully detain for the space of one month the same, or refuse to pay the same when it shall become due, according to the several rates established by the regulations of the service, shall, upon proof thereof before a Court-martial, be discharged from his employment, and shall forfeit eight hundred Company's rupees, and be liable to such further punishment as shall by the Court-martial be awarded, one moiety of such fine to be paid to the informer, and should such informer be a soldier he shall, if he demand it, be discharged from any further service; provided that it shall be lawful for the Governor-general in Council, or the Governor in Council, at the said presidencies respectively, to give orders for withholding the pay of any officer or soldier for any period during which such officer or soldier shall be absent without leave.

Penalties on persons unlawfully having or purchasing military stores

XXXVI. And be it enacted, that any person who shall unlawfully have in his or her pos session or keeping, or who shall knowingly detain, buy, exchange, or receive from any soldier or deserter, or any other person, on any pretence whatsoever, or shall solicit or entice any soldier, or shall be employed by any soldier knowing him to be such, to sell any arms, ammunition, clothes, or military furniture, or any provisions, or any sheets or other articles used in barracks, provided under barracks, provided under barrack regulations, or regimental necessaries, or any article of forage provided for any horses belonging to the service, or shall change the colour of any clothes as aforesaid, shall forfeit for every such offence any sum not exceeding forty Company's rupees, (one moiety to be paid to the informer,) together with treble value of all or any of the several articles of which such offender shall so become possessed; and if any credible person shall prove on oath or solemn declaration before a magistrate, or person exercising the like authority, a reasonable cause to suspect that any person has in his or her possession, or on his or her premises, any property of the description hereinbefore described, on or with respect to which any such offence shall have been committed, the magistrate or person exercising like authority may grant a warrant to search for such property as in case of stolen goods.

Recruits concealing infirmities punishable

XXXVII. And be it enacted, that any person who shall enlist into the Company's forces, and who shall be discovered to be incapable of active service by reason of any infirmity which shall have been concealed by such person, or not declared before the justice of the peace at the time of his attestation, and mentioned at the foot thereof, may be transferred into any garrison or veteran or invalid battalion, or into her Majesty's or Company's marine forces, notwithstanding he shall have been enlisted for any particular regiment, and shall be entitled to receive such portion or residue of bounty only as shall be allowed by the said Company by any regulation made in that behalf, in lieu and instead of the bounty upon which such man shall have been enlisted, anything in any Act or Acts, or any rules or regulations relating to soldiers, to the contrary notwithstanding.

After embarkation all officers and soldiers subject to this Act

XXXVIII. And be it enacted, that all officers and soldiers who shall be enlisted in or transferred to the service of the said Company, and all officers in the said Company's service who may proceed in charge of or be appointed to do duty with such enlisted or transferred officers and soldiers, shall, from and after their embarkation to go abroad to such place whereto they shall be sent in the service of the said Company, be, during their passage, subject to all the provisions and regulations of this Act, and to all such provisions and regulations as officers and soldiers in the pay of the said Company shall from time to time be subject to at the garrison or place to which such officers and soldiers shall be sent.

Offences during passage cognizable after arrival

XXXIX. And forasmuch as it may happen that offences may be committed by the said officers and men after their embarkation, and before their arrival at their place of destination abroad, which nevertheless cannot be tried and punished during their passage in such manner as such offences ought to be tried and punished; be it therefore enacted, that in every such case every such officer or soldier may and shall, after his arrival at his place of destination abroad, be tried and punished for every offence committed after his embarkation and before his arrival, in the same manner as he would have been liable to be tried and punished if such offence had been committed in any place where the offender would have been tried by any Court-martial held under the authority of this Act.

Divers persons, besides officers and soldiers made subject to this Act

XL. And be it enacted, that the provisions of this Act shall apply to all officers and persons who are or shall be serving and hired to be employed, or who shall serve and be hired to be employed, in the artillery, and in the several trains of artillery, and all conductors of stores, and in the department of engineers, and all officers serving or who shall serve in the corps of engineers, and all officers and persons serving or who shall serve as military surveyors or drafts men, or in the corps of sappers and miners or pioneers, and all persons who now are or shall be in the ordnance and commissariat department; and all apothecaries, veterinary surgeons, medical storekeepers, hospital stewards, and others serving in the medical establishment of the army, licensed sutlers and followers, and all storekeepers and other civil officers employed under the ordnance, shall be at all times subject to all the penalties and punishments mentioned in this Act, and shall in all respects whatsoever be holden to be within the intent and meaning of every part of this Act.

Officers and soldiers raised or serving in friendly states subject to martial law

XLI. And be it enacted, that all officers and soldiers of any troops, being mustered and in pay, which shall be raised or serving in any of the possessions or territories which are or may be under the government of the said Company, or places which are or may be occupied by persons subject to the government of the said Company, or by any forces of the said Company, under the command of any officer having a commission immediately from the government of any of the presidencies of the said Company, shall be liable to martial law in like manner as the Company's other forces are.

For the purpose of this Act the presidencies of Fort William to comprise that of Agra

XLII. And be it enacted, that for the purposes of this Act, and of any Articles of War to be made under the same, the presidency of Fort William in Bengal shall be taken and deemed to comprise under and within it all the territories which by law are divisible between the presidencies of Fort William in Bengal and Agra respectively, and shall for all the purposes aforesaid be taken to be the Presidency of Fort William in Bengal.

Governor General in Council empowered to make laws and regulations for securing discipline and punishing offences in the India Navy, as fully as he make other laws under 3&4 W. 4, c. 85

XLIII. And whereas the said Company, for the safety and protection of the territories under their government, in addition to their land forces, maintain a marine establishment, heretofore called "The Bombay Marine," but now called "The Indian Navy;" and by an Act passed in the ninth year of the reign of King George the Fourth, intituled, "*An Act to extend the Provisions of the East-India Mutiny Act to the Bombay Marine*," reciting the said Act of the fourth year of King George the Fourth, and that it was expedient that discipline should be enforced in the said marine establishment in the manner provided by the said Act of the fourth year of King George the Fourth in respect to the other forces of the said Company, it is enacted, that the pro visions of the said Act of the fourth year of King George the Fourth, and the rules and Articles of War made and to be made by virtue thereof, should extend and be applied to the service of "The Bombay Marine;" and that all persons in the service of the said Company belonging to the said Bombay Marine who should be commissioned or in pay as officers, or enlisted or in pay as non-commissioned officers or soldiers respectively, in the said Company's army, should be, to all intents and purposes, liable to the provisions of the said Act of the fourth year of his Majesty King George the Fourth, and to the same rules and Articles of War, and the same penalties, as the officers and soldiers of the said Company's other forces: and whereas it is expedient to provide other means for enforcing discipline in the said marine establishment called "The Indian Navy;" be it enacted, that for the retaining the forces of the said establishment in their duty, the Governor-general of India in Council shall have power to make laws and regulations for securing the observance of an exact discipline in the said service called "The Indian Navy": and for bringing to a more exemplary and speedy punishment than the usual forms of the law will allow all officers, engineers, soldiers, marines, seamen, and all others belonging to the said marine establishment who shall mutiny or stir up sedition, or shall desert the said service, or shall commit any other offence which in its nature would be cognizable by Courts-martial under this Act, or which may be against good discipline in naval service, in the same and as full and ample manner, to all intents and purposes, as by virtue of an Act passed in the session held in the third and fourth years of the reign of his late Majesty King William the Fourth, intituled, "*An Act for effecting an Arrangement with the East-India Company, and for the better Government of his Majesty's Indian Territories till the thirtieth day of April, one thousand eight hundred and fifty-four*," the said Governor-general in Council now has power to make any laws and regulations whatsoever; anything in the said last-mentioned Act, or any other Act or Acts, to the contrary notwithstanding.

Court of Directors, under control may disallow and such laws and regulations

XLIV. Provided always, and be it enacted, that in case the Court of Directors of the East India Company, under the control of the Board of Commissioners for the Affairs of India, shall signify to the said Governor-general in Council their disallowance of any laws or regulations by the said Governor-general in Council made by virtue of this Act, then and in every such case, upon receipt by the said Governor-general in Council of notice of such disallowance, the said Governor-general in Council shall forthwith repeal all laws and regulations so disallowed.

But until repealed they shall be in force

XLV. Provided also, and be it enacted, that all laws and regulations made as aforesaid, so long as they shall remain un-repealed, shall be of the same force and effect, within and throughout the said territories, as any Act of Parliament would or ought to be within the same territories, and shall be taken notice of by all Courts of justice whatsoever within the same territories in the same manner as any public Act of Parliament would and ought to be taken notice of; and it shall not be necessary to register or publish in any Court of justice any laws or regulations made by the said Governor-general in Council.

No law to be made for sentencing to punishment of death European borne subjects, &c

XLVI. Provided also, and be it enacted, that it shall not be lawful for the said Governor-General in Council, without the previous sanction of the said Court of Directors, to make any law or regulation whereby power shall be given to any Court, other than the Courts of justice established by the Charters of the Crown, to sentence to the punishment of death any of her &c. Majesty's natural-born subjects, born in Europe, or the children of such subjects.

Until such law and regulations made, the provisions of this Act to be applicable to the Indian navy

XLVII. Provided also, and be it enacted, that until the said Governor-general in Council shall have made laws and regulations for the good government of the said Indian navy by virtue of the powers by this Act for that purpose given, all the provisions of this Act, and the rules and Articles of War to be made by virtue thereof, shall extend and be applied to the Indian navy. said marine establishment called "The Indian Navy"; and that all persons in the service of the said Company belonging to the said Indian navy, who shall be commissioned or in pay as officers, or enlisted or in pay as non-commissioned officers or soldiers respectively, in thesaid Company's army, shall be, to all intents and purposes, liable to the provisions of this Act, and to the same rules and Articles of War, and the same penalties, as the officers and soldiers of thesaid Company's other forces.

Persons employed under Articles of War to collect effects of officers and soldiers dying in service abroad, may do so without probate or latter of administration

XLVIII. And whereas by an Act passed in the sixth year of the reign of his Majesty King George the Fourth, intituled, "*An Act to amend Two Acts; of the Fifty-eighth Year of his late Majesty, for regulating the Payment of Regimental Debts, and the Distribution of the Effects of Officers and Soldiers dying in Service, and the Receipt of Sums due to Soldiers; and of the Fourth Year of his present Majesty, for punishing Mutiny and Desertion of Officers and Soldiers in the Service of the East-India Company*," [6 G. 4. C. 61], provision is made for the care, application, and distribution of the effects and credits of officers and soldiers in the said Company's service; and it is expedient to render such provisions more effectual; be it enacted, that it shall be lawful for all persons who may be employed or required, by or under the authority of any Articles of War in force for the time being for the European officers or soldiers in the service of the said Company, to take care of, collect, or superintend or direct the collection of the effects of officers or soldiers dying in the service of the said Company out of the United Kingdom, to ask, demand, and receive any such effects, and to commence, prosecute, and carry on any actions or suits for the recovery thereof, and to sell and dispose of the same, without taking out any letters of administration, either with any will annexed or otherwise, in every respect as if such officers or persons employed or required as aforesaid had been appointed executors or had taken out administration of such effects; and no registrar of any Court in the East-Indies, or any person acting under the appointment or authority of such Court, *ad colligenda* or otherwise, shall in any manner interpose in relation to any such effects, unless required and authorized so to do by any such officer or persons employed or required as aforesaid, any Act or Acts, law, statute, or usage, to the contrary notwithstanding.

What debts to be deemed regimental debts, and to have priority accordingly; Military secretary to decide doubts as to regimental debts

XLIX. And be it enacted, that all sums of money due by deceased officers and soldiers in respect of any military clothing, appointments, and equipments, servants' wages due, and household expenses during the current month, or in respect of any quarters, or of any mess or regimental accounts, and all sums of money due to any agent or paymaster or quarter master, or any other officer, upon any such accounts, or on account of any advance made for any such purpose, and also any charges or expenses attending or relating to the illness or funeral of any such officer or soldier, shall be deemed and taken to be regimental debts, and shall be paid out of any arrears of pay or allowances, or out of any prize or bounty money, or the equipage, goods, chattels, and effects of any officer or soldier dying out of the United Kingdom while in the service of the said Company, in preference to any other debts, claims, or demands whatsoever upon the estate and effects of such officer or soldier; and if any doubt shall arise as to whether any claim or demand made in relation to any officer or soldier is a regimental debt or not, or whether such charges or expenses attending or relating to the illness or funeral of such officer or soldier are proper to be allowed, such question shall be decided and concluded by the order or certificate of the military secretary to the government of the presidency to which such officer or soldier shall have belonged; and all such payments shall be good and valid in law; and every person who shall make any such payment out of any such arrears of pay, effects, or proceeds as aforesaid under the provisions of this Act, or in pursuance of any such order or certificate of such military secretary, or into whose hands any such money shall come, shall be and are hereby indemnified for and in respect of such payments, and all other acts, matters, and things done in pursuance of the provisions of this Act, or of the order or certificate of the said military secretary, in relation to the distribution of such assets; anything in any Act or Acts, or law or laws, to the contrary notwithstanding.

Regimental debts to be paid without probate or letter of administration, and the surplus only to be deemed the personal estate to be administered

L. And be it enacted, that all such regimental debts shall and may be paid without probate of any will being obtained, or any letters of administration, or any confirmation of testament, or letters testamentary or dative, being taken out of any person; and the surplus only of such arrears of pay or allowances, prize or bounty-money, equipage, goods, and chattels, or the proceeds thereof, shall be deemed the personal estate of the deceased, for the payment of any duty in respect of any probate, or of any letters of administration or confirmation of testament, or letters testamentary or dative, or for the purpose of distribution as personal estate; and it shall be lawful for the said military secretary to order and direct the payment or distribution of any such surplus in any case in which the same shall not exceed five hundred Company's rupees, without any probate or letters of administration or confirmation of testament, or letters testamentary or dative, or payment of any duty of stamps, or upon legacies or otherwise : and it shall also be lawful for any paymaster or other person to issue any sum not exceeding the value of five hundred

Company's rupees, which may be due to any officer deceased, or to the widow or relative of any officer deceased, or to the representative or representatives of any such officer's widow or relative in India, in like manner without any probate or letters of administration, or confirmation of testament, or letters testamentary or dative, or payment of any duty of stamps, or upon legacies or otherwise, the same to be paid to the person who shall be notified by the said military secretary as aforesaid as being entitled thereto; and all such payments respectively shall be as valid and effectual, to all intents and purposes, as if the same had been made by or to any executor or administrator, or under the authority of any probate or letters of administration, or confirmation of testament, letters testamentary or dative; anything in any Act or Acts, or law or laws, to the contrary notwithstanding.

Effects remitted not deemed assets in the place of which remitted, so as to render administration necessary

LI. And be it enacted, that such effects, or the proceeds or surplus of such effects, of any officer or soldier so dying, when remitted to any person under any order of the military secretary to the government of any of the said Company's presidencies, or to such military secretary, shall not by reason of coming to the hands of such person or military secretary be taken to be assets or effects in the place to which such proceeds or surplus may be remitted, so as to render it necessary that administration should be taken out in respect thereof; and it shall be lawful for the military secretary to the government of the presidency to which the deceased officer or soldier shall have belonged to order that such effects, or the proceeds or surplus of any such effects, shall be remitted to any other place in India where the same can more conveniently be paid over to the person or persons entitled thereto; and the obedience to the orders of such military secretary in respect to the payment and disposal of any such effects, proceeds or surplus of such effects, shall be a discharge from all actions, suits, and demands in respect thereof to any person to whose hands any such effects, proceeds, or surplus shall have come, and which shall have been paid and disposed of under the order of such military secretary.

Mode of administering surplus prescribed; Registrars of Supreme Courts not to take out administration to surplus: Court of Directors may distribute remitted surplus, if b not exceeding £50.

II. And be it enacted, that the effects, or the proceeds or surplus of such effects, of any such officer or soldier dying as aforesaid, which shall remain after satisfying such regimental debts as aforesaid, shall with all convenient speed be transmitted to such military secretary, by the officer or person employed or required to take care of, collect, and receive the same as aforesaid; and such military secretary shall cause the same, or the surplus thereof remaining after satisfying such debts, and after such payment and application as is hereinbefore authorized, to be paid to the executor or legal representative (if in India) of such officer or soldier; or if such executor or legal representative shall not be in India, or shall not within twelve months from the death of such officer or soldier claim such surplus, then and in that case such military secretary shall remit the said surplus to the Court of Directors of the said Company in London, to be by them paid to the executor or legal representative of such officer or soldier so deceased; and such remittance, at the end of twelve months as aforesaid, shall be a discharge to such military secretary from all actions, suits, and demands in respect of such surplus; provided always, that the registrars of her Majesty's several Supreme Courts in India shall not be required or entitled to take out letters of administration, with the will annexed or otherwise, in respect of such surplus; and in all cases in which the surplus so to be remitted by the said military secretary to the said Court of Directors in London shall not exceed fifty pounds it shall be lawful for the said Court of Directors to order and direct the payment and distribution thereof to the parties entitled thereto, without any probate, letters testamentary or dative, or payment of any duty of stamps upon any legacies or otherwise.

Proceedings provisions as to the effects of deceased officers and soldiers extended to the Native

LIII. And whereas it is expedient that the benefit of provisions, similar in principle and extent of operation to those hereby enacted, respecting the collection and conversion into money of the effects of officers or soldiers dying in the service of the said Company out of the United Kingdom, and the nature and priorities of debts of such officers or soldiers, and the general administration of the proceeds or surplus of such effects, should be extended to the Indian navy; be it therefore enacted, that the Governor-general of India in Council shall have power to make laws and regulations in manner aforesaid, to be subject to such disallow remittance as aforesaid, for providing for the due collection and conversion into money, the priorities and discharge of debts out of, and the application, remittance, and distribution of the effects and credits of officers, engineers, soldiers, marines, seamen, and all others belonging to the said marine establishment called the Indian navy, who shall happen to die in the service of the East-India Company out of the United Kingdom; provided that such laws and regulations, so far as the nature and circumstances of the different cases will permit, shall, in principle and substance, be conformable to and in extent of benefit shall not exceed the provisions hereinbefore contained respecting the administration of the effects of officers and soldiers so dying in service as aforesaid; and for the purpose of distribution of the surplus of the effects of such officers, engineers, soldiers, marines, seamen, and all others belonging to the said Indian navy, under any such laws and regulations, in cases in which their legal representatives shall not be in India, such surplus shall be remitted to the Court of Directors of the said Company in London; and in all cases in which the same shall not exceed fifty pounds it shall be lawful for the said Court of Directors to order and direct the payment and distribution thereof to the parties entitled thereto without any probate, letters testamentary or dative, or payment of any duty of stamps upon any legacies or otherwise.

Where troops are serving beyond the jurisdiction of the Court of Request, action of debt, not exceeding 400Company's rupees to be cognizable by a military Court

LIV. And be it enacted, that in all places where the said Company's forces now are or may be employed, or where any body of her Majesty's forces may be serving with the forces of the said Company, situate beyond the jurisdiction of the Court of Requests established at the cities of Calcutta, Madras, and Bombay respectively, actions of debt, and all personal actions against officers, all persons licensed to act as sutlers to any corps or detachment or at any station or cantonment, all persons resident within the limits of a military cantonment, or other persons amenable to the provisions of this Act, shall be cognizable before a Court of Requests composed of military officers, and not elsewhere, provided the value in question shall not exceed four hundred Company's rupees, and that the defendant was a person of the above description when the cause of action arose, which Court the commanding officer of any station or cantonment is hereby authorized and empowered to convene; and the said Court shall in all practicable cases consist of five commissioned officers, and in no instance of less than three, and the president thereof shall in all practicable cases be a field officer, and in no case be under the rank of a captain, and every member having served five years as a commissioned officer; and the president and members assisting at any such Court, before any proceedings to be had before it, shall take the following oath upon the Holy Evangelists, which oath shall be administered by the president of the Court to the other members thereof, and to the president by any member having first taken the oath; (that is to say,)

> I swear, that I will duly administer justice according to "the evidence in the matters that shall be brought before me. So help me God.

And every witness before any such Court shall be examined on oath, which such Courts are hereby authorized to administer, or if natives of the East-Indies, on oath or solemn declaration, as the circumstances of the case may require; and it shall be competent for such Courts, upon finding any debt or damage due, either to award execution thereof generally, or to direct that the whole or any part thereof shall be stopped and paid over to the creditor out of any pay or public money which may be coming to the debtor in the current or any future month, or to be paid by installment on sufficient security; and in case the execution shall be awarded generally, the debt, if not paid forthwith, shall be levied by seizure and public sale of such of the debtor's goods as may be found within the camp, garrison, or cantonment, under a written order of the commanding officer grounded on the judgment of the Court; and the goods of the debtor, if found within the limits of the Company's garrison or cantonment to which the debtor shall belong at any subsequent time, shall be liable to be seized and sold in satisfaction of any remainder of such debt or damages; and if sufficient goods shall not be found within the limits of the camp, garrison, or cantonment, then any public money, or any sum not exceeding the half-pay accruing to the debtor, shall be stopped in liquidation of such debt or damage; and if such debtor shall not receive pay as an officer or from any public department, but be a sutler, servant, or follower, he shall be arrested by like order of the commanding officer, and imprisoned in some convenient place within the military boundaries for the space of two months, unless the debt be sooner paid.

Punishment for giving false testimonies

LV. And be it enacted, that any person wilfully and knowingly giving false testimony on oath or solemn declaration, or affirmation, in any case wherein an oath or solemn declaration is required to be made, shall be deemed guilty of wilful and corrupt perjury, and being thereof duly convicted shall be liable to such pains and penalties as by any law in force in India any persons convicted of wilful and corrupt perjury are subject and liable to ; and every commissioned officer convicted before a general court-martial of perjury shall be cashiered; and every soldier or other person amenable to the provisions of this Act found guilty thereof shall be punished at the discretion of a general or regimental Court-martial.

Limitation of actions; Mode of procedure

LVI. And be it enacted, that any action which shall be brought against any person for anything to be done in pursuance of this Act shall be brought within six months, and it shall be lawful for every such person to plead thereunto the general issue of not guilty, and to give all special matter in evidence to the jury which shall try the issue; and if the verdict shall be for the defendant in any such action, or the plaintiff therein become non-suited, or suffer any discontinuance thereof, the Court in which the said matter shall be tried shall allow unto the defendant treble costs, for which the said defendant shall have the like remedy as in other cases where costs by the laws of this realm are given to defendants; and every action against any person for anything to be done in pursuance of this Act, or against any member or minister of a Court-martial in respect of any sentence of such Court, or of anything done by virtue or in pursuance of such sentence, shall be brought in some of the Courts of Record at the presidency under which such person is serving, or in the Courts of Record at Westminster, or in Dublin, or the Court of Session in Scotland, and in no other Court whatsoever.

Mode of recovering penalties for procuring desertion

LVII. And be it enacted, that all penalties by this Act imposed for persuading or procuring any soldier to desert may and shall be sued for and be recoverable in any Court of Record at the presidency under which such offender shall be resident; provided that no action shall be brought or prosecution carried on by virtue of this Act for the penalties aforesaid, unless the same be commenced within six months after the offence is committed.

Not to affect the royal prerogative

LVIII. Provided always, and be it enacted, that nothing in this Act contained shall in any manner affect her Majesty's royal prerogative of mercy.

Commencement of this Act and repeal of former ACT

LIX. And be it enacted, that this Act shall commence and take effect from and after the first day of January, one thousand eight hundred and forty-one, except where any other commencement is particularly directed; and that from and after such day all powers and pro visions contained in the said Act of the fourth year of the reign of his late Majesty King George the Fourth shall cease and determine, and that the said Act shall be and is hereby repealed.

SCHEDULE to which this Act refers

Form of Oath to be taken by the President and Members of Court-Martial

You shall well and truly try and determine, according to the evidence in the several cases and matters which shall be brought before you, upon the general Court-martial now assembled.

So help you God.

I, ... AB ....., do swear, that I will duly administer justice as a member of the general Court martial now assembled, upon the several cases and matters which shall be brought before the same, according to the rules and articles for the better government of the forces of the East-India Company, and according to an Act of Parliament now in force for the punishment of mutiny and desertion of the said forces, and other crimes therein mentioned, without partiality, favour, or affection; and if any doubt shall arise which is not explained by the said articles or Act, according to my conscience, the best of my understanding, and the custom of war in the like cases: and I further swear, that I will not divulge any sentence of the Court until it shall be duly approved or published in general orders: and I further swear, that I will not, upon any account, or at any time whatsoever, disclose or discover any vote or opinion of any particular member of the Court-martial, unless required to give evidence thereof as a witness by a Court of Justice or a Court-martial in due course of law.

So help me God.

Form of Oath to be taken by the Judge Advocate or Person officiating as such

I, ... do swear, that I will not, upon any account whatsoever, disclose or discover any vote or opinion of any particular member of the Court-martial, unless required to give evidence thereof as a witness by a Court of Justice or Court-martial in due course of law. So help me God.

5 Victoriae. Sess, 2, Cap. XII

An Act for punishing Mutiny and Desertion, and for the better Payment of the Army and their Quarters

[22 April 1842]

An Act under this title and having the same objects is passed annually. The period fixed for the commencement and expiration of the present Act in various parts of the world will be found in section 80, and as its operation in India does not commence until the 1st February, 1844, unless previously promulgated by general orders, the Queen's Forces there will until that period be subject to the Acts passed in former sessions; the provisions of which, however, it is to be observed, correspond with those of the present Act. Another Act exists for the troops of the East-India Company (3 & 4 Vict. cap. 37), but it has no operation within the United Kingdom.

Composition of General Courts-martial

VI. And be it enacted, that a general Court-martial convened in any part of the Queen's dominions, (Bermuda, the Bahamas, Saint Helena, Africa, Jamaica, Honduras, Newfoundland, and the Australian Colonies excepted,) or in the settlements of the East-India Company, shall consist of not less than thirteen commissioned officers; if convened in Jamaica, Newfoundland, Bermuda, or the Bahamas, or out of the Queen's dominions, excepting Saint Helena, Africa, Honduras, and the Australian Colonies, shall consist of not less than seven, and in Saint Helena, Africa, Honduras, and the Australian Colonies of not less than five commissioned officers; and no judgment of death shall pass without the concurrence of two-thirds at the least of the officers present; and the President shall in no case be the officer commanding-in-chief, or Governor of the garrison where the offender shall be tried, nor under the degree of a field officer unless where a field officer cannot be had, nor in any case whatsoever under the degree of a captain.

Powers of General Courts-martial

VII. And be it enacted, that a general Court-martial may sentence any soldier to imprisonment, with or without hard labour, in any public prison, or other place which the Court or the officer commanding the regiment or corps to which the offender belongs or is attached shall appoint, and may also direct that such offender shall be kept in solitary confinement for any portion or portions of such imprisonment, not exceeding one month at a time or three months at different times, with intervals of not less than one month between such times in one year, or of such imprisonment with hard labour, or may sentence any soldier to corporal punishment, not extending to life or limb, for immorality, misbehaviour, and neglect of duty; and a general Court-martial may, in addition to any such punishment as aforesaid, sentence any offender to forfeiture of all advantage as to additional pay and pension on discharge, which might have otherwise accrued from the length of his former service, or to forfeiture of such advantage absolutely, whether it might have accrued from past service or might accrue from future service, according to the nature of the case; and whensoever any general Court-martial by which any soldier shall have been tried and convicted of any offence punishable with death shall not think the offence deserving of capital punishment such Court-martial may, instead of awarding a corporal punishment or imprisonment, adjudge the offender, according to the degree of the offence, to be transported as a felon for life or for a certain term of years, or may sentence him to general service as a soldier in any corps and in any country or place which her Majesty shall thereupon direct, or may, if such offender shall have enlisted for a limited term of years, sentence him to serve for life as a soldier in any corps which her Majesty shall please to direct; and the Court may, in addition to any other punishment, sentence such offender to forfeit all advantage as to increase of pay, or as to pension on discharge, which might otherwise have accrued to such offender from the length of his former service, or to forfeiture of such advantage absolutely, whether it might have accrued from past service or might accrue from future service, according to the nature of the case; provided that in all cases where a capital punishment shall have been awarded by a general Court-martial it shall be lawful for her Majesty, or, if in the East-Indies, for the officer commanding in chief the forces at the presidency to which the offender shall belong, instead of causing such sentence to be carried into execution, to order the offender to be transported as a felon, either for life or for a certain term of years, as shall seem meet to her Majesty, or, if in the East-Indies, to the officer commanding as aforesaid.

Mixture of officers upon Courts-martial

XIII. And be it enacted, that in certain cases, where it may be necessary or expedient, officers of her Majesty's marine forces may sit upon Courts-martial in conjunction with officers of her Majesty's land forces, and such Courts-martial shall be regulated, to all intents and purposes, in like manner as if they were composed of officers of the land forces only, whether the commanding officer by whose order such Court-martial is assembled belongs to the land or to the marine forces; and officers of her Majesty's land forces and officers in the service of the East-India Company, when serving together, may be associated in Courts-martial, which shall, to all intents and purposes, be regulated in like manner as if consisting wholly of officers of her Majesty's land forces, or wholly of officers in the service of the East-India Company; save and except that on the trial of any person in her Majesty's land forces, the provisions of this Act and the oaths thereby prescribed, shall be applicable; and that on the trial of any person belonging to her Majesty's marine forces, the provisions of an Act passed in the present session of Parliament for the regulation of her Majesty's royal marine forces while on shore, and the oaths thereby prescribed, shall be applicable; and on the trial of any officer or soldier in the service of the East-India Company the provisions of an Act passed in the third and fourth years of the reign of her present Majesty, to amend the laws for punishing mutiny and desertion of officers and soldiers in the service of the East-India Company, and the oaths thereby prescribed, shall be applicable, notwithstanding any officer in the actual service of the said Company may have a commission from her Majesty or from his late Majesty King William the Fourth.

Proceedings of Courts-martial

XV. And be it enacted, that in all trials by general Courts-martial to be held by virtue of this Act the President and every member assisting at such trial, before any proceeding be had thereon, shall take the oath in the schedule to this Act annexed, before the Judge Advocate or his Deputy, or person officiating as such, and on trials by other Courts-martial before the President of such Court, who are hereby respectively authorized to administer the same, and any sworn member shall administer the oath to the president; and as soon as the said oaths shall have been administered to the respective members, the President of the Court is hereby authorized and required to administer to the Judge Advocate, or the person officiating as such, the oath in the schedule to this Act annexed; and no proceeding or trial shall be had upon any offence but between the hours of eight of the clock in the morning and four in the afternoon, except in cases which require an immediate example, and except in the East-Indies, where such proceedings or trial may be had between the hours of six in the morning and four in the afternoon: provided also, that all witnesses duly summoned by the Judge Advocate, or the person officiating as such, or by the President of a District or Garrison Court-martial, shall during their necessary attendance in such Courts, and in going to and returning from the same, be privileged from arrest, and shall, if unduly arrested, be discharged by the Court out of which the writ or process issued by which such witness was arrested, or if such Court be not sitting, then by any Judge of the Court of Queen's Bench in London or in Dublin, or the Court of Session in Scotland, or Courts of Law in the East or West Indies or elsewhere, according as the case shall require, upon its being made to appear to such Court or Judge, by any affidavit in a summary way, that such witness was arrested in going to or returning from or attending upon such Court-martial; and that all witnesses so duly summoned as aforesaid who shall not attend on such Courts, or attending shall refuse to be sworn, or being sworn shall refuse to give evidence or to answer all such questions as the Court may legally demand of them, shall be liable to be attached in the Court of Queen's Bench in London or Dublin, or the Court of Session, or Sheriff Depute or Stewarts Depute, or their respective substitutes, within their several shires and stewartries in Scotland, or Courts of Law in the East or West Indies, or in any of her Majesty's colonies, garrisons, or dominions in Europe or elsewhere respectively, upon complaint made, in like manner as if such witness had neglected to attend in a trial in any proceeding in that Court.

Transportation from the colonies

XIX. And be it enacted, that whenever any sentence of transportation heretofore or here after passed by any Court-martial holden in the East-Indies, or in any part of her Majesty's foreign dominions, is to be carried into execution for the term specified in such sentence or for any shorter term, or when sentence of death has been or shall as aforesaid be commuted to transportation, the same shall be notified by the officer commanding in chief her Majesty's forces at the presidency or station, or in his absence by the Adjutant-general for the time being, to some Judge of one of the Supreme Courts of Judicature in the East-Indies, or Chief Justice, or some other Judge, as the case may be, in any part of her Majesty's foreign dominions, who shall make order for the transportation or intermediate custody of such offender, in like manner as for the transportation or intermediate custody of any other convict; and the necessary proceedings shall be taken, according to such order, for the transportation or intermediate custody of such offender; and all Acts in force in such place touching other offenders to be transported shall in all respects apply as well to the offender himself so to be transported as to all other persons whatsoever therein concerned.

Fraudulent confession of desertion

XXIII. And be it enacted, that any person who shall voluntarily deliver himself up as a deserter from her Majesty's forces, or the embodied militia, or the forces of the East-India Company, or who, upon being apprehended for any offence, shall, in the presence of the justice, confess himself to be a deserter as aforesaid, shall be deemed to have been duly enlisted and to be a soldier, and shall be liable to serve in any of her Majesty's forces, as her Majesty shall think fit to appoint, whether such person shall have been ever actually enlisted as a soldier or not; and in case such person shall not be a deserter from the regiment stated in such confession, he shall be liable to be punished as a rogue and vagabond, or may be prosecuted and punished for obtaining money under false pretences; and the confession and receiving subsistence as a soldier by such person shall be evidence of the false pretence and of the obtaining money to the amount of the value of such subsistence, and the value of such subsistence so obtained may be charged in the indictment as so much money received by such person; and in case such person shall have been previously convicted of the like offence, or as a rogue and vagabond for making a fraudulent confession of desertion, such former conviction may be alleged in the indictment, and may be proved upon the trial of such person; and in such indictment for a second offence it shall be sufficient to state that the offender was at a certain time and place convicted of obtaining money under false pretences as a deserter, or as a rogue and vagabond for making a fraudulent confession of desertion, without otherwise describing the said offence; and a certificate containing the substance and effect only (omitting the formal part) of the indictment and conviction for the former offence, purporting to be signed by the clerk of the Court or other officer having the custody of the records of the Court where the offender was first convicted, or by the deputy of such clerk, or by the clerk of the convicting magistrates, shall, upon proof of the identity of the person of the offender, be sufficient evidence of the first conviction, without proof of the signature or official character of the person appearing to have signed the same; and if the person so confessing himself to be a deserter shall be serving at the time in any of her Majesty's forces, he shall be deemed to be and shall be dealt with as a deserter.

Persons subject to this Act

XXXII. And be it enacted, that all the provisions of this Act shall apply to all persons employed on the recruiting service receiving pay in respect of such service, and to the forces of the East-India Company while they shall be in any part of the United Kingdom, and to the officers and persons who are or shall be serving and hired to be employed in the royal artillery and field train, and to master gunners and gunners, and conductors of stores, and to all officers and persons who are or shall be serving in the regiment of royal engineers and the corps of royal sappers and miners, and in the corps of royal military surveyors and draftsmen, and to persons in the ordnance and in the commissariat departments, who are or shall be serving with any part of her Majesty's forces, at home or abroad, under the command of any officer having commission from her Majesty, or from his late Majesty King William the Fourth, and to all storekeepers and other civil officers who are or shall be employed by or act under the ordnance at any of her Majesty's ordnance establishments at foreign stations; provided that nothing in this Act contained shall extend to affect any security which has been given by such storekeeper, barrack master, or other officer, or their sureties, for the due performance of their respective offices, under the provisions of an Act passed in the fiftieth year of the reign of his Majesty King George the Third, to regulate the taking of securities in all offices, but that such bonds and other securities shall be and remain in full force and effect.

Enlisting and swearing of recruits

XXXVI. And be it enacted, that every person who shall receive enlisting money, knowing it to be such, from any person employed in the recruiting service, he being an officer, non-commissioned officer, or an attested soldier, shall be deemed to be enlisted as a soldier in her Majesty's service, and while he shall remain with the recruiting party shall be entitled to be billetted; and every person who shall enlist any recruit shall first ask the person offering to enlist whether he does or does not belong to the militia, and shall within twelve hours after the receipt of the enlisting money cause to be taken down in writing the name and place of abode of such recruit; and (if such recruit shall not reside in or in the vicinity of the town or place where he offered to enlist) the place also at which he shall declare that he intends to sleep, in order that within forty-eight but not sooner than twenty-four hours (any intervening Sunday not included) after his having received the enlisting money, notice of his having so enlisted be given to the recruit or left at his usual place of abode, or at the place where he stated that it was his intention to sleep; and when any person shall be enlisted as a soldier in her Majesty's land service, he shall within four days (any intervening Sunday not included), but not sooner than twenty-four hours after such enlisting, appear, together with some person employed in the recruiting service of the party with which he shall have enlisted, before a justice, or, in Scotland, before any baillie of a royal burgh, residing within the vicinity of the place, and acting for the division or district where such recruit shall have been enlisted, and not being an officer in the army; and if such recruit shall declare his having voluntarily enlisted, the said justice shall put to him the several questions contained in the schedule to this Act annexed, and shall then and there, and in the presence of the said recruit, record or cause to be recorded in writing his answers thereunto; and the said justice is hereby required forthwith to read over, or cause his clerk in his presence to read over, to such recruit, the first and second articles of the second section of the Articles of War against mutiny and desertion, and to administer to such recruit the oath in the schedule to this Act annexed, for limited or unlimited service, or for service in the forces of the East-India Company, as may be applicable to the case of the recruit, and no other oaths, anything in any Acts to the contrary notwithstanding;[1] and the said justice is hereby required to give under his hand the certificate in the schedule to this Act annexed ; and if any such recruit so to be certified shall refuse to take the oath in the schedule to this Act annexed before the said justice, it shall be lawful for the officer or non-commissioned officer with whom he enlisted to detain and confine such person until he shall take the said oath of fidelity.

1 The 50 Geo. 3, cap. 87, prescribes other oaths, the administration of which is thus suspended during the continuance of this Act.

Dissent and relief from enlistment

XXXVII. And be it enacted, that any recruit appearing as aforesaid before such justice shall be at liberty to declare his dissent to such enlisting, and upon such declaration, and returning the enlisting money, and also paying the sum of twenty shillings for the charges expended upon him, together with the full amount of subsistence and beer money which shall have been paid to such recruit subsequent to the period of his having been enlisted, shall be forthwith discharged and set at liberty in the presence of such justice; but if such person shall refuse or neglect, within the space of twenty-four hours after so declaring his dissent, to return and pay such money as aforesaid, he shall be deemed and taken to be enlisted as if he had given his assent thereto before the said justice: provided also, that it shall be lawful for any justice to discharge any person who shall have hastily enlisted, and who shall apply to him to declare his dissent within such four days as aforesaid, upon payment of the sum of money required to be paid by any recruit declaring his dissent under this Act, notwithstanding no person belonging to the recruiting party shall be with the recruit, if it shall appear to such justice, upon proof to his satisfaction, that the recruiting party has left the place where such recruit was enlisted, or that the recruit could not procure any person belonging to such party to go with him before the justice; and the sum paid by such recruit upon his discharge shall be kept by the justice, and paid to any person belonging to the recruiting party entitled thereto demanding the same; provided that no recruit who has been actually, though erroneously, discharged by the justice before the expiration of twenty-four hours after the time of his enlistment shall be liable on that account to be proceeded against as having deserted from her Majesty's service; and the justice who shall discharge any recruit shall in every case give a certificate thereof, signed with his hand, to the recruit, specifying the cause thereof .

Offences connected with enlistment

XXXVIII. And be it enacted, that if any recruit shall receive the enlisting money from any person employed in the recruiting service (knowing it to be such), and shall abscond or refuse to go before such justice, or shall thereafter absent himself from the recruiting party or person with whom he enlisted, and shall not voluntarily return to go before some justice within such period of four days as aforesaid, such recruit shall be deemed to be enlisted and a soldier in her Majesty's service, as fully to all intents and purposes as if he had been duly attested, and may be apprehended and punished as a deserter, or for being absent without leave, under any Articles of War made for punishment of mutiny and desertion; and such recruit shall not be discharged by any justice of the peace after the expiration of such four days as aforesaid, unless it shall be proved to the satisfaction of such justice that the true name and residence of the recruit were disclosed and known to the recruiting party, and that no notice was given to the recruit, or left at his usual place of abode, of his having so enlisted; provided that in every case wherein any recruit shall have received enlisting money, and shall have absconded from the party, so that it shall not be possible immediately to apprehend and bring him before a justice, the officer or non-commissioned officer commanding the party shall produce to the justice before whom the recruit ought regularly to have been brought for attestation a certificate of the name and place of residence of such recruit; and the justice to whom such certificate shall be produced shall, after satisfying himself that the recruit who had absconded cannot be found and apprehended, transmit a duplicate thereof to her Majesty's Secretary at War, in order that, in the event of such recruit being afterwards apprehended and reported as a deserter, the facts of his having received enlisting money, and having absconded after having been enlisted, may be ascertained, before he be finally adjudged to be a deserter; and any recruit who shall enlist into her Majesty's forces, and who shall be discovered to be incapable of active service by reason of any infirmity concealed or not declared by such recruit before the justice at the time of his attestation, may be transferred to any garrison or veteran or invalid battalion or company, or into her Majesty's marine forces, not withstanding he shall have enlisted for any particular regiment, and shall be entitled to receive such proportion or residue of bounty only as her Majesty may allow in that behalf, instead of the bounty upon which such man shall have been enlisted, anything in any Act or Acts, or any rules and regulations relating to soldiers, to the contrary notwithstanding; and it shall be lawful for any two justices before whom such recruit shall be brought, and who shall be

proved upon oath, before them, to have concealed his having been a soldier and discharged, or to have concealed his having been discharged upon any prior enlistment, or to have willfully concealed any such infirmity upon being attested, or to have designedly made any false representation as aforesaid, to adjudge such person, if in England or Ireland, to be a rogue and vagabond, and to sentence him to such punishment as by any law in force may be inflicted upon rogues and vagabonds and vagrants and incorrigible rogues; and to adjudge such person, if in Scotland, to be imprisoned in any prison or house of correction for any period not exceeding six months, and with or without hard labour; and any recruit who shall designedly make any false representation of any particular contained in the oaths and certificates in the schedule to this Act annexed, before the justice, at the time of his attestation, and shall obtain any enlisting money or bounty for entering into her Majesty's service, or any other money, shall be deemed guilty of obtaining money under false pretences within the true intent and meaning, if in England, of an Act intituled, "An Act for consolidating and amending the Laws in England relative to Larceny and other Offences connected therewith;" (7&8 G. 4, c. 29) and if in Ireland, of an Act passed in the ninth year of the reign of his Majesty King George the Fourth, intituled, "An Act for consolidating and amending the Laws in Ireland relative to Larceny and other Offences connected therewith:" (9 G. 4, c. 55) and such recruit, if in Scotland, shall be deemed guilty of falsehood, fraud, and wilful imposition; and the production of such certificate, and proof of the handwriting of the justice giving such certificate, shall be sufficient evidence of such party having represented the several particulars contained in the oath sworn by him, and specified in the certificate of the justice at the time of his being attested; and that proof by the oath of one or more credible witnesses that the person so prosecuted hath voluntarily acknowledged that at the time of his enlistment he belonged to the militia, or to any regiment in her Majesty's service, or to her Majesty's ordnance, navy or marines, shall be deemed and taken as evidence of the fact so by him acknowledged, without production of any roll or other document to prove the same; and such proof of such acknowledgment shall be certified to the Secretary at War by the justice before whom such proof shall have been given; and any man having been enrolled to serve in the militia at the time of offering to enlist who shall deny that he is a militia man, then actually enrolled and engaged to serve, or shall deny to the justice before whom he shall be attested that he belongs to the militia, shall, on conviction thereof before any one justice in the United Kingdom, either upon oath of one witness or upon his own confession, or upon the production of the attestation, and the before-mentioned acknowledgment of such person, certified by the Secretary at War or Deputy Secretary at War, be committed to the common gaol or House of Correction, there to remain without bail or main prize for and during any time not exceeding six calendar months, over and above any penalty or punishment to which such person so offending may be otherwise liable, and shall from the day on which his engagement to serve in the militia shall end, and not sooner, belong as a soldier to the corps of her Majesty's regular forces, or of the East-India Company's forces, into which he shall have so enlisted; provided that every such person shall be liable to serve within the United Kingdom of Great Britain and Ireland, in any regiment, battalion, or corps of her Majesty's regular forces, or of the East-India Company's forces, in which he has so enlisted, during all the time the militia to which he shall belong shall remain disembodied, or shall not be called out for training or exercise, and shall during all such time be subject to all the provisions of this Act, and liable to be apprehended and dealt with and punished as a deserter from the corps in which he shall have so enlisted, if he shall neglect or refuse to join and serve in such corps as aforesaid.

Penalty on officers offending against laws regarding enlistment

XXXIX. And be it enacted, that every military officer who shall act contrary to the provisions of this Act in any respect regarding the enlisting and attesting of recruits of her Majesty's service or for the service of the East-India Company, shall, upon proof thereof upon oath by two witnesses before a general Court-martial, be cashiered, and disabled to hold any civil or military office or employment in her Majesty's service.

Apprentice enlisting to be liable to serve after the expiration of his apprenticeship

XLII. And be it enacted, that any person duly bound as an apprentice who shall enlist as a soldier in her Majesty's or the East-India Company's service, and shall state to the magistrate before whom he shall be carried and attested that he is not an apprentice, shall be deemed guilty of obtaining money under false pretences within the true intent and meaning of the before-recited Acts, and shall, after the expiration of his apprenticeship, whether he shall have been so convicted and punished or not, be liable to serve as a soldier in any of her Majesty's regular forces, or in the forces of the East-India Company, according to the terms of the enlistment; and if on the expiration of his apprenticeship he shall not deliver himself up to some officer authorized to receive recruits, may be taken as a deserter from her Majesty's forces.

Claims of masters to apprentices

XLIII. And be it enacted, that no master shall be entitled to claim an apprentice who shall enlist as a soldier in her Majesty's or the East-India Company's service, unless he shall, within one calendar month after such apprentice shall have left his service, go before some justice, and take the oath mentioned in the schedule to this Act annexed, and produce the certificate of such justice of his having taken such oath, which certificate such justice is required to give in the form in the schedule to this Act annexed; and unless such apprentice shall have been bound, if in England, for the full term of seven years, not having been above the age of fourteen when so bound, and, if in Ireland or in the British Isles, for the full term of five years at the least, not having been above the age of sixteen when so bound, and if in Scotland, for the full term at least of four years, by a regular contract or indenture of apprenticeship, duly extended, signed, and tested, and binding on both parties by the Law of Scotland, prior to the period of enlistment, and unless such contract or indenture in Scotland shall, within three months after the commencement of the apprenticeship, and before the period of enlistment, have been produced to a justice of the peace of the county in Scotland whereinthe parties reside, and there shall have been indorsed thereon by such justice a certificate or declaration signed by him, specifying the date when and the person by whom such contract or indenture shall have been so produced, which certificate or declaration such justice of the peace is hereby required to indorse and sign; and unless such apprentice shall, when claimed by such master, be under twenty-one years of age; provided that any master of an apprentice indentured for the sea service shall be entitled to claim and recover him in the form and manner above directed, notwithstanding such apprentice may have been bound for a less term than seven, five, or four years as aforesaid; and any such master who shall give up the in dentures of apprenticeship within one month after the enlisting of such apprentice shall be entitled to receive to his own use so much of the bounty payable to such recruit, after deducting therefrom two guineas to provide him with necessaries, as shall not have been paid to such t recruit before notice given of his being an apprentice.

Punishment of apprentices enlisting

XLIV. And be it enacted, that no apprentice claimed by his master shall be taken from any corps or recruiting party but under a warrant of a justice residing near, and within whose jurisdiction such apprentice shall then happen to be, before whom he shall be carried, and such justice shall inquire into the matter upon oath, which oath he is hereby empowered to administer, and shall require the production and proof of the indenture, and that notice of the said warrant has been given to the commanding officer, and a copy thereof left with some officer or non-commissioned officer of the party, and that such person so enlisted declared that he was no apprentice; and such justice, if required by such officer or non-commissioned officer, shall commit the offender to the common gaol of the said place, and shall keep the indenture to be produced when required, and shall bind over such person as he may think proper to give evidence against the offender, who shall be tried at the next or at the sessions immediately succeeding the next general or quarter sessions of the county, division, or place, unless the court shall on just cause put off the trial; and the production of the indenture, with the certificate of the justices that the same was proved, shall be sufficient evidence of the said indenture; and every such offender, in Scotland, may be tried by the judge ordinary in the county or stewartry, in such and the like manner as any person may be tried in Scotland for any offence not inferring a capital punishment; provided that any justice not required as aforesaid to commit such apprentice may deliver him to his master.

How and where troops may be billeted

LII. And whereas by petition of right in the third year of King Charles the First it is enacted and declared, that the people of the land are not by the laws to be burthened with the sojourning of soldiers against their wills; and by a clause in an Act of the Parliament of England, made in the thirty-first year of the reign of King Charles the Second, for granting a supply to his Majesty of two hundred and six thousand four hundred and sixty-two pounds seventeen shillings and three-pence, for paying and disbanding the forces, it is declared and enacted, that no officer, civil or military, nor other person whosoever, should thenceforth presume to place, quarter, or billet any soldier upon any subject or inhabitant of this realm, of any degree, quality, or profession whatsoever, without his consent, and that it shall be lawful for any subject or inhabitant to refuse to quarter any soldier, notwithstanding any warrant or billetting whatsoever: and whereas by an Act passed in Ireland in the sixth year of the reign of Queen Anne, intituled, "An Act to prevent the Disorders that may happen by the marching of Soldiers and providing Carriages for the Baggage of Soldiers on their March," [6 Ann. (I)] it was enacted, that no officer, soldier, or trooper in the army, nor the servant of any officer, nor any attendant on the train of artillery, should at any time thereafter be allowed any quarters in any part of Ireland, save only during such time as he or they should be and remain in some seaport town in order to be transported, or during such time as there should be any commotion in any part of Ireland, by reason of which emergency the army should be commanded to march from any part of Ireland to another; but forasmuch as at this time, during the continuance of this Act, there is and may be occasion for the marching and quartering of regiments, troops, and companies in several parts of the United Kingdom of Great Britain and Ireland, be it enacted, that it shall be lawful for all constables of parishes and places, and other persons specified in this Act, in England and Ireland, and they are hereby required to billet the officers and soldiers in her Majesty's service and persons receiving pay in her Majesty's army, and the horses belonging to her Majesty's cavalry, and also all staff and field officers' horses, and all bat and baggage horses belonging to any of her Majesty's other forces, when on actual service, not exceeding for each officer the number for which forage is or shall be allowed by her Majesty's regulations, in victualling houses and other houses specified in this Act (taking care in Ireland not to billet less than two men in any one house, except only in case of billetting cavalry as specially provided); and that they shall be received by the occupiers of such houses in which they are so allowed to be billetted, and be furnished by such victuallers with proper accommodation in such houses, or if any victualler shall not have sufficient accommodation in the house upon which a soldier is billetted, then in some good and sufficient quarters to be provided by such victualler in the immediate neighbourhood, and in England with diet and small beer, and with stables, hay, and straw for such horses as aforesaid, paying and allowing for the same the several rates hereinafter provided; and at no time when troops are on a march shall any of them, whether infantry or cavalry, be billetted above one mile from the place mentioned in the route; and in all places where cavalry shall be billetted in pursuance of this Act, the men and their horses shall be billetted in one and the same house, except in case of necessity; and in no other case whatsoever shall there be less than one man billetted where there shall be one or two horses, nor less than two men where there shall be four horses, and so in proportion for a greater number; and in no case shall a man and his horse be billetted at a greater distance from each other than one hundred yards; and the constables are hereby required to billet all soldiers and their horses on their march in a just and equal proportion upon the keepers of all houses within one mile of the place mentioned in the route, although some of such houses may be in the adjoining county, in like manner in every respect as if such houses were locally situate within such place; provided that nothing herein contained shall be construed to extend to authorize any constable to billet soldiers out of the county to which such constable belongs when the constable of the adjoining county shall be present and undertake to billet the due proportion of men in such adjoining county.; and no more billets shall at any time be ordered than there are effective soldiers and horses present to be billetted; all which billets, when made out by such constables, shall be delivered into the hands of the commanding officer present; and if any person shall find himself aggrieved by having an undue proportion of soldiers billetted in his house, and shall prefer his complaint, if against a constable or other person not being a justice, to one or more justices, and if against a justice, then to two or more justices, within whose jurisdiction such soldiers are billetted, such justices respectively shall have power to order such of the soldiers to be removed, and to be billetted upon other persons, as they shall see cause; and when any of her Majesty's cavalry or any horses as aforesaid shall be billeted upon the occupiers of houses in which officers or soldiers may be quartered by virtue of this Act, who shall have no stables, then and in such case, upon the written requisition of the commanding officer of the regiment, troop, or detachment, the constable is hereby required to billet the men and their horses, or horses only, upon some other person or persons who have stables by this Act liable to have officers and soldiers billetted upon them; and upon complaint being made by the person or persons to whose house or stables the said men and horses shall have been so removed to two or more justices within whose jurisdiction such men or horses shall be so billetted, it shall be lawful for such justices to order a proper allowance to be paid by the person relieved to the persons receiving such men and horses, or to be applied in furnishing the requisite accommodation; and commanding officers may exchange any man or horse billetted in any place with another man or horse billetted in the same place, for the benefit of the service, provided the number of men and horses do not exceed the number at that time billetted on such houses; and the constables are hereby required to billet such men and horses so exchanged accordingly; and it shall be lawful for any justice, at the request of any officer or non-commissioned officer commanding any soldiers requiring billets, to extend any routes or enlarge the districts within which billets shall be required, in such manner as shall appear to be most convenient to the troops; provided that, to prevent or punish all abuses in billeting soldiers, it shall be lawful for any justice within his jurisdiction, by warrant or order under his hand, to require any constable to give him an account in writing of the number of officers and soldiers who shall be quartered by such constable, together with the names of the persons upon whom such officers and soldiers are billetted, stating the street or place where such persons dwell, and the sign, if any, belonging to those houses; and it shall be lawful to billet officers and soldiers in Scotland according to the provisions of the laws in force in Scotland at the time of its union with England; and no officer shall be obliged to pay for his lodging where he shall be regularly billetted, except in the suburbs of Edinburgh.[2]

Supply of carriages

LVII. And be it enacted, that for the regular provision of carriages for her Majesty's forces, and their baggage in their marches, in England and Ireland, all justices of the peace within their several jurisdictions, being duly required thereunto by an order from her Majesty, or the general of her forces, or the master general or lieutenant general of her Majesty's Ordnance, or other person duly authorized in that behalf, shall, on production of such order to such justices by some

2 By 50 Geo. 3, cap. 87, sec. 3, all the powers, authorities, provisions, &c., in any Act of Parliament in force for the time being, relating to the quartering, billetting, and provisioning of soldiers and officers of the Crown and to allowances in respect thereof, as well as to the providing of carriages for the use of such soldiers, are extended to soldiers enlisted for or transferred to the service of the Company.

officer or non-commissioned officer of the regiment so ordered to march, issue a warrant to any constable having authority to act in any place from, through, near, or to which the troop shall be ordered to march, (for each of which warrants the fee of one shilling only shall be paid,) requiring him to provide the carriages, horses, and oxen, and drivers therein mentioned, and allowing sufficient time to do the same, specifying the places from and to which the said carriages shall travel, and the distance between the places, for which distance only so specified payment shall be demanded, and which distance shall not, except in cases of pressing emergency, exceed a day's march prescribed in the order of route, and shall in no cases exceed twenty-five miles ; and the constables receiving such warrants shall order such persons as they shall think proper, having carriages, to furnish the requisite supply, who are hereby required to furnish the same accordingly ; and when sufficient carriages cannot be procured within the proper jurisdiction, any justice of the next adjoining jurisdiction shall, by a like course of proceeding, supply the deficiency; and in order that the burthen of providing carriages may fall equally, and to prevent inconvenience arising from there being no justice near the place where troops may be quartered on the march, any justice residing nearest to such place may cause a list to be made out once in every year of all persons liable to furnish such carriages, and of the number and description of their said carriages, (which list shall at all seasonable hours be open to the inspection of the said persons,) and may by war. rant under his hand authorize the constable within his jurisdiction to give orders to provide carriages, without any special warrant for that purpose, which orders shall be valid in all respects; and all orders for such carriages shall be made from such lists in regular rotation, as far as the same can be done.[3]

Penalty on unlawful recruiting

LXVII. And be it enacted, that all the persons (except such recruiting parties as may be stationed under military command) who shall cause to be advertised, posted, or dispersed bills for the purpose of procuring recruits or substitutes for the line, embodied militia, or East India Company's service, or shall open or keep any house, place of rendezvous, or office, or receive any person therein under such bill or advertisement, as connected with the recruiting service, or shall directly or indirectly interfere therewith, without permission in writing from the adjutant general, or from the Directors of the East-India Company, (as the case may be) shall forfeit for every such offence the sum of twenty pounds.

Duration of Act

LXXX. And be it enacted, that this Act shall be and continue in force within Great Britain from the twenty-fifth day of April, one thousand eight hundred and forty-two, inclusive, until the twenty-fifth day of April, one thousand eight hundred and forty-three; and shall be and continue in force within Ireland, and in Jersey, Guernsey, Alderney, Sark, and Isle of Man, and the islands thereto belonging, from the first day of May, one thousand eight hundred and forty-two, inclusive, until the first day of May, one thousand eight hundred and forty-three; and shall be and continue in force within the garrison of Gibraltar, the Mediterranean, and in Spain and Portugal, from the first day of August, one thousand eight hundred and forty-two, inclusive, until the first day of August,

3 See note on section 52.

one thousand eight hundred and forty-three; and shall be and continue in force in all other parts of Europe where her Majesty's forces may be serving, and in the West-Indies and America, from the first day of September, one thousand eight hundred and forty-two, inclusive, to the first day of September, one thousand eight hundred and forty-three; and shall be and continue in force within the Cape of Good Hope, the Isle of France or Mauritius and its dependencies, Saint Helena, and the Western Coast of Africa, from the first day of January, one thousand eight hundred and forty-three, inclusive, to the first day of January, one thousand eight hundred and forty-four; and shall be and continue in force in all other places from the first day of February, one thousand eight hundred and forty-four, inclusive, to the first day of February, one thousand eight hundred and forty-five: provided that this Act shall, from and after the receipt and promulgation thereof in general orders in any part of her Majesty's dominions beyond the seas, become and be in full force; anything hereinbefore contained to the contrary notwithstanding.

SCHEDULES to which this Act refers

Form of Oaths to be taken by Members of Counts-Martial

You shall well and truly try and determine according to the evidence in the matter now before you. So help you God.

> I, ……. do swear, that I will duly administer justice, according to the rules and articles for the better government of her Majesty's forces, and according to an Act now in force for the punishment of mutiny and desertion, and other crimes therein mentioned, without partiality, favour, or affection, and if any doubt shall arise which is not explained by the said articles or Act, according to my conscience, the best of my understanding, and the custom of war in the like cases: and I further swear, that I will not divulge the sentence of the Court, until it shall be duly approved; neither will I, upon any account, at any time whatsoever, disclose or discover the vote or opinion of any particular member of the Court martial, unless required to give evidence thereof as a witness by a Court of Justice or a Court-martial in due course of law. So help me God.

Form of Oath of a Judge Advocate

> I, …….. do swear, that I will not, upon any account whatsoever, disclose or discover the vote or opinion of any particular member of the Court-martial, unless required to give evidence thereof as a witness by a Court of Justice or a Court-martial in a due course. So help me God.

QUESTIONs to be put separately by the JUSTICE to a RECRUIT

Enlisting for unlimited Service

1. What is your name?
2. In what parish, and in or near what town, and in what county were you born?
3. What is your age?

4. What is your trade or calling?

5. Are you an apprentice?

6. Are you married?

7. Are you ruptured or lame; have you ever been subject to fits; or have you any disability or disorder which impedes the free use of your limbs, or unfits you for ordinary labour?

8. Are you willing to be attested to serve in the .... regiment of ...... until you shall legally be discharged?

9. On what day, at what hour, and by whom were you enlisted?

10. For what bounty did you enlist?

11. Do you now belong to the Militia?

12. Do you belong to any other regiment, or to the marines, ordnance, or navy?

13. Have you ever served in the army, marines, ordnance, or navy?

Note.—The Justice is directed in putting the eleventh question to the recruit, and before he receives his answer, distinctly to apprize the recruit that if he belongs to the militia, and denies the fact, he is liable to six months' imprisonment.

Enlisting for either Her Majesty's or the East-India Company's Service

Question 8 is to be put by the Justice as follows:

8. Are you willing to be attested to serve in her Majesty's army, or in the forces of the East-India Company, according as her Majesty shall think fit to order, until you shall be duly and legally discharged?

Enlisting for the East-India Company's Service

Question 8 to be put by the Justice as follows:

8. Are you willing to be attested to serve the East-India Company until you shall be legally discharged? [Or, if the recruit enlist for limited service, then insert, for the period of twelve years, (if the person enlisting is of the age of eighteen years or upwards, but if under eighteen years then the difference between his age and eighteen to be added to such twelve years, as the case may be, and such period to be inserted instead of twelve years,) provided the said Company should so long require your service?]

OATH to be taken by a RECRUIT enlisting for unlimited or limited service

I, ... do make oath, that the above questions have been separately put tome; that the answers thereto have been read over to me; and that they are the same that I gave, and are true.

I do also make oath, that I will be faithful and bear true allegiance to her Majesty, her heirs and successors, and that I will, as in duty bound, honestly and faithfully defend her Majesty, her heirs and successors, in person, crown, and dignity, against all enemies, and will observe and obey all orders of her Majesty, her heirs and successors, and of the generals and officers set over me. So help me God.

Witness my hand.

---------- Signature of Recruit

---------- Witness present

Sworn before me at …….. this day of ------ one thousand eight hundred and at ----- o'clock.

Signature of Justice

If enlisting for either her Majesty's or the East-India Company's Service, the following addition is to be made to the foregoing Oath

And that if her Majesty, her heirs or successors, shall please to appoint me to serve in the forces of the East-India Company, then I swear that I will also be true to the said Company, and will duly observe and obey all their orders, and the orders of their generals and officers who shall be lawfully set over me.

If enlisting for the East-India Company's Service, the following is to be added to the Oath

And that I also will be true to the said Company, and will duly observe and obey all their orders, and the orders of their generals and officers who shall be lawfully set over me.

CERTIFICATE TO BE GIVEN BY THE JUSTICE

Description of …………

Age, apparently ……….

Height, …….. Feet ……… Inches

Complexion, ……….

Eyes, ……….

Hair, ………

Any distinctive Mark …………….

I, ... one of her Majesty's Justices of the Peace of do hereby certify, that the above is the description of the recruit .... and in my presence all the foregoing questions were put to the said .... ; that the answers written opposite to them are those which he gave to me; and that the first and second Articles of the second section of the Articles of War were read over to him; that he took the oath of allegiance and fidelity; that he received the sum of .... on being attested this day; and that I have given him a duplicate of this certificate, signed with my name.

------------Signature of Justice

5 VICTORIAE. Sess, 2. Cap. XIII

AN Act for the Regulation of her Majesty's Royal Marine Forces while on Shore

22nd April, 1842

Composition of general Courts-martial

VI. And be it enacted, that a general Court-martial, convened in any part of the Queen's dominions, (Bermuda, the Bahamas, Saint Helena, Africa, Jamaica, Honduras, Newfound land, and the Australian Colonies excepted,) or in the settlements of the East-India Company, or elsewhere, shall consist of not less than thirteen commissioned officers, and if convened in Jamaica, Newfoundland, Bermuda, or the Bahamas, or out of the Queen's dominions (excepting Saint Helena, Africa, Honduras, and the Australian Colonies), shall have not less than seven, and in Saint Helena, Africa, Honduras, and the Australian Colonies not less than five commissioned officers; and in all cases to judgment of death shall pass without the concurrence of two-thirds at the least of the members present; and the President shall in no case be the officer commanding in chief or Governor of the garrison where the offender shall be tried, nor under the degree of a field officer, unless where a field officer cannot be had, nor in any case whatsoever under the degree of a captain,

Proceedings of Courts-martial

VIII. And be it enacted, that in all trials by general Courts-martial to be held by virtue of this Act the President and every member of such Court shall, before any proceedings be had thereupon, take the oaths for that purpose set forth in the schedule to this Act annexed, before the Judge-Advocate or person officiating as such, and on trials by other Courts-martial before the President thereof, who are hereby respectively authorized to administer the same; and so soon as such oaths shall have been administered to the respective members, the President of the Court (having himself taken the said oath, to be administered to him by any sworn member) is hereby authorized and required to administer to the Judge-Advocate, or the person officiating as such, the oath in the schedule to this Act for that purpose annexed; and that no proceeding or trial shall be had upon any offence but between the hours of eight of the clock in the morning and four in the afternoon, except in cases which may require an immediate example, and except in the East-Indies, where such trial may be held between the hours of six in the morning and four in the afternoon.

Duration of Act

LXVII. And be it enacted, that this Act shall continue in force within Great Britain from the twenty-fifth day of April, one thousand eight hundred and forty-two, until the twenty-fifth day of April, one thousand eight hundred and forty-three, inclusive; and within Ireland, and in Jersey, Guernsey, Alderney, Sark, and the Ise of Man, and the islands thereto belonging, from the first day of May, one thousand eight hundred and forty-two, until the first day of May, one thousand eight hundred and forty-three, inclusive; and within the garrison of Gibraltar, and in Spain and Portugal, from the twenty-fifth day of July, one thousand eight hundred and forty-two, until the twenty-fifth day of July, one thousand eight hundred and forty-three, inclusive; and in all other parts of Europe where royal marine forces may be serving, and the West Indies, and North America and Cape of Good Hope, from the twenty-fifth day of September, one thousand eight hundred and forty-two, to the twenty-fifth day of September, one thousand eight hundred and forty-three, inclusive; and in all other places from the twenty fifth day of November, one thousand eight hundred and forty-two, to the twenty-fifth day of November, one thousand eight hundred and forty-three, inclusive.

Act No. XVIII of 1844

Passed on the 6th June 1844

Any Officer who may convene or confirm Courts Martial for the Queen's Troops, or for any of the East India Company's Troops may convene or confirm Courts Martial under his actual Command

AN Act to remove doubts as to the proper authority by which in certain cases, Courts Martial may be appointed and convened, and the Sentences thereof confirmed, in the East Indies and elsewhere; and it is important to the Maintenance of good order and Military Discipline that such doubts should be removed; be is therefore enacted by the Queen's most excellent majesty, by and with the Advice and Consent of the Lords Spiritual and Temporal, and Commons, in the present Parliament assembled, and by the Authority of the same, That and Law, Custom, Usage, Statute, Regulations, Articles of War, or warrant to the contrary notwithstanding, any General or other Officer who may from time to time have power to appoint or convene General or District or other Courts Martial for the trial of offences committed by any one of the officers, or Soldiers, in the Service of Her Majesty, or by the any of the Officers, Soldiers, or Followers in the service of the east India Company, not being Natives of the East Indies or other places within the limits aforesaid, shall without any further or other Authority or Warrant, have power and Authority to appoint or convene General or District or other Courts Martial (as the case may be) to be holden for the trail of offences committed by any Officer, Soldiers, or Followers in any of the said Services, who may be in the actual command or who may be or come within the local limits of the Command such General or other Officer, although the power of such officer as to appointing or convening Courts Martial might but for this Act extend to One or more of the said Services only, or to some only of the Forces belonging to any One or more of such Services; and in like manner any General or other Officer who may from Time to Time have Power to confirm Sentences of General or District or Other Courts Martial for the Trial of Offences committed by any of the Officers or Soldiers in the service of Her Majesty, or any of the Officers, Soldiers, or Followers in the service of the East India Company, not being Natives as aforesaid, or by any of the Officers, Soldiers, or Followers in Service of the East India Company, being such Natives as aforesaid, shall, without any further or other Authority of Warrant, have Power and Authority to confirm Sentences of General or District or other Courts Martial (as the case may be) held for the Trial of any Officer or Soldier or Follower in any of the said Services, who may under the actual Command or who may be or come within the local Limits of the Command of such General or other Officer, although the power of such Officer, as to confirming the Sentences of Courts

Martial, might be for this Act extend to One or more of the said Services, or to some only of the Forces belonging to any One or more of such Services.

Offenders may be tried wheresoever they may be serving or the Offence may have been committed

II. And be it enacted, That, the said several Powers may be exercised as aforesaid to whichsoever of the Presidencies of Fort William, Fort St George, or Bombay the offender may belong, or whether the General or other Officer appointing or convening the Court Martial, or confirming the Sentence, may be the Officer Commanding-in-Chief in India, or at the Presidency to which the Offender may belong, r at any other Presidency, or may hold his Command or his power to appoint, convene or confirm the Sentences of Courts martial from or under the Officer Commanding-in-Chief in India, or at the Presidency, or may hold such Command or Power from or under any other Authority whatsoever, or whether the Offence shall have been committed before or after the Officer appointing or convening the Court or confirming the Sentence shall have taken the Command, or before or after the Offender shall have been under the Command of such officer or, before or after the Offender shall have been or shall have come within the local Limits of the Command of such Officer, or wheresoever, whether within the Presidency to which the Offender may belong, or within any other Presidency, Possessions, or Territories under the Government of the said Company, or on the High Seas, or elsewhere the Offender may be serving, or the Offence shall have been committed, or the Court Martial shall be appointed, convened, or held.

Her Majesty may authorize Commander-in-Chief to delegate Power of confirming sentences of General Courts martial

III. And be enacted, That any Articles of war or Usage to the contrary notwithstanding, Her Majesty may grant Warrant under Her Sign Manual severally empowering the Officer Commanding-in-Chief the forces in India, and the General or other Officer Commanding the Forces at each or any of the Presidencies of Fort William, Fort St George, or Bombay for the time being, to authorize any General or other Officer not below the rank of a Field Officer, having the Command of any Body of the troops of Her Majesty or of the said Company serving in the Possessions or Territories which are or may be under the Government of the said Company or elsewhere to confirm the Sentences of General Courts Martial which shall be holden for the Trial of Offences committed by any Officer, Soldier, or Follower of or belonging to such Troops; and the Officer Commanding-in-Chief the Forces in India, or the General or other Officer Commanding the Forces at any of the said Presidencies, being so empowered, may authorize any such General or other Officer to confirm such Classes of Sentences only, or Sentences passed for such Classes of Offences only, or on such Classes of Persons only, as he may think fit, reserving to himself the power of confirming Sentences in all such cases and such General or other Officer may not authorize to confirm, or may think fit to send for the decision of such Officer Commanding-in-Chief the Forces in India, or such Officer Commanding the Forces at any one of the said Presidencies.

No other Confirmation necessary, except in certain Cases

IV. And be it enacted, That when, by any Act of Parliament or Articles of War, the Sentence of Court Martial is not to be carried into execution until confirmed by the general or other Officer Commanding in Chief at the Presidency in the Territories subordinate to which the Offender shall have been tried, with the concurrence of the Governor General in Council or Governor in Council, or Governor of such Presidency, it shall not be necessary, in any such Case that a Sentence so confirmed, with such Concurrence, should, in addition, be reported or approved or confirmed by the General or other Officer Commanding-in-Chief the Forces of the Presidencies to which the Offender may belong; and the Officer confirming the Sentence, with such Concurrence, and in all other cases the Officer authorized under the Provisions in the said Act contain to confirm the Sentence of any Court Martial, shall have Power to cause the same to be put in into execution, or to suspend, mitigate, or remit the same.

Confirmation of Sentences of Death on Commissioned Officers

V. And be it enacted, That nothing in this Act contained shall empower any Person not otherwise duly authorized in that behalf to confirm any Sentence of Death, Transportation or Cashiering on any Commissioned Officer employed upon Her Majesty's Staff, or serving in any of Her Majesty's regular Regiments; and that nothing in this Act contained shall empower any Officer, other than those hereinafter mentioned, to confirm the Sentence of Death, Transportation, or Cashiering on a Commissioned Officer of the east India Company's Service; (that is to say), the General, or Other Officer Commanding-in-Chief at the Presidency within which, or in the Territories subordinate to which, the Offender shall have been tried, or the General Commanding-in-Chief the Army to which the such Division, Brigade, or Party in which the Offender may be serving shall belong or be attached.

Act not otherwise affect laws now in force

VI. provided always, and be enacted, That, save as hereinbefore is expressly provided, this Act shall not alter or affect the laws, Statutes, Regulations, Articles of War, Usages, or Customs which now are or hereafter may be in Force with respect t Her Majesty's Forces or the Forces of the said east India Company, whether natives or not of the east Indies, or other places within the Limits of the said Company's charter; Provided also, that this Act shall not be construed as declaring or interpreting the Extent of Her Majesty's Royal Prerogative, or the meaning of any former Act or of any Article of War.

Act extend only to the East Indies

VII. And be it enacted, That the Provisions of this Act shall apply to all such Persons as may from Time to Time be liable to Martial Law under the Provisions of any Act of Parliament or Articles of War, and who may from Time to Time be serving or may be come within the Limits of the Charter of the east India Company, construing the same as extending to all Places and Seas eastward of the Cape of Good Hope to the Straits of Magellan.

Continuance of Act as to her Majesty's Forces

VIII. And be enacted, That, so far as regard Officers and Soldiers in her Majesty's Service, this Act shall continue in force so long only as there may be in force some Act for punishing Mutiny and Desertion, and for the better Payment of the Army and their Quarters.

Note: Under the Act No. VIII of 1844, passed on 9 April 1844, the Governments of the three Presidencies at Fort William in Bengal, Fort St. George and Bombay, were authorized to remove Native Officers, Soldiers and Followers imprisoned under sentence of a Court Martial from one Prison to another. The Act provided, "It is hereby enacted, that whenever any Native Officer or Soldier, or Follower, belonging to the Forces of the East India Company, shall be a prisoner in any public prison or other place within the territories subject to the Government of the said Company under sentence of any Court Martial, it shall be lawful for the Governor or Governor in Council (as the case may be) of the Presidency, in which such public opinion or other place may be situated, to give an order in writing to the Gaoler thereof, or other person in charge thereof, commanding him to deliver up such prisoner to the person producing such order, and such Gaoler or other person shall deliver up such prisoner at any period of his imprisonment to the person producing such order either for his discharge or in order that he may be removed in Military custody to undergo the remainder of his sentence, to such other public prison or such other place as such Governor or Governor in Council (as the case may be) may direct; Provided that such other public prison or other place shall be within the Presidency subject to the Government of the Governor or Governor in Council (as the case may be) who shall have given such order; And provided that the time of imprisonment on removal from one prison to another, or while the prisoner is in custody for any intermediate period shall be reckoned as part of the original period of imprisonment for which such prisoner shall have been sentenced."

Articles of War

Act XX of 1845

(Passed on the 6th September 1845)

An Act providing Articles of War for the Government of the Native Officers and Soldiers in the Military Service of the East India Company.

Whereas by an Act passed in the third and fourth years of the reign of His Majesty King William the Fourth, intituled, "An Act for effecting an arrangement with the East India Company and for the better government of His Majesty's Indian Territories till the Thirtieth day of April, One Thousand Eight Hundred and Fifty-four," it was, amongst other things, enacted, that it should be lawful for the Governor-General of India in Council, from time to time, to make Articles of War for the government of the Native Officers and Soldiers in the Military Service of the Company, and for the administration of justice by Courts Martial to be holden on such Officers and Soldiers, and such Articles of War from time to time to repeal or vary and amend, and that such Articles of War should be made and taken notice of in the same manner as all other the Laws and Regulations to be made by the said Governor General under the said Act, and should prevail and be in force and should be of exclusive authority over all the Native Officers and Soldiers in the said Military Service, to whatever Presidency such Officers and Soldiers might belong, or wheresoever they might be serving : Provided, nevertheless, that, until such Articles of War should be made by the said Governor-General in Council, any Articles of War for, or relating to, the Government of the Company's Native forces, which at the time of the said Act coming into operation should be in force and use in any part or parts of the territories under the Government of the said Company should remain in force:

It is hereby enacted, in pursuance of the above recited authority, that the following Articles of War shall, from and after the seventh day of October, 1845, be the Articles of War for the government of the said Native Officers and Soldiers in the Military Service of the said Company, and for the administration of justice by Courts Martial to be holden on such Officers and Soldiers.

ARTICLES OF WAR

SECTION I

OF ENLISTING AND DISCHARGES

Article 1.—Every Recruit, prior to being enrolled in his Regiment, shall have the First Four Articles of the Second Section of these Articles of War read and explained to him, after which such Declaration as is now used, if any, in the respective Presidencies, shall be made to him by the

Officer Commanding, in front of the Regiment or Corps, in presence of the Native Officers and Soldiers, and an oath or declaration shall then be required from him, according to the forms of his religion, such oath and declaration to be the like as are now used in the respective Presidencies.

* Article 2.—No Commissioned Officer shall be dismissed except by the Sentence of a General Court Martial. No Non-Commissioned Officer or Soldier shall be discharged as a punishment except by the Sentence of a Court Martial, or by order of the Commander-in-Chief at the Presidency to which he may belong. Every such dismissal or discharge shall include forfeiture of all claim to pension. Provided that no Sentence of discharge awarded by a Court Martial inferior to General shall be carried into effect without the concurrence of the Commander-in-Chief, or the General or other Officer Commanding the Division, Field Force, District or Brigade, in which the prisoner may be serving ; Provided also, that the Governor-General in Council in his executive capacity, and the Governor in Council of any Presidency to which a Commissioned or Non-Commissioned Officer or Soldier may belong, shall have power to order his dismissal or discharge.

Article 3. —All Non-Commissioned Officers and Soldiers discharged the Service, shall be furnished by the Commanding Officer of the Regiment with a Discharge Certificate, made out in the Vernacular Language of the individual discharged, with an English Translation, expressing the authority for, and cause of such discharge, and the period of his entire Service in the Army.

* Article 4.—No Non-Commissioned Officer or Soldier shall enlist himself in any other Regiment without a regular discharge from his former Regiment, under the penalty of being reputed a Deserter, and suffering accordingly.

SECTION II

CRIMES AND PUNISHMENT

Crimes punishable with Death, Transportation, Corporal Punishment or Dismissal

Article 5.—Any Officer, or Soldier, who shall begin, excite, cause, or join in any Mutiny or Sedition in the Regiment or Corps to which he belongs, or in any other Corps or Regiment whatsoever, on any pretence whatever; or who, being present at any Mutiny or Sedition, shall not use his utmost endeavours to suppress it ; or who, coming to the knowledge of any Mutiny, intended Mutiny, or concealed combination against the State, shall not without delay give information thereof to his Commanding Officer ;—or

Article 6.—Who shall strike his Superior Officer, or shall draw, or offer to draw, or lift up any weapon, or use or offer any violence against him ; whether on or off duty, and under all circumstances in which his Superior Officer may be distinguishable as such in any manner;—or

Article 7.—Who shall disobey any lawful command of his Superior Officer; —or

Article 8. —Who shall desert from the East India Company's Service, (whether or not he shall re-enter or re-enlist in the same;—or

Article 9.—Who, being a Sentry, in time of war or alarm, shall sleep upon his post, or shall leave it before regularly relieved or without leave;—or

Article 10.—Who shall shamefully abandon or deliver up any Garrison, Fortress, Post or Guard committed to his charge, or which it was his duty to defend ; or who shall use means to induce any other Officer or Soldier so to abandon or deliver up any such Garrison, Fortress, Post or Guard ;—or

Article 11.—Who shall treacherously make known the watchword to any per son not entitled to receive it, according to the Rules and Discipline of War; —or

Article 1 2.—Who shall hold correspondence with or give intelligence to the Enemy, or any person in arms against the State, either directly or indirectly ; or who coming to the knowledge of such correspondence or communication, shall not discover it immediately to the Commanding Officer ; —or

Article 13.—Who shall, directly or indirectly, assist or relieve the Enemy, or persons in arms against the State, with money, victuals or ammunition ; or shall | knowingly harbour or protect any Enemy or Person in arms against the State; —or

Article 14,—Who shall treacherously release, wilfully aid, or connive at the escape of any Enemy, or person in arms against the State, placed as a prisoner under his charge ;—or

Article 15.—Who shall misbehave himself before the Enemy, or persons in arms against whom he is led, or use means to induce others so to misbehave ;—or

Article 16.—Who shall, in presence of an Enemy, or of persons in arms against whom he is led, shamefully cast away his arms or ammunition;—or

Article 17.—Who shall leave his Commanding Officer, or his Post, or Party, in time of action, to go in search of plunder ;—or

Article 18.—Who, in time of War, shall do violence to any person bringing provisions or other necessaries to the Camp or Quarters of the Forces ; or shall force a Safeguard ; or break into any house, or other place for plunder ; or plunder fields or gardens 6r other property;—or

Article 19.—Who, in time of War, shall, by discharging Fire Arms, drawing swords, beating drums, making signals, using words, or by any means whatever, intentionally occasion false alarms, in Action, Camp, Garrison or Quarters;—or

Article 20. —Who shall, without proper authority, release any State Prisoner, or, through carelessness or neglect, shall suffer any such Prisoner to escape; —or

Article 21.--- Who, being a Sentry placed over any State Prisoner, or over Treasure, or over a Magazine or Dock Yard, shall quit his Post, without being regularly relieved, or without leave or shall sleep upon his Post ;—

Shall, if an Officer on conviction, suffer Death, or Transportation for life, or be dismissed the service:

And, if a Soldier, shall, on conviction, suffer Death, or Transportation for life, or imprisonment, with or without hard labour, for life, or for any term of years : and with or without solitary confinement for any portion or portions of the term of imprisonment, not exceeding twenty-eight days at a time, nor eighty-four days in any one year, with intervals between the periods o/ solitary confinement of not less duration than such periods of solitary confinement ; or shall suffer Corporal Punishment; or dismissal from the Service ; as by a General Court Martial shall be awarded.

Crimes not punishable with Death or Transportation

Article 22.—Any Officer or Soldier who shall in operations in the field, spread Reports, by Words or Letters, calculated to create unnecessary alarm in the Troops or in the vicinity, or in rear of the Army;—or

Article 23. —Who shall, in Action or previously to going into Action, use words tending to create Alarm or Despondency;—or

Article 24.—Who shall be drunk when on or for duty or on Parade or on the Line of March; or

Article 25.—Any Soldier who shall be grossly insubordinate or insolent in the Ranks; or grossly insubordinate and violent in the presence of a Court Martial;

Shall, if an Officer, on conviction, be sentenced to be dismissed the Service, or to be suspended from Rank, and Pay, and Allowances:

And, if a Soldier, shall, on conviction before a General, or District, or Garrison Court Martial, be sentenced to suffer such punishment as a General, or District, or Garrison Court Martial is, by these Articles of War, respectively empowered to award.

Provided, that such Offender shall not be sentenced to Death, or Transportation, or imprisonment with Hard Labour.

Article 26.—Any Officer who shall behave in a manner unbecoming the character of an Officer; (the fact or facts whereon the charge is grounded being clearly specified therein;)—or

Article 27.—Any Officer or Soldier, who being under arrest or in confinement, shall leave his arrest or confinement before he is set at liberty by competent authority;—or

Article 28.—Who shall advise or persuade any other Officer or Soldier to desert, or who shall connive at such desertion ; or who shall knowingly receive and entertain any Deserter, and shall not immediately on discovery give notice to his superior Officer ; or shall not cause such Deserter to be apprehended by the Civil Power;—or

Article 29.—Who shall obtain or attempt to obtain, for himself or for any Officer or Soldier, or for any other person whatsoever, any Pension or Allowance, by any false Statement, Certificate, or Document, or by the omission of the true Statement, or Certificate, or Document;—or

Article 30.—Who shall knowingly make a false Return or Report, to any his Superior Officer authorized to call for a Return or Report, of the state of the men under his Command, or of Arms, Ammunition, Clothing or other Stores there unto belonging or of which he may have charge;—or

Article 31.—Who shall malinger, feign, or intentionally produce disease or infirmity; or intentionally delay his cure; or intentionally aggravate his disease or infirmity;—or

Article 32. —Who, at any post, or on the march, shall illegally and against the will of the parties, extort money or property of any description, as fees, or duties, or on any pretence whatever; or shall, without authority, exact from Villagers or others carriage, porterage, or provisions:—or

Article 33.—Who shall wantonly and intentionally defile any place dedicated to religious worship, or shall wantonly and intentionally insult the religious prejudices of other persons;—or

Article 34.—Who shall, without orders, commit any waste, or spoil, or plunder, or shall injure or destroy any property;—or

Article 35.—Any Soldier who shall, contrary to orders, when off duty, appear in or about Camp or Cantonments, or on occasion of visiting Towns or Bazars, carrying a sword, bludgeon, or other weapon ;—or

Article 36.—Who shall sell, pawn, designedly, or through neglect, lose or injure his horse, arms, clothes, accoutrements, or regimental necessaries; or any of the above articles entrusted or belonging to any other Soldier;—

Shall, if an Officer, on conviction, be sentenced to be dismissed the Service, or to be suspended from Rank, and Pay, and Allowances:

And, if a Soldier, shall, on conviction before a General, District or Garrison Court Martial, be sentenced to suffer such punishment as a General or District or Garrison Court Martial is by these Articles of War respectively empowered to award:

Provided that such Offender shall not be sentenced to Death, or Transportation, or Corporal Punishment.

Crimes punishable with fine or loss of pay, in addition to other Punishments

Article 37.—Any Officer, or Soldier, who shall embezzle or frauduletly misapply any money entrusted to him on the public account, or for any Military purpose; or any Provisions, Forage, Arms, Clothing, Ammunition, or Military Stores, of whatever kind or description, the property of Government, entrusted to his charge; or who shall wilfully spoil such property or suffer it to be spoiled, or shall be concerned in or connive at any such embezzlement or fraudulent misapplication:— .

Shall, on conviction before a General Court Martial, be dismissed the service, and fined to the extent of his arrears of Pay and Allowances ; and further liable to suffer imprisonment with or without hard labour, for a term which may extend to three years, and with or without solitary confinement to be regulated as aforesaid.

Article 38.—Any Soldier who shall be guilty of disgraceful conduct, in wilfully maiming or injuring himself, or any other Soldier, at the instance of such Soldier, with intent to render himself or such Soldier unfit for the Service, or with intent to take his own life ;—or

Article 39.—In purloining or selling Government Stores;—or

Article 40.—In stealing money or goods, the property of a Soldier, or of a Military Officer, or of any Military Mess, or of any person or persons belonging to or serving with or attached to the Army; —or

Article 41.—In embezzling or fraudulently misapplying public money entrusted to him for any Military purpose;—or

Article 42.—In committing any petty offence of a fraudulent nature, to the injury of or with intent to injure any person, Civil or Military;—or

Article 43.—Who shall be guilty of any other disgraceful conduct, being of a cruel, indecent, or unnatural kind:

Shall, on conviction before a General, or District, or Garrison Court Martial, be liable to suffer such punishment as any such Courts are by these Articles of War respectively empowered to award for disgraceful conduct.

And every such offender shall, if not dismissed the service, further be put under stoppages, by sentence of the Court, not exceeding half of his monthly Pay and Allowances; until the amount be made good of any loss or damage arising out of his misconduct.

And if such offender shall be dismissed the service, he shall further be sentenced to forfeit his arrears of Pay and Allowances due at the time of his discharge, or in such proportion as may be required to make good such loss or damage.

Crimes not Punishable with Corporal Punishment or Imprisonment with Labor

Article 44.—Any Officer, or Non-Commissioned Officer who shall strike or otherwise ill-treat any Soldier;—or

Article 45.—Any Sentry who, in time of peace, shall sleep upon his Post, or shall leave it before regularly relieved or without leave;—or

Article 46 —Any Officer, or Soldier, who shall knowingly enlist a Deserter, or connive at his enlistment;—or

Article 47.—Who, directly or indirectly, shall require or accept a bribe, present or gratification, on the pretence of or ns a consideration for procuring leave of absence, promotion, or any other advantage or indulgence for any Officer or Soldier;—or

Article 48.—Who, being in Command at any Post, or on the march, on complaint made to him of any person under his command beating or otherwise ill-treating any person ; or extorting from him more than he is obliged to furnish by authority; or disturbing fairs or markets, or committing any kind of riot, shall not see reparation done to the party or parties injured ; or, if that be impracticable, shall not report the same to his superior Officer;—or

Article 49.—Who, being in Command of a Guard, shall refuse to receive any prisoner duly committed to his charge ; or shall, without proper authority, release any prisoner, or shall suffer, through carelessness or neglect, any prisoner to escape;—or

Article 50.—.Who shall quit his Guard or Picquet in time of peace, without being regularly relieved, or without leave;—or

Article 51.—Who shall impede the Provost Marshal, or his Assistants, or any other Officer or person legally exercising authority:—or refuse to assist him when requiring his aid in the execution of his duty;—or

Article 52.—Wh8, being on leave of absence, shall have received information from the Head Quarters of his Regiment, or from other competent authority, that his Regiment has been ordered on service, and shall not rejoin without delay;—or

Article 53.—Who, in time of peace, shall by discharging fire arms, drawing swords, beating drums, or by any other means whatever, intentionally occasion false alarms in Camp, Garrison, or Cantonments;—or

Article 54.—Who shall fail to repair at the time fixed to the parade, or place appointed for exercise or duty, if not prevented by sickness or some other sufficient cause;—or

Article 55.—Who shall, without urgent necessity, or without leave of his superior Officer, quit his Company or Troop or the parade;—or

Article 56. —Who shall absent himself without leave; or shall, without sufficient cause, overstay the period for which leave may have been granted him;—-or

Article 57.—Any Soldier who shall be found two miles from the Camp contrary to orders ;—or

Article 58. —Who shall, contrary to orders, be absent from his Cantonment after tattoo, or from Camp after retreat beating;—or

Article 59.—Who shall sell, lose, or designedly, or through neglect, waste the ammunition delivered out to him;

Shall, if an Officer, on conviction, be sentenced to suspension from Rank and Pay and Allowances; or to be reprimanded in such manner as the Commander-in-Chief may direct:

And, if a Soldier, shall, on conviction before a General, or District, or Garrison, or Regimental Court Martial, be sentenced to suffer such punishment as any such Courts Martial are by these Articles of War respectively empowered to award;

Provided that such offender shall not be liable to be sentenced to suffer Corporal Punishment or Imprisonment with Hard Labor.

Article 60. —All crimes not capital, and all disorders or neglects which Officers or Soldiers may be guilty of, to the prejudice of good order and Military discipline, though not specified in these Articles, are to be taken cognizance of by Courts Martial, and to be punished according to the nature and degree of the offence, by the Sentence of a General, or District, or Garrison, or Regimental Court Martial ; Provided that a Soldier shall not for any such offences be liable to be sentenced to suffer Corporal Punishment or Imprisonment with Hard Labor.

Crimes incident to Courts Martial

Article 61.—Any person amenable to these Articles of War, who, when duly summoned before a Court Martial, shall not attend, or shall refuse to be sworn, or to make affirmation, or to answer any lawful question ; or who shall induce any other person so to offend ;

Shall be punished according to the Sentence of the same or another Court Martial, with dismissal or suspension from Rank and Pay and Allowances, if a Commissioned Officer; with dismissal or reduction to the ranks, if a Non-Commissioned Officer ; or with dismissal or imprisonment, if a Soldier;

Provided that such person, being a Commissioned Officer, shall not be liable to be punished by any but a General Court partial ; and that no offender punished under the provisions of this Article of War shall be sentenced to suffer Imprisonment with Hard Labor, or Corporal Punishment.

Article 62.—Any person not amenable to these Articles of War, who, having been summoned upon any Court Martial, shall refuse or neglect to attend, or who attending shall refuse to be sworn, or to make affirmation, or to answer any lawful question, or shall give such testimony as, if given in a Criminal Court, would render him guilty of perjury ; or who shall induce any other person so to offend;—

Shall be delivered to a Magistrate to be proceeded against according to law.

Article 63.—Any person using menacing or disrespectful words, signs or gestures, in the presence of a Court Martial, then sitting, or causing any disorder or riot so as to disturb their proceedings;—

Shall be punished, according to the condition of the offender and the nature and degree of his offence, by the sentence of the same or another Court Martial, if he be amenable to these Articles of War: Provided that such offender shall not be liable to be sentenced to Corporal Punishment or to Imprisonment with Hard Labor; and if not amenable to these Articles of War, the offender shall be delivered over to a Magistrate, to be proceeded against according to law.

Article 64.—Any Officer, or Soldier, who shall be found guilty of willfully and knowingly giving false evidence on oath or affirmation on any trial before any General, or other Court Martial, or any Military Court entitled to administer an oath ; or of inducing any other person so to offend;—

Shall be dismissed the service, and shall be further subject to fine, to the amount of his arrears of Pay and Allowances, or to Imprisonment which may ex tend to three years;—according to the Sentence of a General, District, or Garrison Court Martial.

Crimes admitting of less serious notice

Article 65.—Whereas it may be advisable that some of the offences which by the foregoing Articles are directed to be tried by a General, or District, or Garrison Court Martial, should, in certain cases which admit of less serious notice, be tried by District, or Garrison, or Regimental Court Martial respectively, in such cases the Officer Commanding the Regiment or Corps to which the offender belongs shall lay a particular statement of the case before the General or other Officer having authority to convene General, or District, or Garrison Courts Martial, under whose command such offender may be serving, with an application, so to proceed; and such General or other Officer will exercise his discretion in complying or not with such application ; but the permission of such General or other Officer so to proceed,

shall be entered upon the proceedings at the trial of such offender.

Provided that Mutiny shall not be considered one of the offences admitting of such discretionary investigation.

And that in cases where offences designated "Disgraceful Conduct" in these Articles of War, and admitting of less serious notice, shall be permitted to be tried by Regimental Courts Martial, the term Disgraceful Conduct shall be omitted in the Charge.

Offences on the Line of March or on board Vessels

Article 66.—For offences committed on the Line of March, or on board any ship or other vessel, the Officer in command of the Troops is hereby authorized to try any Soldier by a Regimental, or Detachment Court Martial, and to confirm and execute the Sentence, and in all cases of Mutiny or Gross Insubordination to carry the Sentence into execution on the spot;—

Provided that such Sentence shall in no case exceed that which a Regimental Court Martial is competent to award;—and that the proceedings held in all such cases shall be specially reported for the information of the Commander-in-Chief.

SECTION III

ADMINISTRATION OF JUSTICE

Article 67.—Whenever any Officer or Soldier shall commit a crime deserving punishment by Court Martial, he shall, by his Commanding Officer, be put under arrest, if an Officer ; or if a Soldier, be confined, until he shall be either tried by a Court Martial, or shall be lawfully discharged by a proper authority; and no Officer or Soldier who shall be put in such arrest or confinement shall continue in his confinement longer than may be actually unavoidable.

And such process of arrest or confinement, or an attempt to effect such process, shall in no case be omitted where it may be practicable;—but where resistance maybe made, or from other circumstances such process may be impracticable, the offender or offenders shall be liable to trial and punishment at any subsequent period, within the limitations provided in these Articles of War.

Article 68.—No person shall be liable to be tried or punished for any offence against these Articles, which shall appear to have been committed more than three years previous to the order directing the assembly of the Court Martial whereby he is to be tried, unless the person accused, by reason of his absenting himself, or some other manifest impediment, shall not have been amenable to justice within that period ; in which case such person shall be liable to be tried, at any time not exceed ing two years after the impediment shall have ceased.

Article 69.—Any -person amenable to these Articles of War, who may commit any offence against the same, may be tried and punished for such offence in any place within the British Territories, or elsewhere, where he may have come after the commission of the offence, in the same manner as if the offence had been committed where such trial shall take place.

Article 70.—The Commander-in-Chief at the Presidencies of Fort William, Fort Saint George, and Bombay respectively for the time being, may appoint General or other Courts Martial, and confirm, mitigate or remit the Sentences of such Courts: and may issue his Warrant to any General or other Officer having the Command of a Body of Troops in the service of Her Majesty or of the East India Company, empowering such Officer to appoint General, or District, or Garrison Courts Martial as occasion may require, for the trial of offences committed by any of the Officers or Soldiers or Followers in the said Company, being Natives of the East Indies, or of other places within the limits of the said Company's Charter, and confirm, mitigate, or remit the sentences of such Courts Martial.

Article 71.—A General Court Martial shall not consist of less than thirteen Commissioned Officers, unless it be held out of the East India Company's Territories, where such Court Martial may consist of seven Commissioned Officers, if a greater number cannot be conveniently assembled. And no sentence of a General Court Martial shall be put in execution until after a report shall have been made of the whole proceedings to the Commander-in-Chief, or to some other person duly authorized to confirm the same, and until his directions shall have been signified thereupon.

Powers of a General Court Martial

*Article 72.—A General Court Martial may sentence any Officer or Soldier to Death or Transportation, for any crimes which are by these Articles of War expressly made liable to sentence of Death or Transportation, and for such crimes only.

And when a Commissioned Officer shall be convicted of any offence, of which the punishment is not defined in these Articles of War, or is left discretionary, a General Court Martial may adjudge such Officer to be dismissed the service;—or to be suspended from Rank and Pay and Allowances, for a stated period;—or to be placed lower on the list of his rank, by an alteration of the date of his Commission, thereby losing the corresponding benefit of length of service ; and the Court shall in every such sentence specify the extent or degree of suspension or reduction, which they shall so adjudge ;—or the Court may sentence such Officer to be reprimanded in such manner as the Commander-in-Chief may direct.

And a General Court Martial may sentence any Non-Commissioned Officer to be reduced to the ranks;—or may sentence any Non-Commissioned Officer or Soldier to be dismissed the service ;—or to be placed lower in the list of the rank which be holds ;—or may sentence any Soldier to suffer Corporal Punishment not exceeding Two Hundred Lashes;—or Imprisonment with or without hard labor not exceeding two years;—and to be kept in solitary confinement for any portion or portions of such Imprisonment, not exceeding twenty-eight days at a time, nor eighty-four days in any one year, with intervals between the period of solitary confinement, of not less duration than such periods of solitary confinement.

And a General Court Martial may, in addition either to Corporal Punishment or to Imprisonment as aforesaid, sentence a Soldier to forfeiture of all advantage as to additional Pay and to Pension on discharge, which might have otherwise accrued from the length or nature of his former service; or to forfeiture of such advantage absolutely, whether it might have accrued from past service, or might accrue from future service, according to the nature of the case, for disgraceful conduct.

And a General Court Martial may, in addition to the punishment of dismissal, sentence any Officer or Soldier to forfeit his arrears of Pay and Allowances due at the time of his discharge, or such proportion thereof as may be required, to make good any loss or damage arising out of his misconduct;—And in addition to any punishment not involving dismissal from the service, may sentence any Officer or Soldier to be put under stoppages not exceeding two-thirds of his Pay and Allowances in the case of an Officer, and not exceeding half of his Pay and Allowances in the case of a Non-Commissioned Officer or Soldier, until the amount of such low or damage be made good.

Confirmation and Commutation of Sentence, by the Commander-in-Chief

Article 73.—In cases wherein a Sentence of Death shall have been awarded by General Court Martial, for any offence against discipline for which sentence of Death is awardable under these Articles of War, the Commander-in-Chief may confirm such Sentence and cause it to be carried into effect, or may, instead of causing such Sentence to be carried into effect, order the offender, if an Officer, to be transported for life, or to be dismissed, and if a Soldier, to be transported for life, or to be imprisoned with or without Hard Labor either for life, or for a certain term of years, and with or without Solitary Confinement, to be regulated as aforesaid, as to the Commander-m-Chief may seem meet.

In cases of Commissioned Officers sentenced to Transportation the Commander-in-Chief may, in lieu thereof, order the offender to be dismissed. And in cases of Commissioned Officers sentenced to be dismissed from the service, the Commander-in-Chief may, in lieu of such punishment, direct that the offender be suspended from Rank and Pay and Allowances for a certain period, to be distinctly specified by the Commander-in-Chief.

And the Commander-in-Chief may commute a Sentence of Transportation passed on a Soldier, to Imprisonment, with or without Hard Labor and with or without Solitary Confinement, to be regulated as aforesaid; and such Imprisonment may be either for the same period for which Transportation shall have been awarded, or for any lesser period.

And the Commander-in-Chief may commute a Sentence of Corporal Punishment to Dismissal from the Service ; or, in the case of a Non-Commissioned Officer, may mitigate such Sentence to reduction to the ranks ; or in the case of a Non-Commissioned Officer or Soldier may commute such Sentence to Imprisonment without Hard Labor, and with or without Solitary Confinement (to be regulated as aforesaid,) for any period not exceeding two years, if the sentence shall exceed one hundred and fifty lathes; not exceeding one year, if it shall exceed one hundred lashes; and not exceeding liar months, if it shall be less than one hundred ladies;—but the term of such commuted Imprisonment may be for any lesser periods respectively, at the discretion of the Commander-in-Chief.

In cases of Non-Commissioned Officers sentenced to be dismissed from the service, the Commander-in-Chief may, in lieu of such punishment, direct that the offender be reduced to the ranks, or placed lower in the list of the rank which he holds.

And in cases of offenders sentenced to Imprisonment with Hard Labor, the Commander-in-Chief may mitigate such Sentence by causing the offender to be reduced to the ranks, in the case of a Non-Commissioned Officer ; or in the case of a Non-Commissioned Officer or Soldier by directing that he be dismissed from the service; or suffer Imprisonment without Hard Labor, and with or without Solitary Confinement, (to be regulated as aforesaid) for any period not exceeding that for which he shall have been Sentenced to such Imprisonment with Hard Labor.

Article 74.—A District or Garrison Court Martial shall consist of not less than Seven Commissioned Officers, except in situations where that number cannot be conveniently assembled, when such Court may consist of not less than five Commissioned Officers. And such District, or Garrison Court Martial may be composed of Officers of the same Regiment, and shall be assembled in conformity with the orders of the Commander- in Chief.

And the Sentence of a District, or Garrison Court Martial shall be confirmed by the Commander-in Chief, or by some Officer duly authorized to confirm the same.

Commutation of Sentence

And the Commander-in-Chief is empowered to remit or mitigate or commute the Sentences of such Courts Martial, in the same manner as the Sentences of General Courts Martial; and to delegate or withhold the power to Commanding Officers of convening such Courts Martial, and of confirming, remitting, mitigating or commuting the Sentences of such Courts (not including forfeiture of Pay or Pension or other advantage,) as the Commander-in-Chief may deem to be most expedient.

And in case of any Sentence, including forfeiture of additional Pay or of Pension on Discharge, or of any prospective advantage, such Sentence shall not be carried into effect until confirmed by the Commander-in-Chief; and all forfeitures of any present or prospective advantage shall be restorable by the same authority.

Powers of a District or Garrison Court Martial

*Article 75.—District or Garrison Courts Martial may Sentence any Non-commissioned Officer to be reduced to the ranks,—or may Sentence any Non-Commissioned Officer or Soldier to be dismissed from the Service; or to be placed lower in the list of the rank which he holds; or may Sentence any Soldier to suffer Corporal Punishment not exceeding one hundred and fifty lashes ; or Imprisonment, with or without Hard Labor, not exceeding One Year, and to be kept in Solitary Confinement, to be regulated as aforesaid.

And such Court Martial may, in addition either to Corporal Punishment or to Imprisonment as aforesaid, sentence a Soldier to forfeiture of all advantage as to additional Pay, and to Pension on Discharge, which might have otherwise accrued from the length or nature of his former service, or to forfeiture of such advantage absolutely, whether it might have accrued from past service, or might accrue from future service, according to the nature of the case for disgraceful conduct.

And such Court Martial may, in addition to the punishment of Dismissal, sentence any Non-Commissioned Officer or Soldier to forfeit his arrears of Pay and Allowances due at the time of his discharge, or such proportion thereof as may be required to make good any loss or damage arising out of his misconduct; and, in addition to any punishment not involving Dismissal from the service, may sentence any

Non-Commissioned Officer or Soldier to be put under Stoppages, not exceeding half of his Pay and Allowances, until the amount of such loss or damage be made good.

Article 76.—A Regimental Court Martial shall consist of not less than Five Commissioned Officers, (unless it be found impracticable to assemble that number, ihen Three may be sufficient:) and shall be assembled by order of the Officer Commanding the Regiment. And no Sentence of a Regimental Court Martial shall be of force until the Commanding Officer shall have confirmed the same. Provided that such Commanding Officer shall have power to remit all Sentences whatever passed by such Court, and thereupon to cause the offender to be released and to return to his duty.

Commutation of Sentence

And such Commanding Officer shall have power to mitigate all Sentences whatever passed by such Court ; and to commute a Sentence of Corporal Punishment to Imprisonment without Hard Labor, and with or without Solitary Confinement, to be regulated as aforesaid, for any period for which such Court is competent to Sentence an offender to suffer Imprisonment, and in the same manner ; and to mitigate a Sentence of Dismissal in the case of a Non-Commissioned Officer, to Reduction to the Ranks;—and to commute a Sentence of Imprisonment with Hard Labor, or with Solitary Confinement, or both, to Dismissal; or to mitigate such Sentence to Reduction to the Ranks; or to Imprisonment without Hard Labor.

But no Sentence of Corpora! Punishment, or of Imprisonment with Hard Labor, passed by a Regimental Court Martial and confirmed in full by such Commanding Officer, or confirmed and mitigated by him ; and no Sentence of Dismissal confirmed, and no commutation of Dismissal for Imprisonment made as aforesaid, by such Commanding Officer, shall be carried into effect, without the sanction and authority of the Officer Commanding the Division or Field Force or District or Brigade, (being the Senior Officer on the spot) in which the Regiment may be serving, who is hereby empowered to cause such sentence to be inflicted in accordance with the confirmation thereof, in full or in mitigated degree, by the Officer Commanding the Regiment, or such dismissal to be carried into effect, or to direct the release of the offender and his return to duty as he may deem expedient.

Provided that in detached situations, or when on service in the field, the Officer Commanding the Regiment shall have power to carry into effect any Sentence of a Regimental Court Martial, in cases where an immediate example is necessary, and reference cannot be had to superior authority without detriment to the service.

Powers of a Regimental Court Martial

* Article 77.—A Regimental Court Martial may sentence any Non Commissioned Officer to be reduced to the ranks;—or may sentence any Non-Commissioned Officer or Soldier to be dismissed from the service ;—or to be placed lower in the list of the rank which he holds—or may sentence any Soldier to suffer Corporal Punishment not exceeding one hundred lashes; or Imprisonment, with or without Hard Labor, for any period not exceeding six calendar months ; and to be kept in solitary confinement, to be regulated as aforesaid.

Any such Court Martial may, in addition to the punishment of dismissal, sentence any Non-Commissioned Officer or Soldier to forfeit his arrears of Pay and Allowances due at the time of his discharge, or such proportion thereof as may be required to make good any loss or damage arising out of his misconduct; and in addition to any punishment not involving dismissal from the service, may sentence any Non-Commissioned Officer or Soldier to be put under Stoppages, not exceeding half of his Pay and Allowances, until the amount of such loss or damage be made good.

Article 78.—An Officer Commanding any Detachment of his own Regiment may assemble Regimental Detachment Courts Martial;—and an Officer Commanding a Detachment consisting of men of different Corps may assemble Detachment or line Courts Martial;—and all such Courts shall be constituted in the same manner as Regimental Courts Martial under the provisions of these Articles of War, and shall have the like powers.

And the provisions of these Articles of War relating to Courts Martial held in Regiments shall be taken to apply to Courts Martial held in Detachments, in all practicable cases.

Provided that no Officer on detached Command of less than four Troops or Companies, or of Detachments numerically equal to four Troops or Companies, shall carry into effect any punishment awarded by a Court Martial held by his order, until the Sentence shall have been confirmed by the Officer Commanding the Regiment to which the offender belongs, or by the nearest superior Officer holding a Command of not less than a Regiment;—(who is hereby authorized to confirm the same, in like manner as an Officer Commanding a Regiment is empowered to do, and with the same restrictions;) —except in cases where an immediate example is necessary, and reference cannot be made to such Commanding or Superior Officer without detriment to the Service.

Article 79.—At all Courts Martial, it shall be competent to the Officer convening the Court to instruct the Court, that, should the prisoner be found guilty, and Imprisonment form a part of the Sentence, no portion of the Imprisonment should be Solitary:— or, should Corporal Punishment be awardable to the offender, that it shall not be awarded in the particular case; and the Court will govern itself accordingly.

Execution of Sentences of Courts Martial

Article 80.—In every sentence of death awarded by a General Court Martial, the Court shall specify that the offender shall "suffer death by being hanged by the neck until he be dead," or "by being shot to death," as the Court in their discretion shall deem expedient; and such sentence, if confirmed, shall be carried into effect accordingly.

Article 81.—Whenever the sentence of a General Court Martial shall adjudge Transportation, or sentence of Death shall be commuted by competent authority to Transportation, any of the Sudder Courts shall give effect to such sentence or commuted sentence, on the same being certified to the Court under the authority of the Commander-in-Chief.

And whenever any sentence of a Court Martial shall adjudge imprisonment with labor, or with solitary confinement, or both, or whenever the sentence of a Court Martial shall be commuted to any such imprisonment, it shall be the duty of every Judge, Magistrate, Sheriff, or other officer in charge of a Jail, to give effect to such sentence, on the offender being delivered into his custody, and on being furnished with a copy of the sentence by the Officer Commanding the Division, Field Force, District, or Brigade, within which the trial is held.

Article 82.—Whenever any Soldier shall be sentenced to imprisonment for life, or a sentence of death shall be commuted to imprisonment for life, it shall be lawful for the Commander-in-Chief to order such offender to be transported beyond sea for life, unless there should be special reasons inducing the Commander-in-Chief to think such prisoner not a proper subject for transportation.

Article 83.—Persons sentenced to imprisonment by Courts Martial shall be imprisoned in a public prison, or in any other fit place which the Commander-in-Chief shall from time to time direct.

Article 84.—Every Soldier sentenced to imprisonment with hard labor shall, previous to undergoing such punishment, be struck off the strength of his Corps from the date of confirmation of such sentence ; and no Soldier who has undergone such punishment for any period shall be capable of being re-admitted in the ranks, or of receiving pension on discharge.

Article 85.—Offenders sentenced to dismissal for disgraceful conduct;

And offenders subject to Corporal Punishment or to Imprisonment with Hard Labor for disgraceful conduct shall, on any such sentence being confirmed, be dismissed with ignominy.

Article 86.— In every case wherein a fine or stoppages shall be adjudged by a Court Martial, any arrears of pay or public money due to the offender shall be available, under an order from the Commander-in-Chief, for the payment of the amount so adjudged.

And no Soldier sentenced to pay a fine or to stoppages, to make good any loss or damage arising out of his misconduct, shall be continued under forfeiture or stop pages under any one such sentence for any period exceeding one year ; and no Soldier shall be at any one time placed under forfeiture or stoppages exceeding in the whole the amount of half of his Pay and Allowances, nor be liable to be put under stop pages prospectively while actually under stoppages to the amount of half of his Pay and Allowances.

Forms of Proceeding

Article 87.—Trials by Courts Martial may be carried on between the hours of six in the morning and four in the afternoon, and not otherwise, except in cases which may require an immediate example.

Article 88.—At General Courts Martial a Judge Advocate, or a European Officer of not less than ten years service, shall be appointed to conduct the proceedings.

At all Courts Martial inferior to General, a European Officer of not less than four years standing in the service, except in cases where no Officer of that standing may be available, or the Adjutant of the Regiment shall be appointed to conduct the proceedings.

Article 89.—An Interpreter shall be appointed to all Courts Martial; and any Interpreter available at the Station where the Court Martial may sit shall be appointed as occasion may require by the Officer Commanding at such Station, on application from the Judge Advocate or Superintending Officer at such Court Martial. But in situations where the services of an Interpreter are not available, the Superintending Officer at the Court Martial shall perform the duty of Interpreter.

Article 90.—At all Courts Martial the Senior Officer shall sit as President without being so appointed by Warrant. Provided that all Subadar Majors are to take precedence according to the dates of their Commissions, and above all Native Officers holding the rank of Subadar or Jemadar ; and that Sirdar Bahadoors and Bahadoors shall rank only according to their respective Commissions of Subedar Major, Subadar, or Jemadar. Rissaldars will take rank with Subadars, and Naib Rissaldars with Jemadars, according to the dates of their respective Commissions.

In case of the death or unavoidable absence of the President, the next Senior Member shall take the place of President, and the trial shall proceed, provided that the Court shall still consist of at least the number of Members of which such Court U directed to consist by these Articles of War.

Article 91.—No Finding or Sentence of a Court Martial shall be revised more than once, and no Evidence shall be received on such revision. For the purpose of such revision the President and all the Members shall be convened, if possible. But if any of them should be unavoidably absent, the remaining Members may proceed with such revision, provided they are not fewer than the smallest number directed in these Articles respectively. When all the same Members do not meet, the circumstances are to be duly certified on the face of the proceedings.

Manner of Voting

Article 92.—All the Members of a Court Martial are to preserve order, and in giving their votes upon all matters are to begin with the youngest; and in all cases where a sentence of death may not be awarded, the decision shall be by the majority of Members present, provided the number of Members present be not less than that required by the preceding Articles; but in case of an equality of votes, the decision shall be in favor of the prisoner; the President at a Court-Martial shall vote with the other Members, but shall have no casting vote. Provided, that in cases of an equality of votes upon other questions than the finding and the sentence, the President shall have a casting vote.

Article 93.—No sentence of death shall be given against any offender by a Court-Martial, unless two-thirds of the Members present concur therein, or four, where the Court consist of five Members, or five where the Court consist of seven.

Affirmations

Article 94. —On the assembly of a Court Martial, the Judge Advocate or Superintending European Officer shall administer to the Interpreter the following Solemn Affirmation:

> "I, A. B., solemnly affirm, in the presence of Almighty God, that I will faithfully interpret and translate the proceedings of the Court, and that I will not divulge the sentence until it shall have been published by authority; and further that I will not disclose or discover the vote or opinion of any particular member of the Court, unless required to give evidence thereof by a Court of Justice or Court-Martial, in due course of Law."

In case of the unavoidable absence of an Interpreter, the European Superintending Officer of a Court Martial inferior to General, shall make the Solemn Affirmation prescribed for the Interpreter.

The Judge Advocate or Superintending Officer shall then cause the following Solemn Affirmation to be made by each Member:

> "I, A. B., solemnly affirm, in the presence of Almighty God, that I will duly administer justice according to the Articles of War without partiality, favor, or affection, and, if any doubt shall arise, then according to my conscience, the best of my understanding, and the custom of War in the like cases, and that I will not divulge the sentence of the Court until it shall be published by authority; and further, that I will not disclose or discover the vote or opinion of any particular Member of the Court, unless required to give evidence thereof by a Court of Justice or a " Court Martial, in due course of Law."

The following Solemn Affirmation shall then be administered by the Interpreter to the Judge Advocate or Superintending Officer:

> "I, A. B., solemnly affirm, in the presence of Almighty God, that I will not upon any account whatsoever disclose or discover the vote or opinion of any particular Member of the Court Martial, unless required to give evidence thereof as a witness by a Court of Justice, or a Court Martial, in due course of law, and that I will not, unless it be necessary for the due

discharge of my official duties, disclose the sentence of the Court, until it shall be published by authority."

Provided, that it shall be necessary to re-administer these solemn Affirmations on the commencement of fresh trials before the same Court.

Article 95.—All persons who give evidence at a Court Martial are to be examined on Oath, according to the forms of their respective religions, or on affirmation — and persons of the Hindoo or Mahomedan persuasion shall make Affirmation to the following effect:

"I solemnly affirm, in the presence of Almighty God, that what I shall state shall be the truth, the whole truth, and nothing but the truth."

And if any person, making such Affirmation as aforesaid, shall wilfully and falsely state any matter or thing, which, if the same had been sworn, would have amounted to perjury, every such offender shall be subject to the same punishment to which persons convicted of perjury are subject.

Summoning Witnesses not amenable to these Articles

Article 96.—In all cases where persons required as witnesses before a Court Martial, may not be amenable to Military Law, the Judge Advocate or Commanding Officer shall transmit, to the Magistrate within whose jurisdiction the witness may reside, his summons for the attendance of such person, and the Magistrate shall cause the witness to be duly summoned.

Powers and Duties of Provost Marshal

Article 97.—For the prompt and instant repression of all irregularities and crimes which may be committed by Troops in the Field and on the Line of March, Provosts Marshal shall be appointed by the Commander-in-Chief, and their powers shall be regulated according to the established Usages of War and Rules of the Service. Their duties are to take charge of Prisoners confined for offences of a general description; to preserve good Order and Discipline; to prevent Breaches of both by Soldiers and Followers of the Army, and to punish on the spot, on the same day, those whom they may find in the immediate act of committing Breaches of good Order and Military Discipline. Provided, that the punishment be limited to the necessity of the case, and shall accord with the orders which the Provosts may from time to time receive from the Commander of the Forces in the Field; and, whatever may be the crime, the Provost Marshal or his Assistant shall see the offender commit the act, for which summary punishment may be inflicted, or if the Provost Marshal or his Assistant should not see the offender actually commit the crime, but that sufficient proof can be established of the offender's guilt, a Report shall be made to the Commander of the Army in the Field, who is hereby empowered to deal with the case as he may deem most conducive to the maintenance of good Order and Military Discipline. The duties of Provosts Marshal being limited to the punishment of offenders whom they may detect in the actual commission of any crime, the General Commanding the Forces in the Field will cause them to exercise the powers entrusted to them in such manner and under such circumstances as he may consider best calculated to prevent and instantly to repress crimes injurious to the discipline of the East India Company's Army and the Public Service.

Trials by European Courts Martial

Article 98.—At any Presidency where the Native Troops have hitherto been authorized to claim to be tried by European Courts Martial, every person amenable to these Articles of War, and who may be under orders for trial by a Court Martial, shall have the right to claim to be tried by European Officers; and should he make such claim, the Court, whether General, or District, or Regimental, shall be composed of European Commissioned Officers, and the number of Members and the proceedings shall be governed in all respects by the provisions of these Articles.

And it shall be competent to the Governor General of India in Council by a General Order to authorize the Native Troops of any of the Presidencies to claim to be tried in like manner by European Courts Martial.

SECTION IV

Effects of the Dead

* Article 99.—When any Officer or Soldier, or any person receiving public pay drawn by any Officer in charge of a Public Department belonging to the Army, may die, or be killed in the service, the Commanding Officer of the Regiment or Party, or Officer in charge of the Department, shall, if no Heir or Executor be present, secure his Effects, and direct an inventory thereof to be taken, a duplicate of which is to be lodged in the office of the Adjutant, or Officer in charge of the Department.

* Article 100.—If there be no Heir or Executor on the spot the Effects are to be publicly sold; the Commanding Officer of the Regiment, or Party, or Officer in charge of the Department, after discharging the debts of the deceased, viz., the expense of Funeral Ceremonies, his Debts in Camp or Quarter, and Regimental Debts of every description, shall account for the residue to the Heir or Heirs declared by will, whether written or verbal, or nominated in the Regimental Register, or, in failure of such, to the legal representative of the deceased ; and in the event of no Executor, Heir, or other representative of the deceased attending and establishing his claim within twelve months from the date of the casualty, the amount in the hands of the Officer having charge of the Estate is to be remitted to the General Treasury at the Presidency.

SECTION V

Miscellaneous

Article 101.—The Effects of Deserters are to be publicly sold, and the proceeds, after payment of Regimental Debts, remitted by the Officer Commanding the Corps to which the Deserter belongs, to the General Treasury at the Presidency.

Article 102.—All powers and provisions contained in these Articles relating to the Commander-in-Chief shall be construed to extend to the Commander-in-Chief at any Presidency, and to the Officer Commanding the Forces for the time being at any Presidency, unless when otherwise provided.

All powers and provisions contained in these Articles relating to Soldiers, shall be construed to extend to Non-Commissioned Officers, unless when otherwise provided.

Article 103.—When any portion of the Troops belonging to one Presidency shall be serving within the limits of another Presidency, such Troops shall be considered as placed, during such service, under the orders and authority of the Commander-in-Chief, or Commanding Officer of the Forces of the Presidency within which they are serving, for all- the purposes of these Articles of War, in the same manner as though they belonged to such Presidency ; and all the provisions of these Articles of War, which relate to the trial and punishment of offenders belonging to the Presidency within which the trial is held, are hereby declared applicable to the trial and punishment of offenders amenable to these Articles of War serving within such Presidency. Provided always, that it shall be lawful for the Governor General in Council in his executive capacity, to direct that the Troops, or any part thereof of any Presidency, whilst serving without the limits of such Presidency, shall continue under the orders and authority of the Commander-in-Chief, or Commanding Officer of Forces of the Presidency to which they belong, for all purposes of these Articles.

Article 104.—Any Officer Commanding any portion of the East India Company's Troops which may at any time be serving in any place out of Her Majesty's Dominions, or of the possessions or Territories which are or may be under the Government of the said Company, or of the Territories of those States in alliance with the said Company, in which the said Company's Forces are permanently stationed, shall, upon complaint made to him of any offence committed against the property or person of any inhabitant or resident in any such countries, by any person serving with or belonging to the Company's Army, being under the immediate command of any such Officer, summon and cause to assemble a General Court Martial, which shall consist of not less than three Officers at the least, for the purpose of trying any such person, notwithstanding any such Officer shall not have received any Warrant empowering him to assemble Courts Martial; and every such Court Martial shall have the same powers, in regard to summoning and examining witnesses, trial of, and sentence upon any such offenders as are granted by these Articles to General Courts Martial; provided that no sentence of any such Court Martial shall be executed until the General Commanding-in-Chief the Army to which the Division, Brigade, Detachment, or Party to which any person so tried, convicted and adjudged to suffer punishment shall belong, shall have approved and confirmed the same; except where such sentence shall not exceed the power granted by these Articles to a District, or Garrison Court Martial, in which case the Officer by whom the Court is convened is hereby authorized to confirm, or commute, or mitigate, or remit the same; reporting the proceedings to the said General Commanding-in-Chief.

Article 105.—General Courts Martial only shall have the power to try Commissioned Officers; or to pass Sentence of Death or Transportation on any offenders.

Article 106. —No person, being acquitted or convicted before a Court Martial of any offence, shall be liable to be tried a second time by the same or any other Court Martial for the same offence. Provided always, that after a Soldier shall have been found guilty by a Court Martial of any Military offence, such Court Martial shall inquire into and receive evidence of any previous conviction of such Soldier before a Court Martial or a Court of Justice, and shall inquire into the general character of such Soldier; for the purpose of affixing the punishment to which he is liable to be sentenced for the offence of which he has been so found guilty.

Provided that no such evidence shall in any case be received until the Court shall have ascertained that such Soldier had previously to his trial received notice of the intention to produce such evidence on the same. And it is hereby directed that such notice shall be given to all Soldiers previous to trial.

* Article 107.—No Non- Commissioned Officer shall be reduced to the ranks but by the sentence of a Court Martial, or by order of the Commander-in-Chief of the Presidency to which the offender shall belong. Provided that no Non-Commissioned Officer shall be reduced to the ranks for any limited period ; nor suspended from his rank ; nor reduced from a higher to a lower grade of Non-Commissioned Officer ; nor sentenced to suffer Corporal Punishment, or imprisonment without being first reduced to the ranks.

* Article 108.—Any Officer or Soldier thinking himself wronged by his Superior or other Officer, is to complain thereof to the Commanding Officer of his Troop or Company, by whom if the grievance be not redressed, such Officer, Non-Commissioned Officer, or Soldier, may complain to the Commanding Officer of his Regiment, who is hereby required to examine into such complaint, or remit it to his superior authority as the circumstances may require; but if the complaint should appear to be frivolous or groundless, the party preferring it shall be liable to be punished according to the sentence of a General or other Court Martial in manner hereinbefore mentioned; provided that such offender shall not be liable to be sentenced to dismissal nor to suffer Corporal Punishment or Imprisonment with hard labor.

Article 109.—In case of light offences, a Commanding Officer may, without the intervention of a Court Martial, award extra drill, with or without pack, for a period not exceeding fifteen days; restriction to Barrack limits not exceeding fifteen days; confinement in the Quarter Guard, or Defaulter's Room, not exceeding seven days; removal from Staff situations or acting appointments; or may order Soldiers to be employed in piling and unpiling shot; and in cleaning accoutrements of men in Hospital ; but none of these descriptions of punishment shall be awardable by Sentence of a Court Martial. And a Commanding Officer may award solitary confinement not exceeding seven days.

Provided that Soldiers in confinement shall be liable to be ordered to attend ordinary drill.

Article 110.— Any Officer, or Soldier, who shall be taken prisoner by the Enemy, shall forfeit all claim to pay and allowances during the period of his remaining a prisoner, and until he shall again return to the service ; when, if he can establish, before a Court Martial, that he was unavoidably taken prisoner in the course of service, and resisted as long as he was able, and that he hath riot served with or assisted the Enemy, and that he hath returned as soon as possible to the service, he shall be entitled to receive either the whole, or such a portion of his arrears of pay and allowances as the Government of the Presidency to which he may belong shall deter mine, after the opinion or finding of such Court Martial shall have been confirmed by the Commander-in-Chief.

SECTION VI

Mode of dealing with Offences not Military

Article 111.—In all places within the jurisdiction of any Civil Judicature established by appointment of Her Majesty or of the said Company, Officers and Soldiers accused of capital crimes, or of violence, or of offences against person and property, punishable by such Civil Judicature, shall be delivered over to a Magistrate to lie proceeded against according to Law.

And all Officers and Soldiers are hereby required to assist the Officers of Justice in apprehending and securing any person so accused.

Crimes to be tried by Courts Martial where no regular Criminal Tribunals exist

Article 112.—In any place within the limits of the Charter of the East India Company, whether in or out of the British Territories, where there may be no Civil Judicature appointed by Her Majesty or the said Company for the trial of persons accused of offences ordinarily cognizable by Civil Tribunals, such offences, when committed by Officers or Soldiers, shall be cognizable by Court Martial.

Article 113.—General Courts Martial shall have cognizance, ordinarily, of offences punishable with Death;

Transportation for Life;

Imprisonment for Life;

Imprisonment for a period which may extend to 1 4 years;

Imprisonment for a period which may extend to 7 years.

Article 114.—District, or Garrison Courts Martial shall have cognizance, ordinarily, of offences punishable with imprisonment for a period which may extend to three years, and, by special order, of offences ordinarily cognizable by General Courts Martial not liable to the punishment of death or transportation, with power to sentence persons convicted of such offences to imprisonment for any period not exceeding three years.

Article 115.—Regimental, Detachment, of- Line Courts Martial, shall have cognizance, ordinarily, of offences punishable with imprisonment for a period not exceeding six calendar months, and, by special order, of offences ordinarily cognizable by District or Garrison Courts Martial, with power to sentence persons convicted of such offences to imprisonment for a period not exceeding six calendar months.

General Court Martial

Punishment of Death

Article 116.—Any Officer or Soldier who shall be convicted by a General Court Martial of the crime of "Murder," shall be sentenced to suffer death, by being hanged by the neck until he be dead.

If any injury intended against one person shall, through mistake or accident, light upon another person, and kill him, such killing shall be deemed to be murder, whensoever it would have been murder had the person against whom such injury was intended been killed.

Whensoever death shall result from any injury wilfully caused by an offender, but without his intending such injury to light on any person in particular, such offender shall be guilty of murder, if the offence would have been murder had he intended to do the injury to the person killed.

Offences punishable by Transportation for Life

Article 117.— Any Officer or Soldier who shall be convicted by a General Court Martial of any of the offences hereinafter mentioned, accompanied with an attempt to commit murder, or with wounding or other corporal injury to any person endangering the life of such person: That is to say,

1st.—Breaking or attempting to break by day or night into any Dwelling House, Tent, Boat, or other habitation, or into any building or place used for the preservation of property, with the intent to rob or steal.

2nd.—Robbery or attempt to rob.

3rd.—Stealing or attempting to steal in a house, or from the person:—

Shall be sentenced by such General Court Martial to imprisonment with or without hard labour and transportation for life.

Offences punishable by Imprisonment which may extend to 14 Years

Article 118.—Any Officer or Soldier who shall be convicted by a General Court Martial of any of the offences specified in the last Article, accompanied with wounding or other corporal injury to any person not endangering the life of such person:—or

Article 119.—Of wounding with intent to murder, whether the person wounded be the person whom the offender intended to murder or another;—or

Article 120—Of Robbery, by open violence or Dacoity, that is to say, going forth in the day or in the night with an offensive weapon, or in a gang, with or without an offensive weapon, with the intention of committing robbery, and by force or intimidation, robbing or attempting to rob any person in any place, or attacking by open violence any house or place of habitation, or any place in which property may be kept, for the purpose of robbery; — or

Article 121.—Of breaking into any Dwelling House, Tent, Boat, or other place of habitation, between sunset and sunrise, with intent to rob or steal:— or

Article 122.—Of breaking into any such place of habitation, or into anyplace used for the preservation of property, and stealing therefrom property the value of which shall exceed 100 Company's Rupees;—or

Article 123.—Of purchasing or receiving plundered or stolen property knowing it to have been obtained by robbery, by open violence, or by theft or robbery aggravated as described in Article 118 or Article 119;—

Shall be sentenced by such General Court Martial to imprisonment, with or without Hard Labor, for a period not exceeding 14 years.

Offences punishable by Imprisonment not exceeding Seven Years

Article 124. — Any Officer or Soldier who shall be convicted by a General Court Martial of culpable Homicide not amounting to wilful murder; --or

Article 125.—Of premeditated affray, attended with Homicide, or severe wounding, or other aggravating circumstances;---or

Article 126.—Of intentionally wounding, maiming, or otherwise doing corporal injury to any person;-- or

Article 127.—Of accidentally wounding, maiming, or otherwise doing corporal injury to any person, with the intention of doing such injury or to another person;--or

Article 128.—Of breaking into any Dwelling House, Tent, Boat, or other place of Habitation, or into any place used for the preservation of property, between sunrise and sunset, with intent to steal therein;---or

Article 129.—Of stealing from any habitation, or from any person, any property exceeding Three Hundred Company's Rupees in value;--- or

Article 130.—Of having purchased any property so stolen exceeding in value Three Hundred Company's Rupees, knowing it to have been stolen;--- or

Article 131.—Of Arson; ---or

Article 132.—Of an Unnatural Crime;--- or

Article 133.—Of Rape;--- or

Article 134.—Of enticing and taking away, or of causing to be enticed or taken away for any unlawful purpose any unmarried woman under the age of 15 years;--- or

Article 135.—Of stealing a child under the age of 8 years:—Shall be Sentenced by such General Court Martial to suffer Imprisonment, with or without Hard Labor, for any period not exceeding seven years.

District or Garrison Courts Martial

Offences punishable by Imprisonment not exceeding Three Years

Article 136.—-It shall be competent to the Commander-in-Chief, and to any Officer having authority to convene District, or Garrison Courts Martial, to cause offenders, not being Commissioned Officers, accused of any of the offences specified in the preceding Articles of War, for which the punishment of Death or Imprisonment or Transportation for Life is not provided therein, to be tried for such offence before a District, or Garrison Court Martial, and such Court shall have power, on conviction, to sentence any such offender to Imprisonment, with or without Hard Labor, for any period not exceeding three years.

Article 137.—Any Officer or Soldier who shall be convicted by a General, District, or Garrison Court Martial, of stealing from any habitation, or from the person, any property, of value not exceeding Three Hundred Company's Rupees, but exceeding- Fifty Company's Rupees;——or

Article 138.—Of having purchased or received any stolen property of value not exceeding Three Hundred Company's Rupees, knowing it to have been stolen, but not under aggravating circumstances;--- or

Article 139.—Of having stolen property in his possession, and of having kept possession of such property after becoming aware of its having been stolen:—

Shall be sentenced by such Court to suffer Imprisonment, with or without Hard Labor, for any period not exceeding three years.

Regimental, Detachment, or Line Courts Martial

Offences punishable by Imprisonment not exceeding Six Months

Article 140.--- It shall be competent to any Officer having authority to convene a Court Martial, to cause offenders, not being Commissioned Officers, accused of any of the offences specified in the preceding Articles of War, for which nopunishment exceeding Imprisonment with Hard Labour for three years is therein provided, to be tried before Regimental, or Detachment, or Line Courts Martial, and any such Court shall have power, on conviction, to sentence any such offender to suffer Imprisonment, with or without Hard Labor, for any period not exceeding six calendar months.

Offences punishable by Imprisonment from six months to one year, according to the description of Court

Article 141.—Any Officer or Soldier who shall be convicted of stealing property to the value of Fifty Company's Rupees, or of less value;-- or

Article 142.—Of Assault or Affray, unattended with homicide, severe wounding, or aggravating circumstances;—

Shall be Sentenced to suffer Imprisonment, with or without Hard Labor, for any period not exceeding one year, by the award of a General, or District, or Garrison Court Martial; or, for any period not exceeding six calendar months, by the award of a Regimental, or Detachment, or Line Court Martial.

Offences punishable by Imprisonment from six months to two years, according to the description of Court

Article 143.—Any Officer or Soldier who shall be convicted resisting the process of a Magistrate or Police Officer; or

Article 144.—Of having committed any offence against person or property, for which provision is not already made in the preceding Articles of War;—

Shall be Sentenced to suffer Imprisonment, for any period not exceeding two years, by the award of a General Court Martial, not exceeding one year, by the award of a District, or Garrison Court Martial ; and not exceeding six calendar months, by the award of a Regimental, or Detachment, or Line Court Martial.

Article 145.—Any Officer or Soldier who shall be convicted by a General, or District, or Regimental Court Martial, of having been present, aiding and abetting, or of having caused, instigated, or procured, the commission of any of the offences specified in any of the preceding Articles, shall be sentenced by such Court to the punishment therein provided for such offence, and awardable by General, or District, or Regimental Courts Martial, respectively.

Article 146.—No sentence of death shall be carried into effect until confirmed by the Commander-in-Chief, nor if the trial shall have been held within the British Territories forming part of either of the Presidencies of Fort William, Fort St. George, and Bombay, respectively, until such confirmation shall have been concurred in by the Government of the Presidency where such trial shall have been held.

Article 147.—The Commander-in-Chief is authorized at his discretion to confirm any sentence of death, or to remit such sentence, or to commute it into imprisonment with hard labour and transportation for life, or into imprisonment with Hard Labor for any term of years.

Article 148.—No sentence of transportation shall be carried into effect until confirmed by the Commander-in-Chief, and the Commander-in-Chief is authorized at his discretion to confirm any such sentence, or to commute it into imprisonment, with or without Hard Labor, for any period of time.

Article 149.—It shall be competent to any Officer having authority to confirm the sentences of a General or other Court Martial, to remit any sentence passed by such Court Martial, or to mitigate such sentence, by substituting simple imprisonment for imprisonment with hard labor, or by reducing the period of imprisonment, or by directing the discharge of the offender in lieu of any imprisonment.

Article 150.—But no sentence of imprisonment with hard labor, passed by a Regimental, or Detachment, or Line Court Martial, and confirmed either in whole or in part by the Commanding Officer; and no award of discharge substituted for other punishment, as aforesaid, by such Commanding Officer, shall be carried into effect, without the sanction and authority of the Officer Commanding the Division or Field-Force, or District, or Brigade, (being the Senior Officer on the spot,) in which the offender may be serving, or of the Senior Officer on the spot in the field.

Article 151.—A person who may have been tried for any offence by a Court Martial, under the authority of these Articles of War, shall not be tried for the same in any other Court whatsoever, and no person who shall have been acquit ted or convicted of any offence Joy a Court of Civil Judicature shall be punished by a Court Martial for the same, otherwise than by Cashiering or Dismissal from the service.

Article 152.—The Regulations at present in force at any Presidency, by which the office and powers of Commissariat Officers, or Officers in charge of the Police or Superintendents of Bazars, are defined and controled ; or by which Punchaycts are constituted and guided ; or by which, jurisdiction is given to Courts Martial over offences committed by persons amenable to the Articles of War, within certain limits beyond or around Cantonments; are hereby declared to be in full force, and the same shall continue to be observed at the several Presidencies respectively.

SECTION VII

Application of the Articles

Article 153.— All Officers and Soldiers, all Drivers, Farriers, Trumpeters and Drummers ; all Hospital Attendants, Sub-Assistant Surgeons, Native Doctors, and Dressers; all Artificers and Labourers, Sutlers, Followers, public and private, or others attached to or serving with any part of the Army, are to be governed by these Articles and subject to trial by Courts Martial.

Provided, that persons of European descent, (whether on the side of their father or mother) professing the Christian religion, shall not be amenable to these Articles; but if belonging to the descriptions mentioned in this Article, (and not being Her Majesty's natural born subjects, born in Europe, or the children of such subjects,) shall be tried and punished in the same manner as persons are who are subject to the Mutiny Act and Articles of War in force for the better government of the Officers and Soldiers in the European Service of the East India Company.

Promulgation of the Articles

Article 154.—These Articles are to be translated into the several languages of the different Presidencies, and the parts following, viz., the second Section, together with the following Articles in other Sections which are marked with an* (Asterisk) *viz.* 2, 4, 72, 75, 77, 99, 100, 107, and 108, are to be read once every six months at the head of every Regiment, Troop or Company mustered in the Service, and to every Recruit at the period of his enlistment.

Act No. XIX. of 1847

Passed on the 18th December 1847

An Act to make certain Amendments in the Articles of War for the government of the Native Officers and Soldiers in the Military Service of the East India Company: Passed by the Governor-General of India in Council, on the 18th December, 1847.

WHEREAS it is expedient to make certain amendments in the Articles of War provided by Act XX of 1845, for the government of the native officers and soldiers in the military service of the East-India Company, and for the administration of justice by Courts-martial to be holden on such officers and soldiers:

Repeal of Act XX of 1845

I. It is therefore hereby enacted, that from and after the First day of March 1848, the Articles of War provided by Act XX of 1845 are repealed.

Enactment of the following Articles of War

II. And it is enacted, that the following Articles of War shall, from and after the said day, be the Articles of War for the government of the said Native Officers and Soldiers in the Military Service of the said Company, and for the administration of justice by Courts-martial to be holden on such Officers and Soldiers. Provided always, that all crimes and offences committed against the Articles of War provided by Act XX of 1845, aforesaid, may be inquired of and punished in like manner as if they had been committed against the Articles of War hereby provided; and that every Warrant for holding any Court-martial under the Articles of War provided by the Act XX of 1845 aforesaid shall remain in full force, notwithstanding the repeal of such Articles ; and that all proceedings of any Court-martial upon any trial begun under such Articles shall not be discontinued by the repeal of the same.

ARTICLES OF WAR

SECTION I

OF ENLISTING AND DISCHARGES

Enlisting

Article 1.—Every Recruit, prior to being enrolled in his Regiment, shall have the First Four Articles of the Second Section of these Articles of War read and explained to him, and when reported fit for duty in the ranks, such declaration as is now used, if any, in the respective

Presidencies, shall be made to him by the Officer Commanding, in front of the Regiment or Corps, in presence of the Native Officers and Soldiers, and an oath or declaration shall then be required from him, according to the forms of his religion, such oath and declaration to be the like as are now used in the respective Presidencies.

Dismissal and discharge

*Article 2.—No Commissioned Officer shall be dismissed except by the Sentence of a General Court-martial. No Non-Commissioned Officer or Soldier shall be discharged as a punishment except by the Sentence of a Court-martial, or by order of the Commander-in-Chief at the Presidency to which he may belong. Every such dismissal or discharge shall include forfeiture of all claim to pension. Provided also, that the Governor General in Council in his executive capacity, and the Governor in Council of any Presidency to Which a Commissioned or Non-Commissioned Officer or Soldier may belong, shall have power to order his dismissal or discharge.

Discharge

Article 3.—All Non-Commissioned Officers and Soldiers discharged the Service, shall be furnished by the Commanding Officer of the Regiment with a Discharge Certificate, made out in the Vernacular language of the individual discharged, with an English translation, expressing the authority for, and cause of such discharge, and the period of his entire Service in the Army.

Re-enlisting

*Article 4.—No Non-Commissioned Officer or Soldier shall enlist himself in any other Regiment without a regular discharge from his former Regiment, under the penalty of being reputed a Deserter, and suffering accordingly.

SECTION II

CRIMES AND PUNISHMENTS

Crimes punishable with Death, Transportation, Corporal Punishment, Imprisonment, or Dismissal

Crimes

Article 5 —Any officer, or soldier, who shall begin, excite, cause, or join in any mutiny or sedition in the Regiment or Corps to which he belongs, or in any other Corps or Regiment whatsoever, on any pretence whatever; or who, being present at any mutiny or sedition, shall not use his utmost endeavours to suppress it; or who, coming to the knowledge of any mutiny, intended mutiny, or concealed combination against the State, shall not without delay give information thereof to his Commanding Officer;—or

Article 6—Who shall strike his superior Officer, or shall draw, or offer to draw, or lift up any weapon, or use or oiler any violence against him, whether on or off duty, and under all circumstances in which his superior Officer may be distinguishable as such in any manner;—or

Article 7—Who shall disobey any lawful Command of his superior Officer;—or

Article 8—Who shall desert from the East India Company's Service, (whether or not he shall re-enter or re-enlist in the same;)—or

Article 9—Who, being a Sentry, in time of war or alarm, shall sleep upon his post ; or shall leave it before regularly relieved, or without leave ; or shall plunder or injure the property placed under his charge;—or

Article 10— Who shall shamefully abandon or deliver up any Garrison, Fortress, Post, or Guard, committed to his charge, or which it was his duty to defend ; or who shall use means to induce any other Officer or Soldier so to abandon or deliver up any such Garrison, Fortress, Post Or Guard;—or

Article 11—Who shall treacherously make known the watch-word to any person not entitled to receive it, according to the Rules and Discipline of War;—or

Article 12—Who shall hold correspondence with or give intelligence to the Enemy, or any person in arms against the State, either directly or indirectly ; or who, coming to the knowledge of such correspondence or communication, snail not discover it immediately to the Commanding Officer;—or

Article 13—Who shall, directly or indirectly, assist or relieve the Enemy, or persons in arms against the State, with money, victuals, or ammunition ; or shall knowingly harbour or protect any Enemy or person in arms against the State;—or

Article 14—Who shall treacherously release, wilfully aid or connive at the escape of any enemy or person in arms against the State, placed as a prisoner under his charge;—or

Article 15.—Who shall misbehave himself before the enemy, or persons in arms against whom he is led, or use means to induce others so to misbehave ;—or

Article 16—Who shall, in presence of an enemy, or of persons in arms against whom he is led, shamefully cast away his arms or ammunition;—or

Article 17 —Who shall leave his Commanding Officer, or his Post, or Colours, or party, in time of action, to go in search of plunder;—or

Article 18—Who, in time of war, shall do violence to any person bringing provisions or other necessaries to the Camp or quarters of the forces ; or shall force a safeguard ; or break into any house, or other place for plunder; or plunder fields, or gardens, or other property ;—or

Article 19—Who, in time of war, shall, by discharging fire arms, drawing swords, beating drums, making signals, using words or by any means whatever, intentionally occasion false alarms, in Action, Camp, Garrison, or Quarters; —or

Article 20—Who shall without proper authority, release any State Prisoner, or, through carelessness or neglect, shall suffer any such prisoner to escape : or shall connive at the plunder or injury of property in time of War, or the plunder or injury of Treasure, or of a Magazine, or Dock Yard, by the sentry or Guard in whose charge such property, or Treasure, or Magazine, or Dock lard is placed;—or

Article 21—Who, being a Sentry placed over any State Prisoner, or over Treasure, or over a Magazine, or Dock Yard, shall quit his post without being regularly relieved, or without leave ; or shall sleep upon his post; or shall plunder or injure the property placed under his charge;

Punishment

Shall, if an Officer, on conviction, suffer Death, or Transportation for life, or be dismissed the Service;

And, if a Soldier, shall, on conviction, suffer Death or Transportation for life; or Imprisonment, with or without hard labour, for life, or for any term of years ; and with or without solitary confinement for any portion or portions of the term of imprisonment, not exceeding twenty-eight days at a time, nor eighty-four days in any one year, with intervals between the periods of solitary confinement of not less duration than such periods of solitary confinement; or shall suffer Corporal Punishment ; or Dismissal from the Service ; as by a General Court-martial shall be awarded. Provided that no Soldier shall be kept in solitary confinement more than eighty-four days in any one year, whether by the sentence of one or more Courts-martial, or by order of his Commanding Officer.

Crimes punishable by General Court-martial with Dismissal or Suspension of Officers, or by General or District Court-martial with Dismissal, Reduction, Corporal Punishment, or simple Imprisonment, with or without solitary confinement, or Loss of Standing on the Roll of Non-Commissioned Officers and Soldiers

Crimes

Article 22.—Any Officer or Soldier who shall in operations in the field, spread reports, by words or letters, calculated to create unnecessary alarm in the Troops, or in the vicinity, or in rear of the Army;—or

Article 23.—Who shall, in Action or previously to going into Action, use words tending to create Alarm or Despondency;—or

Article 24.—Who shall be drunk when on, or for duty, or on Parade, or on the Line of March;—or

Article 25. —Who shall strike or force any Sentry:—-or

Article 26.—Any Soldier who shall be grossly insubordinate or insolent to his superior Officer in the execution of his Office; or grossly insubordinate and violent in the presence of a Court-martial ;—or

Article 27.—Who, being on actual Service, shall refuse to assist in making field works;

Punishment

Shall, if an Officer, on conviction, be sentenced to be dismissed the Service, or to be suspended from Rank and Pay and Allowances; And, if a Soldier, shall, on conviction, before a General, or District, or Garrison Court-martial, be sentenced to suffer such punishment as a General, or District, or Garrison Court-martial is by these Articles of War respectively empowered to award.

Provided, that such Offender shall not be sentenced to Death or Transportation or Imprisonment with hard labour.

Crimes punishable by General Court-martial with Dismissal or Suspension of Officers or by General or District Court-martial, with Dismissal, Reduction, Imprisonment, with or without hard labour, and with or without solitary confinement, or Loss of Standing on the Roll of Non-Commissioned Officers and Soldiers

Crimes

Article 28.—Any Officer who shall behave in a manner unbecoming the character of an Officer; (the fact or facts whereon the charge is grounded being clearly specified therein;—or

Article 29.—Any Officer or Soldier who shall advise or persuade any other Officer or Soldier to desert, or who shall connive at such desertion; or who shall knowingly receive and entertain any Deserter, and shall not immediately on discovery give notice to his superior Officer ; or shall not cause such Deserter to be apprehended by the Civil Power;—or

Article 30.—Who shall obtain or attempt to obtain for himself, or for any Officer or Soldier, or for any other person whatsoever, any Pension or Allowance, by any false Statement, Certificate, or Document, or by the omission of the true Statement, or Certificate, or Document;—or

Article 31. —Who shall knowingly make a false Return or Report, to any his Superior Officer authorized to call for a Return or Report, of the state of the men under his Command, or of Arms, Ammunition, Clothing, or other Stores thereunto belonging, or of which he may have charge;—or

Article 32.—Who, at any post, or on the march, shall illegally and against the will of the parties extort money or property of any description, as fees or duties, or on any pretence whatever; or shall, without authority, exact from villagers or others, carriage, porterage, or provisions;—or

Article 33.—Who shall wantonly and intentionally defile any place dedicated to religious worship, or shall wantonly, and intentionally insult the religious prejudices of other persons;

Punishment

Shall, if an Officer, on conviction, be sentenced to be dismissed the Service, or to be suspended from Rank and Pay and Allowances;

And, if a Soldier, shall, on conviction before a General, District or Garrison Court-martial, be sentenced to suffer such punishment as a General, or District, or Garrison Court-martial is by these Articles of War respectively empowered to award.

Provided, that such Offender shall not be sentenced to Death, or Transportation, or Corporal Punishment.

Crimes punishable by General Court-martial with Dismissal or Suspension of Officers, or by any Court-martial with Dismissal, Reduction, Imprisonment, with or without hard labour, and with or without solitary confinement, or Loss of Standing on the Roll of Non-Commissioned Officers and Soldiers

Crimes

Article 34.—Any Officer or Soldier, who, being under arrest or in confinement shall leave his arrest or confinement before he is set at liberty by competent authority;—or

Article 35.—Who shall malinger, feign or intentionally produce disease or infirmity; or intentionally delay his cure; or intentionally aggravate his disease or infirmity;—or

Article 36.—Who shall, without orders, commit any waste or spoil, or plunder, or shall injure or destroy any property;—or

Article 37.—Any Soldier who shall, contrary to orders, when off duty, appear in or about Camp or Cantonments, or on occasion of visiting Towns or Bazars, carrying a Sword, Bludgeon or other Weapon;—or

Article 38.—Who shall sell, pawn, or designedly or through neglect lose or injure his Horse, Arms, Clothes, Accoutrements or Regimental Necessaries; or any of the above Articles entrusted or belonging to any other Soldier;

Punishment

Shall, on conviction before a General, District, or Garrison, or Regimental Court-martial, be sentenced to suffer such punishment as such Courts-martial respectively are by these Articles of War empowered to award.

Provided that such offender shall not be sentenced to Death, or Transportation, or corporal punishment.

Embezzlement, punishable by General Court-martial with Dismissal, Fine, and Imprisonment, with or without hard labour, and with or without solitary confinement, of Officers and Soldiers

Crime

Article 39.—Any Officer, or Soldier, who shall embezzle or fraudulently misapply any money entrusted to him on the public account, or for any Military purpose; or any Provisions, Forage, Arms, Clothing, Ammunition, or Military Stores, of whatever kind or description, the property of Government, entrusted to his charge; or who shall wilfully spoil such property, or suffer it to be spoiled, or shall be concerned in or connive at any such embezzlement or fraudulent misapplication;

Punishment

Shall, on conviction before a General Court-martial, be dismissed the Service, and fined to the extent of his arrears of Pay and Allowances : and be further liable to suffer Imprisonment, with or without hard labour, for a term which may extend to three years, and with or without solitary confinement (to be regulated as aforesaid.)

Disgraceful Conduct; punishable by General or District Court-martial, with Corporal Punishment, or Imprisonment, with or without hard labour and solitary confinement, and, in addition, with forfeiture of additional Pay and of Pension on discharge, and stoppages, of Non-Commissioned Officers and Soldiers

Crimes

Article 40.—Any Soldier who shall be guilty of disgraceful conduct; in wilfully maiming or injuring himself, or any other Soldier, at the instance of such Soldier, with intent to render himself or such Soldier unfit for the Service, or with intent to take his own life ;—or

Article 41.—In purloining or selling Government Stores;—or

Article 42.—In stealing money or goods, the property of a Soldier, or of a Military Officer, or of any Military Mess, or of any person or persons belonging to or serving with or attached to the Army;—or

Article 43.—In plundering or injuring property placed under his charge as Sentry, or in charge of his Guard, or in conniving at the plunder or injury of such property ;—or

Article 44.—In embezzling or fraudulently misapplying public money entrusted to him for any Military purpose;—or

Article 45.—In committing any petty offence of a fraudulent or dishonest nature, to the injury of or with intent to injure the Government, or any person, Civil or Military;—or

Article 46.—Who shall be guilty of any other disgraceful conduct, being of a cruel, indecent, or unnatural kind;

Punishment

Shall, on conviction before a General, or District, or Garrison Court-martial, be liable to suffer such punishments as any such Courts are by these Articles of War respectively empowered to award for disgraceful conduct.

And every such offender shall, if not dismissed the service, further be put under stoppages, by sentence of the Court, not exceeding half of his monthly Pay and Allowances ; until the amount be made good of any loss or damage arising out of his misconduct.

And if such offender shall be dismissed the Service, he shall further be sentenced to forfeit his arrears of Pay and Allowances due at the time of his discharge, or in such proportion as may be required to make good such loss or damage.

Crimes punishable by General Court-martial with Suspension or Reprimand of Officers or by any Court-martial with Dismissal, Reduction, or Simple Imprisonment, with or without solitary confinement, or Loss of Standing on the Roll, of Non-Commissioned Officers and Soldiers

Crimes

Article 47.—Any Officer, or Non-Commissioned Officer who shall strike or otherwise ill-treat any Soldier;--- or

Article 48.—Any Sentry who, in time of peace, shall sleep upon his Post; or shall leave it before regularly relieved or without leave;—or

Article 49.—Any Officer, or Soldier, who shall knowingly enlist a Deserter, or connive at his enlistment;—or

Article 50.—Who, directly or indirectly, shall acquire or accept a bribe, present, or gratification, on the pretence of, or as a consideration for, procuring leave of absence, promotion, or any other advantage or indulgence for any Officer or Soldier; —or

Article 51. —Who, being in Command at any Post, or on the March, on complaint made to him of any person under his Command beating or otherwise ill-treating any person ; or extorting from him more than he is obliged to furnish by authority, or disturbing fairs or markets, or committing any kind of riot ; shall not see reparation done to the party or parties injured ; or, if that be impracticable, shall not report the same to his Superior Officer;—or

Article 52.—Who, being in Command of a Guard, shall refuse to receive any Prisoner duly committed to his charge ; or shall without proper authority, release any prisoner, or shall suffer, through carelessness or neglect, any prisoner to escape;—or

Article 53.—Who shall quit his Guard, or Picquet, in time of peace, without being regularly relieved, or without leave;—or

Article 54.—Who shall impede the Provost Marshal, or his Assistants, or any other Officer or person legally exercising authority;—or refuse to assist him when requiring his aid in the execution of his duty;—or

Article 55. —Who, being on leave of absence, shall have received information from the Head Quarters of his Regiment, or from other competent authority, that his Regiment has been ordered on service, and shall not rejoin without delay;—or

Article 56.—Who, in time of peace, shall, by discharging fire arms, drawing swords, beating drums, or by any other means whatever, intentionally occasion false alarms in Camp, Garrison, or Cantonments;—or

Article 57.—Who shall fail to repair at the time fixed to the parade, or place appointed for exercise or duty, if not prevented by sickness or some other sufficient cause;—or

Article 58.—Who shall, without urgent necessity, or without leave of his Superior Officer, quit his Company, or Troop, or the Parade;—or

Article 59.—Who shall absent himself without leave; or shall, without sufficient cause, overstay the period for which leave may have been granted him; or

Article 60. —Any Soldier who shall be found two miles from the Camp contrary to orders;—or *

Article 61.—Who shall, contrary to orders, be absent from his Cantonment after tatoo, or from Camp after retreat beating;—or

Article 62.—Who shall sell, lose, or designedly, or through neglect, waste the ammunition delivered out to him;

Punishment

Shall, if an Officer, on conviction, be sentenced to Suspension from Rank and Pay and Allowances; or to be Reprimanded in such manner as the Commander-in-Chief may direct;

And, if a Soldier, shall on conviction before a General, or District, or Garrison, or Regimental Court-martial, be sentenced to suffer such punishment as any such Courts-martial are by these Articles of War respectively empowered to award;

Provided, that such offender shall not be liable to be sentenced to suffer Corporal Punishment, or Imprisonment with hard labour.

Crimes not specified

Article 63.—All crimes not capital, and all disorders or neglects which Officers or Soldiers may be guilty of, to the prejudice of good order and Military discipline, though riot specified in these Articles, are to be taken cognizance of by Courts-martial, and to be punished according to the nature and degree of the offence, by the Sentence of a General, or District, or Garrison, or Regimental Court-martial; provided that a Soldier shall not for any such offences be liable to be sentenced to suffer Corporal Punishment, or Imprisonment with hard labour.

Crimes incident to Courts-martial; punishable by General Court-martial with Dismissal or Suspension of Officers, and by any Court-martial with Dismissal or Reduction of Non-Commissioned Officers, and with Dismissal or Simple Imprisonment of Soldiers

Crime

Article 64.—Any person amenable to these Articles of War, who, when duly summoned before a Court-martial, shall not attend, or shall refuse to be sworn, or to make affirmation, or to answer any lawful question; or who shall induce any other person so to offend;

Punishment

Shall be punished according to the Sentence of the same or another Court-martial, with Dismissal, or Suspension from Rank and Pay and Allowances, if a Commissioned Officer ; with Dismissal, or Reduction to the Ranks, if a Non-Commissioned Officer ; or with Dismissal, or Imprisonment, if a Soldier;

Provided, that such person, being a Commissioned Officer, shall not be liable to be punished by any but a General Court-martial ; and that no offender punished under the provision of this Article of War shall be sentenced to suffer Imprisonment with hard labour, or Corporal Punishment.

Persons not amenable to Articles of War to be delivered over to magistrate

Article 65.—Any person not amenable to these Articles of War, who, having been summoned before any Court-martial, shall refuse or neglect to attend ; or who, attending, shall refuse te be shown, or to make affirmation, or to answer any lawful question ; or shall give such testimony as, if given in a Criminal Court, would render him guilty of perjury ; or who shall induce any other person so to offend;

Shall be delivered to a Magistrate to be proceeded against according to law.

Contempt of court

Article 66.—Any person using menacing or disrespectful words, signs, or gestures, in the presence of a Court-martial then sitting, or causing any disorder or riot so as to disturb their proceedings;

Shall be punished according to the condition of the offender and the nature and egree of his offence, by the sentence of the same or another Court-martial, if he be amenable to these Articles of War; provided that such offender shall not be liable to be sentenced to Corporal Punishment or to Imprisonment with hard labour; and if not amenable to these Articles of War, the offender shall be delivered over to a Magistrate to be proceeded against according to law.

Perjury; punishable by General or District Court-martial with Dismissal, and in addition with Fine, or simple Imprisonment, of Officers and Soldiers

Perjury

Article 67.—Any Officer, or Soldier, who shall be found guilty of wilfully and knowingly giving false evidence on oath or affirmation on any trial before any General or other Court-martial, or any Military Court entitled to administer an oath: or of inducing any other person so to offend;

Punishment

Shall be dismissed the Service, and shall be further subject to Fine, to the amount of his arrears of Pay and Allowances, or to Imprisonment which may extend to three years;—according to the Sentence of a General, or District, or Garrison Court-martial.

Crimes admitting of less serious notice

Minor crimes

Article 68.—Whereas it may be advisable that some of the offences which by the foregoing Articles are directed to be tried by a General, or District, or Garrison Court-martial, should, in certain cases which admit of less serious notice, be tried by District, or Garrison, or Regimental Courts-martial—in such cases the Officer Commanding the Regiment or Corps to which the offender belongs may, if he thinks it expedient and for the good of the Service, order the offender to be tried by Regimental Court-martial, for any offence ordinarily cognizable by District, or Garrison Court-martial ; making however a report in every such case, for the information of the General Officer Commanding the Division, of the reasons of his having so proceeded ; or such Commanding Officer may lay a particular statement of the case before the General, or other Officer having authority to convene General, or District, or Garrison Courts-martial, under whose command such offender may be serving, with an application for permission to try the offender by District, or Garrison, or Regimental Court-martial; and such General or other Officer will exercise his discretion in complying or not with such application; but the permission of such General or other Officer so to proceed, shall be entered upon the proceedings at the trial of such offender.

Provided, that Mutiny shall not be considered one of the offences admitting of such discretionary investigation.

And that in cases where offences designated "Disgraceful Conduct" in these Articles of War, and admitting of less serious notice, shall be tried by Regimental Courts-martial, the term "Disgraceful Conduct" shall be omitted in the Charge; and the offender shall, on conviction, be liable to suffer such punishment as a Regimental Court-martial is by these Articles of War empowered to award.

Offences on the Line of March or on board Vessels

Offences on the line of march or on board vessels

Article 69.—For offences committed on the Line of March, or on board any Ship or other Vessel, the Officer in Command of the Troops is hereby authorized to try any Soldier by a Regimental, or Detachment Court-martial, and to confirm and execute the Sentence on the spot;

Provided, that such Sentence shall in no case exceed that which a Regimental Court-martial is competent to award;—and that the proceedings held in all such cases shall be transmitted for the information of the Commander-in-Chief.

SECTION III

ADMINISTRATION OF JUSTICE

Arrest or confinement

Article 70.—Whenever any Officer or Soldier shall commit a crime deserving punishment by Court-martial, he shall, by his Commanding Officer, be put under arrest, if an Officer or Non-Commissioned Officer; or if a Soldier, be confined, until he shall be either tried by a Court-martial, or shall be lawfully discharged by a proper authority; and no Officer or Soldier who shall be put in such arrest or confinement shall continue in his confinement longer than may be actually unavoidable.

Resistance to arrest

And such process of arrest or confinement, or an attempt to effect such process, shall in no case be omitted where it may be practicable;—but where resistance may be made, or from other circumstances such process may be impracticable, the offender or offenders shall be liable to trial and punishment at any subsequent period, within the limitations provided in these Articles of War.

Limitation of time

Article 71.—No person shall be liable to be tried or punished for any offence against these Articles, which shall appear to have been committed more than three years previous to the order directing the assembly of the Court-martial whereby he is to be tried, unless the person accused, by reason of his absenting himself, or some other manifest impediment, shall not have been amenable to justice within that period; in which case such person shall be liable to be tried, at any time not exceeding two years after the impediment shall have ceased.

Offender may be tried elsewhere than where the offence was committed

Article 72.—Any person amenable to these Articles of War, who may commit any offence against the same, may be tried and punished for such offence in any place within the British Territories, or elsewhere, where he may have come after the commission of the offence, in the same manner as if the offence had been committed where such trial shall take place.

Powers of Commander-in-Chief in respect of courts-martial

Article 73.—The Commander-in-Chief at the Presidencies of Fort William, Fort Saint George, and Bombay respectively for the time being, may appoint General or other Courts-Martial and confirm, and mitigate, or commute, or remit the Sentences of such Courts; and may issue his Warrant to any General or other Officer having the command of a body of troops in the service of Her Majesty, or of the East India Company, empowering such Officer to appoint General, or District, or Garrison Courts-Martial as occasion may require, for the trial of offences committed by any of the Officers, or Soldiers, or Followers in the service of the said Company, being Natives of the East Indies, or of other places within the limits of the said Company's Charter, and to confirm, and mitigate or commute, or remit the sentences of such Courts-Martial.

Constitution of a general court-martial

Article 74.—A General Court-Martial shall not consist of less than thirteen Commissioned Officers, unless it be held out of the East India Company's Territories, where such Court-Martial may consist of seven Commissioned Officers, if a greater number cannot be conveniently assembled. And no sentence of a General Court-Martial shall be put in execution until after a report shall have been made of the whole proceedings to the Commander-in-Chief, or to some other person duly authorized to confirm the same, and until his directions shall have been signified thereupon.

Powers of a General Court-martial

Death or transportation

*Article 75.—A General Court-martial may sentence any Officer or Soldier to Death or Transportation, for any crimes which are by these Articles of War expressly made liable to sentence of Death or Transportation, and for such crimes only.

Dismissal or suspension

And when a Commissioned Officer shall be convicted of any offence, of which the punishment is not defined in these Articles of War, or is left discretionary, a General Court-martial may adjudge such Officer to be Dismissed the Service;—or to be suspended from Rank and Pay and Allowances, for a stated period;—or to be placed lower on the list of his rank, by an alteration of the date of his Commission, thereby losing the corresponding benefit of length of service and the Court shall in every such sentence specify the extent or degree of Suspension or Reduction, which they shall so adjudge;—or the Court may sentence such Officer to be reprimanded in such manners the Commander-in-Chief may direct.

Reduction to ranks or dismissal/ corporal punishment, imprisonment, imprisonment or solitary confinement

And a general court-martial may sentence any non-commissioned officer to be reduced to the ranks; or may sentence any non-commissioned officer or soldier to be dismissed the service, or to be placed lower in the list of the rank which he holds (which shall not involve any forfeiture of service or other advantage, except that of standing), or may sentence any Corporal punish soldier to suffer corporal punishment not exceeding fifty lashes;—or imprisonment with or without hard labour not exceeding two years;—and to be kept in solitary confinement for any portion or portions of such imprisonment not exceeding twenty-eight days at a time, nor eighty-four days in any one year, with intervals between the periods of solitary confinement of not less duration than such periods of solitary confinement. Provided that no soldier shall be kept in solitary confinement more than eighty-four days in any one year, whether by the sentence of one or more courts-martial, or by order of his commanding officer.

Forfeiture of pay and pension

And a General Court-martial may, in addition either to Corporal Punishment, or to Imprisonment, as aforesaid, sentence a Soldier to forfeiture of all advantage as to additional Pay and to Pension on discharge, which might have otherwise accrued from the length or nature of his former service; or to Forfeiture of such advantage absolutely, whether it might have accrued from past service, or might accrue from future service, according to the nature of the case, for disgraceful conduct.

Forfeiture of arrears and allowances

And a General Court-martial may, in addition to the punishment of Dismissal, sentence any Officer or Soldier to forfeit his arrears of Pay and Allowances due at the time of his discharge, or such proportion thereof as may be required, to make good any loss or damage arising out of his misconduct; — And, in addition to any punishment not involving Dismissal from the service, may sentence any Officer or Soldier to be put under Stoppages not exceeding two-thirds of his Pay and Allowances in the case of an Officer, and not exceeding half of his Pay and Allowances in the case of a Non-Commissioned Officer or Soldier, until the amount of such loss or damage be made good.

Confirmation and Commutation of Sentence by the Commander-in-Chief

Sentence of death

Article 76. — In cases wherein a Sentence of Death shall have been awarded by a General Court-martial, for any offence against discipline for which Sentence of Death is awardable under these Articles of War, the Commander-in-Chief may confirm such Sentence, and cause it to be carried into effect, or may, instead of causing such Sentence to be carried into effect, order the offender, if an Officer, to be transported for life, or to be imprisoned for any term of years, or to be dismissed; and, if a Soldier, to be transported for life, or to be imprisoned, with or without Hard Labour, either for life, or for a certain term of years, and with or without solitary confinement, to be regulated as aforesaid, as to the Commander-in-Chief may seem meet.

Transportation of officers/ Dismissal of officers

In cases of Commissioned Officers sentenced to *Transportation*, the Commander-in-Chief may, in lieu thereof, order the offender to be imprisoned for any term of years, or to be dismissed. And in cases of Commissioned Officers sentenced to be dismissed from the service, the Commander-in-Chief may, in lieu of such Punishment, direct, that the offender be suspended from Rank and Pay and Allowances for a certain period, to be distinctly specified by the Commander-in-Chief.

Transportation of soldiers

And the Commander-in-Chief may commute a Sentence of *Transportation* passed on a Soldier, to Imprisonment with or without Hard Labour, and with or without Solitary Confinement (to be regulated as aforesaid) ; and such Imprisonment may be either for the same period for which Transportation shall have been awarded, or for any lesser period.

Corporal punishment

And the Commander in-Chief may commute a Sentence of Corporal Punishment to Dismissal from the service; or, in the case of a Non-Commissioned Officer, may mitigate such Sentence to Reduction to the ranks; or in the case of a Non-commissioned Officer or Soldier may commute such Sentence to Imprisonment without Hard Labour, and with or without Solitary Confinement (to be regulated as aforesaid), for any period not exceeding two years.

Dismissal of non-commissioned officers

In cases of Non-Commissioned Officers sentenced to be dismissed from the service, the Commander-in-Chief may, in lieu of such punishment, direct that the offender be reduced to the ranks, or placed lower in the list of the rank which he holds; (which shall not involve any forfeiture of service or other advantage, except that of standing).

Imprisonment with hard labour

And in cases of offenders sentenced to Imprisonment with Hard Labour, the Commander-in-Chief may mitigate such Sentence by causing the offender to be reduced to the ranks, in the case of a Non-Commissioned Officer ; or in the case of a Non-Commissioned Officer or Soldier by directing that he be dismissed from the service : or suffer Imprisonment without Hard Labour, and with or without Solitary Confinement, (to be regulated as aforesaid), for any period not exceeding that for which he shall have been Sentenced to such Imprisonment with Hard Labour.

Constitution of a district court-martial

Article 77.—A District, or Garrison Court-martial shall consist of not less than seven Commissioned Officers, except in situations where that number cannot be conveniently assembled, when such Court may consist of not less than Five Commissioned Officers. And such District, or Garrison Court-martial may be composed of Officers of the same Regiment, and shall be assembled in conformity with the orders of the Commander-in-Chief.

Confirmation of their sentence

And the Sentence of a District, or Garrison Court-martial shall be confirmed by the Commander-in-Chief, or by some Officer duly authorized to confirm the same.

Commutation of Sentence

Power of Commander-in-Chief to commute sentence

And the Commander-in-Chief is empowered to remit, or mitigate, or commute the Sentences of such Courts-martial, in the same manner as the Sentences of General Courts-martial; and to delegate to, or withhold from, Commanding Officers the power of convening such Courts-martial, and of confirming, remitting, mitigating, or commuting the Sentences of such Courts (not including forfeiture of pay or pension or other advantage,) as the Commander-in-Chief may deem to be most expedient.

And in case of any Sentence, including forfeiture of additional Pay or of Pension on Discharge, or of any prospective advantage, such Sentence shall not be carried into effect until confirmed by the Commander-in-Chief; and all forfeitures of any present or prospective advantage shall be restorable by the same authority.

Powers of a District or Garrison Court-martial

Powers of a district or garrison court-martial

*Article 78.—A District or Garrison Court-martial may sentence any Non-Commissioned Officer to be reduced to the ranks,—or may Sentence any Non-Commissioned Officer or Soldier to be dismissed from the Service ; or to be placed lower in the list of the rank which he holds (which shall not involve any forfeiture of service or other advantage, except that of standing); or may Sentence any Soldier to suffer Corporal Punishment not exceeding fifty lashes; or Imprisonment, with or without Hard Labour, not exceeding one year, and to be kept in Solitary Confinement (to be regulated as aforesaid).

And such Court-martial may, in addition either to Corporal Punishment or to Imprisonment as aforesaid, Sentence a Soldier to forfeiture of all advantage as to additional Pay, and to pension on Discharge, which might have otherwise accrued from the length or nature of his former service, or to forfeiture of such advantage absolutely, whether it might have accrued from past service, or might accrue from future service, according to the nature of the case, for disgraceful conduct.

And such Court-martial may, in addition to the Punishment of Dismissal, Sentence any Non-Commissioned Officer or Soldier to forfeit his arrears of Pay and Allowances due at the time of his discharge, or such proportion thereof as may be required, to make good any loss or damage arising out of his misconduct; and in addition to any punishment not involving Dismissal, from the service may Sentence any Non-Commissioned Officer or Soldier to be put under Stoppages not exceeding half of his Pay and Allowances, until the amount of such loss or damage be made good.

Regimental court-martial, Commutation of sentence

Article 79.—A Regimental Court-martial shall consist of not less than Five Commissioned Officers, (unless it be found impracticable to assemble that number when Three may be sufficient), and shall be assembled by order of the Officer Commanding the Regiment. And no Sentence of a Regimental Court-martial shall be of force until the Commanding Officer shall have confirmed the same. Provided that such Commanding Officer shall have power, to remit all Sentences whatever, passed by such Court, and thereupon to cause the offender to be released and to return to his duty.

And such Commanding Officer shall have power to confirm and carry into effect or to mitigate all Sentences whatever passed by such Court ; and to commute a Sentence of Corporal Punishment to Imprisonment without Hard Labour, and with or without Solitary Confinement, (to be regulated as aforesaid,) for any period for which such Court is competent to Sentence an offender to suffer Imprisonment and in the same manner; and to mitigate a Sentence of Dismissal in the case of a Non-Commissioned Officer, to Reduction to the Ranks;—and to commute a Sentence of

Imprisonment with Hard Labour, to Dismissal; or to mitigate such Sentence to Reduction to the Ranks; or to Imprisonment without Hard Labour.

Powers of a regimental court-martial

* Article 80. —A Regimental Court-martial may Sentence any Non-Commissioned Officer to be reduced to the ranks;—or may sentence any Non-Commissioned Officer or Soldier, to be dismissed from the service;—or to be placed lower in the list of the rank which he holds (which shall not involve any forfeiture of service or other advantage, except that of standing),—or may Sentence any Soldier to suffer Corporal Punishment not exceeding fifty lashes; or Imprisonment, with or without hard labour, for any period not exceeding six calendar months; and to be kept in solitary confinement (to be regulated as aforesaid.)

Any such Court-martial may, in addition to the punishment of Dismissal, sentence any Non-Commissioned Officer or Soldier to forfeit his arrears of Pay and Allowances due at the time of his discharge, or such proportion thereof as may be required to make good any loss or damage arising out of his misconduct; and in addition to any punishment not involving Dismissal from the service, may Sentence any Non-Commissioned Officer or Soldier to be put under Stoppages not exceeding half of his Pay and Allowances, until the amount of such loss or damage be made good.

Detachment court-martial

Article 81.—An Officer Commanding any Detachment of his own Regiment may assemble Regimental Detachment Courts-martial;—and an Officer Commanding a Detachment consisting of men of different Corps, may assemble Detachment or lane Courts-martial;—and all such Courts shall be constituted in the same manner as Regimental Courts-martial under the provisions of these Articles of War, and shall have the like powers.

And the provisions of these Articles of War relating to Courts-martial held in Regiments, shall be taken to apply to Courts-martial held in Detachments, in all practicable cases.

Provided that no Officer on detached Command of less than four Troops or Companies, or of Detachments numerically equal to four Troops or Companies, and not being on the line of march or on board any ship or other vessel, shall carry into effect any punishment awarded by a Court-martial held by his order, until the Sentence shall have been confirmed by the Officer Commanding the Regiment to which the offender belongs, or by the nearest Superior Officer holding a command of not less than a Regiment;—(who is hereby authorized to confirm the same, in like manner, as an Officer Commanding a Regiment is empowered to do);—except in detached situations beyond Sea or out of the British Territories, or when on Service in the field, or in cases were an immediate example is necessary, and reference cannot be made to such Commanding or superior officer without detriment to the Service; when the Officer Commanding such Detachment may exercise the powers which are vested in an Officer Commanding a Regiment.

Powers of officers convening courts-martial

Article 82.—At all Courts-martial, it shall be competent to the Officer convening the Court to instruct the Court, that, should the Prisoner be found guilty, and Imprisonment form a part of the Sentence, no portion of the Imprisonment should be Solitary ;—or, should Corporal Punishment be awardable to the offender, that it shall not be awardable in the particular case ; and the Court will govern itself accordingly ; and such instruction shall be in writing and shall be attached to the proceedings of the Court.

Execution of Sentences of Courts-martial

Execution of sentence of death

Article 83.—In every sentence of Death awarded by a General Court-martial, the Court shall specify that the offender shall "suffer death by being hanged by the neck until he be dead," or "by being shot to death," as the Court in their discretion shall deem expedient; and such sentence, if confirmed, shall be carried into effect accordingly.

Transportation

Article 84.—Whenever the sentence of a General Court-martial shall adjudge Transportation, or Sentence of Death shall be commuted by competent authority to Transportation, any of the Sudder Courts shall give effect to such sentence, or commuted Sentence, on the same being certified to the Court under the authority of the Commander-in-Chief.

Imprisonment

And whenever any Sentence of a Court-martial shall adjudge Imprisonment with Hard Labour, or with Solitary Confinement, or both, or whenever the Sentence of a Court-martial shall be commuted to any such imprisonment, it shall be the duty of every Judge, Magistrate, Sheriff, or other Officer in charge of a Jail, to give effect to such Sentence, on the offender being delivered into his custody, and on being furnished with a copy of the Sentence by the Officer Commanding the Station or Regiment or Detachment, within which the trial is held.

Imprisonment for life

Article 85.—Whenever any Soldier shall be sentenced to Imprisonment for life or a Sentence of Death shall be commuted to Imprisonment for life, it shall be lawful for the Commander-in-Chief to order such offender to be transported beyond Sea for life and such order shall thereupon be made, unless there should be special reasons inducing the Commander-in-Chief to think such prisoner not a proper subject for Transportation.

Place of imprisonment

Article 86.—Persons sentenced to Imprisonment by Courts-martial shall be imprisoned in any public prison, or in any other fit place which the Commander-in-Chief shall from time to time direct.

Dismissal from service

Article 87.—Every Soldier sentenced to Imprisonment with Hard Labour, shall, previous to undergoing such punishment, be struck off the strength of his Corps from the date of confirmation of such Sentence ; and no Soldier who has undergone such punishment for any period shall be capable of being re-admitted in the ranks, or of receiving Pension on discharge.

Dismissal with ignominy

Article 88.—Offenders sentenced to dismissal for disgraceful conduct;

And offenders subject to Corporal Punishment, or to Imprisonment with Hard Labour for disgraceful conduct, shall, on any such Sentence being confirmed, be dismissed with Ignominy.

Stoppage of pay

Article 89.—In every case wherein a fine, or forfeiture of arrears of pay, or stoppages shall be adjudged by a Court-martial, any pay or public money due to the offender, or that may become due to him, shall be available, with the sanction of the Commander-in-Chief, for the payment of the amount so adjudged.

Limitation

And no Soldier sentenced to pay a fine or to stoppages to make good any loss or damage arising out of his misconduct, shall be continued under forfeiture or stoppages under any one such Sentence for any period exceeding one year; and no Soldier shall be at any one time placed under forfeiture or stoppages exceeding in the whole the amount of half of his Pay and Allowances, nor be liable to be put under stoppages prospectively while actually under stoppages to the amount of half of his Pay and Allowances.

Forms of Proceeding

Hours of court sitting

Article 90.—Trials by Courts-martial may be carried on between the hours of six in the morning and four in the afternoon, and not otherwise, except in cases which may require an immediate example.

Judge advocate

Article 91.—At General Courts-martial a Judge Advocate, or an European Officer of not less than ten years' service, shall be appointed to conduct the proceedings.

At all Courts-martial inferior to General, an European Officer of not less than four years' standing in the service, except in cases where no Officer of that standing may be available, or the Adjutant of the Regiment, shall be appointed to conduct the proceedings.

Interpreter

Article 92.—An Interpreter shall be appointed to all Courts-martial; and any Interpreter, or other competent person available at the Station where the Court-martial may sit, shall be appointed as occasion may require by the Officer Commanding at such Station, on application from the Judge Advocate or Superintending Officer of such Court-martial. But in situations where the services of an Interpreter of other competent person are not available, the Superintending Officer at the Court-martial shall perform the duty of Interpreter.

President

Article 93.—At all Courts-martial the Senior Officer shall sit, as President, without being so appointed by Warrant. Provided, that all Subadar Majors are to take precedence according to the dates of their Commissions, and above all Native Officers holding the rank of Subadar or Jemadar; and that Sirdar Bahadoors and Bahadoors shall rank only according to their respective Commissions of Subadar Major, Subadar or Jemadar, Rissaldars and Rissaidars will take rank with Subadars, and Naib Rissaldars with Jemadars, according to the dates of their respective Commissions.

In case of the death or unavoidable absence of the President, the next Senior Member shall take the place of President, and the trial shall proceed, provided that the Court shall still consist of at least the number of Members of which such Court is directed to consist by these Articles of War.

Revision of sentence

Article 94.—No Finding or Sentence of a Court-martial shall be revised more than once, and no Evidence shall be received on such revision. For the purpose of such revision the President and all the Members shall be convened if possible. But if any of them should be unavoidably absent, the remaining Members may proceed with such revision, provided they are not fewer than the smallest number directed in these Articles respectively. When all the same Members do not meet, the circumstances are to be duly certified on the face of the proceedings.

Manner of Voting

Manner of voting

Article 95.—All the Members of a Court-martial are to preserve order, and in giving their votes upon all matters are to begin with the youngest ; and in all cases where a Sentence of Death may not be awarded, the decision shall be by the majority of Members present, provided the number of Members present be not less than that required by the preceding Article ; but in case of an equality of votes, the decision shall be in favor of the prisoner ; the President at a Court-martial shall vote with the other Members, but shall have no casting vote. Provided, that in cases of an equality of votes upon other questions than the Finding and the Sentence, the President shall have a casting vote.

Sentence of death

Article 96.—No sentence of death shall be given against any offender by a Court-martial, unless two-thirds of the Members present concur therein, or four, where the Court consist of five Members, or five where the Court consist of seven.

Affirmations

Interpreter's affirmation

Article 97.—On the assembly of a Court-martial, the Judge Advocate or Superintending European Officer shall administer to the Interpreter the following Solemn Affirmation:—

"I, A. B., solemnly affirm, in the presence of Almighty God, that I will faith fully interpret and translate the proceedings of the Court, and that I will not divulge the Sentence until it shall have been published by authority; and further, that I will not disclose or discover the vote or opinion of any particular Member of the Court, unless required to give evidence thereof by a Court of Justice or Court-martial, in due course of Law."

In case of the unavoidable absence of an Interpreter, the European Superintending Officer of a Court-martial inferior to General shall make the Solemn Affirmation prescribed for the Interpreter.

Member's affirmation

The Judge Advocate or Superintending Officer shall then cause the following Solemn Affirmation to be made by each Member:—

"I, A. B., solemnly affirm, in the presence of Almighty God, that I will duly administer justice according to the Articles of War, without partiality, favour, or affection, and, if any doubt shall arise, then, according to my conscience, the best of my understanding, and the custom of War in the like cases, and that I will not divulge the Sentence of the Court until it shall be published by authority; and further, that I will not disclose or discover the vote or opinion of any particular Member of the Court, unless required to give evidence thereof by a Court of Justice or a Court-martial in due course of Law."

Judge advocate's affirmation

The following Solemn Affirmation shall then be administered by the Interpreter to the Judge Advocate or Superintending Officer:—

"I, A. B., solemnly affirm, in the presence of Almighty God, that I will not upon any account whatsoever disclose or discover the vote or opinion of any particular Member of the Court-martial, unless required to give evidence thereof as a witness by a Court of Justice, or a Court-martial in due course of Law, and that I will not, unless it be necessary for the due discharge of my official duties, disclose the Sentence of the Court, until it shall be published by authority."

Provided, that it shall be necessary to re-administer these Solemn Affirmations on the commencement of fresh trials before the same Court.

Witness' oath or affirmation

Article 98.— All persons who give evidence at a Court-martial are to be examined on Oath according to the forms of their respective religions, or on Affirmation—and persons of the Hindoo or Mahomedan persuasion, and other persons making Affirmation, shall make Affirmation to the following effect :—

"I solemnly affirm, in the presence of Almighty God, that what I shall state shall be the truth, the whole truth, and nothing but the truth."

And if any person making such Affirmation as aforesaid, shall wilfully and falsely state any matter or thing, which, if the same had been sworn, would have amounted to perjury, every such offender shall be subject to the same punishment to which persons convicted of perjury are subject.

Summoning Witnesses not amenable to these Articles

Summoning witnesses not military

Article 99.—In all cases where persons required as witnesses before a Court-martial may not be amenable to military law, the Judge Advocate or Commanding Officer shall transmit to the Magistrate within whose jurisdiction the witness may reside, his summons for the attendance of such person, and the Magistrate shall cause the witness to be duly summoned.

Powers and Duties of Provost Marshals

Powers and duties of provost marshals

Article 100.—For the prompt and instant repression of all irregularities and crimes which may be committed by Troops in the Field and on the Line of March, Provost Marshals shall be appointed by the Commander-in-Chief, and their powers shall be regulated according to the established usages of war and rules of the service; their duties are to take charge of prisoners confined for offences of a general description; to preserve good order and discipline; to prevent breaches of both, by Soldiers and Followers of the Army, and to punish on the spot, on the same day, those whom they may find in the immediate act of committing breaches of good order and Military discipline; Provided, that the punishment be limited to the necessity of the case, and shall accord with the orders which the Provost Marshals may from time to time receive from the Commander of the Forces in the Field, and that whatever may be the crime, the Provost Marshal or his Assistant shall see the offender commit the act for which summary punishment may be inflicted, or if the Provost Marshal or his Assistant should not see the offender actually commit the crime, but that sufficient proof can be established of the offender's guilt, a Report shall be made to the Commander of the Army in the Field, who is hereby empowered to deal with the case as he may deem most conducive to the maintenance of good order and military discipline. The duties of Provost Marshals being limited to the punishment of offenders whom they may detect in the actual commission of any crime, the General Commanding the Forces in the Field will cause them to exercise the powers entrusted to them in such manner and under such circumstances as he may consider best calculated to prevent and instantly to repress crimes injurious to the discipline of the East India Company's Army and the Public Service.

Trials by European Courts-martial

Trial by European courts-martial

Article 101.—At any Presidency where the Native troops have hitherto been authorized to claim to be tried by European Courts-martial, every person amenable to these Articles of War, and who may be under orders for trial by a Court-martial, shall have the right to claim to be tried by European Officers; and should he make such claim, the Court, whether General, District, or Garrison, or Regimental, shall be composed of European Commissioned Officers, and the number of Members and the proceedings shall be governed in all respects by the provisions of these Articles.

And it shall be competent to the Governor General of India in Council, by a General Order, to authorize the Native troops of any of the Presidencies to claim to be tried in like manner by European Courts-martial.

SECTION IV

Effects of the Dead

Effects of the dead

*Article 102.—When any Officer or Soldier, or any person receiving public pay drawn by any Officer in charge of a Public Department belonging to the Army, may die, or be killed in the service, the Commanding Officer of the Regiment or Party, or Officer in charge of the Department, shall, if no Heir or Executor be present, secure his effects, and direct an inventory thereof to be taken, a duplicate of which is to be lodged in the office of the Adjutant, or Officer in charge of the Department.

Sale of effects

*Article 103.—If there be no Heir or Executor on the spot, the Effects are to be publicly sold; the Commanding Officer of the Regiment or Party, or Officer in charge of the Department, after discharging the debts of the deceased, viz., the expense of Funeral Ceremonies, his Debts in Camp or Quarters, and Regimental Debts of every description, shall account for the residue to the Heir or Heirs declared by Will, whether written or verbal, or nominated in the Regimental Register, or in failure of such, to the legal representative of the deceased; and in the event of no Executor, Heir, or other representative of the deceased attending and establishing his claim within twelve months from the date of the casualty, the amount in the hands of the Officer having charge of the Estate, is to be remitted to the General Treasury at the Presidency.

SECTION V

Miscellaneous

Sale of deserter's effects

Article 104.—The Effects of Deserters are to be publicly sold, and the proceeds, after payment of Regimental Debts, remitted by the Officer Commanding the Corps to which the Deserter belongs, to the General Treasury at the Presidency, or appropriated according to the rules obtaining at such Presidency.

Construction of Articles

Article 105.—All powers and provisions contained in these Articles relating to the Commander-in-Chief, shall be construed to extend to the Commander-in-Chief at any Presidency, and to the Officer Commanding the Forces for the time being at any Presidency, unless when otherwise provided.

All powers and provisions contained in these Articles, relating to Soldiers, shall be construed to extend to Non-Commissioned Officers, unless when otherwise provided.

Of troops serving out of their own presidency

Article 106.—When any portion of the Troops belonging to one Presidency shall be serving within the limits of another Presidency, such Troops shall be considered as placed, during such service, under the orders and authority of the Commander-in-Chief or Commanding Officer of the Forces of the Presidency within which they are serving, for all the purposes of these Articles of War, in the same manner as though they belonged to such Presidency; and all the provisions of these Articles of War, which relate to the trial and punishment of offenders belonging to the Presidency within which the trial is held, are hereby declared applicable to the trial and punishment of offenders amenable to these Articles of War serving within such Presidency. Provided always, that it shall be lawful for the Governor General in Council in his executive capacity, to direct that the Troops, or any part thereof of any Presidency, whilst serving without the limits of such Presidency, shall continue under the orders and authority of the Commander-in-Chief, or Commanding Officer of the Forces of the Presidency to which they belong for all purposes of these Articles.

Of assembling courts-martial in foreign territories

Article 107.—Any Officer Commanding any portion of the East India Company's Troops which may at any time be serving in any place out of Her Majesty's Dominions, or of the possessions or territories which are or may be under the Government of the said Company, or of the territories of those States in alliance with the said Company, in which the said Company's Forces are permanently stationed, shall, upon complaint made to him of any offence committed against the property or person of any inhabitant or resident in any such countries, by any person serving with or belonging to the Company's Army, being under the immediate Command of any such Officer, summon and cause to assemble a General Court-martial, which shall consist of not less than three Officers, for the purpose of trying any such person, notwithstanding any such Officer shall not have received any Warrant empowering him to assemble Courts-martial, and every such Court-martial shall have the same powers in regard to summoning and examining witnesses, trial of, and sentence upon any such offenders as are granted by these Articles to General Courts-martial; Provided that no sentence of any such Court-martial shall be executed, until the General Commanding-in-Chief of the Army to which the Division, Brigade, Detachment, or Party to which any person so tried, convicted, and adjudged to suffer punishment, shall belong, shall have approved and confirmed the same; except where such sentence shall not exceed the powers granted by these Articles to a District, or Garrison Court-martial, in which case the Officer by whom the Court is convened is hereby authorized to confirm or commute, or mitigate, or remit the same ; reporting the proceedings to the said General Commanding-in-Chief.

Trial of commissioned officers

Article 108.—General Courts-martial only shall have the power to try Commissioned Officers; or to pass Sentence of Death or Transportation on any offenders.

No person to be tried a second time for the same offence

Article 109.—No person, being acquitted or convicted before a Court-martial of any offence, shall be liable to be tried a second time by the same or any other Court-martial for the same offence. Provided always, that after a Soldier shall have been found guilty by a Court-martial of any military offence, such Court-martial shall inquire into and receive evidence of any previous conviction of such Soldier before a Court-martial or a Court of Justice, and shall enquire into the general character of such Soldier; for the purpose of affixing the punishment to which he is liable to be sentenced for the offence of which he has been so found guilty.

Provided, that no such evidence shall in any case be received until the Court shall have ascertained that such Soldier had, previously to his trial, received notice of the intention to produce such evidence on the same. And it is hereby directed that such notice shall be given to all Soldiers previous to trial.

Trial of non-commissioned officers

*Article 110. —No Non-Commissioned Officer shall be reduced to the ranks but by the Sentence of a Court-martial, or by order of the Commander-in-Chief of the Presidency to which the offender shall belong. Provided, that no Non-Commissioned Officer shall be reduced to the ranks for any limited period; nor suspended from his rank; nor reduced from a higher to a lower grade of Non-Commissioned Officer; nor sentenced to suffer Corporal Punishment or Imprisonment, without being first reduced to the ranks.

Of complaints against superior officers

*Article 111. —Any Officer or Soldier thinking himself wronged by his superior or other Officer is to complain thereof to the Commanding Officer of his Troop or Company, by whom, if the grievance be not redressed, such Officer, Non-Commissioned Officer, or Soldier, may complain to the Commanding Officer of his Regiment, who is hereby required to examine into such complaint, or remit it to his superior authority as the circumstances may require; but if the complaint should appear to be frivolous or groundless, the party preferring it shall be liable to be punished according to the sentence of a General or other Court-martial in manner hereinbefore mentioned; provided that such offender shall not be liable to be sentenced to Dismissal, nor to suffer Corporal Punishment or Imprisonment with Hard Labour.

Extra drill, &c

Article 112.—In case of light offences, a Commanding Officer may, without the intervention of a Court-martial, award extra drill, with or without pack, for a period not exceeding fifteen days ; restriction to Barrack limits not exceeding fifteen days ; confinement in the Quarter Guard or Defaulter's Room, not exceeding seven days; removal from Staff situations or acting appointments; or may order Soldiers to be employed in piling and unpiling shot; and in cleaning accoutrements of men in Hospital ; but none of these descriptions of punishment shall be awardable by Sentence of a Court-martial. And a Commanding Officer may award solitary confinement not exceeding seven days.

Provided that soldiers in confinement shall be liable to be ordered to attend ordinary drill.

Prisoners of war

Article 113.—Any Officer, or Soldier, who shall be taken prisoner by the Enemy, shall forfeit all claim to pay and allowances during the period of his remaining a prisoner, and until he shall again return to the service; when, if he can establish before a Court-martial, that he was unavoidably taken prisoner in the course of service, and resisted as long as he was able, and that he hath not served with or assisted the Enemy, and that he hath returned as soon as possible to the service, he shall be entitled to receive either the whole, or such portion of his arrears of pay and allowances as the Government of the Presidency to which he may belong shall determine, after the opinion or finding of such Court-martial shall have been confirmed by the Commander-in-Chief. [*And every Officer or Soldier in imprisonment under the sentence of a Court-martial, or a commuted sentence, or under the sentence of a Court of Criminal Judicature, shall, during the term of such imprisonment, receive subsistence only, to the amount of his pay proper, according to the rates of Pay granted to Officers and Soldiers of the Bengal Army.*][1]

SECTION VI

Mode of dealing with offence not Military

Persons charged with offences cognizable by the civil power to be delivered over to the magistrate

Article 114.—In all places within the Jurisdiction of any Civil Judicature, established by appointment of Her Majesty or of the said Company, Officers and Soldiers accused of capital crimes, or of violence, or of offences against person and property, punishable by such Civil Judicature, shall be delivered over to a Magistrate to be proceeded against according to Law.

1 Repealed by Act XXXVI of 1850.

And all Officers and Soldiers are hereby required to assist the Officers of Justice in apprehending and securing any person so accused.

Crimes to be tried by Courts-martial where no regular Criminal tribunals exist

Crimes to be tried by courts-martial where no regular criminal tribunals exist

Article 115.—In any place within the limits of the Charter of the East India Company, whether in or out of the British Territories, where there may be no Civil Judicature appointed by Her Majesty or the said Company for the trial of persons accused of offences ordinarily cognizable by Civil Tribunals, such offences, when committed by Officers or Soldiers, shall be cognizable by Courts-martial.

General courts-martial

Article 116.—General Courts-martial shall have cognizance, ordinarily, of offences punishable with Death; Transportation for Life; Imprisonment for Life; Imprisonment for a period which may extend to fourteen years; and Imprisonment for a period which may extend to seven years.

District or garrison courts-martial

Article 117.—District, or Garrison Courts-martial shall have cognizance, ordinarily, of offences punishable with Imprisonment for a period which may extend to three years, and, by special order, of offences ordinarily cognizable by General Courts-martial not liable to the punishment of Death or Transportation, with power to sentence persons convicted of such offences to Imprisonment for any period not exceeding three years.

Regimental, detachment, or line courts-martial

Article 118.—Regimental, Detachment, or Line Courts-martial, shall have cognizance, ordinarily, of offences punishable with Imprisonment for a period not exceeding six calendar months, and by special order, of offences ordinarily cognizable by District, or Garrison Courts-martial, with power to sentence persons convicted of such offences to Imprisonment for a period not exceeding six calendar months.

General Court-martial

Punishment of Death

Punishment of death

Article 119.—Any Officer or Soldier who shall be convicted by a General Court-martial of the crime of "Murder," shall be sentenced to suffer Death, by being hanged by the neck until he be dead.

If any injury intended against one person shall, through mistake or accident, light upon another person, and kill him, such killing shall be deemed to be murder, whensoever it would have been murder had the person against whom such injury was intended been killed.

Whensoever death shall result from any injury wilfully caused by an offender, but without his intending such injury to light on any person in particular, such offender shall be guilty of murder, if the offence would have been murder had be intended to do the injury to the person killed.

Offences punishable by Transportation for Life

Offences punishable by transportation for life

Article 120.—Any Officer or Soldier who shall be convicted by a General Court-martial of any of the offences hereinafter mentioned, accompanied with an attempt to commit murder, or with wounding or other Corporal injury to any person, endangering the life of such person: That is to say,—

1st.—Breaking, or attempting to break, by day or night, into any Dwelling House, Tent, Boat, or other habitation, or into any building or place used for the preservation of property, with the intent to rob or steal ;

2nd.—Robbery or attempt to rob;

3rd.—Stealing or attempting to steal in a house, or from the person;

Shall be sentenced by such General Court-martial to Imprisonment, with or without Hard Labour, and Transportation for life.

Offences punishable by Imprisonment which may extend to fourteen years

Offences

Article 121.—Any Officer or Soldier who shall be convicted by a General Court-martial of any of the offences specified in the last Article, accompanied with wounding or other Corporal injury to any person, not endangering the life of such person;—or

Article 122.—Of wounding or administering poison with intent to murder whether the person wounded or to whom poison is administered, be the person whom the offender intended to murder or another; —or

Article 123.—Of Robbery by open violence, or dacoity, that is to say, going forth in the day or in the night with an offensive weapon, or in a gang, with or without an offensive weapon, with the intention of committing robbery, and by force or intimidation robbing or attempting to rob any person in any place, or at tacking by open violence any house, or place of habitation, or any place in which property may be kept, for the purpose of robbery;—or

Article 124.—Of breaking, or attempting to break, into any Dwelling House, Tent, Boat, or other place of habitation, between sunset and sunrise, with intent to rob or steal ;—or

Article 125.—Of breaking into any such place of habitation, or into any place used for the preservation of property, and stealing therefrom property the value of which shall exceed One Hundred Company's Rupee ;—or

Regimental, Detachment, or Line Courts-martial

Offences punishable by Imprisonment not exceeding six months

Regimental, detachment, or line courts-martial

Article. 145.—It shall be competent to any Officer having authority to convene a Court-martial, to cause offenders, not being Commissioned Officers, accused of any of the offences specified in the preceding Articles of War, for which no punishment exceeding Imprisonment with Hard Labour for three years is therein provided, to be tried before Regimental, or Detachment, or Line Courts-martial, and any such Court shall have power, on conviction, to sentence any such offender to suffer Imprisonment, with or without Hard Labour, for any period not exceeding six calendar months.

Offences punishable by Imprisonment from six months to one year, according to the description of the Court

Offence

Article 146.—Any Officer or Soldier who shall be convicted of stealing property to the value of Fifty Company's Rupees, or of less value;—or

Article 147.—Of Assault or Affray, unattended with Homicide, severe wounding, or aggravating circumstances:

Punishment

Shall be sentenced to suffer imprisonment, with or without Hard Labour, for any period not exceeding one year, by the award of a General, or District, or Garrison Court-martial; or, for any period not exceeding six calendar months, by the award of a Regimental, or Detachment, or Line Court-martial.

Offences punishable by Imprisonment from six months to two years, according to the description of the Court

Offence

Article 148.—Any Officer or Soldier who shall be convicted of resisting the process of a Magistrate or Police Officer;—or

Article 149. —Of having committed any offence against person or property for which provision is not already made in the preceding Articles of War;

Punishment

Shall be sentenced to suffer Imprisonment for any period not exceeding two years, by the award of a General Court Martini; not exceeding one year, by the award of a District, or Garrison Court-martial and not exceeding six calendar mouths, by the award of a Regimental, or Detachment, or Line Court-martial.

Offence of aiding and abetting

Article 150.—Any Officer or Soldier who shall be convicted by a General, or District, or Garrison, or Regimental Court-martial, of having been present, aiding and abetting, or of having caused, instigated, or procured, the commission of any of the offences specified in any of the preceding Articles, shall be sentenced by such Court to the punishment therein provided for such offence, and awardable by General, or District, or Garrison, or Regimental Courts-martial, respectively.

Sentence of death

Article 151.—No Sentence of Death shall be carried into effect until confirmed by the Commander-in-Chief, nor, if the trial shall have been held within the British Territories forming part of either of the Presidencies of Fort William, Fort St. George, and Bombay, respectively, until such confirmation shall have been concurred in by the Government of the Presidency where such trial shall have been held.

Confirmation or commutation

Article 152.—The Commander-in-Chief is authorized at his discretion to confirm any Sentence of Death, or to remit such Sentence, or to commute it into Imprisonment with Hard Labour and Transportation for 'life, or into Imprisonment with Hard Labour for any term of years.

Transportation

Article 153.—No Sentence of Transportation shall be carried into effect until confirmed by the Commander-in-Chief, and the Commander-in-Chief is authorized at his discretion to confirm any such Sentence, or to commute it into Imprisonment, with or without Hard Labour, for any period of time.

Remission or mitigation

Article 154.—It shall be competent to any Officer having authority to confirm the Sentence of a General or other Court-martial to, remit any Sentence passed by such Court-martial, or to mitigate such Sentence by substituting simple Imprisonment for Imprisonment, with Hard Labour, or by reducing the period of Imprisonment, or by directing the discharge of the offender in lieu of any Imprisonment.

No person to be tried again for the same crime, after trial under this section

Article 155.—A person who may have been tried for any offence by a Court-martial under the authority of these Articles of War, shall not be tried for the same in any other Court whatsoever, and no person who shall have been acquitted or convicted of any offence by a Court of Civil Judicature shall be punished by a Court-martial for the same, otherwise than by Cashiering or Dismissal from the service.

Rules respecting bazar and cantonment police, and punchayets, declared in force

Article 156.—The Regulations at present in force at any Presidency, by which the office and powers of Commissariat Officers, or Officers in charge of the Police, or Superintendents of

Bazars, are defined and controlled ; or by which Punchayets are constituted and guided ; or by which jurisdiction is given to Courts-martial over offences committed by persons amenable to the Articles of War, within certain limits beyond or around Cantonments ; are hereby declared to be in full force, and the same shall continue to be observed at the several Presidencies respectively.

SECTION VII

Application of the Articles

Application of the articles

Article 157. —All Officers and Soldiers, all Drivers, Farriers, Trumpeters, and Drummers; all unattested Recruits; all Hospital Attendants, Sub-Assistant Surgeons, Native Doctors, and Dresser; all Artificers and Labourers, Sutlers, Followers, public and private, or others attached to or serving with any part of the Army, are to be governed by these Articles, and subject to trial by Courts-martial.

Provided, that persons of European descent, (whether on the side of their father or mother), professing the Christian religion, shall not be amenable to these Articles; but if belonging to the descriptions mentioned in this Article, (and not being Her Majesty's natural born subjects born in Europe, or the children of such subjects), shall be tried and punished in the same manner as persons are who are subject to the Mutiny Act and Articles of War in force for the better Government of the European Officers and Soldiers in the service of the East-India Company.

Promulgation of the Articles

Promulgation of the articles

Article 158.—These Articles are to be translated into the several languages of the different Presidencies, and the parts following, viz., the second Section, together with the following Articles in other Sections which are marked with an* (Asterisk), viz., 2, 4, 75, 78, 80, 102, 103, 110, and 111, are to be read once every three months at the head of every Regiment, Troop, or Company mustered in the service and to every Recruit at the period of his attestation.

AD 1849, ACT XIV

An Act to punish tampering with the Army or Navy: Passed by the Honourable the President of the Council of India in Council, on 25 August 1849, with the Assent of the Most Noble the Governor General of India

Preamble

WHEREAS the laws in force for punishing mutiny and sedition do not sufficiently provide for the punishment of all persons endeavouring to stir up mutiny and sedition among the forces of the East-India Company, or to seduce them from their allegiance and duty, it is enacted as follows:

Punishment for seducing military or naval persons form their allegiance, or for exciting mutiny or sedition

I. Every person who maliciously and advisedly endeavours to seduce any person or persons, serving or engaged to serve in the military or naval forces of the East-India Company, from his or their allegiance to Majesty, or duty to the said Company, or who endeavours to stir up any person or persons belonging to either of the said services, to commit any act of mutiny, or to make or endeavour to make any mutinous assembly, or to commit any traitorous or mutinous practice whatsoever, shall, on conviction, suffer transportation for life, or imprisonment, with or without hard labour, for any term not longer than seven years, as the court shall adjudge.

Committal and trial of persons charged with offences under this Act

II. Any person charged with any offence punishable under this Act, may be committed by any magistrate within the territories under the Government of the East-India Company, and shall be tried by the Court of Sessions, or if the offender be not within the ordinary jurisdiction of the Court of Sessions, by the Supreme Court of Judicature established by royal charter within the presidency in which he is in custody.

No futwa required

III. No court shall, on the trial of any offence under this Act, require any futwa from any law officer.

Provision of this Act not to exempt from trial by court-martial

V. This Act shall not exempt any person governed by the Articles of War from being tried by a court-martial, and punished according to the Articles of War, nor any person belonging to the Indian navy from being tried by a court-martial, and punished according to the laws for the observance of discipline in the Indian navy; but no person shall be tried for the same offence under the said Articles or Laws, and also under this Act.

AD 1850, ACT VI

An Act for enabling the Commander-in-Chief to pardon Military Offences: Passed by the Governor-General of India in Council, on the 15th of March, 1850

Preamble

WHEREAS the power of pardoning persons under sentence of a court-martial, for offences which are not punishable by any other authority, may be entrusted to the Commander-in-Chief of the military forces in the service of the East-India Company in each presidency, but in all other cases ought to belong only to the Supreme Government, it is enacted as follows:

Commander-in-Chief may pardon convicts or remit part of sentence

I. The Commander-in-Chief of the military forces in the service of the East-India Company in each presidency shall have power to pardon any person belonging to the said forces, convicted by sentence of a court-martial of any offence against the Articles of War framed for the government of the native officers and soldiers in the military service of the East-India Company, which, wherever committed, is not punishable otherwise than by sentence of a court-martial; or, instead of granting a full pardon to any such person, may remit any part of the punishment awarded for such offence.

Warrant to be issued,

II. In such cases, the Commander-in-Chief shall issue a warrant under his hand, setting forth the offence, and a copy of the warrant or other instrument by which the offender is kept in custody in execution of the sentence, and pardoning or remitting such part of the punishment awarded for the offence as to him shall seem fit.

And countersigned by magistrate or judge

III. The said warrant shall he countersigned by the magistrate of the zillah or city in which the offender is undergoing his sentence; or, if he is confined in any prison belonging to one of the Supreme Courts of Judicature established by royal charter, shall be countersigned by a judge of such court, if it shall appear to such magistrate or judge that the offence, wherever committed, is not punishable by any authority other than that of a court-martial, but not otherwise.

Authorities in charge of gaols to give effect to warrant

IV. All sheriffs, gaolers, and other persons having custody of any offender under sentence of a court-martial, shall obey and give effect to any warrant of the Commander-in-Chief, countersigned by a magistrate or judge of the Supreme Court as aforesaid, for the pardon and release of any offender in their custody respectively, or for the remission of any part of his sentence.

An Act for punishing Mutiny and Desertion, and for the better Payment of the Army and their Quarters

[18 VICTORIAE, CAP. XI]

16 March 1855

WHEREAS the raising or keeping a Standing Army within the United Kingdom of Great Britain and Ireland in Time of Peace unless it be with the consent of Parliament, is against Law: And whereas it is adjudged necessary be Her Majesty and this present Parliament that a Body of Forces should be continued for the safety of the United Kingdom, the Defence of the Possession of Her Majesty's Crown, and the Preservation of the Balance of Power in Europe, and that whole Number of such Forces should consists of One hundred and ninety-three thousand five hundred and ninety-five (193,565) men, exclusive of the Officers and Men belonging to the Regiments employed in the Territorial possession recruiting for those Regiments: And whereas no man can be forejudged of Life or Limb, or subjected in Time of Peace to any Kind of Punishment within this Realm, by Martial Law, or in any other manner than by Judgement of his Peers, and according to the known and established Laws of this Realm; yet nevertheless it being requisite, for the retaining all the before-mentioned Forces in their Duty, that an exact Discipline be observed, and that Soldiers who shall mutiny or stir up Sedition, or shall desert Her Majesty's Service, or be guilty of Crimes and Offences to the Prejudice of good Order and Military Discipline, be brought to a more exemplary and speedy Punishment than the usual Forms of the Law will allow; Be it therefore enacted by the Queen's most Excellent Majesty, by and with the Advice and Consent of the Lords Spiritual and Temporal, and Commons, in this present Parliament assembled, and by the Authority of the same, That--

I. Articles of war made by Her Majesty to be judicially taken notice of, and Copies printed by the Queen's Printer to be transmitted to Judges, &c.

It shall be lawful for Her Majesty to make Articles of War for the better Government of Her Majesty's Forces, which Articles shall be judicially taken notice of by all Judges and in all Courts whatsoever; and Copies of the same, printed by the Queen's Printer, shall, as soon as may be after the same shall have been made and established by Her Majesty, be transmitted by Her Majesty's Secretary-at-War to the Judges of Her Majesty's Superior Courts at Westmimter, Dublin, and Edinburgh respectively, and also to the Governors of Her Majesty's Dominions abroad; provided that no Person within the United Kingdom of Great Britain and Ireland, or the British Isles, shall by such Articles of War be subject to be transported as a Felon, or to suffer any Punishment extending to Life or Limb, except for Crimes which are by this Act expressly made liable to such Transportation or to such Punishment as aforesaid, or shall be subject, with reference to any

Crimes made punishable by this Act, to be punished in any Manner which shall not accord with the Provisions of this Act.

II. Persons subject to this Act

All the Provisions of this Act shall apply to all Persons who are or shall be commissioned or in Pay as an Officer, or who are or shall be listed or in Pay as a Non-commissioned Officer or Soldier, and to all Persons employed on the Recruiting Service receiving Pay in respect of such Service, and to the Officers and Soldiers belonging to the Forces of the *East India Company* while such Officers or Soldiers shall be in any Part of the United Kingdom, and to the Officers and Persons who are or shall be serving and hired to be employed in the Royal Artillery and Field Train, and to Master Gunners, and Gunners, and Conductors of Stores, and to all Officers and Persons who are or shall be serving in the Regiment of Royal Engineers and the Corps of Royal Sappers and Miners, and in the Corps of Royal Military Surveyors and Draftsmen, and to Persons in the Ordnance and Commissariat Departments, who are or shall be serving with any Part of Her Majesty's Forces at home or abroad, under the Command of any Officer having Commission from Her Majesty or from His late Majesty King William the Fourth, and to all Storekeepers and other Civil Officers who are or shall be employed by or act under the Ordnance at any of Her Majesty's Ordnance Establishments in the Islands of *Jersey*, *Guernsey*, *Alderney*, *Sark*, and *Man*, and the Islands thereto belonging, or at Foreign Stations ; provided that nothing in this Act contained shall extend to affect any Security which has been given by such Storekeeper, Barrack Master, or other Officer, or their Sureties, for the due Performance of their respective Offices, under the Provisions of an Act passed in the Fiftieth Year of the Reign of His Majesty King George the Third, to regulate the taking of Securities in all Offices, but that such Bonds and other Securities shall be and remain in full Force and Effect.

III. Act to extend to Jersey, Guernsey, &c.

This Act shall extend to the Islands of *Jersey*, *Guernsey*, *Alderney*, *Sark*, and *Man*, and the Islands thereto belonging, as to the Provisions therein for enlisting of Recruits, whether Minors Guernsey, or of full Age, and swearing and attesting such Recruits, and for mustering and paying, and to the Provisions for the Trial and Punishment of Officers and Soldiers who shall be charged with Mutiny and Desertion, or any other of the Offences which are by this Act declared to be punishable by the Sentence of a Court martial, and also to the Provisions which relate to the Punishment of Persons who shall fraudulently confess themselves to be Deserters, or who shall conceal Deserters, or shall knowingly buy, exchange, or otherwise receive any Arms, Clothes, Military Furniture, or Regimental Necessaries from any Soldier or Deserter, or who shall cause the Colour of any such Clothes to be changed, or who shall aid in the Escape of a Prisoner from a Military Prison, or who shall introduce forbidden Articles into such Prison, or shall carry out any such Articles, or who shall assault any Officer of such Prison, and also to the Provisions for exempting Soldiers from being taken out of Her Majesty's Service for not supporting or for leaving chargeable to any Parish any Wife or Child or Children, or on account of any Breach of Contract to serve or work for any Employer, or on account of any Debts under Thirty Pounds in the said Islands.

IV. Foreign Troops in this Country

All Officers and Soldiers of any Troops being mustered and in Pay, which shall be raised and serving in any of Her Majesty's Dominions abroad, or in Places in possession of or occupied by Her Majesty's Subjects under the Command of any Officer having any Commission immediately from Her Majesty, shall be subject to the Provisions of this Act and of Her Majesty's Articles of War, in like Manner as Her Majesty's other Forces are ; and if such Officers and Soldiers, having been made Prisoners, be sent into England or Ireland, although not allowed to serve therein, all the Provisions of this Act in regard to billeting Soldiers shall apply to such Officers and Soldiers.

V. Militia and Yeomanry

Nothing in this Act contained shall in anywise be construed to extend to any' Militia Forces or Yeomanry or Volunteer Corps in Great Britain or Ireland, excepting only in such Cases wherein, by any Act or Acts for regulating any of the said Forces or Corps, the Provisions contained in any Act for punishing Mutiny and Desertion shall be specifically made applicable to the said Corps.

VI. Power to constitute Courts-martial

For the Purpose of bringing Offenders against this Act and the Articles of War to Justice, Her Majesty may from Time to Time, in like Manner as has been heretofore used, grant Commissions under the Royal Sign Manual for the holding Courts-martial within the United Kingdom of Great Britain and Ireland, and may grant Commissions or Warrants under the said Royal Sign Manual to the Chief Governor or Governors of Ireland, the Commander of the Forces, or the Person or Persons commanding in chief, or commanding for the Time being, any Body of Her Majesty's Forces, as well within the United Kingdom of Great Britain and Ireland and the British Isles, as in any of Her Majesty's Garrisons and Dominions or elsewhere beyond Seas, for convening Courts-martial, and for authorizing any Officer under their respective Commands to convene Courts-martial, as Occasion may require, for the Trial of Offences committed by any of the Forces under the Command of any such last-mentioned Officer, whether the same shall have been committed before or after such Officer shall have taken upon him such Command; the Officer so authorized not being, however, below the Degree of a Field Officer, except in the Settlements on the Western Coast of Africa, where a Captain may be authorized to convene District or Garrison Courts-martial; and any Person subject to this Act who shall, in any Part of Her Majesty's Dominions or elsewhere, commit any of the Offences for which he may be liable to be tried by Court-martial by virtue of this Act or of the Articles of War, may be tried and punished for the same in any Part of Her Majesty's Dominions or elsewhere where he may have come or be after the Commission of the Offence, as if the Offence had been committed where such Trial shall take place.

VII. General Courts-martial

A General Court-martial convened in Saint Helena, the Settlements on the Western Coast of Africa, Honduras, New Zealand, the Australian Colonies, Hong Kong, and the Settlements on the Coast of China, and Prince of Wales Island, Singapore, and Malacca, shall consist of not less than Five Commissioned Officers; if convened in Jamaica, the Windward and Leeward Islands, British Guiana, Newfoundland, Bermuda, the Bahamas, the Cape of Good Hope or other Settlements in

Southern Africa, or in any Part out of the Queen's Dominions, excepting the Ionian Islands and the Parts before mentioned, it shall consist of not less than Seven, and if convened in any other Part of the Queen's Dominions, or in the Ionian Islands or in the Settlements of the East India Company it shall consist of not less than Thirteen Commissioned Officers; and shall have Power to sentence any Officer or Soldier to suffer Death, Transportation, or any other Punishment which shall accord with the Provisions of this Act.

VIII. District or Garrison Courts-martial

A District or Garrison Court-martial shall consist of not less than Seven Commissioned Officers, except in Bermuda, the Bahamas, the Cape of Good Hope or other Settlements in Southern Africa, Saint Helena, Jamaica, Honduras, Newfoundland, New Zealand, the Australian Colonies, the Windward and Leeward Islands, British Guiana, Hong Kong, and the Settlements on the Coast of China, where it may consist of not less than Five Commissioned Officers, and in the Settlements on the Western Coast of Africa, where it may consist of not less than Three Commissioned Officers; and such Court-martial shall have the same Power as a General Court-martial to sentence any Soldier to such Punishments as shall accord with the Provisions of this Act: Provided always, that such Court-martial shall not have Power to try a Commissioned Officer, nor to pass any Sentence of Death or Transportation.

IX. Regimental or Detachment Court-martial

A Regimental or Detachment Court-martial shall consist of not less than Five Officers, unless it is found to be impracticable to assemble that Number, when Three may be sufficient, and shall have Power to sentence any Soldier to Corporal Punishment, or to Imprisonment, and to Forfeiture of Pay, in such Manner as shall accord with the Provisions of this Act.

X. Courts-martial on Line of March or in troop Ships

In Cases of Mutiny and gross Insubordination or other Offences committed on the Line of March, or on board any Transport Ship, Convict Ship, Merchant Vessel, or Troop Ship, not in Commission, the Offender may be tried by a Regimental or Detachment Court-martial, and the Sentence confirmed and carried into execution on the Spot by the Officer in the immediate Command of the Troops, provided that the Sentence shall not exceed that which a Regimental Court-martial is competent to award.

XI. Courts-martial in special Cases out of the Queen's Dominions

It shall be lawful for an Officer commanding any Detachment or Portion of Her Majesty's Troops which may at any Time be serving out of Her Majesty's Dominions, upon Complaint made to him of any Offence committed against the Property or Person of any Inhabitant of or Resident in any such Countries, by any Person serving with or belonging to Her Majesty's Armies, being under the immediate Command of any such Officer, to convene a Detachment General Court-martial, which shall consist of not less than Three Officers, for the Purpose of trying any such Person; and every such Court-martial shall have the same Powers in regard to Sentence upon Offenders as are granted by this Act to General Courts-martial: Provided always, that no Sentence of any such

Court-martial shall be executed until the General commanding the Army to which the Division, Brigade, Detachment, or Party to which any Person so tried, convicted, and adjudged to suffer Punishment shall belong shall have approved and confirmed the same.

XII. Mixed Courts-martial in case of Marines and East India Company

Where necessary or expedient, Officers of Her Majesty's Royal Marines, or Officers in the Service of the East India Company, or Officers of both such Services, may sit on Courts-martial together with Officers of Her Majesty's Land Forces, whether the Commanding Officer by whose Order such Court-martial is assembled belongs to the Land or to the Marine Forces; and when the Person to be tried shall belong to the Land Forces, then the Proceedings of such Court shall be regulated, to all Intents and Purposes, as if the Court was composed of Officers of Her Majesty's Land Forces only, and the Provisions of this Act, and the Oaths hereby prescribed, shall be applicable to the Proceedings of such Court; but where the Person to be tried shall belong to Her Majesty's Royal Marines, then the Provisions of an Act passed in the present Session of Parliament, for the Regulation of Her Majesty's Royal Marine Forces while on shore, and the Oaths therein prescribed, shall be applicable; and where the Person to be tried shall be in the Service of the East India Company, the Provisions of an Act passed in the Twelfth and Thirteenth Years of Her present Majesty, to amend the Laws for punishing Mutiny and Desertion of Officers and Soldiers in the Service of the East India Company, and the Oaths thereby prescribed, shall be applicable, notwithstanding any Officer, though in the actual Service of the said Company, may hold a Commission from Her Majesty or from His late Majesty King William, the Fourth.

XIII. President of Courts-martial

The President of every Court-martial shall be appointed by the Authority convening such Court, and shall in no case be the Confirming Officer or the Officer whose Duty it has been to investigate the Charges on which the Prisoner is to be arraigned; nor in the Case of a General Court-martial under the Degree of a Field Officer, unless a Field Officer cannot be had; nor in any Case whatever under the Degree of a Captain, save in the Case of a Detachment General Court-martial holden out of Her Majesty's Dominions, or of a Regimental or Detachment Court-martial holden on the Line of March, or on board any Transport Ship, Convict Ship, Merchant Vessel, or Troop Ship not in Commission, or on any Foreign Station where a Captain cannot be had: Provided always, that in the Case of a Detachment General Court-martial holden out of Her Majesty's Dominions, the Officer convening such Court may be the President thereof.

XIV. Proceedings at Trial

In all Trials by Court-martial, as soon as the President and other Officers appointed to serve thereon shall be assembled, their Names shall be read over in the Hearing of the Prisoner, who shall thereupon be asked if he objects to being tried by the President or by any of such Officers; and if the Prisoner shall then object to the President, such Objection shall be referred to the Decision of the Authority by whom such President shall have been appointed; but if he object to any Officer other than the President, such Objection shall be decided by the President and the other Officers so as aforesaid appointed to form the Court; and when the Place of the President or other Officer in respect of whom any Challenge shall have been made and allowed shall be supplied by some Officer in respect of whom no Challenge shall have been made or allowed, or if no Challenge whatever shall have been made, or, if made, not allowed, the President and the other Officers composing a General Court-martial shall take the Oaths in the Schedule to this Act annexed before the Judge Advocate General or his Deputy, or Person officiating us Judge Advocate, and on Trials by other Courts-martial before the President of such Court, who are hereby respectively authorized to administer the same, and any sworn Member may administer the Oath to the President ; and as soon as the said Oaths shall have been administered to the respective Members, the President of the Court is hereby authorized and required to administer to the Judge Advocate, or the Person officiating as such, the Oath in the Schedule to this Act annexed; and no Proceeding or Trial shall be had upon any Offence but between the Hours of Eight of the Clock in the Morning and Four in the Afternoon, except in Cases which require an immediate Example, and except in the East Indies, where such Proceedings or Trial may be had between the Hours of Six in the Morning and Four in the Afternoon.

XV. Swearing and summoning Witnesses

All General and other Courts-martial shall have Power and Authority, and are hereby required, to administer an Oath to every Witness or other Person who shall be examined before such Court in any Matter relating to any Proceeding before the same; and every Person, as well Civil as Military, who may be required to give or produce Evidence before a Court-martial, shall, in the Case of General Courts-martial, be summoned by the Judge Advocate General, or his Deputy, or the Person officiating as Judge Advocate, and in the Case of all other Courts-martial, by the President of the Court; and all Persons so summoned and attending as Witnesses before any Court-martial shall, during their necessary Attendance in or on such Courts, and in going to and returning from the same, be privileged from Arrest, and shall, if unduly arrested, be discharged by the Court out of which the Writ or Process issued by which such Witness was arrested, or if such Court be not sitting, then by any Judge of the Superior Courts of Westminster or Dublin, or of the Court of Session in Scotland, or of the Courts of Law in the East or West Indies, or elsewhere, according as the Case shall require, upon its being made to appear to such Court or Judge, by any affidavit in a summary Way, that such Witness was arrested in going to or attending upon or returning from such Court-martial ; and all Witnesses so duly summoned as aforesaid who shall not attend on such Courts, or attending shall refuse to be sworn, or being sworn shall refuse to give Evidence or not produce the Documents under their Power or Control required to be produced by them, or to answer all such Questions as the Court may legally demand of them, shall be liable to be attached in the Court of Queen's Bench in London or Dublin, or in the Court of Session, or Sheriff Depute or Stewards Depute, or their respective Substitutes, within their several Shires and Stewartries in Scotland, or in Courts of Law in the East or West Indies, or in any of Her Majesty's Colonies, Garrisons, or Dominions, in Europe or elsewhere respectively, upon Complaint made, in like Manner as if such Witness, after having been duly summoned or subpoenaed, had neglected to attend upon a Trial in any Proceeding in the Court in which such Complaint shall be made: Provided always, that nothing in this Act contained shall be construed to render an Oath necessary in any Case where by Law a solemn Affirmation may be made instead thereof.

XVI. Previous Convictions to be put in evidence

After a Prisoner has been found guilty of any Charge or Charges, the Court before which any such Prisoner shall have been tried may, before passing Sentence on such Prisoner, and for the Purpose only of affixing Punishment, receive in Evidence against him any previous Convictions by Courts-martial, and in like Manner and for the like Purpose the Court shall receive in Evidence any previous Conviction of such Prisoner by a Court of ordinary Criminal Jurisdiction, where the Offence charged in the Indictment, so far as the Charge of which he was convicted, was of a felonious, fraudulent, or unnatural Nature; and in the Case of Convictions by Courts-martial, duly confirmed, the Court-martial Book or the Regimental or Company's Defaulters Book, and when none of those Books can conveniently be produced, a Certificate, which shall purport to contain a Copy of the Entry of such Convictions in such Books, or any of them, and which shall be signed by the Adjutant, or other Officer having the Custody of the Court-martial Book or of the Defaulters Book of the Regiment or Company to which the Prisoner belongs, shall be sufficient Evidence of such Conviction; and it shall not be necessary to prove the Signature or official Character of the Person appearing to have signed such Certificate, nor, if the Court be satisfied from all the Circumstances of the Case that the Prisoner under Trial is the Person mentioned in any such Certificate, shall it be necessary to give other Proofs of the Identity of the Person of the Offender; and in the Case of a Conviction by a Court of ordinary Criminal Jurisdiction, any Certificate transmitted as herein- after provided to the Officer commanding a Regiment by the Clerk of any such Court or other Officer having Custody of the Records of such Court, or the Deputy of such Clerk, containing the Substance and Effect of any Indictment, omitting the formal Part, together with the Judgment of the Court thereon, and purporting to be signed by such Clerk or other Officer, or by the Deputy of such Clerk, or if such Certificate cannot conveniently be obtained, a Copy thereof, duly certified by the Officer producing it, shall be sufficient Evidence of such last-mentioned Conviction; and it shall not be necessary to prove the Signature or official Character of the Person appearing to have signed such last-mentioned Certificate, nor, if the Court be satisfied from all the Circumstances of the Case that the Prisoner under Trial is the Person mentioned in such Certificate, shall it be necessary to give other Proofs of the Identity of the Person of the Offender: Provided always, that before any such Evidence shall be received it shall be proved to the Satisfaction of the Court that the said Prisoner had previously to his Trial received Notice of the Intention to produce such Evidence against him; provided also, that the Court shall in no Case award to him any other Punishment or Punishments than may by this Act and by the Articles of War be awarded for the Offence of which he shall have been so found guilty.

XVII. Report of Proceedings of General and District Courts-martial

Every Judge Advocate, or Person officiating as such at a General Court-martial, and the President of every District or Garrison Court-martial, where the Offender shall be a Non- commissioned Officer or Soldier belonging to Her Majesty's Land Forces, are required to transmit, with as much Expedition as the Opportunity of Time and Distance of Place can admit, the original Proceedings and Sentence thereof to the Judge Advocate General in London, in whose Office they shall be carefully preserved; and any Person tried by a General Court-martial, or any Person on his Behalf, shall be entitled, on Demand, to a Copy of such Sentence and Proceedings (paying reasonably for the same), whether such Sentence shall be approved or not, at any Time not sooner than Six Months if the Trial took place at Gibraltar, or in the Mediterranean, Three Months if at any other Station within Europe, and Twelve Months if elsewhere in Her Majesty's Dominions; provided that such Demand as aforesaid shall have been made within the Space of Three Years from the Date of the Approval or other final Decision upon the Proceedings before such General Court-martial.

XVIII. No Second Trial but Revision allowed

No Officer or Soldier, being acquitted or convicted of any Offence, shall be liable to be tried a Second Time by the same or any other Court-martial for the same Offence; and no Finding, Opinion, or Sentence given by any Court-martial, and signed by the President thereof, shall be revised more than once, nor shall any additional Evidence be received by the Court on any Revision.

XIX. Crimes punishable with death

If any Person subject to this Act shall at any Time during the Continuance of this Act begin, excite, cause, or join in any Mutiny or Sedition in Her Majesty's Land or Marine Forces, or shall not use his utmost Endeavours to suppress the same, or coming to the Knowledge of any Mutiny or intended Mutiny shall not, without Delay, give Information thereof to his Commanding Officer; or shall hold Correspondence with or give Advice or Intelligence to any Rebel or Enemy of Her Majesty, either by Letters, Messages, Signs, or Tokens, in any Manner or Way whatsoever; or shall treat or enter into any Terms with such Rebel or Enemy without Her Majesty's Licence or Licence of the General or Chief Commander; or shall misbehave himself before the Enemy; or shall shamefully abandon or deliver up any Garrison, Fortress, Post, or Guard committed to his Charge, or which he shall have been commanded to defend; or shall compel the Governor or Commanding Officer of any Garrison, Fortress, or Post to deliver up to the Enemy or to abandon the same; or shall speak Words or use any other Means to induce such Governor or Commanding Officer, or others, to misbehave before the Enemy, or shamefully to abandon or deliver up any Garrison, Fortress, Post, or Guard committed to their respective Charge, or which he or they shall be commanded to defend; or shall desert Her Majesty's Service; or shall leave his Post before being regularly relieved ; or shall be found sleeping on his Post; or shall strike or shall use or offer any Violence against his Superior Officer, being in the Execution of his Office, or shall disobey any lawful Command of his Superior Officer ; or who being confined in a Military Prison shall offer any Violence against a Visitor or other his superior Military Officer, being in the Execution of his Office; all and every Person and Persons so offending in any of the Matters before mentioned, whether such Offence shall be committed within this Realm or in any other of Her Majesty's Dominions, or in Foreign Parts, upon Land or upon the Sea, shall suffer Death or such other Punishment as by a Court-martial shall be awarded: Provided always, that any Non-commissioned Officer or Soldier enlisted or in Pay in any Regiment, Troop, or Company, who shall, without having first obtained a regular Discharge therefrom, enlist himself in any other Regiment, Troop, or Company, may be deemed to have deserted Her Majesty's Service, and shall be liable to be punished accordingly.

XX. Judgment of Death

No Judgment of Death by a Court-martial shall pass unless Judgment Two Thirds at least of the Officers present shall concur therein.

XXI. Commutation of Death for Transportation

Whensoever any General Court-martial by which any Soldier shall have been tried and convicted of any Offence punishable with Death shall not think the Offence deserving of Capital Punishment, such Court-martial may adjudge the Offender, accord- Owning to the Degree of the Offence, to Penal Servitude, or to be transported as a Felon for Life, or for a certain Term of Years, not less than Fourteen, or may sentence him to general Service as a Soldier in any Corps and in any Country or Place which Her Majesty shall thereupon direct, or may, if such Offender shall have enlisted for a limited Term of Years, sentence him to serve for Life as a Soldier in any Corps which Her Majesty shall please to direct: Provided always, that in all Cases where a Capital Punishment shall have been awarded by a General Court-martial or Detachment General Court-martial it shall be lawful for Her Majesty, or, if in the East Indies, for the Officer commanding in chief the Forces in India, or if out of Her Majesty's Dominions (the Ionian Islands excepted) for the Officer commanding in chief Her Majesty's Forces there serving, instead of causing such Sentence to be carried into execution, to order the Offender to be kept to Penal Servitude or to be transported as a Felon, either for Life or for a certain Term of Years, not less than Fourteen, or to suffer such Term of Imprisonment, either with or without Hard Labour, as shall seem meet to Her Majesty, or, if in the East Indies, or out of Her Majesty's Dominions (the Ionian Islands excepted), to the Officers commanding as aforesaid.

XXII. Embezzlement punishable by Transportation

Every Paymaster or other Commissioned Officer of Her Majesty's Forces, or any Person employed in the Ordnance or Commissariat Department, or in any Manner in the Care or Distribution of any Money, Provisions, Forage, or Stores, who shall embezzle or fraudulently misapply, wilfully damage, steal, or he concerned in or connive at the Embezzlement, fraudulent Misapplication, wilful Damage, or Theft of any Money, Provisions, Forage, Arms, Clothing, Ammunition, or other Military Stores belonging to Her Majesty's Forces or for Her Majesty's Use, may be tried for the same by a General Court-martial, which may adjudge any such Offender to Penal Servitude or to be transported as a Felon for Life or for any certain Term of Years not less than Fourteen, or to suffer such Punishment of Fine, Imprisonment, Dismissal from Her Majesty's Service, and Incapacity of serving Her Majesty in any Office, Civil or Military, as such Court shall think fit, according to the Nature and Degree of the Offence ; and every such Offender shall, in addition to any other Punishment, make good at his own Expense the Loss and Damage sustained, which shall have been ascertained by such Court-martial; and in every such Case the Court is required to ascertain by Evidence the Amount of the Loss or Damage incurred, and to declare by their Sentence that such Amount shall be made good by such Offender; and the Loss and Damage so ascertained as aforesaid shall be a Debt to Her Majesty, and may be recovered in any of Her Majesty's Courts at Westminster or in Dublin, or the Court of Exchequer in Scotland, or in any Court in Her Majesty's Colonies where the Person sentenced by such Court-martial shall be resident, after the said Judgment shall be confirmed and made known; and every Commissioned

Officer sentenced to Penal Servitude or to be transported as a Felon, when such Sentence shall be confirmed, shall thereupon cease to belong to Her Majesty's Service, and for ever be incapable of serving Her Majesty in any Military Capacity.

XXIII. Execution of sentence of Transportation in the United Kingdom

Whenever Her Majesty shall intend that any Sentence of Penal Servitude or of Transportation heretofore or hereafter passed upon any Offender by any Court-martial shall be carried into execution for the Term specified in such Sentence or for any shorter Term, or shall be graciously pleased to commute as aforesaid to Penal Servitude or to Transportation any Sentence of Death passed by any such Court, the Sentence, together with Her Majesty's Pleasure thereupon, shall be notified in Writing by the Officer commanding in chief Her Majesty's Forces in Great Britain and Ireland, or in the temporary Absenceof such Officer by the Adjutant General, or when there shall not be any Commander-in-Chief of Her Majesty's Forces in Great Britain and Ireland, then by the Secretary-at-War or his Deputy, to any Judaic of the Queen's Bench, Common Pleas, or Exchequer in England or Ireland, and thereupon such Judge shall make an Order for the Penal Servitude or Transportation of such Offender in conformity with such Notification, and shall also do all such other Acts consequent upon such Notification as such Judge is authorized to do by any Act in force touching the Penal Servitude or Transportation of other Offenders; and the Person in whose Custody such Offender shall at that Time be, and all other Persons whatsoever whom the said Order may concern, shall be bound to obey and shall be assistant in- the Execution thereof, and shall be liable to the same Punishment for Disobedience, or for interrupting the Execution of such Order, as if the Order had been made under the Authority of any such Act as aforesaid ; and every Person so ordered to Penal Servitude or to be transported shall be subject to every Provision made by Law and in force concerning Persons convicted of any Crime and under Sentence of Penal Servitude or of Transportation ; and from the Time when such Order of Penal Servitude or of Transportation shall be made every Act in force touching the Escape of Felons, or their afterwards returning or their being at large without Leave, shall apply to such Offender, and to all Persons aiding and abetting, contriving or assisting in any Escape or intended Escape, or returning without Leave, of any such Offender; and the Judge who shall make any Order of Penal Servitude or of Transportation as aforesaid shall direct the Notification of Her Majesty's Pleasure, and his own Older made thereupon, to be filed and kept of Record in the Office of the Clerk of the Crown of the Court of Queen's Bench; and the said Clerk shall have a Fee of Two Shillings and Six pence only for filing the same, and shall, on Application, deliver a Certificate in Writing (not taking more than Two Shillings and Six pence for the same) to such Offender, or to any Person applying in his or Her Majesty's Behalf, showing the Christian and Surname of such Offender, his Offence, the Place where the Court was held before whom he was convicted, and the Conditions on which the Order of Penal Servitude or of Transportation was given; which Certificate shall be sufficient Proof of the Conviction and Sentence of such Offender, and also of the Terms on which such Order for his Penal Servitude or Transportation was given, in any Court and in any Proceeding wherein it may be necessary to inquire into the same.

XXIV. In the Colonies

Whenever any Sentence of Penal Servitude or of Transportation heretofore or hereafter passed upon any Offender by any Court-martial holden in the East Indies, or in any Part of Her Majesty's Foreign Dominions, or elsewhere beyond the Seas, is to be carried into execution for the Term specified in such Sentence or for any shorter Term, or when Sentence of Death has been or shall as aforesaid be commuted to Penal Servitude or to Transportation, the same shall be notified by the Officer commanding Her Majesty's Forces at the Presidency or Station where the Offender may come or be, or in his Absence by the Adjutant General for the Time being, to some Judge of One of the Supreme Courts of Judicature in the East Indies, or Chief Justice, or some other Judge, as the Case may be, in any Part of Her Majesty's Foreign Dominions, who shall make Order for the Penal Servitude or Transportation or intermediate Custody of such Offender, in like Manner as for the Penal Servitude or Transportation or intermediate Custody of any other Convict; and upon any such Order being made it shall be duly notified to the Governor of the Presidency if in the East Indies, or to the Governor of the Colony if in any of Her Majesty's Colonies, or to the Person who shall for the Time being be exercising the Office of Governor of such Presidency or Colony, who, on Receipt of such Notification, shall cause such Offender to be removed to some Colony or Place in obedience to the Directions for the Removal of Convicts which shall from Time to Time be transmitted from Her Majesty through One of Her Principal Secretaries of State to such Presidency or Colony; and such Offender on being so removed shall undergo the Sentence of Penal Servitude or of Transportation which has been passed upon him in the Colony or Place to which he has been so removed or sent, and whilst such Sentence shall remain in force shall be liable to be there imprisoned, and kept to Hard Labour, and otherwise dealt with under such Sentence in the same Manner as if he had been sentenced to be imprisoned, with Hard Labour, during the Term of his Penal Servitude or of his Transportation, by the Judgment of a Court of competent Jurisdiction in the Colony or Place to which he has been so removed or sent: Provided always, that in any Case where a Sentence of Penal Servitude or of Transportation shall have been awarded by a General or Detachment General Court-martial it shall be lawful for Her Majesty, or, if in the East Indies, for the Officer commanding in chief the Forces in India, instead of causing such Sentence to be carried into execution, to order that the Offender be imprisoned for a Term not exceeding Two Years, either with or without Hard Labour, and Solitary Confinement not exceeding the Period herein-after prescribed.

XXV. Power to inflict Corporal Punishment

Any Court-martial may sentence any Soldier to Corporal Punishment not extending to Life or Limb for disgraceful Conduct as herein-after mentioned Misbehaviour, or Neglect of Duty; provided that no such Sentence of Corporal Punishment exceed Fifty Lashes.

XXVI. Power to inflict Corporal Punishment and Imprisonment

It shall be lawful for any General, District, or Garrison Court-martial, in addition to any Sentence of Corporal Punishment to award Imprisonment, with or without Hard Labour, and with or without Solitary Confinement.

XXVI. Power to commute Corporal Punishment

In all Cases in which Corporal Punishment shall form whole or any Part of the Sentence awarded by any Court-martial it shall be lawful for Her Majesty, or for the General or other Officer authorized to confirm the Sentences of Courts-martial, to commute such Corporal Punishment to Imprisonment, either solitary or with or without Hard Labour, for any Period not exceeding Forty two Days, or to mitigate such Sentence, or instead of such Sentence to award Imprisonment, either solitary or with or without Hard Labour, for any Period not exceeding Twenty Days, and Corporal Punishment, to be inflicted in the Prison, not exceeding Twenty-five Lashes ; provided that such Commutation of Punishment to Solitary Confinement shall in no Case exceed the Period herein-after prescribed.

XXVII. Forfeiture of Pay and Pension by Sentence of Court-martial

Any General Court-martial may, in addition to any other Punishment which it may be competent to award, sentence any Offender to Forfeiture of all Advantage as to additional Pay, Good conduct Pay, and to Pension on Discharge, which might have otherwise accrued from the Length of his former Service, or to Forfeiture of such Advantage absolutely, whether it might have accrued from past Service or might accrue from future Service, or to Forfeiture of the Annuity and Medal which may have been granted for former meritorious Service, or of the Gratuity and Medal awarded for former good Conduct, according to the Nature of the Case; and any District or Garrison Court-martial may also, in addition to any Sentence which such Court may award, sentence any Offender to such Forfeiture for Desertion or for disgraceful Conduct,—

In wilfully maiming or injuring himself or any other Soldier, whether at the Instance of such other Soldier or not, or of causing himself to be maimed or mutilated by any other Person, with Intent thereby to render himself or such other Soldier unfit for Service;

In tampering with his Eyes with Intent thereby to render himself unfit for the Service;

In wilfully doing any Act, or wilfully disobeying any Orders, whether in Hospital or otherwise, thereby producing or aggravating Disease or Infirmity, or delaying his Cure;

In malingering or feigning Disease;

In stealing or embezzling Government Property or Stores, or in receiving the same knowing the same to have been stolen;

In stealing any Money or Goods, the Property of a Comrade, of a Military Officer, or of any Military or Regimental Mess or Band, or in receiving any such Money or Goods knowing the same to have been stolen;

In making any false or fraudulent Accounts, Returns, Matters, or Entries, or assisting or conniving at the same being made, or producing the same as true, knowing the same to be false or fraudulent In stealing or embezzling or fraudulently misapplying Public Money intrusted to him;

Or in committing any other Offence of a felonious or fraudulent Nature, to the Injury of or with Intent to injure any Person, Civil or Military;

Or for any other disgraceful Conduct, being of a cruel, indecent, or unnatural Kind.

XXIX. Forfeiture of Pay on Conviction of Desertion or Felony

Every Soldier who shall be found guilty by a Court-martial of Desertion, of wilfully maiming or injuring himself or any other Soldier, whether at the Instance of such other Soldier or not, or of causing himself to be maimed or mutilated by any other Person, with Intent thereby to render himself or such other Soldier unfit for Service, of tampering with his Eyes with Intent thereby to render himself unfit for Service, such Finding having been confirmed, or of Felony in any Court of ordinary Criminal Jurisdiction in England or Ireland, or of any Crime or Offence in any Court of Criminal Judicature in any Part of the United Kingdom, or in any Dominion, Territory, Colony, Settlement, or Island belonging to or occupied by Her Majesty out of the United Kingdom, which would, if committed therein amount to Felony, shall thereupon forfeit all Advantage as to additional Pay, Good-conduct Pay, and to Pension on Discharge, which might have otherwise accrued from the Length of his former Service, in addition to any Punishment which such Court may award.

XXX. Forfeiture of Pay when in Confinement under Sentence

If any Non-commissioned Officer or Soldier, by reason of his Imprisonment, whether under Sentence of a Court-martial or of any other Court duly authorized to pass such Sentence, or by reason of his Confinement for Debt, or by reason of his Desertion, or, being an Apprentice, by reason of his being allowed to serve out his Time with his Master, shall have been absent from his Duty during any Portion of the Time limited by his Enlistment or Re-engagement or Prolongation of Service as herein-after provided, such Portion of his Time shall not be reckoned as a Part of the limited Service for which such Non-commissioned Officer or Soldier was enlisted or re-engaged, or for which his Term of Service may have been prolonged, and no Soldier shall be entitled to Pay, or to reckon Service towards Pay or Pension, when in Confinement under a Sentence of any Court, or during any Absence from Duty by Commitment or Confinement under any Charge of which he shall be afterwards convicted, either by Court-martial or by any Court of ordinary Criminal Jurisdiction, or whilst in Arrest for Debt ; and when any Soldier shall be absent as a Prisoner of War he shall not be entitled to Pay, or to reckon Service towards Pay or Pension, for the Period of such Absence; but upon rejoining Her Majesty's Service due Inquiry shall be made by a Court-martial, and unless it shall be proved to the Satisfaction of such Court that the said Soldier was taken Prisoner through wilful Neglect of Duty on his Part, or that he had served with or under or in some Manner aided the Enemy, or that he had not returned as soon as possible to Her Majesty's Service, he may thereupon be recommended by such Court to receive either the whole of such Arrears of Pay or a Proportion thereof, and to reckon Service during his Absence; and any Soldier who shall be convicted of Desertion, or of Absence without Leave, shall, in addition to any Punishment awarded by the Court, forfeit his Pay for the Day or Days during which he was in a State of Desertion, or during his Absence without Leave ; and if any Soldier shall absent himself without Leave for any Period not exceeding Five Days, and shall not account for the same to the Satisfaction of the Commanding Officer, or if any Soldier shall be guilty of any other Offence which the Commanding Officer may not think necessary to bring before a Court-martial, the Commanding Officer may, in addition to any minor Punishment he is authorized to award, order that such Soldier shall be imprisoned for any Period not exceeding One hundred and sixty-eight Hours, with or without Hard Labour, or with or without Solitary Confinement, as the said Commanding Officer may think fit, and such Soldier shall forfeit his Pay for any Day or Days on which he may be so imprisoned ; and the said Commanding Officer may moreover order that, in addition to or instead of such Imprisonment and Forfeiture, or any other Punishment which he has Authority to inflict, any Soldier who shall have so absented himself as aforesaid shall forfeit his Pay for the Day or Days on which he shall have so absented himself, and in pursuance of any such Order as aforesaid the Pay of the Soldier shall be accordingly forfeited : Provided always, that such Soldier shall not be liable to be afterwards tried by a Court-martial for any Offence for which he shall have been so punished, ordered to suffer Imprisonment, Punishment, or Forfeiture as aforesaid: Provided also, that any Soldier who shall be so ordered to suffer Imprisonment or Forfeiture of Pay shall, if he so request, have a Right to be tried by a Court-martial for his Offence, instead of submitting to such Imprisonment or Forfeiture: Provided also, that when any Sentence shall have been wholly remitted, and the Offence pardoned by competent Authority, the Soldier shall be entitled to receive his Pay for the Days he may have been in Confinement or Arrest previous to Trial, and until such Decision had been pronounced : Provided also, that it shall be lawful for Her Majesty's Secretary-at-War to order or withhold the Payment of the whole or any Part of the Pay of any Officer or Soldier during the Period of Absence by any of the Causes aforesaid.

XXXI. Forfeiture of Pay for Drunkenness on Duty

A General, District, or Garrison Court-martial may sentence any Soldier for being drunk on Duty under Arms, and any Court-martial may sentence any Soldier for being drunk when on any Duty not under Arms or for Duty or on Parade or on the Line of March, to be deprived of a Penny a Day of his Pay for any Period not exceeding Thirty Days, in addition to any other Punishment which such Court may award.

XXXII. Forfeiture of Pay and Liquor for habitual Drunkenness

Any General, Garrison, or District Court-martial before which any Soldier shall be convicted of habitual Drunkenness shall deprive such Soldier of such Portion of his Pay, for such Period not exceeding Two Years, and under such Restrictions and Regulations, as may accord with Her Majesty's Articles of War, subject to Restoration on subsequent good Conduct; and every Regimental or Detachment Court-martial shall deprive a Soldier, convicted of a Charge of habitual Drunkenness, of such Portion of his additional or regular Pay for such Period not exceeding Six Months, and under such Restrictions and Regulations, as may accord with Her Majesty's Articles of War, subject to Restoration on subsequent good Conduct; and in addition to such Deprivation of Pay, the Court may, if it shall think fit, sentence such Offender to any other Punishment which the Court may be competent to award: Provided always, that a Soldier so sentenced to the Forfeiture of Pay, who shall be quartered at or removed to a Station where Liquor forms Part of his Ration and is issued in Kind, shall be deprived of his Liquor in Kind instead of being deprived of One

Penny of his daily Pay for so long a Time as he shall remain at such Station, and such Sentence of Forfeiture of Pay shall remain in force.

XXXIII. Stoppages

In addition to any other Punishment which the Court may award, a Court-martial may further direct that any Offender may be put under Stoppages until he shall have made good—

Any Loss or Damage occasioned by him in any of the Instances of disgraceful Conduct herein-before specified;

Any Loss or Destruction of, or Damage or Injury to, any Property whatsoever, occasioned by his wilful or negligent Misconduct;

Any Loss or Destruction of, or Damage or Injury to, his Horse, Arms, Clothing, Instruments, Equipments, Accoutrements, or Regimental Necessaries, or any extra Article of Clothing or Equipment that he may have been put in possession of and ordered to wear on the Recommendation of the Surgeon for the Benefit of his Health, or making away with or pawning any Medal for Service in the Field or for general good Conduct which may have been granted him by Order of Her Majesty, or by Order of the *East India Company*, or any Loss or Destruction of, or Damage or Injury to, the Arms, Horse, Clothing, Instruments, Accoutrements, or Regimental Necessaries of any Officer or Soldier, occasioned by his wilful or negligent Misconduct;

Any Expense necessarily incurred by his Drunkenness or other Misconduct;

Provided always, that, except in the Case of the Loss or Destruction of any Arras, Clothing, Instruments, Equipments, Accoutrements, or Regimental Necessaries, in which Case the Court may by its Sentence direct that the said Stoppages shall continue till the Cost of replacing the same be made good, the Amount of any Loss, Destruction, Damage or Injury, or Expense, shall be ascertained by Evidence, and the Offender shall be placed under Stoppages for such an Amount only as shall be proved to the Satisfaction of the Court : Provided also, that after satisfying the Charges for his Messing and Washing, so much only of the Pay of the Soldier may be stopped and applied as shall leave him a Residue at the least of One Penny a Day.

XXXIV. Discharge with Ignominy

Whenever any Soldier shall have been convicted of any such disgraceful Conduct herein-before described, or of Desertion, and the Court in respect thereof shall have made the Forfeiture of all Claim to Pension on Discharge a Part of the Sentence passed on such Soldier, such Court may further recommend that he be discharged with Ignominy from Her Majesty's Service.

XXXV. Marking Deserters

On the first and on every subsequent Conviction of Desertion the Court-martial, after awarding such Punishment as it may think fit, may order the Offender to be marked on the Left Side, Two Inches below the Arm-pit, with the Letter D, such Letter not to be less than an Inch long, and to be marked upon the Skin with some Ink or Gunpowder, or other Preparation, so as to be visible and conspicuous, and not liable to be obliterated.

XXXVI. Power of Imprisonment by different Kinds of Courts-martial

A General, Garrison, or District Court-martial may sentence any Soldier to Imprisonment, with or without Hard Labour, and may also direct that such Offender shall be kept in Solitary Confinement for any Portion or Portions of such Imprisonment not exceeding Fourteen Days at a Time, nor Eighty-four Days in any One Year, with Intervals between the Periods of Solitary Confinement of not less Duration than such Periods ; and when the Imprisonment awarded shall extend beyond Three Months, the Court-martial shall imperatively order that the Solitary Confinement shall not exceed Seven Days in any One Month of the whole Imprisonment awarded, with Intervals between the Periods of Solitary Confinement of not less Duration than such Periods ; and any Regimental or Detachment Court-martial may sentence any Soldier to Imprisonment, with or without Hard Labour, for any Period not exceeding Forty-two Days, and may also direct that such Soldier may be kept in Solitary Confinement for any Portion or Portions of such Imprisonment, not exceeding Fourteen Days at a Time, with an Interval between them of not less Duration than such Periods of Solitary Confinement ; provided that when any Court-martial, whether General, Garrison, or District, or Regimental or Detachment, shall direct that the Imprisonment shall be solitary only, or when any Sentence of corporal Punishment shall have been commuted to such Imprisonment only, the Periods shall in no Case exceed Fourteen Days.

XXXVII. Imprisonment of Offenders already under Sentence for previous Offence

Whenever Sentence shall be passed by a Court-martial on an Offender already imprisoned under Sentence of a Court-martial for any Offence of which he has been before convicted, be lawful for the Court to award Imprisonment for the Offence for which he is under Trial, upon Conviction thereof, to commence at the Expiration of the Imprisonment to which such Offender shall have been previously sentenced; and where such Offender shall be already under Sentence, either of Imprisonment, of Penal Servitude, or of Transportation, the Court, if empowered to pass Sentence of Penal Servitude or of Transportation, may award such Sentence for the Offence for which he is under Trial to commence at the Expiration of the Imprisonment, Penal Servitude, or Transportation to which such Offender shall have been previously sentenced, although the aggregate of the Terms of Imprisonment, Penal Servitude, or Transportation respectively may exceed the Term for which either of those Punishments would be otherwise awarded.

XXXVIII. Term and Place of Imprisonment

Save as herein-before specially provided, every Term of Penal Servitude, Transportation, or of Imprisonment under the Sentence of a Court-martial, whether original or revised, shall be reckoned as commencing on the Day on which the original Sentence and Proceedings shall have been signed by the President ; and the Place of Imprisonment under the Sentences of General Courts-martial shall be appointed by the Officer commanding the District, Garrison, Island, or Colony, and under the Sentence of any other Court-martial shall be appointed by the Officer confirming the Proceedings of such Court-martial, and in default of such Appointment then the

Place of Imprisonment shall be appointed by the Officer commanding the Regiment or Corps to which the Offender belongs or is attached.

XXXIX. Military Prisons

It shall be lawful for the Secretary-at-War to set apart any Buildings now erected or which may hereafter be erected, or any Part or Parts thereof, as Military Prisons, and to declare that any Building, or any Two or more separate and detached Buildings, shall be, and thenceforth such Building or Buildings shall be deemed and taken to be, a Military Prison; and every Military Prison, whether the same now exist or may hereafter be established, which shall be, or which, under the Provisions of any former Act of Parliament, have been, so as aforesaid set apart or declared, shall be deemed to be a public Prison within the Meaning of this Act ; and all and every the Powers and Authorities with respect to County Gaols or Houses of Correction which now are or which may hereafter be vested in any of Her Majesty's Principal Secretaries of State shall, with respect to all such Military Prisons, belong to and may be exercised by the Secretary-at-War; and it shall be lawful for the Secretary-at-War from Time to Time to make, alter, and repeal Rules and Regulations for the Government and Superintendence of any such Military Prison, and of the Governor, Provost Marshal, Officers, and Servants thereof, and of Offenders confined therein; and it shall be lawful for the Secretary-at-War from Time to Time to appoint an Inspector General and Inspectors of Military Prisons, and a Governor, or Provost Marshal, and all other necessary Officers and Servants for any such Military Prison, and, as Occasion may arise, to remove the Governor or Provost Marshal, Officer or Servant of any such Military Prison; and the General or other Officer commanding any District or Foreign Station within which may be any such Military Prison, or such General or other Officer, and such other Person or Persons as the Secretary-at-War may from Time to Time appoint, shall be a Visitor or Visitors of such Prison; and the Secretary-at-War may authorize any General Officer commanding on a Foreign Station to appoint periodically Visitors to any Military Prison within his Command and the Secretary-at-War shall transmit to the Visitor or Visitors of every Military Prison established by his Authority a Copy of the Rules and Regulations which are to be observed and enforced, and the same shall accordingly be observed and enforced, within such Prison; and every Inspector, Visitor, and Governor of any such Military Prison respectively shall, subject to such Rules and Regulations as may from Time to Time be made by the Secretary-at-War, have and exercise in respect of such Prison, and of the Governors, Officers, and Servants thereof, and of the Prisoners confined therein, all the Powers and Authorities, as well in respect of administering Oaths as otherwise, which any Inspector, Visiting Justice, or Governor of a County Gaol or House of Correction may respectively exercise as such.

XL. Custody of Prisoners under Military Sentence in Common Gaols

Every Governor, Provost Marshal, Gaoler, or Keeper of any public Prison or of any Gaol of House of Correction in any Part of Her Majesty's Dominions shall receive into his Custody any Military Offender under Sentence of Imprisonment by a General or other Court-martial, upon Delivery to him of an Order in Writing in that Behalf from the Officer commanding the Regiment or Corps to which the Offender belongs or is attached, which Order shall specify the Period of Imprisonment which the Offender is to undergo, and the Day and Hour of the Day on which he is to be released ; and such Governor, Provost Marshal, Gaoler, or Keeper shall keep such Offender in a proper Place of Confinement, with or without Hard Labour, and with or without Solitary Confinement, according to the Sentence of the Court and during the Time specified in the said Order, or until he be discharged or delivered over to Military Custody before the Expiration of that Time under an Order duly made for that Purpose ; and whenever Troops are called out in aid of the Civil Power, or are stationed in Billets, or are on the Line of March, every Governor, Provost Marshal, Gaoler or Keeper of any public Prison, Gaol, House of Correction, Lock-up House, or other Place of Confinement, shall receive into his Custody any Soldier for a Period not exceeding Seven Days, upon Delivery to him of an Order in Writing on that Behalf from the Officer commanding such Troops.

XLI. Provision for Removal of Prisoners

In the Case of a Prisoner undergoing Imprisonment under the Sentence of a Court-martial in any public Prison other than the Military Prisons set apart by the Authority of this Act, or in any Gaol or House of Correction in any Part of Her Majesty's Dominions, it shall be lawful for the Officer who confirmed the Proceedings of the Court, or for the Officer commanding the District, Garrison, Island, or Colony, to give, as often as Occasion may arise, an Order in Writing directing that the Prisoner be discharged, or be delivered over to Military Custody, whether for the Purpose of being removed to some other Prison or Place, there to undergo the Remainder or any Part of his Sentence, or for the Purpose of being brought before a Court-martial either as a Witness or for Trial; and such Prisoner shall accordingly, on the Production of such Order, be discharged or be delivered over, as the Case may be: Provided also, that the Time during which any Prisoner under Sentence of Imprisonment by a Court-martial shall be detained in Military Custody shall be reckoned as Imprisonment under the Sentence, for whatever Purpose such Detention shall take place.

XLII. Their Subsistence in Common Goals

The Gaoler, or Person having the immediate Inspection of any public Prison, Gaol, House of Correction, Lock-up House, or other Place of Confinement in any Part of Her Majesty's Dominions, shall diet and supply every Soldier imprisoned by the Sentence of a Court-martial or as a Deserter with Fuel and other Necessaries according to the Regulations of such Place of Confinement, and shall receive on account of every Soldier, during the Period of his Imprisonment, Sixpence per Diem, which the Secretary-at-War shall cause to be issued out of the Subsistence of such Soldier, upon Application in Writing signed by any Justice within whose Jurisdiction such Place of Confinement shall be locally situated, together with a Copy of the Order of Commitment, and which Sum of Sixpence per Diem shall be carried to the Credit of the Fund from which the Expense of such Place of Confinement is defrayed.

XLIII. Expiration of Imprisonment in Common Gaols

Every Gaoler, or Person having the immediate Inspection of any public Prison, Gaol, House of Correction, or other Place of Confinement, to whom any Notice shall have been given, or who shall have Reason to believe or to know, that any Person in his Custody for any Offence, Civil or Military, is a Soldier liable to serve Her Majesty on the Expiration of his Imprisonment, shall give, if in Great Britain to the Secretary-at-War, and if in Ireland to the General commanding Her Majesty's Forces in Ireland, One Month's Notice of the Period of such Expiration of Imprisonment, or if there shall not be sufficient Time for a Month's Notice then the longest practicable Notice thereof.

XLIV. Musters and Punishment for false Musters

Musters shall be taken of every Regiment, Troop, or Company in Her Majesty's Service, twice at least in every Year, at such Times as shall be appointed; and no Soldier shall be absent from such Musters unless properly certified to be employed on some other Duty of the Regiment, or to be sick, or in Prison, or on Furlough; and every Officer who shall make any false or untrue Muster of Man or Horse, or shall wittingly or willingly allow or sign the Muster Roll wherein such false Muster is contained, or any Duplicate thereof, or who shall directly or indirectly take or cause to be taken any Money or Gratuity for mustering any Soldiers, or for signing any Muster Rolls or Duplicates thereof, or shall knowingly muster any Person by a wrong Name, upon Proof thereof upon Oath made by Two Witnesses before a General Court-martial, shall for such Offence be forthwith cashiered, and shall be thereby utterly disabled to have or hold any Civil or Military Office or Employment within the United Kingdom of Great Britain and Ireland, or in Her Majesty's Service.

XLV. Trials for Desertion after subsequent Re-enlistment

Every Soldier shall be liable to be tried and punished for Desertion from any Corps into which he may have unlawfully enlisted, although he may of right belong to another Corps and be a Deserter therefrom, and whether such Soldier shall be tried for deserting from the Corps to which he may of right belong, or for deserting from the Corps into which he may have unlawfully enlisted, or for any other Desertion, every Desertion previous or subsequent to that for which he may at the Time be taking his Trial may, if duly stated in the Charges, be given in Evidence against him on such Trial.

XLVI. Apprehension of deserters in the United Kingdom and Colonies

Upon reasonable Suspicion that a Person is a Deserter it shall be lawful for any Constable, or if no Constable can be immediately met with, then it shall be lawful for any Officer or Soldier in Her Majesty's Service, to apprehend or cause such suspected Person to be apprehended, and to bring or cause him to be brought before any Justice living in or near such Place, and acting for the County or Borough wherein such Place is situate, or for the County adjoining such first-mentioned County or such Borough; and such Justice is hereby authorized and required to inquire whether such suspected Person is a Deserter, and if it shall appear by the Testimony of One or more Witnesses, taken upon Oath, or by the Confession of such suspected Person, confirmed by some corroborative Evidence, or by the Knowledge of such Justice, or by Evidence sufficient to satisfy such Justice that there are reasonable Grounds for believing that such suspected Person is a Deserter, such Justice shall forthwith cause him to be conveyed in civil Custody to the Head Quarters or Depot of the Regiment to which he belongs, if stationed within Five Miles of the Place of Apprehension, or if such Head Quarters or Depot shall not be stationed within Five Miles, then to the nearest or most convenient public Prison (other than a Military Prison set apart under the Authority of this Act) or Police Station legally provided as a Lock-up House for temporary Confinement of Persons taken into Custody, whether such Prison or Police Station be in the County or Borough in which such suspected Person was apprehended, or in which he was committed, or not; or if the Deserter shall have been apprehended by a Party of Soldiers of his own Regiment in charge of a Commissioned Officer, such Justice may deliver him up to such Party, unless the Officer shall deem it necessary to have the Deserter committed to Prison for safe Custody; and such Justice shall transmit an Account thereof, in the Form prescribed in the Schedule annexed to this Act, to the Secretary-at-War, specifying therein whether such Deserter was delivered to his Regiment or to the Party of his Regiment in order for his being taken to the Head Quarters or Depot of his Regiment, or whether such Deserter was committed to Prison, to the end that the Person so committed may be removed by an Order from the Office of the said Secretary-at-War, and proceeded against according to Law, and such Justice shall also send to the Secretary-at-War a Report, stating the Names of the Persons by whom the Deserter was apprehended and secured; and the Secretary-at-War shall transmit to such Justice an Order for the Payment to such Persons of such Sum not exceeding Forty Shillings as the Secretary-at-War shall be satisfied they are entitled to according to the true Intent and Meaning of this Act; and for such Information, Commitment, and Report as aforesaid the Clerk of the said Justice shall be entitled to a Fee of Two Shillings and no more; and every Gaoler and other Person into whose Custody any Person charged with Desertion is committed shall immediately upon the Receipt of the Person so charged into his Custody pay such Fee of Two Shillings, and also upon the Production of a Receipt from the Medical Practitioner who, in the Absence of a Military Medical Officer, may have been required to examine such suspected Person, a Fee of Two Shillings and Sixpence, and shall notify the Fact to the Secretary-at-War, and transmit also to the Secretary-at-War a Copy of the Commitment, to the end that such Secretary-at-War may order Repayment of the same ; and when any Person shall be apprehended and committed as a Deserter in any of Her Majesty's Colonies the Justice shall forthwith cause him to be conveyed to some public Prison, if the Regiment to which he is suspected to belong shall not be in the Colony, or, if the Regiment be in the Colony, the Justice may, if within reasonable Distance, deliver him into Custody at the nearest Military Post, although the Regiment to which such Person is suspected to belong may not be stationed at such Military Post; and such Justice shall in every Case transmit to the General or other Officer commanding in the Colony a Description Return in the Form prescribed, to the end that such Person may be removed by Order of such Officer, and proceeded against according to Law.

XLVII. Temporary Custody of Deserters in Gaols

Every Gaoler, or Person having the immediate Inspection of any public Prison, Gaol, House of Correction, Lock-up House, or other Place of Confinement in any Part of Her Majesty's Dominions, is hereby required to receive and confine every Deserter who shall be delivered into his Custody by any Soldier conveying such Deserter under lawful Authority, on Production of the Warrant of the Justice of the Peace on which such Deserter shall have been taken, or some Order from the Office of the Secretary-at-War, which Order shall continue in force until the Deserter shall have arrived at his Destination; and such Gaoler or Person shall be entitled to One Shilling for the safe Custody of the said Deserter while halted on the March, and to such Subsistence for his Maintenance as shall be directed by Her Majesty's Regulations.

XLVIII. Desertion of Recruits

Any Recruit who shall desert prior to joining the Regiment for which he has enlisted shall, on being apprehended, and committed for such Desertion by any Justice of the Peace upon the Testimony of One or more Witnesses upon Oath, or upon his own Confession, be liable to be transferred to any Regiment or Depot nearest to the Place where he shall have been apprehended, or to any other Regiment to which Her Majesty may deem it more desirable that he should be transferred: Provided always, that all Cavalry Recruits so committed for Desertion shall be transferred to Cavalry Regiments, and Infantry Recruits to Infantry Regiments; and that such Deserters thus transferred shall not be liable to other Punishment for the Offence, or to any other Penalty except the Forfeiture of their personal Bounty reserving only for them that Part of the Bounty which is applicable to and required for the Provision of Necessaries.

XLIX. Fraudulent Confession of Desertion

Any Soldier who, while serving in any of Her Majesty's Forces, or the Embodied Militia, or the Forces of the East India Company, shall to any Officer or Non-commissioned Officer fraudulently confess himself to be a Deserter, shall be liable to be tried by Court-martial, and any Person who shall voluntarily deliver himself up and confess himself to be a Deserter from Her Majesty's Forces, or the Embodied Militia, or the Forces of the East India Company, or who, upon being apprehended for any Offence, shall, in the Presence of the Justice, confess himself to be a Deserter as aforesaid, shall be deemed to have duly enlisted and to be a Soldier, and shall be liable to serve in any of Her Majesty's Forces, as Her Majesty shall think fit to appoint, whether such Person shall have been actually enlisted as a Soldier or not; or in case such Person shall not be a Deserter as aforesaid, he shall be liable to be taken before Two Justices of the Peace, and on Proof that any such Confession as aforesaid was false, shall by them be adjudged to be punished, if in England as a Rogue and Vagabond, and if in Scotland or Ireland by Commitment to some Prison or House of Correction, there to be kept to Hard Labour for any Time not exceeding Three Months, or he deemed guilty of obtaining Money under false Pretences, within the true Intent and Meaning, if in England, of an Act passed in the Seventh and Eighth Years of His Majesty King George the Fourth, intituled *An Act for amending and consolidating the Laws in England relative to Larceny and other Offences connected therewith* [7 & 8 G. 4. C. 29], and if in Ireland of an Act passed in the Ninth Year of the Reign of His Majesty King George the Fourth, intituled *An Act for consolidating and amending the Laws in Ireland relative to Larceny and other Offences connected therewith* [9 G. 4. c. 55] or shall be deemed guilty, if in Scotland, of Falsehood, Fraud, and wilful Imposition; and every Person so deemed to be guilty of obtaining Money under false Pretences, or of Falsehood, Fraud, and wilful Imposition, as the Case may be, shall be liable to be proceeded against and punished accordingly; and the Confession and receiving Subsistence as a Soldier by such Person shall be Evidence of the false Pretence, or of the Falsehood, Fraud, and Imposition, as the Case may be, and of the obtaining Money to the Amount of the Value of such Subsistence, and the Value of such Subsistence so obtained may be charged in the Indictment as so much Money received by such Person; and in case such Person shall have been previously convicted of the like Offence, or shall have been summarily convicted and punished, in England, as a Rogue and Vagabond, or in Scotland or Ireland by Commitment, for making a fraudulent Confession of Desertion, such former Conviction may be alleged in the Indictment, and may be proved upon the Trial of such Person; and in such Indictment for a Second Offence it shall be sufficient to state that the Offender was at a certain Time and Place convicted of obtaining Money under false Pretences as a Deserter, or for making a fraudulent Confession of Desertion, without otherwise describing the said Offence; and a Certificate containing the Substance and Effect only (omitting the formal Part) of the Indictment and Conviction for the former Offence, purporting to be signed by the Clerk of the Court or other Officer having the Custody of the Records of the Court where the Offender was first convicted, or by the Deputy of such Clerk, or by the Clerk of the convicting Magistrates, shall, upon Proof of the Identity of the Person of the Offender, be sufficient Evidence of the First Conviction, without Proof of the Signature or official Character of the Person appearing to have signed the same; and if the Person so confessing himself to be a Deserter shall be serving at the Time in any of Her Majesty's Forces, he shall be deemed to be and shall be dealt with by all Justices and Gaolers as a Deserter.

L. Extension of Furlough in case of Sickness

When there shall not be any Military Officer of Rank not inferior to Captain, or any Adjutant of Regular Militia, within convenient Distance of the Place where any Non-commissioned Officer or Soldier on Furlough shall be detained by Sickness or other Casualty rendering necessary any Extension of such Furlough, it shall be lawful for any Justice who shall be satisfied of such Necessity to grant an Extension of Furlough for a Period not exceeding One Month; and the said Justice shall by Letter immediately certify such Extension and the Cause thereof to the Commanding Officer of the Corps or Detachment to which such Non-commissioned Officer or Soldier belongs, if known, and if not then to the Agent of the Regiment, in order that the proper Sum may be remitted to such Non-commissioned Officer or Soldier, who shall not during the Period of such Extension of Furlough be liable to be treated as a Deserter : Provided always, that nothing herein contained shall be construed to exempt any Soldier from Trial and Punishment, according to the Provisions of this Act, for any false Representation made by him in that Behalf to the said Justice, or for any Breach of Discipline committed by him in applying for and obtaining the said Extension of Furlough.

LI. No Person acquitted or convicted by the Civil Magistrate or by a Jury to be tried by Court-martial for the same offence

No Person subject to this Act, having been acquitted or convicted of any Crime or Offence by the Civil Magistrate, or by the Verdict of a Jury, shall be liable to be again tried for the same Crime or Offence by a Court-martial, or punished for the same otherwise than by cashiering; and whenever any Officer or Soldier shall have been tried by any Court of ordinary Criminal Jurisdiction, the Clerk of such Court or other Officer having the Custody of the Records of such Court, or the Deputy of such Clerk, shall, if required by the Officer commanding the Regiment to which such Officer or Soldier shall belong, transmit to him a Certificate, containing the Substance and Effect only of the Indictment, omitting the formal Part, and containing also a Copy of the

Entry of the Judgment of the Court thereon if such Officer or Soldier shall have been convicted, or of the Acquittal of such Officer or Soldier, and shall be allowed for such Certificate a Fee of Three Shillings.

LII. Soldiers liable to be take out of Her Majesty's Service only for Felony, Misdemeanor, or for Debts amounting to 30 pounds and upwards

Any Person enlisted into Her Majesty's Service as a Soldier, Or serving as a Non-commissioned Officer or Drummer on the permanent Staff of the Disembodied Militia, shall be liable to be taken out of Majesty's Service only by Process or Execution on account of any Charge of Felony or of Misdemeanor, other than the Misdemeanor of refusing to comply with an Order of Justices for the Payment of Money, or on account of an original Debt proved by Affidavit of the Plaintiff or of some one on his Behalf to amount to the Value of Thirty Pounds at the least, over and above all Costs of Suit in the Action or Actions, such Affidavit to be sworn, without Payment of any Fee, before some Judge of the Court out of which Process or Execution shall issue, or before some Person authorized to take Affidavits in such Court, of which Affidavit, when duly filed in such Court, a Memorandum shall, without Fee, be endorsed upon the Back of such Process, stating the Facts sworn to, and the Day of filing such Affidavit; but no Soldier or other Person as aforesaid shall be liable by any Process whatever to appear before any Justice of the Peace or other Authority whatever, or to be taken out of Her Majesty's Service by any Writ, Summons, Warrant, Order, Judgment, Execution, or any Process whatsoever issued by or by the Authority of any Court of Law, or any Magistrate, Justice or Justices of the Peace, or any other Authority whatsoever, for any original Debt not Families, or amounting to Thirty Pounds, or for not supporting or maintaining, or for not having supported or maintained, or for leaving or having left his Family or any Part thereof chargeable to any Parish, Township, or Place, or to the Common Fund of any Union, any Relation or Child which such Soldier or Person might, if not in Her Majesty's Service, be compellable by Law to relieve or maintain, or for neglecting to pay to the Mother of any Bastard Child, or to any Person who may have been appointed to have the Custody of such Child, any Sum to be paid in pursuance of an Order on that Behalf, or for the Breach of any Contract, Covenant, Agreement, or other Engagement whatever, by Parol or in Writing, or for having left or deserted his Employer or Master, or his Contract, Work, or Labour, except in the Case of an Apprentice, or of an indentured Labourer, as herein-after described; and all Summonses, Warrants, Commitments, Indictments, Convictions, Judgments, and Sentences, on account of any of the Matters for which it is herein declared that a Soldier or other Person as aforesaid is not liable to be taken out of Her Majesty's Service, shall be utterly illegal, and and void, to all Litents and Purposes ; and any Judge of any such Court may examine into any Complaints made by a Soldier or by his Superior Officer, and by Warrant under his Hand discharge such Soldier, without Fee, he being shown to have been arrested contrary to the Intent of this Act, and shall award reasonable Costs to such Complainant, who shall have for the Recovery thereof the like Remedy as would have been applicable to the Recovery of any Costs which might have been awarded against the Complainant in any Judgment or Execution as aforesaid, or a Writ of Habeas corpus ad subjiciendum shall be awarded or issued, and the Discharge of any such Soldier out of Custody shall be ordered thereupon; provided that any Plaintiff, upon Notice of the Cause of Action first given in Writing to any Soldier, or left at his last Quarters, may proceed in any Action or Suit to Judgment, and have Execution other than against the Body ; provided also, that nothing herein contained relating to the leaving or deserting a Master or Employer, or to the Breach of any Contract, Agreement, or Engagement, shall apply to Persons who shall be really and bond fide Apprentices, duly bound, under the Age of Twenty-one Years, or to indentured Labourers, as herein-after prescribed.

LIII. Officers not liable to take Parish Apprentices

No Officer of Her Majesty's Forces residing in Barracks or elsewhere under Military Law shall be deemed liable to have any Parish poor Child bound Apprentice to him.

LIV. Officers not liable to be Sheriffs or Mayors

No Person who shall be commissioned and in Full Pay as an Officer shall be capable of being nominated or elected to be Sheriff of any County or other Place, or to be Mayor, Portreeve, Alderman, or shall be capable of holding any Office in any Municipal Corporation in any City, Borough, or Place in Great Britain or Ireland.

LV. Enlisting and swearing of Recruits

Every Person who shall receive Enlisting Money, knowing it to be such, from any Person employed in the Recruiting-Service, and being an Officer, Non-commissioned Officer, an attested Soldier, or an Out-Pensioner of Chelsea Hospital authorized to enlist Recruits, shall be deemed to be enlisted as a Soldier in Her Majesty's Service, and while he shall remain with the Recruiting Party shall be entitled to be billeted; and every Person who shall enlist any Recruit shall first ask the Person offering to enlist whether he does or does not belong to the Militia, and shall within Twelve Hours after the Receipt of the Enlisting Money cause to be taken down in Writing the Name and Place of Abode of such Recruit, and (if such Recruit shall not reside in or in the Vicinity of the Town or Place where he offered to enlist) the Place also at which he shall declare that he intends to sleep, in order that within Forty-eight but not sooner than Twenty-four Hours (any intervening Sunday not included) after his having received the Enlisting Money Notice of his having so enlisted be given to the Recruit in the Form prescribed in the Schedule to this Act annexed, or left at his usual Place of Abode, or at the Place where he stated that it was his Intention to sleep; and when any Person shall be enlisted as a Soldier in Her Majesty's Land Service he shall, within Ninety-six Hours (any intervening Sunday not included), but not sooner than Twenty-four Hours after such enlisting, appear, together with some Person employed in the Recruiting Service of the Party with which he shall have enlisted, before any Justice or other Magistrate residing in the Vicinity of the Place where such Person shall have enlisted, or before any Justice or other Magistrate acting for the Division, District, or Place where such Recruit shall have been enlisted, and not being an Officer in the Army; and if such Recruit shall declare his having voluntarily enlisted, the said Justice shall put to him the several Questions contained in the Schedule to this Act annexed, and shall then and there, and in the Presence of the said Recruit, record or cause to be recorded in Writing his Answers thereunto; and the said Justice is hereby required forthwith to read over, or cause his Clerk in his Presence to read over, to such Recruit, the Fortieth and Forty-sixth Articles of the Articles of War against Mutiny and Desertion, and to administer to such Recruit the Oath in the Schedule to this Act annexed,, or for Service in the Forces of the East India Company, as may be applicable to the Case of the Recruit, and no other Oaths ; and the Fee for administering each Oath shall be One Shilling and no more; and the said Justice is hereby required to give under his Hand the Certificate in the Schedule to this Act annexed; and if any such Recruit so to be certified shall refuse to take the Oath in the Schedule to this Act annexed before the said Justice, it shall be lawful for the Justice, at the Request of the Officer or Non-commissioned Officer with whom he enlisted, to detain and confine such Person until he shall take the said Oath of Fidelity.

LVI. Dissent and Relief from Enlistment

Any Recruit appearing as aforesaid before such Justice shall be at liberty to declare his Dissent to such enlisting, and upon such Declaration, and returning the Enlisting Money, and also paying the Sum of Twenty Shillings as Smart Money, together with the full Amount of any Pay which shall have been paid to such Recruit subsequent to the Period of his having been enlisted, shall be forthwith discharged and set at liberty in the Presence of such Justice; but if such Person shall refuse or neglect, within the Space of Twenty-four Hours after so declaring his Dissent, to return and pay such Money as aforesaid, he shall be deemed and taken to be enlisted, as if he had given his Assent thereto before the said Justice: Provided always, that it shall be lawful for any Justice to discharge any Person who shall have hastily enlisted, and who shall apply to him to declare his Dissent within such Ninety six Hours as aforesaid, upon Payment of the Sum of Money required to be paid by any Recruit declaring his Dissent under this Act, notwithstanding no Person belonging to the Recruiting Party shall be with the Recruit, if it shall appear to such Justice, upon Proof to his Satisfaction, that the Recruiting Party has left the Place where such Recruit was enlisted, or that the Recruit could not procure any Person belonging to such Party to go with him before the Justice; and the Sum paid by such Recruit upon his Discharge shall be kept by the Justice, and after deducting One Shilling as the Fee to his Clerk for reporting the Payment to the Secretary-at-War and Inspecting Field Officer of the District, shall be paid to any Person belonging to the Recruiting Party entitled thereto demanding the same; and no Recruit who has been actually, though erroneously, discharged by the Justice before the Expiration of Twenty-four Hours after the Time of his Enlistment, shall be liable on that Account to be proceeded against as having deserted from Her Majesty's Service ; and the Justice who shall discharge any Recruit shall in every Case give a Certificate thereof, signed with his Hand, to the Recruit, specifying the Cause thereof.

LVI. Offences connected with Enlistment

If any Recruit shall receive the Enlisting Money from any Person employed in the Recruiting Service (knowing it to be such), and shall abscond or refuse to go before such Justice, or shall thereafter absent himself from the Recruiting Party or Person with whom he enlisted, and shall not voluntarily return to go before some Justice within such Period of Ninety-six Hours as aforesaid, such Recruit shall be deemed to be enlisted and a Soldier in Her Majesty's Service, or in the Service of the *East India Company*, as fully to all Intents and Purposes as if he had been duly attested, and may be apprehended and punished as a Deserter, or for being absent without Leave, under any Articles of War made for Punishment of Mutiny and Desertion; and such Recruit shall not be discharged by any Justice of the Peace after the Expiration of such Ninety-six Hours as aforesaid, unless it shall be proved to the Satisfaction of such Justice that the true Name and

Residence of the Recruit were disclosed and known to the Recruiting Party, and that no Notice was given to the Recruit, or left at his usual Place of Abode, of his having so enlisted, or that the true Name and Residence of the Recruit were not taken down in Writing : Provided always, that in every Case wherein any Recruit shall have received Enlisting Money, and shall have absconded from the Party, so that it shall not be possible immediately to apprehend and bring him before a Justice, the Officer or Non-commissioned Officer commanding the Party shall produce to the Justice before whom the Recruit ought regularly to have been brought for Attestation a Certificate of the Name and Place of Residence of such Recruit; and the Justice to whom such Certificate shall be produced shall, after satisfying himself that the Recruit who had absconded cannot be found and apprehended, transmit a Duplicate thereof to Her Majesty's Secretary-at-War, in order that in the event of such Recruit being afterwards apprehended and reported as a Deserter, the Facts of his having received Enlisting Money, and having absconded after having been enlisted, may be ascertained before he be finally adjudged to be a Deserter; and any Recruit who shall have enlisted into and been attested for Her Majesty's Forces, and who shall be discovered to be incapable of active Service by reason of any Infirmity concealed or not declared by such Recruit before the Justice at the Time of his Attestation, may be transferred to any Garrison or Veteran or Invalid Battalion or Company, notwithstanding he shall have enlisted for any particular Regiment, and shall be entitled to receive such Proportion or Residue of Bounty only as Her Majesty may allow in that Behalf, instead of the Bounty upon which such Man shall have been enlisted, anything in any Act or Acts, or any Rules and Regulations relating to Soldiers, to the contrary notwithstanding; and it shall be lawful for any Two Justices acting for the County, District, City, Burgh, or Place where any such Recruit shall at any Time happen to be when any such Recruit shall be brought, and shall be proved upon Oath before them upon being attested to have concealed his having been a Soldier and discharged, or to have concealed his having been discharged upon any prior Enlistment, or to have willfully concealed any such Infirmity, or to have designedly made any false Representation, to adjudge such Recruit, if in England, to be a Rogue and Vagabond, and to sentence him to such Punishment as by any Law in force may be inflicted upon Rogues and Vagabonds, and to adjudge such Person, if in Scotland or Ireland, to be imprisoned, with Hard Labour, in any Prison or House of Correction for any Period not exceeding Three Months ; and any Recruit who shall designedly make any false Representation of any Particular contained in the Oaths and Certificates in the Schedule to this Act annexed, before the Justice, at the Time of his Attestation, and shall obtain any Enlisting Money or Bounty for entering into Her Majesty's Service, or into the Service of the East India Company, or any other Money, shall be deemed guilty of obtaining Money under false Pretences, within the true Intent and Meaning, if in England, of an Act passed in the Seventh and Eighth Years of His Majesty King George the Fourth, intituled *An Act for consolidating and amending the Laws in England relative to Larceny and other Offences connected therewith*, and if in Ireland, of an Act passed in the Ninth Year of the Reign of His Majesty King George the Fourth, intituled *An Act for consolidating and amending the Laws in Ireland relative to Larceny and other Offences connected therewith*, and such Recruit, if in Scotland, shall be deemed guilty of Falsehood, Fraud, and wilful Imposition; and any attested Recruit who shall in any Part of Her Majesty's Dominions or elsewhere have committed any of the before-mentioned Offences regarding Enlistment may be summarily punished or prosecuted, tried and convicted, for any such Offence, at any Time during the Continuance of the Service for which he shall have enlisted, and in any County or Place where he may happen to be when such summary Proceeding or Prosecution shall be instituted; and the Production of the Oath in the Schedule to this Act annexed, taken by the Recruit on his Attestation, and the Certificate then signed by the Justice before whom the Recruit was attested, certifying that the Questions and Answers contained in the Attestation were in his Presence put to and given by such Recruit, shall, in the Absence of Proof to the contrary, be deemed and taken to be sufficient Evidence of such Recruit having represented the several Particulars as in the Oath sworn by Lim ; and Proof by the Oath of One or more credible Witnesses that the Person so prosecuted hath voluntarily acknowledged that at the Time of his Enlistment he belonged to any Regiment in Her Majesty's Service, or to Her Majesty's Ordnance, Navy, or Marines, or to the Forces of the East India Company, shall be deemed and taken as Evidence of the Fact so by him acknowledged, without Production of any Roll or other Document to prove the same; and such Proof of such Acknowledgment shall be certified to the Secretary-at-War by the Justice before whom such Proof shall have been given; and any Man having been enrolled as a Volunteer under the Act Fifteenth and Sixteenth Victoria, Chapter Fifty, or any subsequent Acts, to serve in the Militia, who at the Time of offering to enlist into Her Majesty's Forces, Army, Ordnance, or Marines, or into the Forces of the East India Company, or to enter into Her Majesty's Navy, shall deny that he is a Militia Man then actually enrolled and engaged to serve in the Militia, and who shall not have completed his Engagement by Attestation or by being entered on the Books of the Navy, shall, upon Conviction thereof before any One Justice of the Peace in the United Kingdom, either upon the Oath of One Witness or upon his own Confession, be committed to the Common Gaol or House of Correction for any Time not exceeding Fourteen Days; and any Man enrolled as aforesaid who may have denied or shall hereafter deny, or who may have confessed or shall hereafter confess, to the Justice before whom he shall have been or shall be attested for the Army, Ordnance, or Marine Forces, or for the Forces of the East India Company, or who may have denied or shall hereafter deny, or who may have confessed or shall hereafter confess, on the Completion of his Engagement to enter the Navy, that he belongs to the Militia, shall not be liable to Imprisonment for such Offence, but shall, upon Conviction thereof before any One Justice in the United Kingdom, or before a Regimental or Naval Court of Inquiry, either upon his own Confession or upon the Oath of One Witness, forfeit all Militia Bounty which would have become payable to him during the Period of his belonging to Her Majesty's Regular Forces, or to the Forces of the East India Company, or to the Royal Navy, if he had not therein enlisted or entered, and be subjected to a Stoppage of One Penny a Day from his Pay for Eighteen Calendar Months, to be applied as the Secretary-at-War shall direct; or if enrolled in the Militia as a balloted Man or Substitute shall, if convicted before any One Justice as aforesaid, be committed to the Common Gaol or House of Correction, there to remain without Bail or Mainprise for and during any Time not exceeding Six Calendar Months, over and above any Penalty or Punishment to which such Person so offending may be otherwise liable; and such Person, whether he shall have been enrolled as a Volunteer or a balloted Man or Substitute, shall, from the Day on which his Engagement to serve in the Militia shall end, and not sooner, belong as a Soldier to the Corps of Her Majesty's Regular Forces, or of the *East India Company*'s Forces into which ho shall have so enlisted, or to the Navy into which he shall have entered: Provided always, that every such Person so enlisted shall be liable to serve within the United Kingdom of Great Britain and Ireland in any Regiment, Battalion, or Corps of Her Majesty's Regular Forces, or of the East India Company's Forces, in which he has so enlisted, during all the Time the Militia to which he shall belong shall remain disembodied, or shall not be called out for Training or Exercise, and shall during all such Time be subject to all the Provisions of this Act, or if he had entered the Navy to the Rules and Regulations by which that Force is governed, and liable to be apprehended and dealt with and punished as a Deserter from the Corps in which he shall have so enlisted, or from the Navy, if he shall neglect or refuse to join and serve in such Corps, or in the Navy, as aforesaid.

LVIII. Punishment of officers offending against Laws regarding Enlistment

Every Military Officer who shall wilfully act contrary to the Provisions of this Act in any respect regarding the enlisting and attesting of Recruits for Her Majesty's Service or for the Service of the *East India Company* shall, upon Proof thereof upon Oath by Two Witnesses before a General Court-martial, be cashiered, and disabled to hold any Civil or Military Office or Employment in Her Majesty's Service.

LIX. Enlistment and Re-enlistment abroad

And whereas it is expedient that Provision should be made for enlisting and attesting of Soldiers desirous of re-enlisting and others desirous of enlisting abroad: Be it therefore enacted, That it shall be lawful for Her Majesty, by any Warrant signed by the Secretary-at-War in that Behalf, to authorize the Governors of Colonies, and of the several Presidencies in India, to appoint any Person, not being a General Officer nor holding any Regimental Commission, to enlist or attest, or for any Justice of the Peace or Magistrate acting for the Place of such Re-enlistment or Enlistment, and not being a General Officer, nor holding any Regimental Commission, to enlist and attest, out of Great Britain or Ireland, any Soldiers or Persons desirous of enlisting or re-enlisting into Her Majesty's Service; and any Person so appointed shall have the same Powers in that Behalf as are given to Justices in the United Kingdom for all such Purposes of Enlistment and Attestation; and all such Appointments, past and future, and everything done or to be done under them, shall be valid and of full Effect, notwithstanding the Expiration of this Act or of any other Act of Parliament; and any Person so enlisted or reenlisted shall be deemed to be an attested Soldier; and as often as any Corps shall be relieved or disbanded at any Station beyond the Seas it shall be lawful for any Officers thereunto authorized by the Officer commanding in chief at such Station to receive as Transfers as many of the Soldiers belonging to the Corps leaving the Station as shall be willing and fit for Service for any Corps appointed to remain; and every Soldier so transferred is hereby deemed to be discharged from his former Corps, and an attested Certificate of Transfer shall be delivered to the Soldier; and every Infantry Soldier consenting to be transferred to the Cavalry or Artillery shall upon such Transfer become liable to serve the limited Period prescribed for the Cavalry or Artillery, as the Case may be, notwithstanding his original Engagement to serve in the Infantry for a shorter Period.

LX. Enlisting of Negroes

All Negroes or Persons of Colour who, although not born in any of Her Majesty's Colonies, Territories, or Possessions, shall have voluntarily enlisted into Her Majesty's Service, shall, while serving, be deemed to be Soldiers legally enlisted into Her Majesty's Service, and entitled to all the Privileges of natural-born Subjects; and all Negroes purchased by or on account of Her Majesty previous to the total Abolition of Slavery throughout the British Colonies, and serving in any of Her Majesty's Forces, and all Negroes who have been seized and condemned as Prize under the Slave Trade Acts, and appointed to serve in Her Majesty's Army, shall be deemed to be and shall be entitled to all the Advantages of Negroes or Persons of Colour voluntarily enlisted to serve as Soldiers in any of Her Majesty's Colonial Forces.

XLI. Apprentice enlisting to be liable to serve after expiration of his Apprenticeship

Any Person duly bound as an Apprentice in Great Britain or Ireland, or as an indentured Labourer in any of Her Majesty's Colonies or Possessions abroad, who shall enlist as a Soldier in Her Majesty's or the East India Company's Service, and shall state to the Magistrate before whom he shall be carried and attested that he is not an Apprentice or indentured Labourer as aforesaid, shall be deemed guilty of obtaining Money under false Pretences within the true Intent and Meaning of the before-recited Acts, if in England or in Ireland, or in the Colonies or Possessions aforesaid, and of Falsehood, Fraud, and wilful Imposition, if in Scotland, and shall after the Expiration of his Apprenticeship, or of his Indenture as a Labourer, whether he shall have been so convicted and punished or not, be liable to serve as a Soldier in any of Her Majesty's Regular Forces, or in the Forces of the East India Company, according to the Terms of the Enlistment, and if on the Expiration of his Apprenticeship, or of his Indenture as a Labourer, he shall not deliver himself up to some Officer authorized to receive Recruits, may be taken as a Deserter from Her Majesty's Forces.

LXII. Claims of Masters to Apprentices

No Master shall be entitled to claim an Apprentice or an indentured Labourer as aforesaid who shall enlist as a Soldier in Her Majesty's or the East India Company's Service, or shall be serving in the Embodied Militia, unless he shall, within One Calendar Month after such Apprentice or indentured Labourer shall have left his Service, go before some Justice, and take the Oath mentioned in the Schedule to this Act annexed, and produce the Certificate of such Justice of his having taken such Oath, which Certificate such Justice is required to give in the Form in the Schedule to this Act annexed, and unless such Apprentice shall have been bound, if in England, for the full Term of Seven Years, not having been above the Age of Fourteen when so bound, and if in Ireland or in the British Isles, for the full Term of Five Years at the least, not having been above the Age of Sixteen when so bound, and if in Scotland, for the full Term at least of Four Years, by a regular Contract or Indenture of Apprenticeship, duly extended, signed, and tested, and binding on both Parties by the Law of Scotland, prior to the Period of Enlistment, and unless such Contract or Indenture in Scotland shall, within Three Months after the Commencement of the Apprenticeship, and before the Period of Enlistment, have been produced to a Justice of the Peace of the County in Scotland wherein the Parties reside, and there shall have been endorsed thereon by such Justice a Certificate or Declaration signed by him, specifying the Date when and the Person by whom such Contract or Indenture shall have been so produced, which Certificate or Declaration such Justice of the Peace is hereby required to endorse and sign, and unless such Apprentice shall, when claimed by such Master, be under Twenty-one Years of Age: Provided always, that any Master of an Apprentice indentured for the Sea Service, or of any indentured

Labourer in Her Majesty's Colonies or Possessions abroad, shall be entitled to claim and recover him in the Form and Manner above directed, notwithstanding such Apprentice or indentured Labourer may have been bound for a less Term than Seven, Five, or Four Years as aforesaid : Provided also, that any Master who shall give up the Indentures of his Apprentice or of his Labourer as aforesaid within One Month after the enlisting of such Apprentice or indentured Labourer shall be entitled to receive to his own Use so much of the Bounty payable to such Recruit, after deducting therefrom Two Guineas to provide him with Necessaries, as shall not have been paid to such Recruit before Notice given of his being an Apprentice or an indentured Labourer.

LXIII. Punishment of Apprentices enlisting

No Apprentice or indentured Labourer as aforesaid claimed by his Master shall be taken from any Corps or Recruiting Party but under a Warrant of a Justice residing near, and within whose Jurisdiction such Apprentice or indentured Labourer shall then happen to be, before whom he shall be carried; and such Justice shall inquire into the Matter upon Oath, which Oath he is hereby empowered to administer, and shall require the Production and Proof of the Indenture, and that Notice of the said Warrant has been given to the Commanding Officer, and a Copy thereof left with some Officer or Non-commissioned Officer of the Party, and that such Person so enlisted declared that he was no Apprentice or indentured Labourer; and such Justice, if required by such Officer or Non-commissioned Officer, shall commit the Offender to the Common Gaol of the said Place, and shall keep the Indenture to be produced when required, and shall bind over such Person as he may think proper to give Evidence against the Offender, who shall be tried at the next or at the Sessions immediately succeeding the next General or Quarter Sessions of the County, Division, or Place, unless the Court shall on just Cause put off the Trial; and the Production of the Indenture, with the Certificate of the Justices that the same was proved, shall be sufficient Evidence of the said Indenture; and every such Offender, in Scotland, may be tried by the Judge Ordinary in the County or Stewartry, in such and the like Manner as any Person may be tried in Scotland for any Offence not inferring a Capital Punishment: Provided always, that any Justice not required as aforesaid to commit such Apprentice or indentured Labourer may deliver him to his Master.

LXIV. Wages of Servants Listing

It shall be lawful for the Justice before whom any Recruit shall be attested before the Expiration of the Term of Service for which he had been hired by his Master to adjudge to such Recruit a reasonable Proportion of his Wages for the Time he has actually served ; and the said Justice shall make an Order for the Payment of the Amount so awarded, and in case of Neglect or Refusal to pay the same within Four Days shall issue his Warrant for levying the same by Distress and Sale of the Goods and Chattels of the Master.

LXV. Removal of doubts as Attestation of Soldiers

And whereas certain Soldiers who have heretofore been duly enlisted, and who have voluntarily taken the Oath of Allegiance and Fidelity, and are now receiving Her Majesty's pay, have been sworn and attested, but Doubts have arisen whether the Justices before whom the said Soldiers have been so sworn and attested were duly qualified to administer to such Soldiers the Oaths prescribed by the several Acts passed for the punishing Mutiny and Desertion, and for the better Payment of the Army and then- Quarters: In every Case where any such Soldier, having been duly enlisted, shall have been so attested and sworn, and shall not have claimed to be discharged on or before the Seventeenth Day of March One thousand eight hundred and forty-six, he shall not be entitled to his Discharge by reason of such Informality, but shall be liable to all the Provisions of this Act, and of the Act passed during the last Session of Parliament for the punishing Mutiny and Desertion, and for the better Payment of the Army and their Quarters, where in force, and shall be entitled to the full Benefit of his past Service, and to all Pay and Pension in respect thereof, to all Intents and Purposes and in like Manner as if he had been duly attested and sworn.

LXVI. Authorized Deductions only to be made from the pay of the Army

No Secretary-at-War, Paymaster General of the Army, Paymaster, or any other Officer whatsoever, or their under Officers, shall receive any Fees or make any Deductions whatsoever, out of the Pay of any Officer or Soldier in Her Majesty's Army, or from their Agents, which shall grow due from and after the Twenty-fifth Day of April One thousand eight hundred and fifty-five (25 April 1855), other than the usual Deductions, or such other necessary Deductions as shall from Time to Time be required by Her Majesty's Regulations, or by Her Majesty's Order signified by the Secretary-at-War; and every Paymaster or other Officer having received any Officer's or Soldier's Pay who shall unlawfully detain the same for the Space of One Month, or refuse to pay the same when it shall become due, according to the several Rates and agreeably to the several Regulations established by Her Majesty's Orders, shall, upon Proof thereof before a Court-martial, be discharged from his Employment, and shall forfeit One hundred Pounds, and the Informer, if a Soldier, if he demand it, shall be discharged from any further Service; provided, as aforesaid, that it shall be lawful for Her Majesty's Secretary-at-War to give Orders for withholding the Pay of any Officer or Soldier for any Period during which such Officer or Soldier shall be absent without Leave, or improperly absent from his Corps and from his Duty, or, in case of any Doubt as to the proper Issue of Pay, to withhold it from the Parties aforesaid until Her Majesty's Orders shall have been signified by the Secretary-at-War.

Articles LXVII to LXXXVII dealing with Suspension of operations of Recited Acts, Billeting of Guards, Supply of carriage, etc, have not been included in this work.

LXXXVIII. Penalty for inducing soldiers to desert

Any Person who shall in any Part of Her Majesty's Dominions, by Words or by any other Means whatsoever, directly or indirectly procure any Soldier to desert, or shall by Words or by any other Means whatsoever attempt to procure or persuade any Soldier to desert, and any Person who, knowing that any Soldier is about to desert, shall aid or assist him in deserting, or, knowing any Soldier to be a Deserter, shall conceal such Deserter, or aid or assist such Deserter in concealing himself, shall be deemed guilty of a Misdemeanor, and shall, on Conviction thereof, be liable to be punished by Fine or Imprisonment, or both, as the Court before which such Conviction shall take place may adjudge.

LXXXIX. Penalty for forcible Entry in Pursuit of Deserters

Any Officer or Soldier who shall forcibly enter into or break open any Dwelling House or Outhouse, or shall give any Order under which any Dwelling House or Outhouse shall be forcibly entered into or broken open, without a Warrant from One or more Justices of the Peace, shall, on Conviction thereof before Two Justices of the Peace, forfeit a Sum not exceeding Twenty Pounds.

XC. Penalties on aiding Escape or Attempt to escape of prisoners, etc

If any Person shall convey or cause to be conveyed into any Military Prison appointed to be a public Prison under this Act any Arms, Tools, or Instruments, or any Mask or other Disguise, to facilitate the Escape of any Prisoner, or shall by any Means whatever aid and assist any Prisoner to escape or in attempting to escape and on from such Prison, whether an Escape be actually made or not, such Person shall be deemed guilty of Felony, and upon being convicted thereof shall be transported beyond the Seas for any Term not exceeding Fourteen Years; and if any Person shall bring or attempt to bring into such Prison, in contravention of the existing Rules, any spirituous or fermented Liquor, he shall for every such Offence be liable to a Penalty not exceeding Twenty Pounds and not less than Ten Pounds, or to Imprisonment, with or without Hard Labour, for any Time not exceeding Three Calendar Months; and if any Person shall bring into such Prison, to or for any Prisoner, without the Knowledge of the Governor, any Money, Clothing, Provisions, Tobacco, Letters, Papers, or other Articles not allowed by the Rules of the Prison to be in the Possession of a Prisoner, or shall throw into the said Prison any such Articles, or shall by Desire of any Prisoner, without the Sanction of the Governor, carry out of the Prison any of the Articles aforesaid, he shall for every such Offence be liable to a Penalty not exceeding Five Pounds, or to Imprisonment, either with or without Hard Labour, for any Time not exceeding One Calendar Month; and if any Person shall assault or violently resist any Officer of such Prison in the Execution of his Duty, or shall aid or excite any Person so to assault or resist any such Officer, he shall for every such Offence be liable to a Penalty not exceeding Five Pounds, or to Imprisonment, either with or without Hard Labour, for any Time not exceeding One Calendar Month, or, if the Offender be a Soldier already under Sentence of Imprisonment, he shall be liable to be sentenced for every such Offence to be imprisoned, either with or without Hard Labour, upon Conviction thereof by a Board of not less than Three of the Visitors of the Prison, for any Time not exceeding Six Calendar Months, or upon Conviction thereof by a single Visitor for any Time not exceeding Seventy-two Hours, in addition to so much of the Time for which he was originally sentenced as may then be unexpired; or if such Soldier shall, within Forty-eight Hours of the Expiration of his Sentence, be guilty of any Offence against the Rules of the Prison, he may, on Conviction thereof by a single Visitor, be imprisoned, either with or without Hard Labour or Solitary Confinement, for a Period not exceeding Seventy-two Hours in addition to his original Sentences; and all the Provisions of any Act or Acts of Parliament for the Regulation or better ordering of Gaols, Houses of Correction, or Prisons in *England* and *Wales* to shall be deemed to apply to all Military Prisons, so far as any Provision relates to such Offences; and it shall be lawful for the Governor, Provost Marshal, Officer, or Servant of any Military Prison to use and exercise all the Powers and Authorities given by any such Act to the Gaoler, Keeper, or Turnkey of any Prison, or to his or their Assistants, to apprehend or to cause Offenders to be apprehended, in order to their being taken before a Justice or Justices of the Peace; and all the Powers and Authorities given by such Act to any Justice or Justices of the Peace to convict Offenders in any of the above Cases, together with the Forms of Convictions contained in any such Act, shall be applicable to the like Offences when committed in respect of Military Prisons; and all the Provisions contained in any such Act relating to Suits and Actions prosecuted against any Person for anything done in pursuance of such Act shall be deemed to apply to all Suits and Actions prosecuted against any Person acting in pursuance of such Act in respect of Military Prisons.

XCI. Penalty for keeper of Prison for refusing to confine military offenders

Any Governor, Provost Marshal, Gaoler, or Keeper of any public Prison, Gaol, House of Correction, Lock-up House, or other Place of Confinement, who shall refuse to receive and to confine, or to discharge or deliver over, any Military Offender in the Manner herein-before prescribed, shall forfeit for every such Offence the Sum of One hundred Pounds.

Articles **XCII and CIII** not included. And not considered relevant.

CIV. Offences against former Mutiny and Articles of war

All Crimes and Offences which have been committed against any former Act for punishing Mutiny and Desertion, and for the better Payment of the Army and their Quarters, or against Acts and any of the Articles of War made and established by virtue of the same, may, during the Continuance of this Act, be tried and punished in like Manner as if they had been committed against this Act; and every Warrant for holding any Court-martial under any former Act shall remain in fidl Force, and all Proceedings of Courts-martial convened and held under any such Warrant shall be continued, notwithstanding the Expiration of such Act: Provided always, that no Person shall be liable to be tried or punished for any Offence against any of the said Acts or Articles of War which shall appear to have been committed more than Three Years before the Date of the Warrant for such Trial, unless the Person accused, by reason of his having absented himself, or of some other manifest Impediment, shall not have been amenable to Justice within that Period, in which Case such Person shall be liable to be tried at any Time not exceeding Two Years after the Impediment shall have ceased.

CV. Duration of this Act

This Act shall be and continue in force within Great Britain from the Twenty-fifth Day of Ajml One thousand eight hundred and fifty-five inclusive until the Twenty-fifth Day of April One thousand eight hundred and fifty-six; and shall be and continue in force within Ireland, and in Jersey, Guernsey, Alderney, Sark, and Isle of Man, and the Islands thereto belonging, from the First Day of May One thousand eight hundred and fifty-five inclusive until the First Day of May One thousand eight hundred and fifty-six; and shall be and continue in force within the Garrison of Gibraltar, the Mediterranean, and in Spain and Portugal, from the First Day of August One thousand eight hundred and fifty-five inclusive until the First Day of August One thousand eight hundred and fifty-six; and shall be and continue in force in all other Parts of Europe where Her Majesty's Forces may be serving, and in the West Indies and America, from the First Day of

September One thousand eight hundred and fifty-five inclusive to the First Day of September One thousand eight hundred and fifty-six; and shall be and continue in force within the Cape of Good Hope, the Isle of France or Mauritius and its Dependencies, Saint Helena, and the Settlements on the Western Coast of Africa, from the First Day of January One thousand eight hundred and fifty-six inclusive until the First Day of January One thousand eight hundred and fifty-seven; and shall be and continue in force in all other Places from the First Day of February One thousand eight hundred and fifty-seven inclusive until the First Day of February One thousand eight hundred and fifty-eight: Provided always, that this Act shall, from and after the Receipt and Promulgation thereof in General Orders in any Part of Her Majesty's Dominions or elsewhere beyond the Seas, become and be in full Force, anything herein stated to the contrary notwithstanding.

Form of Oaths to be taken by Members of Courts-martial

You shall well and truly try and determine according to the Evidence in the Matter now before you. So help you GOD.

I .... do swear, That I will duly administer Justice according to the Rules and Articles for the better Government of Her Majesty's Forces, and according to an Act now in force for the Punishment of Mutiny and Desertion, and other Crimes therein mentioned, without Partiality, Favour, or Affection, and if and Doubt shall arise which is not explained by the said Articles or Act, according to my Conscience, the best of my Understanding, and the Custom of War in the like Cases: And I further swear, That I will not divulge the Sentence of the Court until it shall be duly approved; neither will I, upon any account, at any Time whatsoever, disclose or discover the Vote or Opinion of any particular Member of the Court-martial, unless required to give Evidence thereof as a Witness by a Court of Justice or a Court-martial in due Course of Law. So help me GOD.

Act No. VIII of 1857

[Passed on 16 May 1857]

An Act to amend Act XIX of 1847

Whereas it is expedient to facilitate the trial and punishment of offences against the Articles of War for the Native Army; it is enacted as follows:—

I. It shall be lawful for the Governor General of India in Council, from time to time, by Order in Council, to empower every General or other Officer having the command of Troops in the service of Her Majesty or of the East India Company, or any of such General or other Officers, to appoint General or District or Garrison Courts Martial, as occasion may require, for the trial of any of the Officers, Soldiers, or followers of the East India Company, being natives of the East Indies or of other places within the limits of the said Company's Charter, and amenable to the Articles of War for the Native Troops, who may be charged with any offence punishable by the said Articles of War, which, in the judgment of such General or other Officer, requires to be punished without delay ; and also to confirm and carry into effect immediately or otherwise, any sentence of such Court Martial ; or to commute, mitigate, or remit any such sentence ; or, in case he shall deem it necessary so to do, to refer any such sentence to the Commander-in-Chief for his orders thereon.

II. Any General Court Martial, which may be appointed under the authority of this Act, shall be appointed by the senior Officer on the spot, and shall consist of not less than five Commissioned Officers, the number to be fixed by the General or other Officer appointing the Court Martial. The Order in Council may direct that a General Court Martial to be appointed under the provisions of this Act shall consist wholly of European Commissioned Officers or of Native Commissioned Officers; and in such case, the Officer appointing the Court Martial shall determine whether the same shall consist of European Officers or of Native Officers. Every General Court Martial appointed under the authority of this Act shall have all the powers of a General Court Martial specified in the 75th Article of War for the Native Army: and sentence of death, or other punishment to which the offender is liable by the said Articles of War, may be given by such Court Martial, if a majority of the members present concur in the sentence.

III. General Order No. 677 of 1857, made by the Governor General in Council in the Military Department, and bearing date the 14th of May 1857, is hereby confirmed; and the same shall have the force and effect of law, and shall be deemed to have had such force and effect from the date thereof.

IV. It shall be lawful for the Governor General in Council to countermand or alter the said General Order, or any Order in Council which may be issued under the authority of this Act.

Act No. XI of 1857

[Passed on 30 May 1857]

I. All persons owing allegiance to the British Government who, after the passing of this Act shall rebel, or wage war against the Queen or the Government of the East India Company, or shall attempt to wage such war, or shall instigate or abet any such rebellion or the waging of such war, or shall conspire so to rebel or wage war, shall be liable, upon conviction, to the punishment of death, or to the punishment of transportation for life, or of imprisonment with hard labor for any term not exceeding fourteen years; and shall also forfeit all their property and effects of every description.

Provided that nothing contained in this Section shall extend to any place subject to Regulation XIV of 1827 of the Bombay Code.

II. All persons who shall knowingly harbour or conceal any person who shall have been guilty of any of the offences mentioned in the preceding Section shall be liable to imprisonment, with or without hard labour, for any term not exceeding seven years, and shall also be liable to fine.

Act No. XIV. of 1857

[Passed on 6 June 1857]

An Act to make further provision for the trial and punishment of certain offences relating to the Army, and of offences against the State.

Whereas it is necessary to make further provision for the trial and punishment of persons who endeavour to excite mutiny and sedition among the Forces of the East India Company, and also for the trial of offences against the State; It is enacted as follows :—

I. Whoever intentionally seduces or endeavours to seduce any Officer or Soldier in the service or pay of the East India Company from his allegiance to the British Government or his duty to the East India Company, or intentionally excites or stirs up, or endeavours to excite or stir up, any such Officer or Soldier, or any Officer or Soldier serving in any part of the British Territories in India in aid of the Troops of the British Government, to commit any act of mutiny or sedition ; and whoever intentionally causes, or endeavours to cause, any other person to commit any such offence—shall be liable upon conviction to the punishment of death, or to the punishment of transportation for life, or of imprisonment with hard labor for any term not exceeding fourteen years ; and shall forfeit all his property and effects of every description.

II. Whoever shall knowingly harbour or conceal any person who shall have been guilty of any offence mentioned in the preceding Section, shall be liable to imprisonment, with or without hard labor, for any term not exceeding seven years, and shall also be liable to fine.

III. It shall be lawful for the Governor General of India in Council, from time to time, by Order in Council, to empower every General or other Officer having the command of Troops in the service of Her Majesty or of the East India Company, or any of such General or other Officers, to appoint General Courts Martial for the trial of any person or persons charged with having committed an offence punishable by this Act or by Section I or Section II of Act XI of 1857, and also to confirm and carry into effect any sentence of such Court Martial.

IV. Any General Court Martial, which may be appointed under the authority of this Act, shall be appointed by the senior Officer on the spot, and shall consist of not less than five Commissioned Officers, the number to be fixed by the General or other Officer appointing the Court Martial. The Order in Council may direct that a General Court Martial to be appointed under the provisions of this Act shall consist wholly of European Commissioned Officers or wholly of native Commissioned Officers, or partly of European Commissioned Officers and partly of native Commissioned Officers ; and in such case the Officer appointing the Court Martial shall determine whether the same shall consist wholly of European Officers or wholly of native Officers, or partly of European Officers and partly of native Officers.

V. Sentence of death or other punishment to which the offender is liable by law, may be given by such Court Martial, if a majority of the members present concur in the sentence; and any such sentence may be confirmed by, and carried into effect immediately or otherwise by order of, the Officer by whom the Court Martial shall have been appointed, or, in case of his absence, by the senior Officer on the spot.

VI. It shall be lawful for the Governor General in Council to countermand or alter any Order in Council which may be issued under the authority of this Act.

VII. It shall be lawful for the Governor General in Council, or for the Executive Government of any Presidency or place, or for any person or persons whom the Governor General in Council may authorise so to do, from time to time to issue a Commission for the trial of all or any persons or person charged with having committed within any district described in the Commission, whether such district shall or shall not have been proclaimed to be in a state of rebellion, any offence punishable by Sections I and II of Act XI of 1857, or by this Act, or any other crime against the State, or murder, arson, robbery, or other heinous crime against person or property.

VIII. The Commissioner or Commissioners authorised by any such Commission, may hold a Court in any part of the district mentioned in the Commission, and may there try any person for any of the said crimes committed within any part thereof, it being the intention, of this Act that the district mentioned in the Commission shall, for the purpose of trial and punishment of any of the said offences, be deemed one district.

IX. Any Court held under the Commission shall have power, without the attendance or futwa of a Law Officer, or the assistance of Assessors, to pass upon every person convicted before the Court of any of the aforesaid crimes any sentence warranted by law for such crime; and the judgment of such Court shall be final and conclusive; and the said Court shall not be subordinate to the Sudder or other Court.

X. If a Commission be issued under the authority of this Act, any Magistrate or other Officer having power to commit for trial within the district described in the Commission may commit persons charged with any of the aforesaid crimes within such district for trial before a Court to be held under this Act.

XI. Nothing in this Act shall extend to the trial or punishment of any of Her Majesty's natural-born subjects born in Europe, or of the children of such subjects.

XII. This Act shall not extend to the trial or punishment of any person for any offence for which he is liable to be tried by the Articles of War.

XIII. The word "Soldier" shall include every person subject to any Articles of War.

XIV. This Act shall continue in force for one year.

Act No. XVI. of 1857

[Passed on 13 June 1857]

An Act to make temporary provision for the trial and punishment of heinous offences in certain Districts

Whereas it is expedient to make temporary provision for the trial and punishment of heinous offences in certain Districts; It is enacted as follows:—

I. Whoever shall commit or attempt to commit any heinous offence in any district or place in which Martial Law hath been or shall be established, or in any district or place to which this Act shall be extended by order of the Governor General of India in Council shall be liable, on conviction, to the punishment of death, or to the punishment of transportation for life, or of imprisonment with hard labor for any term not exceeding fourteen years ; and shall forfeit all his property and effects of every description.

II. The words "heinous offence" shall be deemed to include an attempt to murder, rape, maiming, dacoity, robbery, burglary, knowingly receiving property obtained by dacoity, robbery, or burglary, breaking and entering a dwelling-house and stealing therein, intentionally setting fire to a village, house, or any public building, stealing or destroying any property provided for the conveyance or subsistence of Troops, and all crimes against person or property attended with great personal violence, and all crimes committed with, the intention of assisting those who are waging war against the State or forwarding their designs.

III. Every person who shall be guilty of murder or any of the offences above described, may be tried either by Court Martial appointed under Act XIV of 1857, or by a Commissioner or Commissioners authorised by a Commission issued under the said Act, or by the ordinary Courts of Judicature.

IV. Nothing in this Act shall extend to the trial or punishment of any of Her Majesty's natural-born subjects born in Europe, or of the children of such subjects.

V. This Act shall continue in force for one year.

Act No. XVII of 1857

[Passed on 20 June 1857]

An Act to provide temporarily for the apprehension and trial of Native Officers And Soldiers for Mutiny and Desertion

Whereas it is expedient to make temporary provision for the apprehension and trial of mutineers and deserters amenable to the Articles of War for the Native Troops of the East India Company; It is enacted as follows:—

I. It shall be lawful for every Sessions Judge, and for every person exercising the same powers as a Sessions Judge, and for any person or persons whom the Governor General of India in Council, or the Executive Government of any Presidency or place, or the Chief Commissioners of the Punjab and Oude respectively, or the Commissioner of Nagpore, may, from time to time, invest with such power, to try for mutiny or desertion, wheresoever the offence may have been committed, any person subject to the Articles of War for the Native Troops of the East India Company, who, in the judgment of such Officer or other person, ought to be tried and punished without delay ; and such Officer or other person may, on conviction of the offender, sentence him to such of the following punishments as might by the said Articles of War be awarded against him by a General Court Martial—that is to say, if the offender be an Officer, to death or transportation for life ; and if a Soldier, to death, transportation for life, or imprisonment, with or without hard labor, for life or for any term of years. Such sentence shall be final and conclusive; and if a sentence of death be passed, the same may be carried into execution immediately or at such time as such officer or other person shall direct. The Sessions Judge or other Officer by whom the sentence shall be passed may, if he think proper, report the case to the Governor General in Council or to the Executive Government of the Presidency, together with any remarks or recommendation which he may think fit to make thereon; and the Governor General in Council or the Executive Government of the Presidency may either pardon the offender or commute the sentence to any less punishment.

II. It shall be lawful for the Governor General in Council, or the Executive Government of any Presidency or place, or any of the said Commissioners, to authorise any person or persons to issue a Commission for the trial of mutiny and desertion by any person or persons amenable to the said Articles of War; and every person authorised by such Commission shall have all the powers vested by this Act in a Sessions Judge.

III. It shall be lawful for any Police Officer or other person to apprehend without warrant any person upon reasonable suspicion that he is a mutineer or deserter and amenable to the Articles of War for the Native Troops of the East India Company.

IV. Every person who shall be apprehended as a mutineer or deserter under the provisions of this Act shall be conveyed without delay before a Magistrate or an Officer exercising any of the powers of a Magistrate in or near to the place where such person shall have been so apprehended, and may in the mean time be detained in custody ; and if the said Magistrate or other Officer shall be satisfied that such person is a mutineer or deserter and amenable to the Articles of War for the Native Troops, ho shall cause him to be delivered, together with any depositions and papers relative to the case, to the Commanding Officer of some Military Station, in order that he may be dealt with according to law ; or the Magistrate or other Officer may commit him for trial before any Officer or other person authorized by or under the provisions of this Act to try him for such offence, if the Magistrate or other Officer shall see good and sufficient reason for so doing ; or if the Magistrate or other Officer shall be authorised under the provisions of this Act to try for mutiny or desertion, he may, if he think fit, proceed forthwith to try the offender.

V. The provisions of Sections V and VI of Act XI of 1856 are hereby extended to all Officers, Soldiers, and other persons amenable to the Articles of War for the Native Troops.

VI. All Zemindars, Talookdars and other persons who, by Regulation VI 1810 of the Bengal Code, are declared to be accountable for the early communication of intelligence respecting the resort to their estates of the classes of offenders therein specified, are hereby declared to be accountable for the early communication of intelligence of the resort to any place within the limits of their estates of any person against whom there shall be reasonable suspicion of his having been guilty of mutiny or desertion ; and all the provisions of the said Regulation shall have the same force and effect as if persons guilty of mutiny and desertion had been especially included in the classes of offenders specified in that Regulation. Provided that no proceeding 'shall be taken against any Zemindar, Talookdar, or other person by virtue of this Section for anything done or omitted to be done by him within fourteen days after the passing of this Act.

VII. The word "Magistrate" shall include persons exercising the powers of a Magistrate, Police Magistrates and Justices of the Peace.

VIII. This Act shall continue in force for one year.

Act No. XXXII of 1857

[Passed on 25 November 1857]

An Act to amend the Articles of War for the Native Army

Whereas it is expedient that, on every conviction of mutiny or desertion, the Government or the Court or other lawful authority by which the offender shall be convicted should have power to order the offender to be marked : It is enacted as follows :—

I. It shall be lawful for the Government, by any general or special order, to direct that all or any persons or person subject to the Articles of War for the Native Army, who have been or shall be convicted of mutiny or desertion, shall be marked on the left side two inches below the armpit with the letter **M** in the case of a conviction of mutiny, and the letter **D** in the case of a conviction of desertion, either alone, or together with such other mark as the Government may consider necessary for the purpose of identifying the offender at any future time or of denoting the punishment to which he has been sentenced. The letter shall not be less than an inch long;

and such letter and other mark shall be made upon the skin, with some ink, gun powder or other preparation, so as to be visible and conspicuous and not liable to be obliterated.

II. It shall also be lawful for the Court, or other lawful authority by which any person subject to the Articles of War for the Native Army may be convicted of mutiny or desertion, to order, as part of the sentence on such person, that he be marked with the letter **M** or **D** as the case may be, which letter shall be made in the manner herein-before directed.

III. The word "Government," as used in this Act, shall mean the Governor General of India in Council, or the Executive Government of the Presidency within which the offender shall have been tried.

V. Any sentence or order, by which any person subject to the Articles of War for the Native Army may, upon conviction of mutiny or desertion, have been ordered to be marked, shall be deemed valid.

Act No. XXII of 1858

[Passed on 2 June 1858]

An Act to continue in force for a further period Acts XIV of 1857,
XVI of 1857, and XVII of 1857, and to authorize in certain
cases the transportation of offenders
sentenced to imprisonment

Whereas it is expedient that Acts XIV of 1857, XVI of 1857 and XVII of 1857 should continue in force until the end of the year 1859 ; and that, in certain cases, offenders sentenced to imprisonment under the said Acts should be transported beyond the Sea ; It is enacted as follows :—

I. Acts XIV of 1857, XVI of 1857, and XVII of 1857 shall continue in force until the end of- the year 1859.

II. Unless the Governor General in Council shall otherwise order, whenever any Court or other Officer shall sentence an offender under any of the said Act to imprisonment for a term exceeding three years, it shall be lawful for such Court or other Officer at the same time to order that the offender be transported beyond Sea for such term.

Act No. XXVI of 1858

[Passed on 7 July 1858]

An Act to make further provision for the trial and punishment of offences against the State

WHEREAS it is expedient to make further provision for the trial and punishment of offences against the State; It is enacted as follows:—

I. If any person, owing allegiance to the British Government, shall collect men, arms, or ammunition, or otherwise prepare to levy war, with the intention of either levying or being prepared to levy war against the Queen or the East India Company, or shall instigate any other person to commit such offence, or shall knowingly aid in the commission thereof, such person shall be liable to the punishment of death, or to the punishment, of transportation for life or of imprisonment with hard labor for any term not exceeding fourteen years; and shall also forfeit all his property and effects of every description.

II. Whoever shall knowingly harbour or conceal any person who shall have been guilty of any of the offences mentioned in the preceding Section, shall be liable to imprisonment, with or without hard labor, for any term not exceeding seven years; and shall also be liable to fine.

III. If any person, having knowledge of the commission of any of the offences mentioned in Section I, Act XI of 1857 or in Section I of this Act, shall conceal the fact or shall neglect to declare and make known the same to the Governor General in Council, or to the Executive Government of the Presidency or place, or to the Magistrate or person exercising the powers of a Magistrate in the District in which such offence shall be committed or such person shall be, he shall be liable to imprisonment, with or without hard labor, for a term not exceeding seven years; and shall also be liable to fine.

IV. All the provisions of Acts XI of 1857, XIV of 1857, and XXII of 1858, applicable to offences included in Sections I and II Act XI of 1857, shall be applicable to the offences specified in this Act.

V. Nothing in this Act contained shall extend to the trial or punishment of any of Her Majesty's natural born subjects born in Europe, or of the children of such subjects.

VI. This Act shall continue in force until the end of the year 1859.

Act No. XXVII of 1859

[Passed on 14 December 1859]

An Act to continue in force for a further period Acts XIV of 1857,
XVI of 1857, and XVII of 1857

Whereas it is expedient that Act XIV of 1857 (to make further provision for the trial and punishment of certain offences relating to the Army, and of offences against the State), Act XVI of 1857 (to make temporary provision, for the trial and punishment of heinous offences in certain Districts), and Act XVII of 1857 (to provide temporarily for the apprehension and trial of Native Officers and Soldiers for Mutiny and Desertion) should continue in force until the end of the year 1860;

It is enacted as follows:—

I. Acts XIV of 1857, XVI of 1857, and XVII of 1857 shall continue in force until the end of the year 1860.

The Government of India Act, 1858

Act 95 of 1858

(21 and 22 Vict., c. 106)

Effective 2 August 1858

An Act for the better Government of India

Whereas by an Act of the Session holden in the Sixteenth and Seventeenth Years of Her Majesty, Chapter Ninety-five, "to provide for the Government of India", the Territories in the Possession and under the Government of the East India Company were continued under such Government, in trust for Her Majesty, until Parliament should otherwise provide, subject to the Provisions of that Act and of other Acts of Parliament, and the Property and Rights in the said Act referred to are held by the said Company in trust for Her Majesty for the purposes of the said Government: And whereas it is expedient that the said Territories should be governed by and in the Name of Her Majesty: Be it therefore enacted by the Queen's most Excellent Majesty, by and with the Advice and Consent of the Lords Spiritual and Temporal, and Commons in this present Parliament assembled, and by the Authority of the same, as follows; that is to say, Transfer of the Government of India to Her Majesty.

SECTION 01: TERRITORIES UNDER THE GOVERNMENT OF THE EAST INDIA COMPANY TO BE VESTED IN HER MAJESTY AND POWERS TO BE EXERCISED IN HER NAME

The Government of the Territories now in the Possession or under the Government of the East India Company, and all Powers in relation to Government vested in or exercised by the said Company in trust for Her Majesty, shall cease to be vested in or exercised by the said Company; and all territories in the possession or under the government of the said Company, and all rights vested in or which if this Act had not been passed might have been exercised by the said Company in relation to any territories, shall become vested in Her Majesty, and be exercised in her name; and for the purposes of this Act India shall mean the territories vested in Her Majesty as aforesaid, and all Territories which may become vested in Her Majesty by virtue of any such Rights as aforesaid.

SECTION 02: INDIA TO BE GOVERNED BY AND IN THE NAME OF HER MAJESTY

India shall be governed by and in the Name of Her Majesty, and all rights in relation to any territories which might have been exercised by the said Company if this Act had not been passed shall and may be exercised by and in the name of Her Majesty as rights incidental to the government of India; and all the territorial and other revenues of or arising in India, and all tributes and other payments in respect of any territories which would have been receivable by or in the name of the said Company if this Act had not been passed, shall be received for and in the name of Her Majesty, and shall be applied and disposed of for the purposes of the government of India alone, subject to the provisions of this Act.

SECTION 03: SECRETARY OF STATE TO EXERCISE POWERS NOW EXERCISED BY THE COMPANY, ETC

Save as herein otherwise provided, one of Her Majesty's Principal Secretaries of State shall have and perform all such or the like powers and duties in anywise relating to the government or revenues of India, and all such or the like powers over all officers appointed or continued under this Act, as might or should have been exercised or performed by the East India Company, or by the Court of Directors or Court of Proprietors of the said Company, either alone or by the direction or with the sanction or Approbation of the Commissioners for the Affairs of India in relation to such government or revenues, and the officers and servants of the said Company respectively, and also all such powers as might have been exercised by the said Commissioners alone: Countersigning of warrants-and any warrant or writing under Her Majesty's Royal Sign Manual, which by the Government of India Act, 1854, or otherwise is required to be countersigned by the President of the Commissioners for the Affairs of India, shall in lieu of being so countersigned be countersigned by one of Her Majesty's Principal Secretaries of State.

SECTION 07: COUNCIL OF INDIA ESTABLISHED

For Purposes of this Act a Council shall be established, to consist of 15 Members, and to be styled the Council of India; and henceforth the Council of India now bearing that Name shall be styled the Council of the Governor General of India.

SECTION 28: AS TO COMMUNICATION OF SECRET DESPATCHES FROM INDIA

Any Despatches to Great Britain which might if this Act had not been passed have been addressed to the Secret Committee of the Court of Directors be marked, 'Secret' by the Authorities sending the same; and such Despatches shall not be communicated to the Members of the Council, unless the Secretary of State shall so think fit and direct.

SECTION 33: OTHER APPOINTMENTS AND ADMISSIONS TO SERVICE VESTED IN HER MAJESTY

All Appointments to Cadetships, Naval and Military, and all Admissions to Service not herein otherwise expressly provided for, shall be vested in Her Majesty; and the Names of Persons to be from Time to Time recommended for such Cadetships and Service shall be submitted to Her Majesty by the Secretary of State.

SECTION 34: REGULATIONS TO BE MADE FOR ADMITTING PERSONS TO BE EXAMINED FOR CADETSHIPS IN ENGINEERS AND ARTILLERY

With all convenient Speed after the Commencement of this Act, Regulations shall be made for admitting any Persons being natural-born Subjects of Her Majesty (and of such Age and Qualifications as may be prescribed in this Behalf) who may be desirous of becoming Candidates for Cadetships in the Engineers and in the Artillery, to be examined as Candidates accordingly, and for prescribing the Branches of Knowledge in which such Candidates shall be examined and generally for regulating and conducting such Examinations.

SECTION 35: NOT LESS THAN ONE TENTH OF PERSONS RECOMMENDED FOR MILITARY CADETSHIPS TO BE SELECTED FROM SONS OF PERSONS WHO HAVE SERVED IN INDIA

Not less than One Tenth of the whole Number of Persons to be recommended in any Year for Military Cadetships (other than Cadetships in the Engineers and Artillery) shall be selected according to such Regulations as the Secretary of State in Council may from Time to Time make in this Behalf from among the Sons of Persons who have served in India in the Military or Civil Services of Her Majesty, or of the East India Company.

SECTION 36: NOMINATIONS FOR CADETSHIPS TO BE MADE BY SECRETARY OF STATE AND MEMBERS OF COUNCIL

Except as aforesaid, all Persons to be recommended for Military Cadetships shall be nominated by the Secretary of State and Members of Council, so that out of Seventeen Nominations the Secretary of State shall have Two and each Member of Council shall have One; but no Person so nominated shall be recommended unless the Nomination be approved of by the Secretary of State in Council.

SECTION 37: REGULATIONS AS TO APPOINTMENTS AND ADMISSIONS TO SERVICE

Save as herein-before provided, all Powers of making Regulations in relation to Appointments and Admissions to Service and other Matters connected therewith, and of altering or revoking such Regulations, which if this Act had not been passed might have been exercised by the Court of Directors or Commissioners for the Affairs of India, may be exercised by the Secretary of State in Council, and all Regulations in force at the Time of the Commencement of this Act in relation to the Matters aforesaid shall remain in force subject nevertheless to Alteration or Revocation by the Secretary of State in Council as aforesaid.

SECTION 38: REMOVAL OF OFFICERS BY HER MAJESTY

Any Writing under the Royal Sign Manual, removing or dismissing any Person holding any Office, Employment, or Commission, Civil or Military, in India, of which, if this Act had been passed, a Copy would have been required to be transmitted or delivered within Eight Days after being signed by Her Majesty to the Chairman or Deputy Chairman of the Court of Directors shall, in lieu thereof, be communicated within the Time aforesaid to the Secretary of State in Council.

SECTION 39: REAL AND PERSONAL PROPERTY OF THE COMPANY TO VEST IN HER MAJESTY FOR THE PURPOSES OF THE GOVERNMENT OF INDIA

All Lands and Hereditaments, Monies, Stores, Goods, Chattels and other Real and Personal Estate of the said Company subject to the Debts and Liabilities affecting the same respectively, and the Benefit of all Contracts, Covenants, and Engagements, and all Rights to Fines, Penalties, and Forefeitures and all other Emoluments which the said Company shall be seized or possessed of, or entitled to at the Time of the Commencement of this Act, except the Capital Stock of the said Company and the Dividend thereon, shall become vested in Her Majesty, to be applied and disposed of, subject to the Provisions of this Act, for the Purposes of the Government of India.

SECTION 54: WHEN ORDER TO COMMENCE HOSTILITIES IS SENT TO INDIA, THE FACT TO BE COMMUNICATED TO PARLIAMENT

When any Order is sent to India directing the actual Commencement of Hostilities by Her Majesty's Forces in India, the Fact of such Order having been sent shall be communicated to both Houses of Parliament within Three Months after the sending of such Order, if Parliament be sitting, unless such Order shall have been in the meantime revoked or suspended, and if Parliament be not sitting at the end of such Three Months, then within One Month after the next Meeting of Parliament.

SECTION 55: EXCEPT FOR REPELLING INVASION, THE REVENUES OF INDIA NOT APPLICABLE FOR ANY MILITARY OPERATION BEYOND THE FRONTIERS

Except for preventing or repelling actual Invasion of Her Majesty's Indian Possessions, or under other sudden and urgent Necessity, the Revenues of India shall not, without the Consent of both Houses of Parliament, be applicable to defray the Expenses of any Military Operation carried on beyond the external Frontiers of such Possessions by Her Majesty's Forces charged upon such Revenues.

SECTION 56: INDIAN MILITARY AND NAVAL FORCES TO REMAIN UNDER EXISTING CONDITIONS OF SERVICE

The Military and Naval Forces of the East India Company shall be deemed to be the Indian Military and Naval Forces of Her Majesty, and shall be under the same Obligations to serve Her Majesty as they would have been under to serve the said Company, and shall be liable to serve within the same territorial Limits only, for the same Terms only, and be entitled to the like Pay, Pensions, Allowances, and Privileges, and the like Advantages as rewards Promotion and otherwise, as if they had continued in the Service of the said Company; Such Forces and all Persons hereafter enlisting in or entering the same shall continue and be subject to all Acts of Parliament, Laws of the Governor General of India in Council, and Articles of War, and all other Laws, Regulations, and Provisions relating to the East India Company's Military and Naval Forces respectively, as if Her Majesty's Indian Military and Naval Forces respectively had throughout such Acts, Laws, Articles, Regulations and Provisions been mentioned or referred to, instead of such Forces of the said Company; and the Pay and Expenses of and incident to Her Majesty's Indian Military and Naval Forces shall be defrayed out of the Revenues of India.

SECTION 57: PROVISIONS FOR PERSONS HEREAFTER ENTERING HER MAJESTY'S INDIAN FORCES

Provided that it shall be lawful for Her Majesty from Time to Time by Order in Council to alter or regulate the Terms and Conditions of Service under which Persons hereafter entering Her Majesty's Indian Forces, shall be commissioned, enlisted, or entered to serve; and the Forms of Attestation and of the Oath or Declaration to be used and taken or made respectively on attesting

Persons to serve in Her Majesty's Indian Forces shall be such as Her Majesty with regard to the European Forces, and the Governor General of India in Council with regard to the Native Forces, shall from Time to Time direct: Provided, that every such Order in Council shall be laid before both Houses of Parliament within Fourteen Days after the making thereof, if Parliament be sitting, and, if Parliament be not sitting, then within Fourteen Days after the next Meeting thereof.

SECTION 58: OFFICERS, ETC. IN EMPLOY OF THE COMPANY AT THE COMMENCEMENT OF THIS ACT TO BE DEEMED TO HOLD OFFICES UNDER HER MAJESTY

All Persons who at the Time of the Commencement of this Act shall hold any offices, Employments, or Commissions whatever under the said Company in India shall thenceforth be deemed to hold such Offices, Employments and Commissions under Her Majesty as if they had been appointed under this Act, and shall be paid out of the Revenues of India; and the Transfer of any Persons to the Service of Her Majesty shall be deemed to be a Continuance of his previous Service and shall not prejudice any Claims to Pension, or any Claims on the various Annuity Funds of the several Presidencies in India, which he might have had if this Act had not been passed.

SECTION 74: COMMENCEMENT OF ACT

Save as herein otherwise provided, this Act shall commence and take effect on the Expiration of Thirty Days after the Day of the passing thereof.

SECTION 75: PROVISION AS TO PROCEEDINGS IN INDIA BEFORE THE ACT IS PROCLAIMED THERE

This Act shall be proclaimed in the several Presidencies and Governments of India as soon as conveniently may be after such Act has been received by the Governor General of India; and until such Proclamation be made all Acts, Matters, and Things done, ordered directed, or authorised in India in the Name of the East India Company, or otherwise in relation to the Government of India, shall be as valid and effectual as if this Act had not been passed.

(Sections of the Charter relevant to the subject of this book have only been included)

ACT No. XXIX OF 1861

PASSED BY THE LEGISLATIVE COUNCIL OF INDIA.

(Received the assent of the Governor-General on the 7th September 1861)

An Act to consolidate and amend the Articles of War for the government of the Native Officers and Soldiers in Her Majesty's Indian Army

Preamble

WHEREAS is expedient to consolidate and amend the Articles of War for the government of the Native Officers and Soldiers in Her Majesty's Indian Army; It is hereby enacted as follows:-

Repeal of Acts

Act XXIII of 1839 (for authorizing sentences of imprisonment with or without hard labour by Courts Martial in certain cases), Act II of 1840 (for regulating the execution of sentences passed by Courts Martial in certain cases), Act XXVIII of 1841 (for extending Act XXIII of 1839 to Camp Followers), Act XIX of 1847 (to make certain amendments in the Articles of War for the government of the Native Officers and Soldiers in the Military Service of the East India Company), Act VI of 1850 (for enabling the Commander-in-Chief to pardon Military Offences), Act XXXVI of 1850 (to amend Article CXIII of the Native Army), Act III of 1854 (to amend the 38th Article of War for the Native Army), Act X of 1856 (to repeal the 122nd Article of War for the Native Army and to substitute a new Article in lieu thereof), Act VIII of 1857 (to amend Act XIX of 1847), Act XXXII of 1857 (to amend the Articles of War for the Native Army), and Act VI of 1860 (to amend Act XIX of 1847), shall be repealed from the day on which this Act shall come into operation, except in so far as they repeal any other Act or Acts.

Enactment of the following Articles

II. The following Articles of War shall, from the day appointed for them **to** come into operation, be the Articles of War for the government of the Native Officers and Soldiers in the Military Service of Her Majesty, and for the Administration of Justice by Courts Martial to be holden on such Officers and Soldiers.

Proviso

Provided that all crimes and offences committed against the Articles of War contained in any Act repealed by this Act may be enquired into and punished in like-manner as if they had been committed against the Articles of War contained in this Act; and that every Warrant for holding any Court Martial under the Articles of War provided by any Act repealed by this Act shall remain in full force notwithstanding the repeal of such Act, and that no proceedings of a Court Martial upon any trial begun under any Articles so repealed shall be discontinued owing to the repeal of the same, but that every such trial shall proceed and be completed in the, same manner as if this Act had not been passed.

ARTICLES OF WAR

CHAPTER I

Of Enlisting and Discharges

ARTICLE 1

Enlisting

Every Recruit, prior to being enrolled in any Regiment or Corps, shall have the 5th, 6th, 7th, and 8th, and 48th of these Articles of War read and explained to him. When reported fit for duty in the ranks, any usual declaration or charge shall be made to him by the Officer Commanding, in front of the Regiment or Corps, in presence of the Officers and Soldiers; and the recruit shall then, in front of the guns or colors, or, if attached to the Corps of Sappers and Miners, in front of such portion of the Corps as shall be present, make the subjoined affirmation:-

"I ….., solemnly affirm in the presence of Almighty God, that I will be faithful to Her Majesty the Queen, and will go wherever I am ordered by land or sea, and will obey all commands of the Officers set over me, and will defend these guns (or colors) with my life."

In the case of a Sapper and Miner, the words "and defend these guns (or colors) with my life," shall be omitted.

ARTICLE 2

Dismissal and discharge

No Commissioned Officer shall be dismissed, except by the sentence of a General Court Martial; but the Governor-General of India in Council, or the Governor in Council, or the Commander-in-Chief of the Presidency to which a Commissioned Officer belongs, shall have power to order his discharge. Every such dismissal or discharge of a Commissioned Officer shall involve forfeiture of all claim to pension.

ARTICLE 3

Discharge and discharge

A Non-Commissioned Officer or Soldier shall be liable to dismissal or discharge by order **of** the Governor-General of India in Council, or **of** the Governor in Council, or the Commander-in-Chief of the Presidency to which he belongs.

Discharge and reduction by Commanding Officer

The Commanding Officer of a Regiment or Corps shall have power to dismiss or discharge any Soldier below the rank of a Non-Commissioned Officer; and to dismiss, discharge, or reduce to the ranks any Non-Commissioned Officer belonging to such Regiment or Corps.

Every such dismissal or discharge shall involve forfeiture of claim to pension.

Proviso as to reduction and suspension

No Non-Commissioned Officer shall be reduced to the ranks for any stated period; nor suspended from his rank; nor reduced from a higher to lower grade of Non-Commissioned Officer

Certificate of discharge

Every Non-Commissioned Officer or Soldier discharged the service shall be furnished by the Commanding Officer of the Regiment or Corps to which he belonged with a discharge Certificate in the Vernacular language of such Non-Commissioned Officer or Soldier. Such Certificate shall express the authority for, and cause of, the discharge, and the period of the entire service in the Army of such Non-Commissioned Officer or Soldier, and shall be accompanied with an English translation.

ARTICLE 4

Re-enlisting

No Non-Commissioned Officer or Soldier, until he shall hare received his discharge from the Regiment or Corps to which he belongs, shall enlist in any other Regiment or Corps; and any Non-Commissioned Officer or Soldier who shall so enlist, shall be considered a deserter, and shall suffer punishment accordingly.

Any Non-Commissioned Officer or Soldier who shall have been dismissed or discharged from any Regiment or Corps, and shall enlist in any other Regiment or Corps, without at the time of such enlistment stating the fact of his dismissal or discharge, or showing his discharge certificate, may be dismissed the service by the Officer Commanding the Regiment or Corps in which he has enlisted.

CHAPTER II

Crimes ans Punishmnets

Crimes punishable by General Court Martial.

ARTICLE 5

Mutiny and Sedition

Any Officer or Soldier

Who shall begin, excite, cause, or join any mutiny or sedition in the Regiment or Corps to which he belongs, or in any other Regiment or Corps, on any pretence whatever; or who, being present at any mutiny or sedition, shall not use his utmost endeavours to suppress the same; or who, coming to the knowledge of any mutiny, intended mutiny, or combination against the State, shall not give immediate information thereof to his Commanding Officer;---or

ARTICLE 6

Striking Superior Officer, &c,

Who shall strike his Superior Officer, or shall draw or offer to draw, or lift up any weapon, or use or offer any violence against him, whether on or off duty, and under any circumstances in which his Superior Officer may be distinguishable as such in any manner;---or

ARTICLE 7

Disobeying Superior Officer

Who shall disobey any lawful command of his Superior Officer;---or

ARTICLE 8

Desertion

Who shall desert from Her Majesty's Service, whether he shall have re-enlisted or not;---or

ARTICLE 9

Sentry in time of war or alarm, sleeping upon or deserting his post, &c

Who, being a sentry, in time of war or alarm, shall sleep upon his post; or shall quit his post without being regularly relieved, or without leave; or shall plunder or injure the property placed under his charge;---or

ARTICLE 10

Abandoning Garrison,, or Post, &c

Who shall shamefully abandon or deliver up any Garrison, Fortress, Post, or Guard, committed to his charge, or which it was his duty to defend; or who shall use means to induce any other Officer or Soldier so to abandon or deliver up any such Garrison, Fortress, Post, or Guard ;---or

ARTICLE 11

Making known watch word

Who shall treacherously make known the watchword to any person not entitled to receive it according to the rules and discipline of war;---or

ARTICLE 12

Communicating with enemy

Who shall, directly or indirectly, hold correspondence with or communicate intelligence to the enemy, or to any person in, arms against the State, or who, coming to, the knowledge of such correspondence or communication, shall omit to discover it immediately to his Commanding Officer;---or

ARTICLE 13

Assisting or protecting enemies

Who shall, directly or indirectly, assist or relieve the enemy, or any person in arms against the State, with money, victuals, or ammunition, or in any other way; or shall knowingly harbour or protect any enemy or person in arms against the State;---or

ARTICLE 14

Releasing or conniving at the escape of an enemy

Who shall treacherously release, wilfully aid, or connive at the escape of any enemy or person in arms against the State, placed as a prisoner under his charge;---or

ARTICLE 15

Misbehavior before the enemy

Who shall, in the presence of an enemy or any person in arms against whom it is his duty to act, misbehave or use means to induce any other person so to misbehave;---or

ARTICLE 16

Casting away arms, &c, in presence of an enemy

Who shall, in presence of an enemy, or of any person in aims against whom it is his duty to act, shamefully cast away his arms and ammunition;---or

ARTICLE 17

Leaving post &c, in time of action for search of plunder

Who shall, in time of action, leave his Commanding Officer, or his Post, or Colors, or Party, to go in search of plunder;---or

ARTICLE 18

Using violence in camp or Quarter to person bringing provisions

Who shall, in time of war, do violence to any person bringing provisions or other necessaries to the Camp or Quarters of the Force with which he is serving;; or shall force a safeguard; or shall break into any house or other place for plunder or shall plunder any field or garden or other property;---or

ARTICLE 19

Discharging any fire-arms in time of war

Who shall, in time of war, by discharging any fire-arms, drawing a sword, beating a drum, making any signal, using any word, or by any means whatever, intentionally occasion ...arm in action, camp, garrison, or quarters;---or

ARTICLE 20

Release or conniving at plunder or release of state prisoner

Who shall, without proper authority, release any State prisoner, or shall, through carelessness, or neglect, suffer any such prisoner to escape; or shall connive at the plunder or injury of any property in time of war, or the plunder or injury treasure, or of any magazine or dock-yard, by the sentry or guard in charge such property, treasure, magazine, or dock-yard is placed;---or

ARTICLE 21

Who, being a sentry placed over any State prisoner, or over any treasure, or over any magazine or dock-yard, shall quit his post without being regularly relieved, or without leave, or shall sleep upon his post; or shall plunder or injure any property placed under his charge;---or

Shall, on conviction----

Punishment, if an officer

If an Officer, suffer death; or transportation for life, or for a period not less than seven years; or such other punishment as a General Court Martial is by these Articles empowered to award:---

Punishment, if a Soldier

If a Soldier, suffer death; or transportation for life, or for a period not less than seven years; or imprisonment, with or without hard labor, for a period which may extend to fourteen years, and may be with or without solitary confinement; or such other punishment as a General Court Martial is by these Articles empowered to award.

Embezzlement, punishable by General Court Martial

ARTICLE 22

Embezzlement

Any Officer or Soldier---

Who shall embezzle or fraudulently misapply any money entrusted to him on the Public account, or for any Military purpose; or any provision, forage, arms, clothing, ammunition, or Military stores, of whatever kind or description, the property of Government, entrusted to his charge; or shall be concerned in or connive at any such embezzlement or fraudulent misappropriation;---

Wilful injury to certain Government property

Who shall wilfully injure any property of Government entrusted to him on the Public account, or for any Military purpose, or shall suffer such property to be injured;---

Punishment

Shall, on conviction before a General Court Martial, be dismissed the service, and fined to the extent of his arrears of pay and allowances ; and be further liable to suffer imprisonment with or without hard labor for a term which may extend to three years, and may be with or without solitary confinement.

ARTICLE 23

Officers misbehaving themselves

Any Officer---

Who shall behave in a manner unbecoming the character of an Officer (the fact or facts whereon the charge is grounded being clearly specified therein);---or

ARTICLE 24

Spreading reports calculated to create alarm

An officer or Soldier---

Who shall, in any operation in the field, spread any report, by any word or letter calculated to create unnecessary alarm in the troops, or in the vicinity, or in rear of the army;---or

ARTICLE 25

Using words tending to create alarm

Who shall, in action or previously to going into action, use any word tending to create alarm or despondency;--- or

ARTICLE 26

Being drunk

Who shall be drunk when on or for Duty, or on Parade, or on the Line of march;---or

ARTICLE 27

Striking a Sentry

Who shall strike or force any sentry;----or

ARTICLE 28

Advising or persuading desertion

Who shall advise or persuade any other Officer or Soldier to desert, or who shall connive at such desertion;; or who shall knowingly receive and entertain any deserter, or who knowing of any other Officer or Soldier having deserted, or knowing of any deserter having been received or entertained by any other Officer or Soldier, shall not immediately give notice to his own Superior Officer, or do his best to cause such deserter to be apprehended by the Civil power;---or

ARTICLE 29

Obtaining pension by false statement

Who shall obtain, or attempt to obtain for himself, or for any other Officer or Soldier, or for any other person whatsoever, any pension or allowance, by any false statement, certificate, or document, or by the omission of any true statement, certificate, or document;---or

ARTICLE 30

Making false return to Superior Officer

Who shall knowingly make a false return or report to any Officer authorized to call for a return or report of the state of the men under his command, or of any arms, ammunition, clothing, or other stores belonging to such men, or of which he has charge;---or

ARTICLE 31

Extortion

Who at any post; or on the march, shall unlawfully extort any money or property of any description as a fee or duty, or on any pretence whatever, or shall, without authority, exact from any villager, or any other person; any carriage, porterage, or provision;---or

ARTICLE 32

Defiling place of religious worship

Who shall wantonly and intentionally defile any place dedicated to religious worship, or shall wantonly and intentionally insult the religious prejudices of any person;---or

ARTICLE 33

Breaking arrest or confinement

Who, being under arrest or in confinement, shall leave his arrest or confinement before he is set at liberty by proper authority;---or

ARTICLE 34

Committing waste, &c.

Who shall, without orders, commit any waste, or spoil, or plunder, or shall injure or destroy any property;---or

ARTICLE 35

Enlisting a deserter

Who shall knowingly enlist a deserter, or connive at his enlistment;---or

ARTICLE 36

Demanding or accepting bribe

Who, directly or indirectly, shall require or accept a bribe, present, or gratification, on the pretence of, or as a consideration for, procuring leave of absence, promotion, or any other advantage or indulgence for any Officer or Soldier;---or

ARTICLE 37

Those in command of post, &c, not seeing reparation done to injured parties, &c

Who being in command of any post, or on the march, shall not, on complaint made to him of any one under his command beating or otherwise ill-treating any person, or extorting from such person more than he is obliged to furnish, or disturbing any fair or market, or committing any kind of riot, see reparation done to the person injured; or, if that be impracticable, report the same to his Superior Officer;---or

ARTICLE 38

Those in command of guard refusing to receive prisoner

Who, being in command of a guard, shall refuse to receive any prisoner duly committed to his charge; or shall, without proper authority, release any prisoner; or shall suffer, through carelessness or neglect, any prisoner to escape;---or

ARTICLE 39

Quitting guard or picquet in time of peace

Who, in time of peace, shall quit his guard or picquet without being regularly relieved or without leave;---or

ARTICLE 40

Impeding Provost Marshal

Who shall impede a Provost Marshal or an Assistant of a Provost Marshal, or any person lawfully exercising authority; or refuse when called upon to assist him when requiring his aid in the execution of his duty;---or

ARTICLE 41

Those on leave of absence neglecting to rejoin their Regiment when ordered on service

Who, being on leave of absence, and having received information from the Commanding Officer of his Regiment or Corps, or from other proper authority, that his Regiment or Corps has been ordered on service, shall not rejoin without delay;---or

ARTICLE 42

False alarm in camp in time of peace

Who shall, in time of peace, by discharging any fire-arms, drawing a sword, beating a drum, or by any other means whatever, intentionally occasion a false alarm in camp, garrison, or cantonment;---or

ARTICLE 43

Failure to attend parade, &c

Who shall, without sufficient cause, fail to report at the fixed, to the parade, or place appointed or exercise or duty;---or

ARTICLE 44

Quitting company or parade without leave

Who shall, without urgent necessity, or without leave of his Superior Officer, quit his company, or troop, or the parade;---or

ARTICLE 45

Absence without leave, &c

Who shall absent himself without leave; or shall, without sufficient cause, overstay the period for which leave may have been granted him;---or

ARTICLE 46

Striking or ill-treating a Soldier

Any Officer or Non-Commissioned Officer---

Who shall strike or otherwise ill-treat any Soldier;---or

ARTICLE 47

Insubordination

Any Soldier---

Who shall be grossly insubordinate or insolent to his Superior Officer in the execution of his office;---or

ARTICLE 48

Refusal to assist in making field or other work

Who shall refuse to assist in the making of any field work, or other Military work of any description ordered to be made, either in quarters or in the field;---or

ARTICLE 49

Going armed contrary to order

Who, when off duty, shall, contrary to orders, appear in or about camp or cantonments, or on occasion of going to or returning from, or in or about any town or bazaar, carrying a sword, bludgeon, or other weapon;---or

ARTICLE 50

Pawning, losing, or injuring horse, arms, accoutrements, &c.

Who shall sell, pawn, or designedly or through neglect lose or injure his horse, arms, clothes, accoutrements, or Regimental necessaries; or any such articles entrusted or belonging to any other Soldier; or who shall make away with or pawn any medal or decoration granted to him by order of Her Majesty or of the East India Company, or by order of the Government, for service in the field or for general good conduct;---or

ARTICLE 51

Sentry in time of peace sleeping upon post

Who, being a Sentry, in time of peace, shall sleep upon his post; or shall leave it before being regularly relieved or without leave;---or

ARTICLE 52

Soldier found 2 miles from camp contrary to orders

Who, contrary to orders, shall be found 2 miles from the camp;---or

ARTICLE 53

Absent, losing, or wasting ammunition

Who, contrary to orders, shall be absent from his cantonment after- tattoo, or from camp after retreat beating;---or

ARTICLE 54

Selling, loosing or wasting ammunition

Who shall sell, lose, or designedly, or through neglect, waste any ammunition delivered out to him;---or

Punishment

Shall, on conviction before a General or other Court Martial, be sentenced to suffer such punishment as such Court Martial is by these Articles empowered to award.

Disgraceful conduct; punishable by General or District Court Martial, with Corporal punishment, or Imprisonment with or without hard labor and solitary confinement, and in addition with Forfeiture of additional Pay and of Pension on Discharge, and Stoppage, of Non-Commissioned Officers and Soldiers

ARTICLE 55

Disgraceful conduct

Any Soldier who shall be guilty o f disgraceful conduct:--

In wilfully maiming or injuring himself, or any other Soldier at the instance of such soldier, with intent to render himself or such other Soldier unfit for the service, or with intent to take his own life;---or

ARTICLE 56

Malingering &c

In malingering, feigning, or intentionally producing any disease or infirmity; or intentionally delaying his cure; or intentionally aggravating his disease or infirmity;---or

ARTICLE 57

Stealing or selling Government stores

In purloining or selling my Government stores;---or

ARTICLE 58

Selling property of soldiers and others

In stealing any money or goods, the property of any Officer or Soldier, or any Military Mess, or of any person belonging to or serving with or attached to the Army;---or

ARTICLE 59

Plundering property under his charge as sentry &c

In plundering or injuring any property placed under his charge as sentry, or in charge of his guard, or in conniving at the plunder or injury of any such property;---or

ARTICLE 60

Embezzling Public money

In embezzling or fraudulently misapplying any public money entrusted to him for any Military purpose;---or

ARTICLE 61

Fraud or dishonestly

In committing any petty offence of a fraudulent or dishonest nature, to the injury of or with intent to injure the Government, or any person, Civil or Military;---or

ARTICLE 62

Cruelty, indecency, &c

Who shall be guilty of any other disgraceful conduct, of a cruel, indecent, or unnatural kind;---

Punishment

Shall, on conviction before a General or District or Garrison Court Martial, be liable to such punishment as such Court Martial is by these Articles of War empowered to award for disgraceful conduct.

Every offender so convicted, if not dismissed the service, shall, by sentence of the Court, be put under stoppage not exceeding half of his monthly pay and allowances, until the amount of any loss or damage arising out of his misconduct be made good.

If such offender be dismissed the service, he shall further be sentenced to forfeit any arrears of pay and allowances due at the time of his dismissal, towards making good any loss or damage arising out of his misconduct; or to forfeit any portion of such arrears that may be required to make good such loss or damage.

A copy of every sentence of dismissal for disgraceful conduct passed by any Court Martial shall, after its confirmation, be transmitted by the Adjutant General of the Army to the Chief Civil Officer of the district wherein the village or other place to which the offender belongs is situated; and such Chief Civil Officer shall thereupon publish such sentence by affixing a copy thereof in the village or place, or otherwise as may be usual in the locality.

Crimes incident to Courts Martial, punishment by General or other Court Martial according to the nature and degree of offence

ARTICLE 63

Refusal of a person amenable to Articles of War to attend Court Martial or to be sworn, &c

Any person amenable to these Articles of War, who shall, when duly summoned to attend as a witness before a Court Martial, neglect to attend, or shall refuse to be sworn, or to make affirmation, or to answer any question, or who shall instigate any other person so to offend;---

Shall, on conviction, be sentenced by the same, or another Court Martial, to such punishment as any such Court Martial is by these Articles empowered to award.

ARTICLE 64

Refusal of a person not amenable to Articles of War to attend Court Martial, or to be sworn, &c

Any person not amenable to these Articles of War, who shall, when duly summoned to attend as a witness before a Court Martial, refuse or neglect to attend; or shall refuse to be sworn, or to make affirmation, or to answer any question; or who shall, when he has been duly sworn, or has solemnly affirmed that he will speak the truth, make any statement which is false, and which he either knows or believes to be false, or does not believe to be true; or who shall instigate any other person so to offend; Shall be delivered over to a Magistrate, who shall proceed against the offender in the same manner as if the offence had been committed before a Criminal Court.

ARTICLE 65

Contempt of Court

Any person using any menacing or disrespectful word, sign, or gesture, in the presence of a Court Martial then sitting; or causing disorder or riot so as to disturb the proceedings of such Court Martial; or being grossly insubordinate or violent in the presence of a Court Martial;

Shall, if amenable to these Articles of War, be punished, according to the condition of the offender and the nature and degree of his offence, by the sentence of the same or another Court Martial;

and if not amenable to these Articles of War, be delivered over to a Magistrate, who shall proceed against the offender in the same manner as if the offence had been committed before a Criminal Court.

The offence of giving false evidence, punishable by General or District Court Martial, with dismissal and fine or imprisonment

ARTICLE 66

Perjury

Any Officer or Soldier-

Who shall give false evidence as defined in Article 64 before any General or other Court Martial, or any Military Court entitled to take evidence on oath or affirmation; or who shall instigate any other person so to offend; Shall, on conviction before a General, District, or Garrison Court Martial, be dismissed the service ; and shall further be sentenced to forfeit any arrears of pay and allowances due at the time of his dismissal, and may be sentenced to imprisonment with or without hard labor for a term which may extend to three years.

ARTICLE 67

Crimes admitting of less serious notice

When the Officer Commanding a Regiment or Corps considers that any Soldier under his command, who is charged with any offence declared by the foregoing Articles to be triable by a District or Garrison Court Martial, should be tried by a Regimental Court Martial, he may order the offender to be tried by such Court Martial, and shall report the case to the Officer Commanding the Division, stating the reason, for such order,

When the Officer Commanding a Regiment or Corps considers that any Soldier under his Command, who is charged with any offence declared by the foregoing Articles to be triable by a General Court Martial, should be tried by a District or Garrison or Regimental Court Martial, such Commanding Officer may lay a statement, of the case before the General or other Officer having authority to convene General Courts Martial, under whose command the offender may be serving, with an application for permission to try the offender by District or Garrison or Regimental Court Martial, and such General or other Officer shall comply with or refuse such application at his discretion. The order of such General or other Officer, when the application is complied with, shall be entered upon the proceedings at the trial of such offender.

Provided that mutiny shall not be considered one of the offences admitting of such discretionary investigation.

ARTICLE 68

Offences on the line of march or on board vessels

For any offence committed on the line of march, or on board any ship or other vessel, the Officer in command of the Troops may try any Soldier by a Regimental or Detachment Court Martial, and may confirm and execute on the spot any sentence that may be passed.

Provided that such sentence shall in no case exceed that which a Regimental Court Martial is competent to award;--and that the proceedings held in all such cases shall be transmitted for the information of the Commander-in-Chief of the Presidency to which such Troops belong, and to the Commander-in-Chief of the Presidency within which such troops shall be serving or to which they are proceeding.

ARTICLE 69

Crimes not specified

Any crime not punishable with death, and any disorder or neglect of which any Officer or Soldier is guilty, to the prejudice of Good Order and Military Discipline, may, though not specified in these Articles, be taken cognizance of by Court Martial, and punished, according to the nature and degree of the offence, by the sentence of a General, or District, or Garrison, or Regimental Court Martial.

CHAPTER III

Administration of Justice

ARTICLE 70

Arrest or confinement

Whenever any Officer or Soldier is accused of any crime which the Commanding Officer of such Officer or Soldier considers should be tried by Court Martial, such Commanding Officer shall order the accused, if he be an Officer or Non-Commissioned Officer, to be put under arrest, or if a Soldier, to be confined until he can be tried by a Court Martial, or discharged by proper authority. No such Officer or Soldier shall be detained in arrest or confinement longer than is avoidable.

Resistance to arrest

When, in consequence of any resistance, or, from any other circumstance, such arrest or confinement is impracticable, the offender shall be liable to trial and punishment at any subsequent period within the limitations provided in these Articles of War.

ARTICLE 71

Limitation of time

No person shall be liable to be tried or punished for any offence against the Articles of War, which shall appear to have been committed more than three years previous to the order directing the assembly of the Court Martial whereby he is being, or is to be tried, unless it shall appear that the person accused, by reason of his absenting himself, or some other manifest impediment, could not be brought to trial within that period; in which case such person shall be liable to be tried at any time not exceeding two years after such impediment shall have ceased.

ARTICLE 72

Offenders may be tried elsewhere than where the offence was committed

Any person amenable to these Articles of War, who commits any offence against them, may be tried and punished for such offence in any place where he is, in the same manner as if the offence had been committed in such place.

ARTICLE 73

Powers of the Commander-in-Chief to appoint Courts Martial

The Commander-in-Chief of the Presidency may appoint a General or other Court Martial, and may confirm, and mitigate, or commute or remit the sentence of such Court. He may issue his warrant to any General or other Officer under his command having the command of any body of troops in the service of Her Majesty, empowering such Officer to appoint General, or District, or Garrison Courts Martial as occasion may require, for the trial of any offence committed by any Officer or Soldier or follower in the service of Her Majesty, not being a European British subject of Her Majesty; and to confirm and mitigate, or commute or remit the sentence of any such Court Martial. No sentence, including forfeiture of additional pay, or of claim to pension on discharge, or of any prospective advantage, shall be carried into effect until confirmed by the Commander-in-Chief of the Presidency to which the offender belongs. The Commander-in-Chief may remit any forfeiture awarded, and may order the restoration of any advantage of which the offender has been deprived by such forfeiture.

ARTICLE 74

Appointment Courts Martial for trial of Troops not attached to any Presidency.

Whenever any Native Troops subject to these Articles of War are not attached to the forces of any Presidency, the Governor-General of India in Council shall authorize the Commander-in-Chief of any Presidency to issue his warrant to the General or other Officer having the Command of such troops to appoint Courts Martial in conformity with this Act.

Composition of Courts Martial

ARTICLE 75

Constitution of General Court Martial

Except as hereinafter provided, a General Court Martial shall not consist of less thirteen Commissioned Officers, unless it be held out of the British Territories in India. When a Court Martial is held out of the British Territories in India, it may consist of seven Commissioned

Officers, if a greater number cannot be conveniently assembled. No sentence of a General Court Martial shall be put in execution until after a report shall have been made of the whole proceedings to the Commander-in-Chief of the Presidency or to some other person authorized to confirm the same, and until the directions of such Commander-in-Chief or other person as aforesaid shall have been signified thereupon.

ARTICLE 76

Constitution of District or Garrison Court Martial

A District or Garrison Court Martial shall consist of not less than seven Commissioned Officers when that number can be conveniently assembled. When that number cannot be conveniently assembled, such Court may consist of not less than five Commissioned Officers.

A District or Garrison Court Martial may be composed of Officers of the same Regiment or Corps as the accused, or of any other Regiment or Corps.

The sentence of a District or Garrison Court Martial shall be subject to confirmation by the Commander-in-Chief of the Presidency, or by some Officer duly authorized to confirm the same.

ARTICLE 77

Constitution of Regimental Court Martial

A Regimental Court Martial shall consist of not less than five Commissioned Officers when such number can be assembled. When such number cannot be assembled, such Court may consist of three Commissioned Officers. Such Court shall be assembled by order of the Officer Commanding the Regiment. No sentence of a Regimental Court Martial shall be of force until the Commanding Officer shall have confirmed the same. Such Commanding Officer shall have power to remit all sentences whatever passed by such Court, and to cause the offender to be released and to return to his duty.

Powers of Court Martial

ARTICLE 78

Death, transportation, or Imprisonment

A General Court Martial may sentence---for any crime which by these Articles is made liable to such sentence---any Officer to death or to transportation for life, or for any period not less than seven years, or in cases falling under Article 22 or Article 66, to imprisonment with or without hard labor for any period not exceeding three years, and with or without solitary confinement; or may sentence any Soldier to death; or to transportation for life, or for any period not less than seven years, or to imprisonment for any period not exceeding fourteen years, for any crimes which are by these Articles of War expressly made liable to any such sentence, and for such crimes only. No Court Martial inferior to a General Court Martial shall have power to pass a sentence of death or transportation or imprisonment for any longer period than three years.

Punishments of Commissioned Officers

A General Court Martial may sentence a Commissioned Officer to be Dismissed the service; or to be suspended from rank and pay and allowances for a stated period; or to be placed one or more steps lower in the list of his rank, by an alteration of the date of his Commission, and such Officer shall lose the corresponding benefit of length of service.

No Court Martial inferior to a General Court Martial shall have power to try **a** Commissioned Officer.

Punishments of Non- Commissioned Officers and Soldiers

A General or District or Garrison or Regimental Court Martial may sentence a Non-Commissioned Officer to be reduced to the ranks;---or may sentence a Non-Commissioned Officer or soldier to be dismissed the service ;---or to be placed one or more steps lower in the list of the rank which he holds, whereby such Non-Commissioned Officer or Soldier shall lose the benefit of the corresponding length of service ;---or to suffer corporal punishment not exceeding fifty lashes;---or to imprisonment, which may be with or without hard labor; and which may include solitary confinement for any portion or portions of such imprisonment, not exceeding fourteen days at a time, nor eighty-four days in any one year, with intervals between the periods of solitary confinement of not less duration than such periods of solitary confinement.

No Soldier shall be kept in solitary confinement more than eighty-four days in any one year, whether by the sentence of one or more Courts Martial, or by order of the Commanding Officer of the Regiment or Corps to which such Soldier belongs.

No sentence of imprisonment shall be awardable by **a** General Court Martial for any period exceeding two gears (except when otherwise expressly provided); nor by a District or Garrison Court Martial for any period exceeding one year; nor by a Regimental Court Martial for any period exceeding six calendar months.

No Non-Commissioned Officer shall be sentenced to imprisonment or corporal punishment without being first reduced to the ranks.

Punishment for "Disgraceful Conduct"

Forfeiture of pay or pension in addition to Corporal punishment or imprisonment

A General or District or Garrison Court Martial may, in addition to corporal punishment or to imprisonment, sentence a Soldier convicted of disgraceful conduct to forfeiture of all advantage as to additional pay and claim to pension on discharge, which otherwise might have accrued from the length or nature of his former service; or to forfeiture of such advantage absolutely, whether it may have accrued from past service, or might accrue from future service.

No Soldier shall be tried for disgraceful conduct by any Court Martial inferior to a District or Garrison Court Martial.

Forfeiture and stoppage in addition to dismissal

A Court Martial may, in addition to any punishment involving dismissal or discharge, sentence any Officer or Soldier whom it is authorized to try, to forfeiture of arrears of pay and allowances due at the time of dismissal or discharge, or of such portion thereof as may be required to make good any loss or damage arising out of his misconduct. A Court Martial, in addition to any punishment not involving dismissal or discharge, may sentence any Officer or Soldier to be put under stoppages not exceeding, in the case of an Officer, two-thirds of his pay and allowances, and in the case of a Non-Commissioned Officer or Soldier, one-half of his pay and allowances, until any loss or damage arising out of his misconduct be made good.

Forfeiture of pay during confinement

Every Soldier subjected to confinement in the Quarter Guard, or Defaulter's Room, or in a Solitary Cell, or in any other place of imprisonment, shall forfeit all claim to pay and allowances during such confinement, and shall be entitled to receive subsistence only according to the rates laid down in the Regulations.

ARTICLE 79

Second sentence of imprisonment on an offender already under sentence of imprisonment

Whenever sentence shall be passed by a Court Martial on an offender already under sentence of imprisonment, such Court may award sentence of imprisonment to commence at the expiration of the imprisonment to which the offender shall have been so previously sentenced, although the aggregate of the terms of imprisonment may exceed the term for which imprisonment could otherwise be awarded by such Court Martial.

Confirmation and Commutation of Sentences

ARTICLE 80

Sentence of death

When a sentence of death shall have been awarded by a General Court Martial, the Commander-in-Chief of the Presidency may confirm such sentence, and cause it to be carried into effect; or may in lieu thereof order the offender, if an Officer, to be transported for life, or for a term not less than seven years: or to be imprisoned for any period not exceeding fourteen years ; or if a Soldier, to be transported for life, or for a term not less than seven years, or to be imprisoned with or without hard labor, and with or without solitary confinement, for any period not exceeding fourteen years.

Sentence of transportation

In cases wherein a sentence of transportation has been awarded by a General Court Martial, the Commander-in-Chief of the Presidency may, in lieu thereof, order the offender, if an Officer, to be imprisoned for any period not exceeding fourteen years; or if a Soldier, to be imprisoned with or without hard labor and with or without solitary confinement for any period net exceeding fourteen years. Provided that in any such case, if the sentence, of transportation be for any less period than fourteen years, the imprisonment in commutation shall not be for a longer period.

Sentence of dismissal

In lieu of a sentence of dismissal, in the case of an Officer, the Commander-in-Chief of the Presidency may order the offender to be suspended from rank and pay and allowances for a stated period.

Corporal Punishment or imprisonment with hard labor

Any Officer having authority to confirm the sentence of a Court Martial, may commute a sentence of corporal punishment, to dismissal from the service, or to imprisonment without hard labor, and with or without solitary confinement, for any period not exceeding one year, for which such Court might have sentenced the offender for the offence;--or may commute a sentence of imprisonment with hard labor to imprisonment without hard labor, with or without solitary confinement, for the same or for a less period---or to dismissal from the service.

Corporal punishment, imprisonment, with hard labor or dismissal

Any Officer having authority to confirm the sentence of a Court Martial, may in commutation of a sentence on Non-Commissioned Officer, of corporal punishment, or imprisonment or of dismissal, direct that such Non-Commissioned Officer be reduced to the ranks, or placed lower, in the list of the rank which he holds, whereby such Non-Commissioned Officer shall lose the corresponding benefit of length of service.

ARTICLE 81

Powers of Commanding Officers of Native Regiments in punishing offences committed by Non-Commissioned Officers and Soldiers and Native Camp Followers

The Commanding Officer for the time being of any Regiment or Corps may summarily try any offence against these Articles of War committed by any person subject to these Articles (not being a Commissioned Officer,) and, on conviction, may sentence the offender and carry out such sentence without confirmation or any further authority; provided that such sentence shall not exceed the sentence which a District or Garrison Court Martial might pass.

A Commanding Officer holding a trial under this Article shall be deemed a Court Martial, and the words "Court Martial" in these Articles of War shall be deemed to include a Commanding Officer holding a trial.

The proceedings on such trials by the Commanding Officer shall be conducted in the presence of two or more European or Native Commissioned Officers and shall be recorded in the English language, and the evidence shall be taken on oath or affirmation, and interpreted by an interpreter upon affirmation. The Commanding Officer shall record the finding and sentence, and the proceedings shall then be signed by such Commanding Officer, and by the Officers in whose presence the trial is held, and shall, without delay, be forwarded to the Officer Commanding the Division, who is hereby authorized to set aside the trial for reasons based on the merits of the case, but not on any merely technical grounds. Every sentence so awarded by a Commanding Officer may be carried out without waiting for its approval by the reviewing Officer.

ARTICLE 82

Powers of Officers Commanding Detachments, in punishing offences

An Officer Commanding a Detachment of his own Regiment or Corps may assemble a Regimental Detachment Court Martial;---and an Officer Commanding a Detachment consisting of men of different Regiments or Corps, may assemble a Detachment or Line Court Martial. Every Court so assembled shall be constituted in the manner provided for **a** Regimental Court Martial under the provisions of-these Articles of War, and shall have the like powers.

The provisions of these Articles of War, which relate to a Court Martial held in a Regiment or Corps, shall, in all practicable cases, be taken to apply to a Court Martial held in a Detachment.

No Officer on detached command of less than three troops or companies, or of a Detachment numerically equal to three troops or companies, and not being on the line of march or on board a ship or other vessel, shall carry into effect any punishment awarded by a Court Martial held by his order, until the sentence shall have been confirmed by the Officer Commanding the Regiment or Corps to which the offender belongs, or by the nearest Superior Officer holding a Command of not less than a Regiment, who is hereby authorized to confirm every such sentence in like manner as an Officer Commanding a Regiment or Corps might do. Provided that in detached situations beyond the Sea or out of the British Territories in India, or when on service in the field, or in cases where an immediate example is necessary and reference cannot be made to such Commanding or Superior Officer without detriment to the service, the Officer Commanding such Detachment may exercise the powers which are vested in an Officer Commanding a Regiment or Corps.

The Commanding Officer of such Detachment, and the Commanding Officer of any European Detachment to which native details of less strength than three troops or companies are attached; and any Commissary of Ordnance or other Officer in charge of any arsenal, ordnance establishment, or any camp quipage depot, may summarily try any offence against these Articles of War, committed by any person under his command, who is subject to such Articles (not being a Commissioned Officer); and may on conviction sentence such offender, and carry out such sentence without confirmation or any further authority; provided that such sentence shall not exceed the powers of a Regimental Court Martial.

Such Commanding Officer or other Officer holding a trial under this Article shall be deemed a Court Martial, and the words "Court Martial," in these Articles of War, shall be deemed to include such Commanding Officer or other Officer holding a trial.

The proceedings on such summary trial shall be conducted, so far as may be practicable, and shall be recorded, in the same manner as is provided in Article 81 for summary trials by an Officer Commanding a Regiment or Corps, and shall, in like manner, be signed and forwarded to the Officer Commanding the Division within which such Detachment shall be at the time, who is hereby authorized to set aside the trial for the same reasons that an Officer Commanding a Division is authorized by Article 81 to set aside a trial by an Officer Commanding a Regiment or Corps. Provided that every sentence so awarded by an Officer Commanding any such Detachment, or by any other Officer holding a trial under this Article, may be carried out without waiting for its approval by the reviewing Officer.

ARTICLE 83

Punishment of light offences

For light offences, a Commanding Officer may, without the intervention of a Court Martial, award extra drill, restriction to barrack limits or within the lines of the, Regiment or Camp, confinement in the Quarter Guard or Defaulters Room or in Solitary Cell, removal from Staff situations, or acting appointments; or may order any soldier to be employed in piling and unpiling shot, and in cleaning accoutrements of men in hospital. But none of these punishments shall be awarded by sentence of a Court Martial. Any soldier, while undergoing punishment under this, Article, shall be liable to be ordered to attend ordinary drill.

The Commander-in-Chief of the Presidency shall prescribe the period not exceeding which offenders shall be liable to drill or confinement or restriction to local limits, as authorized by this Article.

ARTICLE 84

Punishment for breach of cantonment Regulations

For any offence in breach of the Rules and Regulations of any Cantonment, the Commanding Officer of such Cantonment may sentence the offender (provided he be not a European British subject or an Officer or Soldier), notwithstanding he is neither amenable to any Articles of War, nor under the Military command of such Commanding Officer, to pay a fine not exceeding fifty Rupees; and in default of payment of such fine, and in lieu thereof, to imprisonment for any period not exceeding thirty days, if the fine be not sooner paid; and the Officer in charge of any jail, on the delivery of him of the person of the offender accompanied by a warrant under the hand of such Commanding Officer, shall give effect to such imprisonment.

ARTICLE 85

Punishment of offences committed by Camp followers

For any breach of good order, a Cantonment Officer of any Regiment, Corps, or Detachment, may sentence any follower of such Regiment, Corps, or Detachment under his command to imprisonment for any period not exceeding seven days; or, if the offender be not of a degree superior to that of a menial servant, to undergo Corporal punishment not exceeding twelve strokes of a rattan; or if the offender to be of a degree superior to that of a menial servant, to fine not exceeding fifty Rupees, and in default of payment to imprisonment for a period of thirty days, if such fine be not sooner paid.

Execution of Sentences of Court Martial

ARTICLE 86

Sentence of Death

In awarding a sentence of death, a General Court Martial, shall specify that the offender shall "suffer death by being hanged by neck until he be dead" or "by being shot to death" as the Court in their discretion shall deem expedient, and such sentence, if confirmed, shall be carried into effect accordingly.

ARTICLE 87

Transportation

Whenever the sentence of a General Court Martial shall adjudge transportation, or sentence of death shall be commuted by competent authority to transportation, the offender shall be delivered over to the Officer in charge of the nearest Jail, and such Officer, in giving effect to the sentence, shall be guided by such order as he shall receive from the local Government.

Imprisonment with hard labor or solitary confinement

Whenever any sentence of a Court Martial shall adjudge imprisonment with or without hard labor, or with solitary confinement or both, or whenever the sentence of a Court Martial shall be commuted to any such imprisonment, it shall be the duty of every Officer in charge of a Jail, to give effect to such sentence on the offender being delivered into his custody, with an authenticated copy of the sentence passed on the offender.

ARTICLE 88

Place of imprisonment

The Commander-in-Chief of the Presidency may, from time to time, direct that any person sentenced to imprisonment by a Court Martial, may be imprisoned in any public Jail or in any other fit place.

ARTICLE 89

Local Government may cause removal to another place of imprisonment

When any person subject to these Articles of War is confined in any public Jail or other place not under Military control under a sentence of imprisonment passed by a Court Martial, the local Government of the Presidency or place in which such place of confinement is situate, may order the removal of such person from such place of confinement to any other public Jail or other fit place of confinement within the Territories of such local Government. The period for which such person is in custody during such removal shall be reckoned as part of the original period of imprisonment for which such person was sentenced. The Governor-General of India in Council may order the removal of any such person from any place of confinement in British India to any other place of confinement therein.

ARTICLE 90

Powers of Commander-in-Chief of a Presidency to pardon certain offenders

The Commander-in-Chief of any Presidency shall have power to pardon any person belonging to the Military Forces of such Presidency, who shall have been convicted by a Court Martial of any offence against the Articles of War, which offence, wherever committed, is not punishable otherwise than by sentence of a Court Martial. Instead of granting a full pardon to any such person, the Commander-in-Chief of the Presidency may remit any part of the punishment awarded for the offence.

In any such case the Commander-in-Chief of the Presidency shall, together with a copy of the warrant or other instrument under which the offender is kept in custody in execution of the sentence, issue a warrant under his own hand, setting forth the offence of which the offender has been convicted, and pardoning or remitting such part of the punishment awarded for such offence as to him shall seem fit.

The said warrant shall be countersigned by the Magistrate of the zillah or city in which the offender is undergoing his sentence; or, if he is confined in any prison within the limits of a Supreme Court of Judicature, shall be countersigned by a Judge of such Court; if it shall appear to such Magistrate or Judge that the offence, wherever committed, is not punishable by any authority other than that of a Court Martial; but not otherwise.

Every Sheriff, Jailor, or other person having custody of any offender under sentence of a Court Martial, shall obey and give effect to any warrant of the Commander-in-Chief of the Presidency, duly countersigned as aforesaid, for the pardon and release of any offender in' his custody, or for the remission of any part of the sentence of any such offender.

ARTICLE 91

Dismissal from service

Every Soldier sentenced under these Articles of War to imprisonment with hard labor for either a Military or Non-Military offence, shall be struck off the strength of the Regiment or Corps to which he belongs from the date of confirmation of such sentence; and no Soldier who has undergone such imprisonment for any period, shall be capable of being re-admitted in the ranks, or of receiving pension on discharge.

ARTICLE 92

Dismissal with ignominy

Any Soldier sentenced for disgraceful conduct, to dismissal, or to corporal punishment, or to imprisonment with hard labor, shall, on any such sentence being confirmed, be dismissed with ignominy.

ARTICLE 93

Stoppage of pay

In every case wherein a fine or forfeiture of arrears of pay, or stoppages, shall be adjudged by a Court Martial, any pay or public money due to the offender or that may become due to him, shall be available, with the sanction of the Commander-in-Chief of the Presidency for the payment of the amount so adjudged.

Limitation

No Soldier sentenced to pay a fine, or to stoppages to make good any loss or damage arising out of his misconduct, shall be continued under forfeiture or stoppages under any one such sentence, for any period exceeding one year; and no Soldier shall be at any one time placed under forfeiture or stoppages exceeding in the whole the amount of half his pay and allowances, nor be liable to be put under further stoppages while actually under stoppages to the amount of half of his pay and allowances.

ARTICLE 94

Time for trial by Court Martial

Trials by Courts Martial may be carried on at any time without restriction. The hour of original assembly of the Court shall be named by the Officer convening the Court, but the adjournment of the Court and the hour of its re-assembly shall be determined by the Court itself.

Forms of Proceedings

ARTICLE 95

Judge Advocate

Except as hereinafter provided, a Judge Advocate, or a European Officer of not less than ten years' service, shall be appointed to conduct the proceedings at every General Court Martial, and European Officer of not less than four years' service, or any Adjutant of a Regiment where such Officer is available, shall be appointed to conduct the proceedings at all other Courts Martial.

ARTICLE 96

Interpreter

An interpreter shall be appointed to every Court Martial. If no interpreter is available at the Station where the Court Martial sits, the Officer Commanding at such Station shall appoint any competent person under his command to perform the duty of interpreter. Where no interpreter or other competent person is available, the Superintending Officer at the Court Martial shall perform the duty of interpreter.

ARTICLE 97

President

At every Court Martial the Senior Officer shall sit as President without being appointed by warrant. Rissaldar Majors and Subadar Majors are to take precedence according to the dates of their Commissions, and above all Native Officers holding the rank of Subadar or Rissaldar. Sirdar Bahadoors and Bahadoors are to take rank only according to their respective Commissions of Rissaldar Major, Subadar Major, Rissaldar, Subadar, or Jernadar. Rissaldars and Rissaidars are to take rank with Subadars, according to the dates of their respective Commissions.

Death or absence of President

In case of the death or unavoidable absence of the President, the next Senior Member shall take the place of President, and the trial shall proceed, if the Court shall still consist of not less than the smallest number of Members of which such Court is directed, to consist by these Articles of War.

ARTICLE 98

Revision of sentence

No finding or sentence of a Court Martial shall be revised more than once, and no evidence shall be received on such revision except evidence relating to previous convictions and general character. For the purpose of such revision, the President and all the Members shall be convened if possible. But if any of them should be unavoidably absent, the remaining Members may proceed with such revision, provided they are not fewer than the smallest number for each description of Court Martial directed in these Articles respectively. When all the same Members do not meet, the circumstances are to be duly certified on the face of the proceedings.

ARTICLE 99

Manner of voting

The Members of a Court Martial are to preserve order, and in giving their votes upon all matters are to begin with the junior in rank. In all cases where a sentence of Death is not awarded, the decision shall be by the majority of Members present, provided the number of members present be not less than that required by the preceding Articles. In case of an equality of votes, the decision shall be in favor of the prisoner. The President at a Court Martial shall vote with the other members, and shall have no casting vote, except upon questions other than the finding and the sentence.

ARTICLE 100

Sentence of death

No Court Martial shall pass a sentence of Death unless two-thirds of the Members present concur in such sentence, or four concur where the Court consist of five Members, or five concur where the Court consist of seven Members.

Affirmations

ARTICLE 101

Interpreter's affirmation

On the assembly of a Court Martial, the judge Advocate or European Superintending Officer shall administer to the interpreter the following affirmation:-

I ….. , solemnly affirm in the presence of Almighty God, that I will faithfully interpret and translate the proceedings of the Court, and that I will not divulge the sentence until it shall have been published by authority; and, further, that I will not disclose or discover the vote or opinion of any particular Member of the Court, unless required to give evidence thereof by a Court of Justice or Court Martial, in due course of law."

In case of the unavoidable absence of an interpreter, the European Superintending Officer of a Court Martial other than a General Court Martial shall make the affirmation prescribed for the interpreter.

Member's affirmation

The Judge Advocate or Superintending Officer shall then cause the following affirmation to be made by each Member:-

"I ….., solemnly affirm in the presence of Almighty God, that I will duly administer justice according to the Articles of War, without partiality, favor, or affection, and, if any doubt shall arise, then , according to my conscience, the best of understanding, and the customs of War in like cases; and that I will not divulge the sentence of the Court until it shall be published by – authority; and, further, that I will not disclose or discover the vote or opinion of any particular Member of the Court, unless required to give evidence thereof by a Court of Justice or a Court Martial in due course of law."

Judge Advocate's affirmation

The following affirmation shall then be administered by the interpreter to the Judge Advocate or Superintending Officer:-

"I ….., solemnly affirm in the presence of Almighty God, that I will not, upon any account whatsoever, disclose or discover the vote or opinion of any particular Member of the Court Martial, unless required to give evidence thereof as a witness by a Court of Justice or a Court

Martial in due course of law, and that I will not, unless it be necessary for the due discharge of my official duties, disclose the sentence of the Court, until it shall be published by authority."

It shall be necessary to administer the foregoing affirmations on the commencement of every fresh trial before the same Court.

ARTICLE 102

Witness' oath or affirmation

Every person who gives evidence at a Court Martial shall be examined on oath or affirmation where an affirmation is allowed.

The affirmation shall be to the following effect:-

"I ....., solemnly affirm, in the presence of Almighty God, that what I shall state shall be the truth, the whole truth, and nothing but the truth."

If any person after making such affirmation shall wilfully and falsely state any matter or thing which amounts to the offence of giving false evidence as defined in Article 64, such person shall be subject to the same punishment as persons convicted of that offence.

ARTICLE 103

Summoning witness not amenable to these Article

When any person required as a witness before a Court Martial is not amenable to Military Law, the Judge Advocate or Officer Commanding shall apply to the Magistrate within whose jurisdiction the witness resides to cause his attendance before such Court Martial. Such Magistrate shall issue his summons to such witness to attend before such Court Martial in the same manner as if the witness were required in the Court of such Magistrate.

ARTICLE 104

Record in the Regimental Books of absence without leave and of the declaration of a Court of Enquiry thereon, to have the same effect as a conviction for desertion

If any Officer or Soldier subject to these Articles of War shall have been illegally absent from his duty for the space of two months, a Regimental Court of Enquiry composed of three Commissioned Officers, of whom all may be European or all Native, or one or more may be European and one or more Native, shall forthwith assemble, and having received proof of the fact on oath or affirmation, shall declare such absence and the period thereof; and the Officer Commanding the Regiment or Corps shall record the declaration of such Court of Enquiry thereon in the Regimental Books; and if such Officer or Soldier shall not afterwards surrender or be apprehended, such record shall have the legal effect of a conviction for desertion. If such Officer or Soldier shall surrender or be apprehended after such record shall have been so entered, such record, or copy thereof, purporting to bear the signature of the Officer having the custody of the Regimental Books, shall, on the trial of such Officer or Soldier on a charge for desertion, be admissible in evidence of the facts therein recorded; and on proof of the identity of the prisoner with the Officer or Soldier therein mentioned, he may be found guilty of desertion.

ARTICLE 105

Proof of absence without leave for two months to be sufficient presumptive evidence of desertion

If, upon the trial of any Officer or Soldier for desertion, it shall be proved that such Officer or Soldier has been absent without leave, or has overstayed his leave, for the space of two months, such proof shall be deemed sufficient presumptive evidence of the desertion of such Officer or Soldier, and shall be sufficient to convict him of the offence of desertion, unless he shall prove that such unauthorized absence was not wilful on his part, or shall otherwise rebut the presumption of desertion arising from proof of his absence without leave.

ARTICLE 106

Reference to Government Officer as to the truth **of** statement concerning cause of absence

If upon the trial of such Officer or Soldier for desertion or for absence without leave, he shall state in his defence that his unauthorized absence was not wilful, or that he was detained in his village from sickness, or shall advance any other sufficient excuse for his absence, or any matter sufficient to rebut any presumptive evidence of desertion, and shall refer to any European, Civil or Military Officer of Government in support of his statement; or if it shall appear to the Court Martial that the truth or falsehood of such statement may be ascertained by reference to any such Civil or Military Officer of Government, it shall be the duty of the Court to address such Civil or Military Officer on the subject, and to adjourn the proceedings until the reply of such officer is received. The reply of such Officer, if favorable to the prisoner, shall be admissible in evidence, and have the same effect as if the statement had been made before the Court by such Officer in person on oath or affirmation, and proof of the handwriting of such Officer shall not be necessary. Should any Court before which a prisoner is being tried be dissolved prior to the receipt of the reply to any communication made under this Section to any Civil or Military Officer, a fresh Court may be ordered, and the trial shall be commenced anew before such Court.

ARTICLE 107

Powers and Duties of Provost Marshal

For, the prompt and instant repression of irregularities and crimes which may be committed by troops in the field and on the march, Provost Marshals shall be appointed by the Commander-in-Chief of the Presidency or the Officer Commanding the forces in the field, and the powers of such Provost Marshals shall be regulated according to the established usages of War and Rules of the service.

The duties of the Provost Marshal so appointed are to take charge of prisoners confined for offences of a general description; to preserve good order and discipline; and to prevent breaches of the same by Soldiers and followers of the Army. The Provost Marshal may punish on the spot, on the same day, any Soldier or follower who, in his view, or in the view of any of his assistants, shall commit any breach of good order and Military discipline: Provided that the punishment be limited to the necessity of the case, and accord with the orders which the Provost Marshal may, from time to time, receive from the Officer commanding the troops. If the Provost Marshal or any of his assistants shall not see the offender actually commit the crime, but sufficient proof can be obtained of the offender's guilt, a report shall be made to the Commander of the troops; who is empowered to deal with the case as he may deem most conducive to the maintenance of good order and Military discipline.

ARTICLE 108

Trial by European Court Martial

In any Presidency where the Native Troops have hitherto been authorized to claim to be tried by European Courts Martial, every person amenable to these Articles of War who is under orders for trial by a Court Martial may, as of right, claim to be tried by European Officers. When such claim is made, the Court, whether a General, District, Garrison, or Regimental Court Martial, shall be composed of European Commissioned Officers, aid the number of Members, and the proceedings shall be governed in all respects by the provisions of these Articles.

It shall be competent to the Governor General of India in Council by a General Order to extend the privilege of claiming to be tried by European Courts Martial to any Native Troops.

It shall further be competent to the Governor-General of India in Council, or to the Governor in Council of the Presidency an Order in Council, to direct that any Court Martial may be composed of European Commissioned Officers. The proceedings of such Courts Martial shall be regulated in every respect as directed in these Articles of War far, Native Courts Martial, except that it shall not be necessary to appoint an Officer to conduct the proceedings of such Court Martial.

ARTICLE 109

Governor-General in Council may by order empower Generals, &c, to appoint General or District or Garrison Courts Martial

It shall be competent to the Governor-General of India in Council or the Governor in Council of any Presidency, from time to time, by an order in Council, to empower every General or other Officer having the Command of troops in the service of Her Majesty, or any such General or other Officer, to appoint General or District or Garrison Courts Martial, as occasion may require, for the trial of any Officers, Soldiers, or Followers, subject to these Articles of War, who may be charged with any offence punishable by the said Articles, which, in the judgment of such General or other Officer, requires to be punished without delay; and also to confirm and carry into effect, immediately or otherwise, any sentence of such Court Martial, or to commute, mitigate, or remit any such sentence ; or if he shall deem it necessary, to refer any such sentence to the Commander-in-Chief of the Presidency for his orders.

Any General Court Martial, which may be appointed under the authority of this Article, shall be appointed by the Senior Officer on the spot, and shall consist of not less than five Commissioned Officers, the number to be fixed by the General or other Officer appointing the Court Martial. The order in Council may direct that a General Court Martial to be appointed under the provisions of this Article shall consist wholly of European Commissioned Officers or of Native Commissioned Officers; and in such case, the Officer appointing the Court Martial shall determine whether the same shall consist of European Officers or of Native office. Every General Court Martial appointed under the authority of this Article shall have all the powers of a General Court Martial specified in the 78th Article, and sentence of death, or other punishment to which the offender is liable by these Articles, may be awarded by such Court Martial, if a majority of the Members present concur in the sentence.

It shall not be necessary to appoint a Judge Advocate to conduct the proceedings of a European Court Martial under this Article.

CHAPTER IV

Effects of the Dead

ARTICLE 110

Commanding Officer to secure the effects of the dead and to direct an inventory to be taken

When any Officer or Soldier dies or is killed in the service, or any other person receiving public pay who is subject to these Articles of War in any department belonging to the Army dies or is killed in the field, the Officer Commanding the Regiment, Corps, or Detachment, or the Officer in charge of the department to which such Officer or Soldier or other person belongs, shall, if no heir or executor be present, secure his effects, and direct an inventory thereof to be taken. **A** duplicate shall be lodged in the Office of the Adjutant, or Officer in charge of the department to which such Officer, Soldier, or other person belongs.

ARTICLE 111

Sale of effects

If there be no heir or executor on the spot, the effects are to be publicly sold. The Officer Commanding the Regiment or Corps or Detachment, or the Officer in charge of the department to which the deceased Officer, Soldier, or other person belonged, after discharging the debts of the deceased, namely, the expense of funeral ceremonies, his debts in camp or quarters, and Regimental debts of every description, shall account for the residue to the heir or heirs declared by will, whether written or verbal, or nominated in the Regimental register, or in failure of such to the legal representative of the deceased; and in the event of no executor, heir, or other representative of the deceased attending and establishing his claim within twelve months from the date of the casualty, the amount in the hands of the Officer having charge of the estate shall be remitted to the General Treasury at the Presidency.

ARTICLE 112

Sale of deserter's effects

The effects of deserters are to be publicly sold, and the proceeds, after payment of Regimental debts, remitted by the Officer Commanding the Regiment or Corps to which the deserter belongs, to the General Treasury at the Presidency, or appropriated according to the rules obtaining in such Presidency.

CHAPTER V

Miscellaneous

ARTICLE 113

Construction of the Articles as regards a Commander-in-Chief

All powers and provisions contained in these Articles relating to a Commander-in-Chief shall, unless when otherwise provided, be construed to extend to the Officer Commanding the forces for the time being in any Presidency.

ARTICLE 114

Construction of the Articles as regards Soldiers

All powers and provisions contained in these Articles relating to Soldiers shall be construed to extend to Non-Commissioned Officers, unless when otherwise provided.

ARTICLE 115

Troops serving out of their own Presidency

When any portion of the troops belonging to any Presidency shall be serving within the limits of any other Presidency, such troops shall be considered as placed, during such service, under the orders and authority of the Commander-in-Chief or other Officer Commanding the forces of the Presidency within which they are serving, for all the purposes of these Articles of War, in the same manner as if they belonged to such Presidency; and all the provisions of these Articles of War, which relate to the trial and punishment of offenders belonging to the Presidency within which the trial is held, are hereby declared applicable to the trial and punishment of offenders serving within such Presidency. Provided that it shall be lawful for the Governor-General of India in Council to direct that the troops, or any part thereof, of any Presidency, whilst serving without the limits of such Presidency, shall continue under the orders and authority of the Commander-Chief or Officer Commanding the forces of the Presidency to which they belong for all the purposes of these Articles.

ARTICLE 116

Assembling Courts Martial in foreign territories

Any Officer Commanding any portion of Her Majesty's troops serving in any place out of Her Majesty's Territories, or out of the Territories of those States in alliance with Her Majesty in which Her Majesty's forces are permanently stationed, shall, upon complaint made to him of any offence committed against the property or person of any inhabitant or resident in any such place by any person serving with, or belonging to, Her Majesty's Army, being under the immediate Command of such Officer, summon and cause to assemble a General Court Martial, which shall consist of not less than three Officers, for the purpose of trying any such person, notwithstanding such Officer shall not have received any warrant empowering him to assemble Courts Martial; and every Court Martial so assembled shall have the same powers in regard to summoning and examining of witnesses, the trial of, and sentence upon such person, as are granted by these Articles to General Courts Martial. Provided that no sentence of any such Court Martial shall be executed until the Officer Commanding-in-Chief the force to which the person so convicted and sentenced belongs, shall have approved and confirmed the same; except where such sentence shall not exceed the pourers granted by these Articles to a District or Garrison Court Martial, in which case the Officer by whom the Court is convened is authorized to confirm, and commute, or mitigate, or remit the same; reporting the proceedings to the Officer Commanding-in-Chief.

ARTICLE 117

No person to be tried a second time for the same offence

No person who shall have been acquitted or convicted by a Court Martial of any offence, shall be liable to be tried a second time by the same or any other Court Martial for the same offence. Provided that any person may be tried for the offence of murder, and punished for that offence, notwithstanding he may have been tried and punished for the act which caused death, if at the time of his conviction for the said act death shall not have resulted or shall not have been known by the Court which passed sentence to have resulted.

When any person subject to these Articles of War shall have been found guilty by a Court Martial of any Military offence, such Court Martial shall enquire into and receive evidence of any previous conviction of such person before a Court Martial or a court of Justice, and shall enquire into the general character of such person, if a Soldier, for the purpose of apportioning the punishment to which he is liable, to be sentenced for the offence of which he has been so found guilty. But no such evidence shall, in any case, be received until the Court shall have ascertained that such person had previously to his trial received notice of the intention to produce such evidence on the same. And it is hereby directed that such notice shall be given to all persons previous to trial.

ARTICLE 118

Complaints against Superior Officer

Any Officer or Soldier, who thinks himself wronged by his Superior or other Officer, is to complain thereof to the Officer Commanding his troop or company; and if his grievance be not redressed, may further complain to the Officer Commanding the Regiment or Corps to which he belongs, who is hereby required to examine into such complaint, or remit it to his Superior Authority, as the circumstances may require. If the complaint so preferred to the Commanding Officer should appear to be frivolous or groundless, the Officer Soldier preferring it shall be liable to be punished according to the sentence of a General or other Court Martial; provided that such Officer or Soldier shall not on such account be liable to be sentenced to dismissal, nor to suffer corporal punishment or imprisonment with hard labor.

ARTICLE 119

Prisoners of War

Any Officer or Soldier, who shall be taken prisoner by the enemy, shall forfeit all claim to pay and allowances during the period of his remaining a prisoner, and until he shall again return to the service. If such Officer or Soldier can then establish, before a Court Martial, that he was unavoidably taken prisoner in the bourse of service, that he resisted as long as he was able, that he did not serve with or assist the enemy, and that he returned as soon as possible to the service, he shall be entitled, after the finding of such Court Martial shall have been confirmed by the Commander-in-Chief of the Presidency, to receive either the whole or such portion of his arrears of pay and allowances as the local Government shall determine.

ARTICLE 120

Subsistence allowance to prisoner not dismissed

Every Officer or Soldier or follower in receipt of any public pay, who is imprisoned under the sentence of a Court Martial, or a commuted sentence, or under the sentence of a Court of Criminal Judicature, shall, during the term of such imprisonment, if such imprisonment does not involve dismissal under Article 91, receive subsistence only, to the amount of his pay proper, according to the rates laid down in the Regulations.

ARTICLE 121

Sentences of transportation for a term of years, passed for offences, punishable with transportation for life, rendered valid

When before the passing of these Articles of War any Court Martial or any Special Commissioner shall have sentenced any person subject to the Articles of War for the Native Army in force at the date of such sentence, to transportation for any term less than the term of his life, for an offence punishable under the Articles then in force with transportation for life, such sentence, to the extent of the punishment awarded thereby, shall be deemed as valid and effectual is if the offender had been sentenced to transportation for life.

ARTICLE 122

Sentence to imprisonment with hard labor passed for offences punishable with simple imprisonment

When before the passing of these Articles of War any Court Martial or any Special Commissioner shall have sentenced any person subject to the Articles of War for the Native Army in force at the date of such sentence to imprisonment with hard labor, for an offence for which by the Articles of War then in force a sentence of simple imprisonment could lawfully be passed, such sentence shall be deemed valid and effective; and all persons are hereby indemnified for anything done in pursuance of such sentence.

ARTICLE 123

Officers Commanding Regiment exercising Magisterial powers

Sentences passed by When before the passing of these Articles of War any Officer Commanding a Regiment or Corps and exercising Magisterial powers, shall have sentenced to punishment any person subject to the Articles of war for the Native Army in force at the date of such sentence, such sentence shall deemed valid, and shall be carried into effect, notwithstanding that such sentence was passed by such Officer in any part of the British Territories where he was not authorized, to exercise such Magisterial powers. Provided such sentence be one which it would have been within the competency of such Officer to pass within the Territories where he was authorized to exercise such powers.

CHAPTER VI

Mode of dealing with offences not Military

ARTICLE 124

Persons charged with offences cognizable by criminal court to be handed over to the Magistrate

When an officer or Soldier, in any place within the jurisdiction of any Criminal Court established by Her Majesty or the Government of India or any local Government, is accused of any offence triable by such Court, he shall be delivered over to a Magistrate to be proceeded against according to law. All Officers and Soldiers are hereby required to assist the Officers of Justice in apprehending and securing any person so accused.

ARTICLE 125

Crimes to be tried by Court Martial where no regular Criminal Tribunal exists

In any place out of the British Territories in India, such offences, when committed by Officers or Soldiers, shall be cognizable by Court Martial.

ARTICLE 126

Offences cognizable by General Courts Martial

General Courts Martial shall have cognizance of offences punishable with:-

Death;

Transportation;

Imprisonment for a period that may extend to seven years or to fourteen years.

ARTICLE 127

Offences cognizable by District or Garrison Courts Martial

District or Garrison Courts Martial shall have cognizance, ordinarily, of offences punishable with imprisonment for a period which may extend to three years. District or Garrison Courts Martial shall also by special order of the Officer Commanding the forces have cognizance of offences of which a General Court Martial may take cognizance (not punishable with death or transportation for life), with power to sentence to imprisonment for any such offence for a period, which hay extend to three years.

ARTICLE 128

Offences cognizable by Regimental, Detachment or Line Courts Martial

Regimental, Detachment, or Line Courts Martial, shall have cognizance, ordinarily, of offences punishable with imprisonment for a period not exceeding six calendar months, and, by special order of the Officer Commanding the forces, of offences ordinarily cognizable by District or Garrison Courts Martial, with power to sentence persons convicted of such offences to imprisonment for a period not exceeding six calendar months.

General Courts Martial

ARTICLE 129

Punishment of death

Any Officer or Soldier who shall be convicted by a General Court Martial of causing death, shall be deemed to have committed murder:---

1st. If the act by which death was caused, was done with the intention of causing death; or

2nd. If it was done with the intention of causing such bodily injury as the offender knew to be likely to cause the death of the person to whom the harm was caused; or

3rd. If it was done with the intention of causing bodily injury to any person, and the bodily injury intended to be inflicted was sufficient in the ordinary course of nature to cause death; or

4th. If the person committing the act, knew that it was so imminently dangerous that it must in all probability cause death, or such bodily injury as is likely to cause death, and if lie committed such act without any excuse for incurring the risk of causing death or such injury as aforesaid.

Any Officer or Soldier convicted of murder shall be sentenced to be hanged by the neck till he is dead, or to transportation for life.

ARTICLE 130

Offences punishable by imprisonment or transportation for life

Any Officer or Soldier who shall he convicted by a General Court Martial of any of the offences hereinafter mentioned, accompanied with an attempt to commit murder, or with wounding or other corporal injury to any person endangering the life of such person; that is to say:---

1st. Breaking, or attempting to break, by day or night, into any dwelling-house, tent, boat, or, other habitation, or into any building or place used for the preservation of property, with the intent to rob or steal;

2nd. Robbery or attempt to rob;

3rd. Stealing or attempting to steal in a house, or from the person--

Shall be sentenced by such General Court Martial to transportation for life, or for any period not less than seven years, or to imprisonment with hard labor for a period that may extend to fourteen years.

ARTICLE 131

Robbery, &c., accompanied with wounding, &c., not endangering life

Any Officer or Soldier who shall be convicted by **a** General Court Martial:---

Of any offence specified in Clauses **1,** 2, and **3** of the last Article, accompanied with wounding or other corporal injury to any person not endangering the life of such person;--- or

ARTICLE 132

Robbery by open violence or dacoity

Of robbery by open violence, or dacoity, that is to say, going forth in the day or in the night with an offensive weapon, or in a gang with or without an offensive weapon, with the intention of committing robbery, and by force or intimidation robbing or attempting to rob any person in any place, or attacking by open violence any house, or place of habitation, or any place in which property may be, kept, for the purpose of robbery;---

ARTICLE 133

House-breaking by night

Of breaking, or attempting to break into any dwelling-house, Cent; boat, or other place of habitation, between sunset and sunrise, with intent to rob or steal;---or

ARTICLE 134

House-breaking and stealing

Of breaking into any such place of habitation, or into any place used for the preservation of property, and stealing there-from property the value of which shall exceed one hundred Rupees;--or

ARTICLE 135

Buying or receiving stolen property

Of purchasing or receiving plundered or stolen property, knowing it to have been obtained by robbery, by open violence, or by theft or robbery, aggravated as described in Article 130 or Article 131;---or

ARTICLE 136

Unnatural crime

Of an unnatural crime;--or

ARTICLE 137

Rape

Of Rape;-

Shall be sentenced by such General Court Martial to imprisonment with hard labour for a period not exceeding fourteen years.

ARTICLE 138

Culpable homicide not amounting to murder

Any Officer or Soldier who shall be convicted by a General Court Martial---

Of the offence of culpable homicide not amounting to murder;---or

ARTICLE 139

Wounding with intent to murder

Of the offence of wounding, or otherwise causing any corporal injury to any person with intent to murder, whether the person wounded or otherwise injured to be the person whom the offender intended to murder, or another; or of attempting to commit murder by any means whatsoever;---

Shall be sentenced by such General Court Martial to imprisonment with or without hard labor for a period not exceeding fourteen years.

ARTICLE 140

Premeditated affray attended with Culpable Homicide

Any Officer or Soldier who shall be convicted by a General Court Martial:---

Of premeditated affray, attended with culpable homicide not amounting to murder, or severe wounding, or other aggravating circumstance;---or

ARTICLE 141

Intentionally doing corporal, injury

Of intentionally wounding, maiming, or otherwise doing corporal injury to any person;---or

ARTICLE 142

Accidently doing corporal injury to one person when intended to be done to another

Of accidentally wounding, maiming, or otherwise doing corporal injury to any person with the intention of doing such injury to another person;---or

ARTICLE 143

House-breaking by night

Of breaking into any dwelling-house, tent, boat, or other place of habitation, or into anyplace used for the preservation of property, between sunrise and sunset, with intent to steal therein;---or

ARTICLE 144

Theft in a dwelling-house

Of stealing from any, habitation, or from any person, any property exceeding three hundred Rupees in value;---or

ARTICLE 145

Buying or receiving stolen property33 Rupees in value

Of having purchased or received any property so stolen, exceeding in value three hundred Rupees, knowing it to have been stolen;---or

ARTICLE 146

Arson

Of Arson;---or

ARTICLE 147

Enticing unmarried women under 15 years

Of enticing and taking away, or of causing to be enticed or taken away for any unlawful purpose, any unmarried woman under the age of fifteen years;---or

ARTICLE 148

Stealing children under 8 years

Of stealing a child under the age of eight years;---

ARTICLE 149

Counterfeiting or fabricating Deed, &c

Of counterfeiting, or causing or procuring the fraudulent fabrication or alteration of any written deed, or printed paper of any description ; or any counterfeit seal or signature thereto; or the illicit imitation of any public stamp or stamped paper issued by Government; or of using, selling, or disposing of such stamped paper, knowing the same to be counterfeit ; or of fraudulently issuing and publishing as true, or of fraudulently giving effect to any fabricated deed or paper knowing it to be a forgery;---or

ARTICLE 150

Counterfeiting Coin &c

Of forging or procuring to be forged any counterfeit coin, in imitation of any of the gold, silver, or copper coin of the Government of India, or of any coin usually received as money in the British Territories in India; or of clipping, filing, drilling, or defacing any such coin; or of paying or tendering in payment counterfeit Coin, Bank Motes, or other Securities for money, knowing the same to be counterfeit, although such Notes or Securities shall be incomplete;---

Shall be sentenced by such General, Court Martial to suffer imprisonment with or without hard labor for any period not exceeding seven years.

District or Garrison Courts Martial

ARTICLE 151

Powers of District or Garrison Courts Martial

It shall be competent to the Commander-in-Chief of the Presidency, and to any Officer having authority to convene District or Garrison Courts Martial, to cause offenders, not being Commissioned Officers, accused of any of the offences specified in these Articles of War, except offences for which the punishment of death or transportation for life is provided, to be tried for such offences before a District or Garrison Court Martial, and such Court shall have power, on conviction, to sentence any such offender to imprisonment with or without hard labor for any period not exceeding three years.

ARTICLE 152

Stealing property not exceeding 300 Rupees, but exceeding 50 Rupees in value

Any Officer or Soldier who shall be convicted by a General, District, or Garrison Court Martial:---or

Of stealing from any habitation, or from the person, any property of value not exceeding three hundred Rupees, but exceeding fifty Rupees;---or

ARTICLE 153

Buying or receiving stolen property not exceeding 300 Rupees in value

Of having purchased or received any stolen property of value not exceeding three hundred Rupees, knowing it to have been stolen, but not under aggravating circumstances:---or

ARTICLE 154

Dishonestly having stolen property in possession

Of dishonestly having stolen property in his possession, and of having dishonestly kept possession of such property after becoming aware of its having been stolen;-

Punishable with imprisonment not exceeding three years

Shall be sentenced by such Court to suffer imprisonment with or without hard labor for any period not exceeding three years.

Regimental, Detachment, or Line Courts Martial

ARTICLE 155

Offences punishable by imprisonment not exceeding six months

It shall be competent to any Officer having authority to convene a Regimental, Detachment, or Line Court Martial, to cause offenders, not being Commissioned Officers, accused of any of the offences specified in these Articles of War, for which no punishment exceeding imprisonment with hard labor for three years is therein provided, to be tried before Regimental, Detachment, or Line Courts Martial, and any such Court shall have power, on conviction, to sentence any such offender to suffer imprisonment with or without hard labor for any period pot exceeding six calendar months.

ARTICLE 156

Stealing property not exceeding 50 Rupees in value

Any Officer or solder, who shall be convicted;---

Of stealing property not exceeding fifty Rupees in value;---or

ARTICLE 157

Simple assault or affray

Of assault or affray, unattended with homicide, severe wounding, or aggravating circumstances:--

Punishable with imprisonment not exceeding one year if awarded by General, District, or Garrison Court Martial for not exceeding six months if awarded by a Regimental, Detachment, or Line Court Martial

May be sentenced to suffer imprisonment with or without hard labor for any period not exceeding one year, by the award of a General, or District, or Garrison Court Martial; or for any period not exceeding six calendar months, by the award of a Regimental, or Detachment, or Line Court Martial.

Offences punishable by imprisonment from six months to two years according to the description of the Court

ARTICLE 158

Resisting process of a Magistrate or Police Officer

Any Officer or Soldier, who shall be convicted:--

Of resisting the process of a Magistrate or Police Officer;---or

ARTICLE 159

Committing any offence not already provided for

Of having committed any offence against person or property for which provision is not already made in the preceding Articles of War;

Punishable with imprisonment not exceeding two years by the award of a General Court Martial, not exceeding one year by the award of a District or Garrison Court Martial, and not exceeding six calendar months by the award of a Regimental, or Detachment, or Line Court Martial

May be sentenced to suffer imprisonment for any period not exceeding two years by the award of a General Court Martial, for any period not exceeding one year by the award of a District or Garrison Court Martial, and for any period not exceeding six calendar months by the award of a Regimental, or Detachment, or Line Court Martial.

ARTICLE 160

Offence of aiding and abetting

Any Officer or Soldier, who shall be convicted by a General, or District, or Garrison, or Regimental Court Martial, of having been present, aiding and abetting, or of having caused, instigated, or procured, the commission of any of the offences specified in any of these Articles, shall be sentenced by such Court to any punishment in these Articles provided for such offence, and within the competency of such Court to award.

ARTICLE 161

Sentence of death

No sentence of death shall be carried into effect until confirmed by the Commander-in-Chief of the Presidency to which the person on whom such sentence is passed belongs; or if such person is attached to the force of any Presidency, but is serving with a force in any place out of British India, until it be confirmed by the Officer Commanding such force; or if such person belongs to a force in any part of India not under the Commander-in-Chief of any Presidency, until confirmed by the Officer Commanding such force.

ARTICLE 162

Confirmation, remission and commutation

The Commander-in-Chief or other Commanding Officer as provided in last Article is authorized at his discretion to confirm any sentence of death, and to remit such sentence, or to commute it to transportation for life, or for a period not less than seven years or to imprisonment with hard labor for any period not exceeding fourteen years.

ARTICLE 163

Transportation

No sentence of transportation shall be carried into effect until confirmed by the Commander-in-Chief, or other Commanding Officer as provided in Article 161, and the Commander-in-Chief or such other Commanding Officer, is authorized at his discretion to remit such sentence or to confirm it, or to commute it to imprisonment with or without hard labor for any period not exceeding fourteen years. Provided that, if the sentence of transportation be for any period less than fourteen years, the imprisonment in commutation shall not be for any longer period.

ARTICLE 164

Remission or mitigation

It shall be competent to any Officer having authority, to confirm the sentence of a General or other Court Martial, and to remit any sentence passed by such Court Martial, or to mitigate such sentence by substituting simple imprisonment for imprisonment with hard labor, or by reducing the period of imprisonment, or by directing the discharge of the offender in lieu of any imprisonment.

ARTICLE 165

No person to be tried a second time for the same offence

Any person who shall have been tried by a Court Martial for any offence under the authority of these Articles of War, shall not be tried for the same offence for any other Court whatsoever except as provided in Article 119; and no person who shall have been acquitted or convicted of any offence by any Court of Judicature, shall be punished for the same offence by a Court Martial. But such person may be discharged from the service.

ARTICLE 166

Regulations respecting Bazar and Cantonment Police, and Punchayets declared in force

The Regulations by which in any Presidency, the office and powers of Commissariat Officers in charge of the Police in any Cantonment, or Superintendents of Military Bazars, are at present defined and controlled; or by which punchayets are constituted and guided; or by which jurisdiction is given to Courts Martial over offences committed by persons amenable to the Articles of War, within certain limits beyond or around Cantonments; shall continue to be in full force, and to be observed at the several Presidencies respectively.

CHAPTER VII

Application of the Article

ARTICLE 167

Persons amenable to the Articles

All Officers and Soldiers, Drivers, Farriers, Trumpeters, Drummers, unattested Recruits, Sub-Assistant Surgeons, Native Doctors, Hospital Attendants, Dressers, Artificers, and Laborers, Sutlers, Followers, public and private, or others attached to or serving with any part of the Army, are to be governed by these Articles, and to be subject to trial and punishment by Courts Martial.

Provided that all Drivers, Farriers, Trumpeters, Drummers, Recruits, Sub-Assistant Surgeons, Native Doctors, Hospital Attendants, and Dressers, hereafter enlisted, shall be attested according to the Regulations of the Presidency to which they belong.

Persons of European descent (whether on the side of their father or mother) professing the Christian religion, if belonging to the descriptions mentioned in this Article (and not being Her Majesty's natural-born subjects born in Europe, or the children of such subjects,) shall be tried for Military offences by Courts Martial composed of European Officers only, and punished according to these Articles of War. For Criminal or Non-Military offences such persons shall not be amenable to these Articles of War, but shall be tried and punished in the same manner as persons who are subject to the Mutiny Act and Articles or War in force for the better government of the European Officers and Soldiers of Her Majesty's Indian forces.

ARTICLE 168

Promulgation of the Articles

These Articles are to be translated into the several languages of the different Presidencies; and the following Articles, namely, the 2nd, 3rd, and 4th, the 5th to the 69th, both included; the 78th, 81st, 82nd, 110th, and 118th, are to be read once every three months at the head of every Regiment or Corps, Troop or Company in the service, and to every recruit at the period of his attestation.

ARTICLE 169

Commencement of Act:

These Articles of War shall take effect on and from the 1st day of November 1861.

ACT No. V of 1869 [1]

THE INDIAN ARTICLES OF WAR

TABLE OF CONTENTS

1 A Collection of The Acts passed by the Governor General of India in Council, in the year 1869, Calcutta: Officer of Superintendent Printing, 1870, p. 73-144.

TITLE II. MILITARY OFFENCES

CHAPTER I. *Crimes punishable with Death or Transportation.*

Article 7. Mutiny and sedition.

Article 8. Violence to superior.

Article 9. Disobedience,

*Article*10. Desertion.

Article 11. Re-enlistment without having been discharged.

Article 12. Sentry sleeping on or quitting post in time of war.

Article 13. Sentry plundering.

Article 14. Abandoning garrison.

Article 15. Betraying watchword.

Article 16. Corresponding with enemy.

Article 17. Assisting enemy.

Article 18. Releasing prisoners.

Article 19. Misbehaviour in presence of enemy.

Article 20. Seeking plunder during action.

Article 21. Quitting guard in time of war.

Article 22. Assaulting persons bringing provisions.

Article 23. Causing alarm in time of war.

Article 24. Punishment for the foregoing offences.

CHAPTER II. Crimes punishable otherwise than by Death or Transportation

Article 25. Unbecoming behaviour.

Article 26. Intoxication on duty.

Article 27. Striking sentry.

Article 28. Harbouring deserter.

Article 29. Enlisting deserter.

Article 30. Absence without leave.

Article 31. Failure to rejoin.

Article 32. Failure to attend parade.

Article 33. Quitting parade *or* division.

Article 34. Quitting guard in time of peace.

Article 35. Refusing to receive or releasing prisoners.

Article 36. Leaving arrest.

Article 37. Insubordination.

Article 38. Refusal to superintend military works.

Article 39. Impeding Provost Marshal.

Article 40. Striking subordinates.

Article 41 . Extortion.

Article 42. House-breaking or plundering in time of peace.

Article 43. Neglecting to compensate person injured by subordinates.

Article 44. Defiling places of worship.

Article 45. Taking bribes.

Article 46. Causing false alarm in time of peace.

Article 47. Making away with regimental necessaries,

Article 48. Attempting suicide.

Article 49. Appearing armed in camp.

Article 50. Sentry sleeping on post in time of peace

Article 51. Absence from camp.

Article 52. Absent from cantonment after tattoo.

Article 53. Punishment for offences mentioned in Articles 25 to 52.

CHAPTER III. *Crimes to be punished with Dismissal from the Service.*

Article 54. Embezzlement.

Article 55. Destruction of Government property.

Article 56. Giving false evidence.

Article 57. Punishment for offences mentioned in Articles 54, 55, 56.

CHAPTER IV. *Disgraceful Conduct*

Article 58. Malingering.

Article 59. Wilfully causing hurt.

Article 60. Theft.

Article 61. Embezzlement of Government property not entrusted on public account.

Article 62. Obtaining pension by false statement.

Article 63. Furnishing false returns.

Article 64. Other fraudulent offences.

Article 65. Cruelty or indecency.

Article 66. Penalties for offences specified in Articles 58 to 65.

CHAPTER V. *Offences against Courts Martial.*

Article 67. Refusal to attend or be sworn.

Article 68. Contempts.

Article 69. Punishment for offences specified in Articles 67 and 68.

CHAPTER VII. *Unspecified Offences.*

Article 70. Unspecified offences.

Article 71. Abetment

TITLE III. JURISDICTION

CHAPTER I. *Court Martial.*

Article 72. Kinds of Courts Martial.

(1). *General Court Martial.*

Article 73. Appointment of General Court Martial.

Article 74. Composition of such Court.

Article 75. Composition of such Court appointed under orders in Council.

Article 76. Powers of such Court.

(2). *Detachment General Court Martial.*

Article 77. Appointment of such Court Martial.

Article 78. Its composition and powers.

(3). *District Court Martial and*

(4). *Garrison Court Martial.*

Article 79. Appointment of such Court

Article 80. Composition of such Court.

Article 81. Officers composing such Courts.

Article 82. Powers of such Courts.

(5). *Regimental Court Martial*

Article 83. Appointment of such Court

Article 84. Composition of such Court.

Article 85. Powers of such Courts.

(6). *Regimental Detachment Court Martial and*

(7). *Detachment Court Martial.*

Article 86. Appointment of Regimental Detachment Court Martial.

Article 87. Appointment of Detachment Court Martial.

Article 88. Composition of such Courts.

Article 89. Powers of such Courts.

(8). *Summary Courts Martial.*

Article 90. Summary Courts Martial.

Article 91. Constitution of such Courts.

Article 92. Persons triable by such Court.

Article 93. Offences triable by such Court.

Article 94. Its powers.

Article 95. Trial of grave offences by inferior Courts.

Article 96. Courts composed of European Officers.

Article 97. Claim to be tried by European Officers.

CHAPTER II. *Procedure.*

Article 98. Limitation of trials.

Article 99. Place of trial.

Article 100. Arrest or confinement of accused.

Article 101. Judge Advocate.

Article 102. Interpreter.

Article 103. President.

Article 104. Conduct of proceedings.

Article 105. Precedence of Native Officers.

Article 106. Time of trial, adjournment and re-assembly.

Article 107. Challenges.

Article 108. Interpreter's oath.

Article 100. Oaths of president and members.

Article 110. Judge Advocate's oath.

Article 111. Oaths of witnesses. .

Article 112. Oaths *to* be binding on conscience

Article 113. Re-swearing in case of several trials.

Article 114. Presumptive evidence of desertion.

Article 115. Reference by prisoner to

Article 116. Trial for desertion.

Article 117. Evidence of previous conviction and general character.

Article 118. Voting of members.

Article 119. Majority requisite to sentence of death.

Article 120. Revision of finding or sentence.

Article 121. Procedure to be generally followed.

Article 122. Summoning witnesses.

Article 123. Contempt of Court.

Article 124. Privilege of witnesses.

Summary Courts Martial.

Article 125. Persons to attend Summary Court Martial.

Article 126. Proceedings of such Courts.

Article 127. Oaths of interpreter and officer holding trial.

Article 128. Evidence.

Article 129. Signature and transmission of proceedings.

Article 130. Of General Courts Martial.

Article 131. Of General, District or Garrison Courts Martial.

Article 132. Reduction, dismissal, corporal punishment and imprisonment.

Article 133. Limit of imprisonment.

Article 134. Solitary confinement.

Article 135. Reduction to ranks.

Article 136. Forfeiture of pay and pension.

Article 137. Forfeiture of arrears of pay.

Article 138. Stoppages.

Article 139. Extent of stoppages.

Article 140. Sentence of transportation or imprisonment on person already sentenced..

*Article*141. Form of sentence of death,

CHAPTER IV. *Confirmation and Commutation of sentence.*

Article 142. Sentences to be confirmed or otherwise disposed of.

Article 143. Sentence of death.

Article 144. Sentence of penal servitude or transportation.

Article 145. Sentence of dismissal on Commissioned Officers, etc.

Article 146. Any sentence on commissioned Officers, etc.

Article 147. Sentence of corporal punishment.

Article 148. Sentence of imprisonment with, hard labour.

Article 149. Sentence of reduction with corporal punishment or imprisonment.

Commutation of sentence of dismissal on Non-Commissioned Officers.

CHAPTER V. *Execution of Sentence*

Article 150. Transpiration.

Article 151. Imprisonment with hard labour.

Article 152. Place of imprisonment.

Article 153. Transfer to military custody.

Article 154. Forfeiture of pay during imprisonment.

Article 155. Striking convict off strength of regiment.

Article 156. Non-re-admission of convict.

Article 157. Dismissal with ignominy..

Article 158. Publication of sentence for disgraceful conduct.

Article 159. Sentences of Summary Courts Martial.

CHAPTER VI. *Pardons and Remissions.*

Article 160. Pardon of person convicted of military offence.

Article 161. Release of prisoners.

CHAPTER VII. *Regimental Courts of Inquiry.*

Article 162. Regimental Courts of Enquiry.

Article 163. Persons absent *as* prisoners of war.

TITLE IV. POWERS OF OFFICERS INDEPENDENTLY OF TRIAL.

Article 164. Reduction to ranks.

Article 165. Minor punishments.

Article 166. Offences of Native followers.

Article 167. Complaints against Officers.

Article 168. Provost Marshals.

Article 169. Their deputies and powers.

TITLE V. NON-MILITAILY OFFENCES.

Article 170. Offences committed within jurisdiction of Criminal Court in British India.

Article 171. Offences committed out of British India.

Article 172. General Court Martial for trial of such offences.

Article 173. Sentences of such Court.

Article 174. Confirmation of sentences.

Article 175. Commutation of sentences and provision as to prisoners.

TITLE VI. EFFECTS OF DECEASED MEN AND DESERTERS.

Article 176. Effects of deceased men and of deserters.

Article 177. Sale of effects and discharge of debts.

Article 178. Remittal of surplus to General Treasury.

Article 179. Sale of effects of deserters.

Remittal of proceeds.

PART III. MISCELLANEOUS.

(a). Prohibition of second trial.

(b). Prohibition of arrest for debt.

(c). Breach of cantonment rules.

(d). Capture of deserters.

(e). Apprehension of military offenders.

(f). Presumption as to signatures.

(g). Native troops serving out of their own presidency.

(h). Power to make orders and issue warrants.

(i). Limitation of certain powers.

(j). Power to make rules.

(k). Articles to be read periodically.

ACT No. V OF 1869.

PASSED BY THE GOVERNOR GENERAL OF INDIA IN COUNCIL.

(Received the assent of the Governor General on 26th February 1869).

An Act to consolidate and amend the Articles of War for the government of Her Majesty's Native Indian Forces.

Preamble.

WHEREAS it is expedient to consolidate and amend the Articles of War for the government of the Native Officers, Soldiers and other persons in Her Majesty's Indian Army; It is hereby enacted as follows:--

PART I. PRELIMINARY.

(a).---Short Title.

This Act may be called "The Indian Article of War."

(b).---Commencement of Act.

This Act shall come into operation on the first day of June 1869.

(c) .---Repeal of Enactments.

From such day the first section of Act No. XXV of 1857 *(to render Officers and Soldiers in the Native Army liable to forfeiture of property for Mutiny and to provide for the adjudication and recovery of forfeiture of property in certain cases)*, Act No. XXIX of 1861 *(to consolidate and amend the Articles of War for the government of the Native Officers and Soldiers in Her Majesty's Indian Army), Act No. V of 1863 (to amend Act XXIX of 1861), and Act No, XXVI of 1865 (to amend Act XXIX of 1861) shall be repealed:*

Provided that all crimes and offences committed against any Articles of War repealed by this Act may be enquired into and punished in like manner as if they had been committed against the Articles of War contained in this Act, and that any warrant for holding Courts Martial, issued under any Act hereby repealed, shall remain in full force, not withstanding such repeal:

Provided also, that no proceedings in any trial begun under any Articles so repealed, shall be discontinued owing to such repeal, but every such trial shall proceed and be completed in the same manner, as if this Act had not been passed.

References to any Act hereby repealed, or any Act passed subsequently thereto, shall be read as if made to this Act.

(d).---Application of Articles.

The Articles contained in Part II of this Act shall apply to all

Commissioned Officers,

Sub-Assistant Surgeons,

Hospital Assistants,

Native Doctors,

Warrant Officers,

Non-Commissioned Officers,

Hospital Attendants of any class,

Trumpeters, Buglers, Drummers,

Musicians,

Soldiers,

Unattested Recruits,

Lascars, Mahouts, Drivers,

Farriers, Syces, Grass-cutters,

Artificers, Labourers,

Sutlers, Followers, whether public or private, and all other persons attached to or serving with any portion of the said Army;

Proviso.

Provided that nothing in the said Part (other than Article 123) shall render any British-born subject of Her Majesty, or any legitimate Christian lineal descendant of such subject, whether in the paternal or maternal line, triable or punishable under the said Part, but all such persons belonging to Her Majesty's Indian Army shall be triable and punishable as if they belonged to Her Majesty's British Forces.

And that nothing in the said Part shall render any American and any Christian European not being British-born, or any Christian legitimate lineal descendant of such American or European, whether in the paternal or maternal line, triable by a Court Martial composed of Native Commissioned Officers; but all such persons belonging to Her Majesty's Indian Army shall be triable by Courts Martial composed of European officers only. Save as aforesaid, such persons shall be subject to this Act as if they were Natives of British India.

(e).---Interpretation-clause.

In this Act, unless there be something repugnant in the subject or contest-

"Army" means Her Majesty's Indian Amy, and "service: means service in such Army:

"Commissioned Officer" includes all Officers holding Commissions in the Native ranks of the Army, whether they be of purely Native or of a mixed European and Native extraction:

"European Officers" includes all European Officers holding Commissions in such rmy or in her Majesty's British Army:

"Commanding Officer" or "Officer Commanding" means the European Officer in actual command for the time being of any Force, Division, District, Regiment, Corps, Detachment, or Depot, as the case may be:

"Judge Advocate" includes and European Officer duly authorized to officiate as Judge Advocate:

"Court Martial" means a Court Martial held under this Act, and in Articles 67, 68, 69 and 123 shall include a Court Martial held under the Act for punishing mutiny and desertion, and for the better payment of the Army and their quarters for the time being in force:

"Soldier" and "Soldiers" include Non-Commissioned Officers and all armed persons doing duty in the ranks of the Amy:

"Attested" means attested under the Articles contained in Part II of this Act:

"Deserter" means a person subject to such Articles, who has deserted from the Army:

"Government" means, in the case of the Madras Army, the Governor of Fort Saint George in Council, in the case of the Bombay Army, the Governor of Bombay in Council, and in the case of any other part of Her Majesty's Indian Army, the Governor General of India in Council;

And the expressions "assault," "criminal force," "dishonestly," "extortion," "fraudulently," "grievous hurt," "hurt," "theft," "voluntarily causes hurt," "voluntarily causes grievous hurt," "reason to believe," "wrongful gain," and "wrongful loss," shall be severally taken to have the meanings assigned to them respectively in the Indian Penal Code, and quoted in Part I of the appendix to this Act.

(f).---Savings of certain Regulations.

Nothing in this Act affects any regulations by which the respective offices and powers of Cantonment Magistrates, Commissariat Officers, Officers in charge of the Police in Cantonments, and Superintendents of Military Bazars are defined and controlled, or by which Panchayats are constituted and guided.

PART II. THE ARTICLES OF WAR.

TITLE. ENLISTMENT, DISMISSAL AND DISCHARGE.

CHAPTER I. Enlistment.

Articles to be read to Recruits.

Article 1. Every person prior to being enrolled in any Regiment or Corps shall have the 7th, 8th, 9th, l0th, 11th, 24th, 38th and 53rd of these Articles read and explained to him,

Affirmation.

When reported fit for duty, such declaration or charge as may be usual shall be made to him, by the Officer Commanding, in front of the Regiment or Corps, or of such portion thereof as shall be present; and the person shall then make the following affirmation :--

" I............., inhabitant of........., son of ...., solemnly affirm in the presence of Almighty God that I will be faithful to Her Majesty the Queen, Her heirs and successors, and will go wherever I am ordered, by land or sea, and will obey all commands of the Officers set over me, even to the peril of my life."

Attestation.

Article 2. All persons of the following classes, hereafter enlisted or enrolled under these Articles, shall be attested accordingly to the regulations of the government to which they are respectively subject:--Sub-Assistant Surgeons. Hospital Assistants, native Doctors, Warrant Officers of any department, Trumpeters, Buglers, Drummers, Musicians, Lascars, mahouts, Drivers, Farriers, Syces and Grass-cutters.

Articles 3,4,5,7 to 71 (both inclusive), 90 to 94 (both inclusive), 130 to 139 (both inclusive), 154, 167 and 170 shall be read to every person enlisted or enrolled under these Articles at the time of his attestation.

CHAPTER II. *Dismissal and Discharge.*

Dismissal of Commissioned Officers

Article 3.—A Commissioned Officer shall be liable to dismissal from the service by the sentence of a General Court martial, or by order of the Governor General of India in Council, or of the Commander-in-Chief of the Presidency to which he belongs, or, if the Officer belongs to either of the Presidencies of Fort St. George or Bombay, of the Governor in Council of such Presidency.

Every Commissioned Officer dismissed under these Articles shall forfeit all claims of pension.

Dismissal of other Persons.

Article 4. Any person subject to these Articles, other than a Commissioned Officer, shall be liable to dismissal from the service

by the sentence of any Court Martial empowered to try him,

or, by order of the Governor General of India in Council, or of the Commander-in-Chief of the Presidency to which he belongs,

or, if he belongs to either of the Presidencies of Fort St. George or Bombay, by order of Governor in Council,

or, if he belongs to a Force not attached to any such Presidency, by order of the Officer Commanding such Force.

Every such person so dismissed shall forfeit all claims to pension.

Attested person dismissed and re-enlisting.

Article 5. Every, attested person of or below the rank of Non-Commissioned Officer who has been dismissed or discharged from the service, and who subsequently re-enters the service without at the time stating the fact of his dismissal or discharge, or showing his certificate of dismissal or discharge, may be dismissed the service by the Officer Commanding the regiment or corps with which he is serving.

Certificate to person dismissed.

Article 6. Every attested person who is dismissed or discharged from the service, shall be furnished by his Commanding Officer with a certificate, in the English language and in the mother-tongue of such person (when his mother-tongue is not English), setting forth:

(a) the authority dismissing or discharging him,

(b) the cause of his dismissal or discharge, and

(c) the full period of his service in the Army.

TITLE II. MILITARY OFFENCES.

CHAPTER I.---Crimes punishable with Death or Transportation.

Mutiny and Sedition.

Article 7. Any person subject to these Articles-

Who begins, excites, causes or joins in any mutiny or sedition in any regiment, corps, detachment, or guard;

or who, being present at any mutiny or sedition, does not use his utmost endeavours to suppress the same, or who, knowing or having reason to believe in the existence of any mutiny, or of any intention to mutiny, or, of my conspiracy against the State,

does not, without delay, give information thereof to his Commanding or other superior Officer;---or

Violence to superior

Article 8. Who uses or attempts to use criminal force to, or commits an assault on, his superior Officer, or whether on or off duty, under any circumstances in which the superior Officer is distinguishable as such in any manner;---or

Disobedience.

Article 9. Who disobeys the lawful command of his superior Officer;---or

Desertion.

Article 10. Who deserts the service;---or

Re-enlistment without having been discharged.

Article 11. Who, without having first obtained a regular discharge from the regiment or corps to which he belongs, enlists, or enrols himself in any other regiment or corps;---or

Sentry sleeping on orquitting post in time of war.

Article 12. Who, being a-sentry in time of war or alarm, or over any State-prisoner, treasure, magazine, or dockyard, sleeps upon his post, or quits it without being regularly relieved, or without leave;---or

Sentry plundering.

Article 13. Who, being a sentry, or on guard, plunders or wilfully destroys or injures any property placed under his charge, or under charge of his guard;---or

Abandoning garrison.

Article 14. Who shamefully abandons or delivers up any garrison, fortress, post or guard committed to his charge, or which it is his duty to defend;---or

Betraying watch-word.

Article 15. Who treacherously makes known the watch-word to any person not entitled to receive it according to the rules and discipline of war;---or

Corresponding with enemy.

Article 16. Who directly or indirectly holds correspondence with, or communicates intelligence to the enemy, or any person in arms against the State, or who, coming to the knowledge of any such correspondence or communication, omits to discover it immediately to his commanding or other superior Officer;---or

Assisting enemy.

Article 17. Who directly or indirectly assists or relieves with money, victuals or ammunition, or knowingly harbours or protects any enemy, or person in arms against the State,---or

Releasing prisoners.

Article 18. Who, without proper authority releases any State-prisoner, enemy, or person taken in arms against the State, placed under his charge, or who negligently suffers any such prisoner, enemy or person to escape;---or

Misbehaviour in the presence of enemy.

Article 19. Who, in presence of an enemy, or of any persons in arms against whom it is his duty to act, shamefully casts away his arms or ammunition, or intentionally uses words or any other means to induce any Officer or Soldier to abstain from acting against the enemy or to discourage such Officer or Soldier from acting against the enemy, or who otherwise misbehaves;---or

Seeking plunder during action.

Article 20. Who, in time of action, without authority, leaves his Commanding Officer, or his post, or colours, or party to go in search of plunder ;---or

Quitting guard in time of war.

Article 21. Who, in time of war, quits his guard, picquet, party or patrol, without being regularly relieved or without leave;---or

Assaulting persons bringing provisions.

Article 22. Who, in time of war, or during any military operation, uses criminal force to, or commits an assault on, any person bringing provisions or other necessaries to the camp or quarters of any of Her Majesty's forces,

or forces a safeguard, or, without authority, breaks into any house or other place for plunder; or plunders, injures or destroys any field, garden or other property of any kind;---or

Causing false alarm in time of war.

Article 23. Who in time of war, or during any military operation, intentionally occasions a false alarm in action, camp, garrison or quarters, or spreads reports by words or by letters calculated to create alarm or despondency,

Punishment for the foregoing offences.

Article 24. Shall, on conviction, suffer, death, or transportation for life or for a term of not less than seven years,

or imprisonment (with or without hard labour, and with or without solitary confinement) for a term which may extend to fourteen years,

or such other punishment as a General Court Martial is, by these Articles, empowered to award.

Whenever any person is convicted under this section of an offence punishable with death, all his property, moveable and immoveable, shall be forfeited to Government.

CHAPTER II. *Crimes punishable otherwise than by Death or Transportation.*

Unbecoming behaviour.

Article 25. Any Officer, Sub-Assistant Surgeon, Hospital Assistant, Native Doctor, Warrant Officer, who behaves in a manner unbecoming his position and character;---and

Intoxication on duty.

Article 26. Any person subject to these Articles, who is in a state of intoxication when on or for any duty, or on parade, or on the line of march;---or

Striking sentry.

Article 27. Who strikes, or forces or attempts to force any sentry;---or

Harbouring deserter.

Article 28. Who knowingly harbours any deserter; or who, knowingly, or having reason to believe, that any other person has deserted, or that any deserter has been harboured by any other person, does not immediately give notice to his own or some other superior Officer, or use his utmost endeavours to cause such deserter to be apprehended;---or

Enlisting deserter.

Article 29. Who knowing, or having reason to believe, that a person is a deserter enlists him;--or

Absent without leave.

Article 30. Who absents himself without leave, or, without sufficient cause, overstays leave granted to him;---or

Failure to rejoin.

Article 31. Who, being on leave of absence and having received information from proper authority that his regiment or corps has been ordered on service, fails, without sufficient cause, to rejoin without delay;---or

Failure to attend parade..

Article 32. Who, without sufficient cause, fails to appear at the time fixed at the parade or place appointed for exercise or duty;---or

Quitting Parade or division.

Article 33. Who, when on parade, or on the line of march, without sufficient cause, or without leave from his superior Officer, quits the parade or line of march;---or

Quitting guard in time of peace.

Article 34. Who, in time of peace, quits his guard, picquet, or patrol without being regularly relieved, or without leave;---or

Refusing to receive or releasing prisoners.

Article 35. Who, being in command of a guard, picquet, or patrol, refuses to receive any prisoner duly committed to his charge, or without proper authority releases any prisoner, or negligently suffers any prisoner to escape;---or

Leaving arrest.

Article 36. Who, being under arrest, or in confinement, leaves his arrest or confinement before he is set at liberty by proper authority;---or

Insubordination.

Article 37. Who is grossly insubordinate or insolent to his superior Officer in the execution of his office;---or

Refusal to superintend military work.

Article 38. Who refuses to superintend or assist in the making of any field-work, or other military work of any description, ordered to be made either in quarters or in the field;---or

Impeding Provost Marshal.

Article 39. Who impedes a Provost Marshal or an Assistant Provost Marshal, or any person lawfully exercising authority, or refuses when called upon to assist such person when requiring aid in the execution of his duty;--or

Striking subordinates.

Article 40. Who strikes or ill-treats any soldier or other person attested under these Articles being his subordinate in rank or position;---or

Extortion.

Article 41. Who commits extortion;; or, without proper authority, exacts from any person carriage, porterage, or provisions;---or

House-breaking or plundering in time of peace.

Article 42. Who, in time of peace, commits house-breaking for the purpose of plundering; or plunders, destroys, or damages any field, garden, or other property;---or

Neglecting to compensate person injured by subordinate.

Article 43. Who, being in command at any post, or on the march, and receiving a complaint that any one under his command has beaten, or otherwise maltreated or oppressed any person, or has disturbed any fair or market, or committed any riot or trespass, fails to have due reparation made to the injured person, or to report the case to the proper authority;---or

Defiling places of worship.

Article 44. Who, by defiling any place of worship, or otherwise, intentionally insults the religion or wounds the religious feelings of any person;---or

Taking bribes.

Article 45. Who, directly or indirectly, requires, accepts, or obtains, or agrees to accept, or attempts to obtain, for himself or for any other person, any gratification as a motive or reward for procuring the enlistment or enrolment of any person, or leave of absence, promotion, or any other advantage or indulgence for any person in the service;---or

Causing false alarm in time of peace.

Article 46. Who, in time of peace, by any means whatever, intentionally occasions a false alarm in camp, garrison, or cantonment;---or

Making away with regimental necessaries.

Article 47. Who designedly or through neglect kills, injures or loses his horse, or who dishonestly or fraudulently removes, conceals or delivers to any person, or who designedly or through neglect injures or loses his arms, clothes, tools, musical or surgical instruments, equipments, ammunition, accoutrements, or regimental necessaries, or any such articles entrusted to him, or belonging to any other person,

or who sells, pawns, destroys or defaces any medal or decoration granted to him by order of Her Majesty, or of the East India Company, or of the Governor General of India in Council for service in the field, or for general good conduct;---or

Attempting suicide.

Article 48. Who attempts to commit suicide, and does any act towards the commission of such offence;---and

Appearing armed in camp.

Article 49. Any person subject to these Articles below the rank of Warrant Officer---

Who, when off duty, appears, without proper authority, in or about camp or cantonments, or in or about, or when going to, or returning from, any town or bazaar, carrying a sword, bludgeon, or other offensive weapon;---or

Sentry sleeping on post in time of peace.

Article 50. Who, being a sentry, in time of peace, sleeps upon his post, or leaves it before being regularly relieved, or without leave;---or

Absence from camp.

Article 51. Who, without proper authority, is found two miles or upwards from camp;---or

Absence from cantonment after tattoo.

Article 52. Who, without proper authority, is absent from his cantonment or lines after tattoo, or from camp after retreat-beating;

Punishment for offences mentioned in Articles 25-55.

Article 53. Shall, on conviction by any Court Martial competent to try him, be sentenced to such punishment, other than death or transportation, as such Court is, by these Articles, empowered to award.

CHAPTER III. Crimes to *be punished with dismissal from the service.*

Enabezzlement.

Article 54. Any person subject to these Articles---

Who dishonestly misappropriates or converts to his own use any money, provisions, forage, arms, clothing, ammunition, tools, instruments, equipments or military stores of any kind, the property of Government, entrusted to his charge on the public account, or for any military purpose,

or who dishonestly, uses or disposes of such property in violation of any direction of a proper authority,

or who dishonestly receives or retains any such property, knowing or having reason to believe the same to have been dishonestly misappropriated or converted;---or ,

Destruction of Government property.

Article 55. Who wilfully destroys or injures any property of Government entrusted to him on the public account, or for any military purpose;---or

Giving false evidence.

Article 56. Who, having been duly sworn or affirmed before any Court Martial, or other Military Court competent to administer an oath or affirmation, makes any statement which is false, and which he either knows or believes to be false, or does not believe to be true;

Punishment for offences mentioned in Articles 25-55.

Article 57. Shall, if convicted by a General Court Martial, be sentenced to be dismissed the service and to forfeit any arrears of pay and allowances due to him at the time of dismissal ; and shall be punishable also with imprisonment (with or without hard labour, and with or without solitary confinement) for a term which may extend to three years : and shall, if convicted by a District or Garrison Court Martial, be liable to any or all of the penalties which such Court may inflict for disgraceful conduct.

CHAPTER IV. *Disgraceful Conduct.*

Malingering.

Article 58. Any person subject to these Articles---

Who malingers, or feigns, or produces disease or infirmity in himself, or intentionally delays his cure or aggravates his disease or infirmity;---or

Wilfully causing hurt.

Article 59. Who, with intent to render himself or any other person unfit for service, voluntarily causes hurt or voluntarily causes grievous hurt to himself or any other person;---or

Theft.

Article 60. Who commits theft in respect of any property of Government, or of any Officer or Soldier, or of any other person in the service, or of any military mess or band, or of any person serving with or attached to the Army, or who dishonestly receives or retains any such property, knowing or having reason to believe it to be stolen;---or

Embezzlement of Government property not entrusted on public account.

Article 61. Who dishonestly misappropriates or converts to his own use any property of Government entrusted to him for any purpose not provided for in Articles 54 and 56,

or who dishonestly receives or retains any such property knowing or having reason to believe it to have been dishonestly misappropriated or converted;-or

Obtaining pension by false statement.

Article 62. Who obtains or attempts to obtain for himself, or for any other person, any pension, allowance, or other advantage or privilege by a statement which is false, and which he knows or has reason to believe to be false, or does not know to be true, or by making or using a false entry in any book or record, or by making any document containing a false statement, or by omitting tomake a true entry or document containing a true statement;---or

Furnishing false returns.

Article 63. Who knowingly furnishes a false return or report of the number or state of any men under his command or charge, or of any money, arms, ammunition, clothing, equipments, stores or other property in his charge, whether belonging to such men, or to Government, or to any person in or attached to the Army, or who, through design or culpable neglect, omits or refuses to send any return or report of the matters aforesaid;---or

Other fraudulent offences.

Article 64. Who does any other thing with intent to defraud, or to cause wrongful gain to one person, or wrongful loss to another person;---or

Cruelty of Indecency.

Article 65. Who commits any other offence of a cruel, indecent, or unnatural kind, or attempts to commit ally such offence and does any act towards its commission;

Penalties for offences specified in Articles 58-65.

Article 66. May be tried for disgraceful conduct, and shall, on conviction by a General, District or Garrison Court Martial, be liable to ally or all of the penalties awardable by such Court for disgraceful conduct.

CHAPTER V. *Offences against Courts Martial.*

Refusal to attend or be sworn.

Article 67. Any person subject to these Articles who, when duly summoned to attend as a witness before a Court Martial, intentionally omits to attend, or refuses to be sworn or make affirmation, or to answer any question, or to produce or deliver up any book or document which he may have been duly warned and called upon to produce or deliver up, or prevaricates;---or

Contempts.

Article 68. Who intentionally offers any insult or causes any interruption or disturbance to, or uses any menacing or disrespectful word, sign or gesture or is insubordinate or violent in the presence of a Court Martial while sitting;

Punishment for offences specified in Articles 67 and 68.

Article 69. Shall, on conviction by the same or by any other Court Martial which, is competent to try the offender, be liable to such punishment as the convicting court is, by these Articles, empowered to award.

CHAPTER VI. *Unspecified offences.*

Article 70. All offences not punishable with death, all neglects to obey any garrison or other orders, and all acts and omission, of which any person subject to these Articles is accused, shall, though not specified in these Articles, if they are prejudiced to good order and discipline, be taken cognizance of and punished according to the nature and degree of the offence, act or omission by any Court Martial empowered to try the person guilty of such offence, act or omission.

Abetment.

Article 71.---Every person subject to these Articles who abets, within the meaning of the Indian Penal Code, sections 107 and 108, any of the offences specified in Articles 7, 8, 10, 13, 14, 18 and 19, may be punished with the punishment hereinbefore provided for such offence.

Every such person who abets, within the meaning of the Indian Penal Code, sections 107 and 108, any other offence punishable under this Act, shall be punished

with imprisonment of any description provided by this Act for the offence so abetted for a term which may extend to one half of the longest term of such imprisonment,

or with one-half of any other penalty awardable by the Court by which he is convicted,

or, if the offence is punishable death or transportation for life, with transportation for a term not less than seven years or with imprisonment (with or without hard labour, and with or without solitary confinement) for a term which may extend to ten years.

The said sections of the Indian Penal Code are set forth in Part II of the Appendix to this Act.

TITLE III.—JURISDICTION.

CHAPTER I. *Kinds of Courts Martial.*

Article 72. For the purposes of these Articles, there shall be eight kinds of Courts Martial, (that is to say),-

(1). General Courts Martial.

(2). Detachment General Court Martial.

(3). District Court Martial.

(4). Garrison Court Martial.

(5). Regimental Court Martial.

(6). Regimental Detachment Courts Martial.

(7). Detachment Courts Martial, and

(8). Summary Courts Martial.

(1).—*General Court Martial.*

Appointment of General Court Martial.

Article 73. A General Court Martial may be appointed---

(a). By the Commander-in-Chief of a Presidency;

(b). By any Officer authorized to appoint General Courts Martial by warrant of the Commander-in-Chief of a Presidency;

(c). By any Officer in actual command of Native troops who is authorized to appoint General Courts Martial by order of the Governor General of India in Council, the Governor of Fort St. George in Council, or the Governor of Bombay in Council;

(d). By any Officer commanding Native troops not attached to the forces of a Presidency who is authorized to appoint General Courts Martial by warrant which the Governor General of India in Council has empowered the Commander-in-Chief in India to issue.

Composition of such Courts.

Article 74. Except as hereinafter provided, every General Court Martial shall, if held in British India, consist of not less than nine Commissioned Officers, but may, if held out of British India, consist of seven Commissioned Officers, if a greater number cannot be conveniently assembled.

Composition of such Court appointed under Orders in Council

Article 75. A General Court Martial appointed under the authority of an Order in Council shall consist of not less than five Commissioned Officers, and shall, if SO provided in the Order, be composed either of European or of Native Commissioned Officers at the discretion of the Officer appointing it.

Powers of such Court.

Article 76. A General Court Martial shall have power to try all persons subject to these Articles accused of mutiny or of any other offence punishable under this Act, and to pass sentences of death,

Transportation for life or for any period not less than seven years,

Imprisonment (with or without hard labour, and with or without solitary confinement) for any term not exceeding fourteen years,

Dismissal from the service,

Suspension from rank, pay and allowances for any stated period,

Degradation,

Loss of standing,

Reduction to the ranks,

Corporal punishment not exceeding fifty lashes,

Forfeiture of additional pay, good conduct pay, and claim to pension,

Forfeiture of arrears of pay and allowances,

Stoppages,

Whenever any person is convicted of any offence for which he shall be transported or sentenced to imprisonment for a term of seven years or upwards, the Court may adjudge that all the rents and profits of his moveable and immoveable estate during the period of his transportation or imprisonment shall be forfeited to Government, subject to such provision for his family and dependents as the Government may think fit to allow during such period.

(2). Detachment General Court Martial.

Appointment of such Court Martial.

Article 77. When any portion of Her Majesty's troops is serving in any place not in British India, and not within the dominions of the Princes and States of India in alliance with Her Majesty, wherein Her Majesty's forces are permanently stationed, a Detachment General Court Martial may be appointed:-

(a). By the Commander-in-Chief of a Presidency;

(b). By any Officer authorized to appoint Detachment General Courts Martial by warrant of the Commander-in-Chief of a Presidency;

(c). By the Officer in actual command of such troops, upon complaint being made of an offence against the person or property of any resident of such place, committed by any person under such Officer's command and subject to these Articles. '

Its Composition and Powers

Article 79. Such Court Martial shall consist of not less than three Commissioned Officers, and shall have the same powers as General Court Martial.

(3). District Court Martial, and

(4). Garrison Court Martial.

Appointment of such Courts.

Article 79. A District or Garrison Court Martial may be appointed---

(a). By the Commander-in-Chief of a Presidency;

(b). By any Officer authorized to appoint District or Garrison Courts Martial (as the case may be) by warrant of the Commander-in-Chief of any Presidency;

(c). By an Officer in actual command of Native troops, authorized to appoint District or Garrison Courts Martial (as the case may be) by order of the Governor General of India in Council, the Governor of Port St. George in Council, or the Governor of Bombay in Council:

(d). By any Officer commanding Native troops not attached to the forces of a Presidency authorized to appoint District or Garrison Courts Martial (as the case may be) by warrant which the Governor General of India in Council has empowered the Commander-in-Chief in India to issue.

Composition of such Courts.

Article 80. *(a).* Except as hereinafter provided, a District or Garrison Court Martial shall consist of seven Commissioned Officers, unless that number cannot conveniently be assembled, in which case such Court may consist of not less than five such Officers.

(b). A District Court Martial appointed under the authority of an Order in Council, may consist of any number of Commissioned Officers not less than thee; and may, if so provided in the Order, be composed either of European or of Native Commissioned Officers at the discretion of the Officer appointing it.

Officers composing such Courts.

Article 81. A District or Garrison Court Martial may, when necessary, be composed wholly of Officers of the regiment or corps to which the accused belongs; Provided that on the trial of a Sub-Assistant Surgeon, Hospital Assistant, Native Doctor or Warrant Officer, not more than two Officers of the same regiment, corps, detachment, depot or department as the accused shall sit upon any such Court.

Powers of such Courts.

Article 82. A District or Garrison Court Martial shall have power to try all persons subject to these Articles, other than Commissioned Officers, for any offence other than mutiny made punishable by these Articles, and to pass sentences of---

Imprisonment (with or without hard labour, and with or without solitary confinement) for a term not exceeding one year,

Dismissal from the service,

Suspension from rank, pay and, allowances,

Degradation,

Loss of standing,

Reduction to the ranks,

Corporal punishment not exceeding fifty lashes,

Forfeiture of additional pay, good-conduct pay and claim to pension,

Forfeiture of arrears of pay and allowances,

Stoppages.

(5). Regimental Court Martial.

Appointment of such Courts.

Article 83. A Regimental Court Martial may be appointed by the Officer commanding any regiment or corps.

Composition of such Courts.

Article 84. A Regimental Court Martial shall consist of not less than five Commissioned Officers, unless that number cannot conveniently be assembled, in which case such Court may consist of not less than three such Officers.

Powers of such Court.

Article 85. A Regimental Court Martial shall have power to try---

(a). All persons subject to these Articles, other than Commissioned Officers, Sub-Assistant Surgeons, Hospital Assistants, Native Doctors and Warrant Officers, for any offence other than mutiny, desertion or disgraceful conduct, punishable under these Articles, when committed on the line of march, or on board any vessel:

(b). Any offence punishable under this Act, and not within the ordinary jurisdiction of a Regimental Court Martial, other than mutiny, desertion and disgraceful conduct, when the Officer the Division or District directs it to be tried by a Regimental Court Martial; and

(c). by offence punishable under these Articles, other than offences not within the ordinary jurisdiction of a Regimental Court Martial---

and to pass sentences of--

Dismissal,

Loss of standing,

Reduction to the ranks,

Imprisonment (with or without hard labour and with or without solitary confinement) for a term not exceeding six months,

Corporal punishment not exceeding fifty lashes,

Forfeiture of arrears of pay and allowances,

Stoppages.

(6). Regimental Detachment Court Martial, and

(7). Detachment Court Martial.

Appointment of Regimental Detachment Court Martial.

Article 86. A Regimental Detachment Court Martial may be appointed by the Officer commanding a detachment of his own regiment or corps.

Appointment of Detachment Court Martial.

Article 87. A Detacmnent Court Martial may be appointed,---

(a). By the Officer commanding any Station, Force or Detachment of men of different regiments or corps;

(b). By the Officer in command of any detachment when any offence not within the ordinary jurisdiction of a Regimental Court Martial (other than mutiny, desertion, or disgraceful conduct), is committed on the line of march, or on board any vessel.

Composition of such Courts.

Article 88. A Regimental Detachment Court Martial and a Detachment Court Martial shall consist of not less than five Commissioned Officers, unless that number cannot conveniently be assembled, in which case such Court may consist of not less than three commissioned Officers.

Powers of such courts.

Article 89.---A Regimental Detachment Court Martial and a Detachment Court Martial shall have the same powers as a Regimental Court Martial.

(8).-Summary Courts Martial.

Article 90. (a). Subject to the provisions and restrictions contained in Articles 91, 92, 93, 94, 125 and 126, a Summary Court Martial may be held by the European Commissioned Officer who is in actual command, for the time being, of any regiment or corps,

or of any detachment consisting of, or equivalent in strength to, three troops or companies,

or of any European corps or detachment to which, Native details subject to these Articles are attached,

or who is in charge of any arsenal, ordnance establishment, or camp equipage depot.

(b). In -detached situations, beyond sea, or out of British India, or on service in the field, or under any circumstances where, immediate example being necessary, a Detachment Court Martial cannot be assembled as provided in Article 87, and reference cannot be made to superior authority without detriment to the service, a Summary Court Martial may be held by the European Commissioned Officer commanding a detachment of any strength;

Provided that if the Officer is of less than five years' standing, he shall not carry into effect any sentence by such Court Martial, until it has received the approval of the nearest superior Military Officer holding a command of not less than a regiment.

Constitution of such Courts.

Article 91. At every Summary Court Martial, the Commanding Officer holding it shall alone constitute the Court.

Persons triable by such Court.

Article 92. No Commanding Officer shall have power to try by a Summary Court Martial any Commissioned Officer, Sub-Assistant Surgeon, Hospital Assistant, Native Doctor, or Warrant Officer, or any person who is not liable to trial by Courts composed of Native Commissioned

Officers; but all other persons subject to these Articles shall be liable to trial and punishment by a Summary Court Martial:

Provided that no person shall be so tried unless he is under the command of the Officer holding the trial.

Offences triable by such Courts

Article 93. Any offence against these Articles, except mutiny, may be tried and punished by Summary Court Martial:

Provided that, when there is no emergent reason for immediate action, and reference can, without detriment to discipline, be made to superior military authority, a Commanding Officer shall not try by Summary Court Martial, without such reference, any of the following offences :-

Offences under Articles 8 to 23 both inclusive, ordinarily punishable by General Court Martial only:

Disgraceful offences under Articles 54, 55, 56, 60, 61 and 64; and

Offences against such Commanding Officer.

Its powers.

Article 94. A Summary Court Martial held by any Officer Commanding a regiment or corps may award any sentence not exceeding that awardable by a District Court Martial.

A Summary Court Martial held by any Commanding Officer other than the Officer Commanding a regiment or corps, may award any sentence not exceeding that awardable by a Regimental or Detachment Court Martial.

Trial of grave offences by inferior Courts.

Article 95. Save, as provided by Article 85, clauses *(a)* and (b) and Article 89, no Commanding Officer shall try by a Regimental or Detachment Court Martial offences which are by these Articles declared to be punishable by a General, District or Garrison Court Martial only. But, as it may be expedient that some such offences should be tried by inferior Courts Martial, the Commanding Officer of any Regiment, Corps or Detachment shall, in every such instance, submit the case for the orders of the Officer Commanding the Division or District in which he is serving, and the Officer Commanding such Division or District, whether on or without such application, may direct trial by such kind of Court Martial as he thinks fit:

Provided that mutiny shall in no case be tried save by a General Court Martial, and that desertion and disgraceful conduct shall in no case be tried by any Court Martial inferior to a District or Garrison Court Martial.

The permission to try grave offences by District or Garrison, Regimental or Detachment Courts Martial, shall be entered upon the proceedings of such Court, and in the monthly return of trials furnished to Army Head Quarters.

Courts composed of European Officers.

Article 96. The Governor General of India, or the Governor of any Presidency, may, by an order in Council, direct that any Court Martial appointed under these Articles, shall be composed of European instead of Native Commissioned Officers, or authorize any General or other Officer to appoint Courts Martial so composed at his discretion.

Any such Court Martial shall in such case be constituted accordingly, but shall in all other respects be governed by these Articles.

Article 97. With the exception of cases of trial by Courts Martial appointed under Orders in Council, every person subject to these Articles, who is under orders for trial by Court Martial, may claim to be tried by European Officers.

When any such claim is made, the Court, whether a General, District, Garrison, Regimental or Detachment Court Martial, shall be composed of European instead of Native Commissioned Officers ; but shall in all other respects be governed by these Articles.

CHAPTER II. *Procedure.*

Limitation of trials.

Article 98. No person subject to these Articles shall be tried or punished by a Court Martial for any military offence after the expiration of three years from the date of such offence, unless the offender, by reason of absence or of some other manifest impediment, could not be arrested or confined and brought to trial within that period; in which case he shall be liable to be tried at any time not exceeding two years after such impediment shall have ceased.

Place of trial.

Article 99. Any person subject to these Articles who commits any offence against them, may be tried and punished for such offence in any place whatever in the same manner as if the offence had been committed in such place.

Arrest or confinement of accused.

Article 100. Whenever any person subject to these Articles is accused of any military offence which his Commanding or other superior Officer considers should be tried by Court Martial, such officer shall order the accused, if not below the rank of Non-Commissioned Officer, to be placed in arrest, or if below such rank, to be put in confinement, until he can be tried by a Court Martial, or discharged by proper authority,

No such person shall be detained in arrest or confinement longer than is necessary for the purposes of justice.

Judge Advocate.

Article 101. It shall not be necessary to appoint a Judge Advocate to any General Court Martial appointed under the authority of an Order in Council. But every other General Court Martial shall be attended by a Judge Advocate, who shall conduct the proceedings; and every District or Garrison, Regimental or Detachment Court Martial, composed of Native Commissioned Officers shall be attended by an European Superintending Officer of not less than four years' service, who shall conduct the proceedings.

Interpreter.

Article 102. An Interpreter shall be appointed to every Court Martial, and shall, when the Court is composed of Native Officers, form part of such Court.

If no duly qualified Interpreter is available at the station or place where the Court Martial sits, the Officer appointing the Court, or the Officer Commanding in the Division, District, or place within or at which the trial is to be held, shall appoint any competent person to perform the duty of Interpreter.

When no other qualified or competent person is available, the Superintending Officer, or in the case of an European Court, the President, shall perform the duty of Interpreter.

No Interpreter shall, as such, have a vote upon any matter.

President.

Article 103. At every Court Martial, whether composed of European or Native Commissioned Officers, the senior Officer shall sit as President, without special appointment as such.

In case of the death or unavoidable absence of the President, the next senior member shall take the place of President, without special appointment as such, and the trial shall proceed if the Court be still composed of the smallest number of members of which it is required by these Articles to consist.

Conduct of Proceedings.

Article 104. In the case of any General Court Martial appointed under an Order in Council, or of any other Court Martial composed of European Commissioned Officers under Article 96 or 97, the President shall conduct the proceedings.

Article 105. Risaldar Majors and Subahdar Majors shall take precedence according to the dates of their commissions, and above all Subahdars or Risaldars.

Sirdar Bahadurs and Bahadurs shall take rank only according to their respectivc commissions of Risaldar Major, Subadar Major, Risaldar, Risaldar Sbahadar, or Jemadar.

Risaldars shall take rank with Subahdars, according to the dates of their commissions as Risaldars, or if they have not been Risaldars then according to the dates of their commissions as Risaldahrs.

Time of Trial, Adjournement and Re-assembly.

Article 106. Trials by Courts Martial may be carried on at any time without restriction.

The date and hour of the Court's original assembly shall be fixed by, or under the orders of the convening Officer; but the adjournment and re-assembly of a Court Martial shall be determined by the Court itself.

Challenges.

Article 107. At all trials by Courts Martial, other than Courts Martial appointed under an order in Council or Summary Courts Martial, as soon as the Court is assembled, the names of the President and Members shall be read over to the prisoner, who shall thereupon be asked by the Officer conducting the proceedings, whether he objects to being tried by any Officer sitting on the ' Court.

If the prisoner objects to any such Officer, his objection, and also the reply thereto of the Officer objected to, shall be heard and recorded, and the remaining Officers of the Court shall, in the absence of the challenged Officer, decide on the objection.

When no challenge is made, or when challenge has been wade and disallowed, or the place of every Officer successfully challenged has been filled by another Officer to whom no objection is made or admitted, the Court shall proceed as hereinafter provided.

Interpreter's oath.

Article 108. The Officer conducting the proceedings shall then administer to the Interpreter, or, when necessary, shall himself make as interpreter, an affirmation or oath as follows:--

"I ..... solemnly affirm, in the presence of Almighty God, that I will faithfully interpret and translate the proceedings of this Court; and that I will not divulge the sentence until it shall have been published by authority; and, further, that I will not disclose or discover the vote or opinion of any particular member of the Court unless required to give evidence thereof by a Court of Justice or Court Martial in due course of law."

When oath is made instead of affirmation, the oath shall commence:--

"I ..... do swear that I will faithfully interpret," & etc, and shall be in all other respects in the above form, and shall end with the words, " So help me God."

Oaths of President and Members.

Article 109. The Interpreter, or the Officer conducting the proceedings, shall then administer to the President and each of the Members of the Court Martial an affirmation or oath in such of the following forms as shall be appropriate:--

For European Officers.

"I ..... solemnly affirm, in the presence of Almighty God, that **I** will duly administer justice, according to the Indian Articles of War, without partiality, favour or affection ; and if any doubt shall arise, then, according to my conscience, the best of my understanding, and the custom of war in the like cases; and that I will not divulge the sentence of the Court until it shall be published by authority; and, further, that I will not disclose or discover the vote or opinion of any particular member of the Court, unless required to give evidence thereof by a Court of Justice or a Court Martial, in due course of law."

When oath is made instead of affirmation, the oath shall commence---

"I ..... do swear that I will duly administer justice," & etc., and shall be in all other respects in the above form, and shall end with the words, " So help me God."

For Native Officers of the Mussalman or Hindu religion,
or of any other religion for which it may be appropriate.

"I ..... solemnly affirm, in the presence of Almighty God, that I will duly administer justice according to the Indian Articles of War without partiality, favour or affection; and if any doubt shall arise, then, according to my conscience, the best of my understanding, and the custom of war in the like cases; and that I will not divulge the sentence of the Court until it shall be published by authority; and, further, that I will not disclose or discover the vote or opinion of any particular member of the Court, unless required to give evidence thereof by a Court of Justice or a Court Martial, in due course of law."

Judge Advocate's Oath.

Article 110. The Interpreter, or any other European Officer of the Court, shall then administer to the Judge Advocate, or Superintending Officer, the following affirmation or the following oath :-

"I solemnly affirm, in the presence of Almighty God, that I will not, upon any account whatsoever, disclose or discover the vote or opinion of any particular member of the Court Martial, unless required to give evidence thereof as a witness by a Court of Justice or a Court Martial, in due course of law; and that I will not, unless it be necessary for the due discharge of my official duties, disclose the sentence of the Court until it shall be published by authority.'

When oath is made instead of affirmation, the oath shall commence I do swear that I will not, upon any account whatsoever, disclose," & etc, and shall be in all other respects in the above form, and shall end -with the words, " So help me God."

Oaths of Witnesses.

Article 111. Every person giving evidence at a Court Martial shall be examined on oath, or on affirmation, where affirmation is appropriate and admissible, and shall be duly sworn affirmed in such of the following forms as may be appropriate:--

For European and persons professing the Christian religion.

"I ..... do swear that what I shall state shall be the truth, the whole truth, and nothing but the truth. So help me God." Or

"I ..... solemnly affirm, in the presence of Almighty God, that what I shall state shall be the truth, the whole truth, and nothing but the truth."

For Mussulman, Hindyu or other Native Witnesses.

" I ..... solemnly affirm, in the presence of " Almighty God, that what I shall state shall be the truth, the whole truth, and nothing but the truth."

Oaths to be binding on conscience.

Article 112. If none of the forms of oath or affirmation prescribed in Articles 108 to 111, both inclusive, are appropriate to any officer of a Court Martial or any witness, such Officer or witness shall make oath or affirmation to the purport hereinbefore prescribed, in such form as the Court ascertains to be according to his religion or otherwise binding on his conscience.

Re-swearing in case of several trials.

Article 113. When more trials than one are held by the same Court Martial, every officer of the Court and every witness before the Court, shall make a fresh oath or affirmation, as hereinbefore prescribed, notwithstanding any previous oath or affirmation.

Presumptive evidence of desertion.

Article 114. If at any trial for desertion, it is proved that the person tried has been absent without authority for the space of two months, such proof shall be deemed sufficient presumptive evidence of desertion; and the Court may thereupon convict him of desertion, unless he proves that his absence was not wilful, or otherwise rebuts the presumption of desertion arising from the proof of his unauthorized absence.

Reference by prisoner to Government Officer.

Article 115. If at any trial for desertion, absence without leave, overstaying leave, or not rejoining when warned for service, the person tried states, in his defence, any sufficient or reasonable excuse for his unauthorized absence, and in support thereof to any Officer in the Civil or Military service of Government, or if it appears that any such officer is likely to prove or disprove the said statement in the defence, the Court shall address such Officer, and adjourn until his reply is received.

The written reply of any Officer so referred to shall, if signed by him, be received in evidence, and have the same effect as if made on oath or affirmation.

If the Court is dissolved before the receipt of such reply, or if the Court omits to comply with the provisions of this Article, the convening officer may, at his discretion, annul the proceedings and order a fresh trial by the same or another Court Martial.

Trial for desertion.

Article 116. On any trial for desertion the accused may be found guilty either of desertion or of absence without leave.

Evidence of previous convictions and general character.

Article 117. When any person subject to these Articles has been convicted by a Court Martial of any military offence, such Court Martial shall enquire into, and receive and record evidence of any previous convictions of such person, either by a Court Martial; or by a Court of Justice; and shall further, in the case of any person below the rank of a Warrant-officer, enquire into and record the general character of such person.

Evidence received under this Article may be either oral, or in the shape of entries in, or certified extracts from, the Court Martial Books; and it shall not be necessary to prove the signature to such certified extract, nor shall it be necessary to give notice before trial to the person tried that evidence as to his previous convictions or character will be received.

Voting by Members.

Article 118. The members of a Court Martial shall preserve order; and in giving their votes upon any matter, shall begin with the junior in rank.

Except where otherwise specially provided, every decision shall be passed by a majority of votes; and where there is an equality of votes, as to either finding or sentence, the decision shall be in favour of the person tried.

In matters other than the finding or sentence, the President shall have a casting vote.

Majority requisite to sentence of death.

Article 119. No sentence of death shall be passed by any General Court Martial, other than a General Court Martial held under an Order in Council, unless such sentence is concurred in by at least two-thirds of the officers composing the Court, or by five out of seven, or few out of five Officers, when the Court consists of either of those numbers.

A General Court Martial held under an Order in Council may, by the votes of a majority of such Court, pass a sentence of death.

Revision of finding or sentence.

Article 120. The finding or sentence of any Court Martial may be revised by order of the Officer authorized to dispose of the proceedings.

But no finding or sentence of a Court Martial shall be revised more than once; nor shall any evidence, save evidence as to previous convictions or general character, be received on a revision.

The Court, on revision, shall consist of the same, and the same number of Officers as were present when the original decision was passed, unless any such Officer or Officers shall be unavoidably absent.

In case of such unavoidable absence, the cause thereof shall be duly certified in the proceedings, and the Court shall proceed with the revision, provided it still consists of the smallest number of Officers of which such Court is by these Articles required to consist.

Procedure to be generally followed.

Article 121. The procedure laid down in the Articles 106 to 119 (both inclusive) shall be adopted at all trials by Courts Martial save when otherwise specially ordered or provided.

Summoning witnesses.

Article 122. The Judge Advocate, in the case of a General Court Martial, and the Officer ordering the trial in the case of any other Court Martial may, by summons under his hand, require the attendance before the Court, at a time and place to be mentioned in the summons, of any person, either to give evidence or to produce documents.

In the case of a witness amenable to military authority, the summons shall be sent to the Officer in actual command of the corps to which he belongs, and such Officer shall serve it upon him accordingly.

In the case of any other witness, the summons shall be sent to the Magistrate within whose jurisdiction he may be, or resides, and such Magistrate shall give effect to the summons as if the witness were, required in the Court of such Magistrate.

When a witness is required to produce any particular document in his possession or power, the summons shall describe it with convenient certainty.

Contempts of Court.

Article 123. Any witness duly summoned, or any other person who commits any contempt of Court in the presence of a Court Martial, or who commits any of the offences described in Articles 56, 67, or 68, shall, if subject to these Articles, be proceeded against as they direct; and shall, if not so subject, be delivered over to a Magistrate, who shall proceed against the offender in the same manner as if the offence had been committed before or towards a Court of Criminal Justice.

Privilege of witnesses.

Article 124. Every witness, while proceeding to, attending-on, or returning from, any Court Martial before which he has been summoned, shall be privileged from arrest in any civil suit or proceeding ; and if arrested in any such suit or proceeding, may be discharged by order of such Court Martial.

Persons to attend Summary Court Martial.

Article 125. Every Summary Court Martial shall be attended by two Commissioned Officers, European or Native, exclusive of the Commanding Officer holding the trial.

An Interpreter shall, in every case, attend at a Summary Court Martial; but when no other competent Interpreter is available, the Officer holding the trial, or one of the Officers in attendance thereat, may perform the duty of Interpreter.

No Interpreter shall, as such, have a vote upon any matter.

Proceedings of such Courts.

Article 126. The proceedings of every Summary Court Martial shall be conducted in presence of all the Officers specified in Article 125, and shall be recorded in the English language in the manner usual at other Courts Martial.

Oath of Interpreter and Officer holding trial.

Article 127. The Interpreter at a Summary Court Martial shall first make oath or affirmation, as provided by Article 108, down to the words "published by authority;" and the Commanding Officer holding the trial shall then make oath or affirmation, as provided in Article 109, down to the words "custom of war in the like cases."

The Officers in attendance shall not as such be sworn or affirmed.

Evidence.

Article 128. All evidence at a Summary Court Martial shall be taken on oath or affirmation, as provided by Article 111.

Any previous convictions on record against the offender, and his general character, shall be recorded by the Commanding Officer as of his own knowledge, or proved as provided by Article 117.

Signature and transmission of proceedings.

Article 129. The proceedings in every case in which a Regimental Court Martial or a Detachment Court Martial tries an offence not within the ordinary jurisdiction of a Regimental Court Martial, committed on the line of march or on board a vessel, shall be sent for the information of the Commander-in-Chief of the Presidency to which the Regiment or Detachment belongs, and of the Presidency within which they may be, or to which they are proceeding.

The proceedings of every Summary Court Martial shall, when closed, be signed by the Commanding Officer and the Officers attending the trial, and shall, without delay, be forwarded to the Officer Commanding the Division or District in which the trial was held; and such Officer, or the Commander-in-Chief in India, or of the Presidency in which the trial was held, is hereby authorized to set aside the trial for reasons based on merit of the case, but not, on any merely technical grounds.

When a Summary Court Martial is held in a force not attached to any Presidency, the Officer Commanding such force may exercise the powers given in this Article in regard to setting aside trials.

The proceedings of every other Court Martial shall, when closed, be signed by the members, and shall without delay, be forwarded or delivered to the Officer under whose orders the trial has been held.

CHAPTER III. *Sentence.*

Of General Courts Martial.

Article 130. (a). Any General Court Martial may, for any offence falling under Articles 7 to 23, both inclusive, and for such offences only, sentence any person subject to its jurisdiction to death, or to transportation for life, or for any period not less than seven years, or to imprisonment (with or without hard labour, and with or without solitary confinement) for any period not exceeding fourteen years.

(b). Any General Court Martial may, for any offence falling under Article 54, 55 or 56 of these Articles, sentence any person as aforesaid to the penalties attached to such offences in Article 57, and may, for any other disgraceful conduct, award the penalties attached to that offence in Articles 136, 137 and 138.

(c). Any General Court Martial may, in any case where no special punishments are prescribed, or, in addition to any special punishment, where so authorized, sentence any person amenable thereto to any punishment specified in Articles 131, 132, 133, 135, 137 and 138.

(d). No Court Martial, other than a General Court Martial, shall have power to award a sentence of death, transportation, or imprisonment exceeding one year.

Any General Court Martial may sentence any Commissioned Officer to be dismissed the service or to be suspended from rank, pay and allowance for any stated period; or to be placed one or more steps lower in the list of his rank.

No Court martial, other than a General Court Martial, shall have power to try or punish a Commissioned Officer.

Of General, District or Garrison Courts Martial.

Article 131. Any General, District, or Garrison Court Martial may sentence a Sub-Assistant Surgeon, Hospital Assistant, Native Doctor or Warrant Officer to be dismissed the service; or to be suspended from rank, pay and allowances for any stated period; or to be reduced to a lower grade or class in his Department, or to be placed one or more steps lower in the list of his rank.

No Court Martial inferior to a District or Garrison Court Martial shall have power to try or punish any Sub-Assistant Surgeon, Hospital Assistant, Native Doctor or Warrant Officer.

Reduction, Dismissal, Corporal punishment and Imprisonment.

Article 132. Any Court Martial may sentence a Non-Commissioned Officer to be reduced to the ranks; or to be placed one or more steps lower in the list of his rank;

Or may sentence any person subject to these Articles below the rank of Warrant Officer, to be dismissed the service; or to suffer corporal punishment not exceeding fifty lashes; or to imprisonment with or without hard labour, and with or without solitary confinement, for such periods as are hereinafter prescribed.

Limit of Imprisonment.

Article 133. Except in the cases provided for in Articles 24 and 57, the limit of imprisonment, whether with or without hard labour and solitary confinement, awardable by Courts Martial under these Articles, shall be for General Courts Martial two years; for District or Garrison Courts Martial one year; and for Regimental or Detachment Courts Martial six months.

Solitary Confinement.

Article 134. No person shall, under any such sentence, or under one or more sentences, be kept in solitary confinement more than eighty-four days in one year, or more than fourteen days at one time, and there shall be, between the periods of solitary confinement, intervals of ordinary imprisonment at least equal to the period of solitary confinement.

Reduction to ranks.

Article 135. No Non-Commissioned Officer shall be sentenced by any Court Martial to imprisonment or to corporal punishment, without being first sentenced to reduction to the ranks.

Forfeiture of pay and pension.

Article 136. On a conviction of any disgraceful conduct, a General, District or Garrison Court Martial may, in addition to any other punishment which it is empowered to award, sentence the offender to forfeit all advantage as to additional pay, good-conduct pay and claim to pension on discharge, which might otherwise have accrued from the length or nature of his former service; or to forfeit all such advantage absolutely, whether it has accrued from former service or may accrue from future service.

Forfeiture of arrears of pay.

Article 137. On any conviction of disgraceful conduct, if the offender be sentenced to dismissal from the service, or if his sentence involve dismissal under Article 155 or Article 157, he shall further be sentenced to forfeit any arrears of pay and allowances, or other public money, due to him at the time of his dismissal, or such portion thereof as may be required to make good any proved loss or damage arising out of his misconduct.

Any Court Martial may, in addition to dismissal, or to any punishment involving dismissal under Article 157, sentence any person whom it is authorized to try, to forfeit any arrears of pay and allowances, or other public money, due to him at the time of his dismissal, or such portion thereof as may be required to make good any proved loss or damage arising out of his misconduct.

Stoppages.

Article 138. Every offender convicted of disgraceful conduct, whose dismissal from the service is not so awarded or involved as aforesaid, shall, in addition to any other punishment, be sentenced by the Court to be put under stoppages, to the extent provided by Article 139, until the amount of any proved loss or damage arising out of such conduct be made good.

And any Court Martial, in addition to any punishment other than, or not involving, dismissal, may sentence any person as aforesaid to be put under stoppages to the extent specified in Article 139, until any proved loss or damage arising out of his misconduct be made good.

Extent of Stoppages.

Article 139. Stoppages under Article 138 shall not be awarded, whether under one or more than one sentence, to a greater extent than, in the case of an Officer, two-thirds, or in the case of any other person, one-half of his monthly pay and allowances; and shall not be so awarded as to extend beyond one year.

Any public money issued to the offender within the said period of one year; shall, for the purposes of this Article be deemed to be pay and allowances.

Sentence of Transportation or Imprisonment on person already sentenced.

Article 140. Whenever a sentence of transportation or imprisonment is passed by any Court Martial upon an offender already under sentence of transportation for a limited term, or of imprisonment, the Court may award transportation or imprisonment to commence on the expiration of such previous sentence; notwithstanding that the aggregate of any terms of imprisonment may thus exceed the limit of imprisonment which such Court is by these Articles empowered to award.

Term of sentence of death.

Article 141. In awarding a sentence of death, a General Court Martial shall, at its discretion, direct that the offender shall "suffer death by being hanged by the neck until he be dead," or shall "suffer death by being shot to death."

CHAPTER IV. CONFORMATION AND COMMUTATION OF SENTENCES.

Sentences to be confirmed or otherwise disposed of.

Article 142. Save in the case of a Summary Court Martia l, no decision or sentence of any Court Martial shall be carried into effect until confirmed or otherwise disposed of by--

(*a*). In the case of any Court Martial for the trial of any person within his command---the Commander-in-Chief of a Presidency; or

(*b*). In the case of any Court Martial for the trial of any person under his command---any Officer authorized in this behalf by warrant of the Commander-in-Chief of any Presidency, but subject to any restrictions contained in the warrant; or

(*c*). In the case of any Court Martial for the trial of any person under his command-any Officer in actual command of troops who is authorized in this behalf by the Governor General of India in Council, the Governor of Fort Saint George in Council, or the Governor of Bombay in Council;

(*d*). In the case of any Court Martial for the trial of any person under his command---any Officer commanding Native troops not attached to the forces of a Presidency who is authorized in this behalf by warrant of the Commander-in-Chief in India;

(*e*). In the case of a Detachment General Court Martial held beyond the limits of British India, and not within the dominions of the Princes and States of India in alliance with Her Majesty-the Officer appointing such Court Martial, unless the sentence of such Court Martial exceeds that awardable by a District or Garrison Court Martial; in which case the Commander of Her Majesty's forces with which the offender is serving, shall alone have power to confirm, remit, commute or annul such sentence;

(*f*). In the case of a Regimental Court Martial for the trial of any person under his command-the Officer appointing such Court Martial;

(*g*). In the case of a Regimental or other Detachment Court Martial for the trial of any person under his command, where the detachment consists of, or is equal in strength to, three troops or companies---the Commanding Officer;

(*h*). But when any such Court Martial is held in a Detachment of less than, or not equal in strength to, three troops or companies, the sentence shall be submitted for confirmation to the Officer Commanding the prisoner's Regiment, or to the nearest superior Officer holding a command of not less than a Regiment, who is hereby empowered to dispose of such sentence in like manner as if the trial had been held by his own order;

Provided that in detached situations beyond sea, or out of British India, or on service in the field, or in cases where immediate example is necessary and reference cannot be made to such Regimental or other superior Commanding Officer without detrimental to the service, the Officer Commanding any Detachment, whatever its strength, may dispose of and carry out the sentence of any Detachment Court Martial held by his order.

(*i*). Any Commander-in Chief or Officer mentioned in clauses (a), *(b)*, (c), (d), (e), (f) and *(g)* of this Article may, subject to the provisions of these Articles, and to the restrictions (if any) in the warrant (if any) by which he is authorized in this behalf, mitigate, remit, commute or annul any sentence to the execution of which his confirmation is necessary.

Sentence of death.

Article 143. when a sentence of death has been passed by any General Court Martial, the Officer so authorized, in accordance with these Articles, may confirm such sentence and cause it to be carried into effect, or may, in lieu thereof, sentence the offender to transportation for life, or for any term not less than seven years, or to imprisonment (with or without hard labour, and with or without solitary confinement) for any term not exceeding fourteen years.

Sentence of penal servitude or transportation.

Article 144. Notwithstanding anything hereinbefore contained, whenever any person, being an European or American or a legitimate lineal descendant of an European or American, is convicted of an offence punishable under these Articles with transportation, the Court shall sentence the offender to penal servitude instead of transportation, according to the provisions of Act No. XXIV of 1855.

When a sentence of transportation has been awarded by any General Court Martial, the Officer authorized, in accordance with these Articles, may confirm the sentence and cause it to be carried into effect, or may, in lieu thereof, sentence the offender to imprisonment (with or without hard labour, and with or without solitary confinement) for any term not exceeding fourteen years, and not exceeding the term of transportation awarded by the Court.

Sentence of dismissal on Commissioned Officers.

Article 145. A sentence of dismissal from the service passed by any Court Martial under these Articles upon a Commissioned Officer, Sub-Assistant Surgeon, Hospital Assistant, Native Doctor or Warrant Officer, may be commuted by the Officer duly authorized to confirm or otherwise dispose of such sentence, to suspension from rank, pay and allowances for any stated period.

Any sentence on Commissioned Officers, & c.

Article 146.---Except on foreign service, or when reference cannot, without detriment to discipline, be made to superior military authority, no decision or sentence passed upon any Commissioned Officer, Sub-Assistant Surgeon, Hospital Assistant, Native Doctor or Warrant Officer, shall be carried into effect until confirmed or otherwise disposed of by the Commander-in-Chief of the Presidency to which the offender belongs, or, when the offender is serving in a Presidency, by the Commander-in-Chief of such Presidency, or, when the offender belongs to a force not attached to any Presidency, by the Officer Commanding the force.

Sentence of corporal punishment.

Article 147. A sentence of corporal punishment passed by any Court Martial may be commuted, by the Officer authorized to confirm or otherwise dispose of such sentence, to dismissal from the service, or to imprisonment without hard labour, and with or without solitary confinement, for any period not exceeding one year, which might have been awarded by such Court Martial.

Sentence of imprisonment with hard labour.

Article 148. A sentence of imprisonment with hard labour passed by any Court Martial may be commuted, by the Officer authorized to confirm or otherwise dispose of such sentence, to dismissal from the service, or to imprisonment without hard labour, and with or without solitary confinement, for the term mentioned in the sentence, or for any shorter term.

Sentence of reduction with corporal punishment or imprisonment.

Article 149. The Officer duly authorized to confirm or otherwise dispose of the sentence of any Court Martial may, in the case of a Non-Commissioned Officer sentenced by any such Court, mitigate a sentence of reduction to the ranks followed by corporal punishment or imprisonment to reduction only,

Commutation of sentence of dismissal on Non-Commissioned Officers.

or may commute a sentence of dismissal from the service to reduction to the ranks.

CHAPTER V. EXECUTION OF SENTENCE.

Transportation.

Article 150. Whenever the sentence of a General Court Martial awarding transportation is duly confirmed, or whenever a sentence of death is duly commuted to transportation, the offender shall be delivered over with a warrant of commitment, containing an authenticated copy of the sentence or commuted sentence, to the Officer in charge of the nearest jail; and such Officer shall give effect to the sentence accordingly, under such order as he may receive from the Local Government.

Imprisonment with hard labour.

Article 151. Whenever the duly confirmed sentence of any Court Martial awards imprisonment with hard labour, or whenever the sentence of any Court Martial is duly commuted to such imprisonment, the offender shall be delivered over with a warrant of commitment, containing an authenticated copy of the said sentence or commuted sentence, to the Officer in charge of the nearest jail; and such Officer shall detain the offender, under the rules in such jail, according to the exigency of the warrant, or until he is discharged by due course of law.

Place of imprisonment.

Article 152. The Commander-in-Chief of a Presidency may, as occasion requires, direct that any person under his command and sentenced under these Articles to imprisonment, shall be confined in any jail or other fit place for confinement, situate within the local limits of such command, or may order his removal from any place of confinement under military control to any other such place, or to any jail or other fit place of confinement situate within such local limits.

The Officer Commanding any force not attached to any Presidency, shall have like powers so far as regards persons under his command and jails or other places of confinement situate within the local Limits of such command.

Article 153. When any person subject to these Articles is confined in any jail or other place not subject to military control, under a sentence of transportation or imprisonment,, whether passed by a Court Martial or by a Court of Criminal Justice, the Government of India, or the Local Government of the Presidency or place wherein such person is confined, may order his transfer to military custody.

Or may order his removal from one to any other such place of confinement within the territories of such Government.

The period during which such person is in custody during his removal shall be reckoned as part of his term of transportation or imprisonment.

Forfeiture of pay during imprisonment.

Article 154. Any person subject to these Articles in receipt of public pay, who is imprisoned in any place under the sentence, or commuted sentence, of a Court Martial, or a Court of Criminal Justice, shall, during such imprisonment, if his sentence does not involve dismissal under Article 155 or Article 157, forfeit all pay and allowances, and be entitled to subsistence only, according to the rates prescribed in the regulations of the Government to which he is subject.

And any such person in confinement in any place whatsoever, whether as a punishment by his Commanding Officer, or under any charge of which he is subsequently convicted, shall, during such confinement, forfeit all pay and allowances, and be entitled to subsistence only, according to the regulations of the Government to which he is subject.

Striking Convict off strength of Regiment.

Article 155. Every person sentenced by any Court Martial, or by any Court exercising jurisdiction in criminal cases, to transportation or to imprisonment with hard labour for any term exceeding three months, shall, in the case of **a** sentence by a Court Martial, from the date of confirmation of such sentence, and in the case of a sentence by a Criminal Court, from the date of such sentence, be struck off the strength of the regiment, corps or department to which he belongs.

Non-re-admission of Convict.

Article 156. No person who has undergone any such period of transportation or imprisonment with hard labour, shall be re-admitted to the service, or be entitled to any pension;

Provided that in the case of any illegal sentence duly annulled as aforesaid, or of a pardon under Article 160, such person may, by order of the Government when the offence is non-military, or by order of the Commander-in-Chief of the Presidency when the offence is military, be re-admitted to service, or pension, as the case may be.

Dismissal with ignominy.

Article 157. Any person below the rank of Warrant Officer sentenced under these Articles to dismissal, or to imprisonment with hard labour, or to corporal punishment for disgraceful conduct, shall, on the confirmation of such sentence, be dismissed with ignominy from the service.

Publication of sentence for disgraceful conduct.

Article 158. A copy of every confirmed sentence of dismissal, imprisonment with hard labour, or corporal punishment for disgraceful conduct, and of the orders passed thereupon, shall be sent by the Adjutant General of the Army to the Chief Civil or Political Officer of the District wherein the offender's place of residence is situated ; and such Officer shall publish the sentence and orders at the said place in such manner as may there be usual.

Sentences of Summary Courts Martial.

Article 159.-Any sentence awarded by a Summary Court Martial may be carried into effect forthwith on the Commanding Officer's own authority, and all provisions contained in Articles 151, 152, 153, 154, 155, 156, 157, 158, 160 and 161 as to execution of sentences and disposal of prisoners, shall equally apply to persons sentenced by Summary Court Martial.

CHAPTER IV. PARDON AND REMISSION.

Pardon of persons convicted of military offence.

Article 160. The Governor General of India in Council, as regards any person subject to these Articles who has been convicted by a Court Martial of a military offence, and the Governors of Fort St. George in Council, and of Bombay in Council, and the Commander-in-Chief of any Presidency, as regards any such person within the territories subject to such Government, or under the command of such Commander-in-Chief, shall have power to pardon such person, and may, instead of granting a full pardon to any such person, remit wholly or in part any punishment awarded to him by a Court Martial.

and may order the restoration to such person of any service or other advantage forfeited under his sentence.

Release of prisoners.

Article 161.---Any Officer in charge of a jail, on receiving a notification under the hand of a Secretary to the Government of India, or to the Government of Fort St. George, or to the Government of Bombay, or under the hand of the Commander-in-chief of any Presidency or of the Officer Commanding any force not attached to a Presidency, or any Division or District, that the sentence under which any person subject to these Articles is imprisoned in such jail, has been annulled or remitted, or that any such person has been pardoned under Article 160, shall, on the authority of such notification alone, immediately release the prisoner or return him to military custody.

CHAPTER VII. *Regimental Courts of Enquiry.*

Article 162. If any person subject to these Articles is, without due authority, absent from his duty for two months, a Regimental Court of Enquiry, composed of European or Native Commissioned Officers, or of both in conjunction, shall forthwith assemble, and having received proof on oath or affirmation of the unauthorized absence, shall declare the same, and the period thereof; and the Officer Commanding the Regiment or Corps shall record such declaration in the regimental books.

If the person absent does not afterwards surrender or is not apprehended such record shall have the legal effect of a conviction of desertion.

If he surrenders or is apprehended, such record, or a copy thereof, purporting to bear the signature of the Officer having the custody of the regimental books, shall, on the trial of such person for desertion, be presumptive evidence of the facts therein recorded; and on proof of the identity of the prisoner with the person therein-mentioned, he may be found guilty of desertion.

Persons absent as Prisoners of War.

Article 163. No person subject to these Articles shall be entitled to any pay or allowances or other public money, or to reckon service during any absence as a prisoner of war.

But when such person rejoins the service, enquiry shall be made by a Court Martial into the circumstances of his absence; and unless it is proved to the satisfaction of such Court that he was taken prisoner through his own willful neglect of duty, or that he had served with or under, or aided the enemy, or that he had not, as soon as possible, returned to the service, he may be recommended by the Court to receive either the whole or any portion of the arrears due to him, and to reckon his service.

Such recommendation duly confirmed by the Commander-in-Chief of the Presidency, or by the Officer Commanding any force not attached to a Presidency, to which the said person belongs, shall entitle him to receive such arrears and reckon service accordingly.

TITLE IV. POWERS OF OFFICERS INDEPENDENTLY OF TRIAL.

Redaction to ranks.

Article 164. The Commander-in-Chief of a Presidency, and the Officer Commanding any force not attached to a Presidency, shall have, respectively, power to reduce to the ranks Non-Commissioned Officers under their respective command.

Minor Punishments.

Article 165. The Commander-in-Chief in India shall, under the authority of the Governor General in Council, prescribe the minor punishments to which persons subject to these Articles shall for light offences be liable, without the intervention of a Court Martial, and shall specify the Officer or Officers by whom, and the extent to which, such minor punishments may be awarded.

No such minor punishment shall be awarded by a Court Martial; and, unless otherwise specially provided by the said Commander-in-Chief, no Commissioned Officer, Sub-Assistant Surgeon, Hospital Assistant, Native Doctor or Warrant Officer, shall be liable to any such minor punishment.

Good-conduct pay shall not necessarily be forfeited on the infliction of a minor punishment, but forfeiture thereof may be awarded as a substantive punishment, either by order of the Commanding Officer or by sentence of a Court Martial, as may from time to time be prescribed in the General Orders of the Commander-in-Chief in India or of the Commander-in-Chief of the Presidency, as the case may be.

Whenever a Soldier is convicted by a Court Martial, his good-conduct pay shall cease.

Forfeiture of good-conduct pay may be awarded in addition to any other minor punishment.

Offences of Native Followers.

Article 166. For any offence in breach of good order, the Commanding Officer of any regiment, corps or detachment, whether European or Native, in camp, or at any frontier post at which troops are stationed, and to which this Article may be specially extended by the Governor General of India in Council, the Governor of Fort St. George in Council, the Governor of Bombay in Council, or any other Local Government, may sentence any Native follower of such regiment, corps or detachment, if above the degree of a menial servant, to pay a fine not exceeding fifty rupees, or, in default of payment, or in lieu thereof, to imprisonment for any period not exceeding thirty days; or if the Native follower be not above the degree of a menial servant, to imprisonment not, exceeding seven days, or to corporal punishment not exceeding twelve strokes of a rattan.

Imprisonment awarded under this Article may be carried out in a military guard, or in a jail, as ordered by the said Commanding Officer; and the Officer in charge of any jail shall, on the delivery to him of the person of the offender, with a warrant under the hand of the said Commanding Officer, detain the offender according to the exigency of the warrant, or until he is discharged by due course of law.

Complaints against Officers

Article 167. Any person subject to these Articles, who deems himself wronged by any superior or other Officer, may, if not attached to a troop or company, complain to the Officer under whose command or orders he is serving; and may, if attached to a troop or company, complain to the Officer Commanding the same.

Then the Officer complained against is the Officer to whom any other complaint should, under this Article, be preferred, the aggrieved person shall complain to such Officer's nest superior office.

No such complaint shall be made to any Officer other than those indicated in the former part of this Article.

Every Officer receiving any such complaint shall examine into it, and, when necessary, refer it to superior authority.

Every such complaint shall be preferred through such channels as may be from time to time prescribed by proper authority; and any person preferring a frivolous or groundless complaint shall be liable trial by any Court Martial competent to try him, and to such punishment, other than dismissal, corporal punishment, or imprisonment with hard labour, as the Court is empowered by these Articles to award.

Provost Marshals.

Article 168. For the prompt and instant repression of irregularities and offences committed in the field or on the line of march, Provost Marshals shall be appointed by the Commander-in-Chief of the Presidency, or the Officer Commanding the Forces in the field; and the powers and duties of such Provost Marshals shall be regulated according to the established custom of war and the rules of the service.

Their duties and powers.

Article 169. The duties of a Provost Marshal so appointed are to take charge of prisoners confined for offences of a general description, to preserve good order and discipline, and to prevent breaches of the same by persons belonging or attached to the Army.

The Provost Marshal may punish, corporally, then and there, any person amenable to these Articles below the rank of Warrant Officer, who, in his view or in the view of any of his assistants, commits any breach of good order and military discipline;

Provided that such punishment shall be limited to the necessity of the case, and shall accord with the orders which the Provost Marshal may from time to time receive from the Officer Commanding the troops;

Provided also that the orders of the said Commanding Officer shall in no case authorize such corporal punishment in excess of that awardable sentence of a Court Martial.

If the actual commission of the offence is not witnessed by the Provost Marshal, or any of his assistants, but sufficient proof can be obtained of the offender's guilt, he shall report the case to the Commander of the Troops, who shall deal with the case as he may deem most conducive to the maintenance of good order and military discipline.

TITLE. V. NON-MILITARY OFFENCES

Offences committed within jurisdiction of Criminal Court.

Article 170. Any person subject to these Articles, who, at any place in British India within the jurisdiction of any Court of Criminal Justice established by Her Majesty, or by the Government of India, or by the Local Government, is accused of any offence against the Indian Penal Code, and not included in the foregoing Articles, shall be delivered over to the nearest Magistrate to be proceeded against according to law.

All persons in, or attached to, the Army, are hereby required, upon application duly made-to them for that purpose, to assist the Officers of Justice in apprehending and securing any such accused person.

Any person in, or attached to, the Army, wilfully neglecting or refusing so to assist shall be punished with any punishment, other than death or transportation, awardable under these Articles.

Offences committed out of British India.

Article 171. In any place out of British India, offences against the Indian Penal Code, and not included in the foregoing Articles shall, when committed by any person amenable to these Articles, be cognizable by a General Court Martial to be convened by any Officer who is empowered by warrant, or Order in Council, or by Article 77, to appoint General Courts Martial.

General Court Martial for trial of such offences.

Article 172. The provisions of these Articles as to the composition and procedure of General Courts Martial, shall, with the exception of those contained in Article 117, apply to General Courts Martial for the trial of non-military offences;

Provided that such General Courts Martial shall, in every case, be attended by a Judge Advocate.

Sentences of such Court.

Article 173. A General Court Martial held for the trial of a non-military offence, shall, on the conviction of any award punishment in accordance with the provisions of the Indian Pond Code.

Article 174. No decision or sentence passed by any such General Court Martial shall be carried into effect until confirmed or otherwise disposed of by the authority which, under these Articles, is empowered to confirm or otherwise dispose of the sentence of such General Court Martial; and no sentence of death shall be carried into effect until confirmed by the Commander-in-Chief of the Presidency to which the offender belongs, or, when the offender is beyond the limits of British India, until confirmed by the Officer Commanding Her Majesty's Forces with which the offender is serving, or when the offender does not belong to any Presidency, until confirmed by the Commander-in-Chief in India.

Commutation of Sentences.

Prisoners.

Article 175. All the provisions contained in Articles 143, 144, 148, 150, 151, 152, 153, 154, 155, 156 and 161, relating to the disposal of sentences and of sentenced prisoners, shall apply to persons sentenced by a General Court Martial for a non-military offence.

TITLE VI. EFFECTS OF DECEASED MEN AND OF DESERTERS.

Article 176. When any person subject to these Articles dies, or is killed in the field, the Officer Commanding the regiment, corps or detachment, or the Officer in charge of the department to which such person belonged, shall, if no representative in interest of such person be on the spot, secure his effects in camp or quarters, and cause an inventory thereof to be made, and a duplicate of such inventory to be lodged with the Officer Commanding, or in charge of, the regiment, corps, detachment or department to which the deceased belonged.

Sale of effects and discharge of debts.

Article 177. If there be no representative on the spot, or readily accessible, such Officer shall, without any representation taken out, publicly sell such parts of the effects of the deceased in camp or quarters as do not consist of money, and shall pay thereout the debts of the deceased in camp or quarters, the expense of his funeral ceremonies, and his regimental debts of every description; and shall pay the surplus (if any) to the representative in interest of the deceased.

Remittal of Surplus.

Article 178. In the event of no claim for the surplus of the deceased person's estate being made and established within twelve months of his death, the amount in the hands of the Officer in charge of the estate shall be remitted to the Controller General of Accounts at Calcutta, or to the Accountant General to the Government of Fort St. George or of Bombay; or, if the deceased shall have belonged to a force not under any Presidency, to the Controller General of Accounts at Calcutta.

Sale of effects of Deserters.

Article 179. The effects in camp or quarters of a deserter shall be publicly sold, and the proceeds, after payment thereout of all regimental or departmental claims, shall be remitted by the Officer Commanding, or in charge of, the regiment, corps, detachment or department to which the deserter belongs, to the Controller General of Accounts at Calcutta, or to the Accountant General to the Government of Fort St. George or of Bombay.

Remittal of proceeds.

If the deserter belongs to a force not attached to any Presidency, then the said proceeds shall be remitted to the Controller General of Accounts at Calcutta.

PART III. MISCELLANEOUS.

Prohibition of Second Trial.

(*a*). Persons subject to the Articles contained in Part II of this Act, who have been acquitted or convicted, either by a Court Martial or by a Court of Criminal Justice, of any offence, whether military or non-military, shall not be again tried or punished for the said offence by any Court whatsoever.

But any such person may be dismissed the service.

Prohibition of Arrest for Debt.

(*b*). No person attested under this Act or any previous Articles of War for Her Majesty's Indian Army, shall, so long as he belongs to such Army, be liable to be arrested for debt under any process issued by, or by the authority of, any Court of Law.

The Judge of any such Court may examine into any complaint made by such person or his superior Officer, of the arrest of such person contrary to the intent of this Act, and may by warrant under is hand discharge such person, and shall award reasonable costs to the complainant, who may recover such costs in like manner as he might have recovered costs awarded to him by a decree against the person obtaining such process.

The arms, horse, clothes, equipments, regimental accoutrements and necessaries of any such attested person shall not be seized, nor shall his pay and allowances or any part thereof be attached, in satisfaction of any judgment against him or any person whom he may represent.

Breach of Cantonment Rules.

(*c*). When any offence in breach of any duly authorized Cantonment rule or regulation is committed by any person not subject to the said Articles, and not an European British subject or an Officer or Soldier, the Officer Commanding the Cantonment may, where there is no Cantonment Magistrate, summon or order the apprehension of the offender; and such Officer may (after personally investigating the case) sentence the offender to pay a fine not exceeding fifty rupees; or in default of payment of, or in lieu of, such fine, to imprisonment in any jail or military guard for a period not exceeding thirty days.

The Officer in charge of any jail shall, on the delivery to him of the person of the offender, with a warrant under the hand of the said Commanding Officer, detain the offender according to the exigency of the warrant, or until he is discharged by due course of law.

Capture of Deserter.

(*d*). Whenever any person subject to the said Articles deserts, the Commanding Officer of the regiment, corps or detachment to which he belongs, shall give written information of the desertion to such Civil, Political, or Police authorities as, in his opinion, may be able to afford assistance toward capture of the deserter; and such authorities shall thereupon take steps for the apprehension of the said deserter, in like manner as if he were a person for whose capture a warrant had been issued by a Magistrate, and shall deliver the deserter when apprehended to military custody.

Such authorities shall also, by such means as appear to them best adapted for the purpose, prevent persons reasonably suspected to be subject to the said Articles from travelling through the districts subject to their jurisdiction, unless on duty, or furnished with a certificate of leave or discharge.

Any Police Officer may arrest, without warrant, any person so suspected, and shall bring him without delay before the nearest magistrate or the nearest Military Commanding Officer when no Magistrate is readily accessible, to be dealt with according to law.

Apprehension of Military Offenders.

(*e*). Whenever any person subject to the said Articles, who is accused of any military offence, is within the jurisdiction of any Civil, Political, or Police Officer, such Officer shall aid in the apprehension and delivery to military custody of such person upon receipt of a written application to that effect, signed by his Commanding Officer.

Presumption as to signatures.

(*f*). In any proceeding under this Act, any application, certificate, warrant, reply or other document purporting to be signed by an Officer in the civil or military service of Government shall, on production, be presumed to have been duly signed by the person and in the character by whom and in which it purports to have been signed, until the contrary is shown.

Native Troops serving out of their own Presidency.

(*g*). When any portion of the Native troops belonging to any Presidency is serving within the limits of any other Presidency, such troops shall, during such service, for all the purposes of the said Articles, be under the authority and orders of the Commander-in-Chief -of the Presidency in which they are serving;

Provided that it shall be lawful for the Governor General of India in Council to direct that, for the purposes of the said Articles, Native troops serving out of their own Presidency shall continue subject to the authority and orders of the Commander-in-Chief of the Presidency to which such troops belong.

Power to make Orders and issue Warrants.

(*h*). The Governor General of India in Council,

The Governors of Fort St. George and Bombay in Council,

The Commander-in-Chief of any Presidency,

may respectively make all orders and issue all warrants for holding Courts Martial or otherwise, which appear necessary for the purposes of this Act; and in the case of military offences requiring to be disposed of without delay, the Governor General of India in Council, and the Governors of Fort St. George and Bombay in Council may respectively further authorize any Officer empowered by Order in Council to confirm, commute, remit or annul sentences in such cases, to refer such sentences for orders to the Commander-in-Chief of the Presidency.

Limitation of Powers.

(i). Nothing hereinbefore contained shall empower the Commander-in-Chief of a Presidency to re-admit to service or pension any person not within his command, or to authorize any Officer to appoint, or to confirm, commute, remit or annul the sentences of Courts Martial for the trial of any person not within the command of such Commander-in-Chief, except in the case specified in the proviso in clause *(g)* of this Part,

or shall empower any Government to give directions as to the composition, of, or to authorize the appointment of, Courts Martial in any place for the time being subject to any other Government.

Nothing in this Act shall be deemed to affect the authority conferred on the Commander-in-Chief in India by any Act of Parliament or by Royal warrant or commission.

Power to make Rules.

(j). It shall be lawful for the Governor General of India in Council from time to time to make rules consistent with this Act, for the guidance of Officers, whether Military, Civil, or Political, in all matters connected with its enforcement,

All such rules shall be published in the *Gazette of India,* and shall thereupon be deemed to have the force of law.

The Commander-in-Chief in India, as regards the Presidency of Fort William and Forces not attached to any Presidency, may, with the previous sanction of the Governor General of India in Council, and the Commanders-in-Chief of the Presidencies of Fort Saint George and Bombay, as regards their respective Presidencies, may, with the previous sanction of the Local Government, from time to time substitute for the forms of affirmation given in Articles 109 and 111 as appropriate to Native Officers and witnesses, such other forms as may be thought appropriate to Native Officers and witnesses of any religion.

Articles to be read periodically

(k). The following Articles, namely, Articles 3, 4, 5, 7 to 91, both inclusive, 90, 91, 92, 93, 94, 125, 126, 130, 131, 132, 133, 135, 136, 139, 138, 139, 154, 167 and176, shall be read once in every three months at the head of every regiment, corps, troop, or company in the service.

[Note: APPENDIX PART I, containing definitions in the Indian Penal Code sections 23, 24, 25, 26, 319, 320, 321, 322, 349, 350, 351, 378, 383; and APPENDIX II, containing provisions of the Indian Penal Code sections 107 and 108 not included in this publication.]

The Unattested Sepoys Act, 1875

(V of 1875)

WHEREAS doubts have arisen as to the rights and liabilities of certain native soldiers who have been enrolled without having been attested, and it is expedient to remove such doubts; it is hereby enacted as follows:-

Validation of enlistment

1. Every person who has for the space of six months been in the receipt of military pay and borne on the rolls of any regiment, corps, depot, ordnance, establishment, or department of Her Majesty's Indian Army (of which the last pay-statement, if produced, shall be evidence), shall be deemed to have been duly enlisted, enrolled, and attested, and shall not be entitled to claim his discharge on the grounds of illegality or irregularity in his enlistment, enrolment, or attestation, or on any other grounds[1] save as such may be recognised by the orders and customs of the service.

1 If there are any other grounds "recognised by the orders and customs of the service", the onus of proving their existence would, on the principle underlying s. 105 of the Indian Evidence Act, 1872, rest of the person pleading them.

The Indian Articles of War

Amendment Act, 1894

ACT No. XII OF 1894

[PASSED BY THE GOVERNOR GENERAL IN COUNCIL]

(Received the assent of the Governor General on the 12th October 1894)

An Act to amend the Articles of War for the Government of Her Majesty's Indian Forces.

WHEREAS it is expedient to amend the Articles of War for the Government of Her Majesty's Indian Forces; It is hereby enacted as follows:

Title and commencement

1. (1) This Act may be called the Indian Articles of War Amendment Act.

(2) It shall come into force on such date as the Governor General in Council may by notification in the Gazette of India fix in that behalf.

Repeal of clause (c) of Part I of Indian Articles of War

2. Part I, clause (c), of the Indian Articles of War, hereinafter called "The said Articles" is hereby repealed.

Substitution of new clause for clause (d) of Part I

2. Part I, clause (d), of the said Articles the following shall be substituted:-

"(d) Application of Articles

"These Articles shall apply to all---

(a) Persons to whom they actually apply at present;

(b) Persons commissioned or gazetted as Native officers, or Gazetted as warrant officers, of Her Majesty's Indian Forces;

(c) Medical subordinates;

(d) Unattested recruits;

(f) Persons enrolled under these Articles;

(g) Persons, not otherwise subject to military law, who, on active service, in camp, on the march, or at any frontier post specified by the Governor General in Council by notification in this behalf, are employed by, or are in the service of, or are followers of, or accompany any portion of, His Majesty's Indian Forces:

Provided as follows:

if any person claims to belong to a class to which the Army Act is, and these Articles are not, applicable, the burden of proving that he belongs to that class shall lie upon him."

Substitution of a new clause for clause (e) of Part I

4. For Part I, clause (e), of the said Article the following shall be substituted, namely:

"(e) Definitions

"In these Articles, unless there is something repugnant in the subject or context:--

(1) 'Notification' means a notification published in the official Gazette.

(2) 'Prescribed' means a prescribed by rules made by the Governor General in Council or by any other authority empowered by him in this behalf.

(3) 'British officer' means an officer holding a commission in Her Majestty's land forces, but does not include an honourary commissioned officer.

(4) 'Native officer' means an officer commissioned or gazette as an officer holding a Native rank in Her Majesty's Indian Force.

(5) 'Officer' mans a British officer or Native officer, but does not include a warrant officer or non-commissioned officer.

(6) 'Medical subordinate' mans a senior hospital assistance, a hospital assistance of the first, second or third class, and a sub-hospital assistance, but does not include an officer.

(7) 'Superior officer,' when used in relation to a person subject to these Articles, includes a warrant officer and a non-commissioned officer, and acting non-commissioned officer.

(8) "Soldier', includes a non-commissioned officer and any armed person doing duty in the ranks of Her Majesty's Indian Forces.

(9) 'Recruit' means a person entitled for enrolment in any corps or department as a soldier.

(10) 'Corps' mean a unit of command, such as a regiment of cavalry, a regiment or battalion of infantry, a battery of artillery, and any other separate body of troops which is declared by the Governor General in Council by general or special order to be corps for the purposes of these Articles; it also includes an army hospital and a transport corps.

(11) 'Department' includes any division or branch of a department.

(12) 'Military reward' means any gratuity or annuity for long or service or good conduct; it also includes any good-conduct pay or pension and any other military pecuniary reward.

(13) 'Enemy' includes all armed mutineers, armed rebel, armed rioters and pirates.

(14) 'Active service', as applied to a person subject to these Articles, means the time during which such person is attached to, or forms part of, a force which is engaged in operations against an enemy, or is engaged in military operations in, or is on the line of march to, a country or place wholly partly occupied by an enemy, or is in military occupation of a foreign country.

(15) The expression 'India' means a British India, together with any territories of any Prince of Chief under the suzerainty of Her Majesty exercised through the Governor General in Council of through an Governor in Council or other officer subordinate to the Governor General in Council: and the expression 'British India' means all territories and places within Her Majesty's dominion which are for the time being governed by Her Majesty through the Governor General in Council through any Governor in Council or other subordinate to the Governor General in Council.

(16) The expression 'general officer commanding' means the general officer commanding the forces in a Command: and the expression 'Command' means one of the principal portion into which the army of India is, for the time being, divided.

(17) 'Commanding officer' when used in any provision of these Articles, with reference to any separate portion of Her Majesty's forces or to any department, means the British officer whose duty it is under the Army Regulations, India, or, in the absence of any such Regulations, by the custom of the service to discharge with respect to that portion of the forces or that department the functions of a commanding officer in regard to matters of the description referred to in that provision.

(18) 'Military custody' means the arrest or confinement of a person, according to the usages of the service.

(19) 'Court-martial' means a court-martial held under these Articles.

(20) 'Criminal court' mans a court of ordinary criminal justice in British India, or established or continued elsewhere by the authority of the Governor General in Council.

(21) 'Civil offence' means an offence which if committed in British India would be triable by a criminal court.

(22) 'Offence' means any act or omission punishable under these Articles and includes a civil offence as hereinbefore defined.

(23) Expressions occurring in the Indian Penal Code (Act XLV of 1860) and used in these Articles and not herein otherwise defined shall have the meaning respectively assigned to them by the Code."

5. For Part I, clause (f), of the said Articles the following shall be substituted, namely:

"(f)—Saving of certain Regulations

"Nothing in these Articles shall affect any regulations by which the respective offices and powers of cantonment magistrates and officers in charge of the police in cantonment are defined and controlled."

6. For Part II, Title I, of the said Articles the following shall be substituted, namely,--

"TITLE I

ENROLMENT, ATTESTATION, DISMISSAL AND DISCHARGE

"Enrolment and attestation

Article 1. (1). The Governor General in Council may, by notification, declare what persons or classes of persons shall be enrolled only, or both enrolled and attested respectively.

(2) A person shall be deemed to be enrolled under these Articles when his name has, with the consent, been entered in the prescribed manner on the list of a corps or department of Her Majesty's Indian Armed Forces.

(3) Subject to the provisions of this Article with respect to recruits, every person to be attested under these Articles shall be taken before the prescribed civil or officer, and that officer shall read and explain to him, or cause to be read and explained to him in his presence, the questions set forth in the prescribed form of attestation, and such other matters (if any) as may be prescribed; and, after having cautioned him that if he makes a false answer to any question set forth in the attestation form he will be liable to be punished as provided by these Article, shall record the answer to each question, and shall, if he is satisfied that the person fully understand the questions, and that the answer has been correctly recorded opposite each question, and if he perceives no impediment, administer to the person an affirmation or oath in the prescribed form.

(4) The form of oath or affirmation under this Article shall contain a promise that the person attested will be faithful to Her Majesty, Her Heirs and successors, and that he will serve in Her Majesty's Indian Forces and go wherever he is ordered by land or sea, and that he will obey all commands of any officer set over him, even to the peril of his life.

(5) When recruit is reported fit for duty, an affirmation or oath in the same form shall be administered to him in the prescribed manner by the commanding officer in front of corps or such portion thereof or such members of the department as shall be present.

(6) After administering the affirmation or oath, the officer shall authenticate the attestation paper by his signature, and the person shall then be deemed to have been attested.

Treatment of enrolment and attestation as of same effect in certain cases

(7) Subject to any rules which may be prescribed, the Commander-in-Chief in India, or the general officer of the Command, may direct that any persons to whom these Articles apply

as attested person shall, for the purposes of these Articles, be deemed to be enrolled, and that any persons to whom these Articles apply as enrolled persons shall, for the purpose of these Articles, be deemed to be attested.

Rank and subordination

Article 2. (1) Subject to the provisions of the Army Act, the Governor General in Council may, by notification, direct that persons of any class subject to these Articles shall, for any of the purposes of these Articles, be deemed to be Native officers, warrant officers or non-commissioned officers.

(2) Subject as aforesaid, any prescribed authority may issue an order giving alike direction with respect to any such person.

(3) Any notification or order issued under this article may be cancelled by the authority issuing the same, and

(4) Subject as aforesaid, any portion of the said classes with respect to whom no such notification or order is in force shall, so far as mat be, deemed for all the purposes of these Articles to be a rank inferior to that of a non-commissioned officer.

(5) Should any question arise as to the rank of any other person subject to these Articles, or as to whether any such person is above or below a specified rank, the decision of the Governor General in Council shall be conclusive.

(6) Every person subject to these Articles shall, for the purposes thereof, be deemed to be under the commanding officer of the corps or department (if any) to which he is attached, and, if not attached to any corps or department, under any officer who may for the time being be named as his commanding officer by the general or other officer commanding the force with which such person may for the time being serving, or of any other prescribed officer, or, if no such officer is named or prescribed, under the said general or other officer commanding:

Provided that a general or other officer commanding shall not take place any person under an officer of official rank inferior to that of such person if there is present at the place where such person is any officer of higher rank under whom he can be placed.

Dismissal and discharge of commissioned officers

"Article 3. (1) Every Native officer shall be liable to be dismissal from the service by the sentence of a general court-martial, and to dismissal or discharge by order of the Governor General in Council, or the Commander-in-Chief in India, or of the general officer of the Command to which he belongs.

(2) A Native officer dismissed under these Articles shall forfeit all claims of pension.

Dismissal and discharge of other persons

Article 4. (1) Every person subject to these Articles, other than a Native officer, shall be liable to:-

(a) Dismissal from the service by the sentence of any court-martial empowered to try him; and

(b) Dismissal or discharge from the service, by order of the Governor General in Council, or the Commander-in-Chief in India, or of the general officer of the Command to which he belongs or of the officer commanding the division or district in which he is serving, or if he belongs to a force not attached to a command, be order of the officer commanding such force.

(2) Every person so dismissed shall forfeit all claims to pension.

Attested persons dismissed or discharge and re-enlisting and or making false answer at his attestation

Article 5. (1) Every attested person of or below rank of non-commissioned officer who has been dismissed or discharged from the service, and who subsequently re-enters the service without at the time stating the fact of his dismissal or discharge, or showing his certificate of dismissal or discharge, amy be dismissed the service by the officer commanding the corps or department with which he is serving, and

(2) Every attested person of or below rank of non-commissioned officer who is discovered to have made a willful false answer to any question set forth in the attestation paper which has been put to him by, or by direction of, the officer before whom he appears for the purpose of being attested, shall, on conviction by court martial, be liable to suffer imprisonment (with or without hard labour) or such less punishment as is in these Article mentioned.

Certificate to person dismissed or discharged

"Article 6. Every attested person who is dismissed or discharged from the service shall be furnished by his commanding officer with a certificate, in the English language and in the mother-tongue of such person (when his mother-tongue is not English), stating forth:

(a) The authority dismissing or discharging him;

(b) The cause of his dismissal or discharge; and

(c) The full period of his service in the army."

Repeal of portion of Article 7

7. In Article 7, sentence I, of the said Article, the words, "in any regiment, corps, detachment or guard" are repealed.

Substitution of new sentence for third sentence of same article

8. For the third sentence of the last-mentioned article the following shall be substituted, namely:

> "or who, knowing or having reason to believe in the existence of any mutiny or sedition or of any intention to mutiny or create sedition, or of any conspiracy against the State."

Amendment to Article 8

9. In article 8 of the said Articles, for the words under any circumstances in which the superior officer is distinguishable as such in any manner" the words "knowing or having reason to believe him to be such" shall be substituted.

10. For articles 10 and 11 of the said Articles the following shall be substituted, namely:

"Desertion

> Article 10. Who deserts or attempts to desert the service;--or
>
> "Re-enlisting without having been discharged
>
> Article 11. Who, without having first obtained a regular discharge from the corps or department to which he belongs, enlists or enrolls himself in any other corps or department, or"

Amendment of Article 24

11. For the last paragraph of article 24 of the said Articles the following shall be substituted, namely:

> "Whenever any person is convicted of an offence specified in article 7 and punishable with death under this article, all his property, movable and immovable, shall be forfeited to the Government."

Substitution of new articles for articles 25 and 26

12. For articles 25 and 26 of the said Articles the following shall be substituted, namely:

"Unbecoming conduct

> Article 25. Any officer, medical subordinate or warrant officer who behaves in a manner unbecoming of his position and character; and

"Intoxication on duty

> Article 26. Who is in state of intoxication when on or after having been warned for any duty, or n parade, or on the line of march, or"

Substitution of new article for article for 31

13. For article 31 of the said Articles the following shall be substituted, namely:

"Failure to rejoin

Article 31. Who having been on leave of absence and having received information from proper authority that his corps or department has been ordered on service, fails, without sufficient cause, to rejoin without delay; or

Substitution of new article for article for 39

14. For article 39 of the said Articles the following shall be substituted, namely:

"Impeding Provost-marshal

Article 39. Who impedes a provost-marshal or an assistant provost-marshal, or any officer or non-commissioned officer or other person, legally exercising authority under or on behalf of a provost-marshal, or, when called on, refuses to assist, in the execution of his duty, the provost-marshal, assistant provost-marshal, or any such officer, non-commissioned officer or other person; or"

Amendment of Article 40

15. In article 40 of the said Articles the words "enrolled or" shall be inserted between the word "person" and the word "attested."

Substitution of new article for article for 47

16. For article 47 of the said Articles the following shall be substituted, namely:

"Making away with regimental necessaries

"Article 47. Who:-

(a) Designedly or through neglect kills, injures, makes away with or loses his horse or ill-treats any animal used in the public service; or

(b) Dishonestly or fraudulently removes, conceals or delivers to any person, or designedly or through neglect injures or loses his arms, clothes, tools, musical or surgical instruments, equipments, ammunition, accoutrements or regimental necessaries, or any such articles entrusted to him or belonging to any other person; or

(c) Sells, pawns, destroys or defaces any medal or decoration granted to him by order of Her Majesty or of the Governor General in Council for service in the field or for general good conduct; or"

Substitution of new article for article 57

17. For article 57 of the said Articles the following shall be substituted, namely:

"Punishment for offences mentioned in Articles 54, 55 and 56

"Articles 57. Shall, if convicted by a general court-martial, be sentenced to be dismissed the service and to forfeit any arrears of pay and allowances due to him at the time of dismissal, and shall be punishable also with imprisonment (with or without hard labour), and with or without solitary confinement, for a term which may extend to two years; and shall , if convicted by a district court-martial, be liable to any or all of the penalties which such court is competent to inflict."

Amendment of article 65

18. In article 65 of the said Articles the word "other" shall be omitted.

Substitution of new article for article 66

19. For article 66 of the said Articles the following shall be substituted, namely:

"Penalties for the offences specified in articles 58 to 65

"Article 66. Shall, on conviction by a general or district court-martial, be liable to any or all of the punishments, other than death or transportation, which the court-martial is competent to award."

Amendment of article 69

20. In article 69 of the said Articles, for the words "such punishments as" to the end, the words "and any or all of the punishments, other than death or transportation, which the court-martial is competent to award" shall be substituted.

Substitution of new article for article 71

21. For article 71 of the said Articles the following shall be substituted, namely:

"Abetment

"Article 71. Every person who abets, within the meaning of the Indian Penal Code, an offence punishable under these Articles may be punishment hereinbefore provided in these Articles for such offence."

Substitution of new article for article 72

22. For article 72 of the said Articles the following shall be substituted, namely:

"Court-martial and the kinds thereof

Article 72. For the purposes of these Articles, there shall be five kinds of courts-martial, that is to say—

(1) General courts-martial

(2) District courts-martial

(3) Regimental courts-martial

(4) Summary general courts-martial

(5) Summary courts-martial

The first three courts-martial hereinafter are called ordinary courts-martial, while the last two are called extra-ordinary courts-martial.

Substitution of new articles for articles 73 and 74

23. For articles 73 and 74 of the said Articles the following shall be substituted, namely:

"Ordinary Court-martial

"Article 73. (1) The following authorities shall have power to convene general or district courts-martial, namely:--

(a) The Commander-in-Chief in India

(b) The general officer on the command

(c) Any officer empowered in that behalf by warrant of the Commander-in Chief in India or the general officer of the command.

(2) The power of convening general or district courts-martial may be granted under clause (1), sub-clause (c), subject to such restrictions, reservations, exceptions and conditions as the Commander-in-Chief in India or the general officer of the command granting the power may think fit.

(3) Any warrant under this article for convening general or district courts-martial, or either of them, may be addressed to an officer by name, or be designation of his office, or partly in one way and partly in the other, and may or may not, according to the terms thereof and the mode in which it is addressed, be limited to an officer named or be extended to any person for the time being performing the duties of such officer, or to the successors in command of such officer."

Composition of general courts-martial

"Article 74. A general court-martial shall, if held in British India, consist of not less than seven officers, unless that number, due regard being had to the public service, is not available, in which case the court may consist of not less than five officers"

Repeal of articles 75, 77, 78 and 79

24. Articles 75, 77, 78 and 79 of the said Articles are hereby repealed.

Amendment of article 76

25. In article 76 of the said Articles, for the words "reduction to the ranks" the words "reduction to a lower grade or to the ranks" shall be substituted.

Substitution of new articles for articles 80 and 81

26. For articles 80 and 81 of the said Articles the following shall be substituted, namely

"Composition of district court-martial

80. A district court-martial shall consist of not less than five officers, unless that number, due regard being had to the public service, is not available, in which case the court may consist of not less than three officers

81. A district court-martial may, when necessary, be composed wholly of officers of the corps or department to which the accused belongs."

Amendment of article 82

27. In article 82 of the said Articles the words "one year" and the words "other than mutiny" shall be omitted.

Further amendment of the same article

28. In the last-mentioned article, for the words "one year" the words "two years" and for the words "reduction to the ranks" the words "reduction to a lower grade or to the ranks" shall be respectively substituted.

Insertion of new article after article 82

29. After article 82 of the said articles the following article shall be inserted, namely:-

Convening order to state if larger number of officers is not available

"Article 82A. Whenever a general or district court-martial is ordered to be composed of the smaller number of officers specified in article 74 or 80, the order convening the court shall expressly state that the larger number of officers is not, due regard being had to the public service, available; and that statement shall be conclusive evidence of the fact so stated."

Substitution of new articles for articles 83, 84 and 85

30. For articles 83, 84 and 85 of the said Articles the following shall be substituted, namely:

"Appointment of regimental court-martial

Article 83. A regimental court-martial may be appointed by the officer commanding any corps or department or detachment thereof or by any officer when in command of two or more corps or departments or detachments thereof.

Composition of regimental court-martial

Article 84. A regimental court-martial shall consist of not less than three officers.

Power of such court

85. A regimental court-martial shall have power to try all persons subject to these Articles and not above the rank of non-commissioned officer—

(a) For any offence triable by a court-martial under these Articles, except an offence punishable under articles 7 to 23 (both inclusive), articles 54 to 65 (both inclusive), or articles 171 to 173 (both inclusive), and

(b) With the previous sanction of the prescribed authority, for any of the offences so expected.

Power as to sentence of such courts

85A. A regimental court-martial shall have the power to pass any sentence which might have been passed by a district court-martial for the like offence other than suspension from the rank, pay and allowances:

Provided that no sentence of imprisonment for a term exceeding six months, nor any of the additional punishments specified in Articles 135, shall be passed by a regimental court martial."

Substitution of new articles for articles 86 and 89

31. For articles 86 to 89 (both inclusive) of the said Articles the following shall be substituted, namely:

"Native and British officers when to be nominated

"Article 86. (1) The officers composing a court martial convened under the forgoing provisions shall, except as hereunder provided, be Native officers.

(2) The Governor General in Council, or the Commander-in-Chief in India, or the general officer of the Command, or any officer empowered in that behalf by warrant of the Commander-in-Chief in India, or the general officer of the Command, may direct that any court-martial convened under these Articles shall be composed of British instead of Native officers.

(3) Any person subject to these Articles, who is under orders for trial by any court-martial, may claim to be tried by British officers.

(4) In all cases of the right of making such a claim shall, before the court is convened, be explained to the persons under orders for trial by the commanding officer, or some officer deputed by him in this behalf, and, when such a claim is made, the court shall be constituted accordingly.

(5) A court-martial convened for the trial of any person subject to these Articles, and serving with any British corps or detachment, may be composed of British officers if, in the opinion of the officer convening the court (such opinion to be expressed in the order convening the

court and to be conclusive), Native officers are not available with due regard to the public service for service on the court.

Judge Advocate and appointment of superintending officer for native court-martial

Article 87. (1) Every general court-martial shall be attended by a judge advocate.

(2) If no officer of the judge advocate general's department is available, the officer convening the court shall appoint a fit person to act as judge advocate.

(3) No person under orders for trial or under trial by any court-martial may, without the leave of the court, object to any person acting or professing to act as judge advocate.

(4) A British officer of not less than four years' service, hereinafter called the superintending officer, shall be appointed to superintendent the proceedings of every court-martial composed of Native officers which is not attended by a judge advocate.

President

Article 88. (1) At every court-martial the senior officer shall sit as president without special appointment as such.

(2) In case of the death or unavoidable absence of the president, the next senior officer shall take the place of the president, without special appointment as such, and the trial shall proceed if the court is still composed of not less than the smallest number of officers of which it is required by these Articles to consist.

Article 89. No finding or sentence of a general, district or regimental court-martial shall be valid, except so far as it may be confirmed as provided by these Articles.

By whom findings and sentences may be confirmed or otherwise disposed of

Article 89A. (1) The following authorities shall have power to confirm the findings and sentences of general and district courts-martial:

(a) The Commander-in-Chief in India.

(b) The general officer of the Command, as regards troops under his command wherever stationed.

(c) The officer commanding a force not attached to a Command.

(d) Any officer empowered I that behalf by warrant of the Commander-in-Chief in India or the general officer of the Command:

Provided that, except on active service or beyond the limits of India, no warrant issued under this article shall be deemed to empower an officer to confirm any finding or sentence in case of an officer, medial subordinate or warrant officer, or a sentence of death, transportation or imprisonment for a term exceeding seven years in any case whatever.

(2) The provisions of article 73m clauses (2) and (3), shall, with the necessary modification, apply to warrants issued under this article.

(3) The officer who convenes a regimental court-martial or the officer having authority to convene such court-martial, at the date of the submission of the finding and sentence thereof, shall have power to confirm the same.

Power of confirming officer to mitigate, remit or commute sentence

Article 89B. Subject to such restrictions as may be contained in any warrant issued under the lase preceding article, the confirming officer may, when confirming the sentence of a court-martial, mitigate or remit the sentence of a court-martial, mitigate or remit the punishment thereby awarded, or commute that punishment for any less punishment or punishments to which the offender might have been sentenced by the court-martial:

Provided that a sentence of transportation shall not be commuted for a sentence of imprisonment for a term exceeding the term of transportation awarded by the court."

Substitution of new article for articles 90 to 97

32. For articles 90 to 97 (both inclusive) of the said Articles the following shall be substituted, namely:

Extraordinary Courts-martial

Article 90. The following authorities shall have power to convene a summary general court-martial, and such a court-martial may be convened:--

(a) In any place, whether or within or beyond British India, by an officer empowered in this behalf by an order of the Governor General in Council or of the Commander-in-Chief in India or of the general officer of the Command.

(b) By an officer commanding any detached portion of Her Majesty's troops upon active service when, in his opinion, it is not practicable, with due regards to discipline and the exigencies of the service, that an offence should be tried by an ordinary general court-martial.

Composition of summary general court-martial

Article 91. (1) A summary general court-martial shall consist of not less than three officers, who may be either British or Native, or both British and Native officers, as the officer convening the court thinks fit.

(2) Such court may be convened and the proceedings thereof be recorded in accordance with the form in the Second Appendix to these Articles with such variations as the circumstances of each case may require:

Provided that the convening officer may, in respect of any such trial by such court, specially order that the evidence, together with the prisoner's statement in defence, to be fully recorded in writing.

Powers of a summary general court-martial

Article 92. A summary general court-martial shall have all powers of a general court-martial, and subject to any instructions contained in the order convening the court, its sentence shall be valid, and may be carried out forthwith in case it does not exceed that which a district court-martial is empowered to pass, and in any other case when confirmed by the authority convening the court.

Convening and constitution of, and persons triable by, a summary court-martial

Article 93. (1) A summary court-martial may be held:--

(a) By the commanding officer, being a combatant officer, of any corps or department of Her Majesty's Indian Forces, or of any detachment of those forces.

(b) By the commanding officer of any British corps or detachment to which Native combatant details subject to these Articles are attached.

(2) At every summary court-martial the officer holding the trial shall alone constitute the court, but the proceedings shall be attended throughout by two other officers, British or Native, who shall not, as such be, affirmed or sworn.

(3) The proceedings shall be recorded in the English language, and, when closed, shall be signed by the officer holding the trial, and by the officers attending thereat.

(4) A summary court-martial mat try any person subject to these Articles and under the command of the officer holding the court, except an officer, medical subordinate or warrant officer.

(5) Any member of an army hospital corps may be tried by summary court-martial by any officer authorized in this behalf by the officer commanding the division, district, brigade or station to which the alleged offender belongs.

Offfences triable by a summary court-martial

Article 94. A summary court-martial may try any offence punishable under any of these Articles:

Provided that when there is no grave reason for immediate action, and reference can, without detriment to discipline, be made to superior authority, a summary court-martial shall not try without such reference any offence punishable under any of the following offence, namely:--

(a) Any offence punishable under any of the Articles 7 to 23 (both inclusive), or Articles 54 to 65 (both inclusive, or Article 171;

(b) Any offence against the officer holding the court.

Powers of a summary court martial

95. (1) A summary court-martial may be held try by the commanding officer of a corps or department may pass any sentence which can be passed under these Articles, except a sentence of death or transportation, or imprisonment for a term exceeding the one year.

(2) A summary court-martial held by any other officer may pass any sentence which can be passed under these Articles, except a sentence of death or transportation, or of imprisonment for a term exceeding one year.

Finding and sentence of a summary court martial

Article 96. The finding and sentence of a summary court-martial shall not require to be confirmed, but may be carried out at once;

Provided that, if the officer holding the trial is of less than five years of service, he shall not, except on active service, carry into effect any sentence until it has received the approval of a superior military officer commanding not less than a corps.

Transmission of proceedings of summary courts-martial

Article 97. The proceedings of every summary court-martial shall, without delay be forwarded to the officer commanding the district, or the division or brigade, within which the trial was held, or to the prescribed officer: and such officer, or the Commander-in-Chief in India, or the general officer commanding the Command, or when the court is held in a force not attached to a Command, the officer commanding the force, may, for reasons based on the merits of the case, but not any merely technical grounds, set aside the proceedings."

Substitution of new article for article 100

33. For Article 100 of the said Articles the following shall be substituted, namely--

"Arrest of confinement of accused

Article 100. (1) Whenever any person subject to these Article is accused of any offence which his commanding or other superior officer consider should be tried by court-martial, such officer shall order the accused to be placed in military custody until he can be tried by a court-martial or is discharged by proper authority.

(2) No such person shall be detained I military custody longer than is necessary for the purposes of justice."

Repeal of article 101.

34. Article 101 of the said Articles is hereby repealed.

Substitution of new article for article 102

35. For article 102 of the said Articles the following shall be substituted, namely:

"Interpreter

Article 102. (1) An interpreter shall be appointed to every court-martial.

(2) If no duly qualified interpreter is available at the station or place where the court martial sits, the officer appointing the court, or the officer commanding the district or place within or at which the trial is to be held, shall appoint any competent person to perform the duty of interpreter.

(3) When no other qualified or competent person is available, the superintending officer, or, in the case of an European court, the president, shall perform the duty of interpreter.

(4) In the case of a trial be a summary court- martial, the officer holding the trial, or one of the officers in attendance thereat, may perform the duty of interpreter if no other competent interpreter is available.

(5) No interpreter shall, as such, have a vote upon any matter."

Substitution of new article for article 103

36. For article 103 of the said Articles the following shall be substituted, namely:

"Dissolution of courts

Article 103. (1) When a court-martial after the commencement of the trial is reduced below the smallest number of officers which it is by these Articles required to consist, it shall be deemed to be dissolved.

(2) If, on account of illness of the prisoner before the finding, it is impossible to continue the trial, a court-martial shall be dissolved.

(3) Where a court-martial is dissolved under this article, the accused may be tried again."

Power to clear court

Article 103A. The president of a court-martial may, on any deliberation among the members, cause to court to be cleared of all other persons.

Power to view place

Article 103B. The court may, when it thinks fit, view any place"

Amendment of article 104

37. In article 104 of the said Articles the words "general court-martial appointed under an Order in Council, or any other" and the words and figures, "under articles 96 or 97" shall be omitted.

Amendment of article 107

38. In article 107 of the said Articles, for the words "courts-martial, other than courts-martial appointed under an Order in Council or summary" the word "ordinary" shall be substituted.

Insertion of new article for article 108

39. After article 108 of the said Articles the following article shall be inserted, namely:

"Affirmation or oath of interpreter

108A. At a summary court-martial the interpreter shall make affirmation or oath down to the words 'published by authority' only"

Repeal of Article 114

40. Article 114 of the said Articles is hereby repealed.

Substitution of new article for article 116

41. For article 116 of the said Articles the following shall be inserted, namely:

"Conviction of one offence permissible on charge of another

116. (1) A prisoner charged before a court-martial with desertion may be found guilty of attempting to desert or of being absent without leave.

(2) A person charged before a court-martial with attempting to desert may found guilty of desertion or of being absent without leave.

(3) A person charged before a court-martial with any one of the following offences, that is to say, theft, dishonest misappropriation or conversion, criminal breach of trust, or dishonestly receiving or retaining stolen property, may be found guilty of any other of those offences.

(4) A person charged before a court-martial with any other offence under these Articles may, on failure of proof of an offence having been committed under circumstances involving a more severe punishment, be found guilty of the same offence as having been committed in circumstances involving a less severe punishment."

Substitution of new article for article 117

42. For article 117 of the said Articles the following shall be inserted, namely:

"Evidence of previous convictions and general character

Article 117. (1) When any person subject to these Articles has been convicted by a court-martial of any offence, such court-martial may inquire into, and receive and record evidence of any previous convictions of such person, either by a court-martial or by a criminal court, and shall further enquire into and record the general character of such person.

(2) Evidence received under this Article may be either oral, or in the shape of entries in, or certified extracts from, court-martial books or other official records; and it shall not be necessary to prove the signature of such certified extracts, nor shall it be necessary to give notice before trial to the person tried that evidence as to his previous convictions or character will be received.

(3) At a summary court-martial the officer holding the trial may, if he thinks fit, record any previous convictions against the offender, his general character, as of his own knowledge, instead of requiring them to be proved under the foregoing provisions of this Article.

General rule as to evidence

Article 117A. Subject to the provisions of the last foregoing article, the Indian Evidence Act, 1872, subject to such modifications thereof and to such additional rules of evidence as the Governor General in Council may, by notification, direct, shall apply to all proceedings before a court-martial."

Substitution of new articles for articles 119 and 120

43. For articles 119 and 120 of the said Articles the following shall be inserted, namely:

"Majority requisite to sentence of death

Article 119. No sentence of death shall be passed by any court-martial without concurrence of two-thirds at least of the members of the court.

Revision of finding or sentence

Article 120. (1) The finding or sentence of any court-martial may be once revised by order of the officer authorized to dispose of the proceedings, and, such revision, the court, if so directed by him, may take additional evidence.

(2) The court, on revision, shall consist of the same officers as were present when the original decision was passed, unless any of those officers shall be unavoidably absent.

(3) In case of such unavoidable absence the cause thereof shall be duly certified in the proceedings, and the court shall proceed with the revision, provided it still consists of smallest number of officers of which such court is by these Articles required to consist."

Substitution of new article for articles 122 to 124

44. For articles 122 to 124 (both inclusive) of the said Articles the following shall be inserted, namely:

"Summoning of witnesses and production of documents

Article 122. (1) The judge advocate in the case of general court-martial, and the officer ordering the trial in the case of any other court-martial, may by summons under his hand, require the attendance before the court, at a time and place to be mentioned in the summons, of any person either to give evidence or to produce any document or other thing.

(2) In the case of a witness amenable to military authority, the summons shall be sent to the officer actually commanding of the corps, department or detachment to which he belongs, and such officer shall serve it upon him accordingly.

(3) In the case of any other witness, the summons shall be sent to the magistrate within whose jurisdiction he may be or reside, and such magistrate shall give effect to the summons as if the witness were required in the court of such magistrate.

(4) When a witness is required to produce any particular document or other thing in his possession or power, the summons shall describe it with convenient certainty.

(5) Nothing in this section shall be deemed to affect the Indian Evidence Act, 1872, sections 123 and 124, or to apply to any letter, post-card, telegram or other document in the custody of the postal or telegraph authorities.

(6) If any document in such custody is, in the opinion of any district magistrate, chief presidency magistrate, high court or court of session, wanted for the purpose of any court-martial, such magistrate or court may require the postal or telegraph authorities, as the case may be, to deliver such document to such person as such magistrate or court may direct.

(7) If any document in such custody is, in the opinion of any other magistrate or of any commissioner of police or district superintendent of police, wanted for any such purpose, he may require the postal or telegraph authorities, as the case may be, to cause search to be made for an to detain such document pending the orders of any such district magistrate, chief presidency magistrate or court.

Contempt of court

Article 123. (1) any witness duly summoned, and any person who commits any contempt of court in the presence of court-martial, or any offence described in articles 56, 57 or 68, shall, if subject to these Articles, be proceeded against as the court may direct.

(2) If any such witness or person is not subject, the president of the court-martial may certify the offence under his hand to the court of any magistrate within the local limits of whose jurisdiction it was committed, and the magistrate may thereupon take cognizance of the case, and after hearing anything which the accused may desire to say, dispose of it as if the offence had been committed in a proceeding in the court of such magistrate.

Privileges of persons attending courts-martial

Article 124.

(1) No president or member of a court-martial, no judge advocate or superintending officer, no party to any proceeding before a court-martial, or his legal practitioner or agent, and no witness acting in obedience to a summons to attend a court-martial, shall, while proceeding to, attending on or returning from, a court-martial, be liable to arrest under civil or revenue process.

(2) If any such person is arrested under any such process, he may be discharged by order of the court-martial."

Repeal of articles 125 to 129

45. Articles 125 to 129 (both inclusive) of the said Articles are hereby repeled.

Amendment of article 130

46. In article 130, clause (d), sentence 1, of the said article, for the words "one year) the words "two years" shall be substituted.

Substitution of new article for article 131

47. For articles 131 of the said Articles the following shall be inserted, namely:

"Dismissal

Article 131. Dismissal from the service may accompany any other sentence passed by a court-martial."

Insertion of words in article 132

48. In article 132 of the said Articles, after the word "reduced" the words "to a lower grade or" shall be inserted.

Substitution of new articles for articles 133 to 137

"Solitary confinement

Article 133. (1) In executing a sentence of solitary confinement, such confinement shall in no case exceed fourteen days at a time, with intervals between the period of solitary confinement of not less duration than such periods; and, when the imprisonment awarded shall exceed three months, the solitary confinement shall not exceed seven days in ant one month of the whole imprisonment of the whole imprisonment awarded, with intervals between the periods of solitary confinement of not less duration than such periods.

Reduction on non-commissioned officers to ranks

Article 134. A non-commissioned officer sentenced by court-martial to any punishment specified in the second paragraph of article 132 shall be deemed to be reduced to the rank.

Forfeiture of pay and pension

Article 135. On a conviction of any offence, a general, summary general or district court-martial may, in addition to any other punishment which it is empowered to award, sentence the offender to forfeit all advantaged as to additional pay and claim to pension on discharge which might otherwise have accrued from the length or nature of his former service, to forfeit all such advantage absolutely, whether it has accrued from former service or may accrue from future service, or to forfeit service for the purpose of promotion, increased pay or pension or any other prescribed purpose, or to forfeit any military decoration or reward.

Stoppage of good-conduct pay on conviction

Article 136. Whenever a person subject to these Articles is convicted by a general court-martial, his good-conduct pay shall, subject to any ules or orders which may from time to time be made with the previous sanction of the Governor General in Council, cease.

Forfeiture of arrears of pay

Article 137. On a conviction for any offence, if the offender is sentenced to dismissal from the service, or if his sentence involves such dismissal, he may further be sentenced to forfeit, if the court shall so direct:-

(a) All or any arrears of pay and allowances or other public money due to him at the time of his dismissal.

(b) Such portion thereof as may be required to make good any proved loss or damage arising out of his offence.

Amendment of article 138

50. The first paragraph of article 138 of the said Articles, and the word "and" st the beginning of the second paragraph of the same article, are hereby repealed.

Amendment of article 139

51. In article 139 of the said Articles, for the words "in the case of an officer, two-thirds, or in the case of any other person, one-half of his" the words "one-half of the offender's" shall be substituted.

Repeal of articles 142 to 149

52. Articles 142 to 149 (both inclusive) of the said Articles are hereby repealed.

Amendment of article 150 and 151

53. In articles 150 and 151 of the said Articles, after the words "the offender shall" the words "as soon as may be convenient" shall be inserted, and for the words "the nearest jail" the words "a Jail" shall be substituted

Addition to article 151

54. To the last-named article the following proviso shall be added, namely:

"Provided that in the case of a sentence of such imprisonment for a period not exceeding three months, the confirming or superior authority or, in the case of a summary court-martial, the commanding officer holding the trial may direct that the sentence shall be undergone in military custody"

Amendment of article 152

55. To article 152 of the said Articles the words "Subject to the control of the Commander-in-Chief in India" shall be prefixed; and for the words "the Commander-in-Chief of a Presidency" the following words shall be substituted, namely: "the general officer of the Command."

Further amendment of same article

56. To the second paragraph of the last-mentioned article the words "Subject as aforesaid" shall be prefixed, and in the same paragraph for the words "any Presidency" the words "a Command" shall be substituted.

Insertion of new words in article 155

57. In article 155 f the said Articles, after the words "from the date of such sentence" the words "or, if an appeal be preferred against such sentence and fail, from the date of the disposal of such appeal," shall be inserted.

Addition to same article

58. To the last-mentioned article the following shall be added, namely:

> "Provided that on active service any such person may, by order of the officer empowered under these Articles to confirm or otherwise dispose of the proceedings of the trial, be retained to serve in the ranks, and his service therein shall be reckoned as part of his term of transportation or imprisonment."

Repeal of articles 156 to 159

59. Articles 156 to 159 (both inclusive) of the said Articles are hereby repealed.

Substitution of new article for article 160

60. For articles 160 of the said Articles the following shall be substituted, namely:

"Pardons and remissions

Article 160. When any person subject to these Articles has been convicted by a court-martial of any offence,--

(a) The Governor General in Council, or

(b) When the person has been convicted of any offence other than civil offence, the Commander-in-Chief in India or, the general officer Command, may--

(1) Pardon the person;

(2) Remit wholly or in part any punishment awarded to him;

(3) Order the restoration to him of any service or other advantage forfeited under his sentence, or

(4) Re-admit him to the service when he has been dismissed therefrom:

Provided that the general officer of the Command shall not exercise the powers conferred by this section in respect of any person, unless—

(1) The person was under his authority when sent sentenced; and

(2) The person is still in the service, or, if the person has been dismissed from the service, the corps or department from which he was dismissed has since continued under the authority of that officer."

Amendment of article 161

61. In article 161 of the said Articles the words "or to the Government of Fort St. George, or to the Government of Bombay," shall be repealed; and for the words "Commander-in-Chief of any Presidency or of the officer commanding any force not attached to a Presidency: the following words shall be substituted, namely: "Commander-in-Chief in India or the general officer of the Command, or of the officer commanding any force not attached to a Command."

Addition of new article after article 161

62. After article 161 of the said Articles the following shall be inserted, namely:

"Preservation of proceedings of court-martial

Article 161A. (1) The proceedings of all general courts-martial shall be preserved by the judge advocate general for not less than seven years, and the proceedings of summary general courts-martial and district courts-martial for not less than three years, from the date of the confirmation of the finding and sentence.

(2) The proceedings of regimental and summary courts-martial shall be preserved for three years with the records of the corps or department to which the prisoner belonged.

(3) Every person tried by a court-martial shall be entitled, on demand at any time after the confirmation of the finding and sentence where such confirmation is required, and before the proceedings are destroyed, to obtain from the officer or person having the custody of the proceedings a copy thereof, including the proceedings upon revision, if any, upon payment for the same at the prescribed rate."

Substitution of new article for article 162

63. For article 162 of the said Articles the following shall be substituted, namely:

"Enquiry on absence of person subject to Articles

Article 162. (1) When any person subject to these Articles has been absent without due authority from his duty for a period of sixty days, a court of inquiry shall, as soon as practicable, be assembled and upon affirmation or oath administered in the prescribed manner, shall inquire respecting the absence of the person, and the deficiency, if any, of property, of the Government entrusted to his care, or of his arms, ammunition, equipments, instruments, clothing or necessaries; and, if satisfied of the fact of such absence without due authority or other sufficient cause, the Court shall declare such absence and the period thereof, and the said deficiency, if any; and the commanding officer of the corps or department to which the person belongs shall enter in the court-martial book of the corps or department a record of the declaration.

(2) If the person declared absent does not afterwards surrender, or is not apprehended, the record shall have the legal effect of a conviction of desertion.

(3) If the person declared absent surrenders or is apprehended, the record or a copy thereof purporting to bear the signature of the officer having the custody of the court-martial book shall, on the trial of the person for desertion, be presumptive evidence of the facts therein recorded; and, on the proof of the identity of the prisoner with the person therein mentioned, he may be found guilty of desertion and the deficiency, if any, therein recorded."

Amendment of article 163

64. For the last paragraph of article 163 of the said Articles the following shall be substituted, namely:

"Such recommendation, duly confirmed by the Commander-in-Chief in India, or by the general officer of the Command, or the officer commanding any force not attached to a command to which he belongs, or by any general officer under whose command the person is serving, shall entitle him to receive such arrears and reckon service accordingly."

Substitution of new article for article 164

65. For article 164 of the said Articles the following shall be substituted, namely:

"Reduction to lower grade or ranks

Article 164. The Commander-in-Chief in India, the general officer of the Command, the officer commanding any force not attached to a command, and the officer commanding any district or division or brigade, shall respectively have the power to reduce to a lower grade or to the ranks any non-commissioned officer under his command."

Amendment of article 165

66. In article 165 of the said Article, for the words "No such minor punishment shall be awarded by a court-martial," to the end of the article, the following shall be substituted, namely:--

"Unless otherwise specially provided by the said Commander-in-Chief, no Native officer, medical subordinate or warrant officer shall be liable to any such minor punishment.

Good-conduct pay shall not necessarily be forfeited on the infliction of a minor punishment, but forfeiture thereof may be awarded as a substantive punishment, by order of the commanding officer, as may from time to time be prescribed in the General Orders of the Commander-in-Chief in India.

Forfeiture of good-conduct pay may not be awarded in addition to any other minor punishment."

Amendment of article 166

67. In article 166 of the said Article, for the words "the Governor of Fort St. George in Council, the Governor of Bombay in Council, or any other Local Government" shall be omitted.

Amendment of article 168

68. In article 168 of the said Article, for the words "the Commander-in-Chief of the Presidency" the words "the Commander-in-Chief in India or the general officer of the Command" shall be substituted.

Amendment of article 169

69. In the second paragraph of article 169 of the said Articles, for the words, "warrant officer" the words "non-commissioned officer" shall be substituted.

Repeal of part of article 170

70. The second and third paragraph of article 170 of the said Articles are hereby repealed.

Substitution of new articles for articles 171 to 175

71. For articles 171 to 175 (both inclusive) of the said articles the following shall be substituted, namely:

"Civil offences

Military jurisdiction with respect to civil offences

Article 171. Every person subject to these Articles who at any place beyond British India, commits any civil offence shall be deemed to be guilty of an offence against military law, and, if charged therewith under this article shall, subject to the provisions of these Articles, be liable to be tried for the same by court-martial at any place, whether within or beyond British India, and on conviction to be punished as follows, that is to say:—

(a) If the offence is one which would be punishable under the law of British India with death or with transportation, or with imprisonment for a term exceeding three years, he shall be liable to any punishment assigned for the offence by the law of British India; and

(b) In other cases, he shall be liable to suffer any punishment assigned for the offence by the law of British India, or such punishment as might be awarded to him in pursuance of these Articles in respect of an act prejudice to good order and military discipline.

Extension of article 171 to certain civil offences

Article 172. The Governor General in Council may, by notification, extend the last foregoing article to civil offences or any class of those offences committed by a person subject to these Articles when on active service in British India, and may cancel any such notification.

Certain offences when triable by military law

Article 173. Every person subject to these Articles who, whether within or beyond British India, commits or attempts to commit or abets the commission of any of the following offences against any person subject to military law, that is to say, murder, culpable homicide or any offence punishable under any of the sections 323 to 335 (both inclusive), or section 506 of the Indian Penal Code, shall be deemed to be guilty of an offence against military law, and, if charged under this Article with any such offence, shall, subject to the provisions of these Article, be liable to be tried by court-martial at any place whether within or without British India, and on conviction shall be liable to suffer any punishment assigned for the offence by the said Code.

Jurisdiction over certain offences

Article 174. When under any of the foregoing Articles a criminal court and a court-martial have each jurisdiction in respect of an offence, it shall be in the discretion of the prescribed military authority to decide before which court the proceedings shall be instituted, and, if that authority decides that they should be instituted before a court-martial, to direct that the accused person shall be detained in military custody.

Power of criminal court to required delivery of offender

Article 175. (1) When a criminal court having jurisdiction is of opinion that proceedings ought to be instituted before itself in respect of any alleged offence, it may, by written notice, require the convening authority or the prescribed military authority at his option, either to deliver over the offender to the nearest magistrate to be proceeded against according to law or to postpone proceedings pending a reference to the Governor General in Council.

(2) In every such case the said authority shall either deliver over the offender in compliance with the requisition or shall forthwith refer the question as to the court before which the proceedings are to be instituted for the determination of the Governor General in Council, whose order upon such reference shall be final.

Substitution of new article for articles 176 to 179

72. For articles 176 to 179 (both inclusive) of the said Articles the following shall be substituted, namely:

"TITLE VI: PROPERTY OF DECEASED PERSON AND DESERTERS

Property of deceased persons

Article 176. The following rules are enacted respecting the disposal of the property of every person who belongs to a class subject to these Articles who dies, is killed in field or deserts:--

(1) The commanding officer shall secure all the moveable property that is on the spot, and cause an inventory thereof to be made, and draw up pay and allowances due to the deceased or deserter.

(2) In the case of a deceased person who has left in a Government savings bank (including any post office savings bank, however named) a deposit not exceeding one thousand rupees, the commanding officer may, if he thinks fit, require the secretary or other proper officer of the bank to pay the deposit to him forthwith, notwithstanding anything in any departmental

rules; and after the payment thereof in accordance with such requisition, no person shall have any right in respect of the deposit except as hereinafter provided.

(3) In the case of a deceased person whose representative is on the spot and has given security for the payment of the regimental or other debts (if any) of the deceased, the commanding officer shall deliver over any property and the amount of the deposit (if any) received under clauses (2) of this article to that representative.

(4) In the case of a deceased person whose estate is not dealt with, under clause (3), and in the case of any deserter, the commanding officer shall cause the moveable property to be sold by public auction, and shall pay the regimental and other debts in camp or quarters (if any), and, in the case of a deceased person, the expenses of his funeral ceremonies, from the proceeds of the sale and from the amount of the deposit (if any) received under clause (2) of this article.

(5) The surplus, if any, shall, in the case of a deceased person, be paid to his representative, if any, or in the event of no claim to such surplus being established within twelve months after the death, then the same shall be remitted to the prescribed person.

(6) In the case of the sale of the effects of a deserter, the amount remaining in the hands of the commanding officer shall be forthwith remitted to the prescribed officer.

Disposal of cert property without production of probate, etc

Article 177. Property deliverable and money payable to the representative of a deceased person under the last foregoing article may, if the total value or amount thereof does not exceed one thousand rupees, and if the prescribed person thinks fit, be delivered or paid to any person appearing to him be entitled to receive it or to administer the estate of the deceased, without requiring the production of any probate, letters of administration, certificate or other such conclusive evidence of title; and such delivery or payment shall be a full discharge to those ordering or making the same and to the Secretary of State for India in Council from all further liability in respect of the property or money; but nothing in this article shall affect the rights of any executor or administrator or other representative, or of any creditor, of a deceased person against any person to whom such delivery or payment has been made.

Meaning of desertion in article 176

Article 178. A person shall be deemed to have deserted within the meaning of article 176 who has been convicted of desertion, or who has been illegally absent from duty for a period of sixty days and has not subsequently surrendered or been apprehended

Application of Article 176 to lunatics

179. The provisions of the last-mentioned article shall, so far as they can be made applicable, apply in the case of a person subject to these Articles becoming insane, such allowance being made for his support as is authorized by the Military Lunatics Act, 1877 [Act XI of 1877]."[1]

1 For text of Military Lunatics Act, 1877, see page xxx.

Substitution of new Part for Part III

73. For Part III of the said Articles the following shall be substituted, namely:

PART III: MISCELLANEOUS

"Prohibition of second trial

Article 180. When any person subject to these Articles has been acquitted or convicted of an offence by a court-martial or by a criminal court, or has been summarily dealt with for an offence under the sections 165 or 166, he shall not be liable to be tried again for the same offence by a court-martial or dealt with summarily in respect of it under either the said Articles.

Exemption from arrest for debt

Article 181. (1) No person subject to these Articles shall, so long as he belongs to Her Majesty's Indian Forces, be liable to be arrested for debt under any process issued by, or by the authority of, any civil or revenue court or revenue officer.

(2) The judge of any such court may examine into any complaint made by such person or his superior officer of the arrest of such person contrary to the provisions of this article, and may, by warrant under his hand, discharge the person, and award reasonable costs to the complainant, who may recover those costs in like manner as he might have recovered costs awarded to him by a decree against the person obtaining the process.

(3) For the recovery of such costs no fee shall be payable to the court by the complainant.

Property exempted from attachment

Article 182. Neither the arms, clothes, equipment, accoutrements or necessaries of any person subject to these Articles, nor any animal used by him for the discharge of his duty, shall be seized; nor shall the pay and allowances of any such person or any part thereof be attached, by direction of any civil or revenue court or any revenue officer, in satisfaction of any decree or order enforceable against him.

Application of the last two foregoing articles to reservists

Article 183. Every person belonging to the Indian Reserve Forces shall, when called out for or engaged upon or returning from training or service, as an officer or soldier, be entitled to all the privileges accorded by the last two foregoing articles to a person subject to these Articles.

Priority of hearing by courts of cases in which Native officers and soldiers are concerned

Article 184. (1) On the representation to any court by or on behalf of any person subject to these Articles of a certificate, from the proper military authority, of leave of absence having been granted to or applied for which by him for the purpose of prosecuting or defending any suit or other and proceeding in such court, the court shall, on the application of such person, arrange, so far as may be possible, for the hearing and final disposal of such suit or other proceeding within the period of the leave so granted or applied for.

(2) The certificate from the proper military authority must state the first and last day of the leave or intended leave, and set forth a description of the case with respect to which the leave was granted or applied for.

(3) No fee shall be payable to the court in respect of the presentation of any such certificate, or in respect of any application by or on behalf of any such person for priority for the hearing of his case.

(4) Where the court is unable to arrange for the hearing and final disposal of the suit or other proceeding within the period of such leave or intended leave as aforesaid, it shall record its reasons for having been unable to do so, and shall cause a copy thereof to be furnished to such officer or soldier on his application, without any payment whatever by him in respect either of the application for such copy or of the copy itself.

(5) If in any case a question arises as to the proper military authority qualified to grant such certificate as aforesaid, such question shall be at once referred by the court to an officer commanding a corps, whose decision shall be final.

Capture of deserters

Article 185. (1) Whenever any person subject to these Articles deserts, the commanding officer of the corps, department or detachment to which he belongs shall give written information of the desertion to such civil, political or police authorities as, in his opinion, may be able to afford assistance towards the capture of the deserter; and such authorities shall thereupon take steps for the apprehension of the said deserter in like manner as if he were a person for whose apprehension a warrant had been issued by a magistrate, and shall deliver the deserter, when apprehended, to military custody.

(2) Such authorities shall also, by such means as appear to them best adapted for the purpose, prevent persons reasonably believed to be subject to these Articles from travelling through the areas subject to their jurisdiction, unless on duty, or furnished with a certificate of leave or discharge.

(3) Any police officer may arrest, without warrant, any person reasonably believed to be subject to these Articles and to be travelling without authority, and shall bring him without delay before the nearest magistrate, or the nearest military commanding officer when no magistrate is readily accessible, to be dealt with according to law.

Apprehension of military offender

Article 186. Whenever any person subject to these Articles, who is accused of any military offence, is within the jurisdiction of any civil, political or police officer, such officer shall aid in the apprehension and delivery to military custody of such person upon receipt of a written application to that effect signed by his commanding officer.

Presumption as to signatures

Article 187 In any proceeding under these Articles, any application, certificate, warrant, reply or other document purporting to be signed by an officer in the service in the civil or military service of the Government shall, on production, be presumed to have been duly signed by the person and in the character by whom and in which it purports to have been signed, until the contrary is shown.

Portion of the forces under an Army Command

Article 188. (1) The Governor General in Council may direct that for the purposes of these Articles:--

(a) Any portion of Her Majesty's Indian Forces belonging to a Command shall, when serving beyond the ordinary limits of the Command, continue subject to the authority of the general officer of the Command; or

(b) Any portion of those forces not belonging to a Command shall be attached to a Command and shall be subject to the authority of the general officer of the Command.

(2) Except as may be directed under clause (1) of this article, any portion of the said forces shall, when serving in a Command, be for the purposes of these Articles subject to the authority of the general officer of that Command.

Saving of authority of Commander-in-Chief in India

Article 189. Nothing in these Articles shall be deemed to affect the authority conferred on the Commander-in-Chief in India by any Act of Parliament or by Royal Warrant or Commission.

Power to make rules

Article 190. (1) The Governor General in Council may, by notification, make rules consistent with these Articles to regulate the procedure of courts-martial and officers, military, civil or political, having any jurisdiction or authority under these Articles, and for the purpose of carrying these Articles into execution, so far as relates to the investigation, trial and punishment of offences triable under them.

(2) Rules under this article may provide among other matters for the following:

(a) The assembly and procedure of courts of inquiry;

(b)The convening and constituting of courts-martial;

(c) The adjournment, dissolution and sittings of courts-martial;

(d) The procedure to be observed in trials by courts-martial;

(e) The confirmation and revision of the findings and sentences of courts-martial;

(f) The carrying into effect sentences of courts-martial;

(g) The forms of orders to be made under the provisions of this Act relating to courts-martial, transportation or imprisonment.

(3) The Governor General in Council may by any such rule confer on any court-martial or officer any power (other than a power to try an accused person or pass a sentence) conferred on a court of original jurisdiction by the Code of Criminal Procedure, 1882.

Power to apply Articles to certain forces under the Government of India

Article 191. (1) The Governor General in Council may, by notification, apply all or any of the provisions of these Articles to any force raised and maintained in India under the authority of the Governor General in Council, and may cancel or modify any such notification.

(2) While any of the provisions of these Articles, apply to any such force, the Governor General in Council may, by notification, direct by what authority any jurisdiction, powers or duties incident to the operation of those provisions shall be exercised or performed in respect to that force."

Addition of second Appendix to Articles

74. After the Appendix to the said Articles the Second Appendix set out in the Schedule to this Act shall be added [schedules not included].

ACT VIII of 1911[1]

THE INDIAN ARMY ACT, 1911

CONTENTS

CHAPTER I

PRELIMINARY

1 This Act was further amended by the Act No. 33 of 1934. The copy of the amending Act is also available in this book at page xxx.

Attestation

11. Persons to be attested.

12. Mode of attestation.

CHAPTER III

DISMISSAL AND DISCAHRAGE

13. Dismissal by Governor General in Council and Commander-in-Chief in India.

14. Dismissal by officer commanding army, division, brigade, etc.

15. *Repealed.*

16. Discharge,

17. Certificate to person dismissed or discharged.

18. Discharge, etc., out of India.

CHAPTER IV

SUMMARY REDUCTION AND PUNISHMENTS OTHERWISE THAN BY ORDER OF COURT-MARTIAL

19. Reduction of non-commissioned officers.

20. Minor punishments.

21. Collective fines.

22. Punishment of certain Indian followers.

Provost-Marshals

23. Appointment.

24. Duties and powers.

CHAPTER V

OFFENCES

Offences in respect of Military Service

25. Offences punishable with death.

26. Offences not punishable with death.

Mutiny and Insubordination

27. Offences punishable with death

28. Offences not punishable with death

Desertion, Fraudulent Enrolment and Absence without Leave

29. Desertion.

30. Harbouring deserter, absence without leave, etc.

Disgraceful Conduct

31. Disgraceful conduct.

Intoxication

32. Intoxication.

Offences in relation to Persons in Custody

33. Offences punishable with death

34. Offences not punishable with death

Offences in relation to Property

35. Offences in relation to property

Offences in relation to False Documents and Statements

36. False accusations and offences in relation to documents

37. False answers on enrolment

Offences in relation to Courts-martial

38. Offences in relation to courts-martial

Miscellaneous Military Offences

39. Miscellaneous military offences

39A. Attempts

Abetment

40. Abetment.

Civil Offences

41. Civil offences committed outside British India or on active service in British India.

42. Certain civil offences triable by military law

CHAPTER VI

PUNISHMENTS

43. Punishments

44. Lower punishments

45. Field punishment

46. Position of corporal punishment in scale

47. Combination of punishments

48. Solitary confinement

49. Reduction of non-commissioned officers to ranks

49A. Retention in the ranks of a person convicted on active service

CHAPTER VII

PENAL DEDUCTIONS

60. Deductions from pay and allowances

51. Deductions from public money other than pay

52. Remission of deductions.

52A. Provision for dependants of prisoners of war

CHAPTER VIII

COURTS-MARTIAL

Constitution and Dissolution of Courts-martial

53. Courts-martial and the kinds thereof

54. Power to convene general courts-martial

55. Power to convene district courts-martial

56. Contents of warrant issued under section 54 or section 55

57. Composition of general courts-martial

58. Composition of district courts-martial
59. Convening order to state if larger number of officers is not available
60. Composition of general or district courts-martial
61. Claim to trial by British officers.
62. Convening of summary general courts-martial
63. Composition of summary general court-martial
64. Summary courts-martial.
65. Dissolution of courts.

Jurisdiction of Courts-martial

66. Prohibition of second trial
67. Limitation of trial
68. Place of trial

Adjustment of jurisdiction of Courts-martial and Criminal Courts

69. Order in case of concurrent jurisdiction
70. Power of criminal court to require delivery of offender
71. Trial by court-martial no bar to subsequent trial by criminal court

Powers of Courts-martial

72. Powers of general and summary general courts-martial
73. Powers of district court-martial
74. Offences triable by summary court-martial
75. Persons triable by summary court-martial.
76. Sentences awardable by summary court-martial

Procedure at Trials by Courts-martial

77. President
78. Judge Advocate
79. Superintending officer
80. Challenges

81. Voting of members

82. Oaths of president and members

83. Oaths of witnesses

84. Summoning witnesses and production of documents

85. Commissions

86. Conviction of one offence permissible on charge of another

87. Majority requisite to sentence of death

Evidence before Courts-martial

88. General rule as to evidence.

89. Judicial notice.

90. Presumption as to signatures.

91. Enrolment paper.

9lA. Presumption as to certain documents

92. Reference by accused to Government officer.

93. Evidence of previous convictions and general character

Confirmation and Revision of Findings and Sentences

94. Finding and sentence invalid without confirmation

95. Power to confirm finding and sentence of general court-martial.

96. Power to confirm finding and sentence of district court-martial.

97. Contents of warrant issued under section 95 or section 96.

98. Confirmation of finding and sentence

99. Power of confirming officer to mitigate, remit or commute sentences

99A. Confirmation of finding and sentence on board ship

100. Revision of finding or sentence.

101. Finding and sentence of a summary court-martial

102. Transmission of proceedings of summary courts-martial

103. Substitution of valid for invalid sentence

103A. Provision in the case of accused being lunatic

CHAPTER IX

EXECUTION OF SENTENCES

104. Form of sentence of death.

103. Imprisonment to be in military custody.

106. Commencement of sentence of transportation or imprisonment.

107. Execution of sentence of transportation or imprisonment

108. Execution of sentence of imprisonment in special cases

108A. Offenders sentenced to transportation how dealt with until transported

109. Communication of certain orders to civil prison officers.

110. Limit of solitary confinement

111. (Instrument of Corporal punishment) Repealed

111A. Execution of sentence of fine

CHAPTER X

PARDONS AND REMISSIONS

112. Pardons and remissions.

CHAPTER XI

RULES

113. Power to make rules.

CHAPTEE XII

PROPERTY OF DECEASED PERSONS, DESERTERS AND LUNATICS

114. Property of deceased persons and deserters; Meaning of desertion

115. Disposal of certain property without production of probate, etc.

116. Application of section 114 to lunatics.

CHAPTER XIII

MISCELLANEOUS

Military Privileges

117. Complaints against officers

118. Privileges of persons attending courts-martial

119. Exemption from arrest for debt

120. Property exempted from attachment

121. Application of the last two foregoing sections to reservists

132. Priority of hearing by courts of cases in which Indian officers and soldiers are concerned.

Deserters and Military Offenders

123. Capture of deserters

124. Arrest by military authorities

125. Arrest by civil authorities

126. Inquiry on absence of person subject to Act

Disposal of Property

126A. Order for custody and disposal of property pending trial in certain cases.

126B. Order for disposal of property regarding which offences committed.

Repeal

127. (Repeal) Repealed

THE SCHEDULE

Repeal of Enactments

Repealed

ACT No. VIII OF 1911

[16th March 1911]

An Act to consolidate and amend the law relating to the Government of His Majesty's Indian[2] Forces.

WHEREAS It is expedient to consolidate and amend the law relating to the Government of the Indian officers, soldiers and other persons in His Majesty's Indian[3] Forces; It is hereby enacted as follows:-

CHAPTER I

PRELIMINARY

Short Title and commencement

1. (1). This Act may be called the Indian Army Act, 1911.

(2). It shall come into force on such date [The 1st January, 1912] as the Governor General in Council may, by notification in the Gazette of India, direct in this behalf.

Persons subject to Act

2. (1). The following persons shall be subject to this Act, namely:-

(*a*) Indian officers and warrant officers;

(b) Persons enrolled under this Act;

(c) Persons not otherwise subject to military law, who, on active service, in camp, on the march, or at any frontier post specified by the Governor General in Council by notification in this behalf, are employed by, or are in the service of, or are followers of, or accompany any portion of, His Majesty's Forces

(2). Every person subject to this Act under sub-section (1), clause (*a*) or (*b*), shall remain so subject until duly discharged or dismissed.

Special provisions as to rank in certain cases

3. (1). The Governor General in Council may, by notification, direct that any persons or class of persons subject to this Act under section 2, sub-section *(1),* clause (c), shall be so subject

2 The word "Native" was repealed by s. 26 and Schedule of the Indian Army (Amendment) Act, 1918 (11 of 1918).

3 For the expressions "native" and "a native" wherever they occur in this Act, the expressions "Indian" and "an Indian' were substituted respectively by s. 2 of the Indian Army (Amendment) Act, 1918 (11 of 1918).

as Indian officers, warrant officers or non-commissioned officers, and may authorize any officer to give a like direction with respect to any such person and to cancel such direction.

(2). All persons subject to this Act other than officers, warrant officers and non-commissioned officers shall, if they are not persons in respect of whom a notification or direction under sub-section (1) is in force, be deemed to be of a rank inferior to that of a non-commissioned officer.

Commanding officer of persons subject to military law under section 2, clause (c)

4. Every person subject to this Act under section 2, sub-section (1), clause (c), shall, for the purposes of this Act, be deemed to be under the commanding officer of the corps, department or detachment (if any) to which he is attached, and if he is not attached to any corps, department or detachment, under the command of any officer who may for the time being be named as his commanding officer by the officer commanding the force with which such person may for the time being be serving, or of any other prescribed officer, or, if no such officer is named or prescribed, under the command of the said officer commanding the force:

Provided that an officer commanding a force shall not place a person under the command of an officer of official rank inferior to that of such person if there is present at the place where such person is any officer of higher rank under whose command he can be placed.

Powers to apply Act to certain forces under the Government of India

5. (1) The Governor General in Council may, by notification apply all or any of the provision b of this Act to any force raised and maintained to in India under the authority of the Governor General in Council.

(2) While any of the provisions of this Act apply to any such force, India, the Governor General in Council may, by notification, direct by what authority any jurisdiction, powers or duties incident to the operation of these provisions shall be exercised or performed in respect of that force.

Officers to exercise powers in certain cases

6. (1) Whenever persons subject to this Act are serving—

(a) Out of India under an officer not subject to the authority of the Governor General in Council, or

(b) In India under an officer commanding any military organization not in this section specifically named, and being, in the opinion of the Governor General in Council, not less than a brigade,

the Governor General in Council may prescribe the officer by whom the powers which, under this Act, may be exercised by officers commanding armies, army corps, divisions and brigades, shall, as regards such persons, be exercised.[4]

4 This sub-section was substituted by s. 3 of the Indian Army (Amendment) Act. 1918 (11 of 1918).

(2) The Governor General in Council may confer such powers either absolutely, or subject to such restrictions, reservations, exceptions and conditions as he may think fit.

Definitions

Definitions

7. In this Act, unless there is something repugnant in the subject or context,—

(1) "British officer" means a person holding a commission in His Majesty's land forces,[and includes, in relation to a person subject to this Act when serving under such conditions as may be prescribed, a person holding a commission in His Majesty' s Air Force];[5]

(2) Indian officer" means a person commissioned, gazetted or in pay as an officer holding an Indian rank in His Majesty's Indian Forces;

(3) "Warrant officer " means a person appointed, gazetted or in pay as an Indian warrant officer in His Majesty's Indian Forces;

(4) 'Non-commissioned officer" means a person attested under this Act holding an Indian non-commissioned rank in His Majesty' s Indian Forces, and includes an acting non-commissioned officer;

(5) "Officer" means a British officer or Indian officer, but does not include a warrant officer or non-commissioned officer;

(6) "Commanding officer," when used in any provision of this Act with reference to any separate portion of His Majesty's forces or to any department, means the British officer whose duty it is under the regulations of the army, or, in the absence of any such regulation by the custom of the service, to discharge with respect to portion of the forces or that department the functions of commanding officer in regard to matters of the description referred to in that provision;

(7) "Superior officer," when used in relation to a person subject to this Act, includes a warrant officer and a non-commissioned officer; and, as regards persons placed under his orders, a warrant officer or noncommissioned officer subject to the Army Act or the Air Force Act;

(8) "Army," "army corps," "division," and "brigade" mean respectively an army, army corps, division or brigade which is under the command of an officer subject to the authority of the Governor General-in-Council or, when on active service, an army, army corps, division or brigade under the command of an officer holding a commission in His Majesty's Land Forces;[6]

(9) "Corps" means any separate body of persons subject to this Act or the Army Act which is prescribed as a corps for the purposes of all or any of the provisions of this Act;

5 These words were added by s. 2 of the Indian Army (Amendment) Act, 1923 (33 of 1923).

6 This clause was substituted by s. 4 of the Indian Amy (Amendment) Act, 1918 (11 of 1918) .

(10) "Independent brigade" means a brigade which does not form part of a division;

(11) "Department" includes any division or branch of a department;

(13) "Enemy" includes all armed mutineers, armed rebels, armed rioters, pirates and any person in arms against whom it is the duty of a person subject to military law to act;

(13) "Active service," as applied to a person subject to this Act, means the time during which such person is attached to, or forms part of, a force which is engaged in operations against an enemy, or is engaged in military operations in, or is on the line of march to, a country or place wholly or partly occupied by an enemy, or is in military occupation of any foreign country;

(14) "Military custody" means the arrest or confinement of a person according to the usages of the service;

(15) "Military reward" includes any gratuity or annuity for long service or good conduct, any good conduct pay, good service pay or pension, and any other military pecuniary reward;

(16) "Court Martial" means a court-martial held under this Act;

(17) "Criminal Court" means a court of ordinary criminal justice in British India, or established elsewhere by the authority of the Governor General in Council;

(18) "Civil offence" means an offence which, if committed in British India, would be triable by a criminal court;

(19) "Offence" means any act or omission punishable under this Act, and includes a civil offence as hereinbefore defined;

(20) "Notification" means a notification published in the Gazette of India:

(21) "Prescribed " means prescribed by rules made under this Act; and

(22) All words and expressions used herein and defined in the Indian Penal Code [Act XLV of 1860] and not hereinbefore defined shall be deemed to have the meanings respectively attributed to them by that Code.

CHAPTER II

ENROLMENT AND ATTESTATION

Enrolment

Procedure before enrolling officer

8. Upon the appearance before the prescribed enrolling officer of person desirous of being enrolled, the enrolling officer shall read and explain to him, or cause to be read and explained to him, in his presence, the conditions of the service for which he is to be enrolled; and shall put to him the questions set forth in the prescribed form of enrolment, and shall, after having cautioned

him that if he makes a false answer to any such question he will be liable to punishment under this Act, record or cause to be recorded his answer to each such question.

Enrolment

9. If, after complying with the provisions of section 8, the enrolling officer is satisfied that the person desirous of being enrolled fully understands the questions put to him and consents to the conditions of service, and if he perceives no impediment, he shall sign and shall also cause the person to sign the enrolment paper, and the person shall then be deemed to be enrolled.

Presumption of enrolment in certain cases

10. Every person who has for the space of six months been in the receipt of military pay and been borne on the rolls of any corps or department shall be deemed to have been duly enrolled, and shall not be entitled to claim his discharge on the ground of illegality or irregularity in his enrolment.

Attestation

Persons to be attested

11. The following persons shall be attested, namely:--

(a) All persons enrolled as combatants;

(b) All other enrolled persons prescribed by the Governor General in Council.

Mode of attestation

12. (1) When a person who is to be attested is reported fit for duty, or has completed the prescribed of period of probation, an oath or affirmation shall be administered to him in the prescribed form by his commanding officer in front of his corps or such portion thereof or such members of his department as may be present or by any other prescribed person.

(2) The form of oath or affirmation prescribed under this section shall contain a promise that the person to be attested will be faithful to His Majesty, His heirs and successors, and that he will serve in His Majesty's Indian Forces and go wherever he is ordered by land or sea, and that he will obey all commands of any officer set over him, even to the peril of his life.

(3) The fact of an enrolled person having taken the oath or affirmation directed by this section to be taken shall be entered on his enrolment paper, and authenticated by the signature of the officer administering the oath or affirmation.

CHAPTER III

DISMISSAL AND DISCHARGE

Dismissal by Governor General in Council and Commander-in-Chief in India

13. The Governor General in Council or the Commander-in-Chief in India may dismiss from the service any person subject to this Act.

Dismissal by officer commanding army, division, brigade, etc

14. An officer commanding an army, army corps, division or brigade, or any prescribed officer, may dismiss from the service any person serving under his command other than an Indian officer.

Dismissal of convicts

15. Repealed by s. 26 and Schedule of the Indian Army (Amendment) Act, 1918 (XI of 1918).

Discharge

16. The prescribed, authority may, in conformity with any rules prescribed in this behalf, discharge from the service any person subject to this Act.

Certificate to person dismissed or discharged

17. Every enrolled person who is dismissed or discharged from the service shall be furnished by his commanding officer with a certificate, in the English language and in the mother tongue of such person (when his mother tongue is not English), setting forth—

(a) The authority dismissing or discharging him;

(b) The cause of his dismissal or discharge;

(c) The full period of his service in the army.

Discharge, etc., out of India

18. (1) Any person enrolled under this Act who is entitled under the conditions of his enrolment to be discharged, or whose discharge is ordered by competent authority, and who, when he is so entitled or ordered to be discharged, is serving out of India, and requests to be sent to India, shall, before being discharged, be sent to India with all convenient speed.

(2) Any person enrolled under this Act who is dismissed from the service and who, when he is so dismissed, is serving out of India, shall be sent to India with all convenient speed;

Provided that, where any such person is sentenced to dismissal combined with any other punishment, such other punishment, or in the case of a sentence of transportation or imprisonment, a portion of such other punishment, may be inflicted before he is sent to India.[7]

7 This proviso was added by s. 7 of' the Indian Army (Amendment) Act, 1918 (11 of 1918).

CHAPTER IV

SUMMARY REDUCTION AND PUNISHMENT OTHERWISE THAN BY ORDER OF COURT MARTIAL

Reduction of non-commissioned officers

19. (1) The Commander-in-Chief in India, an officer commanding an army, army corps, division or brigade, or any prescribed officer, may reduce to a lower grade or to the ranks any non-commissioned officer under his command.

(2) The commanding officer of an acting non-commissioned officer may order him to revert to his permanent grade as a non-commissioned officer or, if he has no permanent grade above the ranks, to the ranks.

Minor punishments

20. (1) The Commander-in-Chief in India may, subject to the control of the Governor General in Council, specify the minor punishments to which persons subject to this Act shall be liable without the intervention of a court-martial, and the officer or officers by whom, and the extent to which, such minor punishments may be awarded.

(2) Imprisonment in military custody and in the case of persons subject to this Act on active service any prescribed field punishment may be specified as minor punishments, provided that:-

(a) The term of such imprisonment or field punishment [8] shall not exceed twenty-eight days; and

(b) It shall not be awarded to any person of or above the rank of non- commissioned officer, or who, when he committed the offence in respect of which it is awarded, was of or above such rank.

Collective fines

21. Whenever any weapon or part of a weapon forming part of the equipment of a half squadron, battery, company or other similar unit is lost or stolen, the officer commanding the army, army corps, division or independent brigade to which such unit belongs may, after obtaining the report of a court of inquiry, impose a collective fine upon the Indian officers, non-commissioned officers and men of such unit, or upon so many of them as, in his judgment, should be held responsible for such loss or theft.

Punishment of certain Indian followers

22. (1) For any offence, in breach of good order, the commanding officer of any corps or detachment on active service, in camp, on the march, or at any frontier post specified by the

8 'Field punishment' was inserted by s. 6 of the Indian Army (Amendment] Act; 1918 (11 of 1918).

Governor General in Council by notification in this behalf at which, troops are stationed, may punish any Indian follower of such corps or detachment who is subject to this Act under section 2, sub-section (1), clause (c)—

(a) If such follower is not a menial servant, with imprisonment; for a term which may extend to thirty days, or with fine which may extend to fifty rupees;

(b) If such follower is a menial servant, with imprisonment for a term which may extend to seven days, or, if on active service, with corporal punishment not exceeding twelve strokes of a rattan.

(2) Imprisonment awarded under this section may be carried out in a military guard, or in a jail, as ordered by the said commanding officer; and the officer in charge of any jail shall, on the delivery to him of the person of the offender, with a warrant, under the hand of the said commanding officer, detain the offender according to the exigencies of the warrant or until he is discharged by due course of law.

Marshals

Appointment

23. For the prompt and instant repression of irregularities and offences committed in the field or on the march, provost-marshals may be appointed by the Commander-in-Chief in India or an officer commanding an army, army corps, division or independent brigade or an officer commanding the forces in the field; and the powers and duties of such provost-marshals shall be regulated according to the established custom of war and the rules of the service.

Duties and powers

24. (1) The duties of a provost-marshal so appointed are to take charge of prisoners confined for offences of a general description, to preserve good order and discipline, and to prevent breaches of the same by persons belonging or attached to the army. [He may at any time arrest and detain for trial any person subject to this Act who commits an offence and may also carry into effect any punishments to be inflicted in pursuance of the sentence of a court-martial.][9]

[(2) A provost-marshal may punish with any punishment mentioned in section 22, sub-section (1), clause (b), any follower who is subject to this Act under section 2, sub-section (I), clause (c) and is a menial servant and who on active service and in his view, or in the view of any of his assistants, commits any breach of good order and military discipline.][10]

9 These words were added by s. 3 of' the Indian Army (Amendment) Act, 1920 (37 of 1920)..

10 This sub-section was substituted for original sub-section (2) and (3) by s.3 of the Indian Army (Amendment) Act, 1920 (37 of 1920).

CHAPTER V

OFFENCES

Offences in respect of Military Service

Offences punishable with death

25. Any person subject to this Act who commits any of the following offences, that is to say,—

(a) shamefully abandons or delivers up any garrison, fortress, post or guard committed to his charge, or which it is his duty to defend; or

(b) in presence of an enemy, shamefully casts away his arms or ammunition, or intentionally uses words or any other means to induce any person subject to military law to abstain from acting against the enemy, or to discourage such person from acting against the enemy, or misbehaves in such manner as to show cowardice; or

(c) directly or indirectly holds correspondence with, or communicates intelligence to, the enemy, or any person in arms against the State, or who, coming to the knowledge of any such correspondence or communication, omits to discover it immediately to his commanding or other superior officer; or

(d) Treacherously makes known the watchword to any person not entitled to receive it; or

(e) Directly or indirectly assists or relieves with money, victuals or ammunition, or knowingly harbours or protects, any enemy or person in arms against the State; or

(f) In time of war, or during any military operation, intentionally occasions a false alarm in action, camp, garrison or quarters, or spreads reports calculated to create alarm or despondency; or

(g) Being a sentry in time of war or alarm, or over any State prisoner, treasure, magazine or dockyard, sleeps upon his post, or quits it without being regularly relieved or without leave; or

(h) In time of action, leaves his commanding officer or his post or party to go in search of plunder; or

(i) In time of war, quits his guard, picquet, party or patrol without being regularly relieved or without leave; or

(j) In time of war or during any military operation, uses criminal force to, or commits an assault on, any person bringing provisions or other necessaries to the camp or quarters of any of His Majesty's forces, or forces a safeguard, or breaks into any house or any other place for plunder, or plunders, injures or destroys any field, garden or other property of any kind; or

(k) On active service commits any offence against the property or person of any inhabitant of, or resident in, the country in which he is serving;[11]

shall, on conviction by court-martial, be punished with death, or with such leas punishment as is in this Act mentioned.

Offences not punishable with death

26. Any parson subject to this Act who commits any of the following offences, that is to say,—

(a) Strikes, or forces or attempts to force, any sentry; or

(b) In time of peace, intentionally occasions a false alarm in camp, garrison or cantonment; or

(c) Being a sentry, or on guard, plunders or wilfully destroys or injures any property placed under his charge of his guard; or

(d) Being a sentry, in time of peace, sleeps upon his post, or quits it without being regularly relieved or without leave;

shall, on conviction by court-martial, be punished with imprisonment, or with such less punishment as is in this Act mentioned.

Mutiny and Insubordination

Offences punishable with death

27. Any person subject to this Act who commits any of the following offences, that is to say,—

(a) Begins, excites, causes, or conspires with any other persons to cause or joins in any mutiny; or

(b) Being present at any mutiny, does not use his utmost endeavours to suppress the same; or'

(c) Knowing or having reason to believe in the existence of any mutiny, or of any intention to mutiny, or of any conspiracy against the State, does not, without delay, give information thereof to his commanding or other superior officer; or

(d) Uses or attempts to use criminal force to, or commits an assault on, his superior officer, whether on or off duty, knowing or having reason to believe him to be such; or

(e) Disobeys the lawful command of his superior officer;

shall, on conviction by court-martial, be punished with death, or with such leas punishment as is in this Act mentioned.

11 Clause (k) was added by s. 8 of the Indian Army (Amendment) Act, 1918 (11 of 1918).

Offences not punishable with death

28. Any person subject to this Act who commits any of the following offences, that is to say—

(a) Is grossly insubordinate or insolent to his superior officer in the execution of his office; or

(b) Refuses to superintend or assist in the making of any field-work or other military work of any description ordered to be made either in quarters or in the field; or

(c) Impedes a provost-marshal or an assistant provost-marshal, or any officer or non-commissioned officer or other person, legally exercising authority under or on behalf of a provost-marshal, or, when called on, refuses to assist, in the execution of his duty, the provost-marshal, assistant provost-marshal, or any such officer, non-commissioned officer or other person;

shall, on conviction by court-martial, be punished with imprisonment, or with such less punishment as is in this Act mentioned.

Desertion, Fraudulent Enrolment and Absence without Leave

Desertion

29. Any person subject to this Act who deserts or attempts to desert the service shall, on conviction by court-martial, be punished with death, or with such less punishment as is in this Act mentioned.

Harbouring deserter, absent without leave

80. Any person subject to this Act who commits any of the following offences, that is to say,—

(a) Knowingly harbours any deserter, or who, knowing, or having reason to believe, that any other person has deserted, or that any deserter has been harboured by any other person, does not without delay give information thereof to his own or some other superior officer, or use his utmost endeavours to cause such deserter to be apprehended; or

(b) Knowing, or having reason to believe, that a person is a deserter, procures or attempts to procure the enrolment of such person; or

(c) Without having first obtained a regular discharge from the corp or department to which he belongs, enrols himself in the same or any other corps or department; or

(d) Absents himself without leave or without sufficient cause overstays leave granted to him; or

(e) Being on leave of absence and having received information from proper authority that any corps or portion of a corps, or any department, to which he belongs, has been ordered on active service, fails, without sufficient cause, to rejoin without delay; or

(f) Without sufficient cause fails to appear at the time fixed at the parade or place appointed for exercise or duty; or

(g) When on parade, or on the line of march, without sufficient cause or without leave from his superior officer quits the parade or line of march; or

(h) In time of peace, quits his guard, picquet or patrol without being regularly relieved or without leave; or

(i) Without proper authority is found two miles or upwards from camp; or

(j) Without proper authority is absent from his cantonment or lines after tattoo, or from camp after retreat-beating;

shall, on conviction by court-martial, be punished with imprisonment, or with such less punishment as is in this Act mentioned.

Disgraceful Conduct

Disgraceful Conduct

31. Any person subject to this Act who commits any of the following offences that is to say,—

(a) Dishonestly misappropriates or converts to his own use any money, provisions, forage, arms, clothing, ammunition, tools, instruments, equipments or military stores of any kind, the property of Government, entrusted to him; or

(b) Dishonestly receives or retains any property in respect of which an offence under clause (a) has been committed, knowing or having reason to believe the same to have been dishonestly misappropriated or converted; or

(c) Wilfully destroys or injures any property of Government entrusted to him; or

(d) Commits theft in respect of any property of Government, or of any military mess, band or institution, or of any person subject to military law, or serving with, or attached to, the army; or

(e) Dishonestly receives or retains any, such property as is specified in clause (d) knowing or having reason to believe it to be stolen; or

(f) Does any other thing with intent to defraud, or to cause wrongful gain to one person or wrongful loss to another person; or ,

(g) Malingers or feigns or produces disease or infirmity in himself, or intentionally delays his cure or aggravates his disease or infirmity; or

(h) With intent to render himself or any other person unfit for service, voluntarily causes hurt to himself or any other person; or

(i) Commits any offence of a cruel, indecent or unnatural kind, or attempts to commit any such offence and does any act towards its commission;

shall, on conviction by court-martial, be punished with imprisonment, or with such less punishment as is in this Act mentioned.

Intoxication

Intoxication

32. Any person subject to this Act who is in a state of intoxication, whether on duty or not on duty, shall, on conviction by court-martial, be punished with imprisonment, or with such less punishment as is in this Act mentioned.

Offences in relation to Persons in Custody

Offences punishable with death

33. Any person subject to this Act, who without proper authority, releases any State prisoner, enemy or person taken in arms against the State, placed under his charge, or who negligently suffers any such prisoner, enemy or person to escape, shall, on conviction by court-martial, be punished with death, or with such less punishment as is in this Act mentioned.

Offences not punishable with death

34. Any person subject to this Act who commits any of the following offences, that is to say,—

(a) Being in command of a guard, picquet or patrol, refuses to receive any prisoner or person duly committed to his charge; or

(b) Without proper authority releases any prisoner or person placed under his charge, or negligently suffers any such prisoner or person to escape; or

(c) Being in military custody, leaves such custody before he is set at liberty by proper authority;

shall, on conviction by court-martial, be punished with imprisonment, or with such less punishment as is in this Act mentioned.

Offences in relation to Property

Offences in relation to Property

35. Any person subject to this Act who commits any of the following offences, that is to say,—

(a) Commits extortion, or without proper authority exacts from any person, carriage, porterage or provisions; or

(b) In time of peace, commits house-breaking for the purpose of plundering, or plunders, destroys or damages any field, garden or other property; or

(c) Designedly or through neglect kills, injures, makes away with, ill-treats or loses his horse or any animal used in the public service; or

(d) Makes away with, or is concerned in making away with, his arms, ammunition, equipments, instruments, tools, clothing or regimental necessaries; or

(e) Loses by neglect anything mentioned in clause (d); or

(f) Wilfully injures anything mentioned in clause (d) or any property belonging to Government, or to any military mess, band or institution, or to any person subject to military law, or serving with, or attached to the army; or

(g) Sells, pawns, destroys or defaces any medal or decoration granted to him;

shall, on conviction by court-martial, be punished with imprisonment, or with such less punishment as is in this Act mentioned.

Offences in relation to False Documents and Statements

False accusations and offences in relation to documents

36. Any person subject to this Act who commits any of the following offences, that is to say:--

(a) Makes a false accusation against any person subject to military law, knowing such accusation to be false; or

(b) In making any complaint under section 117, knowingly makes any false statement affecting the character of any person, subject to military law, or knowingly and wilfully suppresses any material fact; or

(c) Obtains or attempts to obtain for himself, or for any other person, any pension, allowance or other advantage or privilege by a statement which is false, and which he either knows or believes to be false or does not believe to be true, or by making or using a false entry in any book or record, or by making any document containing a false statement, or by omitting to make a true entry or document containing a true statement; or

(d) Knowingly furnishes a false return or report of the number or state of any men under his command or charge, or of any money, arms, ammunition, clothing, equipments, stores or other property in his charge, whether belonging to such men or to Government or to any person in or attached to the army, or who, through design or culpable neglect, omits or refuses to make or send any return or report of the matters aforesaid;

shall, on conviction by court-martial, be punished with imprisonment, or with such less punishment as is in this Act mentioned.

False answers on enrolment

37. Any person having become subject to this Act who is discovered enrolment, to have made a wilfully false answer to any question set forth in the prescribed form of enrolment which has been put to him by the enrolling officer before whom he appears for the purpose of being enrolled, shall, on conviction by court-martial, be punished with imprisonment, or with such less punishment as is in this Act mentioned.

Offences in relation to Courts-martial

Offences in relation to Courts-martial

38. Any person subject to this Act who commits any of the following offences, that is to say,—

(a) When duly summoned to attend as a witness before a court-martial, intentionally omits to attend, or refuses to be sworn or affirmed or to answer any question, or to produce or deliver up any book, document or other thing which he may have been duly warned and called upon to produce or deliver up; or

(b) Intentionally offers any insult or causes any interruption or disturbance to, or uses any menacing or disrespectful word, sign or gesture, or is insubordinate or violent in the presence of, a court-martial while sitting; or

(c) Having been duly sworn or affirmed before any court-martial or other military court competent to administer an oath or affirmation, makes any statement which is false, and which he either knows, or believes to be false or does not believe to be true;

shall, on conviction by court-martial, be punished with imprisonment, or with such less punishment as is in this Act mentioned.

Miscellaneous Military Offences

Miscellaneous Military Offences

39. Any person subject to this Act who commits any of the following offences, that is to say,—

(a) Being an officer or warrant officer, behaves in a manner unbecoming his position and, character; or

(b) Strikes or otherwise ill-treats, any, person subject to this Act being his subordinate in rank or position; or

(c) Being in command at any post or on the march, and receiving a complaint that any one under his command has beaten, or otherwise maltreated or oppressed any person, or has disturbed any fair or market, or committed any riot or trespass, fails to have due reparation made to the injured person or to report the case to the proper authority; or

(d) By defiling any place of worship, or otherwise, intentionally insults the religion or wounds the religious feelings of any person; or

(e) Attempts to commit suicide and does any act towards the commission of such offence; or

(f) Being below the rank of warrant officer, when off duty, appears, without proper authority, in or about camp or cantonments, or in or about, or when going to or returning from any town or bazaar, carrying a sword, bludgeon, or other offensive weapon; or

(g) Directly or indirectly accepts or obtains, or agrees to accept or attempts, to obtain, for himself on for any other person, any gratification as a motive or reward for procuring the enrolment of any person, or leave of absence, promotion or any other advantage or indulgence for any person in the service; or

(h) Neglects to obey any general or garrison or other orders; or

(i) Is guilty of any act or omission which, though not specified in this Act, is prejudicial to good order and military discipline;

shall, on conviction by court-martial, be punished with imprisonment, or with such less punishment as is in this Act mentioned.

Attempts

39A. Whoever attempts to commit an offence punishable by this Act or to cause such an offence to be committed, and in such attempt does any act towards the commission of the offence may, where no express provision is made by this Act for the punishment of such attempt, be punished with the punishment provided in this Act for such offence.[12]

Civil Offences

Civil offences committed outside British India or on active service in British India

41. Every person subject to this Act who at any place beyond British India, or when on active service in British India, commits any civil offence shall be deemed to be guilty of an offence against military law, and, if charged therewith under this section shall, subject to the provisions of this Act, be liable to be tried for the same by court-martial, and on conviction to be punished as follows, that is to say:—

(a) If the offence is one which would be punishable under the law of British India with death or with transportation, he shall be liable to suffer any punishment [other than whipping][13] assigned for the offence by the law of British India; and

(b) In other cases, he shall be liable to suffer any punishment [other than whipping][14] assigned for the offence by the law of British India, or such punishment as might be awarded to him in pursuance of this Act in respect of an act prejudicial to good order and military discipline.

Certain civil offences tiable by military law

42. Every person subject to this Act who commits or attempts to commit or abets the commission of an offence punishable under Chapter VI of the Indian Penal Code [Act XLV of 1860], or any of the following offences against any person subject to military law, that is to say, murder, culpable homicide or any offence punishable under any of the sections 323 to 335 (both inclusive), or section 506 of the said Code, shall be deemed to be guilty of an offence against military law, and, if charged under this section with any such offence, shall, subject to the provisions of this Act,

12 This section was inserted by s. 10 of the Indian Army (Amendment) Act, 1918 (11 of 1918).

13 These words were inserted by s, 4 of the Indian Amy (Amendment) Act, 1920 (37 of 1920).

14 These words were inserted by s, 4 of the Indian Amy (Amendment) Act, 1920 (37 of 1920).

be liable to be tried by court-martial, and on conviction shall be liable to suffer any punishment assigned for the offence by the said Code.

CHAPTER VI

PUNISHMENTS

Punishments

43. Punishments may be inflicted in respect of offences committed by persons subject to this Act, and convicted by court-martial, according to the scale following, that is to say;—

(a) Death;

(b) Transportation for life or for any period not less than seven years;

(c) Imprisonment [either rigorous simple][15], for any term not exceeding fourteen years;

(d) Dismissal from the service;

(e) In the case of officers and warrant officers, suspension from rank, pay and allowances for a period not exceeding two months;

(f) Reduction, in the case of a warrant officer, to a lower grade or class (if any) of warrant officer, or in the case of a noncommissioned officer, to a lower grade or to the ranks;

(g) In the case of officers, warrant officers and non-commissioned officers, forfeiture of seniority of rank;

(gg) In the case of officers, reprimand or severe reprimand;[16]

(h) Forfeitures and stoppages as follows, namely:—

(i) Forfeiture of service for the purpose of promotion, increased pay, pension or any other prescribed purpose;

(ii) Forfeiture of any military decoration or military reward;

(iii) Forfeiture, in the case of a person sentenced to dismissal from the service of all arrears of pay and allowances and other public money due to him at the time of such dismissal;

(iv) Stoppages of pay and allowances until any proved loss or damage occasioned by the offence of which he is convicted is made good;

(v) On active service forfeiture of pay and allowances for a period not exceeding three months.[17]

---

15 These words were substituted for the words and brackets "(with or without solitary confinement) by s. 11(1) of the Indian Army (Amendment) Act, 1918 (11 of 1918).

16 This clause was added by s. 11 of the Indian Army (Amendment) Act, 1918 (11 of 1918).

17 This clause was added by s. 11 of the Indian Army (Amendment) Act, 1918 (11 of 1918).

Lower punishments

44. Where in respect of any offence under this Act there is specified a particular punishment or such less punishment as is in this Act mentioned, there may be awarded in respect of that offence instead of such particular punishment (but subject to the other provisions of this Act as to punishments and regard being had to the nature and degree of the offence) any one punishment lower in the above scale than the particular punishment.

Field punishment[18]

45. Where any person, subject to this Act and under the rank of warrant officer, on active service is guilty of any offence, it shall be lawful for a court-martial to award for that offence any such punishment, other than flogging as may be prescribed as a field punishment. Field punishment shall be of the character of personal restraint or of hard labour but shall not be of a nature to cause injury to life or limb.

Position of corporal punishment in scale

46. Field punishment [substituted for the term "corporal punishment"] shall, for the purpose of commutation, be deemed to stand in the scale of punishment next below dismissal.

Combination of punishments

47. A sentence of a court-martial may award, in addition to or without any one other punishment, any one or more of the punishments specified in clauses (d), (f), (gg) and (h) of section 43.

47A. Whenever an Indian commissioned officer is sentenced to transportation or imprisonment, the court shall by its sentence, sentence such officer to be cashiered.[19]

Solitary confinement

48. Whenever any person is sentenced to rigorous imprisonment, the court may, by its sentence, order that the offender shall be kept in solitary confinement for any portion or portions of the imprisonment to which he is sentenced, not exceeding three months in the whole, according to the following scale, that is to say,—

(a) A time not exceeding' one month if the term of imprisonment does not exceed six months;

(b) A time not exceeding two months if the term of imprisonment exceeds six months and does not exceed one year;

18 This section was substituted by s. 5 of the Indian Army (Amendment) Act, 1920 (37 of 1920). Section 45, dealing with "Corporal Punishment" before its substitution read as:

Corporal Punishment:

45. Where any person, subject to this Act and under the rank of warrant officer---

(a) On active service is guilty of any offence; or

(b) At any time is guilty of the offences specified in clause (d) of section 31; or

(c) At any time is guilty of a civil offence which would be punishable with whipping under the law of British India, and is triable by court-martial under this Act,

it shall be lawful for a court-martial to award for that offence corporal punishment not exceeding thirty lashes.]

19 Section 47A was added by s. 16 of the Indian Amy (Amendment) Act, 1934, (33 of 1934).

(c) A time not exceeding three months if the term of imprisonment exceeds one year.

Reduction of non-commissioned officers to ranks

49. A non-commissioned officer sentenced by court-martial to transportation, imprisonment, field punishment or dismissal from the service, shall be deemed to be reduced to the ranks.

Retention in the ranks of a person convicted on active service

49A. When any person on active service has been sentenced by court-martial to dismissal or to transportation or imprisonment, whether combined with dismissal or not, the prescribed officer may direct that such person may be retained to serve in the ranks, and where such person has been sentenced to transportation or imprisonment, such service shall be reckoned as part of his term of transportation or imprisonment.[20]

CHAPTER VII

PENAL DEDUCTIONS

Deductions from pay and allowances

50. The following penal deductions may be made from the pay and allowances of a person subject to this Act, that is to say,—

(a) All pay and allowances for every day of absence either on desertion or without leave, or as prisoner of war, and for every day of imprisonment awarded by a criminal court, a court-martial, or an officer exercising authority under Section 20 or of field punishment awarded by a court-martial or such officer;

(b) All pay and allowances for every day whilst he is in custody on a charge for an offence of which he is afterwards convicted by a criminal court or court-martial, or on a charge of absence without leave for which he is afterwards awarded imprisonment or field punishment by an officer exercising authority under section 20;

(c) All pay and allowances for every day on which he is in hospital on account of sickness certified by the medical officer attending on him to have been caused by an offence under this Act committed by him;

(cc) for every day on which he is in hospital on account of sickness certified by the medical officer attending on him to have been caused by his own misconduct or imprudence, such sum as may be specified by order of the Commander-in-Chief in India;[21]

(d) All pay and allowances ordered by a court-martial to be suspended or forfeited under section 43;

(e) Any sum ordered by a court-martial to be stopped under section 43;

20 This section was added by s. 13 of the Indian Amy (Amendment) Act, 1918, (11 of 1918).

21 This clause was inserted by s. 14 of the Indian Amy (Amendment) Act, 1918, (11 of 1918).

(f) Any sum required to make good such compensation for any expenses caused by him, or for any loss of or damage or destruction done by him to any arms, ammunition, equipment, clothing, instruments, regimental necessaries or military decoration, or to any buildings or property, as may be awarded by his commanding officer;

(g) Any sum required to pay a fine awarded by a criminal court, a court-martial exercising jurisdiction under section 41 or section 42, or an officer exercising authority under section 20 or section 21:

Provided that the total deductions from the pay and allowances of a person subject to this Act made under clauses (e) to (g), both inclusive, shall not (except in the case of a person sentenced to dismissal) exceed in any one month one-half of his pay and allowances for that month.

Explanation.—For the purposes of clauses (a) and (b)—

(i) Absence or custody for six consecutive hours or upwards, whether wholly in one day or partly in one day and partly in another, may be reckoned as absence or custody for a day;

(ii) Absence or custody for twelve consecutive hours or upwards may be reckoned as absence or custody for the whole of each day during any portion of which the person' was absent or in custody; and

(iii) Any absence or custody for less than a day may be reckoned as absence or custody for a day if such absence or custody prevented the absentee from fulfilling any military duty which was thereby thrown upon some other person.

Deductions from public money other than pay

51. Any sum authorized by this Act to be deducted from the pay and allowances of any person may, without prejudice to any other mode of recovering the same, be deducted from any public money due to him other than a pension.

Remission of deductions

52. Any deduction from pay and allowances authorized by this Act may be remitted in such manner and to such extent and by such authority as may from time to time be prescribed.

Provision for dependents of prisoners of war

52A. (1) In the case of all persons subject to this Act, being prisoners of war, whose pay and allowances have been forfeited under section 50, but in respect of whom a remission has been made under section 52, it shall be lawful, notwithstanding any provision in any enactment or any rule of law to the contrary, for proper provision to be made by the prescribed authorities out of such pay and allowances for any dependants of such persons, and any such remission shall in that case be deemed to apply only to the balance thereafter remaining of such pay and allowances.

(2) Any payments hitherto made to dependants by way of deductions from pay and allowances which, if this section had been in force, could have been validly made are hereby validated.[22]

CHAPTER VIII

COURTS-MARTIAL

Constitution and Dissolution of Courts-martial

Courts-martial and the kinds thereof

53. For the purposes of this Act there shall be four kinds of courts-martial, that is to say :—

(1) General courts-martial;

(2) District courts-martial;

(3) Summary general courts-martial; and

(4) Summary courts-martial.

Power to convene general courts-martial

54. A general court-martial may be convened by the Commander-in-Chief in India, or by any officer empowered in this behalf by warrant of the Commander-in-Chief in India.

Power to convene district courts-martial

55. A district court-martial may be convened by any officer having power to convene a general court-martial or by any officer empowered in this behalf by warrant of any such officer.

Contents of warrant issued under section 54 or section 55

56. A warrant issued under section 54 or section 55 may contain such restrictions, reservations or conditions as the officer issuing it may think fit.

Composition of general courts-martial

57. A general court-martial shall consist of not less than seven officers unless that number, due regard being had to the public service, is not available, in which case the court may consist of not less than five officers.

Composition of district courts-martial

58. A district court-martial shall consist of not less than three officers.

Convening order to state is larger number of officers is not available

59. Whenever a general court martial is ordered to be composed of smaller number of officers specified in section 57, the order convening the court shall state that the larger number of officers is

22 This section was inserted by s. 2 of the Indian Amy (Amendment) Act, 1917, (10 of 1917).

not, due regard being had to the public service, available, and such statement shall be conclusive evidence of the fact so stated.

Composition of general or district courts-martial

60. The officers composing a general or district court-martial shall, at the discretion of the convening officer, but subject to the provisions of section 61, either a British or [Indian][23] officers, but shall not be partly British and Partly [Indian] officers.

Claim to trial by British officers

62. (1) Any person subject to this Act who is under orders for trial by general or district court-martial may claim to be tried by British officers.

(2) In all other cases the right of making a claim shall, before the court is convened, be explained to the person under orders for trial by the commanding officer, or some officer deputed by him in this behalf, and, when such a claim is made, the court shall be constituted accordingly.

Convening of summary general courts-martial

62. The following authorities shall have power to convene a summary general court-martial namely-

(a) An officer empowered in this behalf by an order of the Governor General in Council or of the Commander-in-Chief in India;

(b) On active service, the officer commanding the forces in the field, or any officer empowered by him in this behalf;

(c) An officer commanding any detached portion of the His Majesty's troops upon active service when, in his opinion, it is not practicable, with due regard to discipline and the exigencies of the service, that an offence should be tried by an ordinary general court-martial.

Composition of summary general courts-martial

63. A summary general court-martial shall consist of not less than three officers.

Summary courts-martial

64. (1) A summary courts-martial may be held---

(a) By the commanding officer of any corps or department of His Majesty's Indian Forces, or of any detachment of those forces.

(b) By the commanding officer of any British corps or detachment to which details subject to this Act are attached.

23 The word "Native" was repealed by s. 26 and Schedule of the Indian Army (Amendment) Act, 1918 (11 of 1918).

(2) At every summary court-martial the officer holding the trial shall alone constitute the court, but the proceedings shall be attended throughout by two other officers who shall not, as such be, sworn or affirmed.

Dissolution of courts

65. (1) If a court-martial after the commencement of a trial is reduced below the smallest number of officers which it is by this Act required to consist, it shall be dissolved.

Provided that a general court-martial shall not be dissolved under the provision of this sub-section unless it is reduced below five officers.

(2) If, on account of illness of the accused before the finding, it is impossible to continue the trial, a court-martial shall be dissolved.

(3) Where a court-martial is dissolved under this section, the accused may be tried again.

Jurisdiction of Courts-martial

Prohibition of second trial

66. When any person subject to this Act has been acquitted or convicted of an offence by a court-martial or by a criminal court, or has been summarily dealt with for an offence under the sections 20 or section 22, he shall not be liable to be tried again for the same offence by a court-martial or dealt with summarily in respect of it under either the said sections.

Limitation of Trial

67. No trial by court-martial of any person subject to this Act for any offence (other than an offence of mutiny, desertion or fraudulent enrolment) shall be commenced after expiration of three years from the date of such offence, and no trial for such an offence of desertion (other than desertion on active service) of fraudulent enrolment shall be commenced if the person in question has, subsequently to the commission of offence, served continuously in an exemplary manner for not less than three years with any portion of His Majesty's regular forces.

Explanation---For the purpose of this section, 'mutiny' means any of the offences specified in clauses (a), (b) and (c) of section 27.[24]

Power of criminal court to require delivery of offender

70. (1) When a criminal court having jurisdiction is of opinion that proceedings ought to be instituted before itself in respect of any alleged offence, it may, by written notice, require the prescribed military authority at its option either to deliver over the offender to the nearest Magistrate to be proceeded against according to law, or to postpone proceedings pending a reference to the Governor General in Council.

24 This section, which was originally substituted by s. 2 and Sch. I of the Repealing and Amending Act, 1919 (18 of 1919), was substituted by s. 8 of the Indian Army (Amendment) Act, 1920 (37 of 1920).

(2) In every such case the said authority shall either deliver over the offender in compliance with the requisition, or shall forthwith refer the question as to the court before which the proceedings are to be instituted for the determination of the Governor General in Council, whose order upon such reference shall be final.

Trial by court-martial no bar to a subsequent trial by criminal court

71. (1) Notwithstanding anything contained in section 26 of the General Clauses Act, 1897, or in section 403 of the Code of criminal Procedure, 1898, a person convicted or acquitted by a court –martial may be afterwards tried by a criminal court for the same offence or on the same facts.

(2) If a person sentenced by a court-martial in pursuance of this Act to punishment for an offence is afterwards tried by a criminal court for the same offence or on the same facts, that court shall, in awarding punishment, have regard to the military punishment, he may already have undergone.

Powers of Courts-martial

Powers of general and summary general courts-martial

72. A general or summary general court-martial shall have power to try any person subject to this Act for any offence made punishable therein and to pass any sentence authorized by this Act.

Powers of district court-martial

73. A district court-martial shall have, power to try any person subject to this Act other than an officer for any offence made punishable therein, and to pass any sentence authorised by this Act other than a sentence of death, or transportation, or imprisonment for a term exceeding two years.

Powers of summary courts-martial

74. A summary court-martial may try any offence punishable under any of the provisions of this Act:

Provided that when there is no grave reason for immediate action and reference can without detriment to discipline be made to the officer empowered to convene a district court-martial or on active service a summary general court-martial for the trial of the alleged offender, an officer holding a summary court-martial shall not try without such reference any offence punishable under any of the following offence, namely:---

(a) An offence punishable under sections 25, 27, clauses (a), (b) or (c), 33, 41 or 42, or

(b) Any offence against the officer holding the court.

Persons triable by summary court martial

75. A summary court-martial may try any person subject to this Act and under the command of the officer holding the court, except an officer or warrant officer.

Sentences awardable by summary court martial

76. (1) A summary court-martial may pass any sentence which can be passed under this Act, except a sentence of death or transportation, or imprisonment for a term exceeding the one year.

(2)[25]

Procedure for trial by Court-martial

President

77. At every general, district or summary general court martial the senior member shall sit as the president.

Judge Advocate

78. Every general court-martial shall, and every district court-martial may, be attended by a judge advocate, who shall be either an officer belonging to the department of the Judge Advocate General in India, or, if no such officer is available, an officer appointed by the convening officer.

Superintending officer

79. A British officer of not less than four years' service, hereinafter called the superintending officer, shall be appointed to superintendent the proceedings of every court-martial composed of Indian officers which is not attended by a judge advocate.

Challenges

80. (1) At all trials by general, district or summary general court-martial, as soon as the court is assembled, the names of the president and members shall be read over to the accused, who shall thereupon be asked whether he objects to being tried by any officer sitting on the court.

(2) If the accused objects to any such officer, his objection, and also the reply thereto of the officer objected to, shall be heard and recorded, and the remaining officers of the court shall, in the absence of the challenged officer, decide on the objection.

(3) If the objection is allowed by one-half or more of the votes of the officers entitled to vote, the objection shall be allowed, and the member objected to shall retire, and his vacancy may be filled in the prescribed manner by another officer, subject to the same right of the accused to object.

(4) When no challenge is made, or when challenge has been made and disallowed, or the place of every officer successfully challenged has been filled by another officer to whom no objection is made or allowed, the court shall proceed with the trial.

25 This Sub-section was repealed by s. 4 of the Indian Army (Amendment) Act, 1917 (10 of 1917).

Voting of members

81. (1) Every decision of a court-martial shall be passed by an absolute majority of votes; and where there is an equality of votes, as to either the finding or the sentence, the decision shall be in favour of the accused.

(2) In matters, other than a challenge or the finding or sentence, the president shall have a casting vote.

Oaths of president and member

82. An oath or affirmation in the prescribed manner shall be administered to every member of every court-martial and to the judge advocate or superintending officer before the commencement of the trial.

Oaths of president and members

83. Every person giving evidence before a court-martial shall be examined on oath or affirmation, and shall be duly sworn or affirmed in the prescribed form.

Summoning witnesses and production of documents

84. (1) The convening officer, the presiding officer of a court, the judge advocate or the commanding officer of the accused person, may, by summons under his hand, require the attendance before the court, at a time and place to be mentioned in the summons, of any person either to give evidence or to produce any document or other thing.

(2) the case of a witness amenable to military authority, the summons shall be sent to the commanding officer of the corps, department or detachment to which he belongs, and such officer shall serve it upon him accordingly.

(3) In the case of any other witness, the summons shall be sent to the Magistrate within whose jurisdiction he may be or reside, and such Magistrate shall give effect to the summons as if the witness were required in the Court of such Magistrate.

(4) When a witness is required to produce any particular document or other thing in his possession or power, the summons shall describe it with convenient certainty.

(5) Nothing in this section shall deemed to affect the Indian Evidence Act, 1872, sections 123 and 124, or to apply to any letter, postcard, telegram or other document in the custody of the postal or telegraph authorities.

(6) If any document in such custody is, in the opinion of any District Magistrate, Chief Presidency Magistrate, High Court or Court of Session, wanted for the purpose of any court-martial, such Magistrate or Court may require the postal or telegraph authorities, as the case may be, to deliver such document to such person as such Magistrate or Court may direct.

(7) If any document in such custody is, in the opinion of any other Magistrate or of any Commissioner of Police or District Superintendent of Police, wanted for any such purpose,

he may require the postal or telegraph authorities, as the case may be, to cause search to be made for an to detain such document pending the orders of any such District Magistrate, Chief Presidency Magistrate or Court.

Commissions

85. (1) Whenever, in the course of a trial by court-martial, it appears to the court that the examination of a witness is necessary for the ends of justice, and that the attendance of such witness cannot be procured without an amount of delay, expense or inconvenience which, in the circumstances of the case, would be unreasonable, such court may address the Judge Advocate General in order that a commission to take the evidence of such witness may be issued.

(2) The Judge Advocate General may then, if he thinks necessary, issue commission to any District Magistrate or Magistrate of the first class, within local limits of whose jurisdiction such witness resides to take the evidence of such witness.

(3) When the witness resides in the territories of any prince or chief in India in which there is an officer representing the British Indian Government, the commission may be issued to such officer.

(4) The Magistrate or officer to whom the commission is issued, or if he is the District Magistrate, he or such Magistrate of the first class as he appoints in this behalf, shall proceed to the place where the witness is or shall summon the witness before him and shall take down his evidence in the same manner, and may for this purpose exercise the same powers, as in trials of warrant cases under the Code of Criminal Procedure, 1898.

(5) Where the commission is issued to such officer as is mentioned in sub-section (3), he may delegate his powers and duties under the commission to any other officer subordinate to him whose powers are not less than those of a Magistrate of the first class in British India.

(6) When the witness resides out of India, the commission may be issued to any British consular officer, British Magistrate or other British official competent to administer an oath or affirmation in the place where such witness resides.

(7) The prosecutor and the accused person in any case in which a commission is issued may respectively forward any interrogatories in writing which the court may think relevant to the issue, and the Magistrate or officer to whom the commission is issued shall examine the witness upon such interrogatories.

(8) The prosecutor and the accused person may appear before such Magistrate or officer by pleader or, except in the case of an accused person in custody, in person, and may examine cross-examine and re-examine (as the case may be) the said witness.

(9) After a commission issued under this section has been duly executed, it shall be returned, together with the deposition of the witness examined there-under to the Judge Advocate General.

(10) On receipt of a commission and deposition returned under sub-section (9) the Judge Advocate General shall forward the same to the Court at whose instance the commission was issued, or if such court has been dissolved, to any other court convened for the trial of the accused person; and the commission, the return thereto and the deposition shall be open to inspection by the prosecutor and the accused person, and may, subject to all just exceptions, be read in evidence in the case by either the prosecutor or the accused, and shall from part of the proceedings of the court.

(11) In every case in which a commission is issued under this section the trial may be adjourned for a specified time reasonably sufficient for the execution and return of the commission.

Explanation:---In this section, the expression "Judge Advocate General" means the Judge Advocate General in India, and includes a Deputy Judge Advocate General.

Conviction of one offence permissible on charge of another

86. (1) A person charged before a court-martial with desertion may be found guilty of attempting to desert or of being absent without leave.

(2) A person charged before a court-martial with attempting to desert may found guilty of being absent without leave.

(3) A person charged before a court-martial with any of the following offences specified in section 31, that is to say, theft, dishonest misappropriation or conversion to his own use of property entrusted to him, or dishonestly receiving or retaining property in respect of which any of the aforesaid offences has been committed knowing or having reasons to believe it to have been stolen or dishonestly misappropriated or converted, may be found guilty of any other offences with which he might have been charged.

(4) A person charged before a court-martial with an offence punishable under section 41 or section 42 may be found guilty of any other offence of which he might have been found guilty if the provisions of the Code of Criminal Procedure, 1898, were applicable.

(5) A person charged before a court-martial with any other offence under this Act may, on failure of proof of an offence having been committed in circumstances involving in more severe punishment, be found guilty of the same offence as having been committed in circumstances involving a less severe punishment.

(6) A person charged before a court-martial with any offence under this Act may be found guilty of having attempted to commit or of abetment of that offence, although the attempt or abetment is not separately charged.

Majority requisite to sentence of death

87. No sentence of death shall be passed by any court-martial without concurrence of two-third at the least of the members of the court.

Evidence before Courts-martial

General rule as to evidence

88. The Indian evidence Act, 1872 (I of 1872), shall, subject to the provisions of this Act, apply to all proceedings before a court-martial.

Judicial Notice

89. A court-martial may take judicial notice of any matter within the general military knowledge of the members.

Presumption as to signatures

90. In any proceeding under this Act, any application, certificate, warrant, reply or other document purporting to be signed by an officer in the service in the civil or military service of the Government shall, on production, be presumed to have been duly signed by the person and in the character by whom and in which it purports to have been signed, until the contrary is shown.

Enrolment paper

91. Any enrolment paper purporting to be signed by an enrolling officer shall, in proceedings under this Act, be evidence of the person enrolled having given the answers to questions which he is therein represented as having given. The enrolment of such person may be proved by the production of a copy of his enrolment paper purporting to be certified to be a true copy by the officer having the custody of the enrolment paper.

Presumption as to certain documents

91A. (1) A letter, return or other document respecting the service of any person in, or the dismissal or discharge of any person from, any portion of His Majesty's Forces, or respecting the circumstances of any person not having served in, or belonged to, any portion of His Majesty's Forces, if purporting to be signed by or on behalf of the Governor General in Council or the Commander-in-Chief in India or by any prescribed officer, shall be evidence of the facts stated in such letter, return or other document.

(2) An Army List or Gazette purporting to be published by authority shall be evidence of the status and rank of the officers or warrant officers there in mentioned, and of any appointment held by such officers or warrant officers and of the corps, battalion or arm or branch of the services to which such officers or warrant officers belongs.

(3) Where a record is made in any regimental book, in pursuance of this Act or of any rules made there under or otherwise in pursuance of military duty, and purports to be signed by the commanding officer or by the officer whose duty it is to make such record, such record shall be evidence of the facts therein stated.

(4) A copy of any record in any regimental book purporting to be certified to be a true copy by the officer having custody of such book shall be evidence of such record.

(5) Where any person subject to this Act is being tried on a charge of desertion or of absence without leave, and such person has surrendered himself into the custody of, or has been apprehended by, a provost-marshal, assistant provost-marshal or other officer, or any portion of His Majesty's Forces, a certificate purporting to be signed by such provost-marshal, assistant provost-marshal or other officer, or by the commanding officer of that portion of His Majesty's Forces and stating the fact, date and place of such surrender or apprehension, shall be evidence of the matters so stated.

(6) Where any person subject to this Act is being tried on a charge of desertion or of absence without leave, and such person has surrendered himself into the custody of, or has been apprehended by, a police officer not below the rank of an officer in charge of a police station, a certificate purporting to be signed by such police-officer and stating the fact, date and place of such surrender or apprehension, shall be evidence of the matters so stated.[26]

(7) Any document purporting to be a report under the hand of any Chemical Examiner to Government upon any matter or thing duly submitted to him for examination or analysis and report may be used as evidence in any proceeding under this Act.[27]

Reference by accused to Government officer

92. (1) If at any trial for desertion or absence without leave, overstaying leave or not rejoining when warned for service, the person tried states in his defence any sufficient or reasonable excuse for his unauthorized absence, and refers in support thereof to any officer in the civil or military service of the Government, or if it appears that any such officer is likely to prove or disprove the said statement in the defence, the court shall address such officer and adjourn the proceedings until his reply is received.

(2) The written reply of any officer so referred to shall, if signed by him, be received in evidence and have the same effect as if made on oath before the court.

(3) If the court a dissolved before the receipt of such reply, or if the court omits to comply with the provisions of this section, the convening officer may, at his discretion annul the proceedings and order a fresh trial by the same or another court-martial.

Evidence of previous convictions and general character

93. (1) When any person subject to this Act has been convicted by a court-martial of any offence, such court-martial may inquire into, and receive and record evidence of any previous convictions of such person either by a court-martial or by a criminal court, or may further inquire into and record the general character of such person, and such other matters as may be prescribed.

(2) Evidence received under this section may be either oral, or in the shape of entries in, or certified extracts from, court-martial books or other official records; and it shall not be

26 This Section: (1) to (6) was inserted by s. 18 of the Indian Army (Amendment) Act, 1918 (11 of 1918).

27 This Sub-section was added by s. 3 of the Indian Army (Amendment) Act, 1923 (33 of 1933).

necessary to give notice before trial to the person tried that evidence as to his previous convictions or character will be received.

(3) At a summary court-martial the officer holding the trial may, if he thinks fit, record any previous convictions against the offender, his general character, and such other matters as may be prescribed, as of his own knowledge, instead of requiring them to be proved under the foregoing provisions of this section.

Confirmation and Revision of Findings and Sentences

Finding and sentence invalid without confirmation

94. No finding or sentence of a general or district court-martial shall be valid except so far as it may be confirmed as provided by this Act.

Power to confirm finding and sentence of general court-martial

95. The findings and sentences of general courts-martial may be confirmed by the Commander-in-Chief in India, or by any officer empowered in this behalf by warrant of the Commander-in-Chief in India.

Power to confirm finding and sentence of district court-martial

96. The findings and sentences of district courts-martial may be confirmed by any officer having power to convene a general court-martial, or by any officer empowered in this behalf by warrant of any such officer.

Contents of warrant issued under section 95 or 96

97. A warrant issued under section 95 or section 96 may contain such restrictions, reservations or conditions as the officer issuing it may think fit.

Confirmation of finding and sentence

98. (1) The finding and sentence of a summary general court-martial shall require to be confirmed by the convening officer or if the convening officer so directs, by an authority superior to the convening officer—

(a) In the case of the trial of an officer,

(b) In the case of an acquittal or a sentence of death or transportation or imprisonment for a term exceeding two years, and

(c) In any other case if so ordered by the convening officer.

(2) Save as provided in sub-section (1), a sentence passed by a summary general court-martial shall not require to be confirmed, but may be carried out forthwith

Power of confirming officer to mitigate, remit or commute sentences

99. Subject to such restrictions as may be contained in any warrant issued under section 95 or section 96, a confirming officer may, when confirming the sentence of a court-martial, mitigate or remit the punishment thereby awarded, or commute that punishment for any less punishment or punishments to which the offender might have been sentenced by the court-martial:

Provided that a sentence of transportation shall not be commuted for a sentence of imprisonment for a term exceeding the term of transportation awarded by the court.

Confirmation of finding and sentence on board ship

99A. When any person subject to this Act is tried and sentenced by court-martial while on board ship, the finding and sentence so far as not confirmed and executed on board ship may be confirmed and executed in like manner as if such person had been tried at the port of disembarkation.[28]

Revision of finding or sentence

100. (1) Any finding or sentence of a court-martial which requires confirmation may be once revised by order of the confirming authority; and on such revision, the court, if so directed by him, may take additional evidence.

(2) The court, on revision, shall consist of the same officers as were present when the original decision was passed, unless any of those officers are unavoidably absent.

(3) In case of such unavoidable absence the cause thereof shall be duly certified in the proceedings, and the court shall proceed with the revision, provided that, if a general court-martial, it still consists of five officers, or, if a district court-martial, of three officers.

Finding and sentence of a summary court-martial

101. The finding and sentence of a summary court-martial shall not require to be confirmed, but may be carried out forthwith.

Provided that, if the officer holding the trial is of less than five years' service, he shall not, except on active service, carry into effect any sentence until it has received the approval of an officer commanding not less than a corps.

Transmission of proceedings of summary court-martial

102. The proceedings of every summary court-martial shall without delay be forwarded to the officer commanding the division or brigade within which the trial was held, or to the prescribed officer; and such officer, or the Commander-in-Chief in India, or the officer commanding the army, or army corps, in which the trial was held, may, for reasons based on the merits of the case, but not any merely technical grounds, set aside the proceedings or reduce the sentence to any other sentence which the court might have passed.

28 This section was inserted by s. 20 of the Indian Army (Amendment) Act, 1918 (11 of 1918).

Substitution of valid for invalid sentence

103. Where a sentence passed by a court-martial which has been confirmed, or which does not require confirmation, is found for any reason to be invalid, the authority who would have had power under section 112 to commute the punishment awarded by the sentence if it had been valid may pass a valid sentence:

Provided that the punishment awarded by a sentence so passed shall not be higher in the scale of punishments than, or in excess of, the punishment awarded by invalid sentence.

Provision in the case of accused being lunatic[29]

103A. (1) Whenever, in the course of a trial by court-martial, it appears to the Court that the person charged is of unsound mind and consequently incapable of making his defence, or that such person committed the act alleged but was by reason, of unsoundness of mind incapable of knowing the nature of the act or that it was wrong or contrary to law, the Court shall record a finding accordingly, and the President of the Court or the officer holding the trial, as the case may be, shall forthwith report the case to the confirming officer, or, in the case of a court-martial whose finding does not require confirmation, to the prescribed officer.

(2) A confirming officer to whom a case is reported under sub-section (1) may, if he does not confirm the finding, take steps to have the accused person tried by the same or another court-martial for the offence with which he was originally charged.

(3) A prescribed officer to whom a case is reported under sub-section (1) and a confirming officer confirming a finding in any case so reported to him shall order the accused person to be kept in custody in the prescribed manner, and shall report the case for the orders of the Governor General in Council.

(4) On receipt of a report under sub-section (3), the Governor General in Council may order the accused person to be detained in a lunatic asylum or other suitable place of safe custody.

(5) Where an accused person, having been found by reason of unsoundness of mind to be incapable of making his defence, is in custody or under detention, the prescribed officer may—

(a) If such person is in custody under sub-section (3), on the report of a medical officer that he is capable of making his defence, or

(b) If such person is detained under-sub-section (4), on a certificate such as is referred to in section 473 of the Code of Criminal Procedure, 1898,

take steps to have such person tried by the same or another court-martial, for the offence with which he was originally charged or, provided that the offence is a civil offence, by a Criminal Court.

29 This section was inserted by s. 4 of the Indian Army (Amendment) Act, 1923 (33 of 1923).

(6) A copy of every order made by the prescribed officer under sub-section (5) shall forthwith be sent for the Governor General in Council.

CHAPTER IX

EXECUTION OF SENTENCES

Form of sentence of death

104. In awarding a sentence of death a court-martial shall, in its discretion, direct that the offender shall suffer death by being hanged by the neck until he be dead, or shall suffer death by being shot to death.

Imprisonment to be in military custody

105. Whenever any person is sentenced, under this Act to simple imprisonment, such sentence shall be carried out by confinement in military custody.

Commencement of sentence of transportation or imprisonment

106. Whenever any person is sentenced under this Act to transportation or imprisonment, the term of his sentence shall, whether it has or not, be reckoned to commence on the day on which the original proceedings were signed by the president or, in the case of a summary court-martial, by the court.

Execution of sentence of transportation or imprisonment

107. Whenever any sentence of transportation or rigorous imprisonment is passed under this Act, or whenever any sentence so passed is commuted to transportation or to rigorous imprisonment, the commanding officer of the person under sentence, or such other officer as may be prescribed, shall forward a warrant in the prescribed form to the officer in charge of the civil prison in which such person is to be confined, and shall forward him to such prison with the warrant:

Provided that, in the case of a sentence of rigorous imprisonment for a period not exceeding three months, the confirming officer, or in the case of a sentence which does not require confirmation, the court, may direct that the sentence shall be carried out by confinement in military custody:

[Provided further that on active service a sentence of rigorous imprisonment may be carried out by confinement in such place as the officer commanding the forces in the field may, from time to time, appoint.][30]

Execution of sentence of imprisonment in special cases

108. Whenever, in the opinion of an officer commanding an army, army corps, division or independent brigade, any sentence or portion of a sentence of imprisonment cannot, for special reasons, conveniently be carried out in accordance with the provisions of section 106 or section

30 This proviso was added by s. 21 of the Indian Army (Amendment) Act, 1918 (11 of 1918).

107, such officer may direct that such sentence or portion of sentence shall be carried out by confinement in any civil prison or other fit place.

Offenders sentenced to transportation how dealt with until transportation

108A. In every, case in which a sentence of transportation is passed under this Act, the offender, until he is transported, shall be dealt with in the same manner as if sentenced to rigorous imprisonment, and shall be deemed to have been undergoing his sienten.cei of transportation during the term of his imprisonment.[31]

Communication of certain orders to civil prison officers

109. Whenever an order is duly made under this Act setting aside or varying any sentence, order or warrant under which any person is confined in a civil prison, a warrant in accordance with such order shall be forwarded by the prescribed officer to the officer in charge of the prison in which such person is confined.

Limits of solitary confinement

110. In executing a sentence of solitary confinement such confinement shall in no case exceed fourteen days at a time, with intervals between the periods of solitary confinement of not less duration than such periods, and, when the imprisonment awarded exceeds three months, the solitary confinement shall not exceed seven days in any one month of the whole imprisonment awarded, with intervals between the periods of solitary confinement of not less duration than such periods.

Instrument of corporal punishment

111. Whenever any person is sentenced under this Act by court martial to corporal punishment, such punishment shall be inflicted on bare back with the regulation cat. [32]

Execution of sentence of fine

111A. When a sentence of fine is imposed by a court-martial under section 41 or section 42, whether the trial was held within British India or not, a copy of such, sentence, signed and certified by the president of the court or the officer holding the trial, as the case may be, may be sent to any Magistrate in British India, and such Magistrate shall thereupon cause the fine to be recovered in accordance with the provisions of the Code of Criminal Procedure, 1898, for the levy of fines as if it was a sentence of fine imposed by such Magistrate.[33]

31 This section was inserted by s. 22 of the Indian Army (Amendment) Act, 1918 (11 of 1918).

32 Instrument of corporal punishment was repealed by the Indian Army (Amendment) Act, 1920 (37 of 1920).

33 This section was inserted by s. 23 of the Indian Army (Amendment) Act, 1918 (11 of 1918).

CHAPTER X

PARDONS AND REMISSIONS

Pardons and remissions

112. (1) When any person subject to this Act has been convicted by a court-martial of any offence, the Governor General in Council or the Commander-in-Chief in India or, in the case of a sentence which he could have confirmed or which did not require confirmation, the officer commanding the army, army corps, division or independent brigade in which such person at the time of his conviction was serving, or the prescribed officer may,

(a) Either without conditions or upon any conditions which the person sentenced accepts, pardon the person or remit the whole or any part of the punishment awarded; or

(b) Mitigate the punishment awarded, or commute such punishment for any less punishment or punishments mentioned in this Act;

Provided that a sentence of transportation shall not be commuted for a sentence of imprisonment for a term exceeding the term of transportation awarded by the court.

(2) If any condition on which a person has been pardoned or a punishment has been remitted is, in the opinion of the authority which granted the pardon or remitted the punishment, not fulfilled, such authority may cancel the pardon or remission, and thereupon the sentence of the court shall be carried into effect as if such pardon had not been granted or such punishment had not been remitted;

Provided that, in the case of a person sentenced to transportation or imprisonment, such person shall undergo only the unexpired portion of his sentence.

(3) When under the provisions of section 49 a non-commissioned officer is deemed to be reduced to the ranks, such reduction shall, for the purposes of this section, be treated as a punishment awarded by sentence of a court-martial.[34]

CHAPTER XI

RULES

Power to make rules

113. (1) The Governor General in Council may make rules for the purpose of carrying into effect the provisions of this Act.

(2) In particular, and without prejudice, to the generality of the foregoing power, such rules may provide for—

34 This section was inserted by s. 24 of the Indian Army (Amendment) Act, 1918 (11 of 1918).

(a) The discharge from the service of persons subject to this Act;

(b) The amount and incidence of fines to be imposed under section 21;

(bb) The specification of the punishments which may be awarded as field punishments under sections 20 and 45;

(c) The assembly and procedure of courts of inquiry, and the administration of oaths or affirmations by such courts;

(d) The convening anti constituting of courts-martial;

(e) The adjournment, dissolution .and sittings of courts-martial;

(f) The procedure to be observed in trials by courts-martial;

(g) The confirmation and revision of the findings and sentences of courts-martial;

(h) The carrying into effect sentences of courts-martial;

(i) The forms of orders to be made under the provisions of this Act relating to courts-martial, transportation or imprisonment; and

(ii) The constitution of authorities to decide for what persons, to what amounts and in what manner, provision should be made for dependants under section 52A, and the due carrying out of such decisions;

(j) Any matter in this Act directed to be prescribed.

(3) All rules made under this Act shall be published in the Gazette of India, and, on such publication, shall have effect as if enacted in this Act.

CHAPTER XII

PROPERTY OF DECEASED PERSONS, DESERTERS AND LUNATICS

Property of deceased persons and deserters

114. The following rules are enacted respecting the disposal of the property of every person subject to this Act who dies or deserts:—

(1) The commanding officer of the corps, detachment or department to which the deceased person or deserter belonged shall secure all the moveable property belonging to the deceased or deserter that, is in camp or quarters, and cause an inventory thereof to be made, and draw any pay and allowances due to such person.

(2) In the case of a deceased person who has left in a Government savings bank (including any post office savings bank, however named) a deposit not exceeding one thousand rupees, the commanding officer may, if he thinks fit, require the secretary or other proper officer of the bank to pay the deposit to him forthwith, notwithstanding anything in any departmental

rules, and after the payment thereof in accordance with such requisition, no person shall have any right in respect of the deposit except as hereinafter provided.

(3) In the case of a deceased person whose representative is on the spot and has given security for the payment of the regimental or other debts in camp or quarters (if any) of the deceased, the commanding officer shall deliver over any property received under clauses (2) and (3) to that representative.

(4) In the case of a deceased person whose estate is not dealt with, under clause (3), and in the case of any deserter, the commanding officer shall cause the moveable property to be sold by public auction, and shall pay the regimental and other debts in camp or quarters (if any), and, in the case of a deceased person, the expenses of his funeral ceremonies, from the proceeds of the sale and from any pay and allowances drawn under clause (1) and from the amount of the deposit (if any) received under clause (2).[35]

(5) The surplus, if any, shall, in the case of a deceased person, be paid to his representative (if any), or in the event of no claim to such surplus being established within twelve months after the death, then the same shall be remitted to the prescribed person.

(6) In the case of a deserter, the surplus (if any) shall be forthwith remitted to the prescribed person and shall, on the expiry of three years from the date of his desertion, be forfeited to His Majesty, unless the deserter shall in the meantime have surrendered or been apprehended.

Explanation.—A person shall be deemed to be a deserter within the meaning of this section who has without authority been absent from duty for a period of sixty days and has not subsequently surrendered or been apprehended.]

Disposal of certain property without production of probate, etc

115. Property deliverable and money payable to the representative of a deceased person under section 114 may, if the total value or amount thereof does not exceed one thousand rupees, and if the prescribed person thinks fit, be delivered or paid to any person appearing to him be entitled to receive it or to administer the estate of the deceased, without requiring the production of any probate, letters of administration, certificate or other such conclusive evidence of title; and such delivery or payment shall be a full discharge to those ordering or making the same and to the Secretary of State for India in Council from all further liability in respect of the property or money; but nothing in this section shall affect the rights of any executor or administrator or other representative, or of any creditor, of a deceased person against any person to whom such delivery or payment has been made.

Application of section 114 to lunatics

116. The provisions of section 114 shall, so far as they can be made applicable, apply in the case of a person subject to this Act becoming insane, or, who, being on active service, is officially reported missing;

35 This section was substituted by s. 2 of the Indian Army (Amendment) Act, 1914 (15 of 1914).

Provided that, in the case of a person so reported missing, no action shall be taken under sub-sections (2) to (5), inclusive, of the said section, until one year has elapsed from the date of such report.

CHAPTER XIII

MISCELLANEOUS

Military Privileges

Complaints against officers

117. (1) Any person subject to this Act who deems himself wronged by any superior or other officer, may, if not attached to a troop or company, complain to the officer under whose command or orders he is serving; and may if attached to a troop or company, complain to the officer commanding the same.

(2) When the officer complained against is the officer to whom any, complaint, should, under sub-section (1), be preferred, the aggrieved person may complain to such officer's next superior officer,

(3) Every officer receiving any such complaint shall examine into it, and, when necessary, refer it to superior authority.

(4) Every such complaint shall be preferred through such channels as may be from time to lime specified by proper authority.

Privileges of persons attending courts-martial

118. (1) No president or member of a court-martial, no judge advocate or superintending officer, no party to any proceeding before a court-martial, or his legal practitioner or agent, and no witness acting in obedience to a summons to attend a court-martial, shall, while proceeding to, attending on or returning from a court-martial, be liable to arrest under civil or revenue process.

(2) If any such person is arrested under any such process, he may be discharged by order of the court-martial.

Exemption from arrest for debts

119. (1) No person subject to this Act shall, so long as he belongs to His Majesty's Indian Forces, be liable to be arrested for debt under any process issued by, or by the authority of, any civil or revenue court or revenue officer.

(2) The judge of any such court may examine into any complaint made by such person or his superior officer of the arrest of such person contrary to the provisions of this section, and may, by warrant under his hand, discharge the person, and award reasonable costs to the

complainant, who may recover those costs in like manner as he might have recovered costs awarded to him by a decree against the person obtaining the process.

(3) For the recovery of such costs no fee shall be payable to the court by the complainant.

Property exempted from attachment

120. Neither the arms, clothes, equipment, accoutrements or necessaries of any person subject to this Act, nor any animal used by him for the discharge of his duty, shall be seized, nor shall the pay and allowances of any such person or any part thereof be attached, by direction of any civil or revenue court or any revenue officer, in satisfaction of any decree or order enforceable against him.

Application of the last two foregoing sections to reservists

121. Every person belonging to the Indian Reserve Forces shall, when called out for or engaged upon or returning from training or service, be entitled to all the privileges accorded by sections 119 and 120 to a person subject to this Act.

Priority in hearing by courts of cases in which India officers and soldiers are concerned

122. (1) On the representation to any court by or on behalf of any person subject to this Act of a certificate, from the proper military authority, of leave of absence having been granted to or applied for which by him for the purpose of prosecuting or defending any suit or other and proceeding in such court, the court shall, on the application of such person, arrange, so far as may be possible, for the hearing and final disposal of such suit or other proceeding within the period of the leave so granted or applied for.

(2) The certificate from the proper military authority shall state the first and last day of the leave or intended leave, and set forth a description of the case with respect to which the leave was granted or applied for.

(3) No fee shall be payable to the court in respect of the presentation of any such certificate, or in respect of any application by or on behalf of any such person for priority for the hearing of his case.

(4) Where the court is unable to arrange for the hearing and final disposal of the suit or other proceeding within the period of such leave or intended leave as aforesaid, it shall record its reasons for having been unable to do so, and shall cause a copy thereof to be furnished to such person on his application without any payment whatever by him in respect either of the application for such copy or of the copy itself.

(5) If in any case a question arises as to the proper military authority qualified to grant such certificate as aforesaid, such question shall be at once referred by the court to an officer commanding a corps, whose decision shall be final.

Deserters and Military Offenders

Capture of deserters

123. (1) Whenever any person subject to this Act deserts, the commanding officer of the corps, department or detachment to which he belongs shall give written information of the desertion to such civil authorities as, in his opinion, may be able to afford assistance towards the capture of the deserter; and such authorities shall thereupon take steps for the apprehension of the said deserter in like manner as if he, were a person for whose apprehension a warrant had been issued by a Magistrate, and shall deliver the deserter, when apprehended, to military custody.

(2) Any police officer may arrest without warrant any person reasonably believed to be subject to this Act and to be travelling without authority, and shall bring him without delay before the nearest Magistrate, to be dealt with according to law.

Arrest by military authorities

124. (1) Any person subject to this Act who is charged with an offence may be taken into military custody.

(2) Any such person may be ordered into military custody by any superior officer,

(3) The charge against every person taken into military custody shall, without unnecessary delay, be investigated by the proper military authority, and, as soon as may be, either proceedings shall be taken for punishing the offence, or such person shall be discharged from custody.

Arrest by civil authorities

125. Whenever any person subject to this Act, who is accused of any offence under this Act, is within the jurisdiction of any Magistrate or police-officer, such Magistrate or officer shall aid in the apprehension and delivery to military custody of such person upon receipt of a written application to that effect signed by his commanding officer.

Inquiry on absence of persons subject to Act

126. (1) When any person subject to this Act has been absent without due authority from his duty for a period of sixty days, a court of inquiry shall, as soon as practicable, be assembled and upon oath or affirmation administered in the prescribed manner, shall inquire respecting the absence of the person, and the deficiency, if any, of property, of the Government entrusted to his care, or of his arms, ammunition, equipments, instruments, clothing or necessaries; and, if satisfied of the fact of such absence without due authority or other sufficient cause, the court shall declare such absence and the period thereof, and the said deficiency, if any; and the commanding officer of the corps or department to which the person belongs shall enter in the court-martial book of the corps or department a record of the declaration.

(2) If the person declared absent does not afterwards surrender, or is not apprehended, he shall, for the purposes of this Act, be deemed to be a deserter.

Disposal of Property

Order for custody and disposal of property pending trial in certain cases

126A. When any property regarding which any offence appears to have been committed, or which appears to have been used for the commission of any offence, is produced before a court-martial during a trial, the court may make such order as it thinks fit for the proper custody; of such property pending the conclusion of the trial, and if the property is subject to speedy or natural decay may, after recording such evidence as it thinks necessary, order it to be sold or otherwise disposed of.

Order for disposal of property regarding which offence committed

126B. (1) After the conclusion of a trial before any court-martial, the court or the officer confirming the finding or sentence of such court-martial or any authority superior to such officer, or, in the case of court-martial whose finding or sentence does not require confirmation, the officer commanding the army, army corps, division or brigade within which the trial was held, may make such order as it or he thinks fit for the disposal by destruction, confiscation, delivery to any person claiming to be entitled to possession thereof, or otherwise, of any property or document produced before the court or in its custody, or regarding which any offence appeal's to have been committed or which has been used for the commission of any offence.

(2) Where any order has been made under sub-section (1) in respect of property regarding which an offence appears to have been committed, a copy of such order signed and certified by the authority making the same may, whether the trial was held within British India or not, be sent to a Magistrate in any presidency-town or district in which such property for the time being is, and such Magistrate shall thereupon cause the order to be carried into effect as if it was an order passed by such Magistrate under the provisions of the Code of Criminal Procedure [V of 1898], 1898.

Explanation.—In this section the term "property" includes, in the case of property regarding which an offence appears to have been committed, not only such property as has been originally in the possession or under the control of any party, but also any property into or for which the same may have been converted or exchanged, and anything acquired by such conversion or exchange whether immediately, or otherwise.

Repeal

127. [Repeal.] Repealed by s. 2 and Schedule of the Replacing Act 1927 (12 of 1927).

ACT No. II of 1920

[PASSED BY THE INDIAN LEGISLATIVE COUNCIL]

(Received the assent of the Governor General on the 11th February, 1920)

An Act further to amend the Indian Army Act, 1911

WHEREAS it is expedient further to amend the Indian Army Act, 1911; It is hereby enacted as follows:-

Short title

1. This Act may be called the Indian Army (Amendment) Act, 1920.

Amendment of section 116 of Act V of 1911

2. In section 116 of the Indian Army Act, 1911, after the words "becoming insane" the following shall be added, namely:-

> "or, who, being on active service, is officially reported missing:
>
> Provided that, in the case of a person reported missing, no action shall be taken under sub-sections (2) to (6), inclusive, of the said section, until one year has lapsed from the date of such report."

INDIAN ARMY (AMENDMENT) ACT
ACT No. XXXVII of 1920

[PASSED BY THE INDIAN LEGISLATIVE COUNCIL]

(Received the assent of the Governor General on the 9th September, 1920)

An Act further to amend the Indian Army Act, 1911

WHEREAS it is expedient further to amend the Indian Army Ad, 1911; It is hereby enacted as follows: -

Short title

1. This Act may be called the Indian Army (Amendment) Act, 1920.

Amendment of section 20 of Act VIII of 1911

2. In sub-section (2) of section 20 of the Indian Army Act, 1911 (hereinafter referred to as the said Act),--

(1) for the words "Imprisonment in military custody may be specified as such a minor punishment" the words "Imprisonment in military custody and, in the case of persons subject to this Act on active service, any prescribed field punishment may be specified as minor punishments" shall be substituted; and

(2) In clause (a) after the word "imprisonment" the words "or field punishment" shall be inserted.

Amendment of section 24 of Act VIII of 1911

3. In section 24 of the said Act,--

(1) To sub-section (1) the words "He may at any time arrest and detain for trial any person subject to this Act who commits an offence and may also carry into effect any punishments to be inflicted in pursuance of the sentence of a court-martial" shall he added; and

(2) For sub-sections (2) and (3), the following subsection shall be substituted, namely:-

"(2) A provost-marshal may punish with any punishment mentioned in section 22, sub-section (1) clause (b) any follower who is subject to this Act under section 2, sub-section (1), clause (c) and is a menial servant and who on active service and in his view, or in the view of any of his assistants, commits any breach of good order and military discipline."

Amendment of section 41 of Act VIII of 1911

4. In section 41 of the said Act,--

(1) In clause (a) after the word "punishment," and

(2) In clause (b) after the word "punishment," where it first occurs, the words "other than whipping" shall be inserted.

Substitution of new section for section 45 of Act VIII of 1911

5. For section 45 of the said Act the following section shall be substituted, namely:-

"Field Punishment

45. Where any person, subject to this Act and under the rank of warrant officer, on active service is guilty of any offence, it shall be lawful for a court-martial to award for that offence any such punishment, other than flogging as may be prescribed as a field punishment. Field punishment shall be of the character of personal restraint or of hard labour but shall not be of a nature to cause injury to life or limb."

Amendment of section 46 and 49 of Act VIII of 1911

6. In sections 46 and 49 of the said Act, for the words "corporal punishment" the words "field punishment" shall be substituted.

Amendment of section 50 of Act VIII of 1911

7. In section 50 of the said Act-

(1) To clause (a) the words "or of field punishment awarded by a court-martial or such officer" shall be added; and

(2) In clause (b) after the word "imprisonment", the words "or field punishment" shall be inserted.

Substitution of new section for section 67 of Act VIII of 1911

8. For section 67 of the said Act the following section shall be substituted, namely:-

"67. No trial by court-martial of any person subject to this Act for any offence (other than an offence of mutiny, desertion or fraudulent enrolment) shall be commenced after the expiration of three years from the date of such offence, and no such trial for an offence of desertion (other than desertion on active service) or of fraudulent enrolment shall be commenced if the person in question has, subsequently to the commission of the offence, served continuously in an exemplary manner for not less than three years with any portion of His Majesty's regular forces.

Explanations:--For the purpose of this section, 'mutiny' means any of the offences specified in clauses (a), (b) and (c) of section 27."

Amendment of section 113 of Act VIII of 1911

9. After clause (b) of sub-section (2) of section of the said Act the following clause shall be inserted, namely:-

"(bb) the specification of the punishments which may be awarded as field punishments under sections 20 and 45."

Repeal of section 111 of Act VIII of 1911

10. Section 111 of the said Act is hereby repealed.

ACT No. XXXIII OF 1934

[PASSED BY THE INDIAN LEGISLATURE]

(Received the assent of the Governor General on the 8th September 1934)

An Act further to amend the Indian Army Act, 1911, for certain purposes

WHEREAS it is expedient further to amend the Indian Army Act, 1911, for the purposes hereinafter appearing; It is hereby enacted as follows:-

1. This Act may be called the Indian Army (Amendment) Act, 1934.

2. In the preamble to the Indian Army Act, 1911 (hereinafter referred to as the said Act), for the words "Indian officers" the words "Indian commissioned officers, Viceroy's commissioned of officers" shall be substituted.

3. In section 2 of the said Act;---

(a) In clause (a) of sub-section (1), for the words "Indian officers" the words "Indian commissioned officers, Viceroy's commissioned officers" shall be substituted; and

(b) In sub-section *(2),* for the words "discharged or dismissed" the words "retired, discharged, cashiered, removed or dismissed from the service" shall be substituted.

4. In sub-section (1) of section **3** of the said Act, for the words "Indian officers" the words "Indian commissioned officers, Viceroy's commissioned officers" shall be substituted.

5. In section **7** of the said Act,--

(a) For clause (1) the following clause shall be substituted, namely:-

"(1) 'British officer' means a person holding His Majesty's commission in His Majesty's Land Forces or in the Royal Marines or in the Territorial Army, and includes, in relation to a person subject, to this Act when serving under such conditions as may be prescribed, a person holding a commission in His Majesty's Naval Forces or Royal Air Force."

(b) For clause (2) the following clauses shall be substituted, namely:-

"(2) Indian commissioned officer' means a person commissioned, gazetted or in pay as an officer holding His Majesty's commission in the Indian Land Forces, and includes, in relation to a person subject to this Act when serving under such conditions as may be prescribed, a person holding a commission in the Indian Air Force;

(2A) 'Viceroy's commissioned officer' means a person commissioned, gazetted or in pay as a Viceroy's commissioned officer in the Indian Army;"

(c) For clause (5) the following clause shall be substituted, namely:-

"(5) 'officer' means an officer of any of His Majesty's Military Forces, and includes, in relation to a person subject to this Act when serving under such conditions as may be prescribed, an officer of any of His Majesty's Naval or Air Forces, but does not include a warrant officer, petty officer or non-commissioned officer;"

(d) In clause (6), after the words "British officer" the words "or Indian commissioned officer" shall be inserted;

(e) In clause (7), for the words "a warrant officer or non-commissioned officer subject to the Army Act or the Air Force Act" the words "an officer, warrant officer, petty officer or non-commissioned officer of any of His Majesty's Naval, Military or Air Forces" shall be substituted;

(f) To clause (8) the words "His Majesty's Indian Forces" shall be added; and

(g) In clause (14), after the word "service" the word; "and includes air force custody" shall be inserted.

6. In section 10 of the raid Act, after the words "military pay" the words "as an enrolled person" shall be inserted.

7. Section 13 of the said Act shall be re-numbered as sub-section (1) of section 13, and in that section as so re-numbered,-

(a) The words "or the Commander-in-Chief in India" shall be omitted, and

(b) The following sub-section shall be added, namely:-

"(2) The Commander-in-Chief in India may dismiss from the service any person subject to this Act other than an Indian commissioned officer."

8. In section 14 of the said Act, the word "Indian" shall be omitted.

9. In sub-section (1) of section 19 of the said Act,-

(a) After the words "to the ranks" the words "any warrant officer or" shall be inserted; and

(b) The following proviso shall be added, namely:-

"Provided that a warrant officer reduced to the rank shall not be required to serve in the ranks as a sepoy."

10. In section 21 of the said Act, for the words "Indian officers" the words "Viceroy's commissioned officers, warrant officers" shall be substituted.

11. In clause (b) of section 36 of the said Act, after the word and figures and letter "or section 117A" shall be inserted.

12. (1) Section 41 of the said Act shall be re-numbered as sub-section (1) of section 41.

(2) In the said section as 90 re-numbered,--

(a) After the words "Every person subject to this Act, who" the words "either within British India or" shall be inserted;

(b) The words ", or when on active service in British India," shall be omitted; and

(c) The following proviso shall be added, namely:-

"Provided that a person subject to this Act who at any place within British India or at any place, other than such frontier posts as may be specified by the Governor General in Council by notification in this behalf, in which the Governor General in Council exercises jurisdiction by virtue of the Indian (Foreign Jurisdiction) Order in Council, 1902, and while not on active service, commits the offence of murder or culpable homicide not amounting to murder in relation to a person not subject to military law or the offence of rape, shall not be deemed to be guilty of an offence against military law and shall not be tried by court-martial."

(3) To the said section as so re-numbered and amended the following sub-section shall be added, namely:-

"(2) The powers of a court-martial to try and to punish any person under this section shall not be affected by reason of the fact that the civil offence with which such person is charged is also a military offence."

13. Section 42 of the said Act shall be omitted.

14. In section 43 of the said Act,-

(a) After clause (c) the following clause shall be inserted, namely: -

"(cc) In the case of Indian commissioned officers, cashiering;"

(b) Clause (0) shall be omitted;

(c) For clause (f) the following clause shall be substituted, namely:-

"(f) Reduction, in the case of a warrant officer, to a lower grade or class or place in the list of his rank, or to the ranks; or in the case of a non-commissioned officer, to **a** lower grade or a lower rank or to the ranks:

Provided that a warrant officer reduced **to** the ranks shall not be required to serve in the ranks as a sepoy;"

(d) In clause (g), for the words "of seniority of rank" the words "in the prescribed manner of seniority of rank and service for the purpose of promotion." shall be substituted;

(e) In clause (gg), after the word "officers" the words "warrant officers and non-commissioned officers," shall be inserted; and

(f) In clause (h),-

(i) in sub-clause (i), the word "promotion," shall be omitted,

(ii) sub-clause (ii) shall be omitted, and

(iii) in sub-clause (iii), after the words "sentenced to" and after the word "such" the words "cashiering or" shall be inserted.

15. In section 47 of the said Act, for the words "any one or more of the punishments specified in clauses (d), (f), (gg) and (h) of section 43" the following words shall be substituted, namely: -

"the punishment specified in clause (cc) or clause (d) and any one or more of the punishments specified in clauses *(f)*, (g), (gg) and *(h)* of section 43."

16. After section 47 of the said Act the following section shall be inserted, namely:-

"47A. Whenever an Indian commissioned officer is sentenced to transportation or imprisonment, the court shall by its sentence, sentence such officer to be cashiered."

17. In section 49 of the said Act, for the words "A non-commissioned officer" the words "A warrant officer or non-commissioned officer" shall be substituted.

18. In section 49A of the said Act, for the words "any person" the words "any enrolled person" shall be substituted.

19. (1) Section 50 of the said Act shall be re-numbered as sub-section (2) of section 50 and in that section as so re-numbered, after the words "a person subject to this Act", in both places where they occur, the words "other than an Indian commissioned officer" shall be inserted.

(2) The following sub-section shall be inserted as sub-section (1) of section 50, namely:-

"(1) The following penal deductions may be made from the pay and allowances of an Indian commissioned officers, that is to say,--

(a) All pay-and allowances for every day of absence without leave, unless a satisfactory explanation has been given through his Commanding officer and has been approved by the Governor General in Council.

(b) Any sum required to make good such compensation for any expenses, loss, damage or destruction occasioned by the commission of any offence as may be determined by the court-martial by whom he is convicted of such offence;

(c) Any sum required to make good the pay of any person subject to this Act which he has unlawfully retained or unlawfully refused to pay;

(d) Any sum required to make good any loss, damage or destruction of public or regimental property which after due investigation appears to the Governor

General in Council to have been occasioned by any wrongful act or negligence on the part of the Indian commissioned officer;

(e) Any sum ordered by a court-martial to be stopped under section 43.

20. For section 57 of the said Act the following section shall new section for be substituted, namely:-

"57. A general court-martin1 shall consist of not less than five British officers or Indian commissioned officers, each, of whom has held a commission for not less than three whole years and whom not less than four are of a rank not below that of Captain."

21. In section 58 of the said Act, for the word "officers" the words "British officers or Indian commissioned officers" shall be substituted.

22. Section 59 of the said Act shall be omitted.

23. For section 60 of the said Act, the following section shall be substituted, namely:-

"60. A general, summary general or district court-martial may be composed of either British officers or Indian commissioned officers or of both British officers and Indian commissioned officers."

24. Section 61 of the said Act shall be omitted.

25. In section 63 of the said Act, for the word "officers" the words "British officers or Indian commissioned officers" shall be substituted.

26. In section 65 of the said Act, the proviso to sub-section (1) shall be omitted.

27. In section 67 of the said Act, after the words "the person in question" the brackets and words "(not being an Indian commissioned officer)" shall be inserted.

28. To section 73 of the said Act the following proviso shall be added, namely:-

"Provided that a district court-martial shall not award to a warrant officer any punishment other than the punishment specified in clause (h) of section 43 or, either in addition to or in substitution for any such punishment, the punishment specified in clause (d) or the punishment specified in cause (f) of that section."

29. In clause (a) of the proviso to section 74 of the said Act for the figures and word "41 or 42" the word and figures "or 4" shall be substituted.

30. Section 79 of the said Act shall be omitted.

31. In section 82 of the said Act, the words "or superintending officer" shall be omitted.

32. In sub-section (1) of section 84 of the said Act, the words "before the court" shall be omitted.

33. In sub-section (4) of section 86 of the said Act, the words and figure "or section 42" shall be omitted.

34. Section 105 of the said Act shall be omitted.

35. In section 107 of the said Act, the word "rigorous," wherever it occurs, shall be omitted.

36. In section 108 of the said Act, the words and figures "section 105 or" shall be omitted.

37. In section 111A of the said Act, the words and figures "or section 42" shall be omitted.

38. In sub-section (3) of section 112 of the said Act, before the words "a non-commissioned officer" the words "a warrant officer or" shall be inserted.

39. In clause (a) of sub-section (2) of section 113 of the said Act, for the word "discharge", the words "removal, retirement or discharge" shall be substituted.

40. In section 117 of the said Act,--

(a) In sub-section (1), after the words **"Any** person subject to this Act" the words "other than an Indian commissioned officer" shall be inserted; and

(b) To sub-section (3), the following proviso shall be added, namely: -

"Provided that a decision by an authority competent to dispose of the matter complained of shall be final."

41. After section 117 of the said Act the following shall be inserted, namely: -

"117A. Any Indian commissioned officer who deems himself wronged by his Commanding Officer or any superior officer and who on due application made to his Commanding Officer does not receive the redress to which he considers himself entitled, may complaint to the Governor General in Council."

42. In sub-section (1) of section 118 of the said Act, the words "or superintending officer" shall be omitted.

Indian Army (Suspension of Sentences) Act, 1920

ACT No XX OF 1920

(PASSED BY THE INDIAN LEGISLATIVE COUNCIL)

(Received the assent of the Governor General in Council on the 23th March 1920)

Act to consolidate and amend the law relating to the suspension of sentences passed by Courts-martial under the Indian Army Act, 1911.

WHEREAS it is expedient to consolidate and amend the law relating to the suspension of sentences of imprisonment or transportation passed by Courts-martial on persons subject to the Indian Army Act, 1911 (VIII of 1911); It is hereby enacted as follows:-

Short title and construction

1. This Act may be called the Indian Army (Suspension of Sentences) Act, 1920, and shall be construed as one with the principal Act.

Definitions

2. In this Act, unless there is anything repugnant in the subject or context,--

(a) "Committed" means committed to prison or to confinement in military custody;

(b) "Competent military authority means a superior military authority, or any general or other officer not below the rank of field officer duly authorised by a superior military authority;

(c) "Imprisonment" includes confinement in military custody;

(d) "Principal Act" means the Indian Army Act, 1911 (VIII of 911);

(e) "Sentence" means a sentence of transportation or imprisonment whether originally passed on a person subject to the principal Act, or passed by way of reduction or commutation; and "sentenced" has the corresponding meaning; and

(f) "Superior military authority" means the Commander-in-Chief in India or any officer empowered under the principal Act to convene general Courts-martial or summary general Courts-martial.

Suspension of sentences

3. (1) Where a person subject to the principal Act is sentenced, the confirming officer when confirming the sentence, or, in the case of **a** sentence which does not require confirmation, the officer holding the trial or the President of the Court-martial when passing sentence may, notwithstanding anything in the principal Act, direct that such person be not committed until the orders of a superior military authority have been obtained.

(2) A superior military authority may, in the case of any such offender so sentenced,-

(a) Direct that, until his orders have been obtained, such offender shall not be committed; and

(b) Suspend the sentence whether or not the offender has already been committed.

(3) Where, in accordance with any order passed under sub-section (2), a sentence is suspended, the offender shall, whether he has been committed or not, forthwith be released.

Calculation of periods of sentence under suspension

4. Any period during which, a sentence is under suspension shall be reckoned as part of the term of such sentence.

Power to set aside suspension or order remission

5. **A** superior military authority may at any timr whilst a sentence is suspended under this Act, order;--

(a) That the offender be committed to undergo the unexpired portion of the sentence, or

(b) That the sentence be remitted.

Periodical review of suspended sentences

6. Where a sentence has been suspended under this Act, the case may at any time, and shall at intervals of not more than four months, be re-considered by a competent military authority, and if, on any such re-consideration, it appears to such authority that the conduct of the offender since his conviction has been such as to justify a remission of the sentence, he shall, if he is not also a superior military authority, refer the case to a superior military authority.

Procedure on further sentence of offender whose sentence is suspended

7. Where an offender, while a sentence on him is suspended under this Act, is sentenced for any other offence, then-

(a) If the further sentence is also suspended under this Act, the two sentences shall run concurrently;

(b) If the further sentence is for a period of three months or more and is not suspended under this Act, the offender shall also be committed on the unexpired portion of the previous sentence, but both sentences shall run concurrently; and

(c) If the further sentence is for **a** period of three months or less and is not suspended under this Act, the offender shall be committed on that sentence only, and the previous sentence shall (subject to any order which may be passed under section 5 or section 6) continue to be suspended.

Saving of section 112

8. The powers conferred by this Act shall be in addition to, and not in derogation of, any powers as to the mitigation, remission or commutation of sentences conferred by the principal Act, and a superior military authority shall, as regards persons subject to that Act, be an authority having power to mitigate, remit or commute sentences under section 112 of that Act.

Provision as to dismissal

9. Where in addition to any other sentence the punishment of dismissal has been awarded by a Court-martial, and such other sentence is suspended under this Act, then, notwithstanding anything contained in the principal Act or in any rules made there-under, such dismissal shall not take effect until so ordered by a superior military authority:

Provided that, if a sentence is remitted under this Act, the punishment of dismissal shall also be remitted.

Repeal of Act IV of 1917

10. The Indian Army (Suspension of Sentences) Act, 1917, and the Indian Army (Suspension of Sentences) Amendment Act, 1918, are hereby repealed, and all sentences which are suspended there-under at the commencement of this Act shall be deemed to have been suspended under this Act, and the provisions of this Act shall apply accordingly:

Provided that all such sentences shall, on, the expiry of six months from the commencement of this Act, if still under suspension, be deemed to be remitted.

The Indian Reserve Forces Act, 1888

(ACT No. IV OF 1888)

AN ACT TO REGULATE THE INDIAN RESERVE FORCES

WHEREAS it is expedient to provide for the government, discipline and regulation of the Indian Reserve Forces; It is hereby enacted as follows:—

Sections

1. Title and commencement

(1) This Act may be called the Indian Reserve Forces Act, 1888; and

(2) It shall come into forces on such day as the Central Government may, by notification in the Official Gazette, appoint in this behalf.

2. Division of Reserve Forces into Regular and Supplementary Reserves

The Indian Reserve Forces shall consist of the Regular Reserve and the Supplementary Reserve.

3. Locality of service of Reserves

A person belonging to the Indian Reserve Forces shall be liable to serve beyond the limits of India as well as within those limits.

4. Power to make rules for regulation of Reserve Forces

The Central Government may make rules and orders for the government, discipline and regulation of the Indian Reserve Forces.

5. Liability of Reserve Forces to military law

Subject to such rules and orders as may be made under section 4, a person belonging to the Indian Reserve forces shall as an officer or soldier, as the case may be, be subject to military law in the same manner and to the same extent as a person belonging to the Regular Army.

6. Punishment of certain offences by persons belonging to Reserve Forces

(1) If a person belonging to the Indian Reserve Forces—

(a) When required by or in pursuance of any rule or order under this Act to attend at any place fails without reasonable excuse to attend in accordance with such requirement, or

(b) Fails without reasonable excuse to comply with any such rule or order, or

(c) Fraudulently obtains any pay or other sum contrary to any such rule or order

he shall be liable—

(i) On conviction by a Court-martial to such punishment other than death (imprisonment for life) or imprisonment for a term exceeding one year as such Court is by the Army Act 1950, empowered to award, or

(ii) On conviction by a Presidency Magistrate or a Magistrate of the first class, to imprisonment for a term which may extend, in the case of a first offence under this section, to six months, and, in the case of any subsequent offence thereunder, to one year.

(2) Where a person belonging to the Indian Reserve Forces is required by or in pursuance of any rule or order under this Act to attend at any place, a certificate purporting to be signed by an officer appointed by such a rule or order in this behalf, and stating that the person so required to attend failed to do so in accordance with such requirements, shall, without proof of the signature or appointment of such officer, be evidence of the matters stated therein.

(3) Any person charged with an offence under this section, may be taken into and kept in either military or civil custody, or partly into and in one description of custody and partly and in the other, or be transferred for one description of custody to the other.

7. Reinstatement in civil employ of persons belonging to Reserve Forces on termination of Period of training, muster or army service

(1) If a person belonging to the Indian Reserve Forces is, during the period of his employment under an employer, called up for training, muster or army, service in pursuance of his liability under any rule or order under this Act, it shall be the duty of every such employer to reinstate the person in his employment on the termination of the period of his training, muster or army service in an occupation and under conditions not less favorable to him than those which would have been applicable to him had his employment not been so interrupted.

Provided that if the employer refuses to reinstate such person or denies his liability to reinstate such person, or if for any reason reinstatement of such person is represented by the employer to be impracticable, either party may refer the matter to the authority prescribed in this behalf by rules made under this Act, and that authority shall after considering all matters which may he put before it and after making such further inquiry into the matter as may be prescribed in the said rules, pass an order—

(a) Exempting the employer from the provision of this section, or

(b) Requiring the employer to re-employ such person on such terms, as the authority thinks suitable, or

(c) requiring the employer to pay to such person by way of compensation for failure or inability to re-employ a sum not exceeding an amount equal to six months remuneration at the rate at which his last remuneration was payable to him by the employer.

(2) If any employer fails to obey the order of any such authority as is referred to in the proviso to sub-section (1), he shall be punishable with fine which may extend to one thousand rupees, and the court by which an employer is convicted under this section shall order him (if he has not already been so required by the said authority) to pay to the person whom he has failed to re-employ a sum equal to six months' remuneration at the rate at which his last remuneration was payable to him by the employer, and any amount so required to be paid either by the said authority or by the court shall be recoverable as if it were a fine imposed by such court.

(3) In any proceeding under this section it shall be a defense for an employer to prove that the person formerly employed did not apply to the employer for reinstatement within a period of two months from the termination of the period of his training, muster or army service.

(4) The duty imposed by sub-section (1) upon an employer to reinstate in his employment a person such as is described in that sub-section shall attach to an employer who, before such person is actually called up for training, muster or army service, terminates his employment in circumstances such as to indicate an intention to evade the duty imposed by that sub section, and such intention shall be presumed until the contrary is proved, if the termination takes place after the issue of orders calling him up for training, muster or army service under this Act.

8. Preservation of certain rights of persons belonging to Reserve Forces when called up for training, muster or army service

When any person belonging to the Indian Reserve Forces and called up for training, muster or army service in pursuance of his liability under any rule or order under this Act has any rights under any provident fund or superannuation fund or other scheme for the benefit of employees maintained in connection with the employment he relinquishes, he shall continue, so long as he is engaged in training, muster or army service and if he is reinstated, until such reinstatement under the provisions of this Act, to have in respect of such fund or scheme such rights as may be prescribed by rules made under this Act.

Rules (1925) under the Indian Reserve Forces Act, 1888

The following rules and orders have been made by the Governor General in Council the government, discipline and regulation of the Indian Reserve Forces under section 4 of the Indian Reserve Forces Act, 1888:—

1. These rules and orders may be called the Indian Reserve Forces Rules, 1925.

2. In these rules and orders "Commanding Officer" means the officer in command of reserve centre or of the corps or portion of a corps to which a reservist is attached for training or muster:

Provided that in the case of a reservist of the Indian Hospital Corps, who is attached for training or muster to a unit of his corps, his Commanding Officer will be :—

(a) When the reservist is not called up for training, or muster, the Officer in charge, Indian Hospital Corps Records.

(b) When the reservist is called up for training, or muster, the Commanding Officer of the unit to which he is attached for such a training, or muster.

3A. The reserve shall consist of:—

(a) Junior Commissioned officers who have been or may be transferred to the reserve either with their own consent or in pursuance of, the conditions of their Commission. (SRO 291/62)

(b) Viceroy's Commissioned officers commissioned under Rules 4A and 4B.

(c) Indian Warrant Officers appointed under Rule 4B.

(d) Persons enrolled under the Indian Army Act, 1911, and transferred to the Reserve either with their own consent or in pursuance of the conditions of their enrolment.

(e) Persons enrolled under the said Act for service in the reserve.

3B. Every reservist other than a reservist of the Indian Supplementary Reserve, shall be subject to military law until duly discharged or dismissed.

3C. A reservist of the Indian Supplementary Reserve shall be subject to military law only when called out for service or when carrying out the annual trade test.

4A. (a) Commissions as Risaldars or Jemadars in the Reserve of the Indian Army Service Corps may be granted to gentlemen of influence who being not more than 30 years of age are pronounced medically fit for service.

(b) Such Viceroy's Commissioned officers will ordinarily be retired on attaining 45 years of age.

(c) When called out for army service or for training, such Viceroy's Commissioned officers will, for the purposes of pay, allowances and other concessions in cash and kind, be on the same footing as Viceroy's Commissioned officers of corresponding rank serving of the active list in A. T. units with the exception that they will not be entitled to clothing allowance for the period of training in peace. For the purposes of disability and family pensions they will be governed by the same rules as are applicable to the corresponding ranks mentioned above.

(d) Viceroy's Commissioned officers of the Reserve will rank among themselves according to the dates of their commissions and, when employed on army service, will rank with Viceroy's Commissioned officers of corresponding rank in the Indian army, but as juniors of each rank, Viceroy's Commissioned officers commissioned under clause (a) will exercise no military command except over persons belonging or attached to the Indian Army Service Corps.

(e) Commissions already granted under the provisions of Military Department Notification No. 112, dated the 10th February 1905, shall be deemed to have been granted under the provisions of this rule.

4B. (a) Gentlemen possessing the requisite medical and other qualifications may be granted commissions as leaders or higher commissioned rank, or may be appointed as warrant officers, in the Indian Medical Department Sub-Assistant Surgeon Reserve.

(b) Such Viceroy's Commissioned officers and warrant officers will serve for a period of five years, which may be further extended by periods of two years at a time, until attaining the age of 55 years.

(c) When called up for periodical training such Viceroy's Commissioned officers and warrant officers will receive pay at the minimum of their rank admissible to regular military sub-assistant surgeons, and when called out for army service they will receive pay at the minimum of their rank as admissible to regular military sub-assistant surgeons, with increments as admissible for each year's completed army service. Pension will be drawn in addition by pensioned military sub-assistant surgeons. For the purpose of disability and family passions they will be under the same rules as regular military sub-assistant surgeons. A gratuity at the rate of one month's pay for each year's army service, based on the rate of pay drawn at the time of release, will be admissible on conclusion of army service.

(d) Viceroy's Commissioned officers and warrant officers of the I.M.D., S.A.S. Reserve will rank with regular Viceroy's Commissioned officers and warrant officers of the sub-assistant surgeon branch of the I.M.D. as follows:—

Viceroy's Commissioned officers—according to the date of joining the Reserve as Viceroy's Commissioned officers, or from the date of promotion to Viceroy's Commissioned officer if promoted on a date subsequent to joining the Reserve.

Warrant officers—from the date of appointment to the Reserve.

(e) Appointments to the Indian Medical Department Sub-Assistant Surgeon (I.M.D., S.A.S.) Reserve already made shall be deemed to have been made under the provisions of this rule.

5A. Every reservist other than a reservist of the I.M.D., S.A.S. Reserve shall come up for service, training or muster, when required to do so by order of his commanding Officer; or for service when required to do so by order of the Commander-in-Chief in India or of any authority empowered by him in this behalf, and shall for this purpose attend at any place specified in such order.

5B. Every reservist of the Indian Medical Department Sub-Assistant Surgeon Reserve shall come up for training when required to do so by order of his commanding officer, or for service when required to do so by a notification in the Gazette of India, and shall for this purpose attend at any place specified in such order or notifications.

NOTE: A reservist in Civil Government employ will, when called for periodical training, receive military pay and allowances. He will also receive the excess, if any, of his civil pay over his military pay, provided that this concession is specifically sanctioned by the Department of the Government of India affected, or its attached and subordinate offices, or by the local Government concerned in whose employ the reservist is serving in his civil capacity, and provided also that (except where his civil pay is also met from the Army Estimates) the extra expenditure involved does not constitute a charge against the Army Estimates. A civil sub-assistant surgeon belonging to the I.M.D., S.A.S. Reserve will, when called up for periodical training, receive civil pay in addition to military pay, Civil pay will not be admissible in addition to military pay for periods or mobilized army service.

The periods spent in training and on the journey to and from the place of training will be treated as duty for purposes of civil leave, pension and increments of civil pay.

6. Every reservist shall inform his commanding officer of his address, and shall, on any change of such address, at once inform the said commanding officer of such change.

7. No reservist shall leave India except with the permission of his commanding officer, and in the case of Indian Medical Department Sub-Assistant Surgeon Reserve, with the permission of the A. G. in India. For the purpose of this Rule, Nepal shall, as regards Gurkha reservists, be deemed to be included in the term "India" except in the case of Gurkha Reservists of the ambulance and nursing sections of the Indian Hospital Corps.

8. A reservist who has, for any reason, failed to attend at any place when required to do so in pursuance of Rule 5-A or 5-B may be required by his commanding officer to attend for medical examination at the nearest military station to his home, and if so required, shall attend at such military station on the date appointed for such examination.

9. Notwithstanding anything contained in Section 126 of the Indian Army Act, 1911, it shall not be necessary to assemble a Court of Inquiry under that section merely because a reservist has failed to attend when required to do so in pursuance of Rule 5-A, 5-B or 8. Such a Court of inquiry may, however, at the discretion of the commanding officer of the reservist, be assembled in such a case.

10.A reservist who fails to attend at any place on the date on which required to do so in pursuance of Rule 5-A, or 5-B, shall be liable, at the discretion of his commanding officer, to forfeit all or a portion of arrears of pay and allowances due to him. In determining the amount of such forfeiture regard shall be had to the length of the reservist's absence and to the cause, whether reasonable or otherwise, to which it is due. The absence continues until the reservist is apprehended or satisfies his commanding officer by surrender or otherwise that he is available to fulfill his obligations as a reservist.

11. (a) A reservist, who is discharged at his own request at any time within three calendar months from the date fixed for the next training or muster, shall forfeit all pay and allowances due to him with effect from the first day of the third calendar month preceding the date of such training or muster, provided that if a reservist is discharged on obtaining permanent civil employment under the central or a provincial government, he shall be eligible for pay and allowances up to the date of discharge.

(b) A reservist who is discharged for misconduct shall forfeit pay and allowances due to him with effect from the date of misconduct or the first day of the third calendar month preceding the date fixed for the next training or muster whichever is earlier.

12. The certificate referred to in clause (2) of Section 6 of the Indian Reserve Forces Act, 1888 may be signed by the commanding officer of the reservist concerned, or, in respect of a reservist who fails to attend for medical inspection when required to do so in pursuance of Rule 8, by the commanding officer of the military station at which such reservist was required to attend.

13. When a person subject to the Indian Army Act, 1911, is to be transferred to the Reserve, his commanding officer shall, previous to such transfer, explain or cause to be explained to him the obligations and restrictions imposed by Rules 5-A to 8 and the forfeiture which may be incurred under Rules 10 and 11. When a person not subject to the said Act is enrolled thereunder for service in a reserve establishment, the officer enrolling him shall explain the aforesaid obligations, restrictions and forfeiture.

14. The authority referred to in the proviso to sub-section (1) of section 7 shall be the chief officer in charge of the revenue administration of the district (whether known as Collector or by any other designation) within the local limits of whose jurisdiction the person claiming reinstatement was employed immediately before he was called up for training, muster or any service under these rules (SRO 400/64).

15. Where a reference is made by any party under the proviso to sub-section (1) of section 7 to the authority referred to in Rule 14, a copy of such reference shall be served upon the opposite party and the said authority shall decide the matter after giving both the parties a reasonable opportunity of being heard and after making such further inquiry, if any, as it thinks fit.

16. When any reservist is called up for training, muster or Army service under these Rules-

(a) He may, at his option, continue to subscribe to any provident or superannuation fund or other scheme for the benefit of employees maintained in connection with the employment which he relinquished immediately before he was called up for training, muster or Army service, at such rates as were applicable to him under the rules of such fund or scheme ;

(b) The employer by whom such reservist was employed shall continue to credit his account in the fund or scheme with the amount subscribed and the interest on the amount in such account in accordance with the rules of the fund of scheme;

(c) Such reservist may, if the rule of the fund or scheme so permit and in accordance with such rules, withdraw sums from the amount standing at his credit in the fund or scheme; and

(d) For the purpose of calculating the amount of contribution or withdrawal admissible, such reservist's salary shall be deemed to be the salary which he would have received had he not been so called up.

AUXILIARY FORCE ACT, 1920

ACT No. XLIX of 1920

[PASSSED BY THE INDIANLEGISLATIVE COUNCIL]

(Received the assent of the Governor General on the 22nd September, 1920)

CONTENTS

SECTIONS

AUXILIARY FORCE ACT, 1920

ACT No. XLIX of 1920

[PASSSED BY THE INDIANLEGISLATIVE COUNCIL]

(Received the assent of the Governor General on the 22nd September, 1920)

An Act to constitute an auxiliary force for service in India

WHEREAS it is expedient to constitute an auxiliary force for service in India; It is hereby enacted as follows:--

Short title, extent and commencement

1. (1) This Act may be called the Auxiliary Force Act, 1920.

(2) It extends to the whole of British India, including British Baluchistan and the Sonthal Pargans, and applies also to European British subjects within the territories of any Prince or Chief in India.

(3) It shall come into force on the first day of October, 1920.

Definitions

2. "Advisory Committee" means an Advisory Committee constituted under section 28 for the prescribed military area, or part of a prescribed military area, within which a person subject to this Act for the time being resides or is serving, as the case may be;

"Competent military authority" means the General or other Officer Commanding the prescribed military area within which a person subject to this Act for the time being resides or is serving, as the case may be;

"Enrolled person" means a person enrolled in the prescribed manner under this Act;

"Enrolling officer" means an officer authorized to enroll persons under this Act;

"Prescribed" means prescribed by rules made under this Act; and "prescribe" has a corresponding meaning;

"Regulation" means a regulation made under section 31; and

"Training year" means a period of twelve months beginning on the first day of April and ending on the thirty-first day of March.

Constitution of an auxiliary force

3. There shall be raised and maintained in the manner hereinafter provided an auxiliary force for service in India to be designated the Auxiliary Force, India.

Classes who may be enrolled

4. Every person who—

(a) Is a European British subject as defined in the Code of Criminal Procedure, 1898, or

(b) Was, on the thirtieth day of September, 1920 enrolled or deemed to be enrolled under the Indian Defence Force Act, 1917 (not being a person enrolled under the provisions of section 12 of the Act), or

(c) Is a British subject of European descent in the male line, or

(d) Not being a British subject, satisfies the conditions prescribed for enrolment of persons of that class,

shall, subject to the provisions of this Act, be eligible for enrolment thereunder.

Enrolment

5. (1) Any person made eligible for enrolment under this Act who has attained the age of sixteen years and is not a member of His Majesty's regular naval, military or air forces or of His Majesty's Royal Indian Marine may apply to be enrolled into the Auxiliary Forces,

India, and if he satisfies the prescribed conditions, may be enrolled therein in the prescribed manner, and shall thereupon become subject to the provisions of this Act.

(2) An applicant for enrolment may apply to be enrolled for service in any particular branch, or in any particular corps or unit located in the prescribed military area within which he for the time being resides.

Liability to undergo military training

6. Every enrolled person shall be liable to undergo military training as provided by or under this Act until discharged from the Auxiliary Force, India, as hereinafter provided.

Liability to perform military service

7. Every enrolled person liable to undergo military training under section 6 shall, on and from the day of first April next following the date on which he attains the age of eighteen years or, if he has already attained the age of eighteen years on and from any later date on which he is enrolled, be liable to perform military service under this Act.

Appointment to corps or unit

8. (1) Every enrolled person shall without unnecessary delay, be appointed by, or under the orders of, the competent military authority to a corps or unit of the Auxiliary Force, India, and on receipt of an order so appointing him shall report himself for the purpose of joining such corps or unit at such time and place as may be specified in the order.

(2) Any person who has been enrolled for service in any particular branch, corps or unit shall be appointed to a corps or unit of that branch or to that corps or unit, as the case may be.

Preliminary training

9. Every enrolled person liable to perform military service under this Act who on becoming so liable has not attained the age of thirty-one years shall, within the training year in which he becomes so liable, undergo the preliminary training specified in Schedule I:

Provided that, if such preliminary training cannot be completed within that training year, it may be completed at the discretion of the competent military authority in the training year next following:

Provided further that any person who has completed the preliminary training required by regulations made under the India Defence Force Act, 1917, or who has served for a period of six months in His Majesty's naval, military or air forces or in His Majesty's Royal Indian Marine, or who is certified by the competent military authority to have undergone adequate military training under the India Defence Force Act, 1917, or under this Act or otherwise, shall be deemed to have completed the preliminary training required by this section.

Periodical training of persons entitled to rank as officers

10. Every enrolled person (other than a commissioned officer of the Auxiliary Force, India) who is entitled to rank as an officer of His Majesty's Forces, shall undergo such periodical training as may be laid down in regulations.

Classification and periodical training

11. Every enrolled person liable to perform military service under this Act (other than a person whom the provisions of section 10 apply) shall be included as hereinafter provided in one or another of the following classes, namely:--

(a) Active Class;

(b) The First (A) Class of the Reserve; or

(c) The Second (B) Class of the Reserve;

and shall undergo periodical training specified in Schedule I for the Class in which he is for the time being included.

Classification

12. (1) Every commissioned officer of the Auxiliary Force, India, shall be included in the Active Class until he relinquishes his commission.

(2) Enrolled persons liable to perform military service under this Act, not being commissioned officers of the Auxiliary Force, India, or entitled to rank as officers of His Majesty's Forces shall be classified as follows, namely:--

(a) Every such person who is required by section 9 to undergo preliminary training and has completed or is deemed to have completed the same shall be included in the Active Class until the end of the training year in which he attains the age of thirty-one years;

(b) Every such person who has completed the period of service in the Active Class as required by clause (a) or is enrolled after attaining the age of thirty-one years and before attaining the age of forty years shall be included in the First (A) Class of the Reserve until the end of the training year in which he attains the age of forty years;

(c) Every such person who has completed the period of service in the First (A) Class of the Reserve as required by clause (b) or is enrolled after attaining the age of forty years shall be included in the second (B) Class of the reserve until discharged from the Auxiliary Force, India, as hereinafter provided.

(3) Any enrolled person who ceases to be entitled to rank as an officer of His majesty's Forces or to be a commissioned officer of the Auxiliary Fore, India, shall thereupon be included in the Class in which he would have been included under this section if the provisions of section 10 or sub-section (1), as the case may be, had not applied to him, and shall undergo periodical training accordingly.

(4) Any person who is under this section included in either Class of the Reserve may apply to the competent military authority to be included for any training year in any other Class for which more periodical training is specified in Schedule I, and shall thereupon be deemed to be included in that Class.

(5) Notwithstanding anything hereinbefore contained, if any person is under this section included in any Class after the commencement of a training year, the competent military authority shall reduce to such extent as he may deem fit, or may remit, the amount of periodical training to be undergone by such person in that year.

Variations of training

13. (1) The competent military authority may, by order in writing:--

(a) On the recommendation of the Advisory Committee, direct the inclusion of any enrolled person in any Class for which less periodical training is specified than that specified for the Class in which he is included under the provisions of section 12, or

(b) On his own motion or on the recommendation of the Advisory Committee, reduce the specified amount of training either in individual cases or in the case of any unit or part thereof for any stated period.

(2) The competent military authority shall grant to each person whose training is reduced under clause (b) of sub-section (1) a certificate setting forth the amount of training to be undergone during the said period.

Medical examination

14. Every enrolled person shall, if and when required by the competent military authority, present himself for such medical examination as may be necessary to determine the extent, if any, to which he is fit to undergo military training or to perform military service, before a medical officer appointed or approved in that behalf by the competent military authority, and for the purposes of such medical examination shall comply with the directions of such medical officer.

Transfers

15. (1) Every person appointed to a corps or unit under section 8 shall remain in that corps or unit until transferred to another corps or unit by, or under the orders of, the competent military authority, but no person shall be transferred from the Infantry branch to another branch or from one unit to another unit located in the same prescribed military area except at his own request.

(2) Any person so transferred from, the Infantry branch to another branch may be required to undergo such further preliminary training, not exceeding eight days, as may be ordered by the competent military authority, and thereafter shall undergo the periodical training specified in Schedule I for the branch to which he is transferred:

Provided that any periodical training already undergone by such person in the training year in which he is transferred shall be deemed to have been undergone in such other branch.

Explanation.--For the purposes of this section and of Schedule I, a day shall be deemed to consist of four hours of actual military drill or instruction, and may be made up of fractions of a day not more than four in number.

Change of residence

16. (1) Any enrolled person who leaves his place of residence in India for the time being and thereby leaves the area commanded by one competent military authority for that commanded by another shall, if he does not intend to return to the area which he leaves, notify the competent, military authority commanding that area of his change of residence.

(2) If such person having intended to return does not return within three months, he shall notify the competent military authority as aforesaid' immediately on the expiry of that period.

(3) The competent military authority on being notified of a change of residence under sub-section (1) or sub-section (2) may, subject to the provisions of section 15, transfer such person from the corps or unit in which he is serving to another corps or unit.

Discharge

17. (1) Any enrolled person who has attained the age of forty-five years or hour years' service from the date of his enrolment shall, on application made by him in the prescribed manner, be entitled to receive his discharge from the Auxiliary Force, India.

(2) An enrolled person who is not entitled to his discharge under sub-section (1) may be discharged by the competent authority on a recommendation of the Advisory Committee in this behalf.

Calling out and embodiment

18. No person liable to perform military service under this Act shall be required to perform such service except---

(a) When called out with any portion of the Auxiliary Force, India, by an order of the senior military officer present either to act in support of the civil power or to provide guards which, in the opinion of such officer, are essential; or

(b) When any portion of the Auxiliary Force, India, to which he belongs has been embodied to support or supplement His Majesty's regular forces in the event of an emergency by a notification directing such embodiment issued by the Governor General in Council or any Local Government empowered by the Governor General in Council in that behalf and published in the Gazette of India or the local official Gazette, as the case may be; or

(c) When attached at his own request to any regular forces.

Territorial limits of liability to military service on calling out and embodiment

19. No person called out under clause (a), or embodied under clause (b), of section 18 shall be required to perform military service beyond the limits of the prescribed military area in which the corps or unit to which he has been appointed or is for the time being attached is located, save when it is, in the opinion of the senior military officer present necessary to proceed beyond those limits in the course of the military operations upon which the corps or unit or any portion thereof is for the time being engaged.

Duration of military service on calling out or embodiment

20. Any portion of the Auxiliary Force, India, which having been called out or embodied under section 18, is performing military service, shall be replaced by regular troops or otherwise as soon as circumstances permit, and shall not be required to perform such service after such replacement has been effected to the satisfaction of the senior military officer present or after the cancellation of the order or notification under clause (a) or (b) as the case may be, of section 18.

Application of the Army Act

21. Every commissioned officer of the Auxiliary Force, India, when doing duty as a commissioned officer and man of the said Force—

(a) When attached to or otherwise acting as part of or with any regular forces, and

(b) When called out by an order, or embodied by a notification, under section 18,

Shall be subject to the provisions of the Army Act and any orders and regulations made there-under, and the said Act, orders and regulations shall apply to every such person in the circumstances aforesaid as if the same were enacted in this Act, and as if such person held the same rank in His Majesty's Army as he holds for the time being the said Force.

Refusal to appear for military service

22. If any person liable to perform military service under this Act fails to comply with an order or notification under section 18 calling him out or embodying him for military service, and District Magistrate or Chief Presidency Magistrate may, on the application of the competent military authority or of an officer empowered by such authority in writing in that behalf, cause such person to be arrested and brought before him, and, if the Magistrate is satisfied that such person has been duly required to perform military service, the Magistrate may, without prejudice to any penalty which such person may have incurred, make over such person in custody to the military authorities.

Penalties for breach of sections 8, 14 and 14

23. An enrolled person who refuses or without lawful excuse (the burden of proving which shall lie upon such person) neglects---

(a) To comply with any order under section 8; or

(b) To attend for medical examination, or to comply with the directions of the medical officer, as required by section 14, or

(c) To notify any change of residence as required by section 16

shall be punishable with fine which may extend to fifty rupees.

Other offences

24. An enrolled person commits an offence if he, in circumstances when he is not subject to military law, does any of the following acts, namely---

(1) When on parade or undergoing military training or wearing His Majesty's uniform---

(a) Strikes, or uses or offers violence to or uses threatening or insubordinate language to, or behaves with contempt to, his superior officer; or

(b) Disobeys any standing order of, or lawful command given by, his superior officer; or

(c) Neglects to obey a general or garrison order made specially applicable to the Auxiliary Force, India, by the competent military authority; or

(d) Is in a state of intoxication; or

(e) Being a non-commissioned officer strikes or ill-treats any person subject to military law or to this Act, or to the Indian Territorial Force Act, 1920, who is his subordinate in rank or position;

(2) Without sufficient cause fails to appears at the place pf parade at the time fixed or to attend at any place in his capacity as a member of the Auxiliary Force, India, when duly required so to attend, or when on parade without sufficient cause quits the ranks;

(3) Without sufficient cause fails to perform any part of the training which by or under this Act he is required to perform;

(4) Strikes or uses or offers violence to, any person whether subject to military law or not in whose military custody he is placed, and whether such person is or is not superior officer;

(5) Resists an escort whose duty it is to arrest him or detain him in military custody;

(6) Being under arrest or detention or otherwise in lawful custody escapes or attempts to escape;

(7) When in charge of any property belonging to Government or to a corps or unit if the Auxiliary Force, India, makes away with, or is concerned in making away with, any such property;

(8) Wilfilly injures, or by culpable neglect loses or causes injury to, any such property as is mentioned in clause (7);

(9) Wilfully ill-treats a horse or other animal used in the public service;

(10) Knowingly furnishes a false return or report of the number or state of men under his command or charge, or of any money, arms or ammunition, clothing, equipment, stores or other property in his charge;

(11) Through design or culpable neglect omits to make or send any return of any matter mentioned in clause (10) which it is his duty to make or send;

(12) When it is his official duty to make a declaration respecting any matter makes a declaration respecting such matter which he either knows or believes to be false or does not believe to be true;

(13) Knowingly makes against any person subject to military law or to this Act or to the Indian Territorial Force Act, 1920, an accusation which he either knows or believes to be false or does not believe to be true;

(14) Falsely personates any other person at any parade or on ant occasion when such other person is required by or under this Act to do any act or attend at any place, or abets any such act or personation.

Punishment for offences under section 24

25. (1) Any person committing any of the offences specified in sub-clauses (b), (c) and (d) of clause (1) or clauses (2), (3), (8), (11), and (14) of section 24 shall be punished with fine which may extend to two hundred rupees.

(2) Any person committing any other offence specified in section 24 shall be punishable with imprisonment which may extend to two months, or with fine which may extend to two hundred rupees, or both.

Dismissal

26. The competent military authority may in his direction dismiss any enrolled person from the Auxiliary Force, India.

Summary and minor punishments

27. The Governor General in Council may prescribe summary and minor punishments for offences under section 24 or for contravention of any rule or regulations made under this Act to which enrolled persons shall be liable without the intervention of a Criminal Court, and the officer or officers by whom and the circumstances in which and the extent to which such summary and minor punishment may be inflicted, and the manner in which any such punishment may be enforced:

Provided that no punishment involving any kind of imprisonment shall be imposed as a summary or minor punishment:

Provided further that not summary punishment shall be inflicted in any case in which the accused claims to be tried by a Criminal Court.

Advisory Committees

28. (1) The Local Government shall constitute for each prescribed military area one or more Advisory Committees each consisting of three or more members, of whom one shall be the competent military authority or a military officers appointed by him in this behalf and the others shall be persons eligible for enrolment in the auxiliary Force, India, within the meaning of section 4, who shall be appointed annually by, or under the orders of, the Local Government.

(2) Any Advisory Committee constituted for a prescribed military area or a part thereof, as the case may be, which includes a Presidency-town or any other place to which the Governor General in Council may, by order in writing, declare this sub-section to apply, shall consist of not less than five members, of whom not more than two shall be persons in the service of Government.

(3) The Governor General in Council shall prescribe the duties, powers and procedure of Advisory Committees and, in particular, the matters in respect of which the competent military authority shall be bound to give the effect to a recommendation of an Advisory Committee unless the Local Government otherwise directs.

Constitution and disbandment of units

29. The Governor General in Council may constitute any corps or unit and may disband any corps or unit constituted under this Act.

Power to make rules

30. (1) The Governor General in Council may make rules to carry out the purposes of this Act.

(2) In particular and without prejudice to the generality of the foregoing powers such rules may:-

(a) Provide for the appointment of enrolling officers;

(b) Prescribe military areas for the purposes of this Act;

(c) Prescribe the manner in which and the conditions subject to which European British subjects and other person may offer themselves for enrolment under this Act;

(d) Define the manner in which and the conditions under which persons or any class of persons liable to military service under this Act may be excused from being called out or embodied;

(e) Prescribe the military training to be undergone by persons liable to military training under section 6 but not to military service under section 7;

(f) Prescribe the rates of pay for, and provide for the grant of allowances to, persons liable to perform military service under this Act;

(g) Prescribe for any military area which is a railway area or for any area beyond the limits of British India the authority which shall be deemed respectively to be the Local Government and the District Magistrate for all or any of the purposes of this Act; and

(h) Provide for any other matter which under this Act is to be or may be prescribed.

(3) Any rule made under this section may provide that a contravention thereof shall be punishable with fine which may extend to fifty rupees.

(4) The power to make rules conferred by this section shall, except on the first occasion of the exercise thereof, be subject to the condition of previous publication.

(5) All rules made under this section shall be published in the Gazette of India, and on such publication shall have effect as if enacted in this Act.

Power to make regulations

31. The Commander-in-Chief of His Majesty's forces in India may make regulations consistent with this Act and the rules made there-under providing generally for details connected with the organisation and personnel of the Auxiliary Force, India, and for the duties, equipment, military training, allowances and leave of enrolled persons.

Certain person subject to this Act to be deemed part of His Majesty's Army for certain purposes

32. For the purposes of sections 128, 130 and 131 of the Code of Criminal Procedure, 1898, all officers, non-commissioned officers and men liable to perform military service under this Act who have been appointed to a corps or unit shall be deemed to be officers, non-commissioned officers and soldiers, respectively, of His Majesty's Army.

Trial of offences

33. Save as otherwise provided by section 27, no offence under this Act shall be tried save by a Court not, inferior to that of a Presidency Magistrate or a Magistrate of the first class.

Exemption from local taxation

34. No enrolled person shall be liable to pay any municipal or other tax in respect of a horse, bicycle, motor-bicycle, motor car or other means of conveyance which he is authorised by a general or special order of the competent military authority to maintain in his capacity as a member of the Auxiliary Force, India.

Amendment of section 1, Act XI of 1878

35. In section 1of the Indian Arms Act, 1878, for the words and figures "a volunteer enrolled under the Indian Volunteers Act, 1869," the words and figures "a member of either of the forces constituted by the Indian Territorial Force Act, 1920, or the Auxiliary Force Act, 1920", and for the word "volunteer" the word "member," shall be substituted.

Repeal

36. On and from the date on which this Act comes into force, the enactments mentioned in Schedule II shall be repealed to the extent specified in the fourth column thereof.

SCHEDULE I

(See sections 9, 11 12 and 15)

TRAINING

1. Preliminary:

(a) For infantry:- 32 days, and the annual musketry course as laid down in regulations.

(b) For other branches:- 40 days, and the annual musketry or gun course as laid down in regulations.

2. Periodical:

(1) Active Class:

(a) For infantry:- 16 days in each training year, and the annual musketry course as laid down in regulations.

(b) For other branches:- 20 days in each training year, and the annual musketry or gun course as laid down in regulations.

(2) First (A) Class Reserve:

(a) For infantry:- 6 days in each training year, and the annual musketry course as laid down in regulations.

(b) For other branches:- 10 days in each training year, and the annual musketry or gun course as laid down in regulations.

(3) Second (B) Class Reserve:

(a) For infantry:- The annual musketry course as laid down for this Class in regulations

(b) For other branches:-The annual musketry course as laid down for this Class in regulations.

Note: (section 15):- A day consists of four hours of actual military drill or instruction, and may be made up of fractions of a day not more than four in number.

Auxiliary Force (Amendment) Act, 1928

ACT No. X OF 1928

[PASSED BY THE INDIAN LEGISLATURE]

(Received the assent of the Governor General on the 27th March, 1928)

An Act further to amend the Auxiliary Force Act, 1920, for certain purposes

WHEREAS it is expedient further to amend the Auxiliary Force Act, 1920, for the purposes hereinafter appearing; It is hereby enacted as follows: -

1. (1) This Act may be called the Auxiliary Force (Amendment) Act, 1928.

(2) It shall come into force on such date, not later than the 1st day of January, 1929, **as** the Governor General in Council may, by notification in the Gazette of India, appoint.

2. In section 4 of the Auxiliary Force Act, 1920 (hereinafter referred to as the said Act);--

(a) Clause (b) shall be omitted;

(b) In clause (c), the word "or" shall be omitted, and the clause shall be re-lettered as clause (b); and

(c) Clause (d) shall be omitted.

3. In section 17 of the said Act,--

(a) In sub-section (2), for the word "may" the word "shall" be substituted; and

(b) The following sub-section shall he added, namely:-

"(3) Any enrolled person may be discharged by such authority, and subject to such conditions, as may be prescribed.

(4) Notwithstanding anything contained in sub-section (2) or sub-section (3), no enrolled person, who is for the time being engaged in military service under the provisions of this Act, shall be entitled to receive his discharge before the termination of such service."

4. In subsection (1) of section 21 of the said Act, words "subject, in the case of an officer, to the terms of his commission and the orders of His Majesty, and, in the case of a non-commissioned officer or man, to the orders of the Governor General" shall be added at the end.

5. After section 27 of the said Act, the following section shall be inserted, namely:-

> "27A. Where any non-commissioned officer or man of the Auxiliary Force is required, by or in pursuance of any rule, regulation or order made under this Act, to attend at any place, a certificate purporting to be signed by the prescribed officer stating that the person so required to attend failed to do so in accordance with such requirement, shall, without proof of the signature or appointment of such officer, be evidence of the matters stated therein."

Indian Territorial Force

ACT No. XLVIII OF 1920

[PASSED BY THE INDIAN LEGISLATIVE COUNCIL]

(Received the assent of the Governor General on 22 September 1920)

An Act to constitute an Indian Territorial Force, and to provide for the enrolment therein of persons other than European subjects:

WHEREAS it is expedient to provide for the constitution of an Indian Territorial Force, and for the enrolment therein persons other than European British subjects who may offer themselves therefor; it is hereby enacted as follows:--

Short title, extent and commencement

1. (1) This Act may be called the Indian Territorial Force Act, 1920.

(2) It extends to the whole of British India, including British Baluchistan and Sonthal Parganas.

Definitions

2. In this Act, unless there is anything repugnant in the subject or context,--

"Advisory Committee" means an Advisory Committee constituted under section 12 for the Province within which a person subject to this Act for the time being resides or is serving, as the case may be;

"Enrolled" means enrolled or re-enrolled in the Indian Territorial Army under this Act;

"European British subject" mans any person who is a European British as defined in the Code of Criminal Procedure, 1898, or is a British subject of European descent in the male line;

"Prescribed" means prescribed by rules made under this Act; and

"University Corps" means any corps of the Indian Territorial Force constituted for the appointment thereto of students of, and other persons connected with, a University established by law in British India or colleges affiliated to such a University.

Constitution of Indian Territorial Force

3. There shall be raised and maintained in the manner hereinafter provided a force to be designated the Indian Territorial Army.

Provided that the Governor General in Council shall establish all or any branches of Force as circumstances may permit from time to time.

Constitution and disbandment of units

4. The Governor General in Council may constitute for any Province one or more of Indian Territorial Force and may disband any corps or unit so constituted.

Enrolment

5. (1)Any British subject (not being a European British subject) or any subject of a State in India may offer himself for enrolment in the Indian Territorial Force, and any such person who satisfies the prescribed conditions may be enrolled in the prescribed manner for such period, not exceeding six years, as may be prescribed.

(2) An applicant for enrolment may apply to be enrolled for service in any particular branch, corps or unit constituted for the Province within which he for the time being resides.

Appointment to corps or units

6. (1) Every person enrolled shall without unnecessary delay be appointed in the prescribed manner to a corps or unit constituted under section 4 for the Province in which for the time being resides.

(2) Any person who has been enrolled for service in any particular branch, corps or unit shall be appointed to a corps or unit of that branch or to that corps or unit, as the case may be.

Transfer and attachment

7. (1) any person appointed to a corps or unit under section 6 may be transferred, whether on disbandment of the corps or unit or otherwise, to another corps or unit of the Indian Territorial Force, in such manner as may be prescribed.

(2) Nothing contained in sub-section (1) shall be deemed to authorize any transfer without his own consent of any person enrolled to a corps or unit constituted for a Province other than that in which he for the time being resides, or of a person enrolled for service in a particular branch to a corps or unit of another branch, or of a person enrolled for service in a particular corps or unit to any other corps or unit.

(3) Any person enrolled may be attached at his own request to any corps or unit of the Indian Territorial Force or to any regular force.

Discharge

8. Every person enrolled shall be entitled to receive his discharge from the Indian Territorial Force on the expiration of the period for which he was enrolled, and any such person may, prior to the expiration of that period, be discharged from the said Force by such authority and subject to such conditions as may be prescribed, and shall be so discharged on a recommendation of the Advisory Committee in this behalf:

Provided that no enrolled person who is for the time being engaged in military service under the provisions of this Act shall be entitled to receive his discharge before the termination of such service.

Liability to serve and perform military service

9. (1) Every person enrolled shall, subject to such conditions as may be prescribed, be bound to serve in any corps or unit of the Indian Territorial Force to which he has been appointed or transferred or is for the time being attached, and shall be subject to all rules and regulations that may be made under this Act relating to such corps or unit.

(2) Every such person enrolled shall be liable to perform military service;---

(a) When called out with any portion of the Indian Territorial Force by an order of the senior military officer present either to act in support of the civil power to provide guards which, in the opinion of such officer, are essential; or

(b) When any portion of the Indian Territorial Force to which he belongs has been embodied to support or supplement His Majesty's regular forces in India in the event of an emergency by a notification directing such embodiment issued by the Governor General in Council and published in the Gazette of India; or

(c) When attached at his own request to any regular forces.

Territorial limits of liability to, and duration of, military service

10. (1) No person embodied under section 9 shall be required to perform military service beyond the limits of India save under a general or special order of the Governor General in Council.

(2) Any portion of the Indian Territorial Force which, having been called out or embodied under section 9, is performing military service shall be replaced by regular troops or otherwise as soon as circumstances permit, and shall not be required to perform such service after such replacement has been effected to the satisfaction of the senior military officer in charge or after that cancellation of the order or notification under clause (a) or (b), as the case may be, of section 9.

Application of Act VIII of 1911

11. (1) Every commissioned officer of the Indian Territorial Force when doing duty as a commissioned officer and every non-commissioned officer and man of the said Force--

(a) When called out or embodied for military service under section 9, or

(b) When attached to, or otherwise acting as part of or with, any regular force,

shall be subject to the Indian Army Act, 1911, and rules made thereunder, whereupon the said Act and rules shall apply to him as if he held the same rank in His Majesty's Indian forces as he holds for the time being in the Indian Territorial Force.

(2) Every commissioned officer, non-commissioned officer and man of the said Force when when embodied for, or otherwise undergoing, military training in the prescribed manner shall be subject to the India Army Act, 1911, and the rules made thereunder:

Provided that the said Act and rules shall in their application to such persons be modified to such extent and in such manner as may be prescribed:

Provided further that officers, non-commissioned officers and men of a University Corps shall, when undergoing military training, be subject only to such disciplinary and other rules as may be prescribed in this behalf.

Advisory Committees

12. (1) The Local Government of each Province for which any unit of the Indian Territorial Force has been constituted shall constitute an, Advisory Committee consisting of three members, of whom one shall be a military officer appointed in the prescribed manner and the others shall be persons who are British subjects (other than European British subjects) not in the service of the Government, appointed annually by, or under the orders of, the Local Government.

(2) The duties, powers and procedure of Advisory Committee shall be as may be prescribed.

Power to make rules

13. (1) The Governor General in Council may, after previous publication, make rules to carry out the purposes of this Act.

(2) In particular and without prejudice to the generality of the foregoing powers, such rules may--

(a) Prescribe the manner in which, and the period for which and the conditions subject to which, persons may be enrolled under section 5;

(b) Prescribe the manner in which persons enrolled may be appointed to corps and units under section6 or transferred under section7;

(c) Prescribe the authorities by which and the conditions subject to which enrolled persons may be discharged under section 8;

(d) Prescribe preliminary and periodical training to be undergone by any persons enrolled and provide for the embodiment of any corps or unit for that purpose;

(e) Prescribe the military and other obligations to which members of a University Corps shall be liable when undergoing military training and provide generally for the maintenance of discipline in such cases;

(f) Provide for the medical examination of persons offering themselves for enrolment under section 5;

(g) Provide for and regulate remuneration, allowances, gratuities or compensation (if any) to be paid to any person or class of persons enrolled or to their dependents; and

(h) Provide for any other matter which under this Act is to be or may be prescribed.

(3) All rules made under this Act shall be published in the Gazette of India, and on such publication shall have effect as if enacted in this Act.

Power to make regulations

(1) The Commander-in-Chief of His Majesty's forces in India may make regulations consistent with this Act and the rules made there under providing generally for all details connected with the organization and personnel of the Indian Territorial Force and for the duties, military training, clothing, equipment, allowances and leave of persons enrolled.

(2) In particular and without prejudice to the generality of the foregoing power, such regulations may specify the courses of training or instruction to be followed by any person or call of persons enrolled.

Certain persons subject to this Act to deemed part of His Majesty's Army for certain purposes

15. For the purpose of sections 128, 130 and 131 of the Code of Criminal Procedure, 1898, all officers, non-commissioned officers and men of the Indian Territorial Force who have been appointed to corps or unit shall be deemed to be officers, non-commissioned officers and soldiers, respectively, of His Majesty's Army.

Exemption from local taxation

16. No person shall be liable to pay any municipal or other tax in respect of any horse, bicycle, motor bicycle, motor car, or other means of conveyance which he is authorized by regulations made under section 14 to maintain in his capacity as a member of the Indian Territorial Force.

The Indian Territorial Force (Amendment) Act, 1928

ACT No IX OF 1928

[PASSED BY THE INDIAN LEGISLATURE]

(Received the assent of the Governor General on 27th March, 1928)

An Act further to amend the Indian Territorial Force Act, 1920, for certain purposes

WHEREAS it is expedient further to amend the Indian Territorial Force Act, 1920, for the purposes hereinafter appearing; It is hereby enacted as follows: -

1. (1) This Act may be called the Indian Territorial Force (Amendment) Act, 1928.

(2) It shall come into force on such date, not later than the 1st day of January, 1929, as the Governor General in Council may, by notification in the Gazette of India, appoint.

2. (1) In the long title of the Indian Territorial Force Act, 1920 (hereinafter referred to as the said Act), the words "and to provide for the enrolment therein of persons other than European British subjects" shall be omitted.

(2) In the preamble to the said Act, the words "and for the enrolment therein of person other than European British subjects who may offer themselves therefor" shall be omitted.

3. In section 2 of the said Act,-

(a) The definition of "Advisory Committee" shall be omitted;

(b) Between the definitions of "European British subject" and "presciibed" the following definitions shall be inserted, namely: -

"Non-commissioned officer means a person holding non-commissioned rank in the Indian Territorial Force, and includes an acting non-commissioned officer;

"Officer" means a senior officer or a junior officer;" and

(c) The definition of "University Corps" shall be omitted.

4. In section 4 of the said Act,--

(a) After the word "more," the word "provincial" shall be inserted;

(b) After the word "disband" the words "or re-constitute" shall be inserted; and

(c) Section 4, as so amended, shall be re-numbered as sub-section (1) and the following sub-sections shall be added,

"(2) The Governor General in Council may constitute for any town or group of towns in a Province one or more urban corps or units of the Indian Territorial Force, to be recruited from persons residing in or near such town or towns, and may disband or reconstitute any corps or unit so constituted. .

(3) The Governor General in Council may constitute for any Province a, University Corps consisting of one or more units of the Territorial Force, for the appointment thereto of students of, and other persons connected with, a University established by law in British India, or colleges affiliated to such a University, and may disband or reconstitute any unit so constituted."

5. After section 4 of the said Act, the following section shall be inserted, namely;--

"4A. (1) There shall be the following classes of officers in the Indian Territorial Force, namely:--

(a) Senior officers, holding commissions granted by the Governor General in the name of His Majesty, with British designation of rank, and

(b) Junior officers, holding commissions granted by the Governor General, with Indian designation of rank.

(2) An officer shall be med to be enrolled in the Indian Territorial Force for so long as he holds a commission in that Force."

6. In section (1) of section 5 of the said Act,-

(a) The words and brackets "(not being a European British subject)" shall be omitted; and

(b) The following proviso shall be added, namely:-

"Provided that no European British subject shall be enrolled in any corps or unit of the Indian Territorial Force other than a University Corps."

7. (1) In sub-section (2) of section 5, in sub-section (1) of section 6, and in sub-section (2) of section 7 of the said Act, after the word "Province", the words "or town or group of towns" shall be inserted.

2) In sub-section (2) of section 7 of the said Act, the words "or of a person enrolled in an urban corps or unit to a provincial corps or unit" shall be added at the end.

8. After section 7 of the said Act, the following section shall be inserted, namely:

"7A. (1) Any enrolled person who leaves his place of residence for the time being and thereby leaves the Province in which the corps or unit in which he is serving is constituted shall, if he does not intend to return to that Province, notify the prescribed authority in that Province of his change of residence.

(2) If such person having intended to return does not return within three months, he shall notify the prescribed authority as aforesaid immediately on the expiry of that period.

(3) The prescribed authority on being notified of a change of residence under sub-section (1) or sub-section (2) may, subject to the provisions of section 7, transfer such person from the corps or unit in which he is serving to another corps or unit."

9. In sub-section (2) of section 9 of the said Act;--

(a) After the word "enrolled" the words "who has attained the age of eighteen years" shall be inserted; and

(b) The following proviso shall be added, namely: -

"Provided that nothing in this sub-section shall apply to persons enrolled in a University Corps."

10. In sub-section (1) of section 10 of the said Act, the following words shall be added at the end, namely:

"and no person for the time being serving in an urban corps or unit shall at any time be required to perform military service beyond the limits of the Province in which the corps or unit in which he is serving is located, save when it is, in the opinion of the senior military officer present, necessary to proceed beyond those limits in the course of the military operations upon which the corps or unit or any portion thereof is for the time being engaged."

11. For section 11 of the said Act, the following section shall be substituted; namely:--

11. (1) Every senior officer of the Indian Territorial Force, when doing duty as such officer, shall be subject to the Army Act, and any orders or regulations made thereunder, whereupon the said Act, orders and regulations shall apply to, him as if he held the same rank in His Majesty's Army as he holds for the time being in the said Force, subject to the terms of his commission and the orders of His Majesty.

(2) Every junior officer of the Indian Territorial Force, when doing duty as such officer, shall be subject to the Indian Army Act, 1911, and the rules and regulations made thereunder, whereupon the said Act, rules and regulations shall apply to him as if he held the same rank in His Majesty's Indian Forces as he holds for the time being in the said Force, subject to the terms of his commission and the orders of the Governor General.

(3) Every non-commissioned officer and man of the Indian Territorial Force,-

(a) When called out or embodied for military service under section 9,

(b) When attached to, or otherwise acting as part of, or with, any regular force, or

(c) When embodied for, or otherwise undergoing, military training in the prescribed manner,

shall be subject to the Indian Army Act, 1911, and the rules and regulations made thereunder, whereupon the said Act, rules and regulations shall apply to him as if he held the same rank in His Majesty's Indian Forces as he holds for the time being in the said Force, subject to the orders of the Governor General:

Provided that the said Act, rules and regulations shall, in their application to such non-commissioned officers and men when embodied for or otherwise undergoing military training, be modified to such extent and in such manner as may be prescribed :

Provided further that non-commissioned officers and men of an urban corps or unit, when undergoing military training, without having been embodied for that purpose, and non-commissioned officers and men of a University Corps when undergoing going training, shall, in respect of such training, be subject only to such disciplinary and other rules as may be prescribed.

(4) Where an offence punishable under the Indian Army Act, 1911, or, as the case may be, under that Act as modified under sub-section (3), has been committed by any person whilst subject to that Act under the provisions of this section, such person may be taken into and kept in military custody and tried and punished for such offence, although he has ceased to be so subject as aforesaid, in like manner as he might have been taken into and kept in military custody, tried or punished, if he had continued to be so subject:

Provided that no such person shall be kept in military custody after he has ceased to belong to the Indian Territorial Force, unless he has been taken into or kept in military custody on account of the offence before the date on which he ceased so to belong; nor shall he be kept in military custody or be tried or punished for the offence after the expiry of two months from that date, unless his trial has already commenced before such expiry."

12. After section I1 of the said Act, the following sections shall be inserted, namely

"11A. In addition to, or in substitution for, any punishment or punishments to which he may be liable under the Indian Army Act, 1911, a junior officer, non-commissioned officer or man of the Indian Territorial Force not being a member of a University Corps, may be punished, either by a Criminal Court or summarily by order of the prescribed authority, for any offence under that Act, or for the contravention of any rule or regulation under this Act, with fine which may extend to fifty rupees, to be recovered in such manner and by such authority as may be prescribed:

Provided that no fine shall be summarily inflicted by order of the prescribed authority in any case in which the accused claims to be tried by a Criminal Court:

Provided further that no Court inferior to that of a Presidency Magistrate or a Magistrate of the first class shall try any offence made punishable by or under this Act.

11B. Where a junior officer, non-commissioned officer or man of the Indian Territorial Force is required, by or in pursuance of any rule, regulation or order made under this Act, to attend at any place, a certificate purporting to be signed by the prescribed officer, stating that the person so required to attend failed to do so in accordance with such requirement, shall, without proof of the signature or appointment of such officer, be evidence of the matters stated therein."

13. For section 12 of the said Act, the following section shall be substituted, namely:-

"12. (1) The Local Government of each Province in which any unit or units of the Indian Territorial Force has or have been constituted shall constitute a Provincial Advisory Committee for all such units, and a Unit Advisory Committee for each of such units.

(2) The Governor General in Council shall constitute a Central Advisory Committee to advise him on matters connected with the Indian Territorial Force generally.

(3) The constitution, powers and procedure of the Advisory Committees shall be such as may be prescribed."

14. In clause (b) of sub-section (2) of section 13 of the said Act, after the word and figure "section 7" the words, figure and letter "or section 7A" shall be added.

THE INDIAN AIR FORCE ACT, 1932

CONTENTS

CHAPTER I
PRELIMINARY

SECTIONS

CHAPTER II

ENROLMENT, ATTESTATION, DISMISSAL, DISCHARGE AND REDUCTION

CHAPTER III

PUNISHMENT AND PENAL DEDUCTIONS

19. Punishments
20. Power to award lower punishments
21. Field punishment
22. Combination of punishments
23. Reduction of non-commissioned offices and warrant officers to ranks
24. Retention in the ranks of person convicted on active service
25. Minor punishments
26. Deductions from pay and allowances
27. Deductions from public money other than pay
28. Remission of deductions
29. Provision for dependants of prisoners of war
30. Unauthorized deductions forbidden

CHAPTER IV

AIR FORCE OFFENCES

31. Service offences punishable with death
32. Service offences punishable with long imprisonment
33. Service offences punishable more severely if committed on active service
34. Service offences punishable with short imprisonment
35. Mutiny
36. Insubordination punishable with long imprisonment
37. Insubordination punishable more severely if committed on active service
38. Insubordination punishable with short imprisonment
39. Desertion
40. Fraudulent enlistment
41. Connivance at desertion
42. Absence from duty without leave
43. Scandalous conduct of officer

44. Scandalous conduct punishable with long imprisonment
45. Scandalous conduct punishable with short imprisonment
46. Intoxication.
47. Permitting escape of prisoner
48. Irregular keeping in custody
49. Escape from custody
50. Offences relating to property
51. False accusation and offences relating to documents
52. False answers on enrolment
53. Offences relating to courts-martial
54. Offences relating to aircraft
55. Miscellaneous air force offences
56. Attempts
57. Abetment
58. Civil offences

CHAPTER V

ARREST AND PROCEDURE BEFORE TRIAL

59. Custody of offenders
60. Arrest by civil authorities
61. Capture of deserters
62. Inquiry on absence without leave
63. Provost-marshals
64. Duties and powers

CHAPTER VI

CONSTITUTION, JURISDICTION AND POWERS OF COURTS-MARTIAL

65. Kinds of courts-martial
66. Power to convene general courts-martial
67. Power to convene district courts-martial
68. Limitation of powers of convening authorities

69. Convening of field general courts-martial
70. Composition of general courts-martial
71. Composition of district courts-martial
72. Composition of field general courts-martial
73. Dissolution of courts-martial
74. Jurisdiction and powers of court-martial generally
75. Jurisdiction and powers of general and field general courts-martial
76. Jurisdiction and powers of district courts-martial
77. Prohibition of second trial
78. Limitation of trial
79. Place of trial
80. Order in case of concurrent jurisdiction of criminal court and court-martial
81. Power of criminal court to require delivery of offender
82. Trial by court-martial no bar to subsequent trial by criminal court

CHAPTER VII

PROCEDURE OF COURTS MARTIAL

83. President
84. Judge Advocate
85. Challenges
86. Voting of members
87. Oaths of president and members
88. Oaths of witnesses
89. The summoning of witnesses and production of documents
90. Commissions to obtain evidence
91. Conviction of one offence permissible on charge of another
92. General rule as to evidence
93. Judicial notice
94. Presumption as to signatures
95. Enrolment paper as evidence

96. Presumption as to certain documents

97. Reference by accused to Government officer

98. Evidence of previous convictions and service character

99. Order for custody and disposal of property pending trial in certain cases

CHAPTER VIII

CONFIRMATION, REVISION, PARDON AND REMISSION OF SENTENCES

100. Finding and sentence invalid without confirmation

101. Power to confirm finding and sentence of general court martial

102. Power to confirm finding and sentence of district court martial

103. Limitation on power of confirming authorities

104. Confirmation of finding and sentence of field general court-martial

105. Power of confirming authority to mitigate, remit or commute sentences

106. Confirmation of finding and sentence on board ship

107. Revision of finding or sentence

108. Substitution of valid for invalid sentence

109. Provision where accused is a lunatic

110. Pardons and remissions

CHAPTER IX

EXECUTION OF SENTENCES AND DISPOSAL OF PROPERTY

111. Sentence of death

112. Commencement of sentence of imprisonment

113. Execution of sentence of imprisonment

114. Execution of sentence of imprisonment in special cases

115. Execution of sentence of detention

116. Communication of certain orders to civil prison officers

117. Offenders sentenced to transportation how dealt with until transported

118. Execution of sentence of fine

119. Order for disposal of property regarding which offence committed

CHAPTER X

SPECIAL RULES RELATING TO PERSONS AND PROPERTY

120. Complaints against superior officers and airmen
121. Privileges of persons attending courts-martial
122. Exemption from arrest for debt
123. Property exempted from attachment
124. Application to reservists
125. Priority of hearing by courts of cases in which persons subject to this Act are concerned
126. Property of deceased persons and deserters, Meaning of deserter
127. Disposal of certain property without production of probate, etc
128. Application to lunatics and persons missing on active service

CHAPTER XI

SUPPLEMENTAL

129. Power to make rules
130. Amendment of certain documents

THE SCHEDULES

(Not included)

ACT NO. XIV OF 1932

[PASSED BY THE INDIAN LEGISLATURE]

(Received the assent of the Governor General on the 8th April, 1932)

An Act to provide for the administration and discipline of the Indian Air Force

WHEREAS it is intended to establish an Indian Air Force;

AND WHEREAS it is expedient to provide for the administration and discipline of that Force and for urposes connected therewith;

It is hereby enacted as follows:-

CHAPTER I

Short title and commencement

1. (1) This Act may be called the Indian Air Force Act, 1932.

(2) It shall come into force on such date as the Governor General in Council may, by notification in the Gazette of India, appoint.

Persons subject to this Act

2. (1) The following persons shall be subject to this Act, namely:

(a) Officers and warrant officers of the Indian Air Force;

(b) Persons enrolled under this Act;

(c) Persons not otherwise subject to military or air force law, who, on active service, in camp, on the march, or at any frontier post specified by the Governor General in Council by notification in this behalf, are employed by, or are in the service of, or are followers of, or accompany any portion of, the Indian Air Force.

(2) Every person who has become subject to this Act under sub-section (1) clause (c), shall remain so subject until duly discharged or dismissed.

Special provision as to rank in certain cases

3. (1) The Governor General in Council may, by notification, direct that any persons or class of persons subject to this Act under section 2, sub-section (1), clause (c), shall be so subject as officers, warrant officers or non-commissioned officers, and may authorise any officer to give a like direction with respect to any such person and to cancel such direction.

(2) All persons subject to this Act other than officers, warrant officers and non-commissioned officers shall, if they are not persons in respect of whom a notification or direction under sub-section (1) is in force, be deemed to be of a rank inferior to that of a non-commissioned officer.

Commanding officer of certain persons

4. Every person subject to this Act under section 2, subsection (1), clause (c), shall, for the purposes of this Act, be deemed to be under the commanding officer of the corps, unit or detachment (if any) to which he is attached, and if he is not attached to any corps, unit or detachment, under the command of any officer who may for the time being be named as his commanding officer by the officer commanding the force with which such person may for the time being be serving, or of any other prescribed officer, or, if no such officer is named or prescribed, under the command of the said officer commanding the force:

Provided that an officer commanding a force shall not place a person under the command of an officer of official rank inferior to that of such person if there is present at the place where such person is any officer of higher rank under whose command he call be placed.

Officers to exercise powers in certain cases

5. (1) Whenever persons subject to this Act are serving within or without India under an officer not subject to this Act, the Governor General in Council may prescribe the officer by whom the powers which, under this Act, may be exercised by officers commanding units, shall, as regards such persons, be exercised.

(2) The Governor General in Council may confer such powers either absolutely or subject to such restrictions, reservations, exceptions and conditions as he may think fit.

Definitions

6. In this Act, unless there is something repugnant in the subject or context:---

(1). "Officer of the Indian Air Force" means a person commissioned, gazetted or in pay as an officer of the Indian Air Force;

(2) "Warrant officer" means a person appointed, gazetted or in pay as a warrant officer in the Indian Air Force;

(3) "Non-commissioned officer" means a person attested under this Act holding a non-commissioned rank in the Indian Air Force, and includes an acting non-commissioned officer;

(4) "Officer" means an officer of any of His Majesty's naval, military or air forces, but does not include a warrant officer or non-commissioned officer;

(5) "Airman" means any person subject to this Act other than an officer;

(6) "Commanding officer", used in relation to a person subject to this Act, means the officer for the time being in command of the unit or detachment to which such person belongs or is attached;

(7) "Superior officer", when used in relation to a person subject to this Act, includes a warrant officer and a non-commissioned officer; and, as regards persons placed under his orders, an officer, a warrant officer or non-commissioned officer of any of His Majesty's naval, military or air forces;

(8) "Corps" means anybody of the Indian Air Force which is prescribed as a corps for the purposes of all or any of the provisions of this Act;

(9) "Unit" means anybody of the Indian Air Force which is prescribed as a unit for the purposes of all or any of the provisions of this Act;

(10) "Enemy" includes all armed mutineers, armed rebels, armed rioters, pirates and any person in arms against whom it is the duty of a person subject to naval, military or air force law to act;

(11) "Active service" as applied to a person subject to this Act, means the time during which such person is attached to, or forms part of, a force which is engaged in operations against an enemy, or is engaged in warlike operations in, or is on the line of march to, a country or place wholly or partly occupied by an enemy, or is in military occupation of any foreign country, and includes, in respect of a person subject to this Act attached to or forming part of a force which is about to be or has recently been on such active service, such time as the Governor General in Council may, by notification in the Gazette of India, declare to, be active service in respect of such force;

(12) "Air force custody" means the arrest or confinement of a person according to the usages of His Majesty's military and air forces, and includes military custody;

(13) "Air force reward" includes any gratuity or annuity for long service or good conduct, any good conduct pay, good service pay or pension, and any other air force pecuniary reward;

(14) "Court-martial" means a court-martial held under this Act;

(15) "Criminal court" means a court of ordinary criminal justice in British India, or established elsewhere by the authority of the Governor General in Council;

(16) "Offence" means any act or omission made punishable by any law for the time being in force;

(17) "Air force offence" means any act or omission made punishable by this Act;

(18) "Civil offence" means an offence which, if committed in British India, would be triable by a criminal court;

(19) "His Majesty's naval forces" include the Indian Marine Service;

(20) "Notification" means a notification published in the Gazette of India;

(21) "Prescribed" means prescribed by rules made under this Act; and

(22) All words and expressions used herein and defined in the Indian Penal Code, (XLV of 1860) and not hereinbefore defined, shall be deemed to have the meanings respectively attributed to them by that Code.

CHAPTER II

ENROLMENT, ATTESTATION, DISMISSAL, DISCHARGE AND REDUCTION

Procedure before enrolling officer

7. Upon the appearance before the prescribed enrolling officer of person desirous of being enrolled, the enrolling officer shall read and explain to him, or cause to be read and explained to him, in his presence, the conditions of the service for which he is to be enrolled; and shall put to him the questions set forth in the prescribed form of enrolment, and shall, after having cautioned him that if he makes a false answer to any such question he will be liable to punishment under this Act, record or cause to be recorded his answer to each such question.

Enrolment

8. If, after complying with the provisions of section 7, the enrolling officer is satisfied that the person desirous of being enrolled fully understands the questions put to him and consents to the conditions of service, and if he perceives no impediment, he shall sign and shall also cause the person to sign the enrolment paper, and the person shall then be deemed to be enrolled.

Conditions of enrolment

9. The enrolling officer shall not cause any person to sign the enrolment, paper unless he is satisfied that such person is a subject of His Majesty or of a Prince or Chief in India, and---

(a) Is of unmixed Indian descent, or

(b) If he is of mixed Indian and non-Indian descent, is domiciled in India, or

(c) If he is of unmixed non-Indian Asiatic descent, is domiciled in India and his father and grandfather were domiciled in India.

Presumption of enrolment in certain cases

10. Every person who has for the space of six months been in the receipt of air force pay and been borne on the rolls of any unit shall be deemed to have been duly enrolled, notwithstanding any illegality or irregularity in his enrolment.

Persons to be attested

11. The following persons shall be attested, namely:--

(a) All persons enrolled as combatants;

(b) All other enrolled persons prescribed by the Governor General in Council.

Mode of attestation

12. (1) When a person who is to be attested is reported fit for duty, or has completed the prescribed of period of probation, an oath or affirmation shall be administered to him in the prescribed form by his commanding officer in front of his unit or such portion thereof as may be present, or by any other prescribed person.

(2) The form of oath or affirmation prescribed under this section shall contain a promise that the person to be attested will be faithful to His Majesty, his heirs and successors, and that he will serve in the Indian Air Force and go wherever he is ordered by air, land or sea, and that he will obey all commands of any officer set over him, even to the peril of his life.

(3) The fact of an enrolled person having taken the oath or affirmation directed by this section to be taken shall be entered on his enrolment paper, and authenticated by his signature and by the signature of the officer administering the oath or affirmation.

Dismissal by Governor General in Council

13. The Governor General in Council may at any time dismiss from the service any person subject to this Act.

Dismissal by the Air Officer Commanding or prescribed officer

14. The Air Officer Commanding His Majesty's Air Forces in India, or any prescribed officer, may at any time dismiss from the service any person subject to this Act other than an officer.

Discharge

15. The prescribed authority may, in conformity with any rules prescribed in this behalf, discharge from the service any person subject to this Act.

Certificate to person dismissed or discharged

16. Every enrolled person who is dismissed or discharged from the service shall be furnished by his commanding officer with a certificate setting forth—

(a) The authority dismissing or discharging him;

(b) The cause of his dismissal or discharge;

(c) The full period of his service in the Indian Air Force.

Discharge and dismissal out of India

17. (1) Any enrolled person who is entitled under the conditions of his enrolment to be discharged, or whose discharge is ordered by competent authority, and who, when he is so entitled or ordered to be discharged, is serving out of India, and requests to be sent to India, shall, before being discharged, be sent to India with all convenient speed.

(2) Any person enrolled under this Act who is dismissed from the service and who, when he is so dismissed, is serving out of India, shall be sent to India with all convenient speed;

Provided that, where any such person is sentenced to dismissal combined with any other punishment, such other punishment, or, in the case of a sentence of imprisonment, a portion of such other punishment, may be inflicted before he is sent to India.

Reduction

18. (1) The Air Officer Commanding His Majesty's Air Force in India, or any prescribed officer, may at any time reduce any warrant officer or any non-commissioned officer to a lower grade or to a lower rank or to the ranks, or any airman other than a warrant officer or non-commissioned officer to a lower class in the ranks.

(2) The commanding officer of an acting non-commissioned officer may order him to revert to his permanent grade as a non-commissioned officer or, if he has no permanent grade above the ranks, to the ranks.

CHAPTER III

PUNISHMENTS AND PENAL DEDUCTIONS

Punishments

19. Punishments may be inflicted in respect of offences committed by persons subject to this Act, and convicted by court-martial, according to the scale following, that is to say,---

(a) Death;

(b) Imprisonment, which shall be of two degrees, namely:--

(i) Long imprisonment, which shall be rigorous and for a term not less than three years and not exceeding fourteen years, and

(ii) Short imprisonment, which may be rigorous or simple, for a term not exceeding two years;

(c) In the case of airmen, detention for a term not exceeding two years ;

(d) Dismissal from the service;

(e) In the case of officers and warrant officers, suspension from rank, pay and allowances for a period not exceeding two months;

(f) Reduction, in the case of a warrant officer, or a non-commissioned officer, to a lower grade, or to a lower rank or to the ranks;

(g) In the case of officers, warrant officers and non-commissioned officers, forfeiture of seniority of rank;

(h) In the case of officers, warrant officers and non-commissioned officers, reprimand or severe reprimand;

Forfeitures and stoppages as follows, namely:-

(i) Forfeiture of service for the purpose of promotion, increased pay, pension or any other prescribed purpose;

(ii) Forfeiture of any military or air-force decoration or military or sir force reward;

(iii) Forfeiture, in the case of a person sentenced to dismissal from the service, of all arrears of pay and allowances due to him at the time of such dismissal;

(iv) Stoppages of pay and allowances until any proved loss or damage occasioned by the offence of which he is convicted is made good;

(v) On active service, forfeiture of pay and allowance for a period not exceeding three months.

Power to award lower punishments

20. Where in respect of any offence under this Act there is specified **a** particular punishment, there may be awarded in respect of that offence instead of such particular punishment (but subject to the other provisions of this Act as to punishments and regard being had to the nature and degree of the offence) any one punishment lower in the above scale than the particular punishment.

Field Punishment

21. (1) Where any person, subject to this Act and under the rank of warrant officer, on active service is guilty of any offence, it shall be lawful for a court-martial to award for that offence any such punishment as may be prescribed as a field punishment. Field punishment shall be of the character of personal restraint or of hard labour but shall not be of a nature to cause injury to life or limb.

(2) Field punishment shall, for the purpose of commutation, be deemed to stand in the scale of punishments next below dismissal.

Combination of punishment

22. A sentence of a court-martial may award, in addition to or without any one other punishment, any one or more of the punishments specified in clauses (d), *(f)*, ***(h)*** and *(i)* of section 19.

Reduction of non-commissioned officers and warrant officers to ranks

23. A warrant officer or non-commissioned officer sentenced by court-martial to imprisonment, detention, field punishment or dismissal from the service, shall be deemed to be reduced to the ranks.

Retention in the ranks of person convicted on active service

24. When any enrolled person on active service has been sentenced by court-martial to dismissal or to imprisonment, whether combined with dismissal or not, the prescribed officer may direct that such person may be retained to serve in the ranks, and where such person has been sentenced to imprisonment, such service shall be reckoned as part of his term of imprisonment.

Minor punishments

25. (1) The Governor General in Council may prescribe the minor punishments to which persons subject to this Act shall be liable without the intervention of a court-martial, and the officer or officers by whom, and the extent to which, such minor punishments may be awarded.

(2) Detention and, in the case of persons subject to this Act on active service, any prescribed field punishment may be specified as minor punishments:

Provided that--

(a) The term of such detention or field punishment shall not exceed twenty-eight days; and

(b) Detention or field punishment shall not be awarded to any person of or above the rank of non-commissioned officer, or who, when he committed the offence in respect of which is awarded, was of or above such rank.

(3) The provisions of sections 77, 78 and 79 shall apply to the proceedings of officers empowered to award minor punishments under this section as if such officers were courts-martial.

Deductions from pay and allowances

26. (1) The following penal deductions may be made from the pay and allowances of an officer of the Indian Air Force, that is to say,--

(a) All pay and allowances due to an officer who absent himself without leave or overstays the period for which leave of absence has been granted to him, unless a satisfactory explanation has been given to his commanding officer and has been approved by the Governor General in Council;

(b) Any sum required to make good such compensation for any expenses, loss, damage or destruction occasioned by the commission of any offence as may be determined by the court-martial by whom he is convicted of such offence;

(c) Any sum required to make good the pay of any officer or airman which he has unlawfully retained or unlawfully refused to pay;

(d) Any sum required to make good any loss, damage or destruction of public or service property which, after due investigation, appears to the Governor General in Council to have been occasioned by any wrongful act or negligence on the part of the officer.

(2) The following penal deductions may be made from the pay and allowances of an airman, that is to say,--

(a) All pay and allowances for every day of absence either on desertion or without leave, or as a prisoner of war, and for every day of imprisonment or detention awarded by a criminal court, a court-martial or an officer exercising authority under section 25, or of field punishment, awarded by a court-martial or such officer;

(b) All pay and allowances for every day whilst he is in custody on a charge for an offence of which he is afterwards convicted by a criminal court or court-martial, or on a charge of absence without leave for which he is afterwards awarded imprisonment, detention or field punishment by an officer exercising authority under section 25;

(c) All pay and allowances for every day on which he is in hospital on account of sickness certified by the medical officer attending on him to have been caused by an offence under this Act committed by him;

(d) For every day on which he is in hospital on account of sickness certified by the medical officer attending on him to have been caused by his own misconduct or imprudence, such sum as may be prescribed;

(e) All pay and allowances ordered by a court-martial to be suspended or forfeited;

(f) Any sum ordered by a court-martial to be stopped;

(g) Any sum required to make good such compensation for any expenses caused by him, or for any loss of or damage or destruction done by him to any arms, ammunition, equipment, clothing, instruments, service necessaries, or military decoration, or to any buildings or property, as may be awarded by his commanding officer;

(h) Any sum required to pay a fine awarded by a criminal court, a court-martial exercising jurisdiction under section 58 or an officer exercising authority under section 25;

Provided that the total deductions from the pay and allowances of a person subject to this Act made under clauses (e) to (g), both inclusive, shall not (except in the case of a person sentenced to dismissal) exceed in any one month one-half of his pay and allowances for that month.

Explanation:--For the purposes of clauses (a) and (b)-

(i) No person shall be treated as absent, imprisoned, or detained, unless the absence, imprisonment, or detention has lasted six hours or upwards, except where the absence prevented the absentee from fulfilling any air force duty which was thereby thrown on some other person;

(ii) A period of absence, imprisonment, or detention which commences before and ends after midnight may be reckoned as a day;

(iii) The number of days shall be reckoned as from the time when the absence, imprisonment, or detention commences; and

(iv) No period of less than twenty-four hours shall be reckoned as more than one day.

Deduction from public money other than pay

27. Any sum authorized by this Act to be deducted from the pay and allowances of any person may, without prejudice to any other mode of recovering the same, be deducted from any public money due to him other than a pension.

Remission of deductions

28. Any deduction from pay and allowances authorized by this Act may be remitted in such manner and to such extent and by such authority as may from time to time be prescribed.

Provision for dependents of prisoners of war

29. In the case of all persons subject to this Act being prisoners of war, whose pay and allowances have been forfeited under section 26, but in respect of whom a remission has been made under section 28, it shall be lawful, notwithstanding any provision in any enactment or any rule of law to the contrary, for proper provision to be made by the prescribed authorities out of such pay and allowances for any dependants of such persons, and any such remission shall in that case be deemed to apply only to the balance thereafter remaining of such pay and allowances.

Unauthorized deductions forbidden

30. The pay of an officer or airman of the Indian Air Force shall be paid without any deduction other than the deductions authorized by this Act or by any other enactment for the time being in force or prescribed by the Governor General in Council.

CHAPTER IV

AIR FOECE OFFENCES

Service offences punishable with death

31. Any person subject to this Act who:--

(a) Shamefully abandons or delivers up any garrison, fortress, post, or guard committed to his charge, or which it is his duty to defend, or

(b) Shamefully casts away his arms, ammunition or tools in the presence of the enemy, or

(c) Treacherously holds correspondence with or gives intelligence to the enemy, or treacherously or through cowardice sends a flag of truce to the enemy, or

(d) Assists the enemy with arms, ammunition, or supplies, or knowingly harbours or protects an enemy not being a prisoner, or

(e) Having been made a prisoner of war, voluntarily serves with or voluntarily aids the enemy, or

(f) Voluntarily does when on active service any act calculated to imperil the success of His Majesty's Forces or any part thereof, or

(g) Treacherously or shamefully causes the capture or destruction by the enemy of any of His Majesty's aircraft, or

(h) Treacherously gives any false air signal or alters or interferes with any air signal, or

(i) When ordered by his superior officer or otherwise under orders to carry out any warlike operation in the air, treacherously or shamefully fails to use his utmost exertions to carry such orders into effect,

shall be punishable with death.

Service offences not punishable with death

32. Any person subject to this Act who, on active service:--

(a) Without orders from his superior officer leaves the ranks in order to secure prisoners or horses, or on pretence of taking wounded men to the rear, or

(b) Without orders from his superior officer willfully destroys or damages any property, or

(c) Is taken prisoner by want of due precaution or through disobedience of orders or wilful neglect of duty, or, having been taken prisoner, fails to rejoin His Majesty's service when able to do so, or

(d) Without due authority either holds correspondence with, or gives intelligence, or sends a flag of truce to the enemy, or

(e) By word of mouth, or in writing, or by signals, or otherwise spreads reports calculated to create unnecessary alarm or despondency, or

(f) In action, or previously to going into action, uses words calculated to create alarm or despondency, or

(g) Negligently causes the capture or destruction by the enemy of any of His Majesty's aircraft, or

(h) When ordered by his superior officer or otherwise under orders to carry out any warlike operation in the air, negligently or through other default fails to use his utmost exertions to carry such orders into effect, or

(i) Misbehaves before the enemy in such manner as to show cowardice,

shall be punishable with long imprisonment.

Service offences punishable more severely if committed on active service

33. (1) Any person subject to this Act who treacherously makes known the watchword to any person not entitled to receive it, or treacherously gives a watchword different from on what he received, shall, if he commits the offence on active service, be punishable with death, and, if he commits the offence not on active service, with short imprisonment.

(2) Any person subject to this Act who-

(a) Without due authority alters or interferes with any air signal, or

(b) Forces a safeguard, or

(c) Forces or strikes a sentinel, or

(d) Breaks into any house or other place in search of plunder, or

(e) Being an airman acting as sentinel, sleeps or is intoxicated, or

(f) Without orders from his superior officer leaves his, guard, piquet, patrol or post, or

(g) By discharging fire arms, making signals, using words, or by any means whatever, intentionally occasions false alarms, or

(h) Being all airman acting as sentinel, leaves his post before he is regularly relieved,

shall, if he commits the offence on active service, be punishable with long imprisonment and, if he commits the offence not on active service, with short imprisonment.

Service offences punishable with short imprisonment

34. Any person subject to this Act who:--

(a) By discharging fire arms, making signals, using words, or by any means whatever, negligently occasions false alarms, or

(b) Makes known the watchword to any person not entitled to receive it, or, without good and sufficient cause, gives a watchword different from what he received, or

(c) Impedes the provost-marshal or any assistant provost-marshal or any officer or non-commissioned officer or other person legally exercising authority under or on behalf of the provost-marshal, or, when called on, refuses to assist in the execution of his duty the provost-marshal, the assistant provost-marshal, or any such officer, non-commissioned officer or other person, or

(d) Uses criminal force to or commits an assault on any person bringing provisions or supplies to the forces, or commits any offence against the property or person of any inhabitant of or resident in the country in which he is serving, or

(e) Irregularly detains or appropriates to his own unit or detachment any provisions or supplies proceeding to the forces, contrary to orders issued in that respect,

shall be punishable with short imprisonment.

Mutiny

35. Any person subject to this Act who,--

(a) Begins, incites, causes or conspires with any other persons to cause any mutiny in any of His Majesty's naval, military or air forces, or

(b) Joins in, or, being present, does not use his utmost endeavours to suppress, any such mutiny, or

(c) Knowing or having reason to believe in the existence of any such mutiny, or of any intention to commit such mutiny, or of any such conspiracy, does not without delay give information thereof to his commanding or other superior officer,

shall be punishable with death.

Insubordination punishable with long imprisonment

36. Any person subject to this Act who--

(a) Uses criminal force to or assaults his superior officer, being in the execution of his office, or

(b) Disobeys in such manner as to show a wilful defiance of authority any lawful command given personally by his superior officer in the execution of his office,

shall be punishable with long imprisonment.

Insubordination punishable more severely if committed on active service

37. Any person subject to this Act who---

(a) Uses criminal force to or assaults his superior officer, or

(b) Uses threatening or insubordinate language to his superior officer, or

(c) disobeys any lawful command given by his superior officer,

shall, if he commits the offence on active service, be punishable with long imprisonment, and, if he commits the offence not on active service, with short imprisonment.

Insubordination punishable with short imprisonment

38. Any person subject to this Act who--

(a) Being concerned in any quarrel, affray or disorder, refuses to obey any officer (though of inferior in rank) who orders him into arrest, or uses criminal force to or assaults any such officer, or

(b) Uses criminal force to or assaults any person, whether subject to this Act or not, in whose custody he is placed, whether he is or is not his superior officer, or

(c) Resists an escort whose duty it is to apprehend him or to have him in charge, or

(d) Being an airman, breaks out of barracks, camp or quarters, or

(e) Neglects to obey any general, local or other orders (not being orders in the nature of a rule or regulation published for the general information and guidance of the Indian Air Force),

shall be punishable with short imprisonment.

Desertion

39. Any person subject to this Act who deserts or attempts to desert the service shall, if he commits the offence when on active service or under orders for active service, be punishable with long imprisonment, and, if he commits the offence under any other circumstances, with short imprisonment.

Fraudulent enrolment

40. Any person subject to this Act who, when belonging to the Indian Air Force, without having obtained a regular discharge therefrom, or otherwise fulfilled the conditions enabling him to enlist, enrol or enter, enrols himself, or enlists in or enters any other of His Majesty's air forces, or any of His Majesty's military or naval forces, or re-enrols himself in the Indian Air Force, shall be deemed to be guilty of fraudulent enlistment, and shall be punishable with short imprisonment.

Connivance at desertion

41. Any person subject to this Act who, being cognizant of any desertion or intended desertion of a person subject to this Act, does not forthwith give notice to his commanding officer, or take any steps in his power to cause the deserter or intending deserter to be apprehended, shall be punishable with short imprisonment.

Absence from duty without leave

42. Any person subject to this Act who--

(a) Absents himself without leave, or

(b) Fails to appear at the time fixed at a parade or place appointed for exercise or duty, or goes from thence without leave before he is relieved, or without necessity quits his duty or duties, or

(c) Being an airman, when in camp or garrison or elsewhere, is found beyond any limits fixed or in any place prohibited by any general, local or other order, without a pass or written leave from his superior officer, or

(d) Being an airman, without leave from his superior officer, or without due cause, absents himself from any school when duly ordered to attend there,

shall be with short imprisonment.

Scandalous conduct of officers

43. Any officer or warrant officer subject to this Act who behaves in a manner unbecoming his position and character shall notwithstanding anything contained in section 20, be dismissed from the service.

Scandalous conduct punishable with long imprisonment

44. Any person subject to this Act who—

(a) Steals any property of Government, or dishonestly misappropriates or converts to his own use any property of Government entrusted to him, or

(b) Dishonestly receives or retains any property in respect of which an offence under clause (a) has been committed, knowing or having reason to believe it to have been stolen or dishonestly misappropriated or converted, or

(c) Willfully destroys or damages any property of Government entrusted to him, or

(d) Steals any property of any air force mess, band or institution, or of any person subject to this Act or serving with or attached to the Indian Air Force, or dishonestly misappropriates or converts to his own use any such property entrusted to him, or

(e) Dishonestly receives or retains any property in respect of which an offence under clause (d) has been committed, knowing or having reason to believe it to have been stolen or dishonestly misappropriated or converted,

shall be punishable with long imprisonment.

Scandalous conduct punishable with short imprisonment

45. Any person subject to this Act who-

(a) Does any act, not otherwise specified in this Act, with intent to defraud, or to cause wrongful gain to one person or wrongful loss to another person, or

(b) Malingers or feigns or produces disease or infirmity himself, or intentionally delays his cure or aggravates his disease or infirmity, or

(c) With intent to render himself or any other person unfit for service, voluntarily causes hurt to himself or any other person, or

(d) Commits any offence of a cruel, indecent or unnatural kind, or attempts to commit any such offence and does any act towards its commission,

shall be punishable with short imprisonment.

Intoxication

46. Any person subject to this Act who is found in a state of intoxication, whether on duty or not on duty, shall be punishable, if an officer, with dismissal from the service, and, if an airman, with short imprisonment:

Provided that where the offence of being intoxicated is committed by an airman not on active service or on duty, the sentence imposed shall not exceed detention for a period of six months.

Permitting escape of prisoner

47. Any person subject to this Act who—

(a) When in command of a guard, piquet, patrol or post, releases without proper authority, whether voluntarily or otherwise, any person committed to his charge, or

(b) Voluntarily or negligently allows to escape any person who is committed to his charge, or whom it is his duty to keep or guard, shall be punishable, if he has acted voluntarily, with long imprisonment, and, if he has not acted voluntarily, with short imprisonment.

Irregular keeping in custody

48. Any person subject to this Act who-

(a) Unnecessarily detains a person in arrest or confinement without bringing him to trial or fails to bring his case before the proper authority for investigation, or

(b) Having committed a person to the custody of any officer, non-commissioned officer, provost-marshal, or assistant provost-marshal, fails without reasonable cause to deliver at the time of such committal, or as soon as practicable, and in any case within twenty-four hours thereafter, to the officer, noncommissioned officer, provost-marshal, or assistant provost-marshal, provost-marshal, into whose custody, the person is committed, an account in writing signed by himself of the offences with which the person so committed is charged, or

(c) Being in command of the guard, does not **as** soon as he is relieved from his guard or duty, or if he is not sooner relieved, within twenty-four hours after a person is committed to his charge, give in writing to the officer to whom he may be ordered to report that person's name and offence so far as known to him, and the name and rank of the officer or other person by whom he was charged, accompanied, if he has received the account as above in this section mentioned, by that account,

shall be punishable with short imprisonment.

Escape from custody

49. Any person subject to this Act, who, being in lawful custody, escapes or attempts to esca.pe, shall be punishable with short imprisonment.

Offence relating to property

50. Any person subject to this Act who--

(a) Commits extortion, or without proper authority exacts from any person carriage, porterage or provisions, or

(b) In time of peace, commits house-breaking for the purpose of plundering, or plunders, destroys or damages any field, garden or other property, or

(c) Voluntarily or negligently kills, injures, makes away with, ill-treats or loses any animal used in the public service, or

(d) Makes away with, or is concerned in making away with, any arms, ammunition, equipments, instruments, tools, clothing or service necessaries issued to him or required to be maintained by him, or

(e) Loses by neglect anything mentioned in clause (d), or

(f) Wilfully damages anything mentioned in clause (d) or any property belonging to Government, or to any air force mess, band or institution, or to any person subject to air force law, or serving with, or attached to the Indian Air Force, or

(g) Sells, pawns, destroys or defaces any medal or decoration granted to him,

shall be punishable with short imprisonment.

False accusations and offences relating to documents

51. Any person subject to this Act who—

(a) Makes a false accusation against any person subject to this Act, knowing such accusation to be false, or

(b) In making any complaint under section 120, knowingly makes any false statement affecting the character of any person subject to this Act, or knowingly and wilfully suppresses any material fact, or

(c) Obtains or attempts to obtain for himself or for any other person any pension, allowance or other advantage or privilege by a statement which is false, and which he either knows or believes to be false or does not believe to be true, or by making or using a false entry in any document or by making any document containing a false statement, or by omitting to make a true entry or document containing a true statement, or

(d) Knowingly furnishes a false return or report of the number or state of any men under his command or charge, or of any money, arms, ammunition, clothing, equipments, stores or other property in his charge, whether belonging to such men or to Government or to any person in or attached to the Indian Air Force, or who, wilfully or negligently, omits or refuses to make or send any return or report of the matters aforesaid,

shall be punishable with short imprisonment.

False answers on enrolment

52. Any person having become subject to this Act who is discovered to have made a wilfully false answer to any question set forth in the prescribed form of enrolment which has been put to him by the enrolling officer shall be punishable with short imprisonment.

Offences relating to court martial

53. Any person subject to this Act who—

(a) When duly summoned to attend as a witness before a court-martial, intentionally omits to attend or refuses fuses to be sworn or affirmed or to answer any question, or to produce or deliver up any document or other thing which he may have been duly warned and called upon to produce or deliver up, or

(b) Intentionally offers any insult or causes any interruption or disturbance to, or uses any menacing or disrespectful word, sign or gesture, or is insubordinate or violent in the presence of, a court-martial while sitting, or

(c) Having been duly sworn or affirmed before any court-martial or other court or officer authorised by this Act to administer an oath or affirmation, makes any statement which is false, and which he either known or believes to be false or does not believe to be true,

shall be punishable with short imprisonment.

Offences relating to aircraft

54. Any person subject to this Act who--

(a) Voluntarily or negligently damages, destroys or loses any of His Majesty's aircraft or aircraft material, or

(b) Is guilty of any act or omission likely to cause such damage, destruction or loss, or

(c) Is guilty of any act or omission (whether voluntary or otherwise) which causes damage to or destruction of any public property by fire, or

(d) Without lawful authority disposes of any of His Majesty's aircraft or aircraft material, or

(e) Is guilty of any act or omission in flying or in the use of any aircraft, or in relation to any aircraft or aircraft material which causes or is likely to cause loss of life or bodily injury to any person, or

(f) During a state of war voluntarily and without proper occasion or negligently causes the sequestration, by or under the authority of a neutral State, or the destruction in a neutral State of any of His Majesty's aircraft,

shall be punishable, if he has acted voluntarily, with long imprisonment, and, if he has not acted voluntarily, with short imprisonment.

Miscellaneous air force offences

55. Any person subject to this Act who—

(a) Strikes or otherwise ill-treats any person subject to this Act being his subordinate in rank or position, or

(b) being in command at any post or on the march and receiving a complaint that any one under his command has beaten or otherwise maltreated or oppressed any person, or has disturbed any fair or market, or committed any riot or trespass, fails to have due reparation made to the, injured person or to report the case to the proper authority, or

(c) By defiling ally place of worship, or otherwise, intentionally insults the religion or wounds the religious feelings of any person, or

(d) Attempts to commit suicide and does any act towards the commission of such offence, or

(e) Being below the rank of warrant officer, when off duty, appears, without proper authority, in or about camp or cantonments, or in or about, or when going to or returning from, any town or bazar, carrying a sword, bludgeon or other offensive weapon, or

(f) Directly or indirectly accepts or obtains, or agrees to accept or attempts to obtain, for himself or for any other person, any gratification as a motive or reward for procuring the enrolment of any person, or leave of absence, promotion or any other advantage or indulgence for any person in the service, or

(g) Is guilty of any act or omission which, though not specified in this Act, is prejudicial to good order and air force discipline,

shall be punished with short imprisonment.

Attempts

56. Any person subject to this Act who attempts to commit an air force offence or to cause such an offence to be committed, and in such attempt does any act towards the commission of the offence may, where no express provision is made by this Act for the punishment of such attempt, be punished with the punishment provided in this Act for such offence.

Abetment

57. Any person subject to this Act who abets the commission of any air force offence, or of any offence punishable under the Army Act, the Air Force Act or the Indian Army Act, 1911, such offence being of the same nature as any air force offence, shall be punishable with the punishment provided in this Act for such air force offence.

Civil offences

58. (1) Any person subject to this Act who at any place in or beyond British India commits any civil offence shall be deemed to be guilty of an air force offence, and, if charged therewith

under this section, shall be liable to be tried by court-martial and to be punished as follows, that is to say:-

(a) If the offence is one which would be punishable under the law of British India with death or with transportation, he shall be liable to suffer any punishment, other than whipping, assigned for the offence by the law of British India; and

(b) In other cases, he shall be liable to suffer any punishment, other than whipping, assigned for the offence by the law of British India, or such punishment as might be awarded to him in pursuance of this Act in respect of an act prejudicial to good order and air force discipline:

Provided that a person subject to this Act who, at any place in British India or at any place in which the Governor General in Council exercises powers and jurisdiction by virtue of the Indian (Foreign Jurisdiction) Order in Council, 1902, and while not on active service, commits an offence of murder or culpable homicide against a person not subject to this Act or an offence of rape, shall not be deemed to be guilty of an air force offence and shall not be tried by court-martial.

(2) The powers of a court-martial to charge and to punish any person under this section shall not be affected by reason of the civil offence with which such person is charged being also an air force offence.

CHAPTER V

ARREST AND PROCEEDINGS BEFORE TRIAL

Custody of offenders

59. (1) Any person subject to this Act who is charged with an offence may be 'taken into air force custody.

(2) Any such person may be ordered into air force custody by any superior officer.

(3) The charge against every person taken into air force custody shall, without unnecessary delay, be investigated by the proper authority, and as soon as may be, either proceedings shall be taken for punishing the offence, or such person shall be discharged from custody.

Arrest by civil authorities

60. Whenever any person subject to this Act, who is accused of any offence under this Act, is within the jurisdiction of any Magistrate or police-officer, such Magistrate or officer shall aid in the apprehension and delivery to air force custody of such person upon receipt of a written application to that effect signed by his commanding officer.

Capture of deserters

61. (1) Whenever any person subject to this Act deserts, his commanding officer shall give written information of the desertion to such civil authorities as, in his opinion, may be able to afford assistance towards the capture of the deserter; and such authorities shall thereupon take steps for the apprehension of the said deserter in like manner as if he were a person for whose apprehension a warrant had been issued by a Magistrate, and shall deliver the deserter, when apprehended, to air force custody.

(2) Any police-officer may arrest without warrant any person reasonably believed to be subject to this Act and to be travelling without authority, and shall bring him without delay before the nearest Magistrate, to be dealt with according to law.

Inquiry on absence without leave

62. (1) When any person subject to this Act has been absent without due authority from his duty for a period of twenty-one days, a court of inquiry shall, as soon as practicable, be assembled and, upon oath or affirmation administered in the prescribed manner, shall inquire respecting the absence of the person, and the deficiency, if any, of property of the Government entrusted to his care, or of his arms, ammunition, equipments, instruments, clothing or necessaries; and, if satisfied of the fact of such absence without due authority or other sufficient cause, the court shall declare such absence and the period thereof, and the said deficiency, if any; and the commanding officer of the unit to which the person belongs shall enter in the court-martial book of the unit a record of the declaration.

(2) If the person declared absent does not afterwards surrender, or is not apprehended, he shall, for the purposes of this Act, be deemed to be a deserter.

Provost Marshal

63. For the prompt and instant repression of irregularities and offences committed in the field or on the march, provost-marshals may be appointed by the Air Officer Commanding His Majesty's Air Forces in India; and the powers and duties of such provost-marshals shall be regulated according to the established custom of war and the rules of the service.

Duties and powers

64. The duties of a provost-marshal so appointed are to take charge of persons in air force custody, to preserve good order and discipline and to prevent breaches thereof by persons subject to this Act.

He may at any time arrest and detain for trial any person subject to this Act who commits an offence and may also carry into effect any punishments to be inflicted in pursuance of the sentence of a court-martial.

CHAPTER VI

CONSTITUTION, JURISDICTION AND POERS OF COURTS-MARTIAL

Kinds of courts-martial

65. For the purposes of this Act there shall be three kinds of courts-martial, that is to say:--

(1) General courts-martial;

(2) District courts-martial; and

(3) Field general courts-martial

Power to convene general courts-martial

66. A general court-martial may be convened by the Governor General in Council, or by any officer empowered in this behalf by warrant of the Governor General in Council.

Power to convene district courts-martial

67. A district court-martial may be convened by any authority having power to convene a general court-martial, or by any officer empowered in this behalf by warrant of any such authority.

Limitation on powers of convening authorities

68. A warrant issued under section 66 or section 67 may contain such restrictions, reservations or conditions as the convening authority issuing it may think fit.

Convening of field general courts-martial

69. The following authorities shall have power to convene a field general court-martial, that is to say--

(a) An authority empowered in this behalf by an order of the Governor General in Council;

(b) On active service, the commanding officer of the forces in the field, or any officer empowered by him in this behalf;

(c) The commanding officer of any detached portion of the Indian Air Force on active service, when, in his opinion, it is not practicable, with due regard to discipline or the exigencies of the service, that an offence should be tried by a general court-martial, and circumstances prevent a reference to higher authority.

Composition of general courts-martial

70. A general court-martial shall consist of not less than five officers each of whom must have held a commission during not less than three whole years and of whom not less than four must be of a rank not below that of a flight lieutenant.

Composition of district courts-martial

71. A district court-martial shall consist of not less than three officers.

Composition of summary general courts-martial

72. A field general court-martial shall consist of not less than three officers.

Dissolution of court-martial

73. (1) If a court-martial after the commencement of a trial is reduced below the smallest number of officers of which it is by this Act required to consist, it shall be dissolved.

(2) If, on account of the illness of the accused before the finding, it is impossible to continue the trial, a court-martial shall be dissolved.

(3) Where a court-martial is dissolved under this section, the accused may be tried again.

Jurisdiction and powers of general and field general courts-martial

75. A general or field general court-martial shall have power to try any person subject to this Act for any offence made punishable therein, and to pass any sentence authorized by this Act.

Jurisdiction and powers of district general courts-martial

76. A district court-martial shall have power to try any person subject to this Act other than an officer for any offence made punishable therein, and to pass any sentence authorized by this Act other than a sentence of death or imprisonment for a term exceeding two years.

Prohibition of second trial

77. When any person subject to this Act has been acquitted or convicted of an offence by a court-martial or by a criminal court, or has been summarily dealt with for an offence under section 25, he shall not be liable to be tried again for the same offence by a court-martial.

Limitation of trial

78. No trial by court-martial of any person subject to this Act for any offence (other than an offence of mutiny, desertion or fraudulent enlistment) shall be commenced after the expiration of three years from the date of such offence, and no such trial for an offence of desertion (other than desertion an active service) or of fraudulent enlistment shall be commenced if the person in question has, subsequently to the commission of the offence, served continuously in an exemplary manner for not less than three years with any portion of His Majesty's regular forces.

Explanation.-For the purposes of this section "mutiny" means any of the offences specified in section 35.

Place of trial

79. Any person subject to this Act who commits any offence against it may be tried and punished for such offence in any place whatever.

Order in case of concurrent jurisdiction of criminal court and court-martial

80. When a criminal court and a court-martial have each jurisdiction in respect of a civil offence, it shall be in the discretion of the prescribed air force authority to decide before which court the proceedings shall be instituted, and, if that authority decides that they shall be instituted before a court-martial, to direct that the accused person shall be detained in air force custody.

Power of criminal court to require delivery of offender

81. (1) When a criminal court having jurisdiction is of opinion that proceedings ought to be instituted before itself in respect of any civil offence, it may, by written notice, require the prescribed air force authority at the option of such authority either to deliver over the offender to the nearest Magistrate to be proceeded against according to law, or to postpone proceedings pending a reference to the Governor General in Council.

(2) In every such case the said authority shall either deliver over the offender in compliance with the requisition or shall forthwith refer the question as to the court before which the proceedings are to be instituted for the determination of the Governor General in Council, whose order upon such reference shall be final.

Trail by court-martial no bar to subsequent trial by criminal court

82. (1) Notwithstanding anything contained in section 26 of the General Clauses Act, 1897, or in section 403 of the Code of Criminal Procedure, 1898, a person convicted or acquitted by a court-martial may be afterwards tried by a criminal court for the same offence or on the same facts.

(2) If a person sentenced by a court-martial in pursuance of this Act to punishment for an offence is afterwards tried by a criminal court for the same offence or on the same facts, that court shall, in awarding punishment, have regard to the air force punishment he may already have undergone.

CHAPTER VII

PROCEDURE OF COURTS-MARTIAL

President

83. At every court-martial the senior member shall sit as president.

Judge Advocate

84. Every general court-martial shall, and every district court-martial may, be attended by a judge advocate, who shall be either an officer belonging to the department of the Judge Advocate General in India, or, if no such officer is available, a fit person appointed by the convening officer.

Challenges

85. (1) At all trials by court-martial, as soon as the court is assembled, the names of the president and members shall be read over to the accused, who shall thereupon be asked whether he objects to being tried by any officer sitting on the court.

(2) If the accused objects to any such officer, his objection, and also the reply thereto of the officer objected to, shall be heard and recorded, and the remaining officers of the court shall, in the absence of the challenged officer, decide on the objection.

(3) If the objection is allowed by one-half or more of the votes of the officers entitled to vote, the objection shall be allowed, and the member objected to shall retire, and his vacancy may be filled in the prescribed manner by another officer, subject to the same right of the accused to object.

(4) When no challenge is made, or when challenge has been made and disallowed, or the place of every officer successfully challenged has been filled by another officer to whom no objection is made or allowed, the court shall proceed with the trial.

Voting of members

86. (1) Every decision of a court-martial shall be passed by an absolute majority of votes; and where there is an equality of votes, as to either finding or sentence, the decision shall be in favour of the accused:

Provided that no sentence of death shall be passed without the concurrence of two-thirds at the least of the members of the court.

(2) In matters other than a challenge or the finding or sentence, the president shall have a casting vote.

Oaths of president and members

87. An oath or affirmation in the prescribed form shall be administered to every member of every court-martial and to the judge advocate at the beginning of the trial.

Oaths of witnesses

88. Every person giving evidence at a court-martial shall be examined on oath or affirmation, and shall be duly sworn or affirmed in the prescribed form.

The summoning of witnesses and production of documents

89. (1) The convening officer, the presiding officer of a court, the judge advocate or the commanding officer of the accused person, may, by summons under his hand, require the attendance before the court, at a time and place to be mentioned in the summons, of any person either to give evidence or to produce any document or other thing.

(2) In the case of a witness amenable to air force or military authority, the summons shall be sent to the officer commanding officer of the corps, unit, department or detachment to which he belongs, and such officer shall serve it upon him accordingly.

(3) In the case of any other witness, the summons shall be sent to the Magistrate within whose jurisdiction he may be or reside, and such Magistrate shall give effect to the summons as if the witness were required in the court of such Magistrate.

(4) When a witness is required to produce any particular document or other thing in his possession or power, the summons shall describe it with reasonable precision.

(5) Nothing in this section shall be deemed to affect the Indian Evidence Act, 1872, sections 123 and 124, or to apply to any document in the custody of the postal or telegraph authorities.

(6) If any document in such custody is, in the opinion of any District Magistrate, Chief Presidency Magistrate, High Court or Court of Session, wanted for the purpose of any court-martial, such Magistrate or Court may require the postal or telegraph authorities, as the case may be, to deliver such document to such person as such Magistrate or Court may direct.

(7) if any document in such custody is, in the opinion of any other Magistrate or of any Commissioner of Police or District Superintendent of Police, wanted for any such purpose, he may require the postal or telegraph authorities, as the case may be, to cause search to be made for an to detain such document pending the orders of any such District Magistrate, Chief Presidency Magistrate or Court.

Commissions to obtain evidence

90. (1) Whenever, in the course of a trial by court-martial, it appears to the court that the examination of a witness is necessary for the ends of justice, and that the attendance of such witness cannot be procured without an amount of delay, expense or inconvenience which, in the circumstances of the case, would be unreasonable, such court may address the Judge Advocate General in order that a commission to take the evidence of such witness may be issued.

(2) The Judge Advocate General may then, if he thinks necessary, issue commission to any Presidency Magistrate, District Magistrate or Magistrate of the first class, within local limits of whose jurisdiction such witness resides, to take the evidence of such witness.

(3) When the witness resides in the territories of any prince or chief in India in which there is an officer representing the British Indian Government, the commission may be issued to such officer.

(4) The Magistrate or officer to whom the commission is issued, or if he is the District Magistrate, he or such Magistrate of the first class as he appoints in this behalf, shall proceed to the place where the witness is or shall summon the witness before him and shall take down his evidence in the same manner, and may for this purpose exercise the same powers, as in trials of warrant-cases under the Code of Criminal Procedure, 1898.

(5) Where the commission is issued to such officer as is mentioned in sub-section (3), he may delegate his powers and duties under the commission to any other officer subordinate to him whose powers are not less than those of a Magistrate of the first class in British India.

(6) When the witness resides out of India, the commission may be issued to any British consular officer, British Magistrate or other British official competent to administer an oath or affirmation in the place where such witness resides.

(7) The prosecutor and the accused person in any case in which a commission is issued may respectively forward any interrogatories in writing which the court may think relevant to the issue, and the Magistrate or officer to whom the commission is issued shall examine the witness upon such interrogatories.

(8) The prosecutor and the accused person may appear before such Magistrate or officer by pleader or, except in the case of an accused person in custody, in person, and may examine cross-examine and re-examine (as the case may be) the said witness.

(9) After a commission issued under this section has been duly executed, it shall be returned, together with the deposition of the witness examined there-under to the Judge Advocate General.

(10) On receipt of a commission and deposition returned under sub-section (9) the Judge Advocate General shall forward the same to the Court at whose instance the commission was issued, or if such court has been dissolved, to any other court convened for the trial of the accused person; and the commission, the return thereto and the deposition shall be open to inspection by the prosecutor and the accused person, and may, subject to all just exceptions, be read in evidence in the case by either the prosecutor or the accused, and shall from part of the proceedings of the court.

(11) In every case in which a commission is issued under this section the trial may be adjourned for a specified time reasonably sufficient for the execution and return of the commission.

Explanation:---In this section, the expression "Judge Advocate General" means the Judge Advocate General in India, and includes a Deputy Judge Advocate General.

Conviction of one offence permissible on charge of another

91. (1) A person charged before a court-martial with desertion may be found guilty of attempting to desert or of being absent without leave.

(2) A person charged before a court-martial with attempting to desert may found guilty of desertion or being absent without leave.

(3) A person charged before a court-martial with using criminal force may be found guilty of assault.

(4) A person charged before a court-martial with using threatening language may be found guilty of using insubordinate language.

(5) A person charged before a court-martial with any of the offences specified in clause (a), clause (b), clause (d) or clause (e) of section 44 may be found guilty of any other of these offences with which he might have been charged.

(6) A person charged before a court-martial with an offence punishable under section 58 may be found guilty of any other offence of which he might have been found guilty of the provisions of the Code of Criminal Procedure, 1898, were applicable.

(7) A person charged before a court-martial with any other offence under this Act may, on failure of proof of an offence having been committed in circumstances involving a more severe punishment, be found guilty of the same offence as having been committed in circumstances involving a less severe punishment.

(8) A person charged before a court-martial with any offence under this Act may be found guilty of having attempted to commit or of abetment of that offence although the attempt or abetment is not separately charged.

General rule as to evidence

92. The Indian Evidence Act, 1872, shall, subject to the provisions of this Act, apply to all proceedings before a court-martial.

Judicial notice

93. A court-martial may take judicial notice of any matter within the general, naval, military or air force knowledge of the members.

Presumption as to signatures

94. In any proceeding under this Act, any application, certificate, warrant, reply or other document purporting to be signed by an officer in the civil, military or air force service of the Government shall, on production, be presumed to have been duly signed by the person and in the character by whom and in which it purports to have been signed, until the contrary is shown.

Enrolment paper as evidence

95. Any enrolment paper purporting to be signed by an enrolling officer shall, in proceedings under this Act, be evidence of the person enrolled having given the answers to questions which he is therein represented as having given. The enrolment of such person may be proved by the production of a copy of his enrolment paper purporting to be certified to be a true copy by the officer having the custody of the enrolment paper.

Presumption as to certain documents

96. (1) A letter, return or other document respecting the service of any person in, or the dismissal or discharge of any person from, any portion of His Majesty's Forces, or respecting the circumstances of any person not having served in, or belonged to, any portion of His Majesty's Forces, if purporting to be signed by or on behalf of the Governor General in

Council or the Commander-in-Chief in India or by any prescribed officer, shall be evidence of the facts stated in such letter, return or other document.

(2) An Army List, Air Force List or Gazette purporting to be published by authority shall be evidence of the status and rank of the officers or warrant officers there in mentioned, and of any appointment held by such officers or warrant officers and of the corps, units, battalion, arm, branch or department of the services to which such officers or warrant officers belongs.

(3) Where a record is made in any regimental book, in pursuance of this Act or of any rules made there under or otherwise in pursuance of the air force duty, and purports to be signed by the commanding officer or by the officer whose duty it is to make such record, such record shall be evidence of the facts therein stated.

(4) A copy of any record in any regimental book purporting to be certified to be a true copy by the officer having custody of such book shall be evidence of such record.

(5) Where any person subject to this Act is being tried on a charge of desertion or of absence without leave, and such person has surrendered himself into the custody of, or has been apprehended by, a provost-marshal, assistant provost-marshal or other officer, or any portion of His Majesty's Forces, a certificate purporting to be signed by such provost-marshal, assistant provost-marshal or other officer, or by the commanding officer of that portion of His Majesty's Forces and stating the fact, date and place of such surrender or apprehension, shall be evidence of the matters so stated.

(6) Where any person subject to this Act is being tried on a charge of desertion or of absence without leave, and such person has surrendered himself into the custody of, or has been apprehended by, a police officer not below the rank of an officer in charge of a police station, a certificate purporting to be signed by such police-officer and stating the fact, date and place of such surrender or apprehension, shall be evidence of the matters so stated.

(7) Any document purporting to be a report under the hand of any Chemical Examiner to Government upon any matter or thing duly submitted to him for examination or analysis and report may be used as evidence in any proceeding under this Act.

Reference by accused to Government officer

97. (1) If at any trial for desertion or absence without leave, overstaying leave or not rejoining when warned for service, the person tried states in his defence any sufficient or reasonable excuse for his unauthorized absence, and refers in support thereof to any officer in the civil, military or air force service of the Government, or if it appears that any such officer is likely to prove or disprove the said statement in the defence, the court shall address such officer and adjourn the proceedings until his reply is received.

(2) The written reply of any officer so referred to shall, if signed by him, be received in evidence and have the same effect as if made on oath before the court.

(3) If the court a dissolved before the receipt of such reply, or if the court omits to comply with the provisions of this section, the convening officer may, at his discretion annul the proceedings and order a fresh trial by the same or another court-martial.

Evidence of previous convictions and service character

98. (1) When any person subject to this Act has been convicted by a court-martial of any offence, such court-martial may inquire into, and receive and record evidence of any previous convictions of such person either by a court-martial established under this Act or any other enactment or by a criminal court, or may further inquire into and record the service character of such person.

(2) Evidence received under this section may be either oral, or in the shape of entries in, or certified extracts from, court-martial books or other official records; and it shall not be necessary to give notice before trial to the person tried that evidence as to his previous convictions or character will be received.

Order for custody and disposal of property pending trial in certain cases

99. When any property regarding which any offence appears to have been committed, or which appears to have used for the commission of any offence, is produced before a court martial during a trial, the court may make such order as it thinks fit for the proper custody of such property pending the conclusion of the trial, and if the property is subject to speedy or natural- decay may, after recording such evidence as it thinks necessary, order it to be sold or otherwise disposal of.

CHAPTER VIII

CONFIRMATION, REVISION, PARDON AND REMISSION OF SENTENCE

Finding and sentence invalid without confirmation

100. No finding or sentence of a general or district court-martial shall be valid except so far as it may be confirmed as provided by this Act.

Power to confirm finding and sentence of general court-martial

101. The findings and sentences of general courts-martial may be confirmed by Governor General in Council or by any officer empowered in this behalf by warrant of the Governor General in Council.

Power to confirm finding and sentence of district court-martial

102. The findings and sentences of district courts-martial may be confirmed by any officer having power to convene a general court-martial, or by any officer empowered in this behalf by warrant of any such authority.

Limitation of the powers of confirming authority

103. A warrant issued under section 101 or section 102 may contain such restrictions, reservations or conditions as the authority issuing it may think fit.

Confirmation of finding and sentence of field general court-martial

104. (1) Save as provided in sub-sections (2) and (3), a finding and sentence of a field general court-martial shall not require to be confirmed and may be carried out forthwith.

(2) The finding and sentence of a field general court-martial shall require to be confirmed

(a) In the case of the trial of an officer,

(b) In the case of an acquittal or a sentence of death or imprisonment for a term exceeding two years, and

(c) In any other case if so ordered by the convening officer.

(3) Such findings and sentence may be confirmed by the convening authority or, if the convening authority so directs, by an authority superior to the convening authority.

Power of confirming officer to mitigate, remit or commute sentences

105. Subject to such restrictions as may be contained in any warrant issued under section 101 or section 102, a confirming officer may, if it confirms the sentence of a court-martial, mitigate or remit the punishment thereby awarded, or commute that punishment for any less punishment or punishments lower in the scale laid down in section 19.

Confirmation of finding and sentence on board ship

106. When any person subject to this Act is tried and sentenced by court-martial while on board ship, the finding and sentence so far as not confirmed and executed on board ship may be confirmed and executed in like manner as if such person had been tried at the port of disembarkation.

Revision of finding or sentence

107. (1) Any finding or sentence of a court-martial which requires confirmation may be once revised by order of the confirming authority; and on such revision, the court, if so directed by the confirming authority, may take additional evidence.

(2) The court, on revision, shall consist of the same officers as were present when the original decision was passed, unless any of those officers are unavoidably absent.

(3) In case of such unavoidable absence the cause thereof shall be duly certified in the proceedings, and the court shall proceed with the revision, provided that, if a general court-martial, it still consists of five officers, or, if a district court-martial, of three officers.

Substitution of valid for invalid sentence

108. Where a sentence passed by a court-martial which has been confirmed, or which does not require confirmation, is found for any reason to be invalid, the authority who would have had

power under section 110 to commute the punishment awarded by the sentence if it had been valid may pass a valid sentence:

Provided that the punishment awarded by a sentence so passed shall not be higher in the scale of punishments than, or in excess of, the punishment awarded by invalid sentence.

Provision where accused is a lunatic

109. (1) Whenever, in the course of a trial by court-martial, it appears to the Court that the person charged is of unsound mind and consequently incapable of making his defence, or that such person committed the act alleged but was by reason, of unsoundness of mind incapable of knowing the nature of the act or that it was wrong or contrary to law, the Court shall record a finding accordingly, and the president of the court shall forthwith report the case to the confirming officer, or, in the case of a field general court-martial, to the prescribed officer.

(2) A confirming officer to whom a case is reported under sub-section (1) may, if he does not confirm the finding, take steps to have the accused person tried by the same or another court-martial for the offence with which he was originally charged.

(3) A prescribed officer to whom a case is reported under sub-section (1) and a confirming officer confirming a finding in any case so reported to it shall order the accused person to be kept in custody in the prescribed manner, and where the confirming authority is not itself the Governor General in Council, shall report the case for the orders of the Governor General in Council.

(4) On receipt of a report under sub-section (1), or sub-section (3), the Governor General in Council may order the accused person to be detained in a lunatic asylum or other suitable place of safe custody.

(5) Where an accused person, having been found by reason of unsoundness of mind to be incapable of making his defence, is in custody or under detention, the prescribed officer may—

(a) If such person is in custody under sub-section (3), on the report of a medical officer that he is capable of making his defence, or

(b) If such person is detained under-sub-section (4), on a certificate such as is referred to in section 473 of the Code of Criminal Procedure, 1898,

take steps to have such person tried by the same or another court-martial, for the offence with which he was originally charged or, provided that the offence is a civil offence, by a Criminal Court.

(6) A copy of every order made by the prescribed officer under sub-section (5) shall forthwith be sent for the Governor General in Council.

Pardons and remissions

110. (1) When any person subject to this Act has been convicted by a court-martial of any offence, the Governor General in Council or the prescribed officer may,

(a) Either without conditions or upon any conditions which the person sentenced accepts, pardon the person or remit the whole or any part of the punishment awarded; or

(b) Mitigate the punishment awarded, or commute such punishment for any less punishment or punishments mentioned in this Act;

(2) If any condition on which a person has been pardoned or a punishment has been remitted is, in the opinion of the authority which granted the pardon or remitted the punishment, not fulfilled, such authority may cancel the pardon or remission, and thereupon the sentence of the court shall be carried into effect as if such pardon had not been granted or such punishment had not been remitted;

Provided that, in the case of a person sentenced to imprisonment, such person shall undergo only the unexpired portion of his sentence.

(3) When under the provisions of section 23 a non-commissioned officer is deemed to be reduced to the ranks, such reduction shall, for the purposes of this section, be treated as a punishment awarded by sentence of a court-martial.

Order for disposal of property regarding which offence committed

119. (1) After the conclusion of a trial before any court-martial, the court or the officer confirming the finding or sentence of such court-martial or any authority superior to such officer, or, in the case of court-martial whose finding or sentence does not require confirmation, the officer commanding the army, army corps, division or brigade within which the trial was held, may make such order as it or he thinks fit for the disposal by destruction, confiscation, delivery to any person claiming to be entitled to possession thereof, or otherwise, of any property or document produced before the court or in its custody, or regarding which any offence appears to have been committed or which has been used for the commission of any offence.

(2) Where any order has been made under sub-section (1) in respect of property regarding which an offence appears to have been committed, a copy of such order signed and certified by the authority making the same may, whether the trial was held within British India or not, be sent to a Magistrate in any presidency-town or district in which such property for the time being is, and such Magistrate shall thereupon cause the order to be carried into effect as if it was an order passed by such Magistrate under the provisions of the Code of Criminal Procedure [V of 1898], 1898.

Explanation.—In this section the term "property" includes, in the case of property regarding which an offence appears to have been committed, not only such property as has been originally in the possession or under the control of any party, but also any property into or for which the same may have been converted or exchanged, and anything acquired by such conversion or exchange whether immediately, or otherwise.

CHAPTER IX

EXECUTION OF SENTENCES AND DISPOSAL OF PROPERTY

Sentence of death

111. In awarding a sentence of death a court-martial shall, in its discretion, direct that the offender shall suffer death by being hanged by the neck until he be dead, or shall suffer death by being shot to death.

Commencement of sentence of imprisonment

112. Whenever any person is sentenced under this Act to imprisonment, the term of his sentence shall, whether it has or not, be reckoned to commence on the day on which the original proceedings were signed by the president.

Execution of sentence of imprisonment

113. Whenever any sentence of imprisonment is passed under this Act, or whenever any sentence so passed is commuted to imprisonment, the commanding officer of the person under sentence, or such other officer as may be prescribed, shall forward a warrant in the prescribed form to the officer in charge of the civil prison in which such person is to be confined, and shall forward him to such prison with the warrant:

Provided that, in the case of a sentence of imprisonment for a period not exceeding three months, the confirming officer, or in the case of a sentence which does not require confirmation, the court, may direct that the sentence shall be carried out by confinement in the air force custody:

Provided further that on active service a sentence of rigorous imprisonment may be carried out by confinement in such place as the officer commanding the forces in the field may, from time to time, appoint.

Execution of sentence of imprisonment in special cases

114. Whenever, in the opinion of the air officer commanding His Majesty's Air Force in India, any sentence or portion of a sentence of imprisonment cannot, for special reasons, conveniently be carried out in accordance with the provisions of section 113, such officer may direct that such sentence or portion of sentence shall be carried out by confinement in any civil prison or other fit place.

Execution of sentence of detention

115. When any sentence of detention is passed under this Act, or when any sentence so passed is commuted to detention, the punishment shall be carried out by detaining the offender in any military or air force detention barracks, detention cell or other military or air force custody.

Communication of certain orders to civil prison officers

116. Whenever an order is duly made under this Act setting aside or varying any sentence, order or warrant under which any person is confined in a civil prison, a warrant in accordance with such order shall be forwarded by the prescribed officer to the officer in charge of the prison in which such person is confined.

Offenders sentenced to transportation how dealt with until transported

117. Where a sentence of transportation is imposed by court-martial under section 58, the offender, until he is transported, shall be dealt with in the same manner as if he had been sentenced to rigorous imprisonment, and shall be deemed to have been undergoing his sentence of transportation during the term of his imprisonment.

Execution of sentence of fine

118. When a sentence of fine is imposed by a court-martial under section 58, whether the trial was held within British India or not, a copy of such, sentence, signed and certified by the president of the court or the officer holding the trial, as the case may be, may be sent to any Magistrate in British India, and such Magistrate shall thereupon cause the fine to be recovered in accordance with the provisions of the Code of Criminal Procedure, 1898, for the levy of fines as if it was a sentence of fine imposed by such Magistrate.

Order for disposal of property regarding which offence committed

119. (1) After the conclusion of a trial before any court-martial, the court or the officer confirming the finding or sentence of such court-martial or any authority superior to such officer, or, in the case of court-martial whose finding or sentence does not require confirmation, the officer commanding the unit within which the trial was held, may make such order as it or he thinks fit for the disposal by destruction, confiscation, delivery to any person claiming to be entitled to possession thereof, or otherwise, of any property or document produced before the court or in its custody, or regarding which any offence appears to have been committed or which has been used for the commission of any offence.

(2) Where any order has been made under sub-section (1) in respect of property regarding which an offence appears to have been committed, a copy of such order signed and certified by the authority making the same may, whether the trial was held within British India or not, be sent to a Magistrate in any presidency-town or district in which such property for the time being is, and such Magistrate shall thereupon cause the order to be carried into effect as if it was an order passed by such Magistrate under the provisions of the Code of Criminal Procedure [V of 1898], 1898.

Explanation.—In this section the term "property" includes, in the case of property regarding which an offence appears to have been committed, not only such property as has been originally in the possession or under the control of any party, but also any property into or for which the same may have been converted or exchanged, and anything acquired by such conversion or exchange whether immediately, or otherwise.

CHAPTER X

SPECIAL RULES RELATING TO PERSONS AND PROPERTY

Complaints against superior officers and airmen

120. (1) If an officer of the Indian Air Force thinks himself wronged by his commanding officer, or other superior officer, and on due application made to his commanding officer does not receive the redress to which he may consider himself entitled, he may complain to the Governor General in Council in order to obtain justice.

(2) If any airman thinks himself wronged in any matter by any officer other than the officer under whose command or orders he is serving, or by any airman, he may complain thereof to the officer under whose command or orders he is serving, and if he thinks himself wronged by the officer under whose command or orders he is serving, either in respect of his complaint not being redressed or in respect of any other matter, he may complain thereof to his commanding officer,

and if he thinks himself wronged by his commanding officer, either in respect of his complaint not being redressed or in respect of any other matter, he may complain thereof to the prescribed officer; and every officer to whom a complaint is made in pursuance of this section shall cause such complaint to be inquired into, and shall, if on inquiry he is satisfied of the justice of the complaint so made, take such steps as may be necessary for giving full redress to the complainant in respect of the matter complained of.

Privileges of persons attending courts-martial

121. (1) No president or member of a court-martial, no judge advocate or superintending officer, no party to any proceeding before a court-martial, or his legal practitioner or agent, and no witness acting in obedience to a summons to attend a court-martial, shall, while proceeding to, attending on or returning from a court-martial, be liable to arrest under civil or revenue process.

(2) If any such person is arrested under any such process, he may be discharged by order of the court-martial.

Exemption from arrest for debts

122. (1) No officer or person enrolled in the Indian Air Force shall be liable to be arrested for debt under any process issued by, or by the authority of, any civil or revenue court or revenue officer.

(2) The judge of any such court may examine into any complaint made by such person or his superior officer of the arrest of such person contrary to the provisions of this section, and may, by warrant under his hand, discharge the person, and award reasonable costs to the complainant, who may recover those costs in like manner as he might have recovered costs awarded to him by a decree against the person obtaining the process.

(3) For the recovery of such costs no fee shall be payable to the court by the complainant.

Property exempted from attachment

123. Neither the arms, clothes, equipment, accoutrements or necessaries of any person subject to this Act, nor any animal used by him for the discharge of his duty, shall be seized, nor shall the pay and allowances of any such person or any part thereof be attached, by direction of any civil or revenue court or any revenue officer, in satisfaction of any decree or order enforceable against him.

Application to reservists

124. Every person belonging to the Indian Air Force Reserve shall, when called out for or engaged upon or returning from training or service, be entitled to all the privileges accorded by sections 122 and 123 to a person subject to this Act.

Priority in hearing by courts of cases in which India officers and soldiers are concerned

125. (1) On the representation to any court by or on behalf of any person subject to this Act of a certificate, from the proper military authority, of leave of absence having been granted to or applied for which by him for the purpose of prosecuting or defending any suit or other and proceeding in such court, the court shall, on the application of such person, arrange, so far as may be possible, for the hearing and final disposal of such suit or other proceeding within the period of the leave so granted or applied for.

(2) The certificate from the proper air force authority shall state the first and last day of the leave or intended leave, and set forth a description of the case with respect to which the leave was granted or applied for.

(3) No fee shall be payable to the court in respect of the presentation of any such certificate, or in respect of any application by or on behalf of any such person for priority for the hearing of his case.

(4) Where the court is unable to arrange for the hearing and final disposal of the suit or other proceeding within the period of such leave or intended leave as aforesaid, it shall record its reasons for having been unable to do so, and shall cause a copy thereof to be furnished to such person on his application without any payment whatever by him in respect either of the application for such copy or of the copy itself.

(5) If in any case a question arises as to the proper air force authority qualified to grant such certificate as aforesaid, such question shall be at once referred by the court to an officer commanding a unit, whose decision shall be final.

Property of deceased persons and deserters

126. The following rules are enacted respecting the disposal of the property of every person subject to this Act who dies or deserts:—

(1) The commanding officer of the corps, detachment or department to which the deceased person or deserter belonged shall secure all the moveable property belonging to the deceased or deserter that, is in camp or quarters, and cause an inventory thereof to be made, and draw any pay and allowances due to such person.

(2) In the case of a deceased person who has left in a Government savings bank (including any post office savings bank, however named) a deposit not exceeding one thousand rupees, the commanding officer may, if he thinks fit, require the secretary or other proper officer of the bank to pay the deposit to him forthwith, notwithstanding anything in any departmental rules, and after the payment thereof in accordance with such requisition, no person shall have any right in respect of the deposit except as hereinafter provided.

(3) In the case of a deceased person whose representative is on the spot and has given security for the payment of the regimental or other debts in camp or quarters (if any) of the deceased, the commanding officer shall deliver over any property received under clauses (2) and (3) to that representative.

(4) In the case of a deceased person whose estate is not dealt with, under clause (3), and in the case of any deserter, the commanding officer shall cause the moveable property to be sold by public auction, and shall pay the regimental and other debts in camp or quarters (if any), and, in the case of a deceased person, the expenses of his funeral ceremonies, from the proceeds of the sale and from any pay and allowances drawn under clause (1) and from the amount of the deposit (if any) received under clause (2).

(5) The surplus, if any, shall, in the case of a deceased person, be paid to his representative (if any), or in the event of no claim to such surplus being established within twelve months after the death, then the same shall be remitted to the prescribed person.

(6) In the case of a deserter, the surplus (if any) shall be forthwith remitted to the prescribed person and shall, on the expiry of three years from the date of his desertion, be forfeited to His Majesty, unless the deserter shall in the meantime have surrendered or been apprehended.

Meaning of deserter

Explanation.—A person shall be deemed to be a deserter within the meaning of this section who has without authority been absent from duty for a period of twenty-one days and has not subsequently surrendered or been apprehended.

Disposal of certain property without production of probate, etc

127. Property deliverable and money payable to the representative of a deceased person under section 126 may, if the total value or amount thereof does not exceed one thousand rupees, and if the prescribed person thinks fit, be delivered or paid to any person appearing to him to be entitled to receive it or to administer the estate of the deceased, without requiring the production of any probate, letters of administration, certificate or other such conclusive evidence of title; and such delivery or payment shall be a full discharge to those ordering or making the same and to the Secretary of State for India in Council from all further liability in respect of the property or

money; but nothing in this section shall affect the rights of any executor or administrator or other representative, or of any creditor of a deceased person against any person to whom such delivery or payment has been made.

Application to lunatic and persons missing on active service

128. The provisions of section 126 shall, so far as they can be made applicable, apply in the case of a person subject to this Act becoming insane or who, being on active service, is officially reported missing:

Provided that, in the case of a person so reported missing, no action shall be taken under sub-sections (2) to (5), inclusive, of the said section, until one year has elapsed from the date of such report.

CHAPTER XI

SUPPLEMENTAL

Power to make rules

129. (1) The Governor General in Council may make rules Power to make rules for the purpose of carrying into effect the provisions of this Act.

(2) In particular, and without prejudice to the generality of the foregoing power, such rules may provide for--

(a) The discharge from the service of persons subject to this Act;

(b) The specification of the punishments which may be awarded as field punishments under sections 21 and 26;

(c) The assembly and procedure of courts of inquiry, and the administration of oaths or affirmations by such courts;

(d) The convening and constituting of courts-martial;

(e) The adjournment, dissolution and sittings of courts-martial;

(f) The procedure to be observed in trials by courts-martial;

(g) The confirmation and revision of the findings and sentences of courts-martial;

(h) The carrying into effect sentences of courts-martial;

(i) The forms of orders to be made under the provisions of this Act relating to courts-martial and imprisonment;

(j) The constitution of authorities to decide for what persons, to what amounts and in what manner, provision should be made for dependants under section 29, and the due carrying out of such decisions; and

(k) Any matter in this Act directed to be prescribed.

(3) All rules made under this Act shall be published in the Gazette of India, and, on such publication, shall have effect as if enacted in this Act.

Amendment of certain enactments

130. The enactments specified in the Schedule are hereby amended to the extent and in the manner mentioned in the fourth column thereof.

THE SCHEDULE

(NOT INCLUDED)

Articles of War[1]

[The 1749 Naval Act]

The following articles of war were established for the 25 December 1749; and are directed to be observed and put in execution, as well in time of peace as in time of war

Divine worship

I. All commanders, captains, and officers, in or belonging to any of His Majesty's ships or vessels of war, shall cause the public worship of Almighty God, according to the Liturgy of the Church of England established by law, to be solemnly, orderly and reverently performed in their respective ships; and shall take care that prayers and preaching, by the chaplains in holy orders of the respective ships, be performed diligently; and that the Lord's day be observed according to law.

Swearing, Drunkenness, scandalous actions, &c.

II. All flag officers, and all persons in or belonging to His Majesty's ships or vessels of war, being guilty of profane oaths, cursings, execrations, drunkenness, uncleanness, or other scandalous actions, in derogation of God's honour, and corruption of good manners, shall incur such punishment as a court martial shall think fit to impose, and as the nature and degree of their offence shall deserve.

Holding intelligence with an enemy or rebel

III. If any officer, mariner, soldier, or other person of the fleet, shall give, hold, or entertain intelligence to or with any enemy or rebel, without leave from the king's majesty, or the lord high admiral, or the commissioners for executing the office of lord high admiral, commander in chief, or his commanding officer, every such person so offending, and being thereof convicted by the sentence of a court martial, shall be punished with death.

Letter or message from an enemy, or rebel

IV. If any letter of message from any enemy or rebel, be conveyed to any officer, mariner, or soldier or other in the fleet, and the said officer, mariner, or soldier, or other as aforesaid, shall not, within twelve hours, having opportunity so to do, acquaint his superior or a commanding officer, or if any superior officer being acquainted therewith, shall not in convenient time reveal the same to the commander in chief of the squadron, every such person so offending, and being

1 Articles contain an Act of Parliament [22 Geo. II, c. 33], intituled, *An Act for amending, explaining, and reducing into one act of parliament, the laws relating to the government of His Majesty's ships, vessels, and forces by sea.*

convicted thereof by the sentence of the court martial, shall be punished with death, or such other punishment as the nature and degree of the offence shall deserve, and the court martial shall impose.

Spies and all persons in the nature of spies

V. All spies, and all persons whatsoever, who shall come, or be found, in the nature of spies, to bring or deliver any seducing letters or messages from any enemy or rebel, or endeavor to corrupt any captain, officer, mariner, or other in the fleet, to betray his trust, being convicted of any such offence by the sentence of the court martial, shall be punished with death, or such other punishment, as the nature and degree of the offence shall deserve, and the court martial shall impose.

Relieving an enemy or rebel

VI. No person in the fleet shall receive an enemy or rebel with money, victuals, powder, shot, arms, ammunition, or any other supplies whatsoever, directly or indirectly, upon pain of death, or such other punishment as the court martial shall think fit to impose, and as the nature and degree of the crime shall deserve.

Papers, &c. found on board of prizes

VII. All the papers, charter parties, bills of lading, passports, and other writings whatsoever, that shall be taken, seized, or found aboard any ship or ships which shall be surprised or taken as prize, shall be duly preserved, and the very originals shall by the commanding officer of the ship which shall take such prize, be sent entirely, and without fraud, to the court of the admiralty, or such other court of commissioners, as shall be authorized to determine whether such prize be lawful capture, there to be viewed, made use of, and proceeded upon according to law, upon pain that every person offending herein, shall forfeit and lose his share of the capture, and shall suffer such further punishment, as the nature and degree of his offence shall be found to deserve, and the court martial shall impose.

Taking money or goods out of prizes

VIII. No person in or belonging to the fleet shall take out of any prize, or ship seized for prize, any money, plate, or goods, unless it shall be necessary for the better securing thereof, or for the necessary use and service of any of His Majesty's ships or vessels of war, before the same be adjudged lawful prize in some admiralty court; but the full and entire account of the whole, without embezzlement, shall be brought in, and judgment passed entirely upon the whole without fraud, upon pain that every person offending herein shall forfeit and lose his share of the capture, and suffer such further punishment as shall be imposed by a court martial, or such court of admiralty, according to the nature and degree of the offence.

Stripping or ill treating prisoners

IX. If any ship or vessel be taken as prize, none of the officers, mariners, or other persons on board her, shall be stripped of their clothes, or in any sort pillaged, beaten, or ill-treated, upon the pain that the person or persons so offending, shall be liable to such punishment as a court martial shall think fit to inflict.

Preparation for fight; Yielding or crying for quarter

X. Every flag officer, captain and commander in the fleet, who, upon signal or order of fight, or sight of any ship or ships which it may be his duty to engage, or who, upon likelihood of engagement, shall not make the necessary preparations for fight, and shall not in his own person, and according to his place, encourage the inferior officers and men to fight courageously, shall suffer death, or such other punishment, as from the nature and degree of the offence a court martial shall deem him to deserve; and if any person in the fleet shall treacherously or cowardly yield or cry for quarter, every person so offending, and being convicted thereof by the sentence of a court martial, shall suffer death.

Obedience to order in battle

XI. Every person in the fleet, who shall not duly observe the orders of the admiral, flag officer, commander of any squadron or division, or other his superior officer, for assailing, joining battle with, or making defense against any fleet, squadron, or ship, or shall not obey the orders of his superior officer as aforesaid in the time of action, to the best of his power, or shall not use all possible endeavours to put the same effectually into execution, every person so offending, and being convicted thereof by the sentence of the court martial, shall suffer death, or such other punishment, as from the nature and degree of the offence a court martial shall deem him to deserve.

Withdrawing or keeping back from fight

XII. Every person in the fleet, who through cowardice, negligence, or disaffection, shall in time of action withdraw or keep back, or not come into the fight or engagement, or shall not do his utmost to take or destroy every ship which it shall be his duty to engage, and to assist and relieve all and every of His Majesty's ships, or those of his allies, which it shall be his duty to assist and relieve, every such person so offending, and being convicted thereof by the sentence of a court martial, shall suffer death.[2]

Forbearing to pursue an enemy, &c

XIII. Every person in the fleet, who though cowardice, negligence, or disaffection, shall forbear to pursue the chase of any enemy, pirate or rebel, beaten or flying; or shall not relieve or assist a known friend in view to the utmost of his power; being convicted of any such offence by the sentence of a court martial, shall suffer death.

2 By Act of Parliament, 19 Geo. III, c. 17 (section 3), this article and the subsequent are explained and amended thus: "And whereas, the restraining of the power of court martial to the inflicting of the punishment of death, in the several cases recited in the said clauses, may be attended with great hardship and inconvenience; be it enacted, that from and after the passing of this Act, it shall and may be lawful in the several cases recited in the said clauses, for the court martial to pronounce sentence of death, or to inflict such other punishment as the nature and degree of the offence shall be found to deserve."

Delaying or discouraging any service

XIV. If when action, or any service shall be commanded, any person in the fleet shall presume or to delay or discourage the said action or service, upon pretence of arrears of wages, or upon any pretence whatsoever, every person so offending, being convicted thereof by the sentence of the court martial, shall suffer death, or such other punishment, as from the nature and degree of the offence a court martial shall deem him to deserve.

Deserting to an enemy, running away with ship store

XV. Every person in or belonging to the fleet, who shall desert to the enemy, pirate, or rebel; or run away with any of His Majesty's ship or vessel or war, or any ordnance, ammunition, stores, or provision belonging thereto, to the weakening of the service, or yield up to the same cowardly or treacherously to the enemy, pirate, or rebel, being convicted of any such offence by sentence of the court martial, shall suffer death.

Deserting and entertaining deserters

XV. Every person in or belonging to the fleet, who shall desert to the enemy, pirate, or rebel; or run away with any of his Majesty's ships or vessels of war, or any ordnance, ammunition, stores, or provision, belonging thereto, to the weakening of the service, or yield up the same cowardly or treacherously to the enemy, pirate, or rebel, being convicted of any such offence by the sentence, of the court martial, shall suffer death.

Deserting and entertaining deserters

XVI. Every person in or belonging to the fleet, who shall desert or entice others so to do, shall suffer death, or such other punishment as the circumstances of the offence shall deserve, and a court martial shall judge fit; and if any commanding officer of any of his Majesty's ships or vessels of war shall receive or entertain a deserter from any other of his Majesty's ships or vessels, after discovering him to be such deserter, and shall not with all convenient speed give notice to the captain of the ship or vessel to which such deserter belongs; or if the said ships or vessels are at any considerable distance from each other, to the secretary of the admiralty, or to the commander in chief, every person so offending, and being convicted thereof by the sentence of the court martial, shall be cashiered.

Convoys

XVII. The officers and seamen of all ships appointed for convoy and guard of merchant ships, or of any other, shall diligently attend upon that charge, without delay, according to their instructions in that behalf; and whosoever shall be faulty therein, and shall not faithfully perform their duty, and defend the ships and goods in their convoy, without either diverting to other parts or occasions, or refusing or neglecting to fight in their defence, if they be assailed, or running away cowardly, and submitting the ships in their convoy to peril and hazard; or shall demand or exact any money or other reward from any merchant or master for convoying any ships or vessels entrusted to their care, or shall misuse the masters or mariners thereof; shall be condemned to make reparation of the damage to the merchants, owners, and others, as the court of admiralty shall adjudge, and also be punished criminally according to the quality of their offences, be it by pains of death, or other punishment, according as shall be adjudged fit by the court martial.

Receiving goods and merchandize on board

XVIII. If any captain, commander, or other officer of any of His Majesty's ships or vessels, shall receive on board, or permit to be received on board such ship or vessel, any goods or merchandises whatsoever, other than for the sole use of the ship or vessel, except gold, silver, or jewels, and except the goods and merchandisers belonging to any merchant, or other ship or vessel which may be shipwrecked, or in imminent danger of being shipwrecked, either on the high seas, or in any port, creek, or harbour, in order to the preserving them for their proper owners, and except such goods or merchandisers as he shall at any time be ordered to take or receive on board by order of the lord high admiral of Great Britain, or the commissioners for executing the office of lord high admiral for the time being; every person so offending, being convicted thereof by the sentence of the court martial shall be cashiered, and be for ever afterwards rendered incapable to serve in any place or office in the naval service of His Majesty, his heirs and successors.[3]

Mutinous assembly; Uttering words of sedition and mutiny; Contempt to superior officers

XIX. If any person in or belonging to the fleet shall make or endeavor to make any mutinous assembly upon any pretence whatsoever, every person offending herein, and being convicted thereof by the sentence of the court martial, shall suffer death: and if any person in or belonging to the fleet shall utter any words of sedition or mutiny, he shall suffer death, or such other punishment as a court martial shall deem him to deserve: and if any officer, mariner, or soldier on or belonging to the fleet, shall behave himself with contempt to his superior officer, being in the execution of his office, he shall be punished according to the nature of his offence by the judgment of a court martial.

Concealing traitorous or mutinous design

XX. If any person in the fleet shall conceal any traitorous or mutinous practice or design, being convicted thereof by the sentence of a court martial, he shall suffer death, or any other punishment as a court martial shall think fit; and if any person, in or belonging to the fleet, shall conceal any

3 By an after clause in this act, it was further enacted, that, from and after the 15th of December 1749, if any captain, commander, or other officer of any of his Majesty's ships or vessels shall receive on board, or permit or suffer to be received on board such ship or vessel, any goods or merchandizes contrary to the true intent and meaning of the 18th article of this Act, every such captain, commander, or other officer, shall, for every such offence, over and above any punishment inflicted by this act, forfeit and pay the value of all and every such goods and merchandizes so received or permitted or suffered to be received on board as aforesaid, or the sum of 500 pounds of lawful money of Great Britain, at the election of the informer or person who shall sue for the same, so that no more than one of these penalties or forfeitures shall be sued for and recovered by virtue of this Act. One moiety of which penalties or forfeitures shall be forfeited and paid to the person who shall inform and sue for the same; and the other moiety thereof, to and for the use of the Royal Hospital at Greenwich; which forfeiture shall be sued for and recovers d by action of debt, bill, plaint, or information, in any of his Majesty's Courts of Record at Westminster, or in tile High Court of Admiralty, at the election of the informer or person who shall sue for the same, and the court shall award such costs to the parties as shall be just; and in all cases where judgment or sentence shall be given against any such offender, the court shall with all convenient speed certify the same to the lord high admiral, or to the commissioners for executing the said office.

traitorous or mutinous words spoken by any, to the prejudice of His Majesty or government, or any words, practice, or design, tending to the hindrance of the service, and shall not forthwith reveal the same to the commanding officer, or being present at any mutiny or sedition, shall not use his utmost endeavours to suppress the same, he shall be punished as a court martial shall think he deserves.

No person on any pretence to attempt to stir up disturbance

XXI. If any person in the fleet shall find cause of complaint of the unwholesomeness of the victual, or upon other just ground, he shall quietly make the same known to his superior, or captain, or commander in chief, as the occasion may deserve, that such present remedy may be had as the matter may require; and the said superior, captain, or commander in chief, shall, as far as he is able, cause the same to be presently remedied; and no person in the fleet, upon any such or other pretence, shall attempt to stir up any disturbance, upon pain of such punishment, as a court martial shall think fit to inflict, according to the degree of the offence.

Striking a superior officer; Quarreling; Disobedience

XXII. If any officer, mariner, soldier or other person in the fleet, shall strike any of his superior officers, or draw, or offer to draw, or lift up any weapon against him, being in the execution of his office, on any pretence whatsoever, every such person being convicted of any such offence, by the sentence of a court martial, shall suffer death; and if any officer, mariner, soldier or other person in the fleet, shall presume to quarrel with any of his superior officers, being in the execution of his office, or shall disobey any lawful command of any of his superior officers; every such person being convicted of any such offence, by the sentence of a court martial, shall suffer death, or such other punishment, as shall, according to the nature and degree of his offence, be inflicted upon him by the sentence of a court martial.

Fighting; Provoking speeches

XXIII. If any person in the fleet shall quarrel or fight with any other person in the fleet, or use reproachful or provoking speeches or gestures, tending to make any quarrel or disturbance, he shall, upon being convicted thereof, suffer such punishment as the offence shall deserve, and a court martial shall impose.

Embezzlement of stores

XXIV. There shall be no wasteful expense of any powder, shot, ammunition, or other stores in the fleet, nor any embezzlement thereof, but the stores and provisions shall be careful preserved , upon pain of such punishment to be inflicted upon the offenders, abettors, buyers and receivers (being persons subject to naval discipline) as shall be by a court martial found just in that behalf.

Burning a magazine, ship

XXV. Every person in the fleet, who shall unlawfully burn or set fire to any magazine or store of powder, or ship, boat, ketch, hoy or vessel, or tackle or furniture thereunto belonging, not then appertaining to an enemy, pirate, or rebel, being convicted of any such offence, by the sentence of a court martial, shall suffer death.

Steering and conducting ships

XXVI. Care shall be taken in the conducting and steering of any of His Majesty's ships, that through willfulness, negligence, or other defaults, no ship be stranded, or run upon any rocks or sands, or split or hazarded, upon pain, that such as shall be found guilty therein, be punished by death, or such other punishment, as the offence by a court martial shall be judged to deserve.

Sleeping, negligence, and forsaking a station

XXVII. No person in or belonging to the fleet shall sleep upon his watch, or negligently perform the duty imposed on him, or forsake his station, upon pain of death, or such other punishment as a court martial shall think fit to impose, and as the circumstances of the case shall require.

Murder

XXVIII. All murders committed by any person in the fleet, shall be punished with death by the sentence of a court martial.

Sodomy

XXIX. If any person in the fleet shall commit the unnatural and detestable sin of buggery and sodomy with man or beast, he shall be punished with death by the sentence of a court martial.

Robbery

XXX. All robbery committed by any person in the fleet, shall be punished with death, or otherwise, as a court martial, upon consideration of the circumstances, shall find meet.

False muster

XXXI. Every officer or other person in the fleet, who shall knowingly make or sign a false muster or muster book, or who shall command, counsel, or procure the making or signing thereof, or who shall aid or abet any other person in the making or signing thereof, shall, upon proof of any such offence being made before a court martial, be cashiered, and rendered incapable of further employment in His Majesty's naval service.

Apprehending and keeping criminals

XXXII. No provost martial belonging to the fleet shall refuse to apprehend any criminal, whom he shall be authorized by legal warrant to apprehend, or to receive or keep any prisoner committed to his charge, or willfully suffer him to escape, being once in his custody, or dismiss him without lawful order, upon pain of such punishment as a court martial shall deem him fit to deserve; and all captains, officers, and others in the fleet, shall do their endeavour to detect, apprehend, and bring to punishment all offenders, and shall assist the officers appointed for that purpose therein, upon pain of being proceeded against, and punished by a court martial, according to the nature and degree of the offence.

Behaving unbecoming an officer

XXXIII. If any flag officer, captain, or commander, or lieutenant belonging to the fleet, shall be convicted before a court martial of behaving in a scandalous, infamous, cruel, oppressive, or fraudulent manner, unbecoming the character of an officer, he shall be dismissed from His Majesty's service.

Mutiny, desertion, disobedience when on shore, in the King's dominions

XXXIV. Every person being in actual service and full pay, and part of the crew in or belonging to any of His Majesty's ships or vessels of war, who shall be guilty of mutiny, desertion, or disobedience to any lawful command, in any part of His Majesty's dominions on shore, when in actual service relative to the fleet, shall be liable to be tried by a court martial, and suffer the like punishment for every such offence, as if the same had been committed at sea on board any of His Majesty's ships or vessels of war.

Crimes committed on shore out of the King's dominions

XXXV. If any person who shall be in the actual service and full pay of His Majesty' ships and vessels of war, shall commit upon the shore, in any place or places out of His Majesty's dominions, any of the crimes punishable by these articles and orders, the person so offending shall be liable to be tried and punished for the same, in like manner, to all intents and purposes, as if the same crimes had been committed at sea, on board any of His Majesty's ships or vessels of war.

Crimes not mentioned in this act

XXXVI. All other crimes not capital committed by any person or persons in the fleet, which are not mentioned in this act, or for which no punishment is hereby directed to be inflicted, shall be punished by the laws and customs in such cases used at sea.

No. II Courts Martial Statutes

Abstract of Sections respecting Courts Martial, contained in the Act of Parliament

[22 Geo. II. c. 33] intituled, An Act for amending, explaining, &c.
reducing into one Act of Parliament the Laws relating to
the Government of His Majesty's Ships, Vessels,
and Forces by Sea; likewise,

Clauses of Amendment in the Act 19, Geo. III. c. 17

Section III

Not more than two years imprisonment

No Person convicted of any Offence shall, by the Sentence of any Court Martial, to be held by virtue of this Act, be adjudged to be imprisoned for a longer Term than the Space of two Years.

Section IV

Jurisdiction of a court martial

That nothing in this Act contained shall extend or be construed to extend to impower any Court Martial to be constituted by virtue of this Act, to proceed to the Punishment or Trial of any of the Offences specified in the several Articles contained in this Act, or of any Offence whatsoever (other than the Offences specified in the 5th, 34th and 35th of the foregoing Articles and Orders) which shall not be committed upon the main Sea or in great Rivers only, beneath the Bridges of the said Rivers nigh to the Sea, or in any Haven, River or Creek within the Jurisdiction of the Admiralty, and which shall not be committed by such persons as at the time of the offence committed shall be in actual service and full pay in the Fleet or Ships of War of His Majesty, his Heirs or Successors, such persons only excepted, and for such offences only as are described in the fifth Article of War.

Section V

No land officer or soldier to be tried

Nothing in this Act contained shall extend or be construed to extend, to impower any Court Martial to be constituted by virtue of this Act, to proceed to the Punishment or Trial of any Land Officer or Soldier on board any Transport Ship, for any of the Offences specified in the several Articles contained in this Act.

Section VI

Commission to be granted to assemble courts martial

The Lord High Admiral of Great Britain or the Commissioners for executing the Office of Lord High Admiral of Great Britain for the time being, shall have full Power and Authority to grant Commissions to any officer commanding-in-chief any Fleet or Squadron of Ships of War, to call and assemble Courts Martial, consisting of Commanders and Captains; and that in case any Officer commanding in Chief any Fleet or Squadron of Ships of War, (who shall be authorized by the Lord High Admiral, or the Commissioners for executing the Office of Lord High Admiral for the time being, to call and assemble Courts Martial in foreign Parts) shall happen to die, or be recalled or removed from his Command, then the Officer upon whom the Command of the said Fleet, or Squadron shall devolve, and so, from time to time the Officer who shall have the Command of the Fleet or Squadron, shall have the same Power to call and assemble Courts Martial, as the first Commander in Chief of the said Fleet or Squadron was invested with.

Section VII

No commander-in-chief in foreign parts to preside at a court martial

No Commander in Chief of any Fleet or Squadron of His Majesty's Ships or Detachment thereof, consisting of more than five Ships, shall preside at any Court Martial in foreign Parts, but that the

Officer next in Command to such Officer commanding in Chief, shall hold such Court Martial and preside thereat; any Law, Custom or Usage to the contrary notwithstanding.

Section VIII

Commanders of detachments to be impowered to hold courts martial

In case any Commander-in-Chief in any Fleet or Squadron of His Majesty's Ships or Vessels of War in foreign Parts, shall detach any Part of such Fleet or Squadron, every Commander in Chief shall, and he is hereby authorized and required, by Writing under his Hands, to impower the Chief Commander of the Squadron or Detachment so ordered on such separate Service (and in case of his Death or Removal, the Officer to whom the Command of such separate Squadron or Detachment shall belong) to hold Courts Martial, during the time of such separate Service, or until the Commander of the said Detachment for the time being shall return to his Commander in Chief, or shall come under the Command of any other his Superior Officer or return to Great Britain or Ireland.

Section IX

Five ships meeting, senior officer may hold courts martial and preside

If any five or more of His Majesty's Ships or Vessels of War shall happen to meet together in foreign Parts, then and in such Case, it shall be lawful for the Senior Officer of the said Ships or Vessels to hold Courts Martial, and preside thereat from time to time, as there shall be Occasion, during so long time as the said Ships or Vessels of War or any five or more of them, shall continue together.

Section X

If a material objection to the second officer in command, the third may be appointed to hold courts martial

That where any material objection occurs, which may render it improper for the Person who is next in Command to the Senior Officer or Commander in Chief of any Fleet or Squadron of His Majesty's Ships of War in foreign Parts to hold courts martial, or preside thereat, in such case it shall be lawful for the Lord High Admiral or Commissioners for executing the Office of Lord High Admiral for the time being, as also the Commander-in-Chief of any such Fleet or Squadron of His Majesty's Ships in foreign Parts, respectively to appoint the third Officer in Command, to preside at, or hold such Court Martial.

Section XI

In Great Britain or Ireland the admiralty may appoint the first, second, or third officer in command in any port to hold courts martial

It shall be lawful for the Lord High Admiral of Great Britain or the Commissioners for executing the Office of Lord High Admiral for the time being, and they are hereby respectively authorized, from time to time, as there shall be Occasion, to direct any Flag Officer or Captain of any of His Majesty's Ships of War, who shall be in any Port of Great Britain or Ireland, to hold Courts Martial in any such Port, provided such Flag Officer or Captain be the first, second or third in Command of such Port, as shall be found most expedient, and for the Good of His Majesty's Service; and such Flag Officer or Captain, so directed to hold Courts Martial, shall preside at such Court Martial, anything herein contained to the contrary notwithstanding.

Section XII

Court martial not to consist of more than thirteen or lea than fove next in seniority to the officer presiding

No Court Martial, to be held or appointed by virtue of this present Act, shall consist of more than thirteen, or of less than five Persons, to be composed of such Flag Officers, Captains or Commanders then and there present, as are next in Seniority to the Officer who presides at the Court Martial.

Section XIII

Particular number not to be ascertained by the admiralty or officer impowered to order or hold courts martial

Nothing herein contained shall extend or be construed to extend, to authorize or impower the Lord High Admiral or the Commissioners for executing the Office of Lord High Admiral, or any Officer impowered to order or hold Courts Martial, to direct or ascertain the particular Number of Persons of which any Court Martial, to be held or appointed by virtue of this present Act, shall consist.

Section XIV

In what cases commander may assist

In case any Court Martial shall, by virtue of this Act, be appointed to be held at any Place where there are not less than three, nor yet so many as five officers of the Degree and Denomination of a Post Captain, or of a superior rank, to be found, then it shall be lawful for the officer, at the Place appointed for holding such Court Martial, who is to preside at the same, to call to his Assistance as many of the Commanders of His Majesty's Vessels, under the Rank and Degree of a Post Captain, as, together with the Post Captains then and there present, will make up the Number of five, to hold such Court Martial.

Section XV

No member to go on shore before sentence be given

No Member of any Court Martial, after the Trial is begun, shall go on shore till Sentence be given, but remain on board the Ship in which the Court shall first assemble, except in case of Sickness, to be judged of by the Court, upon Pain of being cashiered from His Majesty's Service; nor shall the Proceedings of the said Court be delayed by the Absence of any of its Members, provided a sufficient Number doth remain to compose the said Court, which shall and is hereby required to sit from Day to Day (Sunday always excepted) until the sentence be given.[4]

Section XVI

Form of oath to be administered

Upon all trials of offenders by any Court Martial, all the officers present who are to constitute the said Court Martial, shall, before they proceed to such trial, take such Oath as is hereinafter mentioned; upon the Holy Evangelists, before the Court; which Oath the Judge Advocate or his Deputy, or the Person appointed to officiate as such, is hereby authorized and required to administer in the Words following; (that is to say),

> I .....AB .... do swear, that I will duly administer Justice, according to the Articles and Orders established by an Act passed in the twenty second Year of the Reign of His Majesty King George the Second, for amending, explaining and reducing into one Act of Parliament, the Law's relating to the Government of His Majesty's Ships, Vessels and Forces by Sea, without Partiality, Favour or Affection; and if any Case shall arise, which is not particularly mentioned in the said Articles and Orders, I will duly administer Justice according to my Conscience, the best of my Understanding, and the Custom of the Navy in the like Cases; and I do further swear, that I will not upon any Account, at any time whatsoever, disclose or discover the Vote or Opinion of any particular Member of this Court Martial, unless thereunto required by Act of Parliament. So help me GOD.

Oath to be administered to the judge advocate

And so soon as the said oath shall have been administered to the respective Members, the President of the Court is hereby authorized and required to administer to the Judge Advocate or the Person officiating as such, an oath in the following words:

> I A.B. do swear, that I will not upon any Account at any time whatsoever, disclose or discover the Vote or Opinion of any particular Member of this Court Martial, unless thereunto required by Act of Parliament. So help me GOD.

4 It having been found by experience, that the confining members of courts martial to the ships in which such courts martial were ordered to be assembled, until sentence was given, had been attended with great inconvenience and prejudice to the healths of officers summoned to attend as members— By 19 Geo. III. cap. 17. *Section 2, this clause of the act was repealed and made void to all intents and purposes.* Provided always, that the proceedings of any court martial shall not be delayed by the absence of any of its members, when a sufficient number doth remain to compose such court, which is required to sit from day to day (Sunday always excepted) until the sentence be given. And no member of the said court martial shall absent himself from the said court, during the whole course of the trial, upon pain of being cashiered from his Majesty's service, except in case of sickness, or other extraordinary and indispensable occasion, to be judged of by the said court.

Section XVII

Court may punish persons refusing to give evidence or prevaricating, or behaving with contempt

In case any Person in the Fleet, being called upon to give Evidence at any Court Martial, shall refuse to give his Evidence upon Oath, or shall prevaricate in his Evidence, or behave with Contempt to the Court, it shall and may be lawful for such Court Martial to punish every such Offender by Imprisonment, at the Discretion of the Court, such Imprisonment not to continue longer than three Months; in case of such Refusal or Prevarication, nor longer than one Month in the Case of such Contempt; and that all and every Person and Persons who shall commit any wilful Perjury, in any Evidence or Examination upon Oath at any such Court Martial, or who, shall corruptly procure or suborn any person to commit such wilful Perjury, shall and may be prosecuted in His Majesty's Court of King's Bench, by Indictment or Information; and every Issue joined in any such Indictment or Information shall be tried by good and lawful Men of the County of Middlesex or such other County as the said Court of King's bench shall direct; and all and every Person and Persons, being lawfully convicted upon any such Indictment or Information, shall be punished with such Pains and Penalties, as are indicted for the like Offences respectively by two Acts of Parliament, the one [5 Eliz. c. 9] made in the fifth Year of the Reign of Queen Elizabeth, intituled, *An Act for Punishment of such persons as shall procure or commit any wilful Perjury*; and the other [2 Geo. II. c. 25] made in the second Year of the Reign of His present Majesty, intituled, *An Act for the more effectual preventing and further Punishment of Forgery, Perjury and Subornation of Perjury; and to make it Felony to steal Bonds, Notes or other Securities for Payment of Money.*

Section XVIII

The offence only to be set forth in any information

And be it further enacted by the authority aforesaid, That in every Information or Indictment to be prosecuted by Virtue of this Act for any such Offence, it shall be sufficient to set forth the Offence charged upon the Defendant, without setting forth the Commission or Authority for holding the Court Martial, and without setting forth the particular Matter tried or to be tried, or directed or intended to be tried before such Court.

Section XIX

Sentence of death (except in cases of mutiny) not to be executed without directions from the admiralty, &c

No sentence of death given by any Court Martial held within the Narrow Seas, (except in Cases of Mutiny) shall be put in execution till after the Report of the Proceedings of the said Court shall have been made to the Lord High Admiral or the Commissioners for executing the Office of Lord High Admiral, and his or their Directions shall have been given therein; and if the said Court shall have been held beyond the Narrow Seas, then such Sentence of Death shall not be carried into execution but by Order of the Commander of the Fleet or Squadron wherein Sentence was passed; and in Cases where Sentence of Death shall be passed in any Squadron, detached from any other Fleet or Squadron upon a separate Service, then such Sentence of Death (except in Cases of Mutiny) shall not be put in execution, but by Order of the Commander of the Fleet or Squadron from which such Detachment shall have been made, or of the Lord High Admiral or Commissioners for executing the Office of Lord High Admiral; and in Cases where Sentence of Death shall be passed in any Court Martial held by the Senior Officer of five or more of His Majesty Ships, which shall happen to meet together in foreign Parts, pursuant to the Power hereinbefore given, then such Sentence of Death (except in cases of Mutiny) shall not be carried into execution but by Order of the Lord High Admiral or Commissioners for executing the Office of Lord High Admiral.

Section XX

Judge advocate to administer oath to witnesses

The Judge Advocate of any Fleet for the time being or his Deputy, shall have full Power and Authority, and is hereby required to administer an Oath to any Witness at any Trial by Court Martial; and in the Absence of the Judge Advocate and his Deputy, the Court Martial shall have full Power and Authority to appoint any Person to execute the Office of Judge Advocate.

Section XXI

This act to be in force with regard to crews of ships lost; Pay of such ships reserved

All the Powers given by the Articles and Orders established by this Act, shall remain and be in full force with respect to the Crews of such of His Majesty's Ships as shall be wrecked or be otherwise lost or destroyed; and all the Command, Power and Authority given to the Officers of the said Ship or Ships, shall remain and be in full force as effectually as if such Ship or Ships to which they did belong were not so wrecked, lost or destroyed, until they shall be regularly discharged from His Majesty's further Service or removed into some other of His Majesty's Ships of War, or until a Court Martial shall be held, pursuant to the Custom of the Navy in such Cases, to enquire into the Causes of the Loss of the said Ship or Ships: And if upon such Enquiry it shall appear by the Sentence of the Court Martial that all or any of the Officers or Seamen of the said Ship or Ships did their utmost to preserve, get off or recover the said Ship or Ships, and, since the Loss thereof, have behaved themselves obediently to their Superior Officers, according to the Discipline of the Navy and the said Articles and Orders hereinbefore established, then all the Pay and Wages of the said Officers and Seamen, or of such of them as shall have done their Duty as aforesaid, shall continue and go on, and be paid to the time of their Discharge or Death; or if they shall be then alive, to the time of the holding of such Court Martial or Removal into some other of His Majesty's Ships of War; and every such Officer and Seaman of any of His Majesty's Ships of War, who after the Wreck or Loss of his Ship shall act contrary to the Discipline of the Navy, and the several Articles and Orders hereinbefore established or any of them, shall be sentenced by the said Court Martial, and punished as if the Ship to which he did belong was not so wrecked, lost or destroyed.

Section XXII

Continuance of wages to men belonging to ships taken by an enemy

All the Pay and Wages of such Officers and Seamen of any of His Majesty's Ships as are taken by the Enemy, and upon Enquiry at a Court Martial shall appear by the Sentence of the said Court to have done their utmost to defend the said Ship or Ships, and since the taking thereof, to have behaved themselves obediently to their Superior Officers, according to the Discipline of the Navy, and the said Articles and Orders hereinbefore established, shall continue and go on, and be paid, from the time of their being so taken, to the time of the holding of such Court Martial, or until they shall be regularly discharged from His Majesty's Service, or removed into some other of His Majesty's Ships of War, or (if they shall die in Captivity, or not live to the time of the holding of such Court Martial) to the time of their Death, in such manner, and not otherwise, as if the said Ship or Ships to which they did belong respectively was not or were not so taken.

Section XXIII

Persons not to be tried after certain time

No person or persons not flying from justice, shall be tried or punished by any Court Martial for any Offence to be committed against this Act, unless the Complaint of such Offence be made in Writing to the Lord High Admiral, or to the Commissioners for executing the Office of Lord High Admiral for the time being, or any Commander in Chief of His Majesty's Squadrons or Ships impowered to hold Courts Martial, or unless a Court Martial to try such Offender shall be ordered by the said Lord High Admiral, or the said Commissioners, or the said Commander in Chief, either within three years after such Offence shall be committed, or within one year after the Return of the Ship or of the Squadron to which such Offender shall belong, into any of the Ports of Great Britain or Ireland; or within one Year after the Return of such Offender into Great Britain or Ireland.

Section XXIV

Penalty on officers' receiving on board any goods contrary to article 18 of this act; Application of the forfeiture; And method of recovery; The court to certify the lords of the Admiralty the judgment

And whereas by the said Act [8 Geo. I. c. 24.], intituled, *An Act for the more effectual Suppressing of Piracy*; it is, amongst other things, enacted in the following words, That the said Captain, Commander or other Officer of the said Ship or Vessel of War, and all and every the Owners and Proprietors of such Goods and Merchandizes, put on board such Ship or Vessel of War as aforesaid, shall lose, forfeit and pay the Value of all and every such Goods and Merchandizes so put on board as aforesaid; one Moiety of such full Value to such Person or Persons as shall make the first Discovery, and give Information of or concerning the said Offence; the other Moiety of such full Value, to and for the Use of Greenwich Hospital; all which forfeitures shall and may be sued for and recovered in the High Court of Admiralty: Now for making the said in part recited Act more useful and effectual, Be it enacted by the Authority aforesaid, That from and after the twenty fifth Day of December One thousand seven hundred and forty nine, if any Captain, Commander or other Officer of any of His Majesty's Ships or Vessels, shall receive on board, or permit or suffer to be received on board such Ship or Vessel, any Goods or Merchandizes, contrary to the true Intent and Meaning of the eighteenth Article in this Act before mentioned and hereby enacted; every such Captain, Commander or other Officer shall, for every such Offence, over and above any Punishment inflicted by this Act, forfeit and pay the Value of all and every such Goods and Merchandizes so received or permitted, or suffered to be received on board as aforesaid, or the Sum of five hundred Pounds of lawful Money of Great Britain, at the Election of the Informer, or Person who shall sue for the same, so that no more than one of these Penalties or Forfeitures shall be sued for and recovered by virtue of this and the said in part recited Act or either of them, against the same Person, for one and the same Offence; one Moiety of which Penalties or Forfeitures shall be forfeited, and paid to the Person who shall inform or sue for the same, and the other Moiety thereof to and for the Use of the Royal Hospital at Greenwich; which Forfeiture shall be sued for and recovered by Action of Debt, Bill, Plaint or Information, in any of His Majesty's Courts of Record at Westminster, or in the High Court of Admiralty, at the Election of the Informer, or Person who shall sue for the same; and the Court shall award such Costs to the Parties as shall be just; and in all Cases where Judgement or Sentence shall be given against any such Offender, the Court where such Judgment or Sentence shall be given, shall, with all convenient Speed, certify the same to the Lord High Admiral or to the Commissioners for executing the said Office.

Section XXV

Limitation on the powers of this act

Provided always, That nothing in this Act contained shall extend or be construed to extend to, take away from the Lord High Admiral of Great Britain or the Commissioners for executing the Office of Lord High Admiral of Great Britain or any Vice Admiral, or any Judge or Judges of the Admiralty, or his or their Deputy or Deputies, or any other Officers or Ministers of the Admiralty, or any others having or claiming any Admiral Power, Jurisdiction or Authority within this Realm, or any other the King's Dominions, or from any Person or Court whatsoever, any Power, Right, Jurisdiction, Pre-eminence or Authority, which he or they, or any of them, lawfully hath, have or had, or ought to have and enjoy; before the making of this Act, so as the same Person shall not be punished twice for the same Offence.

Clauses of amendment in the Act of 19 Geo. III. c. 17, intituled,

An act to explain and amend an Act, made in the
twenty-second year of the reign of
His late Majesty King George the Second

Preamble; Part of the said act repealed

WHEREAS by an act, made in the twenty-second year of the reign of his late Majesty king George the Second, intituled, *An act for amending, explaining, and reducing into one act of parliament, the laws relating to the government of his Majesty's ships, vessels, and forces by*

Sea; it is, among other things, enacted, That, from and alter the twenty-fifth day of December one thousand seven hundred and forty-nine, no member of any court-martial, after the trial is begun, shall go on shore till sentence be given, but remain on board the ship in which the court shall first assemble, except in case of sickness, to be judged of by the court, upon pain of being cashiered from his majesty's service; nor shall the proceedings of the said court be delayed by the absence of any of its members, provided a sufficient number doth remain to compose the said court, which shall, and is thereby required to sit from day to day (Sunday always excepted) until the sentence be given: and whereas it hath been found by experience, that the confiding members of courts-martial to the ship in which such courts-martial shall first assemble, until sentence be given, hath been attended with great inconveniencies and prejudice to the healths of officers summoned to attend as members of courts-martial; and it is highly necessary and expedient that such inconveniencies should be prevented in future; may it therefore please your Majesty that it may be enacted; and be it enacted by the King's most excellent Majesty, by and with the advice and consent of the lords spiritual and temporal, and commons, in this present parliament assembled, and by the authority of the same, That so much and such part of the said recited act as directs that no member of any court-martial, after the trial has begun, shall go on (bore till sentence be given, but remain on board the ship in which the court shall first, assemble, except in case of sickness, to be judged of by the court, upon pain of being cashiered from his Majesty's service; and that the proceedings of the said court shall not be delayed by the absence of any of its members, provided a sufficient number doth remain to compose the said court, which is thereby required to fit from day to day (Sunday always excepted) until the sentence be given, shall be, and the same is hereby repealed and made void, to all intents and purposes whatsoever.

Proceedings of courts martial not to be delayed by the absence of any members, provided sufficient number remain to make a court; No member to be absent except on some extra ordinary occasion

Provided always, and be it enacted, That the proceedings of any court-martial shall not be delayed by the absence of any of its members, provided a sufficient number doth remain to compose such court, which shall, and is hereby required to sit from day to day (Sunday always excepted) until the sentence be given; any thing hereinbefore contained to the contrary thereof in anywise notwithstanding: and no member of the said court-martial shall absent himself from the said court during the whole course of trial, upon pain of being cashiered from his Majesty's service, except in case of sickness, or other extraordinary and indispensable occasion, to be judged of by said court.

Two clauses in the said Act 22 Geo. II. recited

And whereas, by two clauses in the said act, passed in the twenty-second year of the reign of his late Majesty king George the Second, it is enacted and declared, That every person in the fleet, who, through cowardice, negligence, or disaffection, shall, in time of action, with draw or keep back, or not come into the fight or engagement, or shall not do his utmost to take or destroy every ship which it shall be his duty to engage, and to assist and relieve all and every of his Majesty's ships, or those of his allies, which it shall be his duty to assist and relieve, and being convicted thereof by the sentence of a court martial, shall suffer death ; and also that every person in the fleet, who, through cowardice, negligence, or disaffection, shall forbear to pursue the chase of any enemy, pirate, or rebel, beaten or flying, or shall not relieve of assist a known friend in view, to the utmost of his power, and being convicted of any such offence by the sentence of a court-martial, shall suffer death: and whereas the restraining of the power of the court-martial to the inflicting of the punishment of death, in the several cafes recited in the said clauses, may he attended with great hardship and inconvenience, be it enacted, That, from and after the and altered, passing of this act, it shall and may be lawful, in the several cases recited in the said clauses, for the court-martial to pronounce sentence of death, or to inflict such other punishment as the nature and degree of the offence shall be sound to deserve.

The Naval Discipline Act, 1866

[29 & 30 VICTORIAE, c.109]

10 August 1866

An Act to make provision for the Discipline of the Navy

WHEREAS it is expedient to amend the Law relating to the Government of the Navy, whereon, under the good Providence of God, the Wealth, Safety, and Strength of the Kingdom chiefly depend:

Be it enacted by the Queen's most Excellent Majesty, by and with the Advice and Consent of the Lords Spiritual and Temporal and Commons, in this present Parliament assembled, and by the Authority of the same, as follows:

PART I

ARTICLES OF WAR

Public Worship

1. All Officers in Command of Her Majesty's Ships of War shall cause the Public Worship of Almighty God according to the Liturgy of the Church of England established by Law to be solemnly, orderly, and reverently performed in their respective Ships, and shall take care that Prayers and Preaching, by the Chaplains in Holy Orders of the respective Ships, be performed diligently, and that the Lord's Day be observed according to Law.

Misconduct in the Presence of the Enemy

2. Every Flag Officer, Captain, Commander or Officer commanding subject to this Act who upon Signal of Battle, or on Sight of a Ship of an Enemy which it may be his Duty to engage, shall not,

(1)Use his utmost Exertion to bring his Ship into Action;

(2)Or shall not during such Action, in his own Person and according to his Rank, encourage his inferior Officers and Men to fight courageously;

(3)Or who shall surrender his Ship to the Enemy when capable of making a successful Defence, or who in Time of Action shall improperly withdraw from the Fight, shall, if he has acted traitorously, suffer Death; if he has acted from Cowardice shall suffer Death, or such other Punishment as is herein-after mentioned; and if he has acted from Negligence, or through other Default, he shall be dismissed from Her Majesty's Service, with or without Disgrace, or shall suffer such other Punishment as is herein-after mentioned.

3. Every Officer subject to this Act who shall forbear to pursue the Chase of any Enemy, Pirate, or Rebel, beaten or flying, or shall not relieve and assist a known Friend in View to the utmost of his Power, or who shall improperly forsake his Station, shall, if he has therein acted traitorously, suffer Death; if he has acted from Cowardice, suffer Death or such other Punishment as is herein-after mentioned; if he has acted from Negligence, or through other Default, shall be dismissed from Her Majesty's Service, with Disgrace, or shall suffer such other Punishment as is herein-after mentioned.

4. When any Action or any Service is commanded, every Person subject to this Act who shall presume to delay or discourage the said Action or Service upon any Pretence whatsoever, or in the Presence or Vicinity of the Enemy shall desert his Post or sleep upon his Watch, shall suffer Death or such other Punishment as is herein-after mentioned.

5. Every Person subject to this Act, and not being a Commanding Officer, who shall not use his utmost Exertions to carry the Orders of his Superior Officers into execution when ordered to prepare for Action, or during the Action, shall, if he has acted traitorously, suffer Death; if he has acted from Cowardice shall suffer Death, or such other Punishment as is herein-after mentioned; and if he has acted from Negligence, or through other Default, be dismissed from Her Majesty's Service, with Disgrace, or suffer such other Punishment as is herein-after mentioned.

Communications with the Enemy

6. All Spies for the Enemy shall be deemed to be Persons subject to this Act, and shall suffer Death or such other Punishment as is herein-after mentioned.

7. Every Person subject to this Act who shall-

(1)Traitorously hold Correspondence with or shall give Intelligence to the Enemy;

(2)Or fail to make known to the proper Authorities any Information he may have received from the Enemy;

(3)Or who shall relieve the Enemy with any Supplies,

shall suffer Death, or such other Punishment as is herein-after mentioned.

8. Every Person subject to this Act who shall, without any Treacherous Intention, hold any improper Communication with the Enemy, shall be dismissed with Disgrace from Her Majesty's Service, or shall suffer such other Punishment as is herein-after mentioned.

Neglect of Duty

9. Every Person subject to this Act who shall desert his Post or sleep upon his Watch, or negligently perform the Duty imposed on him, shall be dismissed from Her Majesty's Service, with Disgrace, or shall suffer such other Punishment as is herein-after mentioned.

Mutiny

10. Where Mutiny is accompanied by Violence, every Person subject to this Act who shall join therein shall suffer Death, or such other Punishment as is herein-after mentioned; and every Person subject to this Act who shall not use his utmost Exertions to suppress such Mutiny shall, if he has acted traitorously, suffer Death, or such other Punishment as is herein-after mentioned; if he has acted from Cowardice, shall suffer Penal Servitude or such other Punishment as is herein-after mentioned; if he has acted from Negligence he shall be dismissed from Her Majesty's Service, with Disgrace, or suffer such other Punishment as is herein-after mentioned.

11. Where a Mutiny is not accompanied by Violence, the Ringleader or Ringleaders of such Mutiny shall suffer Death, or such other Punishment as is herein-after mentioned; and all other Persons who shall join in such Mutiny, or shall not use their utmost Exertions to suppress the same, shall suffer Imprisonment or such other Punishment as is herein-after mentioned.

12. Every Person subject to this Act who shall endeavour to seduce any other Person subject to this Act from his Duty or Allegiance to Her Majesty, or endeavour to incite him to commit any Act of Mutiny, shall suffer Death or such other Punishment as is herein-after mentioned.

13. Every Person not otherwise subject to this Act, who, being on board any Ship of Her Majesty, shall endeavour to seduce from his Duty or Allegiance to Her Majesty any Person subject to this Act, shall so far as respects such Offence be deemed to be a Person subject to this Act, arid shall suffer Death or such other Punishment as is herein-after mentioned.

14. Every Person subject to this Act who shall make or endeavour to make any mutinous Assembly, or shall lead or incite any other Person to join in any mutinous Assembly, or shall utter any Words of Sedition or Mutiny, shall suffer Penal Servitude or such other Punishment as is herein-after mentioned.

15. Every Person subject to this Act who shall wilfully conceal any traitorous or mutinous Practice or Design, or any traitorous or mutinous Words spoken against Her Majesty, or any Words, Practice, or Design tending to the Hindrance of the Service, shall suffer Penal Servitude or such other Punishment as is herein-after mentioned.

16. Every Person subject to this Act who shall strike, or with any Weapon attempt to strike, or draw or lift up any Weapon against his superior Officer being in the Execution of his Office, shall be punished with Death or such other Punishment as is herein-after mentioned; and every Person subject to this Act who shall, otherwise than with a Weapon, attempt to strike or use or attempt to use any Violence against his superior Officer being in the Execution of his Office, shall be punished with Penal Servitude or such other Punishment as is herein-after mentioned; and every person subject to this Act who shall strike or attempt to strike, or draw or lift up any

Weapon against, or use or attempt to use any Violence against his superior Officer not being in the Execution of his Office, shall be punished with Penal Servitude or such other Punishment as is herein-after mentioned.

Insubordination

17. Every Person subject to this Act who shall wilfully disobey any lawful Command of his superior Officer, or shall use threatening or insulting Language, or behave with Contempt to his superior Officer, shall be punished with Dismissal with Disgrace from Her Majesty's Service, or suffer such other Punishment as is herein-after mentioned.

18. Every Person subject to this Act who shall quarrel or fight any other Person, whether such other Person be or be not subject to this Act, or shall use reproachful or provoking Speeches or Gestures tending to make any Quarrel or Disturbance, shall suffer Imprisonment or such other Punishment as is herein-after mentioned.

Desertion and Absence without Leave

19. Every Person subject to this Act who shall absent himself from his Ship, or from the Place where his Duty requires him to be, with an Intention of not returning to such Ship or Place, or who shall at any Time and under any Circumstances when absent from his Ship or Place of Duty, do any Act which shows that he has an Intention of not returning to such Ship or Place, shall be deemed to have deserted, and shall be punished accordingly; that is to say,

(1)If he has deserted to the Enemy he shall be punished with Death or such other Punishment as is herein-after mentioned;

(2)If he has deserted under any other Circumstances, he shall be punished with Penal Servitude or such other Punishment as is herein-after mentioned;

and in every such Case he shall forfeit all Pay, Head Money, Bounty, Salvage, Prize Money, and Allowances that have been earned by him, and all Annuities, Pensions, Gratuities, Medals, and Decorations that may have been granted to him, and also all Clothes and Effects which he may have left on board the Ship or at the Place from which he has deserted, unless the Tribunal by which he is tried, or the Admiralty, shall otherwise direct.

20. Every Person subject to this Act who shall endeavour to seduce any other Person subject to this Act to desert shall suffer Imprisonment or such other Punishment as is herein-after mentioned.

21. Every Officer in Command of any Ship of Her Majesty who shall receive or entertain any Deserter from Her Majesty's Military or Naval Forces, after discovering him to be a Deserter, and shall not with all convenient Speed, in the Case of a Deserter from Her Majesty's Naval Forces, give Notice to the Commanding Officer of the Ship to which such Deserter belongs, or, if such Ship is at a Distance, to the Secretary of the Admiralty or to the Commander-in-Chief, or, in case of a Deserter from Her Majesty's| Military Forces, give Notice to the Secretary of War, or the Commanding Officer of the Regiment to which such Deserter belongs, the Officer so offending shall be dismissed from Her Majesty's Service or shall suffer such other Punishment as is herein-after mentioned.

22. If any Person subject to this Act (without being guilty of Desertion) improperly leaves his Ship or Place of Duty, he shall be liable to Imprisonment or to such other Punishment as is hereinafter mentioned, and to such other Punishment by Forfeiture of Wages or of other Benefits as the Admiralty from Time to Time by Regulations prescribe.

23. Every Person subject to this Act who (without being guilty of Desertion or of improperly leaving his Ship or Place of Duty) shall be absent without Leave shall be liable to Imprisonment for any Period not exceeding Ten Weeks, with or without Hard Labour, or such other Punishment as the Circumstances of the Case may require, and to such other Punishment by Forfeiture of Wages or of other Benefits as the Admiralty from Time to Time by Regulations is prescribe.

24. If any Person subject to this Act is absent without Leave for a Period of One Month (whether he is guilty of Desertion or of improperly leaving his Ship or Place of Duty or not), but is not apprehended and tried for his Offence, he shall be liable to Forfeiture of Wages and other Benefits as the Admiralty from Time to Time by Regulations prescribe, and the Admiralty, or, on a Foreign Station, the Commander-in-Chief, may by an Order containing a Statement of the Absence without Leave direct that the Clothes and Effects (if any) left by him on board Ship or at his Place of Duty be forfeited, and the same may be sold, and the Proceeds of the Sale shall be disposed of as the Admiralty or the Commander-in-Chief (as the Case may be) may direct; and every Order under this Provision for Forfeiture or Sale shall be conclusive as to the Fact of the Absence without Leave as therein stated of the Person therein named; but in any Case the Admiralty may, if it seems fit, on sufficient Cause being shown at any Time after Forfeiture and before Sale, remit the Forfeiture, or after Sale pay or dispose of the Proceeds of the Sale or any Part thereof to or for the Use of the Person to whom the Clothes or Effects belonged, or his Representatives.

25. If any Person not subject to this Act assists or procures any Person subject to this Act to desert or improperly absent him-self from his Duty, or conceals, employs, or continues to employ any Person subject to this Act, who is a Deserter or improperly absent from his Duty, knowing him to be a Deserter or so improperly absent, he shall for every such Offence of Assistance, Procurement, Concealment, Employment, or Continuance of Employment; be liable, on summary Conviction thereof before a Justice or Justices, or before any Person or Persons or Court exercising like Authority in any Part of Her Majesty's Dominions, to a Penalty not exceeding Thirty Pounds; and, notwithstanding anything in any Act relating to Municipal Corporations, or to the Metropolitan Police, or in any other Act, every such Penalty shall be applied as the Admiralty direct.

26. If any Person not subject to this Act by Words or otherwise persuades any Person subject to this Act to desert or improperly absent himself from his Duty, he shall for every such Offence be liable, on summary Conviction thereof before a Justice or Justices, or before any Person or Persons or Court exercising like Authority in any Part of Her Majesty's Dominions, to a Penalty not exceeding Twenty Pounds; and, notwithstanding anything in any Act relating to Municipal Corporations, or to the Metropolitan Police, or in any other Act, every such Penalty shall be applied as the Admiralty direct.

Miscellaneous Offences

27. Every Person subject to this Act who shall be guilty of any profane Oath, Cursing, Execration, Drunkenness, Uncleanness, or other scandalous Action in derogation of God's Honour and Corruption of good Manners, shall be dismissed from Her Majesty's Service, with Disgrace, or suffer such other Punishment as is herein-after mentioned.

28. Every Officer subject to this Act who shall be guilty of Cruelty, or of any scandalous or fraudulent Conduct, shall be dismissed with Disgrace from Her Majesty's Service; and every Officer subject to this Act who shall be guilty of any other Conduct unbecoming the Character of an Officer shall be dismissed, with or without Disgrace, from Her Majesty's Service.

29. Every Person subject to this Act who shall either designedly. or negligently or by any Default lose, strand, or hazard, or suffer to be lost, stranded, or hazarded, any Ship of Her Majesty or in Her Majesty's Service, shall be dismissed from Her Majesty's Service, with Disgrace, or suffer such other Punishment as is herein-after mentioned.

30. The Officers of all Ships of Her Majesty appointed for the Convoy and Protection of any Ships or Vessels shall diligently perform their Duty without Delay according to their Instructions in that Behalf; and every Officer who shall fail in his Duty in this respect, and shall not defend the Ships and Goods under his Convoy, without Deviation to any other Objects, or shall refuse to fight in their Defence if they are assailed, or shall cowardly abandon and expose the Ships in his Convoy to Hazard, or shall demand or exact any Money or other Reward from any Merchant or Master for convoying any Ships or Vessels intrusted to his Care, or shall misuse the Masters or Mariners thereof, shall make such Reparation in Damages to the Merchants, Owners, and others as the Court of Admiralty may adjudge, and also shall be punished criminally according to the Nature of his Offence, by Death or such other Punishment as is herein-after mentioned.

31. Every Master or other Officer in Command of any Merchant or other Vessel under the Convoy of any Ship of Her Majesty shall obey the Commanding Officer thereof in all Matters relating to the Navigation or Security of the Convoy, and shall take such Precautious for avoiding the Enemy as may be directed by such Commanding Officer; and if he shall fail to obey such Directions, such Commanding Officer may compel Obedience by Force of Arms, without being liable for any Loss of Life or of Property that may result from his using such Force.

32. Every Officer in Command of any of Her Majesty's Ships who shall receive on board or permit to be received on board such Ship any Goods or Merchandises whatsoever, other than for the sole Use of the Ship, except Gold, Silver, or Jewels, and except Goods and Merchandise belonging to any Merchant, or on board any Ship which may be shipwrecked or in imminent Danger either on the High Seas or in some Port, Creek, or Harbour, for the Purpose of preserving them for their proper Owners, or except such Goods or Merchandise as he may at any Time be ordered to take or receive on board by Order of the Admiralty or his Superior Officer, shall be dismissed from Her Majesty's Service, or suffer such other Punishment as is herein-after mentioned.

33. Every Person subject to this Act who shall wastefully expend, embezzle, or fraudulently buy, sell, or receive any Ammunition, Provisions, or other Public Stores, and every Person subject to

this Act, who shall knowingly permit any such wasteful Expenditure, Embezzlement, Sale, or Receipt, shall suffer Imprisonment or such other Punishment as is herein-after mentioned.

34. Every Person subject to this Act who shall unlawfully set fire to any Dockyard, Victualling Yard, or Steam Factory Yard, Arsenal, Magazine, Building, Stores, or to any Ship, Vessel, Hoy, Barge, Boat, or other Craft, or Furniture thereunto belonging, not being the Property of an Enemy, Pirate, or Rebel, shall suffer Death or such other Punishment as is herein-after mentioned

35. Every Person subject to this Act who shall knowingly make or sign a false Muster or Record or other official Document, or who shall command, counsel, or procure the making or signing thereof, or who shall aid or abet any other Person in the making or signing thereof, shall be dismissed from Her Majesty's Service, with Disgrace, or suffer such other Punishment as is herein-after mentioned.

36. Every Person subject to this Act who shall wilfully do any Act, or wilfully disobey any Orders, whether in Hospital or else-where, with Intent to produce or to aggravate any Disease or Infirmity, or to delay his Cure, or who shall feign any Disease, Infirmity, or Inability to perform his Duty, shall suffer Imprisonment or such other Punishment as is herein-after mentioned.

37. Every Person subject to this Act who shall have any Cause of Complaint, either of the Unwholesomeness of the Victuals or upon any other just Ground, shall quietly make the same known to his Superior, or Captain, or Commander-in-Chief, and the said Superior, Captain, or Commander-in-Chief shall, as far as he is able, cause the same to be presently remedied; and no Person subject to this Act upon any Pretence whatever shall attempt to stir up any Disturbance, upon pain of such Punishment as a Court-martial may think fit to inflict, according to the Degree of Offence.

38. All the Papers, Charter-parties, Bills of Lading, Passports, and other Writings whatsoever that shall be taken, seized, or found aboard any Ship or Ships which shall be taken as Prize shall be duly preserved, and the Commanding Officer of the Ship which shall take such Prize shall send the Originals entire and without Fraud to the Court of Admiralty, or such other Court or Commissioners as shall be authorized to determine whether such Prize be lawful Capture, there to be viewed, made use of, and proceeded upon according to Law, upon pain that every Person offending herein shall be dismissed from Her Majesty's Service, or shall suffer such other Punishment as is herein-after mentioned, and in addition thereto shall forfeit and lose his Share of the Capture.

39. No Person subject to this Act shall take out of any Prize Ship seized for Prize any Money, Plate, or Goods, unless it shall be necessary for the better securing thereof, or for the necessary Use and Service of any of Her Majesty's Ships and Vessels of War, before the same be adjudged lawful Prize in some Admiralty Court; but the full and entire Account of the whole without Embezzlement shall be brought in, and Judgment passed entirely upon the whole, without Fraud, upon pain that every Person offending herein shall be dismissed from Her Majesty's Service, with Disgrace, or suffer such other Punishment as is herein-after mentioned, and in addition thereto forfeit and lose his Share of the Capture.

40. If any Ship or Vessel shall be taken as Prize, none of the Officers, Mariners, or other Persons on board her shall be stripped of their Clothes, or in any sort pillaged, beaten, or evil intreated, upon pain that the Person or Persons so offending shall be dismissed from Her Majesty's Service, with Disgrace, or suffer such other Punishment as is herein-after mentioned.

41. If the Commanding Officer of any of Her Majesty's Ships does any of the following Things, namely, (1) By Collusion with the Enemy takes as Prize any Vessel, Goods, or Thing; (2.) Unlawfully agrees with any Person for the ransoming of any Vessel, Goods, or Thing taken as Prize; or (3) In pursuance of any unlawful Agreement for ransoming or otherwise by Collusion actually quits or restores any Vessel, Goods, or Thing taken as Prize; he shall be liable to Dismissal from Her Majesty's Service, with Disgrace, or to such other Punishment as is herein-after mentioned.

42. If any Person subject to this Act breaks Bulk on board any Vessel taken as Prize, or detained in the Exercise of any Belligerent Right, or under any Act relating to Piracy or to the Slave Trade or to the Customs, with Intent to embezzle anything therein or belonging thereto, he shall be liable to Dismissal from Her Majesty's Service, with Disgrace, or to such other Punishment as herein-after mentioned, and in addition thereto to forfeit and lose his Share of the Capture.

43. Every Person subject to this Act who shall be guilty of any Act, Disorder, or Neglect to the Prejudice of good Order and Naval Discipline, not herein-before specified, shall be dismissed from Her Majesty's Service, with Disgrace, or suffer such other Punishment as is[herein-after mentioned.

44. Any Person subject to this Act committing any Offence against this Act, such Offence not being punishable with Death or Penal Servitude, shall, save where this Act expressly otherwise provides, be proceeded against and punished according to the Laws and Customs in such Cases used at Sea.

Offences punishable by ordinary Law

45. Every Person subject to this Act who shall be guilty of Murder shall suffer Death:

> If he shall be guilty of Manslaughter he shall suffer Penal Servitude, or such other Punishment as is herein-after mentioned;
>
> If he shall be guilty of Sodomy with Man or Beast he shall suffer Penal Servitude;
>
> If he shall be guilty of an indecent Assault he shall suffer Penal Servitude or such other Punishment as is herein-after mentioned;
>
> If he shall be guilty of Robbery or Theft he shall suffer Penal Servitude or such other Punishment as is herein-after mentioned;

If he shall be guilty of any other Criminal Offence which if committed in England would be punishable by the Law of England he shall, whether the Offence be or be not committed in England, be punished either in pursuance of the First Part of this Act as for an Act to the Prejudice of good Order and Naval Discipline not otherwise specified, or the Offender shall be subject to the same Punishment as might for the Time being be awarded by any ordinary Criminal Tribunal competent to try the Offender if the Offence had been committed in England.

46. For all Offences specified or referred to in this Act, if committed by any Person subject thereto in any Harbour, Haven or Creek, or on any Lake or River, whether in or out of the United Kingdom, or anywhere within the Jurisdiction of the Admiralty, or at any Place on Shore out of the United Kingdom of Great Britain and Ireland, or in any of Her Majesty's Dockyards, Yictualling Yards, Steam Factory Yards, or on any Gun Wharf, or in any Arsenal, Barrack, or Hospital belonging to Her Majesty, whether in or out of the said United Kingdom, the Offender may be tried and punished under this Act; and for all Offences herein-before specified under the Headings "Misconduct in the Presence of the Enemy," "Communications with the Enemy," "Neglect of Duty," "Mutiny," "Insubordination," "Desertion and Absence without Leave," or "Miscellaneous Offences," if committed by any Person subject to this Act at any Place on Shore, whether in or out of the said United Kingdom, the Offender may be tried and punished under this Act.

PART II

GENERAL PROVISIONS

47. Where the Amount of Punishment for any Offence under this Act depends upon the Intent with which it has been committed, and any Prisoner is charged with having committed such Offence with an Intent involving a greater Degree of Punishment, a Court-martial may find that the Offence was committed with an Intent involving a less Degree of Punishment, and award such Punishment accordingly.

48. Where any Prisoner shall be charged with Murder, a Court-Martial may find him guilty of Manslaughter, or of a Common Assault; where he shall be charged with Sodomy, a Court-martial may find him guilty of an indecent Assault; where he shall be charged with Theft, a Court-martial may find him Guilty of an Attempt to thieve, or of Embezzlement, or of wrongful Appropriation of Property belonging to another; and generally where any Prisoner shall be charged with any Offence under this Act he may, upon Failure of Proof of the Commission of the greater Offence, be found guilty of another Offence of the same Class involving a less Degree of Punishment, but not of any Offence involving a greater Degree of Punishment.

49. All armed Rebels, armed Mutineers, and Pirates shall be deemed to be Enemies within the Meaning of this Act.

50. Every Officer in Command of a Fleet or Squadron of Her Majesty's Ships, or of One of Her Majesty's Ships, or the Senior Officer present at a Port, may, by Warrant under his Hand, authorise any Person to arrest any Offender subject to this Act for any Offence against this Act mentioned in such Warrant; and any such Warrant may include the Names of more Persons than One in respect of several Offences of the same Nature; and any Person named in any such Warrant may forthwith, on his Apprehension, if the Warrant so directs, be taken on board the Ship to which he belongs, or some other of Her Majesty's Ships; and any Person so authorized may use Force,

if necessary, for the Purpose of effecting such Apprehension, towards any Person subject to this Act.

51. Every Person subject to this Act who shall not use his utmost Endeavours to detect, apprehend, and bring to Punishment all Offenders against this Act, and shall not assist the Officers appointed for that Purpose, shall suffer Imprisonment or such other Punishment as is herein-after mentioned.

PART III

REGULATIONS AS TO PUNISHMENTS

52. The following Punishments may be inflicted in Her Majesty's Navy:

(1) Death;

(2) Penal Servitude;

(3) Dismissal with Disgrace from Her Majesty's Service;

(4) Imprisonment or Corporal Punishment;

(5) Dismissal from Her Majesty's Service;

(6) Forfeiture of Seniority as an Officer for a specified Time, or otherwise;

(7) Dismissal from the Ship to which the Offender belongs;

(8) Severe Reprimand, or Reprimand;

(9) Disrating a Subordinate or Petty Officer;

(10) Forfeiture of Pay, Head Money, Bounty, Salvage, Prize Money, and Allowances earned by, and of all Annuities, Pensions, Gratuities, Medals, and Decorations granted to the Offender, or of any One or more of the above Particulars; also, in the Case of Desertion, of all Clothes and Effects left by the Deserter on board the Ship to which he belongs;

(11) Such minor Punishments as are now inflicted according to the Custom of the Navy, or may from Time to Time be allowed by the Admiralty;

and each of the above Punishments shall be deemed to be inferior in Degree to every Punishment preceding it in the above Scale.

53. The following Regulations are hereby made with respect to the Infliction of Punishments in Her Majesty's Navy:

(1)The Admiralty may, except in case of Sentence of Death, which shall only be remitted by Her Majesty, suspend, annul, or modify any Sentence passed on any Person subject to this Act, or substitute a Punishment inferior in Degree for the Punishment involved in any such Sentence, or remit the whole or any Portion of the Punishment involved in any such Sentence, or remit the whole or any Portion of any Punishment into which the Punishment involved in any such Sentence has been commuted, and any Sentence so modified shall (subject to the Provisions of this Act) be valid, and shall be carried into Execution, as if it had been originally passed, with such Modification, by the Court-martial; but so that the Punishment involved in any Sentence be not increased by any such Modification;

(2)Judgment of Death shall not be passed on any Prisoner unless Four at least of the Officers present at the Court-martial, where the Number does not exceed Five, and in other Cases a Majority of not less than Two Thirds of the Officers present, concur in the Sentence;

(3)Except in case of Mutiny the Punishment of Death shall not be inflicted on any Prisoner until the Sentence has been confirmed by the Admiralty or by the Commander-in-Chief on a Foreign Station;

(4)The Punishment of Penal Servitude may be inflicted for the Term of Life, or for any other Term of not less than Five Years;

(5)The Punishment of Penal Servitude shall in all Cases involve Dismissal with Disgrace from Her Majesty's Service;

(6)A Sentence of Dismissal with Disgrace shall involve in all Cases a Forfeiture of all Pay, Head Money, Bounty, Salvage, Prize Money, and Allowances that have been earned by, and of all Annuities, Pensions, Gratuities, Medals, and Decorations that may have been granted to the Offender, and an Incapacity to serve Her Majesty again in any Military, Naval, or Civil Service, and may also in all Cases be accompanied by a Sentence of Imprisonment;

(7)The Punishment of Imprisonment may be inflicted for any Term not exceeding Two Years;

(8)A Sentence of Imprisonment may be accompanied with a Direction that the Prisoner shall be kept in Solitary Confinement for any Period of such Term, not exceeding Fourteen Days at any One Time, and not exceeding Eighty-four Days in any One Year, with Intervals between the Periods of Solitary Confinement of not less Duration than the Periods of Solitary Confinement; and when the Imprisonment awarded exceeds Eighty-four Days, the Solitary Confinement shall not exceed Seven Days in any Twenty-eight Days of the whole Imprisonment awarded with Intervals between the Periods of Solitary Confinement of not less Duration than such Periods:

(9)A Sentence of Imprisonment may also be accompanied with a Direction that the Prisoner shall be kept to Hard Labour for all or any Part of the Term of Imprisonment, and Corporal Punishment may be awarded in addition to any Sentence of Imprisonment, whether such Imprisonment is or is not to be accompanied with Solitary Confinement and Hard Labour, or either of them;

(10) The Punishment of Imprisonment, whether on board Ship or on Shore, shall involve disrating in case of a Petty Officer and Reduction to the Ranks in case of a Noncommissioned Officer of Marines, and shall in all Cases be accompanied by Stoppage of Pay or Wages during the Term of Imprisonment;

(11) In any Case of Corporal Punishment not more than Forty-eight Lashes shall be inflicted: No Officer shall be subject to Corporal Punishment: No Petty or Non-commissioned Officer shall be subject to Corporal Punishment, except in case of Mutiny;

all other Punishments authorized by this Act may be inflicted in the Manner heretofore in use in the Navy.

54. No Person, unless he be an Offender who has avoided Apprehension or fled from Justice, shall be tried or punished in pursuance of this Act for any Offence committed by him unless such Trial shall take place within Three Years from the Commission of such Offence, or within One Year after the Return of such Offender to the United Kingdom, where he has been absent from the United Kingdom during such Period of Three Years.

55. Subject to the foregoing Regulations, where any Punishment is specified by this Act as the Penalty for any Offence, and it is further declared that another Punishment may be awarded in respect of the same Offence, the Expression"other Punishment" shall be deemed to comprise any One or more of the Punishments inferior in Degree to the specified Punishment, according to the Scale herein-before mentioned; but Corporal Punishment shall be deemed equal in Degree to Imprisonment, and may in all Cases, subject to the foregoing Regulations, be inflicted as a Substitute for or in addition to Imprisonment.

56. Any Offence triable under this Act may be tried and punished by Court-martial; and any Offence triable under this Act, not committed by an Officer (except in the Cases by this Act expressly provided for), and not hereby made Capital, may, under such Regulations as the Admiralty may from Time to Time issue, be summarily tried and punished by the Officer in Command of the Ship to which such Offender belongs, subject to the following Restrictions; (that is to say,)

(1) The Commanding Officer shall not have Power to award the Punishment of Penal Servitude;

(2) The Commanding Officer shall not have Power to sentence a Deserter to Imprisonment for a longer Period than Three Calendar Months, or to sentence any other Offender to Imprisonment for a longer Period than Six Weeks, or to award Solitary Confinement for more than Ten Days at a Time, with Intervals of not less than Seven Days between Two successive Periods of Solitary Confinement;

(3) Except in case of Mutiny, no Man shall be sentenced by the Commanding Officer to Corporal Punishment until his Offence has been inquired into by One or more Officers appointed by such Commanding Officer, and his or their Opinion as to the Guilt or Innocence of the Prisoner reported to such Commanding Officer, and the Commanding Officer shall thereupon act as according to his Judgment may seem right.

57. With respect to the Authorities by whom certain Punishments may be imposed, the following Provisions shall take effect; namely,

(1) With respect to any subordinate Officer, the Punishment of Forfeiture of Time or Seniority may be imposed as follows; namely, by the Admiralty for any Time not exceeding Twelve Months, by the Commander-in-Chief on a Foreign Station for any Time not exceeding Six Months, or by the Commanding Officer for any Time not exceeding Three Months:

(2) With respect to any subordinate Officer, the Commander-in-Chief on a Foreign Station shall have Power to impose the Punishments numbered (7), (8) and (9) in the scale herein-before contained.

PART IV

COURTS-MARTIAL

Constitution of Courts-martial

58. The following Regulations are hereby made with respect to Courts-martial:

(1) A Court-martial shall consist of not less than Five nor more than Nine Officers;

(2) No Officer shall be qualified to sit as a Member of any Court-martial held in pursuance of this Act unless he be a Flag Officer, Captain, Commander, or Lieutenant of Her Majesty's Navy on Full Pay;

(3) A Court-martial shall not be held unless at least Three of Her Majesty's Ships, not being Tenders, and commanded by Captains, Commanders, or Lieutenants of Her Majesty's Navy on Full Pay, are together at the Time when such Court-martial is held;

(4) No Officer shall sit on a Court-martial who is under Twenty-one Years of Age;

(5) No Court-martial for the Trial of a Flag Officer shall he duly constituted unless the President is a Flag Officer, and the other Officers composing the Court are of the Rank of Captain, or of higher Rank;

(6) No Court-martial for the Trial of a Captain in Her Majesty's Navy shall be duly constituted unless the President is a Captain or of higher Rank, and the other Officers com-posing the Court are Commanders or Officers of higher Rank;

(7) No Court-martial for the Trial of any Person below the Rank of Captain in Her Majesty's Navy shall he duly constituted, unless the President is a Captain or of higher Rank, nor unless in addition to the President there are Two other Members of the Court of the Rank of Commander or of higher Rank;

(8) The Prosecutor shall not sit on any Court-martial for the Trial of a Prisoner whom he prosecutes;

(9) The Admiralty shall have Power to order Courts-martial to be held for the Trial of Offences under this Act, and to grant Commissions to any Officer of Her Majesty's

Navy on Full Pay authorizing him to order Courts-martial to be held for the Trial of such Offences;

(10) An Officer holding a Commission from the Admiralty to order Courts-martial shall not be empowered to do so if there is present at the Place where such Court-martial is to be held any Officer superior in Rank to himself, on Full Pay and in command of One or more of Her Majesty's Ships or Vessels, although such last-mentioned Officer may not hold a Commission to order Courts-martial; and in such a Case such last mentioned Officer may order a Court-martial, although he does not hold any Commission for the Purpose;

(11) If any Officer holding a Commission from the Admiralty to order Courts-martial, having the Command of a Fleet or Squadron, and being in Foreign Parts, die, be recalled, leave his Station, or be removed from his Command, the Officer upon whom the Command of the Fleet or Squadron devolves, and so from Time to Time the Officer who shall have the Command of the Fleet or Squadron, shall, without any Commission from the Admiralty, have the same Power to order Courts-martial as the first-mentioned Officer was invested with;

(12) If any Officer holding a Commission from the Admiralty to order Courts-martial, and having the Command of any Fleet or Squadron of Her Majesty's Ships in Foreign Parts shall detach any Part of such Fleet or Squadron, or separate himself from any Part of such Fleet or Squadron, he may, by Commission under his Hand, empower, in the first-mentioned Case, the Commanding Officer of the Squadron or Detachment ordered on such separate Service, and in case of his Death or ceasing so to command, the Officer to whom the Command of such separate Squadron or Detachment shall belong, and in the secondly-mentioned Case the Senior Officer of Her Majesty's Ships on the Division of the Station from which he is absent, to order Courts-martial during the Time of such separate Service, or during his Absence from that Division of the Station (as the Case may be), and every such Authority shall continue in force until revoked, or until the Officer holding it returns to the United Kingdom or until he comes into the Presence of a Superior Officer, empowered to order Courts-martial in the same Squadron, Detachment, or Division of a Station, but so that such Authority shall revive on the Officer holding it ceasing to be in the Presence of such a Superior Officer, and so from Time to Time as often as the Case so requires:

(13) The Officer ordering a Court-martial shall not sit thereon;

(14) The President of every Court-martial shall be named by the Authority ordering the same, or by any Officer empowered by such Authority to name the President;

(15) No Commander or Lieutenant shall be required to sit as a Member of any Court-martial when Four Officers of a higher Rank and junior to the President can be assembled at the Place where the Court-martial is to be holden (but the Regularity or Validity of any Court-martial or of the Proceedings thereof shall not be affected by any Commander or Lieutenant being required to sit, or sitting, thereon, under any Circumstances); and

when any Commander or Lieutenant sits on any Court-martial the Members of it shall not exceed Five in Number;

(16) Subject to the foregoing Regulations, whenever a Court-martial shall be held, the Officer appointed to preside thereat shall summon all the Officers next in Seniority to himself present at the Place where the Court-martial shall be held to sit thereon, until the Number of Nine, or such Number, not less than Five, as is attainable, is complete; subject to this Proviso, that the Admirals and Captains, being Superintendents of Her Majesty's Dockyards, shall not be summoned to sit on Courts-martial unless specially directed to do so by Orders from the Admiralty.

Proceedings of Courts-martial

59. A Court-martial under this Act shall be held on board One of Her Majesty's Ships or Vessels of War.

60. A Court-martial held in pursuance of this Act shall sit from Day to Day, with the Exception of Sundays, until Sentence is given, unless prevented from so doing by Stress of Weather or unavoidable Accident, and its Proceedings shall not be delayed by the Absence of any Member, so that not less than Four are present; and no Member shall absent himself unless compelled so to do by Sickness or other just Cause, to be approved of by the other Members of the Court; and if any Member of a Court-martial shall absent himself therefrom, in contravention of this Section, he shall be dismissed from Her Majesty's Service, or shall suffer such other Punishment as may be awarded by a Court-martial.

61. In the Absence of the Judge Advocate of the Fleet or his Deputy, and in default of any Appointment in this Behalf by the Admiralty, or by the Commander-in-Chief of any Fleet or Squadron, the Officer who is to be the President of the Court-martial shall appoint a Person to officiate as Deputy Judge Advocate at the Trial; and the Judge Advocate of the Fleet for the Time being, or his Deputy, or the Person officiating as Deputy Judge Advocate, at any Trial shall administer an Oath to every Witness appearing at the Trial.

62. As soon as the Court is assembled, the Names of the Officers composing the Court shall be read over to the Prisoner, who shall be asked if he objects to being tried by any Member of the Court; if the Prisoner shall object to any Member, the Objection shall be decided by the Court; if the Objection shall be allowed, the Place of the Member objected to shall be filled up by the Officer next in Seniority who is not on the Court-martial, subject to the Regulations herein-before contained.

The Prisoner may then raise any other Objection which he desires to make respecting the Constitution of the Court-martial, and the Objection shall then be decided by the Court, which Decision shall be final, and the Constitution of the Court-martial shall not be afterwards impeached, and it shall be deemed to have been in all respects duly constituted.

63. Before the Court shall proceed to try the Prisoner, the Judge Advocate of the Fleet, or his Deputy, or the Person officiating as deputy Judge Advocate of the Fleet, shall administer to every Member of the Court the following Oath; that is to say,

I ___________ do swear, That I will duly administer Justice according to Law, without Partiality, Favour, or Affection; and I do further swear, that I will not on any Account, at any Time whatsoever, disclose or discover the Vote or Opinion of any particular Member of this Court-martial, unless thereunto required in due Course of Law. So help me GOD.

64. As soon as the said Oath shall be administered to the Members of the Court-martial, the President shall administer to the Judge Advocate of the Fleet, or his Deputy, or the Person officiating as Deputy Judge Advocate, the following Oath:

I____ do swear, That I will not upon any Account, at any Time whatsoever, disclose or discover the Vote or Opinion of any particular Member of the Court-martial, unless thereunto required in due Course of Law. So help me GOD.

65. The Admiralty may from Time to Time frame General Orders for altering and regulating (subject to the Provisions of this Act) the Procedure and Practice of Courts-martial under this Act; and any such General Orders shall have full Effect if and when approved by Her Majesty in Council, on a Report of the Judicial Committee of the Privy Council, but not sooner or otherwise; and every Order in Council made under this Section shall be laid before both Houses of Parliament.

66. Every Person, Civil, Naval, and Military, who may be required to give Evidence before a Court-martial, shall be summoned by Writing under the Hand of One of the Secretaries of the Admiralty, or by the Deputy Judge Advocate, or the Person appointed to officiate as Deputy Judge Advocate at the Trial; and all Persons so summoned and attending as Witnesses before any Court-martial shall, during their necessary Attendance in or on such Court, and in going to and returning from the same, be privileged from Arrest, and shall, if unduly arrested, be discharged by the Court out of which the Writ or Process issued by which such Witness was arrested, or if such Court be not sitting, then by any Judge of the Superior Courts of Westminster or Dublin, or the Court of Session in Scotland, or of the Courts of Law in the East or West Indies, or elsewhere, according as the Case shall require, upon its being made to appear to such Court or Judge, by any Affidavit in a summary Way, that such Witness was arrested in going to or returning from or attending upon such Court-martial; and all Witnesses so duly summoned as aforesaid who make default in attending on such Courts, or attending refuse to be sworn or make Affirmation, or being sworn or having made Affirmation refuse to give Evidence, or to answer all such Questions as the Court may legally demand of them, or prevaricate in giving their Evidence, shall upon Certificate thereof under the Hand of the President of such Court-martial, be liable to be attached in the Court of Queen's Bench in London or Dublin, or the Court of Session, or Sheriff Depute or Stewarts Depute, or their respective Substitutes, within their several Shires and Stewartries in Scotland, or Courts of Law in the East or West Indies, or in any of Her Majesty's Colonies, Garrisons, or Dominions in Europe or elsewhere, respectively, upon Complaint made, in like Manner as if such Witness after having been duly summoned and subpoenaed had neglected to attend on trial in any Proceeding in the Court in which such Complaint is made, or had refused to be sworn, or on being sworn had refused to give Evidence, or to answer all such Questions as the Court may legally demand, or had prevaricated in giving Evidence, or, if the Court-martial shall think fit, in case any such Person belong to Her Majesty's Navy, being called upon to give Evidence at any Court-martial, shall refuse or neglect to attend to give his Evidence upon Oath

or Affirmation, or shall prevaricate in his Evidence, or behave with Contempt to the Court, such Court-martial may punish every such Offender by Imprisonment not longer than Three Months in case of such Refusal, Neglect, or Prevarication, nor longer than One Month in the Case of such Contempt; and every Person not subject to this Act who may be so summoned to attend shall be allowed and paid his reasonable Expenses for such Attendance, under the Authority of the Admiralty, or of the President of the Court-martial on a foreign Station.

67. Every Person who, upon any Examination upon Oath or upon Affirmation before any Court-martial held in pursuance of this Act, shall wilfully and corruptly give false Evidence, shall be deemed guilty of wilful and corrupt Perjury; and every such Offence, wheresoever committed, shall be triable and punishable in England; and where any such Offence committed out of England is tried in England, all Statutes and Laws applicable to Cases of Perjury shall apply to the Case.

68. Where it shall appear upon the Trial by Court-martial of any Person charged with an Offence that such Person is insane, the Court shall find specially the Fact of his Insanity, and shall order such| Person to be kept in strict Custody in such Place and in such Manner as the Court shall deem fit until the Directions of the Admiralty thereupon are known, and it shall be lawful for the Lords of the Admiralty to give Orders for the safe Custody of such Person during Her Majesty's Pleasure in such Place and in such Manner as they shall think fit.

69. Every Judge Advocate, or Deputy Judge Advocate, or Person officiating as Deputy Judge Advocate, shall transmit with as much Expedition as may be the original Proceedings, or a complete and authenticated Copy thereof, and the original Sentence of every Court-martial attended by him, to the Commander-in-Chief or senior Officer, who shall transmit them to the Secretary of the Admiralty for the Time being, and any Person tried by a Court-martial shall be entitled, on Demand, to a Copy of such Proceedings and Sentence at any Time not sooner than Six Months after the Trial if the same takes place in the Mediterranean, Three Months if at any other Naval Station within Europe, and Twelve Months if elsewhere, (upon Payment for the same at the Rate of Four pence per Folio of Seventy-two Words,) but no such Demand shall be allowed after the Space of Three Years from the Date of the final Decision of such Court.

PART V

PENAL SERVITUDE AND PRISONS

Penal Servitude

70. Whenever any Sentence of Death shall be commuted for Penal Servitude, or whenever Sentence of Penal Servitude shall be passed upon any Offender by any Court-martial, and such Sentence, or any Part thereof, is intended to be carried into effect, the Admiralty shall cause the same to be notified in Writing to any Justice of the Queen's Bench, Common Pleas, or Baron of the Exchequer, and thereupon such Justice or Baron shall make an Order for the Penal Servitude of such Offender upon the Terms and for the Time specified in such Notification, and shall do all such other Acts consequent upon such Notification, as any such Justice or Baron is or may be authorized to make or do by any Statute or Statutes in force at the Time of making any such Order

in relation to Penal Servitude of Offenders sentenced by Courts of Criminal Jurisdiction to Penal Servitude; and such Order and other Acts to be so made and done as aforesaid shall be obeyed and executed by such Person in whose Custody such Offender may at that Time be, and by all other Persons whom it may concern, and shall be as effectual and have all the same Consequences as any Order made under the Authority of any Statute relating to Penal Servitude with respect to any Offender in such Statute mentioned; and every Sheriff, Gaoler, Keeper, Governor, or Superintendent whom it may concern, and all Constables and other Persons, shall be bound to obey the aforesaid Order and Orders, and be assistant in the Execution thereof, and be liable to the same Punishment for Disobedience to or for interrupting the Execution of such Order as they would be if the same had been made under the Authority of any such Statute; and every Person so ordered to be kept in Penal Servitude shall be subject to all the Penalties and Provisions made by Law, and in force for the Time being, concerning Persons under Sentence of Penal Servitude, or receiving Her Majesty's Pardon on Condition of Penal Servitude; and from the Time when such Order of Penal Servitude is made, every Law in force touching the Escape of Felons, or their afterwards returning or being at large without Leave, shall apply to such Offender, and to all Persons aiding, abetting, contriving, or assisting in any Escape or intended Escape, of the returning without Leave of any such Offender; and the Judge or Baron who makes an Order for Penal Servitude as afore-said shall direct the Notification of the Admiralty, and his own Order made thereupon, to be filed and kept of Record in the Office of the Clerk of the Crown of the Court of Queen's Bench, and the said Clerk shall have a Fee of Two Shillings and Sixpence only for filing the same, and shall, on Application, deliver a Certificate in Writing (not taking more than Two Shillings and Sixpence for the same) to such Offender, or to any Person applying in his or the Admiralty's Behalf, showing the Christian and Surname of such Offender, his Offence, the Place where the Court was held before which he was convicted, the Sentence, and the Conditions on which the Order of Penal Servitude was made, and such Certificate shall be sufficient Proof of the Conviction and of the Sentence of such Offender, and also of the Terms on which such Order for his Penal Servitude was made, in any Court and in any Proceeding wherein it may be necessary to inquire into the same.

71. When any Sentence of Death shall have been commuted for Penal Servitude, or when any Person subject to this Act shall have been condemned to Penal Servitude, it shall be lawful for the Admiralty, or any Commander-in-Chief on any Foreign Station, or the Commanding Officer of the Ship to which such Person belongs or has belonged, to cause him to be detained and conveyed to any One of Her Majesty's Ships, or any Gaol or Prison, there to remain in safe Custody until he is removed therefrom by the Order of the Admiralty or any such Commander-in-Chief or other due Authority, or under an Order for his Penal Servitude, to be made by some Justice of the Queen's Bench or Common Pleas or Baron of the Exchequer as aforesaid, and a Certificate of his Sentence (such Certificate to be signed by the Secretary of the Admiralty, or by any such Commander-in-Chief, or such Commanding Officer) shall be a sufficient Authority to the Commanding Officer of the Ship to which he may be sent, or to the Governor, Keeper, or Superintendent of the Gaol or Prison, to receive and detain him.

72. In case any such Offender shall be conveyed to any Prison not being a Naval Prison appointed by virtue of this Act, an Allowance such as the Admiralty shall from Time to Time direct shall

be made to the Governor, Keeper, or Superintendent of the Gaol or Prison for the Subsistence of such Offender during his Detention therein, and such Allowance shall be paid by Order of the Admiralty upon Production by the said Governor, Keeper, or Superintendent of a Declaration, to be made by him before One of Her Majesty's Justices of the Peace of such County, of the Number of Days during which the Offender has been so detained and subsisted in such Gaol or Prison.

73. Whenever Sentence shall be passed by a Court-martial on an Offender already under Sentence either of Imprisonment or of Penal Servitude, passed upon him by a Court-martial for a former Offence, the Court may award Sentence of Imprisonment or Penal Servitude for the Offence for which he is under Trial to commence at the Expiration of the Imprisonment or Penal Servitude to which he has been previously sentenced, although the aggregate. of the Terms of Imprisonment or Penal Servitude may exceed the Term for which either of those Punishments could be otherwise awarded.

Prisons

74. Every Term of Penal Servitude or of Imprisonment in pursuance of this Act shall be reckoned as commencing on the Day on which the Sentence was awarded, and the Place of Imprisonment, whether the Imprisonment was awarded as an original or as a commuted Punishment, shall be such Place as may be appointed by the Court or the Commanding Officer awarding the Punishment or which may from Time to Time be appointed by the Admiralty, or by the Commander-in-Chief or senior Officer present on any Foreign Station, and may be One of the Naval Prisons appointed under this Act, or any Common Gaol, House of Correction, or Military Prison within Her Majesty's Dominions.

75. Whenever it is deemed expedient it shall be lawful for the Admiralty or any such Commander-in-Chief; by any Order in Writing from Time to Time to change the Place of Confinement of any Offender imprisoned or sentenced to be imprisoned or detained in persuance of this Act, and the Gaoler or other Person having the Custody of such Offender shall immediately on the Receipt of such Order remove such Offender to the Gaol, Prison, or House of Correction mentioned in the said Order, or shall deliver him over to Naval Custody for the Purpose of the Offender being removed to such Prison; and every Gaoler or Keeper of such last-mentioned Prison, Gaol, or House of Correction shall, upon, being furnished with a Copy of such Order of Removal, attested by the Secretary of the Admiralty for the Time being, receive into his Custody and shall confine pursuant to such Sentence or Order every such Offender.

76. The Gaoler or other Person removing any Offender in pursuance of such Order shall be allowed for the Charges of such Removal a Sum not exceeding One Shilling a Mile, and when any Offender is not confined in a Naval Prison the Gaoler or other Person in whose Custody any such Offender may be shall receive such an Allowance as the Admiralty shall from Time to Time direct for every Day that such Offender is in his Custody, to be applied towards his Subsistence, and such Sum shall be paid to the said Gaoler or other Person under the Authority of the Admiralty, upon the Application in Writing made to the Secretary of the Admiralty by any Justice for the County or Place in which such Gaol, Prison, or House of Correction shall be situate, with a Copy of the Sentence or Order under which the Prisoner is confined.

77. From and after the passing of this Act, Section One of the Act of the Forty-fourth Year of the Reign of King George the Third (Chapter Thirteen), "to prevent the Desertion and Escape of Petty Officers, Seamen, and others from His Majesty's Service by Means or under Colour of any Civil or Criminal Process," shall be read and have effect as if the Words "One Shilling" were substituted for the Words "Two Shillings;" and any such Sheriff, Gaoler, or other Officer as therein mentioned shall, if required, deliver such Petty Officer, Seaman, or other Person as therein mentioned to any Person authorized to receive him, instead of conducting and conveying him as therein provided.

78. Whenever any Prisoner is undergoing Imprisonment in pursuance of this Act, it shall be lawful, for the Admiralty, or any Commander-in-Chief on any Foreign Station, or where an Offender has been imprisoned by Order of his Commanding Officer, for such Commanding Officer or the Admiralty, or any such Commander in-Chief, to give an Order in Writing directing that the Prisoner be discharged; and it shall also be lawful for the Admiralty, or any such Commander in-Chief, and any Officer commanding any of Her Majesty's Ships, by Order in Writing, to direct that any such Prisoner be delivered over to Naval Custody for the Purpose of being brought before a Court-martial, either as a Witness, or for Trial or otherwise, and such Prisoner shall accordingly, on the Production of any such Order, be discharged, or be delivered over to such Custody.

79. The Time during which any Prisoner under Sentence of Imprisonment is detained in Naval Custody shall be reckoned as Imprisonment under his Sentence for whatever Purpose such Detention takes place; and the Governor, Gaoler, Keeper, or Superintendent who shall deliver over any such Prisoner shall again receive him from Naval Custody, so that he may undergo the Remainder of his Punishment.

80. If any Person imprisoned by virtue of this Act shall become insane, and a Certificate to that Effect shall be given by Two Physicians or Surgeons, the Admiralty shall, by Warrant, direct the Removal of such Person to such Lunatic Asylum or other proper Receptacle for Insane Persons in the United Kingdom as they may judge proper for the unexpired Term of his Imprisonment; and if any such Person shall in the same Manner be certified to be again of sound Mind, the Admiralty may issue a Warrant for his being removed to such Prison or Place of Confinement as may be deemed expedient, to undergo the Remainder of his Punishment, and every Gaoler or Keeper of any Prison, Gaol, or House of Correction shall receive him accordingly.

81. The Admiralty may set apart any Buildings or Vessels, or any Parts thereof, as Naval Prisons, and any Buildings or Vessels, or Parts of Buildings or Vessels, so set apart shall be deemed to be Naval Prisons within the Meaning of this Act, and all Powers and Authorities with respect to County Gaols or Houses of Correction which now are or which may hereafter be vested in any of Her Majesty's Principal Secretaries of State shall, with respect to all such Naval Prisons, belong to the Admiralty; and it shall be lawful for the Admiralty from Time to Time to make, alter, and repeal Regulations for the Government and Superintendence of any such Naval Prison, and of the Officers and Servants thereof, and of Offenders confined therein, and from Time to Time to appoint Inspectors and all other necessary Officers and Servants for any such Naval Prison, and, as Occasion may arise, to remove the Inspectors, Officers, or Servants of any such Naval Prison; and the senior Officer at any Port or Place or on any Station where there may be any such Naval

Prison, or such senior Officer and such other Person and Persons as the Admiralty may from Time to Time appoint, shall be a Visitor or Visitors of such. Prison; and every Inspector, Visitor, or Officer having the Charge or Command of any such Naval Prison respectively shall, subject to such Rules and Regulations as may from Time to Time be made as aforesaid, have and exercise, in respect of such Prison, and of the Officers and Servants thereof, and of the Prisoners confined therein, all the Powers and Authorities as well in respect of administering Oaths as otherwise which any Inspector, Visiting Justice, or Governor of a County Gaol or House of Correction may respectively exercise as such.

82. If any Person shall convey or cause to be conveyed into any such Naval Prison any Arms, Tools, or Instruments, or any Mask or other Disguise, to facilitate the Escape of any Prisoner, or by any Means whatever shall aid any Prisoner to escape or in an Attempt to escape from such Prison, whether an Escape be actually made or not, such Person shall be deemed guilty of Felony, and upon being convicted thereof shall be imprisoned, with or without Hard Labour, for any Term not exceeding Two Years, or suffer Penal Servitude for any Term not exceeding Fourteen Years; and if any Person shall bring or attempt to bring into such Prison, in contravention of the Rules, any spirituous or fermented Liquor, he shall for every such Offence be liable to a Penalty not exceeding Twenty Pounds and not less than Ten Pounds; and if any Person shall bring into such Prison, or to or for any Prisoner, without the Knowledge of the Officer having Charge or Command thereof, any Money, Clothing, Provisions, Tobacco, Letters, Papers, or other Articles not allowed by the Rules of the Prison to be in the Possession of a Prisoner, or shall throw into the said Prison any such Articles, or by Desire of any Prisoner, without the Sanction of the said Officer, shall carry out of the Prison any of the Articles aforesaid, he shall for every such Offence be liable to a Penalty not exceeding Five Pounds; and if any Person shall interrupt any Officer of such Prison in the Execution of his Duty, or shall aid or excite any Person to assault, resist, or interrupt any such Officer, he shall for every such Offence be liable to a Penalty not exceeding Five Pounds, or if the Offender be a Prisoner, he shall, upon Conviction thereof before Two Justices of the Peace, or not less than Three of the Visitors of the Prison, be liable to be sentenced for every such Offence to be imprisoned, either with or without Hard Labour, and with or without Solitary Confinement, for any Time not exceeding Six Calendar Months, in addition to so much of the Time for which he was originally sentenced as may be then unexpired, and every Penalty which may be incurred under this Section shall be recoverable in a summary Manner; and such two Justices or Three Visitors are hereby authorized to issue Warrants of Distress and Sale of the Offender's Goods, and every such Penalty shall be applied as the Admiralty shall direct, any Law, Statute, Charter, or Custom to the contrary notwithstanding.

83. Every Governor, Gaoler, and Keeper of any Prison, Gaol, or House of Correction, and every Officer having the Charge or Command of any Place, Ship, or Vessel for Imprisonment, who shall, without lawful Excuse, refuse or neglect to receive or confine, remove, discharge, or deliver up any Offender against the Provisions of this Act, or any of them, shall incur for every such Refusal or Neglect a Penalty not exceeding One hundred Pounds to be recovered in a summary Manner before Two Justices of the Peace; and such Two Justices are hereby authorized to issue Warrants of Distress and Sale of the Offender's Goods, and every such Penalty shall be applied as the Admiralty shall direct, any Law, Statute, Charter, or Custom to the contrary notwithstanding.

PART VI

SUPPLEMENTAL PROVISIONS

84. This Act may be cited for all Purposes as The Naval Discipline Act, 1866.

85. Except as otherwise provided, this Act shall be in force within the United Kingdom; and as regards The United Kingdom the Enactments described in the Schedule to this Act shall be repealed from and after One Calendar Month from the passing hereof; and as regards elsewhere this Act shall be in force, and said Enactments shall be repealed, from and after Six Calendar Months from the passing hereof.

86. In the Construction of this Act, unless there be something in the Context or Subject Matter repugnant to or inconsistent with such Construction,

"Admiralty," or "the Lords of the Admiralty," shall mean the Lord High Admiral for the Time being of the United Kingdom of Great Britain and Ireland, and when there shall be no such Lord High Admiral in Office, any Two or more of the Commissioners for executing the Office of Lord High Admiral of the United Kingdom:

"Officer" shall mean an Officer belonging to One of Her Majesty's Ships, and shall include a subordinate and a Warrant Officer, but shall not extend to Petty and Non-commissioned Officers:

When the Words "Superior Officer" are used in this Act they shall be held to include all Officers, including Petty and Noncommissioned Officers.

87. Every Person in or belonging to Her Majesty's Navy, and borne on the Books of any One of Her Majesty's Ships in Commission, shall be subject to this Act; and all other Persons hereby made liable thereto shall be triable and punishable under the Provisions of this Act.

88. Her Majesty's Land Forces, when embarked on board any of Her Majesty's Ships, shall be subject to the Provisions of this Act to such Extent and under such Regulations as Her Majesty, Her Heirs and Successors, by any Order or Orders in Council, shall at any Time or Times direct.

89. All other Persons ordered to be received or being Passengers on board any of Her Majesty's Ships shall be deemed to be Persons subject to this Act, under such Regulations as the Admiralty may from Time to Time direct.

90. With respect to hired Vessels in Her Majesty's Service in Time of War, being either armed or under the Command of an Officer in Her Majesty's Naval Service, the following Provisions shall take effect if in any Case the Admiralty think fit so to direct, and where such Direction is given the same shall be specified in the Ship's Articles:

(1) Every Person borne on the Books of any such hired Vessel shall be subject to this Act;

(2) Any Offence committed by any such Person, shall be tried and punished as the like Offence might be tried and punished if committed by any Person in or belonging to Her Majesty's Navy, and borne on the Books of any of Her Majesty's Ships in Commission;

(3) Every such Offender who is to be tried by Court-martial shall be placed under all necessary Restraint until he can be tried by Court-martial;

(4) On Application made to the Lords of the Admiralty, or to the Commander-in-Chief, or senior Officer of any of Her Majesty's Ships or Vessels of War abroad authorized to assemble and hold Courts-martial, the Lords of the Admiralty, Commander-in-Chief, or senior Officer (as the Case may be) shall assemble and hold a Court-martial for the Trial of the Offender;

(5) The Officer commanding every such hired Vessel shall have the same Power in respect of all other Persons borne on the Books thereof, or for the Time being on board the same, as the Officer commanding One of Her Majesty's Ships has for the Time being in respect of the Officers and Crew thereof or other Persons on board the same;

(6) The Naval Commander-in-Chief and senior Naval Officer in Her Majesty's Service shall have the same Powers over the Officers and Crew of every such hired Vessel as they have for the Time being over the Officers and Crew of any of Her Majesty's Ships.

91. When any One of Her Majesty's Ships shall be wrecked or lost or destroyed, or taken by the Enemy, such Ship shall, for the Purposes of this Act, be deemed to remain in Commission until her Crew shall be regularly removed into some other of Her Majesty's Ships of War, or until a Court-martial shall have been held, pursuant to the Custom of the Navy in such Cases, to inquire into the Cause of the Wreck, Loss, Destruction, or Capture of the said Ship.

92. When no specific Charge shall be made against any Officer or Seaman or other Person in the Fleet for or in respect or in con-sequence of such Wreck, Loss, Destruction, or Capture, it shall be lawful to try all the Officers and Crew or all the surviving Officers and Crew of any such Ship, together, before One and the same Court, and to call upon all or any of them when upon their Trial to give Evidence on Oath or Affirmation before the Court touching any of the Matters then under Inquiry, but no Officer or Seaman or other Person shall be obliged to give any Evidence which may tend to criminate himself.

93. When deemed necessary by the Admiralty, or any Officer authorized to order Courts-martial, separate Courts-martial shall be held for the Trial of some One or more of such Officers and Crew for or in respect or in consequence of the Wreck, Loss, Destruction, or Capture of any such Ship.

94. For any Offence or Offences committed by any Officer or Seaman, or Officers and Seamen, after the Wreck, Loss, Destruction, or Capture of any such Ship, a separate Court-martial shall be held for the Trial of such Offender or Offenders.

95. When any Ship of Her Majesty shall be wrecked, lost, or otherwise destroyed, or taken by the Enemy, if it shall appear by the Sentence of a Court-martial that the Crew of such Ship did, in the Case of a Ship wrecked or lost, do their utmost to save her or get her off, and in the Case of a Ship taken by the Enemy did their utmost to defend themselves, and that they have, since the Wreck, Destruction, Loss, or Capture of such Ship, behaved themselves well, and been obedient to their Officers, then all the Pay of such Crews, or of such Portions of such Crews as have behaved them-

selves well and been obedient to their Officers, shall be continued until the Time of their being discharged or removed into other Ships of Her Majesty, or dying.

96. If the Ship of any Officer ordered to command any Two or more of Her Majesty's Ships shall be wrecked, lost, or otherwise destroyed, such Officer shall continue in the Command of any Ship or Ships which at the Time of his Ship being wrecked, lost, or destroyed was or were under his Command, and it shall be lawful for such Officer to order the surviving Officers and Crew of the wrecked, lost, or destroyed Ship to join any other Ship under his Command, or to distribute them among the other Ships under his Command, if more than One, and such Officer shall, until he meets with some other Officer senior to himself, have the same Power and Authority in all respect as if his Ship had not been wrecked, lost, or destroyed.

97. It shall not be lawful for any Person to arrest any Petty Officer or Seaman, Non-commissioned Officer of Marines or Marine, belonging to any Ship of Her Majesty, by any Warrant, Process, or Writ issued in any Part of Her Majesty's Dominions for any Debt, unless the Debt was contracted at a Time when the Debtor did not belong to Her Majesty's Service, nor unless before the issuing of the Warrant, Process, or Writ the Plaintiff in the Suit or some Person on his Behalf has made an Affidavit in the Court out of which it issued that the Debt justly due to the Plaintiff (over and above all Costs) was contracted at a Time when the Debtor did not belong to Her Majesty's Service, nor unless a Memorandum of such Affidavit is marked on the Back of the Warrant, Process or Writ.

98. If any Petty Officer or Seaman, Non-commissioned Officer of Marines or Marine, is arrested in contravention of the Provisions of the last foregoing Section, the Court out of which the Warrant Process, or Writ issues, or any Judge thereof, may, on Complaint by the Party arrested, or by his Superior Officer, investigate the Case on Oath or otherwise, and if satisfied that the Arrest was made in contravention of the Provisions of the last foregoing Section, may make an Order for the immediate Discharge of the Party arrested, without Fee, and may award to the Complainant the Costs of his Complaint, to be taxed by the proper Officer, for the Recovery whereof he shall have the like Remedy as the Plaintiff in the Suit would have on Judgment being given in his Favour with Costs.

PART VII

SAVING CLAUSE

99. Any Person who has committed or may commit, before this Act comes into force, any Offence against The Naval Discipline Act, 1864, or the Act thereby repealed, or against any other Enactment repealed by this Act, for which such Person has not been tried before this Act comes into force, shall be tried and punished under this Act as if such Crime or Offence had been committed against the same, but he shall not suffer any greater Punishment than he was liable to under The Naval Discipline Act, 1864, or the Act thereby repealed, or such other Enactment (as the Case may be); and any Proceeding of any Court-martial, or any other Proceedings under The Naval Discipline Act, 1864, or such other Enactment which may be pending when this Act comes

into force, shall be continued, and the Offender, if found guilty, shall be punished as if the Act or Enactment against which he offended had not been repealed.

100. Nothing in this Act shall take away, abridge, or control, further or otherwise than as expressly provided by this Act, any Right, Power, or Prerogative of Her Majesty the Queen in right of Her Crown, or in right of Her Office of Admiralty or any Right or Power of the Admiralty.

101. Nothing in this Act contained shall be deemed or taken to supersede or affect the Authority or Power of any Court or Tribunal of ordinary Civil or Criminal Jurisdiction, or any Officer thereof, in Her Majesty's Dominions, in respect of any Offence mentioned in this Act which may be punishable or cognizable by the Common or Statute Law, or to prevent any Person being proceeded against and punished in respect of any such Offence otherwise than under this Act.

ACT No. XXXIV OF 1934

[PASSED BY THE INDIAN LEGISLATURE]

(Received the assent of the Governor General on 8 September, 1934)

An Act to provide for the application of the Naval Discipline Act to the Indian Navy

WHEREAS by section 66 of the Government of India Act it is among other things enacted that provision may be made by the Indian Legislature for the application to the naval forces raised by the Governor General in Council of the Naval Discipline Act subject to such modifications and adaptations as may be made by the said Legislature to adapt the Act to the circumstances of India;

AND WHEREAS it is expedient to make such provision;

It is hereby enacted as follows: -

Short title and commencement

1. (1) This Act may be called the Indian Navy (Discipline) Act, 1934.

(2) It shall come into force on such date as the Governor General in Council may, by notification in the Gazette of India, appoint.

Definition

2. In this Act, unless there is anything repugnant in the subject or context:--

"the Indian Navy" means the naval forces and ships raised and provided by the Governor General in Council.

Application of the Naval Discipline Act to the Indian Navy

3. (1) The Naval Discipline Act shall apply to the Indian Navy as if that Act were in the form in which it is set forth in the First Schedule to this Act.

(2) In the application to the Indian Navy of the Naval Discipline Act as so set forth-

(a) "The Indian Navy" has the same meaning as in this Act, and

(b) References to His Majesty's Navy and His Majesty's ships shall be deemed to include the forces and ships constituting the Indian Navy.

4. The enactments mentioned in the Second Schedule are hereby repealed to the extent specified in the fourth column thereof.

THE FIRST SCHEDULE

(See Section 3)

THE NAVAL DISCIPLINE ACT

(29 and 30 Vict C.109)

(As modified for application to the Indian Navy)

An Act to make Provision for the Discipline of the Navy.

WHEREAS it is expedient to amend the law relating to the Government of the Navy, whereon, under the good Providence of God, the wealth, safety, and strength of the Kingdom chiefly depend:

Be it enacted by the King's Most Excellent Majesty, by and with the advice and consent of the Lords Spiritual and Temporal, and Commons, in this present Parliament assembled, and by the authority of the same, as follows:

PART I

ARTICLES OF WAR

Public Worship

Facilities for the performance of religious duties

1. All officers in command of ships of the Indian Navy shall the perform give reasonable facilities for the performance of religious duties by the officers and members of the crews of their respective ships to each man according to his religion.

Misconduct in the Presence of the Enemy

Penalty for misconduct in action

2. Every flag officer, captain, commander or officer commanding subject to this Act who upon signal of battle, or on sight of a ship of an enemy which it may be his duty to engage shall not,

(1) Use his utmost exertion to bring his ship into action;

(2) Or shall not during such action, in his own person and according to his rank, encourage his inferior officers and men to fight courageously;

(3) Or who shall surrender his ship to the enemy when capable of making a successful defence, or who in time of action shall improperly withdraw from the fight,

shall, if he has acted traitorously, suffer death; if he has acted from cowardice, shall suffer death, or such other punishment as is hereinafter mentioned: and if he has acted from negligence or through other default, he shall be dismissed from His Majesty's service with or without disgrace, or shall suffer such other punishment as is hereinafter mentioned.

Penalty for not pursuing the enemy, and not assisting a friend in view

3. Every officer subject to this Act who shall forbear to pursue the chase of any enemy, pirate, or rebel, beaten or flying, or shall not relieve and assist a known friend in view to the utmost of his power, or who shall improperly forsake his station, shall, if he has therein acted traitorously, suffer death; if he has acted from cowardice, suffer death or such other punishment as is hereinafter mentioned; if he has acted from negligence or through other default, shall be dismissed from His Majesty's service, with disgrace, or shall suffer such other punishment as .is hereinafter mentioned.

Penalty for delaying or discouraging the service or deserting his post, etc

4. When any action or any service is commanded, every person subject to this Act who shall presume to delay or discourage the said action or service upon any pretence whatsoever, or in the presence or vicinity of the enemy shall desert his post or slip upon his watch, shall suffer death or such other punishment as is hereinafter mentioned.

Penalty for misconduct of subordinate officers and men in action

5. Every person subject to this Act, and not being a commanding officer, who shall not use his utmost exertions to carry the orders of his superior officers into execution when ordered to prepare for action, or during the action, shall, if he has acted traitorously, suffer death; if he has acted from cowardice, shall suffer death, or such other punishment as is hereinafter mentioned; and if he has acted from negligence or through other default, be dismissed from His Majesty's service, with disgrace, or suffer such other punishment as is hereinafter mentioned.

Communications with the Enemy

Penalty for spies

6. All spies for the enemy shall be deemed to be persons subject to this Act, and shall suffer death or such other punishment as is hereinafter mentioned.

Penalty for corresponding etc., with the enemy

7. Every person subject to this Act who shall—

(1) Traitorously hold correspondence with or shall give intelligence to the enemy;

(2) Or fail to make known to the proper authorities any information he may have received from the enemy;

(3) Or who shall relieve the enemy with any supplies, shall suffer death, or such other punishment as is hereinafter mentioned.

Penalty for improper communication with the enemy

8. Every person subject to this Act who shall, without any treacherous intention, hold any improper communication with the enemy, shall be dismissed with disgrace from His Majesty's service, or shall suffer such other punishment as is hereinafter mentioned.

Neglect of duty

Penalty for abandoning post etc

9. Every person subject to this Act who shall desert his post etc. or sleep upon his watch, or negligently perform the duty imposed on him, shall be dismissed from His Majesty's service, with disgrace, or shall suffer such other punishment as is hereinafter mentioned.

Mutiny

Penalty for mutiny accompanied by acts of violence

10. Where mutiny is accompanied by violence; every person subject to this Act who shall join therein shall suffer death or such other punishment as is hereinafter mentioned; and every person subject to this Act who shall not use his utmost exertions to suppress such mutiny shall, if he has acted traitorously, suffer death, or such other punishment as is hereinafter mentioned; if he has acted from cowardice, shall suffer penal servitude or such other punishment as is hereinafter mentioned; if he has acted from negligence, he shall be dismissed from His Majesty's service, with disgrace, or suffer such other punishment as is hereinafter mentioned.

Penalty for mutiny not accompanied by acts of violence

11. Where a mutiny is not accompanied by violence, the ringleader or ringleaders of such mutiny shall suffer death, or such other punishment as is hereinafter mentioned; and all other persons who shall join in such mutiny, or shall not use their utmost exertions to suppress the same, shall suffer imprisonment or such other punishment as is hereinafter mentioned.

Penalty for inciting mutiny

12. Every person subject to this Act who shall endeavour to seduce any other person subject to this Act from his duty or allegiance to His Majesty, or endeavour to incite him to commit any act of mutiny, shall suffer death or such other punishment as is hereinafter mentioned.

Penalty for civilians endeavouring to seduce from allegiance

13. Every person, not otherwise subject to this Act, who, being on board any ship of His Majesty, shall endeavour to, seduce from his duty or allegiance to His Majesty any person subject to this Act, shall so far as respects such offence be deemed to be a person subject to this Act, and shall suffer death or such other punishment as is hereinafter mentioned.

Penalty for making mutinous assemblies or uttering seditious words

14. Every person subject to this Act who shall make or endeavour to make any mutinous assembly shall lead or incite any other person to join in any mutinous assembly or shall utter any words of sedition or muting, shall suffer penal servitude or such other punishment as is hereinafter mentioned.

Penalty for concealing any mutinous practice, design or words

15. every person subject to this Act who shall willfully conceal any traitorous or mutinous practice or design or any traitorous or mutinous words spoken against His Majesty, or any word, practice, or design tending to hindrance of the service, shall suffer penal servitude or such other punishment as is here-in-under mentioned.

Punishment for striking or attempting to strike, etc., superior officer

16. Every person subject to this Act who shall strike or attempt to strike, or draw or lift up any weapon against, or use or attempt to use any violence against, his superior whether or not such superior is in the execution of his officer, shall be punished with penal servitude or such other punishment as is hereinafter mentioned.

Insubordination

Penalty for disobeying or using threatening language to superior officer

17. Every person subject to this Act who shall quarrel or fight with any other person, whether such other person be or be not subject to this Act, or shall use reproachful or provoking approached or gestures tending to make any quarrel or disturbance, shall suffer imprisonment or such other punishment as is hereinafter mentioned.

Dissertation and Absence without Leave

Penalty for desertion

19. Every person subject to this Act who shall absent himself from his ship, or from the place where his duty requires him to be, with an intention of not returning to such ship or place or from his ship or place of duty, to do any act which shows that he has an intention of not returning to such ship or place, shall be deemed to have deserted, and shall be punished accordingly: that is to say,--

(1) If he has deserted to the enemy, shall be punished with death or such other punishment as is hereinafter mentioned;

(2) If he deserted under any other circumstances, he shall be punished with penal servitude or such other punishment as is hereinafter mentioned;

and in every such case he shall forfeit all pay, head money, bounty, salvage, prize money, and allowances that have been earned by him and all annuities, pensions, gratuities, medals, and decorations that may have been granted to him, and also all clothes and effects which he may have left on board the ship or at the place from which he has deserted, unless the tribunal by which he is tried, or the Governor General in Council, shall otherwise direct.

Penalty for inciting any person to desert

20. Every person subject to this Act who shall endeavour to seduce any other person subject to this Act to desert shall suffer imprisonment or such other punishment as is hereinafter mentioned.

Penalty for entertaining a deserter

21. Every officer in command of any ship of His Majesty who shall receive or entertain any deserter from His Majesty's naval, military, or air forces, after discovering him to be **a** deserter, and shall not with all convenient speed, in the case of a deserter from His Majesty's naval forces, give notice to the commanding officer of the ship to which such deserter belongs, or, if such ship is at a distance, to the Governor General in Council or to the Officer Commanding the Indian Navy, or, in case of **a** deserter from His Majesty's military or air forces, give notice to the Governor General in Council, or the commanding officer of the regiment or unit to which such deserter belongs, the officer so offending shall be dismissed from the His Majesty's service, or shall suffer such other punishment as is hereinafter mentioned.

Punishment for breaking out ship

22. If any person subject to this Act (without being guilty of desertion) improperly leaves his ship or place of duty, he shall be liable to imprisonment or to such other punishment as is hereinafter mentioned, and to such other punishment by forfeiture of wages or of other benefits as the Governor General in Council from time to time by regulations prescribes.

Penalty for absence without leave

23. Every person subject to this Act who (without being guilty of desertion or improperly leaving his ship or place of duty) shall be absent without leave shall be liable in time of war to imprisonment or such other punishment as is hereinafter mentioned, and at other times to imprisonment or detention for any period not exceeding ten weeks, or such other punishment as the circumstances of the case may require, and to such other punishment by forfeiture of wages or of other benefits as the Governor General in Council from time to time by regulations prescribes.

Forfeiture of effects for absence without leave

24. If any person subject to this Act is absent without leave for a period of one month (whether he is guilty of desertion or of improperly leaving his ship or place of duty or not), but is not apprehended and tried for his offence, he shall be liable to forfeiture of wages and other benefits as the Governor General in Council from time to time by regulations prescribes, and the Governor General in Council may by an order containing a statement of the absence without leave direct that the clothes and effects (if any) left by him on board ship or at his place of duty be forfeited, and the same may be sold, and the proceeds of the sale shall be disposed of as the Governor General in Council may direct; and every order under this provision for forfeiture or sale shall be conclusive as to the fact of the absence without leave as therein stated of the person therein named; but in any case the Governor General in Council may, if it seems fit on sufficient cause

being shown at any time after forfeiture and before sale, remit the forfeiture, or after sale pay or dispose of the proceeds of the sale or any part thereof to or for the use of the person to whom the clothes or effects belonged, or his representatives.

Penalty for assisting, etc., desertion

25. If any person not subject to this Act assists or procures any person subject to this Act to desert or improperly absent himself from his duty, or conceals, employs or continues to employ any person subject to this Act, who is a deserter or improperly absent from his duty, knowing him to be a deserter or so improperly absent, he shall for every such offence of assistance, procurement, concealment, employment or continuance of employment, be liable, on conviction in summary trial before a Magistrate empowered under section 260 of the Code of Criminal Procedure, 1898, or before any person or persons or court exercising like authority in any part of His Majesty's dominions, to a penalty not exceeding two hundred rupees; and every such penalty shall be applied as the Governor General in Council directs.

Penalty for persuading to desertion, etc

26. If any person not subject to this Act by words or otherwise persuades any person subject to this Act, to desert or improperly absent himself from his duty, he shall for every such, offence be liable, on conviction in a summary trial before a Magistrate empowered under section 260 of the Code of Criminal Procedure, 1899, or before any person or persons or court, exercising like authority in any part of His Majesty's dominions, to a penalty not exceeding two hundred rupees; and every such penalty shall be applied as the Governor General in Council directs.

Miscellaneous Offences

Penalty for profane swearing and other immoralities

27. Every person subject to this Act who shall be guilty of any profane oath, cursing, execration, drunkenness, uncleanness or other scandalous action in derogation of God's honour and corruption of good manners, shall be dismissed from His Majesty's service, with disgrace, or suffer such other punishment as is hereinafter mentioned.

Penalty on officers for cruelty or oppression

28. Every officer subject to this Act who shall be guilty of cruelty, or of any scandalous or fraudulent conduct, shall be dismissed with disgrace from His Majesty's service; and every officer subject to this Act who shall be guilty of any other conduct unbecoming the character of an officer shall be dismissed, with or without disgrace, from His Majesty's service.

Penalty for suffering ships or aircraft to be improperly lost

29. Every person subject to this. Act who shall either designedly or negligently or by any default lose, strand, or hazard or suffer to be lost, stranded, or hazarded, any ship of His Majesty or in His Majesty's service, or lose or suffer to be lost any aircraft of His Majesty or in His Majesty's

service, shall be dismissed from His Majesty's service, with disgrace, or suffer such other punishment as is hereinafter mentioned.

Penalty for not taking care of and defending ships under convoy

30. The officers of all ships of His Majesty appointed for the convoy and protection of any ships or vessels shall diligently perform their duty without delay according to their instructions in that behalf; and every officer who shall fail in his duty in this respect, and shall not defend the ships and goods under his convoy, without deviation to any other objects, or shall refuse to fight in their defence if they are assailed, or shall cowardly abandon and expose the ships in his convoy to hazard, or shall demand or exact any money or other reward from any merchant or master for convoying any ships or vessels intrusted to his care, or shall misuse the masters or mariners thereof, shall make such reparation in damages to the merchants, owners, and others as the Court of Admiralty may adjudge, and also shall be punished criminally according to the nature of his offence, by death or such other punishment as is hereinafter mentioned.

Master of merchant vessel to obey order of convoying officer

31. Every master or other officer in command of any merchant or other vessel under the convoy of any ship of His Majesty shall obey the commanding officer thereof in all matters relating to the navigation or security of the convoy; and shall take such precautions for avoiding the enemy as may be directed by such commanding officer, and if he shall fail to obey such directions such commanding officer may compel obedience by force of arms without being liable for any loss of life or of property that may result from his using such force.

Penalty for taking any goods on board other than for the use of the vessel except gold, silver, jewel, etc

32. Every officer in command of any of His Majesty's ships who shall receive on board or permit to be received on board such ship any goods or merchandises whatsoever, other than for the sole use of the ship, except gold, silver, or jewels, and except goods and merchandise belonging to any merchant, or on board any ship which may be shipwrecked or in imminent danger, either on the high seas or in some port, creek, or harbour, for the purpose of preserving them for their proper owners, or except such goods or merchandise as he may at any time be ordered to take or receive on board by order of the Governor General in Council or his superior officer, shall be dismissed from His Majesty's service, or suffer such other punishment as is hereinafter mentioned.

Penalty for embezzling public stores

33. Every person subject to this Act who shall wastefully expend, embezzle, or fraudulently buy, sell or receive any ammunition, provisions, or other public stores, and every person subject to this Act, who shall knowingly permit any such wasteful expenditure, embezzlement, sale, or receipt, shall suffer imprisonment or such other punishment as is hereinafter mentioned.

Penalty for injuring any magazine or vessel, etc., not belonging to an enemy

34. Every person subject to this Act who shall unlawfully set fire to any dockyard, victualling yard or steam factory, yard, arsenal, magazine, building, stores, or to any ship, vessel, hoy, barge,

boat, or other craft or furniture thereunto belonging, not being the property of an enemy, pirate, or rebel, shall suffer death or such other punishment as is hereinafter mentioned.

Penalty for making or signing false musters

35. Every person subject to this Act who shall knowingly make or sign a false muster or record or other official document, or who shall command, counsel, or procure the making or signing thereof, or who shall aid or abet any other person in the making or signing thereof, shall be dismissed from His Majesty's service, with disgrace, or suffer such other punishment as is hereinafter mentioned.

Penalty for misconduct in hospital

36. Every person subject to this Act who shall wilfully do any act or wilfully disobey any orders, whether **in** hospital or elsewhere, with intent to produce or to aggravate any disease or infirmity, or to delay his cure, or who shall feign any disease, infirmity, or inability to perform his duty, shall suffer imprisonment or such other punishment as is hereinafter mentioned.

Penalty for endeavouring to stir up any disturbance on account of unworthiness of the victuals or other just grounds

37. Every person subject to this Act who shall have any cause of complaint, either of the unwholesomeness of the victuals or upon any other just ground, shall quietly make the same known to his superior, or captain, or to the officer commanding the Indian Navy, and the said superior, captain, or officer, shall, as far as he is able, cause the same to be presently remedied; and no person subject to this Act upon any pretence whatever shall attempt to stir up any disturbance, upon pain of such punishment as a court-martial may think fit to inflict, according to the degree of offence.

Penalty for not sending to the Court of Admiralty all papers found abroad prize ship

38. All the papers, charter-parties, bills of lading, passports and other writings whatsoever that shall be taken, seized, or found aboard any ship or ships which shall be taken as prize shall be duly preserved, and the commanding officer of the ship which shall take such prize shall send the originals entire and without fraud to the Court of Admiralty, or such other court or commissioners as shall be authorised to determine whether such prize be lawful capture, there to be viewed, made use of, and proceeded upon according to law, upon pain that every person offending herein shall be dismissed from His Majesty's service, or shall suffer such other' punishment as is hereinafter mentioned, and in addition thereto shall forfeit and lose his share of the capture.

Penalty for taking money or other effects out of any prize before the same shall be condemned

39. No person subject to this Act shall take out any prize or ship seized for prize any money, plate, or goods, unless it shall be necessary for the better securing thereof, or for the necessary use and service of any of His Majesty's ships and vessels of war, before the same be adjudged lawful prize in some Admiralty Court; but the full and entire account of the whole without embezzlement shall be brought in and judgment passed entirely upon the whole, without fraud, upon pain that every person offending herein shall be dismissed from His Majesty's service, with disgrace, or suffer

such other punishment as is hereinafter mentioned, and in addition thereto forfeit and lose his share of the capture.

Penalty for stripping or ill-using persons taken on board as prize

40. If any ship or vessel shall be taken as prize, none of the officers, mariners, or other persons on board her shall be stripped of their clothes, or in any sort pillaged, beaten, or evil intreated, upon pain that the person or persons so offending shall be dismissed from His Majesty's service, with disgrace or suffer such other punishment as is hereinafter mentioned.

Penalty on commanders capturing as prize by collusion or collusively restoring ships or goods

41. If the commanding officer of any of His Majesty's ships does any of the following things, namely,

(1) By collusion with the enemy takes as prize any vessel, goods, or thing;

(2) Unlawfully agrees with any person for the ransoming of any vessel, goods, or thing taken as prize; or

(3) In pursuance of any unlawful agreement for ransoming or otherwise by collusion actually quits or restores any vessel, goods, or thing taken as prize;

he shall be liable to dismissal from His Majesty's service, with disgrace, or to such other punishment as is hereinafter mentioned.

Penalty for breaking bulk on board prize ship with a view to embezzlement

42. If any person subject to this Act breaks bulk on board any vessel taken as prize, or detained in the exercise of any belligerent right, or under any Act relating to piracy or to the slave trade or to the Customs, with intent to embezzle anything therein or belonging thereto, he shall be liable to dismissal from His Majesty's service, with disgrace, or to such other punishment as is hereinafter mentioned, and in addition thereto to forfeit and lose his share of the capture.

Penalty for offences against naval discipline not particularly mentioned

43. Every person subject to this Act, who shall be guilty of any act, disorder, or neglect to the prejudice of good order and naval discipline, not hereinbefore specified, shall be dismissed from His Majesty's service, with disgrace, or suffer such other punishment as is hereinafter mentioned.

Crimes to be punished according to laws and customs in use

44. Any person subject to this Act committing any offence against this Act, such offence not being punishable with death or penal servitude, shall, save where this Act expressly otherwise provides, be proceeded against and punished according to :the laws and customs in such cases used at sea.

OFFENCES PUNISHABLE BY ORDINARY LAW

Penalty for offences punishable by ordinary law

45. Every person subject to this Act who shall be guilty of an offence punishable under section 302, 304, 304A, 377, 377 read with 511, 379, 380, 381, 382, or.392 of the Indian Penal Code shall be punishable with the punishment provided in that Code for the offence.

If any such person shall be guilty of any other criminal offence which if committed in British India would be punishable by the law of British India, he shall, whether the offence be or be not committed in British India, be punished either in pursuance of the first part of this Act as for an act to the prejudice of good order and naval discipline not otherwise specified, or the offender shall be subject to the same punishment as might for the time being be awarded by any ordinary criminal tribunal competent to try the offender if the offence had been committed in British India.

Offences when punishable

46. For all offences specified or referred to in this Act, if committed by any person subject thereto in any harbour, haven, .or creek, or on any lake or river, whether in or out of British India, or anywhere within the jurisdiction of the Admiralty, or at any place on shore out of British India, or in any of His Majesty's dockyards, victualling yards, steam factory yards, or on any gun wharf, or in any arsenal, barrack, or hospital belonging to His Majesty or in any other premises held by or on behalf of the Crown for naval or military purposes, or in any canteen or sailors' home or any place of recreation placed at the disposal of or used by officers or men of His Majesty's Navy which may be prescribed by the Governor General in Council, whether in or out of British India, the offender may be tried and punished under this Act; and for offences hereinbefore specified under the headings "misconduct in the presence of the enemy," "communications with the enemy," "neglect of duty," "mutiny," "insubordination," "'desertion and absence without leave," or "'miscellaneous offences," if committed by any person subject to this Act at any place on shore, whether in or out of British India, the offender may be tried and punished under this Act.

Provisions where offender has ceased to be subject to the Act

46A. (1) Where an offence under this Act has been committed by any person while subject to this Act, such person may be taken into and kept in custody and tried and punished for such offence although he has ceased to be subject to this Act in like manner is he might have been taken into and kept in custody, tried, or punished if he had continued so subject:

Provided that where a person has since the commission of' an offence ceased to be subject to this Act, he shall not be tried for such offence, except in case of offences of mutiny or desertion, unless proceedings against him are instituted within three months after he has ceased to be subject to this Act, but this section shall not affect the jurisdiction of a civil court in the case of any offence triable by such court as well as by court-martial.

(2) Where a person subject to this Act is sentenced under this Act to penal servitude, imprisonment, or detention, this Act shall apply to him during the term of his sentence notwithstanding that he is discharged or dismissed from His Majesty's service, or has

otherwise ceased to be subject to this Act, and he may be kept in custody, removed, imprisoned, made to undergo detention and punished accordingly, as if he had continued to be subject to this Act.

PART II

GENERAL PROVISIONS

Power of court-martial to find intent with which offence committed

47. Where the amount of punishment for any offence under this Act depends upon the intent with which it has been committed, and any person is charged with having committed such offence with an intent involving a greater degree of punishment, a court-martial may find that the offence was committed with an intent involving a less degree of punishment, and award such punishment accordingly.

Power of court-martial to find guilty of lesser offence on charge of greater

48. Where any person shall be charged with any offence under this Act he may, upon failure of proof of the commission of the greater offence, be found guilty of another offence of the same class involving a less degree of punishment, but not of any offence involving a greater degree of punishment.

Rebels and mutineers to be deemed enemies

49. All armed rebels, armed mutineers, and pirates shall deemed to be enemies within the meaning of this Act.

Power to arrest offenders

50. Every officer in command of a fleet or squadron of His Majesty's ships or of one of His Majesty's ships, or the senior officer present at a port, or an officer having by virtue of subsection (3) of section fifty-six of this Act power to try offences, may, by warrant under his hand, authorise any person to arrest any offender subject to this Act for any offence against this Act mentioned in such warrant; and any such warrant may include the names of more persons than one in respect of several offences of the same nature; and any person named in any such warrant, may forthwith, on his apprehension, if the warrant so directs, be taken on board the ship to which he belongs, or some other of His Majesty's ships; and any person so authorised may use force, if necessary, for the purpose of effecting such apprehensions, towards any person subject to this Act.

Penalty for not assisting in detection of prisoners

51. Every person subject to this Act who shall not use his utmost endeavours to detect, apprehend and bring to punishment all offenders against this Act, and shall not assist the officers appointed for that purpose, shall suffer imprisonment or such other punishment as is hereinafter mentioned.

PART III

REGULATIONS AS TO PUNISHMENT

Punishments

52. The following punishments may be inflicted in His Majesty's Navy:

(1) Death;

(2) Penal servitude;

(3) Dismissal with disgrace from His Majesty's service:

(4) Imprisonment or corporal punishment;

(4A) Detention;

(5) Dismissal from His Majesty's service;

(6) Forfeiture of seniority as an officer for a specified time, or otherwise;

(7) Dismissal from the ship to which the offender belongs;

(8) Severe reprimand, or reprimand;

(9) Disrating a subordinate or petty officer;

(10) Forfeiture of pay, head money, bounty, salvage, prize money, and allowances earned by, and of all annuities, pensions, gratuities, medals, and decorations granted to, the offender, or of any one or more of the above particulars; also, in the case of desertion, of all clothes and effects left by the deserter on board the ship to which he belongs;

(11) Such minor punishments as are now inflicted according to the custom of the navy, or may from time to time be allowed by the Governor General in Council;

And each of the above punishments shall be deemed to be inferior in degree to every punishment preceding it in the above scale.

Regulations as to infliction of punishments

53. The following regulations are hereby made with respect to the infliction of punishments in His Majesty's Navy:-

(1) The powers to suspend, remit or commute sentences or punishment shall be the powers conferred by and shall be exercised in accordance with the provisions of sections 401 and 402 of the Code of Criminal Procedure, 1898, save that such powers shall not be exercisable by the Local Government, and any sentence so modified shall (subject to the provisions of this Act) be valid, and shall be carried into execution, as if it had been originally passed, with such modification, by the court-martial; but so that neither the degree nor the duration of the punishment involved in any sentence be increased by any such modification.

(2) Judgment of death shall not be passed on any prisoner unless four at least of the officers present at the court-martial, where the number does not exceed five, and in other cases a majority of not less than two-thirds of the officers present, concur in the sentence.

(3) Except in case of mutiny, the punishment of death shall not be inflicted on any prisoner until the sentence has been confirmed by the Governor General in Council.

(4) The punishment of penal servitude may be inflicted for the term of life or for any other term of not less than three years.

(5) The punishment of penal servitude shall in all involve dismissal with disgrace from His Majesty's service.

(6) A sentence of dismissal with disgrace shall involve in all cases a forfeiture of all pay, bead money, bounty, salvage, prize money and allowances that have been earned by, and of all annuities, pensions, gratuities, medals, and decorations that may have been granted to the offender, and an incapacity to serve His Majesty again in any military, naval, air force, or civil service, and may also in all cases be accompanied by a sentence of imprisonment.

(7) The punishment of imprisonment may be inflicted for any term not exceeding two years and may be accompanied with a sentence of dismissal from His Majesty's service.

(8) A sentence of imprisonment may be accompanied with a direction that the prisoner shall be kept in solitary confinement for any period of such term not exceeding fourteen days at any one time, and not exceeding eighty-four days in any one year, with intervals between the periods of solitary confinement of not less duration than the periods of solitary confinement; and when the imprisonment awarded exceeds eighty-four days, the solitary confinement shall not exceed seven days in any twenty-eight days of the whole imprisonment awarded, with intervals between the periods of solitary confinement of not less duration than such periods.

(9) A sentence of imprisonment may be rigorous or simple, or partly rigorous and partly simple, and corporal punishment may be awarded in addition to any sentence of imprisonment, whether such imprisonment is or is not to be accompanied with solitary confinement and hard labour or either of them.

(9A) The punishment of detention may be inflicted for any term not exceeding two years;

Provided that, until naval detention quarters shall have been set apart and declared to be such by the Governor General in Council by notification in the Gazette of India no sentence of detention shall be awarded.

(10) The punishment of imprisonment, or detention whether on board ship or on shore, shall involve disrating in case of a petty officer and reduction to the ranks in case of a non-commissioned officer of marines, and shall in all cases be accompanied by stoppage of pay or wages during the term of imprisonment or detention: Provided

that where the punishment awarded is detention for a term not exceeding fourteen days, the sentence may direct that the punishment shall not be accompanied by stoppage of pay or wages during the term of detention

(11) In any case, of corporal punishment not more than forty-eight lashes shall be inflicted: no officer shall be-subject to detention or to corporal punishment: no petty or non-commissioned officer shall be subject to corporal punishment: except in case of mutiny.

All other punishments authorised by this Act may be inflicted in the manner heretofore in use in the navy.

Substitution of imprisonment for penal servitude in certain cases

53A. (1) Where a person other than a European or American is sentenced to penal servitude, the authority sentencing him shall record such sentence and the term thereof and at the same time shall record an order substituting for such sentence a sentence of transportation which may be for life, or of rigorous imprisonment not exceeding fourteen years.

(2) For the purposes of this Act, unless there is anything repugnant in the subject or context, "penal servitude" includes transportation or rigorous imprisonment substituted for penal servitude in accordance with this section.

Limitation of time for trial

54. No person, unless he be an offender who has avoided apprehension or fled from justice, shall be tried or punished in pursuance of this Act for any offence committed by him unless tiueh trid shall take place within three years from the commission of such offence or within one year after the return of such offender to India, where he has been absent from India during such period of three years.

Scale of punishment

55. Subject to the foregoing regulations, where any punishment is specified by this Act as the penalty for any offence, and it is further declared that another punishment may be awarded in respect of the same offence, the expression "other punishment" shall be deemed to comprise any one or more of the punishments inferior in degree to the specified punishment, according to the scale hereinbefore mentioned; but corporal punishment shall be deemed equal in degree to imprisonment, and may in all cases, subject to the foregoing regulations, be inflicted as a substitute for or in addition to imprisonment.

Authorities having power to try offences

56. (1) Any offence triable under this Act may be tried and punished by court-martial.

(2) Any offence not capital which is triable under this Act, and (except in the cases by this Act expressly provided for) is not committed by an officer, may, under such regulations as the Governor General in Council from time to time issues, be summarily tried and punished by the officer in command of the ship to which the offender belongs at the time either of

the commission or of the trial of the offence, subject to the restriction that the commanding officer shall not have power to award penal servitude or to award imprisonment or detention for more than three months.

(3) The power by this section vested in an officer commanding a ship may—

(a) As respects persons on board a tender **to** the ship, be exercised in the case of a single tender absent from the ship, by the officer in command of such tender, and in the case of two or more tenders absent from the ship in company or acting together, by the officer in immediate command of such tenders; and

(b) As respects persons on board any boat or boats belonging to the ship, be exercised when such boat or boats is or are absent on detached service, by the officer in command of the boat or boats; and

(c) As respects persons subject to this Act on detached service either on shore or otherwise, or such of those persons as are not for the time being made subject to military law by an order under section one hundred and seventy-nine of the Army Act, 1881, be exercised by the officer in immediate command of those persons; and

(d) As respects persons subject to this Act quartered in naval barracks, be exercised by the officer in command of those barracks.

(4) Except in case of mutiny, no man shall be sentenced by the commanding officer to corporal punishment until his offence has been inquired into by one or more officers appointed by such commanding officer, and his or their opinion as to the guilt or innocence of the person charged reported to such commanding officer, and the commanding officer shall thereupon act as according to his judgment may seem right.

Forfeiture of time of seniority

57. The Governor General in Council may impose the punishment of forfeiture of time or seniority of not more than twelve months on any subordinate officer.

Trail of officers for disciplinary offences in time of war

57A. (1) Where any officer borne on the books of any of His Majesty's ships in commission is in time of war alleged to have been guilty of a disciplinary offence, that is to say, a breach of section seventeen, eighteen, nineteen, twenty-two, twenty-three, twenty-seven, or forty-three of this Act, the officer having power to order a court-martial may, if he considers that the offence is of such a character as not to necessitate trial by court-martial, in lieu of ordering a court-martial order a disciplinary court constituted as hereinafter mentioned.

(2) A disciplinary court shall be composed of not less than three nor more than five officers, of whom one shall be commander or of higher rank.

(3) A disciplinary court shall have power to impose any punishment inferior to detention in the scale hereinbefore contained, but no greater punishment.

(4) The Governor General in Council may from time to time frame general orders for regulating the assembling, constitution and procedure and practice of disciplinary courts under this section, and may by those regulations apply, with the necessary modifications, to disciplinary courts the provisions of sections sixty-two to sixty-four and sections sixty-six to sixty-nine of this Act relating to courts-martial, and the regulations shall provide for evidence being taken on oath and empower the court to administer oaths for that purpose.

PART IV

COURTS-MARTIAL

Constitution of Courts-Martial

Constitution of courts-martial

58. The following regulations are hereby made with respect to courts-martial: -

(1) A court-martial shall consist of not less than five nor more than nine officers;

(2) No officer shall be qualified to sit as a member of any court-martial held in pursuance of this Act unless he be a flag officer, captain, commander, lieutenant-commander, or lieutenant of His Majesty's navy on full pay;

(3) A court-martial shall not be held unless at least two of His Majesty's ships, not being tenders, and commanded by captains, commanders, lieutenant commanders, or lieutenants of His Majesty's navy on full pay, are together at the time when such court-martial is held;

(4) No officer shall sit on a court-martial who is under twenty-one years of age;

(5) No court-martial for the trial of a flag officer shall be duly constituted unless the president is a flag officer, and the other officers composing the court are of the rank of captain, or of higher rank;

(6) No court-martial for, the trial of a captain in His Majesty's navy shall be duly constituted unless the president is a captain or of higher rank, and the other officers composing the court are commanders or officers of higher rank;

(7) No court-martial for the trial of a person below the rank of captain in His Majesty's navy shall be duly constituted, unless the president is a captain or of higher rank, nor, if the person to be tried is of the rank of commander, unless in addition to the president two other members of the court are of the rank of commander or of higher rank;

(8) The prosecutor shall not sit on any court-martial for the trial of a person whom he prosecutes;

(9) The Governor General in Council shall have power to order courts-martial to be held for the trial of offences under this Act, and to grant commissions to any officer of His Majesty's

navy on full pay authorising him to order courts-martial to be held for the trial of such offences;

(10) An officer holding a commission from the Governor General in Council to order courts-martial shall not be empowered to do so if there is present at the place where such court-martial is to be held any officer superior in rank to himself on full pay and in command of one or more of His Majesty's ships or vessels, although such last-mentioned officer may not hold a commission to order courts-martial; and in such a case such last-mentioned officer may order a court-martial, although he does not hold any commission for the purpose;

(11) If any officer holding a commission from the Governor General in Council to order courts-martial, having the command of a fleet or squadron, and being in foreign parts, die, be recalled, leave his station, or be removed from his command, the officer upon whom the command of the fleet or squadron devolves, and so from time to time the officer who shall have the command of the fleet or squadron, shall, without any commission from the Governor General in Council, have the same power to order courts-martial as the first mentioned officer was invested with;

(12) If any officer holding a commission from the Governor General in Council to order courts-martial, and having the command of any fleet or squadron of His Majesty's ships in foreign parts shall detach any part of such fleet or squadron, or separate himself from any part of such fleet or squadron, he may, by commission under his hand, empower, in the first mentioned case, the commanding officer of the squadron or detachment ordered on such separate service, and in case of his death or ceasing so to command, the officer to whom the command of such separate squadron or detachment shall belong, and in the secondly-mentioned case the senior officer of His Majesty's ships on the division of the station from which he is absent, to order courts-martial during the time of such separate service, or during his absence from that division of the station (as the case may be), and every such authority shall continue in force until revoked, or until the officer holding it returns to India, or until he comes into the presence of a superior officer, empowered to order courts-martial in the same squadron, detachment, or division of a station, but so that such authority shall revive on the officer holding it ceasing to be in the presence of such superior officer, and so from time to time as often as-the case so requires;

(13) The officer ordering a court-martial shall not sit thereon;

(14) The President of every court-martial shall be named by the authority ordering the same, or by any officer empowered by such authority to name the president;

(15) No commander, lieutenant-commander, or lieutenant shall be required to sit as a member of any court-martial when four officers of a higher rank and junior to the president can be assembled at the place where the court-martial is to be holden (but the regularity or validity of any court-martial or of the proceedings thereof, shall not be affected by any commander, lieutenant-commander, or lieutenant being required to sit, or sitting, thereto under any circumstances); and when any commander, lieutenant-commander or lieutenant sits on any court-martial the member of it shall not exceed five in number;

(16) Subject to the foregoing regulations, whenever a court-martial shall be held the officer appointed to preside thereat shall summon all the officers next in seniority to himself present at the place where the court-martial shall be held to sit thereon, until the number of nine or such number not less than five, as is attainable, is complete; subject to this proviso, that the admirals and captain being superintendents of His Majesty's dockyards, shall not be summoned to sit on courts-martial unless specially directed to do so by orders from the Governor General in Council.

Proceedings of Courts-Martial

Where courts-martial to be held

59. A court-martial under this Act shall be held on board one of His Majesty's ships or vessels of war, unless the Governor General in Council or the officer who ordered the court-martial in any particular case for reasons to be recorded on the proceedings otherwise direct, in which case the court-martial shall be held at a port at such convenient place on shore as the Governor General in Council or the officer who ordered the court-martial shall direct.

As to time of sittings of courts-martial

60. A court-martial held in pursuance of this Act may, if it appears to the court that an adjournment is desirable, be adjourned for a period not exceeding six days, but except where such an adjournment is ordered shall sit from day to day, with the exception of Sundays, until sentence is given, unless prevented from so doing by stress of weather or unavoidable accident, and its proceedings shall not be delayed by the absence of any member, so that not less than four are present; and no member shall absent himself unless compelled so to do by sickness or other just cause, to be approved of by the other members of the court, and if any member of a court-martial shall absent himself there-from, in contravention of this section, he shall be dismissed from His Majesty's service, or shall suffer such other punishment as may be awarded by, a court-martial.

Appointment of officiating judge advocate

61. In the absence of the judge advocate of the fleet or his deputy, and in default of any appointment in this behalf by the Governor General in Council, or by the Officer Commanding the Indian Navy, the officer who is to be the president of the court-martial shall appoint a person to officiate as deputy judge advocate al the trial; and the judge advocate of the fleet for the time being, or his deputy, or the person officiating as deputy judge advocate, at any trial shall administer an oath to every witness appearing at the trial.

Proceedings at trial

62. As soon as the court is assembled, the names of the officers composing the court shall be read over to the person charged, who shall be asked if he objects to being tried by any member of the court; if the person charged shall object to any member, the objection shall be decided by the court; if the objection shall be allowed, the place of the member objected to shall be filled , up by the officer next in seniority who is not on the court-martial, subject to the regulations hereinbefore contained.

The person charged may then raise any other objection which he desires to make respecting the constitution of the court-martial, and the objection shall then be decided by the court, which decision shall be final, and the constitution of the court-martial shall not be afterwards impeached, and it shall be deemed to have been in all respects duly constituted.

Oath to be administered to members of courts-martial

63. Before the court shall proceed to try the person charged, the judge advocate of the fleet, or his deputy, or the person officiating as deputy judge advocate of the fleet, shall administer to every member of the court the following oath; that is to say,

> "I do swear, that I will duly administer justice according to law, without partiality, favour, or affection; and I do further swear, that I will not on any account, at any the whatsoever, disclose or discover the vote or opinion of any particular member of this court-martial, unless thereunto required in due course of law.
>
> So help me God."

Provided that an affirmation to the same effect in such terms as the Governor General in Council may prescribe in this behalf may be substituted for such oath.

Oaths to be administered to judge advocate, etc

64. As soon as the said oath shall be administered to the members of the court-martial, the president shall administer to the judge advocate of the fleet, or his deputy, or the person officiating as deputy judge advocate, the following oath:

> "I do swear that I will not upon any account, at any time whatsoever, disclose or discover the vote or opinion of any particular member of the court-martial, unless thereunto required in due course of law.
>
> So help me God."

Provided that an affirmation to the same effect in such terms as the Governor General in Council may prescribe in this behalf may be substituted for such oath.

Power of Governor General in Council to apply general orders framed by Admiralty for practice of courts-martial

65. The Governor General in Council may apply to Indian Navy such general orders altering and regulating the procedure and practice of courts-martial as may from time to time be framed by the Admiralty and approved by His Majesty in Council subject to such modifications as the Governor General in Council may deem necessary to adapt them to the circumstances of the Indian Navy;

Provided that no modification shall be made which involves any racial discrimination.

Summoning of witnesses

66. Every person, civil, naval, and military, or belonging to the air force who may be required to give evidence before a court-martial shall be summoned by writing under the hand of a Secretary

to the Government of India, or by the deputy judge advocate, or the person appointed to officiate as deputy judge advocate at the trial; and all persons so summoned and attending as witnesses before any court-martial shall, during their necessary attendance in or on such court, and in going to and returning from the same, be privileged from arrest, and shall, if unduly arrested, be discharged by the court out of which the writ or process issued by which such witness was arrested, or if such court be not sitting, then by any judge of the superior courts of Westminster or Dublin, or the court of session in Scotland, or of the courts of law in the East or West Indies or elsewhere, according as the case shall require, upon its being made to appear to such court or judge, by any affidavit in a summary way, that such witness was arrested in going to or returning from or attending upon such court-martial; and all witnesses so duly summoned as aforesaid who make default in attending on such courts, or attending refuse to be sworn or make affirmation, or being sworn having made affirmation refuse to give evidence or to answer all such questions as the court may legally demand of them, or prevaricate in giving their evidence, shall, upon certificate thereof under the hand of the president of such court-martial, be liable to be attached in the Court of Queen's Bench in London or Dublin, or the Court of Sessions, or Sheriff depute or stewarts depute, or their respective substitutes, within their several shires and stewartries in Scotland, or court of law in the East of West Indies, or in any of His Majesty's colonies, upon complaint made, in like manner as if such witness after having been duly summoned and subpoenaed had had neglected to attend on a trial in any proceeding in the court in which such complaint is made, or had refused to be sworn, or on being sworn had refused to give evidence, or to answer all such questions as the court may legally demand, or had prevaricated in giving evidence, or, if the court-martial shall think fit, in case any such person, who is subject to this Act,, being called upon to give evidence at any court-martial; shall refuse or neglect to attend to give his evidence upon oath or affirmation, or shall prevaricate in his evidence, or behave with contempt to the court, such court-martial may punish every such offender by imprisonment, or, if the offender is a liable to be sentenced to detention under this Act, by detention not longer than three months in case of such refusal, neglect, or prevarication, nor longer than one month in the case of such contempt; and every not subject to this Act who may be so summoned to attend shall be allowed and paid his reasonable expenses for such attendance, under the authority of the Governor General in Council, or of the president of the court-martial on a foreign station.

Penalty on person giving false evidence

67. Every person who, upon any examination upon oath or upon affirmation before any court-martial held in pursuance of this Act, shall make any statement which is false and which he either knows or believes to be false or does not believe to be true, shall be deemed to have committed the offence of giving false evidence; and every such offence, wheresoever committed, shall be triable and punishable in British India.

Where persons are insane at the time of offence or trial

68. Where it shall appear upon the trial by court-martial of any person charged with an offence that such person is insane, the court shall find specially the fact of his insanity, and shall order such person to be kept in strict custody in such place and in such manner as the court shall deem fit until the directions of the Governor General in Council thereupon are known, and it shall be

lawful for the Governor General in Council to give orders for the safe custody of such person during His Majesty's pleasure in such place and in such manner as they shall think fit.

Report of proceedings of courts-martial to be transmitted

69. Every judge advocate, or deputy judge advocate, or person officiating as deputy judge advocate, shall transmit with as much expedition as may be the original proceedings, or a complete and authenticated copy thereof, and the original sentence of every court-martial attended by him, to the Officer Commanding the Indian Navy or senior officer, who shall transmit them to the Governor General in Council for the time being, and any person tried by a court-martial shall be entitled on demand, to a copy of such proceedings and sentence (upon payment for the same at the rate of three annas per folio of seventy two words), but no such demand shall be allowed after the space of three years from the date of the final decision of such court.

Evidence of rank, etc, of officers

69A. A Navy List or Gazette purporting to be published by authority and either to be printed by a Government printer or to be issued by His Majesty's Stationery Office, shall be evidence of the status and rank of the officers therein mentioned and of any appointment held by such officers until the contrary is proved.

PART V

PENAL SERVITUDE AND PRISONS

Penal Servitude

Sentence of penal servitude

70. Where a person is in pursuance of this Act convicted by a court-martial, and either is sentenced or has his sentence commuted to penal servitude, such conviction and sentence shall be of the same effect as if such person had been convicted by a civil court in British India of an offence punishable by penal servitude and sentenced by that court to penal servitude, and all enactments relating to a convict so sentenced shall, so far as circumstances admit, apply accordingly; and the said convict shall be removed to some prison in which a convict so sentenced by a civil court in British India can be confined either permanently or temporarily, and the order of the Governor General in Council or of the Officer Commanding the Indian Navy, or of the officer ordering the court-martial by whom such person was convicted, shall be a sufficient warrant for the transfer of the said person to such prison to undergo his sentence according to law, and until he reaches such prison for detaining him in naval custody, or in any civil prison or place of confinement.

Sentence of offender

72. In case any such offender shall be conveyed to any prison, not being a naval prison appointed by virtue of this Act, an allowance such as the Governor General in Council shall from time to time direct shall be made to the governor, keeper, or superintendent of the gaol or prison for

the subsistence of such offender while he is detained therein, and such allowance shall be paid by order of the Governor General in Council upon production by the said governor, keeper, or superintendent of a declaration, to be made by him before a Magistrate, of the number of days during which the offender has been so detained and subsisted in such gaol or prison.

Imprisonment of offender already under sentence for previous offence

73. Whenever sentence shall be passed by a court-martial on an offender already under sentence either of detention, imprisonment, or penal servitude, passed upon him under this Act for a former offence, the court may award sentence of detention, imprisonment, or penal servitude for the offence for which he is under trial to commence at the expiration of the detention, imprisonment, or penal servitude to which he has been previously sentenced, although the aggregate of the terms of detention, imprisonment, or penal servitude may exceed the term for which any of those punishments could be otherwise awarded;

Provided that nothing in this section shall cause a person to undergo imprisonment or detention for any period exceeding in the aggregate two consecutive years, and so much of any term of imprisonment or detention imposed on a person by a sentence in pursuance of this section as would prolong the total term of his punishment beyond that period shall be deemed to be remitted.

Prisons

Term and place of imprisonment

74. (1) Every term of penal servitude, imprisonment, or detention in pursuance of this Act shall be reckoned as commencing on the day on which the sentence was awarded, and the place of imprisonment or detention, whether the imprisonment or detention was awarded as an original or as a commuted punishment, shall be such place as may be appointed by the court or the commanding officer awarding the punishment, or which may from time to time be appointed by the Governor General in Council, and may, in the case of imprisonment, be one of the naval prisons appointed under this Act, or naval detention quarters, or any common gaol, house of correction, or military prison or detention barrack, and may in the case of detention be any naval detention quarters or a military detention barrack within His Majesty's dominions.

(2) Where, by reason of a ship being at sea or of a place at which there is no proper prison, or naval detention quarters, a sentence of imprisonment, or detention, as the case may be, cannot be duly executed, then, subject as hereinafter mentioned, an offender under sentence of imprisonment or detention, as the case may be, may be sent with all reasonable speed to some place at which there is a proper prison or naval detention quarters, or, in the case of an offender under sentence of detention, to some place at which there are naval detention quarters, in which the sentence call be duly executed, and on arrival there the offender shall undergo his sentence, in like manner as if the date of such arrival were the day on which the sentence was awarded, and that notwithstanding that in the meanwhile he has returned to his duty or become entitled to his discharge; and the term of imprisonment or detention, as the

case may be, shall be reckoned accordingly, subject however to the deduction of any time during which he has been kept in confinement in respect of the said sentence.

(3) Where in pursuance of this Act a person is sentenced to imprisonment or detention the order of the Governor General in Council or of the Officer Commanding the Indian Navy, or of the officer ordering the court-martial by which such person was sentenced, or, if he was sentenced by the commanding officer of a ship, the order of such commanding officer, shall, be a sufficient warrant for the sending of such person to the place of imprisonment or detention, there to undergo his sentence according to law, and until he reaches such place of imprisonment or detention for detaining him in naval custody, or in the case of a person sentenced to imprisonment in any civil prison or place of confinement.

Power to suspend sentence

74A. Where a person has been sentenced to penal servitude or imprisonment or detention the Governor General in Council or officer who by virtue of sub-section (3) of section seventy-four of this Act has power to issue an order of committal (hereinafter in this section referred to as "the committing authority") may, in lieu of issuing such an order, order that the sentence be suspended until an order of committal is issued, and in such case--

(a) Notwithstanding anything in this Act, the term of the sentence shall not be reckoned as commencing until an order of committal is issued;

(b) The case may at any time, and shall at intervals of not more than three months, be reconsidered by the Governor General in Council or committing authority, or an officer holding such command as the Governor General in Council may by regulation prescribe, and if on any such reconsideration it appears to the Governor General in Council or committing authority or officer that the conduct of the offender since his conviction has been such as to justify a remission of the sentence the Governor General in Council or committing authority or officer shall remit the whole or any part of it;'

(c) Subject to regulations made by the Governor General in Council, the Governor General in Council or committing authority, or an officer holding such command as the Governor General in Council may by regulation prescribe, may at any time whilst the sentence is suspended issue an order of committal and thereupon the sentence shall cease to be suspended;

(d) Where a person subject to this Act, whilst a sentence on him is so suspended, is sentenced to penal servitude or imprisonment or detention for any other offence then, if he is at any time committed either under the suspended sentence or under any such subsequent sentence, and whether or not any such subsequent sentence has also been suspended, the committing authority may direct that the two sentences shall run either concurrently or consecutively, so, however, as not to cause a person to undergo imprisonment or detention for a period exceeding the aggregate of two consecutive years, and where the sentence for such other offence is a sentence of penal servitude, then, whether or not that sentence is suspended, any previous sentence of imprisonment or detention which has been suspended shall be avoided.

When a person has been sentenced to penal servitude or imprisonment or detention and an order of committal has been issued, the Governor General in Council or the committing authority, or an officer holding such command as the Governor General in Council may by regulation prescribe, may order the sentence to be suspended, and in such case the person whose sentence is suspended shall be discharged and the currency of the sentence shall be suspended until he is again committed under the same sentence, and the foregoing paragraphs (b), (c) and (d) of this section shall apply in like manner as in the case where a sentence has been suspended before an order of committal has been issued.

Where a sentence is suspended, under this section, whether before or after committal, the Governor General in Council or, subject to any regulation or direction which may be issued by the Governor General in Council, the committing authority or officer by whom the sentence is suspended may, notwithstanding anything in section fifty-three of this Act, direct that any penalty which is involved by the punishment of penal servitude or imprisonment or detention either shall be or shall not be remitted or suspended.

Place of imprisonment may be changed

75. Whenever it is deemed expedient it shall be lawful for the Governor General in Council, the Officer Commanding the Indian Navy, or senior naval officer present by any order in writing from time to time to change the place of confinement of any offender imprisoned or sentenced to be imprisoned or detained in pursuance of this Act or of any offender undergoing or sentenced to undergo detention, and the gaoler or other person having the custody of such offender shall immediately on the receipt of such order remove such offender to the gaol, prison, or house of correction, or, in the case of an offender undergoing or sentenced to undergo detention, to the naval detention quarters mentioned in the said order, or shall deliver him over to naval custody for the purpose of the offender being removed to such prison or naval detention quarters; and every gaoler or keeper of such last-mentioned prison, gaol, or house of correction or naval detention quarter shall, upon being furnished with a copy of such order of removal, attested by a Secretary to the Government of India for the time being, receive into his custody and shall confine pursuant to such sentence or order every such offender.

Expenses of removal or subsistence of prisoners

76. The gaoler or other person removing any offender in pursuance of such order shall be allowed for the charges of such removal a sum not exceeding twelve annas a mile, and when any offender is not confined in a naval prison or naval detention quarters the gaoler or other person in whose custody any such offender may be shall receive such an allowance as the Governor General in Council shall from time to time direct for every day that such offender is in his custody, to be applied towards his subsistence and such sum shall be paid to the said gaoler or other person under the authority of the Governor General in Council, upon the application in writing made to the Governor General in Council by the District Magistrate or Presidency Magistrate within whose jurisdiction such gaol, prison, or house of correction shall be situate, with a copy of the sentence or order under which the offender is confined.

77. Omitted

Proviso for discharge of removal of prisoners

78. Whenever any offender is undergoing imprisonment or detention in pursuance of this Act, it shall be lawful for the Governor General in Council or where an offender is undergoing imprisonment or detention by order of his commanding officer, for such commanding officer or the Governor General in Council to give an order in writing directing that the offender be discharged; and it shall also be lawful for the Governor General in Council, and any officer commanding any of His Majesty's ships, by order in writing, to direct that any such offender be delivered over to naval custody for the purpose of being brought before a court-martial, either as a witness, or for trial or otherwise, and such offender shall accordingly on the production of any such order, be discharged; or be delivered over to such custody.

Proviso as to time of detention in naval custody

79. The time during which any offender under sentence of imprisonment or detention is detained in naval custody shall be reckoned as imprisonment or detention under his sentence for whatever purpose he is so detained; and the governor, gaoler, keeper, or superintendent who shall deliver over any such offender shall again receive him from naval custody, so that he may undergo the remainder of his punishment.

In case of insanity prisoners to be removed to some lunatic asylum

80. If any person imprisoned or undergoing detention by virtue of this Act shall become insane, and a certificate to that effect shall be given by two physicians or surgeons, the Governor General in Council shall, by warrant, direct the removal of such person to such lunatic asylum or other proper receptacle for insane persons in British India as he may judge proper for the unexpired term of his imprisonment or detention; and if any such person shall in the same manner be certified to be again of sound mind, the Governor General in Council may issue a warrant for his being removed to such prison or place of confinement or in the case of a person sentenced to detention, such naval detention quarters as may be deemed expedient, to undergo the remainder of his punishment, and every gaoler or keeper of any prison, gaol, or house of correction shall receive him accordingly. This section shall not apply to persons imprisoned in England.

The Governor General in Council may set apart buildings and ship as naval prison

81. (1) The Governor General in Council may set apart any buildings or vessels, or any parts thereof, as naval prisons or naval detention quarters, and any buildings or vessels, or parts of buildings or vessels, so set apart as naval prisons or naval detention quarters, as the case may be, shall be deemed to be naval prisons or naval detention quarters respectively within the meaning of this Act.

(2) The Governor General in Council shall have the same power and authority in respect of naval prisons and naval detention quarters respectively as one of His Majesty's Principal Secretaries of State has in relation to military prisons and detention barracks respectively under section one hundred and thirty-three of the Army Act, 1881, and that section shall apply as if it were herein re-enacted with the substitution of "the Governor General in Council" for " a Secretary of State," and of "naval" for "military," and of "naval detention

quarters" for "detention barrack," and rules and regulations may be made accordingly by the Governor General in Council.

Penalties in aiding escape or attempt to escape of prisoners and on breach of prison regulations

82. If any person shall convey or cause to be conveyed into any such naval prison or any such naval detention quarters any arms, tools, or instruments, or any mask or other disguise to facilitate the escape of any prisoner or person undergoing detention or by any means whatever shall aid any prisoner or person undergoing detention to escape or in an attempt to escape from such prison or naval detention quarters, whether an escape be actually made or not, such person shall be punished with imprisonment, which may be either rigorous or simple, for any term not exceeding two years, or suffer penal servitude for any term not exceeding fourteen years; and if any person shall bring or attempt to bring into such prison or naval detention quarters, in contravention of the rules, any spirituous or fermented liquor, he shall for every such offence be liable to a penalty not exceeding two hundred rupees and not less than one hundred rupees; and if any shall bring into such prison or naval detention quarters or to or for any prisoner or person undergoing detention, without the knowledge of the officer having charge or command thereof, any money, clothing, provisions, tobacco, letters, papers, or other articles not allowed by the rules of the prison or naval detention quarters, to be in the possession of a prisoner or person undergoing detention, or shall throw into the said prison or naval detention quarters, any such articles, or by desire of any prisoner or person undergoing detention, without the sanction of the said officer, shall carry out of the prison or naval detention quarters any of the articles aforesaid, he shall for every such offence be liable to a penalty not exceeding fifty rupees; and if any person shall interrupt any officer of such prison or naval detention quarters in the execution of his duty, or shall aid or excite any person to assault, resist, or interrupt any such officer, he shall for every such offence be liable to a penalty not exceeding fifty rupees, or if the offender be a prisoner or person undergoing detention, he shall be punished with imprisonment, which may be either rigorous or simple, for any time not exceeding six calendar months, in addition to so much of the time for which he was originally sentenced as may be then unexpired, and every such penalty shall he applied as the Governor General in Council shall direct, any law, statute, charter, or custom to the contrary notwithstanding

Penalty as regard gaolers, etc

83. Every governor, gaoler, and keeper of any prison, gaol, or house of correction or of any naval detention quarters, and every officer having the charge or command of any place, ship, or vessel for imprisonment, who shall, without lawful excuse, refuse or neglect to receive or confine, remove, discharge, or deliver up any offender against the provisions of this Act, or any of them, shall incur for every such refusal or neglect a penalty not exceeding one thousand rupees and every such penalty shall be applied as the Governor General in Council shall direct, any law, statute, charter, or custom to the contrary notwithstanding.

PART VI

SUPPLEMENTARY PROVISIONS

Short title

84. This Act may be cited for all purposes as the Naval Discipline Act.

Extent and repeal

85. Except as otherwise provided, this Act shall be in force within the United Kingdom; and as regards the United Kingdom the enactments described in the schedule to this Act shall be repealed from and after one calendar month from the passing hereof; and as regards elsewhere this Act shall be in force and the said enactments shall be repealed, from and after six calendar months from the passing hereof.

Definition and terms

86. In the construction of this Act, unless there be something in the context or subject matter repugnant to or inconsistent with such construction,

"Admiralty," or "the Lords of the Admiralty," shall mean the Lord High Admiral for the time being of the United Kingdom of Great Britain and Ireland, and when there shall be no such Lord High Admiral in office, any two or more of the Commissioners for executing the office of Lord High Admiral of the United Kingdom;

"Officer" shall mean an officer belonging to one of His Majesty's ships, and shall include a subordinate and a warrant officer, other than a warrant officer, Class II, of the Royal Marines, and shall include also a person holding any such position in the Indian Naval Volunteer Reserve during and in respect of the time when he is serving in the Indian Navy, but shall not extend to petty and non-commissioned officers;

When the words "superior officer" are used in this Act they shall be held to include all officers, warrant officers, petty and non-commissioned officers.

Persons subject to this Act

87. Every person in or belonging to His Majesty's Navy, and borne on the books of any one of His Majesty's ships in commission and every member of the Indian Naval Volunteer Reserve during and in respect of the time when he is serving in the Indian Navy, whether for training or exercise or having , been called up for any duty or service for which as a member of such Reserve he is liable, shall be subject to this Act; and all other persons hereby or by any other Act made liable thereto shall be triable and punishable under the provisions of this Act.

Land and air forces embarked as passengers

88. His Majesty's land and air forces, when embarked on board any of His Majesty's ships, shall be subject to the provision of this Act to such extent and under such regulations as His Majesty, His heirs and successors, by any Order or Orders in Council shall at any time or times direct.

Other persons embarked as passengers

89. All other persons ordered to be received or being passengers on board any of His Majesty's ships shall be deemed to be persons subject to this Act, under such regulations as the Governor General in Council may from time to time direct.

Provisions respecting discipline in ships in His Majesty's service in war

90. With respect to vessels in His Majesty's service in time of war, whether belonging to His Majesty, or not, which are not wholly manned by naval ratings, but being either armed or under the command of an officer in His Majesty's naval service, the following provisions shall take effect if in any case the Governor General in Council thinks fit so to direct, and where such direction is given the same shall be specified in the ship's articles:

(1) Every person borne on the books of any such vessel shall be subject to this Act;

(2) Any offence committed by any such person shall be tried and punished as the like offence might be tried and punished if committed by any person in or belonging to His Majesty's Navy and borne on the books of any of His Majesty's ships in commission;

(3) Every such offender who is to be tried by court-martial shall be placed under all necessary restraint until he can be tried by court-martial;

(4) On applicat.ion made to the Governor General in Council, or to the Officer Commanding the Indian Navy or senior officer of any of His Majesty's ships or vessels of war abroad authorised to assemble and hold courts-martial, the Governor General in Council, Officer Commanding the Indian Navy, or senior officer (as the ease may be) shall assemble and hold a court-martial for the trial of the offender;

(5) The officer commanding every such vessel shall have the same power in respect of all other persons on the books thereof, or for the time on board the same, as the officer commanding one of His Majesty's ships has for the time being in respect of the officers and crew thereof or other persons on board the same;

Provided that in the absence of the officer commanding such vessel, the officer commanding the ship or vessel or station in which such person may for the time being be held in custody shall have such power as aforesaid;

(6) The Officer Commanding the Indian Navy and senior naval officer in His Majesty's service shall have the same powers over the officers and crew of every such vessel as they have for the time being over the officers and crew of any of His Majesty's ships.

Relations between military, naval and air forces acting together

90A. (1) Where an officer or non-commissioned officer, not below the rank of sergeant, is a member of a body of His Majesty's military forces acting with, or is attached to any body of His Majesty's naval forces under such conditions as may be prescribed by regulations made by the Admiralty and Army Council, then, for the purposes of command and discipline and for the purposes of the provisions of this Act relating to superior officers, he shall, in relation to such body of His Majesty's naval forces as aforesaid, be treated, and may exercise all such powers (other than powers of punishment), as if he were a naval officer or petty officer, as the case may be.

(1A) Where an officer or non-commissioned officer, not below the rank of sergeant, is a member of a body of His Majesty's air force acting with any body of His Majesty's naval forces under such conditions as may be prescribed by regulations made by the Admiralty and Air Council, then, for the purposes of command and discipline and for the purposes of the command and discipline and for the purposes of the provisions of this Act relating to superior officers, he shall, in relation to such body of His Majesty's naval forces as aforesaid, be treated, and may exercise all such powers (other than powers of punishment), as if he were a naval officer or petty officer, as the case may be.

(2) Where any naval officer or seaman is a member of body of His Majesty's naval forces acting with or is attached to any body of His Majesty's military forces under such conditions as may be prescribed by regulations made by the Admiralty and Army Council, then, for the purposes of command and discipline and for the purposes of the provisions of this Act relating to superior officers, the officers and non-commissioned officers, not below the rank of sergeant, of such military body shall, in relation to him, be treated, and may exercise all such powers (other than powers of punishment), as if they were naval officers and petty officers.

(2A) Where any naval officer or seaman is a member of a body of His Majesty's naval forces acting with any body of His Majesty's air force under such conditions as may be prescribed by regulations made by the Admiralty and Air Council, then, for the purposes of command and discipline and for the purposes of the provisions of this Act relating to superior officers, the officers and non-commissioned officers, not below the rank of sergeant, of such body of the air force shall, in relation to him, be treated, and may exercise all such powers (other than powers of punishment) as if they were naval officers and petty officers.

(3) The relative rank of naval and military and air force officers, petty officers, and non-commissioned officers shall, for the purposes of this section, be such as is provided by the King's Regulations and Admiralty Instructions for the time being in force.

Provisions respecting naval officers and seamen in ships of self-governing Dominions

90B. (1) Any person in or belonging to His Majesty's Navy and any officer or man of the Royal Marines who, by order of the Admiralty or of the Commander-in-Chief or the Senior Naval Officer present on a foreign station, is serving in a ship of or belonging to the naval forces of a self-governing Dominion or of India (provided such ship is not at the time placed at the disposal of the Admiralty), or in a naval establishment of a self-governing Dominion or of India or who is on board such ship or in such establishment as aforesaid awaiting passage or conveyance to any destination shall, for all purposes of command and discipline, be subject to the laws and customs for the time being applicable to the ships and naval forces of such self-governing Dominion or of India.

(2) For the purposes of this section, the expression "self-governing Dominion" includes the Dominion of Canada, the Commonwealth of Australia, the Dominion of New Zealand, the Union of South Africa, and Newfoundland.

Persons serving in a ship of the Royal or Dominion Navy to be subject to the laws and customs therof

90C. (1) Any person in or belonging to the Indian Navy, who, by order of the Governor General in Council, is serving in a ship belonging to His Majesty's Navy or to the naval forces of a self-governing Dominion or in a naval establishment of His Majesty's Navy or a self-governing Dominion, or who is on board any such ship or in any such establishment awaiting passage or conveyance to any destination shall, for all purposes of command and discipline, be subject to the laws and customs, for the time being applicable to the Royal Navy or the ships and naval forces of the self-governing Dominion, as the case may be.

(2) For the purposes of this section, the expression "self-governing Dominion" includes the Dominion of Canada, the Commonwealth of Australia, the Dominion of New Zealand, the Union of South Africa, and Newfoundland.

Crews or ships lost or destroyed

91. When any one of His Majesty's ships shall be wrecked or lost or destroyed, or taken by the enemy, such ship shall, for the purposes of this Act, be deemed to remain in commission until her crew shall be regularly removed into some other of His Majesty's ships of war, or until a court-martial shall have been held, pursuant to the custom of the navy in such cases, to inquire into the cause of the wreck, loss, destruction, or capture of the said ship.

All the officers and crew of lost ship may be tried by one court

92. When no specific charge shall be made against any officer or seaman or other person in the fleet for or in respect or in consequences of such wreck, loss, destruction, or capture, it shall be lawful to try all the officers and crew, or all the surviving officers and crew of any such ship, together, before one and the same court, and to call upon all or any of them when upon their trial to give evidence on oath or affirmation before the court touching any of the matters then under inquiry, but no officer or seaman or other person shall be obliged to give any evidence which may tend to criminate himself.

Or by separate court

93. When deemed necessary by the Governor General in Council or any officer authorised to order courts-martial, separate courts-martial shall be held for the trial of some one or more of such officers and crew for or in respect or in consequence of the wreck, loss, destruction, or capture of any such ship.

For subsequent offence separate court

94. For any offence or offences committed by any officer or seaman, or officers and seamen, after the wreck, loss, destruction, or capture of ally such ship, a separate court-martial shall be held for the trial of such offender or offenders.

Pay of crews of ships lost or taken

95. When any ship of His Majesty shall he wrecked, lost, or otherwise destroyed, or taken by the enemy, if it shall appear by the sentence of a court-martial that the crew of such ship did, in the case of a ship wrecked or lost, do their utmost save her or get her off, and in the case of a ship taken by the enemy did their utmost to defend themselves, and that they have, since the wreck, destruction, loss, or capture of such ship, behaved themselves well, and been obedient to their officers, then all the pay of such crews, or of such portion of such crews as have behaved themselves well and been obedient their officers, shall be continued until the time of their being discharged or removed into other ships of His Majesty, or dying.

When ship of senior officer is lost he may dispose of officers and crew of lost ship

96. If the ship of any officer ordered to command any two or more of His Majesty's ships shall be wrecked, lost, or otherwise destroyed, such officer shall continue in the command of any ship or ships which at the time of his ship being wrecked, lost, or destroyed was or were under his command, and it shall be lawful for the such officer to order the surviving officers and crew of the wrecked, lost, or destroyed ship to join any other ship under his command, or to distribute them among the other ships under his command, if more than one, and such officer shall, until he meets with some other officer senior to himself, have the same power and authority in all respects as if his ship had not been wrecked, lost, or destroyed.

Restriction on arrest of seamen, etc, for debt

97. It shall not be lawful for any person to arrest any petty arrest officer or seaman, non-commissioned officer of marines or marine belonging to any ship of His Majesty, by any warrant, process, or writ issued in any part of His Majesty's dominions for any debt, unless the debt was contracted at a time when the debtor did not belong to his Majesty's service, nor unless before the issuing of the warrant, process, or writ, the plaintiff in the suit or some person on his behalf has made an affidavit in the court out of which it is issued, that the debt justly due to the plaintiff (over and above all costs) was contracted at a time when the debtor did not belong to His Majesty's service, nor unless a memorandum of such affidavit is marked on the back of the warrant, process, or writ.

Discharge from arrest

98. If any petty officer or seaman, non-commissioned officer of marines or marine, is arrested in contravention of the provisions of the last foregoing section, the court out of which the warrant, process, or writ issues, or any judge thereof, may, on complaint by the party arrested, or by his superior officer, investigate the case on oath or and if satisfied that the arrest was made n contravention of the provisions of the last foregoing section, make an order for the immediate discharge of the party arrested, without fee, and may award to the complainant the costs of his complaint, to be taxed by the proper officer, for the recovery whereof he shall have the like remedy as the plaintiff in the suit would have on judgment being given in his favour, with costs.

Liability of seamen, etc, for maintenance of wife and children

98A. (1) A person subject to this Act shall be liable to contribute to the maintenance of his wife and of his children, legitimate or illegitimate, to the same extent as if he were not so subject; but execution in respect of any such liability or any decree or order in respect of such maintenance shall not issue against his person, pay, arms, ammunition, equipments, instruments, or clothing.

(2) Where---

(a) It appears to the satisfaction of the Governor General in Council or any person deputed by him for ,the purpose that a person subject to this Act has deserted or left in destitute circumstances, without reasonable cause, his wife or any of his legitimate children under fourteen years of age; or .

(b) Any decree or order is made under any law for payment by a man who is or subsequently becomes subject to this Act either of the cost of the maintenance of his wife or child, or of the cost of any relief given to his wife or child by way of loan, and a copy of such decree or order is sent to the Governor General in Council or any person deputed by him for the purpose;

the Governor General in Council or the person so deputed may direct to be deducted from the pay of the person so subject to this Act, and to be appropriated towards the maintenance of his wife or children, or in liquidation of the sum adjudged to be paid by such decree or order, as the case may be, in such manner as the Governor General in Council or the person so deputed may think fit, a portion of such pay, at his discretion, but the amount deducted shall not exceed the amount fixed by the decree or order (if any), and shall not be a higher rate than the rates fixed by rules made in this behalf by the Governor General in Council:

Provided that no such deductions from pay in liquidation of a sum adjudged to be paid by a decree or order as aforesaid shall be ordered unless the Governor General in Council, or the person deputed by him is satisfied that the person against whom the decree or order was made has had a reasonable opportunity of appearing himself, or has appeared by a duly authorised legal representative, to defend the case before the court by which the decree or order was made, and a certificate, purporting to be a certificate of the commanding officer of the ship on which he was or is serving, or on the books of which he was or is borne, that the person has been prevented by the requirements of the service from attending at a hearing of any such case shall be evidence of the fact unless the contrary is proved.

Where any arrears have accumulated in respect of sums adjudged to be paid by any such decree or order as aforesaid whilst the person against whom the decree or order was made was serving under this Act, whether or not deductions in respect thereof have been made from his pay under this section, then after he has ceased so to serve an order of committal shall not be made in respect of those arrears unless the court is satisfied that he is able ,or has, since he has ceased to serve, been to pay the arrears or any part thereof and has failed to do so.

(3) Where a proceeding under any law is instituted against 'a person subject to this Act for the purpose of enforcing against him any such liability as above in this section mentioned, the process may be served on the commanding officer of the ship on which he is serving or on the books of which such person is borne, or where, by reason of the ship being at sea or otherwise, it is impracticable to serve the process on such commanding officer, the process may, after not less than three weeks' notice to the Governor General in Council, be served by being sent to a Secretary to the Government of India for transmission to such commanding officer, but such service shall not be valid unless there is left therewith in the hands of such commanding officer or, Governor General in Council such sum of money, if any (to be adjudged as costs incurred in obtaining the decree or order if made against the person on whom the process is issued), as may be fixed by the Governor General in Council as being 'necessary to enable him to attend the hearing of the case and to return to his ship or quarters, and such sum may be expended by the commanding officer for that purpose, and no process whatever under any law in any proceeding in this section mentioned shall be valid against a person subject to this Act if served after such person is under orders for service on a foreign station.

The production of a certificate of the receipt of the process purporting to be signed by such commanding officer as aforesaid shall be evidence that the process has been duly served unless the contrary is proved.

Where, by a decree or order sent to the Governor General in Council or officer in accordance with sub-section (2) of this section, the person against whom the decree or order is made is adjudged to pay as costs incurred in obtaining the decree or order any sum so left with the process as aforesaid, the Governor General in Council may cause a sum equal to the sum so left to be paid in liquidation of the sum so adjudged to be paid as costs, and the amount so paid by the Governor General in Council shall be a public debt from the person against whom the decree or order was made, and, without prejudice to any other method of recovery, may be recovered by reduction from his pay, in addition to those mentioned in sub-section (2) of this section.

(4) This section shall not apply to persons subject to this Act where such persons are officers.

(5) In this section the expression "pay" includes all sums payable to a man in respect of his services other than allowances in lieu of lodgings, rations, provisions, and clothing.

PART VII

SAVING CLAUSE

Nothing to take away prerogative of the Crown, or rights or power of Admiralty

100. Nothing in this Act shall take away, abridge, or control, further or otherwise than as expressly provided by this Act, any right, power, or prerogative of His Majesty the King in right of His Crown, or in right of His Office of Admiralty or any right or power of the Admiralty.

Act not to supersede authority of ordinary courts

101. Nothing in this Act contained shall be deemed or taken to supersede or affect the authority or power of any court or tribunal of ordinary civil or criminal jurisdiction, or any officer thereof, in His Majesty's dominions, in respect of any offence mentioned in this Act which may be punishable or cognizable by the common or statute law, or to prevent any person being proceeded against and punished in respect of any such offence otherwise than under this Act.

PART VIII

PRINTING CLAUSE

Printing and construction of Naval Discipline Act

102. (1) Every enactment and word which is directed by any Act amending this Act to be substituted for or added to any portion of this Act shall form part of this Act in the place assigned it by the amending Act, and this Act and all Acts which refer thereto shall, after the commencement of the amending Act, be construed as if that enactment or word had been originally enacted in this Act in the place so assigned, and, where it is substituted for another enactment or word, had been so enacted in lieu of that enactment or word, and as if this Act had been enacted with the omission of any enactment or word which is directed by the amending Act to be repealed or omitted from this Act, and the expression "this Act" shall be construed accordingly.

(2) A copy of this Act with every such enactment and word inserted in the place so assigned, and with the omission of any portion of this Act directed by any such amending Act as aforesaid to be repealed or omitted from this Act, shall be prepared and certified by the Clerk of the Parliament and deposited with the rolls of Parliament, and His Majesty's printers shall print in accordance with the copy so certified all copies of this Act which are printed after the commencement of such amending Act.

(3) A reference in any enactment, Order in Council, or other document, to the Naval Discipline Act shall, unless the context otherwise requires, be construed as a reference to this Act as amended by any enactment for the time being in force.

The Military Lunatics Act, 1877

ACT No. XI OF 1877

[LEGISLATIVE DEPARTMENT]

THE following Act of the Governor-General of India in Council received the assent of His Excellency the Governor-General on the Thirty-first May 1877, and is hereby promulgated for general information:-

An Act to facilitate the admission of Military Lunatics into Asylums

Preamble

WHEREAS it is expedient to facilitate the admission of European Military Lunatics into asylums, and to amend the law now in force with regard to the admission thereto of Native Military Lunatics; It is hereby enacted as follows:-

Short title

1. This Act may be called the Military Lunatics Act, 1877.[1]

Local extent

It extends to the whole of British India, and, so far as regards subjects of Her Majesty, to the dominions of Native Princes and States in India in alliance with Her Majesty;

Commencement

And it shall come into force on the passing thereof.[2]

Repeal of Act XXI of 1872

2. Act XXI of 1872 (to facilitate the admission of Native Military Lunatics into Asylums) shall be repealed.

1 The Military Lunatics Act, 1877 was applicable as a personal law to British subjects in the feudatory Native States of India, and it extended territorially to the whole of British India, except the Shan States and the Scheduled Districts of the Santhal Parganas, the Pargana of Spiti, Angul, and the Chittagong Hill Tracts.

2 Sections 2 and 9 of the Military Lunatics Act, 1877 were repealed by the Repealing and Amending Act, 1891 (XII of 1891), and ss. 4, 5 and 6 by the Repealing and Amending Act, 1903 (I of 1903). There remained, therefore only ss. 1, 3, 7 and 8.

Procedure in respect of European officer or soldier declared a lunatic

3. Whenever any European officer, Warrant officer, Non-commissioned officer, soldier or other person subject to the provisions of the Act for punishing Mutiny and Desertion and for the better payment of the Army and their quarters for the time being in force has been declared a lunatic, in accordance with the provisions of the military regulations of the Presidency to which he belongs, and has been ordered to be forwarded to any one of the Presidency towns, and it appears to one of the Surgeons-General, either of the British Forces or of the Indian Medical Service, according to the Presidency and the service to which the said lunatic belongs, that it is inexpedient that he should be removed to England, or that he should be detained in military custody until he can be conveniently sent to England, such Surgeon-General may, if he think fit, make an order under his hand for the reception of the said lunatic into the Lunatic Asylum at Bhawanipur, Madras or Bombay, or such other Lunatic Asylum as may be duly authorized for the purpose by the Governor-General in Council; and the officer in charge of such Asylum shall receive the lunatic in the asylum, and detain him therein until he is discharged therefrom, in accordance with the local military regulations in force for the time being, or until the Surgeon-General applies for his transfer to the military authorities in view to his removal to England.

Report in case of Native officer or soldier appearing to be insane

4. Whenever any Native officer, Non-commissioned officer or soldier appears to be insane, the officer commanding the regiment or detachment to which he belongs shall report the case to the general officer commanding the division or district or force in which such regiment or detachment is serving.

Examination of Native by committee

5. Such general officer shall thereupon cause the said Native to be examined by a committee composed of at least two medical officers, or (if this be impracticable) by a regimental committee comprising the officer in command of the wing or squadron to which the Native belongs and the medical officer in charge of the corps or detachment of which such wing or squadron forms part.

Procedure on Native being found by committee to be insane

6. If the said committee or regimental committee (as the case may be) are satisfied that the Native is insane, the officer commanding the division or district or force may, if he think fit, make an order under his hand for the reception of the said Native into a Lunatic Asylum, and shall then send him thither under military escort; and the officer in charge of such asylum shall receive the Native into the asylum and detain him therein until he is discharged therefrom in accordance with the local military regulations in force for the time being.

Procedure for discharge of European or Native military lunatic

7. Whenever it appears to the officer in charge of a Lunatic Asylum that the discharge of a military lunatic, whether European or Native, is necessary, either on account of his recovery, or for any other purpose, such person shall be brought before the visitors of the asylum, and on the visitors recording their opinion that the discharge should be made, the general officer commanding the

division, district, or force, or other officer authorized to order the admission of military lunatics into asylums, shall forthwith direct him to be discharged, and such discharge shall take place in accordance with the local military regulations in force for the time being.

Payment of expenses of lunatic

8. The Paymaster of the military circle within which any such asylum is situate shall pay to the officer in charge of such asylum the expense of the lodging, maintenance, clothing and medicine of every lunatic, whether European or Native, received and detained under this Act.

Legalization of past receptions in asylum

9. All military lunatics heretofore received into Lunatic Asylums shall be deemed to have been so received in accordance with law.

The Armed Forces (Emergency Duties) Act, 1947

ACT NO. 15 OF 1947[1]

[20 March 1947]

An Act to enable duties in connection with vital services to be imposed in an emergency on an Armed Forces [of the Crown].[2]

WHEREAS it is expedient to enable duties in connection with vital services to be imposed in the emergency on the Armed Forces [of the Crown].[3]

It is hereby enacted as follows:—

1. Short title and extend.—This Act may be called the Armed Forces (Emergency Duties) Act, 1947.

2. Emergency duties of Armed Forces.—(1) The Central Government may, by notification in the Official Gazette, declare any specified service [4][in a State] to be a service of vital importance to the community:

Provided that such notification shall remain in force for one month in the first instance, but may be extended, from time to time, by a like notification.

(2) Upon a declaration being made under sub-section (1) and until it is rescinded, it shall be the duty of every person subject to [the Army Act, 1950 (46 of 1950) or the Air Force Act, 1950 (45 of 1950)], or [5] [the Navy Act, 1957 (62 of 1957)],[6] to obey any command given by any superior officer in relation to employment upon or in connection with the service specified in

1 The Act was extended to the new Provinces and merged States by the Merged States (Laws) Act, 1949 (59 of 1949), s. 3 and Schedule to the States of Manipur, Tripura and Vindhya Pradesh by the Part C States (Laws) Act, 1950 (30 of 1950), s. 3, in Pondicherry on 1-10-1963 *vide* Reg. 8 of 1965, s. 3 and the Schedule I; to Lakshadweep (w.e.f. 1 October 1987); vide Reg. 8 of 1965, s. 3 and Schedule, to Goa, Daman and Diu with modifications by Reg. 12 of 1962, s. 3 and the Schedule, and in Dadra and Nagar Haveli (w.e.f. 1 July 1965) by Reg. 6 of 1963, s. 2 and the First Schedule.

2 The words "of the Crown" were omitted by the A.O. 1950.

3 The words "of the Crown" were omitted by the A.O. 1950.

4 Substituted by Act 3 of 1951, s. 3 and the Schedule, for "in a Part A State or a Part C State or, if so requested by the Government of a Part B State any specified service in that State".

5 The words "the Naval Discipline Act, in the form in which it is set forth in the First Schedule to" were omitted by the A.O. 1950.

6 Substituted by Act 58 of 1960, s. 3 and the Second Schedule, for "the Indian Navy (Discipline) Act, 1934".

the declaration; and every such command shall be deemed to be a lawful command within the meaning and for the purposes of the said Acts.

3. Validation of certain past commands.—Every command given after 30 September 1946, and before the commencement of this Act, to any person referred to in sub-section (2) of section 2 by any superior officer in relation to employment upon or in connection with any such service as the central Government may, by notification in the Official Gazette, specify in his behalf, shall be deemed to have been a lawful command within the meaning and for the purposes of the Acts referred to in that sub-section, so, however, that no such person shall be punished by reason only of his not having obeyed any such command.

Bibliography

A Collection of Statutes Relating to the East India Company: with an Appendix containing Acts and parts of Acts Relating to Shipping, Duties, etc, 1810, London: George Eyre and Andrew Strahan, pp. 1174.

Adams Phythians E. G., 1948, The Madras Soldier: 1746-1946, Madras: Government Press, pp. 215.

Adye S. Payne, 1810, A Treatise on Courts Martial, Also An essay on Military Punishments and Rewards, London: A Cundee Printer, pp. 270.

Adam John Prime, The Indian Army's British Officer Corps: 1861-1921, Unpublished Ph D Thesis, University of Leicester, February 2018, pp. 261.

Aitchison Captain John William, 1824, A General Code of the Military Regulations in force under the Presidency of Bombay, Calcutta: Mission School Press, pp. 606.

An Act for punishing Mutiny and Desertion, and for the Better Payment of the Army and their Quarters, 16 March 1855.

Aykes W. H., Vital Statistics of the East India Company's Armies in India, European and Native, *Journal of the Statistical Society of London,* Vol. 10, No. 2, May, 1847, pp. 100-131.

Badenach Walter, 1826, *Inquiry into the State of the Indian Army*, London: William Clowes, pp. 151.

Barat Amiya, 1962, *The Bengal Native Infantry: Its Organization & Discipline 1796-1852*, Calcutta: Firma K. L. Mukhopadhyay, pp. 341.

Barrow Ian, 2-17, *The East India Company 1600-1858: A Short History with Documents*, Cambridge: Hackett Publishing Company, pp. 176.

Bhatia H.S. (ed.), 1977, *Military History of British India (1607-1947)*, New Delhi: Deep and Deep Publications, pp. 256.

Biddulph Colonel J., 1901, *Stringer Lawrence: The Father of the Indian Army*, London: John Murray, pp. 143.

Bourne John Michael, The Civil and Military Patronage of the East India Company, 1784-1858, Ph D Thesis, University of Leicester, 1977, pp. 384.

Bowen Huw V., The East India Company and Military Recruitment in Britain, 1763-71, pp. 78-90. Available at: https://onlinelibrary.wiley.com/doi/10.1111/j.1468-2281.1986.tb01180.x.

Broom Captain Arthur, 1850, *History of the Rise and Progress of the Bengal Army*, Vol. I, Calcutta: W. Thacker and Co., pp. 629.

Bruce Alexander, 1717, *The Institution of Military Law: Ancient and Modern*, Edinburgh, pp. 336.

Buckle Late Captain E., (Ed. by) Kaye J. W., 1852, *Memoir of the Services of the Bengal Artillery: form the formation of the Corps to the present time*, London: Wm H Allen & Co., pp. 592.

Burrough Peter, Crime and Punishment in the British Army, 1815-1870, *The English Historical Review*, Vol. 100, No. 396, July 1985, pp. 545-571.

Byrn, John D. Jr, Crime and Punishment in the Royal Navy: Discipline on the Leeward Islands Station, 1784-1812 (England), 1987, LSU Historical Dissertations and Thesis, 4345.

Cadell Sir Patrick, 1938, *History of the Bombay Army*, London: Longmans, Green & Co., pp. 362.

Callahan Raymond, 1972, *The East India Company and Army Reform 1783-1798*, Harvard University Press, Cambridge, pp. 242.

Cameron Alan Douglas, The Vellore Mutiny, Ph D Thesis, University of Edinburgh, 1984, pp. 355.

Candler Edmund, 1919, *The Sepoy*, London: John Murray, pp. 234.

Cardew Lieut. F. G., 1903, *A Sketch of the Service of the Bengal Native Army to the Year 1895*, [Compiled in the Officer of the Adjutant General in India], Calcutta: Office of the Superintendent of Government Printing, India, pp. 576.

Cardew Alexander, 1929, *The White Mutiny: A Forgotten Episode in the History of the Indian Army*, London: Constable & Co Ltd, pp. 263.

Carnduff H.W.C., 1904, *Military and Cantonment Law in India*, Calcutta: SK Lahiri & Co, pp. (i) to (xxv).

Charter granted by Queen Elizabeth to the East India Company, Dated the 31 December 1600, in the 43rd year of Her Reign.

Chesney General Sir George, 1894, *Indian Polity: A view of the system of administration in India*, London: Longmans, Green and Co., pp. 409.

Cohen Stephen P., 1971, *The Indian Army: Its Contribution to the Development of a Nation*, Bombay: Oxford University Press, pp. 216.

Clarke Richard, 1854, *The Regulations of the Government of Fort William in Bengal in Force at the end of 1853, Vol. III, Acts from 1834 to 1853*, London: J & H Cox, Great Queen Street, pp. 559.

Clode Charled M., 1869, *The Military Forces of Crown: Their Administration and Government*, Vol. I, London: John Murray, pp. 596.

Clode Charled M., 1869, *The Military Forces of Crown: Their Administration and Government*, Vol. II, London: John Murray, pp. 804.

Clode Charles M., 1874, *The Administration of Justice under Military and Martial Law*, London: John Murray, Albemarle Street, pp. 411

Clode Charles M., 1872, *The Administration of Justice under Military and Martial Law*, London: John Murray, pp. 370.

Corrigan Gordon, 2015, *Sepoys in the Trenches: The Indian Corps on the Western Front 1914-1915*, UK: Spellmount, pp. 273.

Cox, Edmund C., 1887, *A Short History of the Bombay Presidency*, Bombay: Thacker & Co. Ltd.

Dacam, John H., 'Wanton and Torturing Punishments': Patterns of Discipline and Punishment in the Royal Navy, 1783-1815, Unpublished Ph D Thesis, the University of Hull, September 2009, pp. 266.

Dalrymple William, 2019, *The Anarchy: The East India Company, Corporate Violence, and the Pillage of an Empire*, New Delhi: Bloomsbury Publishing, pp. 522.

Dalrymple William, 2006, *The Last Mughal: The Fall of a Dynasty, Delhi, 1857*, New Delhi: Penguin, pp. 578.

David Julian Saul Markham, The Bengal Army and the Outbreak of the Indian Mutiny, Ph D Thesis, University of Glasgow, 2001, pp. 328.

David Saul, 2009, *The Bengal Army and the Outbreak of the Indian Mutiny*, New Delhi: Manohar, pp. 399.

Dowell H. H. (ed.), The Company's Marines, *The Cambridge History of India*, Vol. VI, London: Cambridge University Press, 1932, pp. 144-152.

Dowell H., 1922, *Sepoy Recruitment in the Old Madras Army*, Indian Historical Records Commission, pp. 72.

Dodwell H. H., 1932, *The Cambridge History of India, Vol. VI: The India Empire 1858-1918*, Cambridge: University Press, pp. 660.

Dutta Manas, Disciplining the Madras Army during the Early Years of the English East India Company's Dominance in South India, *Social Studies*, Vol. 4, No. 3, 2012, pp. 887-899.

Evolution of British Indian Military Organisation: From Company to Crown, available at: http://shodhganga.inflibnet.ac.in/bitstream/10603/14220/5/05_chapter%201.pdf.

Farwell Byron, 1989, *Armies of the Raj: From the Great Indian Mutiny to Independence, 1858-1947*, London: Viking, pp. 399.

Fatal Case of Military Flogging at Hounslow, (author not mentioned), *Edinb Med Surg J.*, Vol. 66 (169), 01 October 1846, pp. 395-433.

Fawcett Sir Charles, 1934, *The First Century of British Justice in India*, Oxford: Clarendon Press, pp. 269.

Featherstone Donald, A military anomaly—the Army of the East India Company 1757–1857, *The RUSI Journal*, Vol. 138, No. 1, 1993, pp.48-52.

Fisher Michael H., "Multiple meanings of 1857 for Indian in Britain," in *1857: Essays from Economic and Political Weekly*, 2008, Hyderabad: Orient Longman, pp. 81-102.

Fortescue John William, 1899, *A History of the British Army*, Vol. II, London: Macmillan and Co., Limited, pp. 629.

Garrett H.L.O., 2007, *The Trial of Bahadur Shah Zafar*, New Delhi: Roli Books, pp. 450.

Garrisi Diana, Reading dermatology in the Victorian newspaper: The performance of medical vocabulary in *The Times* correspondence column, *Journal of Science Communication*, Vol. 16(03), (2017), pp. 1-13.

Gilbert, Arthur N., Recruitment and Reform in the East India Company Army, 1760-1800, *Journal of British Studies*, Vol. 15, No. 1, Autumn, 1975, pp. 89-111.

Gorham Major, 1887, A Short Course of Military Law as Applicable to Persons Subject to the Mutiny Act, Calcutta: Thacker, Spink, and Co., pp. 217.

Grant M. J., Music and Punishment in the British Army in the Eighteenth and Nineteenth Centuries, The World of Music, new series, Vol. 2, No. 1, 2013, pp. 9-30.

Grodzinski John R., Bloody Provost: Discipline During the War of 1812, Canadian Military History, Vol. 16: Issue 4, Article 3, 2007, available at: http://scholars.wlu.ca/cmh/vol16/iss4/3.

Grose Francis, 1788, Military Antiquities Respecting A History of English Army: From The Conquest to the Present Time, Vol. I, London: S. Hooper, pp. 412.

Grose Francis, 1788, Military Antiquities Respecting A History of English Army: From The Conquest to the Present Time, Vol. II, London: S. Hooper, pp. 621.

Haig Lt Col Wolesley, The Armies of the East India Company, in Dowell H. H. (ed.), The Cambridge History of I*ndia, Vol. VI*, London: Cambridge University Press, 1932, pp. 153-166.

Hannay David, 1914, *Naval Courts Martial,* Cambridge University Press, pp. 210.

Hannay David, 1898, *A Short history of the Royal Navy 1217-1688,* Vol. I, London: Methuen &

Co., pp. 487.

Harriet Sherwood, Indians in the trenches: voices of forgotten army are finally to be heard, *The Guardian*, 27 October 2018.

Heathcote T.A., 2013, *The Military in British India: The Development of British Land Forces in South Asia 1600-1947*, South Yorkshire: The Praetorian Press, pp. 232.

Henderson Robert, "Terror of Example" Crime and Punishment in the British Army in 1812, Part One: Capital Punishment, available at: http://www.warof1812.ca/punish1.htm.

Hoffman Gary L., Court-Martial Jurisdiction and the Constitution: An Historical and Textual Analysis, *Creighton Law Review*, Vol. 21, 1887, pp. 43-107.

Holmes T. Rice, 1904, *A History of Indian Mutiny*, London: Macmillan and Co. Ltd. (fifth edition), pp. 659.

Holwell J.Z., 1778, *A Genuine Narrative of the Deplorable Deaths: 20 June 1756*, London: Strand, pp. 56.

Horbaly Jan, Court Martial Jurisdiction, Ph D Dissertation Yale Law School, 1986, pp. 755.

Hough Captain William, 1834, *The Practice of Courts-Martial and Other Military Courts,* Calcutta: Thacker and Co., pp. 350.

Hough Captain William, 1825, *The Practice of Courts-Martial and the Legal Exposition and Military Explanation of the Mutiny Act and Articles of War,* London: Kingsbury, Pahbury and Allen, pp. 1000.

Hough Major William, 1839, *Military Law Authorities*, Calcutta: W Thacker and Co., pp. 255.

Hough Major William, 1853, *Political and Military Events in British India*, London: WM H. Allem & Co., pp. 344.

Huges Captain R.M., 1845, *The Duties of Judge Advocates*, Compiled from Her Majesty's and the Hon. East India Company's Military Regulations, London: Smith, Elder & Co., pp. 273.

Hunter Sir William Wilson, 1919, *A history of British India*, Vol. I, London: Longman, Green and Co., pp. 476.

Hunter Sir William Wilson, 1920, *A history of British India*, Vol. I, London: Longman, Green and Co., pp. 419.

Ilbert Sir, Courtenay, 1907, *The Government of India: Being a Digest of the Statute Law Relating thereto with Historical Introduction and Explanatory Matter*, Oxford: Claredon Press, pp. 454.

Ilbert Sir Courtenay, 1922, *The Government of India: A brief Historical Survey of Parliamentary Legislation Relating to India*, Oxford: Claredon Press, pp. 144.

Innes Lieut. Col. P. R., 1885, *The History of the Bengal European regiment, now the Royal Munster Fusiliers*, London: Simpkin, Marshall & Co., pp. 572.

Irvin William, 1903, The Army of the Indian Moghuls: Its Organization and Administration, London: Luzac & Co., pp. 32.

James Lunt (ed.), From Sepoy to Subedar, Being the Life and Adventures of Subedar Sita Ram, a Native Officer of the Bengal Army written and related by himself, Translated and First Published by Lieutenant-Colonel Norgate, Bengal Staff Corps at Lahore, 1873, pp. 215.

Kaye John William, 1853, The Administration of The East India Company: A History of Indian Progress, London: Richard Bentley, pp. 712.

Law Commission of India: Fifth Report on British Statutes Applicable to India, 1957, pp. 94.

Lieber G. Norman, Cashiering and Dismissal, Judge Advocate US Army, available at: https://www.forgottenbooks.com/en/download/CashieringandDismissal_10504221.pdf.

Lovett Major A.C. (Painted by), MacMunn Major G. F.(Described by), 1911, The Armies of India, London: Adam and Charles Black, pp. 224.

Low, Charles Rathbone, 1877, *History of the Indian Navy, Vol. I*, 1600-1830, London: Richard Bentley and Son, pp. 542.

Low, Charles Rathbone, 1877, *History of the Indian Navy, Vol. II*, 1831-1863, London: Richard Bentley and Son, pp. 596.

MacMunn Sir George, 1931, *The Indian Mutiny in Perspective*, London: G. Bell & Sons Ltd, pp. 276.

Malleson Colonel G.B., 1891, *The Indian Mutiny of 1857*, London: Seelay and Co. Limited, pp. 412.

Malleson G.B., 1914, *Decisive Battles of India*, third edition, London: Reeves & Turner, pp. 454.

Manual of Military Law, War Office, 1907, London: Harrison and Sons.

Marshall Henry, 1846, *The Military Miscellany; Comprehending a History of the Recruiting of the Army, Military Punishments*, London, pp. 375.

Marston Daniel P. and Chandar S. Sundaram (ed.), 2007, *A Military History of India and South Asia: From the East India Company to the Nuclear Era*, London: Praeger Security International, pp. 235.

Mason Philip, 2004, *A Matter of Honour: An Account of the Indian Army, Its Officers and Men*, Dehradun: Natraj Publishers, pp. 580.

Mawson John (compiled by), 1851, *Records of the Indian Command of General Sir Charles James Napeir*, Calcutta: R. C. Lepage and Company, pp. 244.

McArthur John, 1805, *Principles and Practice of Naval and Military Courts Martial*, Vol. I,

London: J Butterworth, pp. 450.

McArthur John, 1805, *Principles and Practice of Naval and Military Courts Martial*, Vol. II, London: J Butterworth, pp. 573.

McArthur John, 1792, *A Treatise of the Principles and Practice of Naval Courts Martial*, London: Whieldon and Butterworth, pp. 573.

McLean Ridley, Historical Sketch of Military Law, *Journal of Criminal Law and Criminology*, Vol. 8, May 1917-March 1918, p. 27-32.

Mcrindle J.W., 1893, *The Invasion of India by Alexander the Great*, Westminster: Archibald Constable and Company, pp. 432.

Menezes Lt Gen S.L., 1999, Fidelity and Honour: The Indian Army form Seventeenth to the Twenty-first Century, Delhi: Oxford University Press, pp. 701.

Mersky Roy M. and Jacobstein J. Myron (ed.), 1859, Courts Martial, Classics in Legal History, Vol. 18, New York: William S. Hein & Co. pp. 459.

Moor Edward, 1801, A Compilation of Bombay Army (Discipline and Expenditure), Bombay: Courier and Gazette Presses, pp. 600.

Morgan, Edward M., Court-Martial Jurisdiction over Non-Military Persons under the Articles of War, Minnesota Law Review, Vol. IV, No. 2, January 1920, p. 79-116.

Napier Charles J., 1837, Remarks on Military Law and the Punishment of Flogging, London: T. and W. Boone, pp. 276.

Noonan, John T. Jr., The Bribery of Warren Hastings: The Setting of a Standard for Integrity in Administration, Hofstra Law Review, Vol. 10: Issue 4, Article 5, 1982, pp. 1073-1120.

Omissi David, 1994, The Sepoy and The Raj: The Indian Army, 1860-1940, London: Macmillan, pp. 313.

Oram, Gerard, The administration of discipline by the English is very rigid: British Military Law and the Death Penalty (1868-1918), Crime, History & Societies, Vol. 5, No. 1, 2001, pp. 93-110.

Oram, Gerard Christopher, What alternative punishment is there?: Military Executions During World War I, PhD thesis, The Open University, 2000, pp. 354.

Peers Douglas M., Sepoys, soldiers and the Lash: Race, Caste and Army Discipline in India, 1820–50, *The Journal of Imperial and Commonwealth History*, 1995, Vol. 23, No. 2, p. 211-247.

Peers Douglas M., Soldiers, Surgeons and the Campaign to Combat Sexually Transmitted Diseases in Colonial India, 1805-1860, *Medical History*, Vol. 42, 1998, pp. 137-160.

Prendergast Harris, 1855, *The Law Relating to Officers in the Army*, London: Parker, Furnivall, and Parker, pp. 268.

Proceedings of a General Court Martial Held at Bangalore on the Trial of Lieut. Col. John Bell on the Madras Artillery, London: T.C. Savill, 1837, pp. 288.

Ridley McLean, Historical Sketch of Military Law, *J. Am. Inst. Crim. L. & Criminology*, Vol. 8, May 1917 to March 1918, p. 27-32.

Rivett-Carnac, Colonel S., 1890, *The Presidential Armies of India*, London: W. H. Allen & Co, pp. 442.

Roberts Lord, 1901, *Forty-One Years in India*, London: Macmillan and Co, pp. 601.

Rollman Robert O, Of Crimes, Courts-Martial and Punishment—A Short History of Military Justice, *JAG L. Rev*, Vol. XI, No. 2, Spring 1969, p. 211-222.

Roy Kaushik, 2009, *Brown Warriors of the Raj: Recruitment and the Mechanics of Command in the Sepoy Army 1859- 1913*, Delhi: Manohar.

Roy Kaushik, 2009, *The Oxford Companion to Modern Warfare in India: From the Eighteenth Century to Present Times*, New Delhi: OUP, pp. 326.

Roy Kaushik, Spare the Rod, Spoil the Soldier? Crimes and Punishments in the Army of India, 1860-1913, *Journal of the Society for Army Historical Research*, Vol. 84, 2006, pp. 9-33.

Roy Kaushik, "The Beginning of 'People's War in India," in 1857: Essays from Economic and Political Weekly, 2008, Hyderabad: Orient Longman, pp. 136-160.

Rules and Articles for the Better Government of His Majesty's Horse and Foot Guards And all Other His Forces in Great Britain and Ireland, Dominions beyond the Seas, and Foreign Parts, 1749, pp. 32.

Sandhu Amna Mahmood, The Royal Indian Army, Evolution and Organization: An appraisal, Margalla Papers 2011, pp. 49-72.

Sarup Leela, 2007, The Trial of Mangal Pandey: State Papers, New Delhi: Neogi Books, pp. 227.

Sen Amiya, The Structure and Organization of the Bengal Native Infantry with Special Reference to Problems of Discipline (1796-1852), Ph D thesis, University of London, 1961, pp. 509.

Sen Surendra Nath, 1928, The Military System of the Marathas, Bombay: Orient Longman, pp. 266.

Shaw J., 1887, *Charters Relating to East India Company*, Madras.

Sherman Edward F., The Civilianization of Military Law, *Maine Law Review*, Vol. 22, No.3, 1970, pp. 1-103.

Singh Major Madan Paul, 1976, *Indian Army under the East India Company*, New Delhi: Sterling Publishing Company, pp. 268.

Singha Radhika, 1998, *A Despotism of Law: Crime and Justice in Early Colonial India*, New Delhi: Oxford University Press, pp. 372.

Singha Radhika, The Rare Infliction: The Abolition of Flogging in the Indian Army, circa 1835-1920, *Law & Hist. Rev.*, Vol. 34, 2016, p. 783-818.

Stanley Peter Alan, White Mutiny: The Bengal Europeans, 1825-75, A study in military social history, Ph. D. Thesis, The Australian National University, March 1993, pp. 440.

Steppler G. A., British Military Law, Discipline, and the Conduct of Regimental Courts Martial in the Later Eighteenth Century, *The English Historical Review*, Vol. 102, No. 405, Oct., 1987, pp. 859-886.

Strachey Henry, 1773, *Narrative of the Mutiny of the Officers of the Army in Bengal in the year 1766, London: Strand*, pp, 196.

Stuart-Smith James, Military Law: Its History, Administration and Practice, *Law Quarterly Review*, Vol. 85, 1969, p. 478.

Syed Hussain Shaheed Soherwordi, 'Punjabisation' in the British Indian Army 1857-1947 and the Advent of Military Rule in Pakistan', *Edinburgh Papers in South Asian Studies*, Number 24 2010, pp. 34.

Taylor Frank E., Military Courts-Martial Procedure under the Revised Articles of War, *Virginia Law Review*, Vol. 12, No. 6, (April 1926), pp. 463-494.

The Army in India and its Evolution, Including an Account of the Establishment of the Royal Air Force in India, (Reorganization in the Army After the War of 1914-18), 1924, Calcutta: Superintendent Government Printing, pp. 253.

The Background of the Uniform Code of Military Justice, The US Judge Advocate General US Army, 1970, pp. 107.

The King's Regulations and Admiralty Instructions for the Government of His Majesty's Naval Service, 1913, Vol. I, pp. 703.

The Law Relating to India, and The East-India Company, 1841, London: WM. H. Allen & Co Leaden Hall Street, pp. 774.

Tugwell Lieut. Col. W.P.G., 1938, History of the Bombay Pioneers, London: The Sidney Press Limited, pp. 439.

Tytler Alexander Fraser, 1806, *An essay on Military Law and the Practice of Courts Martial*, London: Military Library, pp. 423.

Verma Ashok K, "Genesis and Evolution", in Cardozo Ian (ed.), 2005, Indian Army: A Brief History, New Delhi: USI of India, pp. 1-22.

Walden Harley Derek, Sahib and Sepoy: The British Perspective on the Sepoy Rebellion of 1857, Unpublished thesis, Marshall University, 2011. S-22.

Wheeler J. Talboys, 1886, India under British Rule: From the Foundation of the East India Company, London: Macmillan and Co., pp. 312.

Williams Captain, 1817, *An Historical Account of the Rise and Progress of the Bengal Native Infantry From its First Formation in 1757 to 1796*, London: John Murray, pp. 387.

Williams Matthew, Imperial Venture: The Evolution of the British East India Company, 1763-1813, Thesis, Florida State University Libraries, 2011, pp. 91.

Wilson Lieutenant Colonel W. J., 1882, *History of Madras Army*, Vol. I, Madras: E Keys, Govt Press, pp. 396.

Wilson Lieutenant Colonel W. J., 1882, *History of Madras Army*, Vol. II, Madras: E Keys, Govt Press, pp. 383.

Wilson Lieutenant Colonel W. J., 1883, *History of Madras Army*, Vol. III, Madras: E Keys, Govt Press, pp. 408.

Wilson Lieutenant Colonel W. J., 1888, *History of Madras Army: From 1746-1826*, Vol. IV, Madras: R Hill, Govt Press, pp. 552.

Wilson Lieutenant Colonel W. J., 1889, *History of Madras Army*, Vol. V, Madras: Superintendent, Government Press, pp. 60.

Winthrop William, 1920, *Military Law and Precedents*, Washington: Government Printing Office, pp. 1111.

Wood, Sir Evelyn, 1908, *The Revolt in Hindustan 1857-59*, London: Methuen & Co., pp. 367.

Young H.A., 1937, *The East India Company's Arsenals and Manufactories*, Oxford: Clarendon Press, pp. 243.

Index

F

G

H

I

J

K

L

T

U

V

W

www.ingramcontent.com/pod-product-compliance
Lightning Source LLC
Chambersburg PA
CBHW080939240926
51849CB00004BA/500
* 9 7 8 8 1 9 4 2 8 5 1 0 6 *